ROAD TRIP 1

Pacific Coast

INCLUDING: Olympic National Park 15 • Cape Perpetua 35 • Avenue of the Giants 53 • San Francisco 64 • Hearst Castle 84 • San Diego 110

ROAD TRIP 2

Border to Border

INCLUDING: Jasper National Park 120 • Banff National Park 122 • Sun Valley, Idaho 142 • Extraterrestrial Highway 156 • Las Vegas 154 • Tumacácori 172

ROAD TRIP 3

The Road to Nowhere

INCLUDING: Knife River Indian Village 181 • Sitting Bull Memorial 192 • Buffalo Bill Rodeo 203 • OzFest in Liberal, Kansas 212 • Remember the Alamo! 225 • South Padre Island 230

ROAD TRIP 4

The Great River Road

INCLUDING: Mississippi Headwaters 235 • World's Largest Six-Pack 247 • Mark Twain's Hometown 265 • Elvis Presley's Graceland 283 • Delta Blues Museum 287 • Cajun Country 303

ROAD TRIP 5

Appalachian Trail

INCLUDING: See Live Bears! 322 • Gettysburg 368 • Dinosaur Land 374 • Blue Ridge Parkway 390 • Tallulah Gorge 404

ROAD TRIP 6

Atlantic Coast

INCLUDING: Statue of Liberty 411 • Atlantic City 412 • Wright Bros., Kitty Hawk 430 • Savannah, Georgia 456 • Fountain of Youth 465 • Key West 489

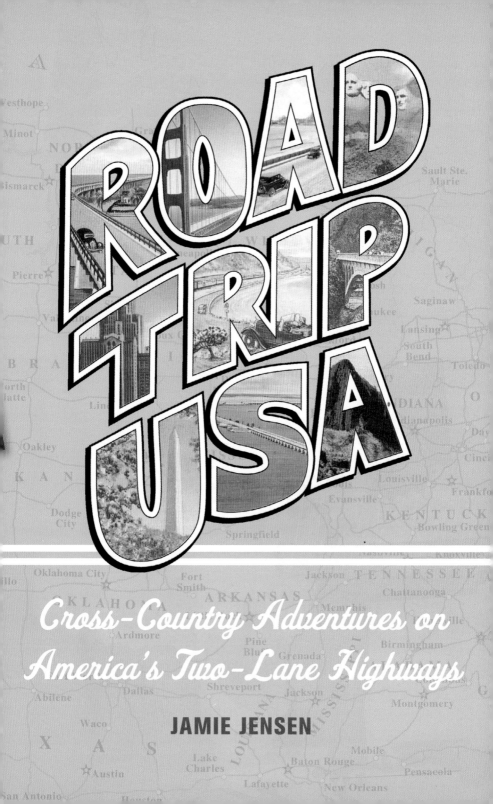

ROAD TRIP USA

Cross-Country Adventures on America's Two-Lane Highways

JAMIE JENSEN

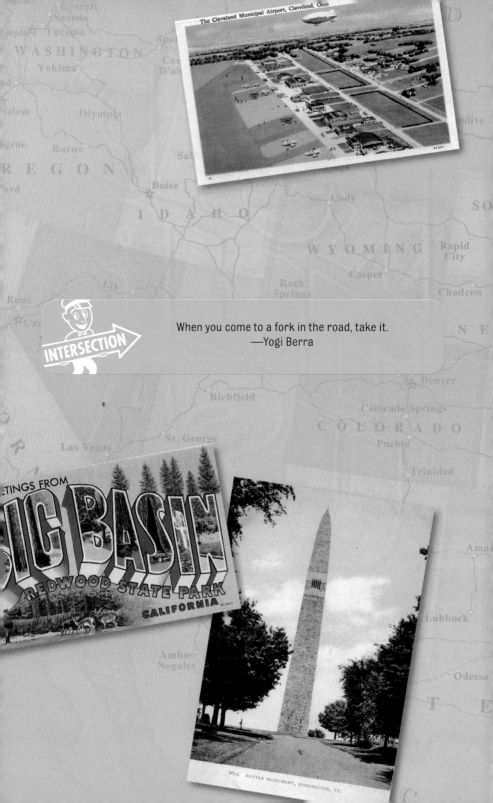

The Cleveland Municipal Airport, Cleveland, Ohio

When you come to a fork in the road, take it.
—Yogi Berra

INTERSECTION

GREETINGS FROM
BIG BASIN
REDWOOD STATE PARK
CALIFORNIA

8671. BATTLE MONUMENT, BENNINGTON, VT.

On the Road

The journeys in this book are as wild and varied as the landscapes they traverse. All celebrate the notion that freedom and discovery await us on the open road. Poets and artists from Walt Whitman to Muddy Waters have long sung the praises of rolling down the highway, and no matter how times have changed we still believe there's nothing more essentially American than hitting the road and seeing the country.

America has always been a nation on the move. From colonial times onwards, each generation pushed relentlessly westward, until the outward frontier finally closed around the turn of the 20th century. Taking advantage of the internal combustion engine, and inspired by the slogan "See America First," Americans began to explore a new frontier, the system of highways that developed between the Atlantic and Pacific coasts. The first transcontinental route, the Lincoln Highway from New York to San Francisco, was completed in 1915, and motor courts, diners, and other new businesses soon sprang up along the roadside to serve the passing trade.

The half-century from the 1920s until the arrival of the Interstate highway system was the golden age of American motor travel, but this book is not especially motivated by nostalgia. Almost all of the places described in Road Trip USA—soda fountains and town squares, neon-signed motels and minor-league baseball teams—are happily thriving in the modern world, and better yet, they are close at hand. The simple act of avoiding the soulless Interstates, with their soggy franchises and identikit chains, opens up a vast, and much friendlier, two-lane world. You'll chance upon monuments marking the actual sites of things you last thought about in high school history classes, or kitschy little souvenir stands flaunting giant dinosaurs outside their doors, and inside still selling the same postcards as they have for decades.

After traveling well over 400,000 miles in search of the perfect stretches of two-lane blacktop, this is the book I wish I'd had with me all along. So whether you're a biker, an RVer, a road warrior, or a Sunday driver, hop on board, turn the key—and hit the highway.

Janie Jen

Contents

PACIFIC COAST 8
Washington · Oregon · California

BORDER TO BORDER 114
Canadian Rockies · Montana · Idaho · Nevada · Arizona

THE ROAD TO NOWHERE 174
North Dakota · South Dakota · Nebraska · Kansas · Oklahoma · Texas

THE GREAT RIVER ROAD 232
Minnesota · Wisconsin · Iowa · Illinois · Missouri · Kentucky ·
Tennessee · Mississippi · Louisiana

APPALACHIAN TRAIL 310
New Hampshire · Vermont · Massachusetts · Connecticut ·
New York · Pennsylvania · Maryland · West Virginia · Virginia ·
North Carolina · Georgia

ATLANTIC COAST 408
New Jersey · Delaware · Maryland · Virginia · North Carolina ·
South Carolina · Georgia · Florida

SCENE ON CADILLAC MOUNTAIN ROAD, ACADIA NATIONAL PARK, MT. DESERT ISLAND, MAINE

Nature's Pulpit, North Dakota Badlands

THE GREAT NORTHERN 492

Washington · Idaho · Montana · North Dakota · Minnesota ·
Wisconsin · Michigan · Canada · Vermont · New Hampshire · Maine

THE OREGON TRAIL 584

Oregon · Idaho · Wyoming · Nebraska · Iowa · Illinois · Indiana ·
Ohio · Pennsylvania · New York · Massachusetts

THE LONELIEST ROAD 704

California · Nevada · Utah · Colorado · Kansas · Missouri ·
Illinois · Indiana · Ohio · West Virginia · Virginia · Maryland

SOUTHERN PACIFIC 800

California · Arizona · New Mexico · Texas · Louisiana · Mississippi ·
Alabama · Georgia

ROUTE 66 864

Illinois · Missouri · Kansas · Oklahoma · Texas · New Mexico ·
Arizona · California

ROAD TRIP RESOURCES 946

INDEX 955

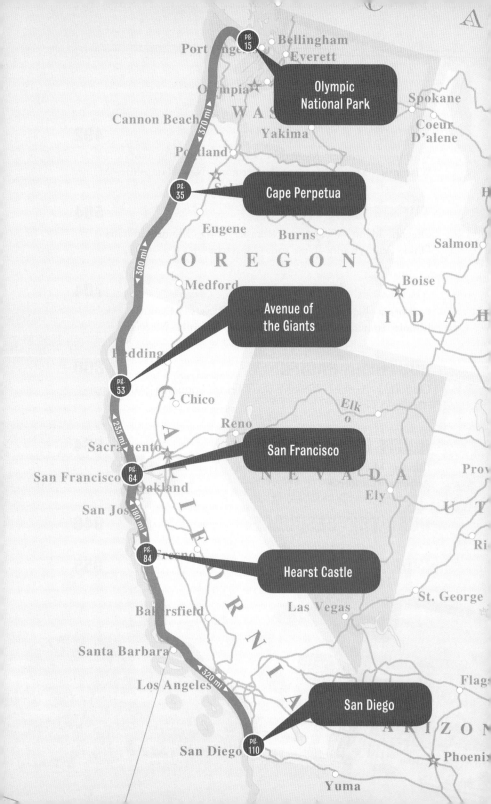

Pacific Coast

CALIFORNIA
1

The amazing thing about the West Coast is that it is still mostly wild, open, and astoundingly beautiful country, where you can drive for miles and miles and have the scenery all to yourself.

Between Olympic National Park and San Diego, California

For some reason, when people elsewhere in the country refer to the Pacific Coast, particularly **California**, it's apparent that they think it's a land of kooks and crazies, an overbuilt suburban desert supporting only shopping malls, freeways, and body-obsessed airheads. All this may be true in small pockets, but the amazing thing about the Pacific Coast—from the dense green forests of western **Washington** to the gorgeous beaches of Southern California—is that it is still mostly wild, open, and astoundingly beautiful country, where you can drive for miles and miles and have the scenery all to yourself.

Starting at the northwest tip of the United States at **Olympic National Park,** and remaining within sight of the ocean almost all the way south to the Mexican border, this 1,650-mile, mostly two-lane route takes in everything from temperate rainforest to near-desert. Most of the Pacific Coast is in the public domain, accessible, and protected from development within national, state, and local parks, which provide habitat for such rare creatures as mountain lions, condors, and gray whales.

Heading south, after the rough-and-tumble logging and fishing communities of Washington State, you cross the mouth of the Columbia River and follow the comparatively peaceful and quiet **Oregon** coastline, where recreation has by and

WASHINGTON

The coast of Washington is a virtual microcosm of the Pacific Northwest, containing everything from extensive wilderness areas to Native American fishing villages and heavily industrialized lumber towns. Starting at splendid **Port Townsend,** US-101 loops west around the rugged Olympic Peninsula, passing near the northwesternmost point of the

continental United States while allowing access to the unforgettable natural attractions—sandy, driftwood-strewn beaches; primeval old-growth forests; and pristine mountain lakes and glaciated alpine peaks, to name just a few—of **Olympic National Park.** The roadside landscape varies from dense woods to clear-cut tracts of recently harvested timber, with large replaced industry, and where dozens of quaint and not-so-quaint communities line the ever-changing shoreline. At the midway point, you pass through the great redwood forests of Northern California, where the tallest and most majestic living things on earth line the "Avenue of the Giants," home also to some of the best (meaning gloriously kitsch) remnants of the golden age of car-borne tourism: drive-through trees, drive-on trees, houses carved out of trees, and much more. The phenomenally beautiful coastline of Northern California is rivaled only by the incredible coast of **Big Sur** farther south, beyond which stretch the beachfronts of Southern California. The land of palm trees, beach boys, and surfer girls of popular lore really does exist, though only in the southernmost quarter of the state.

Along with the overwhelming scale of its natural beauty, the West Coast is remarkable for the abundance of well-preserved historic sites—most of which haven't been torn down, built on, or even built around—that stand as vivid evocations of life on what was once the most distant frontier of the New World. While rarely as old as places on the East Coast, or as impressive as those in Europe, West Coast sites are quite diverse and include the Spanish colonial missions of California, Russian and English fur-trading outposts, and the place where Lewis and Clark first sighted the Pacific after their long slog across the continent.

Last but certainly not least are the energizing cities—**Seattle** and **Portland** in the north, **San Francisco** in the middle, and **Los Angeles** and **San Diego** to the south—which serve as gateways to (or civilized respites from) the landscapes in between them. Add to these the dozens of small and not-so-small towns along the coast, with alternating blue-collar ports and upscale vacation retreats, and you have a great range of food, drink, and accommodation options. Local cafés, seafood grills, and bijou restaurants abound, as do places to stay—from youth hostels in old lighthouses to roadside motels (including the world's first, which still stands in lovely San Luis Obispo, California) to homespun B&B inns in old farmhouses.

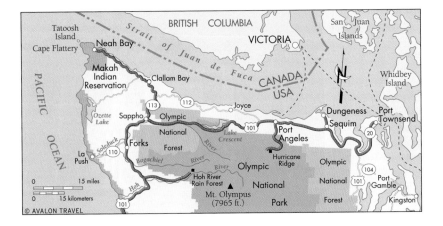

innumerable rivers and streams perhaps the most obvious signs of the immense amount of rainfall (about 12 feet) the region receives every year. Scattered towns, from **Port Angeles** in the north to the twin cities of **Grays Harbor** on the coast, are staunchly blue-collar communities almost wholly dependent upon natural resources—not only trees, but also salmon, oysters, and other seafood. Though the tourism trade has been increasing steadily, visitor services are still few and far between, so plan ahead.

Though it's not on the ocean, the Puget Sound port city of **Seattle** makes a good starting or finishing point to this Pacific Coast road trip.

Port Townsend

Few places in the world can match the concentration of natural beauty or the wealth of architecture found in tiny **Port Townsend** (pop. 9,113). One of the oldest towns in Washington, Port Townsend was laid out in 1852 and reached a peak of activity in the 1880s. But after the railroads focused on Seattle and Puget Sound as their western terminus, the town sat quietly for most of the next century until the 1960s, when an influx of arts-oriented refugees took over the waterfront warehouses and cliff-top mansions, converting them to galleries, restaurants, and comfy B&Bs while preserving the town's turn-of-the-20th-century character.

The Waterstreet Hotel

Port Townsend is neatly divided into two halves: Multi-story brick warehouses and commercial buildings line Water Street and the wharves along the bay, while lovely old Victorian houses cover the bluffs above. It's basically a great place to wander, but there are a couple of sights worth seeing, particularly the landmark **City Hall** (250 Madison St.) along the east end of Water Street. Half of this eclectic gothic pile now houses a local historical museum with three floors of odds and ends tracing Port Townsend history, including the old city jail where Jack London spent a night on his way to the Klondike goldfields in 1897.

Fort Worden, on the north side of Port Townsend, is a retired military base that served as a location for the Richard Gere movie *An Officer and a Gentleman.* Now home to a wonderful natural history museum, the old fort also hosts an excellent series of annual music and arts festivals; contact the Centrum at 360/385-3102 for schedules and more information.

Toward Seattle: Port Gamble

You have a number of options if traveling to or from Port Townsend. You can follow US-101 around the western Olympic Peninsula, or take a ferry via Whidbey Island and explore it and the even prettier San Juan Islands to the north. Last, but not least, you can take a middle route across the Kitsap Peninsula, then catch a ferry to Seattle (see page 498).

This last route, which includes a trip on the very frequent Washington State Ferries between Kingston and Edmonds, has the great advantage of taking you through the lovely old logging town of **Port Gamble,** a slice of New England on the shores of Puget Sound. The entire town is a historic district, with dozens of immaculate Victorian buildings standing along maple tree–lined streets. After wandering past the saltbox houses, have a look inside the large Port Gamble General Store, which includes a seashell museum and a café, or visit the photo-filled **Port Gamble Historic Museum** ($4; 360/297-8078) below the store.

Not surprisingly, considering the extensive tourist trade, Port Townsend has a number of good restaurants and bars. You'll find many of the best places at the east end of town near the corner of Water and Quincy Streets. For breakfast, try the **Salal Cafe** (634 Water St.; 360/385-6532). For lunch or dinner, one of the best seafood places is the **Silverwater Cafe** (237 Taylor St.; 360/385-6448), near the Quincy Street dock. The old waterfront neighborhood also holds a pair of hotels in restored 1880s buildings: **The Waterstreet Hotel** ($50 and up; 635 Water St.; 360/385-5467 or 800/735-9810) and the quieter **The Palace Hotel** ($59 and up; 1004 Water St.; 360/385-0773), where the room names play up the building's past use as a brothel.

The most comfortable accommodations in Port Townsend are the many 1880s-era B&Bs dotting the bluffs above the port area, including the ever-popular **The Old Consulate Inn** ($99 and up; 313 Walker St.; 360/385-6753), where some of the plush rooms come with a view of the Olympic Mountains and all come with a hearty multi-course breakfast. For less-pricey lodging, there's a **campground** (360/344-4400) and the **HI-Olympic Guesthouse & Hostel** ($28 per person; 360/385-0655), with dorm beds in the old Army barracks at Fort Worden, on the coast two miles north of town.

The natural cut of the **Hood Canal** on the east side of the Olympic Peninsula is one of the West Coast's prime oyster-growing estuaries, source of the gourmet Quilcenes, Hama Hamas, and other varieties available at roadside stands, shops, and restaurants throughout the region.

Sequim and Dungeness

Forty minutes southwest of Port Townsend via Hwy-20 and US-101, **Sequim** (pop. 6,606; pronounced "SKWIM") sits in the rain shadow of the Olympic Mountains and so tends to be much drier and sunnier than spots even a few miles west. Though it retains its rural feel, Sequim's historic farming-and-fishing economy is quickly switching over to tourism, with tracts of new homes filling up the rolling, waterfront landscape and a new freeway bypassing the center of town. It's ideal cycling country, for the moment at least, with acres and acres of lavender farms lining quiet country roads.

Sequim lavender fields

Coming in from the east on two-lane US-101, the first thing you pass is the large, modern John Wayne Marina, built on land donated by The Duke's family. The US-101 frontage through town is lined by the usual franchised fast-food outlets and some unique variations, like the 1950s-themed **Hi-Way 101 Diner** (392 W. Washington St.; 360/683-3388), in the heart of town.

The Native American–owned **7 Cedars Casino** stands above US-101 at the foot of Sequim Bay, fronted by totem poles.

Sequim's annual **Irrigation Festival,** held every May, is Washington's oldest continuing community celebration. The **Lavender Festival,** in July, is also very popular.

Just north of US-101, the **Museum & Arts Center in the Sequim-Dungeness Valley** (10 AM–4 PM Tues.–Sun., except the last Sun. of every month; donation; 175 W. Cedar St.; 360/683-8110) houses everything from 12,000-year-old mastodon bones discovered on a nearby farm to exhibits of Native American cultures and pioneer farm implements. From the museum, a well-marked road winds north for seven miles before reaching the waterfront again at **Dungeness,** where a 5.5-mile-long sand spit, the country's longest, protects a shellfish-rich wildlife refuge. All that remains of the abandoned fishing community that existed here through the 1890s is an old schoolhouse and the hit-or-miss local landmark **The 3 Crabs** (360/683-4264), overlooking Dungeness Harbor, which has been serving up fresh fish and local Dungeness crab for over 45 years.

Stay in Sequim at **Groveland Cottage Bed and Breakfast** ($110 and up; 4861 Sequim-Dungeness Way; 360/683-3565), a quaint B&B just a half mile from the harbor, or at the popular waterfront **Juan de Fuca Cottages** ($120 and up; 182 Marine Dr.; 866/683-4433), 2.5 miles to the west.

Port Angeles

A busy, industrial city at the center of the northern Olympic Peninsula, **Port Angeles** (pop. 19,038) makes a handy base for visiting the nearby wilderness of Olympic National Park. The town is slowly but surely recovering from its traditional dependence on logging, and the waterfront, which once hummed to the sound of lumber and pulp mills, is now bustling with tourists wandering along a 6.5-mile walking trail and enjoying the sealife (sea slugs, starfish, and octopuses) on display at the small but enjoyable **Feiro Marine Life Center** (daily during summer, weekends during off-season; $4), on the centrally located Port Angeles City Pier.

Malls, gas stations, and fast-food franchises line the US-101 frontage through town, but life in Port Angeles, for locals and visitors alike, centers on

Olympic National Park

Olympic National Park, in the heart of the Olympic Peninsula, is a diversely beautiful corner of the country, combining features of Maine's rocky coast and the snowcapped peaks of the Rocky Mountains with the unique rain-forests covering the park's Pacific coastal valleys. The rugged, nearly mil-lion-acre landscape, ranging from rocky shores to impassably dense forests, resisted exploitation and development until the turn of the 20th century, when local conservationists persuaded Teddy Roosevelt to declare much of the peninsula a national monument, a movement that eventually resulted in the establishment of Olympic National Park in 1938.

There are no roads and few trails across the peninsula, so you have to choose your points of entry depending upon what you want to see. The dif-ferent areas of Olympic National Park are covered in the surrounding pages, but the most popular part of the park is Hurricane Ridge, which rises high above Port Angeles and offers great views of the silvery peaks and the many glaciers that flank them. (The wildflowers can be spectacu-lar in late spring.)

At the northwestern corner of the park, Lake Crescent sits serenely amidst the forests and peaks, while on the western slopes, the temperate rainforests of the usually wet and rainy river valleys hold some of the world's largest trees, all draped with a thick fabric of mosses. At the western edge of the peninsula, the almost completely undeveloped Pacific Ocean coastline, added to the park in 1953, offers miles of sandy beaches and rocky head-lands, littered only with driftwood logs and vibrant tidepools.

the attractive downtown area, two blocks inland from the waterfront around Lincoln Street and 1st Street. Here cafés like **First Street Haven** (107 E. 1st St.; 360/457-0352) offer great breakfasts and good yet inexpensive soup-and-salad lunches, while amiable bars and pubs like **Peaks,** around the corner (130 S. Lincoln Ave.; 360/452-2802), draw bikers, hikers, and loggers with their pub grub and good beers (more than 50 bottles, plus some intriguing "home brews"). If you're waiting for a boat, or are fresh off of one, more places to eat and drink surround the ferry terminal.

Places to stay in Port Angeles vary. You'll find highway motels, including the **Quality Inn Uptown** ($85 and up; 101 E. 2nd St.; 360/457-9434), and the **Red Lion** ($129 and up; 360/452-9215), on the water at the foot of Lincoln Street. There are also many characterful B&Bs, like the popular **Inn at Rooster Hill** ($99 and up; 360/452-4933).

Weather on the Olympic Peninsula varies widely from place to place. The peaks and coastal valleys of Olympic National Park receive as much as 200 inches of rainfall each year, while the nearby town of Sequim garners an average of just 15–17 inches annually.

Hurricane Ridge

High above Port Angeles, **Hurricane Ridge** provides the most popular access to Olympic National Park. A paved road twists and turns 17 miles up a steep 7 percent grade to the mile-high summit, where, on a clear day, you can gape at the breathtaking 360-degree views of mountain, valley, and sea. A lodge at the crest provides food and drink, and a concession offers ski and snowshoe rentals on winter weekends. Trails lead down into the backcountry, where you're likely to spot marmots, deer, and bald eagles—and if you're lucky, maybe an elk or a mountain lion. From Hurricane Ridge, thrill-seeking drivers and mountain bikers may get a kick out of Obstruction Point Road, a twisting gravel road that continues (without guardrails!) for another eight miles along the crest from the parking lot. In winter, the snowed-in road becomes a popular cross-country skiing trail.

Apart from the area right around Hurricane Ridge, most of the Olympic National Park backcountry is fairly wet and rugged. If you plan to camp overnight, be prepared, and be sure to get a permit from the Olympic National Park **visitors center** (360/565-3130) in Port Angeles, just south of US-101 on the road up to Hurricane Ridge. This is also the best place to pick up general information on the rest of the park, which extends all the way west to the rainforest areas along the coastal valleys.

Lake Crescent

One of the most idyllic spots in the entire Pacific Northwest, the fjord-like **Lake Crescent,** over eight miles long and some 625 feet deep, lies right alongside two-lane US-101, just 18 miles west of Port Angeles. The placid surface reflects the clouds and surrounding peaks, including 4,537-foot Mount Storm King; to appreciate the tranquil beauty, rent a rowboat from the Lake Crescent Lodge and float around under your own steam. Starting from the lodge, a popular mile-long hike follows a well-maintained nature trail up to the delicate cascade of 90-foot **Marymere Falls,** while along the north shore an abandoned railroad grade is open to hikers and mountain bikers.

Ferries to Victoria, British Columbia

From Port Angeles, the Black Ball Ferry Line carries cars and passengers (around $60 per car and driver one-way, plus $16.50 per additional person; 360/457-4491), shuttling across the water to and from pretty Victoria, the provincial capital of British Columbia, one of Canada's most popular destinations. Ships leave Port Angeles at the middle of the attractively landscaped waterfront and arrive very near the center of Victoria, making for a great day trip from either place. At the Port Angeles dock there's a very helpful information center packed with maps and brochures on Victoria and the rest of B.C., or you can call **Tourism Victoria** at 800/663-3883.

Incomparably situated along US-101 on the lake's southeast shore, **Lake Crescent Lodge** (open May–Oct. only, except for the Fireplace Cottages open on the weekends; $110 and up; 360/928-3211) was originally built in 1916 and has been hosting visitors ever since. Fairly rustic rooms are available in the old lodge, which also has a cozy dining room. Other accommodations are available in the adjacent cabins and motel, though the whole place is booked solid on summer weekends, so reserve as soon as you can. Another nice place to stay is the **Log Cabin Resort** ($121 and up; 360/928-3325), three miles north of US-101 on the "sunny northeast shore," with lodge rooms and waterfront A-frame cabins.

In the forested hills above US-101, **Sol Duc Hot Springs Resort** ($160 and up; 360/327-3583) has family-friendly cabins and a restaurant set around a swimming pool and natural hot spring ($12.25 for non-guests).

Hwy-112: Strait of Juan de Fuca

The Strait of Juan de Fuca, the narrow inlet that links the open Pacific with Puget Sound and divides the United States from Canada, was named for the Greek sailor (real name: Apostolos Valerianos) who first mapped it while working for the Spanish Crown in 1592. On a clear day, you can get some great views across the strait from Hwy-112, which runs along the shore from US-101 all the way to the tip of the Olympic Peninsula at Neah Bay. Though it looks like a great drive on the map, Hwy-112 is a very narrow and winding road with some surprisingly steep hills and thick woods that block much of the view, all of which (in addition to the plentiful logging trucks) can make it less than ideal for bicycling or even a scenic drive.

Along Hwy-112, you may pass a pair of fish-headed, human-legged, sneaker-wearing statues. Don't be alarmed.

Neah Bay and Cape Flattery

From the crossroads at **Sappho** on US-101, Hwy-113 leads north, linking up with Hwy-112 on a long and winding 40-mile detour through Clallam Bay to **Cape Flattery,** the northwesternmost tip of the continental United States. The highway is paved as far as the town of **Neah Bay,** a tiny (pop. 865) and somewhat bedraggled community that's the center of the Makah Indian Reservation. Salmon and halibut fish-

Cape Flattery

ing, both by Makah and by visitors, is about the only activity here, though the tribe does have the impressive and modern **Makah Museum** (daily; $5; 360/645-2711), one of the best anthropological museums in the state. Most of the displays are of artifacts uncovered in 1970, when a winter storm exposed the pristine remains of a 500-year-old coastal village that had been buried in a mudslide—the Pompeii of the Pacific Northwest. Other galleries display finely crafted baskets, a full-scale longhouse complete with recorded chants, and a whaling canoe from which fearless Makah harpooners would jump into the surf and sew up the jaws of dying whales, to keep them from sinking. If you want a special souvenir, the museum gift shop displays and sells a variety of high-quality arts and crafts made by Makah people.

In the late 1990s, as part of an effort to preserve tribal traditions and instill pride in younger Makah, the Makah tribe resumed small-scale hunting of migratory gray whales, which they had voluntarily ceased when the whales became endangered a century ago. Though the hunting was largely ceremonial, the news raised the hackles of wildlife organizations, which filed lawsuits and staged loud protests to prevent whales from being killed.

The Hwy-112/113 route twists along the rocky and wooded shore of the Strait of Juan de Fuca, but reaching the actual cape itself isn't difficult. From Neah Bay, the well-maintained western half of the Cape Loop Road winds along the Pacific to a parking area that gives access to a trail that brings you to the top of a cliff overlooking the crashing surf and offshore **Tatoosh Island.** On a sunny day it's a gorgeous vista, but if the weather's less than perfect (which it often is) your time would be much better spent inside the Makah Museum.

Forks

Bending southwest along the banks of the Sol Duc River, US-101 passes through miles of green forests under ever-gray skies to reach **Forks** (pop. 3,532), the commercial center of the northwestern Olympic Peninsula. Named for its location astride the Sol Duc and Bogachiel Rivers, Forks is a die-hard lumber town grappling with the inevitable change to more ecologically sus-

The old-growth forests of **Olympic National Park** *provide prime habitat for the northern spotted owl, an endangered species whose preservation has sparked heated debate throughout the Pacific Northwest.*

tainable alternatives, mainly tourism. Visitors come to fish for steelhead during the late-summer runs, to beachcomb along the rugged coast, or to visit the remarkable rainforests of Olympic National Park. The main attractions in Forks these days are sights related to the wildly popular teenage vampire novels and films of *The Twilight Saga,* which were set here in Forks. Vampires aside, the main event is the quirky, summer-only **Forks Timber Museum** (Tues.–Sat.; 360/374-9663), on US-101 on the south edge of town, packed with handsaws, chainsaws, and other logging gear as well as antique cooking stoves and displays telling the town's characterful history. There's also a forest-fire lookout tower perched outside the upper floor gallery.

With three gas stations and five motels, Forks is not a metropolis by any stretch of the imagination, but it does offer the best range of services between Port Angeles and Aberdeen. **Sully's Burgers** (220 N. Forks Ave.) is a good burger stand on US-101 at the north end of town. There are also a couple of Chinese and Mexican places, plus salmon sandwiches at **The Smoke House Restaurant** and pretty good pies at **Pacific Pizza** (870 S. Forks Ave.). Stay at **The Forks Motel** ($60–160; 351 S. Forks Ave.; 360/374-6243) or a more peaceful B&B, the **Miller Tree Inn Bed and Breakfast** ($115 and up; 654 E. Division St.; 360/374-6806), about half a mile east of Forks's solitary stoplight.

South of Forks along US-101, **Bogachiel State Park** has over 100 forested acres of very nice campsites (with showers!) along the Bogachiel River. Sites are first-come, first-served, and cost around $10 for tents, $15 for RV hookups (360/374-6356).

For more information, contact the Forks **visitors center** (360/374-2531), next to the Timber Museum, which also serves as clearinghouse for *Twilight*-related tourism.

Hoh Rainforest

If you have time to visit only one of the lush rainforest areas of Washington's northwest coast, head for the **Hoh Rainforest,** 12 miles south of Forks and then 18 miles east along a well-signed and well-paved road. Not only is this the most easily accessible of these incredibly lush, old-growth areas, the Hoh Rainforest is also among the least disturbed, with a thick, wet blanket of vibrant green ferns, mosses, and lichens covering every inch of the earth at the foot of massive hemlocks, cedars, and towering Sitka spruce. Displays inside the visitors center tell all about the forest's flora and fauna and how they are affected by the massive rainfall here—upwards of 140 inches every year. There's also a wheelchair-accessible nature trail and a wide range of hiking trails, including the quickest access to the icy summit of 7,965-foot Mt. Olympus, 22 miles away in the glacier-packed alpine highlands at the heart of the park.

If you're very lucky, you might spy one of the rare Roosevelt elk, whose protection was one of the reasons Olympic National Park was established; if you're unlucky, you might also come face-to-face with a mountain lion, which can be dangerous but generally avoids contact with humans.

The closest services to the Hoh Rainforest are in Forks, but budget travelers may want to take advantage of the $10-a-night bunks at the amiable **Rain Forest Hostel** (360/374-2270), 23 miles south of Forks along US-101

Ruby Beach

(between milemarkers 169 and 170), midway between the Hoh Rainforest and the coast at Ruby Beach.

Kalaloch and the Pacific Beaches

Looping around the northern Olympic Peninsula, US-101 finally reaches the coast 27 miles south of Forks at **Ruby Beach,** where wave-sculpted sea stacks frame a photogenic, driftwood-strewn cove. From Ruby Beach, US-101 runs south through the wild coastal section of Olympic National Park, which is almost always foggy and cool, even when the weather's sunny and hot just a mile inland. While almost the entire coast south from Cape Flattery is protected within the national park, this is the only easily accessible stretch. Parking areas along the highway, numbered from Beach 6 to Beach 1 north to south, give access to 20 miles of generally deserted beach, backed by rocky bluffs and packed with tidepools, driftwood castles, and an incredible variety of flotsam and jetsam.

At the southern end of this short but sweet stretch of coastline, between Beach 2 and Beach 3, 25 miles north of Lake Quinault, **Kalaloch Lodge** ($134 and up; 360/962-2271) is a modern resort, with a coffee shop and a nice restaurant overlooking a picturesque cove. There's also a gas station, a summer-only **ranger station** across US-101, and an oceanside **campground** just to the north.

Lake Quinault

Spreading in a broad valley at the southwest corner of Olympic National Park, **Lake Quinault** offers lush rainforest groves within a short walk or drive of most creature comforts. The lake has served for decades as a popular resort destination—cabins, lodges, and stores dating from the 1920s line the southern shore, just outside the park boundary—and the old-growth forests here have survived intact, though the naked tracts of clear-cut timber along US-101 north and south of the lake give a good sense of what the area might have looked like had Teddy Roosevelt and friends not stepped in to protect it around the turn of the 20th century.

From US-101 at **Hoquiam,** Hwy-109 runs west and north along the Pacific Ocean through a series of small fishing ports and beach resorts to the heavily logged lands of the Quinault Indian Reservation.

Before or after the hike, stop at the USFS **ranger station** (360/956-2400) on the south shore, where you can get details of the other excellent hikes in the Lake Quinault area and pick up a map of the guided driving tour around the lake, including the location of the many record-size trees. The roughly four-mile-long **Quinault Loop Trail** winds on a paved path from the ranger station along crashing Cascade Creek up through an old-growth rainforest of alders and bigleaf maples, whose leaves grow upwards of 12 inches across (and provide some splendid "fall color"). Midway along, the trail crosses a raised wooden boardwalk through a fecund cedar swamp, then drops down again along another creek before returning by way of the lakeshore.

On the lakeshore right next to the ranger station, historic **Lake Quinault Lodge** ($79 and up; 360/288-2900) is well worth a look, with a rustic but spacious lobby opening onto lakefront lawns, though the rooms could do with some TLC. The **Rain Forest Resort Village** ($75 and up; 360/288-2535), at the east end of the lake, besides offering comfortable and reasonably priced accommodations (from camping to cabins) and very good food in the Salmon House restaurant, also holds the **World's Largest Spruce Tree,** a 191-foot giant.

Grays Harbor: Hoquiam and Aberdeen

The Olympic Peninsula is cut off from the southern Washington coast by the spade-shaped bay of **Grays Harbor,** named for an early American sea captain and explorer, Robert Gray. Long the state's prime lumber port, Grays Harbor still processes huge piles of trees, but in many ways what's most interesting is the contrast between the two towns here, Hoquiam and Aberdeen.

At the western end of Grays Harbor, tidy **Hoquiam** (pop. 8,726; kind of rhymes with "requiem") celebrates its lumber-based history with an annual Loggers PlayDay bash, complete with ax-throwing and tree-climbing competitions, the second weekend in September. The rest of the year, get a feel for the bygone days of the lumber industry at **Hoquiam's Castle Bed & Breakfast** ($125 and up; 515 Chenault Ave.; 360/533-2005), on a hillside three blocks off US-101, a 20-room mansion built in 1897 by a local lumber baron. Another grand old timber-magnate mansion now houses **The Polson Museum** (Wed.–Sun; donation; 1611 Riverside Ave.; 360/533-5862), on US-101. Not surprisingly, it's devoted to local history, with information on logging.

East of Hoquiam along the Chehalis River at the head of Grays Harbor, **Aberdeen** (pop. 16,896) is much more heavily industrialized and thus has been

The *Lady Washington* is a replica of one of the first American ships to explore the West Coast.

even harder hit by the continuing downturn in the Northwest timber industry. The downtown area has more than a few rough edges, but it also holds one of the more high-profile of the state-sponsored efforts to move from timber to tourism: **Grays Harbor Historical Seaport** (daily; $3; 360/532-8611), a mile south of Hwy-12. A reconstruction of one of American explorer Capt. Robert Gray's ships, the *Lady Washington,* can be toured—when she's not off on one of her regular "goodwill" cruises. The original ship was the first American vessel to visit the area, way back in 1788, and the replica was completed here in 1989 to celebrate the Washington State centennial.

Grunge-rock hero and Nirvana lead singer Kurt Cobain grew up in and around Aberdeen, as did ace road-trip photographer Lee Friedlander.

The region's long-time employer, the Weyerhaeuser pulp mill, located alongside US-101 in the inappropriately named town of Cosmopolis, closed down in 2009. Heading south from Aberdeen, a coastal loop runs along the Pacific via Hwy-105, while US-101 cuts inland, south toward Raymond and Willapa Bay. Heading east from Aberdeen, US-12 cuts inland, passing the defunct Satsop nuclear power plant and one of the most heavily logged areas in Washington before joining the I-5 freeway south of the state capital of Olympia. Midway along, the **Grays Harbor Hostel** in Elma (360/482-3119) has $18-a-night beds (and a small Frisbee golf course!).

Hwy-105: Westport and Tokeland

Between Hoquiam and Raymond, US-101 cuts inland from the coast, while an alternative route, Hwy-105, loops to the west past miles of cranberry bogs (and occasional wild elk) through the salmon-fishing town of **Westport.** Once called "The Salmon Capital of the World," and still a prime place for watching migrating gray whales, Westport is a very busy port—and one of Washington's few good surfing, clam-digging, and surf-kayaking beaches. The whole place really comes to life during the Labor Day seafood festival, but any time of the year the best stop is **Brady's Oysters** (360/268-0077), at the foot of the Hwy-105 bridge from Aberdeen.

At the south edge of the peninsula, absorb more coastal character at the 1885 **Tokeland Hotel** ($43–65; 360/267-7006), off Hwy-105 on the north shore of Willapa Bay, with old-fashioned lodgings (shared bathrooms) and a cozy old dining room.

Willapa Bay: Raymond and South Bend

One of the country's prime oystering grounds, **Willapa Bay** is sheltered from the Pacific by the Long Beach Peninsula and fed by the Nasalle, Willapa, and North Fall Rivers. There are very few towns or even villages on this stretch of US-101, which winds past tidal marshes, cattle ranches, and extensively clear-cut forests—which billboards proclaim to be "America's first industrial tree farm," giving dates of harvest, planting, and re-harvest, on a roughly 40-year cycle.

If the weather's right for a picnic, fresh shellfish can be had at bargain prices—live in the shell, or pre-shucked by the half gallon—from the area's many producers, wholesalers, and roadside stands. Look for them all along US-101 and up the Long Beach peninsula.

At the northeast corner of Willapa Bay, on the south bank of the Willapa River, stand two towns that jointly embody the natural resource–based history and economy of the Pacific Northwest: **Raymond** (pop. 2,882) has the lumber mills, while **South Bend** (pop. 1,637) calls itself the "Oyster Capital of the World." South Bend's other claim to fame is its landmark **Pacific County Courthouse** (Mon.– Fri. only), which since 1910 has loomed like a mini Taj Mahal on a hill just east of US-101. Step inside for a look at the 30-foot stained-glass dome above the rotunda, and wander through the lushly landscaped park next door.

If you want to stretch your legs, Raymond and South Bend are linked by the very nice Chehalis Trail, a walking and cycling path that follows an old railroad right-of-way along the Willapa River, amidst some engaging roadside metal sculptures of people canoeing, bird-watching, cycling, fishing, and generally enjoying the great outdoors.

Long Beach Peninsula

On the western side of Willapa Bay, the **Long Beach Peninsula** stretches for 28 miles of hard-packed sandy beaches along the roiling Pacific Ocean. Away from the few small towns, beaches and breakers abound along here, and you won't have any problem finding peace and solitude. The center of activity on the Long Beach Peninsula is the town of **Long Beach,** two miles from US-101, with a wanderable collection of crafts galleries and souvenir shops. A short walk west from "downtown" Long Beach, a wooden boardwalk winds along the coastal dunes, leading to a very rare sight: the reconstructed skeleton of a gray whale. Lewis and Clark saw similar bones when they passed by 200-plus years ago, and a Discovery Trail linking Corps of Discovery locations runs from here south to Ilwaco, near the mouth of the Columbia River.

If you can bear to stretch your budget a little, Long Beach is home to one of the coast's best B&Bs, historic **The Shelburne Inn** ($115 and up; 4415 Pacific Way; 360/642-2442), located in the Seaview neighborhood (Pacific Way is also known as Hwy-103, the main road). The Shelburne Inn also houses a friendly pub. Long Beach is also the home of the nearly-10-feet-in-diameter "World's Largest Frying Pan," which sits on a rack across from the one-of-a-kind **Marsh's Free Museum** (409 S. Pacific Ave.; 360/642-2188), a totally tacky (and wonderfully kitsch) collection of postcards, peep shows, and old-time arcade games.

"World's Largest Frying Pan"

The rest of the slender Long Beach peninsula is quite quiet, dotted with cranberry bogs and historic fishing and oystering towns. In **Nahcotta,** a dozen miles north of Long Beach, you can stay overnight at the cozy **Moby Dick Hotel and Oyster Farm** ($90–150; 25814 Sandridge Rd.; 360/665-4543), where they grow, harvest, and serve their own bivalve treats. Just north, **Oysterville** is the peninsula's oldest community, with some nifty historic homes dating back to the 1850s. The peninsula comes to an end in the north at **Leadbetter Point State Park,** a great place for watching gulls, hawks, eagles, and migratory seabirds passing through on the Pacific Flyway.

Cape Disappointment

The high headland marking the place where the Columbia River finally merges into the Pacific Ocean, **Cape Disappointment** was named by the early explorer Capt. John Meares, who in 1788 incorrectly interpreted the treacherous sandbars offshore to mean that, despite reports to the contrary, there was neither a major river nor any mythical Northwest Passage here.

Besides the grand view of the raging ocean, the best reason to visit the cape is to tour the small but worthwhile **Lewis and Clark Interpretive Center** (daily; $5; 360/642-3029), incongruously built atop a World War II–era artillery emplacement a short walk from the end of the road. On November 7, 1805, after five months and more than 4,000 miles, the explorers finally laid eyes on the Pacific from this point, and then they sat through nine days of continuous rain before fleeing south to Oregon. Displays inside the museum give the overall context for their journey of discovery, walking you through the different stages of their two-year round-trip. The small "Cape D" lighthouse stands atop a cliff, a half-mile walk from the Lewis and Clark museum, which is 200

Two statues sculpted by chain saws, in a small state park three miles west of the US-101 bridge across the Columbia River, mark the site where Lewis and Clark camped in December 1805 before heading south in search of better weather—which is about the only thing they never found on their epic trip.

feet above the Pacific Ocean. The more impressively photogenic North Head Lighthouse, on the ocean side of the peninsula a mile north of the museum, is the oldest on the West Coast.

The entire 1,882-acre area around the cape, including miles of beaches backed by rugged cliffs, is protected from development within **Cape Disappointment State Park** (360/642-3029), which has hiking, camping, and overnight lodgings in historic quarters next to North Head Lighthouse.

In recent years there have been a number of developments building on the area's Lewis and Clark connections, including the eight-mile Discovery Trail, which heads north to the town of Long Beach, and a series of thought-provoking installations by architect Maya Lin (creator of the Washington, D.C., Vietnam Veterans Memorial). Called the Confluence Project, and located mostly along the riverfront east of the museum, these works all deal with the coming together of the natural and man-made worlds, as well as the interaction of explorers and Native Americans. The installations range from boardwalks and interpretive trails (lined in places by quotations from Lewis and Clark's diaries) to a sculptural basalt "fish-cleaning" table.

The nearest services to Cape Disappointment—gas stations and a couple of cafés—are two miles away, back on US-101 in the rough-and-tumble fishing port of **Ilwaco,** where you can also enjoy the sophisticated yet simple and fresh seafood prepared at **Pelicano Restaurant** (177 Howerton Way SE; 360/642-4034), on the harbor.

Southeast of Ilwaco, toward the Oregon border, US-101 winds along the north bank of the Columbia River, giving good views of the mighty river's five-mile-wide mouth.

OREGON

Rarely losing sight of the Pacific Ocean during its 340-mile jaunt along the Oregon coast, US-101 winds past rockbound coast, ancient forests, and innumerable towns and villages. While the region also has its share of strip towns and places where the timber boom went bust, the beach loops, historic restorations, and more state parks per mile than any place in the country soften its few hard edges. Every 20 miles or so, you'll pass through attractive, if moderately touristy, towns populated by at most a few thousand people, but as a general rule it's the mileage between these hamlets that explains why most people visit: to take in one of the most dramatic meetings of rock and tide in the world.

Starting in the north along the Columbia River at historic **Astoria,** one of the oldest settlements in the western United States, the route winds along the ocean past the very different beachfront hamlets of **Seaside** and **Cannon Beach** before edging slightly inland through the rich dairy lands of **Tillamook County.** Midway along, the popular vacation spots of **Lincoln City, Newport,** and **Florence** form the most developed corridor along the coast, but it's still easy to reach unpeopled stretches, especially at the remarkable **Oregon Dunes** stretching to the south. The dunes end abruptly at the heavily industrial port of **Coos Bay,** beyond which the natural beauty returns with a string of state parks and the diverse coastal towns of **Bandon, Port Orford, Gold Beach,** and **Brookings.**

By state law, there is no self-service gasoline in Oregon; all stations have attendants who pump the gas for you. There's no sales tax, either.

Astoria

The oldest American city west of the Rockies, **Astoria** (pop. 9,477) is an upbeat mix of lovingly preserved past and busy contemporary commerce. Houses perched atop high hills overlook the Columbia River, creating a favorite backdrop for Hollywood movies. Despite its picturesque appearance, Astoria supports an active commercial fishing fleet, and dozens of tugboats guide tankers and container ships across the treacherous sandbars. Founded by and named after fur-trade magnate John Jacob Astor in 1811, Astoria protected the tenuous American claim to the Pacific coast until the opening of the Oregon Trail brought substantial settlement. By the turn of the 20th century, Astoria was still Oregon's second-largest city, but the downturn in both salmon fishing and logging since the end of World War II has caused an economic decline that, as always, town officials look to tourism to overcome.

Much as Forks, Washington, has benefited from its connections with the *Twilight* books and films, Astoria gets a boost in tourism numbers thanks to its starring role in the 1980s Steven Spielberg teen adventure film *The Goonies.*

US-101 crosses the Columbia River on the toll-free, high-level Astoria-Megler Bridge, completed in 1966, which drops you at the west end of the downtown waterfront. To get a sense of the lay of the land, follow the signs along 16th Street up Coxcomb Hill to the **Astoria Column** (daily dawn–dusk; $1 per car) for a view of the Columbia meeting the ocean, the coastal plain south to Tillamook Head, and the snowcapped Cascade Range (including, on a clear day, Mt. St. Helens) on the eastern horizon. A mosaic chronicling local history is wrapped like a ribbon around the column, tracing the many significant events in the town's past. A spiral staircase climbs to the top.

To find out about local issues and current events on the northern Oregon coast, pick up a copy of the excellent **Daily Astorian** newspaper, or tune to commercial-free **KMUN 91.5 FM** for NPR news and diverse programming.

Back downtown **Flavel House Museum** (daily; $5; 441 8th St.) is a Queen Anne–style Victorian showplace restored as an elegantly furnished museum of Astoria's first millionaire, Columbia River pilot George Flavel. A half mile east, near the foot of 17th Street on the north side of waterfront

Marine Drive, the **Columbia River Maritime Museum** (daily; $10; 503/325-2323) displays a large and very impressive collection that tells the story of the lifeblood of this community: the Columbia River.

Fortify yourself at one of the many good seafood places along the water, starting at the funky, ever-popular **Columbian Café** (1114 Marine Dr.; 503/325-2233), where chef Uriah Hulsey prepares all sorts of ultra-fresh food in an impossibly cramped galley kitchen. Meals are massive yet reasonably priced, so be sure to arrive with an appetite; breakfast and lunch are served Wednesday–Sunday, dinner Wednesday–Saturday. Another Astoria eating option is the casual **Ship Inn** (503/325-0033), serving halibut fish-and-chips under the bridge at Marine Drive and 2nd Street. Foodies might want to visit adjacent **Josephson's Smokehouse** (106 Marine Dr.; 503/325-2190) to sample the delicious array of smoked salmon, which is prepared on the premises and sold all over the country.

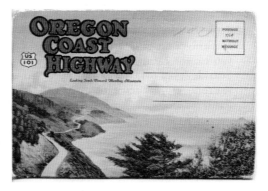

To absorb a full portion of Astoria's addictive ambience, stay the night at the riverview **Crest Motel** ($65 and up; 5366 Leif Erickson Dr.; 503/325-3141), three miles east of town along US-30, or in town at the luxurious and historic **Hotel Elliott** ($129 and up; 357 12th St.; 877/378-1924). Astoria also has a handful of nice B&Bs like the 1890s **Astoria Inn Bed and Breakfast** ($80 and up; 3391 Irving Ave.; 503/325-8153).

Fort Clatsop

In the conifer forests six miles south of Astoria and three miles east of US-101, and part of the extensive Lewis and Clark National Historical Park, the **Fort Clatsop National Memorial** (daily; $3 per person; 503/861-2471) is a credible reconstruction of the encampment Lewis and Clark and company constructed during the winter of 1805–1806. Now the centerpiece of the sprawling, multi-state Lewis and Clark National Historical Park, Fort Clatsop has been fully (and in many ways more accurately) rebuilt after a 2005 fire destroyed the first (circa 1955) replica. The fort itself is joined by a range of exhibits in the visitors center. A longer (13-mile round-trip) trail leads to the coast, and summertime costumed rangers help conjure the travails of two centuries ago. The expedition spent three miserable months here, mingling occasionally with the native Clatsop and Chinook tribes but mostly growing moldy in the incessant rain and damp while being bitten by fleas, sewing new moccasins, and making salt in preparation for the return journey across the continent.

Fort Stevens, off US-101 on the way to Fort Clatsop, was the only continental U.S. fortification bombed during World War II, sustaining a shelling from a Japanese submarine on June 21, 1942.

Gearhart

In between burly Astoria and the boisterous beach resort of Seaside, but a world away from its neighbors in terms of character and ambience, the tiny town of **Gearhart** (pop. 1,462) was the summer vacation home of influential chef and cookbook author James Beard. Beard's culinary legacy lives on in the **Pacific Way Bakery & Cafe** (601 Pacific Way; 503/738-0245), a half mile west of US-101, which offers the coast's best coffees and croissants, along with four-star lunches and dinners. Like many places along the Oregon coast, it's closed Tuesday and Wednesday.

Seaside

Nothing along the Oregon coast prepares you for the carnival ambience of downtown **Seaside** (pop. 6,457), one of Oregon's oldest seafront resorts. Ben Holladay, who built a resort here in the 1870s, included a racetrack, zoo, and plush hotel to lure Portlanders to ride his rail line to the beach. Come during spring break, or on a weekend during July or August, and join the 50,000 or more visitors wandering among the saltwater-taffy stands and video-game arcades along Broadway, or cruising the concrete boardwalk (called The Prom) along the beach.

statue of explorers Lewis and Clark at the end of the trail in Seaside

centennial commemorative stamp

Where Broadway meets the beach, a small traffic circle known locally as The Turnaround is marked by a statue and a sign proclaiming the town "The End of the Lewis and Clark Trail." South of here, between Beach Drive and The Prom, is a replica of the Lewis and Clark salt cairn, where the explorers boiled seawater nonstop for seven weeks to produce enough salt to preserve meat for their return trip east. From the south end of Seaside, you can follow a challenging but very rewarding five-mile trail over Tillamook Head to Ecola State Park.

A half mile north of downtown, housed in a wood-shingled old motor court on the banks of the Necanicum River, the **Seaside International Hostel** (930 N. Holladay Dr.; 503/738-7911) has dorm beds, private rooms, canoes and kayaks, an espresso bar, and nightly movies. There are dozens of motels and a handful of B&Bs in Seaside, booked solid in summer and serene, verging on lonely, come wintertime.

This part of the Pacific Coast marks the beginning of our **Oregon Trail** route, which runs east across the country along a combination of US-6, US-20, and US-26. Coverage of the route begins on page 584; **Portland,** just over an hour or so inland from Seaside and Cannon Beach, is covered on pages 590–591.

Ecola State Park

Just north of Cannon Beach, a mile south of the junction between US-101 and US-26 from Portland, the rainforested access road through **Ecola State Park** (day use only; $5 per car; 503/436-2844) leads you to one of the most photographed views on the coast: Looking south you can see Haystack Rock and Cannon Beach with Neahkahnie Mountain looming above them. Out to sea, the sight of **Tillamook Rock Lighthouse** to the northwest is also striking. Operational from 1881 to 1957, the lighthouse is now used as a repository for the ashes of people who've been cremated.

The rest of Ecola State Park protects a series of rugged headlands stretching for nine miles along the coast, with many forested hiking trails, including some of the most scenic portions of the Oregon Coast Trail system. The park also marks the southernmost extent of Lewis and Clark's cross-country expedition. Clark and a few other members of the Corps of Discovery expedition traversed the area in search of supplements to their diet of hardtack and dried salmon. The word *"ecola"* means whale in the Chinookan tongue and was affixed to this region by the Lewis and Clark expedition, who found one of these leviathans washed up on a beach. They happily bought 300 pounds of tangy whale blubber from local Indians, but these days you'd better bring your own lunch to picnic atop bluffs with sweeping views of the rock-strewn Pacific. The view from the top of **Tillamook Head,** which rises 1,200 feet above the sea at the heart of the park, was memorialized by explorer William Clark as "the grandest and most pleasing prospect" he had ever beheld.

Cannon Beach

Unlike many Oregon coast towns, **Cannon Beach** (pop. 1,690) is hidden from the highway, but it's one place you won't want to miss. Though it's little more than a stone's throw south of boisterous Seaside, Cannon Beach has long been known as an artists' colony, and while it has grown considerably in recent years thanks to its popularity as a weekend escape from Portland, it retains a peaceful, rustic atmosphere.

Cannon Beach

Every summer, Cannon Beach hosts one of the largest and most enjoyable **sand castle competitions** on the West Coast, with some 10,000 spectators and as many as 1,000 participants turning out with their buckets and spades. In terms of traditional tourist attractions, there's not a lot to do, but Cannon Beach is an unbeatable place in which to stop and unwind, or

Haystack Rock

to take long walks along the nine-mile strand and then retreat indoors to the many good galleries, cafés, and restaurants. For breakfast or brunch, fill up on eggs Benedict at **The Lazy Susan Cafe** (closed Tues.; 126 N. Hemlock Street; 503/436-2816); it also serves a stupendous array of ice cream at its "scoop shop" up the street. Another great, casual gourmet place to eat is **Ecola Seafoods** (208 N. Spruce St.; 503/436-9130), which serves locally caught fish and shellfish—including an excellent $5 chowder.

Reasonably priced rooms near the beach and town can be found at the oceanfront **Sea Sprite at Haystack Rock** ($99 and up; 280 S. Nebesna St.; 503/436-2266).

South of Cannon Beach, the beach loop runs along a spectacular grouping of volcanic basalt plugs, notably 235-foot-high **Haystack Rock.** Elsewhere along the Oregon coast, there are at least two more geological outcrops called Haystack Rock, a bigger one off Cape Kiwanda and another down near Bandon.

Neahkahnie Mountain and Oswald West State Park

South of Cannon Beach, US-101 rises high above the Pacific. Nowhere else along the Oregon coast does the roadbed offer such a sweeping ocean view. Soaring another thousand feet above the highway is **Neahkahnie Mountain,** which offers unsurpassed views up and down the coast. About 10 miles south of Cannon Beach at **Oswald West State Park** (800/551-6949), a half-mile trail winds beneath the highway through an ancient forest to driftwood-laden (and surfer-friendly) Short Sands Beach and the tidepools of Smuggler's Cove. Named for an early governor of Oregon who successfully proposed preserving and protecting the beaches of Oregon as state (rather than private) property, Oswald West State Park is a good start for longer hikes, to weather-beaten Cape Falcon or across US-101 to the summit of Neahkahnie Mountain.

South of Neahkahnie Mountain, and thus spared much of the stormy coastal weather (annual rainfall hereabouts averages more than 80 inches), is the upscale resort town of **Manzanita.** Nearby **Nehalem Bay State Park** (503/368-5154) has a large campground with hundreds of sites and plenty of hot showers. US-101 continues through a series of small towns before winding inland past the sloughs and dairy country along Tillamook Bay.

Tillamook

Tillamook (pop. 4,400), where cows outnumber people, sprawls over lush grasslands at the southern end of Tillamook Bay. Its motto, "Land of cheese, trees, and ocean breeze," conjures a clear sense of a place where the high school football team is cheered on by shouts of "Go Cheesemakers!" Tillamook (a Salish word meaning "land of many waters") is dominated by the **Tillamook Cheese Factory** at the north end of town, one of the busiest tourist draws in the state. Inside, a self-guided tour with informational placards traces Tillamook cheese-making from the last century to the present, and a glassed-in observation area lets you watch the stuff being made and packaged.

Tillamook's other attraction is east of US-101 and south of town. One of the world's largest wooden structures—296 feet wide, 1,072 feet long, and nearly 200 feet tall, enclosing more than seven acres of open-span floor space—has been preserved as the **Tillamook Air Museum** (daily; $9 adults; 503/842-1130). Built in 1942, the structure is now a museum telling the story of the World War II surveillance blimps kept here by the U.S. Navy. There

Tillamook Cheese Factory

are also displays about other dirigible craft (like the ill-fated *Hindenburg*) as well as a world-class collection of vintage airplanes (from MiG fighters to an elegant, twin-tailed P-38 Lightning), plus a theater and a restaurant, all making for a fascinating and unusual stop. The building used to be one of a pair of hangars, but the other one burned down in 1992.

Three Capes Loop

US-101 veers inland for 50 miles between Tillamook and Lincoln City, the next sizable town south. If time and weather are on your side, head west along the coast via the well-signed, 40-mile-long **Three Capes Loop.** Running northwest from Tillamook, the loop reaches the mouth of Tillamook Bay at **Cape Meares,** which has a restored 1890 lighthouse and an oddly contorted Sitka spruce known as the Octopus Tree.

Heading south through the coastal villages of **Oceanside** and **Netarts,** the loop proceeds through dairy country until it climbs onto the shoulder of **Cape Lookout,** where a small sign proclaiming Wildlife Viewing Area marks the beginning of a 2.5-mile trail that leads through an ancient forest to the tip of the cape, 100-plus feet above the water. Besides the coastal panorama, in winter and spring this is a prime place to view passing gray whales. From the trailhead, the middle path leads to the cape, while others to the left and

Seven miles south of Tillamook, a turnoff east follows a bumpy, one-mile access road leading to the highest waterfall in Oregon's Coast Range, 319-foot **Munson Creek Falls.** From the parking area at the end of the road, a short trail leads to this year-round cascade.

right lead down to the water. **Cape Lookout State Park** (503/842-4981) has the area's most popular campground, where tent sites, yurts, and cabins come with hot showers and other creature comforts.

The Oregon coast's most famous promontory, **Cape Kiwanda,** sees some of the state's wildest surf battering the sandstone headland. Across from the cape is yet another **Haystack Rock,** this one being a 327-foot-tall sea stack, a half mile offshore. Along the beach south of the cape, surfers ride waves while fisherfolk skid their small dories along the sands most afternoons—a sight worth hanging around to see.

The southernmost settlement on this scenic alternative to US-101 is neighboring **Pacific City,** where two great places to eat, **The Grateful Bread Bakery** (503/965-7337) and the **Riverhouse** (503/965-6722), sit beachside on Brooten Road.

Lincoln City

The most developed section of the Oregon coast stretches for miles along US-101 through **Lincoln City** (pop. 7,930), seven miles of strip malls, outlet stores, fast-food franchises, and motels. With more than 1,000 oceanside rooms, Lincoln City does offer some of the coast's cheapest lodging, especially in the off-season when sign after sign advertises rooms for as low as $35 a night. Along with inexpensive accommodations, Lincoln City has some great places to eat. Start the day with a huge breakfast at **The Beach Dog Café** (1266 SW 50th St.; 541/996-3647), and after a day on the beach or in the forests, tuck into some four-star fish tacos, chowders, or battered seafood at **J's Fish 'N' Chips** (1800 SE US-101; 541/994-4445).

South of Lincoln City, 2.5 miles east of US-101, the **Drift Creek Covered Bridge** is the oldest of some 50 such structures in the state.

One more unforgettable culinary attraction hereabouts sits five miles northeast of Lincoln City, just east of US-101 on Hwy-18, the main road to and from Portland: the **Otis Café** (1259 Salmon River Hwy.; 541/994-2813), which immortalizes American road food, offering excellent waffles and other breakfast treats along with epicurean lunches and fresh berry pies for dessert. The Otis Café is open for breakfast, lunch, and dinner daily.

Seven miles south of Lincoln City, a sign announces the **Salishan Spa & Golf Resort** (800/452-2300), a beautifully landscaped rustic golf resort with a five-star dining room and a surprisingly affordable more-casual restaurant, **The Sun Room.** Down the hill across US-101, **Siletz Bay** is a bird-watcher's paradise, where hawks and herons and thousands of other seabirds (along with chinook salmon and cutthroat trout) are protected within a federal wildlife refuge.

Depoe Bay

Depoe Bay was originally known as Depot Bay, named after a local Siletz Indian who worked at the local U.S. Army depot and called himself Charlie Depot.

Depoe Bay has an appeal, but so much of its natural beauty is obscured from the highway by gift shops or intruded upon by traffic that you've got to know where to look. In his book *Blue Highways,* William Least Heat-Moon wrote "Depoe Bay used to be a picturesque fishing village; now it was just picturesque." While it's true that most of the commercial fishing is long gone, you can still park your car along the highway and walk out on the bridge to watch sportfishing boats move through the narrow channel to what the *Guinness Book of Records* rates as the world's smallest navigable natural harbor. South of the bridge is another record-setter, the Oregon coast's largest secondhand bookstore, the **Channel Bookstore** (541/765-2352).

The **Sea Hag** restaurant (541/765-2734), on US-101 in downtown Depoe Bay, is a time-tested breakfast place, and people drive for miles to enjoy the pies at the **Spouting Horn** (541/765-2261), overlooking the harbor. For a place to stay, try the very popular **Inn at Arch Rock** ($69 and up; 70 NW Sunset St.; 800/767-1835).

Cape Foulweather and the Devil's Punchbowl

Between Depoe Bay and Newport, the roadside scenery along US-101 and the parallel "old road," now signed as the Otter Crest Loop, is dominated by miles of broad beaches and sandstone bluffs, including the 500-foot headland of **Cape Foulweather,** named by Capt. James Cook and offering a 360-degree coastal panorama. The Otter Crest Loop has frequently been closed by slides and reconstruction efforts, but you can reach it from many access roads. With fine old bridges and numerous vistas, it's a great drive—or bicycle route.

Farther south, mid way between Depoe Bay and Newport, the aptly named **Devil's Punchbowl** gives a ringside seat on a frothy confrontation between rock and tide. In the parking area you'll find a small lunch café (a branch of Newport's **Mo's**), whose claim to fame remains a visit from Bruce Springsteen on June 11, 1987.

Newport

Another old fishing community turned tourist nexus, **Newport** (pop. 9,989) became popular in the 1860s on the strength of sweet-tasting Yaquina Bay oysters, which were in demand from San Francisco to New York City and are still available at local restaurants. Oysters, crabs, and clams, along with sea otters, sea lions, sharks, and seabirds, are the inside the aquarium tunnel at the Oregon Coast Aquarium

stars of the show at the large and modern **Oregon Coast Aquarium** (daily; $16; 541/867-3474), south of Newport across the Yaquina Bay Bridge. The aquarium includes an aquatic aviary, where tufted puffins and other shorebirds cavort in a simulated rockbound coastal habitat, and over 40,000 square feet of similarly eco-friendly exhibits, many of them outdoors.

On the north side of the US-101 bridge over Yaquina Bay, turn onto Hurbert Street and head for the bayfront, where boatyards and fish-packing plants service a working harbor. Though it's still one of the state's largest fishing ports, much of Newport's bayfront has been consumed by souvenir shops, a wax museum, a Ripley's Believe It or Not, and other tourist traps. But you'll find the original **Mo's** (622 SW Bay Blvd.; 541/265-2979), a locally famous seafood restaurant.

North of the harbor is **Nye Beach,** an interesting mélange of old-fashioned beach houses and destination resorts on the western side of US-101. Nye Beach is home to hotels, motels, and the bohemian **Sylvia Beach Hotel** ($70–up; 267 NW Cliff St.; 541/265-5428), *the* place to stay in Newport for anyone of literary bent. If you can't afford the private rooms—with decor evocative of different authors—there are dormitory bunk beds for around $40 a night. All rates include breakfast, and sumptuous dinners are available, too.

> The coast and inland forests along the Siletz River near Depoe Bay and Newport were the primary location of the Ken Kesey novels and films *One Flew Over the Cuckoo's Nest* and *Sometimes a Great Notion.*

> The old-growth forests of the **Drift Creek Wilderness** east of Waldport are prime nesting areas for the endangered northern spotted owl, whose numbers are still declining.

Waldport

If you want to avoid lines and general tourist bustle, **Waldport** is a nice alternative to the resort towns surrounding it. Tourism is low-key here, and you can still sense the vestiges of the resource-based economy, a by-product of the town's proximity to rich timber stands and superlative fishing. Stop along

US-101 at the **Alsea Bay Historic Interpretive Center** (541/563-2002) for interesting exhibits on coastal transportation and the local Alsea tribe, as well as a telescope trained on waterfowl and seals in the bay. The center sits at the southwest foot of the modern span that, in 1991, replaced the historic (circa-1936) art deco–style bridge. From the north end of the bridge, you can follow Hwy-34 seven miles upstream to **JD's Café at Kozy Kove** (541/528-3725), a floating restaurant with good food and a bucolic riverside ambience.

A little more than two miles south of Waldport, **Cape Cod Cottages** ($65–185; 4150 SW Pacific Coast Hwy.; 541/563-2106) is a good choice for location and comfort. Four miles south of Waldport, halfway to Yachats, **Beachside State Park** (541/563-3220) has a very popular campground, with hot showers, RV hookups, and a lovely stretch of sandy beach.

Yachats

On the way into **Yachats** (pop. 690; pronounced "YA-hots"), beach loops on either side of the Yachats River give a sense of why the area is called "the gem of the Oregon coast." It's a great place to wander and get lost and found again, especially at the beautiful Ocean Road State Natural Site, where incredible views along a one-mile loop road look out over crashing waves, tidepools, blowholes, and, in winter, gray whales migrating offshore.

Back in town, for the past 30-plus years, **Leroy's Blue Whale** (580 Hwy-101 N., 541/547-3399), on US-101, has been serving breakfast, lunch, and dinner every day, featuring fluffy pancakes, fresh chowders, and fine fish-and-chips.

The word "cottage" is a popular lodging label around Yachats, usually referring to a moderately priced, self-contained cabin or duplex with kitchen. On US-101 there are a half dozen different cottage complexes, each fronting the beach. If you want more than a simple place to spend the night, the **Oregon House** ($65 and up; 541/547-3329) on US-101 nine miles south of Yachats has spacious apartment-like rooms, some with fireplaces and ocean views, and all with access to the well-tended grounds and trails leading down the bluffs to a gem of a sandy cove.

Cape Perpetua

For more than 300 miles along the Oregon coast, US-101 abounds with national forests, state parks, and viewpoints. But unless you have your whole lifetime to spend here, **Cape Perpetua,** two miles south of Yachats, deserves most of your attention. Stop first at the **Cape Perpetua Visitor Center** (541/547-3289), just east of US-101, for seacoast views and exhibits on forestry and area history. From the visitors center, trails lead across the highway past wind-bent trees, piles of seashells and other artifacts left behind by native peoples, excellent tidepools, and two rock formations: Spouting Horn and the Devil's Churn. During stormy seas, both shoot huge spouts of foam into the air. The friendly folks at the visitors center can also point you toward Cape Perpetua's very attractive campground.

You can reach the top of 800-foot-high Cape Perpetua itself by following a two-mile-long road, marked by Cape Perpetua Viewpoint signs and leaving

US-101 100 yards or so north of the visitors center. Once atop the cape, walk the **Whispering Spruce Trail,** a half-mile loop around the rim of the promontory that yields, on a clear day, 150-mile views of the Oregon coast from a rustic, WPA-built stone observation point.

Heceta Head and the Sea Lion Caves

Halfway between Cape Perpetua and Florence, a small bridge just south of Carl G. Washburne Memorial State Park marks the turnoff to **Heceta Head** lighthouse, perhaps the most photographed beacon in the United States. Built in 1894, it was named for the Spanish mariner who is credited with being the first European to set foot in the region. You'll have to be content with gazing at it across the cove from a small but rarely crowded beach, unless you stay at the quaint old lighthouse keeper's quarters, restored as an unforgettable B&B ($133 and up; 541/547-3696).

A half-mile south of Heceta Head lighthouse, 11 miles north of Florence, traffic along US-101 slows to a stop at the gift shop that serves as the entrance to **Sea Lion Caves** (daily; $12). You can ride an elevator down to the world's largest sea cave, the only mainland rookery for the Steller sea lion. Fall and winter offer the best times to see (and smell!) these animals, which throng together here during mating season. When the weather's nice, you can often watch them swimming in the ocean (for free, without the seal smells . . .) from a viewpoint 100 yards up US-101.

Florence

If first and last impressions are enduring, **Florence** is truly blessed. As you enter the city from the north, US-101 climbs high above the ocean; coming from the south, travelers are greeted by the graceful **Siuslaw River Bridge,** perhaps the most impressive of a handful of WPA-built spans designed by

SIUSLAW RIVER BRIDGE, FLORENCE

LOOKING TOWARD TEN MILE LAKE AND SUTTON LAKE

Conde McCullough and decorated with his trademark Egyptian obelisks and art deco stylings. Unfortunately, first impressions feel a little misleading, since much of what you can see from US-101 is a bland highway sprawl of motels, gas stations, and franchised restaurants.

The best part of Florence, **Old Town,** is just upstream from that landmark bridge, along the north bank of the Siuslaw River. Here, among Bay Street's three blocks of interesting boutiques and galleries, you'll find a number of cafés and seafood restaurants. Old Town Florence is also home to the very welcoming **Edwin K B&B** ($125–200; 1155 Bay St.; 541/997-8360), a lovely white Craftsman-style home built in 1914 by one of the town's founders.

Back along US-101, car culture fans will relish the chance to eat burgers and fries at **Bliss' Hot Rod Grill,** a mile north of Old Town (1179 US-101;

541/997-6726), where walls are covered in old road signs and some of the spacious booths are made from classic 1950s American cars.

"Dune Country": Oregon's Sahara

For nearly 50 miles south of Florence, US-101 has an extensive panorama of oceanfront dunes. Though the dunes are often obscured from view by forests, roadside signs indicate access roads to numerous dunescapes on both sides of the highway. Coming from the north, the first of these access points is **Jessie M. Honeyman Memorial State Park,** three miles south of Florence, where rhododendrons line a trail leading to a 150-foot-high dune overlooking a mirage-like lake.

Before setting out on any extended exploration, your first stop should be the USFS-run **Oregon Dunes National Recreation Area Visitors Center** (541/271-3611) at the junction of US-101 and Hwy-38 in **Reedsport,** along the Umpqua River midway between Florence and Coos Bay at the heart of the dunes. The helpful rangers can provide detailed information on hiking and camping throughout the park. Reedsport itself has a line of motels and burger joints—**Don's Main Street Family Restaurant** (2115 Winchester Ave.; 541/271-2032), on US-101, has legions of fans. You'll find one more interesting option just north of Reedsport in the **Gardiner Guest House** (401 Front St.; 541/543-0210), which offers comfortable B&B rooms in a restored Victorian home.

Perhaps the best introduction to the bewildering geography of the dunes region is **Umpqua Dunes,** nine miles south of the Reedsport visitors center. Another popular walk starts from Eel Creek Campground, heading for just under three miles across small marshes and conifer groves en route to the sea, negotiating lunar-like dunes soaring 300–500 feet—some of the tallest in the world. Another nice trek leaves from **Tahkenitch Lake,** a popular largemouth bass fishing spot north of Gardiner, and gives a more in-depth look at the dunes' diverse flora and fauna, including swans and (very rarely!) black bears.

Giant rhododendrons and tumble-down shacks that rent out dune buggies and ATVs line US-101 between Florence and Coos Bay. Dune buggy tours ranging from peaceful to exhilarating are offered by **Sandland Adventures** (541/997-8087), less than a mile south of Florence's Siuslaw River Bridge.

Fans of Frank Herbert's ecological sci-fi saga *Dune* may already know that the stories were inspired by the Oregon Dunes, south of Florence.

Coos Bay

Even if you race right through, it's quite apparent that **Coos Bay** (pop. 15,967), once the world's largest lumber port, retains a core of heavy industry. Many of the big mills have closed, and one has been replaced by **The Mill Casino,** a resort complex operated by native Coquille Indian tribe, but you can still watch huge piles of wood chips, the harbor's number-one export, being loaded onto factory ships in the harbor east of US-101. The chips are sent to Asia, where they're turned into paper. (One chip-ship that didn't make

Behind the Coos Bay visitors bureau, a monument remembers the region's favorite son, middle- and long-distance runner Steve Prefontaine, who electrified the athletic world before his death in a 1975 car wreck, at the age of 24. An annual 10K memorial run is held in September.

it into the harbor, the 640-foot-long *New Carissa,* wrecked in a 1999 storm and sat on the Coos Bay beach for years.)

There's very good seafood and other meals available at **Shark Bites** (240 S. Broadway; 541/269-7475), on US-101, while microbrews are served at the **Blue Heron Bistro** (100 Commercial Ave.; 541/267-3933), across from the visitors bureau. There's no shortage of easy-to-find lodging, including **Motel 6** ($45 and up; 1445 Bayshore Dr.; 541/267-7171) on US-101.

Shore Acres State Park

Nine miles west of Coos Bay, in the busy commercial and sport-fishing port of **Charleston,** you'll be welcomed to town by an unlikely sight: a flipper-waving statue of 1960s-era advertising icon Charlie the Tuna (of StarKist seafood fame).

The historical antecedents for Coos Bay port development were laid a century ago by the Simpson Lumber Company, whose ships transported Oregon logs around the world. The ships returned with exotic seeds that were planted in the Simpson estate's garden, 12 miles west of Coos Bay via the Cape Arago Highway. Though the Simpson house burned to the ground in 1921, the five acres of formal gardens are still a floral fantasia, now open to the public as **Shore Acres State Park** (daily 8 AM–dusk). Besides the formal gardens, which are illuminated during the Christmas holiday season, there's an observation tower above wave-battered bluffs and a trail down to a delightful beach.

On the way to Shore Acres from Coos Bay is **Sunset Bay State Park,** perhaps Oregon's best swimming beach. South of Shore Acres is **Cape Arago State Park,** complete with tidepools and seals (and seal pups in springtime) lounging on offshore rocks. Mostly level trails lead along the coastline from Shore Acres to Sunset Bay and Cape Arago State Parks, and if you're tempted to stay overnight and explore the lovely region, consider taking advantage of one of Oregon's best-kept secrets: the roomy, tent-like **yurts** available for overnight rental (around $40; 800/452-5687) at Sunset Bay and in a dozen other state park beauty spots.

Bandon

There's no sharper contrast on the Oregon coast than the difference between industrial Coos Bay and earthy **Bandon** (pop. 3,066), 24 miles to the south. Here, in the **Old Town** section along the banks of the Coquille River, are several blocks of galleries, crafts shops, and fine restaurants, marked by a gateway arch off US-101. Start a tour of Old Town at the corner of 1st and Baltimore, where Big Wheel General Store houses the **Bandon Driftwood Museum** (daily; free), which gives a good sense of Bandon's back-to-the-land, hippie ethos. A more academic introduction to the town and region can be had at the **Bandon Historical Society Museum** (Mon.–Sat., daily in summer; $2; 270 Fillmore Ave.;

FACE ROCK, CAT AND KITTENS, BANDON BEACH

PHOTO BY WESLEY ANDREWS

541/347-2164), in the old City Hall along US-101. Its exhibits on area history, cranberries, and local color are artfully done, and the building is easy to find, so be sure to stop. South of town, **Beach Loop Drive** runs along a ridge overlooking a fantastic assemblage of coastal monoliths.

For fish-and-chips along the waterfront, the **Bandon Fish Market** (249 1st St. SE; 541/347-4282) is cheap, cheerful, and very very good; a block to the east, looking more like a tackle shop than a restaurant, **Tony's Crab Shack** (541/347-2875) is another local landmark, famous for fish tacos, chowders, and silky crab sandwiches.

Outside of town, the exclusive and expensive (but open to the public) **Bandon Dunes Golf Resort** ($100

Bandon Beach

and up; 541/347-4380 or 888/345-6008) has been drawing raves from golfers, well-heeled vacationers, and landscape architects alike. Designed to preserve and enhance the "natural" scenery in the style of Scottish "links" courses rather than the anodyne green swaths that characterize most suburban country club courses, Bandon Dunes offers golf ($75–225 per round for resort guests), select accommodations, and a nice restaurant.

South of Bandon, 9.5 miles north of Port Orford, **Cape Blanco** is considered—by Oregonians, at least—the westernmost point of land in the contiguous United States. Named by early Spanish explorers for the white shells encrusting the 245-foot cliff face, the cape is also the site of Oregon's oldest (circa-1870) and highest lighthouse. The headland offers great views, and its windswept exposure draws pilots of radio-controlled model planes and gliders. If you need to warm your innards afterwards, stop in at the straightforward **Greasy Spoon Café** (541/348-2514) on US-101 in nearby Langlois for a cup of coffee and some classic biscuits-and-gravy.

Port Orford and Humbug Mountain

Pastoral sheep ranches, cranberry bogs, berry fields, and Christmas tree farms dominate the 25-mile stretch south of Bandon, but as you pull into **Port Orford** (pop. 1,133), you can't help but notice a huge volcanic plug abutting the crescent-shaped shoreline. Known as **Battle Rock,** in memory of a battle (re-enacted every 4th of July) in which early settlers fought off a party of hostile Indians, the rock is impressive from the harbor below, while a trail climbs up to the windblown summit. Due to the southwest orientation, which subjects the harbor to turbulent winds and constant waves, fishing boats have to be lowered into the water by crane, but surfers (and kite-surfers and windsurfers) don't seem to mind.

People who keep track of these things say that tiny Port Orford is the "most westerly incorporated city in the continental United States." Others grant it the less-welcome title of "rainiest place on the Oregon coast."

A nice place to stay in Port Orford is the **Home by the Sea Bed and Breakfast** ($85–115; 444 Jackson St.; 541/332-2855 or 877/332-2855), within walking distance to town along yet another stunning stretch of Oregon coastline.

Six miles south of Port Orford you'll come to **Humbug Mountain State Park,** whose 1,756-foot elevation flanks the west side of the highway. It's one of the coast's highest peaks rising directly off the beach, and its steep contours and tree-covered slopes are best appreciated from the steep but well-maintained three-mile trail that climbs to the summit. The mountain's name may have been bestowed by prospectors who found that tales of gold deposits here were just "humbug"—but the views from the top are splendid.

Prehistoric Gardens

On the west side of the highway, midway between Port Orford and Gold Beach, you'll come across one of the Oregon coast's tackiest but most enduring and enjoyable tourist traps, the **Prehistoric Gardens** (daily; $10 adults; 541/332-4463). Standing out like a sore thumb on this otherwise unspoiled stretch of US-101, brightly colored, more or less life-sized dinosaur sculptures inhabit the evocatively lush green forest. Since 1953, when amateur paleontologist E. V. Nelson sculpted his first concrete *T. rex,* nearly two dozen more have been added to the forest menagerie.

Southern Oregon's coastal forests yield the increasingly rare and disease-threatened Port Orford cedar, a very valuable (up to $50,000 per tree) and very fragrant wood popular for use in Japanese home construction.

Gold Beach

Gold Beach was named for the nuggets mined from the area's black sands during the mid-19th century, but despite its name this is one coastal town where the action is definitely *away* from the beach. The **Rogue River** defines the northern city limits and is the town's economic raison d'être. During salmon season, Gold Beach hotels and restaurants fill up with anglers, while **jet-boat tours** of the wild river are also a draw. **Jerry's Rogue Jets** ($45 and up; 541/247-4571 or 800/451-3645), by the bridge at the north end of town, takes passengers upstream to the isolated hamlet of **Agness,** where a homespun mountain lodge serves family-style fried-chicken lunches and dinners (the food is not included in the price of the jet-boat ride). Other trips head farther upstream to the Rogue River rapids and the roadless wilderness areas of the **Siskiyou National Forest;** these cost $65–90.

Mt. Emily, just east of Brookings, was bombed by a submarine-launched Japanese seaplane in September 1942. Though the Japanese plans to ignite the entire coastline in a massive forest fire fizzled, the attack weakened a short-lived secession movement by southern Oregonians and northern Californians to establish a new state called Jefferson.

The usual motel rooms are available along US-101, but for a more memorable visit, try the **Tu Tu' Tun Lodge** ($135 and up; 96550 North Bank Rogue; 541/247-6664 or 800/864-6357). Set on a hill above the Rogue River, seven miles upstream from the coast, this upscale fishing lodge (pronounced "ta-TWO-tun") has plushly rustic rooms and a great restaurant.

Samuel H. Boardman State Scenic Corridor

Between Gold Beach and Brookings, US-101's windy, hilly roadbed is studded with the cliffside ocean vistas, giant conifers, and boomerang-shaped offshore rock formations of **Samuel H. Boardman State Scenic Corridor.** The park covers 12 of the "Fabulous 50" miles between the two towns, and all of the features come together at Natural Bridges Cove. Located just north of the Thomas Creek Bridge (the highest bridge in Oregon), this turnout is easy to miss despite being well signed because, from the highway, it appears to be simply a parking lot fronting some trees. From the south end of the parking lot, however, a short trail through an old-growth forest leads to a viewpoint several hundred feet above three natural rock archways standing out from an azure cove.

Brookings: Harris Beach State Park

The drive through the malled-over main drag of **Brookings** offers only fleeting glimpses of the Pacific, and if you're hoping for a first or last "Wow!" before or after the 300-plus other miles of coastal Oregon's scenic splendor, these few miles along the California border may be somewhat anticlimactic. That said, Brookings does have beautiful Azalea Park (which is gorgeous during the April–June spring bloom). The popular, welcoming beachfront B&B rooms at **Lowden's Beachfront Bed & Breakfast,** on Wollam Road just west of US-101 ($109 and up; 541/469-7045) offer direct access to a driftwood-strewn beach.

Just north of Brookings, one final piece of Oregon's abundant natural beauty has been preserved at **Harris Beach State Park,** across US-101 from the Oregon Welcome Center. Here you can walk down to a driftwood-laden beach and look out at Bird Island, where rare birds breed.

Heading south, just over the California border from Brookings lies Redwood National Park, truly one of the West Coast's great places.

CALIFORNIA

Stretching along the Pacific Ocean for roughly a thousand miles from top to tail, the California coast includes virgin wilderness, the cutting edge of cosmopolitan culture, and the full spectrum in between. For almost the entire way, coastal roads give quick and easy access to the best parts, with panoramic views appearing so often you'll simply give up trying to capture it all.

Starting in the north, the green forests of the Pacific Northwest continue well beyond the state border, forming a mountainous seaside landscape that lasts until the edge of metropolitan **San Francisco.** Along this stretch you'll find a number of old logging and fishing towns, varying from the burly blue-collar likes of **Eureka** and **Crescent City** to the upscale ambience of **Mendocino,** in and amongst endless acres of redwood forest.

At the approximate midpoint of the California coast sits **San Francisco,** deservedly ranked among the world's favorite cities. The 100 miles of coast stretching south from San Francisco hold numerous remnants of the Spanish and Mexican eras, exemplified by the town of **Monterey** and the beautiful mission at **Carmel.** Beyond here is another stretch of wild coastline, the rugged country of **Big Sur.**

Beyond the southern edge of Big Sur, opulent **Hearst Castle** marks the start of what most people consider Southern California, the rivers and trees of the north giving way to golden beaches, grassy bluffs, and considerably denser populations. A pair of very pleasant small cities, Midwestern-feeling **San Luis Obispo** and ritzy **Santa Barbara,** make excellent stops in themselves, smoothing the transition into the environs of **Los Angeles,** the unwieldy megalopolis that, seen from the I-5 freeway that links Los Angeles and **San Diego,** seems like one monstrous, 100-mile-long suburb. While it's true that the natural beauty that brought so many people to Southern California in the first place is increasingly endangered, some lovely, almost untouched places remain, hidden away but within easy access of the fast lane. We've pointed them out; enjoy them while they last.

Jedediah Smith Redwoods State Park

The northernmost of the great redwood groves, **Jedediah Smith Redwoods State Park** covers nearly 10,000 acres of virgin forest along the banks of the Smith River. Stretching east of US-101, and most easily accessible from US-199, the park offers over 20 miles of usually uncrowded hiking trails through the pristine wilderness; it is considered by many the most perfect of all the redwood forests. One of the most enjoyable trails leads through **Stout Grove,** past tall trees and a number of summertime swimming holes along the Smith River.

There's also a good **campground** (800/444-7275) with hot showers. For fans of roadside kitsch, there's one unique spot along US-101 in the hamlet of Smith River, 15 miles north of Crescent City: **Ship Ashore** (707/487-3141), a gift shop, restaurant, campground and motel along US-101, marked by a grounded but still handsome 1920s yacht, inside which is a gift shop and seashell museum.

The Smith River and Jedediah Smith Redwoods State Park were named in memory of the legendary mountain man Jedediah Strong Smith, who in 1826 at the age of 27 led the first party of Americans overland to California. Smith also blazed the first trail over South Pass through the Rocky Mountains, later used by the Oregon Trail pioneers.

Crescent City

The county seat and only incorporated city in Del Norte County, **Crescent City** (pop. 8,805) is best treated as a base from which to explore the surrounding wilderness. The foggy weather that helps the redwoods thrive makes the city fairly depressing and gray, and what character it developed since its founding in the 1850s has been eroded by storms; a giant tsunami, caused by the 1964 earthquake off Alaska, destroyed much of the city. The more recent tsunami unleashed by the 2011 quake in Sendai, Japan, was less destructive but drowned one man and caused millions in damage to boats moored in the Crescent City harbor.

Crescent City includes the familiar lineup of motels and restaurants, plus local options like the **Beacon Burger** (160 Anchor Way; 707/464-6565), south of downtown. Sugar junkies will want to stop at the **Continental Bakery,** a great doughnut shop on US-101 (503 L St.; 707/465-5652). For overnight, one only-in-California option is the **Curly Redwood Lodge** ($56 and up; 701 S. Redwood Hwy./US-101 S. 707/464-2137), a nicely maintained 1950s motel made from a single, sawn-up redwood tree.

Outside Crescent City, California's most violent long-term criminals are kept behind bars in the state-of-the-art Pelican Bay State Prison, opened in 1989.

Del Norte Coast Redwoods State Park

Spreading south from the Jedediah Smith redwoods, **Del Norte Coast Redwoods State Park** runs along the Pacific Ocean (and US-101) for about eight miles, containing more than 6,000 acres of first- and second-growth redwoods as well as brilliant blooms of rhododendrons, azaleas, and spring wildflowers. Del Norte also protects miles of untouched coastline, the best stretch of which is accessible from the end of **Enderts Beach Road,** which cuts west from US-101 just north of the park entrance. From here, a 30-mile trail follows the coast to Prairie Creek. The state park area is bounded on the south by an undeveloped section of **Redwood National Park.**

Trees of Mystery and Klamath

Hard to miss along US-101, thanks to the massive statues of Paul Bunyan and Babe the Blue Ox looming over the highway, the **Trees of Mystery** (hours vary; $14; 707/482-2251) are literally and figuratively the biggest tourist draws on the Northern California coast. Along the Trail of Tall Tales, chainsaw-cut figures, backed by audiotaped stories, stand in tableaux at the foot of towering redwoods. There's also a SkyTrail gondola lifting passengers up into the treetop canopy, a huge gift shop, and a small free museum of Native American art and artifacts. Across the highway, **Motel Trees** (707/482-3152) has standard rooms (from $75) and a café.

Along the banks of the mighty Klamath River, four miles south of the Trees of Mystery, the town of **Klamath** (pop. 779) is a brief burst of highway sprawl, supported by anglers who flock here for the annual fall salmon runs—provided there are any fish left to catch. Fisherfolk, walkers, and kayakers all avail themselves of the enduringly popular **The Historic Requa Inn** ($89 and up; 866/800-8777), a friendly and very comfortable nearly century-old homestead right on the riverfront. At the south end of Klamath town, take a drive right through the **Tour-Thru Tree** ($5), then cross the Klamath River on a bridge graced by a pair of gilded cement grizzly bears.

All the land along the Klamath River is part of the extensive **Hoopa Valley Indian Reservation,** which stretches for over 30 miles upstream from the Pacific Ocean.

Prairie Creek Redwoods State Park

The largest of the trio of north coast state redwood parks, **Prairie Creek Redwoods State Park** is best known for its large herd of endangered Roosevelt elk, which you can usually see grazing in the meadows along US-101 at the center of the park, next to the main ranger station (707/465-7347). A modern freeway carries US-101 traffic around, rather than through, the Prairie Creek redwoods, so to reach the best sights, detour along the well-signed Newton B. Drury Scenic Parkway, which follows Prairie Creek along the old US-101 alignment through the heart of the park.

Another elk herd can be spotted among the coastal dunes at **Gold Bluffs Beach,** which stretches for 11 miles through untouched wilderness; there are trails leading from US-101, or you can follow Davison Road northwest from US-101, three miles south of the ranger station. Apart from the elk, Prairie Creek offers the usual mix of old-growth redwood trees, which here, more than in the other parks, mingle with dense growths of Sitka spruce and Douglas firs to form a near rainforest of greenery.

Redwood National Park

Established in 1968, and enlarged since then, **Redwood National**

Park protects the last vestiges of the more than two million acres of primeval redwood forest that once covered the entire Northern California coastline. To be honest, alongside the gorgeous groves in the adjacent Smith, Del Norte, and Prairie Creek State Parks, the trees preserved here aren't by any means the oldest, largest, or most beautiful. In fact, much of the federal parkland is second- or third-growth timber, clear-cut as recently as the 1960s. Though redwoods are the fastest-growing softwoods on earth—growing 3–5 feet a year when young—the groves here can look rather disappointing compared to those in nearby areas, but they do serve a valuable role as an environmental buffer zone even if they're not exactly a tree-lover's pilgrimage site.

That said, Redwood National Park does hold two special sights, including the **Lady Bird Johnson Grove,** on Bald Hill Road two miles east of US-101, where the new park was dedicated in 1969. Ten miles farther up this road, and a long hike beyond that, the Tall Trees Grove (free permit required) holds one of the world's tallest trees, the 360-plus-foot Libbey Tree, whose trunk measures over 14 feet in diameter.

At the south end of the park, the roadside-strip town of **Orick** stretches toward the coast, where the main Redwood National Park **visitors center** (707/465-7765) stands at the mouth of Redwood Creek.

The groves of giant trees in Redwood National Park were used as a location for the Star Wars film *Return of the Jedi,* in which the characters cruised through the forest on airborne cycles. Patrick's Point played a starring role in the sequel to *Jurassic Park.*

Patrick's Point State Park

If your idea of heaven is sitting on a rocky headland listening to the roar of the Pacific while watching the sunset or looking for passing gray whales, you won't want to pass by **Patrick's Point State Park** (707/677-3570). Three different 200-foot-high promontories at the heart of the park provide panoramic views, while the surrounding acres hold cedar and spruce forests (no redwoods), open pastures bright with wildflowers, great tidepools, a wide dark-sand beach, and two campgrounds (800/444-7275) with hot showers. There's also the preserved and restored remnants of a Yurok village, a redwood dugout canoe, and a garden of traditional herbs.

Continuing south, US-101 becomes a four-lane freeway along the ocean to Arcata and Eureka, but most of the old US-101 alignment winds along the cliff tops between Patrick's Point and the small town of Trinidad. Along this road you'll find some places to stay, like the **Trinidad Inn** ($75 and up; 1170 Patrick's Point Dr.; 707/677-3349), about three miles south of the park entrance. A little farther down this old stretch of US-101 is **The Larrupin' Cafe** (closed Wed.; 1658 Patrick's Point Dr.; 707/677-0230), which serves up bountiful portions of very fresh all-American food in a friendly, homey ambience—it's California cuisine without the snooty pretense you sometimes find farther south.

The author Bret Harte was run out of Arcata by angry townspeople in 1860, after writing an editorial in the local paper criticizing a massacre of a local Wiyot tribe.

PLEASE DO NOT CLIMB ON ROCKS

Inland from Arcata along scenic US-299, the town of **Willow Creek** claims to be the heart of Bigfoot Country, boasting a large statue of the furry beast to prove it. One of the state's most scenic drives (or bike rides), US-299 continues east over the coast range through the beautiful Trinity Alps to Weaverville, well-preserved site of a mid-1850s gold rush, before linking up with I-5 at Redding.

Arcata

The most attractive and enjoyable town on the far north coast of California, **Arcata** (pop. 15,700) makes the best first (or last, depending upon the direction you're traveling) overnight stop south of the Oregon border. The presence of Humboldt State University's campus on the hills above US-101 accounts for the town's youthful, nonconformist energy. Cafés, bookstores, bars, and crafts shops surround the lively **Arcata Plaza,** two blocks west of US-101 at 9th and G Streets, incongruously graced by palm trees and a statue of President McKinley. The *Utne Reader* once rated Arcata as the most enlightened town in California, and spending even a little time in this vibrant, cooperative Ecotopia may make you wonder whether or not you really do have to race back to the big-city 9-to-5 grind.

You can admire the town's many elaborate Victorian-era cottages, hunt wild mushrooms, clamber over sand dunes, or hike in the redwoods; afterward, relax with a cup of tea or, better yet, a soak in a hot tub at homey **Cafe Mokka,** the coast's only combo sauna and espresso bar, at 5th and J Streets (707/822-2228). Just off the plaza, **Jambalaya** (915 H St.; 707/822-4766) serves burgers, sandwiches, and (of course) jambalaya, while microbrews flow from the taps of Arcata's amiable bars, many of which feature live music. For food, drink, and entertainment all under one roof, head to the very popular "HumBrews," a.k.a. the **Humboldt Brews** (856 10th St.; 707/826-2739). For a complete selection of foodstuffs and supplies, and more insight into the local community, head to the large and stylish **North Coast Co-op** (811 I St.), a block west from the plaza.

For a place to stay, the centrally located **Hotel Arcata** ($85 and up; 708 9th St.; 707/826-0217 or 800/344-1221) is right on the plaza, or you can take your pick of the usual motels along US-101.

Eureka

Evolving into a lively artists' colony from its roots as a fairly gritty and industrial port, **Eureka** (pop. 28,606) was well known to fur-trappers and traders long before it became a

Kinetic Grand Championship

Humboldt County's creative community comes alive every Memorial Day weekend for the world-famous Kinetic Grand Championship, in which participants pedal, paddle, and otherwise move themselves and their hand-made vehicles across land and sea. Part art, part engineering, and part athletic competition, the Kinetic Grand Championship is like nothing you've seen before. Also known as the "Kinetic Sculpture Race" and "The Triathlon of the Art World," the event begins midday Saturday and runs until Monday afternoon, as a mind-boggling array of mobile contraptions—past winners have included everything from dragons and floating flying saucers to Egyptian pyramids (named Queen of Denial) and a Cadillac Coupe de Ville—make their way over land, sand, and sea from the town square of Arcata to the main street of Ferndale, twice crossing chilly Humboldt Bay.

Rule Number One of the Kinetic Grand Championship is that all of the "sculptures" must be people-powered; beyond that, imagination is the primary guide. Many "rules" have developed over the years since the race was first run in 1969, including such pearls as: "In the Event of Sunshine, the Race Shall Proceed," but most of these emphasize the idea that maintaining style and a sense of humor are at least as important as finishing the fastest. Since the Grand Prizes are valued at somewhere around $14.98, racers take part solely for the glory, but prizes are awarded in many categories: First- and last-place finishers are winners, and the racer who finishes in the exact middle of the pack gets the coveted Mediocre Award—historically a broken-down old banger.

Spectators are expected to be active participants, too, so be prepared to shout and scream and applaud the competitors, or even jog or bike or kayak alongside them. There are many great vantage points along the route, but you have to be in the right place on the right day. Before noon on Saturday there's a pre-race lineup around Arcata Plaza, from where racers head through the streets of Arcata out toward the Manila Dunes before spending the first night in downtown Eureka. Sunday morning the racers head across Humboldt Bay from Field's Landing, then camp out overnight on the beach. Monday's trials include another water crossing, and it all culminates in a mad dash down the Main Street of Ferndale, surrounded by cheering multitudes. It's all good fun, and a great focus for a visit to this remarkable corner of the world.

"Just for the Halibut": racing along Samoa Peninsula

booming lumber and whaling port in the 1850s. Thanks to the lumber trade, Victorian Eureka grew prosperous, building elaborate homes, including the oft-photographed but closed to the public **Carson Mansion** along the waterfront at 2nd and M Streets, two blocks west of US-101.

Along with dozens of well-preserved Victorian houses, Eureka has done a fine job of finding new uses for its many ornate commercial buildings, most of which have been preserved to house art galleries, cafés, and restaurants in what's now called **Old Town,** a half dozen blocks between the waterfront and US-101. This historic downtown quarter has a huge number of good places to eat and drink, including **Ramone's Bakery & Cafe** (209 E St.; 707/445-2923), the pub-like **Cafe Waterfront** (102 F St.; 707/443-9190), and the popular **Sea Grill** (316 E St.; 707/443-7187), a block from US-101. And if that's not enough to sate your appetite, for fish-and-chips and a pint or two of ale head along to the **Lost Coast Brewery** (617 4th St.; 707/445-4480).

One unique thing to see in Eureka is the **Romano Gabriel Wooden Sculpture Garden** (315 2nd St.), displayed in a plate-glass showcase. This brilliantly colorful folk-art extravaganza of faces and flowers originally stood in the front yard of local gardener Romano Gabriel, who made them out of discarded packing crates and other recycled materials over a period of some 30 years before his death in 1977.

Accommodation options range from roadside motels to upscale places like the **Carter House Inns** ($159 and up; 301 L St.; 707/444-8062), a re-created Victorian manor with spacious rooms and a big breakfast in the morning. For a more authentic Victorian experience, stay at one of California's most delightful B&Bs, the **Elegant Victorian Mansion** ($135 and up; 1406 C St.; 707/444-3144). A real treasure in a land of nice B&Bs, this magnificently restored 1888 Eastlake-style home has been opulently decorated with real antiques and Bradbury & Bradbury wallpapers by the hospitable Belgian-born innkeeper, Lily Vieyra.

For further information, about Eureka or anywhere in the whole glorious Redwood Empire region, contact the **Humboldt County Convention and Visitors Bureau** (1034 2nd St.; 707/443-5097 or 800/346-3482).

Samoa

Even if you're just passing through, don't miss the chance to visit the old mill town of **Samoa,** across the bay from Eureka but easily reachable via the Hwy-255 bridge. Here on a narrow peninsula between the bay and the open ocean, the unique **Samoa Cookhouse** (707/442-1659) was built in 1890 to feed the many hungry men living and working in the "company town" lumber mill here. The mill is long gone now, but the cookhouse remains in operation as a sort of living history center, packed with logging memorabilia and blue-collar character. So take a seat at one of the 20-foot-long tables (redwood, of course, covered in checkered oilcloth), soak up the history, and dig into the family-style feasts (breakfast, lunch, and dinner daily—all-you-can-eat!). There are no menus, just huge platters of food at very reasonable prices.

Ferndale

Well worth the 10-mile round-trip detour west of US-101, the historic town of **Ferndale** (pop. 1,371) is an odd fish along the woodsy Northern California coast, a century-old dairy town that would look more at home in middle America. The three-block-long, franchise-free Main Street includes a fully stocked general store, the **Golden Gait Mercantile** (421 Main St.), and whitewashed farmhouses dot the pastoral valleys nearby. Ferndale's diverse history is well documented inside the **Ferndale Art & Cultural Center** (hours vary; 580 Main St.; 707/786-4466), where some of the wacky racers that take part in the annual **Kinetic Grand Championship** are displayed.

> The area around Ferndale has been hit by numerous earthquakes, including a destructive tremor in April 1992 that registered 7.2 on the Richter scale.

Ambling along Main Street is the best way to get a feel for Ferndale, and if you build up an appetite, there are many good places to eat. One of the oldest cafés in the West, **Poppa Joe's** (409 Main St.; 707/786-4180), serves great diner food in a no-frills Victorian-era storefront, while one of California's earliest hotels features a family-friendly Italian restaurant, **The Hotel Ivanhoe Restaurant & Saloon** (315 Main St.; 707/786-9000), open for dinner only. On the main road midway between town and US-101 is another fast-foodie landmark: the **No Brand Burger Stand** (1400 Main St.; 707/786-9474), where all the tasty patties are hand-formed from local grass-fed beef. Fab fries and luscious milk shakes, too. Yum.

Along with its good food options, Ferndale is equally well supplied with places to stay. Right off the heart of Main Street is the clean and tidy **Redwood Suites** ($95 and up; 332 Ocean Ave.; 707/786-5000). Also nice is **The Shaw House Inn** ($125 and up; 703 Main St.; 707/786-9958), an 1854 American Gothic masterpiece with B&B rooms for rent.

The Lost Coast

Between Ferndale and Rockport, the main US-101 highway heads inland along the Eel River, but if you have time and a taste for adventure, head west from Ferndale along the narrow, winding Mattole Road, which loops around Cape Mendocino through the northern reaches of the so-called **Lost Coast**, a 100-mile stretch of shoreline justly

> The Lost Coast area was the site of the first oil well in California, which was drilled in the 1860s in the town of **Petrolia** but is now long gone.

famous for its isolated beauty. By road, you can only get close to the ocean at a few points—the few miles south of Cape Mendocino, and again at the fishing resort of **Shelter Cove,** west of Garberville—but hikers can have a field day (or week) exploring the extensive coastal wilderness. Some 50 miles of rugged, untouched coastline, packed with tidepools and driftwood-strewn beaches, have been preserved in a pair of parks, the **King Range National Conservation Area** in the north and the **Sinkyone Wilderness State Park** farther south.

Besides the Hwy-211/Mattole Road, which makes a 70-mile loop between Ferndale and the Rockefeller Forest section of Humboldt Redwoods State Park, a network of rougher and even more remote routes allows auto access to the Lost Coast, linking the hamlet of Honeydew with coastal Hwy-1 near

Rockport. If you do explore this wild (and very rainy) region, take a good map and plenty of food and water, and be careful.

For further information on the Lost Coast, contact the **Bureau of Land Management** (1695 Heindon Rd.; 707/825-2300); its office is off US-101 on the north side of Arcata.

Scotia

Back along US-101, on the banks of the Eel River midway between the coast and the Humboldt Redwoods, **Scotia** was the last true company town left in California. The Pacific Lumber Company (a.k.a. PALCO) built it and for most of the 20th century owned and operated everything, from the two huge wood-cutting mills to the 10 blocks of pastel-painted houses, church, and schools that constituted this little community of about 1,000 people.

The lumber mills used to be the heart and soul of the town, as well as Scotia's main tourist attraction,

but after a 1980s junk-bond leveraged buyout and subsequent asset-stripping PALCO finally went bankrupt in 2007. Since then the town and the mills have struggled to find a way forward, but Scotia is still a proud and photogenic place, well worth a look and a wander.

In summer, the heart of Scotia is the rustic and historic **Winema Theater,** which screens movies on weekend nights (plus an old-fashioned Saturday matinee). The one place to stay in town is the rustic **Scotia Inn** ($75 and up; 100 Main St.; 707/764-5338), which has B&B rooms and a very good restaurant. Part of the old lumber mill has been reconfigured into a biofueled home for

the excellent (and 100 percent organic) **Eel River Brewery,** which operates a popular tasting room and restaurant at its original location near Ferndale, off US-101 in the hamlet of Fortuna (1777 Alamar Way; 707/725-2739).

Humboldt Redwoods State Park

Sheltering the biggest and best collection of giant coastal redwoods anywhere in the world, **Humboldt Redwoods State Park** is an exceptionally breathtaking corner of an exceptionally beautiful region. Covering more than 53,000 acres along the Eel River, this is the true heart of redwood country, containing the largest and most pristine expanses of virgin forest as well as some of the largest, tallest, and most remarkable trees.

The protection of the mighty redwood forests of Northern California was made possible not by the state or federal governments but primarily by the efforts of the **Save the Redwoods League,** a private organization that has raised, since its founding in 1918, millions of dollars to buy or preserve over 185,000 acres of redwood forest. To support these efforts, write to 114 Sansome Street, Suite 1200, San Francisco, CA 94104, or call 415/362-2352.

Even if you're just passing through, be sure to turn onto the amazing **Avenue of the Giants,** 31 miles of old highway frontage between Pepperwood and Phillipsville. This sinuous old road snakes alongside, and sometimes under, the faster and busier US-101

freeway, which is carried on concrete stilts through the park. In and amongst the natural wonders along the Avenue of the Giants are a handful of man-made ones: The **Eternal Tree House** in Redcrest and the **Shrine Drive-Thru Tree** in Myers Flat are just two of the many good-natured "tourist traps" in this neck of the woods. At the north end of the park you'll find an impressive collection of trees in the well-marked **Founder's Grove,** where a half-mile nature trail leads past the 362-foot-tall, possibly 2,000-year-old **Dyerville Giant,** lauded as one of the world's tallest trees before it fell during the winter of 1991.

Once you've done the Avenue of the Giants, if you want to escape the crowds and the freeway rumble, head west from Founder's Grove across US-101, to the 10,000-plus-acre **Rockefeller Forest.** This expansive grove is one of the largest old-growth forests in the world and includes two of the world's champion trees, each over 360 feet tall and some 17 feet in diameter.

The best source of information on the park is the **visitors center** (707/946-2263), midway along the Avenue of the Giants in Weott; there's a pleasant state-run **campground** (800/444-7275) with showers right next door. You may have to drive a ways north (to Ferndale, Eureka, or Arcata) or south (to Garberville) from the park to find an exceptional meal, though there are a few nice places to stay, like the historic **Myers Country Inn** ($180 and up; 707/943-3259), midway along the Avenue of the Giants in Myers Flat. Farther south, the hamlet of Miranda holds the pleasant **Miranda Gardens Resort** ($105 and up; 707/943-3011), with rustic cabins.

Garberville and Redway

Apart from its recurring presence in the national media during the occasional high-profile raids on local marijuana plantations, the redwood country town of **Garberville** is a pretty quiet, peaceful place. The US-101 freeway bypasses the town, and locals walk and talk to each other along the half dozen blocks of Redwood Drive, the well-signed business loop off the highway.

Enjoy an early-morning breakfast with the old-time locals at the **Eel River Cafe** (801 Redwood Dr.; 707/923-3783), or an espresso and healthy food at the **Woodrose Café,** a block south (911 Redwood Dr.; 707/923-3191).

Garberville also has all the motels you could want, including the **Motel Garberville** ($50 and up; 948 Redwood Dr.; 707/923-2422).

Two miles west of Garberville on the old highway, **Redway** is worth the short side trip for an organic burger at **Deb's Great American Hamburgers** (707/923-2244), or a slice of pizza or fine dinner at **The Mateel Cafe** (707/923-2030), a health-conscious gourmet haunt at the center of town.

Along US-101, four miles south of Garberville, one of the region's most characterful places is the stately **Benbow Hotel & Resort** ($100–200; 707/923-2124), a circa-1926 mock Tudor hotel with a nice restaurant offering afternoon tea and scones on a sunny terrace overlooking Lake Benbow.

The Reggae on the River festival, organized by the energetic Mateel Community Center (707/923-3368), attracts world-class performers and thousands of fans every July.

The Garberville/Redway area is home to a pretty unusual community of old hippies and off-the-grid libertarians, who share their music and politics on noncommercial local radio station **KMUD 91.1 FM.**

Leggett: The Chandelier Drive-Thru Tree

No longer even a proverbial wide spot in the road since the US-101 freeway was diverted around it, **Leggett** marks the southern end of the Humboldt redwoods. At the south end of "town," a mile from the US-101/Hwy-1 junction along the old highway, stands one of the redwood region's most venerable and worthwhile roadside attractions, the "original" **Chandelier Drive-Thru Tree** (daily dawn–dusk; $5). In addition to the famous tree, which had the six-foot-nine-inch-tall tunnel cut through it in the 1930s, there's an above-average gift shop with a broad range of books, postcards, and covetably schlocky souvenirs.

Nearby, the 16-acre grounds of **Big Bend Lodge** (summer only, $125 and up; 707/925-2440) has nine very quaint riverfront cabins, perfect for lazy days floating, swimming, or fishing. South of Leggett, US-101 runs inland racing toward San Francisco, while scenic Hwy-1 cuts west over the coastal mountains to Mendocino, winding slowly south along the Pacific.

Rockport and Westport

From US-101 at Leggett, Hwy-1 twists up and over the rugged coastal mountains before hugging the coast through the weatherbeaten logging and fishing communities of **Rockport** and **Westport.** The small and informal **Howard Creek Ranch Inn** ($90 and up; 707/964-6725) in Westport offers comfortable B&B rooms, an outdoor hot tub, and easy access to the driftwood-laden beach. (But be warned: It's a half-hour drive to the nearest restaurants, in Fort

Avenue of the Giants

The stretch of historic US-101 through the redwood country of Humboldt County, frequently called the "Avenue of the Giants," is lined by pristine groves of massive trees and provides boundless opportunities to come face-to-face with your own insignificance in nature's greater scheme of things. If you tire of this display of natural majesty, or simply want to keep it in context with the modern "civilized" world, you're in luck: Every few miles, amongst the stately trees, you'll come upon shameless souvenir stands selling redwood burl furniture and chainsaw sculptures, as well as wonderfully tacky tourist traps like the Legend of Bigfoot. Many of these hyper-tacky attractions now exist only in memory (and on old postcards!), but none of the survivors is big or bold enough to detract from

the main event—the big trees—and since they've been in operation since the early days of car-borne tourism, they're as much a part of the redwood experience as the trees themselves. Most charge only a few dollars' admission, so there's not a lot to lose.

While you're encouraged to stop at any and all of them—at least long enough to buy a postcard

at the end of Leggett, the "original" Drive-Thru Tree

or two—the most tried-and-true attraction is the **Trees of Mystery,** marked by huge statues of Paul Bunyan and Babe the Blue Ox along US-101 in Klamath, well north of the official Avenue of the Giants. In Myers Flat is the **Shrine Drive-Thru Tree,** at 13078 Avenue of the Giants (old US-101), which wagon-borne travelers drove through more than a century ago. Two more classics are found in the south: One of the best stops in redwood country, **Confusion Hill** in Piercy is one of those places where water runs uphill and the rules of physics seem not to apply, and there's also a little railway train here that chugs uphill to a very nice grove of trees. Finally, at the **Chandelier Drive-Thru Tree,** in Leggett off old US-101 on Drive Thru Tree Road, drive your car through a 315-foot redwood tree, still growing strong despite the gaping hole in its belly.

Bragg.) Farther south, **MacKerricher State Park** protects seven miles of rocky coast and waterfront pine forest; there's also a nice campground (800/444-7275). An old logging railroad right-of-way, called Ten-Mile Haul Road, has been brought back into use as a hiking and cycling path that covers most of the eight miles between the north end of MacKerricher and the town Fort Bragg, crossing over Pudding Creek on a recently renovated railroad trestle.

Fort Bragg

Cruising south along Hwy-1, 40 miles from Leggett and US-101, the first real town you come to is **Fort Bragg** (pop. 6,963), whose burly, blue-collar edge comes as something of a shock on the otherwise undeveloped, touristy Mendocino coast. Formerly home to a large Georgia-Pacific lumber mill (plans to redevelop it are still in the works and may include eco-friendly housing and a shopping and light industrial complex), and still home to the region's largest commercial fishing fleet, Fort Bragg takes a mostly no-frills approach to the tourist trade, leaving the dainty B&B scene to its upscale neighbor, Mendocino. However, the coastline is lovely, and there are a few down-to-earth places to eat, starting with the very good omelets and other eggy dishes at the appropriately named **Egghead's Restaurant** (326 N. Main St.; 707/964-5005). Perhaps the most popular place in town is **North Coast Brewing Co.** (455 N. Main St.; 707/964-2739), which serves good food and fine pints of its tasty Red Seal Ale among at least a dozen top-notch brews. As you might expect, Fort Bragg has a number of timeworn bars and taverns, like the **Golden West Saloon** (128 E. Redwood Ave.), two blocks south of the brewery.

From Fort Bragg, the **California Western** railroad runs a number of historic steam- and diesel-powered Skunk Trains over the mountains to Willits and back. Half-day and full-day trips ($34–119; 866/457-5865) run year-round.

Fort Bragg also boasts some unexpected treats: great hot dogs at **Relish** (260 N. Main St.; 707/962-0633), next door to the local legend that is **Cowlick's Ice Cream Café,** and the best pizza for miles, at **D'Aurelios,** a block east of Hwy-1 (438 S. Franklin St.; 707/964-4227).

Fort Bragg also has at least one exemplar of that rare species, the inexpensive (by Mendocino coast standards, at least) motel: the **Beachcomber Motel** ($99 and up; 1111 N. Main St.; 707/964-2402). Handy for the Ten-Mile Haul Road path, this is pretty much the coast's only beachfront accommodation option (apart from camping).

aerial view of Fort Bragg

At the south edge of Fort Bragg, near the Hwy-20 junction and eight miles north of the town of Mendocino, 47 acres of intensely landscaped coastal hillsides tumble down between Hwy-1 and the ocean to form the **Mendocino Coast Botanical Gardens** (daily; $14; 707/964-4352), a nonprofit public space showing off the abundance of plant life that thrives in this mild, lush environment. Cultivated varieties like camellias, azaleas, roses, irises, fuchsias, and dahlias share space with native ferns, pines, redwoods, wildflowers, and wetland plants. It's also the only public garden in the continental USA that fronts right onto the ocean, so you can enjoy crashing waves and maybe even watch a gray whale spout offshore.

Mendocino

Mendocino

One of the prettiest towns on the California coast (as seen in TV shows like *Murder, She Wrote* and numerous movies), **Mendocino** (pop. 894) is an artists' and writers' community par excellence. Now firmly established as an upscale escape for wage-slaving visitors from San Francisco (hence the local nickname, "Spendocino"), the town was originally established as a logging port in the 1850s.

In recent years, Mendocino has successfully preserved its rugged sandstone coastline—great for wintertime whale-watching—while converting many of its New England–style clapboard houses into super-quaint B&B inns. The area is ideal for leisurely wandering, following the many paths winding through **Mendocino Headlands State Park,** which wraps around the town and offers uninterrupted views across open fields, heathers, and other coastal flora to the crashing ocean beyond. For field guides, maps, or a look at Mendocino in its lumbering heyday, stop by the **visitors center** (707/937-5804) in the historic **Ford House** (735 Main St.).

Two miles north of town, one of the north coast's most perfect places is protected as **Russian Gulch State Park** (707/937-5804), where a waterfall, a soaring highway bridge, lush inland canyons, a swimming beach, and a impressive blowhole are yours to enjoy along more than a mile of undisturbed coastline. There's camping, too, and sea kayaking, plus a fairly flat, three-mile paved bike trail and miles of hiking.

Along with its many fine art galleries and bookshops, the town of Mendocino also has a delicious collection of bakeries, cafés, and restaurants. If you're not getting a breakfast at a B&B, come to the very friendly **Mendocino Cafe** (10451 Lansing St.; 707/937-6141), where locals have been starting their days for more than 20 years. Lunch or dinner at **The Moosse Café** (390 Kasten St.; 707/937-4323) is always unforgettable. For a total splurge, try one of California's most famous (and expensive!) restaurants, **Cafe Beaujolais** (961

Ukiah St.; 707/937-5614), two blocks from the waterfront, which serves California cuisine delicacies for dinner nightly starting at 5:30 PM and for lunch Wednesday–Sunday.

Places to stay in Mendocino are rather expensive but generally delightful. The lovely **MacCallum House Inn** ($150 and up; 45020 Albion St.; 707/937-0289) includes a beautiful garden, good breakfasts, and a cozy nighttime bar and restaurant. Another place to stay is the circa-1858 **Mendocino Hotel & Garden Suites** ($129 and up; 45080 Main St.; 707/937-0511), on the downtown waterfront.

Mendocino, as you might expect from a well-heeled artists colony, also has a pretty lively music scene. **Dick's Place** is at the west end of Main Street (707/937-6010), and another long-standing local landmark draws familiar names from all over the world: **The Caspar Inn,** a historic roadhouse nightclub three miles north of town, just past Russian Gulch State Park and just west of Hwy-1 (707/964-5565).

Van Damme State Park

Three miles south of Mendocino at the mouth of the Little River, **Van Damme State Park** stretches along the coastal bluffs and beaches and includes some 1,800 acres of pine and redwood forest. The park's unique attribute is the oddly contorted **Pygmy Forest,** a natural bonsai-like grove of miniature pines, cypress, and manzanita, with a wheelchair-accessible nature trail explaining the unique ecology. There's also a small, very popular campground, concession-guided ocean kayak tours, and a **visitors center** (707/937-0851) housed in a New Deal–era recreation hall.

The nearby hamlet of Little River is home to some rural-feeling, peaceful alternatives to Mendocino's in-town accommodations: the very comfy **The Inn at Schoolhouse Creek** ($140 and up; 800/731-5525), where quaint cottages sit in nine acres of dog- and child-friendly gardens around a historic, oceanview home, and the luxurious, gourmet food-and-wine indulgence of the **Little River Inn** ($130 and up; 707/937-5942), where the same family has been welcoming travelers since 1939.

Anderson Valley

From Hwy-1 south of Mendocino, Hwy-128 cuts diagonally across to US-101 through the lovely **Anderson Valley,** home to numerous fine wineries (including Husch, Navarro, and Kendall-Jackson) and the *Anderson Valley Advertiser,* one of California's most outspoken local newspapers. Anderson Valley also has its own regional dialect, called "Boontling," combining English, Scots-Irish, Spanish, and Native American words into a lighthearted lingo created, some say, simply to befuddle outsiders—or "shark the bright-lighters," in the local lingo.

To find out more, stop in the valley's tiny main town, **Boonville,** at the All That Good Stuff gift shop and ad hoc information center. Fans of local food and wine will want to cross the highway to the **Boonville Hotel** ($185 and up; 14050 Hwy-128; 707/895-2210), a wonderful restaurant (dinner only, alas) and wine bar. The historic building has upstairs rooms filled with art and furniture made by local craftspeople. Beer fans can make a pilgrimage east of town (toward Ukiah) to the partially solar-powered home of the **Anderson Valley Brewing Company** (17700 Hwy-253; 707/895-BEER), where you can sample some of the world's best beers, including the legendary Boont Amber Ale.

© AVALON TRAVEL

Elk

While the coastal scenery is stupendous all the way along the Mendocino coast, one place worth keeping an eye out for on the drive along Hwy-1 is the tiny roadside community of **Elk** (pop. 250), 15 miles south of Mendocino. Elk is a wonderful little wide-spot-in-the-road, with what must be one of the oldest and most characterful service stations in California (the Elk Garage, in business since 1901) alongside a great little veggie-friendly breakfast-and-lunch road-food stop: **Queenie's Roadhouse Café** (707/877-3285). Elk also boasts a general store, some quirky cliffside cabins, and a steep trail leading down to the Pacific shore at Greenwood Cove. If you have the time and means for a splurge, the peaceful oceanfront **Elk Cove Inn** is a delightful small B&B inn ($100 and up; 707/877-3321).

Point Arena and Gualala

With only a few exceptions, the southernmost 40 miles of Mendocino coastline are almost totally undeveloped and virtually uninhabited, with green forests and coastal coves as far as the eye can see. The westernmost point here, **Point Arena,** is about five miles northwest of Hwy-1 via Lighthouse Road (the namesake lighthouse, built in 1870, stands 115 feet tall). Back on Hwy-1, the small town of Point Arena is worth a wander for nice cafés and bakeries; try the fluffy quiches or buttery croissants at *le très* Francophile **Franny's Cup & Saucer** (213 Main St.; 707/882-2500), across the street from the lively Arena Theater, which puts on new-run movies nightly and good live music.

Another 15 miles south, situated at the very southern edge of Mendocino County, the old logging port of **Gualala** (pop. 585) has one truly remarkable feature: the Russian Orthodox domes of **St. Orres** (36601 S. Hwy-1;

707/884-3303), now a B&B inn and $100-a-head gourmet restaurant glowing with polished wood and stained glass, above Hwy-1 on the north side of town.

If you prefer to hang out with locals rather than well-heeled tourists from San Francisco, head instead to local bakeries like **Trinks Café** (707/884-1713) in the Seacliff Center shopping complex, or grab a BBQ brisket sandwich at **Bones Roadhouse** (707/884-1188), just north. Great camping and an incredible coastal panorama can be yours at **Gualala Point Regional Park** ($6 day, $30 camping; 707/785-2377), a mile south of town along the Gualala River.

Sea Ranch

Midway between Mendocino and the San Francisco Bay Area, the vacation-home community of **Sea Ranch** was laid out in the mid-1960s by an enthusiastic group of architects and planners including Lawrence Halprin and the late Charles Moore, who hoped to show that development need not destroy or negatively impact the natural beauty of the California coast. Strict design guidelines, preserving over half the 5,000 acres as open space and requiring the use of muted natural wood cladding and other barn-like features, made it an aesthetic success, which you can appreciate for yourself at the **Sea Ranch Lodge** ($179 and up; 707/785-2371), near the south end of the development.

The rest of Sea Ranch, however, is strictly private, which has raised the hackles of area activists, who after years of lawsuits finally forced through a few coastal access trails in the mid-1980s; these, such as **Walk-On Beach** at milepost 56.5, are marked by turnouts along Hwy-1.

Salt Point State Park

The many sheltered rocky coves of **Salt Point State Park** make it ideal for undersea divers, who come to hunt the abundant abalone. Along these six miles of jagged shoreline, pines and redwoods clutch the water's edge, covering some 6,000 acres on both sides of Hwy-1 to make Salt Point a prime place for hiking and camping. For a guide to the 20 miles of trails, or background on the sandstone mortars and other remnants of the Kashaya Pomo tribal village that stood here until the 1850s, contact the visitors center (707/847-3221).

One of the few positive effects of cutting down the native redwood forests that once covered the Northern California coast has been the emergence of giant-sized rhododendrons in their place. You'll find the most impressive display at the **Kruse Rhododendron State Natural Preserve,** high above Hwy-1 adjacent to Salt Point State Park, where some 300 acres of rhododendrons, some reaching 14 feet in height, burst forth in late spring, usually peaking around the first week of May.

In between Salt Point and Fort Ross, Beniamino Bufano's 93-foot *Peace* statue looms like a shiny silver missile alongside Hwy-1 above craggy Timber Cove, where there's also a nice restaurant and inn ($140 and up; 707/847-3231).

Fort Ross State Historic Park

If you're captivated by California's lively history, one of the most evocative spots in the state is **Fort Ross State Historic Park,** the well-restored remains of a Russian fur-trapping outpost built here in 1812. During a 30-year residen-

Russian Orthodox chapel at Fort Ross

cy, the Russians farmed wheat and potatoes, traded with native tribes, and trapped local seals and sea otters for their furs, which commanded huge sums on the European market. By 1840, the near-destruction of the sea otter population caused the company to shut down operations and sell the fort to Sacramento's John Sutter, who financed the purchase on credit. Later, the abandoned fort was badly damaged by the 1906 San Francisco earthquake and later fires, but the state has completed a high-quality restoration and reconstruction project, using hand-hewn lumber and historically accurate building methods to replicate the original barracks and other buildings, including a luminous redwood chapel.

Bohemian Grove, the world's most exclusive men's club, covers 2,700 acres of redwood forest just south of the Russian River outside the village of Monte Rio.

Fort Ross spreads west from Hwy-1, 20 miles south of Sea Ranch and a dozen miles north of the Russian River. Outside the fort's walls, a modern **visitors center** (daily; $8 per car; 707/847-3286) traces the site's natural, native, and Russian history, and offers information on the park's many fine hiking trails.

Jenner, Guerneville, and the Russian River

South of Fort Ross, Hwy-1 climbs high above the rugged coastline, offering breathtaking vistas of the Pacific Ocean hundreds of feet below. Twelve miles south of Fort Ross, Hwy-1 reaches the low-key resort community of **Jenner** (pop. 170), which stretches along the broad mouth of the Russian River. Harbor seals and sea lions sun themselves on the beach at Goat Rock, houses climb the steep hillsides, and there's also a gas station, a post office, and the excellent **River's End** (closed Tues. and Wed.; 707/865-2484), which has a range of great food (everything from burgers to Indonesian-spiced seafood) and oceanview tables (inside and outside, depending on the weather).

From Jenner, Hwy-116 runs east along the river, passing through forests, vineyards, and popular summertime resort towns, the largest of which is **Guerneville,** 13 miles away, with a number of worthwhile cafés and a largely gay and lesbian summer population. A more traditional place, with a broad but gravelly beach, boat rentals, cabins, and riverfront camping, is **Johnson's Beach & Resort** (16241 1st St.; 707/869-2022). After 35-odd miles, Hwy-116 eventually links up with the US-101 freeway to and from San Francisco, providing a faster alternative to coastal Hwy-1.

the closing of the Russian River ferry, c. 1931

Sonoma Coast State Park

South of Jenner and the Russian River, Hwy-1 hugs the coast along 10 miles of rocky coves and sandy beaches, collectively protected as **Sonoma Coast State Park** (707/875-3483). Starting with Goat Rock at the southern lip of the Russian River mouth, a bluff-top trail leads south past intriguingly named and usually unpopulated pocket strands like Blind Beach, Schoolhouse Beach, Shell Beach, Wright's Beach (site of the park's main beachfront campground), and Salmon Creek Beach.

While hiking along the Sonoma Coast, be careful: Many people have been drowned by "sleeper" waves, which rise unannounced and sweep people off the rocky shore.

At the southernmost end, Sonoma Coast State Park broadens to include the wildflower-covered granite promontory of **Bodega Head,** which juts into the Pacific and provides a great vantage point for watching the gray whale migrations in winter.

Bodega Bay

Protected by the massive bulk of Bodega Head, the fishing harbor of Bodega Bay has grown into an upscale vacation destination, with Sea Ranch–style vacation homes lining the fairways of golf resorts and deluxe hotels overlooking the still-busy commercial wharves. On the waterfront, the **Lucas Wharf Restaurant & Bar** (595 S. Hwy-1; 707/875-3522) dishes up fish-and-chips and clam chowder; nearby **The Tides Wharf Restaurant** (707/875-3652) is bigger and has a large fresh-fish market.

South of Bodega Bay, Hwy-1 cuts inland around the marshy coastal estuaries, passing by the photogenic small town of **Bodega,** whose church Alfred Hitchcock used for many of the scariest scenes in his 1963 movie, *The Birds.* A little later, and a lot more uplifting, in 1976 international artists Christo and Jeanne-Claude used Bodega as a key tableau in their installation *Running Fence,* which draped an 18-foot-high, nearly 25-mile-long fabric curtain across the rolling ranchlands, from the coast to the inland valleys.

Valley Ford

Between Bodega Bay and Point Reyes, Hwy-1 veers inland to avoid the marshy lowlands, and midway between the two bigger destinations the winding two-lane highway brings you to a great road trip stop. **Valley Ford** is a photogenic community that holds a great old family-run roadhouse, **Dinucci's** (707/876-3260), serving huge portions of unreconstructed Italian food—minestrone, fresh bread, salad, and pasta—for around $10 to $20 per person (dinner only, plus lunch on Sun.). More

Bodega's church, used by Alfred Hitchcock in *The Birds*

self-consciously stylish, contemporary fare is on the menu next door at quirky **Rocker Oysterfeller's** (dinner Wed.–Sun., lunch Sat., and brunch Sun.; 707/876-1983), inside the Civil War–era Valley Ford Hotel, which has been renovated with luxurious rooms while retaining old-time charm (quilts on the beds, rocking chairs on the porch, the whole nine yards).

© AVALON TRAVEL

Point Reyes

Between Bodega Bay and the Golden Gate Bridge, Hwy-1 slices through one of the country's most scenically and economically wealthy areas, **Marin County.** Though less than an hour from San Francisco, the northwestern reaches of the county are surprisingly rural, consisting of rolling dairylands and a few untouched small towns; Hwy-1 follows a slow and curving route along the usually uncrowded two-lane blacktop.

> A sign outside the small white garage on Main Street in Point Reyes Station claims it is the oldest Chevrolet dealer in California.

After looping inland south of Bodega Bay, Hwy-1 reaches the shore again at oyster-rich **Tomales Bay,** around which it winds for a dozen or so miles before reaching the earthy but erudite town of **Point Reyes Station.** Here the excellent **Station House Cafe** (closed Wed.; 11180 Hwy-1; 415/663-1515) serves incredibly good breakfasts and delicious lunches that include great-tasting local oysters, on the half-shell or barbecued. The bar is lively and well-stocked, and hosts free live music most Sunday afternoons.

Northwest from town along Sir Francis Drake Boulevard, the 70,000-plus-acre **Point Reyes National Seashore** offers an entire guidebook's worth of hiking and cycling trails, broad beaches, dense forests, and more; stop at the **Bear Valley Visitor Center** (daily; free; 415/464-5100) for more information. The photogenic lighthouse at the tip of Point Reyes gives great views over the coast, and in winter and spring (Dec.–June) the steep headland makes an ideal spot for watching migrating gray whales.

Eight miles from the visitors center, the **HI-Point Reyes Hostel** (1390 Limantour Spit Rd.; 415/663-8811) has dorm beds in an old farmhouse on the road to Drake's Bay.

Dozens of delightful inns and restaurants operate in and around Point Reyes, but because they're a mere 35 miles from San Francisco, they're often booked solid weeks in advance. Everything from treetop rooms to waterfront cabins can be found through **Inns of Marin** (415/663-2000).

Bolinas and Stinson Beach

Sitting at the southern end of the Point Reyes peninsula, **Bolinas** is a small town with a well-earned reputation for discouraging tourists; the signs leading you here from Hwy-1 are regularly torn down by locals bent on keeping the place—little more than a general store, a bakery, and a bar—for themselves. Bolinas also boasts one of the coast's best tidepool areas in **Duxbury Reef,** which curves around the western edge of Bolinas.

In contrast, the broad strands of **Stinson Beach,** four miles south along Hwy-1, are the Bay Area's most popular summertime suntanning spots. A grocery store and deli, the **Live Water Surf Shop** (which rents boards and the essential wetsuits), and a couple of outdoor bar-and-grills along Hwy-1 form a short parade at the entrance to the beach. The best place to eat hereabouts is the **Parkside Cafe** (43 Arenal Ave.; 415/868-1272); if you want to stay overnight, try the basic but cheap **Stinson Beach Motel** ($95 and up; 3416 Hwy-1; 415/868-1712).

If you have the chance to plan ahead, try to book a night at the **Steep Ravine Cabins** (800/444-7275), just over a mile south of Stinson Beach on the ocean side of Hwy-1. Now part of Mt. Tamalpais State Park, these 10 rustic redwood cabins are very basic roof-over-the-head accommodations (bring sleeping bags and food; water faucets are just outside the door) in an absolutely beautiful coastal chasm. These very popular cabins (originally owned by Bay Area bigwigs like Dorothea Lange) sleep up to five people and cost around $75 a night.

Mt. Tamalpais, Muir Woods, and Muir Beach

From the coast, a pair of roads—Panoramic Highway and the Shoreline Highway (Hwy-1)—twist up and over the slopes of **Mt. Tamalpais** (elev. 2,586), the signature peak of the San Francisco Bay Area. Known usually as "Mt. Tam," the whole mountain has been protected in semi-natural state within a series of state and national parks, and its voluptuous slopes offer incredible views of the urbanized Bay Area and the untouched coastline; drive to within 100 yards of the top for a 360-degree panorama, or stop at the Pantoll **ranger station** (415/388-2070) for a map of Mt. Tam's hiking routes and fire roads.

If you plan ahead, you may also be able to spend the night on the mountain, indoors, in the comfort of **The West Point Inn** (around $50 per person; 415/646-0702), a hiker-centric, walk-in only lodge (two miles from Pantoll), that was built back in 1904 as part of a long-vanished scenic railroad, whose right-of-way is now one of Mt. Tam's most popular hiking trails.

A deep, dark valley between the coast and Mt. Tamalpais holds the last surviving stand of Marin County redwoods, preserved for future generations as the **Muir Woods National Monument** (daily 8 AM–dusk; $5) and named in honor of turn-of-the-20th-century naturalist John Muir. A paved, mile-long trail takes in the biggest trees, but since the park is often crowded with busloads of sightseeing hordes making the tour from San Francisco, you may want to explore the farther-flung areas, climbing up Mt. Tamalpais or following Muir Creek two miles downstream to the crescent-shaped cove of **Muir Beach,** along Hwy-1. Besides stunning scenery, Muir Beach is also home to the welcoming **Pelican Inn,** an "Olde English"–style pub serving food and fine beers; overnight guests get cozy rooms and access to a delightful room called "The Snug," with a fireplace (rooms $190 and up; 415/383-6000).

The all-terrain mountain bike, which now accounts for half of all bikes on (and off) the roads, was invented in the late 1970s by a group of daredevil Marin cyclists intent on cruising down the fire roads of Mt. Tamalpais at the highest possible speed.

Another enjoyably ersatz experience awaits at the junction of Hwy-1 and the US-101 freeway, where a historic roadside restaurant has been resurrected as the **Buckeye Roadhouse,** near Mill Valley (15 Shoreline Hwy.; 415/331-2600), where you can feast on fine barbecue, great steaks and burgers, and delicious desserts in a lively, retro–Route 66 atmosphere.

view from atop Mt. Tamalpais

San Francisco

San Francisco is easily the most enjoyable city in the United States. Its undulating topography turns every other corner into a scenic vista, while its many distinctive neighborhoods are perfect for aimless wandering. Museums document everything from Gold Rush history to cutting-edge modern art, while stellar restaurants offer the chance to sample gourmet food from around the world—all in an easily manageable, densely compact small city.

view from inside Fort Point, with the Golden Gate Bridge overhead

If there's one place in the city you should stop to get your bearings, it's **Fort Point,** a massive, photogenic Civil War fort standing along the bay, directly beneath the Golden Gate Bridge. You can wander at will through the honeycomb of corridors, staircases, and gun ports, watch the fearless surfers and windsurfers offshore, and take in a panoramic view of the City by the Bay. From here you can walk up to and across the Golden Gate Bridge, or head west to Land's End or back into town via a popular bayfront walking and cycling trail. Another great place to get a feel for San Francisco is **Golden Gate Park,** which stretches inland from the western edge of the city, including more than 1,000 acres of gardens, a boating lake, and two landmark museums, featuring the copper-clad art of the De Young Museum, and the natural history, aquarium, and planetarium of the grass-roofed Academy of Sciences.

If there's one other place that ought to be on your S.F. itinerary, it's **Alcatraz.** Aptly known as The Rock, this was America's most notorious prison from 1934 until 1963. Now preserved as a historical park, the island is worth a visit as much for the views of San Francisco as for its grim past. To reach Alcatraz, take one of the ferries that leave throughout the day from Pier 41 at the east end of Fisherman's Wharf.

The **San Francisco Giants** (tickets $40 and up; 877/4SF-GTIX) play at retro-modern AT&T Park, along the bay in downtown's South of Market district.

the Conservatory of Flowers in Golden Gate Park

Practicalities

San Francisco is one of the few cities on the West Coast where you really don't need a car, since distances are short and public transportation is quite extensive; the grid street plan makes it easy to find your way around. San Francisco's Municipal Railway's ("Muni"; 415/673-6864) network of public transit buses, trams, and cable cars will take you all over the city.

The only problem for visitors in San Francisco is deciding where to eat—there are so many great places that choosing among them can be a painful process. For breakfast, **Sears Fine Foods** (415/986-1160) at 439 Powell Street on Union Square is a local institution, as is the upscale **Fog City Diner** (415/982-2000) at 1300 Battery Street, which serves gourmet comfort food (and the world's best french toast) in a stainless steel supper club. Two more S.F. culinary landmarks are the **Swan Oyster Depot** (weekdays till 6 PM only; 415/673-1101 or 415/673-2757), a half block north of the California Street cable car at 1517 Polk Street, a simple oyster bar serving the city's freshest shellfish and coldest Anchor Steam beer; and **Sam's Grill** (415/421-0594), downtown at 374 Bush Street, with incredible grilled meat and

view of Alcatraz as seen on approach by boat

fish dishes, melt-in-your-mouth shoestring fries, and ancient-looking 1930s wooden booths that seem like set pieces from a Sam Spade mystery.

Given San Francisco's worldwide popularity, it's no surprise that room rates run pretty high—expect to pay around $200 a night (including taxes). If you're here for a honeymoon or other romantic reason, the nicest place in town is the swanky **Mandarin Oriental** ($350 and up; 415/276-9600) at 222 Sansome Street, which fills the top floors of a Financial District skyscraper and has 270-degree bay views (even from the bathtubs!). The best budget options are the two HI hostels, one on the bay at Fort Mason (415/771-7277), another downtown at 312 Mason Street (415/788-5604); both cost about $25 a night. In between there are some nice motels on the outskirts of downtown, like the nouveau retro **Hotel del Sol** ($129 and up; 415/921-5520), in the Marina District at 3100 Webster Street.

San Francisco, as seen from Yerba Buena Island

The San Francisco Convention and Visitors Bureau (415/974-6900) publishes a good free street map and offers extensive listings of attractions, accommodations, and restaurants.

Marin Headlands

If you can avoid the magnetic pull of the Golden Gate Bridge and San Francisco, take the very last turnoff from US-101 (northbound drivers take the second turnoff after crossing the bridge) and head west to the **Marin Headlands,** a former military base that's been turned back into coastal semi-wilderness. A tortuous road twists along the face of 300-foot cliffs, giving incredible views of the bridge and the city behind it. The road continues west and north to the **visitors center** (415/331-1540), housed in an old chapel, with a reconstructed Miwok shelter and details on hiking and biking routes. And if you're so inclined, on Wednesday–Friday afternoons and the first Saturday of each month you can tour the world's only restored Cold War–era Nike missile silo (free).

Every June since 1905, one of the country's wildest foot races, the **Dipsea,** has followed a rugged 7.4-mile route from the town of Mill Valley to Stinson Beach. For more information, call the Dipsea hotline at 415/331-3550.

Nearby, the barracks of old Fort Barry have been converted into the very peaceful **HI-Marin Headlands Hostel** (415/331-2777), which has dorm beds for around $25 per person as well as private rooms.

Across San Francisco

From the north, Hwy-1 enters **San Francisco** across the glorious **Golden Gate Bridge,** where parking areas at both ends let you ditch the car and walk across the elegant 1.7-mile-long span. South from the bridge, Hwy-1 follows 19th Avenue across Golden Gate Park, then runs due south through the outer reaches of San Francisco, finally reaching the coast again at the often-foggy town of Pacifica. The most scenic alternative is the **49-Mile Drive,** the best part of which heads west from the bridge through the **Presidio,** along Lincoln Boulevard and Camino del Mar, following the rugged coastline to **Lands End,** where you can hike around and explore the remains of Sutro Baths, eat a burger or grilled cheese at **Louis'** (415/387-6330), a historic diner with amazing views, or dine at the wonderful (and not all-that-expensive) **Cliff House** (415/386-3330).

From Lands End, this scenic route runs south along the oceanfront Great Highway, which eventually links back up with Hwy-1 near the small but enjoyable **San Francisco Zoo** (daily; $15; 415/753-7080).

Since driving and parking in San Francisco can be frustrating and expensive (Steve McQueen could never make *Bullitt* in today's traffic!), consider parking out here in the 'burbs and taking public transportation into the center of town. The N Judah Muni trolley line runs between downtown and the coast just south of Golden Gate Park, via the Sunset District neighborhood, where parking is comparatively plentiful.

the opening of the Golden Gate Bridge, 1937

San Francisco is the start of our cross-country road trip along US-50, **The Loneliest Road,** beginning on page 704. The route crosses high mountains and red-rock deserts before winding up at Ocean City, Maryland.

Montara and Princeton

From the San Francisco city limits, Hwy-1 runs along the Pacific Ocean through the rural and almost totally undeveloped coastline of San Mateo County. The first eight miles or so are high-speed freeway, but after passing through the suburban communities of Daly City and Pacifica, the pace abruptly slows to a scenic cruise. **Pacifica,** which has a long pier, a popular surfing beach, a bowling alley, an oceanview Taco Bell, and a handy Holiday Inn Express motel, makes a good edge-of-town base for seeing the San Francisco area. South of Pacifica, two-lane Hwy-1 hugs the decomposing cliff tops of Devil's Slide, where the terrifying old highway is being converted into a cycling and hiking path following completion of a long-delayed new tunnel (decades in the making).

The first real place south of Pacifica is the ramshackle beach town of **Montara,** where the old but still functioning lighthouse has been partly converted into the **HI-Point Montara Lighthouse Hostel** (650/728-7177).

South of Montara, Hwy-1 bends inland around the rugged shores of the **Fitzgerald Marine Reserve** (650/728-3584), a wonderful (but very fragile) tidepool area filled with anemones and other delicate sea creatures. The tidepools are visible at low tide only; look, but don't touch! Hwy-1 continues south past the Pillar Point Harbor at Princeton-by-the-Sea, where you can enjoy a different sort of sealife appreciation: the fresh fish-and-chips (plus nice wines and cold beers) at **Barbara's Fish Trap** (cash only; 650/728-7049).

Half Moon Bay

The first sizable coastal town south of San Francisco, **Half Moon Bay** is 25 miles from the city but seems much more distant. A quiet farming community that's slowly but surely changing into a Silicon Valley exurb, Half Moon Bay (pop. 11,324) still has an all-American Main Street lined by hardware stores, cafés, bakeries, and the inevitable art galleries and B&Bs. The main event hereabouts is the annual **Art & Pumpkin Festival,** held mid-October, which celebrates the coming of Halloween with a competition to determine the world's largest pumpkin—winning gourds weigh more than 1,500 pounds!

Until the construction of the $500-a-night beachfront Ritz-Carlton golf resort, the coastline of Half Moon Bay was almost completely undeveloped, but it's still pretty nice and accessible, with a four-mile-long string of state park beaches at the foot of blufftop vegetable farms and horse

Looking for the world's biggest waves? Head down to **Maverick's,** an offshore reef area off Pillar Point, three miles north of Half Moon Bay. In winter, when conditions are right, megawaves as high as 80 feet draw expert surfers from all over the world. For a report, and a safety advisory to warn off any wannabes, call **Mavericks Surf Shop** (650/560-8088); it's located at Pillar Point Harbor, as near as you can get to the offshore breaks.

ranches. The town also retains its rural feel, but thanks to the presence of so many Silicon Valley billionaires just over the hills, it has significantly better restaurants. The best fish tacos (and great fish-and-chips) can be had at the **Flying Fish Grill** (650/712-1125), off Hwy-92 at the north end of Main Street, while excellent and not outrageously expensive Italian specialties are on the menu at **Pasta Moon** (315 Main St.; 650/726-5125).

Pescadero and Pigeon Point Lighthouse

The 50 miles of coastline between Half Moon Bay and Santa Cruz are one of the great surprises of the California coast: The virtually unspoiled miles offer rocky tidepools and driftwood-strewn beaches beneath sculpted bluffs topped by rolling green fields of brussels sprouts, artichokes, and U-pick berry patches. Access to the water is not always very easy, and while surfers seem to park along Hwy-1 and walk across the fields to wherever the waves are breaking, for visitors it's best to aim for one of the half dozen state parks, like San Gregorio, Pomponio, Bean Hollow, or Año Nuevo.

The biggest town hereabouts, **Pescadero** (pop. 643) is a mile or so inland from Hwy-1 and well worth the short detour for a chance to sample the fresh fish, great pies, and other home-cooked treats at **Duarte's Tavern** (202 Stage Rd.; 650/879-0464), open daily for breakfast, lunch, and dinner at the south end of the block-long downtown.

Less than 10 miles south of Pescadero, the photogenic beacon of **Pigeon Point Lighthouse** has appeared in innumerable TV and print commercials; the graceful, 115-foot-tall brick tower is closed, but the grounds are open for tours (Fri.–Sun. 10 AM–4 PM; donation), and the adjacent lighthouse quarters function as the very popular **HI-Pigeon Point Lighthouse Hostel** (650/879-0633), which has dorms beds, family-friendly private rooms, and a hot tub perched above the crashing surf.

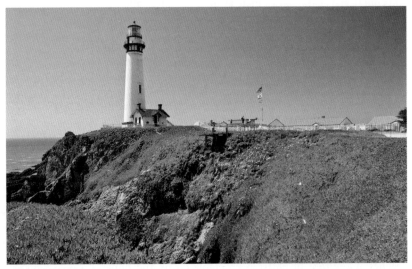

Pigeon Point Lighthouse

Año Nuevo State Reserve

West of Hwy-1, one of nature's more bizarre spectacles takes place annually at **Año Nuevo State Reserve** (8 AM–dusk daily; 650/879-0227), where each winter hundreds of humongous northern elephant seals come ashore to give birth and mate. The males reach up to 13 feet head-to-tail, weigh as much as 4,500 pounds, and have dangling proboscises that inspired their name. These blubbery creatures were hunted almost to extinction for their oil-rich flesh. In 1910, fewer than 100 were left in the world; their resurgence to a current population of more than 100,000 has proved that protection does work.

Two miles north of Davenport, **Swanton Berry Farm** (831/469-8804) is one of the last pick-your-own farms on the California coast. It also sells delicious organic fruit pies year-round.

Every December, after spending the summer at sea, hordes of male elephant seals arrive here at Año Nuevo, the seals' primary onshore rookery, ready to do battle with each other for the right to procreate. It's an incredible show, with the bulls bellowing, barking, and biting at each other to establish dominance; the "alpha male" mates with most of the females, and the rest must wait till next year. Pups conceived the previous year are born in January, and mating goes on through March. During the mating season, ranger-led **tours** ($7; 800/444-4445) are the only way to see the seals; these tours are very popular, so plan ahead and try to come midweek. The three-mile walk from the parking area to the shore is worth doing at any time of year, since it's a very pretty scene and some of the seals are resident year-round.

Midway between Año Nuevo State Reserve and Santa Cruz, the **Davenport Roadhouse at the Cash Store,** on the east side of Hwy-1 in the village of Davenport, serves hearty breakfasts, lunches, and dinners. Tiny Davenport is also the birthplace of the **Odwalla** fresh-fruit-juice company.

The only accommodation option along this stretch of coast is three miles south of the lighthouse, or two miles north of the entrance to Año Nuevo, at **Costanoa** ($89 and up; 650/879-1100). A stylish retro-modern eco-minded resort, open since 1999 on the inland side of Hwy-1, Costanoa has everything from a luxurious lodge to tent cabins (complete with saunas!). There's also a café and an adjacent KOA campground (650/879-7302).

Big Basin Redwoods State Park

The oldest of California's state parks, **Big Basin Redwoods State Park** (831/338-8860) protects some 18,000 acres of giant coastal redwoods. Established in 1902, the park has many miles of hiking and cycling trails high up in the mountains. The heart of the park is most easily accessible from Santa Cruz via Hwy-236, but a popular trail winds up from the coast to the crest, starting from Hwy-1 at **Waddell Beach,** a popular haunt for kite-surfers and sailboarders, who sometimes do flips and loops in the wind-whipped waves.

Santa Cruz

The popular beach resort and college town of **Santa Cruz** (pop. 55,600) sits at the north end of Monterey Bay, a 90-minute drive from San Francisco, at the foot of a 3,000-foot-high ridge of mountains. It's best known for its Boardwalk amusement park, which holds the oldest surviving wooden roller coaster on the West Coast, and for the large University of California campus in the redwoods above. The city was named by Spanish explorer Gaspar de Portolá and shares the name Santa Cruz ("holy cross" in Spanish) with the ill-fated mission settlement begun here in 1777. Modern Santa Cruz was all but leveled by an earthquake in 1989 but has since recovered its stature as one of the more diverting stops on the California coast.

Natural Bridges State Beach, four miles south of Santa Cruz via West Cliff Drive, has a natural wave-carved archway and, in winter, swarms of monarch butterflies.

Santa Cruz has just about fully recovered from the 1989 Loma Prieta earthquake, which had its epicenter in the hills east of the city.

The downtown area lies a mile inland, so from Hwy-1 follow the many signs pointing visitors toward the wharf and the beach, where plentiful parking is available. Walk, rent a bike, or drive along the coastal Cliff Drive to the world's first **Surfing Museum** (open in summer Wed.–Mon. 10 AM–5 PM, the rest of the year Thurs.–Mon. noon–4 PM; donations), which is packed with giant old redwood boards and newer high-tech cutters, as well as odds and ends tracing the development of West Coast surfing. Housed in an old lighthouse, it overlooks one of the state's prime surfing spots, Steamer Lane, named for the steamships that once brought day-tripping San Franciscans to the wharf.

A large part of the Santa Cruz economy still depends upon visitors, and there are plenty of cafés, restaurants, and accommodation options to choose from. Eating and drinking places congregate east of Hwy-1 along Front Street and Pacific Avenue in downtown Santa Cruz, which has a number of engaging, somewhat countercultural book and record shops along with cafés like **Zoccoli's** (1534 Pacific Ave.; 831/423-1711), which has great soups and sandwiches. The best burgers, veggie burgers, and fries are a block west of Pacific at **Jack's Hamburgers** (202 Lincoln St.; 831/423-4421). More good veggie food can be had at the **Saturn Café** (145 Laurel St.; 831/429-8505), while the stylish **Soif** wine bar (105 Walnut Ave.; 831/423-2020) has fine wines and tasty tapas-like treats.

Motels line Hwy-1, and some nice-looking Victorian-era B&Bs stand atop Beach Hill, between the Boardwalk and downtown, where the **Seaway Inn** ($68 and up; 176 W. Cliff Dr.; 831/471-9004) is nice, clean, and reasonably priced. You can also avail yourself of the **HI-Santa Cruz Hostel** (321 Main St.; 831/423-8304)

Surfboard designs have come a long way.

with dorm beds in an immaculate 1870s cottage for less than $30 per person. Among the many nice B&Bs is the rustic **The Babbling Brook Inn** ($157 and up; 1025 Laurel St.; 831/427-2437 or 800/866-1131).

Santa Cruz Beach Boardwalk

The bayfront **Santa Cruz Beach Boardwalk** should really be your main stop; besides the dozens of thrill rides and midway games, it boasts the art deco Cocoanut Grove ballroom and two rides that are such classics of the genre they've been listed as a National Historic Landmark. The biggest thrill is the **Giant Dipper** roller coaster, open since 1924, a senior citizen compared to modern rides but still one of the top coasters in the country— the clattering, half-mile-long tracks make it seem far faster than the 55 mph maximum it reaches. Near the roller coaster is the beautiful Charles Looff **carousel,** one of only six left in the country, with 73 hand-carved wooden horses doing the same circuit they've followed since 1911; grab for the brass rings while listen-

ing to music pumped out by the 342-pipe organ, imported from Germany and over 100 years old.

Along with these and many other vintage arcade attractions, the amusement park also features a log flume ride, a sky ride, a two-story miniature-golf course installed inside the old bathhouse, plus a bowling alley and all the shoot-

Santa Cruz Beach Boardwalk

ing galleries, laser tag, and virtual reality machines you could want. The Boardwalk, which has a concrete concourse but retains a great deal of charm and character, is open daily in summer and weekends only during the rest of the year. Admission is free and individual rides vary in cost, with the Giant Dipper costing $5 a trip and all-day, all-ride passes priced about $30. For more information, call 831/423-5590.

Mystery Spot

In the hills above Santa Cruz, two miles north of Hwy-1, the **Mystery Spot** (daily; $6 per person and $5 per car; 465 Mystery Spot Rd.; 831/423-8897) is one of those fortunate few tourist traps that actually get

people to come back again. Like similar places along the Pacific coast, the Mystery Spot is a section of redwood forest where the usual laws of physics seem not to apply (trees grow in oddly contorted corkscrew shapes, and balls roll uphill). Among those who study vortexes and other odd geomantic places,

© AVALON TRAVEL

the Mystery Spot is considered to be the real thing, but you don't have to take it seriously to enjoy yourself.

Watsonville, Castroville, and Moss Landing

Between Santa Cruz and Monterey, Hwy-1 loops inland through the farmlands fronting Monterey Bay. Part freeway, part winding two-lane road, Hwy-1 races through, and to be honest there's not a lot worth stopping for: The beaches can be dreary, and the two main towns, Watsonville and Castroville, are little more than service centers for the local fruit and vegetable packers, though Castroville does have one odd sight: the "World's Largest Artichoke," a concrete statue outside a very large fruit stand at the center of town.

Back on the coast, midway along Monterey Bay, the port community of **Moss Landing** is a busy commercial fishery, with lots of trawlers and packing plants—not to mention pelicans aplenty. Moss Landing sits alongside Elkhorn Slough, the

Coastal farms along Monterey Bay grow about 75 percent of the nation's artichokes, which you can sample along with other produce at stands along Hwy-1.

In 1947, then-unknown Marilyn Monroe reigned as Miss Artichoke during Castroville's Artichoke Festival, still celebrated each May.

largest and most wildlife-rich wetlands area in Monterey Bay (a busy nursery for baby seals, baby otters, and baby leopard sharks), which you can see in greatest comfort via pontoon boat tour (831/633-5555). Moss Landing is also home to the research arm of the Monterey Bay Aquarium, a nice KOA campground, an obtrusively huge electricity generating plant, and **The Whole Enchilada** (831/633-3038), which has spicy seafood right on Hwy-1, near the power plant.

Much of the bayfront north of Monterey formerly belonged to the U.S. Marine Corps base at Fort Ord. Almost the entire parcel was turned over to the State of California to house the **California State University at Monterey Bay,** which opened its doors in 1994.

San Juan Bautista

Away from the coast, 15 miles inland from Monterey Bay via Hwy-129 or Hwy-156, stands one of California's most idyllic small towns, **San Juan Bautista** (pop. 1,862). It centers upon a grassy town square bordered by a well-preserved mission complex, complete with a large church and monastery, standing since 1812. Two other sides of the square are lined by hotels, stables, and houses dating from the 1840s through 1860s, preserved in their entirety within a state historic park (daily; 831/623-4881).

Completing the living history lesson, the east edge of the square is formed by one of the state's few preserved stretches of El Camino Real, the 200-year-old Spanish colonial trail that linked all the California missions with Mexico. Adding to the interest, the trail runs right along the rift zone of the San Andreas Fault, and a small seismograph registers tectonic activity. (Incidentally, San Juan Bautista was where the climactic final scenes of Hitchcock's *Vertigo* were filmed—though in the movie, they added a much more prominent bell tower with a seemingly endless staircase.)

The town's main street is a block from the mission and is lined by a handful of antiques shops, Mexican restaurants, and cafés like the **Mission Cafe** (300 3rd St. (831/623-2220).

Monterey

The historic capital of California under the Spanish and Mexican regimes, **Monterey** (pop. 27,810), along with its peninsular neighbors Carmel and Pacific Grove, is one of the most satisfying stops in California. Dozens of significant historical sites have been well preserved, most of them concentrated within a two-mile-long walk called the Path of History that loops through the compact downtown area. Park in the lots at the foot of Alvarado Street, Monterey's main drag, and start your tour at **Fisherman's Wharf,** where bellowing sea lions wallow in the water, begging for popcorn from tourists. Next stop should be the adjacent **Custom House,** the oldest governmental building in the state, recently restored as the **Monterey State Historic Park visitors center** (daily; 831/649-7118); here you can pick up maps or join walking tours of old-town Monterey.

From the Custom House, which is now surrounded by the Portola Hotel & Spa, you can follow the old railroad right-of-way west along the water to **Cannery Row,** where abandoned fish canneries have been gussied up into upscale bars and restaurants— most of them capitalizing on ersatz Steinbeckian themes. The one real attraction here is the excellent **Monterey Bay Aquarium** (daily; $29.95; 886 Cannery Row 831/648-4800), housed in a spacious modern building and loaded with state-of-the-art tanks filled with over 500 species of local sealife. The aquarium is rated by many as the best in the world: Displays let visitors touch tidepool denizens,

The internationally famous **Monterey Jazz Festival** is held every September. For performers, dates, and other information, phone 925/275-9255.

jellyfish at the Monterey Bay Aquarium

watch playful sea otters, gaze into the gently swaying stalks of a three-story-tall kelp forest, be hypnotized by brilliantly colored jellyfish, or face truly weird creatures that usually live thousands of feet below the surface of the bay.

Monterey Practicalities

Because Monterey gets such a considerable tourist trade, there's no shortage of restaurants, though good food at reasonable prices can be hard to find. In the historic center of town, one good bet is the **Old Monterey Café** (489 Alvarado St.; 831/646-1021), serving large portions at breakfast and lunch. For breakfast near the aquarium, try **First Awakenings** (125 Oceanview Blvd.; 831/372-1125). For seafood, catch an early-bird special (before 6 PM) at one of the dozen restaurants on the wharf, or head a mile west along the frontage road to the very popular **Monterey's Fish House** (2114 Del Monte Ave.; 831/373-4647).

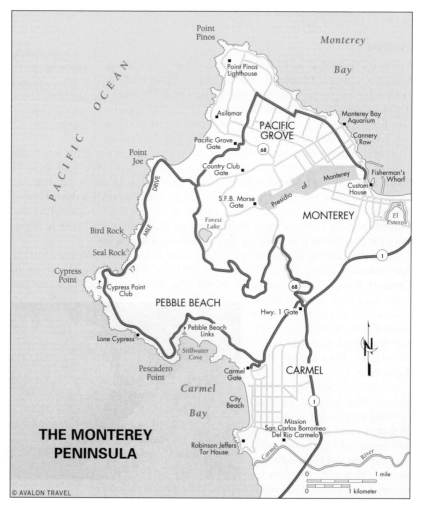

THE MONTEREY
PENINSULA

© AVALON TRAVEL

Places to stay vary widely, starting with the **HI-Monterey Hostel** ($26 per person; 778 Hawthorne St.; 831/649-0375), in historic Carpenters Union Hall off Cannery Row, five blocks from the aquarium. Moderate motels line Munras Street along the old US-101 highway frontage south toward Carmel, while prices in down-

Hotel Del Monte, California, on Road of a Thousand Wonders

town Monterey hover in the $200 range. One exception to the generally high prices is the refurbished and centrally located **Monterey Hotel** ($139 and up; 406 Alvarado St.; 831/375-3184 or 800/966-6490). Near the wharf is the beachfront **Monterey Bay Lodge** ($85 and up; 831/372-8057).

Many other nice places to stay and eat can be found in neighboring Pacific Grove or Carmel. For additional information on destinations from Monterey south to Big Sur, contact the Monterey County **visitors bureau** (831/649-1770 or 877/666-8373).

Pacific Grove

Perched at the tip of the Monterey Peninsula, **Pacific Grove** (pop. 15,041) is a quiet throwback to old-time tourism, dating from the 1870s when the area was used for summertime Methodist revival meetings. The revivalists' tents and camps later grew into the West Coast headquarters of the populist Chautauqua educational movement, based in upstate New York. The town still has a curiously Midwestern feel, from its many small churches to the rows of well-maintained Victorian cottages lining its quiet streets. Besides the many fine old buildings, the best reason to come here is the beautiful, fully accessible shoreline, which boasts some of the coast's best tidepools, sunset views, and endless opportunities for winter whale-watching.

Pacific Grove's main street, Lighthouse Avenue, runs through the 15-mph commercial district of cafés, galleries, movie theaters, and a small but excellent **Pacific Grove Museum of Natural History** (closed Mon.; free), which is a great option for kids or when the weather turns bad. Nearby **Peppers Mexicali Cafe** (170 Forest Ave.; 831/373-6892) serves very good, fresh Mexican food, while a range of fairly

Along Hwy-1 on the northwest edge of Monterey, the elegant **Club Del Monte,** a grand resort that attracted the first wealthy tourists in the 1880s when it was called Hotel del Monte, is now part of the large U.S. Naval Postgraduate School.

The writer John Steinbeck lived in and around the Monterey Peninsula for many years and set many of his stories here, though things have changed so much in recent years that his beloved **Cannery Row** is hard to recognize. Steinbeck was born and is interred in **Salinas,** east of Monterey on US-101; after spurning him for most of his lifetime, the town in 1998 opened the **National Steinbeck Center** (1 Main St.) as a memorial to its literary son.

priced fish dishes are on the menu at **Fishwife** (1996 Sunset Dr.; 831/375-7107), near Asilomar, overlooking the wetsuited surfers riding the waves at Asilomar State Beach.

Places to stay in Pacific Grove are more reasonably priced than in Monterey or Carmel: **Andril Fireplace Cottages** ($140 and up; 569 Asilomar Ave.; 831/375-0994) is a lovingly maintained set of old-fashioned motor-court cabins, all with fireplaces and just two blocks from the ocean. The real landmark place to stay is the rustic **Asilomar Conference Grounds** ($95 and up; 800 Asilomar Ave.; 800/635-5310), on the coast, which has a lovely main lobby (with roaring stone fireplace and heirloom pool tables) and some lovely, woodsy, Julia Morgan–designed cabins and lodge rooms, but is often filled with church groups or convention-goers. For a romantic getaway, it's hard to beat a Victorian-era B&B overlooking the Pacific from Lover's Point: **Seven Gables Inn** ($229 and up; 555 Ocean View Blvd.; 831/372-4341).

> Pacific Grove is the best known of about 20 places in California where millions of migratory monarch butterflies spend the winter months. From October until March, the butterflies congregate on the Butterfly Trees, a grove of pines on Ridge Road off Lighthouse Avenue, well signed from downtown.

The 17-Mile Drive and Pebble Beach

Spanning the coast between Pacific Grove and Carmel, the **17-Mile Drive** is one of the most famous toll roads in the nation. Opened in the 1880s, the route initially took guests of Monterey's posh Hotel Del Monte on a scenic carriage ride along the coast through the newly planted Del Monte Forest between Carmel and Pacific Grove. Guided by Samuel F. B. Morse, son of the inventor, the formerly wild area underwent development beginning in the 1920s, first with golf courses like Pebble Beach and Cypress Point, and since then with resort hotels and posh homes.

MIDWAY POINT, 17 MILE DRIVE

MONTEREY PENINSULA, CALIFORNIA

> One event that brought Pebble Beach to national attention was the annual golf tournament hosted by Bing Crosby; originally an informal get-together, it grew into one of the main events of the professional circuit and is now the **AT&T Pebble Beach National Pro-Am,** held each winter.

Enter the drive at any of the gates, where you'll pay the toll ($9.50; bicyclists are free, and motorcyclists are banned) and be given a map and guide to the route, pointing out all the scenic highlights, especially the trussed-up old **Lone Cypress,** legally trademarked subject of so many Carmel postcards. It's definitely worth doing the drive, if only to say you have, but to be honest, the views from the drive are no more or less splendid than they are from the toll-free drives, like Ocean View Boulevard in Pacific Grove, Scenic Road in Carmel, or Hwy-1 through Big Sur. You do, however, get to stop at the Lodge, where your toll will be deducted from the price of lunch or dinner. If you're in the mood to splurge on wanton luxury, you can also stay overnight at either of two extremely plush golf and tennis resorts: the modern, suburban-style country club of **The Inn at Spanish Bay,** which is also home to an Ansel Adams photography gallery, or stately, old-money **The Lodge at Pebble Beach.** Both resorts charge upwards of $600 a night; for details on accommodations (or Pebble Beach golf fees and tee times), call 800/654-9300.

Carmel

The exclusive enclave of **Carmel-by-the-Sea** (to give its complete name) began life in the early years of the 20th century as a small but lively bohemian colony inhabited by the literary likes of Sinclair Lewis, Mary Austin, and Upton Sinclair. However, with a few arts-and-craftsy exceptions, by the 1950s Carmel had turned into the archly conservative and contrivedly quaint community it is today—a place where Marie Antoinette would no doubt feel at home, dressing down as a peasant, albeit in Chaps by Ralph Lauren. Preserving its rural feel by banning street addresses (and home mail delivery), Carmel simultaneously loves and abhors the many thousands of tourists who descend on it every weekend to window-shop its many designer boutiques and galleries, which fill the few blocks off Ocean Avenue, the main drag through town. Though most of Carmel's many art galleries seem directed at interior decorators, a few are worth searching out, including the **Photography West Gallery** on the southeast corner of Dolores and Ocean, and the **Weston Gallery** on Sixth Avenue near Dolores Street, featuring the works of Edward Weston, Ansel Adams, and other Carmel-based photographers.

Every August for more than 60 years, Pebble Beach has drawn classic car collectors from around the world to show off their immaculately restored automobiles at the annual **Pebble Beach Concours d'Elegance.**

Carmel's leading light, Clint Eastwood, seems ever-present: Besides once serving as mayor, he owns the Mission Ranch resort. As a filmmaker, he used Carmel as the location for one of his most disturbing movies, the psychopathic 1970s *Play Misty for Me.*

Though it's easy to be put off by the surface glitz, Carmel does have a lot going for it. The water is too cold and treacherous for swimming, but broad **Carmel City Beach** at the foot of Ocean Avenue gleams white against a truly azure cove. To the south, aptly named **Scenic Road** winds along the rocky coast, past poet Robinson Jeffers's dramatic **Tor House** (tours Fri. and Sat. 10 AM–3 PM; $10; 831/624-1813). Jeffers, who lived at the house between 1919 and 1962, built much of what you see here out of boulders he hauled up by hand from the beach.

At the south end of the Carmel peninsula, another broad beach, **Carmel River State Beach,** spreads at the mouth of the Carmel River; this usually unpopulated spot is also a favorite spot for scuba divers exploring the deep undersea canyon.

Above the beach, just west of Hwy-1 a mile south of central Carmel, **Carmel Mission,** also known as San Carlos

Big Sur

Stretching 90 miles south of Carmel from Point Lobos all the way to Hearst Castle, Big Sur is one of the most memorable sections of coastline on the planet, with 5,000-foot-tall mountains rising up from the Pacific Ocean. Early Spanish missionaries dubbed it El País Grande del Sur (the Big Country of the South), and the rugged land has resisted development or even much of a population—the current total of around 1,000 is roughly the same as it was in 1900, and for the 3,000 years before that.

Hwy-1, the breathtaking drive through Big Sur, was finally cut across the very steep cliffs in 1937 after 20 years of labor and several fatalities. California's longest and most popular scenic route, it's an incredible trip. Like the Grand Canyon and other larger-than-life natural wonders, Big Sur boggles the mind and, in an odd way, can be hard to handle; you have to content yourself with staring in awestruck appreciation, taking pictures, or maybe toasting the natural handiwork with a cold beer or glass of wine at one of the few but unforgettable cafés and restaurants along the way.

However beautiful the drive along Hwy-1, it's also narrow, twisting, packed with sluggish RVers on holiday weekends, and every few years is closed by mud slides and washouts after torrential winter storms and the even more destructive wildfires that have plagued the coast in recent summers. In 1983, the biggest storm in recent memory closed the road for more than a year, and some scars from the 2008 fires can be seen inland from Big Sur Village.

Big Sur is still a very wild place (with little or no cell phone reception), and there are very few services, with most of the overnight accommodations booked up solidly during the peak summer season. Spring brings wildflowers, while fall gets the most reliably good weather. No matter when you come, even if you just drive through in an afternoon, be sure to stop whenever possible and get out of the car; scenic viewpoints line the roadside, and dozens of trails lead off into the wilds. The best basic guide to Big Sur is an annual free newspaper, *El Sur Grande*, published by Monterey County and available at ranger stations and many other locations in and around Big Sur.

Borroméo de Carmelo (daily; $6.50 donation) was the most important of all the California missions, serving as home, headquarters, and final resting place of Father Junípero Serra, the Franciscan priest who established Carmel and many of the 20 other California missions, and who is entombed under the chapel floor. The gardens—where on weekends wedding parties alight from limos to take family photos—are beautiful, as is the facade with its photogenic bell tower. This is the mission to visit if you visit only one.

Carmel Practicalities

Dozens of good and usually expensive restaurants thrive in Carmel, but one place to see, even if you don't eat there, is the tiny, mock-Tudor **The Tuck Box** (daily; 831/624-6365), on Dolores Street near 7th Avenue. Dollhouse-cute, it serves up bacon-and-eggs breakfasts and dainty plates of shepherd's pie and meatloaf for lunch. If you'd rather join locals than mingle with your fellow tourists, head to **Katy's Place** (daily 7 AM–2 PM; 831/624-0199) on Mission Street between 5th and 6th, serving delicious waffles and some of the world's best eggs Benedict. For great, MSG-free Szechuan Chinese food at low prices (and minimal ambience), check out **Tommy's Wok,** on Mission between Ocean and 7th Avenue (831/624-8518); get your food to go, and wander down to the beach.

Carmel hotel rates average well over $250 a night, and there isn't any real budget option (apart from nearby Monterey). However, if you want to splurge on a bit of luxury, Carmel is a good place to do it. Besides the golf course resorts of nearby Pebble Beach, Carmel also has the commodious, 1920s-era, mission-style **Cypress Inn** at Lincoln and 7th ($225 and up; 831/624-3871), partly owned by dog-loving Doris Day (and featuring posters of her movies in the small bar off the lobby). A relaxing spot away from downtown is the historic, Clint Eastwood–owned **Mission Ranch** ($120 and up; 26270 Dolores St.; 831/624-6436 or 800/538-8221), within walking distance of the beach and mission and offering full resort facilities and a very good restaurant.

Point Lobos State Natural Reserve

82—Rugged Coast on Point Lobos, Carmel Bay in Distance, California

The sculpted headland south of Carmel Bay, now protected as **Point Lobos State Natural Reserve** (daily; $10 per car; 831/624-4909), holds one of the few remaining groves of native Monterey cypress, gnarled and bent by the often stormy coastal weather. The name comes from the barking sea lions (*lobos del mar*) found here by early Spanish explorers; hundreds of seabirds, sea lions, sea otters, and—in winter—gray whales are seen offshore or in the many picturesque, sea-carved coves.

The entrance to the reserve is along Hwy-1, three miles south of Carmel Mission, but in summer the park is so popular that visitors sometimes have to wait in line outside the gates. If possible, plan to come early or during the week. Whenever you can, come: Point Lobos has been lauded as the greatest meeting of land and sea in the world, and crowded or not it's definitely a place you'll want to see. Point Lobos has endless vistas up and down the rocky coast, and if you don't mind a short hike, there are a number of magical beaches hidden away at its southern end.

Garrapata State Park

The northern stretches of Big Sur are marked by the rugged coves, redwood forests, and sandy beach at Garrapata State Park, four miles south of Point Lobos. Though it's just minutes from Carmel, Garrapata could be light-years away from the crowds of shoppers and gallery-goers, but the two-mile-long beach here is pristine and easy to reach, yet generally empty. Winter wildlife-watchers sometimes see gray whales migrating close to shore, and if you really want to stretch your legs try the seven-mile Rocky Ridge Trail through Soberanes Canyon, which includes a steep descent (25 percent grade!) and heads east from Hwy-1 into a lush world of redwood groves, springtime wild-flowers, seasonal streams and amazing views.

The highway clings to the coast for a dozen amazing but uneventful miles, passing a few languid cattle and an occasional vacation home before coming upon one of Big Sur's many unique sights, the massive volcanic hump of Point Sur, 19 miles south of Carmel. Though it's not exactly scenic or beautiful, it definitely helps you keep your bearings. A symmetrical, 361-foot dome, Point Sur is capped by a 120-year-old lighthouse, which has been preserved as a state historic park and is open for tours on Wednesdays, Saturdays and Sundays year-round, and Thursdays during July and August ($10; 831/625-4419).

Andrew Molera State Park

Spreading along the coast at the mouth of the Big Sur River, 20 miles south of Carmel, **Andrew Molera State Park** is a grassy former cattle ranch on the site of one of Big Sur's oldest homesteads. In the 1850s, immigrant Juan Bautista Roger Cooper bought the land and built a cabin in 1861, which still stands along Hwy-1 near the park entrance. Well-blazed but sometimes boggy trails wind along both banks of the river down to the small beach, horses are available for hire (831/625-5486), and there are quite a few nice places to camp (walk-in only). In winter, the park is also a popular resting spot for migrating monarch butterflies.

Big Sur Village

South of Andrew Molera, Hwy-1 cuts inland toward the heart of **Big Sur,** the deep and densely forested valley carved by the Big Sur River. Consisting of lit-tle more than three gas stations, a couple of roadside markets, and a number of lodges and restaurants, the mile-long village of Big Sur (pop. 950) represents the only real settlement between Carmel and Hearst Castle.

At the north end of town, the **Big Sur River Inn** (831/667-2700) has a woodsy, warm, and unpretentious restaurant overlooking the river, and rooms upstairs and across the highway. Next door is a small complex that includes crafts galleries, a grocery store with burrito bar, and the homey **Big Sur Village Pub** (831/667-2355), which features good beers and pub grub. Continuing south, the next mile of Hwy-1 holds Big Sur's nicest group of rustic cabins and campgrounds: Besides a handful of quaint cabins in a quiet location, downhill from the highway and right on the riverbanks, **Ripplewood Resort** (831/667-2242) also has a friendly 1950s café on the east side of Hwy-1, serving very good breakfasts and lunches, as well as a handy gas station and general store.

The photogenic **Bixby Creek Bridge,** 15 miles south of Carmel, was one of the largest concrete bridges in the world when it was built in 1932. The old coast road runs along the north bank of the creek, linking up again with Hwy-1 near Andrew Molera State Park.

At the south end of the Big Sur village, a classic 1950s motor court has been updated and restored to its original glory (now with free Wi-Fi!), as **Glen Oaks Big Sur** ($200 and up; 831/667-2105).

Pfeiffer Big Sur State Park

Roughly a half mile south of Big Sur village, **Pfeiffer Big Sur State Park** is the region's main event, a 1,000-acre riverside forest that's one of the most pleasant (and popular) parks in the state. Besides offering a full range of visitor services—restaurant, lodge, riverside campground, and grocery store—the park includes one of Big Sur's best short hikes, a three-mile loop on the Valley View trail that takes in stately redwoods, a 60-foot waterfall, and a grand vista down the Big Sur valley to the coast. The park also has the main **ranger station** (831/667-2315) for all the state parks in the Big Sur area. Just south of the park entrance, a USFS **ranger station** (831/667-2423) on the east side of Hwy-1 has information on hiking and camping opportunities in the mountains above Big Sur, including the isolated (but poison oak–ridden) **Ventana Wilderness.**

Pfeiffer Beach

South of Pfeiffer Big Sur State Park, halfway up a long, steep incline, a small road turns west and leads down through dark and heavily overgrown Sycamore Canyon, eventually winding up at Big Sur's best beach, **Pfeiffer Beach.** From the lot at the end of the road, a short trail runs through a grove of trees before opening onto the broad white sands, loomed over by a pair of hulking offshore rocks. The water's way too cold for swimming, but the half-mile strand is one of the few places in Big Sur where you can enjoy extended beachcombing strolls. The beach's northern half attracts a clothing-optional crew, even on cool, gray days.

Back along Hwy-1, just south of the turnoff for Sycamore Canyon and Pfeiffer Beach, the excellent **Big Sur Bakery & Restaurant** (831/667-0520) makes its own fresh breads and pastries, brews a rich cup of coffee, and also serves full meals—soups, steaks, and wood-fired pizzas.

Ventana Inn & Spa and the Post Ranch Inn

South of Sycamore Canyon, roughly three miles from the heart of Big Sur village, Hwy-1 passes between two of California's most deluxe small resorts. The larger of the two, **Ventana Inn & Spa** ($400 and up; 831/667-2331 or 800/628-6500), covers 243 acres of Big Sur foothills and offers saunas, swimming pools, and four-star accommodations in 1970s-style cedar-paneled rooms and cabins. There's also a very fine restaurant, with incredible views and reasonable prices, to which guests are ferried in a fleet of electric carts.

The landmark red farmhouse along Hwy-1 at the entrance to Ventana was built in 1877 by pioneer rancher W. B. Post, whose descendants developed the Post Ranch Inn.

Completed in 1992 and directly across Hwy-1 from Ventana, the **Post Ranch Inn** ($595 and up; 831/667-2200 or 888/524-4787), a low-impact but ultra-high-style luxury resort hanging high above the Big Sur coast, is at the forefront of luxury ecotourism. In order to preserve Big Sur's untarnished natural beauty, the Post Ranch Inn is designed to be virtually invisible from land or sea: The 39 guest rooms and two private houses—all featuring a king-size bed and a whirlpool bath with built-in massage table—blend in with the landscape, disguised either as playful tree houses raised up in the branches of the oaks and pines or as underground cabins carved into the cliff top. The Post Ranch restaurant, Sierra Mar, is also excellent, or if you want to have a look and plan for a future escape, free tours of the resort are given Monday–Friday at 2 PM.

In 1987, the mighty California condor was all but extinct in the wild. Now, thanks to a successful captive breeding and reintroduction program, these massive birds can be seen soaring over the Ventana Wilderness that rises above Big Sur.

The hilltop where Nepenthe now stands was previously the site of a rustic cabin that Orson Welles and then-wife Rita Hayworth bought in 1944.

Nepenthe

One of the most popular and long-lived stopping points along the Big Sur coast, **Nepenthe** (831/667-2345) is a rustic bar and restaurant offering good food and great views from atop a rocky headland some thousand feet above the Pacific. Named for the mythical drug that causes one to forget all sorrows, Nepenthe looks like something out of a 1960s James Bond movie, built of huge boulders and walls of plate glass. The food is plenty good—burgers, steaks, and fish dominate the menu—but it's the view you come here for.

Sharing a parking lot, and taking advantage of similar views, the neighboring **Cafe Kevah** (831/667-2344) serves brunch all day, plus good teas and coffees and microbrews on a rooftop deck; you'll find a gift shop downstairs selling top-quality arts and crafts and knitwear by Kaffe Fassett, whose family owns the place.

Right along Hwy-1, at a sharp bend in the road just south of Nepenthe, **The Henry Miller Memorial Library** (closed Tues.; 831/667-2574) carries an erratic but engaging collection of books by and about the author, who lived in Big Sur for many years in the 1950s.

A half mile south of Nepenthe on the east side of the highway, one of the oldest and most atmospheric places to stay is **Deetjen's Big Sur Inn** ($90 and up; 831/667-2377), a rambling and rustic redwood lodge built by a Norwegian immigrant in the 1930s and now a nonprofit, preservationist operation. Though the rooms are not available to families with young children unless you reserve both rooms of a two-room building, Deetjen's also serves Big Sur's best breakfasts and hearty dinners, at which all are welcome.

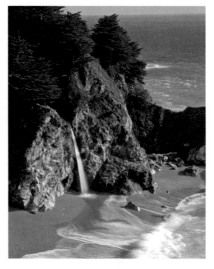

Julia Pfeiffer Burns State Park

If for some untenable reason you only have time to stop once along the Big Sur coast, **Julia Pfeiffer Burns State Park** (dawn–dusk daily) should be the place. Spreading along both sides of Hwy-1, about 14 miles south of Big Sur village, the park includes one truly beautiful sight: a slender waterfall that drops crisply down into a nearly circular turquoise-blue cove. This is the only major waterfall in California that plunges directly into the Pacific.

From the parking area, east of the highway, a short trail leads under the road to a fine view of the waterfall, while another leads to the remnants of a pioneer mill, complete with a preserved Pelton wheel. Other routes climb through redwood groves up to the chaparral-covered slopes of the Santa Lucia Mountains.

Julia Pfeiffer Burns was a Big Sur pioneer whose family lived near Pfeiffer Beach and homesteaded much of this rugged, isolated area. In 1915, she married John Burns, a Scottish orphan who lived with the nearby Post family, and they continued to live and ranch at what is now Julia Pfeiffer Burns State Park until Julia's death in 1928.

About six miles south of Nepenthe, or a mile north of the parking area at Julia Pfeiffer Burns State Park, a steep fire road drops down to **Partington Cove,** where ships used to moor in the protected anchorage. The last stretch of the route passes through a 60-foot-long tunnel hewn out of solid rock.

Esalen and Lucia

Three miles south of Julia Pfeiffer Burns State Park, the New Age **Esalen Institute** takes its name from the native Esselen Indian tribe who were wiped out by European colonizers. Founded in the early 1960s by free-thinking Stanford University graduates inspired by countercultural pioneers like Gregory Bateson and Alan Watts, and set on a breathtaking cliff-top site overlooking a 180-degree coastal panorama, Esalen offers a variety of religious, philosophical, and psychological workshops, but most visitors are drawn to its incredible set of natural hot springs, right above the ocean and open to the public 1–3 PM For information on overnight "personal retreats," or to make reservations for massages or the hot tubs, phone 888/837-2536.

The southern reaches of the Big Sur coast are drier and more rugged, offering bigger vistas but fewer stopping places than the northern half. The road winds along the cliffs, slowing down every 10 miles or so for each of three gas station/café/motel complexes, which pass for towns on the otherwise uninhabited coast. The northernmost of these, nine miles south of Esalen, and 25 miles south of Big Sur village, is **Lucia,** which has wonderful ocean views, a small restaurant, and 10 creaky cabins ($150 and up; 831/688-4884).

High on a hill just south of Lucia, marked by a slender black cross, is the Benedictine **New Camaldoli Hermitage,** open to interested outsiders as a silent retreat. For details, phone 831/667-2456.

Nacimiento-Fergusson Road and Mission San Antonio de Padua

Five miles south of Lucia, the narrow Nacimiento-Fergusson Road makes an unforgettable climb up from Hwy-1 over the coastal mountains. Though ravaged in places by wildfires, it's a beautiful drive, winding through hillside chaparral and dense oak groves before ending up near King City in the Salinas Valley. One real highlight here is **Mission San Antonio de Padua** (daily 10 AM–4 PM; 831/385-4478), a well-preserved church and monastery that is still in use by a Catholic religious community. Because the road passes through sections of Fort Hunter Liggett Army Base, you may need to show valid car registration and proof of insurance. History note: All the land on which the Army base and mission stand belonged at one time to mining magnate George Hearst, whose land stretched from here all the way south and west to the coast at San Simeon, where his only child William Randolph Hearst later constructed Hearst Castle. Hearst's old hunting lodge has been restored and is now operated as an unusual B&B, called the Hacienda ($50 and up; 831/386-2262).

The roadside along Hwy-1 in the southern half of Big Sur has been invaded by thick bunches of pampas grass that crowd out local flora.

Near the foot of the Nacimiento-Fergusson Road is one of the few oceanside campsites in Big Sur, and perhaps the most amazing place to wake up on the West Coast: **Kirk Creek Campground,** operated by the U.S. Forest Service (831/667-2423). The setting is unforgettable, but so are the dastardly raccoons who are fearless in their efforts to eat your lunch before you do.

Continuing south, Hwy-1 runs past **Pacific Valley,** then passes by a number of small but pretty beaches and coves before reaching **Gorda,** the southernmost stop on the Big Sur coast. Just north of Gorda, tucked away on a knoll just east of the highway, **Treebones Resort** ($169 and up; 877/424-4787) offers rustic yurts and a swimming pool.

San Simeon: Hearst Castle

At the south end of Big Sur, the mountains flatten out and turn inland, and the coastline becomes rolling, open-range ranch land. High on a hill above Hwy-1 stands the coast's one totally unique attraction, **Hearst Castle.** Located 65 miles south of Big Sur village and 43 miles northwest of San Luis Obispo,

Hearst Castle is the sort of place that you really have to see to believe, though simple numbers—115 rooms, including 38 bed-rooms in the main house alone—do give a sense of its scale.

Even if Hearst's taste in interior design (or his megalomania, which by all accounts was understated in his fictional portrayal in Orson Welles's *Citizen Kane*) doesn't appeal, Hearst Castle cries out to be seen. One of the last century's most powerful and influential Americans (the Rupert Murdoch of his day), Hearst inherited the land, and most of his fortune, from his mother, Phoebe Apperson Hearst (his father was George Hearst, a mining mogul), and began work on his castle following the death of his mother in 1919. With the help of the great California architect Julia Morgan, who designed the complex to look like a Mediterranean hill town with Hearst's house as the cathedral at its center, Hearst spent more than 25 years working on his "castle"—building, re-building, and filling room after room with furniture—all the while entertaining the great and powerful of the era, from Charlie Chaplin to Winston Churchill.

A small **museum** (daily; free) in the visitors center, next to where you board the trams that carry you up to the house, details Hearst's life and times. If you want to go on a **tour,** the Grand Rooms Tour (which costs $25) gives the best first-time overview, taking in a few rooms of the main house. There's also an Upstairs Suites Tour and a Cottages & Kitchen Tour; each costs $25 and takes around 50 minutes, not including transit time. All tours also come with the option of watching a 40-minute movie giving the background on Hearst and his house-building. Advance reservations (800/444-4445) are all but essential, especially in summer.

Since Hearst Castle is rather isolated, it's a good idea to stay the night before or after a visit at nearby San Simeon, which has grown into a massive strip of motels. There's a $45-and-up-a-night **Motel 6,** or opt for free Wi-Fi at the **San Simeon Lodge** ($49 and up; 9520 Castillo Dr.; 805/927-4601).

William Randolph Hearst

At Piedras Blancas, just north of Hearst Castle, the roadside along Hwy-1 has been taken over by herds of massive, bellowing elephant seals, a once-threatened but clearly resurgent species of massive pinnipeds who congregate here every winter to fight and procreate.

Cambria

Without Hearst Castle, **Cambria** would be just another farming town, but being next to one of the state's top tourist attractions has turned Cambria into quite a busy little hive. Apart from a few hokey, tourist-trapping souvenir shops at the north end of town, it's a casual, walkable, and franchise-free community of arts and crafts galleries, boutiques, and good restaurants; from Hwy-1, Main Street makes a three-mile loop around to the east, running through the heart of town.

Above Cambria, a folk-art landmark known as **Nitt Witt Ridge** ($10; 881 Hillcrest Dr.; 805/927-2690) was built by the eccentric artist Art Beal, who used old Busch beer cans, seashells, roof tiles, and broken-down car parts to build, over 50 years starting in the late 1920s, what is often called a "Poor Man's Hearst Castle." The sprawling three-story house, with great views and intriguing details, is now open for tours.

Back in town, hearty breakfasts are available at the **Redwood Cafe** (2094 Main St.; 805/927-4830), while well-prepared multi-ethnic and vegetarian food is on the menu at **Robin's** (4095 Burton Dr.; 805/927-5007), a half block off Main Street. For barbecue, check out the cash-only **Main Street Grill** (603 Main St.; 805/927-3194). Places to stay range from nice older motels like the **Bluebird Inn** ($90 and up; 1880 Main St.; 800/552-5434) to the spacious suites and cabins at **Cambria Pines Lodge** ($109 and up; 2905 Burton Dr.; 805/927-4200), which has a nice pool high on a hill between town and the beach. For a relaxing overnight, try the lovely little **Bridge Street Inn,** a block from downtown (4314 Bridge St.; 805/927-7653), which offers very reasonable B&B rooms as well as shared HI-approved hostel beds.

Five miles south of Cambria, **Harmony** (pop. 18) is a former dairy town turned arts and crafts colony, with a range of galleries and a small wedding chapel.

Cayucos

Though it doesn't really look like much from Hwy-1, which has grown into a near-freeway to carry all the Hearst Castle traffic, the coastal town of **Cayucos** is definitely worth a look. Sitting along the coast 15 miles south of Cambria, not far from Morro Bay, Cayucos has a nice little beach, a fishing pier, a range of surfing and skateboard shops, and at least two unusual places to eat and drink. If you like tiki-style bars, you'll want to save your thirst for a visit to **Schooners Wharf** (171 N. Ocean Ave.; 805/995-3883), with good mojitos and variable food, served up in a landmark bar room downstairs, or on a oceanview terrace above. For good food, don't miss **Ruddell's Smokehouse,** just off the beach (101 D St.; 805/995-5028), where the no-frills menu features smoked salmon and tuna sandwiches, plus fish, pork, and chicken tacos.

Morro Bay

Marked by the Gibraltar-like monolith of Morro Rock, which was noted by Juan Rodriguez Cabrillo in 1542 and now serves as a peregrine falcon preserve and nesting site, **Morro Bay** (pop. 10,436) surrounds a busy commercial fishing harbor a half mile west of Hwy-1. A thin, three-mile-long strip of sand protects the bay from the Pacific Ocean, forming a seabird-rich lagoon that's included within **Morro Bay State Park,** a mile southeast of Morro Rock. There's an excellent museum ($3) with displays on local wildlife, and the park also contains the friendly **Bayside Cafe** (805/772-1465), serving lunch and dinner. Next door, when the weather's nice, you can rent **kayaks** 805/772-8796) and paddle around the estuary.

The rest of Morro Bay is pretty quiet; one unusual sight is a giant **outdoor chessboard** (with waist-high playing pieces) at the foot of Morro Bay Boulevard on the waterfront in City Park. For clam chowder or fish-and-chips, try **Giovanni's,** in the strollable waterfront neighborhood (1001 Front St.; 805/772-1276). Very good fast Mexican-themed "fusion" food is available at the **Taco Temple,** an often crowded and grandly named fish shack on the land side of the Hwy-1 frontage, a mile north of town (2680 Main St.; 805/772-4965).

The **James Dean Memorial,** 27 miles east of Paso Robles near the junction of Highways 46 and 41, is a stark, stainless steel sculpture near the site where the talented and rebellious actor crashed in his silver Porsche and died on September 30, 1955. The highway has also been signed in Dean's memory.

San Luis Obispo

Located midway between San Francisco and Los Angeles at the junction of Hwy-1 and US-101, **San Luis Obispo** (pop. 44,174) makes a good stopping-off point, at least for lunch if not for a lengthier stay. Like most of the towns along this route, San Luis, as it's almost always called, revolves around an 18th-century mission, here named **Mission San Luis Obispo de Tolosa.** Standing at the heart of town, at Chorro and Monterey Streets, the mission overlooks one of the state's liveliest small-town downtown districts, with dozens of shops and restaurants backing onto Mission Plaza, a two-block park on the banks of Mission Creek.

Besides the mission and the lively downtown commercial district that surrounds it, not to mention the nearly 20,000

Another San Luis landmark, the world's first motel, opened at 2223 Monterey Street in 1925. Originally called the Milestone Mo-Tel, the Spanish revival structure was later renamed the Motel Inn, but it went out of business long ago, and its remnants now stand next to US-101 on the grounds of the Apple Farm restaurant and motel.

El Camino Real and the California Missions

While the American colonies were busy rebelling against the English Crown, a handful of Spaniards and Mexicans were establishing outposts and blazing an overland route up the California coast, along the New World's most distant frontier. Beginning in 1769 with the founding of a fortress and a Franciscan mission at San Diego, and culminating in 1823 with the founding of another outpost at what is now San Francisco, a series of small but self-reliant religious colonies was established, each a day's travel apart and linked by El Camino Real, The King's Highway, a route followed roughly by today's US-101.

Some of the most interesting missions are listed here, north to south, followed by the dates of their founding.

San Francisco Solano (1823). The only mission built under Mexican rule stands at the heart of Sonoma, a history-rich Wine Country town.

San Juan Bautista (1797). This lovely church forms the heart of an extensive historic park, in the town of the same name (see page 72).

San Carlos Borroméo de Carmelo (1771). Also known as **Carmel Mission,** this was the most important of the California missions (see page 77).

San Antonio de Padua (1771). This reconstructed church, still in use as a monastery, stands in an undeveloped valley inland from Big Sur in the middle of Fort Hunter Liggett Army training center. Monks still live, work, and pray here, making for a marvelously evocative visit (see page 84).

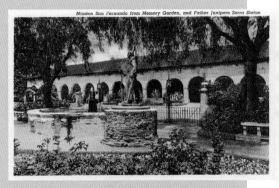

Mission San Fernando from Memory Garden, and Father Junipero Serra Statue

San Miguel Arcángel (1797). This is the only mission not to have undergone extensive renovations and restorations—almost everything, notably the vibrantly colorful interior murals, is as it was.

La Purisima Mission (1787). A quiet coastal valley is home to this church, which was restored in the 1930s using traditional methods as part of a New Deal employment and training project (see page 92).

Santa Barbara (1786). Called the Queen of the Missions, this lovely church stands in lush gardens above the upscale coastal city (see page 94).

San Gabriel Arcángel (1771). Once the most prosperous of the California missions, it now stands quietly and all but forgotten off a remnant of Route 66 east of Los Angeles.

San Juan Capistrano (1776). Known for the swallows that return here each year, this mission has lovely gardens (see page 107).

CALIFORNIA MISSIONS (1769 - 1823)

San Francisco Solano de Sonoma (1823)
San Rafael (1817)
San Francisco de Asis (1776)
Santa Clara (1777)
San Jose (1797)
Santa Cruz (1791)
San Juan Bautista (1797)
San Carlos Borromeo (1770)
Soledad (1791)
San Antonio de Padua (1771)
San Miguel Arcangel (1797)
San Luis Obispo de Tolosa (1772)
La Purisima Mission (1787)
Santa Ynez (1804)
Santa Barbara (1782)
San Buenaventura (1782)
San Fernando Rey (1797)
San Gabriel Arcangel (1771)
San Juan Capistrano (1776)
San Luis Rey (1798)
San Diego (1769)

PACIFIC OCEAN

UNITED STATES
MEXICO

El Camino Real

0   100 miles
0   100 kilometers

© AVALON TRAVEL

students buzzing around the nearby campus of Cal Poly San Luis Obispo, San Luis holds a singular roadside attraction, the **Madonna Inn** ($179 and up; 805/543-3000 or 800/543-9666), which stands just west of US-101 at the foot of town. One of California's most noteworthy pop culture landmarks, the Madonna Inn is a remarkable example of what architecturally minded academic types like to call vernacular kitsch. Created by local contractor Alex Madonna, who died in 2004, the Madonna Inn offers 100 unique rooms, each decorated in a wild barrage of fantasy motifs: There's a bright pink honeymoon suite known as "Love Nest," the "Safari" room covered in fake zebra skins with a jungle-green carpet, and the cave-like "Caveman" Room. *Roadside America* rates it as "the best place to spend a vacation night in America," but even if you can't stay, at least stop for a look at the gift shop, which sells postcards of the different rooms. Guys should head down to the men's room, where the urinal trough is flushed by a waterfall.

A pedestrian walkway in downtown San Luis Obispo, off Higuera Street between Garden and Broad Streets, has become known around the world as **Bubble Gum Alley.** Since the 1950s, local kids have written their names and allegiances on the brick walls, using chewing gum rather than the more contemporary spray paint.

Every Thursday evening, the main drag of San Luis Obispo, **Higuera Street,** is closed to cars and converted into a very lively farmers market and block party, with stands selling fresh food and good live bands providing entertainment.

Though the Madonna Inn has a huge, banquet-ready restaurant—done up in white lace and varying hues of pink—the best places to eat are downtown, near the mission. **Linnaea's Cafe** (1110 Garden St.; 805/541-5888), off Higuera, serves coffee and tea and sundry snack items all day and night; there's also the lively, veggie-friendly **Big Sky Cafe** (1121 Broad St.; 805/545-5401) and the usual range of beer-and-burger bars you'd expect from a college town. For something very special, the heart of SLO holds one of the central coast's great restaurants, **Novo,** serving locally sourced and very fresh Mediterranean-inspired meals on a nice terrace backing onto Mission Plaza (726 Higuera St.; 805/543-3986). Great bar, too.

Along with the Madonna Inn, San Luis has a number of good places to stay, with reasonable rates that drop considerably after the summertime peak season. Besides the national chains, try the **Peach Tree Inn** ($79 and up; 2001 Monterey St.; 800/227-6396) or **La Cuesta Inn** ($89 and up; 2074 Monterey St.; 800/543-2777). There's also the **HI-Hostel Obispo** (1617 Santa Rosa St.; 805/544-4678), 28 beds in a converted Victorian cottage near downtown and the Amtrak station.

Pismo Beach

South of San Luis Obispo, Hwy-1 and US-101 run along the ocean past **Pismo Beach** (pop. 7,655), a family-oriented beach resort where the main attraction is driving or dune-buggying along the sands. Pismo was once famous for its clams, now over-harvested to the point of oblivion, but while you may still see people pitchforking a few small ones out of the surf, you won't find any on local menus. Like the rest of Southern California, the Pismo area has grown significantly in the past two decades, thanks mainly to an influx of retired people housed in red-roofed townhouses, but Price Street, the old main road running through the heart of the old small town, still offers a wide range of motels and restaurants, like the very popular **Cracked Crab** (751 Price St.; 805/773-2722), which has halibut and chips ($17) and a crazy range of fresh crab and other crustaceans (almost all of which come from Alaska). For a close approximation of Pismo's once-abundant clams, walk two blocks from the Cracked Crab, past the bowling alley, to another seafood specialist, the **Splash Café** (197 Pomeroy Ave.; 805/773-4653), which is locally famous for its chowder served up in edible bowls made of freshly baked bread.

At the south end of Pismo Beach, beyond the scruffy farmlands that surround the wide mouth of the Santa Maria River, **Guadalupe-Nipomo Dunes National Wildlife Refuge** holds endless acres of windswept beaches, coastal sand dunes, and boggy bird-friendly marshlands, as well as the buried remains of a movie set used in Cecil B. DeMille's *The Ten Commandments.*

While Pismo is most popular for summer fun, every winter a grove of trees just south of downtown turns into a prime gathering spot for migrating monarch butterflies. The largest groupings, numbering in the tens of thousands though decreasing disturbingly quickly in recent years, are usually found roosting at the North Beach Campground of Pismo State Beach, along Hwy-1 off Dolliver Street.

In 1936, Nipomo was the place where Dorothea Lange took that famous photograph of a migrant mother huddling with her children in a farm-worker camp.

Guadalupe and Santa Maria

South of Pismo Beach, California's coastal highways again diverge. Hwy-1 cuts off west through the still-agricultural areas around sleepy **Guadalupe** (pop. 6,296), where produce stands sell cabbages, broccoli, and leafy green vegetables fresh from the fields. The town itself feels miles away from modern California, with a four-block Main Street lined by Mexican cafés, bars, banks, and grocery stores.

If you opt to follow US-101, shopping malls and tract-house suburbs fill the inland valleys through rapidly suburbanizing **Santa Maria.** Among barbecue aficionados, Santa Maria is famous for its thick cuts of salsa-slathered barbecued beef, which can best be sampled at **Jocko's** (125 N. Thompson Ave.; 805/929-3565) in Nipomo, east of US-101 at the Tefft Street exit, where great steaks (and mouthwateringly moist, inch-thick barbecued pork chops!) highlight the no-frills menu. Barbecue is served from 4:30 PM daily.

Lompoc and La Purisima Mission

The rolling valleys around Lompoc are famed for their production of flower seeds, and consequently the fields along Hwy-1 are often ablaze in brilliant colors. Apart from colorful murals adorning downtown buildings, **Lompoc** as a town is not up to much, despite the unusual nature of the area's two main nonagricultural employers. One is a minimum-security federal prison; the other is Vandenberg Air Force Base, site of numerous missile tests, the aborted West Coast space shuttle port, and the $60 billion "Son of Star Wars" National Missile Defense program.

With its long arcade reaching across the floor of a shallow, grassy valley, **La Purisima Mission** (daily; $6 per car; 805/733-3713) gives a strong first impression of what the missions

Lompoc flower fields

may have looked like in their prime. Four miles northeast of Lompoc, between Hwy-1 and US-101 on Hwy-246, the mission here was originally built in 1812 but fell to ruin before being totally reconstructed as part of a WPA make-work scheme in the New Deal 1930s. During the restoration, workers used period techniques wherever possible, hewing logs with hand tools and stomping mud and straw with their bare feet to mix it for adobe bricks. Workers also built most of the mission-style furniture that fills the chapel and the other rooms in the complex. Other features include a functioning aqueduct, many miles of hiking trails, and a small museum.

Buellton and Solvang

The town of **Buellton,** a block west of US-101 at the Solvang exit, holds one of California's classic roadside landmarks, **Andersen's Pea Soup** restaurant (805/688-5581), advertised up and down the coast. Another Buellton landmark, **The Hitching Post II** restaurant (805/688-0676), starred in the wine-loving road-trip movie *Sideways*.

Four miles east of Buellton and US-101, America's most famous mock-European tourist trap, the Danish-style town of **Solvang** (pop. 5,245), was founded in 1911. Set up by a group of Danish immigrants as a cooperative agricultural community, Solvang found its calling catering to passing travelers. The compact blocks of cobblestone streets and Old World architecture, highlighted by a few windmills and signs advertising the Hamlet Inn among many more suspicious claims to Danishness, now attract tourists by the busload. Many other U.S. towns (Leavenworth, Washington, and Helen, Georgia, to name two) have been inspired by Solvang's success, but to be honest there's nothing much to do here apart from walking, gawking, and shopping for pastries.

The late great pop singer Michael Jackson's **Neverland Ranch** lies here in the foothills of the Santa Ynez Valley, southeast of Solvang via the truly scenic Hwy-154, which loops inland south to Santa Barbara, arriving via a steep and stunning drive over San Marcos Pass.

Just east of Solvang's windmills and gables, the brooding hulk of **Old Mission Santa Inés** stands as a sober reminder of the region's Spanish colonial past. Built in 1804, it was once among the more prosperous of the California missions but now is worth a visit mainly for the gift shop selling all manner of devotional ornaments.

Gaviota State Park and Refugio State Beach

Between Solvang and Santa Barbara, US-101 follows the coast past some of California's most beautiful beaches. Dropping through a steep-sided canyon, US-101 reaches the coast at **Gaviota State Park,** where a small fishing pier and campground are overwhelmed by the massive train trestle that runs overhead. Continuing south, US-101 runs atop coastal bluffs past prime surfing beaches, usually marked by a few VWs pulled out along the west side of the highway. Midway along this stretch of coast, some 22 miles north of Santa Barbara, **Refugio State Beach** has groves of palm trees backing a clear white strand. There's also a small, summer-only store, and a number of attractive campsites with hot showers.

Reservations for camping at Gaviota or Refugio, or at any California state beach, should be made in advance by calling 800/444-7275.

Rancho del Cielo, the ranch of former President Ronald Reagan, spreads along the crest of the coastal hills above Refugio State Beach.

Santa Barbara

The geographical midpoint of California may well be somewhere near San Francisco, but the Southern California of popular imagination—golden beaches washed by waves and peopled by blond-haired surfer gods—has its start, and perhaps best expression, in Santa Barbara. Around 100 miles north of Los Angeles, **Santa Barbara** (pop. 88,410) has grown threefold in the last 60 years, but for the moment, at least, it manages to retain its sleepy seaside charm. Much of its character comes from the fact that, following a sizable earthquake in 1925, the town fathers—caught up in the contemporary craze for anything Spanish Revival—required that all buildings in the downtown area exude a mission-era feel, mandating red-tile roofs, adobe-colored stucco, and rounded arcades wherever practicable. The resulting architectural consistency gives Santa Barbara an un-American charm; it looks more like a Mediterranean village than the modern city that, beneath the surface, it really is.

For a good first look at the city head down to the water, where **Stearns Wharf** sticks out into the bay, bordered by palm tree–lined beaches populated by joggers, in-line skaters, and volleyball players. From the wharf area, follow State Street away from the sands to the downtown district, where Santa Barbarans parade among the numerous cafés, bars, and boutiques. At the

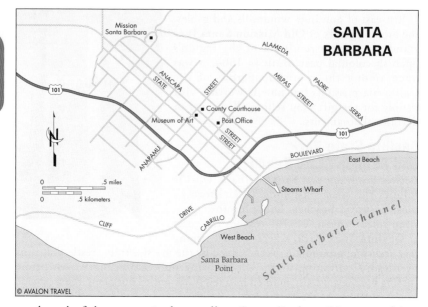

north end of downtown is the excellent **Santa Barbara Museum of Art** (closed Mon.; $9, free Sun.; 1130 State St.; 805/963-4364). A block east on Anacapa Street, the **County Courthouse** is one of the finest public buildings in the state, a handcrafted Spanish Revival monument set in lush semitropical gardens, with an observation tower (8 AM–5 PM weekdays, 10 AM–4:30 PM weekends; free) giving a fine view over the red-tiled cityscape.

Santa Barbara's reigning attraction, **Mission Santa Barbara** (daily; $5; 805/682-4713), stands atop a shallow hill a well-posted mile up from State

Street, looking out over the city and shoreline below. Called the "Queen of the Missions" by the local tourist scribes, Mission Santa Barbara is undeniably lovely to look at, its rose-hued stone facade perfectly complemented by the roses and bougainvillea that frame the well-maintained gardens and lawns.

Santa Barbara is one of many great places along the coast to go on a whale-watching cruise, on the *Condor Express* or other boats, to see migrating gray whales in winter and jumping humpbacks in summer. Trips take a half day or full day, and some head out to the Channel Islands; call 805/963-3564 or 888/779-4253 for details or reservations.

Santa Barbara has perhaps the coast's best variety of places to eat. State Street holds the most lunch and dinner places, like the old-fashioned burgers and beer on tap in the dark-wood dining room of **Joe's Cafe** (536 State St.; 805/966-4638). Great Italian food at fair prices has made a favorite of **Ca'**

Dario, just off State (37 E. Victoria St.; 805/884-9419). There's excellent fresh sushi at **Arigato Sushi** (1225 State St.; 805/965-6074), while some of the world's best hole-in-the-wall Mexican food is served a half mile east of State Street at **La Super-Rica** (622 N. Milpas St.; 805/963-4940), where such distinguished foodies as Julia Child have come to chow down on a variety of freshly made soft tacos and delicious seafood tamales. It's not cheap, but the food is great (fresh tortillas, traditional *adobado*-marinated pork, and spicy chorizo), and the *horchata* is the creamiest you'll taste. Yum.

The city's accommodations, however, are among the central coast's most expensive, especially in summer when even the most basic motel can charge as much as $200 a night. One of the nicest of many motels is **The Franciscan Inn** ($114 and up; 109 Bath St.; 805/963-8845), just a short walk from the beach and wharf. At the top of the scale, the **Simpson House Inn** ($215 and up; 121 E. Arrellaga St.; 805/963-7067 or 800/676-1280) offers comfortable, centrally located B&B rooms. Off the scale completely, money's-no-object visitors can enjoy the deluxe facilities of the **San Ysidro Ranch** ($750 and up; 805/565-1700), in the hills above neighboring Montecito, where Jackie and JFK spent some of their honeymoon. Somewhat ironically, considering the generally high prices here, international budget chain Motel 6 got its start in Santa Barbara, where it now has five area properties, including the recently redesigned original one near the beach ($84 and up; 443 Corona Del Mar; 805/564-1392).

Channel Islands National Park

South of Santa Barbara, US-101 widens into an eight-lane freeway along the coast. Looking out across the Pacific, beyond the partially disguised offshore oil wells, you can't miss seeing the sharp outlines of the Channel Islands, whose rocky, tide-pool-packed shores are protected as a national park. Consisting of eight islands altogether (five are part of the park), they sit from 12 to about 60 miles off the mainland. Numerous scenic cruises around the Channel Islands start from Santa Barbara, but only the closest, Anacapa Island, is easily accessible to the public, via daily trips from Ventura Harbor offered by **Island Packers** ($56; 805/642-1393). Bring water, as none is available on the island; camping is possible, but reservations are required.

CAUSEWAY, COAST HIGHWAY, BETWEEN VENTURA AND SANTA BARBARA

Ventura

Midway between Malibu and Santa Barbara, downtown **Ventura** (pop. 106,433) is an offbeat little place, its three-block Main Street lined by enough thrift shops (seven at last count) to clothe a destitute retro-minded army. Apart from searching out vintage couture, the main reason to stop is the small and much-reconstructed **Mission San**

Ventura is the birthplace and headquarters of the outdoor equipment and clothing company Patagonia, started and still owned by legendary rock climber Yvon Chouinard.

Buenaventura (daily; $2; 211 E. Main St.), standing at the center of Ventura just north of the US-101 freeway. This was the ninth in the California mission chain, and the last one founded by Father Junípero Serra, in 1782. A block from the mission the **Albinger Archaeological Museum** (113 E. Main St.) collects a wide range of artifacts—

the oldest from 1600 BC, the most recent from early American settlers—all excavated from a single city block–sized site alongside the mission.

Ventura doesn't get anything like the tourist trade that Santa Barbara draws, but it does have the very pleasant **Bella Maggiore Inn** ($75 and up; 67 S. California St.; 805/652-0277 or 800/523-8479), offering good-value B&B rooms in a nicely restored 1920s courtyard house between downtown and US-101.

South of Ventura, US-101 heads inland through the San Fernando Valley to Hollywood and downtown Los Angeles, while Hwy-1 heads south through the 10 miles of stop-and-go sprawl that make up the rapidly suburbanizing farming community of **Oxnard** (pop. 197,899), then continues right along the coast through Malibu and West Los Angeles.

Simi Valley

If you opt to follow US-101 rather than coastal Hwy-1 into Los Angeles, be sure to check out the somnolent suburb of **Simi Valley,** 30 miles east of Ventura, where the hilltop **Ronald Reagan Presidential Library** (daily; $12; 805/522-2977) fills 150,000 square feet of Spanish-style stucco with a fascinating array of exhibits and artifacts, most famously a chunk of the Berlin Wall, set in a Cold War–era tableau. Also here, housed in a 200-foot-long glass-walled pavilion, is the actual Boeing 707 used as presidential Air Force One by Nixon, Carter, Ford, Reagan, George H. W. Bush, Clinton, and

George W. Bush. The "Great Communicator" was interred here following his death in 2004; to get to the library, take US-101 to Hwy-23 North (a.k.a. the Ronald Reagan Freeway), exit at Olsen Road, and follow the signs.

The other Simi Valley sight to see is **Bottle Village** (donations; 4595 Cochran St.; 805/583-1627), a complex of small buildings and sculptures built out of glass bottles, TV

Tressa Prisbrey's Bottle Village

sets, hubcaps, and assorted other recycled refuse starting in 1956 by the late Tressa Prisbey. Subject of an ongoing battle between folk-art preservationists and those who think it's a pile of junk, the "village" can be viewed less than a mile south of the Hwy-118/210 freeway between the Tapo Street and Stearns Street exits.

Pacific Coast Highway Beaches

Running right along the beach, the Pacific Coast Highway (Hwy-1) heads south from Oxnard around the rocky headland of **Point Mugu** (pronounced "ma-GOO"), where the U.S. Navy operates a missile testing center and the Santa Monica Mountains rise steeply out of the Pacific Ocean. Most of these chaparral-covered granite mountains have been protected as parkland, with hiking, cycling, and riding trails offering grand views and a surprising amount of solitude. Before or after a hike in the hills (or a Harley ride along the coast, the preferred mode of arrival), the ramshackle **Neptune's Net** restaurant (42505 Pacific Coast Hwy.; 310/457-3095) is a great place to hang out and "star"-gaze while enjoying fresh seafood, served up on paper plates for that down-home Hollywood feel.

South from here, state-owned beaches mark your progress along the coastal road, but this stretch is basically natural wilderness—apart from the highway, of course. Biggest and best of the beaches hereabouts is the lovely **Leo Carrillo State Park** (818/880-0363), which has a sandy strand, some great tidepools, and a sycamore-shaded campground (reservations 800/444-7275). Leo Carrillo (1880–1961) was an actor (he played Pancho in *The Cisco Kid* TV show) and preservationist who was instrumental in expanding the California state parks.

South of Leo Carrillo, which marks the Los Angeles County line, there are many more public beach areas, including (in roughly north-to-south order) **Nicholas Canyon County Beach, El Pescador State Beach,** and **El Matador State Beach** (where episodes of TV's *Baywatch* have been filmed). At big, brash **Zuma Beach County Park,** where volleyball courts and snack bars line the sands, the PCH highway bends inland around the headlands of **Point Dume State Beach,** a great spot for winter whale-watching.

Malibu

South of Zuma Beach, houses begin popping up along Hwy-1 to block the oceanfront views, and more-elaborate multimillion-dollar homes dot the canyons above as well, forming the sprawling exurbia and movie-star playground of **Malibu,** which stretches along Hwy-1 for the next 27 miles into Santa Monica and metropolitan Los Angeles. Unless TV helicopters are flying overhead to document the latest wildfire or other natural disaster, it's hard to get more than a glimpse of the garage doors or wrought-iron gates of these palaces, but this is the address of choice for the movers and shakers of the entertainment world: If you can name them, they probably own property here. Most of the truly huge estates are hidden away on ranches high up in the mountains.

One of these hideaways has been evolving since 1993, when Barbra Streisand

The main route inland from the coast, Malibu Canyon Road, was the setting of the key murder scene in James M. Cain's thriller *The Postman Always Rings Twice.*

donated her 22.5-acre ranch for use as a botanical preserve. Called **Ramirez Canyon Park** (5750 Ramirez Canyon Rd.), it's managed by the Santa Monica Mountains Conservancy and is open by appointment only, thanks to requests from neighbors.

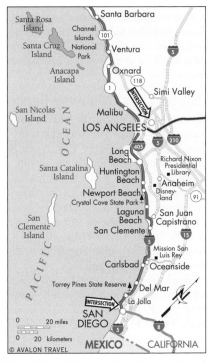

From Hwy-1, the most prominent sight is the **Pepperdine University** campus, which was described by the late, great architect Charles Moore as "an overscaled motel set in obscenely vivid emerald lawns." Below the bluff-top campus, the legendary **Malibu Colony** of celebrity homes stretches along the coast in high-security splendor. Just north of Pepperdine, a short drive up Corral Canyon Road gives access to Solstice Canyon, part of the **Santa Monica Mountains Recreation Area,** where a well-marked, mile-long hiking trail leads through scrubby native chaparral up to a delicate spring waterfall, past numerous signs of the frequent fall wildfires (like the 4,900-acre Corral Fire of November 2007, which destroyed Malibu's oldest home; the remains are preserved in situ).

Malibu Pier at sunset

Away from the mountains, about the only place in Malibu proper where it's fun (and legal) to explore is the area around the landmark **Malibu Pier,** which juts into the ocean at the heart of Malibu's short and rather scruffy commercial strip. North of the pier, which was used most famously in TV's *The Rockford Files,* stretches **Surfrider Beach,** site of most of those Frankie Avalon and Annette Funicello *Beach Blanket Bingo*–type movies made during the 1950s. The pier and the beach are part of **Malibu Lagoon State Park,** which also protects the historic **Adamson House** (Wed.–Sat. 11 AM–3 PM; $7; 23200 Pacific Coast Hwy.; 310/456-8432), a lovely old circa-1930 Spanish Revival courtyard home, right on the beach and full of gorgeous tile work and other architectural features. Tours of the house are given throughout the day, and fascinating exhibits portray Malibu history and the Rindge family, who once owned the entire region.

Just west of the pier and the Adamson House, another great place to get a feel for Malibu is at **Malibu Seafood** (25653 Pacific Coast Hwy.; 310/456-3430), a low-key beach shack drawing local gardeners, pool guys, and Hollywood starlets for BYOB fish-and-chips.

Topanga and the Getty Villa

Between Malibu and Santa Monica, **Topanga Canyon** is one of the last great wild spaces in Los Angeles, with a number of parks, trails, and perhaps the last wild and free waterways—steelhead trout still spawn in the waters of Topanga Creek, which flows down from the mountains to the Santa Monica Bay. Home to an alternative-minded community of some 8,000 hippies and New Agers (Neil Young recorded *After the Gold Rush* in his home here), Topanga was first established as an artists' colony in the 1950s by the likes of Woody Guthrie and actor Will Geer, who played Grandpa in TV's *The Waltons,* long after he'd been blacklisted during the anti-Communist McCarthy witch-hunts. For the past 30 years Geer's old property has been preserved as the **Theatricum Botanicum,** a garden and politically minded 300-seat open-air theater, six miles up the canyon (1419 N. Topanga Canyon Blvd.; 310/455-2322).

South of Topanga, and once again open to the public after a nearly 10-year, $275-million remodeling, are the world-famous antiquities of **The J. Paul Getty Museum.** Over 1,200 priceless classics are displayed in the pseudo-Pompeiian Getty Villa, where the oil magnate's art collection was housed prior to the construction of the massive Getty Center complex above Brentwood. Admission to the Getty Villa is free, but parking reservations ($15 per car; 310/440-7300) are essential.

From the Getty Villa south to Santa Monica, the Pacific Coast Highway (Hwy-1) runs along the wide-open sands of **Will Rogers State Beach,** gifted to the public by the Depression-era humorist.

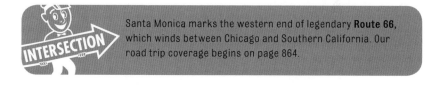

Santa Monica marks the western end of legendary **Route 66,** which winds between Chicago and Southern California. Our road trip coverage begins on page 864.

Crossing Los Angeles

From Malibu and Topanga Canyon, Hwy-1 swoops along the shore, running along the beach as far as the landmark Santa Monica Pier before bending inland through a tunnel and metamorphosing quite unexpectedly into the I-10 Santa Monica Freeway. The second exit off this freeway (which has been officially dubbed the Christopher Columbus Transcontinental Highway, running all the way east to Jacksonville, Florida) takes you to Lincoln Boulevard, which carries the Hwy-1 moniker south through Venice and Marina del Rey to Los Angeles International Airport (LAX), where it runs into Sepulveda Boulevard.

After passing through a tunnel under the airport runways—worth the drive just for the experience of seeing 747s taxiing over your head—Sepulveda

Los Angeles

Love it or hate it, one thing you can't do about L.A. is ignore it. Thanks to Hollywood in all its many guises (movies, television, the music industry), the city is always in the headlines. Without falling too deeply under the spell of its hyperbole-fueled image-making machinery, it's safe to say that L.A. definitely has something for everyone. In keeping with its car-centered culture, however, our suggested tour ignores the many individual attractions and focuses instead on a pair of quintessential L.A. drives.

the Los Angeles skyline, as seen from Mulholland Drive

Winding along the crest of the Hollywood Hills, **Mulholland Drive** is the classic L.A. cruise. Starting in the east within sight of the Hollywood sign and the Hollywood Bowl, this ribbon of two-lane blacktop passes by the city's most valuable real estate, giving great views on both sides, both by day and after dark.

Another classic L.A. cruise, running from the scruffy fringes of downtown all the way west to the coast, **Sunset Boulevard** gives glimpses into almost every conceivable aspect of Los Angeles life. Starting downtown, the historic core of colonial Los Angeles and now a showcase of contemporary architecture thanks to a stunning new cathedral and concert hall, Sunset Boulevard's 27-mile course then winds west past Echo Park and Hollywood to West Hollywood, where it becomes the Sunset Strip, still the liveliest nightclub district in town. Continuing west, Sunset winds through Beverly Hills, Brentwood, and Bel-Air, lined by the largest mansions you're likely to see, before ending up at the edge of the Pacific Ocean.

The **Los Angeles Dodgers** (866/363-4377) play at beautiful Dodger Stadium, on a hill above downtown.

Practicalities

Most flights into Los Angeles arrive at Los Angeles International Airport (LAX), on the coast southwest of downtown, where you'll find all the usual shuttles and rental car agencies. Other useful L.A.-area airports include Bob Hope (BUR) in Burbank and John Wayne (SNA) in Orange County.

Before choosing a place to stay, think about where you want to spend your time and settle near there. High-end places abound, but character can be hard to come by. Along the coast, recommended accommodations range from the handy **Santa Monica HI Hostel** (starts at $27 per person; 1436 2nd St.; 310/393-

The Queen Mary

9913), a block from the beach, to the unique **The Queen Mary** in Long Beach ($104 and up; 877/342-0738), a hotel offering authentic art deco—era staterooms in the fabulous old luxury liner. Midrange with a great mid-city location, try the **Farmer's Daughter Hotel** ($189 and up; 115 S. Fairfax Ave.; 323/937-3930), next to the historic Farmers Market, a very friendly 1950s-style motel with tons of charm and the city's hottest new shopping mall and entertainment complex, The Grove, across the street. Downtown, the most fabulous place to stay is the retro-1960s **The Standard Downtown LA,** ($155 and up; 550 S. Flower St.; 213/892-8080), with the world's coolest rooftop, poolside bar.

For food, one place I always try to stop is **The Apple Pan** (10801 W. Pico Blvd.; 310/475-3585), an ancient (circa-1947) landmark on the West L.A. landscape, serving the best hamburgers on the planet—though I'll admit to being

biased, since I grew up eating them. Take a seat at the counter, and be sure to save room for a slice of the wonderful fruit pies. Late at night, the huge sandwiches and heart-warming soups at **Canter's Deli** (open daily 24 hours; 419 N. Fairfax Ave.; 323/651-2030) draw all kinds of night owls to a lively New York–style deli in the heart of the predominantly Jewish Fairfax District. Downtown, in the heart of old L.A., **Philippe The Original** (1001 N. Alameda St.; 213/628-3781), famous for its French dip sandwiches, is a classic workers' cafeteria, offering good food at impossibly low prices, with character to spare.

The usual array of information about hotels, restaurants, tickets to TV show tapings, and all other L.A.-area attractions is available through the **Los Angeles Convention and Visitors Bureau** (213/689-8822 or 800/228-2452), with an office at 685 South Figueroa Street.

emerges in the Tarantino-esque communities of L.A.'s "South Bay," which utterly lack the glamour of chichi Santa Monica and Malibu. At Hermosa Beach, one of a trio of pleasant if surprisingly blue-collar beach towns, Sepulveda Boulevard changes its name to Pacific Coast Highway, then bends inland to bypass the ritzy communities of the Palos Verdes Peninsula, passing instead through the industrial precincts of San Pedro that border the Los Angeles/Long Beach harbor, one of the busiest on the West Coast.

Since Hwy-1 follows slow-moving Lincoln Boulevard and other surface streets across L.A., if you are in any sort of hurry you should stay on the Santa Monica Freeway (I-10) east to the San Diego Freeway (I-405), and follow that south as far as you're going. Coming from the south, follow these freeways in reverse order—or risk the time-consuming consequences.

Long Beach

Directly south of downtown Los Angeles, the city of **Long Beach** (pop. 462,257) is the second-largest of L.A.'s constituent cities, but it feels more like the Midwest than the cutting-edge West Coast. Long Beach is probably best known as the home of the cruise ship RMS *Queen Mary,* one of the largest and most luxurious liners ever to set sail. Impossible to miss as it looms over Long Beach harbor, the stately ship is open for self-guided tours ($25; 877/342-0738). You can also stay overnight in one of the many staterooms

and cabins, traveling back to a more elegant time for surprisingly reasonable overnight rates.

In place of Howard Hughes's famous "Spruce Goose" airplane, which used to stand next door, there's now a Cold War–era submarine, and across the bay on the main downtown Long Beach waterfront, the **Aquarium of the Pacific** (daily; $24.95; 562/590-3100) explores the diverse ecosystems of the Pacific Ocean, from tropical coral reefs (shown off in an amazing, 350,000-gallon display) to the frigid waters of the Bering Sea. The tanks full of jellyfish of all kinds, colors, and sizes are the main event.

Other Long Beach attractions include the "World's Largest Mural," a 115,000-square-foot painting of migrating gray whales on the outside of the Long Beach Arena, and the self-proclaimed "Skinniest House in the USA" (708 Gladys Ave.).

Long Beach also marks the southern end of L.A.'s reborn streetcar and subway system, and you can ride the Blue Line north to downtown and connect to everywhere else. It's an inexpensive base for exploring the Los Angeles area, especially if you avail yourself of the **HI-South Bay Hostel** (3601 S. Gaffey St.; 310/831-8109), in a peaceful locale on a hill overlooking the harbor area. There's also a **Best Western** ($100 and up; 1725 Long Beach Blvd.; 562/599-5555) directly across from a Blue Line train stop.

Huntington Beach

Winding south and east from Long Beach, Hwy-1 continues along the coast past a series of natural marshlands and small-craft marinas. The first real point of interest is the town of **Huntington Beach** (pop. 189,992), one of the largest communities in Orange County. Incorporated in 1909 and developed by Henry Huntington as a stop along his legendary Pacific Electric "Red Car" interurban railway network, Huntington Beach is best known

as one of the places where **surfing** really took off on the U.S. mainland. To attract Angelenos down to his new town, Huntington hired Hawaiians to demonstrate the sport, which at the time made use of huge solid wooden boards, 15 feet long and weighing around 150 pounds. Huntington Beach, especially around the pier, is still a very popular surfing spot—though contemporary surfers slice through the waves on high-tech foam-core boards, a third the size of the original Hawaiian long boards. The history and culture of West Coast surfing, with examples of boards then and now (plus special collections highlighting surf movies and the creation of surf music by local heroes Leo Fender and Dick Dale), is recounted in the fantastic **International Surfing Museum** (daily; hours vary; donations; 411 Olive Ave.; 714/960-3483), two blocks from the pier in the heart of the lively downtown business district.

Anaheim: Disneyland Resort

Like a little bit of middle America grafted onto the southern edge of Los Angeles, inland Orange County used to feel like a totally different world. Though the area's demographics have changed considerably in the past decade or two, becoming more a part of L.A.'s fast-paced, edgily creative multiethnic stew, Orange County in the 1950s and 1960s was suburban America writ

© DISNEY

inside "it's a small world"

large—mostly white, mostly well-off, and absolutely, totally bland. In short, a perfect place to build the ultimate escapist fantasy, the self-proclaimed "Happiest Place on Earth," **Disneyland.**

The phenomenon of Disneyland has been done to death by all sorts of social critics, but the truth is, it can be great fun—provided you visit out of season, get there early to avoid the crowds, and really immerse yourself in the extroverted, mindless joy of it all. (Being here in the company of appreciative 8- to 12-year-olds is probably the best way to maximize your enjoyment.)

If you haven't been before, or not for a while at any rate, here are some useful tidbits of information: Disneyland is 30 miles south of downtown L.A., right off I-5 in the city of Anaheim—you can see the Matterhorn from the freeway. The park is open daily; in summer, it remains open until midnight. Admission to the park, which includes all rides, costs around $80 per person per day, with discounts for extended visits; kids 9 and under save $6. For further park details, including operating hours, call Disneyland at 714/781-4565.

The major league baseball **Los Angeles Angels of Anaheim** play at Angel Stadium (2000 E. Gene Autry Way; 714/940-2000).

Disneyland opened in 1955, when there was nothing surrounding it; in intervening years, an entire metropolis has grown up around it. In 2001 the park was joined by the much smaller, more grown-up–oriented **Disney California Adventure** theme park. Instead of cuddly cartoon characters, this billion-dollar park has thrill rides like California Screamin', a 55-mph roller coaster, and the excellent Soarin' Over California motion simulator, offering an airborne tour of the Golden State from Yosemite Falls to the Malibu beaches. Disney California Adventure is separate from Disneyland, but a Park Hopper pass allows entry into both for $25 more than a one-park admission. Disney California Adventure hours are shorter than Disneyland's, opening later in the summer and closing earlier year-round.

The whole Disney ensemble includes an upscale resort-hotel complex, surrounded by motels and yet more motels, and it is well worth staying overnight so you can get an early start, go "home" for a while, then come back for the nightly fireworks show. A highly recommended place to stay is the **Sheraton Park Hotel** ($129 and up; 1855 S. Harbor Blvd.; 714/750-1811), a block from Disneyland, offering spacious modern rooms (and a nice pool), with free shuttles every half hour to and from Disneyland.

Richard Nixon Presidential Library

If you've already done the Disneyland thing, or just want a foil to the empty-headed fun, there is one other Orange County attraction you really shouldn't miss: the **Richard Nixon Presidential Library** (daily; $9.95; 18001 Yorba Linda Blvd.; 714/983-9120), 10 miles northeast of Disneyland off Hwy-90. The library is built on the very ground where the former president was born in 1913;

it's also where he and his wife, Pat, are buried, side by side next to the restored Craftsman-style bungalow where Nixon grew up. No matter what your feelings toward him, the spare-no-expense displays do a fascinating job of putting his long career into the distorted perspective you'd expect from the only president ever forced to resign from office. Highlights are many, such as the pictures of the pumpkin patch where Whittaker Chambers concealed the microfilm that Nixon used to put Alger Hiss in prison as a Communist spy, next to photos of Nixon and JFK as chummy freshman U.S. senators sharing sleeping compartments on a train. The best-selling item in the gift shop? Photographs of Nixon greeting Elvis Presley, also available as mousepads, china cups, and fridge magnets.

Newport Beach

Back on the coast, if you want to get a sense of what wealthy Orange Countians do to enjoy themselves, spend some time along the clean white strands of **Newport Beach.** Located at the southern edge of Los Angeles's suburban sprawl, Newport started life in 1906 as an amusement park and beach resort at the southern end of the L.A. streetcar lines. Since then thousands of Angelenos have spent summer weekends at the **Balboa Pavilion,** at the southern tip of the slender Balboa peninsula, where the Fun Zone preserves a few remnants of the pre–video game amusements—a Ferris wheel, a merry-go-round, and those odd Pokerino games in which you win prizes by rolling rubber balls into a series of numbered holes.

Midway along the peninsula, near 23rd Street, Newport Pier is flanked by another holdout from the old days: the dory fleet. For more than a century small boats have set off from the beach here (often around midnight, landing back around 7 AM) to catch rock cod and more exotic fish, which are sold fresh off the boats at an outdoor market right on the sands.

A mile southeast of Balboa Pavilion, next to the breakwater at the very eastern end of Balboa peninsula, **The Wedge** is one of the world's most popular and challenging bodysurfing spots, with well-formed waves often twice as high as anywhere else on the coast.

To return to Hwy-1 from Balboa Peninsula, you can either backtrack around the harbor or ride the **Balboa Island Ferry,** which shuttles you and your car from the pavilion across the harbor past an amazing array of sailboats, power cruisers, and waterfront homes.

Crystal Cove State Park

Midway between Newport and Laguna Beaches, amidst the ever-encroaching Orange County sprawl, **Crystal Cove State Park** (daily dawn–dusk; $15 per car; 949/494-3539) protects one of Southern California's finest chunks of coastline. With three miles of sandy beaches and chaparral-covered bluff lined by well-marked walking trails, it's a fine place to enjoy the shoreline without the commercial trappings. Originally home to Native Americans, the land here was later part of Mission San Juan Capistrano and, until 1979 when the state bought it, the massive Irvine Ranch, which once covered most of Orange County.

The main parking area for Crystal Cove is at **Reef Point** near the south end of the park, where there are bathrooms and showers plus excellent tidepools, a fine beach, and a well-preserved collection of 1930–1950s beach cottages, where you can stay overnight ($33 and up; 800/444-7275). There is also a large section of the park inland from Hwy-1, through the oakland glade of **El Moro Canyon,** which gives a vivid sense of Orange County's rapidly vanishing natural landscape.

Laguna Beach

Compared with much of Orange County, **Laguna Beach** (pop. 24,100) is a relaxed and enjoyable place. Bookstores, cafés, and galleries reflect the town's beginnings as an artists' colony, but while the beach and downtown area are still very attractive, the surrounding hills have been covered by some of the world's ugliest tracts of "executive homes."

During the annual **Pageant of the Masters,** Laguna Beach residents re-create scenes from classical and modern art by forming living tableaux, standing still as statues in front of painted backdrops. Held every summer, it's a popular event and proceeds go to good causes, so get tickets ($15–112; 949/497-6582 or 800/487-3378) well in advance.

Right across Hwy-1 from the downtown shopping district, which is full of pleasant cafés and a wide range of art galleries, Laguna's main beach

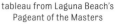

tableau from Laguna Beach's
Pageant of the Masters

(called simply Main Beach) is still the town's main draw, with a boardwalk, some volleyball courts, and a guarded swimming beach with showers.

Many other fine but usually less crowded and quieter beaches are reachable from Cliff Drive, which winds north of downtown Laguna past cove after untouched cove; follow the signs reading Beach Access.

Laguna Beach has a number of nice places to eat; one place worth searching out is the small **Taco Loco** (640 S. Coast Hwy.; 949/497-1635), at the south end of the downtown strip, where the ultra-fresh Mexican food includes your choice of three or four different seafood tacos, from shark to swordfish, in daily-changing specials from about $2 each.

Places to stay are expensive, averaging around $150 a night, and include the beachfront **Laguna Riviera** (825 S. Coast Hwy.; 949/494-1196). At the top end of the scale, the newish **Montage** resort (30801 S. Coast Hwy.; 866/271-6953) has everything you could want from a hotel—all yours for $545 a day (and up!).

South of Laguna Beach, Hwy-1 follows the coast for a final few miles before joining up with the I-5 freeway for the 65-mile drive into San Diego.

San Juan Capistrano

Of the 21 missions along the California coast, **Mission San Juan Capistrano** (daily; $9; 949/234-1300) has been the most romanticized. When the movement to restore the missions and preserve California's Spanish colonial past was at its apogee in the late 1930s, its main theme tune was Leon René's "When the Swallows Come Back to Capistrano," popularizing the legend that these birds return from their winter migration every St. Joseph's Day, March 19. After wintering in Goya, Argentina, they do come back to Capistrano, along with several thousand tourists, but the swallows are just as likely to reappear a week before or a week after—whenever the weather warms up, really.

The mission, which has lovely, bougainvillea-filled gardens, stands at the center of the small, eponymously named town, a short detour inland along I-5 from the coast. Besides the birds, the main attractions include the small **chapel,** the last surviving church where the beatified Father Serra said mass, widely considered the oldest intact church and perhaps the oldest building of any kind in California, and the ruins of the massive **Great Stone Church,** a finely carved limestone structure that collapsed in an earthquake in 1812, just six years after its completion. Many visitors to the chapel are terminally ill patients saying prayers to St. Peregrine, the patron saint of cancer patients.

To get a sense of the huge scale of the Great Stone Church, a church patterned after the fallen building has been constructed behind the mission and now serves as the official mission church, open to visitors except during religious services. Across the street from this church, Mission Basilica, a Michael Graves–designed local **library** gives an intriguing postmodern take on the mission style.

The Coach House (33157 Camino Capistrano; 949/496-8930), two miles south of the mission, is one of Southern California's best small clubs for listening to live music.

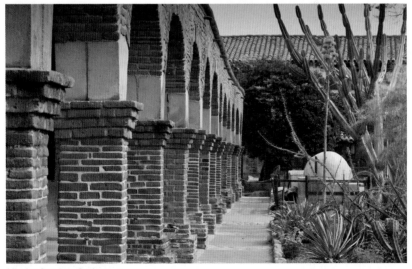

Mission San Juan Capistrano

San Clemente

At the southern tip of coastal Orange County, **San Clemente** marks the midway point between San Diego and Los Angeles. A sleepy beachside community, with frequent Amtrak train service and a nicely undulating stretch of old US-101 (El Camino Real) running through its heart, San Clemente is probably best known as the site of La Casa Pacifica, the one-time "Western White House" of former president Richard Nixon, who lived here following his election in 1968 and during his impeachment in the mid-1970s. The white-walled, mission-style house at the south end of Avenida del Presidente (the western frontage road to I-5) is more easily visible from the beach below, though the 25 acres of trees have grown up to obscure it in recent years.

Within a quick walk uphill from the handful of cafés and bars on and around the pier, **Beachcomber Motel** ($125 and up; 949/492-5457) is a tidy, old-fashioned motor-court motel, facing onto the open ocean. San Clemente also has burger place, **Duke's** (204 S. El Camino Real; 949/481-2040), in the mission-style downtown business district.

Old Mission San Luis Rey de Francia

In the sun-bleached hills above the blue Pacific, four miles east of the ocean off the I-5 along Hwy-76, **Old Mission San Luis Rey de Francia** (daily; $5) was the largest and among the most successful of the California missions. Its lands have been taken over by Camp Pendleton, and most of the outbuildings have disappeared, but the stately church at the heart of the complex survives in fine condition, worth a look for the blue-tinted dome atop the bell tower and for the haunting carved stone skull that looks down from the cemetery gate.

A long but worthwhile detour inland from San Luis Rey brings you to one of the least visited but perhaps most evocative of all the California missions, **Mission San Antonio de Pala** (sometimes closed Mon.; $2; 760/742-1600). Located on the Pala Indian Reservation, 20 miles east of San Luis Rey along Hwy-76, then another 100 yards north along a well-marked side road, Mission San Antonio de Pala is the only California mission still serving its original role of preaching to the native people, and it gives an unforgettable impression of what California's mission era might have been like.

Oceanside

At the southern edge of 125,000-acre Marine Corps Base Camp Pendleton, **Oceanside** (pop. 164,500) is one of the largest cities between Los Angeles and San Diego, but it offers little to attract the casual visitor—apart from a long fishing pier and guided tours of Camp Pendleton's amphibious-assault training exercises. But if you're in the mood to shop for camouflage gear, watch the muscle cars cruise Hill Street, get a $5 G.I. Joe haircut, or drink beer with a gang of young recruits, this is the right place.

Oceanside is also home to one of the last survivors of the old, pre-Interstate, Coast Highway businesses: The **101 Café** (631 S. Coast Hwy.; 760/722-5220) has been open for classic road food since 1928; it often hosts classic car rallies and generally glows with neon-lit nostalgia.

South from Oceanside, all the way to San Diego, a very pleasant alternative to the often-clogged I-5 is the old alignment of US-101, now signed as County Road S21 (and occasionally, Coast Highway 101). Slower than the freeway but still in regular use, the old road is now the main drag of quaint beachfront towns like Carlsbad, Leucadia, Encinitas, and Del Mar. If you have the time, it's a great drive, in sight of the ocean for most of the way.

The northwest corner of San Diego County is taken up by the U.S. Marines Corps's massive **Camp Pendleton** training base, which fills 125,000 acres, running for 17 miles along the coast and about 15 miles inland. Camp Pendleton (the base motto is "No Beach out of Reach") is the largest undeveloped section of the Southern California coast.

Carlsbad: La Costa and Legoland

Named for the European spa town of Karlsbad, in Bohemia of what's now the Czech Republic, **Carlsbad** (pop. 105,328) was established in the 1880s as a spa town and vacation resort. A few remnants of the historic resort area still survive along old US-101 in the center of town. A few flower and strawberry fields surround the town, surviving against the ever-expanding tide of sprawl, and these days Carlsbad's spa-town heritage lives on at **La Costa Resort and Spa** ($249 and up; 760/438-9111), a 500-plus-room complex of luxurious rooms, health spas, golf courses, and tennis courts covering 400 acres of hills on the inland side of I-5.

Some of the best views of the Southern California coastline can be had from the windows of the frequent Coaster commuter trains, which run right along the shore between Oceanside and downtown San Diego.

Carlsbad's other main attraction is the first American outpost of the popular European children's theme park **Legoland** (adults $69, children $59; 760/918-5346). Built out of millions of Lego bricks, and covering 128 acres above the Pacific Ocean, the park is divided up into multiple areas, including Miniland USA, where miniature landscapes modeled on New York, New Orleans, New England, and Southern California have all been constructed using more than 40 million of the trademark plastic bricks.

South Carlsbad State Beach ($8 per car; 760/438-3143) three miles south of town, is one of the nicest and most popular places to camp on the Southern California coast, with its spacious campsites with hot showers ($35–50) spread out along a

model of San Francisco made entirely from Lego blocks

San Diego

San Diego Zoo

Set along a huge Pacific Ocean harbor at the southwestern corner of the country just a few miles from the Mexican border, San Diego embodies the Southern California ideal. Around the turn of the 20th century, it rivaled Los Angeles as a boomtown based on wild real estate speculation, but while L.A. continued to expand by leaps and bounds, San Diego grew comparatively slowly. Instead of Hollywood glamour, San Diego's economy has long been based on the U.S. Navy, as evidenced by the massive former USS *Midway* moored right downtown. (San Diego successfully mixed its military and Hollywood influences in the movie *Top Gun.*) Despite a metropolitan population of more than 3 million people, San Diego still feels small and anything but urban.

The main things to see in San Diego are in **Balboa Park,** a lushly landscaped 1,200-acre spread on downtown's northeast edge, which was largely laid out and constructed as part of the 1915 Panama-California Exposition celebrating the completion of the Panama Canal. The many grand buildings, all built in gorgeous Spanish Revival style by architect Bertram Goodhue, have been preserved in marvelous condition and now house sundry museums, ranging from automobiles to fine art to a functioning replica of Shakespeare's Globe Theatre.

Balboa Park is also home to the **San Diego Zoo** (daily; $40; 619/231-1515), one of the largest and most popular in the world with over 4,000 animals kept in settings that simulate their natural habitats. You can see koalas and komodo dragons, panda bears and polar bears, plus gorillas, giraffes—you name it, if it's anywhere outside in the wild, it'll be here amidst the zoo's lushly landscaped 100 acres.

The **San Diego Padres** (619/795-5000) play at very popular, retro-modern Petco Park, right downtown in the Gaslamp Quarter.

Practicalities

The city of San Diego bends diagonally around its natural harbor, which makes orientation occasionally confusing. The main airport, Lindbergh Field, is on the waterfront just northwest of downtown—and has one of the swiftest final approaches of any urban American airport. Because it is small and relatively compact, San Diego is easy to get around. Downtown is walkable, and on a bike you could see most everything in a day. Buses operated by San Diego Transit (619/234-1060) fan out from downtown, while the light rail San Diego Trolley runs south from downtown to the Mexican border.

Though you may feel the need to duck when planes land at nearby Lindbergh Field, for breakfast try the **Hob Nob Hill** (2271 First Ave.; 619/239-8176), a classic 1940s coffee shop with great pecan waffles. For more all-American fare, head west to Ocean Beach, where **Hodad's,** a great old burger joint, awaits you (5010 Newport Ave.; 619/224-4623). San Diego's Old Town historic park holds some good old-school Mexican places, like the **Old Town Mexican Café** (2489 San Diego Ave.; 619/297-4330). In Balboa Park, soak up San Diego's Spanish Revival splendor while enjoying a meal at **The Prado** (619/557-9441) in the original House of Hospitality.

Places to stay are generally modern, clean, and comfortable, though rates vary with seasons (and conventions). For top-of-the-line accommodations, or just to appreciate the historic architecture, head to the wonderful old **Hotel del Coronado** ($299 and up; 1500 Orange Ave.; 619/435-6611), across the bridge from downtown on Coronado Island. Rising up in turreted glory, this fabulously grand Victorian-era resort hotel still caters, as it always has, to the four-star trade. It has been seen in many movies, including the great Peter O'Toole flick *The Stunt Man.* It's also where England's King Edward VIII is rumored to have first met the femme fatale who inspired him to give up his throne: Mrs. Wallis Simpson, whose first husband was first commanding officer of the local Navy base. The cheapest beds are at the **HI-San Diego Downtown Hostel** ($28 and up per person; 521 Market St.; 619/525-1531), in the historic downtown Gaslamp Quarter, or the hip **500 West Hotel** ($45 and up; 500 West Broadway; 619/234-5252), a boutique restoration of a 1920s YMCA. For more comfort and character, try **The Sofia Hotel,** a restored 1920s hotel ($135 and up; 150 W. Broadway; 800/826-0009). For surfer-friendly accommodations near Ocean Beach and Point Loma, try the **Ocean Villa Inn** ($99 and up; 5142 W. Point Loma Blvd.; 619/224-3481).

The best range of information is available from the **San Diego Convention & Visitors Bureau International Visitor Information Center** (1040 W. Broadway; 619/236-1212).

Balboa Park

sandstone bluff above a broad beach. However, swimming can be dangerous because of strong riptides. If you don't want to camp or pay the parking fee, leave your car at the park entrance, which is well marked on a surviving stretch of the old US-101 highway.

Del Mar and Torrey Pines State Natural Reserve

Most of the time, **Del Mar** (pop. 4,161) is a sleepy little upscale suburb of San Diego, with big houses backing onto more than two miles of fine beach. But in late summer, it comes to life for the thoroughbred racing season at beautiful **Del Mar Racetrack,** built by Hollywood types like Bing Crosby and seen in *The Grifters* and many other Hollywood movies and TV shows. The waves here are well suited to bodysurfing, but the sands can be hard to reach in summer because of a lack of parking—weekdays it's less of a problem.

A Torrey Pine, San Diego, Cal.—9

South along the Camino Del Mar coast road from Del Mar, hang-gliders, tidepoolers, surfers, and beachcombers flock to the nearly 2,000 acres of bluffs and beaches protected in **Torrey Pines State Natural Reserve.** Named for the long-needled pines that grow naturally only here, the reserve is crisscrossed by hiking trails leading down steep ravines between the bluffs and the sands. Besides hang-gliders, Torrey Pines is prime air space for remote-controlled model gliders, which float gracefully in the nearly constant onshore breeze. The primary launching spot is the small city park at the south end of the reserve.

Pacific Beach, one of Southern California's better surfing spots, is home to the friendly, family-run **Paskowitz Surf Camp** (949/728-1000), held every summer since 1972.

Overlooking the Pacific from atop a bluff at the south end of the reserve, the **Salk Institute** is one of the world's most important centers for research in the life sciences. Founded by the late Jonas Salk, designed by Louis Kahn, and modeled in part on the gardens of the Alhambra in Granada, the institute is open for **tours** Monday–Friday at noon (free; 858/453-4100).

Stretching inland and south from the Salk Institute, the hills are covered with faceless business parks around the spacious campus of **University of California at San Diego** (UCSD), beyond which spreads La Jolla and the greater San Diego area. On campus, learn all about local marine biology at the **Birch Aquarium** of UCSD's Scripps Institution of Oceanography ($14; 858/534-3474), from where you can amble along the shore to lovely La Jolla.

La Jolla

The wealthiest and most desirable part of San Diego, La Jolla sits along the coast northwest of the city proper, gazing out over azure coves to the endless Pacific. Besides the gorgeous scenery, great surfing (head to Windansea Beach for the best waves), beachcombing, and skin diving, a big draw here is the recently renovated **Museum of Contemporary Art** (closed Wed.; $10; 700 Prospect St.; 858/454-3541), overlooking the ocean. Tons of good cafés and restaurants have long made La Jolla an all-around great day out, suiting all budgets—especially those with no upper limit.

At **Belmont Park** (3146 Mission Blvd.; 858/488-1549) west of Mission Bay, the Giant Dipper wooden roller coaster survives as the sole remnant of a 1920s beachfront amusement park.

Start the day off right at La Jolla's **The Cottage** (7702 Fay Ave.; 858/454-8409), where delicious food (including a divine buttermilk coffee cake) is served up on a sunny patio. For a memorable lunch or dinner, the very plush **Tapenade** (7612 Fay Ave.; 858/551-7500) is one of the best restaurants in Southern California, offering a deluxe mix of Mediterranean dishes. To continue the swaddled-in-luxury SoCal experience, stay the night at the elegant, Craftsman-style **The Lodge at Torrey Pines** ($350 and up; 11480 N. Torrey Pines Rd.; 858/453-4420), a modern recreation of California's turn-of-the-20th-century Golden Age.

San Diego is also the beginning of our cross-country **Southern Pacific** route, along US-80, which runs east across Arizona all the way to Tybee Island, Georgia. See page 800.

Driving San Diego

From La Jolla south, the US-101 highway is pretty well buried by the I-5 freeway. Old US-101 can still be followed, however, by following Pacific Highway past Mission Bay and Lindbergh Field toward San Diego Bay, where it becomes Harbor Drive—where the light rail San Diego Trolley now runs.

Jasper

pg.
120

Jasper
National Park

Vancouver

172 mi

pg.
122

Calgary

Banff
National Park

Port Angeles
Bellingham
Everett
Seattle
Olympia
Tacoma

Beach

WASHINGTON

Spokane

Coeur
D'alene

Kalispell

Great Falls

Portland

Salem

Olympia

Helena

Helena

Glen

580 mi

Eugene
Burns

OREGON

Salmon

M O N T A N A

Medford

Boise

Sun Valley,
Idaho

I D A H O

pg.
142

Chico

Reno

Carson City

NEVAD

Elk
o

Fresno

land

Las Vega

LIFOR

St. Geor

WYOMING

Rock
Springs

Casper

Rapi
City

Chad

Cheyenne

Boulder

Denver

Extraterrestrial
Highway

Richfield

COLORA DO

Colorado Springs

Pueblo

Las Vegas

Trinidad

Flagstaff

Santa Fe

A R I Z O N A

Albuquerque

oenix

Yuma

Tumacácori

O

Tuc n

Las Cruces

Lubbock

Ambos
Nogales

El Paso

400 mi

170 mi

450 mi

pg.
156

pg.
154

pg.
172

Border to Border

Besides offering up-close looks at mile after mile of almost completely untouched wilderness, US-93 also takes you right through the neon heart of Las Vegas, Nevada.

Between the Canadian Rockies and the Rio Grande

The western half of North America is often described as a land of contrasts, and no route across it gives a sharper sense of the region's extremes than Highway 93. Starting in the north, across the Canadian border at **Jasper National Park** in the heart of the Rocky Mountains, and winding up south of the border in the Sonora Desert twin towns of **Nogales** (one in Arizona, one in Mexico), this route, which retains the number 93 despite the different international jurisdictions, traverses some of the wildest and most rugged lands imaginable: mighty mountains, glaciated valleys, raging rivers, and two very different deserts. Besides offering up-close looks at mile after mile of magnificent and almost completely untouched wilderness, US-93 also takes you right through the neon heart of what is surely the most extreme (and most extremely visual) example of our contemporary "civilization": Las Vegas.

The route divides into two almost unrecognizably different halves. The northern section, from the Canadian Rockies wonderland of **Banff** and **Jasper** south as far as **Sun Valley, Idaho,** is pure alpine majesty. Passing the western flanks of **Glacier National Park,** US-93 runs along river valleys through diverse communities where skiing, hiking, and sightseeing have replaced mining and lumbering as the economic engines. South of **Kalispell,** the highway winds across the **Flathead Indian Reservation** along the western shores of Flathead Lake to **Missoula,** located at the heart of the bountiful country captured in the film *A River Runs Through It.* Western

CANADIAN ROCKIES

At its northernmost extreme high up in the Canadian Rockies, Highway 93 passes through some of the most famous vacation areas in North America: the Canadian national parks of Banff and Jasper. Popular with skiers and snowboarders in winter, and hikers and sightseers in summer, these resort areas have been must-sees for over 100 years and remain among the most beautiful places on earth. Between **Jasper** and **Lake Louise,** Hwy-93 is known as the Icefields Parkway, an amazing drive with endless

Montana's natural beauty reaches a peak in the **Bitterroot Valley,** which stretches south from Missoula all the way to the Idaho border. Besides scenery, the valley also abounds in history, holding many key sites pertaining to the explorers Lewis and Clark, the first whites to set foot in the region, and other sites related to the epic struggle of Chief Joseph and the Nez Percé tribe.

As you pass over the Bitterroots into Idaho across the **Continental Divide,** the scenery remains impressive as US-93 winds along the banks of the Salmon River, all the way to its source in the serrated Sawtooth Mountains, then drops down swiftly into Sun Valley, the oldest and most upscale ski resort in the country.

South of Sun Valley, however, everything changes very suddenly. Roaring rivers and mountain forests give way to lava flows and empty deserts as US-93 races across the inhospitable landscape of the Snake River plain. This was the most difficult portion of the historic Oregon Trail, though the biggest difficulty facing today's travelers is the struggle to stay alert—there's very little to look for, apart from acres of potato farms reclaimed from the arid desert. The one real sight is the **Snake River** itself, which has carved itself into a deep gorge near Twin Falls.

Continuing south into Nevada, US-93 embarks on what is truly, if not officially, the "Loneliest Road in America," traveling across 500 miles of Great Basin Desert. Though not for the faint-hearted (or those with unreliable cars!), it's an unforgettably beautiful journey; after hours (or days) of existential solitude, you drop down into the frenetic boomtown of **Las Vegas.**

Crossing Hoover Dam into Arizona, the route crosses old Route 66 west of the **Grand Canyon,** then races southeast across the lush Sonora Desert—known as the "world's greenest desert" because of its abundant flora and fauna—through **Phoenix** and **Tucson** to the Mexican border. This last stretch is among the most fascinating 200 miles of highway in the country, taking you past such intriguingly diverse and unique sights as the controversial Biosphere 2 scientific research center, the country's only intact Cold War–era missile silo, and a pair of centuries-old churches, two of the most captivating pieces of architecture in the western United States.

panoramas of glaciers and towering peaks, and dozens of turnouts and trailheads to tempt you out from behind the wheel. Over 140 miles (225 kilometers) long, the Icefields Parkway runs right alongside the Continental Divide, the rugged crest that separates the Atlantic and Pacific watersheds. South of the Icefields Parkway, our route passes through the world-renowned resort towns of **Banff** and Lake Louise, taking in their unforgettable alpine scenery—and historic landmark hotels.

Southwest from Lake Louise, Hwy-93 winds through **Kootenay National Park,** another incredible assembly of mountain scenery, before dropping down out of the mountains for the run south to the border, following the broad Kootenay River all the way to Montana.

Town of Jasper

The northernmost point on Hwy-93, at the junction of the Icefields Parkway with the cross-country Yellowhead Highway (Hwy-16), which links Edmonton with Prince Rupert, the town of **Jasper** (pop. 4,700) preserves its frontier character intact. Unlike Banff, which exudes wealth and comfort, Jasper (which became an incorporated entity only in 2001 and is officially referred to as "Town of Jasper" to differentiate it from Jasper National Park) is a rough-and-ready, workaday sort of place. Founded on fur trading and mining, Jasper boomed when a cross-Canada railroad came through in 1911, but since the establishment of the national park in 1930, Jasper has served primarily as a handy base for exploring the wilds that surround it.

Prices in the Canadian sections are given in Canadian dollars, which at time of writing were worth about the same as U.S. dollars. Also, the colloquial Canadian equivalent of "buck" (for a dollar) is "loonie," thanks to the image of a loon (a bird) on the Canadian dollar coin. The two-dollar coin is called a "toonie."

The park's main attractions are covered under the *Jasper National Park* heading, but a few others are located very close to town. First and foremost of these is probably the **Jasper Tramway** (mid-Apr. to Oct. daily; C$30; 780/852-3093), which lifts passengers 3,200 vertical feet up the steep north face of the Whistlers in under 10 minutes. From the upper terminal of the tramway, you can follow a half-mile (0.8-kilometer) path to the 8,100-foot summit for a breathtaking panorama south to the Columbia Icefield and (on a clear

© AVALON TRAVEL

The Last Frontier

The Canadian Rockies are farther north than anything else in *Road Trip USA*, but for indefatigable adventurers there's at least one additional destination: Alaska, "The Last Frontier." It's a mere 1,904 miles from Jasper National Park to Anchorage, via the legendary **Alaska Highway.** Running from the oil- and gas-producing center of Dawson Creek (no connection with the TV show) in British Columbia, the Alaska Highway was constructed in 1942, in just nine months, an amazing engineering feat fueled by fears of a Japanese invasion during World War II. Much improved in the years since, it's now paved all the way but is still quite an adventure, with endless miles (and miles, and miles) of forests, rivers, and mountains.

If you're going, plan ahead carefully and keep a lookout for a few places you won't want to miss. One of these is roughly midway, in Watson Lake right on the British Columbia/Yukon border right along the highway: the world-famous **Sign Post Forest,** a collection of city limits signs from around the globe. The "forest" was started in 1942 by Carl Lindley, a U.S. soldier working to build the highway. When ordered to fix an official road sign, he added another of his own making, pointing the way and the distance to his home in Danville, Indiana. Others followed his lead, and over the years, have added sign upon sign to create the current collection, which at last count totaled more than 71,000.

In the middle of the Signpost Forest is the very helpful **Visitor Information Centre** (daily in summer; 867/536-7469) with practical information and historical exhibits.

day) northwest to Mt. Robson, the highest point of the Canadian Rockies at 13,006 feet (3,964 meters) above sea level.

The other big draw is **Maligne Canyon,** a 100- to 150-foot-deep limestone canyon that's so narrow in places that squirrels can leap from rim to rim. Trails lead around and across it, and in winter you can join an unforgettable guided tour (C\$60; 800/719-2186) and wander along the bottom of the narrow, ice-covered gorge. Beyond Maligne Canyon is one of the prettiest lakes in the Canadian Rockies, **Maligne Lake.** Hiking trails lead along the shore and to panoramic viewpoints, but it is the **cruise to Spirit Island** (C\$60; 800/719-2186) that attracts most visitors.

Jasper's compact center, sandwiched between the west bank of the Athabasca River and a wide bench of land dotted with forest-encircled lakes, holds all the cafés and gift shops you could want within a block of the main drag, Connaught Drive. The **Bear's Paw Bakery** (4 Cedar Ave.; 780/852-3233), off Connaught has cinnamon buns, great fresh-fruit waffles, and anything else you need to start the day off right. **Jasper Pizza Place** (402 Connaught Dr.; 780/852-3225), two blocks north, has wood-fired ovens and walls covered in photos of Jasper in the early days. Another lively spot is the bar and grill on the ground floor of the **Athabasca Hotel** (C$109–175; 510 Patricia St.; 780/852-3386), which also has Jasper's least expensive in-town lodging. Jasper's most expensive place to stay is the **Jasper Park Lodge** (C$249 and up; 780/852-3301), a grand mountain resort dating back to 1921 but now a mostly modern resort offering 446 rooms, plus golfing and horseback riding, on a lovely site across from town on the other side of the Athabasca River.

Budget travelers may want to take advantage of the hostels around Jasper, including the 84-bed **HI-Jasper Hostel** (C$24–30 per person) five miles south of Jasper on the road to the Jasper Tramway, and the smaller and more rustic **HI-Maligne Canyon Hostel** (C$20–30 per person) a short walk from the canyon. Reservations for either hostel, and for other hostels in Jasper National Park, can be made by phone, 780/852-3215. There are also two large **campgrounds,** Whistlers and Wapiti, along Hwy-93 on the south side of Jasper, with over 1,000 sites altogether, some with RV hookups.

For details on hiking and camping options, or to purchase the required entrance passes and backcountry camping permits, go to the Parks Canada **information center** (780/852-6176) in a lovely old stone building off Connaught Drive in Athabasca Park; for complete accommodations information, including listings of rooms available in private homes, talk to the folks at the Jasper **visitors center,** which shares the space (780/852-3858).

Jasper National Park

Running from the Town of Jasper all the way to Lake Louise 144 miles (232 kilometers) to the south, this section of Hwy-93 is known as the **Icefields Parkway.** Like many roads in American national parks, the Icefields Parkway was initially built as a relief project during the Great Depression and was completed in 1940. Without a doubt one of the world's great drives, this sinuous ribbon winds along the banks of a series of icy rivers between glaciers and towering Rocky Mountain peaks, with almost no development to mar the views. The northern half of the highway passes through Jasper National Park, alongside the milky green Athabasca River.

While the Icefields Parkway makes a great drive, a worthwhile detour follows an older alignment of the highway, Hwy-93A, which runs parallel and slightly to the west. One of the best concentrations of scenery surrounds Mt. Edith Cavell, easily reached by Mt. Edith Cavell Road, which turns off Hwy-93A about four miles (six kilometers) south of the Town of Jasper. From the winding road, you can choose from

The four contiguous Canadian Rockies national parks—Jasper, Banff, Yoho, and Kootenay, along with neighboring wilderness areas—jointly protect a 7,000-square-mile (18,000-square-kilometer) area that has been declared a UNESCO World Heritage Site for its ecological importance.

Passes are required for each person entering any of the Canadian Rockies national parks and are available at park gates and at visitors centers. They're valid for one day (C$10 per person) or all year (C$68 per person).

The Brewster Boys

Few guides in the Canadian Rockies were as well known as Jim and Bill Brewster. In 1892, at the ages of 10 and 12, respectively, they were hired by the Banff Springs Hotel to take guests on a tour of local landmarks. As their reputations grew so did their business, which expanded to include a livery and outfitting company, a pair of hotels, and a ski lodge. Today, their legacy lives on in Brewster, where their tour and transportation company has become an integral part of the Canadian Rockies experience for many visitors. The Brewster company operates a fleet of tour buses, a Banff hotel, and the famous Ice Explorers tours, which take tourists out onto the Columbia Icefield.

Athabasca Glacier in the Columbia Icefield

fairly short day hikes up to wildflower-rich alpine meadows, with views of Angel Glacier, or longer overnight treks into the backcountry, including the **Tonquin Valley Backcountry Lodge** (780/852-3909), a 15-mile (24-kilometer) hiking or cross-country skiing trip from the trailhead. Right at the trailhead there's the handy **HI-Mt. Edith Cavell Hostel** (June–Sept.; C$20–24 per person; 780/852-3215).

About 18 miles (30 kilometers) south of the Town of Jasper, Hwy-93A and the Icefields Parkway rejoin at **Athabasca Falls,** where the river is forced through a narrow gorge and over a cliff into a cauldron of roaring water; numerous viewpoints above and below the falls let you get up close and personal with the thundering torrent. There's a rustic **hostel** (877/852-0781) a short walk away from the falls.

At the southern end of Jasper National Park, 67 miles (108 kilometers) south of the Town of Jasper, the massive Columbia Icefield rises high above the west side of the Icefields Parkway.

Columbia Icefield

Rising to the west of Sunwapta Pass, the dividing line between Banff and Jasper Parks, the massive **Columbia Icefield** is what the Icefields Parkway is all about: the largest ice field and most accessible glacier in the Canadian Rockies, seemingly endless square miles of solid ice sitting high atop the Continental Divide. Although it has been visibly shrinking since the 20th century, the ice field is still immense, and you can get an up-close look by joining the very popular Ice Explorer tours (C$50; 800/760-6934) operated by the Brewster company, which leave every 15 minutes and travel out onto Athabasca Glacier.

The Icefields Parkway is kept open year-round, but gas, food, and lodging services are available pretty much only near the towns of Banff, Jasper, and Lake Louise. Wide shoulders and frequent HI hostels along the Parkway make it an excellent bicycling route.

Overlooking the ice field from across the Icefields Parkway is the modern **Columbia Icefield Centre** (daily May–Oct.; free), a mini museum of glacial lore operated by Parks Canada. If you want to experience the ice field up close, buy a ticket and take one of the Ice Explorer tours; don't simply walk across the highway and clamber up, since it only takes one false step to fall to your death into one of the very deep but invisible crevasses that crisscross the glacier.

Banff National Park

Roughly midway along the Icefields Parkway, the Columbia Icefield and Sunwapta Pass mark the boundary between Jasper and Banff National Parks, and the dividing line between the Arctic and Atlantic watersheds. South of the pass, the first worthwhile stop is the **Weeping Wall,** a 350-foot cliff of gray limestone down which a series of waterfalls tumble. Frozen in winter, it's a prime spot for ice-climbing thrill-seekers.

Though it may well sound like empty hyperbole, the list of candidates for the most beautiful sight in **Banff National Park**—and perhaps the entire Canadian Rockies—has to include jewel-like **Peyto Lake,** an iridescently glowing blue-green glacial lake that reflects the surrounding snowcapped peaks. The often mirror-smooth waters of this small, oblong lake change color from a deep blue to jade green as the proportion of glacial silt in the water increases with the snowmelt from summer to fall. The short trail to the usually crowded Peyto Lake overlook starts from the parking area along the Icefields Parkway at 6,803-foot **Bow Summit.**

Bow Summit is one of the highest points reachable by road in Canada; south of here, the Icefields Parkway drops down into the Bow Valley, which is dominated by the sparkling waters of **Bow Lake** and the views across it to

Peyto Lake

Crowfoot Glacier. At the north edge of the lake, historic **Simpson's Num-Ti-Jah Lodge** (C$275–365; 403/522-2167) is a giant octagonal log cabin, with well-priced rooms and a rustic restaurant; it marks the start of a popular trail to **Bow Glacier Falls.** It's a fairly level, 2.5-mile (four-kilometer) one-way hike.

From the lodge, the Icefields Parkway winds along the east shore of Bow Lake, then along the banks of the Bow River, which flows south through Lake Louise, Banff, and on through Calgary, eventually ending up in Hudson Bay.

Yoho National Park

From the village of Lake Louise, the Trans-Canada Highway cuts off from Hwy-93, running west through Kamloops toward Vancouver. The first 25 miles (40

Takakkaw Falls

kilometers) of this highway, west from Lake Louise and the Icefields Parkway, passes through **Yoho National Park,** the smallest and least known, but perhaps most feature-packed, of the contiguous Canadian Rockies parks. It's impossible to do justice to the park in a paragraph or two, but if you like the other parks, and particularly if you enjoy backpacking, think about spending some time here, too.

From Lake Louise, Trans-Canada Hwy-1 climbs quickly over Kicking Horse Pass before reaching the **Spiral Tunnel Viewpoint,** where you can learn about the amazing engineering feat that allowed trains to travel through this rugged region. Five miles (eight kilometers) farther, the next swing north takes you up, and up, and up, along a *very* tight series of hairpin turns, to **Takakkaw Falls,** perhaps the most impressive waterfall in the Canadian Rockies. You can see the 1,250-foot (381-meter) falls from the parking lot, but a short trail leads to the Yoho River, where you can appreciate the view in all its rainbow-refracting glory.

Farther west along Trans-Canada Hwy-1, about a dozen miles (20 kilometers) from the Icefields Parkway in the hamlet of **Field,** you come to the Yoho National Park **information center** (250/343-6783), which can tell you all about the park's natural attractions. **Truffle Pigs Bistro** (250/343-6303), contained in the back of Field's Kicking Horse Lodge, is a charming little eatery serving up fresh and inventive meals.

Three miles (five kilometers) west of Field, a turnoff to the north leads into the wilderness to the **Emerald Lake Lodge** (403/410-7417 or 800/663-6336), a rustic, upscale resort that dates back to 1902. Sitting on the shores of one of the Canadian Rockies' most magnificent lakes, the lodge is open year-round, offering food and lodging (C$375–440 a night, depending on season) as well as swimming, boating, and horseback riding.

Lake Louise

The sight of **Lake Louise,** spreading in a deep aquamarine pool at the foot of silvery snowcapped peaks, is worth traveling around the world to see. Which is exactly what many people do: If you come here in summer, you'll be among an international gaggle of tourists for whom Lake Louise really *is* the Canadian Rockies. A small village with the same name sits along Trans-Canada Hwy-1, but the 1.5-mile-long (2.4-kilometer-long) very cold lake itself is about two miles (three kilometers) west, at the end of Lake Louise Drive. Besides the summer sightseeing, the Lake Louise area offers world-class downhill skiing and snowboarding: Three mountains (over 3,000 vertical feet, 900 vertical meters) are yours for the price of a Lake Louise lift ticket (C$76; 403/522-3555). One of the lifts operates throughout the summer as well, offering a grand Canadian Rockies panorama.

Like the town of Banff to the south, Lake Louise was developed over a century ago as a tourist resort by the Canadian Pacific Railway. As in Banff, the landmark here is a magnificent hotel, the **Fairmont Chateau Lake Louise** (C$329 and up; 403/522-3511), which stands eight stories high above the lakeshore. Taking on a Swiss Alps theme—staff wear lederhosen, while yodelers and harmonica players perform in the hotel lobbies and bars, and all day long a funny old man stands along the shore blowing a 15-foot alpine horn that echoes back and forth in the canyons across the lake—the 550-room Chateau Lake Louise has every service and comfort you could want.

Originally built by the Canadian Pacific Railway, the **Fairmont Banff Springs Hotel, Chateau Lake Louise,** and **Jasper Park Lodge** (and some 25 others across Canada) are all owned and operated by the same company, Fairmont Hotels and Resorts. For rates and reservations, call 800/257-7544.

Of course, there's no charge to explore the hotel or walk along the lake and enjoy the views. You can rent canoes and paddle out onto the lake, and from the hotel a popular trail climbs over 1,000 feet (300 meters) in about two miles (three kilometers) to **Bridal Veil Falls,** continuing a short way farther to **Lake Agnes,** where a rustic teahouse serves sandwiches and tea.

Immediately below the lake, the family-owned **Paradise Lodge and Bungalows** (open May 20–Oct. 2; 403/522-3595) is smaller and friendlier, with cozy log cabins and modern lodge rooms (many with fireplaces) running C$178–389 per night.

Back down in Lake Louise Village, at the northwest end of Village Road, the **HI-Lake Louise Alpine Centre** (403/522-2201) is a very large, modern log-built lodge, with C$30–42 dorm beds and the very nice **Bill Peyto's Cafe,** the area's least expensive place to eat, open daily 7 AM–9 PM May–September and 8 AM–8 PM October–April. There are gas stations, gift shops, a grocery store, cafés, and the popular **Laggan's Mountain Bakery** (great pastries and coffee) in the hard-to-miss Samson Mall. There's also a large **campground** along the Bow River a half mile (0.8 kilometer) south of town. The whole place tends to fill up most days despite having over 400 campsites.

Smaller, less visited, but every bit as spectacular as Lake Louise, **Moraine Lake** sits at the end of a summer-only road, six miles (10 kilometers) south of the midpoint of Lake Louise Drive. Despite the name, Moraine Lake is not in

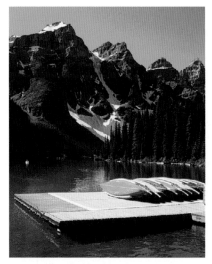
calm, spectacular Moraine Lake

fact formed by a glacial moraine, but by a rockfall; nevertheless it's a gorgeous spot, the placid lake reflecting the jagged surrounding peaks. From the lakeside, a two-mile (three-kilometer) trail climbs up to **Larch Valley,** where you can see fall color extraordinaire courtesy of the namesake trees, which are prolific here.

Town of Banff

Fifteen miles (24 kilometers) southeast of Lake Louise, Hwy-93 and the Trans-Canada Hwy-1 diverge, with Hwy-93 cutting due south through Kootenay National Park across southeastern British Columbia toward the U.S. border. That is the route we follow, all the way south to Mexico eventually, but anyone in his or her right mind will want to make the 15-mile (24-kilometer) trip southeast along Hwy-1 to visit the beautiful Town of Banff, home of the landmark **Fairmont Banff Springs Hotel,** the biggest and most impressive of the grand old Canadian Pacific hotels. When it opened in 1888, this was the largest hotel in the world, with a grand total of 250 rooms; over the years, the hotel has been rebuilt and expanded to currently hold 768 rooms, most of which are booked up months in advance. Spreading between the hotel and Hwy-1, the Town of Banff has grown into the tasteful but bustling commercial center of the Canadian Rockies, with a year-round population of some 7,500 people, plus many times that many visitors daily during the peak summer season. Though the commercialism can detract from the natural splendor, Banff is definitely a very pleasant place to while away some time.

For the most spectacular introduction to Banff, head up Mountain Avenue, where the **Banff Gondola** (daily; C$30; 403/762-2523) will take you 2,300 feet up Sulphur Mountain for a grand view over the entire Bow Valley. The "springs" in the Fairmont Banff Springs Hotel's name refer to actual hot springs; the original hot springs that spurred the growth of Banff have been closed and converted into the **Cave and Basin National Historic Site** (daily; C$4; 403/762-1566), west of town at the end of Cave Avenue, where exhibits detail the underlying geology that makes hot springs happen.

The town's main drag, Banff Avenue, has all the cafés, restaurants,

historic Banff Springs Hotel

and shopping you could want, but if the weather's bad (if it's not, you really ought to be outdoors, enjoying Mother Nature!), you can learn about Banff and the Canadian Rockies in a trio of museums. Best first stop is the **Banff Park Museum** (daily; C$4), near the river at the foot of Banff Avenue, a Victorian-era remnant (it was built in 1903) that displays the taxidermied remains of typical park wildlife. Around the corner, a half block down from pleasant, riverside Central Park, the **Whyte Museum of the Canadian Rockies** (daily; C$8; 111 Bear St.) has an expansive collection of historic books, postcards, paintings, and photographs, all capturing various aspects of the mountains and their inhabitants.

One of many cultural events that take place in Banff is the **Banff Mountain Film Festival** (403/762-6125), where the world's best adventure-travel and mountain-climbing films are shown every November.

Town of Banff Practicalities

So long as you plan ahead, and can afford to enjoy some of Canada's most expensive hotels and restaurants, the Town of Banff makes a great place to visit. Because the Town of Banff is located within the confines of Banff National Park, development has been limited—so much so that summertime accommodations here can be hard to come by, and very expensive. Throughout the summer, hotels are booked up solidly well in advance, and rates start around C$200 for a basic room. (Winter rates are usually less than half that.) A dozen places are within a short walk of downtown: **Brewster's Mountain Lodge** (C$260 and up; 208 Caribou St.; 403/762-2900) has spacious rooms, while rooms at the landmark **Fairmont Banff Springs Hotel** (C$395 and up; 403/762-2211 or 800/441-1414), when available, climb quickly into the four-digit range.

*While Trans-Canada Hwy-1 is faster, the **Bow Valley Parkway** is a more scenic alternative between Banff and Lake Louise. Running parallel and to the east, it also gives access to some very nice spots, including the waterfalls of Johnston Canyon, where **Johnston Canyon Resort** (C$149–315; 403/762-2971) has inexpensive rooms in a quiet, woodland setting.*

If you have trouble finding an affordable room in Banff, consider taking a trip farther east to **Canmore,** a lively little city on Hwy-1, just east of the park's boundary, where the nonprofit Alpine Club of Canada operates the C$27-a-night **HI-Canmore Hostel** (403/678-3200).

Restaurants in Banff are plentiful, good, and wide-ranging—there are over 100, which works out to one for every 70 or so residents. One of the most popular places, with locals and visitors alike, is **Melissa's** (daily; 218 Lynx St.; 403/762-5511) on the west side of downtown. Housed in a 1928 log building with a nice bar and outdoor deck, Melissa's serves great pancakes (with real maple syrup) and beefy burgers. Along with a good Italian place, **Giorgio's** (219 Banff Ave.; 403/762-5114), downtown Banff also has many Japanese restaurants, a Greek café, and the ever-popular **Wild Bill's Saloon,** which has good food and drink (mostly the latter), right at the center of town (201 Banff Ave.; 403/762-0333).

Parks Canada (877/737-3783) operates three **campgrounds** along Tunnel Mountain Road, two miles (three kilometers) east of downtown, which have over 1,000 sites altogether; all the campgrounds have hot showers, and many sites have full or partial RV hookups. Also on Tunnel Mountain Road is the large **HI-Banff Alpine Centre** (C$34–47; 403/762-4123).

For comprehensive information on Banff, head downtown to the large **visitors center** (224 Banff Ave.), which is home to both the commercially oriented Banff/Lake Louise Tourism Bureau (403/762-8421) and the staff of Banff National Park (403/762-1550).

Kootenay National Park

Though Banff and Jasper seem to get all the attention, neighboring **Kootenay National Park** draws travelers who prefer to experience wilderness without having to wait in line. It was originally known as the "Highway Park," since the land was deeded to the federal government in exchange for it building (and paying for!) the 65-mile-long (105-kilometer) Banff-Windermere Highway, which now runs through the heart of the park. Completed in 1922, this was the first road over the Canadian Rockies, and it linked the prairies and the west coast of British Columbia for the first time. Fortunately for visitors, Hwy-1, which runs through Yoho to the north, now carries most of the through traffic.

Kootenay National Park spreads for five miles (eight kilometers) to either side of the highway. As in all the Canadian Rockies parks, grizzly bears still roam the Kootenay backcountry, and black bears, bighorn sheep, and elk are regularly seen along the roadside. A number of stops along the way offer great short hikes. Two of the most enjoyable, **Marble Canyon** and **Paint Pots,** are at the north end of the park, well signed along the north side of the highway. Marble Canyon is an amazing sight (and sound): a 100-foot-deep, very narrow slot canyon carved in the shiny white dolomite limestone by the thundering cascade of Tokumm Creek. A half-mile trail leads back and forth on a series of man-made and natural bridges over the gorge. Two miles south, the Paint Pots are much more sedate, displaying a handful of brightly colored mud puddles dyed varying shades of red and yellow by oxidizing minerals in the natural springs.

Paint Pots in Kootenay National Park

At **Vermilion Crossing** at the center of the park, about 15 miles south of the Paint Pots and 40 miles from Radium, you'll find the park's only overnight accommodations at **Kootenay Park Lodge** ($85–189; 403/762-9196), which in summer has a handful of cabins, a restaurant, a gas station, a visitors center, and a general store. From here south, the road follows the broad banks of the Vermilion and Kootenay Rivers before cutting west over Sinclair Pass, where a viewpoint offers a stunning high-country panorama. At the southern end of the park, the road winds through the narrow gorge of Sinclair Canyon before running suddenly into the roadside sprawl of Radium Hot Springs.

You can drive through Kootenay without charge, but if you want to stop en route you need to buy a park pass (C$10 per person per day) from the entrance stations.

Radium Hot Springs

At the west edge of Kootenay National Park, the town of **Radium Hot Springs** is a swift change from the natural idyll. Motels, cafés, and gas stations line Hwy-93 block after block, and apart from satisfying your fuel-and-food needs, there's not a lot here. The one good place to eat is **The Springs**

Restaurant, west of town on the golf course at family-friendly **Radium Resort** (C$105 and up; 250/347-9311 or 800/667-6444). Standard motels here include the C$100-a-night **Alpen Motel** (250/347-9823).

The actual hot springs from which the town takes its name are just east, inside the park boundary. Unfortunately, the water is heavily chlorinated, and there are no "natural" springs left.

If you're passing through Radium Hot Springs, be sure to stop for a look at the amazing array of signs and sculptures outside Swiss-born artist Rolf Heer's **Radium Wood Carvers,** on a hill just east of the Hwy-93/95 junction.

Fort Steele Heritage Town

South of Radium Hot Springs, Hwy-93 runs along the western foot of the Rocky Mountains, but the natural beauty of the national parks doesn't really return until you cross the border and visit Glacier National Park, a good 200 miles (322 kilometers) away. That said, it's a wide-open drive, passing a few towns, some golf resorts, and two big lumber mills, following the banks of the Kootenay River all the way.

The one real attraction along this stretch of road is the resurrected frontier community of Fort Steele, roughly midway between Radium and the border crossing. Containing more than 60 preserved and reconstructed buildings, **Fort Steele Heritage Town** (daily; C$5; 250/417-6000) re-creates the boomtown that stood here from 1890 until 1898, servicing the silver, gold, and lead mines of the East Kootenays. Along with the buildings, which house interpretive exhibits as well as an ice cream store, a bakery and restaurant, and a general store selling top hats and other period essentials, you can enjoy theater performances or ride on a steam train—though there are extra charges for these activities.

MONTANA

From the Canadian border, US-93 runs south and east along the Tobacco River valley, then cuts through the **Flathead National Forest** to the logging and ski resort towns of **Whitefish** and **Kalispell.** Continuing south along the shores of **Flathead Lake,** the route passes through the college town and cultural nexus of **Missoula,** south of which U passes through some of the beautiful terrain in the country, winding through broad valleys at the foot of the Bitterroot Mountains, past alpine lakes and snowcapped peaks all the way south to the Idaho border. Quite a lot of the old two-lane route has been up-graded into near-freeway status, but US-93 still one of either country's great drives.

Eureka

Like British Columbia, Montana's northwest corner, where Canadian Hwy-93 ends and US-93 begins, is an isolated land of dense forests, broad rivers, and glaciated valleys. Besides providing natural habitat for herds of moose, elk, bison, and bighorn sheep, not to mention mountain lions, wolves, and grizzly bears, the thick groves of cedars, pines, and firs support the Northwest's other endangered species—the logger—whose angular clear-cuts and mono-crop tree plantations are also apparent as you pass through the region.

> Hwy-37 is an official Scenic Byway that winds along the Kootenai River and Lake Koocanusa from Eureka to the town of **Libby,** where it intersects US-2.

The first sizable town, 15 miles south of the border, is **Eureka** (pop. 1,037), a sleepy little place with a pair of gas stations, a couple of cafés, and **Tobacco Valley Historical Village** (open summer only), a fascinating collection of pioneer buildings, preserved and moved to a small park along US-93 at the south end of town.

For a truly unusual experience, spend the night in the former **USFS fire lookout** atop Webb Mountain, 20 miles southwest of Eureka. It's bagpipers at the annual Eureka Rendezvous

very popular and costs around $25 a night. For details and rental availability, contact the USFS ranger station in Eureka (406/883-3636).

Whitefish

A major division point on the historic Great Northern railroad, whose tracks are still in use by Amtrak and the Burlington Northern Santa Fe, **Whitefish** (pop. 6,357) was originally known as Stumptown because of the intensive logging operations centered here. Despite its proud industrial history, the blue-collar base has long since been eclipsed by tourism, and the city now calls itself the "Recreational Capital of Montana," with alpine lakes, fishing streams, hiking trails, great skiing, and endless mountain scenery right on its doorstep. The main attraction in Whitefish, for skiing in winter and hiking and mountain biking in summer, is "The Fish," a.k.a. **Whitefish Mountain Resort,** which surrounds the 6,770-foot peak (with a 2,170-foot vertical drop!) that looms over the northwest shore of Whitefish Lake.

Besides giving access to the surrounding great outdoors, Whitefish is a pleasant place to stop and stretch your legs, and it has everything you could want from a resort town—without the rampant tourist-pandering and real estate speculation that has ruined so many other places. A small **museum** (closed Sunday; free) inside the rustic Great Northern train station, which stands in a pleasant park at the north end of Central Avenue, gives a historical overview of Whitefish. Across the park from the station there's a theater, a library, and the **Great Northern Brewing Company,** whose hoppy products you can sample in a small tasting room or in any Whitefish bar.

The heart of town is a few blocks of Central Avenue, running south from the railroad tracks to Montana's one and only Frank Lloyd Wright building, an early 1950s bank and office complex on the east side of Central Avenue between 3rd and 4th Streets called, directly enough, the Frank Lloyd Wright Building. In between you'll find some great bars and saloons, the Bookworks bookstore on 3rd and Spokane Streets, and art galleries.

The best place to start the day in Whitefish is along 3rd Street, east of Central Avenue, where the **Buffalo Cafe** (514 E. 3rd St.; 406/862-2833) is a popular breakfast and lunch spot, locally famous for its huevos rancheros. Other places line up along Central Avenue, so you can get great burgers or wood-fired pizza or simply quaff a beer or two—all in the same block.

For a place to stay and get to know Whitefish, you can choose from numerous motels along US-93 south of town. The nicest in-town accommodation option is walkably close to downtown: the attractive and comfortable **Garden Wall Inn** ($155 and up; 504 Spokane Ave.; 888/530-1700), a Craftsman-era cottage.

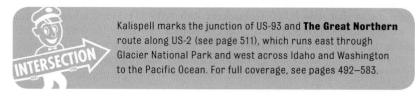

Kalispell marks the junction of US-93 and **The Great Northern** route along US-2 (see page 511), which runs east through Glacier National Park and west across Idaho and Washington to the Pacific Ocean. For full coverage, see pages 492–583.

Kalispell

The nearest thing to an urban center in northwestern Montana, **Kalispell** (pop. 19,927) spreads across the northern Flathead Valley at the junction of the Stillwater, Whitefish, and Flathead Rivers. Cut by two main thorough-fares—east–west US-2 and north–south US-93—it ain't quaint by any stretch of the imagination; at first glance it looks like yet another lumber mill and mining town, but the historic downtown area is full of interesting spots, such as the engaging **Hockaday Museum of Art** (closed Sun. and Mon.; $5), housed in the old Carnegie Library on 3rd Street, two blocks east of Main Street (US-93). Another few blocks east stands the impressive, perfectly pre-served **Conrad Mansion,** built by pioneer trader and Kalispell founder Charles Conrad in 1895 and now open for guided tours (Tues.–Sun.; $8; 406/755-2166).

Breakfasts don't get much better than those served at **Norm's News** (34 Main St.; 406/756-5466), a 1930s soda fountain luncheonette where you can also get killer milk shakes, a wide variety of newspapers and magazines, and more than 500 kinds of candy. (Upstairs is the old Kalispell Opera House.) Kalispell also has an above-aver-age range of taverns, including the venerable **Moose's Saloon** (173 N. Main St.; 406/755-2337), near the junction of US-2 and US-93, fa-mous for pizza and occasional live music. For good old-fashioned roadside fast food, try the popular local mini-chain **Frugals** (1815 S. US-93; 406/257-6710).

Chief Charlo, leader of the Bitterroot Salish, as seen in 1908

There are the usual national motels, but *the* place to stay in Kalispell is the **Kalispell Grand Hotel** ($80 and up; 100 Main St.; 406/755-8100 or 800/858-7422), a conveniently located historic downtown hotel with nice, clean rooms.

Flathead Lake

The largest natural freshwater lake west of the Mississippi River, deep-blue **Flathead Lake** is a magnet for outdoor recreation in western Montana. US-93 winds along the lake's hilly western shore, passing through a number of state parks and small resort communities that enjoy grand views of the Rocky Mountains to the east and the green foothills of the Flathead National Forest to the west.

Along US-93 at the north end of the lake, **Somers** is a neat old timber town with some well-preserved turn-of-the-20th-century buildings, including an old train depot that now holds **Tiebuckers Pub** (406/857-3335), a beer bar and good restaurant. From Somers, you can detour east onto Hwy-82 for a trip along the eastern shore of Flathead Lake, where you can enjoy the upscale resort town of **Bigfork** and the acres of cherry orchards that line the lakeshore, flowering in spring and offering delectable treats in early summer.

Elmo, at the north edge of the Flathead Reservation, hosts the annual **Standing Arrow PowWow** on the third weekend in July. **Arlee,** at the southern edge of the reservation, hosts the **4th of July PowWow,** one of the most popular Native American gatherings in Montana.

Polson: Miracle of America Museum

The southern half of Flathead Lake is surrounded by the Flathead Indian Reservation, home to a mixed population of Flathead Salish, Kootenai, and Caucasians, who make up around 80 percent of the reservation's population. The large reservation covers a 1.2-million-acre area, roughly 35 by 65 miles, hemmed in by the Mission and Cabinet Mountains, but apart from a few small towns, it's mostly prairie and riverside wetlands.

The largest of these towns, **Polson,** at the bottom end of the lake where the Flathead River flows south, is a predominantly white retirement community, with 24-hour gas stations, the area's only ATMs, a Safeway supermarket, and chain motels. Polson is also home to the deluxe lakefront **Best Western KwaTaqNuk Resort** ($72 and up; 303 US-93 E.; 406/883-3636), owned and operated by the Salish-Kootenai tribe, with two pools, an on-site casino, a boat dock, and direct access to the lake.

Just two miles south of Polson along US-93, the bizarre but fascinating **Miracle of America Museum** (daily; $5; 406/883-6804), which calls itself "Western Montana's Largest Museum," displays a mixed bag of kitchen

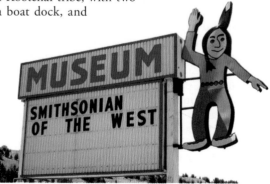

appliances, toys, tractors, armored tanks, and framed newspaper clippings to give a unique (to say the least!) view of America's industrial, military, and cultural history. If you'd enjoy things like a motorized toboggan or a collection of tractor seats, count on spending an hour at least—twice that long if you also like music, because the museum doubles as the Montana Fiddlers Hall of Fame.

South of Polson, US-93 has been realigned and widened in an eco-sensitive, wetlands-friendly fashion, with native plantings, wildlife crossings, and a new name: the Peoples Way.

St. Ignatius and the National Bison Range

The wildly angular Mission Mountains, rising to the east of the Flathead Reservation, were named for a Catholic mission established in the 1850s at **St. Ignatius,** a small town midway between Polson and Missoula. Like most reservation communities, it's a poor and fairly depressed place, worth a look for the imposing **St. Ignatius Mission church** (daily; donations), just east of US-93. Built by Flathead laborers in 1891, the church holds over 55 religious frescoes painted by Fr. Joseph Carignano, the mission cook. Along with the

bison grazing at the National Bison Range

church, St. Ignatius holds the **Flathead Indian Museum and Trading Post** (daily; 406/745-2951), a large gift shop, motel, and drive-through espresso stand right on US-93.

West of St. Ignatius, 18,500 acres of natural rolling prairie have been set aside since 1908 as the **National Bison Range,** protected home of the 500 or so resident bison (a.k.a. buffalo), along with deer, elk, pronghorns, and mountain goats. Allow around two hours to drive a complete circuit of the park; the entrance and visitors center are on the west side of the reserve, off Hwy-200, six miles west of the crossroads town of **Ravalli.**

Missoula

Spreading along the banks of the Clark Fork of the Columbia River at the mouth of Hell Gate Canyon, **Missoula** (pop. 66,788) is an engaging mix of college-town sophistication and blue-collar grit. The two industries that built the city, railroads and lumber mills, have both diminished considerably since their turn-of-the-20th-century heyday but still form the foundation of the local economy. The University of Montana campus has given Missoula a literate and left-leaning air not usually found in this neck of the woods.

The mountains, rivers, and canyons around Missoula are Montana at its best, and downtown Missoula, stretching

The Missoula Ospreys, the only baseball team with a real live animal mascot in residence, play at Allegiance Field (406/543-3300), south of the river and just west of US-93.

A River Runs Through It

Missoula has long been something of a literary center, thanks in part to the late Norman Maclean, whose novella *A River Runs Through It* rhapsodizes over the surrounding Rocky Mountain country and the larger-than-life lives lived there. The book, which was faithfully adapted into a film by Robert Redford, makes a great traveling companion, full of vivid description and insightful humor—Maclean writes that while growing up he soon discovered that the world is "full of bastards, the number increasing rapidly the farther one gets from Missoula, Montana." He lovingly uses the art of fly-fishing as an essential metaphor for a life well lived.

along the north bank of the river, contains a large number of elegant turn-of-the-20th-century brick buildings housing a buoyant range of businesses, from department stores to bike shops. Missoula's other social nexus, the **University of Montana** campus, spreads south of the river at the foot of dusty brown Mt. Sentinel (the one marked with the large "M") and the Sapphire Mountains. It's a pleasant place to walk around—in summer at least, when cyclists and in-line skaters outnumber pedestrians on the many paths—keeping an eye out for posters advertising local events.

East of Missoula, scenic Hwy-200 runs along the **Clearwater River** to Clearwater Junction, where a giant steer welcomes travelers to town.

Missoula's number-one attraction, the **Smokejumpers Base Aerial Fire Depot** (Mon.–Fri. 8:30 AM–5 PM in summer; donations; 406/329-4934), is seven miles west of town at the end of Broadway. Displays include dioramas, old photographs, and antique firefighting gear; hourly guided tours are led by the very people who jump out of airplanes to battle raging forest fires.

Missoula Practicalities

Thanks to the student population, Missoula has a wider than usual range of places to eat, and a truly phenomenal range of places to drink. Start the day at **Bernice's Bakery** (190 S. 3rd St. W.; 406/728-1358), which has good coffee and great pastries. Right downtown (139 W. Main St.), the landmark **Missoula Club** (406/728-3740) is a perfectly preserved 1940s burgers-and-beer bar. For an even grittier Missoula scene, it's hard to beat the round-the-clock **Oxford Saloon** (337 N. Higgins Ave.; 406/549-0117), where men and a few women huddle around nightly poker games, brave souls feast on the house special eggs-and-brains, and everyone drinks too much Bud.

There's no shortage of accommodations in Missoula, though it's always a good idea to book a room in advance. The nicest place to stay is **Goldsmith's** ($124–169; 809 E. Front St.; 406/728-1585), a very comfortable downtown B&B along the river. A half dozen motels line I-90 and US-93 (which follows Broadway west of Missoula and Brooks Street south of town), including the usual national chains.

The Bitterroot Valley

Missoula sits at the north end of the Bitterroot Valley, where **Lewis and Clark** set up camp at what they called **Traveler's Rest** in September 1805 and again on their return in July 1806. A roadside marker off US-93, just south of the US-12 junction, tells more of the story.

If you're a fan of Lewis and Clark, or hot springs, or want to unwind after a day of cross-country skiing, you won't want to miss the idyllic **Lolo Hot Springs Resort** (406/273-2290), in the mountains 26 miles southwest of Missoula via scenic US-12, which runs along the route Lewis and Clark followed on their way west. Moose wander through the wooded grounds, and the natural hot springs (where Lewis and Clark themselves soaked on their way home from the Pacific Ocean) have been extensively but attractively developed.

Continuing south toward the Idaho border, US-93 runs along the banks of the beautiful Bitterroot River through a broad valley lined by groves of cottonwood trees and bordered by parallel ridges of 8,000-foot peaks. In the hamlet of Florence, **Glen's Cafe** (406/273-2534), tucked away just west of the highway, is renowned throughout Montana for its carb-loaded pastries, pancakes, and incredibly good, double-crusted, fresh berry pies.

South of Florence, the **Eastside Highway** (Hwy-203 and Hwy-269), a well-marked alternative route, runs parallel to US-93 a half mile to the east, passing rolling ranch lands, pioneer homesteads—some of which are among the oldest in the state—and occasional prefab trailers. This eastern side of the Bitterroot Valley is mostly open countryside, with a few small hamlets like **Stevensville**, Montana's oldest town. It was founded by Jesuits in 1841 around the still intact **St. Mary's Mission** at the end of 4th Street, two blocks west of Main.

Hamilton

The Bitterroot Valley's sole sizable town, **Hamilton** (pop. 4,443) stands at the southern end of the valley, where US-93 and the Eastside Highway rejoin. Hamilton was laid out in the 1890s as a planned community by the multimillionaire "Copper King" Marcus Daly. Daly's elegant 56-room **Georgian**

mansion, now a museum (daily in summer; $8; 406/363-6004), is set in 50 acres of lushly landscaped gardens.

Hamilton's other main draw is the large **Ravalli County Museum** (closed Sun. and Mon.; free; 406/363-3338), housed in a 100-year-old former courthouse on the corner of 3rd and Bedford, two blocks south of Main Street. Besides an above-average collection of fishing flies, pioneer clothing, and Native American artifacts, the museum has an entire room dedicated to Rocky Mountain spotted fever ticks—Hamilton, home of the Rocky Mountain Laboratories, was where spotted fever was discovered—and you owe it to yourself to study the two-foot-tall tick model and the diagrams tracing the tick's life cycle.

Hamilton has some great places to eat, like the very popular **Coffee Cup Cafe** on US-93 (500 S. 1st St.; 406/363-3822). Great big half-pound burgers ("Best in the Bitterroots") and fresh-cut crispy fries are at **Naps Grill** (220 N. 2nd St.; 406/363-0136), or for something more exotic look for **Spice of Life** (163 S. 2nd St.; 406/363-4433).

One of many highway motels in Hamilton, the **City Center** enjoys a quiet location off US-93 ($60–80; 415 W. Main St.; 406/363-1651). Besides its convenience as a stopover, Hamilton is also the gateway to outdoor activities (hunting, fishing, and riding, mainly) in the Bitterroots. For full details on the huge variety of outdoor recreation hereabouts, contact the **Bitterroot Valley Chamber of Commerce** (105 E. Main St.; 406/363-2400).

Bitterroot Mountains

South of Hamilton, the serrated peaks and forested foothills of the Bitterroot Mountains close in along US-93 as the valley narrows sharply, the towns shrink in size, and woodlands (and campgrounds) replace farmlands (and commerce) along the roadside. Just 17 miles south of Hamilton, the pioneer village of **Darby** has a couple of cafés, a log-cabin public library, and a helpful USFS ranger station (406/821-3913), the best source of information on hiking and camping in the Bitterroots.

The **Big Hole National Battlefield** (406/689-3155), where 800 Nez Percé warriors, women, and children were attacked by the U.S. Army on August 9, 1877, lies east of the Continental Divide near the hamlet of **Wisdom,** 20 miles east of Lost Trail Pass via Hwy-43.

South of Darby, US-93 cuts away from the Bitterroot River at the hamlet of **Sula,** beyond which the highway continues its slow climb up through seven miles of subalpine landscape to another of Montana's many pleasant resorts, **Lost Trail Hot Springs** ($65 and up; 8321 Hwy-93 S.; 406/821-3574), open year-round with hot springs pools, an attractive variety of moderately priced rooms and cabins, and a good on-site restaurant. Lost Trail is especially popular with cross-country skiers, who can traverse many miles of nearby trails, including the route followed by Chief Joseph and the Nez Percé in 1877 while fleeing from the U.S. Cavalry.

From Lost Trail Hot Springs, US-93 climbs up to 6,995-foot **Lost Trail Pass,** which Lewis and Clark crossed in 1805 on their return from the impassable Snake River, and which now marks the border with Idaho. The pass also serves as home to **Lost Trail Powder Mountain,** a low-key downhill ski area ($35; 406/821-3211) with 1,200 vertical feet of groomed runs.

IDAHO

In 1938, the WPA *Guide to Idaho* described the state's section of US-93 as "miles of beautiful mountains, ranging from soft flanks voluptuously mounded to the lean and glittering majesty of toothed backbones." Though the official US-93 route was redirected around the mountains, not much else has changed since then: The old road is still in place and still gives an unmatched tour of the best of what Idaho has to offer.

Entering the state through a historic pass in the beautiful Bitterroot Mountains, the route drops down to follow the mighty Salmon River to its headwaters over 100 miles away near the frontier resort of **Stanley,** high up in the Sawtooth Mountains. South of the Sawtooths, the route plunges into the plush resort community of **Sun Valley,** then races across the Snake River plain through **Twin Falls** to the Nevada border.

Salmon River: North Fork

Beginning at the Montana border, atop Lost Trail Pass, US-93 winds steeply downhill through the 1.7-million-acre Salmon National Forest. Another 26 miles south of the pass, US-93 passes by the village of North Fork—where the friendly folks at the **North Fork General Store** (208/865-2412) run a combination café/motel/post office that has everything a traveler could want, from great pies to an RV park. Here US-93 crosses the Salmon River, which is often called the "River of No Return," because without a jet-boat to help you along, it is navigable only in a downstream direction. Running swiftly for nearly 300 miles west through the heart of the most extensive wilderness left in the lower 48 states, the Salmon River has carved one of the deepest gorges in North America, a full 1,000 feet deeper than the Grand Canyon.

Across Idaho, towns and services are few and far between, and during the peak summer season it's a good idea to make arrangements for accommodations well in advance.

From North Fork, a paved road leads 17 miles west along the riverside to the tiny hamlet of **Shoup,** beyond which a number of rough roads and hiking trails lead to ghost towns and the Frank Church Wilderness, deep in the rugged mountains.

Salmon

Surrounded by ranch lands in a broad valley between the Bitterroot and Yellowjacket Mountains, **Salmon** (pop. 3,300) is a picturesque place that has turned increasingly to tourism and outdoor recreation as its timber and ranching industries have faded. Rafting and fishing guides will take you out into the wilds, and not surprisingly, Salmon makes a better base from which to explore the surrounding scenery than a destination in itself. Main Street, which US-93 follows through town, does have a good variety of places to eat, including the **Salmon River Coffee Shop** (606 Main St.; 208/756-3521) and **Bertram's Brewery** (101 S. Andrews; 208/756-3391).

Salmon River Gorge

South of Salmon, US-93 continues beside the Salmon River, climbing slowly through a landscape that alternates from open meadows to sheer canyons. Nearly 100 miles later, the route arrives at the river's headwaters high up in the Sawtooth Mountains. Apart from a few cottonwoods, there are few trees and no real towns along this stretch of US-93, and traffic still has to stop for the occasional cattle drive, but it's a very pretty drive, and you can stop almost anywhere for a quick walk or picnic along the river. The appearance of the Salmon River canyon varies tremendously, but for most of the way it is dry and brown—a real shock compared to the dense green forests of Montana, just an hour north.

Around Salmon, tune to **KSRA 92.7 FM** or **960 AM** for an eclectic broadcast of oldies, country music, ABC News, and reports on life in the Salmon and Big Hole region.

Challis and the Land of the Yankee Fork State Park

The only town for 50 miles in any direction, **Challis** is an old mining camp that has grown into a miniature version of Salmon—albeit without the water or the tourists. Apart from boasting the all-time Idaho record for least rain in a year (seven inches), Challis is a very quiet market center for local cattle ranchers, with more bars—and barber shops—than you'd expect of a town this small.

On the south side of Challis, at the junction of US-93 and Hwy-75, the excellent, modern **Land of the Yankee Fork State Park visitors center** (daily in summer, closed Sun.

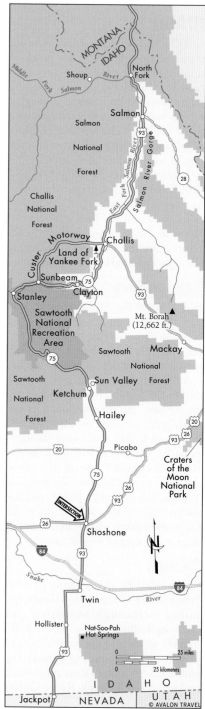

rest of year; 208/879-5244) has extensive displays of local mining history and maps to guide visitors to many evocative ghost towns and other relics sprinkling the surrounding hills. Gold was first discovered in the region in the 1870s, and nearby mines and mining camps boomed for the next 25 years, though by 1905 the last mine had closed. A few gold mines have reopened in recent years, though all of these are hidden away in isolated areas and protected behind high-security walls and fences; none is open to the public.

US-93: Mackay and the Lost River Valley

At Challis, our main route follows the 1940s alignment of US-93, heading west into the Sawtooth Mountains, but today's US-93 swings southeast toward Arco and the Craters of the Moon National Monument through the Lost River Valley. The scenery here remains spectacular, with the mountains towering over the ranches of the valley floor, but it can't compare with the glories of the old road route.

But if you're in a rush, or there's been a recent storm blocking the mountain passes, or you just want to see another corner of Idaho, US-93 will be there for you. Mountaineers follow US-93 on their way to climb 12,662-foot **Mt. Borah,** the highest point in Idaho and a demanding though not technically difficult summit to reach. The trailhead is at the end of the well-signed Borah Peak Access Road, roughly halfway between Challis and Mackay. For details, contact the **USFS ranger station** (208/588-2224) in Mackay.

The rough-and-ready town of **Mackay** (rhymes with wacky; pop. 517) is the valley's hub. You can stay at the **Wagon Wheel** (809 W. Custer St.; 208/588-3331), where rooms with kitchenettes go for as little as $41 a night. Mackay also hosts an annual rodeo, the Custer County Fair, and a mountain bike race, but it's best known for its famous **free barbecue** on the third Saturday in September, when hundreds of people come here for general fun and games and massive amounts of free food (Tons of Meat—Mackay's Treat, say the signs).

South of Mackay, US-93 continues to Arco, then elbows west through the eerie Craters of the Moon, rejoining Hwy-75 at Shoshone.

In 1805, explorers Lewis and Clark became the first Americans to cross the Continental Divide when they climbed over **Lemhi Pass,** 25 miles southeast of Salmon. Hoping to follow the Salmon River west to the Pacific, they found it was impassable, so they continued north over **Lost Trail Pass,** roughly along the route of US-93.

Clayton and Sunbeam

Though US-93 swings to the southeast from Challis, the original alignment, now Hwy-75, winds west into the mountains through the 2,000-foot-deep canyon carved by the Salmon River. You're deep in the forest by the time you

On October 28, 1983, one of the most powerful earthquakes ever to hit North America rumbled the Lost River Valley, instantly dropping the valley floor as much as 14 feet and forming dramatic escarpments still visible in places throughout the region.

reach **Clayton** (pop. 26), a riverside wide spot with a gas station and a biker-friendly tavern. Farther west, some 50 miles upstream from Challis, you come to the small but pleasant year-round resort of **Sunbeam,** which overlooks the confluence of the Yankee Fork and Salmon Rivers. There's a café and campground at the junction, and just a half mile upstream you'll find the area's greatest attraction: the natural **hot springs,** steaming wildly on cold days and forming rock pools of varying temperatures in the Salmon River, marked by a stone bathhouse built during the New Deal 1930s but no longer in use.

From Sunbeam, it's only another 15 miles to Stanley, heart of the glorious Sawtooth Mountains.

Custer Motorway

If you're here in summer and have a few hours to spare, take the rough (no RVs, please!) but very scenic alternative to Hwy-75, built by the Civilian Conservation Corps in the 1930s and called the **Custer Motorway,** which winds west from Challis into the Yankee Fork mining district, passing the remains of old stagecoach stations and stamp mills before reaching the ghost town of **Custer.** Custer now consists of a half dozen mining shacks and log cabins, the Empire Saloon, and a small but engaging museum housed in the old one-room schoolhouse. Beyond Custer, a well-maintained gravel road follows the Yankee Fork of the Salmon River south to Hwy-75, passing an abandoned gold dredge and other relics of mining operations, past and present, before rejoining the highway at Sunbeam, on the banks of the Salmon River.

Further details, and free maps of Custer and the Custer Motorway, are available from the Land of Yankee Fork State Park visitors center (208/879-5244) in Challis.

Stanley

Set in a broad basin at the eastern foot of the angular Sawtooth Mountains, 58 miles west of Challis, **Stanley** (pop. 63; elev. 6,260 feet) is a tiny, isolated town that makes an excellent base for exploring the surrounding two-million-plus acres of alpine forest. In summertime, the population swells to around 500, including visitors, so although it's just 60 miles north of busy Sun Valley there's

still plenty of room to move. Hikers and mountain bikers in summer, and cross-country skiers in winter, should have no trouble finding solitude in the 10,000-foot peaks; the **ranger station** (208/774-3000), four miles south of town on Hwy-75, can supply details of trails and campgrounds as well as rafting trips along the Middle Fork of the Salmon River.

Places to eat, drink, and be merry

stand along Ace of Diamonds Street, the main street of Stanley proper, south-west of the Hwy-21/75 junction. Log cabin breakfasts and great freshly baked goodies are available at **Stanley Baking Company** (250 Wall St.; 208/774-6573), or later in the day make your way to the **BackCountry Bistro** (21 Ace of Diamonds; 208/774-7000), serving steaks and chops Friday and Saturday evenings, as well as barbecue on Monday nights.

If you're not camping, a popular, locally owned, and semi-historic accom-modation is **Danners Log Cabins** ($80–140; 208/774-3539), along Hwy-21 at the center of town. If the log cabins are full, the **Mountain Village Resort** ($60 and up; 208/774-3661) at the junction of Hwy-75 and Hwy-21 offers basic motel rooms, a decent restaurant, and a gas station.

Sawtooth National Recreation Area

Stanley and Sunbeam both stand along the northern border of the 750,000-acre **Sawtooth National Recreation Area,** which extends south for over 20 miles of untrammeled meadows, forests, and lakes and includes the headwaters of many major Idaho rivers. It also holds one of the nicest places to stay in the Rockies: the historic **Redfish Lake Lodge** (May–Oct. only; 208/774-3536), seven miles south of Stanley on Hwy-75 on the east shore of Redfish Lake, which has rustic, log-walled rooms in the main lodge from around $72 a night and spacious cabins for $155–525. The lodge also has a very good restaurant.

There are two main **visitors centers** for the Sawtooth NRA: a summer-only one near Redfish Lake and the headquarters (208/622/5317) on the north side of Ketchum.

South of Redfish Lake, Hwy-75 switchbacks steeply up to 8,752-foot **Galena Summit,** which gives a grand view over the surrounding mountains, before dropping steeply down toward Sun Valley along the headwaters of the Wood River. About five miles south of the pass, 20-odd miles before you reach

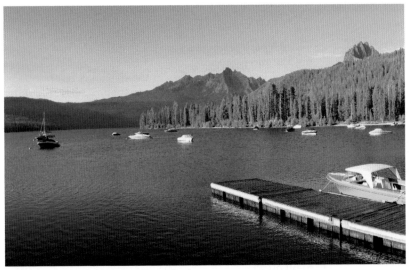

Redfish Lake in Sawtooth National Recreation Area

the resort area, there's one last stop worth making: **Galena Lodge** (208/726-4010), which dates back to the mining era of the 1880s and has been resurrected as a cross-country ski lodge, with food service, ski or snowshoe rentals, and the Sun Valley area's most extensive system of groomed trails. The community-owned lodge also maintains a trio of backcountry "yurts": tent-like structures with wood-burning stoves and bunks for up to eight people for around $125–155 a night.

Sun Valley

The first destination ski resort in the United States, and still among the most famous, **Sun Valley** was developed by Union Pacific railroad tycoon Averell Harriman. In 1936 Harriman built a large mock-Tyrolean chalet, the **Sun Valley Lodge** ($140 and up; 1 Sun Valley Rd.; 208/622-4111 or 800/786-8259), and began to cultivate Sun Valley's exclusive reputation—reinforced to this day by high prices for lift tickets (rapidly approaching $100 a day) and five-star facilities, including golf courses, tennis courts, and gourmet restaurants. Though Colorado's Vail and other resorts now compete for the top-dollar trade, Sun Valley still attracts well-heeled clientele, if the private jets parked at the local airport are any indication.

While the resort itself isn't huge, Sun Valley has come to stand for the larger area, including the towns of Ketchum and Hailey and much of the nearby wilderness, much of which is surprisingly barren and treeless—ideal for skiing, perhaps, though not jaw-dropping beautiful. Besides skiers in winter, Sun Valley also draws golfers and mountain bikers in summer and fall, not to mention anglers, who rate the Wood River as one of the nation's best trout-fishing streams.

Ernest Hemingway is probably the most famous name associated with Sun Valley. Hemingway first came here in the 1930s and worked on *For Whom the Bell Tolls* while staying at the Sun Valley Lodge. He returned in 1960, and a year later shot himself; he's now buried in a simple plot in the middle-rear section of Ketchum's small cemetery. Hemingway is also remembered by a small and surprisingly kitschy memorial along Trail Creek, a mile east of the resort.

Ketchum

Though both places preexisted Sun Valley, the two old mining and sheep-ranching towns of Ketchum and Hailey have more or less lost themselves in the upmarket resort aura of their famous neighbor. **Ketchum** (pop. 2,689), the more touristy of the two, has wall-to-wall art galleries and T-shirt shops lining its traffic-jammed streets. It also supports dozens of very expensive resort hotels and restaurants that cater to Sun Valley's country club set, plus a handful of more interesting and affordable bar-and-grill-type places along Main Street. **Whiskey Jacques'** (251 N. Main Street; 208/726-5297) serves good pizzas and has frequent live music. The Harley-friendly **Casino Club** (220 N. Main St.; 208/726-9901) is a local institution, serving beers and burgers in one of Ketchum's oldest buildings. There's a very good coffeehouse, **Java on Fourth** (191 4th St.), a block west of Main Street.

The most central and affordable of Ketchum's accommodations line up along Hwy-75, including the clean and convenient **Kentwood Lodge** ($100 and up; 180 S. Main St.; 208/726-4114).

Hailey

Hailey, 10 miles south of Ketchum and linked by a popular rail-trail bike path, was founded originally in the 1880s as a supply center for local silver and lead mines and is now the home base of all those workers who make the resorts run smoothly and ski in between shifts. Hailey feels much more friendly and low-key than Ketchum or Sun Valley, and the eating options are much more down-to-earth. For breakfast or lunch, head to diner-style **Shorty's Diner** (126 S. Main St.; 208/578-1293), originally built (but no longer owned) by *Die Hard* actor Bruce Willis. (His ex-wife, movie star Demi Moore, is a local mom about town.) When the sun goes down, you can hang out with the local ski bums and bikers at the venerable **Hailey Hotel** (201 S. Main St.; 208/788-3140), which has a lively bar downstairs.

In contrast to the civic love affair Sun Valley has with the legacy of Ernest Hemingway, Hailey takes little notice of the fact that it was the birthplace (in 1885, in a house that still stands at Pine Street and 2nd Avenue) of another noteworthy literary figure, Ezra Pound. His parents were here working for the U.S. government but fled the snowy winters just two years later.

Hailey Hotel

Shoshone marks the junction of US-93 with our cross-country **Oregon Trail** route (see page 609), which runs along US-20/26 between Boise and the Craters of the Moon National Monument. For full coverage, see pages 584–703

Shoshone: Ice Caves

South of the Sun Valley area, Hwy-75 runs across 60 miles of south-central Idaho's rocky black lava flows. Halfway between Sun Valley and Twin Falls, eight miles north of the town of Shoshone, the **Shoshone Ice Caves** (daily in summer; $8; 208/886-2058) present a series of lava tubes developed into a low-key tourist trap. Just west of the highway, their constant cool temperatures make a pleasant contrast to the often-scorching summer heat. (The "ice" in the name is created by air currents flowing through the tubes, causing subterranean water to freeze.) The only way to explore the caves is through guided tours, which take about 45 minutes. The gift shop and mineral museum, which features lava rocks and local wildlife, will satisfy anyone's needs for tourist-trap trash. (And I mean that in the best possible way.)

Just down the road, **Mammoth Cave** ($8) is much more basic and undeveloped.

dinosaur at Shoshone Ice Caves

The only town along this stretch of road, **Shoshone** (pop. 1,461) is a ranching and railroad center that marks the junction of Hwy-75 with US-93. Some of its buildings have been constructed from local volcanic rock, and though it's a fairly timeworn place, Shoshone looks great at sunset, when its steel water tower glows and places like the neon-signed **Manhattan Cafe** (208/886-2142) on the south side of the railroad tracks look especially appealing.

Minidoka Internment National Monument

Between Shoshone and Twin Falls, the potato-growing Snake River plains hold a surprising remnant of a moment in time many Americans would just as soon forget: the forcible arrest and deportation of 110,000 Americans of Japanese descent during the early 1940s. Moved from their homes in California, Washington, and Oregon—but not Hawaii, where they were a key segment of the workforce—entire families were uprooted and relocated to desolate, middle-of-nowhere places where they were made to live in makeshift shacks. Here at **Minidoka Internment National Monument,** 17 miles northeast of Twin Falls, more than 13,000 American citizens were held as prisoners between 1942 and the end of World War II three years later. The 73-acre site preserves a handful of buildings, including the guard house, but it's the isolation that endures most. The site has no services and can be hard to reach; head east from US-93 along Hwy-25 for 9.5 miles, then north along Hunt Road for another 2.5 miles. (The visitors center is in Hagerman, on US-20 20 miles away.)

Twin Falls

Named for a pair of 200-foot cascades in the Snake River, both of which have long been diverted for irrigation or to generate electricity, **Twin Falls** (pop. 44,125) is the heart of the extensive "Magic Valley" of highly productive irrigated croplands that cover half a million acres of south-central Idaho.

Best known to people outside Idaho as the place where, in 1974, daredevil Evel Knievel tried and failed to ride a rocket-powered motorcycle across the Snake River Canyon, Twin Falls is both a quiet farming community and a busy highway town—with a barrage of backlit and neon signs around the junction of US-93 and the I-84 freeway.

Evel Knievel and the Snake River Canyon

No one who lived through the 1970s could forget the name Evel Knievel (1938–2007), the ultimate thrill seeker who became rich and famous performing dangerous and virtually impossible feats on a motorcycle. Born in Butte, Montana, Knievel dropped out of high school and worked a dozen different jobs before finding his true calling as a motorcycle daredevil. In 1965 he made his first public jump, flying over a caged mountain lion and boxes of rattlesnakes at Moses Lake, Washington. Within a few years he hit the big time: leaping over the fountains at Caesars Palace in Las Vegas and jumping 50 cars at the Los Angeles Coliseum. Though he broke nearly every bone in his body as a result of his numerous crash landings, Knievel's feats were always bigger, better, and more dangerous than the last; as he liked to say, "Where there's little risk, there's little reward."

Banned by the government from attempting a leap over the Grand Canyon, Knievel set his sights on the Snake River Canyon in southern Idaho, leasing the land so no one could stop him, then building a massive ramp and working out the details of his custom-made, rocket-powered Harley-Davidson X-2 Skycycle. On September 8, 1974, some 30,000 people turned out, along with many millions more watching on TV, for Evel's big leap. Unfortunately, one of his parachutes deployed on takeoff, and he floated gently down into the bottom of the gorge, safe and sound and proud of having the guts to try— even if he didn't quite make it.

This lone unique attraction of Twin Falls, the site of **Evel Knievel's** aborted motorcycle jump, is a mile north of town on US-93, south of I-84. There's a large parking area and a visitors center at the south foot of the delicate Perrine Memorial Bridge, and it's well worth stopping for, not only to see the remains of his launch pad (a triangular pile of dirt, on private property a mile or so east of the bridge) or the stone monument that reads Robert 'Evel' Knievel— Explorer, Motorcyclist, Daredevil. The views down into the 500-foot-deep gorge, the floor of which has been irrigated and filled with a bright green golf course, are also impressive, especially at sunset when the whole scene takes on an otherworldly glow.

Though the town can make a good jumping-off point for Sun Valley and the mountain wilderness farther north, there's not a lot to *do* in Twin Falls. The waterfalls for which the town is named are worth a look if you have the time; **Shoshone Falls,** taller than Niagara, may still impress, especially in spring. Check them out from the park at the end of Falls Avenue, seven miles east of US-93. Without its namesake waterfalls, however, Twin Falls has little to offer travelers apart from a chance to fill the gas tank, eat, or get a night's sleep. For breakfast or a burger, head

341. Twin Falls on the Snake River, near Twin Falls, Idaho.

to the **Buffalo Cafe** (218 W. 4th St.; 208/734-0271) or the 24-hour **Depot Grill** (545 S. Shoshone St.; 208/733-0710) along downtown's diagonal main drag, where all-you-can-eat fried chicken is served up every Tuesday night. Sleep at your choice of some two dozen motels around the US-93/I-84 junction.

Nat-Soo-Pah Hot Springs

South of Twin Falls, there's a whole lot of nothing in the 47 miles before you reach the Nevada border at Jackpot. One place worth a stop is the summer-only **Nat-Soo-Pah Hot Springs** ($5; 208/655-4337), halfway to Nevada, where you'll find a 105-degree hot tub, a giant (125-foot by 50-foot!) spring-fed swimming pool, a 90-foot water slide, a tree-shaded picnic area and snack bar, and a $35-a-night **campground.** Nat-Soo-Pah is about a mile south of Hollister, then three miles east on a well-signed road. There are a number of other natural springs in the area, so if you enjoy being in hot water, southern Idaho is a great place to explore.

NEVADA

US-93 runs south along the eastern edge of Nevada for 520 miles, 500 of which take you through an exceptional degree of desolation— endless straight and narrow valleys, two-car traffic jams, and towns few and far between. From the gam-bling oasis of **Jackpot** on the Idaho border to where the highway crosses into Arizona atop Hoover Dam, US-93 is at least as lonely as its Nevada sibling US-50, the official Loneliest Road in America. Towns

If you're heading along US-93 across Nevada, be sure to fill the tank before hitting the road. From Jackpot, the next gas is over an hour away.

like **Wells,** along I-80 in the northern half of the state, are big events; south of here it's 140 miles to the next watering hole, **Ely,** beyond which the old mining camp of **Pioche** and the desert hot springs resort of **Caliente** are the only wide spots in the road before you hit the staggering city of **Las Vegas.**

Jackpot

In every respect but one, **Jackpot** belongs more to Idaho than Nevada—a somewhat incongruous introduction to US-93 in the Silver State. Jackpot's visitors and workers mostly come from Idaho, as do its power and water; even its clocks are set to Idaho time. The one little exception, however, is pure Nevada: border-town gambling. Jackpot was founded in 1954, mere months after Idaho banned slot machines, which didn't, to be sure, reduce the demand. In fact, Jackpot has thrived, as a pit stop in any of the town's casinos will attest. Jackpot is compact enough to give long-distance travelers just enough lights, action, and comfort to satisfy more immediate needs and then send them on their way again.

Cactus Petes ($69–129 and up; 775/755-2321) is the 10-story tower you can see for miles; along with the big casino, it has a great snack bar, a buffet, a sit-down restaurant, and a showroom, and there's more of the same in the **Horseshu** across the street.

Wells

Some lone peaks, a stretch of badlands and buttes, and a couple of north–south ranges usher US-93 down a long basin toward the little junction town of **Wells** (pop. 1,292). Just under 70 miles from Jackpot at the interchange of US-93 and the I-80 freeway, Wells was named by the Central Pacific Railroad, which chose the site for a depot and town to make use of the plentiful springs in the hills a few miles northeast. Despite being hammered by a devastating earthquake in 2008, the old downtown—take a right on 6th

Street and another right at the light—is the most intact abandoned **railroad row** on the entire mainline across northern Nevada. Wells provides an explicit illustration of the West's transition from rail to road to superhighway: The newest action in town is at the east and west exit ramps of I-80; the "strip" between the exits is 6th Street (old US-40), the vintage, pre-Interstate place for action in the 1950s and even 1960s but now derelict around the edges.

East Humboldt Range

The I-80 town of Wells is situated at the northeastern base of the splendidly scenic **East Humboldt Range.** To get into these rugged, glacier-scraped mountains, head briefly west from Wells on I-80 to exit 351, from where Hwy-231 runs 12 miles south and west, climbing to over 8,400 feet before terminating at alluring Angel Lake. For details on the abundance of hiking, camping, and outdoor recreation hereabouts, contact the USFS **ranger station** (140 Pacific Ave.; 775/752-3357) at the west end of Wells.

Continuing down US-93 affords a different view of the East Humboldts. Ten miles south of Wells, you can head west on Hwy-232, which makes a 14-mile loop through luxuriant Clover Valley at the eastern base of the mountains, one of the most bucolic basins in Nevada. About halfway along is a turn leading west up into Week's Creek Canyon. Look up to see **Hole-in-the-Mountain Peak.** The tallest peak in the East Humboldts (11,276 feet), it features a 30- by 25-foot natural window in the thin rock 300 feet below its summit, which gives you a spectacular little patch of blue (or silver, orange, or purple, depending on the time of day) right through the top of the range—compelling.

Wendover

At I-80, US-93 becomes the hypotenuse of an alternative route, which runs for 60 miles southeast to the Utah border at **Wendover,** then another 60 miles southwest to rejoin the mainline US-93 at Lages Station. Wendover, like Jackpot, is a bustling border town, with golf course–view subdivisions and at least five major casino-hotels drawing gamblers from Salt Lake City, 120 miles to the east. Wendover's other claims to fame include **Wendover Will,** the huge cowboy who welcomes you to Nevada along the Utah state line; the **Bonneville Salt Flats** and speedway, where most of the world's land-speed records have been set for almost 100 years; and **Wendover Air Force Base,** where in 1945 the crew of the *Enola Gay* trained to drop an atomic bomb on Japan.

Wendover Will

The Ruby Mountains and Elko

It's a long, solitary, 140 miles from Wells to Ely. US-93 shoots down Clover Valley to the southern edge of the East Humboldts, where Hwy-229, a maintained gravel road, cuts off southwest toward the **Ruby Mountains,** also known as the Nevada Swiss

Bonneville Speedway

Located in the middle of nowhere, west of the Great Salt Lake on the Utah/Nevada border, the vast salt flats of Bonneville cover some 160 square miles. Since the 1930s, Bonneville's broad, hard, flat and unobstructed surface has made it a mecca for efforts to set ever-faster land speed records. The earliest speed records were set at Daytona Beach, Florida, but as top speeds increased, racers needed more room to maneuver safely. In 1931, Ab Jenkins set Bonneville's first world record in his bright red Mormon Meteor, and racers have converged on Bonneville's 10-mile-long drag strip in pursuit of record-breaking speed ever since. Burt Munro's motorcycle speed record was set here at Bonneville in 1967, as depicted in the 2005 Anthony Hopkins movie *The World's Fastest Indian.*

Craig Breedlove, in his car named Spirit of America, was the first to exceed the 400, 500, and 600 mph marks, but in the 1990s problems with water from nearby mining operations dissolving the salt made Bonneville less than ideal, so racers like Richard Noble, whose team set the current record of 763 mph in 1997, opted for the Black Rock Desert, 110 miles north of Reno, Nevada. In recent years the mining companies have worked to restore the salt flats to their historical thickness and size, and once again every August (for Speed Week) and again in October (for the World Finals), hundreds of thrill-seekers descend on Bonneville, racing their hot rods and motorbikes in a series of time trials.

Alps. This is one of Nevada's most scenic ranges: 80 miles long, with more than a dozen peaks over 9,000 feet.

The best access to the Ruby Mountains is 50 miles west of Wells via I-80, through the engaging small city of **Elko** (pop. 18,297), which enjoys the economic benefits of sitting astride one of North America's largest deposits of gold. Besides mining gold and maintaining its traditional Basque culture, Elko is home to the **Western Folklife Center,** in the old Pioneer Building (501 Railroad St.; 775/738-7508), which hosts the very popular Cowboy Poetry Gathering every January, a Cowboy Music Gathering the last weekend in June, and a 4th of July celebration. Take advantage of some of the fine family-style Basque restaurants, like the **Star Hotel** (246 Silver St.; 775/738-9925), near the railroad tracks, which is worth the drive for the delicious lamb chops and other dishes. The Star Hotel has been in business for more than 100 years with few changes, so they must be doing something right.

Back on US-93, between Wells and Ely, US-93 bends away from the heart of the Ruby Mountains, running southeast through Steptoe Valley on a marathon drive down an elongated basin, hemmed in by the Schell Creek Range on the east and the Egan Range on the west. The only signs of civilization on this stretch are two roadhouses: one at **Lages Station** (78 miles south of Wells) and the other at **Schellbourne** (40 miles north of Ely, where there's also an old Lincoln Highway marker, all but abandoned in the sagebrush east of US-93).

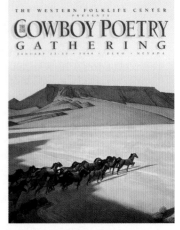

McGill

Tiny **McGill** (pop. 1,148), 128 miles south of I-80 and 12 miles northeast of Ely, is the classic Nevada company town, its workaday life revolving for the first 50 years of the 20th century around a giant copper smelter. Kennecott Minerals mining company officials lived in the fancy houses around the "Circle" at the top of the hill just below the factory, while workers were housed according to their ethnic origins. The saloon and jail were conveniently built right next door to each other, and steam from the copper furnaces was piped to heat the town's houses. The com-

The McGill smelter's last sky-scraping smokestack was felled in September 1993. At 750 feet, it was the tallest structure in Nevada.

pany's been gone for more than 15 years, but the layout remains, along with acres of fenced-off brick factory buildings painted with fading signs encouraging workers to behave safely. A few of McGill's buildings have been converted to current uses, but most are closed and quite forlorn.

One semi-survivor along this short stretch of US-93 is the **McGill Drug Store** (open by appointment or good luck; 775/235-7082), closed since the 1970s but preserved as an ad hoc museum under the care of the White Pine Historical Museum in neighboring Ely. If you can't arrange a tour, peer in through the windows at a soda fountain and shelves stocked full of Nixon-era merchandise.

US-93 intersects with US-50, the legendary **Loneliest Road** in America (see pages 704–799) at **Ely** (described on page 725).

Connors Pass and Majors Place

Southeast of Ely, US-93, spliced together with US-50 and US-6 into a single two-lane highway, continues for 25 miles before crossing the narrow waist of the Schell Creek at **Connors Pass** (elev. 7,722 feet), one of only two areas of Nevada located above the tree line. As you ascend toward the pass, the air cools and freshens, the single-leaf piñon and Utah juniper appear and thicken, and, cresting the summit, the mighty Snake Range, including 13,061-foot Wheeler Peak in Great Basin National Park, comes into view.

At **Majors Place** (where there's a roadhouse), US-93 splits off from US-50 and US-6, the latter two heading east toward Utah, while US-93 cuts south, heading 80 long, solitary miles to the next contact with humans at Pioche. Once again, the highway rolls along taffy-pulled Spring and Lake Valleys, ushered on its way by the Schell Creek, Fairview, Bristol, and Highland Ranges on the west, and the Snake and Wilson Creek Ranges on the east.

Pioche

The only places that are more than a ghostly outline of civilization in the nearly 300 miles of Great Basin Desert that US-93 crosses between Ely and Las Vegas are the wildly different towns of Caliente, Panaca, and Pioche. The oldest and most northerly of the three, **Pioche** (pop. 900; pronounced "pee-OACH," which means pick-ax in French) is a onetime mining boomtown that had its heyday well over a century ago. Now bypassed by the mainline US-93 highway, which runs around the east side of the historic town, Pioche is so remote—back then exponentially more than now—that during the 1870s it descended to a level of anarchy to rival Tombstone, Arizona. In its mining heyday, more than 75 men were killed here before anyone died of natural causes.

Corruption, too, was the order of the day, and you can tour Pioche's "Million Dollar" **Lincoln County Courthouse** on Lacour Street (Hwy-321) for a graphic example of it. Designed in 1871 at an estimated cost of $26,000, the courthouse wasn't completed until 1876, to the tune of $88,000. Then, unable to pay off the principal, the county commissioners kept refinancing the debt, while interest accrued, year after year; by the time it was paid off in 1937, the courthouse had cost a million bucks and been replaced by a more modern structure. Now restored, the old courthouse is open for self-guided **tours** (daily; donations; 775/962-5182) of the offices, the courtroom, and the old jail.

The eclectic **Lincoln County Historical Museum** at the center of town (daily; free; 69 Main St.; 775/962-5207) is another good stop, as are nearby historic buildings such as the Thompson Opera House and the Commercial Club. The rusting remains of the **aerial tramway** that ran through Pioche up through the 1920s, carrying ore to the stamp mills, can be explored—cables, cars, and all—from various points in town. Two state parks to the east (Echo Canyon and Spring Valley, 12 and 20 miles away respectively) round out your Pioche-area sightseeing.

Pioche is a pretty long way from anywhere else, so if you want to stay the night try the characterful **Overland Hotel** ($58–85; 662 Main St.; 775/962-5895), which has a very popular Old West saloon downstairs. There are also a couple of cafés and markets, and a vital gas station, in the photogenically ramshackle downtown.

Panaca and Cathedral Gorge

Panaca, 11 miles south of Pioche and a mile east of US-93 on Hwy-319, was founded in 1864 by Mormon farmers, attracted to the valley by the plentiful water of Panaca Spring, in what was then a part of Utah. The mining strikes at nearby Bullionville and Pioche disturbed their peace briefly, but Panaca—which has a single gas station/minimart, plus a school and lots of houses—has a strong sense of tranquility and timelessness rarely felt in the rest of Nevada.

Cathedral Gorge State Park

Just west of US-93, two miles north of Panaca, **Cathedral Gorge State Park** is a mini Grand Canyon of eroded mud. A lake once covered this deep gully, and silt and clay were washed to the bottom by streams and creeks. The lake dried up, exposing the sediments, and erosion (which never sleeps) sculpted them into the fantastic procession of formations you see today. The campground (775/728-4460) here has shade trees, flush toilets, even showers.

Panaca Spring, a fine local swimming hole with warm, sweet water, is found just outside the town of Panaca: Take 5th Street north past the baseball diamond and a rusty old steam engine, toward a big cottonwood tree about a half mile beyond where the pavement ends.

Caliente

To Pioche's mining and Panaca's farming, **Caliente** (pop. 1,130), 15 miles south, adds railroading. This small town was built around the San Pedro, Los Angeles, and Salt Lake Railroad tracks in the early 1900s, a short while before Las Vegas itself was founded. The **Union Pacific Depot** was built in 1923 and still serves as the nerve center of Caliente, having been restored to house government offices, a local history museum, an art gallery, and a boxcar collection. If you are interested in pre-colonial Nevada, the BLM office here has a good free map and guide to the Caliente region's fantastic array of Native American rock art.

The town supports two gas stations and the enticingly named **Shady Motel** ($53–65; 450 Front St.; 775/726-3106), along US-93. Food offerings are limited to a small but popular pizza place and the very pleasant **Brandin' Iron** café (190 Clover St.; 775/726-3164), across from the train depot.

South from Caliente, US-93 bends due west for 43 miles. Newman Canyon just outside of town has high, sheer, smooth, volcanic-tuff walls. You twist and climb out of the canyon to cross the Delamar Range at **Oak Springs Summit** (6,237 feet), where the juniper trees are a welcome change from the low desert scrub. Beyond is a short interface zone in which the junipers grow right next to Joshua trees, an indication of the change from Great Basin Desert, which lies to the north, to the front edge of the Mojave Desert, which spreads south and west. Pahroc Summit is next (just under 5,000 feet), then Six Mile Flat, and then **Hiko,** where Hwy-318 races north to Ely, and Hwy-375 (a.k.a. "The Extraterrestrial Highway") heads northwest to US-6 and Tonopah.

A nice alternative to US-93 is Hwy-317, south of Caliente through **Rainbow Canyon.** This is one of Nevada's most scenic and least-known drives. Colorful, high volcanic-tuff cliffs hold one of the state's pre-eminent collections of ancient rock art, while railroad trestles, idyllic farms, and ranches line Meadow Wash. The pavement ends after 21 miles, but in dry weather even a rental car can continue 38 miles through Kane Springs Valley to connect back up with US-93.

Ash Springs and Alamo

From the Hwy-375 junction, US-93 turns due south again and enters some unexpectedly lush country, in the midst of which three large and faithful springs provide plentiful water for alfalfa farms and cattle ranches, as well as for the only bona fide lakes that US-93 encounters in more than 400 miles of its Nevada leg. **Ash Springs**—consisting of a single gas station and convenience store called R Place—is named after the nearby water source, which is believed to be part of a vast aquifer underlying much of eastern Nevada.

Twelve miles south of Ash Springs is **Alamo,** whose three motels, two truck stops, and 24-hour Mexican restaurant, Del Pueblo, are the only real services between Caliente and Las Vegas. Four miles south of town is Upper Pahranagat Lake, where an old road runs along the eastern shore, with camping and picnic sites and big cottonwoods—one of the most idyllic spots on the whole Nevada portion of US-93. The water is close enough to the source at Ash Springs that it's relatively warm year-round. Lower Pahranagat Lake, a bit farther south, freezes in the winter.

Upper Pahranagat Lake is also home to the administration and maintenance facilities for the **Desert National Wildlife Refuge,** at 1.5 million acres the largest refuge in the Lower 48. Elusive desert bighorn sheep enjoy protection within this huge habitat, alongside of which US-93 travels for the length of the aptly named Sheep Range. The road descends gradually into rocky and barren desert until finally, 70 miles from Alamo and 125 miles from Caliente, US-93 merges with the I-15 freeway for the high-speed haul into the Big Glow: Las Vegas.

Driving Las Vegas

Las Vegas has to be the easiest city in the world to drive around: Everything lines up along, or in relation to, one big road—**The Strip.** Recently dubbed an official "All-American Highway," along with such scenic landmarks as the Blue Ridge Parkway and the stretch of Hwy-1 through California's Big Sur, this 10-mile-long, traffic-clogged barrage of bright lights and architectural extravagance is also known as South Las Vegas Boulevard and runs parallel to I-15 between the compact downtown area and the airport.

The middle-of-nowhere crossroads of **Hiko,** where Hwy-318 joins US-93 after a long run south from Lund, near Ely, is the finish line for a pair of high-speed road races. Held for the past 25 years with varying degrees of support from official powers-that-be, the **Nevada Open Road Challenge** (in May) and the **Silver State Challenge** (in September) see racers in varying classes of race cars averaging speeds between 100 and 200 mph on the 90-mile course, which is closed to traffic for the day.

The extraterrestrial issues surrounding Area 51 are nothing compared to the actual explosive truth of what has happened there over the years. If you doubt this, visit the **Atomic Testing Museum** (daily; $9–12; 755 E. Flamingo Rd.; 702/794-5150) in Las Vegas.

Las Vegas

Viva Las Vegas! Since its founding more than 100 years ago, Las Vegas has been the biggest, brightest, and brazenest boomtown in the history of the world. Even the real estate crash, which saw property values cut in half amidst the worldwide economic downturn, hasn't really dampened its spirits: In the past 30 years, the Las Vegas population has more than tripled (rapidly approaching two million people in the metropolitan area), and over a dozen major hotels and mega-resorts have re-created everything from ancient Egypt to Venice (complete with canals and gondoliers), Paris (a mock Eiffel Tower), and New York City (with a Coney Island roller coaster and fake steam puffing up from fake sidewalks). More numbers: With more than 150,000 rooms, the city has as many as New York and Chicago combined, and 40 million annual visitors lose more than $8 billion in the casinos here every year.

In addition to gambling, Las Vegas casinos have all the rooms, restaurants, and "recreational opportunities" you can imagine (and then some). If you're staying overnight, you'll enter the wacky and somewhat wicked world of Las Vegas lodging. Rooms are no longer the dirt-cheap bargains they were a generation ago; rates vary depending on the time of year, time of the week, and sometimes even the time of day, but count on spending at least $100 for a decent hotel room, and close to five times that for something special. You should definitely make reservations as early as you can; on Friday nights, or during a big convention or boxing match, the whole town is often sold out. A final note:

If you'll be schlepping a lot of luggage, be aware that Las Vegas hotel rooms are a very long way from its parking spaces, which are in huge high-rise or underground garages. On the upside, parking is free at most hotels.

Here are a few of the many places you can play:

looking up at the Eiffel Tower at Paris, Las Vegas

Caesars Palace (3570 Las Vegas Blvd. S.; 702/731-7110 or 866/227-5938): Long before there was a Mirage; a New York, New York; a Bellagio; or a Venetian, there was Caesars Palace. Though ancient by Las Vegas standards (Caesars opened in 1966 as the first "themed" hotel in Las Vegas), this is still one of the classiest and most famous places in town.

Hard Rock Hotel and Casino (4455 Paradise Rd.; 702/693-5000 or 800/693-7625): For anyone under 60, this is the coolest place in town. It's off the Strip and small by Vegas standards, but where else can you listen to nonstop classic rock 'n' roll while playing Jimi Hendrix slot machines (a line of "Purple Haze" pays $200) or drinking a cocktail at the swim-up bar?

Luxor (3900 Las Vegas Blvd. S.; 702/262-4444 or 877/386-4658): The most distinctive casino, Luxor is housed inside a mammoth (29-million-cubic-foot) glass pyramid at the southern end of the Strip.

The Mirage (3400 Las Vegas Blvd. S.; 702/791-7111 or 800/374-9000): This casino has its own rainforest, a 20,000-gallon saltwater aquarium, and white tigers on display (this is the home of Siegfried and Roy). Next door, at Treasure Island, a theatrical (and free) pirate show is staged right on the Strip every 90 minutes or so in the evenings.

Wynn Las Vegas (3131 Las Vegas Blvd. S.; 702/770-7000 or 877/321-9966): Brought to you by the creator of Mirage and Bellagio, on the site of the historic Desert Inn (where billionaire recluse Howard Hughes used to live), this ultra-fashionable 2,700-suite oasis is the last word in high-end indulgence, with an on-site Ferrari dealership and some of the best restaurants in the country.

The Extraterrestrial Highway

West of US-93, stretching nearly to Death Valley and the California border, the U.S. government has turned the 3.1-million-acre expanse of Nellis Air Force Range into its most top-secret laboratory and testing ground. H-bombs, U-2 spy planes, Stealth bombers, you name it—this is where projects no one is supposed to know about exist.

It's not so surprising that, like Roswell, New Mexico, this lonely corner of the world has become the focus of an ongoing controversy pitting govern-ment secrecy against allegations that the Air Force has been using a cor-ner of the base known as Area 51 to study UFOs and extraterrestrials. Fueled in part by tabloid stories claiming an E.T.-like creature is being kept alive at Area 51 in a high-securi-ty compound underneath Groom Lake—and also by local busi-nesspeople's realization that UFO tourism could mean big money—the hoopla has focused on the tiny village of Rachel, which has become to UFO-spotters what the grassy knoll is to JFK conspiracy theorists.

Rachel (pop. 99), the only community along the 100-mile stretch of Hwy-375 (now offi-cially known as the Extraterrestrial Highway, promoted by the state along the lines of the "Loneliest Road" campaign), is a block-long strip that holds the lighthearted **Little A'Le'Inn** (775/729-2515), a typical back-of-beyond bar and grill where you can munch on Alien Burgers, down drinks like the Beam Me Up, Scotty (Jim Beam, 7UP, and Scotch), or peruse UFO-related key chains, fridge magnets, and T-shirts. The Little A'Le'Inn also has small mobile home trailers available overnight for around $50 a night.

Other roads in Las Vegas are named after the big hotels near their junction with The Strip; hence you have Sahara Avenue, Flamingo Road, and Tropicana Avenue one after another.

Almost everybody who drives into Las Vegas comes by way of the I-15 free-way, which runs between Los Angeles and Salt Lake City, and which connects with US-93 some 20 miles northwest of The Strip. From the south and Hoover Dam, use the new I-515 freeway, which carries US-93 and US-95 on a snaking S-figure between Henderson and Fremont Street in downtown Las Vegas.

US-93 actually bypasses The Strip, veering southeast along Fremont Street and the Boulder Highway—or along I-515—but it's all but required that you

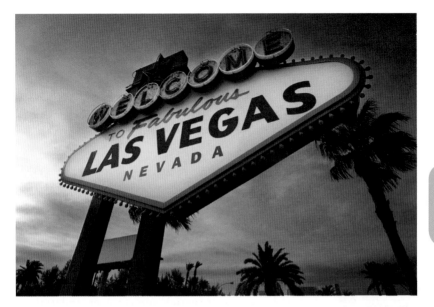

drive at least a little of The Strip before you can say you've been to Las Vegas. Don't expect to get anywhere very quickly, though; The Strip is like one big, slow cruise, with 10 lanes of traffic moving past all those casino lights at about 10 mph, day or night.

Henderson

Southeast of Las Vegas, US-93 joins courses with US-95 along Nevada's newest freeway, I-515, which connects Las Vegas with the rapidly growing industrial city of **Henderson** (pop. 259,573). Henderson itself is relatively young, even by Nevada standards. In 1941, the War Department selected this site, due to its proximity to unlimited electricity generated by the then-six-year-old Hoover Dam, for a giant factory to process magnesium, needed for bombs and airplane components. Within six months, 10,000 workers arrived and the plant and town was built. After the war ended, the factory was subdivided for private industry, and since then, Henderson has grown to be the second-largest city in Nevada, behind only Las Vegas.

Though it doesn't even try to compete with the attractions of Las Vegas, Henderson does have a number of casinos, but it's much more of a place to live than it is a tourist destination. The very good **Clark County Museum** (daily; $2; 1830 S. Boulder Hwy.; 702/455-7955), two miles south of town, has the usual local info plus an enjoyable display on the evolution of motor courts and travel trailers, highlighted by an iconic late 1940s Spartanette.

South of Henderson, US-93/95 climbs up and over 2,367-foot Railroad

Time the drive into Las Vegas so you arrive around dusk, when the western sky sports a purple sunset and the horizon shines brightly from a billion amber streetlights stretching from one end of the valley to the other.

The world's highest amusement park stands atop the **Stratosphere Tower,** where four different roller coasters and thrill rides hang, spin, and twirl you 1,000 feet above the Las Vegas Strip.

Pass, and just beyond is the junction where US-95 cuts south, heading along the Colorado River to Laughlin, Nevada; Needles, California (covered in the *Route 66* chapter); and Yuma, Arizona (which is covered in the *Southern Pacific* chapter). US-93 continues east and loops a little to the north on its way to Boulder City.

See you next time!

Taking their name from extraterrestrial "Area 51," Toronto's Triple A club the Las Vegas 51s play their home games at 10,000-seat Cashman Field, 850 N. Las Vegas Boulevard (702/798-7825).

Boulder City

Like Henderson, **Boulder City** (pop. 15,023) was founded and built by the federal government to house workers at Hoover Dam, what was then the largest construction project ever undertaken. Though the dam was completed in 1935, Boulder City continued under the Feds' ownership and management for another 25 years; in 1960, an Act of Congress conferred independent municipal status on the town. Longtime residents purchased their houses, and alcohol consumption was permitted for the first time in the town's history, though gambling remained forbidden. To this day, almost a half century since "independence," Boulder City remains the only town in Nevada that expressly prohibits gambling, which may explain why it feels more like the Midwest than a suburb of Sin City.

If you're interested in the men and machines involved in building the dam, spend some time at the **Boulder City/Hoover Dam Museum,** inside the historic (and restored) **Boulder Dam Hotel** ($64 and up; 1305 Arizona St.; 702/293-3510). The hotel also has a good dining room. The town has a handful of motels and fast-food outlets—1950s-style cafés and motels line the Nevada Highway/US-93 Business Route through town—but the real draws are just below Boulder City: the dam, of course, and the lake behind it.

Heading south past Hoover Dam into Arizona, you'll pass no towns or services in the 75 miles between Boulder City and Kingman on old Route 66, so stock up and fill up here before proceeding on.

Hoover Dam and Lake Mead

Approaching **Hoover Dam** from the Nevada side, in the eight miles from Boulder City you pass a peculiar parade of electrical generators, transformers, and capacitors all secured by cyclone fencing topped by razor wire and barbs to keep out intruders. A major (10-year, $250 million) reconstruction and road-expansion project was completed in 2010, taking traffic off the dam and moving it onto a bypass and concrete-arch bridge over the Colorado River. One of the biggest and highest in the world, the impressive bridge has been named to honor the memory of Arizona's pro football star Pat Tillman, who volunteered for duty as an Army Ranger in Afghanistan, where he was killed by friendly fire in 2004. There's a small memorial to Tillman, and a pedestrian footpath giving good views of the dam, at the too-small parking area at the foot of the bridge.

Hoover Dam

Because the main US-93 has been diverted around it, if you want to see Hoover Dam up close, make your way to the **Visitor Center** (daily; $8, plus $7 parking; 702/294-3517), which finally opened in 1995 and cost nearly as much as the new bridge. The steep admission price buys you a half-hour film, a self-guided museum tour, and a ride down the $20 million elevators that cut through the rock, ending up inside the dam, where you can gape at the humming turbines, which at peak times generate some 2,000 megawatts of electricity, enough to supply a million homes and still have enough juice left over to light up the Las Vegas Strip. Beyond the visitors center, take a walk across the top of the gargantuan wedge of Hoover Dam: It's nearly a quarter-mile across, 726 feet high, 660 feet thick at the base—all accomplished with a mere seven million tons of concrete.

Upstream from the dam spreads **Lake Mead,** the largest man-made lake in the USA. Containing up to 30 million acre-feet or just over nine *trillion* gallons, Lake Mead irrigates some 2.5 million acres of land in the United States and Mexico, while helping to control the river's seasonal flooding. Recent droughts and increased demands for its water have depleted Lake Mead to less than full capacity, leaving some docks and fishing piers high and dry, but despite the problems the lake is a very popular recreation site, with thousands of water-skiers and others flocking to its 500 miles of shoreline year-round.

Hoover Dam marks the border between Nevada and Arizona, and between the Pacific and Mountain time zones, so set your clocks and watches accordingly (and remember, Arizona does not use daylight saving time).

ARIZONA

Coming into Arizona across the top of Hoover Dam, US-93 cuts southeast across the length, and half the breadth, of the state, covering nearly 500 miles of desiccated desert. Starting at the Nevada border, US-93 makes a diagonal beeline toward the old Route 66 town of **Kingman,** one of the few watering holes in Arizona's northwest quarter. Joshua trees and ghost towns far outnumber gas stations in this part of the state, so fill up before setting off into these great wide-open spaces. From Kingman, the route cuts south across another huge stretch of desert, passing through the dude-ranch resort town of **Wickenburg.** In the middle of Arizona spreads **Phoenix,** the state's capital and largest city. From this sprawling megalopolis, our route bends east into the mountains, following back roads past the otherworldly Biosphere 2 "space station" before hitting **Tucson,** another hugely horizontal city. South of here you'll enjoy the most feature-packed part of the trip, passing by the historic Spanish colonial communities of **Tubac** and **Tumacácori** before winding up at the enjoyable twin border towns of **Ambos Nogales.**

Lake Mead National Recreation Area

Most people come from the Las Vegas area to visit Lake Mead, which covers some 160,000 acres and includes over 500 miles of shoreline, on the extensively developed Nevada side. In contrast, the only access on the Arizona side is from Temple Bar, 19 miles south of Hoover Dam, then another 27 miles northeast on a good paved road. Here you'll find a small marina with boat rentals and a motel (928/767-3211).

Lake Mead

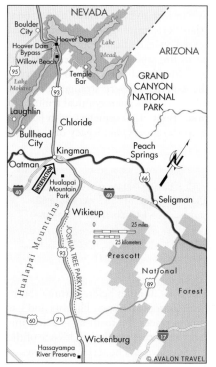

Stretching to both sides of Hoover Dam, the **Lake Mead National Recreation Area** also incorporates the smaller Lake Mojave, clearly visible from US-93 and accessible at **Willow Beach** on the Colorado River, 14 miles south of Hoover Dam and four miles west of US-93.

Laughlin, Nevada

Between Hoover Dam and Kingman, a detour heads west to the Nevada side of the Colorado River to **Laughlin, Nevada,** a place that epitomizes the anything-goes character of Nevada gaming. Laughlin, a booming gambling resort that in many ways seems even more mirage-like than Las Vegas, may lack glitz and pizzazz but makes up for it with cheaper rooms ($35 is not uncommon) and the almost unheard-of attraction of river views from the casino floors.

The history of Laughlin—or rather, the lack of it—is impressive even by Nevada standards. Starting with a run-down bait shop he bought in the mid-1960s, Minnesota-born entrepreneur Don Laughlin envisioned the fantasyland you see today, opening his **Riverside Resort Hotel** ($45 and up; 702/298-2535 or 800/227-3849), which is still a local favorite, in the late 1970s and drawing visitors from all over Arizona and Southern California. Laughlin's independent mini empire was eclipsed in the 1980s by the big shots and big towers with more than 1,000 rooms. First **Harrah's** came, then Circus Circus opened the steamboat-shaped **Colorado Belle,** then came a 2,000-room palace now known as the **Aquarius** (702/298-5111). Fortunes have ebbed and flowed significantly in recent years, but Laughlin is still well worth a look or an overnight stay.

For further information, contact the **Laughlin Nevada Chamber of Commerce** (702/298-2214).

South of Hoover Dam, US-93 runs parallel to the older version of the highway, with numerous old bridges and sections of gravel roadway standing along the modern four-lane freeway.

Laughlin is one of the hottest inhabited places in the country, with an all-time high temperature of 125°F, registered here in 1994.

Chloride

Marked by a big "C" inscribed in the hillside above it, the near–ghost town of **Chloride** (pop. 250), 53 miles south of Hoover Dam and 15 miles north of Kingman, then four miles east of the highway on a paved, well-marked road, is the oldest and among the most evocative former mining camps in Arizona. Following the discovery of silver here in the 1860s, mining activities continued through the 1940s; the town is now preserved by its dedicated residents.

A couple of stores and cafés still cling to life, and occasional festivals and flea markets draw sizable crowds of visitors. Mostly what there is to see are the odd bits of "folk art" so often found in the American desert: strange front-yard sculptures made of rusting metal and odd bits of junk, plus comical tributes to the mythology of the Wild West, like a fake "Boot Hill" cemetery with laconic epitaphs and hand-painted signs playing up the apocryphal legacy of the local "Hangin' Judge" Jim Beam.

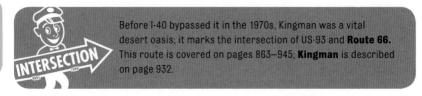

Before I-40 bypassed it in the 1970s, Kingman was a vital desert oasis; it marks the intersection of US-93 and **Route 66.** This route is covered on pages 863–945; **Kingman** is described on page 932.

Joshua Forest Parkway

East from Kingman, US-93 follows I-40 for over 20 miles before turning south, back onto two-lane US-93. Because it's the main route between Phoenix and Las Vegas, US-93 can be very busy, and in many places the roadway is being improved and expanded to handle all the trucks and other traffic, but it's one of the great (and least hyped) drives in the desert Southwest. The scenery improves as you head south from I-40, with chocolate-brown boulders and varnished granite cliffs rising to form impressive canyons above forests of saguaro cactus, Joshua trees, and abundant spring wildflowers. The only real "place" along this stretch of US-93 is a wide spot in the road known as **Wikieup,** 55 miles south of I-40, where a pair of gas stations and trading posts line up around a much-appreciated road-stop: **Joe's BBQ** (closed Wed.; 928/765-2287), famous for its mesquite-smoked ribs and richly textured rib-eye steaks.

Between Wikieup and Wickenburg, the 75-odd miles of US-93 are known as the **Joshua Forest Parkway** because the road passes through one of the world's densest concentrations of these odd trees, which were named by Mormon pioneers. Anthropomorphic, multi-limbed members of the lily family, and found only here in western Arizona and in southern California, Joshua trees can live to 200 years old and reach 50 feet tall.

Wickenburg

In the middle of the Arizona desert, 60 miles northwest of Phoenix and 130 southeast from Kingman, **Wickenburg** (pop. 6,363) grew up as a gold-mining camp in the 1860s and has survived as

The Santa Fe Depot NHR

the Santa Fe Depot, Wickenburg

Spring Training: Cactus League Baseball

The arrival of the Arizona Diamondbacks in 1998 culminated a long but limited history of baseball in the Grand Canyon State. Though it never before had a major league team of its own, Arizona has welcomed out-of-state teams for pre-season spring training since 1947, when the Cleveland Indians and New York Giants first played at Tucson's Hi Corbett Field (springtime home to the Colorado Rockies). Every March, ball players at all levels of the game come to Arizona to try out for places on professional teams. The daily workouts and 250-odd exhibition games of what's known as the Cactus League attract thousands of hard-core baseball fans as spectators.

The metropolitan Phoenix area hosts the bulk of the teams and the tourists, but Tucson gets a fair share as well. Though they're not necessarily played to win, Cactus League games are played in modern 10,000-seat stadia that approach the major leagues in quality, and the smaller sizes allow an up-close feel you'd have to pay much more for during the regular season. (And your chances of snagging balls during batting practice are infinitely better, too.) Most teams have extensive training facilities adjacent to their home stadiums, and morning workouts and practice sessions are usually free and open to the general public.

The best central source of Cactus League schedules, information, and tickets is the Mesa Convention and Visitors Bureau (480/827-4700 or 800/283-6372). Tickets for games cost $5–32 and are available through the teams, through Ticketmaster (800/745-3000), at the stadium box offices, and online. Be aware, however, that March is peak tourist season all over Arizona, so make your accommodation arrangements long before game time.

a low-key resort community. A few crusty prospectors still search for a strike, and cowboys are often seen riding through town, which makes Wickenburg a pleasant place to get a feel for the Old West, especially during the winter months when temperatures are mild and the sun shines nearly every day. If you wander around the compact town, keep an eye out for Gila monsters, tarantulas, and rattlesnakes, but don't worry: If you see one it's likely made of bronze, part of an art installation that has also populated the streets with metal renditions of Wild West outlaws and schoolteachers.

Wickenburg is also home to the gold-mining ghosts of the **Vulture Mine,** which produced some $200 million before its closure in the 1940s.

Wickenburg's Wild West ambience and reliably good winter weather account for the number of **dude ranches** dotting the surrounding desert, most of which are intended for longer stays rather than passing travelers.

Right where US-93 intersects cross-country US-60 at Wickenburg's only stoplight, the **Desert Caballeros Western Museum** (daily; $7.50; 928/684-2272) gives a broad overview of regional history and contains a surprisingly good collection of Western art and sculpture (from George Catlin to Charley Russell), plus the usual rocks and rusty relics.

Most of the places to eat and sleep are lined up along east–west US-60 (Wickenburg Way). Try the **Horseshoe Cafe** (207 E. Wickenburg Way; 928/684-7377). Along with national motels, consider the classic, 1950s-era **Westerner Motel** ($40 and up; 680 W. Wickenburg Way; 928/684-2493).

Hassayampa River Preserve

One of Arizona's very few stretches of riverside ecology preserved in its natural state, the **Hassayampa River Preserve,** three miles southeast of Wickenburg on US-60/89, is a great place to break a journey. For most of its way, the Hassayampa River runs underground, but here it rises to irrigate a dense forest of willows and cottonwood trees, which in turn shelter an amazing variety of birds—over 200 species, from songbirds to raptors, are listed in the preserve's birders' guide. Lots of lizards are here, too, along with bobcats.

The Nature Conservancy, which owns and operates the preserve, runs a small **visitors center** (Wed.–Sun. 8 AM–5 PM in winter, limited hours in summer; $5; 928/684-2772), where you can pick up trail guides and maybe join a guided walk.

Across Phoenix

From the northwest, our route arrives in ever-growing metropolitan **Phoenix** by way of US-60/89, which passes through the retirement communities of Surprise and Sun City. The historic route follows Grand Avenue all the way to the downtown area, where you can follow the old main road, Van Buren Street, but if you're in a hurry hop onto the freeway system and hope you don't get too lost—it's a crazy and confusing city, so spread out it can seem to take forever to get anywhere.

Superstition Mountains and the Apache Trail

East of Phoenix, US-60 runs as a four-lane freeway through suburban Tempe and Mesa, but the sprawl fades as you approach the angular **Superstition Mountains,** some 40 miles east of downtown. Protected within the massive **Tonto National Forest,** this area of volcanic crags, desert cactus, and ponderosa pines is best seen by traveling along Hwy-88, the scenic **Apache Trail,** which winds along the Salt River, the region's lifeblood. Named for the Indian tribe that dominated the area a century ago, and now an official National Scenic Byway, the Apache Trail is a 78-mile, four-hour loop, but even a short trip along it will take you far away from the fast lane.

A mere five miles north of US-60, the Phoenix suburbs give way to the wild desert of **Lost Dutchman State Park** ($3 in the summer; 480/982-4485), named for a legendary gold mine located nearby. Two miles farther is the overlook for the 4,535-foot phallus of Weaver's Needle, beyond which the road passes several reservoirs before reaching the entertaining tourist-trap hamlet of **Tortilla Flat** (pop. 6), 18 miles from US-60 and named after the Steinbeck novella—which has nothing to do with Arizona, but who cares?

Beyond Tortilla Flat, the road turns to dirt and twists and turns through spectacular desert country for the next 27 miles to Roosevelt Dam, then heads southeast to rejoin US-60 near Globe, at the western edge of the San Carlos Apache Indian Reservation, 50 miles east of Phoenix.

In springtime in particular, another great attraction of the Apache Trail region is the **Boyce Thompson Arboretum State Park** (daily; $7.50; 520/689-2811), the state's oldest and largest botanical exhibit, covering 323 acres with a full array of Sonora Desert cactus and wildflowers. The arboretum is right on US-60, 20 miles west of Globe near the copper-mining town of Superior.

Picacho Peak

Looming like a giant battleship alongside the I-10 "fast road," 75 miles southeast of Phoenix and 45 miles northwest of Tucson, 3,374-foot **Picacho Peak** has served as a Sonora Desert landmark for as long as there have been people here. Native Americans, Spanish explorers, American pioneers, you name it; they've used the volcanic peak to keep them on track. Now a state park, Picacho Peak also played a role in the Civil War; the official westernmost battle of the War Between the States was fought here on April 15, 1862, when a dozen Union soldiers skirmished with 17 Confederate cavalrymen. These days, people come here to enjoy the saguaro cactus and the desert wildflowers (in March mainly, when they're at their most colorful), or to hike to the summit for a desert panorama (two miles each way, with a roughly 1,500-foot elevation gain). The park ($7 per car; 520/466-3183) is open for day use and camping.

Along the freeway at the foot of Picacho Peak, a sprawling ostrich farm lets you feed the ungainly beasts or purchase a variety of ostrich-derived products.

Hwy-79: Florence and Casa Grande Ruins National Monument

If you have enough time to avoid the I-10 freeway and follow a slower but more scenic older road, consider Hwy-79, which cuts off south from Apache Junction and US-60. The first stop is **Florence,** one of Arizona's oldest towns, but now best known as the site of the state's largest prison. Florence has a pleasant,

Phoenix

More than four million people have settled in and around the Arizona capital, Phoenix, all but obliterating any sense that the land here ever was, and still is, a desert. Golf courses, swimming pools, lakes, and fountains are everywhere, with only a few carefully coiffed cacti remaining here and there to testify to the natural state of things. But there is something oddly charming about the place—an anything-goes, Wild West spirit manifest in one of the highest rates of car theft in the country and a truly phoenix-like ability to grow and thrive despite the almost total lack of natural advantages.

Zebra Swallowtail at the Desert Botanical Gardens' Butterfly Pavilion

Get an unforgettable sense of the desert's natural beauty at the magical **Desert Botanical Garden,** in Papago Park east of downtown between Scottsdale and Tempe (daily; $10; 480/941-1225). Especially in spring, when the wildflowers are in bloom and the Butterfly Pavilion is open, the gardens here offer an intense and aesthetic distillation of this harsh but intricate environment.

The best thing about downtown Phoenix is the marvelous **Heard Museum** (daily; $15; 2301 N. Central Ave.; 602/252-8344), among the best museums anywhere devoted to the native cultures of the Southwestern United States. The permanent galleries trace the history and diversity of prehistoric peoples and contemporary tribes, while changing exhibitions focus on specific themes.

Don't miss the amazing collection of Hopi kachina dolls, collected by hotelier Fred Harvey and the late U.S. senator Barry Goldwater. Downtown Phoenix is also home to Chase Field, the retractable-roofed stadium where the **Arizona Diamondbacks** (602/462-6500) play in the only major league ballpark with its own outfield swimming pool.

Another treat is **Taliesin West** (daily except major holidays; $24 and up; 480/627-5340), at 12345 Taliesin Drive at the east end of Cactus Road. Every winter from 1937 until his death in 1959, Frank Lloyd Wright lived, worked, and taught here, handcrafting this complex of studios, theaters, and living quarters, which survives as an architecture school.

Practicalities

Phoenix really is a sprawling mess, covering some 500 square miles and expanding by many acres every day—with no end (or beginning or middle, for that matter) in sight. The I-10 freeway cuts through the center, and a spaghetti bowl of local freeways, such as the Hwy-202 Loop, Hwy-51, and the US-60 "Superstition Freeway" complete the high-speed overlay. Though there is a skeletal bus service along with a handy light rail train ($3.50 all day) connecting downtown with Mesa and Tempe, trying to get around town without a car is hazardous to your health. In a word, drive.

Phoenix is actually made up of many separate surrounding cities, each of which has its own character—Mesa, for example, was founded by Mormons and is now bigger than Minneapolis and Miami. Not surprisingly, considering its well-deserved reputation as a winter oasis, the Phoenix area is home to a number of gorgeous resort hotels; rates quoted here are for winter, and summer prices are much lower. The historic **Arizona Biltmore** ($149 and up; 602/955-6600 or 800/950-0086), on the north side of Phoenix at 24th and Missouri Streets, is an absolutely beautiful, Frank Lloyd Wright–style resort complex tucked away on spacious grounds.

Fun for families can be had at the many water park–style resorts, like the **Pointe Hilton Tapatio Cliffs Resort** ($89 and up; 11111 N. 7th St.; 602/866-7500), next to the open expanses of North Mountain Park, which has suites and water slides and eight swimming pools. Downtown, the **Hotel San Carlos** ($79 and up; 202 N. Central Ave.; 602/253-4121) is a well-maintained older hotel with a rooftop swimming pool, and the **HI-Phoenix Hostel** (1026 9th St.; 602/254-9803) has dorm beds for around $20 a night.

The classic road-food stop in Phoenix is the **Tee Pee** (4144 E. Indian School Rd.; 602/956-0178), a characterful and always-crowded place serving huge and very cheap plates of old-style American-Mexican food. For something a bit hotter, brave the salsa at **Los Dos Molinos** (8646 S. Central Ave.; 602/243-9113), in the old Tom Mix house.

On the north side of downtown, next to a Lube 'n' Tune car repair shop, **Sierra Bonita Grill** (6933 N. 7th St.; 602/264-0700) is a very welcoming, unpretentious restaurant offering an interesting mix of Southwestern and pan-American influences (pork loin alongside vegetables and roasted potatoes with a vanilla bean serrano pepper butter sauce) and excellent desserts. Phoenix also boasts an unexpected treat: **Pizzeria Bianco** (Tues.–Sat. 11 AM–10 PM; 623 E. Adams St.; 602/258-8300), where transplanted New Yorker Chris Bianco cooks up delicious wood-fired designer pizzas in a historic downtown storefront.

non-touristy Main Street of bars, general stores, and junk shops, parallel to and a half mile west of the highway. The penal history is documented in gruesome detail at the **Pinal County Historical Museum** (Sept. 1–July 15, Tues.–Sat. 11 AM–4 PM, Sun. noon–4 PM; donations; 715 S. Main St.; 520/868-4382), where an actual hangman's noose and chairs from the retired gas chamber are displayed along with photos of people put to death.

the "big house" at Casa Grande Ruins National Monument

West of Florence, some of the state's largest and most perplexing prehistoric remains are preserved in the **Casa Grande Ruins National Monument** (daily; $5; 520/723-3172), off Hwy-287 midway between Florence and I-10. A small visitors center at the entrance gives some background on the Hohokam people, who built the four-story "big house" and the surrounding village, but no one knows what it was used for or why it was abandoned.

South of Florence, Hwy-79 follows the Pinal Pioneer Parkway, the old main road between Phoenix and Tucson. The route is now lined by a series of signs pointing out palo verde trees, saguaros, and other desert flora. Cowboy actor Tom Mix died here on October 12, 1940, when he crashed his 1937 Cord 812 Phaeton into a ditch along Hwy-79 and was decapitated by his suitcase. The site is marked by a statue of a riderless horse, in a rest area 18 miles south of Florence.

Biosphere 2

One of the most ambitious, controversial, and just plain bizarre schemes to hatch at the millennial end of the 20th century was **Biosphere 2,** which stands in the Arizona desert at the northern foot of snowcapped Mt. Lemmon. Developed in the 1990s by a New Age group called Synergia Ranch and funded by Texas billionaire Ed Bass, Biosphere 2 was originally intended to simulate the earth's entire ecosystem, in order to test the possibility of building self-sustaining colonies on other planets. A crew of four "biospherians" spent two not entirely self-sustained years sealed inside, but amidst allegations of corruption and deceit, the project imploded. The University of Arizona eventually took over running the domes, and has since redirected the focus onto research into the effects of greenhouse gases and other ecosystem changes. The surrounding land has been sold and is slated to become yet another upscale housing development, but Biosphere 2 itself should stay open for self-guided **tours** (daily; $20, kids under 5 free; 520/838-6200). To reach Biosphere 2, follow Hwy-79 to Oracle Junction, 25 miles north of Tucson, then turn east onto Hwy-77 for six miles and follow the signs.

BIOSPHERE 2

The environmental activist and author Edward Abbey, who died in 1989, spent his last years living in the Arizona desert near Oracle Junction.

Tucson marks the junction of the US-93 route with our cross-country **Southern Pacific** route along US-80 (see pages 800–863). **Saguaro National Park, Tombstone,** and more of the area around Tucson are covered on pages 811–815.

Across Tucson

The fastest way across Tucson is I-10, which runs diagonally along the western and southern edges of the city. Some of the more interesting "old road" routes around town include the Miracle Mile, north of downtown, and 6th Avenue, the main highway before the Interstate was built. South of Tucson, 6th Avenue becomes the Old Nogales Highway, the old road to Mexico, which veers in various alignments among extensive pecan groves while crisscrossing I-19.

Mission San Xavier del Bac

Among the most strikingly memorable of all the Spanish colonial missions in the Southwest, **Mission San Xavier del Bac** was built more than 200 years ago and still serves the native Tohono O'odham (a.k.a. Papago) people. Known as the "White Dove of the Desert" because of the gleaming white plaster that covers its adobe walls, balustrades, and twin bell towers—one of which is domed, the other not—this landmark edifice was designed and built by Spanish missionaries beginning in 1783.

The Triple A Tucson Padres play their home games at Kino Stadium, south of downtown along I-10 at 2500 E. Ajo Way (520/434-1367).

Rising up from the flat desert plain, San Xavier presents an impressive silhouette, but what's most unforgettable is the Mexican folk-baroque interior, covered in intensely wrought sculptures and paintings of saints and religious imagery. Currently under restoration, these paintings and figurines are among the country's finest examples of folk art, using painted mud to simulate marble, tiles, and crystal chandeliers.

The mission (daily; donations; 520/294-2624) is well signed and easy to reach, just 10 miles south of downtown Tucson off I-19 exit 92, then a half mile west. Across the plaza from the church is a small Tohono-owned and -operated complex of craft galleries, plus a very good taco stand.

Titan Missile Museum

In just 15 miles south of San Xavier, you can travel from the colonial 1700s to the Cold War 1960s by stopping at the **Titan Missile Museum,** the only Intercontinental Ballistic Missile (ICBM) silo preserved intact and open to the public anywhere in the world. On the north side of the sprawling stucco retirement community of Green Valley (pop. 21,391), just west from I-19 off exit 69

Tucson

Though it's less than half the size of Phoenix, Tucson (pop. 520,116) is perhaps twice as nice a place to visit. With a lively university community, some of the most beautiful desert landscapes anywhere on earth, and more palpable history than anywhere in the Southwest outside New Mexico, Tucson is well worth taking the time to get to know. It also makes an excellent jumping-off point for visiting the Wild West towns of Tombstone and Bisbee in the state's southeast corner.

However, with daytime temperatures averaging over 100°F, Tucson is hotter than heck during the summer months (early May to late September), so try to visit during the rest of the year. Spring is especially nice, with wildflowers blooming and spring training baseball bashing away, but this is also the most expensive time to be here—room rates in March are easily double those the rest of the year.

Many of Tucson's biggest attractions are outside the city limits and covered under various road trips: Biosphere 2 and Mission San Xavier del Bac are north and south of Tucson along US-93, while the two-part Saguaro National Park is east and west of downtown (and covered with the US-80 Southern Pacific route). But unlike many modern desert cities, downtown Tucson is worth a wander for the many historic buildings that have been spared the redeveloper's wrecking ball, including a wonderfully restored Roaring 1920s movie palace, the Fox Tucson Theatre on Congress Street, which has frequent movies and great live concerts.

The other center of activity is two miles north and east from downtown, where the nicely landscaped, 380-acre **University of Arizona** campus spreads between Speedway Boulevard and 6th Street. The campus holds the engaging historical exhibits of the **Arizona State Museum** (closed Sun.; $5; 520/621-6302) and one of the country's preeminent photography collections in the **Center for Creative Photography** (donation; 1030 N. Olive Rd.; 520/621-7968).

On the southeast side of Tucson, off I-10 at the Kolb Road exit, Davis-Monthan Air Force Base holds one of the very strangest sights in the entire Southwest desert: rows and rows and rows of surplus military aircraft, lined up for what seems like miles. The official name for this desert facility is the Aerospace Maintenance and Regeneration Group (AMARG), but it's best known as **"The Boneyard"** because of its role as a salvage yard for aircraft long past their production era. You can glimpse dozens of the planes from the highway, but for the full experience you have to sign up for one of the very popular tours (hours vary; $6–7; 520/574-0462). The tours are offered by the **Pima Air and Space Museum,** which has another extensive exhibit of aircraft, including JFK's Air Force One, nearby, and also operates the unique Titan Missile Museum south of Tucson.

The foothills of the Santa Catalina Mountains, which rise north of Tucson, are blessed by **Sabino Canyon** (daily; 520/749-2861), 12 miles east of downtown, well signed off Tanque Verde Road. With its seasonal waterfalls and a nearly year-round creek, Sabino Canyon is a great place to stretch your legs while getting a sense of how pretty and vibrant the desert can be.

West of Tucson, beyond where Speedway Boulevard climbs over Gates Pass, Tucson Mountain is home to a section of **Saguaro National Park** and the excellent **Arizona Sonora Desert Museum** (daily; $12–14.50; 520/883-2702). Apart from spending a lifetime in the desert, there's really no better place to get a sense of the abundant flora and fauna of the Sonora Desert than this creatively presented zoological park.

Practicalities

The main I-10 freeway runs diagonally from northwest to southeast along the usually dry Santa Cruz River at the western edge of town. Tucson stretches east from here for over 10 miles, and north toward the foothills of the Santa Catalina Mountains. The main east–west route across town is Speedway Boulevard, along with numerous parallel roads.

In addition to the usual highway motels, Tucson has some characterful places to stay, from restored downtown hotels to luxurious vacation resorts. One of the latter is the **Hacienda del Sol** ($100 and up; 5501 N. Hacienda del Sol Rd.; 520/299-1501), a historic guest ranch built as a posh girls' school in

Bird's-Eye View of Tucson, Arizona

the 1920s and now a quiet, intimate getaway, with a pool, tennis courts, great sunset views, and one of Tucson's best restaurants (The Grill). Another historic property, the **Arizona Inn** ($149 and up; 2200 E. Elm St.; 520/325-1541 or 800/933-1093), is perhaps the classic Arizona resort, little-changed since the 1930s, when it was a favorite winter haunt of the Rockefellers and other elites. The Arizona Inn offers very comfortable accommodations on lovingly landscaped grounds near the university campus.

One of the most enjoyable places to eat in Tucson is the quirky **Cafe Poca Cosa,** right downtown (110 E. Pennington St.; 520/622-6400). Adventurously creative Mexican food, served up in large portions at reasonable prices, is the specialty here—try anything in a mole sauce, and you won't be disappointed. Nearby, the **Little Cafe Poca Cosa** (151 N. Stone St.) is open for breakfast and lunch versions of the same delicious stuff. On the west side of downtown is **El Charro** (311 N. Court Ave.; 520/622-1922), "the oldest family-operated Mexican restaurant in the USA," so they say, serving up inexpensive food (and margaritas) since 1922 in a turn-of-the-20th-century house.

the Titan II missile in the silo at the Titan Missile Museum

on Duval Mine Road, the silo was in active use from 1963 until 1982, was declared a National Historic Landmark in 1994, and is now open for **tours** (daily; $9.50; 520/625-7736). The tours, which take around an hour, involve donning a hard hat and descending stairs into the control room of the hardened silo, which still contains a 110-foot-tall Titan missile (sans warhead!). If you like these sorts of things, a longer, much more in-depth tour (around $75) lets you climb all the way down into the silo.

Tubac

Another good place to stop between Tucson and the Mexican border is **Tubac,** 45 miles from Tucson, just east of I-19 at exit 34. One of the first European outposts in what's now Arizona, Tubac was established as a Spanish presidio (fort) in 1751, and a century later boomed with the opening of gold mines nearby.

Scattered around a dusty central plaza, just west of the presidio park, Tubac has developed into a small but diverting arts-and-crafts colony, with a number of good shops and cafés. Local artists are frequently showcased in the Tubac Center for the Arts on the north side of the plaza, near the peaceful, pleasant **Secret Garden** B&B inn ($125 and up; 520/398-9371).

Tumacácori National Historic Park

The preserved ruins of an impressive Spanish colonial mission stand at the center of **Tumacácori National Historic Park** (daily; $3; 520/398-2341), 42 miles from Tucson, 19 miles north of Nogales, and just three miles south of Tubac, off I-19 exit 29. The site was used by missionaries as early as 1691, but it wasn't until 1800 that they set to work building the massive adobe church. Though never finished, thanks to Apache raids and the Mexican

Revolution, Tumacácori stands as an impressive reminder of the religious passion of the friars and their efforts to convert local tribes.

Directly across the highway from Tumacácori is a rare sight—a Greek café—and a half mile north is **Wisdom's** (520/398-2397), which serves reliable Mexican and American food.

Nogales

Arizona's busiest border crossing, and birthplace of iconoclastic jazz great Charles Mingus (1922–1979), Nogales is also perhaps the most pleasant of all the "international" cities along the U.S./Mexico border. Despite being divided by an ugly corrugated steel fence, it gets promoted as **Ambos Nogales** (Both Nogales). The twin cities (pop. 20,837 on the Arizona side, 212,533 in Mexico) are economically codependent, especially post-NAFTA, as Mexicans come across to shop at Safeway and Wal-Mart, and Americans while away evenings drinking *cerveza* in south-of-the-border cantinas. The intriguing little **Pimeria Alta Historical Society Museum** (Fri.–Sun. 10 AM–4 PM; donations; 136 N. Grand Ave.; 520/287-4621), which documents cross-border history in the storefront-sized Old City Hall 400 yards north of the border crossing, is one of the few real sights to see on the Arizona side, but if you just want to spend an hour or two shopping for souvenirs and practicing your Spanish, Nogales, Sonora, Mexico, is a very pleasant place in which to do it.

To save hassle (and time) crossing the border, drivers should park on the streets or in the $5-a-day lots on the U.S. side and walk across. Border formalities are minimal, and U.S. dollars are accepted on both sides. There are quite a lot of good taco stands and cantinas, but one place to look for on the Mexican side is the elegant **La Roca,** partly carved out of a cave 300 yards southeast of the border crossing, across the train tracks (Calle Elias 91; 520/313-6313 or 011-52-631/312-0760). Good food at fair prices, stiff margaritas, continuous live music, and a lovely ambience await.

In Amado, just west of I-19 at the Arivaca Road exit, a huge concrete cow's skull marks the entrance to the **Longhorn Bar and Grill** restaurant and cantina (520/398-3955), one in a long series of businesses that have tried to make a go of this unique location.

Knife River
Indian Village
pg. 181

Sitting Bull
Memorial
pg. 192

190 mi

Buffalo Bill
Rodeo
pg. 203

350 mi

OzFest
Liberal, Kansas
pg. 212

295 mi

Remember
the Alamo!
pg. 225

580 mi

South Padre
Island
pg. 230

390 mi

Westhope
Great Falls
Minot
Grand
Forks
Helena
Helena
NORTH
DAKOTA
Bemidji
MO
Bismarck
Fargo
MN
Billings
Mobridge
St. Cloud
Cody
SOUTH
Minneapolis
DAKOTA
WY
Pierre
Sioux
Falls
Rock
Springs
Casper
Chadron
Valentine
Sioux City
Salt Lake City
Cheyenne
NEBRASKA
IOW
rovo
North
Platte
Omaha
De
Mo
UTAH
Buffalo Bill
Lincoln
Richfield
Colorado Springs
akley
St. Joseph
COLORADO
ANSAS
Topeka
MISS
ge
Kansas
City
Pueblo
Dodge
City
Wichita
Jefferson
Trinidad
agstaff
Tulsa
Oklahoma City
Fort
Smith
NA
Albuquer
Amarillo
OKLAHOMA
AR
enix
NEW
Little Ro
MEXICO
Ardmore
Tucson
Lubbock
Las Cruces
Fort Worth
El Paso
Odessa
Abilene
Dallas
Shre
EXAS
Waco
Lake
Charles
Remember
Austin
San ntonio
Houston
Galveston
ME
I
C
O
Lared
Corpus
Christi
Brownsvi

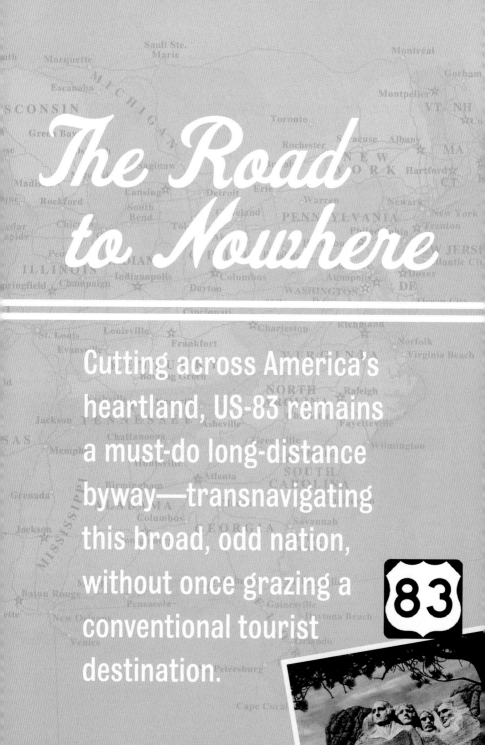

The Road to Nowhere

Cutting across America's heartland, US-83 remains a must-do long-distance byway—transnavigating this broad, odd nation, without once grazing a conventional tourist destination.

83

Between North Dakota and Matamoros, Mexico

Once the only entirely paved route from Canada to "Old Mexico" (as hard-to-find postcards along the route still say), US-83 is still likely the shortest—from Swan River, Manitoba, dead south to Brownsville, Texas, and beyond to Matamoros, Mexico, seemingly without turning once. Its grim moniker, The Road to Nowhere, is alternately unfair and then not severe enough, for the route navigates some of the widest and most aesthetically challenged landscapes in the country—the yawn-inducing rolling grasslands of the northern Great Plains, the beefy expanses of western **Nebraska** and **Kansas,** and the mesmerizing heat of the **Texas/Oklahoma Panhandle**—before following the lower Rio Grande south to the Gulf of Mexico. Yet on US-83 you'll also take in some phenomenal country: verdant farmland dotted with truly small towns, endlessly shifting prairie grassland, winding **Missouri River** roadways, and plain, isolated, where-the-hell-am-I agricultural expanses.

Following roughly along the 100th meridian, US-83 marks the historic divide between the "civilized" eastern United States and the arid western deserts. Physiography aside, this route's cultural landscape centers on small but self-sufficient farm or cattle communities that date back to the last days of the Wild West and that are far enough off the tourist trail to retain an unselfconscious, aw-shucks quaintness. For endless miles in every direction, telephone and power poles provide some of the few signs of life between the highway and the distant horizon, though the towns—where average speeds drop suddenly from 70 mph to radar-enforced 25 mph or slower—are spaced just often enough along the highway to serve your food-and-fuel needs.

Perhaps best of all, US-83 manages to transnavigate this broad, odd nation, albeit north-to-south, without once grazing a conventional tourist attraction. Here along the backbone of the nation, conversations over a daybreak breakfast, afternoons spent cooling off by municipal swimming pools, and twilight American Legion baseball games provide the stuff of truly memorable Road Trip diversions, and for that reason alone, US-83 remains a must-do long-distance byway.

NORTH DAKOTA

Beginning at the U.S. border with Manitoba, Canada, US-83's route across North Dakota is a 265-mile-long rehash of childhood back-of-station-wagon dreamscapes: epic plains too green or golden-hued for your eyes to process rationally, and endless cultivated fields punctuated by umpteen farmers' cooperatives, storage bins, silos, and grain elevators. Hay bales of all shapes and sizes dry perilously close to the roadside, and Stetsoned figures in dusty pickups or mighty tractors amiably lift their index fingers off steering wheels in back-forty greetings.

US-83 doesn't really follow a straight plumb line south—it just seems that way. After meandering from the border across the fertile residuals of ancient Lake Souris near lonely **Westhope,** the route seems to fall straight down the map while crossing the drift prairie south to **Minot.** Continuing south across the viaduct separating giant **Lake Sakakawea** and the much smaller **Lake Audubon,** US-83 winds across slightly more ambitious hills and plateaus along a historic and hardly changed stretch of the mighty Missouri River to **Bismarck,** the state capital and a better-than-expected place to spend some time. South of Bismarck, US-83 cuts away from the riverfront through a pastry-rich pastoral landscape settled around the turn of the 20th century by German immigrants—including the parents of dance-meister Lawrence Welk—while a recommended detour follows the Missouri River across the huge, historic **Standing Rock Indian Reservation** that stretches into South Dakota.

Westhope

US-83 begins winding its way from the Canadian border at the small United States entrance station (daily 8 AM–9 PM only) six miles north of **Westhope** (pop. 429). Westhope, named by an optimistic Great Northern Railway official, is a good example of North Dakota's small agrarian towns. There's the **Gateway Motel** motel/lounge (701/245-6100), cafés, gas stations, a sparse two-block-long downtown, and that's about it.

A half-hour side trip east from US-83 along Hwy-5 brings you to the town of **Dunseith,** where a giant turtle named Wee'l has been constructed out of 2,000 old car and truck tire rims. If you like what you see, nearby Bottineau, North Dakota, has a statue of a giant turtle riding a snowmobile.

Six miles south of Westhope, US-83 zigzags west along Hwy-5 for about 15 miles before sharply banking south. The next 37 miles to Minot are a straight shot south, passing nothing save two sweeping wildlife refuges and a lonely Domino's Pizza, all by itself beneath the occasional B-52s thundering overhead to and from **Minot Air Force Base,** one of the primary bases for the U.S. military's tactical and strategic nuclear

Minot Air Force Base logo

forces. Along with bombers and fighter planes, Minot AFB also controls hundreds of nuclear-tipped Minuteman III ICBM missiles, which are housed in high-security underground silos that look like high-security parking lots amidst the wheat fields all over the northern Great Plains.

Minot

Snug in the Souris River Valley at the junction of US-2 and US-83, **Minot** (pop. 40,888; rhymes with "Why not?") grew so rapidly after the Great Northern Railroad came through in 1887 that it was dubbed "Magic City." Perhaps "Event Capital" would be more apropos today, for despite the city's importance in other areas, most people visit during the huge **state fair** (near the end of July) and during autumn's burgeoning **Norsk Hostfest,** "North America's Largest Scandinavian Festival." The fairgrounds, along the grandly named Burdick Expressway (Business US-2) a half mile east of downtown, also

hold the small **Pioneer Village and Museum** (June–Aug. daily 10 AM–3 PM; by appointment the rest of the year), the usual assembly of turn-of-the-20th-century buildings and artifacts gathered from all over the county.

Minot also has all the traditional, homespun attractions of most Great Plains downtowns, with stores selling cowboy hats and Western wear, along with the world-class collectibles (including baseball cards, old magazines, and more than 120,000 classic comics) on sale at **Tom's Coin & Gem Shop** (2 SW 1st St.; 701/852-4522).

remnant of Minot's Populist past

On US-83 south of town, Minot's newest attraction, **Scandinavian Heritage Park** (1020 S. Broadway) is set in a pleasant, tree-shaded city park and includes all sorts of things tracing—guess what?—Minot's Scandinavian heritage: a 230-year-old house from Sigdal, Norway; a Danish windmill; a statue and eternal flame honoring famous Scandinavian skiers like Casper Oimoen and Sondre Norheim; a number of waterfalls; and a statue of that famous Viking wanderer, Leif Eriksson. Towering over the whole ensemble is a beautiful (and huge!) wooden replica of the medieval Gol Stave Church in Oslo, Norway, and right along US-83 there's a 20-foot-tall red Dala horse, symbolizing Minot's Swedish heritage.

In summer, when daytime highs hover in the mid-90s, Minot's most enticing attractions are the expansive gardens of **Roosevelt Park,** along the banks of the Souris River between the fairgrounds and downtown Minot. Named, like everything else in North Dakota, for Teddy Roosevelt—there's a larger-than-life statue of him, astride a horse in full Rough Rider regalia—the shady green space also holds a large swimming pool with a 350-foot-long water slide, a slacker's dream of a skateboard park, a rideable miniature train, and a 20-acre zoo with a Northern Plains habitat.

East of Minot on US-2, the town of **Rugby** is nearly the geographical center of North America.

To rent bikes and explore the trails of Roosevelt Park, try **Val's Cyclery** (222 E. Central Ave.; 701/839-4817).

Minot Practicalities

Along with the usual crossroads barrage of franchised fast-food places, Minot supports a couple of local cafés, including a retro-styled train car diner, **Kroll's Diner,** just off US-2 (1221 SE 20th Ave.; 701/839-4111), and a great old 24-hour truck stop, **Schatz Econostop Family Restaurant,** farther east on US-2 (1712 SE 20th Ave.; 701/852-5044).

In range for an hour or more in all directions, Minot's **KRRZ 1390 AM** broadcasts oldies from the 1950s and 1960s, along with Minnesota Twins baseball games.

Downtown, the longstanding favorite is **Charlie's Main Street Cafe** (113 S. Main St.; 701/839-6500), just a couple blocks east of US-83, its fluorescent-lit pink vinyl booths full of gossiping Minot ladies. A couple blocks north, across from the old Soo Line train depot, any big-city superiority complex you might bring with you will disappear during a meal at the warm but sophisticated **10 North Main** (10 N. Main St.; 701/837-1010), where a wide range of dishes (from locally raised elk and bison steaks, to exotic, line-caught Tasmanian salmon!) is complemented by fine wines and smart cocktails.

After dark, choose from over a dozen haunts, from bingo parlors and low-stakes casinos to country-western honky-tonks and low-key beer bars like the **Blue Rider** (118 1st Ave. SE; 701/852-9050), a friendly, smoke-free pub with what may be rural North Dakota's best selection of bottled brews—look for the Grain Belt Beer sign.

Motels are scattered along the congested arteries of both US-83 and US-2, so you shouldn't have trouble finding a place to sleep (except perhaps during the state fair). To cope with the extreme weather on the northern Great Plains (winter cold and summer heat), locals seek relief in the Dakota Square Mall, southwest of downtown, where room rates at the "World's Largest" **Sleep Inn**

& Suites, 2400 10th Street ($130 and up; 701/837-3100), include free use of the **Splashdown Dakota Super Slides** water park, which has 24,000-square-feet of water slides, swimming pools, and a 48-person hot tub.

East of downtown Minot near the fairgrounds, there's a nice **Holiday Inn** ($120 and up; 2200 E. Burdick Expressway; 701/852-2504 or 888/465-4329).

The Minot **visitors center** (1020 S. Broadway; 701/857-8206 or 800/264-2626), on US-83 south of downtown near the Scandinavian Heritage Park, has complete listings and detailed information on events and activities. Being so central to the state, Minot hosts everything from chili cook-offs to the state softball championships, and there's usually *something* going on.

Minot marks the junction of US-83 and **The Great Northern** route along US-2 (see page 528), which runs cross-country from Seattle, Washington, to Acadia National Park in Maine. For full coverage of this route, see pages 492–583.

Lake Sakakawea and the Garrison Dam

At 178 miles long and with nearly 1,600 miles of shoreline along the dammed Missouri River, **Lake Sakakawea** is the third largest man-made "lake" in the United States. There are countless things to do on the water, most of them involving fishing. The pleasant town of **Garrison** (pop. 1,453), six miles west of US-83 on Hwy-37, has a pair of red-roofed water towers labeled Hot and Cold, and a photogenic fiberglass statue of Wally-the-26-Foot-Walleye.

Lake Sakakawea is one of many places in the northwestern United States named for the legendary Shoshone Indian woman, also known as Sacagawea, who accompanied the Lewis and Clark expedition across the Rocky Mountains.

At the south end of Lake Sakakawea, and 12 miles west of US-83 via Hwy-200, the Missouri River backs up behind wide but low-slung **Garrison Dam,** the fifth-largest earth-filled dam in the United States. The powerhouse is enmeshed within a labyrinth of huge power stanchions, high-voltage lines, and transformers. In the adjacent **fish hatchery** on the downstream side of the dam, tanks hold hundreds of thousands of walleye, bass, and northern pike, plus rainbow and brown trout.

South of Garrison Dam, roadside interest along US-83 focuses on leviathan testimonials to engineering prowess. Huge tractors and bulldozers raise clouds of dust at the extensive coal mining operations around **Underwood**—the whole area on both sides of US-83 has been strip-mined and restored, though current operations are hard to get a good look at—and some 7.5–8 million tons of the valuable black rock each year ends up at the 1,100-megawatt **Coal Creek Station,** six miles north of Washburn and two miles off the roadway but *readily* apparent. This is one of the largest lignite-fired coal plants in the country, boasting a four-mile-long coal conveyor belt, which passes over the highway in a tube.

However, unless you have an abiding interest in fossil fuels, a more interesting alternative to driving this stretch of US-83 is to follow the Missouri River's western bank south of Lake Sakakawea, where it reverts to its naturally broad and powerful self for the next 75 miles.

Knife River Indian Village National Historic Site

Between Garrison Dam and Washburn, scenic Hwy-200 passes two of North Dakota's most significant historic sites: Fort Clark and the Knife River Indian Village, both of which, though small, saw key scenes of the late 18th- and early 19th-century interactions between Native Americans and interloping European traders and explorers. Downstream from Garrison Dam along the west bank of the Missouri River, the **Knife River Indian Village National Historic Site** (daily; free; 701/745-3300) is one of North Dakota's most fascinating historic places, and the only federally maintained site devoted to preservation of the Plains tribes' cultures.

Knife River Indian Village's earth lodge

Standing above the Missouri floodplain, on the site of what was the largest and most sophisticated village of the interrelated Hidatsa, Mandan, and Arikara tribes, the park protects the remains of dozens of terraced fields, fortifications, and earth lodges, remnants of a culture that lived here for thousands of years until the 1830s, when the tribes were devastated by smallpox and other diseases within a few short years of European contact.

A highlight of the park is an **earth lodge,** reconstructed using traditional materials, which gives a vivid sense of day-to-day Great Plains life. Measuring 40 feet across and 12 feet high at its central smoke hole, the earth lodge looks exactly as it would have when the likes of George Catlin and Karl Bodmer were welcomed by the villagers during the 1830s. Just north of the earth lodge spread circular depressions in the soil—which are all that remain of the Hidatsa community where, in 1804, the Lewis and Clark Corps of Discovery was joined by the French fur-trapper Charbonneau and his wife, Sacagawea.

The modern visitors center, well signed off Hwy-200 at the south edge of the park, has high-quality reproductions of the drawings and paintings that Catlin, Bodmer, and others made of the Knife River Indian Village, along with archaeological and anthropological summaries that help bring to life these intriguing Native American peoples. The center also has information on the many annual events, festivals, and powwows held at Knife River throughout the year, including the **Northern Plains Indian Culture Fest** in late July.

A half mile south of the visitors center, the tiny town of **Stanton** (pop. 366) has two cafés, two bars, and two gas stations along its three-block main drag. For breakfast or lunch before or after a hike around the Knife River Indian Village site, stop off at **Glo's Kitchen** (701/745-3535) on Hwy-31 in tiny,

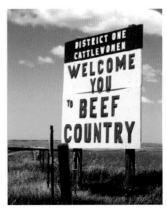

The Lewis and Clark Expedition

Following the instructions of President Thomas Jefferson, Meriwether Lewis and William Clark set off across the continent in 1804 to explore the vast territory recently acquired from France in the Louisiana Purchase. Part of their mission was to find a viable trade route from the Mississippi River to the Pacific Ocean.

Sharing command of what was officially known as the Corps of Discovery, which included 33 soldiers and experienced "mountain men," plus the legendary Sacagawea, her husband Toussaint Charbonneau, and their infant Pomp, not to mention Lewis's Newfoundland dog, Seaman, Lewis and Clark blazed a route up the Missouri River, crossed the Rocky Mountains, and made their way west down the Columbia River, returning to St. Louis after two and a half years and over 8,000 miles of unprecedented travel.

Meriwether Lewis

Along with their copious journals, many good books have been written documenting the Lewis and Clark expedition and tracing their route, which has been declared the **Lewis and Clark National Historic Trail.** Much of the land they traversed has been altered beyond recognition, though thanks to recent bicentennial celebrations, numerous historic sites along

Fort Clatsop · Fort Canby · Portland
Columbia River
Traveler's Rest
Knife River Indian Villages
Fort Mandan
Bismarck
Tillamook Head
Lemhi Pass
Snake River
On-a-Slant Indian Village
Mississippi
Boise
ROCKY MOUNTAINS
Missouri River
Floyd Monument
New York
San Francisco
Denver
Jefferson National Expansion Memorial
ST. LOUIS
River

0 ———— 800 miles
0 ———— 800 kilometers

Land Acquired Through Louisiana Purchase

© AVALON TRAVEL

William Clark

the way have been preserved or protected as parks or museums. The best of these are covered here.

Museum of Westward Expansion is an excellent museum underneath the Gateway Arch in St. Louis (see page 272).

The Sergeant Floyd Monument,In Sioux City, is a concrete-core stone obelisk marking the grave of the only expedition member to lose his life— from appendicitis (see page 634).

On-A-Slant Indian Village has been reconstructed atop the remains of a Mandan village (see page 189).

Fort Mandan, where the expedition spent the winter of 1804–1805, has been reconstructed downstream from the original site (see page 184).

Knife River Indian Village National Historic Site, along the banks of the Missouri River, holds the remains of the Hidatsa village where Sacagawea lived before joining the Corps of Discovery (see page 181).

Lemhi Pass, on the Idaho/Montana border, is where the expedition first crossed the Continental Divide (see page 139).

The River of No Return is an impassable portion of the **Salmon River** (see page 137).

Traveler's Rest, in the Bitterroot Valley south of Missoula, was such an idyllic spot that the Corps of Discovery camped here on both the outbound and return legs of their journey (see page 135).

Fort Canby, now called **Cape Disappointment State Park,** overlooking the mouth of the Columbia River, has a small museum on the spot where the expedition first saw the Pacific Ocean (see page 24).

Fort Clatsop, a full-scale reconstruction of the wooden fort where the expedition spent a miserable winter in 1805–1806, sits in lush forest along the Oregon coast (see page 27).

Tillamook Head, rising high above the Pacific Ocean, is the farthest point the expedition reached (see page 29).

tidy "downtown" Stanton; Glo's specializes in homemade ice cream sundaes but also dishes up a mean sandwich or boxed lunch for those more inclined to pack up a picnic to nosh on down by the river. The **Mercer County Courthouse** (8 AM–4 PM Mon.–Fri.; 1021 Arthur St.), at the center of Stanton, displays arrowheads and other Indian artifacts.

Fort Clark

Seven miles downstream from the Knife River site, well signed off Hwy-200, **Fort Clark State Historical Site** (daily May–Sept.; free) is as eerily isolated as can be. One of three major fur-trading posts on the upper Missouri River, Fort Clark was founded by the American Fur Company circa 1831, primarily to trade with the Mandan Indians. The fort was visited by other tribes, as well as the usual roll-call of adventurers, explorers, and frontier luminaries, such as Prince Maximilian, George Catlin, and Karl Bodmer; unfortunately, the steamboats that plied the waters to bring supplies also brought smallpox, and in one tragic winter in 1837, the Mandan tribe's population was cut by 90 percent. After the fur trade declined, Fort Clark was abandoned in 1860.

Today the tranquil site, approached on a narrow gravel-and-dirt road, is devoid of anything—it's a somber, quiet piece of history stretching out on a grassy, flat-topped bluff overlooking the Missouri River. Unfortunately, the silence and emptiness of the place are marred by the presence of a smoky Basin Electric Power Company coal plant up the river. A walking trail has markers designating the locations of eight original buildings, and depressions from an earth lodge village and primitive fortifications are still apparent, but you really need to use your imagination to see very much.

Fort Mandan

Back on the east bank of the Missouri River, north of Washburn and two miles west of US-83, **Fort Mandan** is a reconstruction of Lewis and Clark's winter quarters in 1804–1805. Arriving here at the end of October after a tediously difficult six-month slog upstream from St. Louis, the expedition set up camp, which consisted of rough-hewn log cabins arranged to form a triangular palisade, surrounded by an 16-foot-high wall. Here the 33 men spent the winter, making friendly contact with nearby Indian tribes, most significantly those of the Knife River site—where Lewis and Clark hired the French fur-trapper Charbonneau and his young wife, the legendary Sacagawea, who helped guide them across the Rockies.

As it flows across the south-central corner of North Dakota, the **Missouri River** also marks the dividing line between the central and mountain time zones.

The actual site of Lewis and Clark's encampment, some 10 miles upstream across the river from the site of Fort Clark, was long ago washed away by the ever-shifting Missouri River, but this full-scale, historically accurate replica fort was built in the 1970s by local history buffs, and recently restored and expanded as part of the Lewis & Clark Interpretive Center in Washburn. Constructed and furnished, with some original pieces, to look how it did when Lewis and Clark camped here, the fort gives a good sense of the difficulties the explorers faced. History aside, the wild Missouri River frontage is a great place

Detour: The Enchanted Highway

Standing out against the badlands of western North Dakota, the world's largest collection of roadside statuary enlivens an otherwise unexciting swath of the northern Great Plains. Standing along a quiet country road outside the town of Regent (pop. 160), some 32 miles south of I-94 exit 72, the unexpected visual delights of the Enchanted Highway have earned it a place in the *Guinness Book of Records* (as the World's Largest Scrap Metal Sculpture), as well as in the hearts of many a long-distance road-tripper. Created beginning in 1991 by former schoolteacher and self-taught metal sculptor Gary Greff, these are some of the largest works of art in the world—a flock of geese reaches over 100 feet into the air, while the *Tin Family* stands some 50 feet tall along the roadside. The Enchanted Highway is, well, simply enchanting, and definitely worth the detour.

to play Tom Sawyer—on summer afternoons you'll see barefoot kids, shirtless in overalls, fishing and mucking along the banks. Another insight into local life is provided by the visitors center, which is constructed almost entirely out of recycled by-products of the coal-mining industry.

Washburn: Lewis & Clark Interpretive Center

Now a tranquil little highway town, **Washburn** (pop. 1,246) was once a frenetic Missouri River ferry crossing, served by steamboats from St. Louis, the last of which has been mounted on a concrete pedestal at the base of the bridge that helped to make it obsolete. In addition to nearby Fort Clark, across the river, and Fort Mandan, two miles to the northwest—not to mention the **Lewis and Clark Cafe** right downtown, where you can rent a canoe or a kayak to experience the Missouri River as closely as possible to how the Corps of Discovery did—Washburn has the excellent **Lewis & Clark Interpretive Center** (daily; $7.50; 701/462-8535). It's at the intersection of US-83 and North Dakota Hwy-200A, an ideal jumping-off point for your exploration of the lower Missouri River valley. Offering the hard-to-find combination of informative exhibits (including a full set of the detailed watercolors painted in the 1830s by explorer-artist Karl Bodmer), great Missouri River views, an excellent gift shop, and impeccably clean restrooms, this is a place you will want to linger for at least an hour (or maybe two). The highly interactive museum exhibits let curious Corps of Discovery enthusiasts try on a buffalo robe, program their own museum-browsing background music (selecting from a variety of period fiddle music and Native American chant tracks), or trace the dramatic shifts in the river's course over the past 200 years.

Part of the promotional campaign for the 2004–2006 bicentennial celebrations of the Corps of Discovery's amazing expedition, billboards all around North Dakota relayed the slogan "Lewis & Clark Slept Here—146 Times."

Cross Ranch State Park

Across the Missouri River, a little more than eight miles south of Washburn via Hwy-1806, **Cross Ranch State Park** ($5 per car) is set among 589 acres of cottonwood-shaded free-flowing Missouri River bottomland with numerous hiking trails, canoe rentals, and fine camping, with sites for RVs and tents. There are also furnished **log cabins and yurts,** in which you can stay for around $65 a night for a cabin and around $50 for a yurt; for details, phone the park **visitors center** (701/794-3731 or 800/807-4723), which also has canoe and kayak rentals and information on the annual **Missouri River Bluegrass Festival and Kid Fest,** held here in the middle of June.

Across Hwy-1806 from the state park, the remains of the pioneer town of **Sanger** stand as a mute memorial to Great Plains history. Founded in 1879, Sanger was the county seat and a major steamboat and railroad town, with a population of some 400 people. By World War II, Sanger had effectively been bypassed by the modern age, and the post office closed down in the mid-1950s. By 1985, just three residents remained, but a half dozen buildings still line Main Street, urgently awaiting some visionary effort to preserve and protect them for future generations.

From the state park, enticing trails lead into The Nature Conservancy's 5,600-acre **Cross Ranch Nature Preserve** (daily dawn–dusk; free; 701/794-8741). One of the richest surviving native Missouri River valley ecosystems, the preserve includes floodplain prairie and riparian forest, plus a resident herd of bison and some undisturbed Native American archaeological sites.

Bismarck

In his best-selling travelogue *Travels with Charley,* writer John Steinbeck wrote about Bismarck:

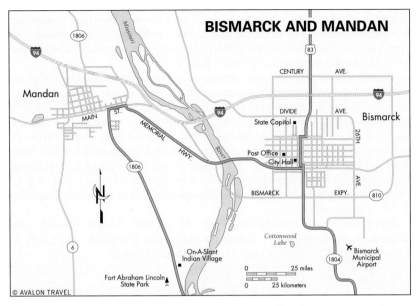

BISMARCK AND MANDAN

Mandan

Bismarck

MAIN ST.

MEMORIAL HWY.

Missouri River

CENTURY AVE.

DIVIDE AVE.

State Capitol ■

Post Office ■ ▪
City Hall ■

26TH

BISMARCK EXPY.

AVE.

Cottonwood
Lake

On-A-Slant
Indian Village
■

Fort Abraham Lincoln ▲
State Park ‡

✕ Bismarck
Municipal
Airport

0   25 miles

0   25 kilometers

© AVALON TRAVEL

Here is where the map should fold. Here is the boundary between east and west. On the Bismarck side it is eastern landscape, eastern grass, with the look and smell of eastern America. Across the Missouri on the Mandan side it is pure west, with brown grass and water scorings and small outcrops. The two sides of the river might well be a thousand miles apart.

Like many towns across the Great Plains, **Bismarck** (pop. 61,272) was named after a wealthy European, in this case the chancellor of Germany, in order to lure much-needed capital investment. The town grew exponentially following booms in the railroad industry, Black Hills gold, and most recently, oil, gas, and bio-fuels, but it's still economically and culturally dependent upon its status as North Dakota's state capital. It's one of the smallest of the 50 in the United States, but as state capitals go, Bismarck rates quite highly for its size, with thousands of parkland acres, well-preserved historic districts, and an old-time boat ride along the Missouri River.

Bureaucratic Bismarck seems intent on glossing over its bawdy historical peccadilloes by building monuments to modernity, like the capitol building, 19 stories of angular art deco nicknamed the "Skyscraper of the Prairies." The white limestone and classical symbolism seem out of place on the plains, but free **tours** highlight the ornate interior's woodwork, stonecarving, and metalsmithing.

On the grounds you'll find the usual memorial statues of noteworthy North Dakotans, starting with a large statue of **Sacagawea,** the guide of Lewis and Clark, carrying her newborn baby Pomp and looking sternly forward. Nearby is another popular subject, a **buffalo,** here rendered out of rusty steel

Thirty-four miles west of Bismarck, the **World's Largest Cow** stands along I-94 in New Salem.

Between the two state capitals of Bismarck, North Dakota, and Pierre, South Dakota, the Missouri River has been dammed to form 231-mile-long **Lake Oahe.**

reinforcing rod. A short walk away, the **North Dakota Heritage Center** has an informative array of historical and cultural exhibits, using dinosaurs and tepees to trace the development of North Dakota from its geological underpinnings to its contemporary culture and industry.

Though Bismarck is the state capital, the selection of places to eat is pretty slim. For a truly otherworldly experience that combines pretty tasty American and Tex-Mex with Jetsonesque, space-age decor, the **Space Aliens Cafe** (1304 E. Century Ave.; 701/223-6220), on the US-83 strip north of I-94, is your logical destination. Earthlings Welcome, proclaims the telltale sign; this lively joint may get a bit too cute with its nomenclature, but it does deliver on flavor with its Planet of the Zombies Taco Burger, Martian Munchies barbecue platter, and Outer Space appetizers. If you want good food rather than a good snigger, you might be better off at the **Pirogue Grill** (121 N. 4th St.; 701/223-3770), near Broadway.

Along with the clusters of motels on the northern fringes of US-83 and along I-94, accommodation options include a nice **Radisson** ($103; 605 E. Broadway; 701/255-6000) a mile south of the state capitol.

Missouri River Tour: Hwy-1806

An outstanding alternative to US-83 between Bismarck and the South Dakota border is the narrow but well-maintained Hwy-1806, which meanders along the Missouri River taking in views of great hillocks and easy bluffs off to the left, or scintillating blue water ribboning beneath stark-white, standing-driftwood trees. Round a bend and you'll see a lagoon. Or admire a great panorama of 2,000-foot buttes to the west, all the way across the state line. Be sure to fill up on gas and supplies before you set off since it's a 100-mile drive with few services along the way.

Mandan

Cross-river sibling to the state capital, **Mandan** (pop. 18,331) is a shipping and warehousing center that grew up swiftly in the years after 1882, when the Northern Pacific railroad completed a bridge from Bismarck. As John Steinbeck pointed out, Mandan marks the beginning of the wild western United States. For a quick trip back to the 1880s, when the Northern Pacific Railroad made its epic push across the Great Plains, visit the **North Dakota State Railroad Museum** (daily 1–5 PM; 3102 37th St. NW; 701/663-9322). In addition to a wide array of old railroad photographs, the museum includes restored cabooses, boxcars, tankers, and flatcars from the Soo, Great Northern, and Burlington Northern lines.

Most everything in Mandan, from cafés to beauty parlors, seems to be named after some-

Theodore Roosevelt, Rough Rider

one related to Lewis and Clark—apart from the string of windowless, cowboy-themed beer bars along Main Street (choose among Silver Dollar Lounge, the Last Call Bar, and a number of others). The other main things to see in Mandan are two statues, one a 25-foot-tall Indian figure carved from a cotton-wood tree (601 SE 6th Ave.), the other the requisite **Teddy Roosevelt,** in front of the train station on Main Street. Alas, one favorite reason to stop in Mandan is no more: As of 2010, there are no more milk shakes, or anything else, available at the Americana-rich Mandan Drug (316 W. Main St.).

Fort Abraham Lincoln State Park

Heading south along Hwy-1806 from Mandan along the west bank of the Missouri River, the first place you'll reach is sprawling **Fort Abraham Lincoln State Park** (daily except winter; $5 per car; 701/667-6340), which was originally established as Fort McKeen in advance of the Northern Pacific Railroad expansion. It eventually fell into the hands of the U.S. Army, which in 1872 changed the fort's name to the present one. Soon afterward, General Custer arrived to take over the reins of command, and in 1876 the fort was placed squarely on the map and in the national press as the departure point for the doomed general and his 262 men, who met their demise at Little Big Horn. Abandoned in 1891, the fort was dismantled by settlers who salvaged the wood and bricks to build their own homes, and most everything here today is a reconstruction.

The modern park covers slightly more than 1,000 acres and contains a number of barracks, stables, and stores, plus a replica of **Custer's house** (daily; $6), where paid syco-phants will lead you around, calling you "General" while conducting guided tours. Best of all is the **On-A-Slant Indian Village,** near the north end of the park, an excavated Mandan village established about 1575 where you can explore four full-scale earth lodges re-created by the Civilian Conservation Corps in 1933–1934.

General George Armstrong Custer

If you like the idea of *not* driving for a change, the **Fort Lincoln Trolley** (daily 1–5 PM in summer; $7; depot at 2000 SE 3rd St.) runs along the river between Mandan and Fort Abraham Lincoln, departing every hour or so for the 4.5-mile trip. You can also stay at the park overnight, either in a small sleeping cabin (summer only; $40) or in the adjacent campground. Make reservations for these well ahead (800/807-4723) so you don't miss out on the Missouri River sunrise views.

Standing Rock Indian Reservation: Fort Yates

Genuinely huge hills start to appear around the **Standing Rock Indian Reservation,** home to approximately 8,500 Sioux and spreading across the state line with a total of 2.3 million acres. For outsiders, the main draw to the reservation, besides the fantastic roadside views and the glitzy Prairie Knights casino (800/425-8277), is the original burial site of Sitting Bull in **Fort Yates** (pop. 184), the reservation headquarters. The unimpressive

The primary tourist attraction on the Standing Rock Indian Reservation is the surreal **Prairie Knights Casino and Resort,** 46 miles south of Mandan on Hwy-1806.

site, marked by a boulder on a dusty side road two miles west of Hwy-1806, is certainly not what one would expect for the great warrior. He is now more suitably interred near Mobridge, South Dakota.

Across from the agency headquarters is another site sacred to the Sioux, the Standing Rock from which the reservation takes its name. In the correct angle of sunlight, the stone resembles a seated woman wearing a shawl. Legend holds that the woman, jealous of her husband's second wife, refused to move when the tribe decamped; a search party later found her, turned to stone.

South of Fort Yates, the scenery and the driving (or riding) are magnificent. Flawless blacktop winds through valleys and up ambitious, swooping hills of grazing land, and you'll be confronted by one gorgeous landscape after another, especially at dusk, when the intense Western sun illuminates the bands of sunflower fields, turns the dry and grassy hills a reddish shade of ochre, and casts angular shadows beneath the darting sandpipers, who whisk their brown-and-white forms along the roadway, buzzing the lone car on the road in an extended game of highway tag. You won't even realize you're in South Dakota until you notice the gold border on the highway signs.

US-83: Linton, Strasburg, and the Lawrence Welk Birthplace

While the scenery is superior along the Hwy-1806 detour, for travelers of a certain age the trek south of Bismarck along US-83 is redeemed by one unique Road Trip destination: the **Ludwig and Christina Welk Farmstead** (Thurs.–Sun. 10 AM to 5 PM; $5; 701/336-7777), boyhood home of Lawrence Welk, a wholesome, middlebrow dance-band maestro who for more than 20 years starting in the mid-1950s had one of the most popular programs on TV. Located a mile north of the town of **Strasburg,** then 2.5 miles west from

US-83 following well-signed dirt roads, the preserved homestead where Welk was born in 1903 is one of the top tourist draws in North Dakota. (Which, to be honest, is not saying a lot; North Dakota is frequently numbered at the very bottom of "Favorite States to Visit.")

Though the Lawrence Welk connection is the main draw for most visitors, the farm is intended as a memorial to his par-

Lawrence Welk leading his band on *The Lawrence Welk Show*

ents, who as part of an exodus of Bavarian-born Catholic farmers fled the Ukraine during the late 1800s when exemptions from Tsarist military service were threatened and emigrated to this country in 1893. The promise of land brought the Welks to North Dakota in the 1890s. The clapboard house that stands today began as a sod house—the mud walls can still be seen in places—and is now full of odds and ends of furniture and memorabilia donated by the Welk family, who still own the place. Hand tools, a windmill, and farming implements are arranged around the yard, while in the hayloft a mannequin dressed as young Lawrence squeezes out polkas on the accordion—apparently, his early playing was so bad that he was banned from practicing in the house, though now his recordings are broadcast nonstop from a speaker system strung around the grounds.

Much of southern North Dakota is still predominantly populated by descendants of the original wave of these immigrant "Germans from Russia" who homesteaded the region in the 1890s. Their influence is clearly apparent in the town of **Linton** (pop. 1,097), on US-83 around 10.5 miles north of the Welk homestead, where the **Model Bakery** (117 N. Broadway; 701/254-4687) bakes up delicious, creamy custard kuchen and German cakes and cookies Tuesday–Friday. In **Strasburg** (pop. 409), Welk's parents are buried in the cemetery behind the absolutely huge Catholic church that dwarfs the tiny town.

The border between North and South Dakota is marked by 720 stone monuments, each seven feet tall but half-buried in the ground every half mile. They were erected by the federal government in 1892; one stands right alongside Hwy-1804, on the eastern shore of Lake Oahe.

Both Linton and Strasburg used to have the only-in-North-Dakota attractions of what must have been the world's smallest bowling alleys: A two-lane bowling alley was tucked away in back of the Linton Cafe (105 N. Broadway), while Strasburg's four-laner was part of the Pin Palace Cafe (714 Main St.). Both were closed at last report; here's hoping they're open when you pass through.

SOUTH DAKOTA

US-83 cuts through South Dakota's broad expanse for 254 miles, crossing mostly level but never slate-flat topography, and passing through what's known as the Great Lakes region of the state, most evident in and around **Pierre.** Instead of a multi-lane, transcontinental highway, US-83 across South Dakota resembles a country road, giving an up-close-and-personal look at farming and grazing lands, with an occasional jutting hill, ravine, or serpentine creek bed to break up the monotony. Classic South Dakota—no pretensions.

To either side of the North Dakota border, US-83 is little more than a beeline across the plains. Sadly, the Missouri River is well out of eyeshot, so we highly recommend following a scenic detour across the river through the huge Standing Rock Indian Reservation, linking up with US-83 again approximately 20 miles east of Mobridge via

Wild pheasants and other beautifully plumed game birds scurry about in the grassy verges along US-83 across the Dakotas.

US-12. After that you'll pass through small farm towns before reaching the state capital, Pierre, at the center of South Dakota.

Standing Rock Indian Reservation: Mobridge

Since US-83's route across northern South Dakota doesn't offer much stimulation for the senses, if you've got the time to spare, detour west along the Missouri River, leaving North Dakota via the Lewis and Clark Highway, Hwy-1806. This scenic route brings you across the middle of Standing Rock Indian Reservation, which falls mainly in South Dakota but stretches about 30 miles over the border.

On Hwy-1806, at tiny **Kenel,** a historical marker points out the site of fur-trading Fort Manuel, where Lewis and Clark's guide Sacagawea may have died of fever in 1812, at the age of 25. South of Kenel, the road runs straight south, away from the winding Missouri River and toward imposing 2,200-foot Rattlesnake Butte. After 26 miles or so, you'll cross on sweeping bridges into **Mobridge** (pop. 3,465), the biggest town between the North and South Dakota capitals.

The name "Mobridge" stems from a hasty telegraph message transmitted in 1906 by an operator who needed a quick and clear reference to the area. He chose, at random, "Mo," for the Missouri River, and "bridge," referring to the one then under construction by the Milwaukee Railroad.

Mobridge, once a village of the Arikara tribe, is heavily dependent on the anglers who come to pluck the lunkers, walleye, and even 20-pound northern pike from Lake Oahe. The area's earlier history and Native American culture are celebrated on the walls inside the **Scherr-Howe Arena** (Mon.–Fri. only; free; 212 Main St.), where bold 16- by 20-foot murals depict Sioux history and culture. These murals were painted as part of the Depression-era Works Progress Administration by native Yankton Sioux artist Oscar Howe (1915–1983).

The most interesting food option is **Rick's Café,** in downtown Mobridge (117 N. Main St.; 605/845-5300), famed for its award-winning chili and burgers. The **Wrangler Motor Inn** ($50 and up; 820 W. Grand Crossing; 605/845-3641), a half mile west on US-12, is the best overnight stop on the stretch, with two dining rooms, a coffee shop, and a heated pool.

Sitting Bull Memorial

A 10-minute trip from Mobridge, back across the Missouri to the Grand River Casino and Resort then south on Hwy-1806, will bring you to the **Sitting Bull Memorial.** This is the final resting place of the great Sioux Indian leader, after his body was disinterred in 1953 from Fort Yates in a surreptitious and still-controversial move. Whatever injustice or disrespect

Sitting Bull Monument

exhuming his body may have incurred, this magnificent view, high atop a palisade hilltop looking southeast over the river, is at least worthier than the previous site. The six-foot granite bust that serves as Sitting Bull's tombstone was carved by the late Korczak Ziolkowski, the sculptor who began the quixotic Crazy Horse Mountain carving near Mt. Rushmore.

US-83: Selby

Twenty-odd miles east and slightly south of Mobridge, US-83 passes through diminutive **Selby** (pop. 642), the kind of sleepy, middle American hamlet with grain elevators and water towers, populated with children riding bikes home at dusk and teenagers rumbling down Main Street in their muscle cars. Downtown Selby has an old "opera house" theater, and the comfortable, inviting **Berens Bar, Hotel & Cafe** (3422 Main St.; 605/649-7621). Berens serves home-cooked meals downstairs in a humble, friendly setting that will make you want to linger as long as you can—overnight, even. It's very welcoming after a long day on the road.

Another place that may encourage you to hang around is on the north edge of town, near the US-12 and US-83 intersection: oasis-like **Lake Hiddenwood State Park** ($4 per person; $6 per vehicle), with picturesque deep swales and oak and cedar trees surrounding, as the name implies, a secluded swimming hole. If you mentally transport yourself back a century and a half, when explorers crossed these bone-dry parts and stumbled accidentally onto this lushness, the name's quite apt.

Hoven, Agar, and Onida

Between Selby and Pierre, there's nothing of dramatic importance. Highway hypnosis is kept at bay by a roadside marker five miles south of Selby, standing on the site of the vanished town of Bangor; farther south, then 13 miles east of US-83, the very large **Cathedral on the Prairie** looms over the hamlet of **Hoven** (pop. 406).

And then, finally, a town—or at least some grain elevators and a turquoise water tower. **Agar** (pop. 76), "Home of the 1977 State B Track Champions," is a classic, single-sidewalk leg-stretch where the Pepsi machine seems as large as the filling station it rests against. The same goes for little **Onida** (pop. 658), with a handsome onion-domed courthouse, a water tower emblazoned with a sunflower, and a cute city park complete with swimming pool and horseshoe courts. You'd hardly guess that this was once a thriving homesteader boomtown, full of transplanted New Yorkers who named it after Oneida, with no apparent reason for the change in spelling.

Pierre

The second smallest and by far the sleepiest state capital in the country, **Pierre** (pop. 13,646; pronounced "PEER") is an odd amalgam of South Dakota characteristics. Part farm town, part railroad town, and best of all, part river town, Pierre accurately embodies South Dakota's dominant activities. Located at nearly the geographic center of the state, quiet, easy Pierre is filled with natural attractions and totally lacking in the usual power-broker trappings of other state-capital cities.

Locally known as Houck's, the **Triple U Buffalo Ranch,** 34 miles northwest of Pierre on Hwy-1806, is a 53,000-acre spread supporting about 2,000 head of bison, some of whom were seen in the movie *Dances with Wolves.* The ranch mainly serves trophy hunters, but there's also a small gift shop (605/567-3624) selling buffalo steaks, jerky, hides, skulls, and other products.

Pierre's one not-to-be-missed stop is the excellent **South Dakota Cultural Heritage Center** (daily; $4; 900 Governor's Dr.; 605/773-3458) built into the side of a hill on the north side of town. A startling and beautiful structure, it is designed to be a modern evocation of a traditional, energy-efficient Native American dwelling. Inside, the museum has the usual interpretive historical displays of native and pioneer cultures, with a focus on the Sioux tribes and the battles for the Black Hills region. A glass case holds the actual lead plate the brothers Louis-Joseph and Francois Verendrye, the first Europeans to explore what's now South Dakota, left behind when they claimed the entire territory for France in 1743.

At the center of town, the **state capitol** grounds are a verdant island of tranquility with an arboretum, walking trails, and the Flaming Fountain Memorial, dedicated to South Dakotans who have fought for their country in time of war. The fountain sits on a lake that is home to thousands of migrating winter waterfowl.

For travel-weary road hogs, especially those traveling with children, the coolest museum has to be the hands-on **South Dakota Discovery Center and Aquarium** (daily; $4; 805 W. Sioux Ave.; 605/224-8295), in the old Pierre Municipal Power & Light building, with loads of science exhibits and an aquarium full of Missouri River fish.

Museums aside, nature is really what draws folks to Pierre. Bordering the town to the south is the long **La Framboise Island Nature Area,** a perfect place to while away time, recuperating from the drive along the beautiful bay. If you're interested in biking or paddling along the Missouri River, you can rent bikes and boats at **Pedal & Paddle** (411 S. Pierre St.; 605/224-8955).

Pierre Practicalities

The nicest place to eat is **La Minestra** (106 E. Dakota Ave.; 605/224-8090), a surprisingly cozy and elegant bistro in a restored 1880s building that during its storied history has housed a funeral parlor, a card room, and a country western saloon. The sophisticated Italian specialties make this one of the nicest restaurants you'll find along the 100th meridian. There's also a pretty good steakhouse next door, **Mad Mary's** (605/224-6469), and if beef is what you live for you'll also want to try the local landmark **Myril Arch's Cattlemen's Club Steakhouse,** one of the country's great cowboy haunts, six miles or so east of town along the river via Hwy-34 (605/224-9774).

There are the usual assorted motels on US-83 as it swoops in from the north and follows the wide landscaped boulevards; west of the state capitol building, you'll find lots of locally owned places: the **Governor's Inn** ($82 and up; 700 W. Sioux Ave.; 605/224-4200 or 800/341-8000) is at the top end of the price and comfort scale, and this same can't-miss-it main drag holds a popular **Days Inn** ($73 and up; 520 W. Sioux Ave.; 605/224-0411).

Fort Pierre

South of Pierre, US-83 crosses the Missouri River, then takes you into **Fort Pierre** (pop. 2,078). It's not much now, but it has a rich history. As far back as 1832, it was known as Fort Pierre Chouteau, an American Fur Company trading post, and before that it was Ree and Arikara tribal lands. Located at the mouth of the Bad (Teton) River, Fort Pierre

Spreading across the plains south of Pierre along both sides of US-83, the 116,000 acres of the **Fort Pierre National Grasslands** are home to deer, pronghorn, jillions of waterfowl, and one of the most pervasive stretches of prairie dog towns in the region. The grassland doesn't offer developed campsites, but it does have great fishing at some of the hundreds of small dams dotting the landscape.

Wall Drug

America's most famous roadside business, Wall Drug began with free ice water. Ted Hustead bought this tiny South Dakota town's drugstore in 1931, and for five years Ted and his wife Dorothy struggled to survive during the depths of the Depression. Then Dorothy had a brainstorm: Hundreds of people drove past Wall every day on US-16, the main route across South Dakota, battling the dusty dirt road and 90°F summer heat. Why not give them an excuse to stop? Once in the store, maybe they'd buy an ice cream, or an aspirin.

So in the summer of 1936, Ted Hustead erected roadside signs to tempt travelers off the highway and into his store. Spaced at intervals along the highway, like the famous Burma-Shave ads, the signs read:

GET A SODA
GET ROOT BEER
TURN THE CORNER
JUST AS NEAR
TO HIGHWAY 16 AND 14
FREE ICE WATER
WALL DRUG

Before he could return to the store, the tourists were already arriving. And they're coming still: some 20,000 per day in the summer—well over a million a year. Proud South Dakotans have covered foreign landscapes with signs proclaiming the mileage to Wall Drug, and the Husteads themselves have advertised on London buses, Amsterdam canals, and French bistros. Before the 1960s era of "highway beautification" banned most billboards, Wall Drug touted its free ice water on 3,000 billboards in all 50 states.

But what's waiting at the end of all those billboards?

Originally, not much, apart from that glass of water. But today's 50,000-square-foot Wall Drug is a different story: It can feed, clothe, and entertain the entire family for hours. Photo opportunities abound, thanks to the 80-foot-long dinosaur, six-foot fiberglass jackalope, Mt. Rushmore replica, a 520-seat café, and shops for everything from postcards to cowboy boots. A younger generation of Husteads still runs Wall Drug, the ice water's still free, and the coffee still costs a nickel. Drop in sometime!

Wall Drug (510 Main St., 605/279-2175) is at the center of Wall, South Dakota (pop. 766), just north of I-90 exit 110. Apart from Wall Drug, one other reason to visit is the chance to tour a real-life nuclear missile silo, at the *Minuteman Missile National Historic Site* (daily; free; 605/433-5552), off I-90 exit 131. The silo and control center are accessible only by very popular guided tours (at 9 AM and 1:30 PM), so sign up as soon as you know you'll be here.

once was a thriving port, but it is better known as the site where Joseph La Framboise, a fur trader, stopped and erected a driftwood shelter out of necessity, establishing the area's first white settlement.

Visit the old fort, now a National Historic Landmark spread out over 1.3 acres near town. In the center of town you'll find the **Verendrye Museum** (daily in summer only; 115 Deadwood St.), which has collections of South Dakota pioneer artifacts and a duplicate of the plate the Verendrye brothers, the first white men to enter South Dakota, planted here in 1743 to claim the land for France. The original plate is in the state Heritage Center in Pierre; the Verendrye brothers themselves are commemorated with a monument in small Centennial Park, off US-83 at the center of town.

Immediately south of Fort Pierre, typical South Dakota topography resumes: rolling black and green hills and twisting creek beds beneath sharp vertical drops of million-year-old geology.

Murdo

One of the duller stretches of US-83 is this 20-mile leg west along the mind-numbing I-90 artery between the Fort Pierre grasslands and **Murdo** (pop. 488). Once a stop on the legendary Texas Cattle Trail and also used by stage-coaches, the town was named for cattle baron Murdo McKenzie, who managed ranches that pushed through some 20,000 head of cattle a year. Today, the town of Murdo still lives on the cattle industry.

If you're thinking about driving along US-83 during August, be aware that you may have to share the road with hordes of Harley riders bound for the annual get-together in **Sturgis,** at the edge of the Black Hills.

The one place that's definitely worth a stop is smack-dab at the diesel-blue polluted confluence of US-83 and I-90, where nostalgists will find the **Pioneer Auto Show** (daily; $10; 605/669-2691), a 10-acre, 42-building collection of about 275 antique cars, with tons of other great items. There's also a nifty White Co. motor home from 1921, one of the earliest RVs, and the General Lee muscle car from TV's *Dukes of Hazzard*. Star of the show: Elvis Presley's 1976 Harley-Davidson Electra Glide 1200 motorcycle. This is pure Americana.

The Pioneer Auto Show also has a very good, 1950s-style ersatz diner. The public swimming pool across the street from the Pioneer will round off your perfectly Middle American Murdo experience.

Rosebud Indian Reservation

There's nothing much south of I-90 and Murdo until you come across a picturesque dale while crossing the White River, sheltering the first grove of trees in too long a time. South of White River, US-83 rolls its way across the **Rosebud Indian Reservation.** After the signing of the Fort Laramie Treaty in 1868, the Sicangu Lakota, under the guide of Spotted Tail, were moved five times before finally being settled on this reservation, one of the smallest on the Great Plains. The first town you'll encounter is **Mission,** the reservation's trading center, where US-83 zigzags through a strip of gas stations, a Subway sandwich store, and the Rosebud Sioux arts and crafts center.

The heart of the reservation is **Rosebud,** five miles west of Mission on US-18, then 10 miles southwest on BIA-1. Most of the reservation's activities, including weekend rodeos and powwows, are centered on the tribal headquarters. The biggest powwow is the **Rosebud Sioux Tribal Fair and Powwow** in late August, where you can feast on a traditional buffalo dinner. Another eight miles southwest is tiny **St. Francis,** which has the **Buechel Memorial Lakota Museum** (daily June–Sept.; free; 350 S. Oak St.; 605/747-2745), a museum dedicated to the Teton Sioux culture and begun by Fr. Eugene Buechel, a German Jesuit, avid botanist, and dedicated student of Plains Indian culture.

Back on US-83, 23 miles south of Mission, is the tribe's most recent economic endeavor, the **Rosebud Casino,** which sits right on the Nebraska state line, showing just where its prospective gamblers are coming from.

NEBRASKA

The 257 miles from South Dakota to Kansas encompass two distinct regions: typical Midwestern wheat and cattle ranches, and the fascinating grass-coated sand dunes of central Nebraska's Sand Hills region. Contrary to a popular belief inspired by the powerhouse college football Cornhuskers nickname, Nebraska isn't mostly corn, but beef—lots and lots of it. US-83 passes by more cattle than it does people, with scant few communities along the way. In the northern corner of the state there are trees, trees, and more trees, especially as you drop down from the scorched plains into the evergreen-studded Niobrara River Valley. Coming from South Dakota, your first stop south of the border is **Valentine,** then US-83 crosses the rolling Sand Hills region toward the railroad town of **North Platte,** former home of "Buffalo" Bill Cody. From North Platte, it's a straight shot south to Kansas.

Thanks to its cupidic name, Valentine is a popular place to mail greeting cards for delivery on February 14. If you want a special "With Love on Valentine's Day" postmark, in early February pack up your stamped, addressed Valentine's cards in a larger envelope and send them to "The Postmaster, Valentine Re-Mailing, Valentine, NE 69201."

Valentine

Just west of the 100th meridian, the small town of **Valentine** (pop. 2,737) is a center of the extensive cattle ranching industry of the Sand Hills region, and the kind of tiny but prideful town that makes road-tripping fun. Seat of enormous Cherry County and situated at the northern edge of the 20,000-square-mile Sand Hills region, Valentine,

Valentine marks the junction of US-83 and the east–west **Oregon Trail** along US-20. For full coverage of this road trip, see pages 584–703.

which takes its name from a U.S. congressman, is a broad, well-maintained place that pays its bills with beef cattle fed to tenderness on the hundreds of species of grasses coating the region.

Considering the long stretches of road ahead, it's prudent to check out what the town's got, and there's quite a bit. Downtown—where the streetlights are hung with red and white banners emblazoned with the unsurprising town motto "Valentine, Heart of the Sand Hills"—the facade of the First National Bank holds the "Largest Brick Mural in Nebraska," with 1,200 square feet of images of longhorn cattle and the building of the transcontinental railroad built out of dark brown bricks.

Four miles southeast of Valentine on US-20/83, an absolutely *huge* old railroad trestle bridges the broad Niobrara River, at the heart of the inviting Fort Niobrara nature reserve.

Valentine has the usual motels scattered along US-20 and US-83, including the 1960s-era **Trade Winds Motel** ($69 and up; 402/376-1600 or 888/376-1601) on the southeast edge of town; there's also a Comfort Inn. The place most people go for a sit-down meal is the **Cedar Canyon Steakhouse** (112 N. Main St.; 402/376-3176), formerly known as the Peppermill, featuring steaks, seafood, and alfresco dining in summer.

Fort Niobrara National Wildlife Refuge

One of Valentine's sightseeing highlights is the massive old railroad bridge over the broad Niobrara River. Just a few miles south of downtown along US-20/83, rising on trestles 150 feet above the water, the bridge now carries the popular "Cowboy Trail" hiker-biker route, which follows the old railroad right-of-way almost all the way across the state. This stretch of the Niobrara River has been protected for nearly 100 years within the nearly 20,000-acre **Fort Niobrara National Wildlife Refuge** (402/376-3789) and offers topnotch canoeing and tubing. The refuge is named for old Fort Niobrara, semi-famous for

railroad bridge over the Niobrara River

never seeing a battle during its 27 years on the Wild West prairie. The diverse environs of the refuge provide a home for a huge variety of native plants and animals; a 3.5-mile, self-guided auto tour lets you watch for resident and migratory birds, while herds of elk, bison, pronghorns, and Texas longhorns roam around the gorgeous green rolling prairies.

Nature-lovers score well at other sites around Valentine. Cyclists and walkers will enjoy the chance to follow the Cowboy Trail, right through town, while seasoned canoeists, kayakers, and keen trout anglers will want to tackle the rough **Snake River** some 23 miles southwest of town, near the short but powerful **Snake River Falls.** A good local outfitter is **Yucca Dune** (148 E. 1st St.; 402/376-3330), in downtown Valentine, which rents bikes, rafts, canoes, and kayaks and sells outdoor clothing and climbing and camping gear.

Nebraska Sand Hills

South of Valentine are two fine natural areas, preserving and highlighting the unique ecosystems of the **Nebraska Sand Hills.** South along US-83 is the large **Valentine National Wildlife Refuge,** which, thanks to water seeped from the world's biggest aquifer, the Ogalala Aquifer, is home to both native rolling dune

view from the Nebraska Sand Hills over the prairies and forests

The Sand Hills of northwestern Nebraska form one of the largest areas of rolling dune geology in the world. They're also the largest tract of mid- to tallgrass prairie in North America, and, in the right light (sunrise or sunset), at the right time of year (spring especially, and in winter when the majestic sandhill cranes are migrating through), they are absolutely beautiful.

prairie and lowlands of lake, marsh, and sub-irrigated meadow. Lots of curlews, sandpipers, terns, and mule deer are found on the drives and hikes through the vaulted hills and long spiny grasses, and along the lakeshores.

Farther south, the Sand Hills occasionally flatten out into simple, absolutely open range, with perhaps a ridge jutting out. Cows fleck the land, as do a few windmills: great, stark, American Gothic windmills, not the pseudo-efficient energy spinners seen elsewhere.

US-83 joins with Hwy-2 approximately 30 miles after leaving the Valentine Wildlife Refuge. Swinging east will take you to one of the three huge districts of the **Nebraska National Forest,** among the largest man-made forest tracts in the world (20,000 acres total), all planted by hand more than a century ago.

Thedford and Scenic Hwy-2

Sleepy little **Thedford** (pop. 188) stretches west of US-83, lining up along the Burlington Northern railroad tracks. The town—not much more than a few little houses, some loud cicadas, a motel or two, and a combination Conoco station and road-food restaurant—does mark the junction of US-83 and Scenic Hwy-2, which runs west–east across the heart of Nebraska, abounding in wildflowers, ultra-quaint but totally unselfconscious small towns, and pastoral beauty from horizon to horizon.

At the south edge of the Sand Hills, 123 miles west of Thedford at the end of Hwy-2, the unique **Carhenge**—the finest Detroit wheels, stacked on top of each other to form a steel Stonehenge— stands just outside the town of Alliance.

South of Thedford, US-83 jumps and descends for another 66 miles or so toward North Platte with very, very little to occupy your time other than scenic overlooks along the Dismal and South Loup Rivers.

North Platte

It can take some time getting into **North Platte** (pop. 24,733), but despite the heavy-industrial initial appearance there is a lot here to enjoy. The northern approach along US-83 crosses over the North Fork of the Platte River, taking a leisurely little swoop up and over it, passing scenic bluffs, then flashing back through a living history of the days when the train was king. Rusty, old, weed-filled tracks and abandoned shops and warehouses lie off to the side, steel and brick remnants of North Platte's blue-collar trade and transportation heyday. From the south the entrance is less memorable, crossing the I-80 strip with its back-lit plastic signs and anonymous franchise architecture.

Originally the site of a Union Pacific construction camp, North Platte nearly expired when the workers decamped for Colorado; however, the town's 300 permanent residents were spared when the railroad chose it as a division point, securing its future. The city is still proud of its **Bailey Yard,** in 1995 deemed by the *Guinness Book of Records* the largest railroad classification yard in the world at 2,850 acres!). A high-tech visitors center (complete with eight-story

Golden Spike Tower) opened on the south side of the tracks in 2008, giving casual visitors and hard-core rail fans a bird's-eye view of the intricate operations; drive west on Front Street from downtown and you can't miss it.

Bailey Yard

Many of the city parks feature railroad displays, including 100-acre **Cody Park** along US-83. Within the confines rests **Big Boy,** one of the world's largest steam locomotives.

Before the railroad came through, North Platte was a key stop on both the Oregon Trail, which followed the Platte River west past Scotts Bluff and into Wyoming, and the Pony Express. At the dawn of the Automobile Age, North

Platte played a starring role along the historic Lincoln Highway, the first transcontinental road, which followed the Oregon Trail route west along what's now US-30, US-50, and I-80, eventually ending up in San Francisco.

But North Platte is most widely known as the home of Buffalo Bill Cody. The huge **Buffalo Bill Ranch State Historical Park** (daily; $4 per car; 308/535-8035), also known as Buffalo Bill Scout's Rest Ranch, is four miles northwest via US-30 and Buffalo Bill Avenue. It includes original dwellings on 25 surviving acres of Buffalo Bill's original 4,000-acre spread. Cody's house and some outbuildings look much the way they did when Buffalo Bill lived here, from 1879 to 1913. This is where Buffalo Bill originated his rodeo with the "Old Glory Blowout" in 1882 and later housed Buffalo Bill's Wild West show when not on the road. The whole town of North Platte still whoops it up with the **Buffalo Bill Rodeo** in June.

Besides Buffalo Bill memorabilia, North Platte has an interesting World War II canteen mock-up (preserved intact from the days when North Platte was a whistle-stop for troop trains), a great Railroad Town, and an eight-million-year-old, 200-pound, fossilized land tortoise, all on display at the **Lincoln County Museum** (daily; 2403 Buffalo Bill Ave.; 308/534-5640), adjacent to the Scout's Rest Ranch.

Downtown North Platte, on the south side of the railroad tracks, has largely been superseded by the surrounding Interstate sprawl, but the brick-paved streets here still hold some grand old buildings and a few nifty old neon signs, including one for the landmark **Fox Theater,** at 5th and Bailey Streets.

Buffalo Bill Cody

Fifty miles east of North Platte, via I-180 or the old Lincoln Highway, the town of **Cozad** has a big sign proudly proclaiming its place along the 100th meridian, the historic dividing line down the middle of America.

Just north of I-80 is one last great Buffalo Bill stop: the giant **Fort Cody Trading Post** (free; 308/532-8081), a massive postcard and souvenir store with a very good selection of books on Western Americana and, best of all, a fabulously detailed miniature working model of Buffalo Bill's Wild West show, complete with dancing bears, jumping horses, and hundreds of cowboys and Indians.

Because I-80 whips through North Platte, there's no shortage of fast food or places to stay. The I-80 route replaced one of the country's first cross-country roads, the Lincoln Highway, and if you've got some time (and an appetite!), take a little trip along the old Lincoln Highway (US-30).

The Great Platte River Road Archway Monument

The north–south US-83 route takes you through the heart of North Platte, but historically the main way through was heading west. First along the Oregon Trail, then along the Pony Express, the Union Pacific railroad, and up to today's I-80 freeway, the Platte River has long been one of the country's most important transportation throughways. Paying tribute to all stages of the

South of North Platte on US-83, you'll pass a country road, going east and south, that leads to the **Sioux Lookout,** one of the highest points above the Platte Valley. The very fine 1930s statue that used to stand here has been moved to downtown North Platte's Lincoln County Courthouse.

river corridor's long history, the **Great Platte River Road Archway Monument** (daily; $10; 308/237-1000) is an expansive interactive museum dedicated to America's freedom of mobility. Exhibits cover everything from Lewis and Clark to the Lincoln Highway; one highlight offers a chance to nail speeders on I-80 with your own radar gun. The $60 million museum actually spans I-80, but to reach it you have to take exit 272, just south of the town of Kearney (pronounced "CAR-knee"), an hour and a half or so east of North Platte, and follow surface streets to the Archway Monument.

Some 22.5 miles southeast of Kearney in Minden is another great monument to America: **The Harold Warp Pioneer Village** (daily; $11; 800/445-4447), a Middle American version of Henry Ford's Greenfield Village, with a much better sense of fun. The 20-acre site preserves dozens of historic structures, along with the proclaimed world's oldest steam-powered merry-go-round; 350 classic cars, trucks, and airplanes; and some 50,000 other items of varying historical interest. Almost everything here dates from 1830–1950, illustrating Mr. Warp's sense of history:

For thousands of years man lived quite simply. Then like a sleeping giant our world was awakened. In a mere hundred and twenty years of eternal time man progressed from open hearth, grease lamps, and ox carts to television, super sonic speed, and atomic power. We have endeavored to show you the actual development of this astounding progress as it was unfolded by our forefathers and by ourselves.

Wellfleet: Dancing Leaf Earth Lodge

South of North Platte, there's nothing much, community-wise, in the 70-odd miles along US-83 until you reach McCook, but the road and rolling landscape will definitely hold your interest. You're privy to the few acres of genuine Nebraska corn, which eventually fold into encroaching knobby little rises, hollows full of oaks, or open range. Though there are no real sights to look out for, a detour east of the highway brings you to one truly unique place: the **Dancing Leaf Earth Lodge** (6100 E. Opal Springs Rd.), located among cottonwood trees along the banks of Medicine Creek, midway between North Platte and McCook in the town of **Wellfleet,** two miles east of US-83. An as-authentic-as-possible re-creation of a Native American dwelling, the 20- by 20-foot lodge is the heart of a cultural learning center that endeavors to give visitors a total immersion into the life ways and spirituality of ancient Plains Indians. Constructed by hand from willows and grasses and plastered with thick mud, the two earth lodges stay cool in summer and warm in winter and provide primitive but comfortable accommodations and an unforgettable experience of what life might have been like before the arrival of European cultures.

Guided **tours** (daily; $7; 308/963-4233) give a good overall introduction to Plains Indian traditions, but nothing beats an overnight stay. Families and groups are especially welcome at the Dancing Leaf, where rates, including a buffalo stew dinner and a soothing session in the sweat lodge, start at $100 a night for up to three people. The lodges each sleep a maximum of 15 people, but this is a re-creation of a ancient lifestyle, not a luxury experience; all guests need to bring a sleeping bag. Even if you don't stay overnight, canoe rentals and hiking trails, plus informal instruction in the crafts of tool-making, basket-weaving, hunting, fishing, and cooking, are also available from the hosts, Les and Jan Hosick.

McCook

Fifteen miles north of the Kansas border, patches of corn grow in the fertile loam of the undulating Republican River Valley around **McCook** (pop. 7,698), the market center for much of southwest Nebraska. With the arrival of the railroad, the town (which is still served by Amtrak's California Zephyr and numerous freight trains) grew into a farm trade center, and it now is a sedate, content-enough place, with at least two good excuses for a brief stop, both of them on the hill above downtown. The **High Plains Museum** (Tues.–Sat.; free; 421 Norris Ave.; 308/345-3661), in a large modern building, includes excellent fossil collections, some World War II prisoner-of-war artwork, a room dedicated to Sen. George Norris, and an old drugstore replicated in the very building where Kool-Aid was developed. Up the street, the **George W. Norris Home** (Tues.–Sat.; $3; 706 Norris Ave.; 308/345-8484) is devoted to McCook's favorite son, the progressive Nebraska senator (born 1861, died 1944) who sponsored legislation forming the Tennessee Valley Authority and

McCook sits at the crossroads of US-83 and US-6, which used to be the longest cross-country highway in the United States, running from the tip of Cape Cod all the way to Long Beach, California.

promoted rural electrification during the New Deal in the 1930s. Norris, who was first elected to Congress as a Republican in 1902, spoke out strongly against U.S. involvement in World War I and was elected to his final term in 1936 as an Independent.

In between the two museums stands Nebraska's only Frank Lloyd Wright–designed house (602 Norris Ave.). Finished in 1908, it is a private residence and not open for tours.

South of McCook, US-83 turns grandly scenic (it's even marked as such on some maps). Just north of the Nebraska/Kansas state line, the highway crosses the Beaver Creek, passing over an old trestle bridge.

KANSAS

Kansas is no mere geographical expression, but a "state of mind," a religion, and a philosophy in one.
    —Carl Becker, *Kansas* (1910)

I like Kansas—that is, natural Kansas— better than I had expected to.
    —Horace Greeley, *An Overland Journey* (1859)

The clichés have told you wrong: US-83 across much of Kansas—surprise, surprise—is actually a treat, not at all the interminable tedium of grain-field stretches you might expect. Yes, the physiography through most of the intrastate span is still predominantly flat, dry northern high plains, but it's compensated for, particularly in the north, with extensive irrigation that coaxes lusher patches of vegetation out of the dark rich soil.

US-83, much of which has been officially proclaimed the "Western Vistas Historic Byway," ushers you along gaping, horizon-filled stretches broken by isolated lakes and occasional oases such as **Oberlin** and **Oakley,** home of the nearly famous Prairie Dog Town. Continuing south across the windblown plains and limestone hills, US-83 passes through the cow towns of **Scott City** and **Garden City** before crossing the Arkansas River into the baked-clay watercolor that stretches south into Oklahoma and Texas. One final Kansas stop is perhaps the best: **Liberal,** the self-declared home of fictional Dorothy from the celluloid *Wizard of Oz.*

Oberlin

All across northwest Kansas, US-83 sweeps across beautiful rolling farmlands, paralleling railroad tracks and passing through low, one-horse towns with towering feed elevators. Funky little **Oberlin,** 12 miles south of the Nebraska state line, is definitely worth a stop. It's a picture-postcard town, with a Social Realist native limestone statue of a pioneering family marking its northern edge and a mini movie theater called the Sunflower (220 N. Penn Ave.; 785/475-3374)—in honor of the Kansas state flower—playing Hollywood hits amid awning-covered storefronts along the two blocks of redbrick downtown streets.

The peace and quiet of today's Oberlin is in stark contrast to its past: Oberlin was the site of the last Indian raid in Kansas on September 30, 1878, after a fierce skirmish had erupted between Chief Dull Knife's Northern Cheyenne, heading to regain their lands in the Dakotas, and an infantry contingent from Fort Dodge at what is today Lake Scott State Park, near Scott City 80 miles to the south. The Oberlin cemetery contains a memorial to the 19 settlers who were killed in the Cheyenne attacks, and the town has the early-October **Mini-Sapa Days,** commemorating the event. Downtown along South Penn Avenue, the worthwhile **Decatur County/Last Indian Raid Museum** (closed Sun., Mon., and holidays; $5; 785/475-2712) has eight preserved buildings, including a sod house.

Oakley

Possibly the most bizarre tourist trap the Midwest has to offer, **Prairie Dog Town** (daily May–Oct.; $8; 785/672-3100), sits along US-83 amid the olfactory assault of the I-70 junction. This collection—Home of the 8,000-lb. Prairie Dog, as the old roadside signs say—is a combination petting zoo and freak show, with collections of the eponymous little dogs as well as dozens of birds, snakes, bobcats, bison, and other Great Plains critters, many taken in as orphans, crammed into cramped cages. There's even a five-legged cow and a six-legged cow.

The rest of **Oakley** (pop. 2,045), south and west of I-70 and lined up along historic US-40, turns out to be an old, big-time ranching and railroad town, featuring lots of utilitarian architecture, massive diesel engines, farm supply stores, and

West of Oakley, on an 80-foot easel along the I-70 freeway in Goodland Kansas, keep an eye out for the World's Largest Van Gogh Sunflower Painting.

railroad tracks. The big event here, the **Fick Fossil Museum** (daily; free; 700 W. 3rd St.; 785/671-4839), just off US-83, features yet more unique exhibits: 11,000 fossilized shark teeth, a sod house, collections of pressed wildflowers, and some perfectly garish mosaics, including the Great Seal of the President of the United States, made entirely out of the aforementioned shark's teeth. It was created by—who else?—Mrs. Fick. The local history and paleontology exhibits are quite good, too.

The I-70 Business Loop (old US-40) offers the usual array of cafés and motels. The favorite local place to go for dinner and a drink is the very friendly **The Bluff** (210 S. Freeman Ave.; 785/671-8892), formerly Scotts Bluff and formerly a private club with great steaks and sandwiches. And there's no better place to hang out and overhear cowgirls, cattlemen, and assorted other bull-shippers shooting the breeze over a beer or two.

Chalk Pyramids/Monument Rocks

South of Oakley, the road bolts straight for over 20 miles, passing between an enormous sea of yellow flowers (in early summer) on one side and expanses of open range on the other. Later, the scenery peters out into a prickly, dry, faintly yellow, rocky desolation that signals the fringes of the Smoky Hills region.

The prime topographical feature of the Smoky Hills is the surreal **Chalk Pyramids,** also known as **Monument Rocks;** they are referred to in the old WPA *Guide to Kansas* as the "Kansas Pyramids." Whatever you call them, these highly eroded geological formations, which reach heights of 70 feet above the plains, are composed of layers of ancient seabed from the Cretaceous period and were originally formed 80 million years ago. The impressive spires,

Monument Rocks

karst-like formations, and shale cliffs farther on have yielded thousands of excellent fossils of sharks, shark teeth, fish, and reptiles. Although the pyramids are on private land, access is not restricted, but there are no facilities. To get there from Oakley, drive 20 miles south on US-83, then east for 4 miles on Jayhawk Road, around 3 miles south and another mile east; from Scott City, drive 18 miles north, turn east on Dakota Road and zigzag east and north for around 9 miles. Don't go in wet weather, however, or you'll get stuck in the mud, and you could be there for some time.

Traveling US-83 across the Midwest, you'll notice that most of the roadside services are found along the east–west crossroads, especially the major old transcontinental highways like US-6, US-30, or US-40, or today's Interstate superslabs. North–south travelers have always been a rare species.

You can get some good maps and directions at the friendly **Keystone Gallery** (620/872-2762), "conveniently located in the middle of nowhere" midway between Oakley and Scott City along US-83; the gallery also has a display of fossils from the Monument Rocks, and you can enjoy a sampling of local art and sculpture as well.

Lake Scott State Park and Scott City

Midway across Kansas, south of the Monument Rocks and west of US-83, **Lake Scott State Park** (daily dawn–dusk; $4.20 per car; 620/872-2061) is a true spring-fed oasis sheltering cottonwood, ash, hackberry, and willow trees in open high-sky rangeland. Beyond offering a lovely and relaxing spot in which to unwind, Lake Scott includes Kansas's most intriguing historical site, **El Cuartelejo** (The Old Barracks), the only Pueblo Indian community in Kansas and the farthest north of any in the country.

Originally settled in the 1660s by Taos Pueblo people fleeing the Spanish in New Mexico, the area became home to the Picuris about 30 years later. Both migrant groups joined with the local Plains Apache clan, but the oasis and the ruined pueblo buildings continued to be used for occasional nomadic squatting by the Pawnee, and later by Spanish and French explorers and traders, before eventually eroding away. In the late 1880s the site was discovered accidentally by Herbert Steele, who stumbled onto the extensive irrigation ducts leading from spring areas to crop patches. Further excavation eventually revealed the pueblo sites, now considered the first permanent-walled structures in the state. The park has a few other historical points of interest, including a marker on the site of the fateful last battle between the U.S. Cavalry and escaping Cheyenne Indians led by Chief Dull Knife. The park also has herds of elk and bison, and visitors can see the preserved home of Herbert Steele, full of pioneer furniture and farming implements.

South of Lake Scott State Park, US-83 continues across the high plains, with not a whole lot to disrupt the continuity until Garden City, another 45 miles south. The only town of any size is **Scott City** (pop. 3,816), with its

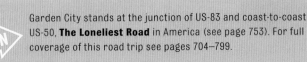

Garden City stands at the junction of US-83 and coast-to-coast US-50, **The Loneliest Road** in America (see page 753). For full coverage of this road trip see pages 704–799.

INTERSECTION

The Dust Bowl

Though it may not have been the biggest migration in U.S. history, it was certainly the most traumatic—entire families packing up their few belongings and fleeing the Dust Bowl of the Depression-era Great Plains. Beginning in 1930 and continuing year after year until 1940, a 400-mile-long, 300-mile-wide region roughly bisected by US-83—covering 100 million acres of western Kansas, eastern Colorado, and the panhandles of Oklahoma and Texas—was rendered uninhabitable as ceaseless winds carried away swirling clouds of what had been agricultural land.

The "Dust Bowl," as it was dubbed by Associated Press reporter Robert Geiger in April 1935, was caused by a fatal combination of circumstances. This part of the plains was naturally grassland and had long been considered marginal at best, but the rise in agricultural prices during and after World War I made it profitable to till and plant. Farmers invested in expensive machinery, but when the worldwide economic depression cut crop and livestock prices by as much as 75 percent, many farmers fell deeply into debt. Then, year after year of drought hit the region, and springtime winds carried away the fragile topsoil, lifting hundreds of tons of dust from each square mile, and dropping it as far east as New York City.

By the mid-1930s, many of the farmers had been forced to abandon their land, and while some were able to rely on a series of New Deal welfare programs, many more fled for California and the Sunbelt states. In this mass exodus, as recorded by photographers like Dorothea Lange and most memorably in John Steinbeck's 1939 novel *The Grapes of Wrath*, some 100,000 people each year packed up their few possessions and headed west, never to return.

Nowadays, thanks to high-powered pumps that can reach down to the Ogalala Aquifer, much of what was the Dust Bowl is once again fertile farmland, no longer as dependent on the vicissitudes of the weather. Much of the rest of the land was bought up by the U.S. government, and some four million acres are now protected within a series of National Grasslands that maintain the Great Plains in more or less their natural state.

miles and miles of cattle fencing, feed lots, innumerable cattle companies, and big American flags greeting you (or waving good-bye) at the town limits. It's a hardy, industrious place, with everyone busy working. Hard.

Garden City

One of the biggest towns in this part of the Great Plains, **Garden City** (pop. 26,658) is perhaps best known for its huge public **swimming pool**: around 330 feet by 220 feet, with 2.2 million gallons of water. It's south of US-50 at the end of 4th Street, near the Arkansas River in Finnup Park, and it only costs $1! Next to the swimming pool is a small historical museum and the nice **Lee Richardson Zoo** (620/276-1250), with rhinos, elephants, giraffes, and zebras. The zoo is free for people on foot but costs $10 for a drive-through tour.

North of the zoo in the brick-paved downtown (which unlike many places shows few signs of businesses fleeing to the highway frontages), you can window-shop (or even buy something) at the department stores and antiques shops, see a movie at the classic **State Theatre** on Main Street, or get a bite to eat at cafés like **Herb's Carry Out** (110 W. Kansas Ave.; 620/276-8021), which has great burgers, freshly made fruit pies, and famous fudge brownies. Yum! Another notable downtown landmark is the Windsor Hotel. After its construction in 1887, this "Waldorf of the Prairies" drew lots of cowpoke-luminaries, including Buffalo Bill Cody. Alas, the classic Windsor Hotel is a hotel no longer.

Garden City supports not only the usual gas stations, motels, and fast food, but also, best of all, the 3,760-acre **Sandsage Bison Range and Wildlife Area,** which may be viewed along the west side of Business US-83, around a half mile south of town.

Farther south, across the often dry-as-a-bone Arkansas River, oil pumps languidly dip their heads. This is where the stereotypical Kansas landscape comes in: either stark desolation or—thanks to money and modernity—vast irrigation efforts. Prior to the advent of reliable irrigation from the Ogalala Aquifer, over-eager farmers almost ruined the region's fortunes plowing up the fragile buffalo grass for a quick cash crop. But the winds then blew the topsoil away, so the hills that stood here prior to the Dust Bowl are gone completely now, and the landscape is endless, see-forever plains, marked by grain elevators and telephone poles.

At the Brookover feed lot along US-83 on the northwest side of Garden City, a huge sign standing atop a pair of grain elevators reads Eat Beef Keep Slim. From the comfort of your car you can hear the thousands of cattle burping and mooing up a storm.

Founded in 1879, Garden City was promoted by C. J. "Buffalo" Jones, one of many larger-than-life characters who populated the Wild West, and who was a pal of writer Zane Grey, who based the novel *Last of the Plainsmen* on Jones's life. One of Jones's many achievements was the capture and preservation of a small herd of buffalo, the descendants of which populate the buffalo preserve on the south side of town.

Liberal

First, the name. It's said that a munificent early settler came and dug a well, and whenever a dusty emigrant would offer money for a drink or the chance to wash his neck, the settler would say, "Water is always free here." One day the reply came, "That is mighty liberal." Rush Limbaugh wouldn't approve the word choice, but the name stuck, and now the town's stuck with it.

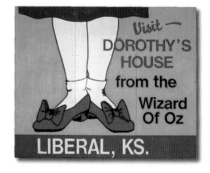

Second, the adjectives: hot, dusty, treeless, flat. The approach into town reveals the drab side of Liberal's oil, gas (the town lies on the eastern edge of an enormous natural gas field), and meatpacking industries.

A dozen miles north of Liberal, the majestic **Rock Island Line Railroad Bridge** *crosses the Cimarron River. The "Mighty Samson," at 1,269 feet long and 100 feet above the river, is among the largest of its kind.*

But the sights do improve. Honest. There is one significant draw, the top-notch **Mid-America Air Museum** (daily; $7; 2000 W. 2nd St.; 620/624-5263), on the site of the old Liberal Army Airfield. It's one of the five largest air museums in the United States and has amassed an astonishingly diverse collection of aircraft covering the entire history of flight, including military fighters and bombers from World War II and the Korean and Vietnam Wars.

Otherwise, there's a lot of "Ozmania" in town, since Liberal claims to be the home of Dorothy from the *Wizard of Oz*. Though there's not even the most tenuous connection between Liberal and the film or the book, apart from them all being set in Kansas, an annual **OzFest** blowout is held at so-called **Dorothy's House**, at the **Coronado House Museum** (daily; $7; 567 E. Cedar St.; 620/624-7624), a block north of US-54. This combination historical museum and re-creation of the movie's Kansas sets displays a mock-up of Dorothy's bedroom from the movie, a mini Yellow Brick Road lined by models of the film's animal heroes, as well as a horse bit left behind by the expedition of Don Francisco Vasquez de Coronado and his troops, who passed through in 1541 searching for the fabled Seven Cities of Cibola.

The city's most unusual attraction happens annually on Shrove Tuesday (a.k.a. Mardi Gras), when it holds its annual, international, soon-to-be-famous **Liberal's International Pancake Day race,** a competition between local housewives and their counterparts from Olney, England. No matter how cold or inclement the weather may be, the ladies of Liberal race a 415-yard, S-shaped course, each carrying a frying pan all the way. The Olney event purportedly dates from 1445, when a woman rushed to church with her pan still in her hand; the Liberal race has taken place since 1950.

US-83 and US-54, which is known as Pancake Boulevard in Liberal, claim the majority of Liberal's places to eat and sleep.

OKLAHOMA

On its beeline to Texas, US-83 doesn't just cross Oklahoma; it forsakes it, merely nipping the panhandle for a 37-mile dash. When crossing the border three miles south of Liberal, among the first things you see are a trailer park, a couple of bars, and a bingo hot spot. They're inauspicious sights at best. And that's not even mentioning the slate-flat, wicked badlands, with temperatures high enough in summer to occlude your vision of the blistering pavement and preclude a drive at top speeds. After a while, you're unable to conjure up synonyms for "endless," though there's plenty of time for it. Even the historical marker you think you eventually see winds up being in Texas.

TEXAS

The old WPA *Guide to Texas* says that "no other route across Texas offers such differences in topography, produce, climate, and people" as does US-83, which is still very true today. Starting at the Oklahoma border on the southern edge of the Great Plains, your route winds along the foot of the Caprock Escarpment, then opens out onto the cattle country of Edwards Plateau, where numerous river canyons provide respite from the mesquite scrubland, and finally ends up some 900 miles later at the Gulf of Mexico. Besides diverse landscapes, US-83 also passes through a virtual survey of Texas history: the prehistoric pictographs of **Paint Rock;** Mexican-American battlegrounds along the **Rio Grande;** 100-year-old frontier towns built of red brick around their central courthouses; and the modern Gulf Coast resort of **South Padre Island.** As you'll soon learn if you're perusing other Texas travel literature, this section of the state is, for the most part, ignored. Thus, you're definitely among an elite company, traveling along truly unbeaten paths.

In its 900-mile-plus crossing of Texas, US-83 is also known as the Texas Vietnam Veterans Memorial Highway. It forms the longest stretch of U.S. highway through any of the lower 48 states.

Perryton

Surrounded by wheat fields and ranch lands, agreeable **Perryton** (pop. 8,211) sits seven miles south of the Oklahoma border. The town was formed in 1919 when the Santa Fe Railroad came through; people in nearby towns simply picked up their stuff—buildings included—and shifted them here. Ochilton, eight miles south off US-83/Hwy-70, was one such town, before some 600 people moved the whole infrastructure. If you ignore the industrial oil-industry litter on the outskirts, Perryton's not bad-looking, with spacious, tree-lined streets. The self-styled "Wheatheart of the Nation," Perryton is also the hometown of Mike Hargrove, 1974 American League Rookie of the Year and later manager of the Cleveland Indians and Seattle Mariners.

Canadian

Exhibiting many of the up- and downsides of the Texas Panhandle region's boom-and-bust economy, **Canadian** (pop. 2,233) was founded in the 1880s as a railroad town, and later got rich developing oil and gas reserves. After an extended dormancy, Canadian is now hoping to grow again as a center for environmentally sensitive tourism, attracting bird-watchers and history-minded travelers who appreciate the brick-paved streets, 100-year-old buildings, and the delicate, walkable, wooden-decked wagon bridge that spans the Canadian River, two miles north of town.

A crossroads town at the junction of US-83 and cross-country US-60, Canadian has dubbed itself "The Oasis of the Texas Panhandle," and its riverside location offers the most trees for miles, as well as opportunities for experiencing some Great Plains hospitality while viewing herds of deer, wild turkeys, and the mating rituals of the odd-looking lesser prairie chicken (a member of the grouse family). In downtown Canadian, the interesting **River Valley Pioneer Museum** (closed Sun. and Mon.; 118 N. 2nd St.; 806/323-6548), on US-83, is the best place to get your bearings.

A dozen miles northeast of Canadian via paved Hwy-2266, the **Black Kettle National Grassland** maintains one of the few surviving portions of the natural landscape that once covered the Great Plains—where the deer and the antelope once played, and millions of buffalo roamed. Camping and hiking are available at Lake Marvin (580/497-2143).

For food, Main Street holds the popular **Our Fillin' Station,** in a 1940s Phillips 66 station (closed Mon.; 217 S. 2nd St.; 806/323-6504), alongside doughnut shops and lunch stands complete with the quintessential advertisement proclaiming "Good Eats." There are motels on the north side of town.

Four miles south of Canadian, along the east side of the suddenly four-lane highway that jointly carries US-60 and US-83, a huge **brontosaurus** stands atop a high bluff. The sculptor, former highway worker Gene Cockrell, named her after his wife, Aud. You may well spot other unique sculptures in and around town.

At Shamrock, US-83 crosses the legendary **Route 66** (see page 897). This full Chicago-to-L.A. odyssey is covered on pages 864–945.

Shamrock

Once a major oil-pumping and refining center, **Shamrock** is a dusty, rusty old industrial town, off I-40 and a mile south of historic Route 66, which survives as the Business Loop of I-40 through town. Though it's not a particularly lovely place, Shamrock does have at least one real highlight: the lovely old **Tower Gas Station** and **U Drop Inn** café, standing together in full art deco glory on the northeast corner of US-83 and Route 66. Following a long-overdue, very contentious $1.7-million state-funded restoration, these landmark buildings look great, but instead

Playing up the Irish connection, Elmore Park in the Route 66 town of Shamrock exhibits a reportedly genuine sliver of the Blarney Stone, encased in a hip-high hunk of green concrete, and there's an annual St. Patrick's Day parade and celebration.

of selling gas or serving food, they now dispense generous portions of helpful advice, courtesy of the friendly local **visitors bureau** (806/256-2501).

To discover more about Shamrock, visit the old brown-brick Reynolds Hotel, south of Route 66 and east of US-83, where the better-than-you-might-expect **Pioneer West Museum** (Mon.–Fri.; free; 204 N. Madden St.; 806/256-3941) has two dozen rooms

full of bygone goodies, including the complete interiors, fixtures, and fittings of a dentist's office, a barber shop, and a general store. There's also an exhibit honoring Apollo astronaut Alan Bean, who lived nearby in his youth.

For a bite to eat, it's hard to do better than **Big Vern's Steakhouse,** right on old Route 66 (200 E. 12th St.; 806/256-2088).

Wellington

South of Shamrock, US-83 passes over the Salt Fork of the Red River, which definitely deserves its name, running a muddy red throughout the rainy season. West of the highway rise the Rocking Chair Mountains, named after a large cattle ranch established west of here in the 1880s by a group of aristocrats, mainly younger sons of noble Scottish families. The only visible sign of their Hibernian legacy survives in place-names like Aberdeen, Clarendon, and **Wellington** (pop. 2,185), 25 miles south of Shamrock. The center of Wellington is west of the highway, where a nifty 1920s Ritz Cinema has been brought back to life ($7; 902 E. Ave.; 806/447-0090), but the US-83 frontage holds all the gas stations and cafés.

Childress

A vintage Texas town built around an old Spanish *zócalo* (town square), **Childress** (pop. 6,674) is an important shipping and supply point for surrounding grain and cattle ranches and serves as the market town for area cotton farmers. Located at the junction of US-83 and US-287, Childress was named after George Childress, the principal author of the Texas Declaration of Independence.

The once-picturesque downtown still houses the small but engaging **Childress County Heritage Museum** (closed Sat. and Sun.; free; 210 3rd St. NW—follow the signs). The downtown is one short step from dry, depressed implosion—the result of every business relocating to the congested, annoying fringe highways—but the elaborate 100-year-old facades provide ample opportunities for nostalgic photography and aimless wandering. Depending on your time of arrival, the brick-cobbled streets and empty shells of formerly grand buildings smack more of a ghost town, but there are a few good antiques shops taking advantage of the historic charm.

The **Goodnight-Loving Trail,** the famed frontier cattle trail, passed through Childress.

Virtually every motel in town lines US-287 (Avenue F) east and west of the junction with US-83, but thanks to their highway-side location ("Midway between Amarillo and Wichita Falls"), they all suffer from a lack of quiet and privacy.

Paducah

Many of the smaller, usually dirt, roads in Texas are labeled "FM," for farm-to-market, or "RM," for ranch-to-market, before their route numbers: e.g., "RM-1208." For simplicity's sake, we have labeled all of them "Hwy-##."

South of Childress, US-83 passes through a magnificent landscape of rich red and gold canyon lands covered with vast groves of trees. **Paducah,** 30 or so miles south of Childress at the junction of US-70, is a modest cotton town proudly arrayed around an art deco central courthouse modeled after an Egyptian temple. Brick-paved streets front abandoned stores and the huge old Cottle Hotel, which stands as a dormant reminder of better times, when harvest season or round-up would bring hundreds of transient field hands, cowboys, and card sharps into town. Nowadays Paducah offers little in the way of restaurants other than a doughnut shop and **Cracker's Steakhouse** (1112 Easley St.; 806/492-3171). You can find a room at three motels west of US-83 along US-70; other options will require more than an hour's drive, so if it's quitting time, check out **The Town House** (1301 Easley; 806/492-3595), the best of the lot.

West of Paducah along US-70 spreads the **Matador Ranch,** once one of the largest in Texas, with acres of hunter-friendly pasture and thirsty gullies amid semiarid canyons dotted with cedars and mesquite.

Hamlin and Anson

Deep in the heart of Texas, surrounded by miles and miles of green grass, red earth, mesquite and juniper trees, windmills, pump supplies, and peanut driers, the tidy town of **Hamlin** (pop. 2,124; "Home of the Pied Pipers") is full of charming folks and streets lined by locust trees.

Eighteen miles southeast of Hamlin, at the junction of US-180, sits **Anson,** named in honor of Dr. Anson Jones, the last President of the Republic of Texas. Anson was also a stop on the legendary Butterfield Stage U.S. Mail route that ran between St. Louis and San Francisco from 1858 to 1861, but these days it feels more like a stage set for *The Last Picture Show,* with handsome blocks of brick-fronted buildings forming a square around the stately Jones County Courthouse at the center of town. Anson is still a center for the local cotton industry, but its main claim to fame is the **Cowboys' Christmas Ball,** described in an 1890 poem by William Lawrence "Larry" Chittenden and recently revived by country-folk singer Michael Martin Murphey. In 1985 Murphey recorded a hit song also called "The Cowboy Christmas Ball," after which he helped recreate the annual dance here in Anson. Murphey has been hosting an annual Christmas party ever since, and also hosts an event at the National Cowboy Hall of Fame in Oklahoma City.

You can see almost all of Anson by driving through on US-83, but if you want to see a scale model of what Anson looked like during its 1900s heyday, or simply want to learn a little something about Texas, stop by the **Anson Jones Museum** (Fri.–Sun. 2–4:30 PM; 1302 Ave. K; 325/823-3683), across from the courthouse.

INTERSECTION

Anson marks the junction of US-83 and US-180, part of the cross-country **Southern Pacific** route (see page 831). For full coverage of this road trip see pages 800–863.

Abilene

At the junction of US-83 and I-20, **Abilene** (pop. 117,063) sits approximately in the geographic center of Texas. Abilene's fundamentalist Christian seminaries and the tame (for Texas) demeanor of its citizens have earned it the much-used nickname, "Buckle of the Bible Belt." Abilene, Texas, originally named after the raucous cowboy town of Abilene, Kansas, grew from nothing once the Texas and Pacific Railway came through in the 1870s. Then, as now, cattle played a predominant economic role, though Abilene's economy has diversified into other classic Texas endeavors, such as a huge U.S. Air Force base and oil refining. Abilene supports big-city amenities, including a symphony, though its indigenous fundamentalism precludes more libertine nocturnal notions; in 1925, the town fathers made it a misdemeanor, in the eyes of the law, to "flirt in a public place."

Abilene's downtown area, marked by a pair of 10-story towers, is not quite gentrified, but obviously galvanized for the attempt. The grand old Hotel Grace has been refurbished as the **Grace Museum** (closed Sun. and Mon.; $6,

Cowboys' Christmas Ball

All along US-83, but especially in the panhandle area of northern Texas, you pass through town after time-worn town that has clearly seen more prosperous times. Stately courthouse squares, massive old hotels, and blocks of all-but-abandoned storefronts testify to the depopulation of many rural areas in the wake of agricultural mechanization and a myriad of related economic and social changes. Looking at the photogenic remains of these once-bustling towns, it's hard not to imagine what life would have been like here during harvest, round-up, or holiday festivities, when every able-bodied man, woman, and child for miles would come to town to buy supplies, sell their goods, and socialize with friends and neighbors. An excerpt from an entertaining poem written about Anson, Texas, in 1890 by William Lawrence "Larry" Chittenden captures the vitality of these occasions, and gives a strong sense of the creative phraseology that animates cowboy poetry to this day.

Way out in Western Texas, where the Clear Fork's waters flow,
Where the cattle are a-browzin' and the Spanish Ponies grow;

free on Thursday evenings; 102 Cypress St.; 325/673-4587), with an art museum, an engaging historical museum, and a children's museum, all air-conditioned and well worth a look. East of downtown, the 13-acre **Abilene Zoo** (daily; $5) features a great exhibit on southwest and Texas Panhandle habitats, comparing veldts and plains of places as diverse as Africa and the United States, as typified by the local habitat of the "Elm Creek Backyard." In between the zoo

and downtown Abilene, you'll find **Frontier Texas,** an impressive high-tech historical museum. West of town is the **Dyess Air Force Base** and its "Linear Air Park," a collection of aircraft from World War II to Desert Storm; it's free and your parents' tax dollars already paid for it, so you may as well check it out. Dyess AFB is home to the bulk of the Strategic Air Command's potent B-1B bomber fleet, and in the 1960s it served as command center for Atlas Missile silos, five of which line the Atlas ICBM Highway (Hwy-604), which loops around the southeast fringes of Abilene.

Abilene Practicalities

Abilene's best place for food is the upscale **Cypress Street Station** (158 Cypress St.; 325/676-3463), next to the museums in the heart of downtown. If you'd prefer to search out some local flavor, aim for the classic Texan BBQ of **Harold's Pit BBQ,** on the north side of town (1305 Walnut St.; 325/672-

Where the Northers come a-whistlin' from beyond the Neutral Strip;
And the prairie dogs are sneezin,' as though they had the grip;
Where the coyotes come a-howlin' round the ranches after dark,
And the mockin' birds are singin' to the lovely medderlark;
Where the 'possum and the badger and the rattlesnakes abound,
And the monstrous stars are winkin' o'er a wilderness profound;
Where lonesome, tawny prairies melt into airy streams,
While the Double Mountains slumber in heavenly kinds of dreams;
Where the antelope is grazin' and the lonely plovers call,
It was there I attended the Cowboys' Christmas Ball.
The town was Anson City, old Jones' county seat,
Where they raised Polled Angus cattle and waving whiskered wheat;
Where the air is soft and balmy and dry and full of health,
Where the prairies is explodin' with agricultural wealth;
Where they print the Texas Western, that Hall McCann supplies
With news and yarns and stories, of most amazin' size…

—Larry Chittenden, *Songs of the Cowboys,* compiled in 1908 by Jack Thorp

4451), three blocks or so west of US-83. **Joe Allen's,** south of downtown in an unpromising industrial district (301 S. 11th St.; 325/672-6082), lost a little of its charm when it moved a few years ago, but the food, especially the rib-eye steaks cut to order as thick as you want 'em, is excellent.

Most of Abilene's accommodation options line up along I-20 or the older US-80 strip along the railroad tracks.

Buffalo Gap

If you're passing through Abilene, don't miss the restored frontier town of **Buffalo Gap** (daily; $7; 325/572-3365), 14 miles southwest of town via Hwy-89. It's not completely a tourist trap; cowpokes still reside here, and a courthouse and jail are just two of 20-odd buildings dating from the late 1800s, when Buffalo Gap, then the county seat, had over 1,200 residents and Abilene was barely a blip on the map. Other buildings are done up as Wild West souvenir stands, and there's at least one good restaurant: **Perini Ranch** (3002 Hwy-89; 325/572-3339), for steak and chicken.

Ballinger

Heading south from Abilene, the first real place you come to among the rolling sheep-herding hills of the Edwards Plateau is **Ballinger** (pop. 4,459), a lively little town with many of its brick and sandstone buildings dating from its inception in

Southwest of Abilene off US-277, about 20 miles beyond Buffalo Gap, Horse Hollow is home to **Horse Hollow Wind Energy Center** and what for a short while was the "World's Largest Wind Farm," where 421 giant turbines together produce as much as 735MW of eco-friendly, zero-emission electricity. At peak times, the wind farm generates enough power to supply 200,000 homes.

1886 as Hutchings, when the railroad came through. Standing along the banks of the Colorado River, the town now supports itself with agriculture. Within a block of the photogenic **Pompeo Coppini's Charles H. Noyes Statue** on the courthouse square, get a taste of Ballinger at the **Texas Grill** (325/365-9900), which has a nifty Texas-shaped neon sign. The courthouse itself is a Texas classic, completed in 1889 in opulent, mansard-roofed Second Empire style.

Paint Rock Pictographs

Fifteen miles or so south of Ballinger, just west of US-83, the **Paint Rock Pictographs** are the largest concentration of prehistoric drawings in Texas, with well over 1,500 brightly colored images covering a limestone bluff along the north bank of the Concho River. These images, which range in size from a few inches to over five feet tall, are on ranchland owned since the 1870s by the family of Kay Campbell, who offers two-hour guided tours through **Paint Rock Excursions** ($6 adults, $3 children, with a $15 minimum; 325/732-4376). Many of the paintings were made in the frontier days of the 19th century, when Comanche Indians lived in the region, but some are believed to date back over 1,000 years, to the time when Kiowa and Apache forebears settled here.

The town of Paint Rock is a relic of sorts itself, with photogenic abandoned buildings and a couple of picturesque churches.

Menard

South of Paint Rock, US-83 winds through another 40 miles or so of scrubby hills before reaching the fascinating old wool-products market

Coppini's statue at
courthouse square in Ballinger

town of **Menard** (pop. 1,491; pronounced "muh-NARD"), standing in a lush valley along the San Saba River. A trading post and stop on the old cattle trails, Menard was originally founded by Franciscan missionaries in 1757, and many of its early structures survive or have been restored.

It's a picturesque little place, with huge trees, solid old brick storefronts, and a wide, wide bridge over the river. **Menardville Museum,** housed in the old Atchison, Topeka and Santa Fe railroad depot, contains a 150-year-old wooden bar from the now-defunct Legal Tender Saloon. A block south of the old main drag, the **Historic Ditch Walk** follows a section of the 10-mile Vaughn Agricultural and Mechanical Canal, a fancy name for an irrigation ditch that has served local farmers since 1876. The canal features remains of the old waterworks and colorful flower plantings, and the walk passes the 1899 Sacred Heart Catholic Church and a vintage Sinclair filling station before finishing up, appropriately enough, at Menard's summer-only outdoor swimming pool.

Several historic limestone buildings in town date to the turn of the 20th century. The Luckenbach Building (built in 1903) contains the **Burnham Brothers Co.** (325/396-4572), the oldest U.S. retailer of game calls, from simple wooden instruments to state-of-the-art computerized devices that lure turkey, deer, elk, ducks, and other animals.

South of Ballinger along US-83, keep an eye out for a 100-foot-tall stainless steel cross, set on a hill east of the highway.

During Menard's annual **Jim Bowie Days** in late September, visitors and residents gather for arts and crafts shows, mock gunfights, live music, and the outdoor production of *Song of Silver,* a musical patterned after Bowie's life story.

On the main highway, **Sideoats Bakery & Café** (509 US-83; 325/396-2069) serves up tasty, health-conscious baked goods and breakfast items, and there are a couple of moderate motels, like the **Motel 83** ($41; 325/396-4549).

San Saba Mission

Two miles west of Menard, off US-190 on the banks of the San Saba River, a cemetery and foundations of a few buildings are all that's left of the **Santa Cruz de San Saba Mission.** Established in 1757 as Spain's northernmost outpost in the Apache and Comanche lands of what is now Texas, the mission was abandoned in 1768 after repeated Comanche attacks. Now a county park next to a golf course along Hwy-29, the rebuilt chapel houses a small museum; portions of a later stone fort, named **Real Presidio de San Saba,** also survive. A simple inscription, "BOWIE," on the stone gate is thought to have been carved by Jim Bowie of Alamo fame. Bowie lived at the presidio ruins while searching for buried Spanish silver during the early 1800s.

Fort McKavett State Historic Site

Farther along US-190, 17 miles west of Menard then another six miles south on Hwy-864, **Fort McKavett** (daily; $4; 325/396-2358) was called the "prettiest post in Texas" by Civil War General William Sherman. Established in 1852 as the "Camp on the San Saba," Fort McKavett served as a first line of defense against Comanche raids along the Texas frontier and provided protection for travelers along the Upper San Antonio–El Paso Trail. Temporarily abandoned in 1859, the post was re-established in 1868 after local residents lobbied for Army protection. All four of the Army's African-American units, whose ranks came to be known as **"Buffalo Soldiers"** by the Indians, eventually served at McKavett, including the famous 9th and 10th Cavalries. Fourteen of the original 40 buildings have been restored, including the officers' quarters, barracks, hospital, school, bakery, and post headquarters. Seven other buildings lie in ruins, and the rest are gone. The hospital ward serves as a visitors center and contains interpretive exhibits explaining the natural and military history of the area. A nature trail, passing through pastures of spring wildflowers, leads to a shady dell around the clear waters of Government Springs.

Junction

After passing through the attractively rugged but shallow canyon lands south of Menard, US-83 crosses high-speed I-10 at the aptly named town of Junction. Once a major crossing where the east–west Chihuahua Trail met a branch of the north–south Chisholm Trail (now I-10 and US-83 respectively),

Junction (pop. 2,688) sits at the edge of Texas's famed Hill Country, where the Edwards Plateau crumbles into limestone canyons and cliffs along the Balcones Escarpment. As in the areas to the immediate north, wool and mohair production are the main means of local livelihood, supplemented by pecan farming (not to mention catering to passing travelers).

From Junction, I-10 heads southeast to San Antonio, passing through the Hill Country town of Kerrville, which hosts the very popular **Kerrville Folk Festival** around Memorial Day. For information, call 830/257-3600.

To continue south along US-83, you can wind along Main Street or follow I-10 southeast for one exit, roughly two miles, to rejoin the old road. Another nice drive is along US-377, which traces a scenic route along the Llano River southwest of Junction, bisecting typical Edwards Plateau tableaus of limestone arroyos studded with mesquite, oak, prickly pear, and yucca. **South Llano River State Park** ($3; 325/446-3994), five miles southwest of Junction off US-377, protects 524 wooded acres and abundant wildlife (white-tailed deer, Rio Grande turkey, blue birds, finches, and javelina) and offers facilities for picnicking, camping, hiking, mountain-biking, canoeing, tubing, and swimming.

Leakey and the Frio Canyon

South of Junction, US-83 continues southward through nearly 62 beautiful miles of rolling ranches and native pecan orchards, entering a verdant, spring-filled region that was one of the last strongholds of the Lipan Apaches and Comanches. The rolling hills around **Leakey** (pop. 343; pronounced "LAY-key"; "Home of the 1975 State Football Champions") hold limestone caves, some of which the Confederates mined for bat guano to make saltpeter—an essential ingredient of gunpowder—during the Civil War. At 1,600 feet above sea level, this is one of US-83's prettiest reaches through Texas, as the road follows the clear, cold Frio River through 17 miles of cypress, pecan, live oak, cedar, walnut, wild cherry, piñon, and mountain laurel. Some areas also have bigtooth maples and sycamores, a major tourist attraction in the late fall when the leaves change color.

The hamlet of **Rio Frio** (pop. 50) boasts the largest live oak tree in Texas. The centuries-old tree stands alongside Hwy-1120 on the east side of the Frio River.

You'll find a dozen or more camps and lodges along this stretch of US-83—including tin-roofed, wooden-sided, bicycle-and-motorcycle only **D'Rose Inn and Cabins** ($75 and up; 830/232-5246) in the center of Leakey, and the peaceful **River Haven Cabins** ($165 and up; 830/232-5400), three miles southeast of town along Hwy-1120.

About 10 miles south of Leakey along US-83, the very pretty and very popular **Garner State Park** (830/232-6132) offers campgrounds, cabins, hiking trails, canoe rentals, pedal boats, river swimming, and a popular summertime dance terrace on the banks of the Frio River.

Texas Hill Country: Lost Maples and Utopia

While the landscape along US-83 is very pleasant, the scenery is much more rugged and beautiful if you detour to the east, into the heart of the Texas Hill Country. East of Leakey via Hwy-337 and then Hwy-187, there's a wonderful drive to **Lost Maples State Natural Area,** where miles of hiking trails take you away from the road into deep canyons carved by the Sabinal River. The "lost maples" of the name refers to a grove of bigleaf maples, which in October provide a taste of New England's famous fall color. The rest of the year Lost Maples is a real oasis: Texas laurels and wildflowers offer spring blooms, while juniper scent and birdsong fill the air. For the best overview, take the East Trail, a 4.2-mile loop that starts at the maple grove and climbs swiftly over a plateau before dropping down to a swimming hole at the foot of limestone cliffs. Camping (with hot showers) is available ($18; 830/966-3413), and a couple of nearby ranches offer characterful accommodations, like the **Foxfire Cabins** ($110 and up with off-season deals; 830/966-2200).

Lost Maples marks the start of the first official bike route in Texas, the **Utopia 100K,** which follows narrow, winding two-lane roads via Utopia to Garner State Park and back. Another popular cycling road is Hwy-337, which gets especially rugged (and popular with proto-Lance Armstrong cyclists) around Medina, midway to San Antonio.

South of Lost Maples, 15 miles east of Rio Frio via Hwy-1050, the Sabinal River town of **Utopia** represents a legacy left by frontier circuit preachers who found this spot a heavenly place to hold camp meetings and save souls. (This is Paradise—Keep it Nice, a sign says.) The **Sabinal Canyon Museum** (Sat.

Lost Maples State Natural Area

10 AM–4 PM, Sun. 1–4 PM; 830/966-3747) on Main Street displays local arts and crafts, including antique handmade quilts, historic photos, farm implements, arrowheads, spurs, and other artifacts that outline Bandera County history. Across from the museum, Utopia's best place to eat is the **Lost Maples Cafe** (830/966-2221).

Uvalde

Forty miles south of Leakey, US-83 crosses US-90 (the former San Antonio–El Paso Trail) at **Uvalde** (pop. 26,405), founded in 1855 and still centered on a broad square that originally served as a wagon yard for teamsters and travelers. Uvalde was the home of a Western legend, the late, great celluloid cowgirl Dale Evans; the town's most famous native son, John Nance "Cactus Jack" Garner, served as Franklin Delano Roosevelt's first- and second-term vice president (1933–1941). After retiring from politics, Garner returned to Uvalde and lived here until his death in 1967 at age 98. His home is now owned by the University of Texas and contains the **John Nance Garner Museum** (closed Sun. and Mon.; 333 N. Park; 830/278-5018), a repository of memorabilia from Garner's fascinating political career. (Renovations temporarily relocated the museum to the First State Bank of Uvalde for much of 2012.)

To get a taste of South Texas culture, tune in to "Tejano 102," **KUVA 102.3 FM,** for nonstop Tejano and traditional country-western tunes.

South of Uvalde: Crystal City

As US-83 continues south from Uvalde, the highway descends farther onto the mostly flat Rio Grande Plain, entering a subtropical zone of seemingly endless chaparral. Amidst this scrubby "brush country"—marked by a mixture of

Detour: The Alamo

One of the great icons of the American Southwest, the Alamo sits about 82 miles east of US-83, at the center of the city of San Antonio. "Remember the Alamo!" was never a question, but a pledge of allegiance that inspired frontier-era Texans to fight and win their independence from Mexico. The significance of the Alamo varies depending upon how you look at it—some see it as the first triumph of Yankee imperialism, others as a sad case of mighty, slave-holding southerners spreading their dominion—but from any angle, the story is quite compelling. The Alamo itself is a small Mexican church, built in 1724 and taken over by a band of Texans and Tejanos, including a band of American mercenaries led by Davy Crockett, in December 1835. Led by Col. William Travis, the volunteers were besieged and held out several months before they were eventually killed by the Mexican Army. Other Americans then defeated the Mexican Army and established the Republic of Texas, which briefly existed as an independent nation before joining the United States in 1845. The **Alamo church** (daily; free; 300 Alamo Plaza; 210/225-1391), right downtown, still stands much as it has for nearly 300 years and is a pilgrimage spot—one of the most visited sites in the country.

To soak it all up, stay the night at the historic **Menger Hotel** ($105 and up; 204 Alamo Plaza; 210/223-4361), across the street. The surrounding city of San Antonio is very attractive in its own right, with the lively River Walk winding through downtown, and numerous other sights and attractions. **Austin,** the Texas state capital, is just a ways up the road from "San Antone." Between San Antonio and US-83, the **Texas Hill Country** is perhaps the most beautiful part of the Lone Star State.

For more information, contact the **San Antonio visitors bureau** (800/447-3372).

thorny cacti, mesquite, dwarf oak, black bush, and huisache—spread large irrigated farms known as the "Winter Garden of Texas" for the bounty of spinach and citrus crops they produce. Nearly 40 miles south of Uvalde sits **Crystal City** (pop. 7,386), the Zavala County seat and self-proclaimed "Spinach Capital of the World," home to a pair of photo-friendly statues of the world's most famous spinach lover: Popeye. One stands on an island in the middle of the main street, Veterans Avenue. The other, older statue is a block away, in front of the City Hall.

Crystal City: "The Spinach Capital of the World"

Laredo

Founded as the first nonmissionary, nonmilitary Spanish settlement in North America in 1755, **Laredo** (pop. 236,091) is surrounded by some of the oldest ranch lands in the United States. With a population that is about 90 percent Hispanic, the city is growing rapidly (more than doubling in the past 20 years) due to its position as the largest international trade center along the U.S.–Mexico border. The I-35 corridor feels as anonymous and fast-paced as anywhere in the United States, but the center of town still holds on to its historic personality.

Eighteen miles north of Laredo, US-83 merges with I-35, then crosses the Rio Grande to meet Mexico 85 (the Pan-American Highway), forming a continuous road between Canada and the Panama Canal, via Mexico and Central America.

At the heart of downtown Laredo, a block north of the Rio Grande, is the **Villa de San Agustín Historical District,** site of the original 1755 Spanish settlement of Villa de San Agustín. Numerous historic buildings surround the plaza, including a small stone building next to La Posada Hotel that served as the

"The Gateway to and from Mexico" in 1892

capitol of the short-lived Republic of the Rio Grande. It now houses a **museum** (closed Sunday and Mon.; $2 and up; 956/727-0977) containing a collection of memorabilia from the separatist movement of 1840.

Built as a high school in 1917, the place to stay to soak up Laredo's substantial if faded character is the plaza's stately **La Posada Hotel** ($109 and up; 956/722-1701), which is also home to a good café and a more expensive Latin American restaurant, the Tack Room. Another old Laredo standout is on the old US-83 route, just west of the I-35 freeway: the timeless **La Reynera Bakery & Restaurant** (1819 San Bernardo Ave.; 956/722-6641), which has been serving breakfast tacos (here called *"mariachis"*), plus *pan dulce* (sweet pastries) and lunch specials since 1928.

Southeast from Laredo: Roma

South of Laredo, US-83 passes through one of the fastest-growing and most Hispanic areas in the United States, following a route parallel to the Rio Grande. The construction from 1950 to 1954 of **Falcon International Reservoir** altered the look and feel of the riverside landscape, but there are still a few places that evoke the past. The surviving 19th-century Spanish- and Creole-style architecture in **Roma,** 40 miles southeast of Zapata, hasn't changed much since it inspired director Elia Kazan to use the town as a film location for the 1952 movie *Viva Zapata!* starring Marlon Brando and Anthony Quinn. Many of the town's buildings have been quietly restored, and the town is *so*

The Texas League San Antonio Missions play Double A baseball at Wolff Municipal Stadium (210/675-7275), five miles west of downtown along US-90.

On the banks of the Falcon Reservoir, **Zapata, Texas** has become a popular starting point for long-distance hang-gliders. Many world hang-gliding records have been set from here, with flights traveling over 400 miles.

quiet you can sometimes hear roosters crowing across the river in the Mexican town of **Ciudad Miguel Alemán,** where the narrow sandstone streets, old churches, and plazas haven't changed in centuries.

Farther south along US-83 comes **Rio Grande City,** where among the historic buildings downtown the renovated **LaBorde House** ($70; 601 E. Main St.; 956/487-5101) is a Creole-style inn designed by Parisian architects in 1893 with construction completed in 1899.

Rio Grande Valley

¡Zapata!

Southeast of Rio Grande City, the river and US-83 curve eastward toward the Gulf of Mexico through a broad delta region known as the **Rio Grande Valley,** despite the fact there are no nearby mountains to make it a true valley. Compared to the rural stretches US-83 passes through for most of its journey, the Rio Grande Valley is a densely developed, chaotic, and generally poverty-stricken region, with little to recommend it apart from warm winter weather. Citrus orchards line the highway, while lush plantings of bougainvillea and poinsettias drape many of the houses in the string of towns and shantytown "colonias" that appear every few miles all the way to the Gulf. The population of the valley, which sits at approximately the same latitude as the Florida Keys, swells with the arrival each winter of over 150,000 "Winter Texans" fleeing colder climes like Canada and Michigan. This snowbird presence is celebrated by weekly square dance festivals, and perhaps the nation's highest concentration of RV and mobile home parks.

While US-83 runs as a multi-lane freeway past one big box mega-mall after another, the main attractions are to the south and west, along the Rio Grande.

The influx of "snowbirds" is perhaps most noticeable at the weekly open-air promenades held each Monday in **McAllen,** in the weeks leading up to February's **Texas Square Dance Jamboree.** As many as 10,000 people take part, making McAllen the unofficial "Square Dance Capital of the World."

The area's unique attraction is **Los Ebanos ferry,** the last hand-pulled ferry across the Rio Grande. The ferry is about midway between Rio Grande City and McAllen, south and west of Sullivan City. To get there from US-83, drive west on the mazelike El Faro road until you hit the river. In service daily 7 AM–3 PM, the ferry can carry three cars and a small number of pedestrians on each crossing, and you can help pull (if you want to). To be honest, there's not a lot at either end, but it's a fun ride.

Another main draw is the potential for bird-watching: About eight miles southwest of McAllen via Hwy-374 (west) and Hwy-2062 (south), **Bentsen-Rio Grande Valley State Park** (956/585-1107) protects precious acres

Crossing the Border

At dozens of sleepy little towns across Southern California, Arizona, New Mexico, and Texas, the temptation to nip across the border and see something of our southern neighbor can be strong. It's only a hop and a skip away, and the crossing is usually simple and hassle-free, but in these days of Homeland Security it's good to know a few things about international customs—small "c" and big "C"—before you go.

For years, all that a U.S. citizen needed to cross the border for 72 hours or less (and be re-admitted to the United States afterward!) was some proof of citizenship. Often, you could get by with just a driver's license, but in this age of increased security new rules have been implemented, so all travelers returning from Mexico or Canada must have a valid, current passport or other documents approved by U.S. Customs and Border Protection to re-enter the United States.

If you're thinking of heading south to stock up on Mexican beers or a rug or other handicrafts, NAFTA did nothing to change what you can bring back: In most cases, merchandise is subject to an $800 duty-free limit, above which U.S. Customs will charge a 10 percent duty based on fair retail value. Alcohol imports by individuals are limited to a whopping liter every 30 days—less than three cans of beer—and it is illegal to import Mexican versions of trademarked items (perfumes, watches, even cans of Coke!) that are also sold in the United States. So don't risk having to leave something behind at the border—ask before you buy.

It's probably a good idea before heading abroad to first to go over the U.S. Customs and Border Protection's pamphlet *Know Before You Go: Regulations for International Travel by U.S. Residents,* which can be downloaded from the agency's website at www.cbp.gov.

Because of insurance and other legal concerns, you should definitely leave your car on the United States side of the border and cross into Mexico on foot. Driving is not worth the hassle, especially with the long lines to cross back into the United States.

of Rio Grande riparian ash and elm woodlands, and it is home to the World Birding Center, which helps bird-watchers find their way around the dozen different wildlife refuges along the lower Rio Grande, where some 500 different species are regularly seen and heard.

Harlingen's **Arts and Heritage Museum** (closed Mon.; $2; 956/216-4901), three miles north of town at Boxwood and Raintree near the Harlingen airport, contains exhibits interpreting the history of the valley. At the private Marine Military Academy prep school, next to the airport, the **Iwo Jima Memorial** is the original sculpture (first made of plaster,

South of McAllen on the Mexican border, the town of **Hidalgo** has proclaimed itself the "Killer Bee Capital of the USA" and has a hundred-times-larger-than-life statue of one of these ferocious-looking critters, in front of the library at the center of town, to prove it.

now protected in fiberglass) from which the famous bronze statue of the flag-raising World War II Marines was made. There's also a small museum (Mon.–Fri.; donations; 956/423-6006) documenting the experience of Iwo Jima veterans.

Brownsville

South of Harlingen, US-83 merges with US-77 for the final 26 miles to **Brownsville,** where you may well feel like you've unknowingly crossed the border into Mexico. One of the most historic cities in Texas, Brownsville retains its Spanish and Mexican heritage more than most places, particularly in the architecture of the downtown district around Elizabeth Street, which runs northwest from the 24-hour border crossing at **Matamoros, Mexico.** U.S.–Mexico trade supports the local economy via a Union Pacific rail terminus connected with Mexico's national railway over the Rio Grande; also, a 17-mile deep-sea channel in the river delta links the city with the U.S. Inland Waterway System and the Gulf of Mexico.

Besides the historic downtown, another must-see is the well-endowed **Gladys Porter Zoo** (daily; $9.50; 956/546-7187) at Ringgold and 6th Streets, named by zoo professionals as one of the country's 10 best zoological facilities.

Sabal Palm Grove Sanctuary

The last remaining grove of the squat, endangered sabal palms in the Rio Grande delta (they are the only palm tree native to the continental United States) is protected for future generations in the 527-acre **Sabal Palm Grove Sanctuary,** run by the National Audubon Society and located about five miles southeast of Brownsville. The palms are nice enough, but the reserve is really for the birds: Bird-lovers flock here to catch a glimpse of the rare green jays, as well as the colorful parakeets and hummingbirds that make their homes in the dense jungle-like growth. Hundreds of species of butterflies are found here as well.

At time of writing the reserve had managed to reopen to the public after a year of closure, which occurred in part because of the economic downturn, but mainly because of Department of Homeland Security plans to build a giant fence between Brownsville and the Sabal Palm preserve, which would have stranded it outside the United States, leaving it effectively part of Mexico. To reach the reserve from Brownsville, take Boca Chica Boulevard (Hwy-4) east, then turn right (south) on Hwy-511/Hwy-3068. From the end of the road, turn right (west) on Hwy-1419 and follow the marked road to the sanctuary. The small **visitors center** (daily; $5; 956/541-8034) has maps and natural history guides to the sanctuary, which is open from dawn to dusk.

South Padre Island

Twenty-six miles or so northeast of Brownsville via Hwy-48 and the Queen Isabella Causeway, **South Padre Island** provides a strong contrast to the sleepy, historic towns of the Rio Grande Valley. Only the southernmost five miles of this 30-mile Gulf of Mexico barrier island are developed; sand dunes and tidal marshes dominate the remainder.

In the developed zone, multi-story hotels and condominiums line white-sand beaches on both the Gulf and Laguna Madre sides of the island. Rooms are easy to come by except during the annual spring break (mid-March),

giant shark at the Seven Seas Gift Shop, on Hwy-100 near South Padre Island

when some 200,000 college kids from all over Texas and the Midwest fill the hotels and beaches with round-the-clock revelry. Gift shops lining Hwy-100, the main route to "SPI," are fronted by giant sea shells, giant sharks, and a 40-foot dinosaur. The main daytime activity is sliding down the slippery chutes at the giant **Schlitterbahn Waterpark Resort** ($43 and up; 33261 Hwy-100; 956/772-7873). Drinking is legal on the beaches here—you have been warned. To dive in, try the **Padre Island Brewery** (3400 Padre Blvd.; 956/761-9585) for great seafood, sports on TV, pool tables, and microbrews; another popular spot is **Louie's Backyard** (2305 Laguna Blvd.; 956/761-6406), a bayside bar "as seen on MTV."

sand dunes on South Padre Island

The Great River Road

Old Man River, Father of Waters, "body of a nation," Big Muddy—by any name the mighty Mississippi River cuts a mythic figure across the American landscape.

Steamer G. W. Hill, Burlington, Iowa.

Mississippi Headwaters
pg. 235

475 mi

World's Largest Six-Pack
pg. 247

325 mi

Mark Twain's Hometown
pg. 265

425 mi

Elvis Presley's Graceland
pg. 283

80 mi

Delta Blues Museum
pg. 287

360 mi

Cajun Country
pg. 303

Between Lake Itasca and the Gulf of Mexico

Old Man River, Father of Waters, "body of a nation," Big Muddy: By any name, the mighty **Mississippi River** cuts a mythic figure across the American landscape. Who hasn't read Mark Twain or listened to *Showboat* and not dreamed of a trip down the Mississippi? If you're tired of waiting for somebody to buy you passage aboard the *Delta Queen* or to help you paddle among the 1,500-ton barges, then do what Huck Finn would have done if he'd had a driver's license: Tag alongside the Mississippi on the Great River Road.

Created in 1938 from a network of federal, state, and local roads, the Great River Road—also known as the River Road, and commonly abbreviated to "GRR"—forms a single route along the Mississippi from head to toe. Designed to show off the 10 states bordering the Mississippi from its headwaters to its mouth, the GRR is nothing if not scenic, and anyone who equates the Midwest with the flat Kansas prairie will be pleasantly surprised. Sure, farms line the road, but so do upland meadows, cypress swamps, thick forests, limestone cliffs, and dozens of parks and wildlife refuges.

Of course it isn't all pretty. There's enough industry along the Mississippi for you to navigate the river by the flashing marker lights on smokestacks, and a half dozen major cities compete with their bigger cousins on the coasts for widest suburban sprawl and ugliest roadside clutter. A pandemic of tacky strip malls has infected the region, too, but apart from the astounding growth in casinos (you'll never be more than 100 miles from a slot machine from one end of the Mississippi to the other) the GRR resists the developers' bulldozers because its meanders are shunned by a century increasingly drawn to the straight, fast, and four-lane.

A full 50 percent longer than the comparable route along the Interstates, the GRR changes direction often, crosses the river whenever it can, dallies in towns every other road has forgotten, and altogether offers a perfect analog to floating downstream. If the road itself isn't your destination, *don't* take it. For those who do travel it, the GRR spares you the fleets of hurtling 40-ton trucks and that Interstate parade of franchised familiarity, and rewards you with twice the local color, flavor, and wildlife (two- and four-legged) found along any alternative route. Lest these tangibles be taken too much for granted, every so often the GRR will skip over to a freeway for a stretch to help you sort your preferences. Savor, and enjoy.

MINNESOTA

The Great River Road begins in **Lake Itasca State Park** and stair-steps along occasionally unpaved but well-graded backcountry roads through a mix of northern boreal forest, tree farms, and hayfields, all the while staying as close to its namesake as possible. By **Grand Rapids,** only 130 road miles from its source, the Mississippi has been transformed from a grassy brook barely deep enough to canoe to an industry-sustaining river fed by a half dozen of the state's 10,000 lakes. Farther south, the red and white pines, paper birch, and bigtooth aspen give way to more farms while the route breaks from the surveyor's section lines to curve with the river across the glacially flattened state. By St. Cloud, the GRR enters an increasingly developed corridor that culminates in the hugely sprawling Twin Cities of **St. Paul** and **Minneapolis,** south of which the road slips into rural Wisconsin.

Lake Itasca State Park

The GRR begins here among the cattails and tall pines, in the park that protects the headwaters of the mighty **Mississippi River.** The small, clear brook tumbling out of the north end of Lake Itasca will eventually carry runoff from nearly two-thirds of the United States and enough silt to make the muddy plume at the river's mouth visible from space. But at its headwaters, 2,550-odd meandering miles from the Gulf of Mexico, you can wade across the Mississippi, and the water is still so clean and clear you can see the bottom.

The Mississippi's humble beginnings were the object of chest-thumping adventurers and the subject of not-so-scholarly debate for decades before explorer Henry Rowe Schoolcraft, led by Ojibwa native

If the rivers were being named today, the Mississippi River would flow into the Missouri River and not vice versa, since the Missouri is by far the longer of the two.

Throughout the upper Midwest, Friday night is the traditional night for a fish fry. Look for the backlit signboards or hand-lettered banners stuck out in front of the local VFW post or social club for a sample of the truly local variety.

© AVALON TRAVEL

Navigating the Great River Road

The Great River Road (or GRR) is identified on signs by a green pilot's wheel with a steamboat pictured in the middle. Quality and quantity of route markers vary considerably from state to state; some states, like Minnesota and Illinois, are well marked, with advance warning of junctions and confirmation after turns, while other states, like Louisiana and Mississippi, seem committed to hiding GRR signs miles from where they would serve any conceivable good. Adding to the confusion are the many variations—signposted as Alternate or State Route—and spurs, denoted by a brown pilot's wheel, which lead off the GRR to various points of interest.

Though most people will be able to find their way along the riverside without too many dead-ends, trying to travel the length of the GRR just by following the signs is not recommended for perfectionists; part of the fun is getting slightly lost and making your own way. To ease your journey, get a detailed map of the entire GRR, along with a guide to local happenings in each of the states along the route, from the **Mississippi River Parkway Commission.** Its very helpful, ad-free website is www.experiencemississippiriver.com.

Ozaawindib, determined this lake to be the true source of the nation's most legendary river in 1832. Schoolcraft's story, the tale of the battle to protect the park against logging, and lots of other Mississippi facts are found at the **interpretive center** just inside the park's north entrance (open year-round; $5 per car; 218/699-7251). Skeptics will also find out why professional geographers don't consider the two smaller lakes and the five creeks that feed Itasca competition for the headwaters title.

The fact that the lakeshore has been "improved" from its naturally marshy state, the surrounding old-growth pine forest—the most extensive stand of virgin timber left in the state—and outdoorsy amenities such as paved bike trails, boat launches, and café near the "official headwaters" all contribute to Itasca's popularity. Bike and boat rentals are available spring through fall (218/266-2150).

Accommodations include the grand turn-of-the-20th-century **Douglas Lodge,** where rooms cost $75–127 a night, and assorted lakeside cabins (all overnight reservations can be made at 866/857-2757). Just steps from the bike path and beach you'll find the immaculate, friendly, and bargain-priced **HI-Mississippi Headwaters Hostel** ($27 per person; 218/266-3415), which has rooms for families and couples as well as single travelers. When not fishing or foraging for your meals, consider the Douglas Lodge dining room, where the menu includes regional blueberries, wild rice, and walleye pike.

No matter when or how long you visit Lake Itasca, or anywhere in Minnesota really, be sure to pack plenty of potent repellent for ticks and mosquitoes.

Between Bemidji and Grand Rapids, the **Great River Road** follows a slower but more scenic parallel to transcontinental US-2 (see page 533). This **Great Northern** route across Minnesota is detailed on pages 492–583.

Bemidji

Less than a century ago, the northern forests of Minnesota were chock-full of lumber boom camps, with hundreds of mills and lumber works whining night and day, and dozens of saloons, brothels, and boardinghouses catering to the rough-and-tumble logging trade. The ravenous cutting wiped out the stands—virtually nothing remains of Minnesota's primeval pine forests—and the camps disappeared as quickly as they sprang up, but the woods have repeatedly grown back, to be harvested on a more sustainable basis while still providing an eye-pleasing backdrop to the region's literally thousands of lakes.

If you're practicing your Lake Wobegon language skills, be sure to say "You bet" in place of "You're welcome."

North Woods Public Radio broadcasts NPR news and other arts and cultural programming on a series of stations across northern Minnesota, including **KAXE 91.7 FM** in Grand Rapids.

From its boomtown roots, **Bemidji** (pop. 13,431) has long since settled down into a picturesque community—i.e., looking just as it did when Hubert Humphrey first ran for Congress—its compact and charismatic business district filling a half dozen blocks along the south shore of lovely Lake Bemidji. With large mills still busily turning trees into wood products, Bemidji is a typically industrious lumber town, remarkable mainly for having assisted in the birth of that well-loved legendary duo of logging lore, Paul Bunyan and his blue ox, Babe.

The main course of the GRR wraps around downtown Bemidji, so be sure to follow the Business Loop (old US-2), which passes up and over both the Mississippi River and Lake Bemidji while winding to downtown and a park where the town's big tourist draw, leviathan statues of **Paul Bunyan** and **Babe the Blue Ox,** have stood along the lakefront since their construction in 1937. Next to that big Paul and Babe on the lakeshore, the Bemidji **visitors center** (800/458-2223) boasts a fireplace made with stones from every U.S. state (apart from Alaska and Hawaii, which weren't states when the fireplace was built) and has displays with odd historical items—including Paul Bunyan's ax and his oversized underwear.

PRICE 15 CENTS

Home of Paul Bunyan

BEMIDJI
MINNESOTA

Invites You

. . . to REST AND RELAX in the LAND OF LAKES AND PINES

Along with Paul and Babe, Bemidji offers endless opportunities for water-skiing, canoeing, fishing, ice-fishing, and autumnal leaf-peeping (it's also the "Curling Capital of the USA"). Bemidji also has the northernmost outpost of a café destined to detain the most discerning road-food aficionado: the **Maid-Rite Diner** (1602 Bemidji Ave.; 218/444-7224), near the

The Legends of Paul Bunyan

Like most other myths born on the American frontier, the legend of Paul Bunyan is obscured in the mists of time. Tall tales describe his life: When he was born it took five storks to deliver him and it took a whole herd of cows to keep him fed; at just a week old he was big enough to wear his father's clothes; he once bent a crowbar and used it as a safety pin to hold his pants together; he was able to fell trees an acre at a time; and he used to whistle through a hollowed-out log. The stories are impossible to trace, though their widespread popularity is due primarily to a public relations man at the Red River Lumber Company, William Laughead.

Beginning in 1914, and continuing for the next 20 years, Laughead and the lumber company, which was owned by the Walker family (founders of the Walker Art Center in Minneapolis), published a series of illustrated booklets recounting the stories already in general circulation around the logging camps. The booklets bore the full title *The Marvelous Exploits of Paul Bunyan as Told in the Camps of the White Pine Lumberman for Generations, During Which Time the Loggers Have Pioneered the Way through the North Woods from Maine to California, Collected from Various Sources and Embellished for Publication*.

The first large statue of Paul and Babe was built in 1937 in Bemidji, where it now stands along the lake. Statues of Paul and Babe were later built in nearby Brainerd, Minnesota, and others can be found in logging towns from coast to coast, like Klamath, California, and Bangor, Maine.

Bemidji State college campus. A classic diner, it's open from 7:30 AM for famous "loose meat" sloppy joe sandwiches and homemade rhubarb pies. Another good fast-food option is **Dave's Pizza** (218/751-3225) at 15th and Irvine on the north side of town, while the old downtown area has a couple of inviting pubs, like **Brigid's Cross** (317 NW Beltrami Ave.; 218/444-0567), serving good food and great beer, two blocks from the lakefront.

Bemidji's many motels include the family-oriented **Hampton Inn** ($130 and up; 1019 Paul Bunyan Dr.; 218/751-3600 or 800/776-3343), situated on the lake, with its own beach and complimentary canoes available to guests.

Walleye pike is a mild whitefish sought by Midwest anglers from May through the cold of February. The walleye found in Minnesota restaurants all come from Red Lake, site of the only commercial walleye fishing allowed by law.

Bemidji to Grand Rapids: The Big Fish

Leaving downtown Bemidji along the edge of the lake, the GRR makes a series of backcountry loops past tree farms and at least six of the state's 10,000 lakes, crossing US-2 twice before snaking into Grand Rapids 100 miles later. The road hugs red pine– and aspen-wooded shores and crosses the ever-widening Mississippi eight times, while numerous signs

Big Fish Supper Club

point to unseen resorts, which in Minnesota don't offer luxury so much as proximity to good fishing. Fishing is serious business hereabouts, as is evident from the frequency of signs advertising Leeches-Minnows-Nightcrawlers.

If you're just passing through, one place to set aside some time for is about halfway along, in the hamlet of Bena. Right along US-2, a 65-foot-long tiger muskie, with a 14-foot-wide mouth, welcomes customers to the popular **Big Fish Supper Club** (218/665-2299). As seen in that classic Chevy Chase road-trip movie *National Lampoon's Vacation,* the friendly café is open for dinner and drinks every day, except during the depths of winter.

Grand Rapids

Navigational headwaters of the Mississippi River, **Grand Rapids** (pop. 10,869) is a small Frank Capra–esque kind of place, known for its four large in-town lakes (there are over 1,000 in this part of the state) and a great bridge over the river. The town—which is proud of its recent rating as the 49th Best Small Town in America—can be a bit confusing in its layout, but its compact size makes sightseeing manageable.

The city sits along the western edge of the famed Mesabi Iron Range and includes viewing sites at a handful of open pit mines. The iron mines are a thing of the past, but Grand Rapids is still a major lumber town, and you can tour the impossible-to-miss **Blandin Paper Mill** (Wed.–Fri.

Cass Lake was home to Ka-Be-Nah-Gwey-Wence, whose Anglicized name was John Smith, an Ojibwa who lived to be somewhere between 129 and 137 years old. It is said he never slept in a bed. It may be unrelated, but the lake enjoys a reputation for having some of the most beautiful and serene camping in the state.

Grand Rapids is very proud of its most famous daughter, Judy Garland, and whoops it up every June with a festival in her honor.

10 AM–3 PM; free; 218/327-6682). One of the world's largest paper producers, Blandin owns most of the surrounding forests and turns the trees into the stock onto which magazines like *Time* and *Sports Illustrated* are printed.

Three miles southwest of Grand Rapids, well signed along the Great River Road and equidistant via US-169 or US-2, the fine **Forest History Center** (daily in summer, weekends only rest of the year; $8; 218/327-4482) is a living-history replica of a 19th-century logging camp, complete with nature trails through the surrounding woods and energetic lumberjacks rolling logs and telling tall tales.

In the center of town, the **Itasca Heritage and Arts Center and Judy Garland Exhibit** ($4; 10 NW 5th St.; 218/326-6431) is housed in a three-story 1890s Romanesque-style grade-school building at the crossroads of US-2 and US-169.

Grand Rapids' real draw is the self-proclaimed "World's Largest Collection of Judy Garland Memorabilia," she of ruby-slipper fame having been born Frances Ethel Gumm in Grand Rapids on June 10, 1922. Truly a cradle-to-grave biographical assembly, the collection displays everything from her first crib to photos of her early performances as part of the Gumm Sisters, a family vaudeville group, to a final shot of her tomb in Hartsdale, New York. There are posters from most of her movies and a copy of her costume from *The Wizard of Oz* (although the ruby slippers were stolen some years ago).

West of Grand Rapids, near Cohasset, a low ridge divides this area of Minnesota and distributes the rivers and streams into three watersheds: south to the Gulf of Mexico, north to the Hudson Bay, and east to the Great Lakes.

All of these artifacts are on display, alongside the house where she was born, at the **Judy Garland Museum** ($8; 2727 S. US-169; 218/327-9276).

Aitkin

South of Grand Rapids, the land rivals Kansas for flatness, yet the mix of farms and forest continues to lend visual interest to what could otherwise be achingly monotonous. The GRR alleviates boredom with its sinuous irregularity, the curves always hinting at the proximity of the Mississippi. For most of the way the river itself remains hidden, although regular signs for boat landings confirm its presence, and on occasion its broad channel and tree-lined banks roll into view.

For nearly 70 miles south of Grand Rapids you will have this rural road to yourself; then at the single stoplight in **Aitkin** (pop. 2,165), the GRR joins busy Hwy-210, at the edge of the mid-state lakes region. Aitkin is best known as the site of the annual **Fish House Parade,** in which ice fishers show off their one-of-a-kind refuges from the winter cold; this unique event is held every year on the Friday following Thanksgiving. Year-round, Aitkin is a nice, all-American town, with a still-in-use 1930s movie palace (The

Rialto, on Minnesota Avenue), and the very good **Aitkin Bakery** (14 NW 2nd St.; 218/927-2019).

Some of the best pies in the land of great pies can be had 20 miles north of Aitkin in the riverside town of Palisade (pop. 167), where the wonderful Palisade Café (210 Main St.; 218/845-2214) sells all sorts of fresh homemade pies.

Crosby

Watch your compass needle for signs of deflection as you proceed to the small but tidy town of **Crosby,** the center of Minnesota's "forgotten" iron range, the Cuyuna. The flood-prone mines have died out, but the surrounding landscape still bears evidence of mining's heyday, with lakes and hills created by subsidence and strip mining, and also by contemporary gravel quarrying. Crosby itself has a nice park fronting onto Serpent Lake, complete with a brightly colored, 50-foot-long sea serpent, while **Croft Mine Historical Park** (daily in summer; tour $3.50; 218/546-5466), well posted on the edge of Crosby, profiles the iron-mining industry, covering immigration and labor issues as well as the actual mining process. Machinery, period buildings, a gift shop, and a simulated underground tour round out the site's features.

Between Grand Rapids and Brainerd, the official GRR takes a slow and somewhat scenic route along country lanes, though you'll save many hours (and not miss that much) by taking US-169 and Hwy-210.

South of Crosby, the GRR leaves the truck traffic and takes to the cornfields and sumac-laced forests again, passing as many barns as houses, the occasional lakeside hideaway, and some rural town halls; for a thumbnail overview of the area's settlement history, keep an eye peeled for the historical markers along the way.

Brainerd

At roughly the geographical center of the state, **Brainerd** (pop. 13,590) is a medium-sized Minnesota town that played a starring role in that offbeat Coen brothers movie, *Fargo.*

A huge Wausau paper mill along the banks of the river notwithstanding, the economy of this part of the state benefits greatly from recreation. In Minnesota this means lakes: over 400 within a 50-mile radius, with over 150 resorts or campgrounds on their shores. Brainerd, the commercial center of it all, began life in 1870 when the Northern Pacific Railroad chose to cross the Mississippi River here. The rail yards are still in the

Twin Cities: Minneapolis and St. Paul

The Twin Cities share the Mississippi River but have little else in common. In general, Minneapolis has fashion, culture, and reflective glass, while St. Paul has a greater small-town feel, more enjoyable baseball, and the state capitol. Together, the Twin Cities are a typically sprawling American metropolis with an atypically wholesome reputation: safe, liberal-minded, welcoming to strangers, and inclined to go to bed early. Don't fret; there's enough to keep the visitor fully entertained.

Walker Art Center

The best place to stop and get a feel for the Twin Cities is at the **Minneapolis Sculpture Garden,** on Lyndale Avenue along I-94 (daily 6 AM–midnight; free). This is one of the city's finer urban oases, with over 40 works of art ranging from Henry Moore to Claes Oldenburg's Pop Art *Spoonbridge with Cherry*. Running over the I-94 freeway, a sculptural footbridge adorned with words from a John Ashbery poem connects the sculpture garden to Loring Park and the pedestrian greenway to downtown (an in-line skater's heaven). Next to the garden is the **Walker Art Center** (closed Mon.; $10; 612/375-7622), rightfully renowned as one of the nation's finest contemporary art museums and an architectural marvel.

Across the Mississippi in St. Paul, at the **Minnesota History Center** (closed Mon.; $10; 345 W. Kellogg Blvd.; 651/259-3000), off I-94, you can dance in a re-created 1940s swing ballroom. Exhausting? Maybe. Worth it? You bet!

Another advantage of visiting the Twin Cities: Baseball fans have two choices, and both are a blast. The major league **Minnesota Twins** play outdoors at **Target Field,** in the lively Warehouse District on 3rd Avenue, between 5th and 7th Streets. The unaffiliated, independent, and generally anarchic **St. Paul Saints** play outdoors at usually sold-out **Midway Stadium,** north of I-94 at the Snelling Avenue exit ($5–10; 1771 Energy Park Dr., 651/644-6659). The fun-loving Saints fans cheer as freight trains rumble past the outfield fences, and they are treated to a fireworks show every Friday night.

Practicalities

The Twin Cities are on opposite sides of the Mississippi River, at the crossing of the I-35 and I-94 freeways. (It was a bridge along the I-35W freeway that collapsed in August 2007, killing 13 people; in typically cooperative Minnesota fashion, the replacement bridge was finished in just over a year.) Located seven miles south, the Minneapolis–St. Paul International Airport (MSP) is served by 10 major airlines, with Northwest Airlines exercising the home field advantage. Drivers here, like all Minnesotans, are friendly and helpful, and the city grids are easy enough to navigate by car, although on-street parking becomes more scarce as you approach the downtown areas. There are many parking garages (called "ramps"), and rates vary considerably.

Eating is perhaps the area where the Twin Cities really show off their multi-cultural vitality to best advantage. There are large Central American, Caribbean, Somali, Kurd, and Hmong populations here, and the traditional dominance of meaty northern and eastern European cuisine is being challenged by a bumper crop of new and different places to eat all over town. For a sample, head to **Chino Latino** (2916 S. Hennepin Ave.; 612/824-7878), where the Sushi Loco selections capture all the complexity and contradiction underlying the Twin Cities' calm surface.

For a taste of old-style Minnesota, there's still **Nye's Polonaise Room** (112 E. Hennepin Ave.; 612/379-2021), just over the bridge from downtown, a dimly lit, plush-boothed, 1950s surf-and-turf restaurant with sing-along polka concerts on the weekends. For another touch of the Twin Cities' past, nearby **Kramarczuk's Deli** (215 E. Hennepin Ave.; 612/379-3018) has fat wursts and borscht, as well as *varenyky, nalesnyky,* and *holubets* (a.k.a. dumplings, crepes, and cabbage rolls), all served up cafeteria-style beneath coffered tin ceilings and the gaze of a giant Miss Liberty holding aloft her lamp.

Without doubt, the best road-food place is the decidedly ungentrified, 24-hour **Mickey's Dining Car** (36 W. 7th St.; 651/698-0259), right in downtown St. Paul opposite the bus station. Haute cuisine it ain't, and half the regulars treat it as a social service agency, but this 1937 O'Mahony is a fine example of what has become an endangered species since the proliferation of double arches.

If you're traveling on an expense account, downtown Minneapolis has the hotel for you: the sleek, modern **Graves 601** ($209 and up; 601 N. 1st Ave.; 612/677-1100 or 866/523-1100). In St. Paul, the **St. Paul Hotel** ($159 and up; 350 Market St.; 651/292-9292 or 800/292-9292), across from the beautiful Ordway Music Theatre, is a 1910 gem built for the city's rail and mill tycoons and has a rooftop gym. For a unique stay, try the **Covington Inn** ($140–235; 651/292-1411), a tugboat B&B moored on the Mississippi opposite downtown St. Paul. Otherwise, look to the Interstate beltways for the national chains, particularly I-494 between the airport and Bloomington's 100-acre **Mall of America,** the nation's largest.

The **Greater Minneapolis Convention and Visitors Association** (250 Marquette Ave.; 612/661-4700) can provide complete information on hotels, restaurants, and attractions.

heart of town beneath the giant water tower, which resembles a Las Vegas–style medieval castle. The historic downtown has been badly "malled" by outlying shopping plazas, but among the discount merchandisers, pawn shops, and empty storefronts there are still a few points of light, such as the **Front Street Cafe** (616 Front St.; 218/828-1102), across the tracks from that faux piece of Camelot. With free seconds on soups, mile-high meringue on the pies, and unbelievably low prices, the Front Street Cafe sets a hip standard for square meals.

South of Little Falls, the GRR continues on its meandering way, but you can switch over to the uglier but much faster US-10 or I-94 freeways for the ride into the Twin Cities without missing anything significant.

East of downtown Brainerd, there is a 27-foot statue of a sitting Paul Bunyan at **Paul Bunyan Land** (daily in summer; 17553 Hwy-18; 218/764-2524), part of the 35-acre kid-friendly rural-history theme park.

The Fourth of July in Brainerd is a big event, with marching bands, rock bands, and parades—plus a rubber duck race down the Mississippi River.

Across the Mississippi from Monticello, 2.5 miles downstream from Elk River off US-10, the **Oliver H. Kelley Farm** living history center preserves the place where the Patrons of Husbandry, an agricultural education and lobbying organization better known as The Grange, was founded in 1867.

Many chain motels are clustered along the GRR (Hwy-371) and on Hwy-210 heading west out of Brainerd.

Crow Wing State Park

South of Brainerd, the GRR speeds along Hwy-371, which yearns to be an Interstate for the 30-odd straight miles it takes to reach Little Falls. Exceedingly flat and awash in a sea of corn, the region gives no hint of the Mississippi River except at **Crow Wing State Park** ($5; 218/825-3075). Native Americans, missionaries, fur-trappers, and lumberjacks made Crow Wing a thriving town until the 1870s, when the forced removal of the Indians and the shift of trade to the rail crossing at Brainerd turned Crow Wing into a ghost town. These days only cellar depressions, a cemetery, and a single surviving home remain around the old townsite, while trails, a picnic area, and campsites spread out beside the confluence of the Mississippi and Crow Wing Rivers.

Little Falls

At **Little Falls** the GRR neatly misses the fast-food and gas claptrap that has sprung up along the busy Hwy-371 bypass, proceeding instead through the heart of town, which would probably still be recognizable to aviator Charles Lindbergh, who spent his boyhood summers here a century ago. Running along the west bank of the river, the GRR passes by the **Charles A. Lindbergh House and History Center** (daily in summer; $7; 1620 Lindbergh Dr. S.; 320/616-5421). The house, which sits a mile south of town on a beautiful stretch of the Mississippi, bears the unusual distinction

Charles A. Lindbergh

of having been restored with the meticulous guidance of "Lucky Lindy" himself. Lindbergh wanted the site to honor his father, a five-term U.S. congressman, as well as himself, and so it does. Exhibits also illustrate the junior Lindbergh's life and achievements after his historic solo flight across the Atlantic in 1927. There is little mention of Lindy's public admiration for Adolf Hitler, but the museum does display Lindy's 1959 VW Beetle, which he drove more than 170,000 miles on four continents.

The Burma-Vita Company, based just west of Minneapolis, began erecting advertising signs along Hwy-61 near Red Wing and Hwy-65 near Albert Lea back in 1925. Over the next 38 years, these signs and their witty rhymes appeared in nearly every state in the United States and made Burma-Shave one of the most recognized brand names in American business.

Driving the Twin Cities

South of Little Falls, agriculture continues to dominate the landscape, but as our route approaches the junction with I-94 at St. Cloud, the loss of farms foreshadows what is to come downriver. For nearly 100 miles, the GRR does its best to offer a scenic alternative, but sprouting subdivisions and suburban minimalls make it hard to enjoy. I-94 parallels the GRR and the Mississippi River all the way through the heart of the Twin Cities, and for better or worse it's pretty much the closest you'll get to a riverside highway. If you were hoping to follow the river through this stretch (by car, at least), you're out of luck.

WISCONSIN

Heading out of St. Paul along the industrialized Mississippi riverbanks, the GRR crosses the St. Croix River at Prescott, Wisconsin, and wends south on Hwy-35 across a portion of the glacial plain whose rolling hills, sown in corn, account for an important part of the nation's breadbasket. The fertile soil here, as throughout the Midwestern grain belt, is a product of drift: pulverized soil left by mile-thick ice sheets scouring the ancient sediments of an inland sea for about two million years. Farther south, however, the GRR enters a very different landscape, known as the **Driftless Region,** an area of limestone bluffs and rocky uplands bypassed by all that rototilling glaciation. Stretching south into Illinois, and covering an area four times the size of Connecticut, the Driftless Region affords dramatic views, wildlife habitat, and a setting for one of the more painful episodes in Native American history, the devastating Black Hawk War.

The GRR follows two-lane Hwy-35 from Prescott south for nearly 100 miles, staying within closer view of the Mississippi for longer stretches than almost anywhere else on the route.

On the Minnesota side of the Mississippi River, US-61 runs as a very fast and fairly scenic freeway, four lanes wide with near-continuous river views almost all the way south to La Crosse, Wisconsin. One place along here worth a linger is the town of **Wabasha**, as seen in the Walter Matthau/Jack Lemmon film *Grumpy Old Men*. Another is **Lake City**, where banners and billboards proclaim it the "Birthplace of Water Skiing."

On an island near Red Wing, Minnesota, the Prairie Island Nuclear Power Plant is the northernmost of a half dozen uranium-powered generating stations located along the Mississippi.

Hwy-35: Main Street USA

At **Maiden Rock,** about 50 miles southeast of St. Paul, Hwy-35 enters the heart of the Driftless Region, picking its way between steep bluffs and the wide Mississippi. Small towns, populations numbering only in the hundreds, cling to the margin, competing for the distinction of having the longest **Main Street** in the nation, if not the world; for some of these long hamlets the GRR is nearly the *only* street. These towns wear their age well, too busy with fishing or loading up barges to make themselves pretty for tourists, or to tear down every old building that no longer seems useful. Most of these towns have at least a gas station, open late, and a roadhouse with Old Style or Pabst neon in the windows, open even later. Along with the riverside scenery, most also have a single tourist attraction: Amish crafts in **Stockholm,** a cheese factory in **Nelson**— and **Alma** has an observation platform and small café over Lock and Dam No. 4, where you can watch river traffic "lock through." In **Pepin,** midway between Maiden Rock and Alma (and roughly midway between Minneapolis and La Crosse), there's a replica of the log cabin where Laura Ingalls Wilder was born in 1867. Her first book, *Little House in the Big Woods,* was set here, though it's hard now to imagine that this was still the wild northwestern frontier back then (but it was).

Trempealeau

At the sleepy hamlet of **Trempealeau** (pop. 1,435), the GRR would have you zigzag right through town, but detour a block down toward the river's edge to find the **Historic Trempealeau Hotel, Restaurant & Saloon** ($110 and up; 608/534-6898), sole survivor of an 1888 downtown fire—maybe that's why the whole joint is smoke-free. The hotel dining room offers a surprisingly eclectic menu, from steak and seafood to Tex-Mex and vegetarian dishes; just head for the neon sign reading Delicious Food. The rooms are nice (and cheap!), and the hotel also sponsors an excellent annual out-

door music series beginning with a **Reggae Sunsplash** the second weekend of May and featuring bands you've heard of throughout the summer (Steppenwolf and Asleep at the Wheel have appeared more than a few times). The hotel rents canoes and bicycles to hardy souls desiring to try either the **Long Lake Canoe Trail** or the 100 miles of paved bikeways that pass through town.

Just south of Trempealeau, the GRR crosses US-53. Consider taking this Interstate-wannabe into La Crosse to avoid the uninteresting 12 miles of stop-and-go traffic through Holman and Onalaska, La Crosse's northern abutters.

La Crosse

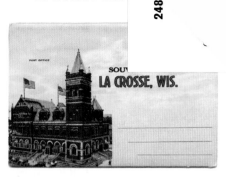

La Crosse (pop. 51,320) was named by fur-traders who witnessed local Winnebago Indians playing the game. It's an attractive place, but you wouldn't know that coming into town from the north; thanks to the town's location astride the I-90 freeway, miles of food-gas-lodging establishments compete for attention. Successfully run the gauntlet and your reward will be finding the century-old downtown, the tidy residential neighborhoods, and the leafy University of Wisconsin—La Crosse campus. Slap *Spartacus* on the theater marquee and the whole place could easily be mistaken for a giant Eisenhower-era time capsule.

Between Minneapolis and La Crosse, Winona State University's **KQAL 89.5 FM** plays an excellent range of commercial-free pop, punk, and world beat music.

The biggest sight to see in La Crosse is the **World's Largest Six-Pack,** right on the GRR on the south side of downtown (1111 S. 3rd St.). La Crosse–based Heileman was widely recognized around the upper Midwest for its Old Style brand beer, and its brewery was famous for its giant fermentation tanks painted to look like the world's largest six-pack. Alas, about 10 years ago Heileman's brewery was bought out by a multinational company, which immediately whitewashed over what had long been a cherished local landmark. Then a local company, City Brewing, took over operations and brought back the big Six Pack, which when full holds enough beer to fill more than seven *million* real-life cans.

The best overview of La Crosse is two miles east of downtown at the end of Main Street: **Grandad Bluff,** a lofty 590 feet over the city, gives a grand view of the Mississippi and the two states along its opposite shore.

La Crosse Practicalities

La Crosse food tends toward the hearty and all-American. For good ol' drive-in burgers, chili dogs, root beers, and milk shakes, nothing beats **Rudy's** (608/782-2200), northeast of downtown at 10th and La Crosse Streets, where roller-skating car-hops feed you 10 AM–10 PM daily, weather permitting. Rudy's sponsors classic car "Cruise Nite" every Tuesday, June–September.

The Pearl, a polished-to-perfection confectionery (207 Pearl St.; 608/782-6655), offers such indulgences as fluorescent Blue Moon ice cream, while the Andrews Sisters harmonize in the background. More grown-up pleasures, in the shape of nearly 400 bottled beers (plus a dozen microbrews on draft), Wi-Fi, and popcorn await you at the awesome **Bodega Brew Pub,** two blocks away (122 S. 4th St.; 608/782-0677). Travelers seeking something wholesome, fresh, and filling should head to the

World's Largest Six-Pack

Six miles east of La Crosse, **West Salem** was the boyhood home of Pulitzer Prize–winning novelist Hamlin Garland, whose bittersweet stories of 1860s Wisconsin farm life have earned him a reputation as one of the finest American authors. His honest, social-realist books include the autobiographical *Son of the Middle Border* and an excellent collection of stories, *Main-Traveled Roads.*

deli of the **People's Food Co-op** (315 S. 5th Ave.; 608/784-5798), between Cass and King.

For accommodations, look to I-90 for the national chains, while local motels line Hwy-35/US-61 (the GRR, sometimes a.k.a. Mormon Coulee Rd.). Just south of downtown, the **Guest House Motel** ($55; 810 S. 4th St.; 608/784-8840) offers British hospitality, comfortable clean rooms, and a café.

For more detailed information, call the **La Crosse Area Convention and Visitors Bureau** (608/782-2366 or 800/658-9424) or visit its information center in leafy green Riverside Park, where a 25-ton, 25-foot-tall statue of Hiawatha greets river traffic with arms crossed.

Spring Green

Architect Frank Lloyd Wright's famous country house and studio, Taliesin (pronounced "tally-ESS-en"), is in **Spring Green,** 70 miles east of Prairie du Chien via Hwy-60. Fully guided tours of the private residence and architecture school he inspired are offered daily April–October; ticket prices vary, depending on what's included in the tour ($17–80; 608/588-7900). Spring Green is also home to the state's biggest tourist trap, the incredible **House on the Rock** (daily; $28.50; 608/935-3639), with its "World's Largest" merry-go-round, kitschy collections of everything from dolls to replicas of the crown jewels, and the eponymous house, standing atop a 450-foot-high rock.

© AVALON TRAVEL

Black Hawk War

One name recurs frequently as you travel along the northern Mississippi River: Black Hawk was the leader of the Sauk and Mesquakie Indians of northern Illinois during the feverish era of American expansion into the newly opened Louisiana Purchase in the late 1820s. Indian fighters were held in high esteem by 19th-century Americans; consider that a number of U.S. Army officers sent against Black Hawk later became president, including William Henry Harrison, Zachary Taylor, Abraham Lincoln, Jefferson Davis, and Andrew Jackson. After Jackson rode his Indian-fighter reputation into the White House, Black Hawk and his people were forced to leave their rich Illinois cornfields as settlers and lead miners moved in.

In 1832, as newspapers around the United States demanded the extermination of any and all Indians, Black Hawk (who was around 65 years old at the time) moved back to Illinois to regain the tribe's lost lands along the Rock River. In response, President Jackson sent in the army, and as Black Hawk and his 300 or so supporters tried to withdraw back across the

statue of Black Hawk in Lowden State Park, near Oregon, Illinois

Mississippi, soldiers and frontier militias attacked them at what became known as the **Battle of Bad Axe,** near the present town of Victory, midway between La Crosse and Prairie du Chien. When Black Hawk and his men came forward under a white flag, an Army gunboat opened fire, while many of the Indian women and children who had succeeded in riding log rafts across the river were slaughtered on the other side. By various accounts, some 150 of Black Hawk's people were killed. Black Hawk himself was soon captured and imprisoned, then paraded around the United States in chains. After Black Hawk died in 1838, his skeleton was displayed in the governor's mansion in Iowa, like a trophy.

Hwy-35

For most of the nearly 60 miles between La Crosse and Prairie du Chien, the GRR (Hwy-35) is again confined to the margin between the tall gray and yellow bluffs and the impressively wide, lake-like Mississippi. At times the roadway is so narrow that the few houses have to climb three stories up the irregular wooded slopes, while the railroad tracks on your right are suspended over the water on viaducts. About halfway along, there's a maze of small islands around the mouth of the Bad Ax River, with the occasional blue heron poised like a Giacometti sculpture in algae-covered sloughs. Dotting the curves alongside the road are a series of historical markers old enough to be artifacts themselves; most are related to the tragic **Black Hawk War** of 1832.

Midway along this scenic stretch of highway, 34 miles north of Prairie du Chien between the riverside hamlets of De Soto and Genoa, the **Great River Roadhouse** (9660 Hwy-35; 608/648-2045) is a great place to stop and stretch your legs—and your stomach, feasting on the roast chickens, good pizza, tangy barbecue, Friday night fish fry, and constant cold beers.

South of Prairie du Chien, across from McGregor, Iowa, is the spot where Louis Joliet and his Jesuit companion, Jacques Marquette, caught their first sight of what became known as the **Mississippi River**. They were coming down the Wisconsin River in 1673, searching for a route to the Orient.

Prairie du Chien

Named by early 19th-century French voyageurs, **Prairie du Chien** (pronounced "duh-SHEEN") could be re-christened Prairie du Kwik-Stop or Prairie du Pabst by the modern traveler cruising along the GRR on downtown's West Blackhawk Avenue. The town's main attraction is the posh **Villa Louis** (daily May–Oct.; $9; 608/326-2721), which embodies the wealth that could be made in the fur trade back when every European dandy's head sported beaver-pelt hats. Built by the state's first millionaire, the house boasts one of the finest collections of domestic Victoriana in the country; signs point you here from all over town.

IOWA

In its 140-mile course across Iowa, the GRR passes swiftly but unmistakably across the cultural and geographical North-South Divide. Separated by the Mississippi River from the rough topography of Wisconsin's Driftless Region, the southeastern corner of Iowa offers instead a taste of the state's trademark rolling plains covered with corn and soybeans. Menus are different, too: Cattle here are raised for meat instead of milk, and Iowa is a leading producer of hogs (one of the state lottery games is called Bring Home the Bacon, while radio ads encourage you to "Eat more pork—the other white meat"). So say goodbye to walleye and hello to barbecue.

Running along the western bank of the Mississippi, our route tends to the tops of the bluffs, too, rather than to their base, which means the river is often spied from a distance and seems unrelated to the rolling landscape; fortunately it continues to guide the curves of the road. Other than **Dubuque,** our route passes through towns so far from the beaten path they don't even rate a fast-food strip or Wal-Mart—appreciate this while it lasts.

Marquette: Effigy Mounds National Monument

Immediately across, and effectively underneath, the long bridges over the Mississippi from Prairie du Chien, **Marquette** is a homey, workaday community that verges on quaint—so long as you manage to turn a blind eye to the garish pink elephant advertising its Isle of Capri Riverboat Casino complex. Unless you're a gambler, the main reason to visit is three miles north of Marquette, right along the riverbank: the **Effigy Mounds National Monument** (daily; free; 563/873-3491), which preserves 2,500 acres of natural riverside ecosystems plus more than 200 distinct burial mounds, many shaped like birds and animals. The unusual mounds are traces of the native people who lived along the Mississippi from around 500 BC to the time of first European contact. The visitors center has exhibits on the archaeology of the

mounds, and a dozen miles of hiking trails reach from the river to restored vestiges of the native tallgrass prairie.

McGregor

Just south of Marquette, near the foot of the "original" Pike's Peak—Zebulon Pike came up the Mississippi before he went out west to Colorado—**McGregor** (pop. 871) is a river town whose enticing old

aerial view of the Great Bear Mounds

Great Bear Mounds on the ground

Forty-six miles west of McGregor is the Bohemian (as in the Czech Republic, not bearded poets) town of **Spillville**, where Antonin Dvorak completed his symphony *From the New World* in 1893. The Main Street house (319/562-3569) where he stayed now leads a double life: Displays on Dvorak are upstairs, while downstairs is an incredible show of wooden clocks carved by the Bily brothers, depicting everything from the Twelve Apostles to Charles Lindbergh.

saloons and storefronts are a fine reason to stop and stretch your legs, watching the boat and barge traffic or simply wandering along the water. A number of browsable antiques-and-collectibles shops line the GRR through the four-block main business district, and McGregor also boasts about the only riverside hotel on the entire Great River Road: the family-friendly **Holiday Shores Motel** ($48–99; 563/873-3449) at the foot of Front Street.

Just south of town, the 500-foot-high limestone bluff known as Pike's Peak is one of the highest points anywhere along the Mississippi River and has been protected at the center of spacious green **Pike's Peak State Park** (563/873-2341), with hiking trails, scenic viewpoints, and a campground with a small store, hot showers, and RV hookups.

Guttenberg

Atop the bluffs, tidy frame farmhouses dot the landscape, with white barns, silos, and farmland aroma accompanying US-18 and US-52 as they loop inland south toward **Guttenberg** (pop. 3,141), another postcard-pretty old river town whose downtown lines the Mississippi. In fact, it's one of the few Mississippi riverfronts where the river itself is not hidden away behind levees, and a long green riverside park, just a quick two blocks east of the main highway, makes the downtown area a particularly pleasant place to stroll.

Guttenberg is indeed named in honor of Johannes Gutenberg, 15th-century inventor of printing from moveable type. Local legend has it that an official of French descent purposely added the extra "t" after German residents won a vote to change the town's name from the original Prairie la Porte. Germanic surnames still predominate in the local phone book, and the two main streets, which run perpendicular to the Mississippi, are named Schiller and Goethe.

McGregor was the hometown of the five children who grew up to found the Ringling Brothers circus.

On the north side of town, the GRR takes an up-close look at the prairie's geological underpinnings as it cuts down to the river's edge. From the downtown area, it's a quick walk upriver to the concrete walls of Lock and Dam No. 10. Besides giving a sense of the massive engineering that attempts to tame the Mississippi, the locks are also home to an aquarium that offers a quick biology lesson through displays of live specimens of many of the river's fish and invertebrate species.

There are great views to be had in the first few miles of Iowa's GRR route south of Guttenberg. About 10 well-signed miles south of Guttenberg, you can take the Cassville ferry across the Mississippi from Millville and visit the unique Dickeyville Grotto, or stay on the Iowa side and cruise through the Germanic eye-blink towns that dot the rolling uplands between Guttenberg and Dubuque. Midway along, tiny **Balltown** in particular is worth a stop to sample the food and decor at **Breitbach's** (563 Balltown

Rd.; 563/552-2220), a bar and restaurant that's so old President Millard Fillmore issued the permit allowing it to open.

Dickeyville Grotto

Dickeyville Grotto

Across the river from Dubuque, the Wisconsin town of Dickeyville is home to one of the most interesting folk-art environments along the Mississippi: the **Dickeyville Grotto** ($1 suggested donation; 305 W. Main St.; 608/568-3119). Started by Father Mathias Wernerus in 1920 as a memorial to three local boys killed in World War I, and worked on as a community project by his followers up through the 1960s, the Dickeyville Grotto consists of a series of caves, alcoves, and shrines made of poured concrete almost completely covered in shells, shards, minerals, and costume jewelry. Along with the expected Catholic religious themes, parts of the grotto also exhibit a unique vein of patriotic Americana—highlighted by the "Patriotism in Stone" memorial to Christopher Columbus, George Washington, and Abraham Lincoln. Maintained as a public park, with almost no commercialization, the grotto is open 24 hours every day, adjacent to the Holy Ghost Catholic Church, a block west of US-61.

Dickeyville can be reached a number of ways. It's a quick shot north along US-151 from Dubuque, or from Prairie du Chien you can follow scenic Hwy-133 along the east bank of the Mississippi. If it's summertime and you want an up-close look at the Mississippi, make your way to Cassville, a historic frontier town that holds one of the river's few surviving car ferries. The ferry has been running since the 1830s and now runs daily in summer, weekends only in May, September, and October ($15 per car; 608/725-5180).

Dubuque

At the southern end of a very enjoyable ride, cruising up and down sculpted hills and winding past miles of Iowa prairie and river towns, the GRR rolls into **Dubuque** (pop. 56,637), named for the 18th-century French voyageur Julien Dubuque,

Different towns along the Iowa stretch of the GRR act as the finish line for the trans-Iowa **RAGBRAI**, a 500-mile, weeklong mass bike ride that sees 10,000 cyclists cruising across the state every July.

who unsuccessfully mined lead on land acquired from the Spanish. Finding lead wasn't the problem—Indians had dug lead by hand as early as 1680 for trade with the English—but getting it to market was. After the steamboat's invention and forced removal of native tribes in the late 1820s, mineral wealth became a major catalyst to settlement of the tri-state area around Dubuque, as town names like Potosi, Mineral Point, New Diggings, and Lead Mine attest. During the Civil War, just five counties around here supplied all the lead for the entire Union war effort.

On the inland side of the compact downtown, a grand view of the city and the Mississippi valley can be had from the top of the **Fenelon Place Elevator,** a historic funicular cable car that proudly holds the title of "World's Steepest, Shortest Scenic Railway" ($2 round-trip; daily Apr.–Nov. only). Still hauled up and down the hill by a 15-hp motor in the head house, the elevator is a mini version of those in Pittsburgh and the Swiss Alps. Hop on at the east end of 4th Street and ride up to the plush residential district on the hilltop.

On the other side of downtown, the Dubuque waterfront has been recharged by the **National Mississippi River Museum and Aquarium** (daily; $15; 350 E. 3rd St.; 563/557-9545), one of the two biggest and best museums dedicated to the history and culture of Old Muddy (the other one is on River Island in Memphis). A large collection of historic riverboats is highlighted by the steamboat *William M. Black,* an official National Landmark, while other galleries include a National Rivers Hall of Fame that tells the stories of explorers and adventurers like Lewis and Clark and John Wesley Powell. The introductory film, *River of Dreams,* is narrated by Mr. Lake Wobegon himself, Garrison Keillor.

Fenelon Place Elevator

Dubuque marks the junction of the Great River Road and our cross-country route US-20, **The Oregon Trail** (see page 638). This road trip is covered in full detail on pages 584–703.

The museum complex is at the heart of the America's River complex, which also has the inevitable casino plus docks for scenic sightseeing and gambling boats, a nice riverside promenade, a café in the restored train depot, and the **Grand Harbor Resort** ($99 and up; 563/690-4000), a deluxe hotel and 25,000-square-foot water park.

Dubuque is a very meat-and-potatoes place when it comes to food, and as in most of the Midwest, you should plan to dine early to catch restaurants before they close. Near the Fenelon Place Elevator, the **Shot Tower Inn** (4 Locust St.; 563/556-1061) is a very popular pizza place with an upstairs deck and beer by the pitcher. The one standout in Dubuque is the **Pepper**

Dubuque Shot Tower

Sprout (378 Main St.; 563/556-2167), where the range of dishes (and the big-city prices) proves that "Midwest fine dining" is not an oxymoron.

East and west of Dubuque, US-20 offers a pair of excellent detours off the Great River Road. The ball field created for the movie *Field of Dreams* has become a minor tourist mecca for rural **Dyersville,** 30 miles due west of Dubuque via US-20 or the surprisingly scenic, gravel-paved Heritage Trail, which runs along an old railroad route.

South of Dubuque, the GRR follows US-52 back up the bluffs past Julien Dubuque's original lead workings and across 45 miles of upland farms and wooded bottoms until the next Mississippi crossing at Sabula.

St. Donatus

Fifteen undulating agricultural miles south of Dubuque, the tiny hamlet of **St. Donatus** (pop. 140) is widely advertised as a historic and picturesque Luxembourg village, mainly thanks to the handsome masonry of the **Gehlen House** (563/773-2480 or 800/280-1177), a 150-year-old home now used as a restaurant and B&B. Other eye-catching structures are the Catholic church and **Pieta Chapel** atop the adjacent Calvary Hill; if you wish to make a pilgrimage up the Way of the Cross, start behind the church burial ground, east of the Kalmes General Store. There's a nice view from the top—the other set of spires across the valley belongs to the German Lutheran St. John's Church.

Bellevue and Sabula

The GRR (US-52) returns to the Mississippi valley at **Bellevue,** with its lengthy Main Street and Riverfront Park beside Lock and Dam No. 12. Bellevue earns its name when you sit on the porch of the restored **Mont Rest B&B** ($150 and up; 300 Spring St.; 563/872-4220 or 877/872-4220) and take in the sweeping 270-degree panorama over the Mississippi.

Continuing south, the GRR stays in sparsely populated wooded lowlands through **Sabula,** an island of a town created by the Corps of Engineers when the pool above Lock and Dam No. 13, 16 miles downstream, flooded out the surrounding plains. Sabula takes its name from the Latin *sabulum* (sand). The river here is nearly four miles wide. Sabula's encompassing levees provide fine wetlands bird-watching, especially for bald eagles.

ILLINOIS, IOWA, AND MISSOURI

The Great River Road route along the middle Mississippi starts in northwestern Illinois, at the southern edge of the Driftless Region, and proceeds through sandy floodplain and fertile prairie, nipping back and forth across the ever-locked and dammed Mississippi between Illinois, southern Iowa, and the generally more-developed Missouri uplands. Here, small towns bypassed by much of the 20th century are more likely to be forlorn than quaint, a prelude to those southern states in which local ordinances appear to require the public display of rusty appliances. With a few exceptions—such as the historic Mormon town of **Nauvoo** or Mark Twain's hometown of **Hannibal**—our route now mostly runs through communities whose best years may have passed. This stretch of the GRR also includes one of the most dramatic sections of the entire route: the 25 miles around **Grafton,** Illinois, at the northern doorstep of **St. Louis.**

Thomson, 20 miles south of Savanna on Hwy-84, is the self-proclaimed "Watermelon Capital of the World" and celebrates its **Melon Days** festival every Labor Day weekend. Country music, carnival rides, watermelon-eating contests, and free watermelon are the traditional highlights.

South of St. Louis, I-55 is the recommended route, as it bypasses a long string of auto dealerships, appliance stores, shopping centers, and other prefab conveniences lining old US-61. Passing by the enticing old river town of **Sainte Genevieve,** the GRR crosses the Mississippi once again, ambling back to the corn, soybeans, and cicadas of southern Illinois. Accents, "Bar-B-Q" signs, and Baptist churches leave no doubt that our route has entered the South; in summer the heat and humidity confirm this with a vengeance. Fortunately, after leaving the "American Bottom" the GRR skirts the edge of the **Shawnee National Forest,** whose shade brings up to 25°F of relief from the temperatures along the roadside fields on a sunny July day. Occasional levees, raised roadbeds, and brackish seasonal ponds are reminders that the mile-wide Mississippi is only temporarily out of sight of the GRR, which finally crosses into Kentucky beside the giant turbid confluence of the Mississippi and Ohio Rivers at Cairo.

View of Mississippi River from Bluffs at SAVANNA Ill.
Publisher for A. O. Elliott, Savanna, Ill.   U. S. 304.

Savanna: Mississippi Palisades

Across the Mississippi from Iowa, **Savanna,** Illinois, is an old railroad town that has grown into an antiques center, offering three antiques mini-malls along the main drag. Savanna maintains a few pretty Victorian mansions up on the heights, but for a truly attractive vista take a detour north along Hwy-84 from the end of the Iowa bridge to the 2,500-acre **Mississippi Palisades State Park** (815/273-2731), with its great eroded bluffs (popular with rock climbers), 13 miles of hiking trails (brilliant fall color in the forested ravines), and fine river views. There's camping, too, with hot showers and RV hookups.

Between Savanna and the I-80 beltway around the Quad Cities are nearly 50 flat miles of river valley, dotted with small historic river and railroad towns mixed in with new commercial and residential construction. Agriculture is conspicuous, too, and the sandy soils between Savanna and Thomson are particularly known for their melon crops. While the Mississippi for the most part stays invisible from the GRR, the industry on its banks is clearly evident, especially at night. River access is at hand via a handful of recreation areas in the Upper Mississippi National Fish and Wildlife Refuge.

Le Claire, Iowa

On the northeastern edge of the Quad Cities, just off the I-80 freeway, lies the little town of **Le Claire** (pop. 3,765), famous once for its river pilots but now best remembered as William F. "Buffalo Bill" Cody's home. The **Buffalo Bill Museum** (daily; $5; 199 N. Front St.; 563/289-5580), on the waterfront, is dedicated to Cody's life. LeClaire is also home to the **Faithful Pilot** (117 N. Cody Rd.; 563/289-4156), on Le Claire's main street (US-67). One of the best restaurants in the entire Quad Cities region, the Faithful Pilot has creative, high-quality cuisine, a good wine list, fine microbrews, and a small bar at the back with views over the river.

The Quad Cities

Straddling the Mississippi at its confluence with the Rock River, the **Quad Cities**—Moline and Rock Island, Illinois, and Davenport and Bettendorf, Iowa—encompass an enormous sprawl of some 400,000 residents. While much of the cityscape is dominated by heavy industry, particularly on the Iowa side, points of interest are sprinkled throughout.

Along the river at the heart of the Quad Cities, adjacent to downtown Rock Island, is the former namesake of that city, now called Arsenal Island for the U.S. Army facility based there. Despite the look of the gatehouse at the southern entrance, the island is open to the public; besides an arsenal museum and Civil War cemeteries, there's a very good **Corps of Engineers visitors center** (daily; free) on the island right next to Lock and Dam No. 15, where the operation of the locks can be seen from a penny-pitch away.

The first railroad bridge over the Mississippi linked Rock Island and Davenport in 1856. The railroad was promptly sued by a steamboat company whose craft was mortally attracted to the bridge piers. The plaintiffs argued that bridges violated their navigation rights; the defense lawyer's elegantly simple—and successful—rebuttal was that a person has as much right to cross a river as to travel upon it. That lawyer was Abraham Lincoln. Today the railroad crosses the river on the upper deck of the old iron Government Bridge, which swings open for the tows entering the locks; cars crossing between Rock Island and Davenport can ride the humming lower deck or take the modern concrete highway span below the dam.

If you come to the Quad Cities looking for a slice of old-fashioned, Middle American humdrum, you're in for a surprise: one of the oldest and most impressive municipal art museums stands at the heart of unassuming Davenport. The **Figge Art Museum** (closed Mon.; $7; 225 W. 2nd St.; 563/326-7804), overlooking the Mississippi, is housed in a beautiful glass gem designed by noted British architect David Chipperfield. The museum shows off the University of Iowa's fine collection of painting and sculpture, and stages events and educational activities as outreach to general public. Another intriguing cultural enterprise is just up the street, where the **River Music Experience** (closed Sun.; free; 129 N. Main St. 563/326-1333) is an interactive museum exploring the many different sorts of music that have grown up along the Mississippi River. Frequent, free live concerts are held on the plaza outside.

Davenport celebrates the music legacy of native son and cornetist Leon Beiderbecke with the annual **Bix Beiderbecke Memorial Jazz Festival,** held at the end of July. A statue of Bix stands along

cornetist Leon Beiderbecke, 1924

the river, next to wonderful old (circa-1930) but thoughtfully modernized Modern Woodmen Park, where the minor-league **Quad Cities River Bandits** (tickets $5–12; 563/322-6348) play their home games. In a nod to the nearby Field of Dreams, before games the home team players run out from a corn field planted down the left field foul line.

Quad Cities Practicalities

In downtown Davenport, the only large Mississippi River city not cut off from Ol' Muddy by a flood wall, look to the historic downtown area around the River Music Experience, where you'll find several good brewpubs and cafés. Away from downtown Davenport, off I-80 exit 292, the original **Iowa Machine Shed Restaurant** (7250 Northwest Blvd.; 563/391-2427) draws families from near and far for its huge portions of roast pork and other Midwest faves (like the famously good pies).

In downtown Moline, a half dozen blocks along 5th Avenue between I-74 and 14th Street hold everything from the unexpectedly excellent French-infused Vietnamese fare of **Le Mekong** (1606 5th Ave.; 309/797-3709) to the extraordinary **Lagomarcino's** (1422 5th Ave.; 309/764-1814), a candy store and soda fountain that serves drinks like phosphates in a setting virtually unchanged since it opened in 1908. Order a hot fudge sundae—it's made with homemade fudge and ice cream.

Rock Island's old downtown, 2nd Avenue, has experienced something of a revival with the appearance of a riverboat casino a block away; one pleasant result is "the District," centered on the 2nd Avenue pedestrian mall. One great place hereabouts is the **Blue Cat Brew Pub** (113 18th St.; 309/788-8247) along the riverside, where salads, seafood, and desserts go way beyond your average pub fare, and the beers range from traditional lagers and ales to more esoteric concoctions (orange coriander *hefe weiss,* anyone?).

For a truly regional diner experience, make your way to a **Maid-Rite Diner;** there's one in Moline (2036 16th St.; 309/764-1196). A strictly upper-Midwest phenomenon whose faded logo, "Since 1926," can often be seen on old brick buildings or historic commercial storefronts as far away as Minnesota, the local Maid-Rites are unusually bright and polished, and they come heartily recommended.

Illinois: The Yellow Banks

Zigzagging for nearly 100 miles south of the Quad Cities, the GRR picks its way along a series of back roads through Illinois floodplain and prairie, where frequent small farming towns serve as reminders of the need for frequent stops by early stages, steamboats, and railroads. Most of the towns seem not to have changed much since the last steamboat or train whistle blew, although now there's neon in the bars, vinyl and aluminum siding on the houses, and farmers with high-powered four-by-fours on the roads.

Nearly 45 miles south of the Quad Cities beltway, the GRR passes tiny **New Boston,** at the mouth of the Iowa River. The town is a historical footnote these days, having been surveyed by the young Abraham Lincoln after his stint in

Mississippi Bridge, Niota

the army—a tour of duty during which his only combat was against mosquitoes, he later recalled. Along the river farther south, near **Keithsburg,** a sign welcomes travelers to **Yellow Bank country,** named for the deep layer of sand exposed in the river valley in this region. Because of this deposit, visitors can find sandburs and even cactus in the Big River State Forest south of town. Keithsburg used to be one of a number of button manufacturing centers located along the middle Mississippi: Freshwater clams were dredged from the river bottom and their shells were used for making pearl buttons.

Snake Alley, the "World's Twistiest Street", in Burlington, Iowa

Burlington and Niota

Across the Mississippi River via an austere modern suspension bridge, **Burlington** was the frontier capital of Iowa, founded in 1808 and holding many Victorian homes and commercial buildings. In 1887 Burlington gave birth to the great American nature writer Aldo Leopold, then in 2004 the city was awarded "Great American Main Street" status from the National Trust for Historic Preservation. Now it has a fun Class A baseball team (the Bees, an Oakland A's farm club), a riverboat casino, a nice bridge over the Mississippi, a great **Maid-Rite diner** (112 W. Division St.), and some very busy downtown rail yards—one-time home base of the Burlington Northern Santa Fe (BNSF) railroad conglomerate.

If you have time to wander away from the river and downtown areas, head up to the 6th Street shopping district on Heritage Hill, following the twists and turns of "Snake Alley," a section of Washington Street that Ripley's Believe-It-Or-Not once called the "Crookedest Street in the World."

At **Niota,** the ghost of a town that marks the next crossing south of Burlington, a nifty old 1920s double-decker swing bridge (trains below, cars on top) crosses the Mississippi, landing on the west bank next to a huge old state prison at the historic town of Fort Madison, Iowa.

The Oakland A's Class A farm team, the Burlington Bees (319/754-5886), play all summer long at Community Field, on Mount Pleasant Street a mile west of the Mississippi River.

Nauvoo

Founded in 1839 by the Church of Jesus Christ of Latter-day Saints (LDS), the town of **Nauvoo**—a Hebrew-sounding word its founding father was told meant "the beautiful location"—was named by Mormon leader Joseph Smith,

Mormons in Illinois

If you're passing through Nauvoo, you'll have plenty of opportunities to learn about Mormon history and religion. Nauvoo is a mecca for Mormons, or Latter-day Saints (LDS), as church members prefer to call themselves. In 1839, a dozen years after receiving their new gospel via the Angel Moroni, the Mormons purchased a large tract of swampy land along the Mississippi River, then set about draining swamps and building a city. Within a few years, Nauvoo was not only the largest LDS settlement in America, but the 10th-largest city in the United States. The emergence of such a powerful little theocracy (with its own well-armed militia) generated resentment among outnumbered neighbors, and even some internal dissent. The friction escalated to violence on both sides, finally culminating in the 1844 arrest of Joseph Smith Jr., church founder and president, for having sanctioned the destruction of printing presses used by some church members to question his leadership. While in the nearby Carthage jail, Smith was lynched by a mob and so became one of the Mormons' first martyrs. Amid ensuing disputes over church succession and renewed hostilities with non-Mormon neighbors, most residents followed Brigham Young across the Mississippi on the famous exodus to Salt Lake City.

Given Smith's martyrdom, the fact that he's buried here, and the Brigham Young migration's roots in the town, it's little wonder that Nauvoo attracts Mormon pilgrims by the busload. The Utah-based LDS have sponsored a massive restoration of old Nauvoo buildings, and the town now ranks as one of the capitals of historic preservation in the United States. Most of old Nauvoo is operated essentially as a big museum, totally free and open to the non-LDS public.

12 years after he received the Book of Mormon from the Angel Moroni. Smith and many of his followers had spent the previous winter jailed in Liberty, Missouri, and by 1846 they were effectively exiled to Utah, but for a few years Nauvoo was among the largest settlements on the western frontier, with hundreds of log cabins and brick buildings and a population of some 6,000 Mormon believers. After 150 years of relative peace and quiet, in the late 1990s the Mormon church started a massive, $30-million program of historic preservation, turning Nauvoo into a top destination for Mormon pilgrims and retirees. The "restoration" of Mormon Nauvoo, and the influx of well-heeled Mormon immigrants, has been on such a big scale that many non-Mormons have felt under siege. Visitors to Nauvoo will certainly have plenty of opportu-

nities to learn about Mormon history and religion, but for the moment at least the part-preserved, part-restored townscape has a broad interest as a mostly noncommercialized reminder of what frontier America looked like in the years before the Wild West was finally "won."

The biggest change in Nauvoo has been the reconstruction of the original Mormon **Nauvoo Temple** (50 Wells St.), which, from the time it was finished in 1846 until it was burned down in 1848, was the largest building west of Philadelphia. An exact replica of the original, the new temple took more than three years to complete and was dedicated in 2002. The temple has a remarkable series of stone capitals carved with sunburst motifs and a 165-foot-high steeple capped by a statue of the Angel Moroni. Other interesting LDS-related sites include the store run by Joseph Smith and the home of Brigham Young. The home and workshop of John Browning, inventor of the repeating rifle, has been restored along Main Street, south of the present downtown area. There's also a massive **outdoor pageant** (8:30 PM Tues.–Sat.; free; 217/453-2429 or 800/453-3860) every July, celebrating the early, pre-Utah years of the LDS community, and all summer long you can take part in mostly free, nonsectarian activities like blacksmithing and horse-drawn carriage rides.

In **Oquawka, Illinois,** 10 miles northeast of Burlington, Iowa, a roadside marker points out the spot where in 1972 a circus elephant (named Norma Jean Elephant!) was killed by lightning.

The annual **Nauvoo Grape Festival,** held each Labor Day weekend at Nauvoo State Park south of town, celebrates the wine business that arose after European immigrants moved onto farms abandoned by the Mormon exodus. Nauvoo also developed a blue-cheese industry in the 1920s, after Prohibition shut down the winemaking trade. The centerpiece of the festival is a combination custom car show and the "Wedding of the Wine and Cheese," a medieval-style pageant borrowed from Roquefort, France.

Nauvoo Practicalities

For a map of the town and visitor information, stop by the huge **LDS Visitors Center** (daily; free; 888/453-6434), at the north end of Main Street. The town operates its own info center, too: the **Nauvoo Chamber of Commerce** (1295 Mulholland St.; 217/453-6648), opposite the historic Hotel Nauvoo.

Restaurants and lodgings are clustered along Mulholland Street (Hwy-96, a.k.a. the GRR) within the few blocks of downtown Nauvoo. For picnic supplies and cinnamon buns, try the **Nauvoo Mill and Bakery** (1530 Mulholland St.; 888/453-6734) near the Shell station. Near the reconstructed temple, the circa-1840s **Hotel Nauvoo** (1290 Mulholland St.; 217/453-2211) is particularly well regarded for its belt-straining buffets and is also the town's most characterful place to stay (rooms run $49–115).

Warsaw

For a scenic dozen miles south of Nauvoo, the GRR returns after long absence to the banks of the Mississippi, shaded by native hickory and oak, and then sidesteps yet another opportunity to enter Iowa, this time via US-136 west to Keokuk. Staying on the east bank, the GRR follows a series of farm roads past gravel pits and fields for most of the 40-mile run down to Quincy.

Warsaw lends its name to a variety of geode found locally in profusion; inside, Warsaw geodes grow calcite crystals. Across the Mississippi, Keokuk geodes grow quartzite crystals inside their stony spheres.

First stop south of Nauvoo is **Warsaw,** where the photogenic old downtown is kept alive by a pair of very welcoming stops: **J. Doggs Bar and Grill** (605 Main St.; 217/256-4088), which is locally famous for juicy pork tenderloins, and the gigantic **Warsaw Brewery,** on the riverfront (900 N. 6th St.; 217/256-4393), which opened in the 1860s, closed in the 1970s, and was resurrected in 2006 as a fine place for a cold beer. At the south end of town the GRR threatens to turn amphibious as it rolls down past a towering grain elevator to the Mississippi's edge, bends south along the base of the bluffs past old house trailers, scruffy fields full of wildlife—including wild turkeys and river turtles waddling along the roadside—and old kilns visible in the limestone. The road passes, finally, back into Illinois's signature cornfields, planted in the fertile floodplain of the Mississippi.

Quincy

Midway between the Quad Cities and St. Louis, **Quincy** (pop. 40,633) is a modest-sized city, Germanic enough in its heritage to consider Pizza Hut an ethnic restaurant. A bastion of abolitionists before the Civil War, Quincy was also home to anti-abolitionist Stephen Douglas, the incumbent Illinois senator whose campaign debates with Abraham Lincoln put that tall country lawyer on the path to the White House.

The GRR follows the riverfront and again the pilot's wheel is missing, but the giant span of the Bayview bridge over the Mississippi will leave no doubt as to which way to turn to stay on track. However, most of the city perches on the tall bluffs above the GRR and is worth a drive-through, if only to sample its textbook variety of residential architecture. Check out the **Gardner Museum of Architecture and Design** (Mar.–Dec. Wed.–Sat. 1–4 PM; $3; 217/224-6873), in the old public library downtown on Maine and 4th, for an overview of both those topics. Then take a walk or drive through the East End, an area roughly bounded by Maine and State Streets between 16th and 24th. Filled with historic mansions along quiet tree-canopied streets, it's the perfect place to practice distinguishing your Queen Anne from Tudor, and your Prairie Style from Gothic Revival.

The World Free Fall, an annual skydiving event, once filled Quincy's skies with thousands of jumpers from all over the planet. It was the legacy of one Thomas Baldwin, whose pioneering parachute jump from a balloon into a Quincy park in 1887 earned him two world exhibition tours.

If you have thus far avoided the tried-and-true cooking of the **Maid-Rite** chain, Quincy gives you a chance to fix this oversight: Perhaps the most intact of all the original Maids is here in Quincy (507 N. 12th St.; 217/222-7527).

If you plan to spend the night, you'll find the national chains downtown out on Broadway near I-172. If you prefer antiques to HBO in your room, try the **Cooper Adams House** in the heart of the historic mansions ($95 and up; 1122 Kentucky St.; 217/430-1884).

For more information, call or drop by the tourist information center in the **Villa Kathrine** (217/224-3688 or 800/978-4748), that hard-to-miss, turn-of-the-20th-century Moroccan-style residence on the bluffs overlooking the Mississippi, just south of the US-24 bridge.

Hannibal

It doesn't take a literature professor to figure out who Hannibal's most famous resident was: His name prefaces half the signs in town, and the names of his characters preface the other half. Cross the Mississippi River on the I-72 Mark Twain Memorial Bridge, shop at the Huck Finn Mall or swim at Mark Twain Lake, then spend the night at Injun Joe's Campground or the Tom N' Huck Motel. Turn onto 3rd Street (the Great River Road) near the Hotel Clemens and park yourself in the heart of historic old Hannibal, and visit the Mark Twain Home and Mark Twain Museum. Take a very expensive ride on the almost miniature *Mark Twain* riverboat, docked at the Center Street Landing; browse through books by and about Twain at the Becky Thatcher Bookshop; or

Twain was a bit of an impractical investor, losing lots of money on lots of harebrained schemes while missing at least one spectacular opportunity, the telephone. Or so hindsight teaches us—but how much would you invest in a new invention by a guy who flies tetrahedral kites and makes devices to detect metal in the body? Twain said no, so Alexander Graham Bell took his invention to J. P. Morgan instead.

eat Mark Twain Fried Chicken at the Mark Twain Dinette. Not to detract from the credit due him, but don't look for any subtlety or modesty surrounding Mark Twain's achievements here.

Most of this Twainery is located downtown, within a few blocks of the Mississippi River, and enjoyment requires at least a passing familiarity with (and fondness for) *Tom Sawyer,* Twain's fictionalized memoir of his boyhood here. A statue of Tom and Huck stands at the foot of Cardiff Hill, and two blocks south, the white picket fence featured in that book still stands in front of the **Mark Twain Boyhood Home** (daily; $9; 208 Hill St.; 573/221-9010), where young Samuel Clemens (Twain's real name) grew up in the 1840s. The historic site preserves a half dozen buildings, including his father's law offices and the drugstore above which the Clemens family also lived. The home of Tom Sawyer's "girl next door," Becky Thatcher, is actually across the street, and the upstairs parlor and bedrooms have been re-created to evoke the era. The main **Mark Twain Museum** (415 N. Main St.) recently moved into a much larger space in an ornate Victorian building two blocks away but is still part of the same operation. Exhibits, including a steamboat pilot's wheel and numerous first editions, bring to life scenes from Twain's Mississippi novels.

A pair of high hills bookend **Hannibal** (pop. 17,757), and climbing up either (or both) gives a grand overview of the town and the broad Mississippi, its historic lifeblood. On the north side, climb up the staircase from the Tom and Huck statue to the top of Cardiff Hill, where the **Mark Twain Memorial Lighthouse,** built in 1935 to celebrate the centenary of Twain's birth, offers a fine view. South of town, **Lover's Leap** is higher and more breathtaking—best visited by car or bike. Farther south of downtown along the GRR (Hwy-79) is Hannibal's most kid-friendly attraction: the **Mark Twain Cave Complex** (daily; $16), where costumed guides spin tales about Tom and Huck on an hour-long tour.

The most popular annual festival is **Tom Sawyer Days,** held the weekend nearest to the 4th of July, when children take part in the National Fence Painting Championship (a whitewashing homage to *Tom Sawyer*), a frog-jumping competition (remembering Twain's Gold Rush–era short story, *The Celebrated Jumping Frog of Calaveras County*), and the very messy Mississippi Mud Volleyball Championships.

Hannibal Practicalities

To immerse yourself fully in the Mark Twain experience, try the Mark Twain memorial chicken (or a Mississippi Mud Malt) served all day at the **Mark**

Twain Dinette (400 N. 3rd St.; 573/221-5511), adjacent to the Mark Twain Home in what looks suspiciously like a converted A&W. A step up the culinary scale, **Ole Planters Restaurant** (316 Main St.; 573/221-4410) has a full range of lunches and dinners; dessert fans will want to sample the German chocolate pie, a specialty of the house. This species, like rhubarb, is predominantly found in pie cases along the middle Mississippi, so if you're planning a scientific sampling, start now.

Consistent with its status as an international tourist attraction, Hannibal has plenty of motels, B&Bs, and campgrounds. The **Best Western** ($90 and up; 401 N. 3rd St.; 573/248-1150) sits downtown at the foot of the old US-36 bridge. The national chains line up along busy US-61 west of downtown.

For a complete list of lodgings, restaurants, events, and tourist traps, pick up a free guide from the Hannibal **visitors center** (505 N. 3rd St.; 573/221-2477 or 866/263-4825).

The Twain mania is so overwhelming that little is made of Hannibal's other famous sons. Baseball lovers searching for some mention of Joseph Jefferson "Shoeless Joe" Jackson will look in vain; there is none. Neither is there much mention of Bill Lear, inventor of the car radio, the eight-track tape, and the Lear jet, who was born here in 1902.

Louisiana and Clarksville

For the first 20-odd miles south from Hannibal, the GRR ascends and descends the densely wooded tops of bluffs, pausing at scenic turnouts for views across the Mississippi Valley, here many miles wide. In October, the upland forests are blazing with fall color that compares with any outside New England, and if you roll down the windows or stop to stretch your legs during the summer, listen for the omnipresent buzz of cicadas in the tangled undergrowth.

Another icon of the lower Mississippi, one that has extended its range north, like the cicadas (and the fire ant), is the huge and pungent chemical plant on the south side of the town of **Louisiana** (pop. 3,743); ironically, considering current concerns about energy supplies, this plant was originally constructed by U.S. Army in the 1940s, to create synthetic alternatives to fossil fuels. The town itself, like a Hannibal without Mark Twain, has one of the Midwest's most intact Victorian-era streetscapes, full of 125-year-old brick cottages and warehouses, but looking like it has just about lost the battle against extinction.

A short ways farther south, **Clarksville** (pop. 438) is another GRR town with more of a past than a future, but some optimistic restorers of the riverfront historic block are counting on tourism to improve the town fortunes.

Claiming preeminence as the highest point along this stretch of the Mississippi River, 900-foot **Pinnacle Peak** is also noteworthy for the rusty remains of its old Sky Ride chair lift, which once carried riders over the GRR all the way to the top. Clarksville also boasts what may be the

If you've been keeping track, you'll have noticed that the lock and dam numbering skipped No. 23 between Hannibal and Clarksville. There are 29 Army Corps of Engineers–operated locks and dams on the Mississippi, from the unnumbered ones in the Twin Cities to No. 27 at St. Louis.

largest concentration of **bald eagles** in the lower 48 states; in winter months they feed by the hundreds below Lock and Dam No. 24, on the northern edge of town.

Swinging away from the river south of Clarksville, the GRR reenters the corn belt in great straight stretches of road, rising and falling over rolling prairie still hilly enough that you can play peek-a-boo with approaching traffic over the miles of ups and downs, passing towns that often comprise little more than a few houses around a gas station and a grain elevator on a rarely used railroad siding. The landscape feels far away from urban anything, yet you're less than a half-hour from downtown St. Louis.

Calhoun County

Wedged between the Mississippi and Illinois Rivers, the rural peninsula of **Calhoun County** is one of the best-kept secrets in the state of Illinois. Cut off from the rest of the "Land of Lincoln" and connected to neighboring Missouri by ferry only, Calhoun County is a world of its own. A third of the state's sub-

stantial peach crop is grown here on farms that have changed hands only a few times, if at all, since they were given out as land grants to veterans of the War of 1812; bypassing the summer farm stands, especially when the baseball-sized, plum-sweet tomatoes are in season, borders on criminal. A lucky few St. Louisians have weekend getaways here, too, alongside shacks and trailers that seem to accumulate debris like the Corps' dams accumulate Mississippi mud.

In the town of **Brussels** (pop. 141), whose public phone booth is possibly the town's sole civic improvement since the Coolidge administration, a few cafés and bars are evidence of its popularity with weekenders from St. Louis. The most popular haunt in Brussels is the venerable **Wittmond's Restaurant** (618/883-2345), across from the water tower and post office at the heart of Brussels. The dining room here serves delicious, all-you-can-eat, family-style meals (very popular on Sunday). It no longer rents rooms, but there's still a timeless bar and an even more ancient-looking general store—complete with dusty old merchandise that looks like it dates back to when the enterprise opened in 1847.

Getting to and around Calhoun County is a bit of an adventure. The main access is from near Grafton, Illinois, across the Illinois River via the state-run, round-the-clock, and (best-of-all) free Brussels Ferry. There's also a bridge at Hardin 14 miles upstream. From the Missouri side north of St. Louis, the only access is via the privately operated *Golden Eagle* ferry (618/535-5759), which runs across the Mississippi River from a landing outside St. Charles to **Golden Eagle,** Illinois. Most of the ferries cease operation in the winter, but during summer they run more or less from dawn to midnight, sell local maps, and can offer basic visitor information. Road signs in Calhoun County are almost nonexistent, but just driving (or cycling!) around, getting lost and found, and lost and found again, is by far the best way to get a feel for this preserved-in-amber island in time.

The Illinois River and Père Marquette State Park

At the south end of Calhoun County, the Brussels Ferry takes all of two or three minutes to cross the narrow **Illinois River,** along which Marquette and Joliet returned to Canada after their failure to find a westward-flowing river to the rich lands of Cathay and the Far East. René-Robert Cavelier, Sieur de La Salle, came down the Illinois eight years later in 1681, on the first expedition to specifically target the Mississippi. It was La Salle who claimed the Mississippi territory for his sponsor, King Louis XIV of France, and who went all the way down to the Gulf of Mexico (Marquette and Joliet turned back after the confluence of the Arkansas River).

While the Mississippi may be muddy and less than pristine, at least one man is working to clean it up: Chad Pregracke spends his days hauling old tires, sunken refrigerators, and other light industrial discards out of the water. You can follow the progress at www. livinglandsandwaters.org.

If you're equipped for some hiking or biking, **Père Marquette State Park** is a short, well-signed, and definitely worthwhile three-mile detour upstream from the Brussels Ferry landing. The handsome **park lodge,** built by the Civilian Conservation Corps in the late 1930s, is noted for its 700-ton stone fireplace, massive tree-trunk roof supports, decorative ironwork, and out-sized chess set. Cabins and lodge rooms are available for reasonable rates (from $99 for two; 618/786-2331). Expect holiday and fall foliage weekends to be booked up a year in advance; camping and tent rentals are also available (618/786-3323).

Following an old railroad route for much of the way, the 20-mile **Sam Vadalabene Bike Trail** between Père Marquette State Park and Alton is un-questionably the best venue for appreciating the scenery, even for a short walk, for Hwy-100 is a fast, divided highway whose drivers don't appreciate slowpokes.

Grafton and Elsah

North of St. Louis on the Illinois side of the Mississippi, the high-speed section of the GRR between **Grafton** and Alton is widely considered one of its most scenic stretches. Towering limestone bluffs, their curving faces pocked with

the Great River Road along the Mississippi River one mile east of Grafton, Illinois

EXCURSION STEAMER "CAPITOL" ON THE MISSISSIPPI.

STRECKFUS STEAMBOAT LINE, SAINT LOUIS.

Atop the bluffs over Elsah is the very Tudor campus of **Principia College.** A Christian Science institution of higher education, the campus and many buildings were designed by arts-and-crafts master architect Bernard Maybeck.

caves and overhangs, push the road to the edge of the broad lake formed by Lock and Dam No. 26.

Speeding along Hwy-100 south of Grafton, it's easy to miss the turnoff for **Elsah,** but even if you have to turn around and come back, it's worth it to check out this tiny hamlet tucked away in a cleft in the palisades. Light years away from St. Louis, but only a half hour's drive away, Elsah is listed in the National Register of Historic Places in its entirety and is an architectural gem, with 19th-century cut-stone and clapboard buildings and narrow lanes reminiscent of some idyllic English country village. Two small B&Bs and the **Green Tree Inn** ($125; 618/374-2821) offer unexpectedly romantic getaways, a taste of New England here in southern Illinois.

South of Elsah, before the bluffs give way to grain elevators at Alton, you'll catch a glimpse of the **Piasa Bird** (pronounced "PIE-a-saw") high on the wall of an old roadside quarry. Marquette and other early explorers mention a pair of huge pictographs on the cliff face, representations of the Illini Indians' legendary "bird that devours men." Faded by the 1840s, the original site was destroyed by quarrying. The current 20- by 40-foot replica, based on various eyewitness descriptions, resembles something from the notebook of an adolescent Dungeons & Dragons fan.

Alton

At **Alton,** 20 miles northeast of St. Louis, the riverfront turns decidedly urban. The GRR races along the water, past busy tugboat docks, sulfurous chemical plants, and towering concrete grain elevators, all along a great protective levee under a thicket of high-tension power lines. The main attrac-

casino boats on the Mississippi

tion here is the vivid green-and-orange (and hugely lucrative) *Argosy Alton* casino boat, formerly the *Alton Belle,* the first in Illinois when riverboat gambling was made legal in 1991.

Inland from the waterfront, however, Alton is surprisingly peaceful and quiet, its redbrick streets lined by mature trees and a range of modest but well-maintained 19th-century houses. Near 5th and Monument Streets at the south end of town, high on a hill above the river-front, Alton's cemetery is dominated by a large column topped by a winged figure—a monument to one of Alton's most important individuals, the abolitionist news-paper editor Elijah Lovejoy. Widely considered to be the nation's first martyr to freedom of the press and freedom of speech, Lovejoy, a newspaper publisher and preacher, was lynched in Alton in 1837 by a mob of pro-slavery Missourians.

Six miles south of Alton, near the village of Hartford, keep an eye out for the signs to the **Lewis & Clark Historical Site,** a reconstruction of the winter campsite of the Corps of Discovery in 1803–1804. Recently expanded with a small state-run museum (closed Mon. and Tues.; free; 618/251-5811), the site sits opposite the confluence of the Missouri and Mississippi Rivers, which roll together in a muddy tide between swampy wooded banks.

The GRR Across St. Louis

The Great River Road has many routes in, around, and across St. Louis, and they're all so poorly marked that you're sure to get lost trying to follow any of them. From Alton, US-67 crosses just below Lock and Dam No. 26, taking first the Clark Bridge (over the Mississippi) and then the Lewis Bridge (over the Missouri River). No priz-es for guessing what *those* names refer to, since coming from the north you enter the city on Lewis and Clark Boulevard (Hwy-367).

A good main, non-freeway route across St. Louis is Kings Highway, which runs north–south past many of the city's main destinations, including Forest Park and the Missouri Botanical Garden, before ending up at Gravois Avenue, part of old Route 66. From here, numerous roads give direct access to I-55 and US-61, both of which link up with the scenic GRR route south to Sainte Genevieve.

In May 2005, an Alton fisherman pulled a 125-pound blue catfish out of the Mississippi River, a world-record catch, and in 2010, an even bigger fish weighed in at over 130 pounds.

A life-sized statue of Robert Pershing Wadlow, the world's tallest human, stands on the campus of the Southern Illinois University Dental School, on College Avenue (Hwy-140) a mile or so east of the river. The Alton-born "gentle giant," who enrolled here in what was then a Baptist seminary in 1938, was 8 feet 1 ¾ inches tall when he died in 1940, at the age of 22.

Get a feel for St. Louis listening habits by tuning in to commercial-free **KDHX 88.1 FM.**

St. Louis is the only city where three of our routes coincide—the **Great River Road, the Loneliest Road,** and **Route 66.** For the intersection with US-50, **The Loneliest Road,** see page 769.

For the junction with **Route 66,** see page 875. Where the **Great River Road** hops onto the I-55 freeway for its final approach into St. Louis, a road clearly marked GRR Spur leads to **Cahokia Mounds,** the remains of the largest prehistoric American city north of Mexico (see page 873).

St. Louis

the Gateway Arch

Founded by French fur trappers in 1764, St. Louis served for most of its first century as a prosperous outpost of "civilization" at the frontier of the Wild West. It was the starting point for the explorations of Lewis and Clark, and much later Charles Lindbergh, whose *Spirit of St. Louis* carried him across the Atlantic. Unfortunately, like many other American cities, St. Louis has suffered from years of decline and neglect; the population, which peaked at over 850,000 in 1950, is now less than half that, and the sale of the city's iconic beer, Budweiser, to the Belgian company InBev didn't exactly thrill many locals. Although it has all the cultural and institutional trappings of a major city, not to mention the landmark Gateway Arch, St. Louis is at heart a city of small neighborhoods, such as bluesy Soulard south of downtown, the Italian-American "Hill" (boyhood home of Yogi Berra), and the collegiate West End district near verdant Forest Park.

One thing you have to see when in St. Louis (you literally cannot miss it) is the **Gateway Arch** (daily; 314/655-1600), on the riverfront at the foot of Market Street. Rising up from the west bank of the Mississippi River, Eero Saarinen's stunning 630-foot stainless steel monument still dominates the city skyline, despite the disrespectful rise of nearby office towers. Under the legs of the arch, which is officially called the Jefferson National Expansion Memorial, the free and fascinating **Museum of Westward Expansion** chronicles the human wave that swept America's frontier west to the Pacific. A small elevator-like tram ($10) carries visitors up the arch to an observation chamber at the very top.

West of downtown around the Washington University campus, in Forest Park's 1,300 beautifully landscaped acres, museums of fine art, history, and science fill buildings that date back to the 1904 World's Fair, St. Louis's world-class swan song.

The **St. Louis Cardinals** (314/421-2400), one of the country's most popular baseball teams, play at retro-modern Busch Stadium, right downtown with views of the river and Gateway Arch. Games are broadcast on **KMOX 1120 AM.**

Practicalities

Freeways and high-speed arteries reminiscent of Los Angeles make a car handy for navigating the St. Louis area—unless you have oodles of money for cab fares—but thanks to the city's sad history of replacing its landmark buildings with blacktop, you'll find plenty of parking lots around downtown.

For food, The Hill neighborhood is hard to beat: **Gian-Tony's** (5356 Daggett Ave.; 314/772-4893), is perhaps the best of a dozen classic neighborhood Italian places. Wherever you go, try the toasted ravioli, a local treat. Near Washington

University, another great place is the slightly kitschy **Blueberry Hill** (6504 Delmar Blvd.; 314/727-4444), a retro-1950s diner that has an excellent juke-box, very good burgers, and enough real-life credibility to sometimes attract the likes of St. Louis–born father of rock 'n' roll, Chuck Berry, to play impromptu gigs.

No one leaves St. Louis without cruising old Route 66 southwest from downtown to **Ted Drewes** (6726 Chippewa Ave.; 314/481-2652), a local institution famous for its many flavors of "concrete"—a delicious frozen dairy-and-egg-custard concoction so thick you can turn it upside down and not spill a drop. Nearby, fried chicken fans flock to **Hodak's** (2100 Gravois Ave.; 314/776-7292). One last Route 66 place has been going strong for more than 60 years: the **Eat-Rite Diner** (622 Chouteau Ave.; 314/621-9621), a plain blue-and-white cube serving up breakfasts and burgers 24 hours daily. As the sign says: "Eat Rite, or Don't Eat at All."

St. Louis doesn't have that much of a tourist trade (the muggy weather here in summer keeps most sensible people far away), so places to stay are relatively cheap. **Hampton Inn at Gateway Arch** ($99 and up; 333 Washington Ave.; 314/621-7900) is one of the more popular downtown hotels. The **Hyatt Regency at the Arch** ($109 and up; 315 Chestnut St.; 314/655-1234) is another. In a historic reincarnation, a quartet of stately old warehouses has been converted to house the **Westin St. Louis** ($160 and up; 811 Spruce St.; 314/621-2000), near the arch, the river, and the baseball stadium.

The **St. Louis Convention & Visitors Commission** (701 Convention Plaza; 314/421-1023 or 800/888-3861) operates a well-stocked information center downtown, near the river and I-70.

ONE OF THE MAGNIFICENT EIGHT-HORSE HITCHES OF INTERNATIONAL CHAMPION CLYDESDALES USED BY THE LARGEST BREWERY IN THE WORLD — ANHEUSER-BUSCH INC., ST. LOUIS, MO. — BREWERS OF THE FAMOUS BUDWEISER, KING OF BOTTLED BEER.

Sainte Genevieve

South of St. Louis, to avoid the sprawling suburbia, take I-55 as far as exit 162, where you can rejoin the GRR by picking up US-61 south. If you don't blink, you may even catch sight of one of Missouri's rare pilot's-wheel signs as the busy road ascends a ridge with a fine western panorama. About 55 miles south of St. Louis's I-270/255 beltway, the GRR reaches the outskirts of **Sainte Genevieve,** one of several French trading posts established along the Mississippi in the wake of La Salle's 17th-century expedition. The town's new trade is tourism, as the antiques shops and upscale restaurants clearly illustrate, but the beauty of Sainte Genevieve lies in its restored 18th- to 19th-century remnants, including a brick belle of a **Southern Hotel** ($80 and up; 146 S. 3rd St.; 573/883-3493), one of the oldest hotels west of the Mississippi River. **Sara's Ice Cream** (124 Merchant St.; 573/883-5890), down toward the water, provides yet more tasteful distractions, with great handmade ice cream cones, old-fashioned soda fountain drinks, and milk shakes.

Since US-61 doesn't enter town, follow the small blue Tourist Information signs down to the old waterfront to find the area's historic places, like the **Bolduc House,** the "most authentic Creole house in the USA." Visit the **Welcome Center** (daily; free; 66 S. Main St.; 573/883-7097 or 800/373-7007) to learn about the town's past and present.

Sainte Genevieve also boasts a way across the river: the **Mississippi River–Modoc Ferry** (daily; $2 one-way for pedestrians, $10 one-way for automobiles; 573/547-8357) to Modoc, Illinois, is three miles out of town; head down Main Street until it dead-ends at the ferry landing. On the Illinois side, 12 rural crop-lined miles from the Modoc Ferry we rejoin the GRR, heading south on Hwy-3 toward Chester.

George Rogers Clark's fame as a war hero, Indian fighter, and explorer put him at the top of Thomas Jefferson's short list for leading an expedition into what became the Louisiana Purchase, but the aging Clark nominated his younger brother instead. Thus did William Clark join Meriwether Lewis for their historic journey to the Pacific.

Kaskaskia, Illinois

Fifteen miles south of Sainte Genevieve, signposted off US-61, is old **Kaskaskia,** the first Illinois state capital and the only Illinois town now *west* of the Mississippi, thanks to an 1881 flood. "Town" is a generous overstatement: Originally consisting of only a church and a handful of farmhouses, the community has been all but washed away numerous times in its 250-year history. Cut off from the Missouri shore by huge levees and a swampy river channel, Kaskaskia is now a ghost town with an illustrious past: It was here, during the American Revolution, that George Rogers Clark and his tiny force of Kentucky "Long Knives" launched their attack against British control of the huge, formerly French territory between the Mississippi and Ohio River valleys, a campaign so stunningly successful that it effectively doubled the size of the United States. After capturing Fort Kaskaskia (now across the river), the victorious Americans rang the 600-pound bell that hung in the French Catholic church; this bell, now in its own spartan iron-barred chapel, is called the Liberty Bell of the West.

Chester: Home of Popeye

The GRR neatly skips around **Chester,** "Home of Popeye," via a pleasant riverbank detour, returning to Hwy-3 on the downstream side of town. **Popeye** first appeared in print in 1929, and a memorial to local boy Elzie Segar, creator of the spinach-guzzling scrapping Sailor Man, stands in a picnic area beside the bridge to Missouri; if you miss it, you'll have to turn around on the other side of the Mississippi. As the story goes, Chester locals Frank "Rocky" Fiegel and William "Windy Bill" Schuchert were the inspiration for Popeye the Sailor and Wimpy the Hamburger Fiend. If you pass through on the second weekend of September, drop by the annual **Popeye Picnic,** with its big flea market of all the Popeye collectibles you never imagined existed.

South of Chester, the GRR passes by a couple of old barns painted with fading signs advertising "Meramec Caverns— US-60—Stanton MO" (see page 876 in the **Route 66** chapter).

Hwy-3: Shawnee National Forest

No town of any consequence impedes the GRR's 90-mile leg along the southern tip of Illinois. The roadside landscape continues to be fields of heat-loving corn and leafy soybean, while the bluffs of the **Shawnee National Forest** appear to the east. Much of the forested uplands are a botanical crossroads: glacier-borne northern species like the sumac and partridge berry; warmth-seeking southern species like the short-leaf pine; eastern species held back by the Mississippi, such as Virginia willow and silver bell; and western species with a toehold in the east, like Missouri primrose and Ozark coneflower. All count southern Illinois as the

Absentminded and lead-footed drivers beware: Some cash-strapped counties of southern Illinois are known to use speed traps to help make ends meet.

edge of their natural ranges. When John James Audubon passed through this region in the early 1800s, he recorded seeing thousands of bright green, red, and yellow-striped parakeets, but these birds are all long extinct.

Jonesboro

Just under 50 miles south of Chester, eight miles east of the GRR via Hwy-146, the small town of **Jonesboro** hosted the third of seven 1858 U.S. Senate campaign debates between challenger Abe Lincoln and incumbent Stephen Douglas, who tried to portray Lincoln as being out of touch with the people over the issue of slavery. Although Illinois was a designated free state, this area had strong sympathies with the South, something it maintains to this day. For proof, enjoy the down-home ambience and delicious smoked pork barbecue at **Dixie Barbecue** (205 W. Broad St.; 618/833-6437). Broad Street, a.k.a. Hwy-146, roughly marks the route of the **Trail of Tears,** the 1838 winter death march of the Cherokee Nation.

In 2003, a $100 million, 100-foot-wide suspension bridge over the Mississippi replaced its narrow, rusting predecessor.

Back on Hwy-3, just north of I-57 and the town of Cairo, the GRR passes **Horseshoe Lake Conservation Area,** an example of what happens when the river shifts to a new channel and leaves an oxbow lake behind. Now prime winter habitat for over a million migrating geese and ducks, its tupelo gum trees, bald cypress, and swamp cottonwoods foreshadow the scenery found downstream among the bayous of the Mississippi Delta.

Cape Girardeau and the Trail of Tears

If you don't have time to follow the GRR's leisurely wind across southern Illinois, the fastest routes between St. Louis and Memphis are west of the Mississippi, where both US-61 and high-speed I-55 make quick work of the 300-mile drive. Along with Sainte Genevieve, another good stop on the Missouri side is the city of **Cape Girardeau** (pop. 37,941), the biggest and most bustling place for miles. Boyhood hometown of right-wing radio talk-show host Rush Limbaugh, whose father and grandfather were both local lawyers, Cape Girardeau dates its founding back to its days as trading post in the early 1700s, when the area was still in the hands of the French. The long history of the town and surrounding region is engagingly portrayed in a mile-long series of large murals (24 different scenes, totaling nearly 20,000 square feet!), painted on the massive concrete flood walls that protect downtown from Mississippi floods.

You can take in some of the murals, and the whole Cape Girardeau experience, while enjoying a meal at **Port Cape** restaurant (19 Water St.; 573/334-0954), while more memorable food is on the menu at **Broussard's Cajun Cuisine,** a block away (120 N. Main St.; 573/334-7235).

One of many scenes portrayed in the Cape Girardeau murals is a truly tragic one. Six years after wiping out Indians of the upper Mississippi in the Black Hawk War, President Andrew Jackson ordered the "Five Civilized Tribes" of the Cherokee, along with all Native Americans across the southeastern United States, to be forcibly removed from their fertile lands in Florida and Georgia and Tennessee, where gold had just been discovered. Some 5,000 Cherokee died along this 1,000-mile journey, during which many Native American men, women, and children crossed the Mississippi River here at Cape Girardeau. Ten miles north of town, the 3,400-acre **Trail of Tears State Park** (573/290-5268) preserves the scene of one moment along this marathon tragedy, with a two-mile section of the historic trail and interpretive plaques marking the wooded, riverside bluffs.

Cairo

"A grave uncheered by any gleam of promise" was but one of Charles Dickens's unsympathetic descriptions of **Cairo** (pronounced "CARE-oh" or "KAY-ro"; pop. 2,831), the town that presides over—and sometimes under—the meeting of the Mississippi and Ohio Rivers. Routinely submerged by floodwaters until the Corps of Engineers ringed the town with a massive stockade of levees and huge steel floodgates, Cairo's star shone briefly in the steamboat era and during the Civil War, when General Grant quartered his Army of the Tennessee here and Union ironclads were berthed along the waterfront. If you enjoy studying historic buildings (more often than not in Cairo they are empty, decaying buildings), you can see many signs of the prosperity that helped Cairo reach a peak population of over 15,000 people: a number of Victorian-era mansions built by merchants and boat captains remain in varying stages of repair, there's a majestic public library, and volunteers have been slowly restoring the stately, circa-1872 **Customs House** (Tues.–Fri.; free; 1400 Washington Ave.; 618/734-9632) into an intriguing (if incomplete) museum.

Along with the historic remnants, Cairo has something else worth seeing: the confluence of the two mighty rivers. Unless there's a flood in progress (as there was so destructively in the spring of 2011), do your watching from a small platform in **Fort Defiance State Park,** at the foot of the bridge that carries US-60 between Missouri and Kentucky, lasting but a quarter mile in Illinois.

While most of Cairo's story is in the past, if you visit you can enjoy one present-day pleasure: the delicious pulled pork sandwiches and other barbecue treats on offer at **Shemwell's** (1102 Washington St.; 618/734-0165), just up from the Customs House.

Metropolis: Home of Superman

The town of **Metropolis,** Illinois (pop. 5,676), along the Ohio River 25 miles northeast of Cairo but most easily accessible via Paducah, Kentucky, takes pride in its adopted superhero son, Superman. An impressive and photogenic 15-foot-tall bronze statue of the Man of Steel stands downtown, on a pedestal promoting "Truth—Justice—The American Way," on the north side of the Massac County Courthouse. Nearby are a quick-change telephone booth and the "offices" of the *Daily Planet* newspaper, and every June a festival celebrates the Man of Steel's crime-fighting efforts. For more information, and a look at one of the most extensive collections of Superman artifacts and memorabilia anywhere, visit the **Super Museum** (daily; $5; 517 Market St.; 618/524-5518).

TRUTH – JUSTICE – THE AMERICAN WAY

Metropolis, Illinois, the hometown of Superman, is also associated with another famous figure: Robert F. Stroud, the "Birdman of Alcatraz," is buried in the Masonic Cemetery.

The other big attraction in town is the 40,000-square-foot **Harrah's Metropolis Casino,** down on the banks of the Ohio River at the base of the railroad bridge.

KENTUCKY AND TENNESSEE

Most of the GRR's 60-odd miles across Kentucky are quite scenic, populated by only a handful of small towns, none of which has been overrun by tacky commercial strips. Continuing south across the Tennessee line, the route retains its rural, slow-road feel as it winds along the cultivated bottomlands around earthquake-created **Reelfoot Lake.** Midway to **Memphis,** the GRR comes back to the modern world, crossing the I-55 freeway then rejoining four-lane US-51 as it races to downtown Memphis, passing pine woods and cotton fields mixed with mobile homes, suburban ranch houses, and gas stations that double as the local video stores.

Wickliffe, Hickman, and New Madrid

Skipping from the banks of the Ohio River, the GRR stays with US-51 southbound through small, thoroughly industrial **Wickliffe** (pop. 794), then takes an attractive 40-mile meander away from the rivers through wooded hill country, returning to the edge of the Mississippi at **Hickman,** a dozen miles from the Tennessee line.

Across from Hickman, on the Missouri side of the river, is the spot where the Army Corps of Engineers blasted a hole in the Mississippi flood wall, taking pressure off the main channel but flooding more than 100,000 of riverside

Reelfoot Lake

farmland around the town of **New Madrid** (pronounced "MAD-rid"). New Madrid, in historical terms, is no stranger to disaster: Besides floods, the town was the epicenter of one of the strongest earthquakes ever to hit the United States, which struck on December 16, 1811. Seismographs and the Richter scale weren't around to measure it, but the quake was felt as far away as Boston, and more than 1,000 aftershocks rattled the region for years.

New Madrid conveniently marks the otherwise invisible line between Kentucky and Tennessee, and from here south the GRR follows Hwy-78 across a 40-mile stretch of low-lying bottomlands, passing the roadhouse bars and bait shops near **Reelfoot Lake,** a 25,000-acre recreation area and wildlife refuge created by the New Madrid earthquake. At **Dyersburg** (pop. 17,177), self-described as "friendly, God-fearing and patriotic citizens living and enjoying

Memphis

Memphis's gifts to American culture include the supermarket, the drive-in restaurant, the Holiday Inn, Elvis Presley, and Federal Express, and if you detect a pattern here you'll understand why the city is at once entertainingly kitsch and supremely captivating. This is not to say Memphis (pop. 646,889) lacks a coherent character—just the opposite—but its charms can have unpredictable side effects.

Beale Street, downtown between 2nd and 4th Streets, has been Memphis's honky-tonk central ever since native son W. C. Handy set up shop in the early 1900s with the blues he'd learned in Mississippi. Beale Street, and much of downtown Memphis, has been sanitized for your protection, turning it into a new! and improved! version of its old self. A massive shopping mall and flashy new arena for the Grizzlies basketball team have transformed the entire south side of downtown Memphis. Slap an adhesive name tag on your lapel and you'll fit right in with the tour bus crowds strolling at night along Beale Street's block of clubs—including **B. B. King's** (143 Beale St.; 901/524-5464), marked by a giant neon guitar.

Fortunately, a number of other music-related museums and attractions capture a more authentic Memphis: The original **Sun Records** studio (daily; $12; 706 Union Ave.; 901/521-0664), where Elvis, Johnny Cash, Roy Orbison, and many others recorded their historic tracks in the 1950s, is a short walk northeast. Even more satisfying for most music obsessives: the site of **Stax Records** studio (daily, closed Mon. in winter; $12; 926 E. McLemore Ave.; 901/942-7685), now an excellent museum documenting the soulful impact of Sam & Dave, Otis Redding, Al Green, and other greats during the 1960s.

If there's one place that shouldn't be missed, it's the eloquent **National Civil Rights Museum** (closed Tues.; $13; 450 Mulberry St.; 901/521-9699), south of Beale Street behind the restored facade of the Lorraine Motel, where Dr. Martin Luther King Jr. was assassinated in 1968. Aided by extensive video

Sun Records

newsreels and life-sized dioramas, museum exhibits let you step as far as you like into the powerful history of the Civil Rights Movement. Across the street, disturbing displays about Dr. King's assassination are housed in the old rooming house where James Earl Ray fired the fatal shots.

On the north side of downtown Memphis, **Mud Island** is a real island in the middle of the Mississippi River, connected to downtown by a pedestrian bridge and a monorail. This 50-acre island holds a five-block-long mock-up of the Mississippi River, with the Gulf of Mexico played by a huge, 1.3-million-gallon public swimming pool. Also here is the excellent **Mississippi River Museum.**

Right in downtown Memphis, but just a step away from the majors, the **Memphis Redbirds** ($5–18; 200 Union Ave.; 901/721-6000), Class AAA farm club for the St. Louis Cardinals, play at AutoZone Park.

Practicalities

As it is with live music, food is one area where Memphis can still surpass just about any other American city, and if your taste buds prefer improvisation and passion to over-refined "perfection," Memphis is sure to satisfy.

Competition among the city's 50 or more rib shacks is fierce. Elvis Presley's favorite barbecue joint, **Charlie Vergo's Rendezvous** (52 S. 2nd St.; 901/523-2746), right downtown, with its main entrance through a downtown alley, is now something of a tourist trap. Main challengers to the title of "Best Barbecue in the Universe" include **Neely's Interstate BBQ** (2265 S. 3rd St.; 901/775-2304), just north of where US-61 crosses I-55, and bare-bones drive-up barbecue stand **Cozy Corner** (745 N. Parkway; 901/527-9158), just east of US-51. For a change of pace from ribs, try the onion rings, burgers, beers, and live blues at another Memphis institution, **Huey's** (77 S. 2nd St.; 901/527-2700), right downtown.

Except during the city's many music and food festivals, Memphis accommodations are priced very reasonably. The whole alphabet of major chains—from Best Western to Super 8—is spread around the I-240 beltway, and again along I-55 in neighboring Arkansas. One landmark place to stay, the **Peabody Hotel** ($209 and up; 149 Union Ave.; 901/529-4000) is Memphis's premiere downtown hotel, whose sparkling lobby is home to the Mississippi's most famous mallards: Twice daily, at 11 AM and 5 PM, the red carpet is rolled out for the Peabody ducks to parade (waddle, really) to and from the lobby fountain. And if you're planning a vigil at Graceland, consider **Elvis Presley's Heartbreak Hotel** ($115 and up; 3677 Elvis Presley Blvd.; 901/332-1000 or 877/777-0606). Owned by his heirs and across from his former lair, the Heartbreak Hotel features a 24-hour in-room Elvis movie channel.

For tourist information contact the friendly and thorough **Memphis Convention and Visitors Bureau** (47 Union Ave.; 901/543-5300 or 888/633-9099), or drop by the information center at 340 Beale Street.

big city conveniences," the Great River Road jumps on to US-51, and from here south to Memphis the route does its level best to mimic an Interstate, rendering the final 75 miles a forgettable blur.

Driving Across Memphis

Fans of pop-culture kitsch will love what the GRR offers in Memphis: The main road from the north (US-51) is Danny Thomas Boulevard; south of downtown, this turns into Elvis Presley Boulevard and runs right past the gates of Graceland. (However, if you're continuing on to the Mississippi Delta, from Graceland you should switch onto US-61, which runs about two miles to the west.)

MISSISSIPPI

Ecologically speaking, the Mississippi Delta is the vast alluvial plain between Cairo and the Gulf of Mexico, but "The Delta" of popular myth is much more circumscribed, occupying the 250-mile-long realm of King Cotton, between Memphis and Vicksburg. As important as its proper boundaries is its legacy as the cradle of nearly every American musical style from gospel,

The word Mississippi comes from the Algonquin word *misezibi*, meaning "water from land all over," or "great water."

blues, and jazz to country and rock 'n' roll. The backbone of our route, US-61, is also legendary as the path of the "Great Migration," the mass exodus to the industrialized northern United States of some five million black sharecroppers in the decades after World War I.

As the Great River Road cuts inland and drops like a plumb line across the cotton fields, we recommend a number of side trips to landmarks of this rich cultural heritage. Where the Delta ends at **Vicksburg's** bluffs, our route begins mingling with ghosts from the South's plantation and Civil War past, then finally rolls into Louisiana.

Mississippi law doesn't require casinos to be riverboats, it merely requires them to float. All appearances to the contrary, the giant Las Vegas–style casinos in Tunica County are indeed floating, mostly in ponds dredged specifically to meet the letter of the law.

All across Mississippi, away from the main roads on the sleepier section of the GRR, the towns are filled with shotgun shacks, low-slung Creole-style bungalows, and old trailers that some people have nicknamed "doghouses" without any attempt at irony. What look like oil drums mounted on garden carts in the odd front yard are smokers, for doing barbecue just right; their presence sometimes implies the proximity of a social club or juke joint that may do only weekend business. Local stores, if they exist, are where men in overalls sit and stand in clusters, keeping an eye on the world. In autumn when the cotton is ready for harvest,

In Search of Elvis

Scratch the surface of Memphis, and you'll always turn up a little Elvis, like pennies and pocket lint in an old sofa. That guy behind the counter? His mom used to give piano lessons to Elvis's stepbrothers. That woman at the next table? Her after-school job was in the Libertyland amusement park, which Elvis would rent out in its entirety just so he could ride the Zippin' Pippin' roller coaster for hours on end. A frequent Graceland visitor during the Elvis years collected fuzz from the shag carpet to give to friends; maybe the woman paying for her coffee still has her tuft. Even the owner of the greasiest old pizza joint will tell you how Elvis would come in with his band, "back when he was nothin'." Get used to it: Elvis is everywhere.

The font of all this meta-Elvis-ness is, of course, **Graceland** (daily; 3734 Elvis Presley Blvd./US-51; 901/332-3322 or 800/238-2000), about a mile south of I-55 amid a clutter of burger joints and muffler shops. At age 21, flush with his early success, Elvis paid $100,000 for Graceland, which was one of the more fashionable houses in Memphis in 1957, and seeing what happens when Elvis's poor-white-boy taste and Hollywood budget run amok is well worth the price of admission. You can buy tickets to each part of the Graceland complex or splurge on a $35 combination Platinum Tour ticket that gives admission to the mansion as well as the other "collections," such as the King's private jet or his car collection. Many of his cars, including his famous pink 1955 Cadillac, are arrayed as if at a drive-in movie, with a big screen playing his race car scenes from *Viva Las Vegas* on a continuous loop—it's my favorite stop in the whole shebang.

A visit to Graceland says very little about Elvis's music (though there is a room showing off an 80-foot wall full of gold and platinum records) but speaks volumes about his mystique. Elvis is buried on the property, alongside his father and mother, in the Meditation Garden.

Elvis's 1955 Cadillac

huge truck-sized bales sit in the cleared muddy margins of the fields, and white fluff accumulates in drifts on the narrow loose shoulder, swirling in small eddies in your wake.

Meanwhile the Mississippi River does its snaky shuffle off to the Gulf of Mexico behind a continuous line of levees, a bayou here and cut-off lake there as proof of past indirections.

Northwest Mississippi: Casino Country

Leaving Memphis via US-61, the GRR enters De Soto and Tunica Counties; the place-names memorialize Hernando de Soto, the first European to see the Mississippi, and the combative Tunica tribe, which forced the Spanish conquistador's mosquito- and snake-bitten expedition to flee across the river hereabouts in 1542. Outfitted with cannons, priests, slaves, pigs, war dogs, and 1,000 soldiers, de Soto spent years marching through southern swamps in quest of gold—but he was 450 years too early. Tunica County, long one of the most destitute places in America, only became a gold mine after the state legalized gambling in 1992. Several billion dollars of investment later, Tunica is the third-largest gambling center in the country, and every big name in the casino business lines the levee here. Bugsy Siegel would be proud, but as ever outsiders have benefited much more than the still-poor local residents.

To aid the influx of people anxious to part with their money, US-61 has been turned into a high-volume, four-lane highway. And motels, fast-food places, and gas stations have popped up like mushrooms after a spring rain.

One non-gaming benefit of all this investment has been the construction of the **RiverPark,** where a two-mile hiking trail winds through Mississippi wetlands, a real riverboat shuttles out onto the Mississippi for an 90-minute-long cruise ($15), and a rooftop gallery gives grand views over the river. (Be aware that ongoing renovations may limit your access.)

South of the casino area along US-61, the GRR brings you to another traditional Mississippi experience: the classic grits-and-gravy, steak-and-potatoes **Blue & White Café** (1355 N. US-61; 662/363-1371). Offering a true taste of the Delta with its buffets and local specialties, including deep-fried pickles, the Blue & White has hardly changed since the day it opened in 1937. South from Tunica, US-61 makes a 35-mile beeline through the cotton fields to Clarksdale.

Moon Lake

Twenty miles south of Tunica's casinos, just west of US-61, **Moon Lake** was home to one of the South's most famous Prohibition landmarks, the Moon Lake Club. Unlike speakeasies associated with thugs and tarts, this club was a family destination where parents could dance and gamble while the kids played by the lake. In a place and time when planes were still so rare the sound of their engines could interrupt work and empty classrooms, the club flew in fresh Maine lobster and Kansas City steak for its clientele of rich, white Memphians.

Moon Lake has a literary history, too, appearing in a number of Tennessee Williams's dramas. Williams knew it well: Not only was the club property owned by a cousin, but as a boy he had been a frequent guest, accompanying his grandfather, the Reverend Dakin, on parish calls throughout the county.

Now known as **Uncle Henry's Place** (662/337-2757), the restaurant is still popular, and cottages are sometimes available.

Helena, Arkansas

About a dozen miles west of the GRR and Moon Lake via US-49 is **Helena, Arkansas,** the most deadly place on the river to Union regiments in the Civil War, stopped in their tracks by the festering malarial swamps that once surrounded the town. It began building a different reputation back in the 1940s when local radio station **KFFA 1360 AM** began broadcasting *King Biscuit Time,* a live blues show, originally hosted by harmonica legend Sonny Boy Williamson; the show is still on the air every weekday at 12:15 PM In early October, the **Arkansas Blues and Heritage Festival** attracts fans by the tens of thousands to hear one of the best lineups of live gospel and blues in the nation. The **Delta Cultural Center** (Tues.–Sat. 9 AM–5 PM; free; 141 Cherry St.; 870/338-4350), in the renovated train depot downtown, with its fine historical displays on the lives of Delta inhabitants, is an equally compelling reason to visit this small river town.

Jetting the Blues

If serious blues hounds sniff around enough, they can still find the kind of swaggering, sweaty, Saturday-night juke joint that will always be synonymous with real Delta blues. You know the place: bottles of Budweiser on ice in a plastic cooler, clouds of cigarette smoke, some rough customers, hot dancing, and honest gut-wrenching blues played with an intensity that rattles your fillings. Yes, such places exist, but they don't run display ads in the local paper or make the list of area attractions given out by local chambers of commerce.

The really homegrown variety announces itself with hand-lettered signs on telephone poles and launderette bulletin boards, if at all. They have no phone numbers and no advance tickets (usually); you have to show up to find out who, if anyone, is playing. Ask around—the convenience store clerk or the person next to you at the barbecue counter. Keep in mind that the blues are rooted in a condition of the Delta's black community that is no bed of roses; voyeurs slumming as tourists-to-hardship will be politely stonewalled at best. Rest assured, though; with perseverance and the proper attitude (and especially for women, a companion), you'll find what you're looking for. Once you get there, out-of-towners needn't worry about the reception: Blues musicians welcome an appreciative audience, period.

Weekends, again mostly Saturday nights, are also about the only time you'll catch blues in the more commercial juke joints and clubs, simply because so many musicians have other jobs during the week. If you really want to be sure of hearing some blues, time your travels to coincide with one of the big annual blues festivals, like these:

Sunflower River Blues and Gospel Festival
mid-August; Clarksdale, Mississippi

Memphis Music and Heritage Festival
Labor Day weekend; Memphis, Tennessee

Mississippi Delta Blues Festival
mid-September; Greenville, Mississippi

King Biscuit Blues Festival
early October; Helena, Arkansas

Clarksdale

The blues were born in the Delta, but they grew up in **Clarksdale.** The census rolls for this small town read like a musical hall of fame: Ma Rainey, W. C. Handy, Bessie Smith, Sam Cooke, Ike Turner, Muddy Waters, Wade Walton, John Lee Hooker, Big Jack Johnson, and many others whose achievements are described—and may be heard—in the **Delta Blues Museum** (closed Sun.; $7; 662/627-6820) in the circa-1918 railroad depot at the heart of Clarksdale's "Blues Alley" district downtown. The museum offers maps of blues landmarks around town and around the state, a calendar of blues events, and all sorts of helpful information. In short, this is the best place to start your journey through the Delta blues world, especially if you can arrange to be here for one of the annual blues and culture festivals, like mid-April's very lively **Juke Joint Festival.**

Thomas Harris, author of *The Silence of the Lambs,* hails from the tiny hamlet of Rich, just east of the junction of US-61 and US-49.

Unlike the spreading deltas of the Orinoco or Nile, the Mississippi cuts a deeper channel as it rolls south, the deceptively smooth surface hiding a flow four times greater than it was at the St. Louis Arch.

Ever since W. C. Handy traded his steady gigs in Clarksdale for a career on Beale Street in Memphis, the Mississippi Delta has exported its blues musicians to places where they receive wider recognition and a living wage, but come on a Friday or Saturday night and you'll see Clarksdale still cooks up some good hot blues. Many of the most "authentic" juke joints are in dilapidated parts of town, but an infusion of cash by the likes of actor Morgan Freeman has created the more accessible **Ground Zero Blues Club** (662/621-9009), offering meals and music a block from the Delta Blues Museum. If you're in town during August, it would be a shame to miss the **Sunflower River Blues and Gospel Festival,** organized by the Delta Blues Museum and staged at venues around town.

The rest of downtown Clarksdale is well worth exploring for its lazy ambience and wealth of history. The old **Delta Cinema** (11 3rd St.), downtown, still shows current releases in a 1920s theater and helps host the Juke Joint Festival. There's also a steamboat-shaped store around the corner, across the street from the Sunflower River, and funky art galleries like **Cat Head Blues and Folk Art** (252 Delta Ave.; 662/624-5992) showcase local culture and events while offering an array of hard-to-find CDs, DVDs and T-shirts.

About 30 miles south of Clarksdale on US-49 is **Parchman,** infamous home to the state prison farm memorialized in songs like bluesman Bukka White's "Parchman Farm." The "Midnight Special," another oft-heard allusion in Delta blues lyrics, was the weekend train from New Orleans that brought visitors to the prison.

Clarksdale has plenty of fast food, but the barbecue is better: Try the **Ranchero** (1907 N. State St.; 662/624-9768), on US-49, or **Abe's Bar-B-Q** (616 State St.; 662/624-9947), in the center of town, cooking up tangy 'cue and pork-filled hot tamales since 1924. For a surprising (and comparatively healthy) dose of Lebanese-Italian food (and

Ground Zero Blues Club sign in Clarksdale, Mississippi

fantastic chocolate cream pies!) amid the pork palaces, check out **Chamoun's Rest Haven** (closed Sun.; 419 N. State St.; 662/624-8601), on US-49 just south of the Big Sunflower River.

US-61, a.k.a. State Street, is also where you'll find Clarksdale's motels, including **Comfort Inn** ($80 and up; 818 S. State St.; 662/627-5122) at the southern end of town. More adventurous visitors might want to consider Clarksdale's old Afro-American Hospital, where blues vocalist Bessie Smith died in 1937 after a car wreck out on US-61. Now called the **Riverside Hotel,** it rents a few minimally updated rooms ($40; 615 Sunflower Ave.; 662/624-9163). For a more comfortable but still definitely down-to-earth Delta experience, spend the night in a renovated sharecropper shack at the one-of-a-kind **Shack Up Inn** ($65 and up; 662/624-8329), on the grounds of the historic Hopson Plantation 10 miles south of Clarksdale. The 14 wooden shacks have plumbing and power but still feel authentic, and you get your own front porch to practice your blues harp or simply take in the Delta dawn.

Oxford

Do you need a break from the Delta yet? Has counting pickup trucks, propane tanks, and barbecued ribs induced a bad imitation drawl? How far would you detour for a well-stocked bookstore, or a restaurant that doesn't immerse everything in boiling oil? Sixty-two miles east of Clarksdale on Hwy-6 is the college town of **Oxford,** whose cultural amenities, though common to college towns from Amherst to Berkeley, set it in a world apart from most of Mississippi. The college in question is "Ole Miss," otherwise known as the **University of Mississippi,** whose pleasant campus holds such treasures as B. B. King's entire personal collection of records, posters, photos, and more in the **Ole Miss Blues Archive** (Mon.–Fri. 8 AM–5 PM), in Farley Hall across from Barnard Observatory. The renovated antebellum astronomical observatory houses the **Center for the Study of Southern Culture** (Mon.–Fri.; 662/232-5993), which sponsors exhibits, lectures, and screenings.

Elsewhere under the leafy old oaks you'll find a large collection of Southern folk art in the **University Museums** (Tues.–Sun. 10 AM–6 PM; free) and a collection of William Faulkner first editions in the J. D. Williams Library. Faulkner was a resident of Oxford for most of his life; readers of his novels will recognize in surrounding Lafayette County (pronounced "luh-FAY-it") elements of Faulkner's fictional Yoknapatawpha. A statue of him was recently placed in the square at the center of Oxford, and **Rowan Oak** (Tues.–Sat. 10 AM–4 PM, Sun. 1–4 PM; $5; 662/234-3284), his house on Old

Taylor Road off South Lamar Avenue, remains as he left it when he died in 1962, with the bottle of whiskey next to the old typewriter in his study almost, but not quite, empty.

Visit Faulkner's gravesite by following the signs from the north side of Courthouse Square. Near the cemetery entrance lie other family members who didn't affect adding the "u" to their surname, including the brother whose untimely death Faulkner mourned in his first novel, *Soldier's Pay*.

Oxford Practicalities

When respects have been paid to Southern culture and it's time to eat, there's a lot to choose from. The west side of central Courthouse Square is home to two good restaurants, ranging from the homespun **Ajax Diner** (118 Courthouse Square; 662/232-8880)—great pies and cobblers!—to the eclectic "New Southern" cuisine of the plush **City Grocery** (152 Courthouse Square; 662/232-8080), where traditional dishes like bread pudding and shrimp and grits are complemented by fine wines and a full bar. And thanks to all the Ole Miss students, you can enjoy a range of fast food, pizza places, and live music along Lamar Street, south of the square.

East of the GRR on Hwy-61 is small **Mound Bayou,** the oldest black town in the state. A man named Isaiah Montgomery, inspired by Booker T. Washington's prescriptions for black self-improvement, founded the all-black community in 1887 with support from his former employer, Jefferson Davis.

Accommodations in Oxford include the **Downtown Oxford Inn and Suites** ($125 and up; 400 N. Lamar; 662/234-3031), a former Holiday Inn north of the courthouse, and the comfortably worn **5 Twelve,** formerly the Oliver-Britt House ($105 and up; 512 Van Buren Ave.; 662/234-8043), a circa-1905 B&B.

The **Oxford Tourism Council** (662/234-4680) will happily provide more information and a calendar of cultural events; it also operates a visitors center in a tiny cottage next to City Hall on the central square. Another good source of information is **Square Books,** on the south side of the same square. This is one of the country's great independent bookstores, with a full range of local and international authors, plus a nice café.

Hwy-1: Great River Road State Park

Between Clarksdale and Greenville, the Great River Road winds west of the much-busier US-61, looping next to the Mississippi River along Hwy-1. It's a rural road, running past soybean, cotton, and "pond cat" farms—catfish farming is big business hereabouts. Midway along, the GRR runs past **Great River Road State Park,** near the town of Rosedale. Located inside the Mississippi River levee, the park offers unique views of the "Father of Waters" from a 75-foot-high overlook tower.

Across the Mississippi from Rosedale in a cotton field off Hwy-1 is **Rohwer, Arkansas,** where 8,500 Japanese Americans were forced from their California homes and imprisoned for the duration of World War II.

Farther south, at the north edge of Greenville, the 1,000-year-old, 55-foot-high earthen cones next to the highway are the remnants of the prehistoric Mound Builder people who lived here a millennium ago. Now preserved as the **Winterville Mounds,** the 11 ancient mounds that still remain here are thought to have been sacred ceremonial sites. Little is known about the enigmatic people who built them (and hundreds of others) along the banks of the Mississippi and Ohio Rivers, but the on-site museum (daily, free) shows off a range of pottery and arrowheads recovered here.

About 30 miles east of Greenville, Moorhead is known in blues geography as the place "where the Southern crosses the Dog," an allusion to the Southern and Yazoo-Delta (a.k.a. Yellow Dog) Railroads. Nearby **Money, Mississippi,** was the location of the notorious 1955 murder of 14-year-old Emmett Till, a key moment in the burgeoning Civil Rights Movement.

Greenville

The Delta's largest city, **Greenville** (pop. 34,927) is one of the largest river ports in the state, but instead of cotton-shipping wharves, its levees are now lined by floating casinos. Hwy-1 through Greenville takes top honors for the least attractive strip of gas stations and minimarts along the GRR, but appearances can be deceiving, as the city has some fine cultural traditions, from the anti–Ku Klux Klan editorializing of Hodding Carter's *Delta-Democrat Times* during the 1950s and 1960s, to the great steaks and hot tamales served up since 1941 at **Doe's Eat Place** (502 Nelson St.; 662/334-3315). Despite being granted a James Beard "American Classic" award in 2007, Doe's is still housed in the same big white building it started in (follow N. Broadway to the brick churches, then turn toward the river).

It's known for good food and good spirits throughout the state—and all over the South. Ten other Doe's Eat Place restaurants have opened, including one in Little Rock, Arkansas, that was made famous by former president Bill Clinton. Though Doe's looks homespun, its prices are not; steaks will set you back a good $25 or more.

For faster, more affordable food, try **Gino's Hamburgers,** off South Main Street (128 W. Reed St.; 662/378-9655).

Second to Clarksdale in the Delta blues galaxy, Greenville comes alive in mid-September during the annual **Mississippi Delta Blues and Heritage Festival** (662/335-3523 or 888/335-3523). For accommodations, look along US-82 near the junction with US-61, east of town.

Hearing Delta blues live can be as big a challenge as finding it on the radio. Helena, Arkansas's historic **KFFA 1360 AM** plays at least half an hour at lunchtime, and you can catch more contemporary music on Greenville's **WBAD 94.3 FM.**

Highway 61 Revisited

Between Greenville and Vicksburg, the GRR continues along Hwy-1 through the cotton-rich bottomlands, the landscape as unvarying as the country music that dominates the radio dial. Before the Civil War, this land was nearly uninhabitable hardwood forests and fever-riddled swamps, home to snakes, panthers, fire ants and mosquitoes. After Reconstruction, the valuable oaks, sweetgum, and hickory were logged off, the swamps drained, and levees built. Now just the snakes and mosquitoes remain. It's a long, slow ride, while US-61 races along to the east.

East of Greenville, just west of US-61, the town of Leland was the boyhood home of Muppet-master Jim Henson. There's now a small and suitably warm-spirited museum, on the north side of US-82 at Deer Creek, honoring him, Kermit the Frog, and his other creations.

The 50 miles of US-82 between Greenville and Greenwood pass through the heart of Delta blues country, and a number of nearby towns feature high on any "blues pilgrimage" itinerary. Holly Ridge holds the grave of **Charley Patton** ("Voice of the Delta," 1891–1934). Robert Johnson (1911–1938) is remembered by a burial marker in Morgan City (one of three alleged grave sites for the blues legend). B. B. King was born in Indianola and is honored in an annual festival the first weekend in June. Farther south on US-61, Rolling Fork was the birthplace of **Muddy Waters** (1915–1983), while the great bass player and songwriter Willie Dixon (1915–1992) was born in Vicksburg.

R.I.P., Robert Johnson

Vicksburg stands at the junction of the Great River Road and our **Southern Pacific** route along US-80 (see page 841). This route, runnings from San Diego to Savannah, is described on pages 800–863.

Vicksburg

The "Red Carpet City of the South," **Vicksburg** (pop. 23,856) didn't roll one out for the Union army during the Civil War. Instead, the city so stubbornly opposed Union efforts to win control of the Mississippi River that it became the target of one of the longest sieges in U.S. military history. After the war ended, Vicksburg suffered once again in 1876, when the city woke up to face a mud flat of flopping fish after the Mississippi River found itself a new streambed—overnight. Thanks to the diligence of engineers who redirected the Yazoo River in 1903, Vicksburg has its waterfront back, now complete with several modern-day sharks, whose slot machines and roulette wheels spin 24 hours a day for your entertainment.

Many of the city's posh antebellum

Birth of the Teddy Bear

About 30 miles north of Vicksburg along US-61, the hamlet of **Onward** has a historical plaque marking the "Birthplace of the Teddy Bear." The original teddy bear was inspired by a cub from the woods near Onward: Tied by a noose to a tree in the canebrakes, the cute fellow was found by President Teddy Roosevelt while hunting here in 1902. His refusal to shoot the defenseless animal, publicized in an editorial cartoon, garnered such popular approval

that a New York firm requested the president's permission to name a stuffed toy after him. The only rub is, T. R. didn't actually refuse to shoot—because, in fact, he wasn't there. But neither was the cub! According to members of the hunting party, the president's guide, Holt Collier, an African American veteran of the Confederate cavalry, was challenged to prove he could lasso a bear. So he did, when one came along through the swamp—an old and rather weak one, as it turned out, that splashed around in a slough before they cut him loose. T. R., however, having tired of waiting for game, had returned to camp and missed the whole episode.

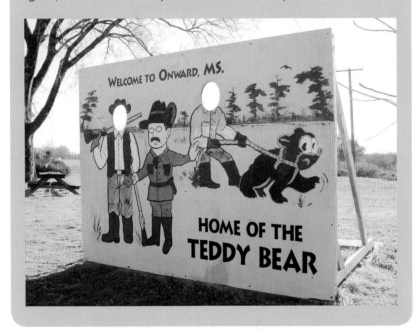

houses survived the Civil War with varying degrees of damage, and during the post-war Reconstruction several additional mansions were added to the bluffs overlooking the river. Most of these homes are open to the public (for around $10 each), and during the fortnight-long "Pilgrimages" in late March and mid-October, slightly discounted multiple-house tours are available. The architecturally varied mansions, many of which double as B&Bs, and their copious inventories of fine antiques are more fascinating to decorative arts aficionados than to history buffs, who may find tours illuminating more for what is omitted than included. Stories of deprivation and Union plundering, cannonballs in parlor walls, and other wartime relics are religiously enshrined, yet only rarely is a word spoken about slavery.

To escape from Vicksburg's indoor onslaught of Chippendale claw feet, road-trippers used to stop by **Margaret's Grocery,** right on the GRR (old US-61) on the north side of town, where an assemblage of huge hand-lettered signs and vividly painted sculptures preach biblically inspired words of wisdom at passersby. But since Miss Margaret died in 2009, her preacher husband Dennis has been in a care home, and their roadside creation has, alas, been left to decay.

The most famous of Vicksburg's antebellum homes turned B&Bs is **Cedar Grove Inn** ($100 and up; 2200 Oak St.; 601/636-1000), south of downtown, which has a spectacular panorama over lush gardens and railroad yards down the bluffs to the broad Mississippi River. Ironically, Cedar Grove was built for a cousin of General Sherman, who used it as a military hospital. Another grand old mansion, **Anchuca** ($125 and up; 1010 E. 1st St.; 601/661-0111), preserves a more complete picture of antebellum life, with well-preserved gardens and slave quarters (plus a very fine café). Dozens more, dating from the 1870s up through the early 1900s, are found throughout Vicksburg's pleasant cobblestone residential areas.

The downtown commercial district, on the bluffs above the river, offers another, more contemporary glimpse into Southern culture. If you've ever tried to imagine a world without Coke, step into the **Biedenharn Coca-Cola Museum,** smack downtown (1107 Washington St.), and see where one man's ingenuity slew all hopes for such a world. Here, in 1894, Joseph Biedenharn conceived of putting the strictly regional soda-fountain drink into bottles, the better to reach new markets. The rest, as they say, is history. Toast worldwide domination with some of the classic stuff, straight up or over ice cream, or pay $3 to view galleries full of old promotional serving trays and the like.

Vicksburg National Military Park

Though the engineering feat that redirected the Yazoo and Mississippi Rivers (and brought Vicksburg more civil engineers per capita than any other U.S. city) is impressive, it's the story of the Civil War campaign to split the Confederacy in half that dominates history here. The battle for Vicksburg, which was known as the "Gibraltar of the Confederacy," reached its dramatic conclusion on July 4, 1863, amid the strategic heights and ravines of the 1,800-acre **Vicksburg National Military Park.** The ins and outs and strategizing behind the 47-day Siege of Vicksburg, and the story behind the 1,300-odd markers and monuments, becomes emotionally compelling after some accounting of the anecdotes of individual valor, of odd courtesies amid the bloodshed, and of the tragedy and

Late in the year when the pecan crop is in, you can buy pecans from vans or shacks beside the highway. Buy pre-shelled ones, or spend hours struggling with a nutcracker.

humanity that lie behind the 16 winding miles of stone. The **visitors center** (daily; $8 per car; 601/636-0583), on the east side of Vicksburg via Clay Street or off I-20 exit 4, has exhibits, maps, brochures, and audio tours with narration and sound effects. Or, you can hire a guide to accompany you in your car and explain everything from battle tactics to the symbolism of the monuments. The advantage to a live guide is the opportunity to ask questions and to delve into whatever suits your curiosity, be it stories of the many women who fought incognito, or of the immigrants who enlisted to win citizenship.

While Vicksburg's surrender allowed President Lincoln to declare that "the Father of Waters now flows unvexed to the sea," local whites stayed vexed for over 80 years: Because the surrender occurred on July 4, until the end of World War II Independence Day in Vicksburg was celebrated only by African Americans.

One of the most unusual sights in the Vicksburg Military Park is the **USS Cairo,** an ironclad paddlewheel battleship that was sunk by a torpedo during the Civil War. Preserved for a century by the Mississippi mud, it was recovered and restored and is now on display in its own museum, above the river at the west end of the park.

Vicksburg also has two military cemeteries, one for each side. The Union cemetery is the largest Civil War burial ground in the country, holding the remains of more than 17,000 soldiers who died here and all over the south; more than 12,000 of the dead are simply marked "unknown." Another 5,000 Confederate dead are buried in the Vicksburg City Cemetery.

Vicksburg Practicalities

Vicksburg has an enormously compelling history, but it's also a very pleasant place to spend some time. For a traditional home-style feast, sit down to the communal round table at **Walnut Hills** (1214 Adams St.; 601/638-4910) and dig into the endless supply of classic regional dishes, from fried pork tenderloin to fried dill pickles. Given the fresh ingredients (and depending on how much of a pig you can be), the moderate prices are a great value, and the overall ambience embodies the essence of Southern hospitality. Deep-fried tamale addicts should seek out **Solly's Hot Tamales,** near the Cedar Grove mansion on US-61 Business (1921 Washington St.; 601/636-2020). Barbecue lovers will want to sample the offerings at **Goldie's Express,** south of I-20 (3313 Pemberton Blvd.; 601/636-2551).

The icon of Southern gentility and refreshment, the mint julep, was allegedly born in Vicksburg: Water from fragrant Mint Springs in what is now the National Military Park was mixed with good Kentucky bourbon brought to town by riverboat captains. It goes without saying that Kentuckians and Tennesseeans consider this pure fiction.

Vicksburg motels, found at the south edge of town along I-20 between the Mississippi River and the Military Park, include a wide selection of the national chains and their local imitators; one of the nicest is the **Deluxe Inn** ($50 and up; 2751 North Frontage Rd.; 601/636-5121).

If you're in the mood, you can play Rhett and Scarlett for a night, pampering yourself with canopied beds in one of the dozen camellia-draped antebellum mansions (including Cedar Grove and Anchuca) that double as plush B&Bs. Any will have you whistling "Dixie," but true history buffs will want to request the Grant Room at Cedar Grove, which is still furnished with the very bed the general used after Union forces occupied Vicksburg. The staff claims Grant was a bedridden drunk for his entire stay, but pay no attention—he was probably a poor tipper at the bar, and folks around here bear grudges for generations over things like that.

You won't notice many people lolling about on grassy lawns or parks in the southern Delta, for the simple reason that this has become the realm of the fire ant, whose stinging bite would shame a wasp into adopting some other line of work.

For thorough information on lodging and attractions, contact the friendly **Vicksburg Convention and Visitors Bureau** (3300 Clay St.; 601/636-9421 or 800/221-3536) opposite the entrance to the National Military Park. If your visit falls during Pilgrimage, don't expect easy pickings on rooms: Most B&Bs are booked up to *two years* in advance for those weeks.

Port Gibson

One of the many little gems of the GRR is 30 miles south of Vicksburg: **Port Gibson,** the town General Grant found "too beautiful to burn." As they did with Savannah, Georgia, the Union Army spared Port Gibson during the Civil War, and decades of economic doldrums have spared the town from the Wal-Mart sprawl that at times seems to have enveloped the rest of the South. Fine homes still grace the pleasantly shaded main drag, but most eye-catching is the giant Monty Python prop known as the **Church of the Golden Hand** because its steeple is topped by a gold-leafed hand, its index finger pointing the way to heaven. Actually, this is the circa-1859 First Presbyterian Church, whose interior is lit by the gasoliers of the famous steamboat *Robert E. Lee,* the record-setting winner of the Great Steamboat Race of 1870. Newspapers of the day reckoned that millions of dollars were wagered on the outcome of the New Orleans-to-St. Louis race, which attracted international attention. The *Lee*'s three-day, 18-hour, and 14-minute victory was an upset for the favored title holder, the *Natchez.*

the Church of the Golden Hand

Across the street from the Golden Hand, next to an Exxon station, stands another unusual building, **Temple Gemiluth Chassed,** an elaborate Moorish-arched temple built in 1892 by Port Gibson's then large and prosperous Jewish community.

For an overview of a nearly vanished Southern culture, spend some time at the **Museum of the Southern Jewish Experience.** Based at a former Jewish summer camp in **Utica,** a half hour to the northeast of Port Gibson, the museum also has a branch exhibit in the basement of Temple B'nai Israel in **Natchez** (213 S. Commerce St.); both are by appointment only (601/362-6357).

Ruins of Windsor and Emerald Mound

From Port Gibson, you can race along the 70-mph US-61 to Natchez or follow a quietly scenic 50-mile detour along kudzu-lined country back roads and the serene Natchez Trace Parkway. The great Mississippi writer Willie Morris said "there is no more haunted, complex terrain in America" than this, and traveling through here you can't help but be aware of the region's many ghostly remnants. The looping first part of this route leaves Port Gibson next to the Exxon station, heading west on Rodney Road (Hwy-552) toward the Mississippi River past abandoned homesteads and picturesque old cemeteries rotting in the woods. After about 13 miles, look for a small sign and follow a short gravel road until you spot giant stone columns poking through the treetops. This is the **Ruins of Windsor.** Once the state's most lavish Greek Revival mansion and landmark to river pilots, it was reduced by an 1890 fire to its bare Corinthian ribs.

Ruins of Windsor

Another enigmatic remain is farther south, nearly invisible in the lush growth: **Emerald Mound,** a prehistoric platform over 400 feet wide and 35 feet tall. The second-largest mound in North America, it was built around AD 1250 and was still in use as a ceremonial center when the first Europeans arrived; Emerald Mound is open daily, located on Hwy-553 just west of Natchez Trace Parkway milepost 10.3.

the only known drawing of Windsor before the fire

Natchez

Before the Civil War, **Natchez** (pronounced "NATCH-iss," rhymes with "matches") had the most millionaires per capita in the United States, and it shows. If luxurious antebellum houses make your heart beat faster, Natchez (which has more than 500 antebellum structures inside the city limits), with its innumerable white columns and rich smorgasbord of Italian marble, imported crystal, and sterling silver, might just put you in the local ICU. That so much antebellum finery still exists is because Natchez, unlike Vicksburg, surrendered to Grant's army almost without a fight. Anti-Yankee sentiment may in fact run higher now than during the war, for Natchez was vehemently opposed to the Confederacy and outspokenly against Mississippi's secession from the Union. Since Natchez was second only to New Orleans as social and cultural capital of a region with two-thirds of the richest people in America, most of whom owed their wealth to slave-picked cotton, its support of the Union might seem a little incongruous.

Of course, such apparent contradictions should come as no surprise from a community raised with genteel cotillions and the Mississippi's busiest red-light district side by side. (Once-disreputable Natchez Under-the-Hill, where the most famous brothel in the South was destroyed by a fire in 1992, is today but a single gentrified block of riverfront bars and restaurants lined up alongside the permanently moored riverboat Isle of Capri casino.

As befits the place that originated the concept, the annual Natchez Pilgrimages (held for five weeks in late spring and two weeks in October) are longer than you will typically find elsewhere. The number of **antebellum mansions** open to the public more than doubles, hoop skirts and brass-buttoned waistcoats abound, and musical diversions like the Confederate Pageant are held nightly. Among the most fascinating homes open year-round is the one that didn't get finished: **Longwood,** on Lower Woodville Road, is the nation's largest octagonal house, capped by a red onion dome. Its grounds are fittingly gothic, too, with moss-dripping tree limbs, sunken driveway, and the family cemetery out in the woods. Information on the Pilgrimages, other house tours (about $10 per house), and the chance to stay in one of many historic B&Bs all comes from the same group, Natchez Pilgrimage Tours (601/446-6631 or 800/647-6742), which also runs horse-drawn carriage tours.

Southern history doesn't merely comprise those Greek Revival heaps and their *Gone With the Wind* stereotypes. Natchez, for example, had a large population of free blacks, whose story is told in downtown's **Museum of Afro-American History and Culture** (Tues.–Sat. 1–4:30 PM; 301 Main St.; 601/445-0728), in the old post office, where you'll also find interesting Black Heritage walking-tour brochures. Large Jewish sections in the **City Cemetery** (follow signs for the National Cemetery; City Cemetery is along the way) also furnish evidence of the South's tapestried past. The marble statuary and decorative wrought iron offer a pleasant outdoor respite for weary mansion-goers, too.

There are no cotton fields around Natchez, because all the cotton that paid for these mansions was grown across the river in the Louisiana bottomlands.

Across the Mississippi from Natchez, the town of **Ferriday, Louisiana,** was where rocker Jerry Lee "Great Balls of Fire" Lewis and his cousin, evangelist Jimmy Swaggart, grew up. The Lewis family home is now a museum (daily; $6; 318/757-2460), with 11 rooms full of old photos, baby clothes, and other mementos.

Natchez Practicalities

As befits a place with a strong tourism trade, Natchez has some great places to eat. Natchez is almost the southern extremity of the Tamale Belt, and you can sit down to a paperboard dish of them (a dozen for $9.50) at **Fat Mama's** (303 S. Canal St.; 601/442-4548). Fat Mama's also serves killer "Knock You Naked" margaritas, a combination that draws large crowds on summer

Natchez Trace Parkway

A mile or so south of Port Gibson, US-61 and the GRR cross the much more relaxed Natchez Trace Parkway, which, like the Blue Ridge Parkway, is a scenic route managed by the National Park Service. The parkway follows the route of the old Natchez Trace, a pre-Columbian Indian path that grew into the major overland route between the Gulf Coast and the upper Mississippi and Ohio River Valleys in the years before steamboats provided a faster alternative. The Natchez Trace appeared on maps as early as 1733, and from the 1780s to the 1820s, when steamboats made it obsolete, the Natchez Trace was one of the nation's most traveled routes. Farmers and craftspeople in the Ohio River Valley would transport their products by raft downstream to Natchez or New Orleans, then return on foot, staying at the dozens of inns along the route while doing battle with swamps, mosquitoes, and bands of thieves.

The entire 430-mile length of the parkway, which runs from Nashville south to the edge of Natchez, with a short break around Jackson, is well paved and makes a delightful driving or riding route, with places of interest marked every few miles. Just north of Port Gibson at milemarker 41.5, the Sunken Trace preserves a deeply eroded, 200-yard-long section of the trail, the canopy of moss-laden cypress trees offering one of the most evocative five-minute walks you can imagine. Between Port Gibson and Natchez, sights along this short (and eminently bikable) stretch include the prehistoric **Emerald Mound,** the second-largest prehistoric structure in the United States, which dates from around AD 1400 and offers a commanding view of the woodlands. **Mount Locust** at milemarker 15.5 is a restored Trace roadhouse and the best place to pick up parkway information; if you're fortunate, you might get a tour guided by park ranger Eric Chamberlain, who was born in the house, and whose family lived there for five generations.

The National Park police keep the parkway under very thorough radar surveillance, by the way, so try to stay within the posted speed limit, often 35 mph with a maximum of 50 mph.

nights (and earned the place a role in Jill Conner Browne's novel *Sweet Potato Queens' Book of Love*).

If you prefer fried catfish, po' boys, and chocolate shakes, head down to the **Malt Shop** (601/445-4843), where Martin Luther King Street (US-61 Business) dead-ends into Homochitto Street. For a change of pace, try **Pearl Street Pasta** (105 S. Pearl St.; 601/442-9284), just off Main Street, whose menu is eclectic, reasonably priced, and laced with vegetables that haven't been boiled to oblivion.

One last Natchez landmark deserves special mention: **Mammy's Cupboard** (601/445-8957), a roadside restaurant in the shape of a five-times-larger-than-life Southern woman, whose red skirts house the small dining room and gift shop. Having survived many incarnations, Mammy's is once again open for business, offering homemade lunches (red beans and rice, sandwiches, iced tea served up in mason jars, and a huge range of scrumptious desserts) 11 AM–2 PM Tuesday–Saturday. Mammy's Cupboard can be found along the east side of four-lane US-61, roughly five miles south of downtown Natchez.

Accommodations in Natchez include a half dozen familiar names scattered along US-61 and US-84 both north and south of downtown. For a more memorable experience, consider staying the night in one of

Mammy's Cupboard, Natchez

those historic mansions, many of which do double-duty as B&Bs. Top of the line is probably **Monmouth Plantation** ($195 and up; 36 Melrose Ave.; 601/442-5852 or 800/828-4531), preserved as it was in its circa-1818 heyday and set amidst 26 acres of lush gardens. Keep in mind that the enormous popularity of Pilgrimage requires seriously advanced bookings during those times.

For an illustrated B&B guide and other useful information contact the **Natchez Convention and Visitors Bureau** (640 S. Canal St.; 800/647-6724), which operates a large orientation center near the Mississippi River bridge (US-84).

Woodville: Rosemont Plantation

Rolling and curving past hay fields and woods, the distinctively red earth of southern Mississippi crowding the soft shoulders, the GRR passes quickly over the 45 miles between Natchez and the Louisiana state line. You won't see it from the highway, but just across the Mississippi is possibly the most significant piece of engineering anywhere along its length: the **Old River Control Project.** More than mere flood control, the project is designed to keep the Mississippi going down to Baton Rouge and New Orleans, rather than finding a route to the Gulf via the Atchafalaya River. This actually happened during the 1948 flood, and there are hydrologists who predict it is only a matter of time before it will happen again—a potential economic catastrophe for downstream cities along both rivers. About 10 miles north of the border, an unprepossessing intersection of gas stations marks the turnoff west for **Woodville** (pop. 995), where a lovely old courthouse sits at the center of a green square full of stately old oak trees and three historic churches line the somnolent streets.

The biggest attraction of Woodville, however, is a mile east of the GRR on US-24, where a small sign along the highway marks the entrance to **Rosemont**

Plantation, the boyhood home of President Jefferson Davis of the Confederacy. Built in 1810 with wooden pegs holding together hand-hewn posts and beams, the house is surrounded by a grove of live oaks and a large rose garden, planted by Davis's mother, after which the plantation takes its name.

LOUISIANA

As the GRR approaches its southern end, land and river begin to merge. With giant levees on one side and standing water on the other, it's easy to imagine the land is sinking—and indeed, by the time you roll off elevated I-10 into New Orleans, you will be 4–6 feet *below* sea level.

From the St. Francisville ferry to the Interstate bridge just west of New Orleans, the GRR crosses the Mississippi four times, threading along rough back roads past a series of fine antebellum plantation homes along what's sometimes called **Plantation Alley.** The GRR also runs among a barrage of industrial giants whose toxic discharges have earned the region another sobriquet: Chemical Corridor. The Great River Road across Louisiana is not without its charms—a vividly painted church out in a field, or wrought iron gates framing exquisitely gnarled live oaks festooned with Spanish moss—but these are all too often overshadowed by the specter of a land being poisoned for profit. End of sermon.

St. Francisville

The past is ever-present in this part of the country, so turn west off US-61 at **St. Francisville** and explore the myriad tales of this fascinating community, which grew up around the graveyard of a frontier-era monastery. Pick up an anecdotally rich walking-tour brochure at the **West Feliciana Historical Society Museum** (daily 9 AM–5 PM; free; 11757 Ferdinand St.; 225/635-6330), for a sample of the architectural charms that draw visitors to this curious little town. All around St. Francisville, there are grand old manor homes, most notably at **Rosedown Plantation** (daily; $10; 225/635-3332), on Hwy-10 just east of US-61, where a 370-acre state-run historic site preserves an 1830s main house, a pair of slave cabins, and lush formal gardens. About five miles southeast of St. Francisville on Hwy-965, the **Audubon State Historic Site** (daily; $4; 225/635-3739) is also known as the Oakley House, where in 1821 naturalist and illustrator John James Audubon came to work as a resident tutor while he compiled his comprehensive *Birds of America*.

Along with the rich history, St. Francisville also has a couple of compelling culinary attractions: the **Magnolia Cafe** (225/635-6528), a wonderful little restaurant housed in the old 3V motor court complex at the corner of Commerce and Ferdinand Streets. The café moved here when its original home (a gas station) burned down in 2003, but it's better than ever, still serving some of the best-tasting po' boys in the state that invented them. The Magnolia doubles as one of the coolest little nightclubs anywhere, drawing big-name alt-folk performers like Dave Alvin and the Bottle Rockets, who stop here in between big-city gigs. There's also a coffeehouse-cum-art gallery and occasional cabins for overnight guests; there's no better place to get a feel for this part of Louisiana. More good food—great fried chicken, pork chops, cornbread and all the other Deep South classics—is available a block

Greenwood Plantation, St. Francisville

away at **Eight Sisters Restaurant** (4712 Commerce St.; 225/635-4000).

Heading on from St. Francisville, race south down US-61 to Baton Rogue or snake west along Ferdinand Street head west across the river on the new John James Audubon Bridge toward Louisiana's legendary Cajun Country.

Baton Rouge

From the lofty vantage point of the I-10 bridge over the Mississippi River, **Baton Rouge** (pop. 229,553) appears to be a largely industrial city, its skyline dominated by smokestacks, a World War II destroyer, a mock–Mississippi Riverboat casino, and the nation's tallest state capitol—essentially a 34-story monument to the populist demagoguery of Huey "Kingfish" Long. Just south of the towering capitol, a life-sized animatronic figure of Long, the state's legendary Depression-era governor, dominates the **Old State Capitol** (Tues.–Sat. 9 AM–4 PM; free), that clearly visible white gothic-style castle—the only thing missing is a moat. Inside the restored 1847 edifice are engaging computer-aided history exhibits, including one about Huey Long's unresolved 1935 assassination: Was the patronage-dealing, road-building, vote-buying potentate the target of premeditated murder, or was then–U.S. Senator Long the victim of his five trigger-happy bodyguards' "friendly fire," aimed at a man who merely punched the boss? Review the evidence and draw your own conclusions.

Another lesson in Louisiana history can be yours at the wonderful **Rural Life Museum**

A dozen miles west of St. Francisville and the Great River Road along Hwy-1, the small town of **Morganza, Louisiana,** was the place where the character played by Jack Nicholson was beaten to death in his sleeping bag in the classic 1960s road movie *Easy Rider.* North of St. Francisville via Hwy-66 is **Angola,** location of a state prison that holds a famous annual rodeo and Louisiana's Death Row, which was featured in the book and movie *Dead Man Walking.*

Along with po' boys and boiled crawdads, Louisiana's roadsides offer another local specialty, the daiquiri bar. Like a high-octane version of a Dairy Queen slush, daiquiris come pre-mixed in a variety of sticky fruit flavors and size up to an eye-crossing 32-ouncer. Most of these bars have drive-up windows: In the eyes of the law, that piece of masking tape across the cup's lid makes it a "sealed container," so it's legal to drive with one in your cupholder, as long as you don't insert the straw.

© AVALON TRAVEL

(daily; 8:30 AM–5 PM; $7; 4560 Essen Ln.; 225/765-2437), managed by Louisiana State University and located east of downtown off I-10 exit 160. This expansive collection of shotgun houses, barns, farming equipment, riverboats, donkey carts, hand tools, and appliances—basically, anything that might have been seen in the state 100 years ago—was assembled on a former plantation by artist Steele Burden. The rest of the plantation is now a picturesque garden that covers 25 acres.

Baton Rouge hosts the **Pennington Balloon Championship** early in August. Besides being a beautiful sight, the hundreds of colorful balloons take part in a target competition, trying to drop beanbags onto a bull's-eye from 1,000 feet in the air.

The popularity of college football shouldn't be underestimated in Baton Rouge: Motel No Vacancy signs light up all over town whenever the **LSU Tigers** play. Basketball, baseball, and other sports are big, too; for tickets, call LSU (800/960-8587).

Baton Rouge Practicalities

If you're looking for a place to eat and absorb a little Baton Rouge ambience, the **Pastime** (252 South Blvd.; 225/343-5490), a few blocks from the Old State Capitol, right under the I-10 interchange, is one of those windowless, smoky sports bars ideally suited for discussing political chicanery over po' boys, fried fish, and beer. Best pizzas in town, too—try the one topped with crawfish tails for some local flavor. Another excellent place to eat a fine meal and get filled in on local life ways is world-famous **Jay's Barbecue** (5734 S. Sherwood Forest Blvd.; 225/293-1232), open every day but Sunday for real good ribs, pulled-pork sandwiches, hickory burgers, po' boys, and—if you're lucky and ask nicely— smoked alligator.

Another bunch of good eating and drinking prospects are clustered around the Highland Avenue entrance to Louisiana State University, a couple of miles south of I-10. **Louie's Cafe** (209 W. State St.; 225/346-8221), across from the Super Fresh shopping plaza, is open 24 hours, so there's no excuse to miss it. Facing the LSU gates is **The Chimes** (3357 Highland; 225/383-1754), a restaurant and oyster bar with 100 beers from 24 countries and frequent live music. Several other bars in the vicinity offer music with some regularity, but be warned that undergraduate projectile vomiting is a serious hazard.

While there are a number of hotels in downtown Baton Rouge and along the highways south and east of town, most of the inexpensive accommodations cluster around exit 151 on I-10, two miles west of the Mississippi in Port Allen. For a memorably characterful overnight, try **The Stockade B&B** ($135 and up; 8860 Highland Rd.; 225/769-7358), a home-style inn on spacious grounds near LSU.

Louisiana is divided into parishes rather than counties, one of many subtle reminders of the original French Catholic settlement of the state.

The bridge that now carries US-190 over the Mississippi was built during the gubernatorial reign of the notorious "Kingfish," Huey P. Long. The structure was designed to be low enough to prevent oceangoing freighters from passing, thus snuffing out the chances of Vicksburg and other upstream cities to compete with the port of Baton Rouge—now the nation's fifth-busiest.

Cajun Country

West of New Orleans and Baton Rouge, a world away from the grand houses lining the Mississippi River, the watery world known as **Cajun Country** spreads along the Gulf of Mexico. If you have the time to explore, the region offers an incredible range of delights for all the senses: antebellum plantation houses and moss-covered monuments set amidst groves of stately old oak trees, with all manner of wildlife (from birds to gators) chirping and squawking away in the oddly still bayous, and the sound of accordions and the aroma of boudin sausages and boiling crawfish emanating from what can seem like every other doorway. Cajun Country is also sugarcane country: Over half a million acres are cultivated each year, rising to 10 feet in height by the end of summer, when the cane is chopped down and made into molasses at the many aromatic mills. The name "Cajun" comes from the French-speaking Catholic Acadians, 10,000 of whom were chucked out of Canada when the English took over in 1755. The Acadians were refused entry by the American colonies on the East Coast and had to make their way to this corner of still-French Louisiana, where they absorbed many other cultural influences while retaining their distinct identity.

US-90, the main route through Cajun Country, follows the route of the Old Spanish Trail, the historic cross-country highway that, in the early days of the automobile, linked San Diego and St. Augustine. Though the main route has

For a dramatic perspective, cross the Mississippi on the Hwy-70 **Sunshine Bridge,** which runs between the GRR at Donaldson and I-10 exit 182. A quick link between Plantation Alley and New Orleans, the Sunshine Bridge was named in honor of "Singing Governor" Jimmy Davis's most famous song, "You Are My Sunshine," now the state's official song.

been widened and "improved" countless times in the past century (it is often signed as Future I-49), many wonderful stretches of old country road still wind along shady bayous.

Wandering aimlessly, getting lost amid the many small backwater towns, is half the fun of spending time here, but there are a number of places where the whole Cajun Country experience comes together in a concentrated dose. One of your main stops should be the historic town of **St. Martinville,** where the **Church of St. Martin de Tours** ($1; 133 S. Main St.; 337/394-6021) stands at the center of many blocks of ornate buildings and majestic oak trees, including the one featured in the Cajun-flavored Longfellow poem "Evangeline."

St. Martinville is just north of **New Iberia,** the home of Tabasco sauce, perhaps Cajun Country's most identifiable product, and just south of another great stop in Cajun Country: **Breaux Bridge,** the "Crawfish Capital of the World," located just off the I-10 freeway, a quick half hour west of Baton Rouge. Next to the bridge in Breaux Bridge, look for **Café des Amis** (140 E. Bridge St.; 337/332-5273), renowned for its Saturday morning Zydeco Breakfast. The music, with a full band, starts bright and early (usually around 8:30 AM).

Plantation Alley

Between Baton Rouge and New Orleans, if you don't have a stomach strong enough to bear miles of industrial blight, hop onto the I-10 freeway, but if your senses can handle the constant juxtaposition of refined domestic design alongside unsightly industrial complexes, with a few trailer parks, upscale vacation homes, and photogenic aboveground cemeteries thrown in for good measure, the Great River Road is full of treats, and this 100-mile traverse of what is promoted as **Plantation Alley** may well be a highlight of your trip. To 19th-century passengers aboard the packet steamboats traveling the lower Mississippi, the great mansions adorning the river bends between Baton Rouge and New Orleans must have made an impressive sight. The houses are no less grand today, but, sadly, their surroundings have been degraded by the presence of enormous petrochemical refineries. These have, by and large, replaced the antebellum sugarcane fields as the region's economic engine, but in late summer when the cane is 10 feet tall and the smell of molasses fills the air, you can *almost* pretend nothing has changed.

To get a real feel for Louisiana's extensive bayous, you have to get out of the car. A number of outfits offer "swamp tours," including Swamp Adventures (504/810-3866) and Munson's Tours on Chacahoula Swamp (985/851-3569) in Schriever.

Giving directions along Plantation Alley is complicated by the winding Mississippi, with its bridges and ferry boats, by the numerous roads and highways, and by the fact that the region is equally easy to explore from Baton Rouge or New Orleans, but it's as a good place as any to get lost and found again, so take your time and enjoy the ride. Nottoway, Houmas House, Oak Alley, and Laura are four of the most popular and memorable plantation estates, but there are many along the way, in varying stages of restoration and decay.

Nottoway

Heading north to south, as the river flows, the first of these riverside manors is **Nottoway** (daily; $20; 225/545-2730), whose 64 rooms place it among the largest plantation homes in the South. Built in the 1850s, it was also one of the last "big houses" to be built. On the western shore of the Mississippi, along Hwy-1 about two miles north of the town of White Castle, Nottoway is a bright white Greek Revival structure enclosing over an acre of floor space, so you'll be glad you don't have to pay the air-conditioning bills or do the dusting. If you like the look of it all, you can stay for lunch in the grand dining room or overnight in one of many lushly appointed rooms ($110 and up).

Two miles south of White Castle, a state-run ferry jogs across the river (every 30 minutes, during commute hours only) to Carville on the other side.

Burnside: Houmas House

The most familiar (and easiest to reach) of Louisiana's plantation homes, **Houmas House** (daily; $20; 40136 River Rd.; 225/473-9380), stands on the east bank of the Mississippi amid 12 acres of manicured grounds. Another of Louisiana's *grandes dames,* Houmas House is a dignified complex of buildings constructed over many generations, mainly between the 1780s and 1840s. The main is composed of white columns and rich red-ochre walls supporting a central belvedere (like a cupola) from which the antebellum owners could survey their domain. Today, the endless seas of sugarcane have been replaced in part by the monstrous sprawl of the neighboring DuPont plant. Once the seat of a massive, 20,000-acre sugarcane plantation, Houmas House may well look strangely familiar: The stately home was used as the setting for Robert

New Orleans

Royal Street in New Orleans' French Quarter

New Orleans has long been famous for its easygoing, live-and-let-live personality, and for placing a high value the good things in life—food, drink, and music, to name a few. Slowly but surely, the Big Easy is getting its groove back after the destruction that followed in the wake of Hurricane Katrina in 2005.

With deep roots going back to the earliest days of European settlement in North America, New Orleans is very proud of its multicultural heritage: Its people, its ornate buildings, and especially its food all reflect a uniquely diverse and resilient culture. The focus of New Orleans, for visitors and locals alike, is the **Vieux Carré,** in the French Quarter, which sits

Royal Street in the French Quarter

on the highest ground in the city and thus escaped the worst of Katrina's floods. Centering on Bourbon Street, lined with tacky souvenir stalls and strip clubs catering to conventioneers, this square mile is full of wrought-iron balconies on picturesque brick buildings. Yes, it's a huge tourist attraction, but it's also the heart of old New Orleans. At the center of the quarter is **Jackson Square,** where a statue of the victor of the Battle of New Orleans, Andrew Jackson, stands in front of St. Louis Cathedral, which was rebuilt in 1850 on top of an original foundation dating back to 1724. The nearby **Old U.S. Mint** (closed Mon.; $6; 400 Esplanade; 504/568-6968), holds excellent collections tracing the history of two New Orleans institutions: jazz and Mardi Gras.

Jackson Square

After dark, there's live music aplenty in all styles and modes, but one stop you have to make is **Preservation Hall** (nightly from 8 PM; $12; 726 St. Peter St.; 504/522-2841), for the redolent ambience and the live traditional Dixieland jazz, still going strong after 50 years.

Practicalities

New Orleans has some of the best and most enjoyable places to eat in the world, so plan to take the time to enjoy yourself here. In the French Quarter, the informal **Acme Oyster House** (724 Iberville St.; 504/522-5973) is the place to go for the freshest bivalves, but it closes early by New Orleans standards— around 10 PM on weeknights and 11 PM on Friday and Saturday. At the other end of the spectrum is expensive, formal **Antoine's** (713 St. Louis St.; 504/581-4422), one of the oldest restaurants in the world, which serves classic French-Creole cuisine to a who's who of New Orleans society. Another very popular spot is **K-Paul's Louisiana Kitchen** (416 Chartres St.; 504/596-2530), where Chef Paul Prudhomme, who popularized Cajun-style "blackened" food all over

the country, saves the very best exam-ples for his own place. Another world-famous place that merits a meal or two is **NOLA** (534 St. Louis St.; 504/522-6652), a comparatively casual setting for celebrated chef Emeril Lagasse's finely crafted Creole fare.

Antoine's Restaurant, 713 St. Louis St., New Orleans

No visit to New Orleans is complete without a stop for coffee and beignets (and some serious people-watching) at busy **Cafe du Monde** (800 Decatur St.; 504/525-4544), open 24 hours a day (ex-cept on Christmas) on the river side of Jackson Square. A wider range of bev-erages, and even more immersive his-tory, is on tap at the legendary **Napoleon House** bar (500 Chartres St.; 504/524-9752).

Except during Mardi Gras, Jazz Fest, or Superdome football games, places to stay in New Orleans aren't *all* that expensive. In the French Quarter, the characterful **Olivier House** ($135 and up; 828 Toulouse St.; 504/525-8456) is a quirky, family-run hotel filling a pair of French Quarter townhouses. Another good bet is **Place d'Armes Hotel** ($100 and up; 625 St. Ann St.; 504/524-4531 or 800/366-2743), right off Jackson Square at the heart of the French Quarter, with rooms facing onto a quiet courtyard.

The best visitor information is provided by the **New Orleans Metropolitan Convention and Visitors Bureau** (504/566-5011).

Aldrich's 1964 gothic Southern horror film, *Hush...Hush, Sweet Charlotte,* starring Bette Davis, Olivia de Havilland, Joseph Cotten, and Bruce Dern. B&B rooms and a restaurant are also available.

Located on Hwy-942 near the hamlet of Darrow, Houmas House is just four miles west of the I-10 freeway via Hwy-22 or Hwy-44, and it is about a dozen miles north of the Sunshine Bridge (Hwy-70) over the Mississippi.

Vacherie: Oak Alley and Laura

Traveling along the GRR, moldering concrete mausoleums, houses with loud colors and louvered French doors, and insouciant pedestrians along the levee (not to mention the dangerously large potholes) may arrest your attention briefly, but **Oak Alley** (daily; $18; 3645 Hwy-18/Great River Rd.; 225/265-2151) will probably stop you in your tracks. This place is to antebellum plantations what Bora Bora is to islands, or the Golden Gate is to bridges: Even if you've managed to avoid seeing Oak Alley on tourist brochures, or in the movies *Interview with a Vampire* or *Primary Colors,* it will look familiar—or rather, it will look exactly like it ought to. Plus, no cooling tower or gas flare mars the immediate horizon. For the full effect of the grand quarter-mile-long allée of arching live oaks, which were planted in the 1700s, nearly a century before the current house was built in the late 1830s, drive past the entrance a short ways. Besides the obligatory tour, there's lodging and a restaurant in buildings on the grounds in back of the main house.

Oak Alley stands on the west bank of the river, three miles north of Vacherie. The house is about 15 miles south of the Sunshine Bridge and eight miles north of the Veteran's Memorial Bridge (Hwy-3213). There's a ferry nearby, too, between Edgard and Reserve, but this runs at very limited hours.

As a colorful antidote to the grand, whitewashed privilege on display at Oak Alley, set aside some time for a tour of nearby Laura plantation as well. Smaller, but seeming more in touch with the realities of sugarcane plantation life, **Laura** (daily; $18; 2247 Hwy-18; 225/265-7690) presents itself as a Creole plantation and plays up the myriad of ethnicities and cultures that came together in Louisiana. Laura is nine miles downriver from Oak Alley, south of Vacherie on the Great River Road.

Oak Alley

Continuing south from Vacherie, scattered housing begins to invade the sugarcane, and traffic starts to pick up as the GRR (Hwy-18) works its serpentine way past a pair of ferry landings, a nuclear power plant, and a huge chemical plant with a photogenic cemetery felicitously occupying its front yard. By the time the GRR is within sight of the stylish, rusty-red I-310 bridge, the tentacles of New Orleans's bustle are definitely apparent. Hop on the Interstate eastbound, and inside of 25 miles you can be hunting for parking in New Orleans's Vieux Carré, or searching for a Sazerac to celebrate the journey.

Driving New Orleans

Assuming you resisted the industrial-strength charms of US-61 and opted to take the I-10 freeway into town, stay on it until you reach downtown, then get off and park the car as soon as you can, and get out and walk. New Orleans rivals Boston for the discomfort it causes drivers, and there are no driving routes that let you see anything you can't see better on foot—or from the St. Charles trolley. Parking in and around the French Quarter is a nightmare, and the small print on the signs can set you up for a ticket or a tow, so play it safe and park in one of the many nearby lots, which typically charge anything from $10 a day (if you can get an early bird rate) to $10 an hour (if you can't).

Because the Mississippi in its natural, pre-Corps state created a raised channel for itself between embankments of silt, the river sits higher than a third of Louisiana. Much of New Orleans, as the world learned during the Hurricane Katrina disaster, is below sea level, and the river has been dredged to a depth of more than 200 feet.

Hwy-23: To the Gulf

From downtown New Orleans, if you really, really want to follow the Mississippi River all the way to its mouth at the Gulf of Mexico, you can. (Well, almost . . .) From the Superdome, take the US-90 bridge south across the river to Gretna, where you can join the Belle Chasse Highway (Hwy-23), which follows alongside the river for about 75 miles, ending up at Venice, still a dozen miles from the Gulf, on the fringes of the Delta National Wildlife refuge. Apart from swamps and giant freighters, the main sight along the route is old **Fort Jackson,** six miles northeast of Venice. Built following the War of 1812 to help protect the river from invasion, Fort Jackson was flooded and badly damaged by the Hurricane Katrina storm surge.

inside Fort Jackson

Appalachian Trail

This driving route parallels the hiking trail, from the top of New England to the heart of Dixie, taking you through continuous natural beauty—without the sweat, bugs, or blisters.

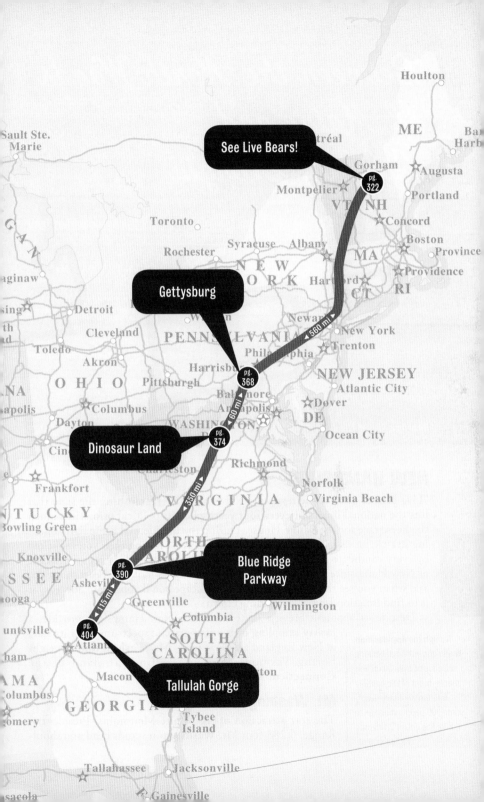

See Live Bears!
pg. 322

Gettysburg
pg. 368

560 mi

60 mi

Dinosaur Land
pg. 374

350 mi

Blue Ridge
Parkway
pg. 390

115 mi

pg. 404

Tallulah Gorge

Between the North Woods of Maine and Atlanta, Georgia

The longest and best-known hiking trail in the country, the **Appalachian Trail** winds from the North Woods of Maine all the way south to Georgia. While you won't earn the same kudos driving as you would by walking, the following scenic roads come very close to paralleling the pedestrian route, taking you through the almost continuous natural beauty without the sweat and blisters. Best of all, this driving route follows magnificently scenic two-lane roads all the way from the top of New England to the heart of Dixie, running past a wealth of fascinating towns and historic sites.

The Appalachian landscape holds some of the wealthiest, and some of the most needy, areas in the entire country. These contrasting worlds often sit within a few miles of one another: Every resort and retirement community seems to have its alter-ego as a former mill town, now as dependent upon tourism as they once were upon the land and its resources.

After an extended sojourn through the rugged and buggy wilds of northern **Maine,** where the hikers' route winds to the top of Mt. Katahdin, our Appalachian

NEW HAMPSHIRE

"Live Free or Die" is the feisty motto of tiny New Hampshire, the state that hits the national limelight every four years when its political primaries launch the horse race for the White House. During the presidential campaign's opening stretch, locals have to turn into hermits to avoid having their votes solicited by every candidate running and their opinions polled by every reporter. Some of New Hampshire's million residents take the state's motto to heart, however, and when you see the ruggedness of the landscape you'll appreciate how easy it is to find isolation from the madding crowd.

Despite its apparent brevity, the route across New Hampshire provides a hearty sampling of the topographic spectrum from its start at New England's highest peak, **Mt. Washington,** to neighboring Vermont amid the rolling farmland of the **Connecticut River Valley.**

Though the **Appalachian Trail** runs within day-hiking distance of over 50 million people, most of the route is intensely solitary—only some 200 people manage to hike the entire 2,175-mile trail each year.

Mt. Washington

The star attraction of the White Mountains' Presidential Range, 6,288-foot **Mt. Washington** stands head and shoul-

Trail driving tour reaches an early high point atop windswept Mt. Washington in the heart of **New Hampshire's Presidential Range.** From these 6,000-foot peaks, the tallest mountains in New England and some of the hardest and most durable rocks on earth, the route winds through **Vermont's Green Mountains,** taking in the idyllic charms of rural New England, with its summer homes and liberal-arts college communities. Beyond the **Berkshires,** the summer destination of the Boston and New York culture vultures and intelligentsia for most of two centuries, towns become even more prissy and pretty as we approach within commuting distance of New York City.

Skirting the Big Apple, our route ducks down through the **Delaware Water Gap** to enter the suddenly industrial Lehigh Valley, former land of coal and steel that's now struggling to find an economic replacement. South of here, we pass through the heart of the world-famous **Pennsylvania Dutch Country,** where the simple life is under the onslaught of package tourism.

South from Pennsylvania, nearly to the end of the route in **Georgia,** the Appalachian Trail runs through continuous nature, with barely a city to be seen. Starting with Virginia's **Shenandoah National Park,** then following the **Blue Ridge Parkway** across the breathtaking mountains of western **North Carolina,** it's all-American scenic highway all the way, with recommended detours east and west to visit such fascinating historic sights as Thomas Jefferson's home, Monticello, outside Charlottesville, Virginia; the most opulent mansion in America, Asheville's Biltmore; the real-life town that inspired TV's *Mayberry RFD*—Mount Airy, North Carolina; or the white water featured in the film *Deliverance*, north Georgia's Chattooga River.

All in all, the Appalachian Trail is an amazing drive, whether or not you come for fall color.

ders above every other peak in New England. East of the Mississippi, only Mt. Mitchell and Mt. Craig in North Carolina's Blue Ridge and Clingman's Dome in Tennessee's Great Smokies are taller. Despite its natural defenses—such as notoriously fierce storms that arise without warning—Mt. Washington is accessible to an almost unfortunate degree. The **Mount Washington Auto Road** (May–mid-Oct. daily, weather permitting; $25 car and driver, $8 each additional adult; 603/466-3988) was first opened for carriages in 1861, earning it the nickname "America's Oldest Man-Made Tourist

Attraction." It still switchbacks up the eastern side, climbing some 4,700 feet in barely eight miles. A marvel of engineering, construction, and maintenance, the Mount Washington Auto Road offers a great variety of impressions of the mountain and wonderful views from almost every turn.

Although clear-day views from the summit of Mt. Washington are amazing, 9 days out of 10 the summit is socked in and cold, and snow can fall any month of the year.

The first automobile ascent of Mt. Washington was made in 1899 by none other than Freelan O. Stanley, piloting one of his namesake Stanley Steamers.

If the weather's clear, you can see the Atlantic Ocean from the top of the mountain; in summer, mornings tend to be clearer, and sunny afternoons turn cloudy and stormy on the summit, complete with lightning and thunder. At the top, be prepared for winter weather any time of year (it can and does snow here every month of the year), and be sure to have a look inside the Summit House, which has displays on the historic hotels and taverns that have graced the top over the years. Visited by hundreds of people every day throughout the summer, since the 1850s the summit of Mt. Washington has sprouted a series of restaurants and hotels—even a daily newspaper. The most evocative remnant of these is the tiny **Tip Top House,** "the oldest mountaintop hostelry in the world," still open for tours, if not food and drink (which is available in the Summit House cafeteria).

Cyclists, runners, and motorists regularly race each other up the road to the summit, but there is another, much easier ride to the top: the **Mount Washington Cog Railway,** which climbs slowly but surely on its steam-powered, coal-fired way, straight up and down the mountain's western slope from Bretton Woods.

historic Tip Top House at the summit of Mount Washington

Pinkham Notch

South from the foot of the Mount Washington Auto Road, Route 16 passes through Pinkham Notch, a mostly undeveloped stretch of the White Mountains lined by forests and a few ski areas. About four miles south of the Auto Road is the area's outdoorsy Grand Central Station: the **Pinkham Notch Visitor Center.** Operated by the venerable Appalachian Mountain Club (AMC), the year-round trailhead facility offers topographical maps, guidebooks, weather updates, and precautionary advice, as well as limited gear. The camp also offers snacks, a cafeteria, a 24-hour hikers' pack room with bath-

Severe Weather on Mt. Washington

A mountain barely over 6,000 feet hardly deserves the same respect as Mount Everest (29,029 feet), or even Mount McKinley (20,320 feet), yet people get into serious and sometimes fatal trouble on the slopes of New Hampshire's Mt. Washington all the same. Easy access invites complacency and a tendency to ignore trailside warnings advising retreat if you're unprepared for bad weather. But do respect the facts of nature: Simply put, the Presidential Range of the White Mountains experiences some of the worst weather in the world, rivaling both Antarctica and the Alaska-Yukon ranges for consistently raw and bone-numbing combinations of gale-force winds, freezing temperatures, and precipitation. Lashings by 100-mph winds occur year-round on Mt. Washington, whose summit holds the title for highest sustained wind speed on the face of the planet (231 mph in April 1934). Cloudy days outnumber clear ones on the peak, where snowstorms can strike any month of the year, and even in the balmiest summer

months the average high temperature at the summit hovers around 50°F. Compounding the weather's potential severity is its total unpredictability: A day hike begun with sunblock and short sleeves can end up in driving rain and temperatures just 10 degrees above freezing—or worse, in a total whiteout above tree line—even as a group of hikers a couple miles away on a neighboring peak enjoys lunch under blue skies and warm breezes.

The bottom line is, listen to what your mother always told you: Be careful, and don't take chances. Be prepared. Don't hike or ski alone. Carry enough water and food. Learn to recognize and prevent hypothermia. Figure out how to read your trail maps and use your compass *before* you get caught in pelting sleet above tree line. It's better to feel foolish packing potentially unnecessary wool sweaters and rain gear for a hike in July than to have your name added to the body count.

rooms and showers, scheduled shuttle van service, and the **Joe Dodge Lodge** (about $84/person bed and board; 603/466-2727), a modern hostel with shared bunk rooms, a few private doubles, and great views from the library.

Along the northeastern side of the White Mountains, between Grafton Notch and Mt. Washington, the Appalachian Trail parallels **The Great Northern** route of US-2 (see page 574). Full coverage is on pages 492–583.

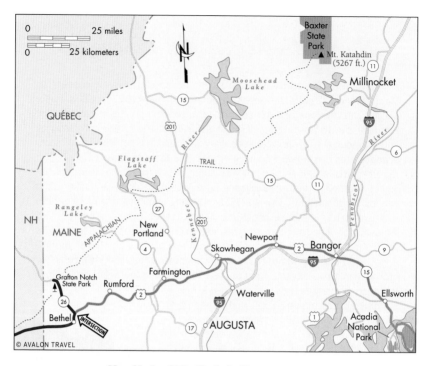

In New England, locals call their highways "routes," and we've followed suit, using Route as a generic term (Route 100, for example, rather than Hwy-100). The Interstates (I-93) and federal highways (US-3) are abbreviated as usual.

North to Mt. Katahdin

North and east of Mt. Washington, the Appalachian Trail runs through one of its toughest sections, rambling through Mahoosuc Notch into Maine, then passing through **Grafton Notch State Park.** There are no real roads anywhere near here, so drivers wanting a quick taste of this impenetrable country will have to join US-2 for the drive through Gorham, New Hampshire, and Bethel, Maine, then wind along the Bear River on scenic Route 26. Beyond Grafton Notch, the hikers' Appalachian Trail passes through ever more extensive wilderness, with fewer services (and many more mosquitoes and black flies!) the closer you get to the trail's northern finish, atop **Mt. Katahdin.**

Though the hiking trail and the nearest roads are like strands of a double helix, both routes take you through some memorable country, especially around Rangeley Lakes and Moosehead Lake, in the deep Maine woods.

Mt. Washington Valley: Jackson

Dropping sharply away to the south of Pinkham Notch is the Ellis River, along whose banks sits the northern gateway to the Mt. Washington valley, resort-dominated **Jackson** (pop. 816). Given the number of lodgings among the attractive century-old clapboard homes, it seems the principal village occupation is innkeeper. The porches, gables, and chimneys hint at standard country

B&B charms: lazy breakfasts in summer, nooks and crannies brimming with roses, and crackling fires in your room at night. A covered bridge beside Route 16, taverns filled with antiques, and winter sleigh rides complete Jackson's postcard image of Merry Olde New England.

The Jackson area is not only pretty but also has a couple of northern New Hampshire's best places to eat, drink, and sleep. At the junction of Route 16 and Route 16A, the **Shannon Door Pub** (603/383-4211) is usually just the right side of crowded—full of skiers, hikers, and other hungry folks enjoying hearty food, good beers, and frequent live folksy, Celtic-tinged music in a jovial setting. In business for nearly 60 years, the pub was a main character in John Sayles's first film, *The Return of the Secaucus Seven*. The grand hotel in Jackson is the stately **Wentworth** ($134 and up; 603/383-9700) at the heart of the village, welcoming travelers since it was established back in 1869.

To park a car at any trailhead in the **White Mountains National Forest,** you'll need to buy a pass from one of the information centers; these passes cost about $5 and are good for seven days.

If you can turn a blind eye to all the retail frenzy, North Conway's central park offers one of the best views of Mt. Washington, and the baseball diamond here hosts some pretty intense games.

Glen

A half mile south of Jackson along Route 16 or Route 16A you pass the picturesque Jackson Covered Bridge, where the two alternative routes rejoin at the north edge of tiny **Glen.** In the short stretch between the bridge and the junction with US-302, Glen has one of the more concentrated barrages of roadside clutter in the White Mountains. Glen is best known not for hiking or sightseeing but as home to the children's theme park **Story Land** (daily in summer only; $28, under 2 free; 603/383-4186), where among its many playfully designed and carefully coiffed acres, the highlights include a boat ride, a raft ride, and a fiberglass cow that gives fake milk when you squeeze its fake udders.

A half mile south of Storyland, Route 16 links up with US-302 at a cluster of shops where the **Red Parka Steakhouse & Pub** (603/383-4344), a jolly, moderate-to-inexpensive place to eat and drink, has live music most weekend nights.

North Conway

If you're overdue for a little retail therapy you might consider continuing south on Route 16 from the US-302 junction toward **North Conway** (pop. 2,349), one of the cornerstones of New England's factory-outlet circuit. City dwellers be warned: Horrible flashbacks to your commute may result if you venture into the shopping mall zone, where half-hour (or longer) crawls along a five-mile stretch of highway are not unheard-of on holidays, weekends, and afternoons, or during summer, spring, and autumn.

Besides factory-outlet stores, North Conway is also home to New Hampshire's most popular scenic railroad, running steam engines throughout summer and during the fall color season. Based out of Conway's downtown depot, the **Conway Scenic Railroad** ($15 and up depending on trip; 603/356-5251) runs historic trains south to Conway, through Bartlett, and all the way to Crawford Notch via the historic Frankenstein Trestle, with special excursions available in addition to these frequent trips.

Although all the tourists may well drive you away from North Conway, there are some good places to eat along Route 16, like **Elvio's Pizzeria and Restaurant!** (2888 White Mountain Hwy.; 603/356-3208), where you can get slices or full pies, submarine sandwiches, and big salads, plus wine and beer. During the day, the place to eat home-style breakfasts or great burgers is family-friendly **Peaches Restaurant** (2506 White Mountain Hwy.; 603/356-5860).

Conway Scenic Railroad

Just over the Maine border, about 10 miles east of North Conway via US-302, the town of **Fryeburg** hosts a weeklong agricultural fair during the first week in October that's one of the most popular in New England—packed with tractor pulls, horse racing, lots of music, even a pig scramble (a contest, not an egg dish).

There are lots of accommodations on and off Route 16, from old cabin courts to anodyne motels, but the most interesting place has to be the **Cranmore Inn** ($85 and up; 80 Kearsarge Rd.; 603/356-5502), a quick walk east of Route 16, which has been welcoming travelers since 1863.

Conway

Conway, five miles down Route 16 from North Conway at the south end of the scenic railroad line, is a nicer, littler town, with a couple of restaurants, a post office, and the very clean and very friendly **HI-White Mountains Hostel** ($23 per person, $58 private rooms; 36 Washington St.; 603/447-1001), in the heart of town. If you have your doubts about hostelling, this place is sure to dispel them; run as a sustainable living center, it's as clean as it is serene, and besides saving money staying here, you're apt to meet like-minded fellow travelers over breakfast or relaxing in the game room.

Up in the hills above Conway, off Route 16 one mile south of the Kancamagus Highway at the edge of the White Mountains National Forest, the **Darby Field Inn and Restaurant** ($140 and up; 603/447-2181) is a B&B open year-round for skiing, hiking, and great après-outdoors meals.

Kancamagus Highway

Running east–west from Conway over the mountains to Lincoln, the 34-mile **Kancamagus Highway** (Route 112) is a National Scenic Byway and one of the most incredible drives in the White Mountains. Much shorter and a lot less traveled than the prime tourist route along US-302 and US-3 through Crawford and Franconia Notches, The Kanc, as it's often called, takes you up and over the crest of the peaks, giving grand vistas over an almost completely undeveloped landscape—great for fall-color leaf-peeping. Fall is definitely prime time for the drive, but any time of year (except maybe winter, when it can be a bit hairy) it's a lovely trip, lined by lupines in early summer and raging waterfalls in the spring.

Near the midpoint of The Kanc, the **Russell-Colbath Historic House** dates from the early 1830s and now houses a small museum (Fri.–Sun. 10 AM–4 PM; free) with exhibits describing the lives of the White Mountains' early settlers. From the house, the short loop Rail N' River Trail explores the effects loggers had on this region in the 1890s, when everything you see along The Kanc (and most everywhere else) was devastated by clear-cuts.

Three miles farther west, just east of the crest and an easy half-mile walk from the well-signed parking area, **Sabbaday Falls** is a lovely little waterfall roaring through a narrow gorge. In a series of noisy, splashing cascades, the river drops down through a polished pink granite gorge, barely 10 feet wide but surrounded by dense forest. It's an ideal picnic spot, and only 10–15 minutes from the road.

Fall foliage is at its best when warm clear days are followed by cold nights that stop the essential pigment-producing sugars from circulating out of the leaves. Sugar production is low on cloudy days, when warm nights allow the sugars to disperse before the brightest colors are produced.

The name Kancamagus honors the local Indian chief who controlled the area when the first European settlers began arriving at the White Mountains in the 1680s. The roadway was not paved until 1964 and was declared a National Scenic Byway in 1989.

Crawford Notch

US-302 between Glen and Twin Mountain winds west around the southern flank of the Presidential Range, then heads north through **Crawford Notch,** another of the White Mountains' high passes and centerpiece of the **Crawford Notch State Park.** The road closely follows the Saco River through new-growth forest; the oaks and white pine of the lower valley give way to more birch and spruce as you gain elevation.

Crawford Notch offers good **day hikes** to various waterfalls and vantage points such as **Frankenstein Cliff,** named for an artist whose work helped popularize the White Mountains, and 140-or-so-foot **Arethusa Falls,** the state's second highest waterfall.

For ambitious and well-prepared hikers, the north end of Crawford Notch is the start of the oldest and perhaps grandest walking trail in the country, the eight-mile **Crawford Path** up towering Mt. Washington. A strenuous, demanding, and potentially dangerous route, the Crawford Path is

The first known ascent of Mt. Washington was made in 1642 by Darby Field of Durham, New Hampshire, who historians believe followed a route near that of today's Crawford Path.

also breathtakingly beautiful, and a walk along it gives an almost complete picture of the White Mountains—sparkling brooks, fields of wildflowers, and glorious mountaintop panoramas.

Mount Washington Hotel and Cog Railway

North of Crawford Notch, the highway joins the Ammonoosuc River headwaters as they flow toward the Connecticut River, passing **Bretton Woods** and the access road for the Mount Washington Cog Railway. The giant **Mount Washington Hotel** ($230 and up; 603/278-1000) dominates the surrounding plain, its Victorian luxury no longer standing in such grand isolation below the peaks of the Presidentials now that a ski resort sits across the highway and motels and condos squat around its skirts. Built at the turn of the 20th century by Pennsylvania Railroad tycoon Joseph Stickney, the Mount Washington Hotel received its most lasting recognition as host of the 1944 United Nations International Monetary Conference, the historic meeting of financiers from 44 nations that established the World Bank and chose the dollar as the global standard for international trade.

Climbing the mountains behind the hotel, the **Mount Washington Cog Railway** was built in 1869 and has a maximum grade of 37.5 percent, surpassed by only one other non-funicular railway in

Mount Washington Cog Railway

the world, high up in the Swiss Alps. One cinder-spewing engine runs on coal, but others have been adapted to run on eco-friendly biodiesel. This historic "Railway to the Moon" takes over an hour to ratchet up the three-mile track to the often windy, cold summit. Trips ($62; 603/278-5404) run year-round; you can ride up and hike (or ski) back down.

Much more active and exciting than the slow chug up the cog railway is the **Bretton Woods Canopy Tour** ($15 and up), which takes you on a tour up into the top of the trees by way of cables, bridges, and ziplines.

Franconia and Sugar Hill

Between Twin Mountain (at the junction of US-302 and US-3) and where US-3 merges with I-93, you'll find the aging face of the area's long association with tourism: a variety of motel courts and "housekeeping cottages" at least as old as you are. Despite their outward dowdiness, several make a virtue of the

Mount Washington Hotel

rustic, but given their prime location most are hardly the bargains you might hope for. More interesting and historic lodging may be had on a 200-acre working farm in **Franconia** (pop. 1,104), where, since 1899, the friendly Sherburn family's **Pinestead Farm Lodge,** on Route 116 south of town, has offered simple rooms and warm hospitality at reasonable rates ($45 and up with shared bath and kitchen; 603/823-8121).

Parking along New Hampshire highways is illegal, so don't be tempted to leave your car beside the road while you take a hike up that nearby hill—you may return to find it's been towed to some town 20 miles away.

Just west of Franconia on Route 117 is **Sugar Hill.** The township is aptly named: The sugarbush (a grove of sugar maples) on Hildex Maple Sugar Farm contributes its unforgettable essence to breakfasts at the very popular **Polly's Pancake Parlor.** Polly's is located in the farm's thrice-expanded 1830 carriage shed (daily 7 AM–2 PM; closed in winter; 603/823-5575). Warning: After trying real maple syrup, you may never be able to go back to Mrs. Butterworth's again.

The most famous farm in the vicinity is certainly **The Frost Place** ($5; 603/823-5510) on Route 116 south of the Franconia village intersection. Besides the 1.5-mile Poetry Trail and the displays of Robert Frost memorabilia from his five-year full-time residency and 19 summers here, there's a regular program of readings by the current poet-in-residence.

Franconia Notch

Franconia Notch is probably the most popular spot in the White Mountains, and, despite the numbers of visitors, it's a fantastic place to spend some time. I-93, the country's only two-lane Interstate, offers easy access; a host of attractions—an aerial tram, the state's own "little Grand Canyon," covered bridges, a powerful waterfall called the Flume, even a trading post with

Cannon Mountain, home slope of World Cup ski champion Bode Miller, was the location of the first aerial tram for skiers in the United States. One of the original aerial tram cars has been preserved among the many attractions at **Clark's Trading Post,** near Lincoln at the south end of Franconia Notch.

The hikers' Appalachian Trail crosses the Franconia Notch Parkway and Pemi Trail at **Whitehouse Bridge,** in between the Basin and the Flume.

trained bears—make it a great place to linger. If you give yourself the time to hike around or just sit still by a mountain stream, you could easily spend a week or more enjoying it all.

The main draw in Franconia Notch used to be one of the most famous landmarks in New England: the Old Man of the Mountain, a series of five granite ledges 1,200 feet above the valley, which, when viewed from certain angles, seemed to resemble an old man's profile. After years of reconstructive surgery, being held together by epoxies and steel reinforcement, the Old Man came tumbling down on May 3, 2003.

Fortunately, the other well-known feature of Franconia Notch is still there: **The Flume** is a granite gorge, 12–20 feet wide and nearly 100 feet high, carved by roaring waters at the south end of the notch. To get there, head to the large **visitors center** (daily May–Oct., 9 AM–5 PM; 603/745-8391), pay the admission fee ($15), and take a short bus ride to near the start of the wooden boardwalk, which runs the length of the 800-foot-long gorge and ends up at the ear-pounding rumble of Avalanche Falls.

Though less famous than the Old Man and The Flume, in between the two sits another favorite Franconia Notch stop: **The Basin,** where a lovely waterfall in the thundering Pemigewassett River has polished a 25-foot-round pothole. Thoreau visited in the 1820s and thought it was remarkable; it's still a peaceful place to sit and picnic and be soothed by the natural white noise.

Clark's Trading Post

Just south of Franconia Notch along US-3, a barrage of deliciously tacky tourist attractions and old-fashioned roadside Americana awaits you. Well-maintained 1930s motor courts line the highway, setting the stage for one of New England's greatest roadside attractions, **Clark's Trading Post** (daily in summer; $18; 603/745-8913), where you can enjoy a slice of good ol' cornpone kitsch. At Clark's, you can ride on a genuine old wood-burning railroad over an authentic 1904 covered bridge (and be chased all the way by a hairy, hilarious Wolfman); admire an immaculate 1931 LaSalle in a vintage gas station; or tour a haunted mansion.

For the past 50 or so years, the main draw at Clark's has been the chance, according to the sign, to **"See Live Bears!"**

House-trained black bears perform a series of entertaining tricks—rolling barrels, shooting basketballs through hoops, and riding scooters—and they clearly seem to enjoy their work (not to mention the ice cream cones they're rewarded with). The trainers and caretakers crack jokes and make wry comments about "bear facts" and how the animals are "bearly" able to behave themselves, but they smile and beam every time the bears do what they're supposed to, giving the performances a feel more akin to a school play than to a professional circus. Many of the bears are born and reared here at Clark's, and although they're captive, they have a much longer life expectancy than wild bears. Across from the enclosure where they perform you can pay respects to the graves of favorite bears who've performed here over the years. Spend any time at Clark's and you'll begin to realize that the bears are regarded as family members (albeit seven-foot-tall, 500-pound family members).

Take those moose-crossing signs seriously. Dozens of collisions occur annually, and you can bet your car won't fare too well if it hits an animal that weighs well over a half ton.

Clark's has been in business since 1928, when it was known as Ed Clark's Eskimo Sled Dog Ranch, and everything about it is very much a family affair. More than a dozen Clarks and close relatives work here throughout the summer, doing everything from training and caring for the bears to making milk shakes. The bear shows at Clark's Trading Post are scheduled irregularly (typically in the afternoons, roughly every two hours or so; the schedule is posted online at www.clarkstradingpost.com). You could happily spend most of a day here, making it well worth the price of admission. If you're just racing through, be sure to at least visit the gift shop, which is stocked with all the wonderfully tacky stuff (wind-up toys, funky postcards, snow domes, and the like) retro-minded road-trippers drive miles to find.

Lincoln sits at the west end of Route 112, the amazing Kancamagus Highway.

In case you're wondering what North Woodstock is north of, there is a much smaller hamlet called **Woodstock,** little more than a collection of cabins, about five miles or so south of North Woodstock along US-3.

Lincoln and North Woodstock

Nine miles south of Franconia Notch, tiny **North Woodstock** (pop. 528) is a good example of what White Mountains towns used to look like before vacation condos popped up like prairie dog colonies; neighboring **Lincoln** (pop. 1,662) is the portrait of "after." North Woodstock is a handful of mostly unpretentious businesses at the junction of US-3 and Route 112, while Lincoln seems to be nothing but a strip of ski-clothing stores, malls, and motels east of I-93 at the base of the Loon Mountain ski resort. When Loon's condo-covered foothills fill to capacity during fall and winter holidays, the weekend population can mushroom more than 20-fold to more than 30,000.

Diner fans will want to check out the **Sunny Day Diner** (closed Tues.; cash only; 603/745-4833), a stainless-steel 1950s icon at the north edge of North Woodstock in Lincoln on US-3. A classic breakfast and lunch place, the Sunny Day makes some fine french toast (including a deeply flavored banana variation that goes great with local maple syrup). The Sunny Day is just south of Clark's Trading Post.

Lost River Gorge

With five main roads and countless minor ones connecting the Franconia Notch area with the Connecticut River Valley, there are nearly endless ways to get between these two places while staying more or less on the path of the hikers' Appalachian Trail, which disappears into the woods for most of the way. All of the roads are partly pretty and partly yucky in about equal degrees, but one of the easiest to follow is Route 112, which runs west from North Woodstock along the Lost River, hopping over the crest and dropping down along the Wild Ammonoosuc. The main stop along this route is the privately owned **Lost River Gorge and Boulder Caves** (daily mid-May–Oct.; $16; 603/745-8031), where you can explore the jumble of glaciated granite boulders that seem to swallow up the river, giving it its name. Many of the big, moss-covered boulders have been given names (Guillotine Rock and Lemon Squeezer, to name two), and you can see these (and smell the fragrant pine trees) from the comfort of a wooden boardwalk or go wild and explore some of the many caves formed by the huge piles of rocks.

Continuing west from Lost River Gorge, which sits at the top of Route 112's spectacular run through wild Kinsman Notch, the highway drops down into the Connecticut River watershed toward the Vermont town of **Wells River,** which happens to be home to the best truck stop in all New England: the **P&H Truck Stop Cafe** (802/429-2141) at I-91 exit 17, where you can enjoy fine chowder, charbroiled cheeseburgers, and great pies—24 hours a day. After eating here, backtrack four miles to the river and follow scenic Route 10 along its east bank, winding south toward Hanover. A parallel route along the Vermont side of the river, along old US-5 through the town of **Fairlee** (which has a nice diner and a unique drive-in movie theater/motel), is another nice alternative to the I-91 freeway.

Route 10: North Haverhill and Lyme

While hikers along the Appalachian Trail have to struggle up and over several mountaintops, we drivers get to amble along a few miles to the west, following scenic Route 10 along the east banks of the lazy Connecticut River. Winding past pastures and cornfields, Route 10 is a nonstop pleasure to drive (or cycle); uneventful, perhaps, but giving seemingly endless pastoral views framed by white rail fences, occasional farmhouses, and the voluptuous peaks that rise to the east and west. The first hamlet you reach along this part of Route 10, **North Haverhill,** is a real museum piece, with a necklace of distinctive colonial-era homes flanking an oval town green, and one of New Hampshire's oldest cemeteries close by.

In case you're worried, Lyme, New Hampshire, is not the place the tick-borne disease was named for; that Lyme is in Connecticut. That said, you still need to be on the lookout for these devilish little creatures.

Farther south spreads Loch Lyme, where the fine restaurant, rustic lodge, and cabins of **Loch Lyme Lodge** ($150

You Can't Get There from Here

One of the first things first-time visitors to New England notice is its compact size: A crow flying 100 miles from almost any treetop outside of Maine will end up in the next state, if not Canada. But map distances bear absolutely no relation to travel time, thanks to the mountain ranges pitched up across northern New England. So if you're sitting in your motel room in New Hampshire or Vermont wondering how far to drive for dinner, look to towns north or south. As a rule these will share the same valley since the rivers and mountains are generally aligned north–south, like compass needles. In contrast, that next town to the east or west may as well be on the opposite side of the state so far as convenience is concerned: Whether winding along erratic streambeds or stitching their ways up the sides of passes between high peaks, east–west roads tend to be a slow grind in even the best weather, truly as tortuous as the wiggling lines on the map suggest. Heavy vehicles, cautious drivers, and foul weather can make the going doubly difficult. Keep this in mind as you consider outings and side trips or you, too, will learn to say, "You can't get there from here."

and up; 800/423-2141) have been welcoming generations of New Englanders since 1946. Swim, sail, or float out on the small lake, which has an idyllic location between the mountains and the river.

A mile south of Loch Lyme Lodge on Post Pond, 10 miles north of Hanover, the tidy town of **Lyme** presents yet another Kodak-worthy scene, with a Civil War Monument standing at the center of a slender green, a large church at one end and an equally large stable at the other.

Hanover: Dartmouth College

Dartmouth College is the principal resident of attractive little **Hanover** (pop. 11,260), and the Ivy League influence shows in the local architecture, fashions, and cultural diversions. When school is in session, the cafés hum with undergraduate discourse, the downtown teems with students, and a varsity air envelops the historic campus and its sturdy neighbors. Between terms, however, the town's metabolism drops toward hibernation levels,

Baker Memorial Library, Dartmouth College

which means there's no line for espresso.

Standing out from all the Georgian-style brick buildings is Dartmouth's **Hood Museum of Art** (closed Mon.; free; 603/646-2808), on the southeast side of the green. Housed in a modern gallery designed in part by Charles Moore, the Hood shows a changing selection from its permanent collection but mainly hosts visiting exhibitions.

Currier and Ives lithograph of the Dartmouth campus, circa 1834

More contentious art can be experienced at the very center of Dartmouth, where, in the lower level reading room of Baker Library, the walls are covered with a set of politically charged frescoes by José Clemente Orozco, *An Epic of American Civilization.*

Although Ivy League Dartmouth has a $4 billion endowment and a conservative reputation, it also has had some interesting students and supporters, including children's stars Dr. Seuss and Mr. Rogers. Although Captain Kangaroo was not technically a student, both of his children were, and he received an honorary doctorate from the College in 1975. The poet Robert Frost also attended Dartmouth, but dropped out.

If it's too nice a day to stay indoors and contemplate society's ills, rent a bike and ride north to Lyme and back, or rent a canoe or kayak from Dartmouth's **Ledyard Canoe Club** ($10/hour; 603/643-6709), located on the river just north of the Route 10A bridge, and play Huck Finn for an afternoon. Or you can take a hike—the Dartmouth Outing Club maintains hundreds of miles of trails, including a part of the Appalachian Trail that runs right through town. There's an AT marker embedded in the sidewalk in front of the Hanover Inn, from where the trail runs west across the bridge to Vermont, and east down Main and Lebanon Streets to the town of Etna, before climbing the 2,280-foot peak of Moose Mountain.

Hanover Practicalities

Generations of Dartmouth students have survived their college years thanks in part to the generous portions served up at **Lou's** (30 S. Main St.; 603/643-3321). Hardly changed since it opened in 1947, and famed for its magical strawberry rhubarb and other freshly baked pies, Lou's does great big breakfasts, lunchtime soups, and burgers. For dinner, head across the street to the popular **Canoe Club Bistro** (27 S. Main St.; 603/643-9660).

For accommodations around Hanover, there's the stately, Dartmouth-run **Hanover Inn** facing the green ($250–350; 603/643-4300); for affordable rooms, however, look in nearby West Lebanon or across the river in White River Junction, Vermont.

The Hanover Inn

Into the Mountains: Norwich, West Hartford, and Pomfret

Just uphill from where the Appalachian Trail crosses the Connecticut River, along Route 10A on a broad low bridge from Hanover, you might want to while away an afternoon in **Norwich** at the interesting **Montshire Museum of Science** (daily; $12; 802/649-2200), which has more than 100 education-al exhibits focusing on natural history, as well as aquariums showcasing fresh- and saltwater creatures. The next town the AT passes through is **West Hartford,** on the banks of the White River upstream from I-91 along Route 14 and just off I-89.

From West Hartford, you can circle around (on unnumbered and rather rough-surfaced country roads) through North Pomfret, **Pomfret,** and South Pomfret, passing dairy farms, quaint barns, and one post office per town, coming in through the back door to upscale Woodstock, where this AT route links up with US-4. From South Pomfret, a quaint little hamlet that's also home to the Suicide Six ski area, the hikers' Appalachian Trail heads up into the mountains through a long, roadless stretch before crossing Route 100 at Sherburne Pass. The only real driving equivalent follows Route 12 south into Woodstock.

Lebanon and West Lebanon

Sitting rather quietly a couple of miles south of Hanover, east of the Connecticut River near the point where US-4 gets submerged beneath the I-89 freeway, historic **Lebanon** (pop. 13,151) has a town green so spacious it seems more like the outskirts of a city park than the center of a town.

Right along the bonny banks of the Connecticut River, three miles or so south of patrician Hanover, the commercial busybody of **West Lebanon** has everything you probably try hard to avoid: shopping plazas, traffic tie-ups, and familiar fast *everything,* all clustered around the two local exits off the I-89 freeway.

VERMONT

Vermont is quintessential New England: pictur-esque villages still served by cluttered country stores, small farms nestled among the granite ridges of the **Green Mountains,** and needle-sharp white church spires rising above forests ablaze with autumn colors. Precocious from birth—its con-stitution was the first in the United States to prohibit slav-ery and establish public schools—Vermont is known for its independent-minded politicians like Jim Jeffords and Bernie Saunders and for its strong liberal traditions (think Howard Dean).

From the Connecticut River, this route across Vermont follows the contours of the land, tagging along fast-running mountain streams or keeping to the valleys between the steep sur-rounding ridges that carry the Appalachian Trail ever southward.

White River Junction

Across the river from Hanover and Dartmouth, turn-of-the-20th-century **White River Junction** (pop. 2,286) used to echo with the sounds of some 50 trains a day traveling over five separate rail lines. The demise of the railroads and arrival of the Interstate cloverleaf on the outskirts of town effectively mothballed the downtown area, but like good vintage clothing, the photogenic historic center has been rediscovered by an art-smart crowd that doesn't mind the holes and missing buttons.

Freight trains still rumble through White River Junction a few times a day (and night!), and Amtrak stops here on its mainline Vermonter route along the Connecticut River from New York City. Apart from the trains, the main signs

of life here are at breakfast and lunch, when the ancient-looking **Polka Dot Diner** (daily 5 AM–7 PM; 7 N. Main St.; 802/295-9722) serves the usual unpretentious, inexpensive grilled and fried foods. The stylish **Tip Top Café,** up the street (closed Sun. and Mon.; 85 N. Main St.; 802/295-3312), offers delicious soups, sandwiches, and an ever-changing variety of bistro-style meals at lunch and dinner.

If you're looking for lodging with more character than the chain motels along the Interstates, consider downtown's **Hotel Coolidge** ($89 and up; 39 S. Main St.; 802/295-3118 or 800/622-1124). In business since the 1920s, it has a nice café downstairs. It is clean, friendly, and definitely good value. Even better value are its bare-bones HI-hostel bunks and rooms, which go for around $25 and up per person.

If you're in the area around mid-June, check out the **Quechee Hot Air Balloon, Craft and Music Festival,** held over Father's Day weekend.

Quechee and Quechee Gorge

In three miles west from White River Junction and the I-91/I-89 freeways, US-4 climbs upstream into the valley of the Ottauquechee (AWT-ah-KWEE-chee) River. You cross **Quechee Gorge** almost without warning, but adjacent parking on both sides of the gorge gives you a chance to take a longer look at the dramatic little canyon or to stretch your legs along the rim-side hiking trails. East of the gorge there's a tacky Quechee Gorge Village souvenir shop, which boasts a tiny train and a well-preserved streamline-style 1946 Worcester pre-fab that's been incorporated into the **Farmers Diner** (802/295-4600), a retro all-American roadhouse serving up locally sourced versions of the usual standards.

Also on the east side of the gorge, **Quechee State Park** (802/295-2990) provides access to the Ottauquechee River and also has camping with hot showers. Next to the park is the nature center of the **Vermont Institute of Natural Science** (daily; $11; 802/359-5000), an outdoor museum dedicated to local wildlife, especially raptors. Enclosures let you get up close and personal with hawks, eagles, owls, and falcons.

QUECHEE GULF BRIDGE OVER OTTAUQUECHEE RIVER AT DEWEY'S MILLS, VT., HEIGHT 164 FT.

ON COOLIDGE MEMORIAL HIGHWAY BETWEEN WHITE RIVER JUNCTION AND RUTLAND, VT.

West of the gorge, you can turn north off US-4 into old **Quechee,** a quaint town famed as the home of renowned glassblower **Simon Pearce's** lumber mill–cum–art gallery. Norman Rockwell-esque Quechee is a fine example of how pleasant life can be once you turn away from the fast lane. Soak up the ambience with a stay (or just a memorable meal) at the **Quechee Inn** ($109 and up; 1119 Main St.; 802/295-3133), a half mile from town.

Woodstock

"The good people of Woodstock have less incentive than others to yearn for heaven," said a 19th-century resident. It's a sentiment readily echoed today. Chartered in 1761, **Woodstock** (pop. 900) remains an exceedingly well-preserved example of small-town New England—tidy Federal-style homes, built by wealthy professionals of the newborn American republic, still ring the classic village green. Now the historic village is home to wealthy retirees and their fortunate sons and daughters. You'll see the signs of this old money throughout the town: well-stocked wine racks at the general store, shady basketball courts along the river, excellent performing arts at the Town Hall Theater, and, most importantly, the wherewithal to refuse any compromising commercial development. To put it mildly, expansion of the tax base is *not* a pressing issue for this community.

During summer and fall, walking tours are an excellent way to take stock of the town's history and architecture. Call or visit the **Information Booth** (802/457-3555) on the

All over southern Vermont, especially along US-4 around Quechee, Woodstock, and up to Killington, the worst floods in state history followed in the wake of Hurricane Irene in August 2011. Streets and buildings were washed away, and many beloved covered bridges were damaged or destroyed.

Notice, as you approach Woodstock Village Green, that there are no overhead power lines on the two main downtown streets, Central and Elm. Laurance Rockefeller paid to have the lines buried back in 1973.

Diners: Fast Food Worth Slowing Down For

Aaaah, the local diner! Throughout New England, these brightly lit establishments are magnets for folks weary of the dull predictability of the fast-food mega-chains. In contrast to the impersonal nature of those billions-serving burger factories, diners are low-key gathering spots where community gossip is shared and politics debated by a gang of regulars assembling each morning. Where waitresses (frequently named Mildred, Blanche, and Edna) wear lace hankies pinned to their aprons and are quick to offer refills on coffee. Where UPS drivers, Methodist clergy, morticians, and middle-school principals perched on adjacent stools know they can score decent hot roast-beef sandwiches or a great piece of fresh fruit pie. And where autumn leaf-peepers and other passers-through can inquire about local attractions or find out which nearby motels or B&Bs might still have empty rooms for that night.

The diner's lineage can ultimately be traced back to horse-drawn lunch carts selling sandwiches and hot coffee along the streets of cities like Providence and Boston beginning in the 1870s. However, the prototypical New England diners are those built from 1906 through 1961 by the Worcester Lunch Car Company: barrel-roofed with colorful porcelain panels on the exterior and plenty of varnished hardwood inside. Other diners came from manufacturers headquartered in New York (DeRaffele) and especially New Jersey (Mountain View, Fodero, Kullman, Paramount, Silk City, O'Mahony, and many more). Each diner-maker trumpeted its own design innovations: streamlined metal exteriors, artful tile work, bits of elegant stained glass, distinctive built-in clocks, and more efficient floor plans. Some diners even came from the factory with all necessary crockery, flatware, and cooking equipment included, so that new owners could begin serving hungry locals on the very day set-up was complete.

green for a schedule. Hiking trails lead up both the summits overlooking the town. A community blackboard at the corner of Central and Elm, a.k.a. the Town Crier, lists local events and activities all year. Even if you're racing through Woodstock, bound for the mountains, be sure to stop long enough to enjoy this quick tour: From the oblong green, cross the Middle Covered Bridge and follow the Ottauquechee downstream along River Street. Then work your way back via Elm Street and **F. H. Gillingham & Sons,** Vermont's oldest country store, which offers locally made food and crafts.

If you've admired the rolling fields and weathered wooden fences, savored

Aficionados will be quick to inform you that real diners are roadside eateries whose component parts were fabricated in a factory, then shipped by road or rail for final assembly on-site. Real diners, they'll insist, always have counters, with at least some cooking done within view of patrons. There'll almost certainly be booths, too, and a definite blue-collar, no-frills ambience. Unlike their urban or roadside truck stop equivalents, few diners are open 24 hours; many in fact serve breakfast and lunch only, opening very early in the morning (around 6 AM) and closing around 2 or 3 PM But not every place with the word "diner" in its name is the genuine article. Many places that call themselves diners are as far removed from the classic prefab as IKEA furniture is from a handcrafted antique, and mavens regard diner-themed restaurants (like Denny's, or Johnny Rockets) with considerable scorn. The smaller, the better, they say, with points deducted for any remodeling that disfigures the original design.

You needn't care about any of this lore, of course, to enjoy yourself. But after visiting your third or fourth diner, you may begin to notice similarities and differences among them. Curious about a particular establishment's history? Quiz the owner—more often than not, he or she will be happy to tell you all about the place, which may have started life with a different name in another town and been moved three or more times before it found its current home. Look for a "tag," the small metal plate (often affixed to the wall over the entry door) listing manufacturer, date, and serial number. The best and most enjoyable way to get to know diners and diner culture is simply to spend time in them, but if you want to learn more, check the authoritative volume, *American Diner Then and Now,* by Richard Gutman, published by Johns Hopkins University Press.

the local apples and sharp cheddar, and enjoyed the scent of mown hay or boiling maple sap, you'll appreciate an even closer look at New England's farms with a visit to the **Billings Farm & Museum** (daily in summer, weekends the rest of the year; $12; 802/457-2355), just off Route 12 north of the village. Frederick Billings, better known as the builder of the Northern Pacific Railroad (Billings, Montana, is named for him), began this working dairy farm in the late 19th century. Its restored farmhouse and huge barns illustrate the rural life in galleries, demonstrations, and hands-on activities.

Across the road, another historic farm is open to the public as the **Marsh-Billings-Rockefeller National Historical Park** (tours daily Memorial Day weekend to late October; $8; 802/457-3368), Vermont's only national park. The property, which includes the former home of Laurance Rockefeller (1910–

2004), who married Frederick Billings's granddaughter, is a study in conservation practice, and its dense woodlands are living proof of the merits of sustainable agriculture. Some 60 miles of trails are open in the winter for cross-country skiing and snowshoeing from the Nordic center at **The Woodstock Inn & Resort** ($18; 802/457-6674).

Woodstock Practicalities

Hungry travelers will find plenty of choices around town. There are also two very interesting if rather bare-bones road-food haunts bookending the town along US-4. At the east end of town, you'll find the white shack housing **Wasp's Snack Bar** (57 Pleasant St.; 802/457-3334), fairly regarded as one of the finest greasy spoons in Creation. On US-4 a half mile west of the green is the **Woodstock Farmer's Market** (802/457-3658), with top-quality produce and deli fare.

Accommodations run the gamut from moderate motels to deluxe inns; at all of them, expect rates to increase during high season, which in Woodstock is most of summer and fall, along with the winter holidays. The main place right in town, the 142-room, Rockefeller-built **Woodstock Inn & Resort** ($230 and up; 802/457-1100) sits on the south side of the green, and although it tries hard to look like a stately old place, the inn was actually built from scratch in 1969. The **Village Inn** ($150 and up; 41 Pleasant St.; 802/457-1255), a lovely Victorian-era B&B, has much more character, yet is still affordable. The modest **Braeside Motel** ($98 and up; 432 Woodstock Rd.; 802/457-1366), along US-4 on the eastern outskirts of town, is about as budget-friendly as you're going to get.

Bridgewater and Killington

The tiny town of **Bridgewater** (pop. 895), stretching along the banks of the Ottauquechee, seems well on the way to the middle of nowhere. But that's what lures many visitors to this region—the fact that so much of it seems to have contentedly hung back with Rip van Winkle. That said, Bridgewater *is* a gateway to one of the state's most important somewheres: the ski resorts of central Vermont. The large woolen mill here has been converted into the Old Mill Marketplace, its water-powered turbines and textile machines replaced by small shops selling a typically Vermont mix of antiques, ski

Pico Alpine Ski Lift, Rutland, Vermont, in the Green Mts.— 98

apparel, New Age books, and gift-packaged Vermont foods to visitors heading for the mountains.

Through the Bridgewater area, US-4 is generously wide-shouldered and level, making it a popular cycling route, especially during the fall color season, when the dense hardwood forests that climb the slopes above the roadway are blazing with autumn hues. When the leaves have fallen and been replaced by snow, this scenic stretch changes character completely, becoming one of the East Coast's most prominent ski resorts, **Killington.** The permanent population of Killington is maybe 50 people, but on winter weekends as many as 10,000 skiers flock to its seven different mountains and many miles of trails (lift tickets around $69 and up; snow info 800/621-6867). The skiers also support a plethora of real estate agencies, restaurants, and bars, especially off US-4 on the main road to the slopes, Killington Road.

Compared to the rest of Vermont, Killington is not an especially attractive place to be in summer, when the parking lots of the time-share condo complexes are empty and the hills are scarred by clear-cut ski trails, but the lack of crowds also means lower prices for accommodations. Options from roadside motels to upscale resorts like the **Inn at Six Mountains** offer their lowest rates when the temperatures are highest.

Gifford Woods State Park

Sitting in the scenic heart of the Green Mountains, at the junction of US-4 and Route 100, **Gifford Woods State Park** (802/775-5354) protects one of the few virgin hardwood forests left in New England, with seven acres of massive sugar maple, birch, and ash trees, some of which are more than 300 years old. There's a nice **campground** with hot showers (around $20), four one-room cabins ($50), and access to many fine trails, including the Appalachian Trail and the Long Trail, which run together across US-4 just west of 2,190-foot Shelburne Pass.

Vermont holds more than 100 covered bridges, several good examples of which are to be seen between Quechee and Bridgewater. Look for the 1836 **Taftsville Bridge** west of Quechee, the **Middle Covered Bridge** in Woodstock (which was totally rebuilt way back in 1969), and the 1877 **Lincoln Bridge** four miles west of Woodstock. The nation's second longest covered bridge, **Cornish-Windsor,** crosses the Connecticut River at Windsor, about 15 miles or so southeast of Woodstock, with a 449-foot span built in 1866.

In the Killington area, tune to "The Peak," **WEBK 105.3 FM,** for the best in alternative pop music—everything from the Grateful Dead to Beck and Bela Fleck.

Route 100: Rochester and Granville Gulf

Route 100 runs north–south through the geographical and spiritual heart of Vermont, winding from curve to curve past cornfields and fat cows lazing in impossibly green pastures, alongside gurgling streams, up and down switch-backing passes, and generally setting the standard for what scenic roads ought to be. Route 100 runs right at the edge of the Green Mountains National Forest, parallel to Vermont's beloved crestline Long Trail, and every so often passes by a picturesque gas station–cum–general store, selling everything you'll need to keep you on the road, from gas to maple-syrup milk shakes. Up and down the whole state of Vermont, Route 100 is a wonder-ful drive, as are just about all of the roads that intersect it.

North of US-4, the first place you come to along Route 100 is **Pittsfield,** an all-in-white hamlet set in a pastoral valley and sur-rounded by hayfields and acres of corn. From here Route 100 edges east into the White River Valley, passing through Stockbridge, which centers on an ancient-look-ing Ford dealership, and a couple more places that seem to exist solely on maps. The next stop is **Rochester,** at the junction with Route 73, which heads west over scenic Brandon Gap. Rochester is a proper Vermont town, with a vil-lage green, a bandstand, and the excellent **Rochester Café & Country Store** (802/767-4302), serving breakfast and lunch (and bread pudding and milk shakes—yum).

Two miles south of Rochester, across the river and away from Route 100, the **Liberty Hill Farm Inn** ($98 per person; 802/767-3926) is a family-friend-ly farmstay B&B and has a working 261-acre dairy where you can hike, bike, fish, or help feed the cows (and the ducks and chickens and cats).

North of Rochester, Route 100 passes through a still-working landscape, with ski club cabins sharing the roadside scene with a few barns and remnants of historic sheep pens. The one don't-miss highlight of this middle section of Route 100 is **Granville Gulf State Preserve,** about 30 beautiful miles north from US-4. The Green Mountains rise steeply to either side of the road, and just off the west side of the road, delicate **Moss Glen Falls** tumble down through craggy cliffs to a gurgling stream. A short boardwalk, built using re-cycled wood products and supermarket plastic bags, leads to the foot of the falls from a small parking turnout.

Plymouth Notch: Calvin Coolidge Country

Running a twisty seven miles south from US-4 and Bridgewater, Route 100A passes through beautiful scenery and **Plymouth Notch,** birthplace of Calvin Coolidge, the only U.S. president born on July 4. The small hilltop clutch of buildings is so little changed by modern times, it's a wonder there aren't horses with carriages parked behind the visitors center instead of Subarus. One of the most evocative and simply beautiful historic sites in New England, the **Calvin Coolidge Homestead District** has been restored to its 1923 appearance, the year Colonel John Coolidge administered the oath of office to his vacationing son, the vice president, after President Harding died unexpectedly in San Francisco. The house, the general store, and the cheese factory are three of the 10 buildings open to the public (daily in summer; $7.50; 802/672-3773). There's also a mile-long nature trail offering fine views of Plymouth Notch and its Green Mountain surroundings.

COLONEL JOHN COOLIDGE, FATHER OF PRESIDENT CALVIN COOLIDGE AND CALVIN JR., PLYMOUTH, VERMONT

Route 100: The Skiers' Highway

Known as the **Skiers' Highway,** serpentine Route 100 manages to pass the base of nearly every major ski resort in southern Vermont. From Ludlow south through Jamaica, Stratton, and West Dover, any doubt that skiing is the cash cow of the state's most lucrative industry—tourism—is quickly dispelled by the wall-to-wall inns, sportswear shops, vacation real estate offices, and restaurants along the way.

In recent years, downhill mountain-bikers and inn-to-inn cyclists riding Route 100 have made the region more of a year-round recreation center, but overall you still get the sense that, pretty as they are with their village greens, old homes, and hand-carved wooden signs, many of these Route 100 towns spend the warm months convalescing.

"Silent Cal" Coolidge was famous—perhaps unjustly—for being a man of few words. A White House dinner guest is said to have bet that she could make the president address her with at least three words; when confronted with this challenge, Coolidge replied, "You lose."

Brigham Young, the man who led the Mormon exodus to Utah, was born in **Whitingham,** fewer than 10 miles south of Wilmington on Route 100, at the south end of the Harriman Reservoir. There's a small commemorative monument and picnic area on the Town Hall Common.

Wilmington and Route 9

Route 100 catches a panoramic view of Mt. Snow as the roadway descends into **Wilmington** (pop. 2,225), a picturesque village of 18th- and 19th-century shops and houses built along the Deerfield River. Wilmington also has some great old-fashioned places to eat, like **Dot's Restaurant** (3 E. Main St.; 802/464-7284), a white-clapboard Vermont institution, famous for its pancakes, burgers, chili, and pies. The chamber of commerce is named after the local Mount Snow ski resort rather than the town, so you know who pays the bills around here. Nevertheless, the warmer months see a fair bit of activity in the galleries and antiques shops, and for classical music lovers, the **Marlboro Music Festival** (802/254-2394 in summer only) marks summer's zenith at Marlboro College, a dozen miles east toward Brattleboro on Route 9. Between mid-July and mid-August several score of the world's finest classical musicians perform here in one of the nation's most distinguished annual chamber music series.

Heading westward toward Bennington, you can continue west on Route 9 to Bennington and follow US-7 south through Williamstown, or you can make your way south through the much less developed areas along Route 8 and Route 100, which take you through the heavy-duty mill town of North Adams.

Bennington

By far the largest Vermont town south of Burlington, **Bennington** (pop. 15,737) is a bustling little manufacturing and commercial center. It was the site of a significant victory against the British-paid Hessians in 1777 during the American Revolution, a sweet morale-booster that contributed to the defeat of General "Gentleman Johnny" Burgoyne's army of Redcoats at Saratoga. In the subsequent centuries, Bennington's name became synonymous with art: the decorative arts of the antebellum United States Pottery Company; the liberal arts of **Bennington College,** one of the nation's most expensive and exclusive private colleges; and the folk art of Mary Robertson "Grandma" Moses.

statue of Seth Warner at the Bennington Battle Monument

The largest public collection of Grandma Moses's beguiling work is on display in the **Bennington Museum** (closed Wed. and the month of Jan.; $10; 75 West Main St.), whose ivy-covered edifice is found up the hill on Route 9

Raspberry and chocolate chip pancakes at the Blue Benn Diner: yum.

in the graceful old part of town. Along with 30 Grandma Moses paintings and the rural schoolhouse she attended two centuries ago, the museum also has a wide variety of historical artifacts, examples of early Bennington pottery, and the sole survivor of the fabulous motor cars once made here in Bennington: a 1925 Wasp.

From the Bennington Museum, walk north toward the 306-foot obelisk that towers over the town: the **Bennington Battle Monument,** completed in 1891 to commemorate the Revolutionary War victory, which actually occurred west of town, over the New York state border. For $2, mid-April–November 1, an elevator will take you to an observation room near the top of the tower for a great view up and down the valley.

Bennington is also the final resting place of poet Robert Frost, whose tombstone in the burial ground alongside the Old First Church, at Church and Monument Streets, says: "I had a lover's quarrel with the world."

If anyone starts erecting monuments to good dining instead of old wars or dead poets, this town would have another tower of stone beside the **Blue Benn Diner** (314 North St.; 802/442-5140), on a bend in US-7 north of town. The fact that it's a vintage 1940s Silk City certainly gives this cozy, nonsmoking joint character. But what earns the seven-days-a-week (from 6 AM) loyalty

Site of the Catamount Tavern, 1767 308

Bennington, Vt.

of its patrons is the top-notch short-order cooking: From baked meat loaf and roast pork to broccoli stir-fry and multigrain pancakes, the food's good, cheap, and served up so fast you'll barely have time to choose your song on the wall-hung jukebox at your table.

Most of Bennington's accommodations are strung along Route 7A to the north and US-7 to the south of downtown, all local names but for the Ramada and Best Western inns found on 7A. If you are in the market for a distinctive B&B, check out the central, historic, and highly regarded **Four Chimneys Inn** ($149 and up; 21 West Rd.; 802/447-3500), which offers 11 rooms and 11 acres of grounds and gardens, and a fine restaurant, west of Bennington on Route 9.

When garnished with Vermont-made Ben & Jerry's ice cream, apple pie à la mode is certainly nothing to sneer at, but if you really want to try apple pie the Vermont way, ask for a slab of sharp cheddar on the side instead of ice cream.

Whether or not you need gas, those interested in old cars and automobilia will want to stop by the full-service, re-created Sunoco filling station and antique car collection at **Hemmings Motor News** (222 Main St.; 802/447-9580) in Bennington.

MASSACHUSETTS

Hemmed in by the daunting topography of its surrounding mountains, the Berkshire region of western Massachusetts is a world apart, blessed with abundant nature and an easygoing small-town character. The region's relaxed, rural charms and its location equidistant from Boston and New York City have long made it a magnet for writers and artists as well as a playground for the rich, so be prepared to experience a little of everything from natural splendors to high-society display. And remember, it never takes more than a few strategic turns to trade plush restaurants and music festivals for splendidly rural forests as deep and undisturbed as any in New England.

North Adams

If you've grown accustomed to the typical tourist New England of village greens and clapboard B&Bs, industrial **North Adams** (pop. 13,708) may come as something of a shock. Nearly from its inception, North Adams tied its fortunes to major manufacturing plants, churning out printed cotton until textiles went south, then rolling out electronics for everything from the first atomic bomb to the television sets of the 1950s and 1960s. When electronics went solid-state and overseas, North Adams nearly died clinging to the belief that some new assembly line would come fill its sprawling complex of massive Victorian-era mill buildings. Finally, the town's long-awaited salvation seems to be taking shape, in the form of art: the Massachusetts Museum of Contemporary Art. Better known as **Mass MoCA** (daily in July and Aug., closed Tues. rest of year; $15; 413/662-2111), the museum galleries fill some 200,000 square feet of heavy-duty industrial buildings with an ever-changing array of cutting-edge art plus the inevitable gift shop, a very nice café, frequent live music, and even its own very stylish B&B, **The Porches** ($180 and up; 231 River St.; 413/664-0400).

By the early 19th century, farmland had replaced 75 percent of Berkshire County's forests. Now forests have reclaimed that 75 percent and more, but innumerable dry stone walls serve as reminders of the once vast cultivated fields.

North Adams is five miles north of the quaint town of Adams, the birthplace of voting rights activist Susan B. Anthony (1820–1906), and once-again home to the recently revived **Miss Adams Diner,** right on Route 8 (53 Park St.; 413/776-7372).

For those who are very interested in the olden days, the region's historic gravy train is faithfully recollected in the **Western Gateway Heritage State Park** (daily May–Oct.; free; 413/663-6312). About a mile southwest of the museum, and occupying the former freight yard of the Boston and Maine Railroad, the park highlights the landmark construction of the five-mile-long Hoosac Tunnel and North Adams's front-row seat on the Boston–Great Lakes rail connection it made possible.

Susan B. Anthony, circa 1890

In northwestern Massachusetts, this Appalachian Trail route crosses **The Oregon Trail** transcontinental road trip along US-20 and other highways (see page 683). The entire coast-to-coast journey, heading east from North Adams along Route 2 (the Mohawk Trail to Boston and Cape Cod) and west from Williamstown through Albany and beyond, is covered on pages 584–703.

Williamstown

To the visitor it appears as if stately **Williamstown** (pop. 4,754) is simply a nickname for the immaculate and graceful campus of Williams College—even the main commercial block is basically the corridor between dorms and gym. From their common 18th-century benefactor, Ephraim Williams (who insisted the town's name be changed from its original West Hoosuck), to the large number of alumni who return in their retirement, "Billsville" and its college are nearly inseparable. The town-gown symbiosis has spawned an enviable

It was during the blasting of the Hoosac Tunnel that nitroglycerin was first used as a construction explosive. And just so you know, the river is the Hoosic, but the mountain range is the Hoosac.

array of visual, performing, and edible arts, yet fresh contingents of ingenuous youth keep all the wealth and refinement from becoming too cloying.

Singer Sewing Machine heir Robert Sterling Clark's huge art collection ended up in Williamstown in part because of the Cold War. In the late 1940s and early 1950s, the threat of a Russian nuclear attack seemed real enough that being as distant as possible from likely bomb targets was a critical factor in choosing a permanent repository. Today **Clark Art Institute** (daily July and Aug., closed Mon. Sept.–June; $15 in summer, free rest of year; 225 South St.; 413/458-2303), in a pastoral setting, is the town's jewel, displaying paintings by Winslow Homer and an extraordinary collection of Impressionist works, including more than 30 Renoirs. Special exhibitions are held in a gorgeous, Tadao Ando–designed gallery built into a nearby hillside. Also worth a look in Williamstown is the excellent and wide-ranging **Williams College Museum of Art** (closed Mon.; free) on Main Street opposite Thompson Memorial Chapel (that mini-Westminster Abbey).

antique piano at the Clark Art Institute

Williamstown can claim another gem, this time in the natural art of relaxation. Luxurious Cunard Lines used to serve its ocean-going passengers water exclusively from Williamstown's

Sand Springs (Memorial Day–Labor Day; $7.50; 158 Sand Springs Rd.; 413/458-5205). A family-friendly swimming pool has been open every summer since the 1950s on the site, on the north side of town, but the complex was for sale at the time of writing.

Williamstown Practicalities

For breakfast, head to US-7 on the north side of town, where the popular **Chef's Hat** (905 Simonds Rd.; 413/458-5120) preserves a 100-year-old counter and other parts of its original diner incarnation. The hands-down best takeout pizza joint is **Hot Tomatoes** (100 Water St.; 413/458-2722), and in mild weather the nearby streamside park is well suited to lolling picnickers. Also good: the Indian-inspired food at **Spice Root** (23 Spring St.; 413/458-5200).

Tony continental dining suitable for starched alumni banquets abounds in Williamstown, but if you're looking for truly fresh, interesting food, skip the inns and go to **Mezze Bistro and Bar** (413/458-0123), which outgrew its original downtown home and moved to more spacious digs along US-7 a mile southwest of town, where the very best locally sourced produce, meats, and fish are featured on a stylish, dinner-only menu.

Williams College Museum of Art

A drive along Main Street (Route 2) will give you a view of most of Williamstown's accommodations, including many small motels out on the eastern edge of town, like the friendly and clean **Maple Terrace Motel** ($99 and up; 555 Main St.; 413/458-9677). For a real treat, consider **The Guest House at Field Farm** ($150 and up; 554 Sloan Rd.; 413/458-3135) in South Williamstown, five miles south along either Route 7 or scenic Water Street (Route 43). Occupying the 316-acre former estate of Pacific Northwest lumber tycoon Lawrence Bloedel, the main house, designed in 1948, is a striking example of American mid-20th-century modern architecture. If you have any love of Frank Lloyd Wright or Charles and Ray Eames, you'll be delighted by this live-in museum of contemporary design, with its huge picture windows, proto-Scandinavian furniture, and meadow-side swimming pool.

Mount Greylock

South of Williamstown, Massachusetts's tallest peak is the centerpiece of 12,500-acre **Mount Greylock State Reservation,** one of the state's largest and most popular possessions. More than 70 miles of trails, including some thigh-burning mountain-bike routes, wander along the reforested slopes, most of which were heavily logged for timber and charcoal back in the 19th century. Rock ledges provide great views of the Hoosic River Valley to the east and the Housatonic Valley to the south, when the namesake mists aren't keeping the 3,491-foot summit wadded up in a damp ball of dingy cotton. The $25 million reconstruction project has been a complete success, and during warm months, access is a cinch: Century-old Notch Road snakes its way up through the birch and spruce from Route 2 on the north side, while Rockwell Road ascends more gently from US-7 along the flanks of Greylock's southern neighbors. Combine these roads' 17 miles and you'll enjoy the most scenic, driveable mountain ascent in New England, although keep in mind that both roads are narrow, enlivened by occasional hairpin turns, and—especially at dusk— prone to wandering wildlife.

If you want to see over the forest, climb the 93-foot **Massachusetts Veterans War Memorial Tower** on the summit. If the weather is good, you'll have a panoramic view from New Hampshire to Connecticut. A stone's throw from the granite tower is the **Bascom Lodge** (413/743-1591), a beautiful old stone and timber structure that offers private rooms (around $125), shared bunk rooms ($35 per person), and good food (and showers!).

Pittsfield

Compared to the carefully preserved Norman Rockwell simplicity of many of the surrounding small towns, the aging industrial cityscape of **Pittsfield** (pop. 44,737) has made it the place most Berkshire weekenders strenuously try to avoid, despite the fact that its size and the valley's topography make this nearly

Hancock Shaker Village

Just five miles west of Pittsfield on old US-20, Hancock Shaker Village is one of the best-preserved remnants of the religious sect known popularly as Shakers, but formally as the United Society of Believers in Christ's Second Appearing, whose utopian communities flourished in the years before the Civil War. Shakers, as outsiders called them because of their occasional convulsions during worship, were dedicated to a

the Round Barn

communal life conspicuous in its equality between men and women, a natural corollary to their belief in parity between a male God and a female Holy Mother Wisdom.

The English-born leader of the group, Ann Lee, was in fact regarded by Shakers as the female, and second, incarnation of Christ. Although Puritan theocracy was ending, preaching this gospel did not endear her to many New Englanders in the decade following her arrival just prior to the American Revolution. During that war, Lee and her "children" sought their Heaven on Earth, as seen in her visions. Mother Ann died near Albany, New York, in 1784, before any communities based on her precepts could be founded.

Hancock Shaker Village, third among the 24 settlements built in the nation by Lee's followers, was founded in 1783 and survived 177 years, outlasting all but two other Shaker communities. It's been preserved as a living museum (daily Apr.–Oct.; $17; 413/443-0188 or 800/817-1137), with exhibits, tours, and working artisans interpreting the rural lifestyle and famous design skills of the Shakers. Appreciation of the efficiency, simplicity, and perfect workmanship consecrated within the "City of Peace" can quickly fill a couple of days if you let it.

The center of Shaker activities was just west of Hancock, along US-20 across the New York border at New Lebanon, where a few buildings still stand today. Other large Shaker communities in New England included Sabbathday Lake in Maine (the only one still "alive"), one at Enfield, New Hampshire (east of Hanover), and another at Canterbury, New Hampshire (south of Franconia Notch).

impossible unless you have a resident's familiarity with the back roads. In contrast to the lives of leisure lived in many Berkshire towns, Pittsfield has always been a busy, hard-working place, resolutely down-to-earth.

Herman Melville

Despite Pittsfield's anything-but-quaint appearance, there are actually some good reasons for travelers to pay the place a visit. Head out to Holmes Road, at the city's rural southern edge, and maybe you will see the resemblance between a leviathan and the imposing outline of Mt. Greylock, particularly if you view it from the study window of Herman Melville's **Arrowhead** (daily in summer; $13; 413/442-1793). That salty masterpiece, *Moby Dick,* was indeed written in this landlocked locale, where Melville moved in 1850 to be near his mentor, Nathaniel Hawthorne. While foremost a literary shrine, the spacious farm is also home to the **Berkshire County Historical Society,** whose well-curated exhibits are always interesting. Serious pilgrims on the path of Ishmael and the great white whale will also want to visit the Melville Memorial Room on the upper level of the **Berkshire Athenaeum,** Pittsfield's public library (1 Wendell Ave.).

As with its other attractions, Pittsfield has some real unexpected gems when it comes to food, with three great places lining up along East Street between downtown and US-7. If you love hot dogs (and who doesn't?), you've probably been dreaming of some day finding a place like **Teo's Hot Dogs** (1410 East St.; 413/447-9592), where you can wash down excellent chili dogs with super-cold $2 beers. For fresh pasta, pizza, and pub grub at a great small-town price,

Arrowhead

You may not know that all of the paper used in all of the money printed in the United States comes from a mill here in the backwoods of Massachusetts, but it does. In fact, Crane & Co. of Dalton makes the 100 percent cotton paper used in United States currency at a series of historic mills along Route 8 just east of Pittsfield.

cruise a half-mile farther west down East Street to the **East Side Cafe** (378 Newell St.; 413/447-9405), just off the main road, a neighborhood bar whose comfort food and convivial atmosphere attract a family clientele. In between these two blue-collar haunts is one great, full-service dinner place: **Elizabeth's** (1264 East St.; 413/448-8244), serving full-flavored Italian classics. All three are cash-only, and very popular.

Lenox: Tanglewood and The Mount

During the late-19th-century Gilded Age, the Berkshires were the inland equivalent of Newport, Rhode Island, with dozens of opulent "cottages" constructed here by newly rich titans of American industry. Built for an era in which "society" was a respectable, full-time occupation for folks with names like Carnegie and Westinghouse, some 75 of these giant mansions still stand, especially around the genteel town of **Lenox** (pop. 5,100). Many of the houses have been converted to palatial B&B inns, full-service health spas, or private schools; others are home to organizations whose presence has made Lenox a seasonal mecca for the performing arts.

The lives and times of the Gilded Age elite were well chronicled by Edith Wharton, who lived in Lenox for many years in a 42-room house she designed and built for herself called **The Mount** (daily in summer only; $16; 413/551-5111). Recently restored and set in three acres of Italianate gardens, The Mount is just south of central Lenox, well signed off Plunkett Street. Wharton, who considered herself better at gardening than writing, was the first woman to win a Pulitzer Prize in the novel category (for her 1920 *The Age of Innocence*). She drew upon local people and incidents in many of her works, including two of her most famous: *The House of Mirth* and *Ethan Frome*.

Lenox is also connected with another great American writer, Nathaniel Hawthorne, who lived here with his family around 1850 and wrote *The House of Seven Gables* at what is now **Tanglewood** (tickets 888/266-1200), the summer home of the Boston Symphony Orchestra, the Mark Morris Dance Group, and visiting pop performers like James Taylor and Earth, Wind and Fire. Besides Tanglewood, the Lenox area also hosts the **Jacob's Pillow Dance Festival** in Becket (413/243-0745) and the **Berkshire Theatre Festival** in Stockbridge (413/298-5576), so you can understand why such a small town is such a big magnet for East Coast culture vultures.

one of the gardens at The Mount, former home of Edith Wharton

Lenox Practicalities

The Berkshires' annual influx of cosmopolitan concert-goers affects everything in southwestern Massachusetts, most obviously the local restaurants, half of which cater to seasonal immigrants from Boston and New York. Try the eclectic (and not too expensive) menu at the tiny but highly regarded "locavore" **Nudel Restaurant** (37 Church St.; 413/551-7183), where the sometimes exotic tastes from the kitchen highlight come from locally sourced ingredients. Many other contenders for the town's gourmet dining crown lie within the same two-block area.

Along with its many good restaurants, Lenox brims with more than 20 handsome B&B inns, all attractively situated amid wide lawns and gardens. Try the historic and very cozy **Birchwood Inn** ($175 and up; 7 Hubbard St.; 413/637-2600), opposite the Church on the Hill, or the **Brook Farm Inn** ($180 and up; 15 Hawthorne St.; 413/637-3013), which offers more than 700 volumes of poetry in the library, poetry on audiotape, poetry readings on Saturday, and poems *du jour* for perusal before breakfast. Another popular option, right at the center of Lenox, is the always charming **Village Inn** ($202 and up; 16 Church St.; 413/637-0020), built in 1771 and featuring clean, comfortable rooms and a very good restaurant.

Stockbridge

On the south side of the I-90 Mass Turnpike from Lenox, the other main center of Berkshires cultural life is **Stockbridge** (pop. 1,947). If Main Street feels familiar, perhaps it's because the town made its way onto Norman Rockwell canvases during the final decades of his career, when he lived and worked here. You may dismiss his illustrations as the epitome of contrived sentimentality, but only people with hearts of solid flint won't find themselves grinning after a stroll through the collection of the **Norman Rockwell Museum** (daily; $16; 413/298-4100). The modern museum is on Route 183 two miles west of town, and the town itself is well worth a stroll, too, particularly past the grand houses along Main Street that seem frozen in an idyllic past.

Know that Rockwell painting of the runaway kid with the policeman? The lunch-counter setting was inspired by **Joe's Diner** (85 Center St.; 413/243-9756) in nearby **Lee,** a Berkshire institution favored by everybody from local factory workers to New York celebrities.

While most of the large estate homes around Stockbridge are not open to the public, one of the county's more extravagant "cottages" is **Naumkeag** (daily in summer only; $15), an 1885 mansion on Prospect Hill Road less than a mile north of downtown. The mansion, designed by Stanford White for Joseph Choate, a lawyer who later served as U.S. ambassador to Britain, amply illustrates why this region was regarded as the state's Gold Coast a century ago. The impressively landscaped grounds are an attraction in their own right.

Stockbridge's Main Street hasn't always been the exclusive province of boutiques for coffee, curtains, and AARP members. Once upon a time it was also home to the eatery immortalized by Arlo Guthrie as the place where "you can get anything you want" in his 1967 folk song, "Alice's Restaurant Massacree."

Sculpture is the highlight of **Chesterwood** (daily in summer; $15), off Route 183 just south of the Norman Rockwell Museum. The residence was the summer home of Daniel Chester French, one of the most popular contributors to the fin-de-siècle American renaissance. French arrived on the art scene with a bang, sculpting Concord's *Minute Man* statue at age 25, but he is best remembered for his statue of the seated president in the Lincoln Memorial in Washington, D.C. A tour of French's studio and house (now a property of the National Trust) or a walk around the 122 wooded acres graced with works of contemporary sculptors quickly confirms why French once called his seasonal visits "six months…in heaven."

Tyringham

Route 8, US-20, and the Mass Turnpike all cross the Appalachian Trail at Greenwater Pond east of Lee, but a much more scenic stretch of the trail can be accessed south of here in the village of **Tyringham** (pop. 420). Site of a Shaker community in the 1800s, and later a popular artist colony, this small hamlet is situated in a delightfully rural landscape of small farms and rolling pastures. The main sight here is an odd one: **Santarella** (tours by appointment only; $5/person with $20 minimum; 413/243-2819), the hand-hewn home and studio of British sculptor Sir Henry Kitson, whose many works include the *Pilgrim Maiden* monument at Plymouth and the *Minuteman* at Lexington Green. His house is a place where Bilbo Baggins of *The Hobbit* would feel at home, with its sculpted rocks, twisting beams, and organic-looking pseudo-thatched roof.

South of Santarella, beyond the ever-quaint center of Tyringham, a signed parking area marks the crossing of the Appalachian Trail, which you can follow on a short (three-mile round-trip) hike through fields of wildflowers up through Tyringham Cobble to a ridge giving a good view over this pastoral valley, which feels far more remote than it really is.

Museum & Gardens

Great Barrington

While most South County towns have been spruced up like precious antiques, **Great Barrington,** with as many hardware stores as chic boutiques, is like Grandma's comfortable old sofa, still too much in daily use to keep under velvet wraps. The town doesn't deplore the few tacky commercial lots around its fringes, perhaps because they can't detract from the handsome buildings at its core. Prime among these buildings, which include stone churches on wide Main Street and imposing Searles Castle, a former Berkshire cottage turned private academy, is the landmark **Mahaiwe Performing Arts Center** (14 Castle St.; 413/528-0100), all marble and gilt

The first black man ever to earn a Ph.D. from Harvard, writer W. E. B. DuBois, was born in Great Barrington in 1868.

Main Street, Great Barrington

trim behind its marquee. Built for vaudeville and recently restored, the Mahaiwe still hosts frequent film, theater, and musical theater productions.

Besides architecture and history, Great Barrington has a lot to offer hungry travelers. Fussy early-risers seeking their cappuccino and muffins will want to check out **RiverBend Cafe,** right on US-7 (403 Stockbridge Rd.; 413/528-0858), which serves up espresso drinks, teas, and bakery items, with the added benefit of the South County's best let's-hang-out atmosphere.

When people think of electricity they think of Thomas Edison and light bulbs, but the roots of your local utility lie here in the nation's first commercial electrical system, created by transformer inventor William Stanley for Great Barrington's downtown in 1886.

Sheffield: Bartholomew's Cobble

Between Great Barrington and the Connecticut state line, US-7 winds through **Sheffield** and is lined by dozens of antiques stores, earning this stretch the nickname "Antique Alley." Sheffield also has a faded gray covered bridge, just 100 yards east of US-7 on the north side of town. At the south edge of Sheffield, just west of US-7 off Weatogue Road, the natural rock garden of **Bartholomew's Cobble** rises up above the west bank of the Housatonic River. Geology and weather have conspired to produce an outstanding diversity of plants and birds—800 species, including beautiful wildflowers—within a relatively small pocket of fern-covered limestone outcrops and broad meadows. At

The mountainous section of US-20, north of the Mass Turnpike between Huntington and Lee, is one of the oldest auto roads in New England, originally called Jacob's Ladder. Older, and in some ways prettier, than the busier and much more famous Mohawk Trail across the state's northwestern tier, Jacob's Ladder is centered on the quaint town of **Chester.**

The last battle of Shay's Rebellion, an uprising of farmers demanding reforms to prevent foreclosures after the American Revolution dried up English credit, was fought in a field south of the village on Sheffield Road. A small stone obelisk marks the spot, coincidentally adjacent to the Appalachian Trail.

the center of the 329-acre state-run reserve ($5), a very pleasant walk up Hulburt's Hill gives a broad view over the surrounding Berkshire scene.

South Egremont: Bash Bish Falls

While US-7 gets the most tourist traffic, a more pastoral way south into Connecticut follows Route 41 via **South Egremont,** another of those well-preserved villages entirely ensconced in the National Register of Historic Places, which is hardly a rare honor in Massachusetts. At the center of town, **The Old Mill** (53 Main St.; 413/528-1421) has been serving great soups, burgers, steaks and more for more than 30 years.

South Egremont is the gateway to the state's remotest corner, the over 4,000 forested acres of **Mount Washington State Forest.** Within its wooded boundaries are miles of hiking trails, including a stretch of the Appalachian Trail climbing up to the 2,624-foot summit of Mt. Everett, but the highlight here is photogenic **Bash Bish Falls,** the highest in Massachusetts. A whopping 60-foot drop, splashing down in a V-shaped pair of cascades, Bash Bish Falls is no Niagara, but it's a nice place to while away a hot summer afternoon.

CONNECTICUT

Anyone who drives its Interstates will appreciate why Connecticut enjoys a solid reputation among New Englanders as "the drive-through state." The high-speed route between Boston and New York City, I-95, is something endured rather than enjoyed, but our route through the scenic northwest corner is as different from the coastal megalopolis

as a tulip is from a truck tire. Like the neighboring Berkshires, Connecticut's **Litchfield Hills** are a traditional retreat for discerning city dwellers. The area is rich in forests, farms, and picturesque little towns laden with antiques and great restaurants. Fast food and discount shopping are as alien to this landscape as affordability, so if your purse strings are tight you'll want to keep moving; otherwise, linger a while and enjoy some of the rural charm so prized by those people you might see on the cover of *Business Week*.

North Canaan and Salisbury

Crossing into Connecticut from the north on US-7, the first thing that will catch your eye is the stainless-steel siding of **Collin's Diner** (100 W. Main St.;

860/824-7040) in **North Canaan.** A classic 1940s prefab O'Mahony diner, Collin's has all the usual diner standards, and its big parking lot (shared with the neighboring historic railroad depot) is frequently full of equally classic cars, whose owners congregate here on summer afternoons. The rest of North Canaan—a couple of clothing stores and an

old movie theater—is anything but prissy, a refreshing change of pace from the overly tidy tourist towns that dominate the surrounding region.

From Collin's and Canaan, US-44 winds east toward Hartford, stopping after 15 miles at another gem of a small town, **Norfolk;** if any town has capitalized on being far removed from trading floors and board meetings, it's this one. With three public parks and the largest private forest in the state, Norfolk has considered its sheer scenic beauty a stock in trade for nearly a century; the town green is worth the drive, so you can see the folksy road sign that points the way with pictures of rabbits and other cute creatures.

After extensive touring around New England, you risk taking white columns, wide porches, picket fences, and the obligatory Congregational steeple for granted. Even then, prim little **Salisbury,** a half dozen miles west of US-7 at the junction of Route 41 and US-44, still may elicit reveries about what small-town America would look like if strip malls ceased to exist. Spend an afternoon munching on cake while sipping cardamom-scented tea in tiny **Chaiwalla,** on US-44 (2 Main St.; 860/435-9758), and see if you disagree that the mass production of food and drink should be declared a misdemeanor.

> Salisbury's Lakeville Furnace was the armory of the American Revolution, supplying George Washington's troops with almost their entire arsenal of artillery and ammunition for the duration of the war.

West Cornwall

Rivers are consistently some of the most attractive driving companions you could ask for, a fact proven once again as US-7 rejoins the Housatonic River east of Lime Rock. The highway's scenic miles are further enhanced by the sudden appearance of a barn-red covered bridge, which since 1864 has served as the one-lane gateway to idyllic **West Cornwall.** This is the kind of place that would tar and feather the first vinyl-siding salesperson to walk into town, lest harm befall its antiquarian bookshop or other clapboard buildings bearing signs from previous commercial lives.

South of town, **Housatonic Meadows State Park** (860/672-6772) offers riverside camping, perfectly

> On Route 112 a couple of miles west of US-7, you'll find **Lime Rock Park,** an automobile racetrack made famous in part by classic car rallies, a mid-May Grand Prix, the Skip Barber Racing School, and the occasional appearance of celebrity drivers like Tom Cruise. The sharp, twisting descent from nearby Lakeville to the raceway is one of many pretty back-road drives in the area.

situated for anyone considering a canoe or kayak rental from adjacent **Clarke Outdoors,** on US-7 a mile south of that covered bridge. Clarke's 10-mile canoe trips (around $50 for two people; 860/672-6365) include a boat, life vests and all the gear, plus van shuttles and hot showers. Remember to bring bug repellent if you're planning to spend time near the water.

Housatonic Meadows State Park also includes a short, three-mile round-trip trail up 1,160-foot Pine Knob, which offers fine views from its summit. Just south of the park boundary, the hikers' Appalachian Trail crosses US-7 and the Housatonic River at the hamlet of Cornwall Bridge, then runs alongside the river for some eight miles, the longest riverside cruise in the trail's entire 2,100 miles.

Kent

Like many of its Litchfield-area neighbors, **Kent** (pop. 2,918) had a thriving iron industry until competition from larger Pennsylvania mines—with better access to post–Civil War markets—forced the local furnace to close. Now it's a bustling, upscale market town, its main street (US-7) lined with antiques shops, galleries, and boutiques that have replaced blacksmith shops and wheelwrights. The area's transition from industry to leisure is implicit in the unusual displays inside the **Sloane-Stanley Museum** (Wed.–Sun. 10 AM–4 PM; $8; 860/927-3849), located along US-7 a mile north of Kent, near the ruins of an early-American iron foundry. The collection consists mainly of old tools—planes of all shapes and sizes, plus handsaws, augers, clamps, and other woodworking devices—all arranged by local artist and author Eric Sloane (1905–1985), whose books and prints are available in the gift shop. The "Stanley" in the museum's name comes (surprise, surprise) from the famous Stanley tool company, based in nearby New Britain, which donated the land and the museum building. Stanley tools make up a significant portion of the collection, but many others are handmade tools, some of which date back to days when colonial-era craftsmen forged their own tools to suit their specific needs.

Kent Falls State Park, along US-7 about four miles north of the museum, is a nice place to take a break from behind the wheel. Along with the namesake cascade, which is most impressive after a rain, the park includes a short path through dense woods.

Running south of Kent, parallel to US-7 for about six miles along the west bank of the Housatonic River, Schaghticoke Road is a slower, much more scenic route that gives an up-close look at the rugged geology beneath the trees. The route crosses the Schaghticoke Indian Reservation and passes an old Indian cemetery before rejoining US-7 via a covered bridge on Bulls Bridge Road, three miles north of Gaylordsville.

The Appalachian Trail crosses the New York state line near Bull's Bridge south of Kent, and so should you, making your way west to Route 22 or the Taconic State

Kent Falls State Park

Parkway if you want to enjoy a landscape that offers more fields and trees than guardrails and parking lots. Technically speaking, there's still a large swath of New England between New York and New Milford, but most of this has more in common with the Indianapolis beltway than with the Vermont countryside.

NEW YORK

According to the map, the Appalachian Trail's corner-cutting path across the southern edge of the state seems well outside **New York City**'s sprawl, but there is no escape from the greater reality of the urban northeast: This part of the Atlantic seaboard is the original megalopolis. The map may not make it obvious that some tens of millions of people live within an hour's drive of this route, but the volume of traffic will.

Between the Connecticut border and the Hudson River, many of the roads along the route of the Appalachian Trail have become heavily developed corridors of suburban malls and Park and Ride lots for Manhattan commuters, but there are also some fascinating parks and other places worth exploring.

West Point

The hikers' Appalachian Trail, and our driving equivalent along old US-6, both cross the Hudson River near West Point, the U.S. Army's famous military academy, located at a point on the west bank of the Hudson, naturally. Even if you're not a military buff, there's a lot of fascinating history here: This is the fortress the traitorous U.S. general Benedict Arnold offered to hand over

Even if you're racing across New York on the I-84 freeway, there's one place you should stop: the town of **Hyde Park,** where the homes of Franklin D. and Eleanor Roosevelt offer a look back at their admirable lives and challenging times.

The Hudson Valley Renegades (845/838-0094) play Class A baseball in Wappingers Falls, north of I-84 along Route 9D.

to the British (for cash and a promotion) during the Revolutionary War. There's a small museum (daily; free) offering guided tours of the grounds; walk up to Trophy Point for a great view of the river and a display of cannons captured during various U.S. wars.

On the north side of West Point, south of Newburgh off Hwy-32, stretch your legs and enjoy a different outlook on life at the pastoral **Storm King Art Center** (Apr.–mid-Nov. only, closed Mon. and Tues.; $12; 845/534-3115), a fabulous 500-acre sculpture park that celebrates the dynamic relationship between nature and culture. The artworks include more than a dozen large metal sculptures by the pioneering David Smith (1906–1965), who learned to weld while working in the Studebaker factory in South Bend, Indiana, and became one of the most influential Abstract Expressionists before his death in a car wreck. The Storm King collection also includes pieces by Alexander Calder, Henry Moore, and Louise Nevelson.

Along the east bank of the Hudson River in the town of Beacon, another unexpected art find is the intriguing **Dia: Beacon** (closed Tues. and Wed.; $10; 845/440-0100), a minimally remodeled 1930s factory full of thought-provoking works by Robert Irwin, Dan Flavin, Donald Judd, Louise Bourgeois, Bernd and Hilla Becher,

© AVALON TRAVEL

and many other influential artists. Metro-North commuter trains run right past the windows, heading down the river from Beacon to NYC's Grand Central Station (about 80 minutes each way; $28 round-trip).

West and south of West Point, the hikers' Appalachian Trail closely follows historic US-6 for a scenic foray through Harriman and Bear Mountain State Parks before heading south and west toward New Jersey and Pennsylvania.

Harriman State Park and Bear Mountain

Rising out of the Hudson Valley, **Harriman State Park** is a mountainous oasis with 31 lakes and some 200 miles of hiking trails; the first section of the Appalachian Trail was opened here in 1923. In utter contrast to the get-out-of-my-way style of later highway construction, the roads across the park, designed in the 1920s for Sunday afternoon family outings in the new-fangled motor car, maximize exposure to the surrounding forests, and even the rustic Romanesque stone arch bridges manage to harmonize with local rock outcroppings.

Closer to the Hudson River, an adjacent state park, **Bear Mountain,** is even more full of old-fashioned pleasures and draws more annual visitors than Yellowstone National Park (no doubt thanks to its location at the north end of the Palisades Parkway). A scenic drive leads near the top of Bear Mountain itself, where a New Deal–era lookout tower gives views over the entire region,

the view east from the Torne encompassing the Bear Mountain Bridge: Anthony's Nose, the 9W overpass to the left, and the Palisades Parkway at the center to bottom right

New York City

STATUE OF LIBERTY, NEW YORK CITY

Some people avoid New York City like the plague, but more than eight million others can't bear to leave the glorious buzzing mosaic that makes New York unique in the world. Love it or hate it, New York is New York, and this great metropolis is undeniably the capital of the capitalist world, with some of the best museums, the best shops, the best sights, and the best restaurants in the world.

There's not much point in our recommending a select few of New York's huge spectrum of attractions, so we'll get straight to offering some practical help. For drivers, to whom all roads must seem to converge upon—and become gridlocked in—New York City, if you value your sanity and your shock absorbers park your car in a long-term lot (not on the streets; city parking regulations are arcane and the fines huge) and walk or take public transportation. New York's subway system, one of the most extensive in the world, is relatively safe and usually the fastest way to get around town; it's also inexpensive ($2.25 per ride, or $8 a day, payable via electronic Metrocard). City buses are generally slower, but you see more of the sights. Taxis are ubiquitous—except when you want one.

The key to a successful visit to New York City is finding a place to stay. Ideally, you'll have an expense account, a friend, or a rich aunt, but lacking that, here are a few suggestions, most in the low-to-moderate range. It's hard to beat the **Holiday Inn Soho** ($225 and up; 138 Lafayette St.; 212/966-8898) for convenience, as it's equidistant from Chinatown, Little Italy, SoHo, and TriBeCa. For families, another good option is the **Embassy Suites** ($299 and up; 102 North End Ave.; 212/945-0100) at Battery Park City, with views of the Statue of Liberty. The least expensive place in town is the very large and popular **HI-New York Hostel** (891 Amsterdam Ave.; 212/932-2300), on the Upper West Side at 103rd Street, with private rooms (around $75) plus dorm beds for less than $29 a night. One of the many fabulous hotels in New York City is the small, stylish, and recently renovated Ian Shrager hotel, **Morgans** ($250 and up; 237 Madison Ave.; 212/686-0300).

Eating out is another way to blow a lot of money very quickly, but there are some great places where you can get both a good meal and a feel for New York without going bankrupt. One such place is **Katz's Delicatessen** (205 E. Houston St.; 212/254-2246), a Lower East Side landmark that's been serving up huge sandwiches (including great pastrami) since 1888. (For movie buffs,

Katz's is where Meg Ryan did her famous fake-orgasm scene in *When Harry Met Sally*.) And if you like diners, check out the **Star on 18** (128 10th Ave.; 212/366-0994), at 18th Street in the Chelsea neighborhood—then take a leisurely walk on the magical High Line, a long-abandoned rail line recently reborn as a stylish pedestrian path, 20 feet above the not-so-mean streets. Another affordable all-American experience can be had at the retro-trendy **Shake Shack,** a high-style burger stand across from the iconic Flatiron Building in Madison Square Park, a leafy oasis off Madison Avenue at East 23rd Street (212/889-6600). On the Upper East Side, between the Metropolitan and Whitney museums, Michelin-starred chef Daniel Boulud serves up exquisitely prepared French bistro fare at his **Cafe Boulud** (20 E. 76th St.; 212/772-2600). The ever-changing menu features a

wide variety of traditional favorites and contemporary inventions, available for lunch and dinner at (comparatively) moderate prices. It's very popular, so make reservations as soon as you can.

The **Statue of Liberty** marks the beginning of our **Atlantic Coast** trip. See page 411.

The High Line, formerly a rail line, now serves as a green pedestrian path.

Bear Mountain Inn

and an interior mural traces local history. In season, there are pedal boats for rent, plus a large swimming pool (or an ice-skating rink). Meals and accommodations are available in the circa-1915 **Bear Mountain Inn** (845/786-2731).

Local literary trivia: At the beginning of Jack Kerouac's *On the Road,* the main character, Sal Paradise, sets off from New York City on an ill-fated attempt to follow US-6 all the way to the West Coast. Hoping to hitch a ride along the "one red line called Route 6 that led from the tip of Cape Cod clear to Ely, Nevada, and there dipped down to Los Angeles," Sal got caught in a rainstorm here at Bear Mountain and had to head home, giving up on the "stupid hearthside idea that it would be wonderful to follow one great line across America instead of trying various roads and routes."

Port Jervis

West of Harriman State Park, the Appalachian Trail and US-6 cross the busy I-87 New York Thruway, then wind through the exurbs of the Big Apple, where town after town seems unsure whether this is country living or not.

Farther west, along I-84 on the tri-state (New York/New Jersey/Pennsylvania) border, **Port Jervis** is a curious mixture of small-town dereliction and commercial bustle. Transportation has clearly been a major historical force here, with the influence of successive eras—the river, the railroad, and the highway—inscribed in the very layout of the town. For a glimpse of the long reign of the iron horse, check out the intriguing artifacts and photos in the restored waiting room of the old **Erie Lackawanna Depot** on Front Street, or stop inside the old **Erie Hotel and Restaurant** next door, which has an ornate bar, a lively restaurant and rooms upstairs (around $59; 845/858-4100).

Port Jervis clearly still believes in the virtues of home cooking: **Homer's Coffee Shop** (2 E. Main St.; 845/856-1712) is a prime example, with its democratic social club of elderly regulars, young tie-wearing businessmen, and tradespeople with company names stitched on their shirt pockets, all drawn to the bargain meals and early-morning doughnuts. Despite the acoustic tile and too-new counter and seating, it's a welcoming spot, with the added attraction of a soda fountain in case you need to wash down that turkey club or beef stroganoff with a Tin Roof Sundae.

About 30 miles northwest of Port Jervis, Max Yasgur's farm outside Bethel, New York, welcomed revelers to the August 1969 Woodstock Festival of Music and Art, starring Jimi Hendrix; Crosby, Stills and Nash; and some 300,000 mud-soaked hippies.

PENNSYLVANIA

The hikers' Appalachian Trail runs across southern New York and western New Jersey, but our road route avoids the Garden State almost entirely, crossing instead the natural chasm of the **Delaware Water Gap,** whose forests, waterfalls, and wildlife are popular with city-dwellers escaping the New York/Philly megalopolis. In its 150-mile length,

this route across Pennsylvania passes through a succession of strikingly different places, starting with the densely populated industrial regions of the Lehigh Valley and the historic little town of **Bethlehem,** which plays up its Christmas connections more than its role as a formerly vital steelmaking center. Farther south, modern industry gives way to the traditional agriculture of **Pennsylvania Dutch Country,** world famous for its anti-technology, Old Order Christian com-

munities. Continuing southwest across the Susquehanna River, you'll follow the route of the old Lincoln Highway through historic **York,** early capital of the United States, now home to the Harley-Davidson motorcycle assembly plant. The last stop on the Pennsylvania leg of the route is the Civil War battlefields at **Gettysburg,** just shy of the Maryland border.

Lackawaxen

The tiny town of **Lackawaxen** (pop. 4,994), along the Delaware River 20 winding, scenic miles northwest of Port Jervis via Hwy-97, holds two fascinating attractions: the preserved home of writer Zane Grey, and a unique suspension bridge completed in 1848 by Brooklyn Bridge designer John Roebling. It comes as something of a surprise to find out that Zane Grey, author of the classic Western novel *Riders of the Purple Sage,* was in fact a fly-fishing, baseball-loving Pennsylvania dentist, but he was. His home was preserved by his family as the **Zane Grey Museum** (in summer daily 10 AM–5 PM; free; 135 Scenic Dr.; 570/685-4871). Now maintained by the National Park Service, the museum offers an unusually intimate look into his life and works. Zane Grey and his wife (and childhood sweetheart) Dolly are buried side-by-side in the small Lackawaxen graveyard.

The Roebling Bridge is about 100 yards downstream from Zane Grey's home and has been preserved by the National Park Service—though it's now used by cars instead of canal boats. For the full experience, stay the night in the circa-1870 canal office, now housing the **Roebling Inn on the Delaware** ($99 and up; 570/685-7900).

Milford

At the west end of US-6's very pleasant run along the river from Port Jervis, just off I-84 at the northern end of Delaware Water Gap National Recreation Area, **Milford** (pop. 1,530) is a cute little town cashing in on the hordes of rafters, campers, and B&B patrons who make the weekend journey to the surrounding Pocono Mountains from New York or Philadelphia.

Milford was the longtime home of sustainable forestry pioneer and two-term Pennsylvania governor Gifford Pinchot (1865–1946), whose **Grey Towers** estate off US-6 is now preserved as a National Historic Site, open in summer for tours ($6; 570/296-9630). Visitors and locals alike converge on the town's culinary landmark, the **Milford Diner** (6 AM–10 PM daily; 301 Broad St.; 570/296-8611).

Delaware Water Gap National Recreation Area

Totaling some 67,000 acres of forest on both banks of the Delaware River, the **Delaware Water Gap National Recreation Area** stretches for 35 miles south of the I-84 freeway along two-lane US-209. Established beginning in 1960, the park is still very much under development, though numerous hiking trails lead through hardwood forests to seasonal waterfalls, and the river itself offers abundant canoeing, swimming, and fishing. Though far from pristine, the natural beauty is surprisingly undisturbed considering the park lies only 50 miles northwest of New York City.

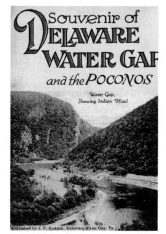

A few remnants of the area's historic agricultural villages have been preserved under the aegis of the park service, but the main attraction is the oddly named Delaware Water Gap itself, a deep cleft carved by the river into the solid rock of the Kittatinny Mountains. Artists, sightseers, and rock-climbers have admired this unique feat of geology for centuries, but unfortunately the natural passageway is crisscrossed by all manner of road and railroad, including the six-lane I-80 freeway, which runs right through it.

A stretch of the Appalachian Trail cuts along a 1,200-foot-high ridge at the southeast corner of the park, crossing the Delaware River on an old bridge at the town of Delaware Water Gap. Get a feel for the trail at the full-service, Appalachian Mountain Club–run **Mohican Outdoor Center** (908/362-5670), outside Blairstown, New Jersey.

The tiny tourist town of **Delaware Water Gap,** south of I-80 at the far southern end of the park, provides the best views of the gap. A visitors center sits along the river, just off I-80 at the first/last New Jersey exit, and offers exhibits on the geology and history of the region. Also in town is **Pack Shack Adventures,** a block off the Appalachian Trail (88 Broad St.; 570/424-8533), where you can rent a canoe, get out on the water, and stretch your arms and legs.

The Poconos

The **Pocono Mountains,** which rise to the west of the Delaware River, hold a number of traditional summer resort hotels spread among the golf courses and ski areas. Like the Catskills "Borscht Belt" of southern New York, the Poconos had their glory days in the 1950s, but some resorts still thrive thanks to the invention here in the 1960s of the couple-friendly, heart- or champagne glass–shaped bath tub, which has turned many a Pocono hotel into a pseudo-Roman honeymoon destination (the *Baltimore Sun* called one a "mini Playboy Mansion"). Many of these passion pits tend to feature all-inclusive package deals (free archery lessons, so you and your beloved can play Cupid with real arrows, etc). If you're interested, try **Caesars Pocono Palace** (800/432-9932) off US-209 five miles northeast of Stroudsburg.

By contrast, a classic "old-school" Pocono resort—the rightly named **Skytop Lodge Resort and Spa** (570/595-7401 or 800/345-7759)—is about 20 miles northwest of Stroudsburg, via Hwy-447. This very grand yet family-friendly 1920s hotel, with just 125 rooms and suites but full resort facilities, sits on 5,500 acres of mountaintop forest, with its own golf course, hiking trails, and hunting preserve.

At the southern edge of the Delaware Water Gap park, **Stroudsburg** has the Poconos' most extensive tourist facilities, clustered along the I-80 freeway corridor.

Easton and Nazareth

South of the Delaware Water Gap, Hwy-611 runs along the Delaware River until its confluence with the Lehigh River, near the town of **Easton.** This historic industrial center is now home to one of the Poconos' most popular family attractions: the **Crayola Crayon Factory Tour** (closed Mon.; $10; 30 Centre Square; 610/515-8000), where you can watch colorful crayons being made and packaged, then scribble away to your heart's content. The actual Crayola factory is a half dozen miles away and not open to the public; this toddler-friendly mini-factory shares a waterfront building with the **National Canal Museum,** which traces the history of the Delaware and Lehigh Canal and other man-made waterways all over the United States. Occasional canal boat trips are offered.

Another more historic American factory tour is in nearby **Nazareth,** where the venerable **Martin Guitar Company** (510 Sycamore St.; 610/759-2837 or 888/433-9177) has been in business since 1833. If you've ever enjoyed strumming a six-string, you'll want to take one of the wonderful tours (Mon.–Fri. 11 AM–2 PM; free) of the family-owned factory. The tours include both a look inside the workshops—where you can watch workers as they bend, carve, inlay, and polish the instruments—and displays of classic Martin guitars.

Along with Martin Guitars, Nazareth is home to **Nazareth Speedway,** home track of the Andretti racing family. Another sporting hero, boxer Larry Holmes, lives in Easton.

Bethlehem

Upstream from Easton along the Lehigh River and US-222, the remarkable small city of **Bethlehem** (pop. 74,982), famous for its Christmas festivals and as a fun place from which to mail Christmas cards, was originally established in 1741 by a group of Moravian missionaries. The missionaries'

Monocacy Creek in Bethlehem

chapel built from 1803 to 1806 still stands at the heart of the compact, gas-lighted downtown district, its cemetery full of 200-year-old headstones laid flat so as not to offend God.

The **Moravian Museum** (Thurs.–Sun. noon–4 PM; $7; 66 W. Church St.; 610/691-6055) is housed inside the circa-1741 **Gemeinhaus,** the oldest building in Bethlehem. Besides showcasing historic artifacts, the museum also offers guided walking tours of the downtown area. Another engaging historic site is the **Sun Inn** (564 Main St.), a well-preserved former tavern "where the leading figures of the Revolutionary era were entertained," says a plaque on the wall.

Every May, Bethlehem hosts a hugely popular **Bach Festival,** rated as one of the best in country. For details, contact the Bach Choir (610/866-4382).

Across the Lehigh River from the tidy homes and shops of downtown Bethlehem, Lehigh University stands above the rusting remains of the Bethlehem Steel Company. Famous for fabricating engineering marvels such as the towers of the Golden Gate Bridge—cast here in sections, then shipped through the Panama Canal and assembled in San Francisco—the mill was in business for over a century before being closed down in 1995. The hulking structure, the massive blast furnace, and most of the cranes and other machinery and equipment are slated for eventual preservation as part of the Smithsonian Institution's National Museum of Industrial History, while the bulk of the complex has been converted into the massive **Sands Casino Resort** ($160 and up; 877/726-3777), where the huge old furnaces are lit up in brightly colored lights as an architectural feature.

Along with the old steel works and the new casino, the Lehigh University neighborhood holds another noteworthy landmark: the nonprofit **Godfrey Daniels Coffee House** (7 E. 4th St.; 610/867-2390), which has been hosting a range of live folk and jazz music for more than 30 years. For a bite to eat, grab a chili dog at **Pete's Hot Dog Shop,** around the corner (400 Broadway; 610/866-6622), or head back across the river into Bethlehem proper, where the bistro-style **Apollo Grill** (85 W. Broad St.; 610/865-9600) is perhaps the nicest place in town for lunch or dinner.

For a place to stay, the large **Hotel Bethlehem** ($139 and up; 437 Main St.; 610/625-5000 or 800/607-2384), overlooking the river, is centrally located.

Allentown

The seat of Lehigh County, **Allentown** (pop. 118,032) spreads west of Bethlehem, across a bend in the Lehigh River. The downtown area has two

The town of **Jim Thorpe**, in the Lehigh Valley 30 miles northwest of Allentown off the Pennsylvania Turnpike (I-476), 10 miles north of the Appalachian Trail, is a former coal-mining town with many 19th-century buildings. The town changed its name from Mauch Chunk in 1954 to honor the great Olympic athlete Jim Thorpe, whose remains lie in a granite mausoleum along Hwy-903 on the northeast side of town.

Midway between Allentown and Reading, every June and July the weeklong **Kutztown Folk Festival** celebrates the arts, crafts, and culture of the local Pennsylvania Dutch communities, which are less austere than their Lancaster County counterparts.

very worthwhile stops, the bigger and better of which is the **Allentown Art Museum** (closed Mon.; $6; 31 N. 5th St.; 610/432-4333). After a recent expansion, you'll find a very good collection of paintings and photography as well as an entire library moved from the Frank Lloyd Wright–designed Little House. Allentown's other main attraction lies two blocks west at Church and Hamilton Streets: the **Liberty Bell Shrine** (Mon.–Sat. noon–4 PM; free; 610/435-4232), an old church that houses a replica of the famous bell that was hidden here for safekeeping during the Revolutionary War battles at Philadelphia.

Another reason to visit: the Class AAA **Lehigh Valley IronPigs**, the Phillies top farm club, play in a nice new ballpark ($6–14; 610/841-7447), south of US-22 near the Allentown airport. Games are broadcast on **ESPN 1230-1320 AM**.

Allentown boasts some great places to eat, thanks to the multiple branches of **Yocco's: The Hot Dog King**; these local landmarks, like the original (625 Liberty St.; 610/433-1950), have been serving up wieners (and a few burgers) bathed in a top-secret chili sauce since 1922. Allentown also has one of the country's oldest, largest collections of roller coasters (and a fine old carousel), in **Dorney Park and Wildwater Kingdom** (daily in summer; around $40; 610/395-3724). There's a water park, too.

Reading

Standing along the eastern banks of the Schuylkill River, **Reading** (pop. 88,082) is more interesting than its somewhat frightening sub-title, "Factory Outlet Shopping Capital of Southeastern Pennsylvania," might lead you to expect. Ornately turreted row houses line 5th Avenue (US-222 Business) through the residential districts, downtown holds a number of well-maintained businesses and signs from the first half of the 20th century, and a very photogenic 72-foot, 100-year-old pagoda offers panoramic views from the summit of Mt. Penn, east of town.

A step below their near neighbors the Ironpigs, Reading is home to another Phillies farm club, the **R-Phils**, who play AA-ball at the very pleasant FirstEnergy Field ($6–10; 610/375-8469). Games are on **ESPN 1240 WIOV AM**.

For history buffs, two worthwhile places to visit sit southeast of Reading along the Schuylkill River. The closer of these is at **Birdsboro**, 10 miles from town and a mile north of US-422. The **Daniel Boone Homestead and Birthplace**

Roadside America

One of the quirkiest tourist attractions in the United States, Roadside America (daily; $7; 610/488-6241) stands alongside the I-78 freeway, 20 miles northwest of Reading in the village of Shartlesville. Built by Reading native Laurence Gieringer, Roadside America is a giant 3/8-to-the-inch scale model of bygone Americana, fleshed out with animated scenes that trace a typical day in the life of the country—circa 1930s, when Roadside America first opened to the public. As you walk around the edges of the 8,000-square-foot exhibit, you can push buttons to make wheels spin, lights flash, and pumps pump, and you'll see a little of everything rural: an 1830s New England village featuring a church and choral music; a canyon and lake complete with waterfalls and resort cabins; a model of Henry Ford's workshop in Dearborn, Michigan, where he built one

of the first "horseless carriages"; various turnpikes, canals, highways, and railroads; a coal mine; and a mock-up of the San Francisco Bay Bridge, the closest Roadside comes to a city scene.

Though it's definitely a fine example of kitsch, Roadside America is also an oddly compelling place, and only the hardest-hearted road-tripper will be able to hold back the tears when, every half hour or so, the sun sets and Kate Smith bursts into "God Bless America."

(closed Mon.; $6; 610/582-4900) marks the site where the great frontiersman was born in 1734.

Well worth the winding five-mile drive south of Birdsboro via Hwy-345, the **Hopewell Furnace National Historic Site** (daily; free) preserves intact an entire iron-making community that thrived here from the colonial era until the mid-1880s. Park rangers fire up the furnace and demonstrate the primitive foundry (melting aluminum rather than iron to take the "heat" off the ancient tools), and exhibits trace the iron-making process—mining the ore, making charcoal, and fabricating the finished product, which here at Hopewell was primarily pig iron and stoves.

The Monopoly Chance card "Take a Ride on the Reading" commemorates the railroad that formerly ran between Reading and Philadelphia.

Ephrata and Lititz

South of Reading, US-222 runs along the western edge of the Amish- and Mennonite-influenced Pennsylvania Dutch Country. The heart of this region is due east of Lancaster, but the area north of Lancaster also holds a number of

The Pennsylvania Dutch Country

East of Lancaster, toward Philadelphia, the old Lincoln Highway (US-30) runs through the heart of what has become internationally famous as the Pennsylvania Dutch Country. This is a very pretty, almost completely rural region, unremarkable apart from the presence here of various Old Order Anabaptist Christian sects, including Amish and Mennonite groups, who eschew most of the trappings and technological advances of the 21st century, including cars, electricity, and irrigation, and retain their simple ways. Long before the Peter Weir movie *Witness* gave Amish low-tech lifestyle the Hollywood treatment, visitors have been coming here to see these anachronistic descendants of German immigrants (Deutsche = Dutch) who settled here in the early 1700s, and to whom all outsiders are known simply as "English."

The best way to get a feel for the Amish and Mennonite ways of life is to follow back roads, by bike if possible, through the gently rolling countryside of Lancaster County, keeping an eye out for their horse-drawn buggies (Amish ones are gray, the

Amish Boys Out for a Drive, Lancaster County, Pa.

Mennonites' are black). You can cross covered bridges and buy produce, related sites often missed by visitors. The most appealing of these is the **Ephrata Cloister** (daily; $9; 632 W. Main St.; 717/733-6600), just west of the town of Ephrata. Founded in 1732 by a communal society of religiously celibate German Pietists, the Ephrata Cloister consists of a half dozen well-preserved 250-year-old wooden buildings, which housed dormitories, bakeries, and a printing shop where the commune produced some of the finest illustrated books of the colonial era. Across from the entrance, the **Cloister Restaurant** (607 W. Main St.; 717/733-2361) serves very good home-style food for breakfast, lunch, and dinner in an overgrown 1940s diner.

If you happen, or can manage, to be in Ephrata on a Friday, there's no more authentic Dutch Country experience than the once-a-week **Green Dragon Farmers Market** (955 N. State St.; 717/738-1117), a chaotic complex of some 400 different fresh fruit and vegetable sellers, sausage and hot dog stands, pizza places, and bakery outlets, covering 30 acres in seven buildings, just over a mile north of town. Many people here are truly Amish, so obey the second commandment and resist the urge to take their photo.

Lititz is the unlikely final resting place of John Sutter, the Swiss immigrant who owned huge chunks of pre-gold rush California. He died here in Pennsylvania while battling the Washington, D.C., bureaucracy, hoping in vain to receive compensation for his confiscated land.

breads, cakes, and shoo-fly pie from the many roadside stands marked by hand-lettered signs. If you're fond of kitsch, don't miss the restored one-room **Weavertown Schoolhouse** ($4; 717/768-3976), populated by "authentic" audio-animatronic Amish schoolkids, along Hwy-340 a mile east of the town of Bird-in-Hand, 2.5 miles west of Intercourse.

Most of the many Amish-style restaurants in the region are huge and forbiddingly full of bus-tour hordes; one exception is **Stoltzfus Farm Restaurant** (May–Nov. Mon.–Sat. 11:30 AM–8 PM; 717/768-8156) on Hwy-772 a quarter mile southeast of Intercourse. A less Amish but very good road-food place is **Jennie's Diner** in Ronks, open 24 hours every day on the north side of US-30 (2575 E. Lincoln Hwy.; 717/397-2507), just east of the Hwy-896 intersection.

Though it won't give you any great insight into the Amish, one unique place to stay is the **Red Caboose Motel and Restaurant** ($85 and up; 888/687-5005 or 717/687-5000), a mile east of Strasburg on Paradise Lane. All the rooms are built inside old railroad cars, and the on-site restaurant simulates a train journey, with whistles blowing and a gentle rocking vibration to ease your digestion. Strasburg is also home to the **Village Greens** miniature golf course (717/687-6933), which is so fun and challenging that it was featured in *Sports Illustrated*.

For complete listings of attractions, restaurants, and hotels, or to pick up handy maps and other information, stop by the helpful **Pennsylvania Dutch Visitor Center** (800/723-8824), on US-30 just east of Lancaster.

Ephrata Cloister

A word to the wise: In Dutch Country, remember that anything claiming to be "authentic Amish" definitely isn't. Please respect the Amish you see and refrain from taking photographs. Drive carefully, too.

West of Ephrata, eight miles north of Lancaster via Hwy-501, the delightful though tiny town of **Lititz** (pop. 9,369) is dominated by the huge **Wilbur Chocolate** candy factory (48 N. Broad St.), which liberally perfumes the air with the smell of hot chocolate. Lititz, which is packed full of stone buildings and carefully tended gardens, also holds the nation's oldest operating pretzel factory, the **Julius Sturgis Pretzel House** (219 E. Main St.), where you can twist your own. Lititz also holds a huge Fourth of July party every year—well worth planning a trip around.

Lancaster

The only place approaching an urban scale in this part of Pennsylvania, **Lancaster** (pop. 59,322) is the region's commercial center, a bustling city that, for a single day during the Revolutionary War, served as capital of the rebellious United States. Though most visitors view it as little more than a handy base for exploring nearby Pennsylvania Dutch Country, Lancaster does have a couple of attractions in its own right, such as the redbrick, pseudo-Romanesque **Central Market** (23 N. Market St.) near King and Queen Streets in the center of town. It hosts the nation's oldest publicly owned, continuously operating farmers market, currently held all day Tuesday and Friday, as well as Saturday mornings and early afternoons. A block south on Queen Street, the ground-floor windows of the local newspaper trace local history through headlines, starting back in 1794 and continuing up through the present day.

Midway between Lancaster and York, the town of **Columbia** holds what is arguably the country's best collection of timepieces in the **National Watch and Clock Museum** (514 Poplar St.). Also in Columbia is a beautiful multi-arched concrete bridge that used to carry the old Lincoln Highway (US-30) across the broad Susquehanna River.

Two miles northeast of Lancaster, the state-run and well-signed **Landis Valley Museum** (daily; $12) is a popular living history park of more than 100 acres preserving and interpreting traditional rural life ways of eastern Pennsylvania.

Hallam: The Shoe House

Many oddball attractions grew up along the old Lincoln Highway, the great cross-country highway that ran coast-to-coast beginning in 1915, and one of the best-beloved is the **Haines Shoe House,** which stands above the modern four-lane US-30 freeway, west of the town of Hallam. This landmark of program-

matic architecture was built in 1948 by Mahlon "The Shoe Wizard" Haines, who owned a successful shoe company that proudly claimed to make boots "hoof-to-hoof," from raising the cattle to selling the finished products. The seven-room structure is shaped like a giant cartoon boot and can be reached by following Hwy-462 (the old Lincoln Highway, which runs just south of current US-30), to Shoe House Road, then winding north for a quarter mile. (The turn-off is easy to miss, so keep an eye out for the Shoe House Mini-Storage, which stands on the corner.) The Shoe House has been bought and sold a number of times over the years. If you're lucky, the owners will be there to let you tour the interior.

Just east of Hallam on US-30, **Jim Mack's Ice Cream** (5745 Lincoln Hwy.; 717/252-2013) has been attracting fans for its ice cream—and its adjacent mini-golf course and mini-zoo, complete with a pair of rather sad-looking brown bears. Next door is a bowling alley.

York

Though it doesn't look like much from the highway, by-passed by both US-30 and the I-83 freeway, the medium-sized town of **York** (pop. 43,718) claims to be the first capital of the United States: Late in 1777, the Articles of Confederation were adopted here by the 13 newly independent former colonies, and (arguably) it's in that document that the name "United States of America" was first used. A significant number of historic buildings still stand in the quiet, low-rise downtown area, including the medieval-looking, circa-1741 Golden Plough Tavern and other colonial-era structures along Market Street at the west edge of the business district.

For all its historic importance, York is best known for its industrial prowess, which is saluted at the **Harley-Davidson assembly plant and museum** (Mon.–Thurs. 9 AM–2 PM; free; 717/852-6590), a mile east of town off US-30 on Eden Road. The guided tours take about two hours and begin with a brief history of the company, which is still based in Milwaukee. The tour then takes you past a lineup of some 40 Harleys past and present, culled from the corporate collection of over 200 motorbikes, then proceeds to the shop floor for a close-up (and very noisy) look and listen as the bikes get put together: Sheets of steel are pressed to form fenders and fairings, and, once assembled, each bike is "road-tested" at full throttle on motorcycling's equivalent of a treadmill. A souvenir store is stocked with all manner of things with the Harley-Davidson logo, from T-shirts to leather jackets.

Downtown York has a handful of cafés and restaurants, and on the west edge of town, where the US-30 bypass rejoins the old Lincoln Highway (Hwy-462), **Lee's Diner** (4320 W. Market St.; 717/792-1300) is a classic early-1950s Mountain View pre-fab diner, still serving up hearty road food. The nicest place to stay has to be the historic **Yorktowne Hotel** ($119 and up; 48 E. Market St.; 717/848-1111), a 1920s landmark.

Two of the main tourist stops in the Dutch Country region are the towns of **Intercourse** (source of many snickeringly allusive postcards) and **Paradise** (the Paradise post office, just north of US-30 at the east end of town, is a popular place for sending mail).

The town of **Hanover,** south of US-30 between York and Gettysburg, is a prime producer of snack foods, from potato chips to the famed pretzels baked by **Snyder's of Hanover** (1350 York St.), which offers free factory tours.

Gettysburg

Totally overwhelmed by the influx of tourists visiting its namesake battleground, the town of **Gettysburg** (pop. 7,620) has survived both onslaughts remarkably unscathed. Despite the presence of sundry tourist attractions—wax museums, various multimedia reenactments of the battle and President Lincoln's Gettysburg Address, even a Lincoln Train Museum displaying over a thousand model trains (including a scale replica of the one Lincoln rode here in)—once the day-tripping crowds have dispersed, Gettysburg is actually a very pleasant place, with rows of brick-fronted buildings lining Baltimore and York Streets at the center of town.

There are, not surprisingly, quite a few places to eat, including the atmospheric **Dobbin House Tavern** (89 Steinwehr Ave.; 717/334-2100), south of town, serving above-average pub food in Gettysburg's oldest building. The dozens of other places to stay include all the usual national chains, plus the circa-1797 **Gettysburg Hotel** ($129 and up; 717/337-2000), on Lincoln Square right at the center of town.

Gettysburg National Military Park

Site of the most famous two-minute speech in U.S. history, and of the bloody Civil War battle that marked the high tide of Confederate fortunes, **Gettysburg National Military Park** surrounds the town of

Abraham Lincoln
Robert E. Lee
George Gordon Meade

cannons at Gettysburg National Military Park

The Lincoln Highway

The main east–west route through Pennsylvania Dutch Country, US-30 is also one of the best-preserved stretches of the old Lincoln Highway, the nation's first transcontinental route. Conceived in 1912 and named soon afterward, the Lincoln Highway linked New York City's Times Square with the Panama Pacific International Exposition in San Francisco, following over 3,000 miles of country road across 12 states. A thousand miles of the original "highway" were little more than muddy tracks, scarcely more visible on the ground than they were on the still-nonexistent road maps, but by the early 1930s the road was finally fully paved, following present-day US-30 as far as Wyoming, then bending south to follow what's now US-50, "The Loneliest Road in America," along the route of the Pony Express across Nevada and most of California.

Originally marked by telephone poles brightly painted with red, white, and blue stripes and a large letter L, in 1928 the Lincoln Highway was blazed by more discreet concrete mileposts carrying a small bust of Lincoln; 3,000 of these were placed, one every mile, by Boy Scout troops across the land, but only around a dozen still stand in the original locations. As with the later Route 66, the Lincoln Highway was replaced by the Interstates, but it does live on, in folk memory as well as the innumerable Lincoln Cafes and Lincoln Motels along its original route, much of which still bears the name Lincolnway. You can become a member of the **Lincoln Highway Association** (815/456-3030), which offers a top-quality quarterly magazine well worth the annual dues.

Gettysburg, protecting the scenes of the struggle as they were July 1–3, 1863, when as many as 51,000 of the 165,000 combatants were killed or wounded. Over a thousand monuments mark the various historic sites around the 6,000 acres of rolling green pasture that form the park. The entire battlefield is evocative and interesting, but to make the most of a visit start your tours at the **visitors center** (daily; free; 1195 Baltimore Pike; 717/334-1124), discreetly hidden away near Hunt Avenue east of Taneytown Road two miles south of town, where an extensive museum puts the battle into context and displays a huge array of period weaponry. Unfortunately, you can no longer watch the battle unfold on the much-loved Electric Map, which looks a lot like a boxing ring but has been superseded by more advanced multimedia displays in the digital age. However, the new visitors center has made space for an even older didactic artifact: the famous circular **Cyclorama,** a 27- by 359-foot painting that evocatively

A 230-acre farm on the southwest fringe of the Gettysburg battlefields was home to U.S. Army general and later president Dwight D. Eisenhower and his wife, Mamie, and is part of the 690-acre **Eisenhower National Historic Site,** now open for guided tours (daily; $7.50; 717/338-9114) that leave from the Gettysburg visitors center.

portrays the final Confederate assault on July 3, 1863. There are also numerous maps and guides available, including an excellent podcast tour of the surrounding battleground.

North from the visitors center, a mile-long and very worthwhile walk leads north to the **Gettysburg National Cemetery,** where President Abraham Lincoln delivered his famous address on November 19, 1863.

MARYLAND

Crossing the Mason-Dixon Line from Gettysburg into Maryland on US-15, our route veers west into the Appalachian foothills of **Catoctin Mountain Park,** site of the presidential retreat Camp David. The landscape here is quite rugged, and signs of life few and far between—an oasis of peace and quiet, under an hour by road from Baltimore or Washington, D.C.

The Maryland state motto, *Fatti Maschii, Parole Femine,* is translated roughly as "Manly Deeds, Womanly Words."

Winding south through the mountains of the Maryland Panhandle (the thin strip of land that stretches for some 75 miles between Pennsylvania and West Virginia), this route again meets the hikers' Appalachian Trail, then detours to visit the battlefield of **Antietam,** the well-preserved site of the worst carnage of the Civil War.

In **Gathland State Park,** on the Appalachian Trail east of Gapland off Hwy-67, the 50-foot terra-cotta arch of the **War Correspondents Memorial** was erected in the late 1880s in honor of journalists killed while covering the Civil War.

Catoctin Mountain Park: Camp David

US-15 continues south from Gettysburg across the Maryland border, and there's little to stop for until **Thurmont** (pop. 6,125), "Gateway to the Mountains." The green expanse of **Catoctin Mountain Park,** fully recovered after previous centuries of logging activity, protects some 5,810 acres of hardwood forest, a handful of 1,500-foot peaks, and the presidential retreat at **Camp David,** hidden away in the woods and strictly off-limits to visitors (for security reasons, Camp David doesn't even appear on park maps). The **Catoctin park visitors center** (daily; 301/663-9388) along Hwy-77 two miles west of US-15 provides information on cabins, camping, and maps of the many hiking trails, including a short trail from the visitors center to the preserved remains of the Blue Blazes whiskey still, where rangers demonstrate moonshine-making on summer weekends.

The name "David" in Camp David was bestowed by President Eisenhower in celebration of his then 5-year-old grandson, who went on to marry Julie Nixon, daughter of Eisenhower's vice president, Richard Nixon. Later in life, young David also inspired John Fogerty of Creedence Clearwater Revival to write the song "Fortunate Son."

Spreading along the south side of Hwy-77, Maryland-run **Cunningham Falls State Park** offers more natural scenery and a very pleasant swimming area in Hunting Creek Lake. There's a snack bar and boats for rent, and a half-mile trail leads to the eponymous cascade.

Washington Monument State Park

From Catoctin Mountain Park, our route heads south on undivided Hwy-6 and two-lane Hwy-17 along the hikers' Appalachian Trail, winding up at **Washington Monument State Park** between the I-70 freeway and the small town of **Boonsboro.** A 30-foot-tall, bottle-shaped mound dedicated to the memory of George Washington stands at the center of the park; Boonsboro citizens completed the monument in 1827, making it the oldest memorial honoring the first U.S. president.

Atop a hill south of the park, across an old alignment of the National Road (US-40), the **Old South Mountain Inn** (301/432-6155) has operated as a tavern and inn since 1732 and now serves dinner Tuesday–Sunday and brunch on Sunday.

Antietam National Battlefield

Between Boonsboro and the Potomac River, which forms Maryland's border with West Virginia, **Antietam National Battlefield** preserves the hallowed ground where over 23,000 men were killed or wounded on the bloodiest single day of the Civil War—September 17, 1862. Atop a shallow hill at the middle of the park, a scant mile north of **Sharpsburg** off Hwy-65, the **visitors center** (daily; $6 per car; 301/432-5124) offers films, museum exhibits, and interpretive programs that put the battle into military and political context. Though there was no clear winner, Antietam is said to have convinced Lincoln to issue the Emancipation Proclamation, officially freeing slaves in Confederate states and effectively putting an end to British support for the southern side.

Clara Barton tended the wounded during and after the Civil War's bloodiest battle at Antietam.

WEST VIRGINIA

In its short run across the eastern tip of West Virginia, US-340 passes through one of the most history-rich small towns in the United

States: **Harpers Ferry,** located at the confluence of the Shenandoah and Potomac Rivers. Lovely mountain scenery surrounds Harpers Ferry, especially during early autumn when the hardwood forests rival Vermont's for vibrant color. South of Harpers Ferry, the hikers' Appalachian Trail runs directly along the Virginia/West Virginia border, east of the Shenandoah River atop the roadless crest of the **Blue Ridge Mountains.** The best route to follow by car, US-340 swings to the west through the historic mountain resort of **Charles Town** before entering Virginia.

Harpers Ferry

Climbing the steep slopes of the Blue Ridge Mountains, **Harpers Ferry** (pop. 286) embodies the industrial and political history of the early United States. Protected since 1963 as a national park, its many well-preserved wood, brick, and stone buildings are palpable reminders of early American enterprise: Besides the country's first large factory, first canal, and first railroad, scenic Harpers Ferry saw abolitionist John Brown's 1859 rebellion against slavery, and it was later a strategic site during the Civil War. Harpers Ferry was also home to Storer College, an African American college that operated here from the 1860s until 1955.

Harpers Ferry is the national headquarters of the **Appalachian Trail Conference,** the nonprofit group that oversees the entire 2,175-mile footpath. For information, contact the group (304/535-6331).

Small museums, housed in separate buildings along Shenandoah and High Streets along the riverfront in the "Lower Town," trace the various strands of the town's past. From the Shenandoah River, the Appalachian Trail winds south down what the third president called "one of the most stupendous scenes in Nature," Jefferson's Rock. Crossing the Potomac River to the north, the AT climbs up to Maryland Heights for more spectacular vistas.

Especially in summer, when cars are banned from lower Harpers Ferry, the best first stop is the small **visitors center** (daily; $6; 304/535-6029) above the town along US-340. Park here and take one of the frequent free shuttles down to the historic area. Although most of Harpers Ferry is preserved as a historic site, there is considerable pressure to "develop" surrounding lands, so get here while it's still nice. The eastern portions along the Potomac riverfront have remained in private hands, and here you can indulge your taste for fast food, wax museums, and schlocky souvenirs. There's excellent cycling, a

downtown Harpers Ferry

couple of companies offer white-water rafting trips, and for another sort of adventure you can head down to the very cute, red clapboard depot and hop onboard one of the **Amtrak/MARC** trains, which serve Washington, D.C., on a very limited schedule. To get the most out of a visit, stay overnight at the lovingly restored, circa-1790s, Federal-style, brick-fronted **Jackson RoseBed and Breakfast** ($120 and up; 1167 W. Washington St.; 304/535-1528).

Charles Town

Founded in 1786, the former colonial resort of **Charles Town** (pop. 5,259) was named in honor of George Washington's younger brother Charles, who surveyed the site on behalf of Lord Fairfax. Many of the streets are named after other family members, over 75 of whom are buried in the cemetery alongside the **Zion Church,** on Congress Street on the east side of town. Charles Town, which shouldn't be confused with the West Virginia state capital, Charleston, later played a significant role in John Brown's failed raid on Harpers Ferry. After Brown was captured, he was tried and convicted of treason in the Jefferson County Courthouse at the corner of George and Washington Streets and hanged a month later. With his last words, Brown noted the inevitable approach of civil war, saying he was "quite certain that the crimes of this guilty land will never be purged away but with blood." A small **museum** (Tues.–Sat. 11 AM–4 PM; $3) operates in the basement of the town library, a block from the old courthouse on Washington and South Samuel Street.

South of Charles Town, US-340 winds along the western slopes of the Appalachians for a dozen miles before entering Virginia east of Winchester.

East of Winchester, Virginia, the Appalachian Trail crosses the transcontinental US-50 highway, **The Loneliest Road** in America (see page 790). Full coverage is found on pages 704–799.

VIRGINIA

The Appalachian Trail covers more ground in Virginia than it does in any other state, following the crest of the Blue Ridge Mountains from Harpers Ferry in West Virginia all the way south to the Tennessee and North Carolina borders. In the northern half of the state, the road route closely follows the hikers' route, and the two crisscross each other through the sylvan groves of **Shenandoah National Park.** Midway along the state the two routes diverge, and hikers turn west while the motor route follows the unsurpassed Blue Ridge Parkway along the top of the world.

Most of the time the route follows the mountain crests, though in many places you'll find fascinating towns and cities a short distance to the east or west. Best among these is **Charlottesville,** a history-rich Piedmont town that's best known as the home of Thomas Jefferson and the University of Virginia. Other suggested stops include the Shenandoah Valley town of **Lexington,** the "natural wonder" of **Natural Bridge,** and the engaging city of **Roanoke.**

Dinosaur Land

Located at the intersection of US-340 and US-522, eight miles southeast of Winchester near the hamlet of White Post, **Dinosaur Land** (daily; $5; 540/869-2222) displays an entertaining and marvelously kitschy collection of man-made sharks, cavemen, and, of course, dinosaurs. It's especially fun for kids, who are welcome to climb on and around the concrete menagerie, and wry-humored adults will enjoy searching through the very large gift shop, which has all manner of cheesy souvenirs.

Front Royal and Little Washington

The town of Front Royal takes its name, perhaps apocryphally, from a Revolutionary War drill sergeant who, since his troops were unable to tell their left from their right, was forced to shout out "Front Royal Oak" to get them to face the same way. **Front Royal** (pop. 14,440) sits just

White Post got its name from—you guessed it—a white post, placed here by a young surveyor named George Washington. The post marked the road to the country estate of Lord Fairfax, which was destroyed in 1858.

Until recently housed in an old feed store off I-81 in Middletown, the **Route 11 Potato Chip Factory** (Mon.–Sat. 9 AM–5 PM; 11 Edwards Way; 540/477-9664) in nearby **Mount Jackson** is said to be the smallest potato chip factory in the country. When it's open, you can watch the spudmasters at work and sample the freshly made chips.

south of I-66 at the entrance to Shenandoah National Park. Because of its key location, Front Royal has grown a little unwieldy in past decades but retains some semblance of its 19th-century self along Chester Street, a well-maintained historic district at the center of town, a block east of US-340. You can also rent a boat and float along the South Fork of the Shenandoah River, thanks to the friendly folks at the **Front Royal Canoe Company,** on US-340 (8567 Stonewall Jackson Hwy.; 540/635-5440).

At the foot of the Blue Ridge Mountains, a bit more than 18 miles southeast of Front Royal via US-522, pristine, colonial **Washington** (pop. 135) was surveyed by the future father of the United States, George Washington, who named many of the streets after friends and family. The main attraction here is the **Inn at Little Washington** at Main and Middle Streets (540/675-3800), which over the past 30 years has grown from modest origins into one of the few Forbes Travel Guide five-star resort hotels in the country. (It has to be said that with room rates starting at $425 and up a night and dinners averaging $200 a head, it's definitely a special-occasion place to stay or eat.) It's worth it, though, especially if someone else is paying the bill: A critic for *The New York Times* said his dinner there was "the most fantastic meal of my life."

Shenandoah National Park

Shenandoah National Park in autumn

One of the most popular national parks in the east, especially during the fall foliage season when seemingly everyone in the world descends upon the place to leaf-peep, **Shenandoah National Park** protects some 300 square miles of hardwood forest along the northernmost crest of the Blue Ridge Mountains. Though the landscape looks natural now, the aboriginal forests were logged out and the landscape was heavily cultivated until the 1920s. During the Depression, when the depleted soils could no longer sustain the residents, thousands of farmers and their families moved out and the government began buying up the land to return it to its natural state.

> Fall foliage in the Blue Ridge Mountains can be stunning, though it is not usually as intense as in New England.

Most people experience the park from the top, by driving along the famously beautiful Skyline Drive. This road climbs up from the Shenandoah Valley but mostly runs along the crest, offering grand vistas (when the air is clear, at least). Besides the hardwood forests, the park also protects numerous waterfalls, wildflower meadows, and understory plants like azaleas and mountain laurels, which bloom brightest in late spring. There is considerable development in the park, with a pair of rustic lodges and enough gas stations and restaurants and campgrounds to handle the thousands of visitors who flock here (especially in October, for the autumn foliage). Despite the crowds, it's not hard to find peace and quiet, especially if you venture off on even the briefest of hikes.

> Pollution from metropolitan areas and from so many car-borne visitors has caused serious problems at Shenandoah National Park, both for the trees—many of which have been poisoned—and for the views people come to see. On an average summer day, visibility is impaired and the surrounding valleys are often shrouded in smoggy haze.

There is a ranger station at each entrance to the park, where you pay your $15 per-car fee (or show your annual parks pass). There's a **visitors center** (540/999-3500) at each end of Skyline Drive, and one in the middle, at Big Meadows (milepost 51). Trails at Big Meadows lead past herds of very tame

Skyline Drive

Most people experience Shenandoah National Park by driving the spectacular Skyline Drive. The drive, which was plotted and surveyed in 1931 and opened in 1939, runs (at 35 mph!) along the crest over 100 miles, winding between the I-66 and I-64 freeways while giving grand vistas at every bend in the road. Mileposts, arranged in mile-by-mile order from north to south, mark your progress along Skyline Drive. The scenic driving is definitely memorable, but by far the best way to really see the park is to get out of the car and walk along the many miles of trails (including more than 100 miles of the Appalachian Trail) that lead through the dense green forests to innumerable waterfalls and overlooks.

A helpful map and brochure is handed out at National Park entrance booths along the route (one at either end and two midway). Here are some more great places to look out for:

Milepost 21.1: A roadside parking area marks the trailhead for a lovely, 3.2-mile hike to Overall Run Falls, the tallest in the park. You can also reach the falls from Matthews Arm campground, just down the road.

Milepost 31.5: Thornton Gap is the junction with US-211.

Milepost 32.4: Mary's Rock Tunnel is a 670-foot-long, 13-foot-wide bore cut through the granite in 1932. RV drivers beware—it is just 12 feet, 8 inches high.

Milepost 50.7: Near Big Meadows, under a mile from the well-marked trailhead, Dark Hollow Falls tumbles over a 70-foot incline. Outside the Byrd Visitor Center, a macho statue of "Iron Mike" commemorates the efforts of the workers who built the trails, overlooks, and campgrounds as part of the New Deal Civilian Conservation Corps.

Milepost 52.8: Milam Gap marks the start of a two-mile walk to Rapidan Camp, where President Hoover established a trout-fishing retreat in 1929.

Milepost 56.4: A short, steep hike scrambles up to the 3,300-foot-high summit of Bearfence Mountain for a 360-degree panorama.

Milepost 84.1: A parking area marks the trailhead for the rewarding 3.6-mile hike to Jones Run Falls, tumbling over a mossy 45-foot cliff.

Milepost 98.9: Near the southern end of Skyline Drive, Calf Mountain provides a grand panorama over the Shenandoah Valley.

Along with multicolored leaves, the autumn months bring hundreds of hawks, eagles, and other birds of prey to the mountains on their annual migration. You'll spot the greatest numbers of raptors in late September.

deer to Dark Hollow Falls, which drops 70 feet over greenish volcanic stone. The **Big Meadows Lodge** was built in 1939 and retains its cozy feel; this is also where the park's largest campground is located. There's another lodge to the north, at Skyland (milepost 42), the highest point on Skyline Drive. There are full-service restaurants at both lodges; all food and lodging (and most everything else in the park) is managed by a private concession, Aramark (540/843-2100 or 888/896-3833).

Luray Caverns

Halfway through Shenandoah National Park, US-211 runs west down to **Luray Caverns** (daily; $23 adults, $11 children; 540/743-6551), the largest and most impressive in the eastern United States—there are 64 acres of caverns to explore. It also boasts the "World's Only Stalacpipe Organ," where rubber mallets make music by banging on the stone stalactites. There's also a large antique car museum and the Luray Valley Museum (included in caverns admission), and a garden maze ($7 adults, $6 children).

Near the caverns, along US-211 a half mile west of town, the **Luray Zoo**

The Blue Ridge Parkway: From Shenandoah National Park to Roanoke

Starting at the southern end of Shenandoah National Park and winding along the crest of the Blue Ridge Mountains all the way to Great Smoky Mountains National Park some 469 miles away, the Blue Ridge Parkway is one of the country's great scenic drives. This is especially true during autumn, when the dogwoods and gum trees turn deep red, and the hickories yellow, against an evergreen backdrop of pines, hemlocks, and firs. Spring is wildflower time, with abundant azaleas and rhododendrons blooming orange, white, pink, and red throughout May and June, especially at the higher elevations.

First proposed in the 1920s, the bulk of the Blue Ridge Parkway was constructed in many stages between 1935 and 1967, during which time it grew from a network of local roads to the current route, along which billboards and commercial traffic are both banned. The last section near Linn Cove Viaduct in North Carolina was completed in the mid-1980s. While the parkway avoids towns and commercial areas to concentrate on the scenery, many interesting towns and other places along the way are well worth a detour. For ease of use, we've divided the Blue Ridge Parkway into three main sections, starting with the drive between Shenandoah National Park and Roanoke. (For the **Roanoke–North Carolina** section, see page 385; for the final run south to the **Great Smoky Mountains,** see page 390-391.)

(daily; $10; 540/743-4113) is an animal rescue center and zoo that's home to one of Virginia's largest collections of scaly creatures, both extinct and living. Cobras, alligators, and 20-foot pythons coexist with tropical birds, big cats, and cheerful, playful monkeys. For younger children, there's also a petting zoo of goats, deer, donkeys, pigs, and all manner of farmyard animals.

Staunton

West of the mountains from the south end of Shenandoah National Park on I-64, tidy **Staunton** (pop. 23,746; pronounced "STAN-ton") was founded in 1732 as one of the first towns on the far side of the Blue Ridge. Unlike much of the valley, Staunton was untouched during the Civil War and now preserves its many 18th- and early-19th-century buildings in a townscape so perfect it was rated among the dozen most distinctive destinations in the United States by the National Trust for Historic Preservation.

Earl Hamner Jr. based his famous 1970s TV series *The Waltons* on vivid memories of growing up during the Depression in the rural village of **Schuyler,** a half hour southwest of Charlottesville. Fans of the show will enjoy visiting the **Walton's Mountain Museum** (Mar.–Nov. daily 10 AM–3:40 PM; $7; 434/831-2000), which re-creates the Waltons' kitchen and living room (and John-Boy's bedroom) in the Schuyler Community Center— Earl Hamner's old elementary school.

Mile 0: Rockfish Gap, at the southern end of Shenandoah National Park's Skyline Drive, marks the northern start of the Blue Ridge Parkway.

Milepost 6.1: Humpback Rocks has a short but strenuous trail (45 minutes each way), leading through a reconstructed farmstead and a visitors center (vistors center at Milepost 5.8; 540/943-4716), ending with a 270-degree view over the mountains.

Milepost 34.4: The Yankee Horse parking area has an exhibit on an old logging railroad, part of which has been restored, and a short trail to Wigwam Falls.

Milepost 63.6: The James River Visitor Center (434/299-5496) offers exhibits and trails along the James River and Kanawha Canal. This is the lowest point on the parkway, at 649 feet, and also the junction with US-501, which runs west along the James River for 15 miles to Natural Bridge.

Milepost 76.5: Great views can be had over both valleys from the highest point on the parkway in Virginia, at 3,950 feet.

Mileposts 84–87: The most popular—and most developed—stretch of the parkway, the Peaks of Otter section includes a visitors center (540/586-4496), gas station, restaurant, and very pleasant lodge ($122 and up; 540/586-1081), open year-round. Three peaks rise above a small lake and give great sunrise and sunset views; many good trails, including a two-mile loop to Fallingwater Cascades, let you escape the sometimes-sizable crowds.

Milepost 105: This section ends at the city of Roanoke.

Detour: Charlottesville

From the southern end of Shenandoah National Park, it's a quick 20 miles east on I-64 to **Charlottesville** (pop. 43,475), a richly historic college town that's

one of the most enjoyable stops in the state. From the rolling green lawns of the University of Virginia campus to neoclassical Monticello on the hills above it, the legacy of Thomas Jefferson dominates Charlottesville. Jefferson lived and worked here for most of his life—when he wasn't out founding the country or serving as its president.

West of the compact downtown district, the **University of Virginia** campus was Jefferson's pride and joy. Not only did he found it (in 1819) and fund its early years, he planned the curriculum and designed the original buildings, a quadrangle of redbrick Palladian villas that the American Institute of Architects declared the most perfect place in the country. Edgar Allan Poe lived and studied here briefly before dropping out in 1826. Poe's room, appropriately, is No. 13 in the West Range, and it's decorated to look like it did a century ago, with a few period belongings visible behind the glass door. When school is in session, free campus tours are offered five times a day by the **University Guides** (434/924-3239).

Charlottesville's other key sight is Jefferson's home, **Monticello**—the domed building that fills the back of the nickel coin—well signed off I-64, exit 121. Recently restored and open for tours (daily; $22; 434/984-9822), Monticello embodies the many different traits of this multifaceted man. The house was designed and built by Jefferson over a period of 40 years (1769–1809) and holds various gadgets he invented—including a double-pen device that made a copy of everything he wrote—and odd things he collected over the years, from elk antlers to recipes for home-brewed beer. Jefferson died here at Monticello on July 4, 1826, and the grounds, which in Jefferson's

time formed an extensive plantation worked by slaves, hold his mortal remains in a simple tomb beyond the vegetable gardens.

Down in the valley below Monticello, **Michie Tavern** (daily; $9; 434/977-1234) is a touristy but interesting inn that opened in 1784 and was moved to the present site in the 1920s. Admission includes a tour of the parlors, bars, and upstairs

Monticello, home of Thomas Jefferson

rooms, as well as a dairy and a gristmill. Michie Tavern is also a restaurant serving "Olde Worlde foode" for the bus-tour hordes, at around $20 a head (plus dessert!) for a "colonial buffet" lunch. (Just so you know, Michie is pronounced "MICK-ee," as in Mantle.)

Practicalities

Like most college towns, Charlottesville provides a broad range of good places to eat, from bare-bones cafés like the **White Spot** (1407 University Ave.; 434/295-9899), right across from campus—this is the place to satisfy those midnight cravings for a cheeseburger with a fried egg on top, known here as a Gus Burger. On the downtown Mall you'll find places like **Rapture Restaurant and Nightclub** (303 E. Main St.; 434/293-9526), which offers eclectic Asian dishes alongside steaks and fish-and-chips. It's also a very popular nightclub, with pool tables, dancing, and a modish bar. Also on the Mall, try the modish versions of diner food at **Bizou** (119 W. Main St.; 434/977-1818), and there's more

great live music at **Miller's Downtown** (109 W. Main St.; 434/971-8511), where alt-rock pop star Dave Matthews used to tend bar. For great barbecued ribs and chicken, head over to **Jinx's Pit Stop** (1307 E. Market St.; 434/293-6904).

Most of Charlottesville's motels line up along Emmett Street (US-29 Business), near the US-250 freeway, including the well-placed **English Inn** ($100 and up; 2000 Morton Dr.; 434/971-9000 or 800/786-5400). For more detailed information on visiting Charlottesville, contact the **visitors center** (434/293-6789 or 877/386-1103), which is hard to miss along I-64 at exit 121.

University of Virginia

Just east of the Skyline Drive, three miles northeast of I-64 exit 107, "Virginia's Best Pizza" has been served up for more than 30 years inside barn-red **Crozet Pizza** (5794 Three Notch'd Rd.; 434/823-2132) on Hwy-240.

One of Staunton's many sizable historic districts surrounds the boyhood home of favorite son Woodrow Wilson. Son of a Presbyterian minister, Wilson was born in 1856 in a stately Greek Revival townhouse, now established as the **Woodrow Wilson Presidential Library and Museum** (daily; $14; 18–24 N. Coalter St.; 540/885-0897), with galleries tracing his life as a scholar—he was president of Princeton University—and as U.S. President during World War I.

Staunton is also the home of the unique **Frontier Culture Museum** (daily; $10; 540/332-7850), right off I-81 exit 222 on the southeast side of town. A rural version of Williamsburg, this living history museum consists of four resurrected working farms, incorporating buildings brought over from Germany, England, and Ireland. The fourth farm, dating from antebellum Virginia, shows how various Old World traditions blended in America. The farms are inhabited by interpreters dressed in (very clean) period costumes busily husking corn, spinning wool, or working in the fields.

While in Staunton, check out the wares available at the **Jolly Roger Haggle Shop** (27 Middlebrook Ave.), a fascinating junk shop ("over 1,000,000 items") across from the train station.

Woodrow Wilson

Staunton holds one of the best places to eat in the Shenandoah Valley, on US-250 just east of I-81 exit 222, near the frontier museum: **Mrs. Rowe's Family Restaurant and Bakery** (540/886-1833), which has been serving excellent, home-style cooking, from pork chops to banana cream pies, for more than 60 years. It's open every day (since 1947) for breakfast, lunch, and dinner—go for the world-famous fried chicken, which is well worth the 25-minute wait.

Staunton is also home to another classic: **Wright's Dairy-Rite** (346 Greenville Ave.; 540/886-0435), with great burgers, hot dogs, and onion rings, served up in your car or a dining room decorated with old menus. Enjoy free Wi-Fi and a free Wurlitzer jukebox.

If you've had enough road food and junk food, try the locally sourced produce and other fine foods at the **Staunton Grocery,** in the heart of downtown (105 W. Beverley St.; 540/886-6880).

All the usual motels cluster around Staunton's I-64/I-81 junction.

Lexington

Founded in 1778, and named for the then-recent Revolutionary War battleground, photogenic **Lexington** (pop. 7,042) is home to an estimable pair of Virginia institutions, the Virginia Military Institute (VMI) and Washington and Lee University, which meld into one another at the center of town.

Numerous old brick buildings, including a typically southern lawyer's row around Courthouse Square, still stand around the town, which you can tour on foot or in one of the horse-drawn carriages that leave from the downtown visitors center.

Animated by an unusually crew-cut version of typical college-town energy, Lexington is redolent with, and intensely proud of, its military heritage. Generals, in fact, have become the town's stock-in-trade: From 1851 until 1861 when he rode off to fight in the Civil War, **Gen. Thomas "Stonewall" Jackson** lived at 8 East Washington Street, now a small **museum** (daily; $8; 540/463-2552); he is buried in the small but well-tended cemetery on the south edge of town. Gen. Robert E. Lee spent his post–Civil War years teaching at Washington and Lee, which was named after him (and his wife's ancestor, George). Lee is entombed in a crypt below the chapel, under a famous statue of his recumbent self, with his trusty horse, Traveller, buried just outside. Another influential old warhorse, Gen. George C. Marshall, is honored in a large eponymous museum (Tues.–Sat. 9 AM–5 PM; $5) on the VMI campus. The museum traces General Marshall's role in planning the D-Day invasions in World War II and salutes his Nobel Peace Prize–winning Marshall Plan for the successful reconstruction of postwar Europe.

There are some good bistros and soup-and-sandwich places along Main Street, and an unusually healthy menu at the **Blue Sky Café** (125 W. Nelson St.; 540/463-6546). There are a number of comfortable and captivating places to stay in and around Lexington, like the **Llewellyn Lodge** ($89–199; 603 S. Main St.; 540/463-3235 or 800/882-1145). Comfortable, convenient, welcoming, and helpful, and within easy walking distance of the campuses and the historic town center, the Llewellyn is everything a B&B should be.

To get a sense of life in the Shenandoah Valley, tune to **WSVA 550 AM** in Harrisonburg, which broadcasts updated farm and livestock prices every hour on the hour.

Spend a summer night in Lexington at the community-run **Hull's Drive In** ($6; 2367 N. US-11; 540/463-2621), a much-loved local Ozoner drive-in theater still showing Hollywood hits. Before a movie, grab a burger at **Kenney's,** off US-11.

Natural Bridge

Held sacred by local Monacan Indians and bought from King George in 1774 by Thomas Jefferson, the 215-foot-high notch of **Natural Bridge** is a remarkable piece of geologic acrobatics. Spanning some 90 feet, the thick stone arch bridges Cedar Creek at the bottom of a steeply walled canyon. To see the Natural Bridge, which is heralded as one of the Seven Natural Wonders of the World (others on the list include Niagara Falls, Yellowstone, and Giant's Causeway in Northern Ireland), you have to buy a ticket (daily; $18; 800/533-1410 or 540/291-2121) from the unbelievably huge souvenir shop that fills the bottom of the old hotel. Natural Bridge is the focus of a once-plush resort complex that has definitely seen better times but still offers some 150 rooms in two hotels, as well as a large cave and a wax museum of Virginia history in which you can watch the wax figures being made, dressed, and posed.

The **Natural Bridge Hotel and Convention Center,** located next to the Natural Bridge entrance, has rooms ($85 and up) and four- to six-room cottages across the road. There's also an Olympic-sized pool, and the colonial dining room serves all meals daily, with outdoor dining on the veranda and popular weekend buffets.

Roanoke

"World's Largest Man-Made Star," on Roanoke's Mill Mountain

Apart from Asheville at its southern end, **Roanoke** (pop. 97,032) is the only real city that can claim it's actually *on* the Blue Ridge Parkway. With block after block of brick-fronted business buildings, most of them adorned with neon, metal, and painted signs that seem unchanged since the 1940s, Roanoke contrasts abruptly with the natural verdancy of the rest of the parkway, but you may find it a welcome change after so many trees. Once a busy, belching, industrial Goliath supported by the railroads, Roanoke has evolved into a sophisticated, high-tech city—the commercial, cultural, and medical center of southwest Virginia.

Southeast of Roanoke, the **Booker T. Washington National Monument** (540/721-2094) preserves the tobacco fields and plantation cabin where the influential African American leader was born. Other buildings on the 207-acre site, 20 miles or so from Roanoke via Hwy-116 and Hwy-122, have been reconstructed.

Roanoke's main visitor attractions lie right downtown in the **Center in the Square** complex (540/342-5700), a restored warehouse that holds a wide variety of cultural offerings, including theaters, an art museum (free), a kid-friendly science museum ($8), and a local history museum ($3). Also worth a look is the **Virginia Museum of Transportation** (daily; $8; 303 Norfolk Ave. SW; 540/342-5670), three blocks west of Center in the Square, which displays lots of old cars and trucks, steam and diesel locomotives, and horse-drawn carriages, plus a complete traveling circus—minus the performers, of course. Steam trains, as documented by Roanoke-based photographer O. Winston Link, are the real highlight of the museum, and a short walk away, inside Roanoke's streamlined 1930s-era Norfolk & Western Railroad passenger station, the new **O. Winston Link Museum** (daily; $5; 101

The Blue Ridge Parkway: Roanoke to North Carolina

South from Roanoke, the Blue Ridge Parkway winds another 100 miles before crossing the North Carolina border. This midsection of the parkway, especially the first 25 miles south of Roanoke, runs at a lower elevation across a more settled and cultivated landscape than the rugged ridge tops followed elsewhere. In place of the spectacular vistas, you'll see many more houses and small farms, a few pioneer cabins (preserved and not), miles of split-rail fences, and some picturesque cemeteries. The southern reaches, approaching the North Carolina border, get better and better.

Milepost 122: This section begins at the city of Roanoke.

Milepost 154.5: A two-mile loop trail leads to a pioneer cabin overlooking the Smart View for which it's named. Blooming dogwoods abound in May.

Milepost 165.2: At Tuggles Gap, the junction with Hwy-8 has a motel, restaurant, gas station, and also a small cemetery right along the parkway.

Mileposts 167–174: The 4,800-acre Rocky Knob area contains a campground (540/745-9662), a visitors center near the Meadows of Dan (540/745-9662), and a strenuous but very rewarding 10-mile round-trip trail (starting at milepost 167.1) leading down through Rock Castle Gorge and over 3,572-foot Rocky Knob.

Milepost 176.1: A short trail leads to Mabry Mill, in use 1910–1935. In summer, interpreters demonstrate blacksmithing and milling skills. A coffee shop, open in summer only, sells old-fashioned pancakes made from stone-ground flour, plus country ham and hamburgers.

Milepost 199–200: This is the junction with US-52, which runs south to Mount Airy, North Carolina, home of Mayberry, RFD.

Milepost 216.9: You've reached the Virginia/North Carolina border.

Shenandoah Ave.; 540/982-5465) displays more than 200 of the photographer's indelible black-and-white images. There's also a neat gallery devoted to the building's legendary designer, Raymond Loewy, who created the Coke bottle, the logo for Lucky Strike cigarettes, and hundreds of other all-American icons.

On Mill Mountain high above Roanoke, the 88.5-foot-tall **World's Largest Free-Standing Man-Made Star** shines nightly, lit by 2,000 feet of red, white and blue neon tubing. You can drive up to the base of it and get a grand view over Roanoke.

For NPR news and noncommercial arts programming, tune to **WVTF 89.1 FM** in Roanoke.

Roanoke Practicalities

Roanoke's most popular place to eat is either **The Roanoker Restaurant** (closed Mon.; 2522 Colonial Ave. SW; 540/344-7746), "The Home of Good Food since 1941," which serves traditional Virginia dishes and also does a tasty bowl of chili, a mile south of downtown off I-581 (Wonju Street exit). Or it's **Thelma's Chicken and Waffles,** right downtown (315 Market St.; 540/343-8888). There's also the unexpected world-beat cuisine at **Carlos' Brazilian and International Cuisine** (4167 Electric Rd.; 540/776-1117) on a hilltop three miles south of town. If you're planning a picnic up in the mountains, be sure to stop first at the historic **farmers market** (free), downtown next to the Center in the Square and active since 1882.

In the mountains west of Roanoke, across I-81 on Hwy-311 in Catawba, excellent home cooking (around $15 for all you can eat: fresh biscuits, fried chicken, incredible fresh fruit cobblers) is served Thursday–Sunday, for dinner only, at **The Home Place Restaurant** (540/384-7252).

Places to stay range from the usual Interstate motels, lined up along Orange Avenue (US-460), to a pair of grand hotels. Oldest and best of these is the **Hotel Roanoke** ($120 and up; 110 Shenandoah Ave.; 540/985-5900 or 800/222-8733), which has anchored downtown for over a century. Now managed as a Doubletree, the hotel has outlasted the railroads that financed it, and even if you stay elsewhere, the lobby, with its Florentine marble floors and vaulted ceiling, is worth a look.

The soft drink Dr. Pepper, which originated in Waco, Texas, was named for a pharmacist who worked in the town of **Rural Retreat, Virginia,** along I-81 near its intersection with the AT.

Floyd

The town of **Floyd,** west of the Blue Ridge Parkway, about an hour southwest of Roanoke, has only one stoplight, so it's easy to find **The Floyd Country Store,** which is famous for grilled cheese sandwiches, bowls of chili, and its weekly Jamboree ($5; 540/745-4563). Every Friday at 6:30 PM, the display cases are pushed aside and the floor given over to *real* country music, square dancing, and shuffling feet.

NORTH CAROLINA

Running along the crest of the Blue Ridge Mountains at the far western edge of the state, this route across North Carolina takes in some of the most beautiful scenery east or west of the Mississippi. Though not as immense as the Rockies or other western landscapes, this part of North Carolina abounds with rugged peaks and deep valleys, pastoral meadows, and ancient-looking mountain villages, some dating back to colonial times. It's all linked by the magnificent Blue Ridge Parkway, perhaps the country's greatest scenic drive.

The border between Virginia and North Carolina was surveyed in 1749 by a team that included Thomas Jefferson's father, Peter.

The region's sole city, **Asheville,** is a proud old resort dominated by the ostentatious Biltmore Estate, the world's largest private house, but everywhere else nature predominates—especially in the majestic **Great Smoky Mountains National Park** in the state's far southwestern corner.

Mount Airy: Mayberry, RFD

Along the Virginia/North Carolina border, 12 miles southeast of Blue Ridge Parkway milepost 200 via US-52, **Mount Airy** (pop. 10,388) was the boyhood home of Andy Griffith, who based much of his long-running TV show *The Andy Griffith Show* and the spin-off sitcom *Mayberry, RFD* on the region. If you have fond memories of Opie, Andy, Barney, and Aunt Bee, you'll definitely want to visit Mount Airy, which has effectively re-created itself in the image of the show. Take a Mayberry Squad Car tour (336/789-6743) and let a wannabe Barney show you the sights. Eat an ever-tender pork chop sandwich, raved about by *Gourmet Magazine* and Oprah, at the very popular **Snappy Lunch** (closed Sun.; 125 Main St.; 336/786-4931) in the compact downtown business district. And don't neglect to admire the 8x10 glossies of Mayberry actors and their local the sheriff's car, parked outside Mayberry

lookalikes at Floyd's Barber Shop, next door. Or head a few blocks west to **Aunt Bea's Barbeque** (425 Old US-52; 336/789-3050). Then stay the night at the comfortable, clean, and inexpensive **Mayberry Motor Inn** ($60 and up; 336/786-4109) across the highway—just look for the black-and-white Mayberry sheriff's car parked out front.

The Mayberry mania reaches a peak during **Mayberry Days** in late September; details on this (and anything to do with Andy Griffith) can be had from the **Mount Airy visitors center** (800/948-0949).

> In the valley below Mount Mitchell, off I-40 northeast of Asheville, **Black Mountain College** was a lively intellectual and artistic nexus during the 1930s, 1940s, and 1950s.
>
> Mount Airy is home to the world's largest open-faced granite quarry.
>
> Just west of Blowing Rock and the Blue Ridge Parkway, the town of **Boone** got put on the map in a big way when its local college, **Appalachian State,** beat the football team of mighty Michigan.

Blowing Rock

A quick two miles south of the Blue Ridge Parkway via US-221 from milepost 291.9 lies the delightful little resort community of **Blowing Rock** (pop. 1,241)—the place to stop if you're only stopping once. The cool summer temperatures have been attracting visitors for centuries, and once you get past the factory outlet mall that welcomes you to town, quaint old Main Street is a great place to stretch your legs while taking in the eclectic range of late Victorian buildings, including some delightful churches. Blowing Rock takes its name from a nearby cliff overlooking John's River Gorge, where updrafts can cause lightweight objects to be blown upwards rather than down; this effect, which earned Blowing Rock a mention in *Ripley's Believe It or Not!* as the only place "Where Snow Falls Upside Down," also inspired the Native American legend of a Cherokee brave who, rather than be forcibly separated from his Chickasaw lover, leapt off the cliff, only to be blown back into the arms of his sweetheart.

North Carolina's oldest tourist attraction, the **Blowing Rock** itself, two miles east of town via winding US-321 (daily; $6), is worth the admission, whether or not the "magic wind" is blowing. Check out the tremendous views from a platform suspended 3,000 feet above the valley below. The nearby area also offers a couple of enjoyable tourist traps, including an apparently gravity-defying **Mystery Hill** just off the parkway, and the toddler-friendly, coal-fired steam trains of the **Tweetsie Railroad,** four miles north of town on US-321.

Downtown Blowing Rock has a number of good places to eat lined up along and around the quaint few blocks of Main Street downtown, like **Crippen's Country Inn** (239 Sunset Dr.; 828/295-3487). Across US-321 from the Blowing Rock, the storybook **Green Park Inn** ($129–229; 828/414-9230) is a large historic resort hotel built in 1882; there's a golf course down the street. More modern conveniences are available at the **Cliff Dwellers Inn** ($80 and

up; 800/322-7380 or 828/295-3122),
right off the parkway on US-321.

Little Switzerland

Another classic mountaintop vacation spot, located midway between
Blowing Rock and Asheville, Little
Switzerland was founded in 1910
around the **Switzerland Inn** ($119
and up; 828/765-2153 or 800/654-
4026), a peaceful and relaxing old
chalet-style resort that also operates a very popular
restaurant right off the Blue Ridge Parkway at milepost 334.

> The hikers' Appalachian
> Trail winds west of the
> Blue Ridge Parkway along
> the North Carolina/
> Tennessee border.

The inn stands on a crest, but the rest of Little
Switzerland sits in the deep canyon to the east, spread
out along Hwy-226 and a number of smaller side roads. The main stop is
Emerald Village (daily Apr.–Nov.; $7; 828/765-6463), on McKinney Mine
Road 2.5 miles from the parkway, where you can tour an old gemstone mine
(above and below ground) and museums displaying everything from gemstones to mechanical music makers.

Asheville

What the English country town of Bath was to Jane Austen's 18-century
London, the mountain resort of **Asheville** (pop. 83,393) was to the pre-jet-
set, pre-air-conditioned Deep South. When summer heat and humidity

The Blue Ridge Parkway: North Carolina to the Smokies

The highest and most memorable parts of the 469-mile Blue Ridge Parkway are the 250 mountainous miles leading along the backbone of North Carolina. Following the southern Blue Ridge Mountains as they fade into the taller and more massive Black Mountains, the parkway skirts three other mountain ranges before ending up at Great Smoky Mountains National Park on the Tennessee border. Spring flowers (including massive rhododendrons), fall colors, songbirds, wild turkeys, numerous waterfalls, and occasional eerie fogs that fill the valleys below all make this an unforgettable trip no matter what the time of year. Take your time and drive carefully, however hard it is to keep your eyes on the road.

A couple of worthwhile detours—to the mountain hamlets of Blowing Rock and Little Switzerland, and to the city of Asheville—are covered in greater detail in the main text. From north to south, here are the mile-by-mile highlights along the North Carolina portion of the Blue Ridge Parkway:

Milepost 216.9: This section starts at the Virginia/North Carolina border.

Milepost 217.5: A very easy half-mile trail leads to the top of 2,885-foot Cumberland Knob. A visitors center marks the location workers began construction of the parkway in 1935.

Mileposts 238.5–244.7: Doughton Park, named for one of the politicians who made the parkway possible, is home to **Bluffs Lodge and Coffee Shop** (336/372-4499), which has nice rooms, a café serving good downhome country cooking, a gas station, and a campground.

Milepost 260.6: An easy mile-long trail leads to the top of Jumpinoff Rocks for a sweeping view.

Mileposts 292–295: Moses H. Cone Memorial Park is a 3,600-acre former private estate, with many miles of mountaintop hiking trails. At Mile 294, Southern Highlands Crafts Guild members demonstrate various Appalachian crafts throughout the summer, on the front porch of the former Cone mansion, which is now the nonprofit Parkway Craft Center.

Milepost 304: The marvelous engineering feat of the Linn Cove Viaduct carries the parkway around rugged Grandfather Mountain. Completed in 1987, this was the last part of the parkway to be built. Dense walls of rhododendrons border the parkway south of the viaduct.

Milepost 305.1: US-221, which used to carry the parkway before the viaduct was built, leads a mile south to 5,946-foot **Grandfather Mountain,** the highest peak in Blue Ridge, now a private park (daily; $15; 828/733-4337 or 800/468-7325) with nature trails, a zoo, and the famous Mile-High Swinging Bridge.

Milepost 308.2: A half-mile nature trail leads to 3,995-foot Flat Rock for a view of Grandfather Mountain.

Milepost 316.3: Linville Falls crashes through a rugged gorge; short trails lead to scenic overlooks.

Milepost 331: At the junction of Hwy-226, the **Museum of North Carolina Minerals** (daily 9 AM–5 PM; free; 828/765-2761) displays all kinds and sizes of local gemstones, which you can watch being polished.

Milepost 355.4: West of the parkway, the 1,650 acres of Mount Mitchell State Park include a mountaintop observation tower. Drive to within 200 yards of the weather-beaten 6,684-foot summit, the highest point east of the Mississippi River.

Milepost 364.6: Best seen in late spring when the rhododendrons are in full bloom, the lush greenery of Craggy Gardens feels like an Appalachian Shangri-La.

Milepost 382: You can check out exhibits and demonstrations of Appalachian arts and crafts in the Folk Art Center (daily 9 AM–5 PM; 828/298-7928).

Milepost 431: At the highest point on the parkway (6,047 feet in elevation), a self-guided nature trail leads through a first-growth spruce and fir forest.

Milepost 469: The southern end of the Blue Ridge Parkway is at the junction with US-441 and the entrance to Smoky Mountains National Park.

Linn Cove viaduct

the Biltmore Estate, "World's Biggest Vacation House"

A dozen miles west of the Blue Ridge Parkway via US-321 and Hwy-194, the village of **Valle Crucis** holds the original **Mast General Store,** which sells a little of everything, from gasoline to Gore-Tex parkas. There is a branch in Blowing Rock, with several other locations throughout the region.

became unbearable, the gentry headed here to stay cool while enjoying the city's many grand hotels and elaborate summer homes.

The presence here of the world's biggest vacation house, the Vanderbilt family's **Biltmore Estate** (daily; around $60; 800/411-3812 or 828/225-1333), is proof of Asheville's primary position in the old-school resort pantheon. The estate now covers 8,000 acres on the south side of town, though at the turn of the 20th century it covered 125,000 acres, stretching all the way up to today's Blue Ridge Parkway. Surrounded by a series of flower gardens planned in part by Frederick Law Olmsted, the estate centers on a truly unbelievable French Renaissance–style mansion built in 1895. The 250-plus rooms hold everything from a palm court and a bowling alley to Napoleon's chess set to paintings by Renoir, Singer Sargent, Whistler, and others. Signs aplenty direct you to the estate, which stands just north of the I-40 exit 50 off Biltmore Avenue, across from the shops and restaurants in **Historic Biltmore Village,** which originally housed the estate's staff and workshops— it's a true "model village," designed in gothic style by Richard Morris Hunt.

The rest of Asheville can't compete with the nouveau riche excess of the Biltmore Estate, and in fact it's a surprisingly homespun city, with a downtown commercial district filled with 1930s-era storefronts housing thrift stores and off-beat art galleries. One truly worthwhile place to see in downtown Asheville is the nondescript old boardinghouse where author Thomas Wolfe grew up from 1900 to 1920, preserved as it was when Wolfe lived here. The rambling house across from the beige modern Radisson Hotel, is officially known as the **Thomas Wolfe Memorial State Historic Site** (daily, closed Mon. in winter;

$1; 48 Spruce St.; 828/253-8304); unfortunately, the house suffered a major fire in 1998, but after restoration is still one of the most evocative of all American literary sites. In the details and, more importantly, in general ambience, it's identical to the vivid prose descriptions of the house he called "Dixieland," the primary setting of his first and greatest novel, *Look Homeward, Angel*. After Wolfe's death from tubercular meningitis in 1938, the house was made into a shrine to Wolfe by his family, who ar ranged it to look as it did during his youth; one room contains his desk, typewriter, and other mementos of his life and work. An adjacent museum tells more of his story.

Two blocks or so south of the Wolfe memorial, where Broadway becomes Biltmore Avenue, **Pack Square** is the center of Asheville, surrounded by the county courthouse, the city hall, a small art museum, and the public library. This is where Thomas Wolfe's father ran a stonecutting shop, on whose porch stood the homeward-gazing angel, now recalled by a statue standing on the square's southwest corner.

Asheville Practicalities

The streets around Pack Square hold many good places to eat, including a trio of bistro-type places with outdoor dining areas, lined up side by side around the **Bistro 1896** (7 SW Pack Square; 828/251-1300). There are more good places around the magical, art deco–era Grove shopping arcade west of the square, and yet more cafés and bakeries line Biltmore Avenue south of Pack Square, where you'll also find Asheville's best nightlife. **The Orange Peel** (101 S. Biltmore Ave.; 828/255-5851) gets an enviable array of nationally known musicians in all genres (from Bob Dylan to the Flaming Lips), while the **Fine Arts Theatre** up the street shows the latest arthouse releases ($8.75; 36 Biltmore Ave.; 828/232-1536). North of downtown, near the UNC-Asheville campus, good microbrews (and $3 evening movies) are available at **Asheville Pizza and Brewing** (675 Merrimon Ave.; 828/254-1281). Another Asheville Pizza and Brewing location is 77 Coxe Avenue (828/255-4077).

The usual chain hotels cluster along the Interstates, and some more characterful older, neon-signed motels line old US-70 between downtown and the Blue Ridge Parkway. For a true taste of Americana, you may prefer the classic 1930s **Log Cabin Motor Court,** six miles north of Asheville ($65–275; 330 Weaverville Hwy.; 828/645-6546).

When Vanderbilt types come to Asheville today, they probably stay at **Grove Park Inn Resort and Spa** ($250 and up; 290 Macon Ave.; 828/252-2711 or 800/438-5800), east of I-26 and north of I-40 and I-240, a lovely rustic inn built in 1913. Newer wings

Asheville's long-standing relationship with visitors explains why the local minor league baseball team is called the **Asheville Tourists.** The Colorado Rockies farm club plays at retro-modern McCormick Field, a mile south of downtown (828/258-0428). Games are broadcast on **WRES 100.7 FM.**

For good commercial-free music and NPR news in and around Asheville, tune to **WNCW 88.7 FM** of Spindale.

Novelist F. Scott Fitzgerald stayed at Asheville's Grove Park Resort and Spa while visiting his wife, Zelda, who had been committed to the adjacent Highland Hospital sanitarium, where she died in a fire in 1948.

Twenty miles southwest of Asheville, the eponymous peak featured in the book *Cold Mountain* rises amidst the Pisgah National Forest, but the Academy Award–winning movie version was filmed on location— in distant Romania.

contain the most modern four-star conveniences, but the original lodge boasts rooms filled with authentic Roycroft furniture, making the Grove Park a live-in museum of arts-and-crafts style. There's also a very plush **Inn on Biltmore Estate** ($200 and up; 828/225-1600), for the full Biltmore Estate experience.

For further information on the Asheville area, contact the **visitors center** (36 Montford Ave.; 828/258-6129).

Profits from Grove's Tasteless Tonic paid for the ultra-tasteful Grove Park Inn.

Maggie Valley

The Blue Ridge Parkway swings south from Asheville through Transylvania County on the approach to Great Smoky Mountains National Park, though you'll save an hour or more by following the I-40 freeway to the junction with US-19, which links up with the south end of the parkway. This stretch of US-19, winding through the **Maggie Valley** over the foothills of the Great Smokies, is a very pretty drive, and absolutely packed with roadside Americana—miniature golf courses, trout farms, souvenir shops, lookout towers alongside pancake houses, barbecue shacks; you name it, it's here.

For years, the biggest and best of many great places to stop in Maggie Valley was the **Ghost Town in the Sky,** an old Appalachian ghost town–themed amusement park with roller coasters, bumper cars, and all the usual suspects, high on the side of the Great Smoky Mountains. Built in the 1960s, the park was plagued by financial problems for years and closed, apparently permanently, in 2009.

You can spot the wild mountains southeast of Asheville in numerous movies, including *Last of the Mohicans,* much of which was filmed around Chimney Rock, east of town along scenic US-64. **Chimney Rock** (800/277-9611 or 828/625-9610) is a great destination, featuring fabulous views and a 26-story elevator carved through solid granite.

Cherokee

West of Maggie Valley, the Blue Ridge Parkway and US-19 join up 40 miles west of Asheville at touristy **Cherokee** (pop. 2,138), commercial center of the 56,000-acre **Cherokee Indian Reservation,** which was established here by a small band of Cherokee Indians in 1866, long after the rest of this once-mighty tribe had been forcibly exiled to Oklahoma on the Trail of Tears. Cherokee is a last gasp of commercialism at the edge of the national park, a traffic-clogged gauntlet of places where you can "See Live Bears," "Eat Boiled Peanuts," "Pan For Gold," or ride the "Rudicoaster" at the pricey but kid-friendly **Santa's Land Theme Park and Zoo** ($20; 828/497-9191). The biggest draw hereabouts is the ever-expanding **Harrah's Casino** ($60 and up; 800/CAESARS or 828/497-7777).

The upscale casino, the region's biggest draw, looms over a fading roadside lined by tacky old-time souvenir stands like the "Big Chief," but amidst the tourist-taunting sprawl is at least one worthwhile stop: the **Museum of the Cherokee Indian** (daily; $10), which traces tribal history from pre-conquest achievements—the Cherokee used a natural version of aspirin centuries before western chemists "discovered" it, for example—to their forced removal after gold was discovered here in the 1830s. There's also a living history village and a big outdoor pageant.

Great Smoky Mountains National Park

The most popular park in the United States, **Great Smoky Mountains National Park** offers a taste of wilderness to more than nine million visitors annually. Knoxville, Nashville, and Atlanta are all within a two-hour drive, and day-trippers visit mostly during late October for the annual display of fall color. Criss-crossed by more than 800 miles of hiking trails, including the Appalachian Trail, the park covers 521,085 acres along the 6,600-foot-high crest of the Great Smoky Mountains, so named for the fogs that fill the deep valleys. Before the park was established, its lands were extensively logged—70 percent of the trees had been clear-cut by 1934, when the lands were protected as a national park. Fortunately, the forests have grown back to obscure any sign of past degradations, and the uncut portions form the most extensive stands of primeval forest in the eastern United States.

Having spent more than 50 years as a living roadside landmark, Cherokee chief Henry Lambert was known as "The World's Most Photographed Indian." Though Chief Henry died in 2007, his image still graces countless Cherokee postcards.

Biologists estimate that some 1,500 native black bears live in the back-country (and campgrounds!) of Great Smoky Mountains National Park.

The Appalachian Trail runs along the crest of the Great Smoky Mountains, crossing Newfound Gap Road at the center of the park. West of the park, the AT crosses another great road, US-129, whose winding route takes in more than 300 twisty corners in less than 12 miles. Dubbed the "Tail of the Dragon," this is one of the country's great driving (and motorcycling) routes.

The many different salamanders native to the Great Smokies range from the tiny pygmy to the massive hellbender, which grows up to two feet long, head to tail. These crawling critters have earned the Great Smokies a reputation as the "Salamander Capital of the World."

The main route through the park is Newfound Gap Road (US-441), which runs northwest from Cherokee to the even more tourist-traveled Gatlinburg and Pigeon Forge in Tennessee. The road winds steeply through dense forests packed with magnificent giant hardwoods, flowering poplar, dogwood, azalea, and rhododendron, and evergreen pines and firs at the highest elevations. Where the highway reaches the crest, a spur road runs parallel to the Appalachian Trail five miles west to 6,642-foot **Clingman's Dome,** the highest point in the park, where you can take a short but steep trail up to a lookout tower.

One of the most extensive natural areas—unlogged, old-growth forest, full of the park's oldest and tallest trees—lies at the very center of the park, off Newfound Gap Road on the north side of the crest. Starting at the popular Chimney Tops picnic area, the well-marked, three-quarter-mile **Cove Hardwood Nature Trail** winds through a sampling of the park's most stately maples and other broadleafed trees—the ones responsible for the best of the fall colors.

Along Little River Road, west of the Sugarlands Visitor Center off US-441 at the park's northern entrance, stands another group of ancient trees. Midway along, trails lead to two marvelous waterfalls, Laurel Falls and Meigs Falls. Little River Road ends up at **Cades Cove,** where the preserved remnants of a mountain community that existed here from the early 1800s until the 1930s give a strong sense of Appalachian folk ways. A church and a number of mills still stand, and interpretive staff offer guided walks and other programs explaining the history and culture of these "hillbilly" people—some 6,000 of whom used to live within the park boundaries. **Bike rentals** are available at the Cades Cove Campground Store near the Cades Cove

Just over the mountains on the Tennessee side of the Great Smokies, Dolly Parton owns, runs, and stars at **Dollywood** (800/365-5996), northeast of Pigeon Forge off US-441, the country's biggest autobiographical theme park.

campground (865/448-9034), and you'll find plenty of opportunities for rides along the old country lanes.

Another popular park destination is **Grotto Falls,** southeast of Gatlinburg via the Roaring Fork Road, where a short, flat trail to the tumbling cascade leads through lush hemlock forest—an ideal environment for mushrooms, and for the 27 to 30 different species of salamanders that slither around underfoot.

The only beds available in the park are at the historic **LeConte Lodge** (865/429-5704), built in the 1920s atop 6,593-foot Mt. LeConte, and located a 6.5-mile hike from the nearest road. There are no phones, no TVs, little privacy, and no indoor plumbing, but the $116 and up nightly rates do come with "family-style" breakfast and dinner. Ten fairly basic **campgrounds** (no

Detour: Chattanooga

Mixing traditional southern hospitality with fascinating history, cultural vitality, and a stupendous natural setting, Chattanooga is an unexpected treat. Best known to older generations as the home base of Glenn Miller's 1940s big band swing anthem "Chattanooga Choo Choo," this midsized city stretches along the banks of the Tennessee River, where a very pleasant promenade of footpaths and bike trails ties an array of tourist attractions into local history. Markers, fountains, and plaques commemorate everything from Civil War battles to the sorry story of the banishment of the native Cherokee westward along the Trail of Tears in the 1830s.

The opening of the ever-expanding **Tennessee Aquarium** (daily; $25 and up; 800/262-0695), one of the largest and most popular in the country, was key to Chattanooga's current renaissance. Along with an **IMAX theater,** the excellent **Hunter Museum of American Art,** and a minor league baseball stadium for Class AA Chattanooga Lookouts, the aquarium has energized a wholesale reconstruction of the Chattanooga riverfront. On a nice summer's day, cross the river on the 121-year-old **Walnut Street Bridge,** gazing down at kayakers and rock climbers before hopping on the dollar-a-ride historic carousel in idyllic **Coolidge Park.**

While the aquarium and related attractions have given the city a new lease on life, one of the country's most enduring tourist attractions, **Rock City,** has been tempting travelers here for nearly a century. Standing six miles south of town atop 2,392-foot-tall **Lookout Mountain,** Rock City is one of the most hyped sights in the United States. From the 1930s through the 1960s, hundreds of rural barns from Michigan to Texas were painted with the words "See Rock City," "World's 8th Wonder," and "See 7 States." (The claim that one can see seven states from Rock City is disputed, but in order of distance they would be Georgia, Tennessee, Alabama, North Carolina, South Carolina, Kentucky, and Virginia.) **Rock City** ($19; 800/854-0675 or 706/820-2531) itself is terrific, with paths winding through oddly shaped limestone canyons at the edge of heart-stopping cliffs. Even better are the other attractions atop Lookout Mountain, especially the beautiful limestone caves, the 150-foot-high underground **Ruby Falls** ($18; 423/821-2544), and the historic **Incline Railroad ($14; 423/821-4224).** All-inclusive tickets are available.

The lively Chattanooga Lookouts, the Double A farm club of the LA Dodgers, play right downtown at riverside AT&T Field (423/267-4849). Games are broadcast on ESPN 105.1FM.

showers or hookups) operate in the park, with reservations taken only for the largest and most popular ones at Cades Cove, Elkmont, and Smokemount (877/444-6777). These three are accessible to RVs up to 35 feet long; for hikers, there are also bear-proofed backcountry shelters along the Appalachian Trail.

For more information, or to pick up the handy brochures describing the park's array of flora, fauna, trails, and other features, stop by either of the two main visitors centers. North of Cherokee at the south entrance, the **Oconaluftee Visitor Center** (828/497-1900) stands alongside a restored pioneer farmstead, where crafts demonstrations are given in summer. From the **Sugarlands Visitor Center** (865/436-1200), two miles south of Gatlinburg, Tennessee, you can take a short hike to Cataract Falls.

South to Georgia: Franklin

South from Cherokee and the Great Smoky Mountains, US-441 runs through the giant **Nantahala National Forest,** which stretches all the way to the Georgia border. It's a fast road, mostly divided, four-lane freeway, passing through a fairly developed corridor of towns and small cities.

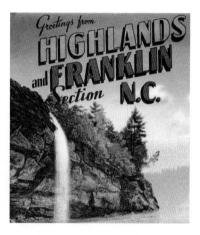

The biggest town in this part of North Carolina, **Franklin** (pop. 3,845) was founded in the mid-1800s on a shallow ridge overlooking the Little Tennessee River. Along with lumber milling, Franklin's main industry has long been the mining of gemstones—garnets, rubies, and sapphires. Now a light industrial center, spread out around the intersection of US-441 and US-64, Franklin has a compact downtown area packed with gemstone and jewelry shops like **Ruby City** (closed Sun.; 130 E. Main St.; 800/821-7829 or 828/524-3967), which also has a small free museum. The **Franklin Motel** ($60; 17 W. Palmer St.; 828/524-4431 or 800/433-5507) has clean, comfortable rooms and a swimming pool.

One of the few radio stations you can hear in mountainous western North Carolina, Franklin's **WPFJ 1480 AM** plays an entertaining combination of local news and contemporary Christian country music.

US-441 races south to Georgia from Franklin, while Hwy-28/US-64 heads southeast through the heart of **Transylvania County,** known as the "Land of Waterfalls" because of its many cascades. The biggest of these is 13 miles or so from Franklin and named, for some unknown reason, **Dry Falls.** From the well-signed parking area, follow a short trail that ends up underneath and behind the impressively raging torrent, a powerful white-noise generator you can hear long before you reach it. Another waterfall, known as **Bridal Veil Falls,** is a mile south from Dry Falls. A portion of old US-64 runs under Bridal Veil Falls, so motorists can drive under the cascade of water.

Two miles south from Bridal Veil Falls, US-64 enters the resort community of **Highlands** (pop. 924). Here Hwy-106 loops back to the southwest, giving grand panoramic views over the forested foothills before rejoining US-441 across the Georgia border in Dillard.

Between Franklin and Highlands, US-64 passes by several waterfalls and has been designated a Mountain Waters Scenic Byway.

GEORGIA

If Georgia brings to mind endless, flat cotton or peanut plantations, you'll be pleasantly surprised by the mountainous wilds of the state's northern tier. The great Appalachian ridge that runs along the East Coast has its southern foot here, high up in the forests of Rabun County, which packs natural wonders, outdoor adventures, and down-home Appalachian spirit into the state's small, isolated corner. Chattooga River white water—made famous by the movie *Deliverance* and rated among the top 10 river runs in the United States—is the biggest draw, and sightseers can take in the spectacular waterfalls of **Tallulah Gorge.** Christmas-tree farms, dairies, and car graveyards dot the old-time mountain towns, but the ongoing "improvement" of US-441 into a four-lane freeway has resulted in a development boom of golf courses and mountain-view estates, increasing exponentially as the route approaches Atlanta's endless suburbs.

Dillard

Just south of the North Carolina border, the highway hamlet of **Dillard** (pop. 339) is a mini fiefdom of the Dillard family, whose name dates back to the 1700s in these parts. For generations, the Dillards have run a local hospitality empire based around the sprawling set of bungalows, lodges, and dining rooms all going by the name **Dillard House** (706/746-5348 or 800/541-0671), on a hill above US-441 at the south edge of town. Heading up the complex is the

Rock City Gardens, Lookout Mountain

SEE SEVEN STATES

If you've seen the 900-odd barn signs urging you to "See Rock City," you may want to detour west to Chattanooga, where **Lookout Mountain** is a capital of roadside kitsch, giving a supposed 150-mile view over seven states.

Atlanta

With a youthful and energetic metropolitan population of more than five million people, Atlanta has emerged as one of the most dynamic communities in the country. State capital of Georgia, and world headquarters of that flagship of American culture, Coca-Cola, Atlanta is the financial and cultural heart of the "New South," having recovered from its total destruction during the Civil War. Despite the sprawling scale of the place, in general people here are gracious and welcoming, so much so they could seem like walking parodies of Southern hospitality—if they weren't so darn sincere.

Atlanta began as a railroad junction (its original name was simply "Terminus"), and the early streetscape has been preserved and restored in **Underground Atlanta** (404/523-2311), a warren of shop fronts underneath the center of the modern city. Abandoned in the 1920s, the buildings here were restored in the late 1980s to form a successful shopping and entertainment district. Numerous plaques and artworks commemorate the area's past, while two blocks to the east stands the gold-domed Georgia state capitol. On the northwest edge of downtown, building on the mixed success of the 1996 Olympics, Atlanta has developed Centennial Park as its new center, opening the $200 million **Georgia Aquarium** (daily; around $30; 404/581-4000), the world's largest aquarium, alongside a showcase for the city's most successful product, **World of Coca Cola** (daily; $16; 800/676-COKE or 404/676-5151). The surrounding area holds the world headquarters of another Atlanta product, CNN, along with the city's huge Georgia World Congress convention center, the Georgia Dome sports arena, and the campus of Georgia Tech university.

whale shark at the Georgia Aquarium

Gone With the Wind still draws thousands to Atlanta.

On the southwest side of downtown, near the I-20/I-85/I-75 junction, the powerhouse **Atlanta Braves** (800/326-4000 or 404/249-6400) play at Turner Field, a.k.a. "The Ted."

Across the wide I-75 freeway, a half mile east of downtown, the **Martin Luther King Jr. National Historic Site** (daily; free; 450 Auburn Ave.; 404/331-6922) sits at the heart of the predominantly black "Sweet Auburn" neighborhood. The four-block area holds many important landmarks in the life of Dr. King: his birthplace (501 Auburn Ave.); the recently renovated Ebenezer Baptist Church (407 Auburn Ave.), where he, his father, and his grandfather all served as pastor; and his tomb, emblazoned with the words "Free at Last, Free at Last," sitting on the grounds of The King Center for Non-Violent Social Change (449 Auburn Ave.).

Atlanta's main museum district is six miles north of downtown, in the upscale Buckhead neighborhood, where the **Atlanta History Center** (daily; $16.50; 130 W. Paces Ferry Rd.; 404/814-4000) is a don't-miss introduction to the city, the state, and the South in general.

Practicalities

Atlanta's airport, Hartsfield-Jackson Atlanta International Airport, one of the busiest in the country, is a dozen miles south of downtown Atlanta, at the junction of the I-85 and I-285 freeways. The usual rental cars, taxis, and shuttle vans are supplemented by the extensive network of Metro Atlanta Rapid Transit Authority (MARTA) trains. The I-75/I-85 freeways cut through the center of Atlanta, while the I-20 freeway skirts its southern edge. Sliced by freeways and spreading Los Angeles—like in a low-level ooze of minimalls, housing tracts, and traffic jams, Atlanta's outlying areas are impossible to make sense of, but the downtown area is compact and manageable. Note also that seemingly every other thoroughfare includes the word "Peachtree" in its name, so check twice before getting completely lost.

Midtown Atlanta has a couple of nice places to stay, including the **Hotel Indigo** ($126 and up; 683 Peachtree St. NE; 404/874-9200), a historic 1920s building upgraded into boutique status by the InterContinental chain, in a handy location across from the landmark Fox Theatre. The adjacent all-suite **Georgian Terrace** ($120 and up; 659 Peachtree St. NE; 404/897-1991) is characterful and spacious.

(continued on next page)

(continued)

East of the Midtown neighborhood, about two miles northeast of downtown, the lively Virginia-Highland district has Atlanta's best range of restaurants, cafés, and bars. There are also some older Atlanta landmarks, like **Mary Mac's Tea Room** (224 Ponce de Leon Ave.; 404/876-1800), serving traditional Southern food (fried chicken, peach cobbler, and sweet iced tea) since 1945. The same street also holds the **Majestic Diner** (1031 Ponce de Leon Ave.; 404/875-0276), a large, lively (and just a little bit seedy) 1940s-style café, open 24 hours for great waffles, burgers, and endless cups of java.

One more north-of-downtown Atlanta landmark deserves mention: **The Varsity** (61 North Ave.; 404/881-1706), near Georgia Tech alongside I-75, is the world's largest drive-in, serving up very good junk food: chili dogs, onion rings, and more Coca-Cola than anywhere else on this earth. Farther north, within a mile of each other off I-85, are two more Atlanta landmarks: Carnivores and blues fans flock to **Fat Matt's Rib Shack** (1811 Piedmont Ave. NE; 404/607-1622), while **The Colonnade Restaurant** (1879 Cheshire Bridge Rd. NE; 404/874-5642) has been serving Southern food (baked ham, fried chicken, and more) since 1962 (at the current location, at least—the original location opened in 1927!).

After dark, enjoy an alfresco movie at the **Starlight Six** ($7, $1 for children under 10; cash only; 2000 Moreland Ave. SE; 404/627-5786), four miles southeast of downtown. Double features are shown every night, rain or shine, starting around 9 PM.

The usual barrage of tourist information can be had from the **Atlanta Convention and Visitors Bureau** (233 Peachtree St. NE; 800/285-2682 or 404/521-6600).

The Varsity

Dillard House restaurant, famous for its all-you-can-eat country cooking and its glass-walled patio, where diners can enjoy plates of classic country ham, fried chicken, pan-fried trout, vegetables, cornbread, and assorted relishes and desserts. The legendary institution may today impress you as more institution than legend—bus tours dominate the clientele—but you never leave hungry. Rooms (round $60 and up) are around back in low-slung lodges scattered near a swimming pool, tennis courts, and a petting zoo.

In addition to the rambling inn, the family oligarchy operates a row of roadside businesses off US-441, selling collectible and keepsake souvenirs.

Black Rock Mountain State Park

At the wind-worn summit of 3,640-foot Black Rock Mountain, a flagstone terrace looks out over a grand Appalachian panorama: If there's no fog, you can see clear to the South Carolina Piedmont 80 miles away and as far as the Great Smokies to the north. The highest state park in Georgia, **Black Rock Mountain State Park** offers hiking trails and accommodations in addition to the splendid vistas. Set off in a ring at the top of the mountain, 10 spacious cottages are removed from lowland civilization—no phones, no TVs, just fireplaces and porch rockers. The cottages cost around $125 and up a night, sleep up to 10 people, and are available for rent year-round—a nice snowy winter retreat. There's also a pair of campgrounds. The park is three miles north of Clayton, well signed to the west of US-441. For information, or for reservations for the cabins or the campgrounds, contact the **visitors center** (706/746-2141 or 800/864-7275) near the summit.

Mountain City: Foxfire Museum

The monolith of Black Rock Mountain imposes an early twilight on **Mountain City** (pop. 1,088), the community that stretches along US-441. Tucked away on the west side of US-441 just south of the turnoff to Black Mountain State Park, the modest **Foxfire Museum** (Mon.–Sat.; $6; 706/746-5828) is part of a radical cultural and educational movement that began here in the mid-1960s when local schoolteacher Eliot Wigginton, frustrated in attempts to motivate his uninspired high-school students, assigned them the task of interviewing their elders about how things were in "the old days." The students, inspired with the newly discovered richness of their Appalachian heritage, assembled the written interviews into a magazine, which they named *Foxfire* after a luminescent local fungus.

The magazine expanded to a series of *Foxfire* books, and more than eight million copies have been sold worldwide. The program's twofold success—educational innovation and folk-life preservation—further broadened as the then-emerging back-to-the-land movement seized upon these books as vital

The rocky crest of Black Rock Mountain marks the eastern Continental Divide—from here waters part to follow a path to either the Atlantic Ocean or the Gulf of Mexico.

The hikers' Appalachian Trail crosses the Georgia/ North Carolina border roughly 10 miles west of Dillard, then veers southeast, coming to a finale at the 3,782-foot summit of **Springer Mountain,** where a photogenic sign marks the end (or the beginning, since most of the 200 or so annual through-hikers travel south to north) of the 2,175-mile trail.

how-to manuals for subsistence farming and generally living off the grid. The Foxfire organization still runs classes and summer programs on a 110-acre campus in the hills above town.

Clayton: *Deliverance*

Slicing through the Appalachian wilderness along the Georgia/South Carolina border, the Chattooga River rates among the nation's top 10 white-water river adventures, attracting some 100,000 visitors a year for rafting, canoeing, kayaking, tubing, swimming, fishing, and riverside hiking. The Wild and Scenic–designated river was seen in the movie *Deliverance,* based on the book by Georgia poet and novelist James Dickey; ever since the movie was released, authorities have been pulling bodies out of the river—not toothless mountaineers but overconfident river-runners who underestimate the white water's power.

The largest town in the area, the down-home mountain community of **Clayton** (pop. 2,047) is a popular base for excursions into the wild forest and Chattooga River areas. US-441 has grown into an exurban morass of Wal-Mart sprawl, but Main Street, a three-block length of wooden storefronts on a sunny rise just west of US-411, still looks like you could hitch a horse at the curb without attracting much attention.

Tallulah Falls and Gorge

Balanced precariously over the precipitous gorge that once held the thundering cascades of the Tallulah River, tiny **Tallulah Falls** (pop. 168) has an illustrious history. As word of the natural wonder spread, crowds were drawn to the breathtaking sight, and by the turn of the 20th century Tallulah Falls was a fashionable resort, with several elite hotels and boardinghouses catering to lowland sightseers. Fortunes changed when the falls were harnessed for hydro-electricity, but recent compromises have brought the falls back to occasional life. On weekends, usually in spring and fall, the waters are again released and can be admired from **Tallulah Gorge State Park** (706/754-7981), a very pleasant park with a local history museum, camping, showers, hiking trails, and a very cool suspension bridge over the river and gorge.

Stretching downstream along the six cascades of Tallulah Falls, the dramatic sheer walls of Tallulah Gorge have both haunted and attracted people for centuries. The wary Cherokee heeded legends that warriors who ventured in never returned, and many a curious settler had a waterfall or pool named in his honor—posthumously, after an untimely slip.

Tallulah Gorge is best seen via staircase-trails leading from the state park, or from the mile-long scenic route (old US-441), which loops off east of the modern highway. Drivers can pull over at numerous parking areas and take one of several rough trails along the gorge's rim, though the best views are from the historic **Tallulah Point Overlook** (daily 9 AM–6 PM; free), a privately owned concession stand midway along the loop.

Clarkesville

The charming little town of **Clarkesville** (pop. 1,733) retains a sophistication dating back to its founding over 150 years ago by lowland Carolina and coastal Georgian plantation families seeking refuge from the oppressive summer

When you take in the sight of **Tallulah Gorge,** imagine walking a tightrope suspended 1,200 feet above the ground across its breadth. "Professor Leon" managed it (despite a stumble) in 1886, and in 1970, the flying Karl Wallenda replicated the feat, walking across on a wire suspended from the Tallulah Point Overlook, where postcards and photos document his effort.

In the mountains northwest of Clarkesville, 15 miles along Hwy-17 and Hwy-75, the tiny town of **Helen** (pop. 510) turned itself into a tourist draw in 1969 by remodeling all the buildings in mock-Bavarian decor and repaving the streets in cobblestones.

downtown Helen

heat. Best known as the home of the renowned country resort Glen-Ella Springs Inn, Clarkesville sits at the lower slope of a river valley that stretches northwest to the faux-Bavarian town of Helen and is surrounded by countryside perfect for a leisurely drive or bike tour past an old mill here, a covered bridge there, and old-time country stores in wooden cabins.

Clarkesville tucks urbane delights into its rustic country setting, with over 40 buildings, most of them former summer homes, listed on the National Register of Historic Places. Downtown, three blocks of wooden storefronts, centering on a shaded plaza where numerous festivals take place, hold cafés and crafts shops.

Hundred-year-old **Glen-Ella Springs Inn** ($150 and up; 877/456-7527 or 706/754-7295), eight miles or so north of Clarkesville on Bear Gap Road off US-441, is northern Georgia's premier country inn. Set on 17 lush acres, the historic two-story lodge holds 16 guest rooms, each of which opens to a porch with rocking chairs.

Athens

If you've got the time and inclination, one of Georgia's most enjoyable destinations is just a slight veer to the east off our route: Athens, the coolest college town in the South. Famed for its lively music scene, which gave the world the

Cornelia, the southernmost Appalachian town, is known for its Big Red Apple monument on Hwy-23 downtown, which pays homage to the apples and apple farmers of the county, and if you're here in fall you can sample them fresh from the tree.

alternative-rock bands B-52s and R.E.M., Athens is the home of the University of Georgia, whose Greek Revival campus sits at the center of town, bordered on the north by a half dozen blocks of cafés, bars, and book and record stores. Besides the dozens of super-sized Bulldogs (the UGA mascot) around town, Athens also holds a classic road trip destination: **"The Tree That Owns Itself,"** a second-generation mighty oak tree standing on a small circle of land at the corner of Finley and Dearing Streets west of campus, whose legal autonomy earned it a place in *Ripley's Believe or Not!*

The main music venue is the **40 Watt Club** (285 W. Washington St.; 706/549-7871), where R.E.M. played their second gig. Good, cheap food is available on the east side of town at **Weaver D's Soul Food BBQ** (1016 E. Broad St.; 706/353-7797), whose enigmatic slogan "Automatic for the People" was enshrined as an R.E.M. album title. R.E.M.'s Michael Stipe owns the building in which you can find the gourmet meat-free restaurant **The Grit** (199 Prince Ave.; 706/543-6592). The best restaurant in Athens, and one of the top 10 in the USA according to *Food & Wine Magazine,* is the **Five & Ten** (1653 S. Lumpkin St.; 706/546-7300), off

Milledge Street two miles southwest of down-town. The Five & Ten is open for dinner nightly and Sunday brunch, serving a range of Southern favorites enlivened by inventive, international touches. (Fried catfish and grits with lemon and arugula, anyone?)

On to Atlanta: Stone Mountain

Midway between Athens and Atlanta, just south of I-85, the top-class Gwinnett Braves play at Coolray Field (678/277-0340).

From the foothills of northern Georgia, it's only an hour by freeway southwest to Atlanta, the cultural and commercial center of the New South, and a fascinating (and fun) place to explore. Unfortunately, Atlanta is surrounded by miles and miles of mega-freeway sub-prime-mortgage sprawl, so you'll have to endure some of the country's craziest driving to get there.

From Athens, Hwy-316 merges into I-85 for the quickest route there, but for a more interesting route follow old US-78 southeast, approaching Atlanta by way of **Stone Mountain,** 16 miles east of downtown. A Confederate Mt. Rushmore and historic KKK rallying point, Stone Mountain (daily; $10 per car; 770/498-5690 or 800/401-2407) consists of the 20-times-larger-than-life figures of Robert E. Lee, "Stonewall" Jackson, and Jefferson Davis carved into an 800-foot-high hump of granite. A 45-minute patriotic laser-and-fireworks extravaganza is shown nightly in summer (May–late Aug.). At the base of Stone Mountain are 3,200 acres of the tackier tourist traps going (riverboat cruises, a scenic railroad, a reconstructed antebellum plantation, a cable car Skylift to the summit, and a treetop Sky Hike rope course and rock-climbing complex—all of which charge separate fees of around $9 each, or $28 for an unlimited day pass. Stone Mountain also holds a number of restaurants and hotels, plus Atlanta's best campground.

"The Tree That Owns Itself"

Atlantic Coast

Starting at the Statue of Liberty and winding up at free-wheeling Key West, these almost 2,000 miles of roadway run within earshot—if not sight— of the Atlantic Ocean.

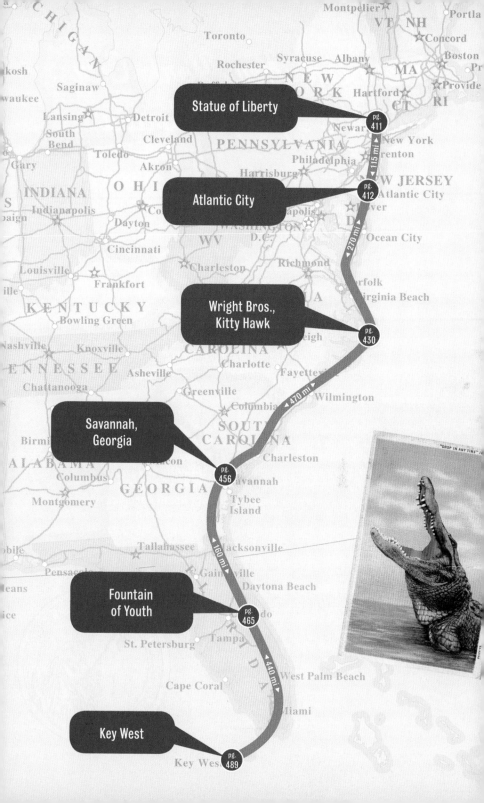

Statue of Liberty — pg. 411

115 mi

Atlantic City — pg. 412

270 mi

Wright Bros., Kitty Hawk — pg. 430

470 mi

Savannah, Georgia — pg. 456

160 mi

Fountain of Youth — pg. 465

440 mi

Key West — pg. 489

"DROP IN ANY TIME"

Between New York City and the Tip of Florida

If your impressions of the East Coast come from driving along the I-95 corridor through nearly nonstop urban and industrial sprawl, following our Atlantic Coast route will open your eyes to a whole other world. Alternating between wildly differing beach resort areas and lengthy stretches of pristine coastal wilderness, the route runs along almost 2,000 miles of two-lane country roads, within earshot, if not sight, of the Atlantic Ocean almost the entire way. In place of the grimy concrete and soulless netherworld of the Interstate, this route passes through innumerable quirky seaside towns and timeless old fishing villages, interspersed with huge swaths of beaches, wetlands, and woodlands that have hardly changed since the first explorers laid eyes on them four centuries ago.

Starting in the north at that all-American icon, the **Statue of Liberty,** and winding up in the south at free-wheeling **Key West,** this route truly offers something for everyone. Those searching for photogenic lighthouses or beachcombing solitude will love the undeveloped and usually deserted strands that stretch for miles along the low-lying islands that make up most of the coast, much of which, as at **Assateague Island** or **Cape Hatteras,** has been protected as national seashore parks. In contrast, the many beach resorts that dot the in-between areas vary from the grand Victorian charms of Cape May to the funky old Coney Island–style attractions of **Ocean City, Maryland,** and **Myrtle Beach, South Carolina,** with their boardwalks full of roller coasters, wax museums, and saltwater taffy stands. And let's not forget the glitzy casino resorts of **Atlantic City.**

Alongside the contemporary attractions are many evocative historic sites, including such unique places as **Roanoke Island, North Carolina,** where the first English-speaking colony in North America vanished without a trace in 1587. Lying south of the Mason-Dixon Line for almost all of its length, the route also visits many important Civil War sites, including **Fort Sumter,** where the first shots were fired, and the vital naval battlegrounds at **Hampton Roads** at the mouth of Chesapeake Bay. Midway along, we also pass one of the key sites of modern history: the windy sand dunes at **Kitty Hawk** where the Wright Brothers first proved that humans could fly.

Though this Atlantic Coast route will bring you to many well-known sights, its real attraction is the traveling, stopping off for fried chicken or barbecue at one of the hundreds of roadside stands, watching the shrimp boats pull into a sleepy dock and unload their day's catch, or simply chatting with locals at the general store or post office in a town that may not even be on the map.

NEW JERSEY

Being so close to New York and Philadelphia, it's not surprising that New Jersey has among the busiest and most densely developed stretches of coastline in the country. It *is* surprising, however, that beyond the boardwalk amusements and flashy gambling casinos of **Atlantic City,** the New Jersey shore offers a whole lot more. As with most of the East Coast, the "shoreline" is actually a series of barrier islands separated from the mainland by wildlife-rich estuaries; these provide fishing and bird-watching opportunities, as well as a break from the ceaseless commercial and residential development along the ocean beaches. Bustling in summer, these beachfront communities—starting with **Margate** near Atlantic City, and running south through vibrant **Wildwood** before winding up at the dainty Victorian-era beach resort of **Cape May**—offer something for everyone, all within a 150-mile stretch of shoreline.

The Statue of Liberty

Raising her lamp beside New York City's immense harbor, the **Statue of Liberty** is one of the most vivid emblems of America. Despite the fact she is French, given to the American people to celebrate the 100th anniversary of the Declaration of Independence, the statue has come to symbolize the Land of the Free and the Home of the Brave. Its spirit has long been evoked by the poem Emma Lazarus wrote in 1883 to help raise funds for installing the Statue of Liberty. Called "The New Colossus," the poem ends with these famous words:

Inspired by the end of slavery following the Civil War, the Statue of Liberty took nearly 20 years to complete. Lady Liberty was sculpted in France, then the 300-plus pieces were put in crates and shipped across the ocean. The statue is just over 150 feet tall, but including her 150-foot stone pedestal, it was the tallest building in New York when dedicated in 1886.

"Keep ancient lands, your storied pomp!" cries she
With silent lips. "Give me your tired, your poor,
Your huddled masses yearning to breathe free,
The wretched refuse of your teeming shore.
Send these, the homeless, tempest-tost to me,
I lift my lamp beside the golden door!"

The Statue of Liberty sits on a 12-acre island and can be visited by ferry only (daily; $13; 877/LADY-TIX). It's about a mile from Manhattan, but much easier to reach from **Liberty State Park** in Jersey City, off New Jersey Turnpike exit 14B. So long as you start your trip before 2 PM, both ferry routes also visit Ellis Island, where some 12 million immigrants entered the United States. There is no admission fee for the Statue of Liberty or Ellis Island, but if you want to climb up onto Lady Liberty's pedestal you need a free, time-stamped Monument Pass, which you can get when you buy your ferry tickets.

All pass-holders can explore the base of the Statue of Liberty and gaze up inside her hollow shell, but access up into the very small viewing area in the crown on her head requires special tickets ($3 extra) and a climb up more than 350 steps. Her torch has been off-limits since 1916. In the security-conscious environment, the welcoming sentiments expressed in the Lazarus poem can seem quite sharply ironic, and sadly, the experience of visiting the statue can end up having more to do with restrictions and limitations than it does with grand concepts like "Liberty."

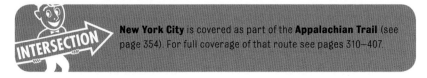

New York City is covered as part of the **Appalachian Trail** (see page 354). For full coverage of that route see pages 310–407.

The New Jersey Shore

The northernmost stretches of the New Jersey shore are not exactly appealing, and visitors bound for the beaches and vacation spots farther south turn a blind eye to the industrial blight. From **Perth Amboy** (Vaseline) to **Asbury Park** (Bruce Springsteen), the region has given the world many distinctive products, and there are a couple of intriguing Victorian-era resorts like **Spring Lake** and **Avon-by-the-Sea,** but to be honest, the attractions increase the farther south you go.

The middle stretch of the Jersey shore is actually the quietest, with the million-acre **Pinelands National Preserve** (daily; free; 609/894-7300) covering the inland area with forest and wetlands, and the coastal **Long Beach Island** dotted with sleepy little fishing and retirement communities. The biggest sight hereabouts is at the northern tip of the island: **Barnegat Lighthouse** (daily; free; 609/494-2016), "Old Barney," whose image appears on personalized New Jersey license plates.

Atlantic City

Midway along the Jersey Shore, the world-famous beach resort of **Atlantic City** (pop. 39,558) has ridden the ups and downs of history. Home of the world's oldest beachfront boardwalk and the first pleasure pier, Atlantic City also spawned the picture postcard and the Miss America beauty contest. Perhaps most significant of all, the street names for Monopoly were taken from Atlantic City, although the city's layout bears little resemblance to the board game (and there's no "Get Out of Jail Free" card, either).

sunset on the beach, Atlantic City

Atlantic City reached its peak at the turn of the 20th century, when thousands of city-dwellers flocked here from New York and Philadelphia each weekend. Later on, as automobiles and airplanes brought better beaches and more exotic locales within reach, Atlantic City went into a half century of decline until **gambling** was legalized in the 1970s and millions of dollars flowed into the local economy from speculating real-estate developers like Donald Trump, whose name is emblazoned on a number of towering resort hotels. These days, the Boardwalk of Atlantic City has been transformed from a derelict relic into a glitzy gambling resort, attracting some 30 million annual visitors and millions of dollars daily to its casinos. It's no Las Vegas, and the population is still comparatively poor and shrinking, but the clattering of slot machines and the buzz of the craps tables continues 24 hours a day year-round.

> To enjoy a day on the sands at many of New Jersey's beaches, you need to buy (and wear) a beach badge, which costs around $2 a day and is available at local tourist offices, shops, and fast-food stands.

The **Boardwalk,** backed by a wall of 25-story casino/hotels, is still the main focus of Atlantic City, running along the beach for over two miles. Few of the remaining pleasure piers offer much of interest, and only the

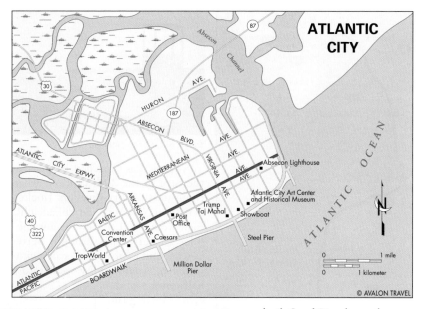

rebuilt **Steel Pier,** located opposite Trump's Taj Mahal, holds the traditional seaside rides and arcade games, plus a sometimes-lively branch of the House of Blues nightclub chain.

Besides constituting Atlantic City's main attractions, the casinos hold most of the places to eat, apart from the dozens of fast-food stands along the Boardwalk. That said, a couple of old favorites stand out from the seedy crowd of ramshackle businesses that fill the nearby

Boardwalk at Atlantic City

streets. One is the birthplace of the "submarine" sandwich, the chrome **White House Sub Shop** (2301 Arctic Ave.; 609/345-1564), open until midnight every day. A block away, but at the other end of the aesthetic and budgetary spectrum, is **Dock's Oyster House** (2405 Atlantic Ave.; 609/345-0092), a white-linen, dinner-only restaurant that's been serving great seafood since 1897. Along with a number of national chains, the casinos also control accommodation options—expect to pay upwards of $100 a night, though off-peak bargains can be found.

Margate: Lucy the Elephant

Immediately south of Atlantic City, tidy **Margate** (pop. 8524) fans out along the shore, its solidly suburban streets lined by grand houses. Margate utterly

Lucy the Elephant

lacks the reckless seaside qualities of its larger neighbor but does include one classic remnant of the Jersey shore's glory days: **Lucy the Elephant** (daily in summer, limited hours rest of the year; $7; 9200 Atlantic Ave.; 609/823-6473). The six-story wood-and-tin pachyderm, a curiosity built by a Philadelphia real-estate speculator in the 1880s to draw customers to his newly laid-out community, looms over the beach. The landmark architectural folly was used around the turn of the 20th century as a tavern and now holds a small museum of local history. Visitors walk through the museum on the way up to an observation deck, which is disguised as a canopied seat on Lucy's back.

Saved from demolition and restored by community efforts in the 1970s, Lucy is ever in need of repair, kept alive by tour monies, donations, and sales of Lucy souvenirs in the small gift shop.

Ocean Drive: Ocean City and Stone Harbor

A series of local roads collectively known as **Ocean Drive** runs along the south Jersey coast, passing through a number of family-oriented beach resorts, starting at Ocean City, "The Greatest Family Resort for a Vacation, or a Lifetime," 10 miles south of Atlantic City. **Ocean City** (pop. 14,699) was founded as a religious retreat in the late 1870s and hasn't strayed far from its roots: Every summer morning (at 9:20 AM, on the dot), life on the Boardwalk promenade comes to a standstill as "The Star-Spangled Banner" blares out from loudspeakers and the American flag is raised at the beachfront amusement park. Located at 6th Street, and known as **Gillian's Wonderland Pier** (daily in summer, weekends only spring and fall; free admission, fee per ride; 609/399-7082), this old-time funfair has over 30 rides, including a giant Ferris wheel and a 1920s carousel. A block south, you can cool off on a hot summer's day at **Gillian's Island** water park.

Vacation homes, marinas, miniature golf courses, and a pair of toll bridges mark Ocean Drive for the next 20 miles. At **Stone Harbor,** five miles north of Wildwood, the **Wetlands Institute** (daily in summer, Tues.–Sat. rest of year; $8; 1075 Stone Harbor Blvd.; 609/368-1211) is one of the best places to experience the abundant natural life of the New Jersey shore. An observation tower looking over 6,000 acres of saltwater marshland provides excellent bird-watching opportunities, and there's also a museum with a touch-tank and aquarium.

Wildwood

On the Jersey Shore, fun in the sun reaches a peak at raucous **Wildwood,** a trio of interconnected towns housing dozens of nightclubs and New Jersey's biggest beachfront amusement parks. The largest of all, **Mariners Landing** on the pier at Schellenger Avenue, has 35 rides including the largest Ferris wheel on the East Coast. At 25th Street is **Morey's Pier,** which has a miniature golf course that takes you through the history of the New Jersey shore. A little farther south is **Morey's Adventure Pier,** which is home to the Great White, the only wooden roller coaster in the U.S. to be built on a pier. All three of these are owned by the Morey family, prime movers behind Wildwood's retro-rediscovery, and an all-ride, all-pier pass (around $60; 609/522-3900) is available for a full day's fun. Batting cages, go-karts, and some of the wilder rides are not included in the pass price.

Away from the sands in the low-key downtown district, Wildwood's local history **museum** (free; 3907 Pacific Ave.; 609/523-0277) is worth a look for its one unique feature: the **National Marbles Hall of Fame,** featuring thousands of glass balls and more marble-shooting paraphernalia than you've ever seen. The museum, which hosts the National Marbles Championship every June, also has a fascinating and informative display of postcards documenting the region's recent past.

For many visitors, the best reason to spend time in Wildwood is that the area boasts an extensive collection of 1950s roadside architecture—mainly motel after motel, all sporting exuberant Las Vegas–style neon signs. Many of these motels are closed in the November–May off-season, but in the warmer months you can step back in the past by staying the night in one of these classic "Doo Wop" motels—like the **Mango Motel** (209 E. Spicer Ave.; 609/522-2067) or the renovated **Lollipop Motel** (2301 Atlantic Ave.; 609/729-2800).

Chili dog lovers will want to chow down at **Maui's Dog House** (806 New Jersey Ave.; 609/846-0444), at the north end of town, while other retro-minded visitors will want to stop for a meal at the chrome-and-glass **Pink Cadillac Diner** (3801 Atlantic Ave.; 609/522-8288), a block south of the main pier.

For more details on places to stay and things to do—like October's massive and rowdy **Thunder on the Beach** monster truck rally—contact the **Wildwood visitors center** (3601 Boardwalk; 800/992-9732).

Cape May–Lewes Ferry

Running between the tip of the New Jersey shore and the heart of the Delaware coast, the Cape May–Lewes Ferry carries cars and passengers on a relaxing ride across the mouth of Delaware Bay. The trip ranges in cost depending upon day and season (summer weekends being most expensive), from about $30 to $45 each way for a car and one passenger, plus fees for each additional passenger. Schedules change seasonally, with boats leaving about every two hours in summer and every three hours in winter. Crossings take about 90 minutes, and if the seas are calm you can often see porpoises playing in the swells.

the *Cape May,* one of the five boats in the fleet

For up-to-date times and other information, call 800/643-3779. Reservations ($5 extra) are a very good idea at peak travel times and should be made at least one day in advance.

Cape May

A world away from the carnival atmosphere of the Wildwoods, **Cape May,** the oldest and most serene of the New Jersey beach towns, sits at the southern tip of the state. First settled in the early 1600s, Cape May's glory years ran from the 1850s to the 1890s as an upper-crust summer resort, when it rivaled Newport, Rhode Island, as the destination of choice for the power brokers of Philadelphia and New York City.

A few modern motels and miniature golf courses spread along Cape May's broad beaches, while the compact downtown district retains all its overwrought Victorian splendor. Century-old cottages now house cafés, boutiques, and art galleries, and it seems as if every other building has been converted into a quaint B&B. The town's ornate gingerbread mansions were constructed in the aftermath of a disastrous 1878 fire; among the better examples is the elaborate **Emlen Physick House** (1048 Washington St.), eight blocks north of downtown, designed by noted Philadelphia architect Frank Furness. It now houses the nonprofit, preservation-oriented **Mid-Atlantic Center for the Arts** and is open as a museum of late Victorian life (daily in summer, weekends only in winter; $8; 609/884-5404).

Pick up walking-tour maps of some of the town's 600 listed historic buildings and do a taste-test of Cape May's many architecturally magnificent, mostly Victorian-era bed-and-breakfasts. These include the mansard-roofed **Queen Victoria** ($115 and up; 102 Ocean St.; 609/884-8702),and the **Mainstay Inn** ($175 and up; 635 Columbia Ave.; 609/884-8690), which has a spacious veranda opening onto gorgeous gardens. Cape May's oldest and most atmospheric place to stay is the Southern gothic **Chalfonte Hotel** ($89–189; 301 Howard St.; 609/884-8409). What the Chalfonte lacks in TVs and telephones it more than makes up for in hospitality: a bank of front-porch rocking chairs, full breakfasts, and huge, down-home dinners are all included in the rates.

Places to eat, including a dozen or so bakeries, cafés, restaurants, and bars, can be found along the pedestrian-friendly few blocks of Washington Street at the center of town, while the seafood restaurants, naturally enough, are near the marina and ferry terminal on the north edge of town, off US-9. One more great option for a hearty all-American breakfast or a Greek-inflected lunch or dinner: **George's Place,** right downtown on the water (cash only; 301 Beach Ave.; 609/884-6088), is perhaps the most popular place in whole Garden State, with lines snaking out the door.

DELAWARE

Across Delaware Bay from Cape May, the Delaware shore is considerably quieter and more peaceful than New Jersey's. Both shores, originally settled by Scandinavian whalers who established port colonies here in the early 1600s, share a common history. But because the Delaware shore is that much

farther from the urban centers, it has been spared the over-development of much of the rest of the coast. Nevertheless, Delaware's statewide population doubles in summer as visitors from Baltimore and Washington, D.C., descend upon its coastal resorts, from historic **Lewes** to lively **Rehoboth Beach** to the untouched sands of **Delaware Seashore State Park,** stretching south to the Maryland border.

Lewes and Cape Henlopen

Sitting at the southern lip of Delaware Bay, **Lewes** is a vacation and sportfishing center that traces its roots back to 1631, when it was settled by the Dutch West India Company as a whaling port. Though this colony lasted only two years, Lewes calls itself the "First Town in the First State," commemorating its history in the false-gabled brick **Zwannendael Museum** at the center of town (closed Mon.; free; 102 Kings Hwy.; 302/645-1148). Lewes also harbors huge sand dunes, a fine stretch of beach, and a **campground** with showers in 3,000-acre **Cape Henlopen State Park** (302/645-8983), east of town at the mouth of Delaware Bay. Expect relative peace and quiet here, since many visitors, arriving off the Cape May ferry, simply rush through Lewes to the beach resorts farther south.

Just north of US-9, look out for **Cafe Azafran** (109 W. Market St.; 302/644-4446), a very welcoming, wholesome, and flavorful trans-European

Zwannendael Museum

café that's open for breakfast, lunch, and dinner, serving good coffee, cold beer, and fine wines along with French cheese, Spanish Serrano ham, Greek olives, and a whole range of regional delicacies.

Rehoboth Beach

Fronting the open Atlantic, **Rehoboth Beach** was founded in the 1870s when church groups bought beachfront land, established the town, and extended a railroad line south from Lewes. The highway frontage along Hwy-1 is over-full of franchise food and factory outlet malls, but the heart of town along Rehoboth Avenue is the place to go. With its summer-only but very lively Sputnik-era **Funland Amusement Park** (302/227-1921, open May–Sept., hours vary), where the attractions include bumper cars, a nighttime haunted house, and a tidy boardwalk running along the broad beach, Rehoboth has somehow retained a small-town feel despite the many thousands of bureaucrats and power brokers who descend upon the place during the summer, escaping the sweltering heat of Washington, D.C.

The D.C. connection helps explain the town's profusion of very good (and some very expensive) restaurants. Lining the main drag are casual, kid-friendly places like **Dogfish Head** (320 Rehoboth Ave.; 302/226-2739), which has great food and killer beers in Delaware's oldest microbrewery. More grown-up palates will be drawn to the gourmet places a

Ever wonder what happens to all those pumpkins that don't get bought by Halloween? In Delaware, they end up as fodder for a unique competition, the **Punkin' Chunkin',** in which the hapless gourds get launched hundreds, even thousands of feet through the air by a variety of mechanical devices. Thousands turn out for the event, which is usually held on a farm at Coverdale Crossroads, 30 miles west of Lewes, on the first weekend in November ($9, intersection of Seashore Hwy. and Chaplains Chapel Rd.).

block south, where the outrageously kitsch **La La Land** (22 Wilmington Ave.; 302/227-3887) fills a pair of old beach houses alongside the eclectic, Mediterranean-inspired and unfailingly yummy **Espuma** (28 Wilmington Ave.; 302/227-4199). There are also the more mainstream delights of **Thrashers French Fries,** and sundry beer-and-burger stands along the boardwalk.

Places to stay include some quaint old B&Bs and a barrage of highway chain motels, plus local ones like the **Beach View** ($70 and up; 6 Wilmington Ave.; 302/227-2999), on the boardwalk.

Delaware Seashore State Park

South from Rehoboth stretches one of the last long stretches of pristine beach on the whole northern East Coast: **Delaware Seashore State Park** (302/227-3071), which contains six miles of open beach with golden-flecked white sand and 2,825 acres of marshland estuary, thronged in season with migrating birds—and bird-watchers (and campers and anglers, too.) The park's many beaches are all easily accessible from beachfront Hwy-1.

The park has camping and nice new cottages (costing $1,800 a week during prime summer season!) and is book-ended by a pair of densely developed resort towns: **Dewey Beach** in the north draws a younger, collegiate crowd, while **Bethany Beach** in the south attracts more families.

Near Maryland, the 1858 **Fenwick Island Lighthouse,** on the bay side of Hwy-1 just south of Hwy-54, marks the state border. This lighthouse is a local landmark, but the waist-high white marker in front of it may be more significant: Placed in 1751, it marked the boundary between Maryland and Pennsylvania, of which Delaware was then a part. Showing respect to the colonial proprietors, the more than 250-year-old marker has the Calvert family coat of arms on the Maryland (south) side and William Penn's family crest on the other.

MARYLAND

Maryland, the most oddly shaped of the lower 48 states, shares the broad "DelMarVa" peninsula with Delaware and a small piece of Virginia. The inland area along the eastern shore of Chesapeake Bay, with its many inlets and tributary rivers, is filled with dozens of small colonial-era towns and fishing villages, while the Atlantic Coast is completely taken up by two very different beasts: the gloriously kitschy beach resort of **Ocean City** and the untrammeled wilds of **Assateague Island National Seashore.** Heading inland around Assateague, the highway passes by a number of historic small towns, including **Berlin** and captivating **Snow Hill.**

Running west from Ocean City across the Eastern Shore and then across the country to California is the US-50 route (see page 799). This **Loneliest Road** in America is covered on pages 704–799.

OCEAN CITY

© AVALON TRAVEL

Ocean City

About the only place left on the entire East Coast that retains the carnival qualities of classic seaside resorts, **Ocean City** (pop. 7,105, swelling to some 400,000 in summer) has by far the best array of old-time funfair attractions in the Mid-Atlantic (well, south of Wildwood, New Jersey, at least). On and around the main pier at the south end of the island, there are enough merry-go-rounds, Ferris wheels, roller coasters (including The Hurricane, which is illustrated with scenes from Ocean City storms past), mini-golf courses, haunted houses, and bumper cars to divert a small army. A block inland, **Trimper's Amusements,** which has been operated by the same family for five generations, since the 1890s, has two more roller coasters, plus a Tilt-a-Whirl, a 100-year-old Hershell carousel, and a spooky haunted house. Places like Trimper's, and the sundry batting cages, go-kart tracks, and zip lines, are threatened by rising property values (and property taxes) and increasingly close to becoming extinct, so enjoy them while you can. Trimpers's local rival, Jolly Roger, also runs a big water park and another amusement park at the north end of town, along the bay at 30th Street.

From the pier north, Ocean City stretches for over three miles along a broad, clean, white-sand beach. A wide, part-wooden boardwalk lines the sands, packed with arcades full of video games and a few nearly forgotten old amusements like Skee-Ball and Pokerino, not to mention midway contests—the kind where, for $1 a try, you can win stuffed animals and other prizes by shooting baskets or squirting water into clowns' mouths. A ramshackle collection of fortune-tellers, T-shirt stands, and burger-and-beer bars completes the scene, forming a busy gauntlet that is among the nation's liveliest promenades.

On summer weekends, Ocean City becomes Maryland's second-largest city,

To go along with its great beaches, Ocean City has a radio station, the excellent **WOCM 98.1 FM,** playing classic rock 'n' roll and broadcasting details of Ocean City's nightclub scene.

Haunted House at Trimper's Amusements, Ocean City

and most of the fun is simply in getting caught up in the garish human spectacle of it all, but there are a couple of specific things worth searching out. For the price of a bumper car ride, you can enjoy the quirky collections of the **Life-Saving Station Museum** (daily May–Oct., weekends only in winter; $3), at the south end of the boardwalk, where alongside displays of shipwrecks and bathing suits you can compare and contrast bowls full of sand from 100 different beaches around the world. The museum also marks the starting point for the open-air trams ($3) that run north along the boardwalk for over two miles.

Ocean City Practicalities

Much of Ocean City's charm is decidedly lowbrow, but the food is better than you might expect, with numerous places offering plates full of shrimp and pitchers of beer for under $10, and freshly fried chicken or crab cakes available from boardwalk stands. **Thrashers Fries** are available (no ketchup; salt and vinegar only!) from a number of counters along the boardwalk, and you can top them off with a cone or milk shake from **Dumser's Ice Cream,** which runs a trio of stands at the south end of the boardwalk.

Places to stay are also abundant, though many of the huge concrete towers you see are actually condominiums and not available for overnight stays. In fact, of all the dozen or more grand, older hotels, only the **Atlantic Hotel** ($80

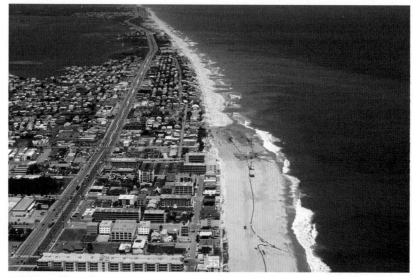
aerial view of Ocean City

and up; 5 Somerset St.; 410/289-9111), on the oceanfront, is still open for business. Modern motels like the **Oceanic** (710 S. Philadelphia St.; 410/289-6494), looking across the inlet to Assateague Island, charge as much as $200 a night for a room that goes for less than $50 off-season.

For help finding lodgings and restaurants, contact the **Ocean City visitors center** (4001 Coastal Hwy.; 410/723-8600 or 800/626-2326), in the Convention Center.

Assateague Island National Seashore

At one time, Assateague Island, the long thin barrier island on which Ocean City sits, stretched in an unbroken line all the way into Virginia. In 1933, a major storm crashed through the sands and created the broad inlet that now divides Ocean City from the near-wilderness of **Assateague Island National Seashore.** One of the few areas of the Atlantic coast protected from commercial development, Assateague Island offers some 37 miles and 10,000 acres of hiking, swimming, camping, canoeing, bicycling, clamming, and bird-watching. Swarms of voracious mosquitoes and a lack of fresh water keep the crowds to a minimum.

To reach the island from Ocean City, follow US-50 west for two miles and turn south on Hwy-611, which loops around Sinexpunt Bay before arriving at the **visitors center** (daily; 410/641-1441). The center has a small aquarium, as well as maps, guides, and up-to-date information about the national seashore.

On the road between Ocean City and Assateague Island, at the junction of US-50 and Hwy-611, the very nice **Wheels of Yesterday** vehicle museum ($5; 410/213-7329) displays more than 30 classic cars and trucks and has a great little gift shop, too.

Berlin and Snow Hill

From Ocean City, the route turns inland around Assateague Island and Chincoteague Bay, following US-50 west for eight miles, then turning south on US-113 through the dark cypress swamps along the Pocomoke River. Just southwest of the US-50/113 junction, the remarkably well-preserved town of **Berlin** offers a look back at a slower-paced era. Redbrick buildings house antiques shops around the 1890s landmark **Atlantic Hotel** ($60 and up; 2 N. Main St.; 410/641-3589), where the rocking chairs along the open-air front porch all but demand that you sit and stay a while. Inside, the very stylish **Drummers Cafe** (open at 11 AM daily) may tempt you to alter your travel plans so you can enjoy the delicious local seafood.

Another 15 miles southwest of Ocean City, detour west from the highway to take a look at the 250-year-old town of **Snow Hill** (pop. 2,409). The **Julia A. Purnell Museum** (Tues.–Sun. Apr.–Oct. only; $2; 208 W. Market St.), housed in an old church, features a range of exhibits tracing Eastern Shore history, including a 200-year-old iron furnace and a one-room schoolhouse. Pick up a walking-tour map of Snow Hill's many significant structures, or if the weather's fine, paddle a canoe or a kayak through the surrounding wild cypress swamps with the **Pocomoke River Canoe Company** (312 N. Washington St.; 410/632-3971), next to the drawbridge.

VIRGINIA

Virginia's Eastern Shore is among the most isolated regions of the country, and its dozens of small towns and villages remain much as they have for centuries. Everything on the Eastern Shore is on a much smaller scale than on the mainland, and the many stands selling fresh corn and tomatoes along the roadside attest to the important role farming plays in the local economy. Although fast-food places, chicken-processing plants, and a couple of modern malls dot US-13, the main route through Virginia's Eastern Shore, the area is still mostly rural and undeveloped, with business loops turning off through the many well-preserved old towns. The numerous historic sites include colonial-era plantations and archaeological remnants of Native American tribes.

The highlight for most visitors is **Chincoteague,** a small commercial and sportfishing port sitting at the entrance to massive Chincoteague National Wildlife Refuge, which faces the Atlantic Coast and offers the only ocean beaches in this part of the state. South of Chincoteague, US-13 runs down the center of the narrow Eastern Shore peninsula, giving access to the Chesapeake Bay waterfront at **Accomac,** then passing through numerous small towns like **Onancock** and **Eastville,** neither of which has changed much since Revolutionary times. Crossing the mouth of the Chesapeake Bay via a 23-mile-long bridge and tunnel brings you to maritime **Norfolk** and the state's main Atlantic resort, **Virginia Beach,** before the route turns inland and south into North Carolina.

Chincoteague

The drive into **Chincoteague** (pop. 4,317; pronounced "SCHINK-a-teeg"), a low-key fishing village, takes you across miles of glowing gold and blue marshlands through a gauntlet of quirky billboards advertising local motels, restaurants, and sportfishing charters. This mix of natural beauty and tacky tourism aptly reflects the character of the town, which is totally dependent upon summertime visitors but seems to wish that we'd all just leave and let the locals go fishing.

A small bridge along Hwy-175, which runs 10 miles east from US-13, drops you at the heart of town, where casual seafood restaurants line the small wharves wild ponies at Chincoteague National Wildlife Refuge

that stretch along the bay. For breakfast, head south of town, where the popular **Mr. Baldy's Family Restaurant** (3441 Ridge Rd.; 757/336-1198) serves up hearty meals across from the "pony swim" landing at Black Point. Near here, at the end of Beebe Street just outside the refuge boundary, you can pitch a tent or park an RV at the very pleasant, privately owned **Tom's Cove Campground** (757/336-6498).

Among the many places to stay are several nice B&Bs and a handful of standard motels like the friendly and central **Birchwood** ($65 and up; 3650 N. Main St.; 757/336-6133).

Chincoteague National Wildlife Refuge

Spreading east of town, the **Chincoteague National Wildlife Refuge** is one of the largest nature preserves along the Atlantic flyway, attracting hundreds of species of birds, including egrets, herons, geese, swans, and snow geese, not to mention thousands and thousands of migrating ducks. A continuation of the Assateague Island National Seashore across the Maryland border, the refuge contains thousands of acres of marshland, excellent beaches, and a number of hiking and cycling trails. The refuge **visitors center** (daily; 757/336-6577) has detailed information on park activities as well as special exhibits on Chincoteague's famous wild ponies, which can usually be seen from the Woodland Trail that loops south from Beach Road.

In summer, stands selling fresh fruit and vegetables—particularly sweet corn and tomatoes— dot roadsides all over the Eastern Shore.

The children's story *Misty of Chincoteague* is set in the area and tells how wild ponies—whose ancestors were sent here by English settlers in the late 1600s—are rounded up from the wildlife refuge on Assateague Island for a forced swim across to Chincoteague. The annual roundup, swim, and auction benefits local firefighters and attracts thousands of spectators. The swim takes place the last Wednesday in July, and the auction follows the next day.

Accomac

One of the most photogenic spots on the Eastern Shore, **Accomac** (pop. 547) is centered on an ancient-looking redbrick courthouse, flanked by a series of wooden sheds converted into professional offices. The old library next door dates from the 1780s and was used for years as a debtors' prison; the library, courthouse, and surrounding buildings together make for a great leg-stretch spot, midway along the Eastern Shore. By way of contrast, Accomac is also home to another Eastern Shore landmark: the huge Perdue Chicken processing plant, right along US-13, which produces and packs more than 12 million birds every year.

Onancock and Tangier Island

The picturesque harbor town of **Onancock** (pop. 1,525; pronounced "o-NAN-cock"), on the Chesapeake Bay two miles west of US-13 via Hwy-179, is one of the nicest towns on the Eastern Shore. A short walking tour of over a dozen historical homes and churches begins at perhaps the finest mansion on the Eastern Shore, the **Ker Place** (Tues.–Sat. 11 AM–4 PM; $8; 69 Market St.; 757/787-8012), built in 1799 and now home to the offices and museum of the Eastern Shore of Virginia Historical Society. Another historical curiosity is the 150-year-old Hopkins and Bros. General Store, on the wharf (2 Market St.), which in the past has sold everything from sweet potatoes to postcards—and now serves as a sort of mini welcome center.

A great taste of Onancock life awaits inside the **Corner Bakery** (36 Market St.; 757/787-4520), where great doughnuts and fresh coffee are served up to a mostly local crowd, or in the evening you can catch a flick at Onancock's nifty 1950s movie theater, the **Roseland** (48 Market St.; 757/787-2209). Dinner and nice rooms are available at the **Charlotte Hotel** (7 North St.; 757/787-7400). Finally, back on US-13, the hamlet of Exmoor has one last road-food stop, the **Exmoor Diner.**

Onancock was born and grew up around its natural deep-water harbor, and the town wharf is still the place to catch the seasonal ferry across Chesapeake Bay to **Tangier Island,** an evocative old place where things seem to have hardly changed since colonial times. The few hundred people who live here year-round have a unique and almost indecipherably archaic accent—which some trace back to 17th-century Cornwall, England—and earn their livelihoods catching crabs and the occasional oyster from Chesapeake Bay. Tangier Island is best known for its soft-shell crabs, which are sold all over the eastern United States.

Visiting Tangier Island is easy but takes some advance planning. From mid-April until October, boats leave once a day Tuesday–Saturday from Onancock Wharf (about $25; 757/891/2505); travel time is one hour and 15 minutes each way, leaving around 10 AM and returning around 3 PM This means visitors returning on the ferry have only about two hours on the island, so staying overnight at a homespun B&B like **Shirley's Bay View Inn** (757/891-2396) or **Hilda Crockett's Chesapeake House** (757/891-2331) is about the only way to have any kind of close encounter with the tourist-shy locals. Hilda's also serves meals, and good seafood can be had at a handful of unpretentious places like the **Fisherman's Corner Restaurant** (757/891-2900), where you may well be served by the person who caught your meal (or his sister).

Bike rentals are available on Tangier Island, no part of which is more than five feet above sea level.

Eastville

You can get a good idea of just how rural and quiet life is on Virginia's Eastern Shore by visiting **Eastville** (pop. 281), the seat of Northampton County. A mile west of US-13 on a well-marked business loop, Eastville centers on the redbrick courthouse and old county jail, with a handful of even older buildings dating back to the mid-1700s. Eastville has an excellent roadside crab shack along US-13: the **Great Machipongo Clam Shack** (757/442-3800) has crabmeat sandwiches, fresh steamed clams, and an astonishing variety of shellfish, most of it grown, caught, or picked by the owners.

Chesapeake Bay Bridge-Tunnel

One of the more impressive engineering feats on the East Coast is the **Chesapeake Bay Bridge-Tunnel,** which opened in 1964 at the mouth of the Chesapeake Bay and was effectively doubled in 1997 by the addition of an extra set of driving lanes. Almost 18 miles long and charging a $12 toll, the structure consists of one high-level bridge, two deep tunnels, four islands, and many miles of raised causeway. Two miles from the southern end of the bridge, a fishing pier and restaurant operate on man-made Sea Gull Island.

Before the Chesapeake Bay Bridge–Tunnel was completed in 1964, ferries linking the Eastern Shore with the mainland docked at Cape Charles, west of US-13 eight miles south of Eastville. Barges still use the harbor, ferrying freight trains across the bay.

The Chesapeake Bay Bridge-Tunnel's unique design allows for ships to pass easily, and makes for a scenic drive, day or evening.

Virginia Beach

From the toll plaza at the southern end of the Chesapeake Bay Bridge, US-60 heads east along Atlantic Avenue, passing through the woodland waterfront of **First Landing State Park** before winding up at the ocean and **Virginia Beach** (pop. 437,994), the state's most populous city and its one and only beach resort. Ten-story hotels line the main drag, Atlantic Avenue, which is plastered with large signs banning cars from "cruising" the mile-long array of funfairs, surf shops, and nightclubs.

The two deepwater harbors near Norfolk at the mouth of the Chesapeake Bay, Newport News and Hampton Roads, are the headquarters of the U.S. Navy's Atlantic Fleet and together form the world's largest naval base.

Unlike many coastal towns, Virginia Beach also boasts a significant history. Virginia's first colonists landed at Virginia Beach on April 26, 1607, before settling upriver at Jamestown; the site is marked by a stone cross at Cape Henry, at the southern lip of Chesapeake Bay. Five miles south, the excellent **Virginia Aquarium** (daily; $21; 717 General Booth Blvd.; 757/385-3474) has nearly a million gallons of sharks, sting rays, barracudas, and sea turtles, plus an IMAX theater ($8–12 extra).

If you see or hear warnings about shark attacks, take them seriously. In recent years many swimmers have been badly injured or killed by sharks, even in very shallow water.

Along with the beaches and the aquarium, one of the big attractions in Virginia Beach is breakfast, thanks to the fantastic range of places up and down Atlantic Avenue, like the **Maple Tree Pancake House** (2608 Atlantic Ave.; 757/425-6796) or **Pocahontas Pancakes** (3420 Atlantic Ave. at 35th St.; 757/428-6352).

But perhaps the best reason to stop at Virginia Beach is that accommodations are so much cheaper here than out on the Outer Banks: Dorm beds at **Angie's HI Hostel** (302 24th St.; 757/491-1830) cost around $20 a night, and

Virginia Beach

the same owners offer reasonably priced rooms at the adjacent **Ocean Cove Motel** ($80 and up; 300 24th St.; 757/491-1830). Other locally run places include the **Golden Sands Inn** ($50–150; 1312 Atlantic Ave.; 757/428-1770), and campers will appreciate the fine facilities, including beaches, coastal wetlands, hiking trails, and kayaking routes, at the nearly 3,000-acre **First Landing State Park** (757/412-2300).

Norfolk

During colonial times, **Norfolk** (pop. 242,803; pronounced "NAW-fik") was the largest city in Virginia and one of the busiest ports in North America. It's still very much connected with the water, which you can experience firsthand at the **Nauticus National Maritime Center** (daily in summer, closed Mon. rest of year; $13.95; 757/664-1000), where the engaging displays inside are dwarfed by the massive hulk of the battleship USS *Wisconsin* moored alongside. Away from the waterfront, Norfolk has a couple more worthwhile destinations, including the lovely **Chrysler Museum** (Wed.–Sun.; free; 245 Olney Rd.; 757/664-6200), on the north side of downtown off Duke Street. The personal art collection of Walter Chrysler, the self-educated engineer who created one of the "Big Three" car companies and built New York's Chrysler Building, is displayed inside a commodious Italianate building. Norfolk, a staunch Navy town, also holds the final resting place of controversial U.S. Army general Douglas MacArthur, preserved alongside his personal papers (and his 1950 Chrysler Imperial limousine) at the **MacArthur Memorial** (Tues.–Sun.; free; 757/441-2965), inside Norfolk's old City Hall building at Bank and Plume Streets downtown.

DOUGLAS MacARTHUR

Even if you're just racing through, bound for the beach, Norfolk has one place where you really ought to stop and eat: **Doumar's Cones and BBQ** (757/627-4163), a half mile north of downtown at 19th Street and Monticello Avenue. Besides being a real old-fashioned drive-in, this place stakes a claim to having invented the ice cream cone, since the owner's uncle, Abe Doumar, sold the first ones at the 1904 St. Louis World's Fair. Doumar's still sells great handmade cones, barbecue sandwiches, and a deliciously thirst-quenching limeade. Pass by at your peril. . . .

Virginia Beach is home to the **Association for Research and Enlightenment** (800/333-4499 or 757/428-3588, 215 67th St.), which is dedicated to continuing the legacy of early American psychic Edgar Cayce, offering classes in ESP—but you already knew that, didn't you?

The **Norfolk Tides** (757/622-2222), Class AAA farm team of the Baltimore Orioles, play at beautiful Harbor Park, off I-264 at Waterside Drive, where you can watch big ships sail past. Games are broadcast on **WGH 1310 AM.**

Stop for a bite at Doumar's.

From Norfolk, you can take US-17 south across the aptly named Great Dismal Swamp or follow the faster Hwy-168, which takes you past a feast of roadside fruit stands, barbecue shacks, and junk shops, straight down to Kitty Hawk and the Outer Banks of North Carolina.

NORTH CAROLINA

Wild Atlantic beaches, a handful of tiny fishing villages, and some of the country's most significant historic sites make coastal North Carolina a great place to visit. A highlight for many vacationers is the **Outer Banks,** miles of barrier islands where busy resort towns like **Nags Head** contrast with the stretches of pristine beaches protected on the **Cape Hatteras National Seashore.** Besides golden

sands, the Outer Banks area includes two evocative historic sites: the dunes at **Kitty Hawk,** where the Wright Brothers first took to the air, and **Roanoke Island,** site of the first ill-fated English effort to colonize the New World. Farther south, beyond the quirky, small city of **Wilmington,** a movie-making mecca, the 300-mile coastal route turns inland around **Cape Fear,** heading toward the South Carolina border.

Kitty Hawk: The Wright Brothers National Memorial

Alternately known as Killy Hauk, Kitty Hock, and Killy Honk before its current name came into general use, **Kitty Hawk** to most people means one thing: the Wright brothers' first powered airplane flight more than a century ago, on December 17, 1903. Lured by the steady winds that blow in from the Atlantic and by the high sand dunes that cover the shore, Wilbur and Orville Wright first came to the Outer Banks in 1900 and returned every year thereafter with prototype kites and gliders built out of bicycle parts, which they fine-tuned to create the world's first airplane. Their tale is truly one of the great adventure and success stories of the modern age, and the site of their experiments has been preserved as the **Wright Brothers National Memorial.** First stop is the **visitors center** (daily; $4; 252/441-7430), which in-

First flight: 120 feet in 12 seconds. Orville mans the plane, Wilbur runs alongside.

Orville Wright   Wilbur Wright

cludes a number of exhibits tracing the history of human efforts to fly. Every hour, rangers give engaging talks alongside a full-sized replica of the Wright brothers' first plane.

The most affecting aspect of the memorial is the unchanged site where the brothers first flew. Each of the first four flights is marked by stones set on the grassy field. The first flight, with Orville at the controls flying into a 25-mph headwind, lasted 12 seconds and covered just 120 feet—barely more than a brisk walking pace. The 90-foot-high sand dune where Wilbur and Orville first took to the air has been planted over with grasses to keep it from blowing away. Paths climb to the top of the dune, where a 60-foot, wing-shaped granite pylon is inscribed with these words:

In commemoration of the conquest of the air by the brothers Wilbur and Orville Wright. Conceived by genius, achieved by dauntless resolution and unconquerable faith.

The park is off US-158, on the inland side of the highway, two miles south of the Wright Memorial Bridge from the mainland. Though the memorial is definitely worth an extended visit, the towns around it are a bit disappointing—both Kitty Hawk and Kill Devil Hills are little more than narrow strips of commercial development.

Jockey's Ridge State Park

The windswept 110-foot-high twin sand dunes of **Jockey's Ridge State Park** (daily; free; 252/441-7132) tower over US-158 between Kitty Hawk and Nags Head. The highest sand dunes on the East Coast, Jockey's Ridge barely survived being bulldozed in the 1970s to form yet another Outer Banks resort; it's now one of the prime hang-gliding spots in the country—remember the Wright brothers! Jockey's Ridge is also a nice place to wander the short boardwalk nature trail that points out the diverse plants and animals of the dune community. You may want to take your shoes off and scamper around the sands barefoot. If you feel especially daring, **Kitty Hawk Kites** across the highway at milepost 10.5 dubs itself the "World's Largest Hang-Gliding School" and offers equipment rentals and lessons ($90 and up; 252/441-4127 or 877/359-8447), plus anything else you might need to make the most of your time here.

Nags Head

The towns of the northern Outer Banks overlap each other so much it can be hard to tell you are in **Nags Head,** six miles south of Kitty Hawk. One of the oldest and most popular resorts in the region, Nags Head also offers the widest range of visitor facilities. Good places to spend a night or two include a beachfront roadside classic at milepost 16.5: the historic **Sea Foam Motel** ($75 and up; 7111 S. Virginia Dare Trail; 252/441-7320), one of the last surviving 1940s motels on the Outer Banks. The pine-paneled walls, vivid tiles, and slamming screen doors will take you back to a simpler time. Nearby, the even more atmospheric **First Colony Inn** ($89 and up; 6715 S. Croatan Hwy.; 252/441-2343), along US-158 at milepost 16, was moved from its valuable oceanfront location to the middle of the island, but it still offers oodles of old-fashioned charm along with a delicious breakfast and afternoon tea.

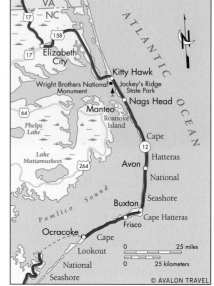

One more long-standing local landmark, **Sam & Omie's** (closed in winter; 7228 S. Virginia Dare Trail; 252/441-7366), near the east end of US-64, has featured inexpensive but well-prepared family fare, three meals a day (plus a full bar), for over 70 years.

Roanoke Island: Fort Raleigh National Historic Site

From an area known as Whalebone Junction at the south end of Nags Head, US-64 runs west over a causeway and bridge to **Roanoke Island,** site of the first English settlement in North America. The legendary "Lost Colony" was first established in 1584 by Sir Walter Raleigh, but the effort was not a success, and the survivors returned to England. In 1587, a larger expedition of 117 colonists arrived, including women and children, but because of the outbreak of war with Spain and the manifold difficulties involved in crossing the Atlantic Ocean, there was no further contact with England until 1590.

By the time the next supply ship returned, the settlers had disappeared without a trace, which prompted numerous theories about their fate. Now, amid an eerily dark forest, the colony's original earthwork fortress has been excavated and reconstructed as the centerpiece of the **Fort Raleigh National Historic Site.** Exhibits inside the **visitors center** (daily; free; 252/473-5772) include a few rusty artifacts and dry displays explaining the historical context of the colonial effort. There are also copies of the many

---

If you're traveling along the Carolina coast in summer, be aware that the hurricane season begins in June and lasts through the end of November. These are deadly serious storms, so take heed of any warnings, and follow the evacuation instructions broadcast over radio and TV networks.

The name Nags Head is derived from the practices of Outer Banks pirates, who tied lanterns around the heads of their horses to simulate boats bobbing at anchor. The lanterns lured passing ships onto shore, where they ran aground on the offshore sandbars.

beautiful watercolors and drawings of native plants, animals, and people produced by the original expedition's two immensely talented scientists, John White and Thomas Hariot.

The historic port of **Manteo** (pop. 1,052; pronounced "MAN-tee-o"), in the middle of Roanoke Island between Fort Raleigh and the beach resorts of the Outer Banks, was named for the Native American who helped Sir Walter Raleigh and the Lost Colony. Manteo is the only county seat in

Raleigh's flagship, *Ark Raleigh*

North Carolina that's located on an island. You can still sense the town's proud seagoing history as you walk along the quiet streets near the tidied-up waterfront. Surrounded by pleasure boats, the main attraction here is the *Elizabeth II* (daily Mar.–Dec.; $8), a full-sized, square-rigged replica of the type of ship that carried colonists here from England 400-odd years ago.

Cape Hatteras National Seashore

The first piece of coastline to be protected as a national park, **Cape Hatteras National Seashore** stretches for 75 miles along the Atlantic Ocean. Starting in the north at Nags Head, and continuing south along slender Bodie, Hatteras, and Ocracoke Islands, the area preserved within Cape Hatteras National Seashore is the largest undeveloped section of coastline on the East Coast, providing an increasingly rare glimpse of nature amid ever-encroaching development. The few old fishing villages that stood here when the seashore was set aside in the 1930s are unfortunately exempt from the anti-development prohibitions of the national seashore; these have grown ugly and unwieldy. Nevertheless, the many miles in between remain almost entirely untouched.

Cape Hatteras Lighthouse

For many visitors, the highlight of the national seashore is the historic **Cape Hatteras Lighthouse,** a mile west of Hwy-12 at the south end of Hatteras Island. Others come here to enjoy the warm waters and strong, steady winds—two areas of Pamlico Sound on the inland side of Cape

Hundreds of ancient ships and unfortunate sailors met their watery end in the shallow waters off Cape Hatteras. The remains of over 2,000 vessels lie along the entire Carolina coastline; a few are visible from shore at low tide.

Throughout the summer, a waterfront theater adjacent to Fort Raleigh presents a popular production of **Lost Colony,** which dramatizes the events of the ill-fated settlement. Call for details or tickets ($20–24 adults, $10 under 12; 252/473-3414).

Warmed by the Gulf Stream currents, the Outer Banks beaches are some of the best in the world, but the waters do not warm up appreciably until south of Oregon Inlet, and swimming in the northern stretches remains quite invigorating until July.

The Outer Banks

The geography of the Outer Banks, a series of barrier islands stretching for over 200 miles along the coast of North Carolina, has changed dramatically over time, thanks to hurricanes and winter storms, not to mention human hands. Until a series of lighthouses was built beginning in the late 18th century, the islands and the offshore shoals were so treacherous they became known as the "Graveyard of the Atlantic."

Nowadays, the same places where pirates once plundered are given over to windsurfing, hang-gliding, kite-surfing, sportfishing, and beach-combing, as the Outer Banks (sometimes abbreviated OBX) have become a tourist and recreation destination par excellence. The resident population of some 33,920 swells to accommodate over six million annual visitors, but unlike its nearest comparison, Cape Cod, the Outer Banks area boasts only a few historic towns. Instead, substantial development during the 1990s building boom has covered the sands with an ugly sprawl of vacation homes and time-share condos perched—often on stilts to protect them from storm damage—directly on the broad Atlantic beaches. Most of the development has taken place in the north along two parallel roads: US-158, usually called The Bypass but also known as Croatan Highway; and ocean-front Hwy-12, a.k.a. Virginia Dare Trail and Beach Road. Mileposts on both roads mark distances from north to south. There's plentiful lodging in the many little towns along Hwy-12; gas stations and fast-food restaurants line US-158. The exception to the commercial sprawl is the magical 75 miles of the Cape Hatteras National Seashore.

Along the northern Outer Banks, bridges link Nags Head and Kitty Hawk with the mainland, though access to the less-developed southern parts of the Outer Banks is limited to ferry boats, all of which carry cars.

The section of Pamlico Sound known as **Canadian Hole,** between the towns of Avon and Buxton, is rated as one of the best windsurfing spots on the East Coast.

Hatteras have been set aside for windsurfers, dozens of whom flock here on summer days to what's considered one of the finest sailboarding and kite-surfing spots in the United States. And of course, there are miles of open beaches, perfect for aimless strolling.

At the north end of Cape Hatteras, eight miles south of Nags Head, there's a national seashore **visitors center** (daily; 252/473-2111) and a nature trail winding along Pamlico Sound at the foot of **Bodie Island Lighthouse,** the first of three historic towers along the Hatteras coast. On the ocean side of Hwy-12, **Coquina Beach** has a broad strand, lifeguards and showers in summer, and the remains of a wooden schooner that was wrecked here in the 1920s.

Continuing south, across the Oregon Inlet (where there's a first-come, first-served campground), Hwy-12 runs through the 5,800-acre **Pea Island National Wildlife Refuge,** which was established in 1937 to protect the nesting grounds of loggerhead sea turtles, as well as the coastal wetlands essential to the survival of the greater snow goose and other migratory waterfowl. South of the refuge, a few short barrages of vacation condos and roadside sprawl—go-kart parks, mini-golf courses, and a KOA Kampground—line the highway between Rodanthe and Salvo, before the road reaches the heart of the park, where high sand dunes rise along 15 miles of undeveloped oceanfront.

Avon and Buxton: Cape Hatteras Lighthouse

At the rough midpoint of Hatteras Island, the vacation town of **Avon** stretches for a couple of miles along Hwy-12 before the road hits the Canadian Hole windsurfing area, two miles south of town. After another few miles of natural dunes, the road bends sharply to the west; continuing south here brings you to the main **Cape Hatteras National Seashore visitors center** (daily in summer only; 252/995-4474) and the famous **Cape Hatteras Lighthouse.** At 210 feet,

Cape Hatteras Lighthouse, Cape Hatteras, N. C.

the black-and-white-striped lighthouse is the tallest brick lighthouse in the United States, visible from as far as 25 miles. However, because the ocean here has been slowly eroding away the beach (when the lighthouse was built in 1870, it was a quarter mile from the waves; by 1995 the coast was a mere 120 feet away from its base), in 1999 the National Park Service succeeded in lifting the 3,000-ton lighthouse onto rails and shifting it a quarter mile inland. If you feel fit, climb the stairs (12 stories' worth, each way; $7) to the top of the lighthouse for a grand view—one that gives the clearest sense of just how narrow and transitive the Outer Banks really are.

Farther along, at the end of this road, there's a summer-only, first-come, first-served campground.

From the Cape Hatteras Lighthouse, Hwy-12 bends west and south through **Buxton** and **Frisco,** where you will find a gauntlet of motels, gas stations, and fast-food restaurants at the commercial center of Cape Hatteras. The very good and very popular **Fish House** (252/995-5151), on Hwy-12 next to Cape Hatteras High School, doesn't look like much from the road, but the fish here is fresh daily. Buxton's motels, like the **Lighthouse View** (252/995-5680 or 800/225-7651), which is right on the beach and also has a good-sized swimming pool, are reasonably priced (around $100 a night in summer) and clean. Ocean beaches here at the very tip of the cape are among the most spectacular anywhere; swimmers should note that because they are south-facing, they tend to pick up some of the most extreme surf—especially when hurricanes hit—which is why Buxton and Frisco are the local surfing capitals.

More restaurants and motels (including a Holiday Inn Express) await you in

The village of Frisco, five miles north of the Hatteras ferry terminal, holds the small but surprisingly good **Native American Museum** (closed Mon.; $5; 252/995-4440), which boasts an extensive collection of artifacts from several tribes, including those from the Cape Hatteras area, and Hopi and Navajo crafts.

Hatteras, at the southern end of the island. From here, state-run ferries (5 AM–midnight; free) shuttle every half hour across to Ocracoke Island, another mostly unspoiled barrier island where you'll find great beaches and the pretty village of Ocracoke, at the island's southern tip.

Ocracoke

About the only Outer Banks town that hasn't lost its small-scale charm, **Ocracoke** is a great place to spend an afternoon or two, walking or cycling along unpaved back streets lined by overgrown gardens and weathered old homes. Since it's easy to reach from the mainland, via ferries from Swan Quarter and from Cedar Island, Ocracoke is a popular destination, but the tourism here is so low-key it still feels like a place you can discover for yourself.

The ferries from the mainland south of Ocracoke drop you at the heart of town. Coming in from the north on Hwy-12, you pass through a short strip of real estate agencies and restaurants like **Howard's Pub** (252/928-4441), a local institution whose rooftop, ocean-view deck is a very pleasant place to eat deep-fried local seafood and sample one or more of its 200 different beers.

From Hwy-12, a number of small back roads (including oak-lined Howard Street and another called simply Back Road, which runs past **Teach's Hole,** a shop dedicated to the pirate Blackbeard) are worth exploring—especially by bike, the best way to get around Ocracoke. Just south of the harbor, Point Road runs west to the squat, whitewashed 1823 Ocracoke Lighthouse.

Ocracoke Practicalities

Ocracoke's small and photogenic harbor is ringed by low-key, low-rise restaurants, bike rental stands, hotels, bars, and B&Bs. Many of the restaurants ringing the Ocracoke harbor morph into bars after dark. All are friendly and informal, and most have some kind of live music during the summer season, making wandering around town a prime visitor activity. Away from the harbor, the **Back Porch** (110 Back Rd.; 252/928-6401) is rated as one of the Outer Banks' best restaurants.

There are no chain hotels on Ocracoke (which may in itself be reason enough to visit!), and local places are generally down-to-earth, not fancy. The oldest lodging option is **Blackbeard's Lodge,** a rambling old motel across from the Back Porch ($80 and up; 111 Back Rd.; 252/928-3421). Another characterful place is the 100-year-old **Island Inn** ($75 and up; 252/928-4351), near the harbor.

Right across from the ferry landing, there's a very helpful **visitors center** (252/928-4531) that has complete information on Ocracoke and the rest of Cape Hatteras. Running between Ocracoke on Cape Hatteras, and two places on the North Carolina mainland (Cedar Island and Swan Quarter), the state-run ferry departs approximately every two hours (every three hours in winter) and takes just over 2.5 hours each way. The cost is about $15 per car, $30 for an RV; call 800/BY-FERRY for current schedules and further information.

From Cedar Island, it's close to an hour's drive along US-70 to the next big city, Beaufort.

Blackbeard the Pirate

Wandering around the idyllic harbor of Ocracoke, it's hard to imagine that the waters offshore were once home to perhaps the most ferocious pirate who ever sailed the Seven Seas—Blackbeard. The archetypal pirate, even in his day, when piracy was common, Blackbeard was famous for his ruthlessness and violence as much as for his long black beard and exotic battle dress, wearing six pistols on twin gunbelts slung over his shoulders and slashing hapless opponents

Capture of the Pirate, Blackbeard, 1718

with a mighty cutlass. His pirate flag featured a heart dripping blood and a skeleton toting an hourglass in one hand and a spear in the other.

For all his near-mythic status, Blackbeard's career as a pirate was fairly short. After serving as an English privateer in the Caribbean during Queen Anne's War, in 1713 Blackbeard (whose real name was Edward Teach) turned to piracy, learning his trade under the pirate Benjamin Hornigold. Outfitted with four stolen ships, 40 cannons, and a crew of 300 men, Blackbeard embarked on a reign of terror that took him up and down the Atlantic coast of the American colonies. After five years of thieving cargoes and torturing sailors, Blackbeard was confronted off Ocracoke by forces led by Lt. Robert Maynard of the Royal Navy, and during a ferocious battle on November 22, 1718, the pirate and most of his men were killed. Blackbeard himself was stabbed 25 times, and his head was sliced off and hung like a trophy on the bowsprit of his captor's ship.

Though there is no evidence that he ever buried any treasure anywhere near Ocracoke, Blackbeard's ship, the *Queen Anne's Revenge,* was discovered in 1996 off Bogue Bank, and some cannons and other objects recovered from the pirate's ship are being preserved by the North Carolina Maritime Museum in Beaufort. Blackbeard's legend, to be sure, lives on.

Cape Lookout National Seashore

If you like the look of Cape Hatteras but want to avoid the crowds, plan a visit to the much wilder **Cape Lookout National Seashore,** another series of barrier islands, which stretch for 55 miles from Ocracoke to the south near Beaufort. It's accessible only by boat, and there are few roads or services once you're there, but it's a lovely place to hike or camp, collect seashells, or just wander along the peaceful shore, exploring the remains of cabins and abandoned villages. Day trips to Point Lookout leave from Beaufort on the "World's Largest Speedboat," the Lookout Express ($15; 252/728-6997), or you can usually arrange a charter from Ocracoke.

Beaufort and Morehead City

Known as Fishtown until it was re-named in 1722, the charming 18th-century town of **Beaufort** (pop. 4,189) has quiet streets lined with churches, cemeteries filled with weather-stained monuments, and whitewashed houses with narrow porches. The nautical-themed shops and restaurants along the water on busy Front Street, three blocks south of US-70, attract tourists and boat-ers traveling along the Intracoastal Waterway. The spacious **North Carolina Maritime Museum** (daily; free; 315 Front St.; 252/728-7317) features many informative ex-hibits on the region's nautical and natural history, as well as a truly im-pressive display of over 1,000 beau-tiful seashells. The museum also sponsors an annual **Wooden Boat Show,** held the last weekend in September.

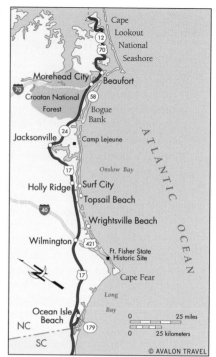

If you're looking for a meal in Beaufort, try **Clawson's** (425 Front St.; 252/728-2133), a burger and seafood place housed in an old grocery store that's been in business since 1905.

While Beaufort may be prettier, you'll find the best food in burly **Morehead City,** three miles west of Beaufort and across the bridge. Try the homemade seafood-cocktail sauce and Tarheel hush puppies at the **Sanitary Fish Market & Restaurant** (501 Evans St.; 252/247-3111); it's easy to find amidst the sportfishing boats a block off US-70. For even more famous burgers (and shrimp burgers, and onion rings, and milk shakes, and more!), head along to **El's Drive-In** (252/726-3002), open since 1959 on US-70, three miles south of Morehead City, a mile south of the bridge to Atlantic Beach.

> Not surprisingly, Beaufort, North Carolina is often confused with Beaufort, South Carolina. The former is pronounced "BO-fort"; the latter is pronounced "BYOO-furd."

Bogue Bank: Fort Macon

More barrier island beach resorts line **Bogue Bank,** which runs south of Morehead City in a nearly east–west orientation for some 25 miles. The half dozen family-oriented resort towns have freely accessible—but quite often crowded—beaches. The largest, **Atlantic Beach,** across a bridge from Morehead City, has a boardwalk backed by a go-kart track and a small amusement arcade. The very enjoyable **State Aquarium** (daily; $8), five miles west of town on Hwy-58, features extensive displays on the local log-gerhead sea turtles.

Hurricanes

If you're traveling along the East Coast in late summer, be aware that the farther south you go the more likely you are to encounter one of Mother Nature's most powerful phenomena, the hurricane. All across the southeastern United States, hurricane season begins in June and lasts through November, and the threat of a storm can put a sudden end to the summer fun. Hurricanes are tropical storms covering upwards of 400 square miles, with winds reaching speeds of 75 to 150 mph or more. These storms form as far away as Africa, and sophisticated warning systems are in place to give coastal visitors plenty of time to get out of harm's way. Radio and TV stations broadcast storm watches and evacuation warnings, and if you hear one, heed it and head inland to higher ground.

Even more dangerous than the high winds of a hurricane is the storm surge—a dome of ocean water that can be 20 feet high at its peak, and 50 to 100 miles wide. Ninety percent of hurricane fatalities are attributable to the high waves of a storm surge, which can wash away entire beaches and intensify flooding in coastal rivers and bays many miles upstream from the shore. The strongest hurricane recorded in the United States was the Labor Day storm of 1935, which killed 500 people and destroyed the Florida Keys Railroad. More recent hurricanes include Hurricane Irene in 2011, the multiple 'canes that pounded Florida in 2004, and Hurricane Andrew in 1992. The levee breaks that flooded New Orleans made August 2005's Hurricane Katrina by far the most costly U.S. storm, at some $85 billion, but the deadliest hurricane on record hit Galveston Island, Texas, early in September 1900, killing more than 6,000 people—in human terms by far the worst natural disaster in United States history.

At the northeast end of Bogue Bank stands **Fort Macon State Park** (daily; free), which centers on a massive pre–Civil War fortress overlooking the harbor entrance. The pentagon-shaped masonry fort, completed in 1834, was captured early in the Civil War by the Confederacy. In April 1862, Union forces retook Fort Mason after a bombardment and controlled Beaufort for the rest of the war.

Camp Lejeune and Jacksonville

Midway between Beaufort and Wilmington, much of the coastline is taken over by the 100,000-acre U.S. Marine Corps base of **Camp Lejeune.**

North Carolina's beaches are prime nesting grounds for endangered loggerhead sea turtles. These huge turtles come ashore mid-May to late August by the light of the full moon. Females lay and bury as many as 100 eggs, then in September–October the tiny hatchlings scramble back into the sea.

Established during World War II and now home to the crack rapid deployment forces and an urban combat training center, Camp Lejeune is open by appointment to groups interested in a nose-to-nose encounter with tanks, humvees, and other lethal machines. (Visting groups should consist of 10–45 people, and must be recognized civic, private, or military organizations.) Sentries will check you in and out at both ends of the surprisingly scenic 25-mile drive across the base along Hwy-172, which serves as a shortcut to looping US-17.

At the northwest corner of Camp Lejeune, **Jacksonville** (pop. 80,542) is little more than a civilian adjunct to the base, with all the gas stations, fast-food franchises, and tattoo parlors Lejeune's 45,000 Marines and their dependents could want. One sobering sight is on the edge of town, just off Hwy-24 (opposite a Sonic Drive-In): the 50-foot-long granite wall of the **Beirut Memorial** remembers the more than 250 Camp Lejeune Marines killed in Beirut in 1983 by a suicide bomber. Alongside a list of their names are the words "They Came in Peace."

Wrightsville Beach

South of Camp Lejeune, US-17 runs through the lushly forested lowlands around Holly Ridge, while Hwy-210 cuts across a series of narrow barrier islands. The waterfront is mostly private, backed by beach house after beach house (rentals aplenty, if you can manage to stay for a full week), but with a few parking areas for passing travelers. The clean strands and clear blue waters continue through sleepy Topsail Beach, home to a homespun hospital for injured loggerhead turtles, the **Karen Beasley Sea Turtle Rescue & Rehabilitation Center** (822 Carolina Blvd.). The 20-odd "patients" are cared for by volunteers at the center downtown, across from the water tower.

Most of this stretch of coastline is dedicated to low-key, by-the-week family vacations, but the town of **Wrightsville Beach** has a bit more going on. Located 10 miles east of US-17 via US-74 or US-76, it's not all that different from dozens of other coastal vacation communities, but proximity to the lively city of Wilmington makes it a great place to stop. Places to stay along the beach include the comfortable **Blockade Runner Resort** ($99–300; 275 Waynick Blvd.; 910/256-2251), which has a good restaurant, two bars, and bicycle, boat, and kayak rentals.

sunrise on Wrightsville Beach, seen from Blockade Runner Resort

Wilmington

Though it's surrounded by the usual miles of highway sprawl, the downtown business district of **Wilmington** (pop. 106,476) is unusually attractive and well preserved, its many blocks of historic buildings stepping up from the Cape Fear River waterfront. The largest city on the North Carolina coast, Wilmington was of vital importance to the Confederate cause during the

U.S.S. *North Carolina*

Civil War, when it was the only southern port able to continue exporting income-earning cotton, mostly to England, in the face of the Union blockade. Wilmington also played an important role before and during the Revolution, first as a center of colonial resistance, and later as headquarters for British general Cornwallis.

Despite its lengthy and involved military history, Wilmington itself has survived relatively unscathed and now possesses one of the country's more engaging small-town streetscapes. Cobblestone wharves and brick warehouses line the Cape Fear River, which also provides moorage for the massive 35,000-ton battleship USS *North Carolina* (daily; $12), across the river. A couple of the warehouses, like the Cotton Exchange at the north end, have been converted to house boutiques and restaurants. A block inland, Front Street is the lively heart of town, a franchise-free stretch of book and music stores, cafés, and other businesses that's often used by film crews attempting to re-create a typically American "Main Street" scene. Films like *Blue Velvet* and TV's teenage soap opera *Dawson's Creek* were shot at Wilmington's massive Screen Gems studio and in surrounding locales.

Thanks in large part to its significant TV and movie-making business, Wilmington has a number of excellent places to eat, like the comfortable **Caffé Phoenix** (35 N. Front St.; 910/343-1395), an excellent Italian bistro serving fresh pasta dishes and pizzas. Within stumbling distance are bars like the rough-hewn **Barbary Coast** (116 S. Front St.; 910/762-8996). For a taste of top-quality traditional Southern food—grits with everything—try the **Dixie Grill** (116 Market St.; 910/762-7280), where you can work off the calories with a game of pool.

Rates at Wilmington's many chain motels and hotels are comparatively low; try the riverfront **Hilton** ($99 and up; 301 N. Water St.; 910/763-5900).

South of Wilmington, US-17 runs inland, so if you want to stick close to

In the book and movie *Gone With the Wind,* dashing southern hero Rhett Butler spent the Civil War as a Wilmington-based blockade runner, evading the U.S. Navy.

Transcontinental I-40 starts in Wilmington and runs west to Southern California. The first stretch is named in honor of local basketball superstar Michael Jordan, and another sign gives the mileage to the road's western destination: Barstow, Calif. 2,554.

the coast, take Hwy-179, which curves along the shore past the rambling towns of **Ocean Isle Beach** and **Sunset Beach** before rejoining US-17 at the South Carolina border.

Cape Fear

Though it has lent its name to two of the most terrifying movies ever made, **Cape Fear** is not at all a scary place—so long as you stay on land. The name was given to it by sailors who feared its shipwrecking shoals, and hundreds of vessels have indeed been wrecked off the cape, including dozens of Confederate blockade-runners sunk during the Civil War embargo of Wilmington harbor.

Between the east and west banks of the Cape Fear River, a ferry (800/ BY-FERRY, www.ncdot.org/ ferry) runs about once an hour between Fort Fisher and Southport.

South of Wilmington, US-421 runs along the east bank of the Cape Fear River through typical barrier island beach resort towns like Carolina Beach and Kure Beach. Near the south end of the island, **Fort Fisher State Historic Site** features the earthwork fortification that enabled Wilmington harbor to remain open to ships throughout most of the Civil War. The fortress looks more like a series of primitive mounds than an elaborate military installation, but its simple sand piles proved more durable against Union artillery than the heavy masonry of Fort Sumter and other traditional fortresses. A **visitors center** (daily; free; 910/458-5538) describes the fort's role, with details of the war's heaviest sea battle, when Union ships bombarded Fort Fisher in January 1865. Surrounding lands have been left wild, and a nice outpost of the State Aquarium has tanks of local sealife.

On the west bank of the Cape Fear River, Hwy-133 winds up at the pleasure-craft harbor of **Southport,** which is the halfway point between New York City and Miami, attracting sailors traveling the Intracoastal Waterway. It's also the site of the large Brunswick nuclear power plant.

Cape Fear itself is formed by **Bald Head Island,** at the mouth of the Cape Fear River, reachable only by boat from Southport. The **Old Baldy Lighthouse** on the island is the state's oldest, built in 1817.

SOUTH CAROLINA

Just beyond the border into South Carolina, you suddenly hit the exuberant mega-tourism of the "Grand Strand," a 25-mile-long conglomeration of resort hotels, amusement arcades, and Coney Island–style Americana that centers on **Myrtle Beach,** the state's number-one tourist destination. South of here things quiet down considerably, as coastal US-17 winds past the lush lowland marshes, passing through historic **Georgetown** and numerous preserved plantations before reaching **Charleston,** one of the most gracious and engaging cities in the southern United States.

Myrtle Beach: The Grand Strand

Standing at the center of the Grand Strand, **Myrtle Beach** (pop. 32,000) is one of the largest and most popular beach resorts in the country, attracting some 13 million visitors every year. It's a huge place, with mile after mile of motels, Wal-Marts, and fast-food franchises lining all the main roads. Long famous for its golf courses (and for having the world's biggest collection of miniature golf courses), in recent years—its landmark Pavilion amusement park was demolished in 2006, to make room for yet another mall—Myrtle Beach has swapped roller coasters and beachfront fun for shopping and merchandising.

Myrtle Beach Practicalities

If you don't mind keeping your tongue wedged firmly in your cheek, the Myrtle Beach area can be fun, and it's definitely a mecca for fans of ersatz "themed" restaurants: Planet Hollywood, NASCAR Café, Hard Rock Cafe, Margaritaville, and Caddyshack all vie for attention in the massive Broadway-at-the-Beach complex on Kings Highway, north of US-501. Owned by the same company that tore down the Pavilion, this is the biggest attraction in Myrtle Beach, but despite the name, Broadway-at-the-Beach is over a mile from the ocean.

If you want a more genuine taste of Myrtle Beach, some of the best places to eat are in Murrells Inlet. One very nice "old-time" Myrtle Beach restaurant, the **Sea Captain's House** (3002 N. Ocean Blvd.; 843/448-8082), has survived the developers' blitz and is still serving three delicious meals a day, just as it has since 1954. The seafood is great, and just about every table has an ocean view.

The spring- and summer-blooming crepe myrtle trees, with long branches of purple and red flowers, gave Myrtle Beach its name. The old beachfront Pavilion in Myrtle Beach was the 1950s birthplace of "The Shag," a sexually explicit slow jitterbug that is now the official South Carolina state dance.

Myrtle Beach boasts more golf courses, including a bewildering array of miniature golf courses, than anywhere else in the country. Most have castaway or pirate themes; one's based upon the TV show *Gilligan's Island*.

Murrells Inlet

There *may* be more picturesque places elsewhere in the state, but the as-yet-unspoiled fishing village of **Murrells Inlet,** 12 miles south of Myrtle Beach, is

South of the Border

If the Grand Strand and Myrtle Beach haven't satisfied your need for roadside kitsch, or if you're bombing along I-95 looking for a place to take a break, head to South of the Border, the world's largest and most unapologetic tourist trap. Located just south of the North Carolina state line at I-95 exit 1, South of the Border is a crazy place with no real reason to exist, yet it draws many thousands of visitors every day to a 135-acre assembly of sombrero-shaped fast-food stands, giant video arcades, souvenir shops, and innumerable signs and statues of the South of the Border mascot, Pedro, including one that's nearly 100 feet tall.

Many roadside businesses suffered when a new Interstate or bypass left them high and dry, but in the case of South of the Border, the opposite is true. It started as a fireworks and hot dog stand along US-301 in the early 1950s, but when highway engineers decided to locate I-95 here, its middle-of-nowhere locale suddenly became prime highway frontage, and owner Alan Shafer (who died in 2001 at the age of 87) made playful use of its location (50 feet south of the state line) to create this pseudo-Mexican "South of the Border" village—cum—roadside rest stop. Though the complex itself is hard to miss, with its sombrero-clad concrete brontosaurus and 20-story Sombrero Tower giving a panoramic view of the Interstate, I-95 drivers from both directions

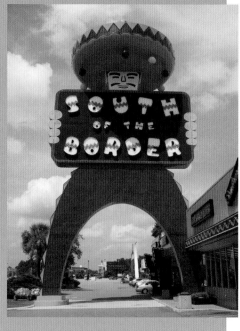

get plenty of notice of their approach, thanks to the hundreds of garish billboards that line the road, saying silly things like "Chili Today, Hot Tamale," the subliminal messages all but forcing you to pull off and chow down on a taco or three and buy some mass-produced keepsake you'll throw away as soon as you get home.

South of the Border is open 24 hours every day, and, along with the myriad of tourist shlock, it also has two gas stations and a pleasant, 300-room motel ($55 and up; 843/774-2411).

The Carolina League Myrtle Beach Pelicans play baseball at BBT Coastal Field (843) 918-6000), off US-17 next to Broadway at the Beach.

definitely worth a stop for the chance to sample the dozens of excellent seafood restaurants lining a short business loop off US-17. For the best and freshest seafood, head to **Flo's Place** (which has great key lime pie) at the north end of town (3797 US-17; 843/651-7222). And if you've got the time and inclination to catch your own seafood, sportfishing charter boats run from the marina, or you can put on some waders and head into the waters in search of clams, mussels, oysters, and crabs.

Brookgreen Gardens and Huntington Beach State Park

One of the most popular and pleasant gardens in South Carolina, **Brookgreen Gardens** (daily; $12), 16 miles south of Myrtle Beach, is a nonprofit, 4,000-acre park on the lushly landscaped grounds of four colonial-era indigo and rice plantations. Oak trees laden with Spanish moss stand alongside palmettos, dogwoods, and azaleas, as well as hundreds of sculptures, including many done by the owner, Anna Hyatt Huntington, who developed the site in the 1930s. Alligators and otters play in the simulated swamp, and many species of birds fly around enclosed aviaries in a section of the gardens set aside as a wildlife park.

Across the highway is the 2,500-acre **Huntington Beach State Park** ($5 per car; 843/237-4440), which sits on land carved out of the Huntington estate

Carry insect repellent and be prepared for mosquitoes, especially late in the afternoon, almost everywhere along the muggy South Carolina coast.

The carnivorous Venus flytrap, which Charles Darwin called "the most wonderful plant in the world," does not grow wild in any part of the world except the seacoast Carolinas.

One of the more unusual radio stations in the country, **WLGI 90.9 FM,** is operated by the Ba'hai faith and broadcasts a commercial-free mix of classic 1970s soul, contemporary jazz, and messages of peace, love, and understanding. To learn more, call 800/228-6483.

The original lyrics to Stephen Foster's song "The Old Folks at Home" began "Way down upon the Pee Dee River," though he quickly changed it to the more sonorous "Suwanee."

that is leased to South Carolina. Besides a nice beach and a popular campground, it features the Moorish-style castle called Atalaya, Anna Huntington's studio.

Pawleys Island and Hobcaw Barony

South of the commercial chaos of Myrtle Beach, travelers in search of serene tranquility have long appreciated **Pawleys Island.** The rope hammocks for which the island is best known aptly symbolize this generally relaxed, weatherworn community, where a few traditional tin-roofed shacks mix with ever-increasing numbers of multi-million-dollar mock-antebellum mansions. It's mostly private, apart from the plush environs of **Litchfield Plantation** ($160 and up; 843/237-5300), a 600-acre resort on the grounds of a colonial-era plantation. The poet and novelist James Dickey, author of *Deliverance,* liked it so much he lived here for his last 25 years and is buried in the small Pawleys Island cemetery.

An even more extensive and intimate (and affordable) taste of the old-fashioned Lowcountry life is available just down the road from Pawleys Island. Spreading along the north bank of the Pee Dee River, a mile north of Georgetown on US-17, **Hobcaw Barony** is a 17,500-acre estate that was once the winter home of 1920s financier and New Deal–era statesman Bernard Baruch and his daughter, Belle. The extensive, mostly undeveloped grounds are home to two university research centers specializing in coastal ecology, and the main homes and plantation buildings have been kept in original condition, complete with one of very few surviving slave streets. Along with preserving these historic quarters and the regional history they represent, the nonprofit educational foundation that runs Hobcaw Barony offers half-day tours to school groups and individuals (Tues.–Fri.; $20; 843/546-4623). Tours start at the **visitors center and museum** (Mon.–Fri.; free) along US-17.

Georgetown

Site of a short-lived Spanish settlement in 1526, the first European outpost in North America, **Georgetown** later became the rice-growing center of colonial America. Bounded by the Sampit and Pee Dee Rivers and the narrow inlet of Winyah Bay, Georgetown is one of the state's few deepwater harbors and home to two huge steel and paper mills along US-17, but its downtown district along Front Street is compact and comfortable, with dozens of day-to-day businesses and a few cafés and art galleries filling the many old buildings.

Three blocks south of US-17, at the east end of Front Street, there's a pleasant waterfront promenade, where the clock-towered old town market now houses the **Rice Museum** (closed Sun.; $7). Dioramas trace South Carolina's little-known history as the world's main rice and indigo producer, a past often overshadowed by the state's later tobacco and cotton trade. The rest of town holds many well-preserved colonial and antebellum houses, churches, and commercial buildings.

A couple of good places to eat in Georgetown include seafood specialties at the **River Room** (801 Front St.; 843/527-4110) and the locals' favorite **Thomas Café** (703 Front St.; 843/546-7776), next to the Rice Museum. For more information, or to pick up a self-guided-tour map of town, contact the **Georgetown County Chamber of Commerce** (531 Front St.; 843/546-8436 or 800/777-7705), on the waterfront.

Hampton Plantation and McClellanville

The Santee Delta region along US-17 between Georgetown and Charleston once held dozens of large and hugely profitable plantations. One of the best preserved of these is now the **Hampton Plantation State Park,** located 15 miles south of Georgetown, then two miles west of US-17. Spreading out along the northern edge of Francis Marion National Forest, the 320-acre grounds feature a white wooden Greek Revival manor house (tours Sat.–Tues. at 1, 2, and 3 PM; $4) that once welcomed George Washington. The manor house was later home

Another South Carolina musical connection: Chubby Checker (of "The Twist" fame) was born inland from Georgetown in Spring Gully, near the town of Andrews.

the south facade of the Hampton Plantation house

to Archibald Rutledge, poet laureate of South Carolina from 1934 until his death in 1973.

South from Hampton Plantation along US-17, a small sign marks the turnoff to the quaint Lowcountry fishing village of **McClellanville** (pop. 413). A short drive past moss-draped oak trees brings you to the town dock, where some of the last portions of South Carolina's shrimp and crab catch get unloaded and shipped to market. But some of the local shellfish doesn't travel very far at all, ending up in the kitchens of **T.W. Graham & Co.,** housed in a former general store just up from the docks (closed Mon.; 810 Pinckney St.; 843/887-4342). Graham & Co. also grills burgers and bakes great pies, so plan to stop and spend some time here.

Cape Romain National Wildlife Refuge

Dense forests stretch west from the highway, while the unspoiled **Cape Romain National Wildlife Refuge** stretches south of McClellanville nearly to Charleston, forming one of the largest and most important sanctuaries for migratory birds on the East Coast. Thousands of great blue herons, pelicans, terns, and ducks join the resident population of wild turkeys, feral pigs, deer, and alligators. To get a glimpse of the diverse life protected here, visit the **Sewee Visitor Center** (daily; free; 843/928-3368), on US-17 at Awendaw. Exhibits inside explain the natural and human history of the region, and trails outside lead to a boardwalk viewing area and an enclosure that's home to native red wolves.

Directly across from the refuge entrance on US-17, you can appreciate other aspects of the area's culture at the homey **SeeWee Restaurant** (4808 N. US-17; 843/928-3609), a general store turned restaurant serving homemade specialties, including a fabulously rich she-crab soup (served with a shot of sherry on the side). The ambience is perfect—tin cans still fill the shelves, and local fishermen stop by to offer their catches—and the low prices and friendly people make it worth planning your trip around.

Fort Moultrie and Mount Pleasant

Sitting at the entrance to Charleston harbor, across from its better-known sibling, Fort Sumter, **Fort Moultrie** (daily; $3) overlooks the Atlantic with good views of passing ships and the city of Charleston. The location alone would make Moultrie well worth a visit, but most come because of its vital role in American military history. Originally built from palmetto logs during the Revolutionary War, and since rebuilt many times, the fort is a testament to the development of coastal defenses. Its well-preserved sections date from every major U.S. war between 1812 and World War II, when Fort Moultrie protected Charleston harbor from roving German U-boats. But the fort is most famous for its role in the events of April 1861, when Fort Moultrie touched off the Civil War by leading the bombardment of Fort Sumter.

Fort Moultrie is easy to reach. From Mount Pleasant, a suburban community on the north bank of the Cooper River across from Charleston, turn south from US-17 onto Hwy-703 and then follow signs along Middle Street to the fort.

Along with Fort Moultrie, **Mount Pleasant** itself is worth visiting for the many African sweetgrass basket-makers who set up shop along US-17. While the roadside is rapidly filling up with suburban tract-house "plantations," in the warmer months women sit and weave these intricate baskets at their ramshackle stands. Like so many other Lowcountry traditions, sweetgrass weaving may soon be a lost art, as younger women are increasingly reluctant to take on this low-paid work; it can take four to five hours to weave a basket that may sell for less than $60.

Fort Sumter National Monument

Commanding an island at the mouth of Charleston Harbor, **Fort Sumter National Monument** marks the site of the first military engagement of the Civil War. On April 12, 1861, a month after Abraham Lincoln's inauguration and four months after South Carolina had seceded from the United States, Confederate guns bombarded the fort until the Federal forces withdrew. The structure was badly damaged, but no one was killed and the fort was held by the Confederates for the next four years, by which time it had been almost completely flattened. Partly restored, but still a powerful symbol of the destruction wrought by the War Between the States, Fort Sumter is a key stop on any tour of Civil War sites.

the USS *Yorktown*, at Patriot's Point

You can visit Fort Sumter by taking your personal boat or by taking a ferry tour boat ($17; 843/722-2628); they leave from the north side of Charleston Bay at Patriot's Point, just off US-17 at the foot of the soaring new cable-stayed bridge across the Cooper River. (Other boats to Fort Sumter dock at the South Carolina Aquarium in downtown Charleston.) Patriot's Point is also the anchorage of the aircraft carrier USS *Yorktown* (daily; $18), centerpiece of an excellent floating maritime museum that also includes World War II–era fighter planes, a destroyer that took part in D-Day, a Coast Guard cutter, and a Cold War–era submarine.

Beaufort

The second-oldest town in South Carolina, **Beaufort** (pop. 12,361; pronounced "BYOO-furd") is a well-preserved antebellum town stretching along

Charleston

The Charleston accent is famous throughout the South. The word "garden" here is characteristically pronounced "gyarden," and "car" is "kyar," while the long "a" of Charleston (usually pronounced "Chaaahrleston") is as distinctive as JFK's "HAAH-vahd."

C.T. 1—The Old Market, Charleston, S. C. "America's Most Historic City"

Established in 1670 as the capital of South Carolina, **Charleston,** more than any other Deep South city, proudly maintains the aristocratic traditions established during the plantation era. Then the elite would flee the heat, humidity, and mosquitoes of their lowland fiefdoms and come here to cavort in ballrooms and theaters. Still ruled by old money, though no longer the state capital, Charleston is both pretentious and provincial; locals like to say that Charleston is the place where the Ashley and Cooper Rivers meet to form the Atlantic Ocean. Though there are clear divides between the haves and have-nots, Charleston is surprisingly cosmopolitan, accommodating a historic ethnic mix of French Huguenots, Catholic Acadians, and Afro-Caribbeans, who collectively introduced the wrought-iron balconies and brightly colored cottages that give the city much of its charm. George Gershwin's opera *Porgy and Bess,* for example, was inspired by life in Charleston's Creole ghetto, specifically Cabbage Row, now a tidy brick-paved alley off Church Street.

Having suffered through a devastating earthquake, two wars, and innumerable hurricanes, Charleston has rebuilt and restored itself many times, yet it remains one of the South's most beautiful cities. Impressive neoclassical buildings line the streets, especially in the older, upmarket sections of town south of Broad Street and along the waterfront Battery. Charleston's many small, lush gardens and parks make it ideal for aimless exploring on foot rather than by car. If you'd like a friendly, intelligent guide to show you around, contact Mr. Ed Grimball (843/762-0056).

Many of the mansions and churches are open to visitors, but it's the overall fabric of Charleston, rather than specific sites, that is most memorable. That said, the 1828 Greek Revival **Edmondston-Alston House** (daily; $10; 21 E. Battery) is definitely worth a look, as is the beautiful spire of **St. Michael's Episcopal Church** (daily; donations; 71 Broad St.), which was modeled on the London churches of Sir Christopher Wren. A quarter mile north, at Church and Market Streets, is the open-air **City Market,** known as the "Ellis Island of Black America," since over a third of all slaves arrived in the colonies here. Once the commercial center of Charleston, the market now houses a range of souvenir shops and touristy restaurants.

Charleston's annual arts-and-opera **Spoleto Festival USA** (843/722-2764) is held over two weeks in May and June.

Charleston Practicalities

Thanks to its considerable tourist trade, Charleston supports a number of excellent eateries at all price ranges. In the center of town, great breakfasts (as well as lunch, dinner, and Sunday brunch) are available at the very popular **Hominy Grill** (207 Rutledge Ave.; 843/937-0930). Around the City Market, you'll find the very popular **Hyman's Seafood** (215 Meeting St.; 843/723-6000), which has a variety of basic but good-value fresh fish entrées for around $10; expect a wait. More sedate and expensive dinner places nearby include the stylish **SNOB** (Slightly North of Broad; 192 E. Bay St.; 843/723-3424) and **Magnolia's** (185 E. Bay St.; 843/577-7771), serving inventive takes on Charleston's traditional Lowcountry food.

Like its restaurants, Charleston's accommodation options tend toward the luxurious and expensive. Of the dozens of old-fashioned but well-appointed B&Bs (all of which charge upwards of $200 a night), the elegant **John Rutledge House** (116 Broad St.; 843/723-7999 or 800/476-9741) offers four-star comfort in a converted 1763 house. On the bay, fronting the Battery, the romantic, Queen Anne–style **Two Meeting Street Inn** (2 Meeting St.; 843/723-7322) has been welcoming guests for over 50 years. Hotels in and around the historic district are similarly expensive, though you'll find a very handy **Days Inn** ($125 and up; 155 Meeting St.; 843/722-8411) downtown.

Outside the historic area a half mile south of US-17, the **Charleston Visitor Center** (daily; 375 Meeting St.; 843/724-7174) is a good first stop. It is free to ride the DASH shuttle buses that follow several routes downtown.

Edmondston-Alston House

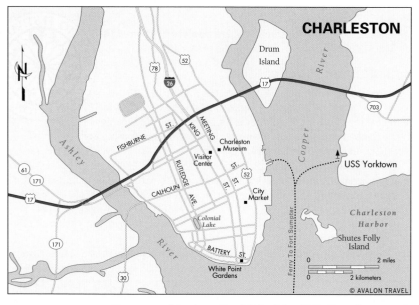

As recently as 1960, the population of South Carolina's Sea Islands was predominantly African American—10 to 1 on average. Now, with all the recent "plantation-style" vacation resorts, the proportions have effectively been reversed. As a last defense against the dark arts of resort developers, traditional African American Gullah culture is celebrated in summer festivals and tourism literature promoting the Gullah-Geechee Heritage Coast.

a fine natural harbor. Established in 1710, Beaufort stands on the largest of some 75 islands near the Georgia border; the town is perhaps best known as the home of the massive U.S. Marine Corps Recruit Depot at nearby Parris Island, where new Marines undergo their basic training. Dozens of colonial-era and antebellum homes line Beaufort's quiet Bay Street waterfront, but only two, the **Verdier House** and the Greek Revival **Elliott House,** a block apart on Bay Street, are open to visitors. Verdier House offers tours, while the Elliott House is open as an art gallery.

Beaufort is a very enjoyable place to wander around and explore, and it has at least one great place to eat: **Blackstone's Cafe** (205 Scott St.; 843/524-4330), off the main street, where fans of the shrimp and grits and corned beef hash include local writer Pat Conroy. Places to stay include the waterfront **Best Western Sea Island Inn** (1015 Bay St.; 843/522-2090 or 800/528-1234) and the state's only four-star B&B, the lovely **Rhett House** ($160 and up; 1009 Craven St.; 843/524-9030), where the film of Conroy's *The Prince of Tides* was shot on location.

South to Savannah: Hilton Head Island

From Beaufort, the easiest way south is to follow Hwy-170 all the way to Savannah or to detour east onto I-95. Otherwise, a pleasant but potentially confusing series of two-lane roads run around Hilton Head Island across the lowlands toward Georgia.

Near the southern tip of South Carolina, **Hilton Head Island** is the largest ocean island between Florida and New Jersey. It was first settled in 1663, but only since the late 1950s, when a bridge to the mainland was completed, has it really been on the map. The deluxe, 500-room, 5,000-acre **Sea Pines Resort** ($250 and up; 32 Greenwood Dr.; 866/561-8802) is an international destination, and upscale golf courses and plantation-style estates abound around the island's 30,000 acres, as do minimalls and all the trappings of suburban America. There's also a very popular, family-friendly **Disney resort** ($175 and up; 22 Harbourside Ln.; 843/341-4100).

Along the Savannah River, which marks the boundary between South Carolina and Georgia, Eli Whitney invented the cotton gin in 1793 at Mulberry Grove plantation.

The "success" of Hilton Head has caused developers to set their sights on the rest of the Lowcountry, as shown by the opening of the super-plush **Palmetto Bluff** resort ($500 and up; 843/706-6500) at nearby Bluffton, where each of 50 waterfront cottages is outfitted with plasma TVs and a Sub-Zero fridge for that quintessential Lowcountry experience.

The beautiful city of Savannah marks the junction of our Atlantic Coast route with the **Southern Pacific** road trip along US-80; some coastal destinations, including the excellent **Tybee Island,** are covered there (see page 862). Full coverage of US-80 is on pages 800–945.

GEORGIA

The marshes and barrier islands that line the Atlantic Ocean along the Georgia coast are among the lesser-known treasures of the eastern United States. Geographically, the coastline consists of mostly road-less and largely unconnected islands, which makes coastal driving nearly impossible; the nearest north–south routes, I-95 and the older US-17, run roughly 15 miles inland, and only a few roads head east to the Atlantic shore. The lack of access has kept development to a minimum and has also been a boon to wildlife—well over half the coastline is protected within state and federal parks, preserves, and refuges.

The "you-can't-get-there-from-here" aspect can make it more than a little frustrating for casual visitors, but if you have the time and inclination, it also makes the Georgia coast a wonderful place to explore. One of the main car-friendly destinations along the Georgia coast is **Tybee Island** in the north, east of Savannah. Farther south, take time to explore the beautiful and history-rich **Golden Isles,** east of Brunswick. Both are great places to visit, and they offer an appetizing taste of the 100 miles of isolated shoreline Georgia otherwise keeps to itself.

Midway: The Smallest Church in America

The section of US-17 south of the Ogeechee River, off I-95 between exits 14 and 12, offers shunpikers (those who shun turnpikes; see www.shunpikers.com) a

24-mile taste of old-style Lowland Georgia. Sometimes called the Old Atlantic Highway, it is a textbook example of how traveling the two-lane highways is superior in almost every way to hustling down the Interstates. Midway along, the coincidentally named town of **Midway** (pop. 1,500) was founded back in 1754 by a band of New England colonists, two of whom (Lyman Hall and Button Guinett) went on to sign the Declaration of Independence as Georgia's self-declared representatives to the Continental Congress. The centerpiece of Midway, then and now, is 200-year-old **Midway Church,** which preserves the original pulpit and slave gallery; keys for the church are available at the adjacent **Midway Museum** (closed Mon. and Sun.; $3; 912/884-5837).

South of Midway along US-17, a small sign on the east side of the highway (a mile south of I-95 exit 67) points travelers toward the "Smallest Church in America," a 12-seat cabin that's open 24 hours. (Please turn the lights out when you leave.) Besides the kitsch value, there's another good reason to keep an eye out for the Smallest Church: six miles east of the church, a mile from the shore down Harris Neck Road, the wonderfully named, nearly world-famous **Old School Diner** (closed Mon.–Tues.; cash only; 912/832-2136) serves up generous portions of fantastically flavorful seafood, barbecue ribs, chicken, and more. Only a half hour from Savannah, it's worth a trip from just about anywhere.

Sapelo Island and Darien

Though coastal Georgia has by and large been spared the worst excesses of real estate development, for an unforgettable taste of the *real* pre–tourist industry

Georgia culture, make your way east to **Sapelo Island,** which stretches offshore between Midway and Darien. The island is a stark, sparsely populated, mostly undeveloped, and generally fascinating place to spend some time, a truly wild landscape where alligators and ferocious feral pigs live free among remnants of colonial-era plantation agriculture and native Creek Indian shell middens dating back 6,000 years. Once a cotton plantation, worked by slaves whose 70-odd descendants live in Hog Hammock, Sapelo's only permanent community, the island is now owned by the state of Georgia and used as a marine biology research center.

There is no real commercial development on Sapelo Island—no stores and no restaurants, so bring your own food and drink—just miles of beaches, marshlands, and open sea. Get there from the mainland hamlet of **Meridian,** where you can catch the state-run ferry for a four-hour guided tour (reservations required; adults $10, under 18 $6; 912/437-3224), which gives a full introduction to Sapelo Island life. For an even more memorable experience, arrange to stay overnight at **The Wallow** (912/485-2206), a small Hog Hammock B&B run by lifelong Sapelo Island resident Cornelia Bailey. There's a communal kitchen, or meals can be arranged in advance.

South of Sapelo Island near the mouth of the Altamaha River, which formed the rough and frequently fought-over boundary between British and Spanish parts of the New World, **Darien** (pop. 1,800) looks a lot like most other coastal Deep South towns, but it boasts a history to match many bigger or more famous destinations. After a small, 16th-century Spanish mission near here was destroyed by Native Americans, Darien was founded in 1736 by Scottish colonists (many named McIntosh, now the name of the surrounding county) near Fort King George, the first British outpost in what became Georgia. Darien later became a center of the lucrative early-19th-century rice trade, surrounded by plantations where the abuse of slaves inspired British actress Fanny Kemble's book-length indictment, *Journal of a Residence on a Georgia Plantation in 1838–39,* an influential abolitionist text.

Despite the many claims it could make to importance, Darien preserves its past in a matter-of-fact manner. The main attraction is the reconstructed **Fort King George,** a state historic site, a mile east of US-17 on Fort King George Drive (closed Mon.; $6).

Another intriguing place to visit is the **Hofwyl-Broadfield Plantation** (Thurs.–Sat.; $6), five miles south of Darien along US-17, where a well-preserved plantation home is surrounded by 1,200 acres of one-time rice fields that have reverted to cypress swamps. Displays inside the visitors center tell the story of how slaves were forced to labor in the sweltering, mosquito-plagued summer heat, building levees and doing the back-breaking work of planting, growing, and harvesting the rice.

The Class A **Savannah Sand Gnats** (912/351-9150), a Washington Nationals farm club, play at WPA-built Grayson Stadium, off US-80 on the south side of town.

A compelling nonfiction account of 1970s Darien, Melissa Fay Greene's *Praying for Sheetrock* describes how locals and legal activists used federal lawsuits to overcome the corrupt regimes of local government and law enforcement officials.

Savannah

Bonaventure Cemetery

Named the "Most Beautiful City in North America" by the Parisian newspaper and style arbiter *Le Monde*, **Savannah** (pop. 136,286) is a real jewel of a place. Founded in 1733 as the first settlement in Georgia, the 13th and final American colony, Savannah today preserves its original neoclassical, colonial, and antebellum self in a welcoming, unselfconscious way. Famous for having been spared by General Sherman on his destructive March to the Sea at the end of the Civil War, it was here that Sherman made his offering of "40 acres and a mule" to all freed slaves.

Before and after the war, Savannah was Georgia's main port, rivaling Charleston, South Carolina, for the enormously lucrative cotton trade, but as commercial shipping tailed off, the harbor became increasingly recreational—the yachting competitions of the 1996 Olympics were held offshore. Savannah, home of writer Flannery O'Connor and songsmith Johnny Mercer, also served as backdrop to the best-selling book *Midnight in the Garden of Good and Evil* and numerous movies, most famously *Forrest Gump*, but it has resisted urges to turn itself into an "Old South" theme park; you'll have to search hard to find souvenir shops or overpriced knickknack galleries.

At the center of Savannah, midway down Bull Street between the waterfront and spacious Forsyth Park, **Chippewa Square** was the site of Forrest Gump's bus bench (the movie prop was moved to the visitors center and may one day be erected in bronze). **Reynolds Square,** near the waterfront, has a statue of John Wesley, who lived in Savannah in 1736–1737 and established the world's first Sunday School here. **Wright Square** holds a monument to Chief Tomochichi, the Native American tribal leader who allowed Georgia founder James Edward Oglethorpe to settle here, and **Forsyth Park,** at the south edge of the historic center, is modeled after the Place de la Concorde in Paris, surrounded by richly scented magnolias.

Another great place to wander is **Factor's Walk,** a promontory along the Savannah River named for the "factors" who controlled Savannah's cotton trade. This area holds the Cotton Exchange and other historic buildings, many of them constructed from 18th-century ballast stones. Linked from the top of the bluffs by a network of steep stone stairways and cast-iron walkways, **River Street** is lined by restaurants, and at the east end there's a statue of a girl waving; it was erected in memory of Florence Martus, who for 50 years around the turn of the 20th century greeted every ship entering Savannah harbor in the vain hope that her boyfriend would be on board.

March is when things get crazy here in Savannah: Thousands of visitors come to the bars along Congress Street for what has grown into the world's second-largest **St. Patrick's Day** celebration—only New York City's is bigger.

One of Savannah's more unusual tourist attractions is the **Juliet Gordon Low Birthplace** (142 Bull St.), a circa-1820 house that was the childhood home of the woman who introduced Girl Scouts to America in 1912. Current Girl Scouts gain a merit badge just by walking in the door.

Savannah Practicalities

Getting around is blissfully easy: Savannah is the country's preeminent walkers' town, with a wealth of historic architecture and a checkerboard of 22 small squares shaded with centuries-old live oak trees draped with tendrils of Spanish moss, all packed together in a single square mile. Savannah's sensible and very attractive modified grid plan makes finding your way so simple that it's almost fun to try to get lost.

St. Patrick's Day celebrators

For an unforgettable midday meal, be sure to stop at **Mrs. Wilkes' Dining Room** (Mon.–Fri. 11 AM–2 PM; 107 W. Jones St.; 912/232-5997), a central Savannah home and former boardinghouse that still offers up traditional family-style Southern cooking—varying from fried chicken to crab stews, with side dishes like okra gumbo; sweet potato pie; red, green, or brown rice; and cornbread muffins. It's worth a trip from anywhere in the state—don't leave Savannah without eating here. For a more upscale take on these Deep South classics, make plans to have lunch or dinner at **The Olde Pink House,** on Reynolds Square (23 Abercorn St.; 912/232-4286). Near the Sand Gnats baseball stadium on the south side of town, right on old US-80, **Johnny Harris** (1651 E. Victory Dr.; 912/354-7810) is Savannah's oldest restaurant and one of the fanciest fried chicken and barbecue places in the world.

Road-food fans may want to head a half mile south of downtown to the **Streamliner Diner** (102 W. Henry St.), a gorgeously restored 1938 Worcester diner operated by (and across the street from) the Savannah College of Art & Design (SCAD), which has taken over many of the city's older buildings and converted them into art studios, galleries, and cafés.

Places to stay in Savannah vary from quaint B&B inns to stale high-rise hotels. For the total Savannah experience, try the **Bed and Breakfast Inn** ($150 and up; 117 W. Gordon St.; 912/238-0518), which has very nice rooms in an 1853 townhouse off Monterey Square. At the **River Street Inn** ($150 and up; 124 E. Bay St.; 912/234-6400 or 800/253-4229), well-appointed rooms fill a converted antebellum cotton warehouse, right on Factor's Walk at the heart of the Savannah riverfront. Nearby, the large **Inn at Ellis Square** ($125 and up; 201 W. Bay St.; 912/236-4440 or 800/325-2525) has good-sized hotel rooms (in a former Days Inn), right across from Factor's Walk.

The **Savannah Visitors Center** (301 Martin Luther King Blvd.; 912/944-0455), in the old Georgia Central railroad terminal just west of the historic center, has free maps and brochures and other information on the city.

Brunswick: The Golden Isles

Along the southeast Georgia coast, a patchwork of islands known as the **Golden Isles** offer a wide range of images and experiences. The largest and best known, **St. Simon's Island,** is a mini Hilton Head, with many vacation resorts and a sizable year-round community. The center of activity on St. Simon's is at the south tip of the island, where the village consists of a central plaza and a few blocks of shops, saloons, and restaurants along Mallery Street, which leads down to the waterfront pier and a circa-1872 lighthouse. Sea kayaks, bicycles, and boats can be rented here, and there are a number of reasonable motels. For a carb-loading breakfast or lunch, or a taste of the Food Network's favorite Five Cheese Grilled Cheese, make your way to the popular **4th of May Café** (321 Mallery; 912/638-5444) just off Ocean Boulevard.

Georgia's most famous 19th-century poet, Sidney Lanier, settled near Brunswick after contracting tuberculosis as a POW during the Civil War. He wrote his most famous poems, including "The Marshes of Glynn," while he sat under an oak tree that stands along US-17, a mile north of town.

Also on St. Simon's, right at the heart of the island, purist wood-smoke barbecue fans flock to **Southern Soul BBQ** (2020 DeMere Rd.; 912/638-SOUL) for juicy, melt-in-the-mouth ribs, pulled pork sandwiches, and an excellent version of Brunswick Stew (pork, chicken, beef, corn, beans, and more mixed up in a rich tomato barbecue sauce).

Apart from the excellent food, the one real "sight" on St. Simon's Island is the **Fort Frederica National Monument,** at the northwest edge of the island, which protects the remains of the village surrounding what was once the largest fortress in the British colonies. Built in 1736 and abandoned in 1763, Fort

St. Simon's Island Light Station

Frederica played a vital role in keeping Georgia British, rather than Spanish; in 1742, a key battle was fought six miles south of the fort, at a site known as "Bloody Marsh."

For the total Golden Isles experience, splurge on a night or two at one of the country's plushest resorts, the five-star **Cloister Hotel** ($400 and up; 912/638-3611 or 888/SEA ISLAND), east of Fort Frederica, which covers adjacent Sea Island with 36 holes of golf courses and 264 Spanish-style rooms. Presidents from Coolidge to Bush have vacationed here, the late JFK Jr. got married here, and the G8 economic summit has been held here, too, which should give you some idea of the elite character of the place.

Back on the mainland, heavily industrialized **Brunswick** (pop. 16,500) feels about as far from the genteel pleasures of the Golden Isles as you can be. Most vacationers pass through quickly on their way to and from the Golden Isles, but there is one great place to stop: the **Georgia Pig** (912/264-6664), southwest of town at the US-17 junction, just east of I-95 exit 29. Tucked away next to a gas station in a scruffy woodland, it looks like it's been there forever; the bare-bones decor—log rafters, pine picnic tables, and creaking front door—disappears when you bite into the juicy ribs and fabulous pulled-pork sandwiches, which are smoked in a hickory-fired oven right behind the counter. Even for non-barbecue fans, Brunswick holds a road food attraction: **Willie's Wee-Nee Wagon** (3599 Altama Ave.; 912/264-1146), a yellow-and-white candy-striped diner, a mile west of US-17 across

from the College of Coastal Georgia. Famous for all sorts of good things—crunchy cole-slaw, chili dogs, pork chops, steak sandwiches, and more—Willie's is something of a Georgia coast institution, and well worth searching for.

Jekyll Island

Southeast of Brunswick, and developed in the late 1880s as a private, members-only resort for New York multimillionaires, **Jekyll Island** now offers a chance for those *not* in control of a Fortune 500 company to enjoy a generous slice of Golden Isles life. Now owned by the state of Georgia, a grand hotel and dozens of palatial vacation "cottages" that would look equally at home in Newport, Rhode Island, are accessible to the general public after a long life spent catering to the richest of the rich.

Around the turn of the 20th century, the 50-odd members of the Jekyll Island Club, which included such names as Rockefeller, Carnegie, Morgan, and Vanderbilt, controlled as much as 20 percent of the world's wealth.

At the center of the island, and the best place to start a visit, is the landmark **Jekyll Island Club Hotel** ($170 and up; 912/635-2600 or 800/535-9547). The very pleasant rooms here aren't *all* that expensive, considering the luxury you're swaddled in, and the setting is superb. Majestic oak trees dangling garlands of Spanish moss cover the 200-acre grounds, and within a short walk, many of the grand old mansions are now open for guided tours ($10). The nearby stables have been converted into a nice little **museum** (daily; free), which tells the whole Jekyll Island story.

Georgia Sea Turtle Center, Jekyll Island

One new development here has been the **Georgia Sea Turtle Center** ($6; 214 Stable Rd.; 912/635-4444), housed in the old Jekyll Island power plant. This is one of the prime places for the study and rehabilitation of these lyrical swimmers, whose native habitats have been threatened by all the housing and resort development along the Atlantic shore.

Less than a mile east, the Atlantic oceanfront is lined by Beachview Drive and a five-mile-long beach—with the least developed stretches at the north and south ends of the island. Bike rentals—which really provide the best way to see the island—are available along Beachview Drive ($5/hr; 912/635-9801).

Cumberland Island National Seashore

Right on the Florida border, and once the private reserve of the Carnegie family, the **Cumberland Island National Seashore** is a 99 percent uninhabited barrier island with miles of hiking trails and primitive backcountry camping along beaches and in palmetto forests. Also here is the unique **Greyfield Inn** (904/261-6408), the Carnegie family mansion now operated (by Carnegie heirs) as an unpretentious 16-room historic lodge that runs around $400 a night for two people, including gourmet meals and transportation from the mainland. (Bring your own bug spray!)

St. Marys, Georgia, the main access to Cumberland Island, is also home to the huge Kings Bay U.S. Navy Base, home port of the nuclear-powered and -armed submarine Atlantic fleet.

Unless you're a guest at the Greyfield, Cumberland Island is only accessible by a twice-daily ferry ($20 round-trip plus a $4 entrance fee) from the town of St. Marys, 10 miles east of I-95 exit 1. For further details, contact the Cumberland Island National Seashore information and reservations center at 912/882-4336.

FLORIDA

Stretching some 600 miles between the Georgia border and Key West at its far southern tip, Florida offers something for everyone, from unsullied nature to the tackiest tourist traps in the land, and everything imaginable in between. More than anywhere else in the United States, the Florida landscape has been designed for tourists, and no matter what your fancy or fantasy, you can live it here, under the semi-tropical sun. The many millions who visit Disney World or flock to fashionable Miami Beach each year are doing exactly what people have come to Florida to do for over a century—enjoy themselves.

In the 1930s, when car travel and Florida tourism were both reaching an early peak of popularity, the roadside landscape was, in the words of the WPA *Guide to Florida,* lined by

. . . signs that turn like windmills; startling signs that resemble crashed airplanes; signs with glass lettering which blaze forth at night when automobile headlights strike them; flashing neon signs; signs painted with professional touch; signs crudely lettered and misspelled. They advertise hotels, tourist cabins, fishing camps, and eating places. They extol the virtues of ice creams, shoe creams, cold creams; proclaim the advantages of new cars and used cars; tell of 24-hour towing and ambulance service, Georgia pecans, Florida fruit and fruit juices, honey, soft drinks, and furniture. They urge the traveler to take designated tours, to visit certain cities, to stop at certain points he must see.

Two men who made millions in the automobile industry have had immeasurable influence over the evolution of the Florida coast. Standard Oil baron Henry Flagler constructed the first railroad and built a chain of deluxe resort hotels from St. Augustine to Miami, while Carl Fisher, the developer of car headlights, promoted Florida's "Route 66," the Dixie Highway, and later helped to found Miami Beach. Their names reappear frequently wherever you travel along the Atlantic coast.

Despite the modern gloss of golf course estates and sprawling retirement communities, which tend to overshadow the substantial stretches of wide open beaches and coastal forest, Florida has a lengthy and fascinating history, with significant native cultures and, in **St. Augustine,** some of the oldest signs of European presence in North America, including the legendary Fountain of Youth. At the other end of the state, on the fringes of the Caribbean, **Key West** is a tropical paradise, founded by pirates four centuries ago and still one of the most lively and anarchic places in the United States. In between, our road-trip route passes through such diverse places as **Daytona Beach,** mecca for race car fans and a magnet for college kids on spring break; the launch pads and mission control centers of the **Kennedy Space Center;** the multicultural melting pots of **Miami** and **Miami Beach;** and, of course, the "Happiest Place on Earth," **Disney World.**

There are three main routes running north–south along Florida's Atlantic coastline, and your travels will likely make use of at least a little of each one. The

Of all the American colonies, only Florida remained loyal to the British crown during the Revolutionary War. After the war, the British ceded Florida to Spain, which eventually swapped it to the United States in 1821 in exchange for $5 million in assumed debt.

fastest route is the I-95 freeway, which races uneventfully along, linking the major cities. The most scenic route is Hwy-A1A, a mostly two-lane highway that runs as close as possible to the shoreline, linking many gorgeous beaches but, because of the very flat topography and the extensive beach-front development, offering only rare glimpses of the open ocean. In between I-95 and Hwy-A1A runs historic US-1, part of the old Dixie Highway, which is lined by reminders of Florida's rich roadside heritage but which also passes through some of the state's less salubrious corners, especially in and around the larger cities. Our suggested route primarily follows coastal Hwy-A1A, but directions from other, faster routes are also given, so you can alternate freely and easily among them all.

Amelia Island

Entering Florida from Georgia across the St. Marys River, which flows east out of the Okefenokee Swamp to the Atlantic Ocean, you may want to skirt around the metropolitan sprawl of Jacksonville by following old US-17, or

Forth Clinch State Park

getting off I-95 at exit 129, to Hwy-A1A, which runs due east to the brilliant white-sand beaches and picturesque historic buildings of **Amelia Island.** The main community on the island is **Fernandina Beach** (pop 12,076), once the main port in northeast Florida. The eastern terminus of the first trans-Florida railroad, and long a popular tourist destination, Fernandina Beach retains many late-Victorian buildings, collected together in a wanderable 30-block historic district along the Amelia Island bayfront.

A local landmark, the **Florida House Inn** ($150 and up; 20 S. 3rd St.; 904/491-3322) is Florida's oldest hotel, welcoming travelers since 1857, while at the center of town the lively **Palace Saloon** (117 Centre St.; 904/491-3332) is another of "Florida's Oldest," with a lovely carved wood bar, very good burgers, and regular live reggae and other warm-weather music.

More history has been preserved at the north end of Amelia Island, adjacent to Fernandina Beach, where the well-preserved remnants of a pre–Civil War brick fortress stand in **Fort Clinch State Park** (daily; $6 per car; 904/277-7274), with 250 acres of marshes, sand dunes, and coastal hammock forests, plus a nice campground, along the edge of Cumberland Sound.

South of Fernandina Beach, Hwy-A1A follows Fletcher Avenue along Amelia Island's gorgeous white beaches, passing upscale resorts (including a Ritz-Carlton) before crossing over a bridge onto Talbot Island. Four miles south of the bridge, there's a turnoff west to the 3,000-acre **Kingsley Plantation** (daily; free; 904/251-

An anhinga female guards a nest on Amelia Island.

3537), the last remaining antebellum plantation in Florida, where you can explore the elegant old lodge and remains of more than 20 slave cabins.

Continuing south, Hwy-A1A winds across the dense native jungles of **Little Talbot Island,** where a large **state park** (daily dawn–dusk; $5 per car; 904/251-2320) has hiking and cycling trails, a nice campground, and a magnificent beach. The scenic road, which has been dubbed the "Buccaneer Trail," eventually ends up at the terminal for the ferry to Mayport (every 30 min.; no RVs) across the St. Johns River.

Henry Flagler: Father of Florida Tourism

Though you've probably never heard of the man, you can't travel very far along the east coast of Florida without coming under the influence of Henry Flagler, who almost single-handedly turned what had been swampy coastline into one of the world's most popular tourist destinations. After making a fortune as John D. Rockefeller's partner in the Standard Oil Company, in the early 1880s Flagler came to St. Augustine with his wife, who was suffering from health problems. He found the climate agreeable, but the facilities sorely lacking, so he embarked on construction of the 540-room Hotel Ponce de León, which opened in 1888. The hotel, the first major resort in Florida, was an instant success, and Flagler quickly expanded his operations, building the first railroad along the coast south to Palm Beach, where he opened the world's largest hotel, the now-demolished Royal Poinciana, in 1894, joined by The Breakers in 1901 and his own palatial home, Whitehall, in 1902.

Meanwhile, Flagler was busy extending his railroad south, effectively founding the new city of Miami in 1897 when he opened the deluxe Royal Palm Hotel. From Miami, he decided to extend his Florida East Coast Railway all the way to Key West, which at the time was Florida's most populous city and the American deep-water port closest to the proposed Panama Canal. At a cost of $50 million and hundreds of lives, this amazing railroad was completed in 1912, but it lasted only two decades before a hurricane destroyed the tracks in 1935. The remnants of Flagler's railroad were used as the foundation for today's Overseas Highway, US-1, but Flagler himself never lived to see it: In 1913, a year after his railroad reached Key West, Henry Flagler fell down a flight of stairs and died at age 84.

Whitehall, formerly Flagler's home in Palm Beach, is now the Henry Morrison Flagler Museum.

Jacksonville Beach

East of Jacksonville, at the mouth of the St. Johns River, Hwy-A1A curves around a large U.S. Navy base (third largest in the U.S., specializing in helicopters, which you'll often see hovering overhead), past the busy Bath Iron Works shipyard and the sizable fishing port of **Mayport,** where you can enjoy a quick bite at seafood shack **Singleton's** (4728 Ocean St.; 904/246-4442) 100 yards west of the ferry landing. From Mayport, Hwy-A1A zigzags inland south and east, reaching the water again at **Jacksonville Beach,** a welcoming, family-oriented community with the usual gauntlet of cafés, mini-golf courses, and video arcades, and a nice beachfront centering on a small pier.

Class AA farm club for the Florida Marlins, the Jacksonville Suns play ball at a very nice $35 million downtown stadium called the Baseball Grounds (904/358-2846).

South of Jacksonville Beach spreads the enclave of **Ponte Vedra Beach,** where country club resorts replace roadside sprawl. Hwy-A1A bends inland through here, so if you want to keep close to the shore (most of which is private), follow Hwy-203 instead, rejoining Hwy-A1A on the edge of town.

South of Ponte Vedra, Hwy-A1A passes a pair of beachfront state parks (the marvelous 12,000-acre **Guana River** and smaller **South Ponte Vedra**), both of which give access to usually uncrowded sands.

Host of the 2005 Super Bowl, **Jacksonville,** which covers over 840 square miles, is the largest city by area in the continental United States.

Fountain of Youth

North of St. Augustine, Hwy-A1A cuts inland from the shore, crossing a bridge over the North River, then following San Marco Avenue south into the center of St. Augustine past the Fountain of Youth. That's right, the Fountain of Youth. Though its efficacy has never been proven in court, there is an actual site where Spanish explorer Ponce de León, searching for a fabled spring that would keep him

forever young, came ashore in 1513. Now a pleasant 20-acre park, facing Matanzas Bay about a mile north of central St. Augustine, the **Fountain of Youth** (daily 10 AM–4 PM; $10; 800/356-8222) preserves a naturally sulfurous spring (which you can drink from using Dixie cups—though there are no guarantees of immortality!), a burial ground, and remnants of a native Timucuan village and an early Spanish settlement.

St. Augustine

If you like history, architecture, sandy beaches, bizarre tourist attractions—or any combination of the above—you'll want to spend some time in St. Augustine. The oldest permanent settlement in the United States—though

Across the street from the Ripley's Believe It or Not!, a coquina stone ball known as the Zero Milepost marks the eastern end of the **Old Spanish Trail,** one of the earliest transcontinental highways. Marked and promoted from here west to San Diego, the Old Spanish Trail, like the Lincoln Highway and the Dixie Highway, preceded the system of numbered highways (Route 66 et al.) and provided a popular cross-country link.

Santa Fe, New Mexico, makes a strong counterclaim to this title—**St. Augustine** was founded in 1565, half a century after Ponce de León first set foot here in 1513, looking for the Fountain of Youth. Under Spanish control, the town's early history was pretty lively, with Sir Francis Drake leveling the place in 1586. The British, after trading Cuba for Florida at the end of the Seven Years' War, took control in 1763 and held St. Augustine throughout the American Revolution—during which Florida was staunchly loyal to King George. It served for many years as capital of Florida under both the British and Spanish, but after the Americans took over, the city lost that status to Tallahassee. St. Augustine subsequently missed out on much of Florida's 20th-century growth and development, which has allowed the preservation of its substantial historical remnants.

The heart of St. Augustine is contained within a walkably small area, centered on the Plaza de la Constitución, which faces east onto Matanzas Bay. Pedestrianized St. George Street runs north and south from here through the heart of historic St. Augustine, while two blocks west stands the city's most prominent landmarks: two grand, early 1900s hotels—the **Ponce de Leon** and the **Alcazar.** They were originally owned and operated as part of Henry Flagler's Florida empire but now respectively house **Flagler College** and the decorative arts collections of the **Lightner Museum** (daily; $10). Both are full of finely crafted interior spaces and well worth a look.

Though it's the compact size and overall historic sheen of St. Augustine that make it such a captivating place to spend some time, there are lots of individual attractions hawking themselves as important "historic sites," usually the oldest this-or-that in Florida, or even in the whole United States. The **Oldest Wooden Schoolhouse** (14 St. George St.), in the heart of historic St. Augustine, dates from 1750 and now features a push-button wax dummy of a schoolteacher, while the **Oldest Store Museum,** a block south of the main plaza (4 Artillery Ln.), has 100,000 items, all of them well past their turn-of-the-20th-century sell-by date. At the north end of St. George Street, an original city gate leads across San Marco Avenue (Hwy-A1A) to another must-see tourist trap: the original **Ripley's Believe It or Not!** museum (daily; $14.95; 904/824-1606), an elaborate Spanish Revival mansion filled since 1950 with Robert Ripley's personal collection of oddities. Outside, in the parking lot, is a four-room "tree house," carved out of a California redwood tree in 1957.

These are fun in a tongue-in-cheek way, but the most impressive historic site is the remarkable **Castillo de San Marcos** (daily; $6), which dominates the St. Augustine waterfront. Built by Spain between 1672 and 1695, the Castillo saw its first battle in 1702, when British forces laid siege for 50 days but were unable to capture it, though they did once again level the adjacent town of St. Augustine. The Castillo was later used by the British to house American POWs during the Revolutionary War, and by the United States to house Native American prisoners captured during the Seminole War of 1835–1842 as well as during the later Indian Wars of the Wild West. Since 1924 it's been a national monument and is open for walks along the ramparts and for frequent ranger-guided tours.

One of many attractive things about St. Augustine is the almost total lack of franchised fast-food restaurants, at least in the historic downtown area. Instead, you can choose from all sorts of local places, like the **Florida Cracker Cafe** (81 St. George St.; 904/829-0397), a casual seafood grill where you can sample the local delicacy, alligator tail. For fish-and-chips, try the **Mill Top Tavern** (19½ St. George St.; 904/829-2329), which boasts good live music and a block-long bar. (Yes, it's a short block.) Another fun place to while away an evening is **Scarlett O'Hara's,** offering beers, burgers, and live music a block from Flagler College(70 Hypolita St.; 904/824-6535). Fun and fairly good value, east of the historic core but right on lovely St. Augustine Beach itself, **Paula's Beachside Grill** (6896 Hwy-A1A; 904/471-3463) is a very popular tiki bar–style burger, sandwich, and beer stand.

Unfortunately for present-day visitors, the grand old Ponce de Léon Hotel no longer welcomes overnight guests, but contemporary St. Augustine does offer a wide variety of accommodations, including the imaginatively named **Beachfront B&B** ($129 and up; 1 F St.; 904/461-8727) in St. Augustine Beach, where you can spend the night in one of six tastefully decorated suites in a historic home, then wake up to watch the porpoises cavorting offshore. In the historic district, the **Kenwood Inn** ($125 and up; 38 Marine St.; 904/824-2116) has 14 rooms in a Victorian-era hotel along the Matanzas River.

For additional listings, maps, and general information, your first stop should be the **St. Augustine visitors center** (904/825-1000 or 800/653-2489), across from the Castillo.

Alligator Farm

From the heart of St. Augustine, Hwy-A1A crosses over the Matanzas River on the lovely, historic Bridge of Lions to Anastasia Island, bound for the Atlantic beaches three miles to the east. On the way to the beach, just two miles south of Old Town St. Augustine on Anastasia Boulevard (Hwy-A1A), sits one of the greatest of Florida's many tourist traps, **Alligator Farm** (daily; $21.95; 904/824-3337). Touted as the world's only complete collection of crocodilians,

Alligator Farm resident

this was the first and is now one of the last of many such roadside menageries. A legitimate historical landmark, Alligator Farm is also a fun and informative place to spend some time—great for kids and anyone who finds gators and crocs (and turtles, iguanas, monkeys, and tropical birds, all of which are here) to be captivating creatures. Start at the largest enclosure, a mossy pond seething with hundreds of baby gators (which you can feed), and be sure to pay your respects to Gomek, the Alligator Farm's massive taxiderm-ied mascot, and to Maximo, a 16-foot Aussie crocodile who's still growing ever-larger.

About three miles north of Marineland, on the inland side of Hwy-A1A, you can see the 16-foot-thick stone walls of **Fort Matanzas,** built by the Spanish around 1736 and never conquered. Now a national historic site, it's open for free tours.

Across from Alligator Farm, a road turns east from Hwy-A1A to **Anastasia State Recreation Area,** the site where the stone for Castillo de San Marcos was quarried, and where in addition to beaches there's an inlet set aside for wind-surfing, hiking trails through coastal hammock forests, and a nice camp-ground (904/461-2033) amid stately live oaks and magnolia trees.

Marineland

Eighteen miles south of St. Augustine, 35 miles north of Daytona Beach, the orig-inal sea-creature amuse-

Sulawesi Red-knobbed Hornbills at Alligator Farm

ment park, **Marineland** (daily; $8.50; 904/471-1111), opened with a "splash" in 1938 and closed down suddenly in 1998, declaring bankruptcy after struggling for years to compete with the much-larger likes of Sea World and Disney World. Marineland, which is credited with the first performing dolphins (and with playing a key role in the sci-fi movie *Creature from the Black Lagoon*), reopened in 2005 on a much smaller scale, with an "edutainment" focus on offering intimate encounters with its famous dolphins. It sounds like a magical experience, but before you mention Marineland to your kids, be warned: these "Swim with a Dolphin" programs cost around $200 per person—and up.

Continuing along the coast south of Marineland, you start to see roadside fruit stands advertising "Indian River Fruit"—something you'll see more of as you travel south. This is a major citrus-growing region. This stretch of Hwy-A1A, around the town of Flagler Beach, is also one of the few where you can actually see the ocean from the road.

Daytona Beach

Offering a heady barrage of blue-collar beach culture, **Daytona Beach** (pop. 68,128) is a classic road-trip destination in every way, shape, and form. The beach here is huge—over 20 miles long, and 500 feet wide at low tide—and there's a small and recently pretty scruffy amusement pier at the foot of Main Street. The rest of Daytona Beach is rather rough at the edges, with boarded-up shops and some lively bars and nightclubs filling the few blocks between the beach area and the Halifax River, which separates the beach from the rest of the town.

The winning car of each year's Daytona 500 remains on display in the Daytona 500 Experience until the following year's race.

Besides being a living museum of pop culture, Daytona Beach has long played an important role in car culture: In the first decades of the 20th century, a real Who's Who of international automotive pioneers—Henry Ford, R. E. Olds, Malford Duesenberg, and more—came here to test the upper limits of automotive performance. The first world land-speed record (a whopping 68 mph!) was set here in 1903, and by 1935 the ill-starred British racer Malcolm Campbell had raised it to 276 mph.

The speed racers later moved west to Bonneville Salt Flats in Utah, and Daytona became the breeding ground for stock car racing—today's Daytona 500 started out as a series of 100- to 200-mile races around a rough four-mile oval, half on the sands and half on a paved frontage road. The circuit races, both for cars and motorcycles, really came into their own after World War II.

Detour: Orlando and Walt Disney World

Entire guidebooks are devoted to covering the mind-boggling array of tourist attractions in and around Orlando, but three words would probably suffice: **Walt Disney World.** Over 50,000 people come here every day to experience the magic of the Magic Kingdom, which is divided into four main areas—the Magic Kingdom amusement park, a new Animal Kingdom animal park, the futuristic EPCOT Center, and the Disney-MGM studio tours. Entrance to any of these will set you back around $80; to see all of them, get a Park Hopper pass, which is valid for four days (about $225) or longer. For further information on admissions and lodging packages call 407/824-4321.

At the time of writing, there's still no law that says you have to go to Disney World just because you've come to Florida, but it is a cultural phenomenon and more than a little fun. While you're in Orlando, you may want to visit other big-time attractions like Sea World and Universal Studios, but there are also some funky, pre-Disney-era tourist traps, with ad budgets small enough that you won't have to fight the crowds. Best of this bunch is probably **GatorLand** (daily; $24; 14501 S. Orange Blossom Trail; 407/855-5496), where thousands of alligators, crocodiles, snakes, and other reptiles are gathered together in a cypress swamp. You enter through a gator's gaping jaws, and inside you can see such sights as live chickens being dangled over a pond, taunting the hungry carnivorous gators just of

---

The town of **Ormond Beach,** which adjoins the north side of Daytona Beach, was also used by early speed-seekers. Prior to that, it was a winter playground of the rich and famous, richest and most famously John D. Rockefeller, who wintered here for years before his death in 1937 at age 97. His mansion, called **The Casements,** is now a museum (25 Riverside Dr.; 386/676-3216) along the east bank of the Halifax River.

In 1947, NASCAR (the National Association for Stock Car Auto Racing) was founded here as the nascent sport's governing body, but the races soon outgrew the sands, and in 1958 they were moved to the purpose-built **Daytona International Speedway,** on US-92 six miles west of the beach, right off I-95 exit 87. Daytona offers "ride-alongs" and on-track driving experiences (for a mere $150 to $2,500). After a visit, you may want to spend some time practicing your skills at the **Speed Park** go-kart and drag racing track across the street (201 Fentress Blvd.; 386/253-3278).

Adding to Daytona's already broad mix of pop culture icons is the **Hamburger Hall of Fame** (tours by appointment; 386/254-8753). This wacky collection of burger-related memorabilia is displayed in the private home of burgermeister Harry Sperl.

out reach below. Continuing south along US-441, past the world headquarters of Tupperware, another sight of offbeat interest is the 100-year-old historic district at the heart of **Kissimmee** (pop. 38,200), where a 50-foot stone and concrete pyramid, constructed in 1943 with rocks from most states, as well as 21 countries, stands in Lake Front Park.

The entertaining design of Disney World doesn't stop at the park gates. *Au contraire.* Perhaps the most memorable aspect of the Disney experience is seeing how the clever folks at Disney deal with "real life," specifically the lodging, dining, shopping, and entertainment options around the park. It doesn't take a Boy Genius to figure out the customer base of Disney World's Jimmy Neutron–themed **Nickelodeon Family Suites** ($125 and up; 877/642-5111), a kid-friendly Holiday Inn with multiple bedroom suites (and a fun but chaotic pool area—avoid the holiday peak times) near Disney World. Another movie spinoff is Disney's extraordinary **Animal Kingdom Lodge** (around $250; 407/939-6244), where a 30-acre savannah landscape, complete with roaming giraffes and zebras you can see from your balconies, offers families and fans of *The Lion King* the chance to take an African safari—without the jet lag. And it's not all just for little kids: sports fans flock to the **All Star Sports Resort,** a sports-themed hotel next to the ESPN/ABC Wide World of Sports complex, spring training home of the Atlanta Braves.

Between Orlando and the Space Coast, the Beeline Expressway (Hwy-528) is a fast, flat toll road, with only three exits in the 30 miles between I-95 and greater Orlando.

Daytona Beach is party central during March and April, when some 300,000 college kids escape from northern climes to defrost and unwind with a vengeance. There has been a concerted effort to keep a lid on things recently, but if you're after peace and quiet you should head somewhere else. The same is true of the springtime **Bike Week** before the Daytona 200 in March, and again in fall during **Biketoberfest,** when thousands of motorcycling enthusiasts descend upon Daytona for a week or more of partying in between races at Daytona Speedway. The granddaddy of all stock car races, the **Daytona 500,** is held around Valentine's Day, but getting one of the 110,000 tickets is all but impossible for casual fans.

Daytona Beach Practicalities

A world apart from the spring break, biker, and race car scenes, but just a block from the beach, the classic 1950s luncheonette **Bertie's** (2575 N. Atlantic Ave.; 386/672-8656) serves breakfasts and good sandwiches.

Daytona has a lot of low-rise motels, and tons of high-rise hotels along the beachfront, like the large and spacious **Holiday Inn** ($125 and up; 930 N. Atlantic Ave.; 386/255-5494).

The Space Coast: Cape Canaveral

It's more than a little ironic that one of the most extensive sections of natural coastal wetlands left in Florida became home to the launch pads of the nation's space program. Though the natural aspects—thousands of seabirds and wide open stretches of sandy beaches—are attractive enough in their own right to merit a visit, many people are drawn here by Cape Canaveral's **Kennedy Space Center.** All the big milestones in the history of the U.S. space program—the Mercury, Gemini, Apollo, and space shuttle launches—happened here, and if names like Alan Shepard, John Glenn, or Neil Armstrong mean anything to you, set aside time for a visit.

Inland from the Space Coast is Florida's biggest tourist attraction, Orlando, home of Walt Disney World. For a Disneyfied view of the ideal American town, visit the Walt Disney Company's very pleasant retro-Victorian planned community of **Celebration** (pop. 11,000 and growing), south of US-192 at the I-4 junction. Contrary to popular belief, this is not the town seen in the Jim Carrey movie *The Truman Show* (that was Seaside, in the Florida Panhandle), but it could have been.

The Kennedy Space Center itself, eight miles west of US-1 via the NASA Parkway (Hwy-405), is open to the public, but only on guided tours. These tours require advance tickets, and all leave from the large **visitors complex** (daily; $20–45; 866/737-5235), where two IMAX theaters show films of outer space

Spring Training: Grapefruit League Baseball

Every February and March, hundreds of baseball players at all levels of expertise head to Florida to earn or keep their places on some 20 different major league teams and their minor league farm club affiliates. The informality and ease of access during this spring training, which is known as the Grapefruit League, attracts thousands of baseball fans as well (more than a million spectators for the month-long "season"). Though they're not necessarily played to win, Grapefruit League games are played in modern 10,000-seat stadia that approach the major leagues in quality, and the smaller size allows an up-close feel you'd have to pay much more for during the regular season. (And your chances of snagging balls during batting practice, or the early morning training sessions, are infinitely better, too.)

Most of the Grapefruit League teams make their springtime homes on the Gulf Coast, but many others locate in cities and towns along Florida's Atlantic coast, and some teams are in the Orlando area, including the Atlanta Braves and the Houston Astros. The teams move around from town to town depending on the deals they can finagle from local taxpayers, but at time of writing, the New York Mets train in Port St. Lucie, the Washington Nationals in the Space Coast town of Viera, while the St. Louis Cardinals and Florida Marlins play in Jupiter.

space shuttle *Endeavor*'s final launch, Cape Canaveral

to get you in the mood. There are also some small museums, a simulated space shuttle mission control center, a half dozen missiles in the Rocket Garden, and an actual space shuttle, which you can walk through. The visitors center also has a couple of fast-food restaurants and a kennel for pets.

To see the Kennedy Space Center up close, board a bus for a tour; these leave every few minutes and visit the Apollo and space shuttle launch pads and other sites, including a mock-up of the International Space Station. On other tours, you can visit the Cape Canaveral Air Force station or the Cape Canaveral Air Station, site of many early space race adventures, or even have lunch with an astronaut and talk about outer space with someone who's actually been there (glass of Tang not included).

To watch a rocket launch at Kennedy Space Center, you can get passes from the visitors center, or simply watch from the many good vantage points: Playalinda Beach, in the Canaveral National Seashore at the west end of Hwy-402 from Titusville; across the Indian River, along US-1 in Titusville; or the beaches west of Hwy-A1A in Cocoa Beach.

One of the best places to eat in this part of Florida is west of the Space Center, in the town of Titusville: **Dixie Crossroads** (daily; 1475 Garden St.; 321/268-5000) is an immense (and immensely popular) place to eat seafood, especially massive plates of shrimp. All-you-can-eat piles of small shrimp cost close to $40, while jumbo shrimp cost around $2 apiece. The Crossroads is away from the water, two miles east of I-95 exit 220.

> At the entrance to the Kennedy Space Center visitors center, the **Astronaut Memorial** is a huge black granite block backed by high-tech mirrors that reflect sunlight onto the surface of the stone, illuminating the engraved names of the men and women who have given their lives exploring space.

Cocoa Beach

The town of **Cocoa Beach,** familiar to anyone who ever watched the 1960s space age sitcom *I Dream of Jeannie,* sits south of the Kennedy Space Center. Long before there were space shuttles, or even NASA, Cocoa Beach was home to the Cape Canaveral Air Station, the launch site for the unmanned space probes of the late 1950s, including the first U.S. satellite (Explorer 1), and the famous "astro chimps" (Gordo, Able, and Miss Baker, who were sent into orbit to test the effects of weightlessness). The air station, which is accessible through the Kennedy Space Center complex, has historical exhibits and dozens of missiles, from today's Patriots back to German V2s (which were fired at England

> East from Hwy-A1A on the south side of Cocoa Beach, I Dream of Jeannie Lane leads down to a nice beachfront park.

during World War II and provided the engineering basis for the American rockets of a decade later). The on-site museum includes early computers and other equipment, housed inside the blockhouse from which the first launches were controlled.

Though space travel is clearly on the minds of many residents, especially personnel stationed at Patrick Air Force Base here, another focus is catching the perfect wave: Cocoa Beach is surf center of the Space Coast. Along with a clean, 10-mile-long beach, the town also holds a batch of good-value motels, located within a short walk of the waves. Choose from chains (including a Motel 6), or check out the garish pink **Fawlty Towers** ($85 and up; 100 E. Cocoa Beach Causeway/Hwy-520; 321/784-3870), which for fans of the eponymous British sit-com is sadly devoid of John Cleese or put-upon Juan. It is, however, walkably close to the beach, and right next door to Cocoa Beach's main event, the massive **Ron Jon Surf Shop** (4151 N. Atlantic Ave.; 321/799-8888), open 24 hours every day, and *the* place to buy or rent surfboards, body boards, or bicycles.

Vero Beach

As a boy growing up in sunny Los Angeles, I could never understand why the Dodgers felt they had to disappear to distant Florida to get in shape during spring training. I knew the weather couldn't be so much better there (after all, didn't L.A. have the heavenly climate?), and I never quite figured out what the big attraction of **Vero Beach,** the Dodgers' historic off-season home, could be. But when I discovered that the Dodgers had started playing here way back in 1948—back when they still called Brooklyn home—it all began to make sense. But all that is now in the past—after 60 years, the Dodgers moved west to Arizona in 2008, and the managers of **Dodgertown,** their former training complex, are looking for a new tenant.

With or without baseball, Vero Beach is a really nice place, with an excellent beach, in South Beach Park at the end of the Palmetto Causeway. This South Beach is family-friendly and about as far as you can get from Miami's South Beach and still be in Florida: The sands here are clean, grainy, and golden, the waves are good-sized, and there are showers and free parking. Vero Beach also has a nice place to stay and eat: the **Driftwood Resort** (3150 Ocean Dr.; 772/231-0550), which has funky 1950s-style motel rooms and the fun and good-value **Waldo's,** a poolside café and bar overlooking the ocean.

Fort Pierce and Jupiter

South of Vero Beach, Hwy-A1A continues along North Hutchinson Island past the **UDT Navy SEALs Museum** (closed Mon.; $8; 772/595-5845), which describes the various roles played by Navy SEAL units, whether it's serving as underwater divers in demolishing enemy property during wartime, or assassinating bad guys like Osama bin Laden. Among the displays of wetsuits and explosives is an Apollo capsule—it was Navy SEALs who rescued returning astronauts after they "splashed down" in the ocean. On either side of the museum, undeveloped stretches of the coast have been preserved in a pair of parks, where you can enjoy uncrowded beaches or wander along boardwalks through thickly forested mangrove swamps.

Bending inland across the North Bridge, Hwy-A1A links up briefly with US-1, the old Dixie Highway, through the town of **Fort Pierce** (pop. 39,365), a market center of the famous "Indian River" produce-growing district. After this half-mile detour, Hwy-A1A returns to the shore, passing along the way by the very good **St. Lucie County Historical Museum** (closed Mon. and Tues.; $4), at the east end of the South Bridge, where broad-ranging displays tell the history of the region, showing off a hand-carved canoe and explaining the "fort" in Fort Pierce (it was built in 1835, during the Seminole Wars).

South of Fort Pierce, Port St. Lucie is the spring training home of the New York Mets (525 NW Peacock Blvd., off I-95; 772/871-2115).

Heading south from Fort Pierce, Hwy-A1A embarks on a nearly 30-mile run along Hutchinson Island, where dense stands of pines block the views of largely undeveloped beachfront. On the coast just north of Palm Beach, the town of **Jupiter** has a landmark lighthouse, which you can climb inside up to the top for a grand view, and Roger Dean Stadium is spring training home of the Marlins and Cardinals, as well as their Class A Florida League farm clubs. Pop culture fans may also want to know that Jupiter has long been home to movie star Burt Reynolds: His achievements (from TV's *Gunsmoke* through movies like *Deliverance* and *Smokey and the Bandit*) are chronicled at his acting school and museum (Thurs.–Sun.; $5; 100 N. US-1; 561/743-9955), though redevelopment threatens to leave Burt's museum and school without a home.

Midway between Jupiter and Palm Beach, the hamlet of **Juno Beach** is home to the entertaining and educational **Loggerhead Marinelife Center** (14200 US-1; 561/627-8280).

Palm Beach

A South Florida sibling to the conspicuous consumption that once defined Newport, Rhode Island, **Palm Beach** (pop. 10,468) has been a winter refuge for the rich and famous since Henry Flagler started work on his fashionable (but long-vanished) resort hotel, the 1,150-room Royal Poinciana. It was the world's largest wood building when completed in 1894, but the site is now an upscale shopping district at the center of town. Away from here, most of Palm Beach is well-guarded private property, off-limits to most mere mortals. The best way for anyone not named Kennedy or Pierpont to get a look at Palm Beach life is to spend some time at the Hearst Castle of the East Coast, the **Henry Morrison Flagler Museum** (closed Mon.; $18; 561/655-2833), on the inland side of downtown Palm Beach, at the north end of Cocoanut Row. Officially known as Whitehall, this opulent 60,000-square-foot mansion was Flagler's private home, and the 50-plus rooms (many of which were taken from

Inland from Palm Beach, you can wave at rhinos, lions, and wildebeests in a 500-acre, drive-through simulation of African ecosystems at **Lion Country Safari** ($28; 561/793-1084), 18 miles west of I-95 via US-98. No convertibles allowed!

European buildings and re-installed here) contain historical exhibits tracing the life of Flagler, the Standard Oil baron (John D. Rockefeller's right-hand man) who made a fortune while making Florida into an immensely popular vacation destination.

Not surprisingly, there are some very good and very expensive restaurants in and around Palm Beach, but happily there's also a very nice, normal, all-American luncheonette just two blocks north of The Breakers: **Green's Pharmacy** (151 N. County Rd.; 561/832- 0304) serves very good diner-style meals.

Even bigger and better than Whitehall is **The Breakers,** a stately resort hotel that faces the ocean at the east end of Palm Beach and retains much of its 1920s Mediterranean style and grace. Rooms will set you back around $350 a night (much more for suites), but you can enjoy the lobby, have a drink or afternoon tea, or take a tour (Wed. at 3 PM only; free; 561/655-6611).

Boca Raton

Whoever named **Boca Raton** (pop. 84,392), which translates literally as "Rat's Mouth," clearly didn't have an ear for future promotional bonanza, but despite the awkward name the town has become one of the more chichi spots in the state. As in Palm Beach, Coral Gables, and Miami's South Beach, the best of Boca dates from the 1920s, when architect and real estate promoter Addison Mizner, flush from his success building Mediterranean-style manors in Palm Beach, created a mini Venice of resorts and canals, which survives mainly in the shocking pink palazzo of the **Boca Raton Resort** ($200 and up; 501 E. Camino Real; 561/447-3000), on the southeast side of town.

Downtown Boca has been turned into a massive stucco shopping mall, but it's worth braving for a look inside the ornate Mizner-designed Town Hall, on US-1 (old Dixie Highway) in Palmetto Park downtown, which now houses the local historical museum (closed Mon.; free).

US-1, the main route through town, also holds the very popular **Boca Diner** (2801 N. Federal Hwy.; 561/750-6744), serving above-average coffee shop fare; the early evening early-bird scene here is straight out of *Seinfeld.* Boca Raton is also home to one of the best sushi places in South Florida: **Daimatsu,** in the heart of Boca's downtown shopping district (271 SE Mizner Blvd.; 561/361-7557).

Hwy-A1A misses most of Boca Raton, cruising past along the densely pine-forested coast. The beaches are accessible but hard to find; one well-marked stop along the way is the **Gumbo Limbo Nature Center** (Mon.–Sat. 9 AM–4 PM, Sun. noon–4 PM; $5 donation; 561/338-1473) on the inland side of the highway, a mile north of Mizner Park. A variety of native Floridian landscapes have been re-created here, letting you wander at will past coastal dunes, mangrove wetlands, and rare sabal palm hammocks. Across Hwy-A1A, **Red Reef Park** is a popular surfing beach.

Fort Lauderdale

Once famed for wild spring break frolics that saw thousands of college kids descending here for an orgy of drunken round-the-clock partying, **Fort**

Fort Lauderdale

Lauderdale (pop. 165,651) is a surprisingly residential city, brought to a more human scale by the many waterways that cut through it. One of the largest cargo ports in the state, Fort Lauderdale also boasts more boats per capita than just about anywhere else in the United States, and over 165 miles of canals, inlets, and other waterways flow through the city.

Downtown Fort Lauderdale has a few big, dull office towers, but along the New River there are some well-preserved historic buildings dating back to 1905, when the city first emerged from the swamps. Find out more by visiting the **Fort Lauderdale History Center** (Tues.–Sun. noon– 4 PM; $10; 231 SW 2nd Ave.), west of US-1, which has lots of old photos and walking-tour maps, or the nifty **Stranahan House** (daily; $12; 335 SE 6th Ave.), off Las Olas Boulevard. This circa-1901 trading post and home, with broad verandas and high ceilings,is one of the most evocative historic places in the state.

Fort Lauderdale is said to be one of the points that form the Bermuda Triangle, so of course there are numerous beachside bars where college kids try to simulate its supernatural effects by imbibing too many margaritas.

Fort Lauderdale's main beachfront bar and nightclub district is along Atlantic Avenue and Las Olas Boulevard, where you'll find some nice sidewalk cafés and fast-food restaurants. One culinary landmark is **Johnny V.'s** (625 E. Las Olas; 954/761-7920), a popular and stylish haunt where traditional American dishes are enlivened by a canny blend of exotic ingredients. For a change of pace from the frenetic tourism, or simply to enjoy good basic fried seafood, cold beer, and live blues, head south down US-1 to **Ernie's BBQ Lounge** (1843 S. Federal Hwy.; 954/523-8636), famous for its conch fritters, calamari rings, and rooftop deck.

Miles of inexpensive motels line Hwy-A1A north of Fort Lauderdale, and unless there's something big going on you shouldn't have trouble finding a room for under $100—half that in summer. One of the nicest places is the moderately priced, family-friendly **TropiRock Resort** ($80 and up; 2900 Belmar St.; 954/564-0523), with tennis courts, a tiki bar, and a pool, just a short walk from the beach.

North of Fort Lauderdale, Hwy-A1A winds in along the coast through a series of funky, friendly beachside communities. South of Fort Lauderdale, Hwy-A1A heads inland and merges into US-1, returning to the coast for the run south to Miami Beach.

North Miami Beach

Between Fort Lauderdale and Miami Beach, Hwy-A1A runs along the shore, first as Ocean Drive and later as Collins Avenue, while US-1 runs inland parallel to (and sometimes as) the old Dixie Highway. There's nothing here to compare with the attractions farther south, but the town of **North Miami Beach** does have one oddity: the **Ancient Spanish Monastery** (hours vary; $8; 16711 W. Dixie Hwy.; 305/945-1461), a 12th-century monastery bought in the 1920s by William Randolph Hearst, who had it dismantled and shipped to the United States for his Hearst Castle complex in California. However, after the stones were confiscated by U.S. Customs and Hearst lost his fortune in the Great Depression, the monastery was finally rebuilt here in Florida—as an Episcopal church.

On the coast, Hwy-A1A runs past a number of indistinct beach towns before hitting **Bal Harbour,** home to one of Miami's biggest and best shopping malls, and one of its biggest beaches, **Haulover Beach.** Besides having a café, lots of tennis courts, and gorgeous sands, Haulover Beach is also famous for attracting the clothing-optional crowd.

From Haulover Beach south to Miami Beach, Collins Avenue (Hwy-A1A) used to be known as "Millionaire's Row" for all the huge estates here, but now the road is lined with towering concrete condos and hotels, including the landmark Morris Lapidus–designed complex of the **Fontainebleau Resort** ($200 and up; 4441 Collins Ave.; 305/538-2000). It's been the setting for several movies: Jerry Lewis filmed *The Bellboy* here in 1959; Sean Connery checked in as James Bond, most famously in the film *Goldfinger;* and Al Pacino hung out by the pool in the quintessential 1980s Miami movie, *Scarface.*

The stately Mediterranean Revival manor where fashion designer Gianni Versace lived and was murdered sits at the heart of South Beach, on Ocean Drive just north of 11th Street.

Miami Beach

Covering a broad island separating downtown Miami from the open Atlantic Ocean, **Miami Beach** (pop. 84,633) has long been a mecca for fans of 1930s art deco architecture and design. More recently, it's also become one of the world's most fashionable and bacchanalian beach resorts, with deluxe hotels and high-style nightclubs and restaurants lining the broad white sands of South Beach, the relatively small corner of Miami Beach that gets 99 percent of the press and tourist attention. Here, along beachfront Ocean Drive and busier Collins Avenue (Hwy-A1A) a block inland, you'll find dozens of glorious art deco hotels, many lighted with elegant neon signs. Guided walking tours (daily; $20) of the district leave from the **Art Deco Welcome Center** (daily; 1001 Ocean Dr.;

Carl Fisher: Father of Miami Beach

Fisher Park, on the bay side of Miami Beach on Alton Road at 51st Street, holds a small monument to the fascinating Carl Fisher, the man most responsible for turning Miami Beach from a mangrove swamp into America's favorite resort. Before building up Lincoln Avenue into Miami Beach's first commercial district, Carl Fisher had played an important role in America's early automotive history. Called the "P. T. Barnum of the Automobile Age," Fisher made millions through the Prest-O-Lite company, which in the early 1900s developed the first functioning car headlight. Around 1910, he invested this fortune in building and promoting the Indianapolis Motor Speedway, then went on to plan and publicize both the Lincoln Highway, America's first transcontinental road, and the Dixie Highway, the first main north–south route in the eastern United States. He invested heavily in Miami Beach property but was ruined by the Great Depression and the sudden drop in land values. He died here, nearly penniless, in 1939, just as the economy was rebounding and the art deco hotels of South Beach were bringing new life to Miami Beach.

305/672-2014), which also rents iPod-based self-guided tours and sells guidebooks, posters, postcards, and anything else you can think of that has to do with the art deco era.

No matter how intoxicating the architecture, beach life, and nightlife along South Beach are, while you're here be sure to set aside an hour or two to explore the fascinating collection of pop culture artifacts on display two blocks inland at the **Wolfsonian** (closed Wed.; $5; 1001 Washington Ave.; 305/531-1001). One of the odder highbrow museums you'll find, the Wolfsonian (officially the Mitchell Wolfson Jr. Collection of Decorative and Propaganda Arts) fills a retrofitted 1920s warehouse with four floors of furniture, sculpture, architectural models, posters, and much more, almost all dating from the "Modern Era," roughly 1885 to 1945. Two areas of excellence are drawings and murals created under the New Deal auspices of the WPA, and similar agitprop artifacts created in Weimar, Germany. Only a small portion of the extensive collection is on display at any one time, and most of the floor space is given over to changing exhibitions—on anything from World's Fairs to Florida tourism to how children's books were used to indoctrinate future soldiers—but it's a thought-provoking and surprisingly fun place, with an unexpressed but overriding theme of how art can counterbalance, or at least respond to, the demands of industrial society.

Miami

Equal parts jet-set glitz and multicultural grit, and with more than half its population coming here from other countries around the globe, Miami (pop. 435,000) really embodies the transitive state of the nation in the early years of the 21st century. Having sprung up from swampland in the 1920s, Miami has weathered hurricanes and race riots, real estate booms and busts, drug running, and endless political intrigue to become one of America's most energetic cities. In her 1987 book *Miami,* Joan Didion describes the city as an economically schizophrenic place where it's possible "to pass from walled enclaves to utter desolation while changing stations on the car radio."

Approaching from Miami Beach past the cruise ship docks along the MacArthur Causeway, or the older and more leisurely Venetian Causeway, you experience the view of Miami made famous by the 1980s television series *Miami Vice*—downtown towers rising above Biscayne Bay. West of downtown, Miami's most engaging district is Little Havana, which focuses along SW 8th Street (a.k.a. Calle Ocho) between 12th and 16th Avenues. Since the 1950s and 1960s, when the first refugees fleeing Castro's regime fetched up here, this neighborhood has been the heart of Cuban-American Miami. Hang out for a while with the old men who congregate in the Domino Park on 8th Street and 14th Avenue, or visit the Martyrs of Giron (a.k.a. Bay of Pigs) Monument along 8th Street between 12th and 13th Streets; you'll definitely get a feel for it. Better yet, stop for something to eat or drink at one of Little Havana's many great Cuban cafés, like **Versailles** (3555 SW 8th St.; 305/444-0240), a favorite haunt of Miami's politically potent anti-Castro Cuban-Americans. Enjoy very good, very traditional Cuban food: toasted chorizo sandwiches, or perhaps a bowl of *ropa vieja* (tender threads of garlicky beef in a black bean soup), finished off with a creamy flan and a cup of super-strong Cuban coffee.

For an entirely different aspect of Miami, check out the two-time wild card World Series champion **Florida Marlins** (305/930-4487), who play at the retractably roofed $700 million stadium on the site of the historic Orange Bowl.

Miami Beach has the best range of stylish hotels, but in downtown Miami the characterful and historic **Miami River Inn** is a well-preserved circa-1908 hotel with B&B rooms (all with private baths) in a slightly dodgy downtown neighborhood ($70–199; 118 SW South River Dr.; 305/325-0045). At the top end of the style and expense spectrum is the **Four Seasons** ($350 and up; 1435 Brickell Ave.; 305/358-3535), offering stunning views from a 64-story tower. Back down to earth, the major chains all have locations on the downtown waterfront; as at all South Florida accommodations, room rates tend to increase considerably during the peak season (Jan.–Apr.).

The best source of information on greater Miami, including Miami Beach, is the **Greater Miami visitors bureau** (701 Brickell Ave.; 305/539-3000 or 800/933-8448).

Miami Beach Practicalities

Not surprisingly, there are scores of cafés and restaurants in and around Miami Beach; some, like exotic **Wish** (801 Collins Ave.; 305/531-2222) in The Hotel, are rated among the best in the world. More down to earth, and just two blocks west of the beach, the **11th Street Diner** (305/534-6373) on 11th and Washington is a 1948 Paramount pre-fab diner, plunked down in 1992 and open 24 hours ever since.

the Domino Park, Calle Ocho

For an unforgettably hedonistic experience, check into one of South Beach's great old art deco hotels, or at least saunter through the lobby and stop for a drink. The **Delano** ($350 and up; 1685 Collins Ave.; 305/672-2000) is a high-style, Shrager/Starck symphony in white, while the **Raleigh** ($250 and up; 1775 Collins Ave.; 305/534-6300) has the coolest pool in South Beach—and that is really saying something. Dozens of these 1930s divas stand out along Ocean Drive and Collins Avenue, but the wonderful architecture, alas, doesn't always manage to mask their elderly bones, nor is the 24-hour hubbub that surrounds them especially conducive to a good night's sleep. Ocean Drive, by the way, is undriveable on weekend nights, since so many cars cruise up and down it, stereos blasting.

Stylish though it is, South Beach is not frequented by many locals, who instead tend to spend time on **Lincoln Road,** a half mile north of South Beach. The

The Latin American influence on Miami is evident everywhere you go, but for proof of just how deep the connections run, consider the fact that two of Cuba's deposed presidents, Gerardo Machado and Carlos Prio Socarras, are buried in Miami's Woodlawn Park Cemetery, a mile west of Little Havana. Former Nicaraguan dictator Anastasio Somoza is buried there, too.

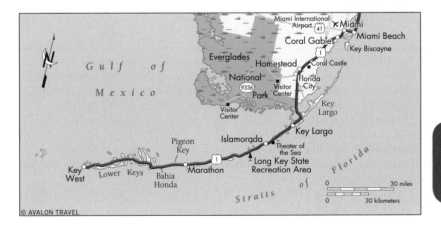

© AVALON TRAVEL

Mediterranean Revival–style commercial district along Lincoln Road, developed in the 1920s by promoter Carl Fisher, was the original main drag of Miami Beach; it has been pedestrianized and nicely landscaped and is now packed with dozens of lively sidewalk cafés. Japanese refinement meets Brazilian passions at the iconoclastic **Sushi Samba Dromo** (600 Lincoln Rd.; 305/673-5337), a fish lovers' paradise.

Across Miami

The I-95 freeway, and the old main route, US-1, both enter Miami north of downtown in the very rough Little Haiti neighborhood, while the infinitely more scenic Hwy-A1A crosses Biscayne Bay from Miami Beach. Around downtown, Biscayne Boulevard winds along the waterfront, merging into historic Brickell Avenue, now lined by flashy postmodern bank and condo towers. From here, detour west on the one-way system along 7th and 8th Streets through Little Havana, then south through Coral Gables, joining the old Dixie Highway (US-1) for the drive south through Homestead to the Florida Keys.

Coral Gables

South of Miami's Little Havana neighborhood, accessible through grand gates off the Tamiami Trail (8th Street), the stately community of **Coral Gables** is one of the few Florida resort towns that survives fairly unchanged since the boom years of the 1920s. Coral Gables boasts many grand boulevards, fine fountains, plazas, and lush gardens, but the landmark to look for is the 26-story **Biltmore Hotel** ($270 and up; 1200 Anastasia Ave.; 305/445-1926 or 800/727-1926), off Granada Boulevard. This opulent hotel, which opened in 1926 and once boasted the world's largest swimming pool (Johnny Weismuller was the original lifeguard!), has been restored to its original glory.

In 1983, the Bulgarian artist Christo wrapped 11 Biscayne Bay islands in bright pink plastic as part of his *Surrounded Islands* installation.

The southern edge of Coral Gables is occupied by the drab campus of the University of Miami, which is bounded by US-1, the old Dixie Highway.

Homestead: Coral Castle

One of the most diverting stops between Miami and the Florida Keys has to be the **Coral Castle** (daily; $12; 28655 S. Dixie Hwy.; 305/248-6345), an amazing house hand-carved out of huge blocks of oolitic coral in the 1930s. Located right along the highway, two miles north of Homestead, the house is filled with furniture also carved from stone—a 3,000-pound sofa and a 500-pound rocking chair—and no one has figured how its enigmatic creator (Ed Leedskalnin) did it all without help or the use of any heavy machinery.

Homestead, along with neighboring Florida City farther south, forms the main gateway to Everglades National Park, and there are tons of reasonably priced motels hereabouts—all the usual suspects line up here along US-1, including the very nice **Best Western Gateway to the Keys** ($90 and up; 305/246-5100).

Florida's other big national park, **Biscayne National Park,** stretches east of Homestead from near Miami to the top of the Florida Keys, but it is almost completely underwater. Privately run snorkeling and diving tours (around $30–35) leave from near the main **Convoy Point visitors center** (305/230-7275), nine miles east of US-1 at the end of 328th Street—near the huge Homestead-Miami Speedway (and a nuclear power plant).

Everglades National Park

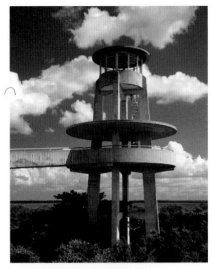

the observation tower in Shark Valley

Covering over 1.5 million acres at the far southwestern tip of mainland Florida, **Everglades National Park** protects the largest subtropical wilderness in the United States. A fair portion of the park is actually underwater, and the entire Everglades ecosystem is basically a giant, slow-flowing river that is 50 miles wide but only a few inches deep. Fed by Lake Okeechobee, and under constant threat by irrigation in-flows and out-flows and by the redirection of water to Miami and other cities, the Everglades still seem to vibrate with life. Some 300 species of birds breed here, as do 600 different kinds of fish and animals, ranging from rare manatees to abundant alligators (not to mention the gazillions of mosquitoes).

The backcountry parts of the Everglades can be visited by boat, but by road there are only two main routes. In the north, the Tamiami Trail (the Tampa to Miami Trail, a.k.a. US-41) heads west from Miami to misnamed **Shark Valley,** where you can rent bikes or take a tram tour ($18.50 for tram tour, $7.50 per hour for bike rentals, $10 entrance fee) on a 15-mile loop through the sawgrass swamps that make up the heart of the Everglades. Gazing at the gators, eagles, and hawks here, it's hard to believe you're barely a half hour from South Beach. Just west of Shark Valley, the **Miccosukee Indian Village** is a somewhat poignant reminder of the plight of

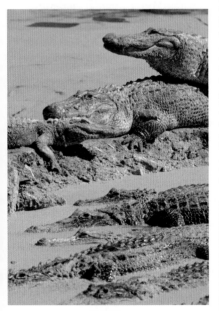

Gators!

In the Everglades, and anywhere in Florida, mosquitoes are intensely annoying pests, so if you're here at any time but the dry middle of winter, bring strong insect repellent—and lots of it. In parts of the Everglades, the bugs are so bad that full-body cover is recommended, in addition to the most potent sprays and lotions you can lay your hands on.

The Overseas Highway

Imagine a narrow ribbon of asphalt and concrete hovering between emerald seas and azure blue skies, and lined by swaying palm trees and gorgeous, white-sand beaches. Add a generous taste of exotic wildlife, including alligators and dolphins; the country's only tropical coral reefs; and a romantic history rich with tales of buccaneering pirates and buried treasure. Hang it off the far southern tip of Florida, and you have the Overseas Highway, one of the country's most fascinating scenic drives.

Running for over 125 miles from the Everglades to the edge of the Caribbean, the Overseas Highway is the southernmost section of US-1, the historic route that winds for over 2,400 miles along the full length of the East Coast. From its very inception, the Overseas Highway has been unique. It was built on top of the legendary Florida and East Coast Railroad, which at the turn of the 20th century linked the great resort hotels of St. Augustine and Palm Beach with Key West and Cuba. An engineering master-piece, the railroad cost $50 million and hundreds of lives to complete in 1912, but it lasted only two decades before the century's most powerful hurricane destroyed the tracks in September 1935. The state of Florida

Between milemarker 106 and milemarker 86, a hiking and bicycling path parallels US-1—sometimes very closely—but it's a rare long-distance route on these tiny islands.

the Everglades native peoples, the Seminoles, whose ances-tors fought off the U.S. Army but who now wrestle alliga-tors, run casinos and souvenir shops, and give airboat tours of their ancestral lands.

The main road access to the Everglades is via Palm Drive (Hwy-9336) from the Florida Turnpike or US-1. This route takes you past the **Ernest Coe Visitors Center** (305/242-7700), where interpretive displays and a pair of nature trails give an appetizing taste of the Everglades (and almost guaranteed sightings of alligators). The road continues nearly 40 miles west to the former town of Flamingo, where both the residents and the namesake birds have all moved on, and the Everglades' only eating and accommodation option, the Flamingo Lodge, closed after suffering damage in the 2005 Katrina hurricane.

Key Largo

The Overseas Highway (US-1) officially starts in Florida City, near the Everglades some 50 miles south of Miami, but doesn't really come alive until it leaves the mainland and lands at **Key Largo,** the first and largest of the dozens of "keys" (from the Spanish word *cayos,* meaning small islands) the highway bought the remnants of the railroad for $650,000 and proceeded to convert it into a two-lane highway, the Overseas Highway, which opened to traffic in 1938. Most of the old road has since been superseded by a more modern highway, but many old bridges and causeways still stand as evocative remnants of an earlier era.

As in much of Florida, ramshackle roadside development has uglified much of the route—in the larger keys towns, like Key Largo, Islamorada, and Marathon, signs hawking restaurants, motels, and snorkel tours are more common than pelicans—but you can't help but be hypnotized by the scenic beauty of what pockets of nature still remain. Many of the best views are from the road itself, and specifically from the bridges, such as the Long Key Bridge and soaring Seven Mile Bridge, which run north and south of Marathon. Two state parks, John Pennecamp on Key Largo and Bahia Honda in the Lower Keys, offer a respite from the commercialism, and all along the Overseas Highways, unmarked roads and driveways lead across the narrow keys down to the waterside, where all manner of sportfishing marinas and Margaritaville-type bars give you another outlook on the true "key experience."

All the way along the Overseas Highway (US-1), the roadside is lined by milemarker (MM) posts counting down the miles from Florida City to Key West, starting at MM 127 and ending up at MM 0; addresses usually make reference to these numbers. Though it's only about 160 miles, be sure to allow at least four hours for the drive between Miami and Key West—plus however many hours you manage to spend out of the car, of course.

links together. The Overseas Highway reaches Key Largo at the very popular **John Pennekamp Coral Reef State Park** (daily; $8; MM 102.5; 305/451-1202). The first place where you can really get a feel for life on the keys, the park is the starting point for a variety of **guided tours** (scuba diving, snorkeling, or in glass-bottomed boats) that offer up-close looks at the only tropical coral reef in the continental United States and all but guarantee that you'll see enough sealife to fill a photo album or two. Along with the adjacent **Key Largo Coral Reef National Marine Sanctuary,** the park gives access to more than 175 square miles of diving spots, including reefs, shipwrecks, and a nine-foot-high bronze statue called *Christ of the Deep*. The visitors center has a replica reef in a 30,000-gallon aquarium full of colorful fish, allowing a quick look at the fascinating underwater world without getting your feet wet; the park also has other on-land attractions, like a boardwalk over a mangrove swamp and a pleasant campground.

Film fans will know that Key Largo was the title and setting of a great 1948 film noir movie starring Bogie, Bacall, and Edward G. Robinson; these days,

Key Largo is home to the **Key Lime Products** store (305/853-0378) at milemarker 95, selling all manner of key lime pies, juice, cakes, cookies, suntan lotions—even key lime trees, though commercial key lime orchards are a thing of the past. (Most key limes today come from Mexico and Honduras.)

it's also home to the co-star of another classic, the boat from the *African Queen,* which is moored next to the Holiday Inn at milemarker 100. Most of Key Largo today, however, is a rather tawdry four-mile stretch of seashell stands, dive shops, boat shops, and margarita bars; there are many good restaurants, including **Mrs. Mac's Kitchen** (closed Sun.; MM 99.4; 305/451-3722), a small and friendly place with inexpensive food and more beers to drink than seats to sit on.

Key Largo also has many good places to stay, from the funky **Sunset Cove Motel** ($115 and up; MM 99.5; 305/451-0705) to the boutique **Azul del Mar** ($175 and up; MM 104.3; 305/451-0337), a relaxing small resort. Also here is the unique **Jules' Undersea Lodge** (packages from $250 per person; 305/451-2353), a two-room motel that's 22 feet beneath the sea—a quick scuba dive down from 51 Shoreland Drive, off MM 103.2.

Islamorada

Continuing south on US-1, Key Largo blends into **Islamorada** (pronounced "EYE-la-mo-RA-da"), the self-proclaimed "Sportfishing Capital of the World," where anglers from all over the world come to try their hand at catching the elusive, hard-fighting bonefish that dwell in the shallow saltwater "flats" and the deep-sea tarpon, marlin, and sailfish. Though now famous for its fishing and fun-in-the-sun, Islamorada (Purple Island) used to be synonymous with death and destruction: On September 2, 1935, a huge tidal wave, whipped up by 200-mile-per-hour hurricane winds, drowned over 400 veterans and local residents trying to escape on what turned out to be the last train ever to travel along the old Florida East Coast Railway. Most of the dead were World War I veterans, members of the "Bonus Army" who had marched on Washington, D.C., in 1934 and had been given jobs working to build the Overseas Highway. A stone pillar at the south end of Islamorada, along US-1 at milemarker 81.6, was erected by the WPA to remember the event.

Entering Islamorada from the north, you are welcomed to town by the "World's Largest Lobster," standing at milemarker 86.1 in front of the Rain Barrel Artisan Village. She hasn't yet been boiled or grilled, so she's a naturally green-brown color, not bright red.

At the center of Islamorada sits one of the older tourist traps in south Florida: the **Theater of the Sea** (daily; $26.95; MM 84.5; 305/664-2431), a funky, friendly place where you can watch performing sea animals or even swim with dolphins.

Islamorada is also home to what may be the most pleasant and plushest accommodation option in the Florida Keys: **The Moorings** ($250 and up; 123 Beach Rd.; 305/664-4708), on the ocean side of milemarker 81.5. The Moorings is an idyllic and much-loved retreat, with 18 self-sufficient wooden cottages on 18 acres, alongside a beautiful 1,100-foot white-sand beach.

The Moorings also has a nice restaurant, **Morada Bay** (81600 Overseas Hwy.; 305/664-0604), serving urbane renditions of traditional key favorites on US-1 at milemarker 81.6. For a more down-to-earth taste of the keys, try the nearby **Green Turtle Inn** (closed Mon.; 305/664-2006), where specialties include shrimp 'n' grits and local fish.

For more information on Islamorada, stop by the little red caboose that holds the **visitors bureau** (MM 82.5; 305/664-4503 or 800/322-5397). Outside, in the parking lot, informational plaques tell the story of the ill-fated railroad that became the Overseas Highway.

Long Key State Park

South of Islamorada, up and over the high "Channel 5" bridge, the roadside scene gets pretty again very fast, especially at the **Long Key State Park** at milemarker 67.5, where boardwalks wind through coastal hammocks (dense stands of mahogany and dogwood trees that bunch together on the small humps of land that lie above the tide line). There's a campground ($36; 305/664-4815) in the park, with showers, and some nice but narrow beaches.

Marathon and Pigeon Key

The second-longest of the many bridges that make up US-1, the elegant multi-arched Long Key Bridge supports a long, flat causeway where the road finally earns its other name, the Overseas Highway. Unobstructed views of the distant horizon are yours in all directions, with the narrow ribbon of highway seemingly suspended between the sky and the sea. Fortunately, turnouts at both ends of the causeway let you take in the vista without worrying about on-coming traffic.

The Long Key Bridge marks the northern end of **Marathon,** a sprawling community that's the second largest in the keys, stretching between milemarkers 65 and 47 over a series of islands. One of the visitor highlights of Marathon is on Grassy Key, where the **Dolphin Research Center** (daily; $19.50; MM 59; 305/289-0002), a rest home for dolphins who've been kept in captivity for too long, is marked by a 30-foot-tall statue of a leaping dolphin. You can swim with a dolphin for around $175.

Accessible by tram from a visitors center in Marathon, **Pigeon Key** (daily; $11; MM 48; 305/743-5999) is one of the least famous but perhaps most fascinating spots along the Overseas Highway. A national historic district, preserving substantial remnants of the clapboard construction camp that housed some 400 workers employed on the original Seven Mile Bridge from 1912 to 1935, Pigeon Key offers a glimpse of blue-collar keys history the likes of which you'll find nowhere else.

Lower Keys: Bahia Honda

The old Seven Mile Bridge, which carried first the railroad and later US-1 over Pigeon Key between Marathon and Big Pine Key, was replaced in the early 1980s by a soaring new bridge that gives another batch of breathtaking ocean-to-gulf views. (The old bridge, which was seen in the Arnold Schwarzenegger/ Jamie Lee Curtis movie *True Lies,* still stands below the new one but is now used as a very long fishing pier.)

On Bahia Honda Key, near milemarker 37, you can see a double-decker remnant of the original keys railroad, with the 1938 Overseas Highway supported atop the trestle. Widening the rail bed to accommodate cars was impossible, so a new deck was added to the top of the bridge.

The south end of the Seven Mile Bridge, near milemarker 40, marks the start of the Lower Keys, which are considerably less commercial than the others. The best of the Lower Keys is yours to enjoy at milemarker 36.5, where the entrance to **Bahia Honda State Park** (305/872-2353) leaves the highway behind and brings you back to the way the keys used to be: covered in palms and coastal hardwood hammocks, with white-sand beaches stretching for miles along blue-water seas. Facilities are limited to a few cabins (around $122.50 off season, $162.50 peak season), a general store, and a snorkel rental stand, but it's a great place to spend some time fishing, beachcombing, sunbathing, or swimming in the deep, warm waters of the Atlantic Ocean or Gulf of Mexico. Camping overnight, the best way to enjoy the sunset, sunrise, and everything in between, costs around $38.50 a night.

From Bahia Honda, US-1 bends along to Big Pine Key, second largest of the keys and suffering from a bout of suburban mini mall sprawl. Though it looks about as far from natural as can be, Big Pine Key happens to be part of the **National Key Deer Refuge,** set up to protect the increasingly rare key deer, the "world's smallest deer" at around three feet tall. Some 800 key deer now live on the island.

white sands, clear water, blue skies: Bahia Honda State Park

The last big key before Key West is Sugarloaf Key, formerly full of pineapple plantations but now known for its **Perky Bat Tower,** a national historic landmark alongside US-1 at milemarker 17. Built by a man named Perky in 1929, the 35-foot tower was designed to house a colony of bats, who were supposed to feast on the plentiful mosquitoes here; however, the bats stayed away, and the mosquitoes stayed put. Sugarloaf Key is also home to the wild **Mangrove Mama's** (MM 20; 305/745-3030), a roadhouse tucked away south of the bridge. The seafood and key lime pie are as good as it gets, and there's often live music in the evenings.

Key West

Closer to Cuba than to the U.S. mainland, and still proudly preserving the anarchic spirit of a place that was founded by pirates, **Key West** (pop. 22,463) is definitely a world unto itself. The main drag, Duval Street, has been overrun by tacky souvenir shops, but the rest of Key West is still a great place for aimless wandering.

Just a block from the official Mile Zero end of US-1, one of Key West's most popular stops is the **Hemingway House** (daily 9 AM–5 PM; $12.50; 907 Whitehead St.; 305/294-1136), an overgrown mansion on Hwy-A1A, where the burly writer produced some of his most popular works, including *To Have and Have Not* and *For Whom the Bell Tolls.* Writing in a small cabin connected to the main house by a rope bridge, and spending his nights in the roughneck bar (originally called Sloppy Joe's, now known as Captain Tony's) that still survives at 428 Greene Street, "Papa" Hemingway lived in Key West for about 10 years until his divorce in 1940, when he moved to Havana.

Just so you know, the seashell that's been adopted as a Key West emblem, the conch, is pronounced "KONK."

At sunset over the Gulf of Mexico, keep your eyes open for the visual effect known as the "green flash," when the sky and the sea seem to explode in a bright flash of green.

Hemingway House

BIRD'S EYE VIEW, SHOWING P. & O. DOCKS AND FLORIDA EAST COAST TERMINAL, KEY WEST, FLA.

Though Key West is the southwestern end of the Overseas Highway, the name is thought to derive from a corruption of the Spanish Cayo Hueso (Island of Bones). When the first explorers set foot here, they found piles of human bones.

A half mile away, at Whitehead and South Streets, a brightly painted buoy marks the "Southernmost Point in the USA"; next to this is the Southernmost House. (There's also a Southernmost Motel.)

At the other end of Duval Street, one place you ought to go—especially if you can time it to be there around sunset—is Mallory Square, which faces west across the Gulf of Mexico and the open Caribbean Sea. Street performers juggle and play music on the broad, brick-paved plaza all day and much of the night. This historic waterfront area is lined by old warehouses and the **Mel Fisher Maritime Museum** (daily; $12.50; 200 Greene St.), which displays many millions of dollars worth of jewels, silver, and gold recovered from a pair of 17th-century Spanish shipwrecks.

Key West Practicalities

Amid the tourist clutter, Key West holds a range of fabulous restaurants, enough to suit all tastes and budgets. Capturing the eccentric Key West spirit for over 20 years, kid-friendly **Camille's** (1202 Simonton St.; 305/296-4811) serves crisp waffles, sandwiches, and delicious dinners every day. For a memorable dinner, **Antonia's** (615 Duval St.; 305/294-6565) has truly excellent Italian food: great fresh pastas, perfect lasagnas, and awesome grilled meats. But for a real taste of Key West, you can't beat **B.O.'s Fish Wagon,** a ram-

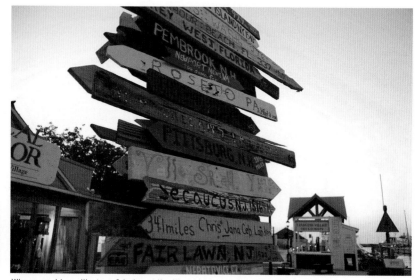

Where would you like to go? A sign at Key West Marina on Duval Street gives directions and distances to dozens of places around the world.

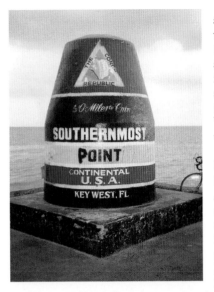

shackle fish stand a block from the water and three blocks north of Duval (801 Caroline St.; 305/294-9272)— soft-shell crab and oyster po' boys, fresh mahi fish-and-chips, cold beer, and frequent live blues bands make this a great place to soak up Key West's party-hardy-at-the-end-of-the-world ambience.

The **Southernmost Motel in the USA** ($95 and up; 1319 Duval St.; 305/296-6577) has a poolside bar and AAA-rated rooms. A surprisingly desirable option is the **Crowne Plaza** ($150 and up; 430 Duval St.; 305/296-2991), which plasters its chain-hotel name on the facade of the La Concha Hotel, one of Key West's oldest and largest hotels, but otherwise preserves the historic 1920s character; you can't get more central than this. There are also many nice old B&Bs around Key West, like the landmark **Old Town Manor** ($150 and up; 511 Eaton St.; 305/292-2170), an 1880s Greek Revival mansion with a gorgeous garden.

Key West is the end of the Overseas Highway, but it's not the end of the sightseeing opportunities, so if you don't want to turn around and head home just yet, you don't have to. You can board a sunset cruise, or take a seaplane tour of historic **Fort Jefferson,** a photogenic 150-year-old fortress and

> The official end of US-1 is marked by a zero milepost sign in front of the Key West post office, on Truman Avenue.

prison located on an island in **Dry Tortugas National Park,** 68 miles west of Key West. Prisoners held here included the hapless doctor Samuel Mudd, who set the broken leg of Lincoln assassin John Wilkes Booth.

Fort Jefferson

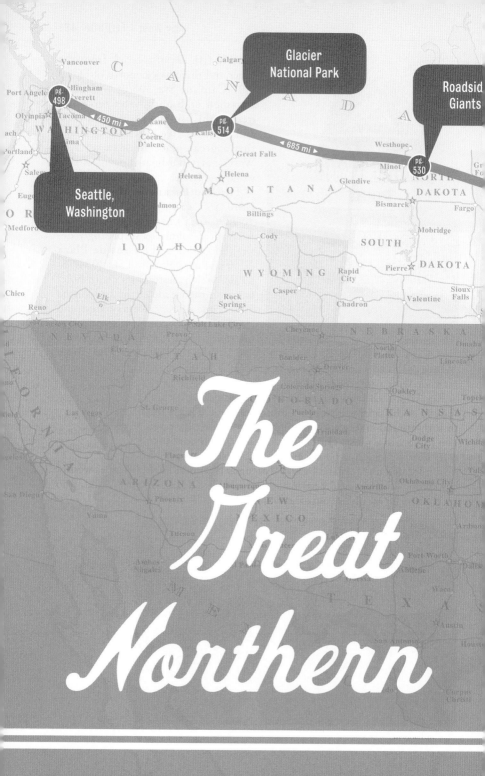

Vancouver

Calgary

Glacier
National Park

Roadside
Giants

Port Angeles
pg.
498

llingham
everett

Olympia
Tacoma

◄ 450 mi ►

Kane

pg.
514

◄ 685 mi ►

Westhope

pg.
530

ach

Olympia
Tacoma

WASHINGTON

Coeur
D'alene

Great Falls

Minot

Gr
Fo

ortland

ima

NORTH

Salem

Helena
Helena

DAKOTA

Eug

Salmon

MONTANA

Glendive

Bismarck

Fargo

Seattle,
Washington

Billings

OR

lmon

Medfor

IDAHO

Cody

SOUTH

Chico

Reno

Elk
o

WYOMING

Rapid
City

Pierre

DAKOTA

Casper

Chadron

Valentine

Sioux
Falls

NEVADA

Provo

Cheyenne

NEBRASKA

Ely

Bonlder

North
Platte

Omaha

Lincoln

Richfield

Denver

Oakley

Topek

Las Vegas

St. George

OLORADO

KANSAS

Colorado Springs

Pueblo

Dodge
City

Wichit

Flag

Trinidad

ARIZONA

lbuquerque

Amarillo

Oklahoma City

OKLAHOM

San Diego

Yuma

Phoenix

NEW

MEXICO

Ardmo

Tucson

Fort Worth

Dalla

Nogales

Waco

TEXAS

Austin

San Antonio

Housto

Corpus
Christi

The
Great
Northern

Michigan's Upper Peninsula

pg. 540

◄ 605 mi ►

The Big Nickel

pg. 553

◄ 375 mi ►

◄ 700 mi ►

Acadia National Park

pg. 583

COOLER
NORTHERN VACATION
ROUTE

US 2

THEODORE
ROOSEVELT
HIGHWAY

U. S. HIGHWAY 2 ASSOCIATION

Following US-2 through wide-open spaces is guaranteed to bring new meaning to the expression "getting away from it all."

Between Seattle, Washington, and Acadia National Park

Though many come close, no other cross-country route takes in the variety and extremity of landscape that US-2 does. Dubbed the Great Northern in memory of the pioneer railroad that parallels the western half of the route, US-2 is truly the most stunning and unforgettable, not to mention longest, of all the great transcontinental road trips.

Starting in the west near the beautiful Pacific port city of Seattle, US-2 runs steeply up and over the volcanic **Cascade Range,** climbing from sea level to alpine splendor in around an hour. From the crest, the road drops down onto the otherworldly **Columbia Plateau,** a naturally arid region reclaimed from sagebrush into fertile farmland by New Deal public works projects like the great **Grand Coulee Dam,** one of the largest pieces of civil engineering on the planet. From **Washington,** US-2 bends north, clipping across the top of the **Idaho Panhandle** before climbing up into western **Montana,** a land of forests, rivers, and wildlife that culminates in the bold granite spectacle of **Glacier National Park.**

WASHINGTON

The 350 miles of US-2 across Washington State contain enough contrasting landscapes to fill many states. West to east, the route begins at the industrial fringes of **Seattle** and Puget Sound, passing through a couple of Victorian-era towns before climbing steeply up toward the towering peaks, dense forests, and pristine

lakes of the Cascade Mountains. East of the Cascade crest, the rugged volcanic landscape suddenly becomes drier and much more sparse, the dense forests fading first into lush farmlands and orchards reclaimed from the natural desert, then continuing across increasingly barren sagebrush plains into Idaho.

Midway between Seattle and Everett, the town of Edmonds has frequent Washington State Ferry service (206/464-6400 or 888/808-7977) across Puget Sound to Kingston on the Olympic Peninsula, the start of our **Pacific Coast** road trip, which begins on page 8.

On the eastern flank of the Rockies, the route drops suddenly to the windswept prairies of the northern **Great Plains.** Though empty to look at—especially when you're midway along the 1,000-mile beeline across Montana and **North Dakota,** wondering how long it will be until you see the next tree or peak—this is a land rich in history, where the buffalo once roamed freely, where Plains tribes like the Shoshone, Blackfeet, Sioux, and Cheyenne reigned supreme, and where the Lewis and Clark expedition followed the Missouri River upstream in search of a way west to the Pacific.

Midway across the continent, the Great Plains give way to the **Great North Woods** country of **Minnesota**—birthplace of both Paul Bunyan and Judy Garland—and then to the rugged lumber and mining country of **Wisconsin** and **Michigan's Upper Peninsula.** Continuing due east, the route crosses the border into **Ontario, Canada,** running through the francophile environs of **Montreal** before returning to the United States near lovely **Lake Champlain** in upstate **New York.**

From there, US-2 passes through the hardwood forests of **Vermont's Green Mountains** and the rugged granite peaks of **New Hampshire's White Mountains,** two very different ranges, though only 50 miles apart. The route winds down to the coast of **Maine,** reaching the Atlantic Ocean at Bar Harbor and **Acadia National Park.**

Landscapes, rather than cities and towns, play the starring roles on this route. For nearly 2,000 miles at the heart of the route, between Seattle and the Canadian capital city of Ottawa, the biggest cities along the route are Spokane and Duluth. Still, after a few days spent following US-2 through small towns and wide-open spaces, you'll probably consider Duluth bustling and fast-paced; driving even a short stretch of the Great Northern highway is guaranteed to bring new meaning to the expression "getting away from it all."

Though traffic can be heavy on long summer weekends, and also in winter in the Cascades section, along US-2 it is usually light, since most of the 18-wheelers and other heavy vehicles follow the parallel I-90 freeway, 25 miles to the south.

Everett

Thirty-odd miles north of downtown Seattle via the I-5 freeway or the older, funkier Hwy-99, at the west end of transcontinental US-2, busy **Everett** (pop. 103,109) is a thoroughly blue-collar place that feels a lot farther from Seattle's high-tech flash than the mere half hour it is. A heavy industry center economically dependent upon two of the largest livelihoods in the Pacific Northwest—wood products and aircraft manufacturing—Everett has a few large turn-of-the-20th-century mansions overlooking the all-business waterfront, where a Kimberly-Clark paper mill shares space with a big U.S. Navy base that's home port to the aircraft carrier USS *Abraham Lincoln,* the ship on which

If a Boeing tour doesn't get your blood flowing, maybe a baseball game will: The always-entertaining **Everett AquaSox** (425/258-3673), Class A affiliate of the Seattle Mariners, play at 39th and Broadway, off I-5, exit 192. Games are broadcast on **KRKO 1380 AM.**

East of Monroe, just west of the town of **Sultan**, a dollhouse-sized church stands along US-2 as a roadside rest stop and mini shrine. Sultan is also home to an annual **Summer Shindig and Logging Show** every July.

George W. Bush made his "Mission Accomplished" speech during the Iraq War. The old-fashioned downtown, a half mile west of I-5 around Hewitt and Colby Avenues, has some neat antiques and junk shops, plus a dozen or so roughneck bars and taverns around the historic **Everett Theatre** (2911 Colby Ave.). For milk shakes or great fish-and-chips, stop by **Ray's Drive-In** (1401 Broadway; 425/252-3411), two miles north of downtown.

Everett's one big tourist draw is the huge **Boeing assembly plant** on the southwest edge of town, well-marked from I-5 exit 189, at the west end of Hwy-526. The factory, where they make the world's biggest planes—747s through 787 Dreamliners—is worth a look if only for the 11-story, quarter-mile-long building, which is the largest in the world by volume. These "Future of Flight" tours (daily 8:30 AM–5:30 PM; $16–20; 800/464-1476 or 360/756-0086) leave every half hour until 3:30 PM in the summer.

US-2 leaves Everett on Hewitt Avenue, which crosses I-5 then takes a historic old drawbridge over the Snohomish River before winding for a half dozen miles across low-lying fields toward the town of Snohomish.

Snohomish

Though they're spreading fast, Seattle's suburbs haven't yet reached the tidy Victorian town of **Snohomish** (pop. 9,098), a century-old former logging center that lines the north bank of the Snohomish River, 25 miles upstream from Puget Sound. Six blocks of well-preserved warehouses and commercial buildings stand along 1st Street, across the river from a whining old sawmill, while the blocks above hold dozens of charming homes and quite a few impressively steepled churches. One of these old homes has been restored and now houses the **Blackman House Museum** (Sat.–Sun. noon–3 PM; donations; 118 Ave. B; 360/568-5235). The museum features period-style furnishings and displays on the town's early history. The range of antiques shops, taverns, and cafés in the historic center has made Snohomish a popular day trip from Seattle. Pastry fans come here for the fantastic apple, pecan, cherry, and other slices available at the **Pie Company** (915 1st St.; 360/568-3589), while beer-drinkers converge upon **Fred's Ale House,** on the river (1114 1st St.; 360/568-5820). Snohomish has maintained an admirable balance of history and commerce and is well worth a short stop if you're passing by.

Around Snohomish, the old US-2 road has been replaced by a four-lane freeway that loops around to the north, so follow signs for the Historic Center.

Gold Bar and Index

Surprisingly little of the route traversed by US-2 on its way between the flatlands and Stevens Pass high up in the Cascades is given over to ski shops, bike shops, and espresso stands—except for the section around **Monroe,** where a mile-long gauntlet of megamalls and fast-food franchises catering to Seattleites racing to and from the slopes comes as a shock to the system. East of Monroe, the one-time mining, logging, and railroad camp of **Gold Bar** stretches along US-2, halfway between Stevens Pass and Puget Sound. Besides all the gas stations and cafés you could want, Gold Bar also holds the well-posted trailhead (follow 1st Street north from the center of town) for the 3.5-mile hike to 250-foot **Wallace Falls,** one of the tallest in the northern Cascades, tantalizingly visible from US-2.

Farther east, **Index,** on a side road a mile north of US-2, sits at the western foot of the Cascade Mountains at the point where the scenery changes suddenly from pastoral to alpine. Besides **River House Coffee Shop** (425/883-9039), you'll find a general store/post office, a neat little historical museum featuring Great Northern Railroad photographs, and constant trains rumbling over the swimmably deep (but often freezing cold) Skykomish River.

You'll see reminders around town of Index's early industry: a granite quarry that cut the steps used in the state capitol. There's a giant saw blade in a park at the center of town and the Index Town Wall, a 400-foot sheer granite cliff that attracts Seattle rock climbers and quite a few peregrine falcons.

Skykomish and Deception Falls

Lining the busy Burlington Northern Santa Fe railroad tracks, a block south of US-2, **Skykomish** is a quirky and engaging place that seems to belong somewhere else, some long time ago. If you like the idea of being lulled to sleep by the rumble of trains, spend a night at the historic **Cascadia Inn** (210 E. Railroad Ave.; 360/677-2030). The inn also has a café and cocktail bar,

Seattle

The Two Sentries,
The 42 story L. C. Smith Building and Mt. Rainier,
SEATTLE
U.S.A.

An engaging and energetic combination of scenic beauty, blue-collar grit, and high-tech panache has made Seattle one of the most popular cities in the United States, for visitors and residents alike. A young city, historically and demographically, Seattle has managed to preserve much of its heavy industrial heritage as parks and museums, if not as economic engines. The eco-conscious, civic-minded city spreads over a series of hills, surrounded by the waters of Puget Sound (be sure to ride a ferry or two!), with a backdrop of the snowcapped Cascade and Olympic Mountains. The evergreen Seattle can be an entrancing city—at least when the sun comes out, which no matter what people say is likely to happen at least once during your stay.

The heart of downtown Seattle, **Pike Place Market** is a raucous fish, crafts, and farmers market with some 500 different stalls and stores filling an early-1900s municipal-feeling building that steps along the waterfront. For a respite from the hubbub, head two blocks south to the postmodern **Seattle Art Museum** (closed Mon. & Tues.; $15; 1300 1st Ave.; 206/654-3100) and enjoy the amazing collection of regional Native American art and artifacts on display. Downtown's other piece of noteworthy recent architecture is the shiny **Seattle Central Library** (1000 4th Ave.), a fantastic (and free!) high-tech (some say hermetic) space whose multifaceted glass diamond exterior steps down between two city blocks.

At the south edge of downtown, a little under a mile from Pike Place Market, the 20-some-block **Pioneer Square** historic district preserves the original core of the city, which boomed in the late 1890s with the Klondike Gold Rush. Just south of Pioneer Square, spectators can enjoy downtown views and Puget Sound sunsets at Safeco Field ballpark, where the **Seattle Mariners** (206/346-4001) play.

Another essential place to go is the **Seattle Center** (206/684-7200), a mile north of downtown at Broad Street and 5th Avenue North, built for the 1962 World's Fair, and featuring Seattle's Space Age icon, the Space Needle ($18). The Seattle Center, which you can reach via a quick ride on Seattle's short monorail, is the primary location for Seattle's excellent annual Labor Day arts and music festival, **Bumbershoot,** and is also home to the intriguing Experience Music Project, now better known as **EMP** (daily; $18; 206/770-2700), a hands-on musical exploration that includes a living memorial to the city's native-born guitar genius, Jimi Hendrix. A don't-miss photo opportunity: a statue of Chief Seattle with the Space Needle rising behind him.

Besides funding EMP, Microsoft billionaire Paul Allen has indulged his taste for Space Age adventure by subsidizing the private rocketship SpaceShipOne, and closer to home by renovating the world's last intact **Cinerama** theater (2100 4th Ave.; 206/448-6680), an early 1960s icon.

Practicalities

Seattle's main airport is Seattle–Tacoma International Airport ("Sea-Tac"), a half-hour drive south of downtown Seattle via the I-5 freeway. Seattle's freeways are often filled to capacity most of the day, but the best drive-through tour of Seattle follows old US-99 along the Alaskan Way Viaduct, a concrete freeway that cuts along the downtown waterfront, runs through a tunnel, then follows Aurora Avenue on a soaring bridge over the west end of Lake Union. (By the way, under the Aurora Bridge sits one of Seattle's biggest pieces of auto-art: the **Fremont Troll,** caught in the act of capturing an old VW Beetle.)

Most everything of visitor interest in Seattle is within the walkably compact downtown, where an extensive bus system runs in a fare-free zone; there's also a 1.2-mile-long monorail ($2 one-way), linking 5th Avenue and Pine Street downtown with the Seattle Center and Space Needle.

The niftiest place to stay is the **Hotel Ändra** ($189 and up; 2000 4th Ave.; 206/448-8600), a fully modernized 1920s hotel just a short walk from Pike Place Market. At the other end of the scale, the cheapest place to stay has to be the newly renovated **HI-Seattle at the American Hotel,** just east of Pioneer Square (520 S. King St.; 206/622-5443), which offers clean and comfortable dorm beds for around $30.

Seafood, not surprisingly, is the thing Seattle restaurants do best, and the city is full of great places to eat fish. The sushi here is as good as it gets, outside Japan. Try **Maneki** (304 6th Ave. S.; 206/622-2631), which has been serving fresh sushi for over 100 years in the International District. For fish-and-chips or cheap, fresh oysters (and Washington produces more oysters than anywhere else in the United States), head down to **Emmett Watson's Oyster Bar** (206/448-7721) at the north end of Pike Place Market. More down-home fare is served up for breakfast, lunch, and dinner at the **5 Spot** (1502 Queen Anne Ave. N.; 206/285-7768), in the residential Queen Anne district, about two miles northwest of downtown high above Lake Union.

The best source of advance information on visiting Seattle is **Seattle's Convention and Visitors Bureau** (206/461-5840).

view of the Seattle skyline from Queen Anne Hill

popular with kayakers and trout-fishers who come for its access to the river, and with skiers who like its easy access to the slopes at Stevens Pass, 16 miles farther east.

Around eight miles east of Skykomish, midway to Stevens Pass, a well-marked turnout along US-2 gives access to one of the region's prettiest and most historically significant sites. On the north side of the highway, the parking area's interpretive exhibits tell the story of the Great Northern Railroad, the transcontinental railroad that was completed on this spot in 1893. A plaque displays a photograph showing the driving of the traditional golden spike, while other exhibits discuss the construction and importance of the railroad in the growth of Puget Sound.

If you're not interested in railroad lore, head along the 100-yard-long paved trail that loops back under the highway to the powerful cascade of **Deception Falls.** If you can stand the usually bone-chilling snowmelt, you'll be pleased to find a number of deep and clean swimming holes in the area.

Stevens Pass

At the crest of the Cascades, US-2 climbs over 4,061-foot **Stevens Pass,** the highest and northernmost Cascade pass that's kept open year-round. Stevens Pass was also a historically vital railroad crossing, though Amtrak and other trains now avoid the pass, detouring instead through an eight-mile-long tunnel cut through the mountains in 1929. In 1910, before the completion of the tunnel—the longest still in use in the western hemisphere—the pass was the site of the worst avalanche disaster in U.S. history: 96 passengers and railroad workers were killed by a mile-long snow slide.

Stevens Pass was named in honor of John F. Stevens, the Great Northern Railroad engineer who also plotted the Panama Canal.

Besides providing grand views of the nearby peaks and more distant valleys, Stevens Pass is also a very popular **ski area** (206/634-1645) with 10 chair lifts, reasonable rates, a terrain park, and a 1,800-foot vertical drop. In summer, the slopes convert to a mountain biking terrain park.

Tumwater Canyon

Heading east through the Cascades from Stevens Pass, US-2 runs through the forests of **Tumwater Canyon,** a breathtaking place when fall color sweeps through it, and quite scenic any other time of year. Much of the surrounding wilderness was badly burned by wildfires, but most of the area right along US-2 survived pretty much unscathed.

All along this stretch, US-2 winds along the raging Wenatchee River through evergreen conifer forests highlighted by occasional aspens. The river is a very popular rafting and kayaking spot, whose challenges vary with the water levels and intensity of the snowmelt. There are also some nice late-summer swimming holes, easily accessible from US-2, but the roadside is basically undeveloped, with one exception: At Coles Corner, 15 miles west of Leavenworth, the blue-roofed **'59er Diner** (509/763-2267) is a popular road-food restaurant, with great juicy burgers, crispy fries, milk shakes, and a jukebox.

Leavenworth

Sitting in the eastern foothills of the Cascades, 125 miles from Seattle, **Leavenworth** (pop. 1,965) has successfully transformed itself from an economically depressed railroad town into one of the most popular day-trip destinations in the Pacific Northwest. After the local lumber mills closed down in the mid-1960s, the town took advantage of its spectacular location and re-created itself as an ersatz Bavarian village; it has been drawing huge crowds of tourists ever since—over a million visitors annually. Check out the old photographs on the walls of **Der Markt Platz** shopping center, on the corner of 8th and Commercial Streets, for the whole story.

Bavarian architecture in Leavenworth

Over a dozen blocks of half-timbered pseudo-chalets and Tyrolean shopping malls house a range of low-budget craft galleries, sausage-and-beer gardens, and T-shirt stores, which you can escape by walking two blocks south to an attractively landscaped park along the Wenatchee River. Eat and drink at the **Heidleburger Drive-In,** near the west end of town (12708 W. US-2; 509/548-5471), or at the elaborate mock-Bavarian McDonald's. Perhaps the best place to eat and drink is the **Munchen Haus** (709 Front St.; 509/548-1158). One pleasant and moderately priced place to stay is the **Linderhof Inn** ($93 and up; 690 US-2; 509/548-5283 or 800/828-5680).

> Leavenworth's faux-European reconstruction was inspired in part by Danish-flavored Solvang, California.

Cashmere

At the heart of the Wenatchee Valley, surrounded by apple orchards and bare-brown eastern Cascade foothills, **Cashmere** (pop. 3,063) has an attractive downtown district, its unusual red columns and brown-shingled awnings both shading the sidewalks and giving the town some visual identity. The main sight here is the large **Chelan County Historical Museum** (daily; $4.50), off US-2 at the east end of town, with an excellent collection of Native American artifacts and a free outdoor Pioneer Village made up of 18 different historic structures from around the county.

> Two miles northwest of Cashmere, right along US-2, the sandstone slabs and spires of **Peshastin Pinnacles State Park** provide a popular rock-climbing spot—but no camping.

Cashmere is also the home of **Aplets and Cotlets,** fruit-and-nut candy, started here in the 1920s by two Armenian immigrants. These sweet treats are so dominant in the local scheme of things that the main route into town has been renamed Aplets Way. The Liberty Orchards factory, across from the railroad depot, is open daily for free tours and samples.

For road food (good milk shakes!), stop by **Rusty's Drive-In** (700 Cotlets Way; 509/782-2425) at the east edge of town near the big Tree Top apple juicery, or head to the block-long downtown district, where you'll find a handful of cafés and taverns and the **Village Inn** ($59–99 and up; 229 Cottage Ave.; 509/782-3522).

Ohme Gardens County Park

Overlooking the confluence of the Wenatchee and Columbia Rivers on a bluff above the US-2/US-97 junction, **Ohme Gardens County Park** (daily Apr. 15–Oct. 15; $7; 509/662-5785) maintains nine acres of immaculate greenery that offer a cool contrast to eastern Washington's arid terrain. Created beginning in 1929 by the Ohme family, the lush plantings of ferns and evergreens have transformed an otherwise rugged Cascade crest. Stone pathways wind past waterfalls and rocky pools, culminating in a rustic lookout that gives sweeping views of Wenatchee and the surrounding Columbia River valley.

Wenatchee

Just south of US-2, **Wenatchee** (pop. 30,229) is the commercial center of the Wenatchee Valley, one of the world's most productive apple- and pear-growing regions—it's responsible for about half the nation's annual crop. The **Washington Apple Commission Visitor Center,** a block north of US-2 below the Ohme Gardens, is the place to go to find out all about the state's apple industry, and to enjoy free apples and apple juice (not to mention potent air-conditioning).

Wenatchee stretches south from US-2, with three miles of shopping malls, car dealerships, and anonymous highway sprawl before you reach the downtown business district. Many large fruit warehouses and a nice park line the railroad tracks along the riverfront. One place worth stopping is the excellent **Wenatchee Valley Museum and Cultural Center** (closed Sun.; $5; 127 S. Mission St.), which contains extensive displays tracing the region's prehistoric and pioneer past, from native rock art to a working, HO gauge model of the Great Northern Railway route over the Cascades. An adjacent building houses a large exhibit on Washington's apple industry, including an antique but fully functioning apple sorting and packing line.

Along with every fast-food franchise known to humankind, Wenatchee also has some great local haunts, including **Dusty's In-N-Out** (1427 N. Wenatchee Ave.; 509/662-7805), fa-

SweeTango apples in Wenatchee

mous for burgers and shakes (and words of wisdom on its sign) since 1949. There are also lots of motels, ranging from the inexpensive **Avenue Motel** ($55 and up; 720 N. Wenatchee Ave.; 509/663-7161) to the business-oriented **Coast Wenatchee Center Hotel** ($79–125; 201 N. Wenatchee Ave.; 509/662-1234).

Lake Chelan

From Wenatchee, US-97A runs north along the west bank of the Columbia River to beautiful **Lake Chelan,** at the southern edge of the North Cascades National Park. Edged by wilderness and surrounded by tall mountain peaks, fjord-like Lake Chelan offers quick and comfortable escape from the modern world, thanks to the *Lady of the Lake* tour boat (open year-round; daily Apr.–Oct.; $34.50–59 round-trip; 509/682-4584), which crosses the waters to the peaceful hamlet of Stehekin, on the lake's road-free northern shore. If you want an unusual adventure, or more time to explore the surrounding wilderness, you can fly across the lake on a seaplane (around $160; 509/682-5555).

Lake Chelan

From Stehekin, where there is a **national park visitors center** (360/856-5700), you can hike deep into the volcanic

Stehekin Landing Resort

wilds of the North Cascades, ride bikes along old mining trails, fish or swim in the glacial lake, and stay the night at the 28-unit **Stehekin Landing Resort** ($82–185; 509/682-4494), one of a handful of tourist facilities in this delightfully isolated neck of the woods.

If you don't have much time but still want to savor the Lake Chelan experience, head to **Campbell's Resort** (509/682-2561), which has nice rooms and a great restaurant on the easier-to-reach south shore.

Waterville

Standing at the center of fertile wheat fields 10 miles east of the Columbia River, the compact farming town of **Waterville** (pop. 1,185) was laid out in 1885 around the stately, whitewashed brick **Douglas County Courthouse,** which still stands at Birch and Rainier Streets. Most of downtown Waterville has been declared a national historic district, and the four franchise-free blocks of attractive brick buildings still house banks, cafés, and grocery stores—making it a very nice place to stop on a journey across the state. There's a photogenic, sign-painted barn at the west end of town, and midway along US-2's zigzag through town, the **Douglas County Museum and Historical Society** (closed Mon.; donation; 124 W. Walnut St.; 509/745-8435) has an intriguing display of objects tracing regional history, including Native American artifacts and a perfectly preserved pioneer post office.

Across US-2 from the museum, the attractive **Waterville Historic Hotel** ($49–149; 102 East Park St.; 509/745-8695) has been nicely restored and offers unexpectedly characterful and comfortable accommodations; it's like stepping back a century or so, to a time when Teddy Roosevelt was president. For a bite to eat, head a block north from the museum to the welcoming **Coyote Pass Café,** on US-2 (104 W. Locust St.; 509/745-9999).

Moses Coulee

One of the last vestiges of eastern Washington's natural, unirrigated landscape, protected in its untrammeled splendor by the nonprofit Nature Conservancy, **Moses Coulee** is an 800-foot-deep gorge bounded by vertical walls of ruddy brown volcanic basalt, brightened by splashes of green and orange lichen. From the rolling plains above, US-2 cuts down into the coulee, then back up the other side, passing through some of the Columbia River Basin's sole surviving sagebrush and giving a strong sense of how profoundly irrigation has changed the region.

Coulee City and Dry Falls

A shipping center for the wheat farms of eastern Washington, **Coulee City** (pop. 562) calls itself the "Friendliest Town in the West." Despite this claim, there's no more reason to stop now than there was during the pioneer days of the 1860s, when it was said that transfer times on stagecoaches and trains were arranged so that travelers were forced to spend the night in Coulee City, like it or not. If you find yourself here, you can choose from a pair of motels and three gas stations.

Northwest of Coulee City, the large **Dry Falls Dam** impounds Columbia River water to form Banks Lake; Hwy-155 runs along its sluggish shores on the way to the Grand Coulee Dam. Though you can see the coulee's towering basalt walls from this road, to get a sense of what the Grand Coulee looked like before the dams were built, follow Hwy-17 four miles south from Coulee City to where the **Dry Falls** escarpment stands out as the most impressive reminder of the region's tumultuous geology. Interpretive exhibits along the highway explain that during the last ice age, when the Columbia River flowed over the falls, this was the most powerful waterfall on the planet: twice as high as Niagara, and over three miles across.

Grand Coulee Dam

The centerpiece of the massive project of dams and canals that have "reclaimed" the Columbia Basin, the **Grand Coulee Dam** is one of the civil engineering wonders of the world. Built from 1933 to 1942 under the auspices of FDR's New Deal, at a cost of many millions of dollars and 77 lives, the dam is one of the largest concrete structures in the world: 550 feet high, 500 feet thick at its base, and nearly a mile across. The combined generating capacity is more than 6,450 megawatts—half of which comes from the Third Powerplant, added in 1975. Exhibits on the construction and impact of the dam fill the large, modern **Visitor Arrival Center** (daily; free; 509/633-9265) just down-stream. On summer evenings a free, half-hour laser light show is projected onto the spillway of the dam.

There are three small towns—Coulee Dam, Grand Coulee, and Electric City, re-spectively, east to west from the dam—all of which service the needs of boaters, anglers, and other visitors. The best place to see the Grand Coulee Dam light show is the very pleasant **Columbia River Inn** ($105 and up; 509/633-2100), across from the visitors center.

In **Electric City,** along Hwy-155 a mile southwest of Coulee Dam, take a look at the **Gehrke Windmill Garden,** a whimsical collection of whirligigs and windmills made by folk artist Emil Gehrke, who lived here until his death in 1979.

The Columbia Basin: Wilbur and Davenport

The 150-mile stretch of rolling farmland that lies to the east of the Cascades is a natural desert, receiving an average of 10 inches of annual rainfall. Though small-scale farming limped along here for over a century, the region underwent a wholesale change after World War II, when irrigation water from reclamation projects along the Columbia River and its many tributaries turned the sagebrush plains into the proverbial amber waves of grain, spreading toward the hori-zon against an (almost) always-clear blue sky.

US-2 runs directly across the heart of this sparsely populated, nearly treeless region, passing through a few very small towns. In **Wilbur,** at the turnoff to Coulee Dam, an old service station has been brought back to life as a drive-by espresso stand, and **Billy Burgers** has good food and great milk shakes, right on US-2 (804 SE Main St.; 509/647-5651). Eight miles east is the blink-and-you'll-miss-it community of **Creston** ("Home of 1982 and 1984 Girls State B Champions"), where daily life revolves around the **Corner Café** at the center of town.

Twenty miles east of Creston, **Davenport,** one of the oldest towns in east-ern Washington, has a nifty old courthouse on a hill just north of US-2, a handful of quaint old houses, as well as the small **Lincoln County Historical Museum** (509/725-6711), located a block south of US-2 at Park and 7th Streets. Davenport also boasts a pair of burger-and-shake places along US-2 at either end of town.

Spokane

The only real city in eastern Washington, **Spokane** (pop. 208,916) feels even bigger than it is, thanks to its location amidst the prosperous agricultural

In summer, enjoy a Class A **Spokane Indians** (509/535-2922) baseball game at Avista Stadium, on the county fairgrounds off Broadway. Games are broadcast on **KGA 1510 AM.**

hinterlands of the Columbia River Basin. First established as a fur-trading outpost around 1810, Spokane began to grow when railroads arrived in the 1870s and has boomed since the advent of irrigation in the 1940s. The second largest city in Washington, and the biggest between Seattle and Minneapolis, Spokane is economically dependent on warehousing and transportation, taking advantage of its busy railroads as well as its location at the junction of US-2, US-395, and I-90.

Though downtown Spokane boasts a number of grand buildings—one guidebook calls Riverside Street between Jefferson and Lincoln "the loveliest three blocks in the Pacific Northwest"—Spokane really came of age when it hosted the 1974 World's Fair, for which much of the riverfront was cleared and converted to the attractive, 100-acre **Riverfront Park.** Designed by Frederick Law Olmsted a mere century earlier, but never implemented, the park gives good views of tumbling **Spokane Falls,** which form a deep canyon at the center of downtown. Besides an opera house and a convention center, other remnants of the fair include numerous kiddie rides, a summer-only **gondola** sky ride (daily; $7.25) that drops down to the base of the falls, a 1909 **Looff Carousel** ($2) complete with hand-carved wooden horses, an IMAX theater, and a landmark sandstone clock tower that's the sole reminder of the Great Northern rail yards that lined the riverfront for most of the previous century.

One of Spokane's most popular roadside attractions is the giant-sized **Radio Flyer wagon,** 12 feet tall with a slide down the "handle," near the clock tower in Riverfront Park.

Riverfront Park is right at the heart of downtown, and a quick walking tour can take in dozens of well-preserved, creatively reused architectural treats, like the Spokane **City Hall,** which faces the southwest corner of Riverfront Park (808 W. Spokane Falls Blvd.)—the only government I know of that's housed in a converted Montgomery Ward department store, a terra-cotta gem dating from 1929. Another worthwhile stop is **Auntie's Bookstore,** a full-service independent bookstore with a popular café (402 W. Main Ave.; 509/838-0206).

Northeast of downtown, across the Spokane River via Division Street (US-2), the best-known dropout of **Gonzaga University,** Bing Crosby, is fondly remembered in a museum in the Crosby Student Center at the heart of the small campus.

Spokane's other center of visitor interest is **Browne's Addition,** a turn-of-the-20th-century residential district a mile or so west of downtown with many stately homes. The highlight here is the wonderful MAC, the **Northwest Museum of Arts and Culture** (closed Mon.–Tues.; $18; 2316 W. 1st Ave.; 509/456-3931), which houses extensive collections of artifacts tracing Native American and regional history and culture.

Spokane Practicalities

There's no shortage of good places to eat in Spokane, from hearty and homespun to eclectic and expensive. Spokane's best breakfast is served up in a unique setting: the former presidential carriage of the Northern Pacific Railroad is now **Frank's Diner** near downtown (1516 W. 2nd Ave.; 509/747-8798). Spokane's youthful, outdoorsy population also supports numerous bistro-style restaurants and brewpubs, like **Hills',** serving great Reuben sandwiches and a full range of food and beer (401 W. Main Ave.; 509/747-3946), across from Auntie's Bookstore. In Browne's Addition, west of downtown, another good bet is the **Elk Public House** (1931 W. Pacific Ave.; 509/363-1973), with yet more good bistro-style food (and a soda fountain).

Motels line the main highways in and out of Spokane, especially along I-90, and Spokane also has a great place to stay at the heart of downtown: the fabulous **Davenport Hotel** ($100–150; 10 S. Post St.; 800/899-1482) has luxurious rooms in the fully renovated circa 1914 original, and in a brand-new tower.

> Some people in Spokane insist that, rather than dying in a shootout in South America, Wild West legend Butch Cassidy actually lived for years in Spokane, under the name William Phillips, until his death at age 70 in 1937.

Newport

Northeast of Spokane, US-2 crosses a few miles of suburban sprawl before winding through 35 miles of beautiful forested uplands and occasional crossroads communities on the Idaho border. Straddling the state line, **Newport** (pop. 2.126) began as a small trading post on the Idaho side in 1889, then moved to Washington when the Great Northern Railroad arrived in 1892. The original town site, overlooking the Pend Oreille (pronounced "PON-doo-ray") River, holds the business district, while the railroad legacy still defines much of the main part of town. Two depots face each other along US-2 at the south end of the three-block main street, Washington Avenue, one holding the offices of a lumber company, the other housing the small but enjoyable **Pend Oreille County Museum** (daily May–Oct.; donations), which has farming and mining artifacts—plus a pencil collection.

IDAHO

Even though the route zigzags for some 75 miles along the Kootenai and Pend Oreille Rivers, it doesn't take long for US-2 to cross the narrow neck, known as the Panhandle, of northern Idaho. Following the Pend Oreille River east from Washington, the route passes a pair of struggling but proud old logging communities, then pauses at the resort town of **Sandpoint** before threading the deep gorge of the Kootenai River upstream toward Montana.

Sandpoint

Located at the junction of US-2 and US-95 at the northern end of Idaho's largest lake, Pend Oreille, **Sandpoint** (pop. 8,159) is a resort community with a relaxed, welcoming feel. The highly regarded **Schweitzer Mountain Resort** (208/263-9555 or 800/831-8810) north of Sandpoint attracts adventurous off-piste skiers in winter and daredevil mountain bikers in summer. The mix of Rocky Mountain scenery and abundant rec-

reation has made Sandpoint a popular place to visit and live, yet despite the dozens of real estate agents and other signs of potential despoliation, it still feels like a small town.

As you might guess from the name, Sandpoint boasts a fine, quarter-mile-long beach, **City Beach,** just a few blocks' walk from downtown at the east end of Bridge Street, complete with volleyball courts and a dock where you can board tour boats to cruise the lake.

South of downtown, summer visitors in search of burgers and soft-serve cones flock to **Dub's Drive In** (703 US-2; 208/263-4300). Downtown, the main business district along 1st Avenue fills a half dozen blocks around the landmark **Panida Theater** (208/263-9191), where big names and locals still perform. You'll find a number of good cafés here, plus **Eichardt's** (212 Cedar St.; 208/263-4005), a beer-drinker's delight with great food (burgers, sand-wiches, fish-and-chips). Two blocks east, the **Cedar Street Bridge** was rebuilt in 1983 to house a funky range of boutiques, cafés, and food stalls, inspired by the Ponte Vecchio in Florence. Besides the $150-a-night rooms at Sandpoint's resorts, there are many more moderate motels, like the slightly faded but well-located **Best Western Edgewater Resort** ($85–200; 56 Bridge St.; 208/263-3194), right on the lakefront.

Naples and Bonners Ferry

North from Sandpoint, US-2 and US-95 run together through broad flat val-leys dotted with small timber towns. The largest of these, **Naples,** is still a lit-tle bit notorious because of its connections to the 1990s battles between the FBI and local neo-Nazi sympathizers around nearby Ruby Ridge. These days things are pretty quiet, but travelers are drawn to Naples's friendly **Northwoods Tavern,** on US-2, a great place to meet locals over a beer and a game of pool (or three). There's a handy general store next door, and not too far away is the **Naples Inn** (208/267-5964).

Ten miles north of Naples, and named after a ferry service across the Kootenai River that started here in 1864, **Bonners Ferry** (pop. 2,543) is a busy blue-collar town with a natural resource–based (read: logging and farming, especially hop-growing) economy. The **Kootenai River Inn** ($115 and up; 7169 Plaza St.; 208/267-8511) is an Indian-run casino and Best Western.

Away from the highway, the Bonners Ferry area has an unusual accommodation option: the **Shorty Peak Fire Lookout,** 45 miles from town, and a two-mile hike from the nearest road, way up in the wild Selkirk Mountains, where two people can spend the night and take in the panoramic views for around $25 a night. For reservations, and information on hiking in the surrounding wilderness, contact the USFS **ranger station** (208/267-5561) on US-2/95 at the south edge of town.

Between Bonners Ferry and the Montana state line, US-2 crosses the once-wild, now-dammed Moyie River on a 450-foot-high bridge.

MONTANA

Crossing northern Montana roughly 30 miles south of the Canadian border, US-2 gives an up-close look at two very different parts of this huge state. The western quarter, on the slopes of the Rocky Mountains, offers incredible scenic beauty and innumerable options for outdoor recreation, culminating in magnificent **Glacier National Park.** East of Glacier, it's like a completely different world as two-lane US-2 (popularly known as the "Hi-Line") races across glaciated Great Plains range lands along the many tributaries of the broad Missouri River. A few low buttes and cylindrical grain silos rise up in sharp silhouettes, but the horizon is the dominant aspect, stretching for what feels like hundreds of miles in all directions. Apart from dozens of one-side-of-the-road blink-stops, the towns along US-2 in the eastern stretches of Montana—Culbertson, Wolf Point, Glasgow, Malta, and Havre—are few and far between. It's here you realize what the "Big Sky Country" is all about: cruising along at 70

The Idaho/Montana line marks the boundary between the Pacific and mountain time zones, so adjust your clocks and watches accordingly.

How big is Montana? It stretches for over 560 miles east to west, covering an area larger than New England and New York put together, but it has a total population smaller than that of Hartford, Connecticut.

The many roadside crosses you'll see while driving through Montana each mark a traffic fatality. Since 1953, they have been placed along the roads by the American Legion; many are now elaborate shrines to lost loved ones.

mph, pacing a freight train and waving at the engineer, and *never* passing a gas station when the tank's less than half full.

Troy: Kootenai Falls

On the banks of the broad Kootenai (pronounced "KOOT-nee") River, 14 miles east of the Idaho border, the mining and lumber-milling town of **Troy** (pop. 940) is at very nearly the state's lowest elevation—1,892 feet above sea level. There's not a lot to the place, apart from a short stretch of motels, gas stations, taverns, churches, and cafés—the best of which is the family-friendly **Silver Spur,** right in town (120 US-2; 406/295-2033)—plus a small historical museum at the east end of town. Some seven miles west of Troy, there's a nice USFS campground at the confluence of the Yaak and Kootenai Rivers.

Though the only sign says simply Historic Point, the nicest spot to stop is nine miles west of Libby, two miles east of Troy, where the thundering cascade of **Kootenai Falls** drops down a half-mile-long series of terraces. Two hiking trails leave from the well-marked roadside parking area, one leading 400 yards upstream to the main falls, the other heading downstream to a rickety old swinging bridge that sways from cables suspended 50 feet above the green water.

For most of the way between Troy and Libby, US-2 is bordered by marked turnouts where trails lead to the narrow, twisting old highway, preserved as a hiking and cross-country skiing trail through the dense forest.

Writer and resident Rick Bass has documented the isolated Yaak River Valley, north of US-2 via the scenic Hwy-508, in a trio of compelling books: the nonfiction titles Winter: Notes from Montana *and* The Book of Yaak, *and a 1998 novel,* Where the Sea Used to Be.

Libby

The lumber town of **Libby** (pop. 2,640) was first founded as a gold-mining camp but grew into its present, elongated form after the Great Northern railroad came through in 1892. On the south bank of the Kootenai River, Libby is just downstream from the Libby Dam, which was built in 1972 and forms the Lake Koocanusa Reservoir, stretching north into Canada. Despite the fact that Libby is the hometown of former Montana governor and Republican Party national chairman Mark Racicot, the town has suffered one of the worst cases of toxic pollution in recent U.S. history. From the 1940s up until 1990, mining company W. R. Grace dug millions of tons of asbestos-laced vermiculite rock out of a local mountain, covering Libby in toxic dust that has caused more than 1,200 people (almost half the current population) to suffer from serious lung diseases. The EPA has spent more than $50 million to clean up Libby's streets, gardens, and houses, though company officials were eventually cleared of criminal charges.

Despite the occasional media interest in the asbestos case, Libby looks like a pretty typical Montana mountain town. Alongside the railroad tracks, Libby strings for a few miles along US-2 frontage, where you can find casinos and gas stations galore, plus a Subway and a Pizza Hut. A half dozen motels, including the **Sandman** ($50–68; 406/293-8831) offer rooms, and locally owned places to eat, like **Beck's Montana Cafe** at the west end of town (2425

Libby Dam on the Kootenai River

W. US-2; 406/293-6687), round up the food options. Off the highway, the old center of town, north of US-2 toward Libby Dam, holds the **Past Time Bar** (216 Mineral Dr.; 406/293-6097), which has been serving beer since 1916 and hosting Thursday night karaoke for as long as anyone can remember.

A number of pleasant **campgrounds** operate in and around Libby, including excellent spots in the nearby **Cabinet Mountains Wilderness.** Libby's most interesting accommodation option is spending a night or two in the **Mount Baldy Fire Lookout,** 20 miles north of town. The popular lookout sleeps up to five people and costs $25 a night; for details contact the Libby ranger station (406/293-7773) or Kootenai National Forest (406/293-6211).

Between Libby and the busy mini metropolis of the Columbia Falls/Whitefish/Kalispell area, US-2 traverses 70 miles of Kootenai National Forest, an all but uninhabited area, sections of which have been badly charred by forest fires. A small display at milepost 63 explains the role of fire in the natural scheme of things.

West of Glacier National Park, US-2 crosses US-93, the **Border to Border** route, which runs through the towns of Whitefish and Kalispell (see page 131). This road trip is described fully on pages 114–173.

Columbia Falls and Hungry Horse

Two intriguingly named towns line US-2 between Kalispell and Glacier National Park. A roadside collection of gas stations and industrial plants, including a massive Plum Creek lumber mill, make up the much larger town of **Columbia Falls** (pop. 4,688), where, despite the name, there are no falls.

There are, however, a ton of entertaining roadside attractions right on US-2, from go-karts to mini-golf, and a couple of very good, low-frills restaurants, including the MSG-free Chinese food at **Tien's Place** (329 W. 9th St.; 406/892-1585) and great rotisserie chicken and ribs a block away at the **Back Room** (522 W. 9th St.; 406/892-9944).

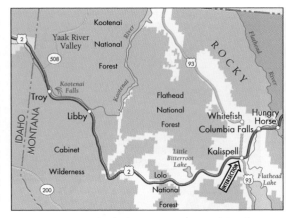

If you like homespun Americana and roadside kitsch, you're in for a big treat as you head east along US-2. The town of **Hungry Horse** (pop. 826), a service center for the large reservoir to the southeast, proclaims itself "The Friendliest Dam Town in the Whole World," and boasts ever bigger roadside attractions, starting with the **House of Mystery** ("Montana's Only Vortex"), on the north side of US-2 (daily Apr.–Sept. only; $8; 406/892-1210). Located three miles east of Columbia Falls, along the Flathead River at the mouth of Bad Rock Canyon (which Native Americans thought was haunted), this is among the more credible of these places where, to quote from the brochure, "the laws of physics are bent, if not broken altogether…where birds won't fly and trees grow at odd angles. Could it be a bearing point for extraterrestrial visits centuries ago? . . . Nobody knows!" It's as fun as these places get (which is to say, very, if you get into the spirit of the place), and well worth the minimal admission fee; there's a good gift shop, too.

> If you're a fan of local newspapers, check out old copies of the *Hungry Horse News*, Pulitzer Prize–winning organ of record about life in the Glacier National Park region (now online-only).

The stretch of US-2 between Hungry Horse and the turnoff to Glacier National Park holds one more "attraction" after another, but even if you're appalled by the brashness of all this hucksterism, you'll want to stop in Hungry Horse for a piece of pie or a milk shake at the **Huckleberry Patch** (8868 E. US-2; 406/387-5000), at the center of town. In summer it also has a full-service restaurant, boasting over 25 different fresh berry and cherry concoctions.

West Glacier

Like many tourist towns on the edges of our national parks, **West Glacier** has its share of tackiness, but here it's on a tolerably small scale and limited to the approach along US-2 from the west. After all the billboards advertising scenic helicopter rides, taxidermy museums, and "The World's Greatest Maze," the actual town of West Glacier seems serenely quiet and peaceful, with little more than a couple of restaurants and comfortable motels, including the **West Glacier** ($85 and up; 406/888-5662), right on the Flathead River (and the railroad tracks!). There's also a large visitors center for Glacier National Park.

For many visitors, especially those who love trains, the main highlight in West Glacier is the landmark **Belton Chalet** ($99 and up and up; 406/888-5000), built by the Great Northern in 1910 and fully, lovingly restored in 2000. Rooms are small but have balconies with nice views, and the restaurant is one of the best in the Glacier region.

Belton Chalet

Essex:
The Izaak Walton Inn

Avoiding the most extreme alpine scenery and the heavy winter snows, US-2 winds around the southern edge of Glacier National Park, climbing over the Continental Divide at 5,216-foot **Marias Pass,** the lowest of the Rocky Mountain passes. Though the road and the railroad are kept open year-round, there's very little visible development, and numerous trailheads access the southern reaches of the Glacier National Park backcountry.

One place that's well worth a stop, or better yet an extended stay, is the **Izaak Walton Inn** ($115 and up; 406/888-5700), midway between East and West Glacier, a half mile south of US-2 in the railroad village of **Essex.** Especially in winter, when the inn overlooks miles of cross-country ski trails, this is one of the best stops in the state. A more humble version of the grand Glacier Park lodges, the inn was built to house railroad workers (which it still does) and is now a popular, year-round alternative to the often-overbooked accommodations within the park. The inn also serves very good food for breakfast, lunch, and dinner (try the huckleberry pie).

Another place worth a stop in early summer is the so-called **Goat Lick** on US-2, near milepost 182 about five miles east of the Essex turnoff, where, in April and May especially, dozens of shaggy white mountain goats congregate around a mineral-rich spring.

Glacier National Park

The wildest and most rugged of all the Rocky Mountain national parks, Glacier National Park protects some 1,500 square miles of high-altitude scenery, including the glaciers for which the park is named, more than 200 lakes, and countless rivers and streams. Knifelike ridges of colorful sedimentary rock rise to over 10,000 feet, looming high above elongated glacier-carved valleys. Grizzly bears, black bears, bighorn sheep, mountain

GOING-TO-THE-SUN HIGHWAY, GLACIER NATIONAL PARK, MONT.

lions, and wolves roam the park's wild backcountry, which is crisscrossed by some 700 miles of hiking and riding trails.

The park's main features are reached via 50-mile-long **Going-to-the-Sun Road,** a magnificent serpentine highway that is arguably the most scenic route on this planet. Climbing up from dense forests to the west and prairie grasslands to the east, this narrow road (built in 1932, and currently undergoing a restoration project by the National Park Service) is the only route across the park's million acres. Note that the road's middle section—everything east of Lake McDonald, basically—is usually closed by snow from late October until early June. RV drivers

Going-to-the-Sun Road

note: No vehicles or combinations over 21 feet are allowed on the Going-to-the-Sun Road.

On the west side of the park, lovely Lake McDonald is Glacier's largest lake, and also the most developed area, with an attractive lodge, two restaurants, a gas station, and a nice campground. A boat offers hour-long narrated tours throughout the summer. Between the lake and Logan Pass, **Avalanche Creek** is the most beautiful short hike in the park, winding through dense groves of cedar and fir alongside a creek that cascades noisily down a sharp cleft in the deep red rock. The two-mile trail ends up at Avalanche Lake, hemmed in by 1,500-foot-high cliffs.

The heart of the park is **Logan Pass,** a 6,680-foot saddle straddling the Continental Divide, which comes alive when the snow melts to reveal a rainbow of brightly colored wildflowers. Two very popular trails run from the large visitors center: The shorter but more strenuous one heads south on a wooden boardwalk across an alpine meadow to a viewpoint overlooking Hidden Lake, while the fairly flat High Line Trail runs north, high above the Going-to-the-Sun Road, leading to the backcountry **Granite Park Chalet,** where you can stay overnight (around $85 per person; 888/345-2649).

Along with the extensive facilities along US-2 at West Glacier, East Glacier, and St. Mary, you'll find a couple of rustic lodges and motels within the park. Apart from the chalets, all lodging (and everything else) in Glacier is run by the same concessionaire, Glacier Park Inc. (406/892-2525). The nicest place to stay is the intimate, comfortable **Lake McDonald Lodge,** with a lovely lobby filled with comfy chairs arrayed around a fireplace, and lots of bearskin and buffalo rugs. In the park's northeast corner, the **Many Glacier Lodge** is a circa-1915 pseudo-Swiss

(continued on next page)

(continued)

chalet on the shores of Swiftcurrent Lake, looking up at Grinnell Point. There are over a dozen campgrounds in Glacier, but they fill up fast.

Besides the grand lodges, a few other relics of Glacier Park's early days as a "Grand Tour" destination still survive: bright red, open-top 1930s vintage touring cars (expensively overhauled to be as eco-friendly as possible) run along the Going-to-the-Sun Road, providing enjoyable guided tours as well as a shuttle service for hikers.

For a complete overview of the park, stop in at one of three main visitors centers, located in West Glacier, at Logan Pass (summer only), and at the eastern entrance in the town of St. Mary. Or call the park headquarters (406/888-7800).

Avalanche Creek

East Glacier Park

Situated along US-2 at the southwest edge of the Blackfeet Indian Reservation, the town of **East Glacier Park** is, as the name suggests, the eastern gateway to Glacier National Park. It's a tiny place, barely more than a wide spot in the road, with a couple of general stores and gas stations, plus **Serrano's,** a good Mexican restaurant just south of US-2 (29 Dawson Ave.; 406/226-9392). North of US-2, on the way to Glacier National Park, there's more good food available at the **Whistle Stop Restaurant** (1024 Hwy-49; 406/226-9292).

With the main park entrance over 30 miles to the northeast at St. Mary, East Glacier Park is not an especially convenient base, though it does have one compelling attraction: the **Glacier Park Lodge** (406/892-2525), the grandest of all the historic park lodges. Built by the Great Northern Railroad to attract visitors to the park (and to its trains), the lodge centers on a magnificent lobby built of 40-foot-tall Douglas fir logs—each of which runs floor to ceiling, with the bark still on it. It's an impressively rustic space, and well worth a look.

St. Mary

Located on the Blackfeet Indian Reservation, 30 miles north of US-2 at the east entrance to Glacier National Park, the town of **St. Mary** makes a great alternative to the in-park lodges. At the east end of the historic Going-to-the-Sun Road, St. Mary has a large Glacier National Park visitors center and the clean, modern **St. Mary Lodge** ($139–399; 406/732-4431) resort. Before or after a big day on the trails, you'll be pleased to find the excellent **Park Cafe and Grocery** (406/732-4482), which serves mega-breakfasts and yet more great berry pies, a half mile north of the park turnoff. The Park Café is worth planning your day around, as the berry pies are every bit as amazing as Glacier's Rocky Mountain scenery.

St. Mary makes an especially handy base for visiting the comparatively quiet Many Glacier section of Glacier National Park, and for seeing the sights of adjacent **Waterton Lakes National Park,** across the border in Canada.

Blackfeet Indian Reservation

The 1.5-million-acre **Blackfeet Indian Reservation,** stretching north to the Canadian border along the eastern border of Glacier National Park, is a weather-beaten land home to 7,500 members of what was once the most powerful tribe on the Northern Plains. The Blackfeet, whose nomadic lives took them all over the plains in pursuit of buffalo, were feared and respected for their fighting and hunting abilities, though contact with white traders brought smallpox, alcoholism, and other diseases that devastated the tribe. Their strength in battle won the Blackfeet concessions from the encroaching U.S. government, including a huge swath of land that, in 1855, included everything north of the Yellowstone River between the Dakotas and the Continental Divide. Much of this land, including what's now the eastern half of Glacier National Park, was later bought back or simply taken away; the tribe now earns most of its income from ranching, and from oil and natural gas leases.

Thirteen miles east of Browning, or 22 miles west of Cut Bank, a much-abused monument along US-2 points out the most northerly point reached by Lewis and Clark on their cross-country expedition. On July 23, 1806, Meriwether Lewis, searching for the headwaters of the Marias River, made it to a spot four miles north of US-2, which he called **Camp Disappointment,** before turning back because of bad weather.

The Blackfeet's tribal headquarters and main commercial center is **Browning** (pop. 1,016), located on US-2 near the eastern entrance to Glacier National Park. Like many reservation towns, Browning has a desolate and depressing feel to it, but there are a couple of places worth stopping, including the **Museum of the Plains Indian** (daily in summer, Mon.–Fri. rest of the year; $4), near the west end of town at the junction of US-2 and US-89. Operated by the U.S. government's Bureau of Indian Affairs, the bland building contains a small collection of Plains Indian arts and crafts, mostly blankets and jewelry. Browning, which comes alive during the annual **North American Indian Days PowWow** in mid-July also has a couple of cafés, a very small casino, and a pair of concrete tepees.

teepees in Browning

Cut Bank

It's hard for travelers heading west along US-2 to believe that, despite having covered over 1,000 miles of undulating Great Plains, they have yet to reach the mountains. It isn't until **Cut Bank** (pop. 2,869) that the see-forever glaciation looks like it might be waning. You crest a hill and suddenly there they are: the rugged Rocky Mountains. Popularly known as the coldest city in the United States, as measured at the local U.S. Weather Service monitoring station, Cut Bank is a friendly and pretty enough place, bisected neatly by US-2 and the railroad tracks.

Downtown, on US-2, the **Highway Two Café and Grill** (13 W. Main St.; 406/873-4010) is great for rubbing shoulders with the locals at breakfast or lunch. At the east end of town, Cut Bank's iconic 27-foot-tall penguin stands next to the **Glacier Gateway Inn and Plaza** ($63–80; 1130 E. Main St.; 406/873-5544 or 800/851-5541), the town's nicest motel.

Shelby

By northern Great Plains standards, bustling **Shelby** (pop. 3,376) is a hive of activity, mainly due to the busy I-15 Interstate freeway, which crosses US-2 here, 25 miles south of the Canadian border. Even so, Shelby's activity—typical truck-jockey, blue-smoke activity—is relegated to the area immediately around the I-15 exit and to the busy multimodal depot along the Burlington Northern tracks. Otherwise, it's an oversized version of all the other Great Northern Railroad towns, one that extends farther than most along the tracks, with wide streets and a much-appreciated hill flaring up to the south of downtown.

Shelby is not rowdy, but neither does it roll up its sidewalks by 8 PM Shelby has an impressive lineup of bars along Main Street (The Mint Bar, the Montana Club, the Alibi Lounge, and the Tap Room, to name a few), but the town's major claim to fame is that it hosted the 1923 world heavyweight fight between Jack Dempsey and Tommy Gibbons, a 15-round decision for Dempsey that was closer than it should have been. The match was produced as a publicity stunt to lure people to the oil boomtown, and Shelby built a 40,000-seat arena, but after Dempsey's managers hemmed and hawed about canceling the bout, only 7,000 showed up.

A replica arena and a room full of artifacts from the fight are among the many intriguing items on display at the summer-only **Marias Museum of History and Art** (closed Sun.; donations; 406/424-2551), in a former residence at the corner of 12th Avenue and 1st Street North. It feels much more like a home than a museum, which adds a welcome amount of weirdness to the usual battery of dusty old stuff. Best of all, the museum is across the street from the local **swimming pool,** an essential rest stop on a hot midsummer afternoon.

Shelby boasts the last good range of services for the 100-plus miles between here and Havre, so be sure to fill up the tank before setting off. There are a handful of cafés, like **The Griddle** (311 Main St.; 406/434-7260), and an absolutely huge Motel sign marks the entrance to **O'Haire Manor** ($40 and up; 204 S. 2nd St.; 406/434-5555).

Heading east, US-2 eases into its long grind across the bare Great Plains, the level horizon broken by grain bins, wheat farms, and the occasional remnants of Cold War–era missile silos. Though the road meanders a little along the banks of the Milk and Mission Rivers, it's mostly a thumb-on-wheel, greased-lightning, straight-shot road, miles and miles of your own wandering thoughts.

For great shotgun-seat reading along the way, William Least Heat-Moon's *Blue Highways* contains an honest, lyrical account of the highs, lows, and endless in-betweens along this stretch, including a brief account of a day in Shelby.

Up until the oil crisis of 1974, when federal lawmakers enacted a national speed limit of 55 mph, Montana law stipulated only that drivers should travel at a reasonable and prudent speed, with no legal maximum. In 1996 federal legislation returned speed-limit control to the states, and for a few years—until Montana set a statewide 70-mph limit in 1999—this meant you could drive as fast as you wanted.

bitterroot,
state flower of Montana

Havre

The largest town along eastern US-2, **Havre** (pop. 9,575; pronounced "HAV-ver") was founded by the Great Northern Railroad and named, for no good reason, after the French port Le Havre, though you'd never tell by the pronunciation. Havre retains more than a little of its Wild West feel and has enough unusual attractions to merit an extended stop. West of town is a large area of eroded badlands, and just north of US-2, behind the Holiday Village Shopping Center, is **Wahkpa Chu'gn "Buffalo Jump" Archaeological Site** (daily 9 AM–2 PM May–Sept.; $6; 406/265-6417). Dating back to prehistoric times, the area has been used by many cultures, including Plains Indian tribes, to drive bison to their deaths. Many of the artifacts recovered from the area are displayed inside nearby **H. Earl Clack Memorial Museum** (Tues.–Sat. 11 AM–6 PM May–Sept.; donations; 406/265-4000), which manages the site.

Havre itself, home to popular Governor Brian Schweitzer, is engaging and also a little rowdy. Numerous poker clubs (everything has "casino" tacked onto it) and cowboy bars line the compact downtown area, underneath which is a defunct underground world of illicit bordellos and opium dens, all part of the whiskey trail that flourished a century ago and again during Prohibition, when copious quantities of bathtub gin from Canada, a stone's throw north, were run through. Relaxed but informative tours ($12) are available through **Havre Beneath the Streets** (120 3rd Ave.; 406/265-8888).

Along 1st Street (US-2) you'll find all the usual fast-food suspects, as well as Chinese at **Canton Restaurant** (439 W. 1st St.; 406/265-6666). There's also the smaller, fresher **Lunch Box** deli/café (213 3rd Ave.; 406/265-6588), south of US-2. For a place to stay, the plushest of Havre's handful of motels is the **Best Western Great Northern Inn** (1345 1st St.; $90 and up; 406/265-4200).

Chinook and Chief Joseph

Chinook (pop. 1,386) takes its name from the Northwest intertribal patois for the warm southerly winds that rip through the area in January and February, raising temperatures some 50°F in a matter of hours, melting the winter snow, and allowing cattle to forage. Now a small cattle-ranching town, Chinook is best known for its proximity to the surrender site of Nez Percé **Chief Joseph** to the U.S. Army in 1877—which effectively marked the end of the Indian Wars of the Plains. The very good **Blaine County Museum** (free; 501 Indiana St.; 406/357-2590), four blocks south of US-2, includes an impressive collection of fossils and local pioneer artifacts, as well as an informative multimedia presentation on the events leading up to the final surrender of Chief Joseph.

If the weather's fine and you can spare half a day, the actual site where the Nez Percé were captured is now preserved (with an interpretive trail and a few plaques, but otherwise unchanged) as **Nez Perce National Park and Nez Perce National Historic Trail,** 16 miles south of Chinook via Hwy-240.

Fort Belknap Indian Reservation

Between Chinook and Malta, US-2 runs along the northern border of the **Fort Belknap Indian Reservation,** which covers some 650,000 acres stretching south to near the Missouri Breaks, a rock-and-sagebrush landscape that

Chief Joseph and the Nez Percé

The odyssey of Chief Joseph and his 600 followers is perhaps the most familiar tale of the final days of freedom of the North American Indians. Having led his band over 1,000 miles throughout the summer from their lands in Idaho, from which they were forcibly removed by the U.S. government (which had "renegotiated" an initial treaty, in effect reducing the Nez Percé's holdings by 90 percent), Joseph and the ragtag, exhausted Nez Percé, thinking the cavalry farther south and Canada closer north than either really was, chose to camp and rest near Chinook, Montana, in 1877.

The U.S. Army, in hot pursuit, sent ahead a 400-man contingent, which reconnoitered the tribe and camped 12 miles to the southeast on September 28. The Nez Percé awoke to attack on September 30. The Army, expecting to prevail on the basis of surprise, instead met fierce resistance, and a five-day siege ensued. After losing their herd of horses, 30 warriors, and three chiefs, and suffering high casualties among the women and children, the Nez Percé gave up. Chief Joseph's words upon surrendering were an eloquent and tragic encapsulation of the Native American experience:

Our chiefs are killed; the little children are freezing to death. My people have no blankets, no food.... I want to have time to look for my children and see how many I can find.... Hear me, my chiefs. I am tired. My heart is sick and sad. From where the sun now stands, I will fight no more forever.

After receiving promises from the U.S. commanders that the Nez Percé would be allowed to return to Idaho, Chief Joseph instead suffered the government's forked-tongue duplicity. Most of the Nez Percé were dispersed to several reservations, eventually winding up in Oklahoma. In 1885, through the Herculean efforts of Chief Joseph and with help from his old nemesis Colonel Miles, some 120 Nez Percé were allowed to return to Idaho. Chief Joseph, however, was never allowed to see his homeland again, finishing out his days in exile on the Colville Reservation in Washington, where he is buried.

provided perfect hiding spots for outlaws like Kid Curry, Butch Cassidy, and the Hole-in-the-Wall Gang.

The Fort Belknap reservation was established in 1887 to contain the surviving members of the once-feared Gros Ventre and Assiniboine Indians who, before siding with the U.S. Army against the Blackfeet, were one of the major powers on the northern Plains. The tiny town of **Fort Belknap,** just south of US-2 about 25 miles east of Chinook, is the main reservation crossroads. The town hosts the annual **Milk River Indian Days** at the end of July, featuring athletic contests as well as dances and country-fair festivities.

Malta

Twenty miles east of the Fort Belknap reservation is **Malta,** named for the Mediterranean island but otherwise just another ranching town that grew up along the Great Northern Railway. Along with the above-average **Phillips County Museum** in the old Carnegie Library ($5; daily; 431 US-2 E.; 406/654-1037), Malta holds the region's best place to eat, drink, and sleep: the landmark **Great Northern Hotel** ($69 and up; 2 S. 1st St. E.; 406/654-2100), which has a bar-cum-steakhouse and a café with good breakfast specials.

Butch Cassidy

Malta, where the eastbound and westbound trains of Amtrak's Empire Builder pass each other, is just one of dozens of flyspeck US-2 Montana towns with names borrowed at random by Great Northern Railway promoters from all over the globe. Heading along the highway, you pass near or through Dunkirk, Kremlin, Havre, Zurich, Harlem, and Tampico, all of which were founded by the railroad and settled in the main by Northern and Eastern European immigrants enticed here around the turn of the 20th century by the railroad's offers of farmlands and homesteads.

> At the tiny farming town of **Saco,** 28 miles east of Malta, pride of place is given to the one-room schoolhouse where TV journalist Chet Huntley received his education. Saco is also proud of the fact that, in 1999, the town cooked up a world-record-sized hamburger, weighing in at more than three tons.

Milk River Valley

East of Malta, the road and the railroad cross and recross the banks of the sluggish and narrow Milk River. Highway signs proclaim your entrance to Beef Country; just check out the menu options in the cafés and you'll know you've arrived. US-2 continues its jaunt over the Milk River tributaries, winding along the swampy **Lake Bowdoin National Wildlife Refuge,** once the state's best duck-hunting grounds and now warm-weather home to pheasants, grouse, and sage hens as well as pelicans, ibises, and herons.

Unless you're a keen bird-watcher, the main place worth stopping along this stretch is 10 miles west of Saco and four miles north of US-2. Here, the large and enticing **Sleeping Buffalo Hot Springs** resort ($50 and up; 406/527-3370) offers a huge naturally heated swimming pool, as well as hot tubs—as hot as 106°F!

Glasgow

Glasgow (pop. 3,250), on the north banks of the Milk River 50 miles west of Wolf Point, is one of the few Hi-Line towns that's more than a collection of grain elevators, though its own dominant visual aspects are spreads of com-

Fort Peck Dam and the Missouri River

bines and threshers. Founded as a railroad town by the Great Northern Railroad in 1889, Glasgow is now the largest town in northeastern Montana. In summer, stop in for a look at the tremendously cluttered, diorama-filled **Valley County Historical Museum** on US-2 at 8th Avenue, worth a look for its barroom exhibit.

Fort Peck and Fort Peck Dam

Fifteen miles south of Glasgow and US-2 via Hwy-24, the enormous Fort Peck Lake collects the waters of the Missouri River behind massive **Fort Peck Dam,** one of the largest construction projects of the New Deal era and still the world's second-largest earthen dam. From 1933 until 1940, a friendly invasion of ultimately 10,000 civilian workers, earning between $0.50 and $1.20 per hour, hacked, dug, poured, sweated, and wrested a sea out of High Plains desolation. As a result, 20 million acre-feet of water can be impounded behind the nearly four-mile-long dam, corralled to a maximum depth of 220 feet and with a serpentine shoreline longer than California's—1,600 miles! Ongoing drought since 1998 means levels are well below average, hurting recreation and leaving boat ramps high and dry; the lake is also home to a huge array of wildlife, including elk, bighorn sheep, pronghorn, and migrating waterfowl, all protected within the **Charles M. Russell National Wildlife Refuge.** The Fort Peck area also has one of the world's biggest concentrations of fossils; dinosaur bones, including

Roughly 20 miles north of US-2, the 15,500-acre **Black Coulee National Wildlife Reserve** shelters one of the few nesting areas of the white pelican in the northwestern United States.

In winter, northeastern Montana suffers some of the worst weather in the lower 48 states, as arctic storms cause wind chills to drop as low as -80°F.

In the premier issue of *Life* magazine (Nov. 23, 1936), documentary photographer Margaret Bourke-White profiled the town of Fort Peck as well as the other 18 boomtowns that sprang up in the surrounding area during construction of Fort Peck Dam.

skulls of a triceratops and T. rex, can be seen inside the **Fort Peck Dam Interpretive Center and Museum** (daily in summer; free; 406/526-3493), at the base of the dam. Fort Peck Lake is most easily approached via Hwy-117, 15 miles south from US-2 at the town of Nashua; you can also reach it from Glasgow via Hwy-24.

Fort Peck Theatre

Besides the dam and lake, the area's best surviving example of New Deal spirit is the snug town of **Fort Peck** (pop. 233), built from scratch to house the construction workers, though its current population is but a small fraction of the number that once called it home. A few of the old buildings still stand, including the landmark **Fort Peck Theatre** (406/228-9219) on Hwy-24, a huge draw in the area with its summertime plays and musicals. One of the greatest places to stay near US-2 in Montana is the original **Fort Peck Hotel** (closed Jan.–Mar.; 406/526-3266), long dormant but recently taken over and touchingly (with nary an ounce of avarice) brought back into a semblance of its classic old self. Rates are very reasonable, and the restaurant is by far the best in the area.

Because trees are scarce on the eastern Montana plains, early settlers built homes by impaling slabs of sod over thin poles. A few of the museums in towns along US-2 display mock-ups of these sod houses.

The tiny town of Ismay (pop. 26), 120 miles south of US-2, unofficially changed its name in 1993 to **Joe,** in honor of 1980s 49ers football superstar Joe Montana. Which makes one wonder which Montana town will try to change its name to Hannah, with hopes of attracting pre-teen girls.

Fort Peck Indian Reservation

The sprawling **Fort Peck Indian Reservation,** Montana's second-largest, stretches for nearly 100 miles along US-2, and for 50 miles north. Home to 6,800 Assiniboine and Yanktonai Sioux, but co-owned by non-Indians as a result of unscrupulous land dealings encouraged by the 1887 Dawes Act, the reservation offers few sights or services to outsiders. Travelers interested in tribal life can best experience it at weekend events like the annual **Red Bottom** celebrations (held every June in Frazer, west of Wolf Point); the **Wild Horse Stampede** rodeo in July, the oldest rodeo in Montana; or the **Wadopana PowWow** (early August). The latter two events are held in Wolf Point, the reservation's largest town.

The site of the Montana Cowboy Hall of Fame, **Wolf Point** is halfway across the Fort Peck reservation, and home to cafés and motels like the **Sherman Inn** ($75 and under; 200 E. Main St.; 406/653-1100), which has clean rooms and a decent restaurant.

Another 55 miles east of Wolf Point down US-2, nearly at the North Dakota border, **Culbertson** (pop. 714) is a quiet town with a disproportionate number of farm-implement and feed dealers. Located a mile east of town, the **Montana Visitor Center** (406/787-6320) houses a good local history museum. There are also a couple of cafés in town, including the classic three-meals-a-day **Wild West Diner** (20 E. 6th St.; 406/787-5374), right on US-2. The **King's Inn** ($69–86; 408 E. 6th St.; 406/787-6277) is a clean, modern motel.

NORTH DAKOTA

Apart from the likeable small city of **Grand Forks,** at the state's eastern border, much of North Dakota's landscape lives up to those nondescript clichés from childhood family trips: It hems and rolls and yawns *forever.* Montana may be Big Sky Country, but North Dakota sure seems to be High Sky Country, the land where, if you tire of watching dancing golden wheat mirages, you can exercise your finger channel-surfing on the radio. It's a long, flat, and (dare we say it?) dull drive across the state, divided four-lane almost all the way, with little but plains or pseudo-prairie, and even the most epic side trip offers minimal relief.

> Crossing between Montana and North Dakota, you switch between central and mountain time zones, so set your clocks and watches accordingly.

The state has done what it can to help out bored travelers by eliminating roadside mowing to encourage wildflowers for most of the trip across, opting for native prairie and a potential refuge for wildlife—and roadkill. That said, the 300 miles across the state do hold a few points of interest, including **Fort Union,** an evocative outpost of the early frontier; popular **Devils Lake** recreational areas; and the geographical center of North America, marked by a stone monument in the town of **Rugby.**

Fort Union Trading Post

Astride the Montana/North Dakota border, standing proud atop the banks at the confluence of the Yellowstone and Missouri Rivers, the **Fort Union Trading Post National Historic Site** was once the largest and busiest outpost

Fort Union Trading Post National Historic Site

on the upper Missouri River. Despite the "fort" in its name, it was never a part of the U.S. military; it was, however, the most successful and longest-lived of all the frontier trading posts. In 1804, Lewis and Clark visited the site, which they called "a judicious position for the purpose of trade." Twenty-five years later, John Jacob Astor's American Fur Company proved them right, establishing an outpost here in a successful attempt to end the Hudson Bay Company's monopoly on northwest trade. Linked by steamboat with St. Louis some 1,800 miles away, Fort Union reigned over the northern plains. Its bon vivant overseer, Kenneth McKenzie, the "King of the Missouri," kept the fine china polished and the wines cool in the cellar, offering a taste of displaced civilization to such luminary explorers as George Catlin, Prince Maximilian, and John James Audubon.

The fort was abandoned as the fur trade declined in the 1850s, and portions of original buildings and walls were taken down by the U.S. Army in 1867 to construct Fort Buford, a mile to the east. In the late 1980s, the park service reconstructed the buildings atop the original foundations, giving a palpable if somewhat overly polished idea of how the old fort looked. McKenzie's old home and office, **Bourgeois House,** is now a visitors center (daily; donations; 701/572-9083) with some surprising artifacts. The fort hosts occasional reenactments of boisterous frontier life: Mid-June, for example, brings the annual **Fort Union Rendezvous,** a rollicking re-creation of fur-trapper gatherings to trade, talk, and compete in wilderness skills.

Fort Buford

Built in 1866 and now a state historic site, **Fort Buford** is eerily quiet, with only the stone powder magazine and a museum in an original soldiers' quarters open for viewing. South of Fort Union, and once home to a company of "Buffalo Soldiers," as the Sioux called the black cavalrymen, the fort is best known for its sad contribution to the U.S. campaign to exterminate Native Americans: It was here that Chief Sitting Bull surrendered to the U.S. Army in 1881, and here that Chief Joseph of the Nez Percé was brought after his "I will fight no more forever" surrender in Montana.

wild prairie rose,
state flower of North Dakota

Williston

Just north of the Missouri River, a dozen miles east of the Montana line, **Williston** (pop. 14,716) has always been a boom or bust kind of place, and in recent years it has been thoroughly enjoying the recent boom in its primary industries—wheat-growing and oil-pumping—so much so that by some measures it is the fastest-growing small town in the USA. Motels are often booked up by "fracking" oil field workers, but the downtown area is still an all-American scene straight out of *Our Town*.

Apart from filling the tank before a trip to Fort Union or farther afield, one more good thing to do in Williston is eat: Responding to an impromptu breakfast poll, locals will likely recommend **Gramma Sharon's** (1501 W. 16th St.; 702/572-1412) as the eatery of choice; it's right on the US-2/US-85 bypass, on the east edge of town.

Epping: Buffalo Trails Museum

Like many other North Dakota rural communities, the old Great Northern railway town of **Epping** (pop. 100) has all but disappeared thanks to automobiles, changes in farming practices, the railway's move to diesel instead of steam, and sundry other common complaints. Here, however, the rapidly vanishing Great Plains life ways have been partially preserved, thanks to the efforts of a local preacher who single-handedly preserved the abandoned buildings and artifacts as the **Buffalo Trails Museum** (closed Mon.; $3.50; 701/859-4361), which has grown to encompass almost the entire town. Main Street is still dusty dirt, lined by a general store, a hardware store, a pool hall, the Sons of Norway Hall, and other essential elements. Most of these old buildings have been converted to house an amazing array of animated dioramas (papier-mâché dummies dressed up like dentists and patients) and the usual old tools and other junk, but it's a great place to stop.

In the past, the historic sites of **Fort Buford** and neighboring **Fort Union** used to be more easily reached from Montana, though recent roadwork has made them accessible from either side of the border. Signs point the way south from US-2.

Roughly 65 miles southeast of Williston via US-85, the north unit of **Theodore Roosevelt National Park** preserves one of the largest surviving contiguous areas of semi-natural Great Plains landscape.

Across western North Dakota, tune to **KMHA 91.3 FM** for commercial-free country music and rock alternative as well as community news and features from the **Fort Berthold Indian Reservation,** home to descendants of the Native American Mandan, Arikara, and Hidatsa tribes.

Ross and Stanley

East of Epping toward Minot, US-2 twists up and through a hundred miles of gentle, chocolate-drop hillocks, residuals of the great Ice Age glaciers, with some beautiful rises and plateaus capped by an occasional abandoned squad of dwellings. Along the way, podunk villages whiz by, full of boarded-up buildings, grain silos, and occasional surprises: **Ross** (pop. 97), for example, is a typically funky old town with some dilapidated, boarded-up buildings and huge grain elevators that look more like spacecraft engines, but this unlikely-looking place is home to the **first mosque built in the USA.** Constructed by a Syrian farmer back in 1929, the original mosque was replaced by a newer, nicer temple in 2005, next to a cemetery holding the remains of Ross's early Muslim settlers.

The one sizable place, **Stanley** (pop. 1,458), resting along the horizon-straight railroad tracks seven miles east of Ross and 47 miles west of Minot, is worth a stop to sample the world's last working Whirl-a-Whip milk shake machine at the old-fashioned soda fountain inside the **Dakota Drug Store** (107 S. Main St.; 701/628-2255), a mile north of US-2. There's also a municipal campground at the north end of town.

Minot marks the junction of US-2 and US-83, **The Road to Nowhere,** which runs from Canada to Mexico and is described on pages 174–231. The many attractions of **Minot** are described on pages 178–180.

Rugby: Geographical Center of North America

The landscape along the North Dakota stretch of US-2 consists of immense stretches of hay fields typical of the Great Plains, and only occasional highlights of miniature cattails, goldenrod, and sunflowers. The place-names here are decidedly Anglocentric, with towns named Leeds or York after the hometowns of English investors who, during the 1880s, pumped the fledgling towns full of cash. The general population, however, has always been decidedly Scandinavian.

Midway between Devils Lake and Minot, **Rugby** (pop. 2,876) is an important agricultural hamlet, known to road wanderers as the town nearest to the geographical center of North America. The exact spot is marked with a two-story stone cairn along the south side of US-2, in front of a café and gift shop (formerly the Conoco

marker at the geographical center of North America

station) and across from a Dairy Queen. Nearby is the **Geographical Center Pioneer Village Museum** (summer only; $3), featuring 27 restored buildings—train depot, schoolhouse, even a reconstruction of a railroad hobo camp—relocated here from around the county, as well as an exhibit on the life of an over-eight-foot-tall local man, Clifford Thompson.

Devils Lake and Fort Totten

The wetlands south of the eponymous town of **Devils Lake** (pop. 7,141), 60 miles east of Rugby and 85 miles west of Grand Forks, are one of the biggest natural draws in the state, with bird-watching, hunting, and fishing opportunities aplenty. However, the waters of what is the largest body of water in North Dakota have no natural outlet, and, true to its name, for the past 20 years Devils Lake has been wreaking havoc. Lake levels have risen by more than 30 feet, flooding farmland, threatening homes, and forcing the raising and rebuilding of US-2 into a sort of causeway. Despite the threat, the town still takes good care of its blocks of tidy brick buildings, one of which houses the artsy **Liquid Bean** café (Mon.–Sat.; 316 NE 4th Ave.; 701/662-1065) and the popular **Old Main Street Café,** around the corner (416 NE 4th St.; 701/662-8814).

Historic **Fort Totten** (daily; $4), 14 miles south of town on Hwy-57, is one of the country's best-preserved 19th-century military forts, with numerous restored buildings set around a spacious central square, as well as a museum and a theater (productions Wed., Thurs., Sat., and Sun. in July). A rodeo and pow-wow, featuring highly competitive Native American dances, are held during **Fort Totten Days** the last weekend in July. Next to the fort is **Sullys Hill National Game Preserve,** a more-than-1,600-acre refuge for bison, elk, deer, and other wildlife, which you may spot while hiking the nature trail.

Both the fort and the nature preserve are located on the 137,000-acre **Fort Totten Sioux Indian Reservation,** centering on the mission village of **St. Michael's,** four miles east of the fort. The main attraction is the **Spirit Lake Casino and Resort,** formerly known as Dakotah Sioux Casino, "North Dakota's First and Finest," standing 18 miles southeast of downtown Devils Lake.

Grand Forks

The oldest and second-largest community in North Dakota, and frequently rated one of the "Top 10 Most Livable Places" in the country, **Grand Forks** (pop. 52,838) gained a place in the national headlines during the terrible floods that devastated the city in April 1997. Following one of the worst winters on record, during which blizzard after blizzard dumped over eight feet of snow and ice on the

Midway between Minot and Rugby, the tiny town of **Denbigh** is the burial site of Sondre Norheim, a Norwegian national hero who in the 1860s invented the telemark turn and introduced the words "ski" and "slalom" into the English language. Royals have paid their respects—you can, too.

Many places along the Missouri River are named for the intrepid and enigmatic Shoshone woman who guided explorers Lewis and Clark across the Plains in 1804. Sacagawea is alternatively rendered as Sakakawea or Sacajawea and translated either as "Bird-Woman" or "Boat-Launcher."

Long the commercial center of northern Great Plains agriculture, Grand Forks became the birthplace of Cream of Wheat cereal in 1893.

Roadside Giants of North Dakota

It may be the long cold winters, the endless flat landscape, or the incredible solitude of life on the northern Great Plains, but there's something about North Dakota that makes people do strange things. The most obvious signs of this odd behavior are the many giant sculptures that stand along the roadside all over the state. Bigger and better than their cousins elsewhere in the United States, the roadside giants of North Dakota quite simply have to be seen to be believed. Here are a few of the biggest and best:

World's Largest Turtle: Nicknamed W'eel, this giant turtle was made in 1982 out of more than 2,000 old steel wheels, and it stands along Hwy-5 near Dunseith, north of Rugby near the Turtle Mountains.

World's Largest Cow: "Salem Sue" stands along I-94 in New Salem, 30 miles west of Bismarck.

World's Largest Buffalo: Built in 1959, and fixed up nicely in 2007, this 60-ton giant looms over I-94 in Jamestown, 100 miles south of Devils Lake.

surrounding plains, Grand Forks prepared for the worst floods the Northern Plains had ever seen. The Red River of the North, which forms the state border between North Dakota and Minnesota, was expected to crest at more than twice its usual peak. In the aftermath of a hurricane-force rain- and snowstorm, the river rose an inch every hour, two feet a day, day after day, while volunteers and relief workers struggled to protect the town.

Under the watchful eyes of the national news media, the river continued to rise, finally breaching its sand-bagged banks and inundating the town. The entire population was evacuated, and over 75 percent of the homes and buildings were flooded; many were partially submerged for more than a month until the waters finally receded and cleanup could begin. The worst destruction occurred in the downtown core, where electrical short-circuits set off fires that raged for days and turned historic landmarks into scorched, empty shells. Total damage reached over $1 billion, but, miraculously, not a single death was attributed to the floods. Signs of flood and fire are still visible everywhere in

Grand Forks, but what is most remarkable is how quickly and energetically the community set about rebuilding itself. A lone obelisk along the riverside shows the high-water mark.

Many century-old downtown buildings have been renovated, including the landmark **Empire Theater** (415 DeMers Ave.; 701/746-5500), now an arts center. Another of Grand Forks' liveliest institutions is the 11,000-student University of North Dakota, whose pretty brick campus spreads north of DeMers Avenue (old US-2). A former campus gym is now home to the **North Dakota Museum of Art** (daily; donations; 701/777-4159), which survived the flood unscathed and houses the state's only contemporary art collection.

Grand Forks Practicalities

For weary road-trippers, one place you'll definitely want to stop is legendary **Whitey's Cafe and Lounge** (121 DeMers Ave.; 218/773-1831), across the river on the new "boardwalk" of East Grand Forks. Though legally in Minnesota, this is a true Grand Forks institution, a genuine speakeasy dominated by the fabulous art deco–style "Wonderbar"—a horseshoe-shaped, stainless steel sculpture, surrounded by comfy booths with individual jukeboxes. The food and drink—try the pan-fried walleye, best washed down with a bottle of microbrewed Summit Ale—is excellent, but the ambience alone would be worth the visit. Another characterful old Grand Forks landmark, **The Kegs** (901 N. 5th St.; 701/775-4993) is an outdoor root-beer stand supported by, you guessed it, a massive pair of bright orange wooden-looking kegs. Look for them north of downtown; order a sloppy joe and a side of onion rings, and people will think you belong here.

Right downtown, the best bet for food and drink is the **Toasted Frog,** a popular sandwich and martini bar (4 PM–1 AM; 124 N. 3rd St.; 701/772-3764) near the landmark Empire Theater. Downtown Grand Forks also houses a great natural foods grocery, the **Amazing Grains Natural Food Market,** on the west side of the Red River bridge (214 DeMers Ave.), where you can pick up organic foods, baked goods, and even prepared foods for a quick-fix picnic lunch.

Accommodation options include the usual range of national chain motels out around the junction of US-2 and I-29; close to downtown there's also the very attractive **GuestHouse Inn** ($65–85; 710 1st Ave. N; 701/746-5411 or 800/867-9797), with an indoor pool and on-site miniature golf course.

MINNESOTA

In its trek across northern Minnesota, US-2 offers nearly 250 miles of open road before winding up in the busy but surprisingly attractive lakefront city of **Duluth.** Midway across the state, after the endless wheat fields of the west, the scenery turns slightly turbid with the remnants of old iron mines and a series of still-busy lumber and paper mills. Opportunistic little cells of roadside community crop up to serve the beer-and-bait needs of those bound for the myriad recreational opportunities of Minnesota's "Lake

Country" along the headwaters of the mighty Mississippi River. At either edge of this summertime playground, two largish towns, **Grand Rapids** and **Bemidji,** serve as gateways to the gaping spreads of **Chippewa National Forest** and many of Minnesota's 10,000 lakes.

Fisher

The first town east of the North Dakota state line, tiny **Fisher** (pop. 435) doesn't look like much, but it was once a bustling frontier port, thanks to its location at the navigational headwaters of the Red River of the North. River traffic has all but disappeared, but the local sugar-beet industry pulls in a billion dollars a year, which may explain the town's prosperous air.

Near Fisher stretches the **Malmberg Prairie,** one of the few extant virgin prairies left. Protected by the Nature Conservancy, 80 acres of wild prairie roses, blue gentians, and bright yellow sunflowers shine in late summer. Once home to herds of bison, the land here has never been plowed, and it looks all the more special, surrounded as it is by acres and acres of industrial-scale agriculture. To reach the preserve from US-2, take US-75 south to Hwy-9, then turn south onto Hwy-56 and drive for two miles until you see the Nature Conservancy sign.

The Minnesota Welcome Center, 11 miles east of the North Dakota border on US-2, has a full range of maps and information on both states.

The tiny town of **Fosston,** midway between Erskine and Bagley, holds one of two stoplights on this 100-mile stretch of US-2. Fosston also marks the sudden switch between the Great Plains and the Great North Woods; the town motto is unusually appropriate: "Fosston, Where the Prairie Meets the Pines."

Crookston

Crookston (pop. 7,891), 25 miles east of the North Dakota border, has a series of bridges over the meandering and tree-lined Red Lake River, which winds along the south side of the compact downtown business district. There's a statue of a hearty pioneer in front of the community center on US-2, and the small **Polk County Historical Museum** (daily June–Sept.; donations) contains the usual slew of 19th-century stuff alongside the "World's Largest Ox-Cart," (celebrated in August's Ox-Cart Days).

pink and white lady slipper,
state flower of Minnesota

Erskine

In the 100 miles east of the North Dakota border, US-2 spreads into a divided four-lane highway, climbing out of the fecund Red River Valley of the North (not to be confused with the *other* Red River Valley, down in Texas) onto the flat glaciated plains, while the roadside colors alternate between the dark reds and greens of sugar beets and the buff and leafy tones of the wheat, soy beans, and potatoes for which the area is known.

Continuing east, US-2 passes occasional isolated pockets of trees, planted as windbreaks amidst the furrowed fields. In the tiny village of **Erskine** (pop. 503), a classic one-horse Midwest town, you'll find **Joe DiMaggio's Grill and Pizza,** southeast of downtown along the US-2 frontage (218/687-2100), which is neither a misprint nor the genuine article. (The owner, Mr. D., used to get oodles of phone calls meant for the legendary Yankee Clipper. Not surprisingly, his place is full of baseball memorabilia.) Erskine also has a swimming beach on Lake Cameron and takes civic pride in being the home of the "World's Largest Northern Pike." (There's a 40-foot-long statue on the pretty downtown lakefront.)

Between Bemidji and Grand Rapids, US-2 runs parallel to the slower but more scenic **Great River Road,** which winds along the Mississippi River from Lake Itasca all the way south to New Orleans (see page 237). The entire route is detailed on pages 232–310.

Skyline Parkway and Hwy-61

One of the greatest loop trips in the country, **Skyline Parkway** is a 25-mile (over 30 with side trips) bucolic wind along the bluffs above Duluth. Accessed from West Duluth off I-35, the parkway takes in numerous historical sites, but it's mostly just jaw-dropping scenery, especially **Hawk Ridge,** which offers perfect wind conditions for viewing up to 30,000 hawks, eagles, and falcons daily in fall; also along the ridge is a fantastic network of trails, boarding stations, and observation posts. The parkway, which was started in 1889 and completed in 1929, connects at its north end with famed Hwy-61, which, if you've got the time to spend, is an even more beautiful jaunt along Lake Superior's granite cliffs to Grand Portage and Canada, 150 miles to the northeast. Along the way are some of the region's best places to eat: numerous smokehouses touting their smoked fish, plucked from the frigid waters of the great lake.

On Hwy-33, 11 miles south of US-2 and 15 miles west of Duluth on the edge of the Fond Du Lac Indian Reservation, the town of **Cloquet** boasts the only gas station ever designed by famed architect Frank Lloyd Wright. Cloquet also has a large, Fond du Lac Indian–owned casino.

Duluth

Though it doesn't get a lot of positive press, **Duluth** (pop. 86,265) has to be one of the most beautiful and underappreciated travel destinations in the Midwest, "a Lilliputian village in a mammoth rock garden," the old WPA *Guide to Minnesota* aptly noted. Gracefully etched into the side of tough, 800-foot granite slopes and gazing over the dark harbor hues, Duluth, from the attractively redone redbrick paving of gentrified Superior and Michigan Streets downtown

102-D Bird's-Eye View from Skyline Drive, Duluth, Minn.

to the grittier heights atop the bluff, quietly goes about its business, usually with foghorns belching in the background. It is a city of maritime and timber history, but it is a city of stunning, pervasive, pristine, *healthy* wilderness as well.

Tracts of forest, harbor preserves, shoreline, and parks flourish in the city, and there are dozens of interesting Great Lakes or historical museums, mansions, lakefront walks, boat or foot tours, and festivals—from Native American powwows (in the summer) to midwinter dogsled races. Many visitors start at Duluth's landmark, the **Aerial Lift Bridge,** a 385-foot-tall monster connecting the mainland to the mouth of the harbor. The waterfront around here has been gently redeveloped, with the **Lake Superior Maritime Visitor Center** (daily; free; 218/727-2497) within a short stroll. Best of all is another landmark of Great Lakes maritime industry, the truly huge hulk of the **SS *William A. Irvin*** (daily; $10; 218/722-7876), a former U.S. Steel ore ship that stretches over two football fields long.

The Aerial Lift Bridge over Duluth's harbor can be raised 138 feet in under a minute to let ships pass underneath. When it's down, cross the bridge and continue for a quarter mile for a real treat: a long, clean, sandy beach stretching along the shores of Lake Superior.

Hwy-61 north of Duluth is the road that inspired the title of Bob Dylan's album *Highway 61 Revisited.* Dylan himself was born in Duluth and grew up in the nearby iron-mining town of **Hibbing,** which is also where Greyhound Bus Lines got its start, shuttling between the mines and the town. Home-run hitter Roger Maris was another Hibbing product.

In Minnesota and Wisconsin, the "On or Off" and "Off Sale" signs on many bars and roadhouse restaurants designate whether they can sell beer and wine for consumption on or off the premises.

SS *William A. Irvin*

Another good stop, the **St. Louis County Heritage and Arts Center,** a.k.a. "The Depot," across I-35 but walkably close to the waterfront (506 W. Michigan Ave.), is an enormous, magnificently restored example of early city architecture as well as home to many of the city's artistic and cultural centers. Around it are the historic locomotives of the Lake Superior Railroad Museum, and two dozen shops re-creating early 20th-century Duluth, right down to the old ice cream parlor.

A fun and filling place to eat, **Grandma's Saloon** (522 S. Lake Ave.; 218/727-4192) serves up heaps of Italian-American food at the foot of the Aerial Lift Bridge. Stay overnight on the lakefront at the **Inn on Lake Superior** ($159 and up; 350 Canal Park Dr.; 218/726-1111).

WISCONSIN

US-2's brief stint across Wisconsin navigates wisely, for it takes in the lovely Lake Superior cap of Wisconsin's northern region and includes a majestic 140-mile detour along the rough-and-tumble **Lake Superior** shoreline, home of rich history, gorgeous boreal forest, and pastoral and littoral scenery.

Superior

Both rival and best friend of bigger Duluth across the harbor, despite the "superior" name, **Superior** (pop. 26,960) is often the butt of jokes, usually regarding its comparatively lower geography (which means Superior catches all of Duluth's flotsam), its blue-collar mentality, its forests of grain elevators

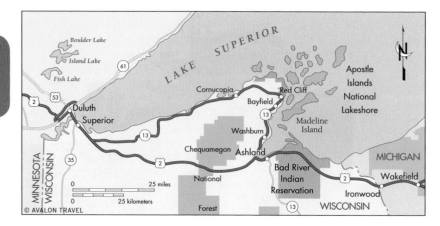

Northern Wisconsin is in the heart of big snow country, a promontory jutting into the maw of bad-tempered Gitcheegumee, where 35 inches of snow a month during the winter don't begin to crease a frown on a native Wisconsinite's face. Play it safe if you're traveling along Lake Superior then.

After starring in the bodybuilding docudrama *Pumping Iron* in 1979, the future *Terminator* movie star and former California "Governor" Arnold Schwarzenegger got a BA degree from the UW-Superior business school.

(rather than trees), and its mountains of coal. It is also proud, along with Duluth, of being one of the busiest harbors in the nation, shipping millions of tons of ore a year from the nation's most-inland port.

Superior's lack of pretense is perhaps its biggest attraction. The route on US-2 through the city is decidedly industrialized, featuring a seemingly endless amount—almost 30 miles—of bay shore crowded with trains, tracks, elevators, and spindly working piers jutting out into the lake almost to the horizon. The city itself is sedate but offers a few things of historical or Great Lakes interest, including its biggest draw, **Fairlawn Mansion** (daily; $8), the sprawling 42-room ex-residence of a lumber and mining baron, once an orphanage and now the main local-history museum. The main stretch of US-2 through town is looked over by a stern statue of an early industrial magnate, James J. Hill, "The Empire Builder," who made a fortune building and running the Great Northern railroad, whose tracks still parallel US-2 west to Puget Sound.

There are plenty of places to stay along the main strip through town, including a nice **Days Inn** (around $50; 715/392-4783) a couple of blocks north of the junction of US-2 and Hwy-53. For food, try the **A & W Drive In,** a full service, family-oriented café on US-2, across from the UW-Superior campus (701 Belknap St.; 715/392-6125).

Hwy-13 Loop: Cornucopia

One of the best alternative routes on the Upper Midwest stretch of US-2 is Hwy-13's 100-mile loop along the shores of Lake Superior. The 45 miles that this loop adds to your journey across the state are without question worth it, taking in the superlative Apostle Islands, charming peninsula communities, and unbeatable roadside vistas. Each little hill you climb reveals a new view of the expansive lake, groves of trees, or mosaics of farmland bordered by vacation cabins and archaic farming equipment. An occasional black bear may cross the road as you whiz by the tottering, one-eyed cabins hardly larger than hunting shacks, their grainy, weather-beaten shingled siding obscured by weeds.

Starting in the west at the blue-collar harbor town of Superior, Hwy-13 zigzags northeast to the lakeshore and follows it to picturesque **Cornucopia,** the northernmost community in Wisconsin. If you're here on a Friday evening, be sure to stop for the traditional Scandinavian fish boil, held at the **Village Inn Restaurant** (715/742-3941), which also has rooms for around $65–85.

East of Cornucopia, the road veers away from the water, emerging again onto the lakefront at the peninsula's main Ojibwa Indian town, **Red Cliff,** which has a marina and boat slip, a lakeside campground within view of Basswood and Madeline Islands, a big casino, and an annual 4th of July powwow. The outskirts of Red Cliff include some lake views and some great views of open pastureland meshed with dense evergreen forests on what appears to be slight tableland. Boats and canoes are ever-present, scattered among rural jetsam, decades-old Chevys and Ford pickups, their sculpted sheet metal rusting mutely in the cattails.

From Red Cliff, Hwy-13 turns south, immediately entering the outskirts of Bayfield.

Bayfield and Apostle Islands National Lakeshore

The nerve center of Hwy-13's sinuous trip through the Apostle Islands region is the diminutive, laid-back resort village of **Bayfield** (pop. 487). Bayfield itself dates from 1856 and looks at first glance about as Lilliputian as you can get, with a curvy (10 mph on the corners) narrow road winding beside impeccably tailored cottages and modest local-brownstone mansions. Virtually every hairpin turn offers an outstanding glimpse of the Apostle Islands and the boats plying the waters, especially on the far northern edge of town. While the waterfront area draws most visitors, the best views of the town and lake can be had from the blocks of dainty Victorian homes that line the hills above.

There are plenty of classy or quaint places to stay in Bayfield, from cottages and motels to the ritzy **Old Rittenhouse Inn** ($99–219; 301 Rittenhouse Ave.; 715/779-5111), famed for its comfy rooms and multi-course gastronomic feasts. Hearty meals for the common man and woman have been served up since the Civil War at **Greunke's** (17 Rittenhouse Ave.; 715/779-5480), across from the marina, which is famous throughout the state for

A unique draw in the summer is Washburn's **Big Top Chautauqua** ($4–65; 715/373-5552 or 888/244-8368), a revival of old traveling tent shows that offers great concerts, plays, and musical revues most evenings.

In northern Wisconsin, tune your radio to **WOJB 88.9 FM,** run by the Lac Court Oreille Ojibwa Nation and featuring excellent, eclectic music as well as National Native News and NPR news.

Canoes tour Squaw Bay Sea Caves in Apostle Islands National Lakeshore.

its whitefish livers, weekend fish boils, and generally funky feel. From the marina, there are plenty of ferries (windsleds over the ice in winter!) to **Madeline Island** or some of the Apostle Islands, which are sprinkled out to the north across the chilly waters of Lake Superior. The headquarters of the **Apostle Islands National Lakeshore** (daily; 715/779-3397), located in the old Bayfield Town Hall, offers the best introduction to these undeveloped islands, which are served by the **Apostle Island Cruise Service** (715/779-3925). The islands offer hiking trails, photogenic lighthouses, and wilderness camping. If you don't have time for an extended visit, you can hike along the Lakeshore Trail on the mainland, which runs along the northern tip of the Bayfield Peninsula, starting from Little Sand Bay Visitor Center, midway between Cornucopia and Red Cliff.

South of Bayfield, Washburn is a pleasant little community, less pretty than Bayfield, perhaps, but with cheaper accommodations; try the **Super 8** ($59 and up; 715/373-5671). Downtown Washburn's parks offer great lake vistas and a lakeshore walking trail.

Ashland

It's not until you enter Ashland on US-2, roughly midway between the Minnesota and Michigan borders, that Lake Superior finally pokes its great nose at you. A big fish in sparsely populated north-woods Wisconsin, **Ashland** (pop. 8,695) likes to call itself the "Garland City of the Inland Seas," but it's really a town full of trestles, all the roads dipping and drooping under the mud-brown wood framework or plain faded steel of Soo Line bridges. Built up on an ever-so-slight rise above the lake, the town has an attractive Main Street with many well-preserved old buildings and a lakeshore lined with great parks and frigid-looking beaches. And you can gaze at the gargantuan **Ashland Soo Line Ore dock,** the largest of its kind in the world—so long as this huge wooden fortress hasn't been demolished or converted into a heritage park.

Another sign of Ashland's historic importance is the grand **Hotel Chequamegon** (pronounced "shuh-WAH-muh-gun"; $79–209; 101 W. Lakeshore Dr.; 715/682-9095), at the junction of US-2 and Hwy-13. Following a 1955 conflagration that destroyed the structure, the reconstruction has managed to capture the decorative charm and original grandeur, and it has a fine restaurant to boot.

Another big attraction, in interest if not actual size, is the newish **Northern Great Lakes Visitor Center** (daily; free; 715/685-9983), 2.5 miles west of downtown, along US-2 at the Hwy-13 junction. The spacious building is full of interpretive exhibits tracing local history and industry; outside there's a nature trail through 180 acres of mixed forest and wetlands, and a five-story tower gives a panoramic view.

For a change of pace, head 50 miles south from Ashland to Phillips, where the **Wisconsin Concrete Park** (free; N8236 S. Hwy-13; 715/339-6371) preserves the hundreds of creative concrete-and-glass sculptures of Paul Bunyan, Abe Lincoln, and lots of farm animals, all made in the 1950s by former logger and self-taught artist Fred Smith.

Bad River Indian Reservation and Superior Falls

Home to one of Wisconsin's six Ojibwa communities, the **Bad River Indian Reservation** encompasses 124,234 acres owned by approximately 1,800 descendants of the original Ojibwa Loon Clan who settled near the delta confluence of the Bad and White Rivers. The tribe holds its annual **Manomin Powwow** in late August, its wood-products factory builds log-home kits, and of course there's a large casino.

From the eastern edge of the reservation, it's another 20 miles to the Michigan border. The main highlight of this stretch is about midway along: a very nice vista point, overlooking the lakeshore from a parking area just west of the Hwy-122 junction. If you're up for a short detour, follow

Just west of the border with Michigan, a Wisconsin liquor store proffers travelers a giant corkscrew statue, beckoning you to imbibe.

Hwy-122 north for a half dozen miles to the shores of Lake Superior, where beautiful **Superior Falls** plummet more than 50 feet at the end of the Montreal River. There's a parking area near the small power plant, and the sunsets here can be spectacular.

MICHIGAN

There are two main routes across **Michigan's Upper Peninsula** (the "U.P."), which stretches for nearly 300 miles between Canada and Wisconsin, wedged between Lake Superior and Lake Michigan.

Between Ironwood in the west and Sault Ste. Marie on the Canadian border in the east, you can choose **US-2** along the north shore of Lake Michigan or the slightly more direct option, **Hwy-28,** which runs near the south shore of Lake Superior near **Pictured Rocks National Lakeshore.** Either way takes most of a day, and this is not a place to try to make up time.

In either case, you're privy to one of the greater finds of the Midwest, the sparsely populated and thoroughly underappreciated (especially by the "trolls" of southern Michigan) land of the "Yoopers," as the proud residents have christened themselves, many still ensconced in the logging and mining enclaves their forebears founded. The U.P. is a surprisingly mountainous and larger-than-it-looks place, dotted with boom-to-bust towns relying on summer tourism and one or more of the industrial triumvirate up here: timber, mining, and fishing. More than three quarters of the land here is protected to varying degrees within national and state parks and forests, and it's no surprise that the best places tend to be farthest away from the main roads; though the roadside scenery is plenty pretty, the more remote areas are as wild and ruggedly beautiful as anywhere in North America.

Ironwood and Environs: The Gogebic Range

The westernmost U.P. town is **Ironwood** (pop. 6,293), which, along with sleepy Bessemer and rough-and-tumble Hurley over the Wisconsin border, was the center of the Gogebic Range iron-mining district. The area's population now is about a fifth of what it was during the 1920s peak, and these mountain towns have moved on from mining to a more leisurely occupation: downhill skiing. Within a few miles are some of the Midwest's largest ski resorts, all benefiting from the vertiginous topography and the average 200 inches of annual snowfall. Most of these ski areas, like **Indianhead** (906/229-

2229), double as summer mountain biking centers, and rental shops line US-2.

The center of Ironwood is easy to miss, but it's worth the quick trip along the US-2 Business Loop to see the old-fashioned business district, which fills a few blocks around the art deco Ironwood Theatre movie palace. In a small hillside park just south of downtown, don't miss the absolutely huge, 52-foot-high statue of **Hiawatha,** the fictional hero of Henry Wadsworth Longfellow's famous poem.

The place to eat in Ironwood is **Joe's Pasty Shop,** two blocks off US-2 (116 Aurora St.; 906/932-4412), serving pasties since 1946; it's open daily for breakfast (try the pasties filled with eggs and cheese) and lunch.

Black River Road and the Porcupine Mountains Wilderness

From Hwy-28 at Bessemer, Hwy-513 heads north toward the shores of Lake Superior, forming one of the U.P.'s many lovely scenic drives. Best known as the **Black River Road,** this 15-mile-long, densely wooded two-laner runs along the banks of the Black River, which drops over a series of well-signed waterfalls as it approaches the lakeshore; a good trail starts at a parking area about 13 miles from Bessemer. Nearby, the **Copper Peak Ski Flying Hill** is the world's tallest ski-jumping facility, its 25-story towers rising high above the forest. In summer, visitors with no fear of heights can ride a chairlift, then an elevator, then take stairs to the top for a great view of the forest, Lake Superior, three states, and Canada ($14; 906/932-3500).

East of the Black River area, Michigan's largest state park, the **Porcupine Mountains Wilderness,** covers 60,000 acres of serrated ridges and dense pine forests, including the largest swaths of virgin forest in the Midwest. The main outposts of civilization here (motels, restaurants, bars, etc.) are the lakefront towns of Silver City and **Ontonagon;** the latter is home to the park headquarters (906/885-5275). Both towns are about 20 miles north of Hwy-28, via Hwy-64 or US-45, respectively.

US-2: Crystal Falls

At the eastern edge of the vast Ottawa National Forest, **Crystal Falls** (pop. 1,469) is a charming, postcard kind of place built into a bluff near a rivulet waterfall on the Paint River. Time seems to stand still here, the town sporting

Besides ski areas, Bessemer is also home to what a large plaque claims is "The Most Scenic Little League Baseball Stadium in America," located just a block north of US-2.

All over the U.P. you'll see signs advertising pasties. The quintessential miner food, the Cornish pasty (which rhymes with "nasty," not "tasty"—hang onto the vowel a bit, like a true Yooper) was introduced to Copper Country 100-odd years ago by immigrant Cornish miners. These dense, baked crust-pockets, stuffed with minced meat and vegetables, are ubiquitous in U.P. cafés and restaurants.

East of Ironwood, at the town of Wakefield, our route divides: US-2 runs south along Lake Michigan, while Hwy-28 veers north along Lake Superior.

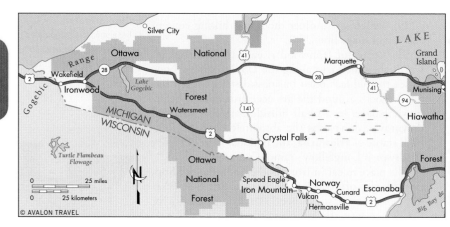

original (read: *old*) street signs still pointing the way, and huge trees overhanging US-2 as it slowly hairpins through town. The only "sights" here are the local courthouse, won in a poker game in the 1880s, and a water-filled old pit mine outside of town.

Southeast from Crystal Falls, US-2 passes numerous rock and ore formations jutting out of the hillsides. The road sweeps into the **Copper Country State Forest,** which gives every appearance of symmetrical reforestation, then flits through 15 miles of northern Wisconsin before re-entering the U.P. just west of Iron Mountain.

Iron Mountain and Norway

Though separated by a half dozen blacktop miles of US-2, the sister towns of Norway and Iron Mountain both grew up with the lumbering and iron-mining industry, producing over 300,000 tons annually from three big mines. The larger of the two towns, **Iron Mountain** (pop. 7,624), backs up against the easy grade of its eponymous mountain and seems casually

strewn about in parts: The east side is minimall sprawl, while the west side is older, traditional "downtown." The must-see here, everyone will tell you, is the **Cornish Pump and Mining Museum** (daily May–Sept. $5; 906/774-1086), two blocks off US-2 on Kent Street. This comprehensive local-history museum has as its star attraction the most enormous steam-driven pump engine you could imagine—it's 54 feet tall and weighs in at over 700 tons. There are also displays about the old Ford Motor Company factory complex in Kingsford, which fabricated such innovations as the "Woody" station wagon, charcoal briquettes, and World War II gliders. The *real* must-see is the freebie, the **Pine Mountain Ski Jump,** west of town off US-2 along Pine Mountain Road. This 120-meter jump hosts annual international competitions in late January or early February and is the site of the current U.S. distance record.

apple blossom,
state flower of Michigan

The mines at **Norway** (pop. 2,845) were so close together and so active that the village once caved in and they had to rebuild it down the hill. Gritty Norway—which once produced more wood shingles than anywhere else, as shown by the numerous houses still coated with them—also boasts the beautiful **Piers Gorge,** a couple of miles south via US-8, where the raging whitewater of the Menominee River scraped out this fascinating, 70-foot-deep gorge on the border between Michigan and Wisconsin. West of Iron Mountain, the Menominee River also provides a backdrop to one of the area's most pleasant places to stay: the **Edgewater Resort** ($90 and up; 4128 N. US-2; 906/774-6244), 10 family-friendly one-, two-, and three-bedroom log cabins with kitchens, right on the river.

Escanaba

Midway along US-2's route across far northern Michigan, **Escanaba** (pop. 12,616)—with picture-perfect placement where the Escanaba River pours into the Little Bay de Noc—was born in typical U.P. fashion, out of the country's insatiable need for timber and ore. At one time its docks contributed to the largest ore-shipping operation of its kind in the United States, work that continues today as Escanaba feeds the steel mills of Indiana, across Lake Michigan. To get a feel for lake life, head to the renovated 1867 **Sand Point Lighthouse** ($3; 906/789-6790) along the lushly landscaped waterfront. The annual **U.P. State Fair,** held here the third week in August, is great fun.

Hiawatha National Forest: Fayette State Park

Between Escanaba and Manistique, US-2 broadens into a fast four-lane highway along both Big and Little Bay de Noc, where you'll pass through a slew of lakefront "resorts," some with their own beaches and all famous for their

Around Iron Mountain in the 1920s, car maker Henry Ford created an industrial complex named **Kingsford** that supplied, among other products, fuel for his factories. This came in the form of charcoal briquettes, the same ones now essential for summer barbecues.

Fifteen miles west of Escanaba, at the eastern edge of the tiny Potawatomi Indian Reservation, you pass between the central and eastern time zones. Adjust your clocks and watches accordingly.

fall colors on Michigan's Upper Peninsula

fishing. Between the bays, the landscape reverts to trees and more trees in the chevroned conifers of the 879,000-acre **Hiawatha National Forest.** The flyspeck communities here haven't changed much—ubiquitous flashing yellow lights, matchbox dwellings attached to bulbous propane gas tanks, and, in a few communities, forlorn old Soo Line railcars aging gracelessly on the tracks right off the highway.

Jutting south from US-2, two quiet peninsulas stick their thumbs out into Lake Michigan. Both have forests, fruit orchards, and a few lighthouses, but the best destination here has to be **Fayette Historic State Park,** the extant ghost of an iron smelting community with a few dozen stone and wooden buildings kept almost totally in their original 1890s condition, not renovated but preserved in varying states of repair. The park is an impressive, sometimes eerie place, situated on sheer limestone cliffs along Hwy-183, 17 miles south of US-2 from the crossroads community of Garden Corners.

US-2: Along Lake Michigan

The route that US-2 follows along Lake Michigan between Escanaba and St. Ignace is one of the U.P.'s best autumn scenic drives. The true heart of U.P. lies here, with patches of pine or birch woodland followed by brief lakeshore, then a dormant ore mine, a trailer park, or a long-abandoned fishing camp. The only sizable town between St. Ignace and Escanaba, **Manistique** (pop. 3,097) tends to underwhelm, apart from its Lake Michigan frontage. Mountains of gravel and mini smokestacks line the road into town on the east side, and the sweetly pungent smell of paper permeates the air.

From the flyspeck town of Gulliver, 13 miles east of Manistique, a road leads southeast to Michigan's most picturesque lighthouse, at **Seul Choix Pointe.**

Driving between Manistique and St. Ignace, the scenery

becomes increasingly gorgeous. Bay views give way only occasionally to small towns or groves of trees, but most of the way the lake breaks through fully as US-2 skims along a beachside causeway bordered by huge sand dunes with green tufts of mixed grasses.

St. Ignace

Coming into St. Ignace from the west along US-2, travelers are tempted by a number of "scenic overlooks," each proffering a chance to stretch and view the often fog-shrouded Mackinac Bridge over blue Lake Michigan. Coming from the east, the approach is slightly diminished by the busy I-75 freeway, and from the south the build-up is truly unforgettable, riding high on the elegant Mackinac Bridge. No matter how you get here, picturesque **St. Ignace** (pop. 2,452; pronounced "IG-nus") is more important than its obviously tourism-contrived loveliness would indicate, situated as it is at the crossroads of the upper and lower regions of Michigan, with Mackinac Island just across the bay. The town is busy and cheerful, in places gentrified and meticulously maintained; downtown you can stroll along a bright lake promenade lined with gift shops, motels, and restaurants.

St. Ignace sits at the north end of what locals like to call the "Eighth Wonder of the World," the **Mackinac Bridge,** one of the longest suspension bridges in the world at 7,400 feet (with its approaches, the total length is over five miles). Lots of scenic views are found throughout St. Ignace and from Straits State Park, west of town.

Downtown, the city-run **Museum of Ojibwa Culture** (daily May–Oct.; donations; 500 N. State St.; 906/643-9161) traces over three centuries of life along the Straits of Mackinac, detailing the native Ojibwa and Huron life ways. The museum, on the site of Father Marquette's original mission, also hosts a number of summer powwows; the largest takes place over Labor Day weekend. Attending one is an unforgettable way to experience the tribe's heritage.

Sample yet more local culture by heading north from downtown along the lakeshore to **Bessie's Original Homemade Pasties** (1106 N. State St.; 906/643-8487), where you can sample the U.P.'s local delicacy, the Cornish pasty, brought over by immigrant miners from England over a century ago.

Mackinac Island

The main attraction around St. Ignace is anachronistic **Mackinac Island,** one of the top draws in the Midwest. Pronounced "MACK-i-naw," this flyspeck island is almost completely car-free, and walking and cycling trails loop around its 2,200 acres (even UPS delivers parcels by bike!). Now billed as a sort of by-gone-days living museum, during the early 19th century Mackinac Island was the headquarters of John Jacob Astor's early fur-trading empire. For two centuries before then, its coveted position at the heart of the Great Lakes meant that French, British, and, later, Americans frequently fought over it. Historic sites and beauty spots abound, so be sure to move quickly through the Main Street commercial area around the ferry landing, which is oversupplied with fudge shops (an island specialty since Victorian times).

horse-drawn carriage on Mackinac Island

Apart from slabs of fudge, the biggest tourist attraction on Mackinac has to be the aptly named **Grand Hotel,** which has been in business since 1887. Famous for its 660-foot-long "World's Longest Front Porch," packed with potted plants and comfy chairs, the hotel is definitely deluxe; room rates are pretty high (starting at around $249 a night, including dinner; 906/847-3331), but you can explore the place and enjoy a drink or high tea, or pay for a self-guided tour ($10). Room rates elsewhere on the island start around $150 at most of the many nice hotels and B&Bs, like the **Main Street Inn,** at the heart of town (906/847-6530). No matter where or how

long you stay, Mackinac Island is a great place to rent a bike (or take a horse-and-buggy ride), cruise around, and forget about your daily grind.

Passenger ferry services (about $22 round-trip) from the docks in St. Ignace are fast (20 minutes each way) and frequent from April through October; call Arnold Line (800/542-8528) or Star Line (800/638-9892) for times and rates.

Hwy-28: Marquette

Midway across the Upper Peninsula along Hwy-28, the U.P.'s biggest and, in many ways, most attractive city is **Marquette** (pop. 21,355), a Lake Superior ore port with a lovely lakeside setting. Blocks of 100-year-old beaux arts buildings fill the business district above the heavy industrial harbor, and the presence of government offices and the region's main college (Northern Michigan University) has given it a lively, prosperous feel.

Other aspects of U.P. life are documented down the road in neighboring **Negaunee,** eight miles west along Hwy-28/US-41, where the excellent **Iron Industry Museum** (daily May–Oct.; free; 906/475-7857) tells the full story of the $48 billion Michigan iron mining industry. Farther west, the lighter side of U.P. life is the theme of **Yooperland** (daily; free; 906/485-5595), a.k.a. "Da

Yoopers Tourist Trap," a gigantic gift shop–cum-cultural museum along Hwy-28/US-41 in Ishpeming. (Just look for the "World's Largest Snowplow" parked out front.) If you're looking for comic postcards of giant pasties and similar oddities, this is the place to come.

Every February, Marquette hosts the start and finish of the **U.P. 200,** a sled dog race to Escanaba and back that draws some 15,000 spectators.

The Huron Mountains

Stretching north and west from the Marquette region, the **Huron Mountains** hold the highest point in Michigan (1,979-foot Mt. Arvon), but almost all of this rugged 50- by 25-mile area is privately owned and pretty much off-limits. It's also one of the wildest corners of a wild part of the country; the private owners (with last names like McCormick, founders of International Harvester, and Miller, of Miller Beer infamy) keep it pretty much as it has always been—before the miners and loggers had their way with the rest of the Upper Peninsula. The best place to get a feel for the Huron Mountains region is the hamlet of Big Bay on Lake Superior, 25 miles northwest of Marquette.

Pictured Rocks National Lakeshore

If travel time is not an issue for you, there is at least one excellent reason to by-pass US-2 across the Upper Peninsula and to follow Hwy-28 instead. **Pictured Rocks National Lakeshore,** a lovely, 40-mile-long stretch of undisturbed sand dunes, beaches, and colorful bluffs, lines Lake Superior in the northeast-

ern quadrant of the Upper Peninsula. For casual visitors, the lakeshore is best visited by boat, since roads here are few, far between, mostly unpaved, and all but invisible; in summer, three-hour **cruises** leave about every two hours from the pier in **Munising,** right on Hwy-28 at the west edge of the park. Even better, if you're feeling fit, is a self-powered kayak trip; try **Northern Waters** (129 E. Munising Ave.; 906/387-2323), which offers daylong guided tours.

Besides being the gateway to the Pictured Rocks, Munising is also the main departure point for glass-bot-tomed-boat tours of the many ship-wrecks that lie along this treacherous stretch of coastline. Well preserved by the cold Lake Superior waters, the wrecks are also legally protected within the 113-square-mile **Alger Underwater Preserve.**

Munising Falls is one of more than a dozen waterfalls in the Pictured Rocks region.

Tahquamenon Falls State Park

Tahquamenon Falls State Park and Paradise

East of the Pictured Rocks National Lakeshore, about 40 miles west of Sault Ste. Marie, you come to a real gem: **Hwy-123,** a must-do loop road (particularly during autumnal color sweeps) that heads north from Hwy-28 past the outstanding—and popular—**Tahquamenon Falls State Park.** The 50-foot-high, 200-foot-wide Upper Falls here were mentioned in Longfellow's *Song of Hiawatha.* Hwy-123 also passes through the lakefront vacation village of **Paradise,** where Whitefish Point Road runs 11 miles north up to some of the best and most isolated beaches in the U.P., and the oldest lighthouse (circa 1849) on the Great Lakes.

From Longfellow to Lightfoot: In Whitefish Point, north of Paradise, visit the **Great Lakes Shipwreck Museum** (daily May–Oct.; $13; 877/492-3747 or 906/492-3747), to learn about the wreck of the 725-foot lake freighter *Edmund Fitzgerald,* subject of Canadian balladeer Gordon Lightfoot's 1970s pop song. The ship suddenly went down 20 miles offshore—without a distress call, but with all 29 crew members on board—in November 1975.

Sault Ste. Marie, Michigan

Michigan's oldest community, **Sault Ste. Marie** (pop. 14,144; pronounced "SOO-saynt-ma-REE") was home to an Ojibwa Indian community for hundreds of years before the first fur-trappers and French-Catholic colonists arrived in the late 17th century. Known historically for the tussles over the area between the French and British, and as the closest land link between the United States and Canada for hundreds of miles, "The Soo" is a great place to break a journey and catch up on the region's complicated past, present, and future.

Beneath the steel-span International Bridge, which links this Michigan town with Ontario's twin "Soo," the raging torrents that impelled French Fr. Jacques Marquette to dub the newly established mission Le Sault de Sainte Marie, literally "falling waters of Saint Mary," are no longer readily apparent.

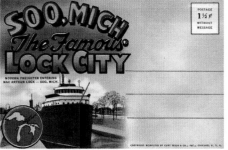

The U.S. Army Corps of Engineers long ago corralled and tamed the rapids between 20-foot-higher Lake Superior and Lake Huron with four enormous locks, the largest and busiest in the world. During their 1920s mining heydays, the locks conveyed many times the tonnage of the Panama and Suez Canals combined—with no tolls paid. The locks area is worthy of at least an hour's siesta; lush parks and a walkway line the locks, with observation points letting you get within a few feet of the massive lake freighters that pass through around the clock. If you want to "lock through" yourself, join a **Soo Lock boat tour** ($22; 800/432-6301).

A handful of nice cafés and restaurants line Water Street and Portage Avenue within a few blocks of the locks; this is also where you'll find the art deco **Ramada Plaza Hotel Ojibway** ($120 and up; 240 Portage Ave.; 906/632-4100).

CANADA

Between **Sault Ste. Marie** and **Ottawa,** the capital of Canada, our route winds along the north shore of Lake Huron then cuts inland to follow a series of broad rivers. The main highway here, Hwy-17, is a section of the busy Trans-Canada Highway; it is also part of the "Voyageurs Trail," roughly retracing the route taken by the early fur-traders between their winter trapping grounds—the wilderness of forests, lakes, and streams to the northwest—and Montreal, the summer fur market. The scenery varies from rivers and forests to paper mills and coal mines, and most of the way Hwy-17 is a two-lane road with a 90-kph (55-mph) maximum and

the International Bridge that joins Sault Ste. Marie, Michigan and Sault Ste. Marie, Ontario

occasional passing lanes to help you get around the timber trucks. Towns here tend to sprawl along the roadside, with a few "chip stands," selling fried potatoes, among the franchised American fast-food joints, but there are expansive sections of natural wilderness within easy reach.

East of Ottawa, it's a short run to French-speaking **Montreal,** Canada's second-largest city and one of the most European places in North America. The change between bilingual Ontario and French-speaking Quebec is

Driving in Canada

Between the United States and Canada, the rules of the road don't really change, but the measurements do. Both countries drive on the right, and the speed limits are similar: In Canada it's generally 80 kilometers (50 miles) per hour on two-lane roads, 100 kph (63 mph) on freeways. All cars are required to have their headlights illuminated night and day; to the un-accustomed, a daytime traffic jam can look like a massive funeral procession. Other rules: All passengers must wear seat belts, and turning right on red is no longer illegal in the Province of Quebec, but it is on Montreal Island; in the rest of Canada, turning right on red is legal so long as you stop first. Deciphering parking zones, especially in French-speaking Quebec, can really test your interpretive abilities.

Gas (*essence* in Quebec) north of the border tends to be more expensive than in the States, and it's priced by the liter (3.785 liters equal 1 U.S. gallon). Some gas stations accept U.S. currency, and almost all accept credit cards, but often they give you a less-than-favorable rate of exchange.

Crossing the border, there are brief checkpoints (and sundry duty-free shops) on both sides. Customs officers usually do a cursory check, asking your address, reason for travel, when you last visited the country, and whether you are carrying firearms, tobacco, or alcohol. The rules are subject to change, but all travelers need to have a passport, even U.S. or Canadian citizens. People of other nationalities should double-check their visa status well before attempting to cross the border, otherwise it may be difficult (or impossible) to return to the United States, and border officials have been known to confiscate vehicles and arrest people they suspect are trying to enter the United States illegally.

bilingual stop sign in Ottawa, near the Parliament Building

sudden and sometimes surreal, as if England and France were divided by a river, not the English Channel.

Sault Ste. Marie, Ontario

Across the busy harbor from Michigan, the "other" **Sault Ste. Marie** (pop. 81,000) is a much bigger, much grittier, and comparatively depressed Canadian sibling. Fortunately, the main visitor attraction offers a quick escape from all the heavy industry. From the Algoma Central Railway Terminal, well signed downtown, the **Agawa Canyon Tour Trains** (daily; C$79 and up; 129 Bay St.; 705/946-7300 or 800/242-9287) depart throughout the summer and early fall (fall color season is the prime time to come). These daylong train trips take you north through a roadless wilderness featuring narrow river canyons and spectacular views. An hour and a half stop above the canyon lets you get out and have a picnic or stretch your legs with a walk to a waterfall. From January through March there is a Snow Train for the hardy, and there's also an End of the Line Tour (to Hearst, Ontario), which takes around two days (and does return, despite the name).

St. Joseph Island

East of Sault Ste. Marie, Hwy-17 winds along Lake Huron's North Channel waterfront for most of the way to Sudbury. South and east of Bar River, a turnoff heads south to St. Joseph Island, part of the Manitoulin Island chain. The main sight here lies at the island's south end: **Fort St. Joseph National Historic Park.** When the fort was built by the British in 1796, it was the westernmost outpost of their Canadian empire. At first the fort protected the fur trade; it then served as a base for attacking the Americans during the War of 1812. The Americans burned the fort in 1814, and the park is built around its scenic remains.

At the island's north end is the tiny town of **Richards Landing;** the café at the dock serves good burgers and a variety of entrées.

Along Lake Huron

Twelve miles east of the St. Joseph Island turnoff lies the town of **Bruce Mines,** founded in 1846 around some small copper mines. As in the U.P., and mining areas all over the world, many of the earliest settlers were unemployed tin and copper miners from Cornwall in England. Two smaller islands offshore from Bruce Mines are home to the very pleasant **Bruce Bay Cottages and Lighthouse** (C$75 and up; 705/785-3473).

East of Bruce Mines, the road then runs slightly inland, returning to the lakeside a dozen miles later at **Thessalon,** where you can stay the night along the beachfront at the very popular **Carolyn Beach Motor Inn** (C$104 and up;

Unless otherwise noted, prices in the Canadian sections of this book are given in Canadian dollars (C$). The Canadian colloquial equivalent of "buck" (for a dollar) is "loonie," for the image of a bird (the loon) that adorns the dollar coin. The $2 coin is called a "toonie."

The double suspension bridge linking the Canadian and American Sault Ste. Maries gives memorable views of the Algoma Steel Mill, one of the largest in Canada. Flags in the middle of the bridge mark the boundary between the two nations.

The highway town of **Bar River** is home to the Big Loonie, a very large statue of the Canadian dollar coin, right along Hwy-17.

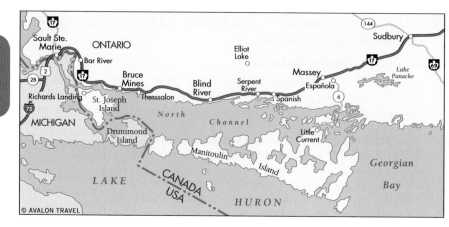

705/842-3330). The on-site restaurant is open all day and nearly always has fresh fish on the menu.

Following Hwy-17 east along the lakeshore toward Massey, the landscape is generally flat with occasional rocky outcrops. Just west of the settlements of Spanish and Serpent River, you have a great view across the North Channel, an arm of Lake Huron, to Manitoulin Island in the distance.

Massey and Manitoulin Island

Massey, "The Home of Chutes Provincial Park and Lots of Friendly People," sits at the confluence of the Sauble and Spanish Rivers. The main attraction hereabouts is just north of Hwy-17: **Chutes Provincial Park** offers swimming, camping, picnicking, and several scenic waterfalls along the Sauble River.

Twenty miles east of Massey, 40 miles west of Sudbury, Hwy-17 intersects with Hwy-6, which heads south toward **Manitoulin Island,** the world's largest freshwater island, set in the northern end of Lake Huron. Manitoulin is a popular vacation spot, ringed with picturesque harbors at Meldrum Bay, Providence Bay, and South Baymouth.

Manitoulin Island is one of the largest freshwater islands in the world, and it still has a substantial First Nation population.

Around Sudbury, a rare alternative to the often over-earnest CBC (Canadian Broadcasting Corporation) radio is offered by Laurentian University's **CKLU 96.7 FM**—wacky, ad-free, and often very funny college radio.

Sudbury

The biggest city between Ottawa and Duluth, **Sudbury** (pop. 157,857) lies in the middle of a geological basin that contains one of the world's largest concentrations of nickel, as well as numerous other precious metals. Originally an Ojibwa tribal settlement, the town began to develop after the 1883 arrival of the railway and boomed when nickel and copper were discovered here three years later. Uncontrolled development followed—mines and processing plants sprang up all over the landscape—and soon the area was a classic industrial-era ecological disaster. No trees grew for miles around, and a haze of toxic smoke choked the inhabitants, who lived in narrow valleys below the mine heads.

A beaver, national animal of Canada, adorns the Parliament Building.

In the early 1950s, Sudbury undertook a massive urban renewal and land reclamation project to return the land to its original beauty and clean up the air, with great success. For older residents, the city has changed dramatically for the better; the air is cleaner and trees dot the landscape. Today, Sudbury is still Canada's most important mining community, producing tons and tons of nickel and copper, but it's an infinitely healthier place than its polluted past may suggest.

As it passes around Sudbury, the Trans-Canada Highway (Hwy-17) bypasses the city's center, so turn north onto Hwy-80 toward Sudbury's real visitor draw: **Science North.** Located at the edge of downtown Sudbury, along manmade Lake Ramsey, Science North is one of Canada's most popular attractions, a state-of-the-art science and technology museum featuring many hands-on displays for kids and adults alike (daily; C$20–45; 705/522-3701 or 800/461-4898). Inside the snowflake-shaped structure, you can experience a simulated hurricane, watch flying squirrels fly, enjoy a butterfly aviary, talk to ham radio operators around the world, enjoy a show (recently featuring grizzly bears) in the IMAX theater, or take a virtual-reality voyage to Mars. The newest attraction here is **Dynamic Earth,** which simulates an underground mine. Outside Science North, you can see Sudbury's famous **Big Nickel,** moved here in 2003—the Big Nickel is exactly what it sounds like, a 30-foot-tall replica of a Canadian nickel.

Science North also has some of Sudbury's better places to eat—the **LakeHouse Restaurant**—which says a lot about

Big Nickel

East of Sudbury, Hwy-17 enters the narrow Veuve River Valley, lined with scraggly pines and picturesque rock outcroppings. Apart from a couple of very small towns, it's mostly dairy farming country for the 130 kilometers (80 miles) of Hwy-17 between Sudbury and North Bay.

Ottawa

Royal Canadian Mounted Police

Originally an Algonquin settlement, Ottawa (pop. 900,000) was a small fur-trading and lumber-milling outpost until the 1850s, when Queen Victoria chose the city to be the national capital, a compromise answer to the bitter rivalry between Montreal and Toronto. Construction of the Parliament buildings began the following year, but government only became the largest employer after World War II, when the lumber mills began to decline. Today the train tracks and factories have been replaced by telecom and computer companies. Miles of parks and greenbelts, and the boating (or ice skating) along the Rideau Canal, make Ottawa one of the most peaceable and pleasant of the world's capitals.

Orientation within Ottawa is easy: **Parliament Hill,** which holds the most prominent buildings, is on the north edge of town, with its back turned on the Ottawa River and the French-speaking province of Quebec. Getting around is easy, since most of the sights are gathered together around Parliament Hill and the adjacent ByWard Market. To see Ottawa, you should definitely park the car, get out, and walk (or bike, or rollerblade) around town.

Parliament Hill is home to the three buildings that compose Parliament, Canada's seat of federal government. The architecture is reminiscent of England's Houses of Parliament as redesigned by the cartoonist Charles Addams: Elegant, Gothic-style carved stone walls rise to copper mansard roofs topped with fantastically filigreed wrought iron. On the lawns of the Parliament buildings, the **Changing of the Guard** ceremony (late June–late Aug. daily at 10 AM; free) is extremely popular with tourists.

East of Parliament Hill stands the **National Gallery of Canada** (May–Oct. daily, Nov.–Apr. closed Mon.; $9–15; 380 Sussex Dr.). Along with many floors of painting and sculpture from colonial times up to the present, including George Segal's automobilia assembly *The Gas Station,* there's also a large collection of Asian and Inuit art. Another striking piece of modern architecture stands upstream, west of Parliament Hill: the new riverfront **Canadian War Museum** (daily; C$12), which documents Canadian soldiers' bravery in war- and peace-making.

Practicalities

Ottawa's airport, with flights from most major U.S. hubs, is 20 minutes south of the city. The major east–west access is via Hwy-17, the Trans-Canada

Highway; within town, this becomes the Hwy-417 freeway. From the south, Hwy-31 links up with Hwy-401, the Interstate freeway along the north shore of Lake Ontario.

ByWard Market, east of Parliament Hill across the Rideau Canal, is the place to go for food. The market stalls offer a variety of fresh produce, cafés are abundant, and the restaurants and bars lively

Ottawa's Château Laurier hotel

and generally pretty good. **Blue Cactus Bar & Grill** (2 ByWard Market; 613/241-7061) is one of many good restaurants here, featuring Tex-Mex food in a cheery ambience and a late-night supper club. There's a popular Streamline-style American diner, **Zak's** (14 ByWard Market; 613/241-2401), open 24 hours seven days a week, and the very nice **Cafe Shafali,** on the east edge of ByWard Market (308 Dalhousie St.; 613/789-9188), serving tandoori chicken, lamb madras, and other East Indian specialties in a soothing saffron-colored room.

Places to stay in Ottawa are centrally located and not all that expensive—the capital of Canada is not really a major tourist destination. **Fairmont Château Laurier** (C$199 and up; 1 Rideau St.; 613/241-1414), situated in an opulent tower directly across from Parliament Hill, is a luxurious landmark. Much more affordable, **Albert House Inn** (C$104–185; 478 Albert St.; 613/236-4479) is a large mansion converted into one of Ottawa's nicest bed-and-breakfast inns. Finally, one of the most interesting budget options anywhere has to be the **HI-Ottawa Hostel** (C$32 and up; 75 Nicholas St.; 613/235-2595), which occupies the old Ottawa jail a 10-minute walk from Parliament Hill. Guests sleep on bunks in the old cells; solitary confinement is now the laundry room.

An overwhelming quantity of visitor information on Ottawa is available from the **Capital Infocentre** (90 Wellington St.; 613/239-5000).

National War Memorial on Parliament Hill

the town's culinary offerings. (Sudbury's other "best place to eat," **Curious Thymes Bistro** (1200 Paris St.; 705/522-3500), is next door to Science North.

Among the many Sudbury hotels is **Travelodge Hotel Sudbury** (C$136 and up; 1401 Paris St.; 705/522-1100), a half mile south of Science North.

North Bay

North Bay (pop. 53,966; "Gateway to Opportunity") was originally a fur-trading post that boomed after the 1882 arrival of the railway. These days North Bay is still a trade and transportation center, and its fur auctions are among the largest in the world. Many tourists use the city as a jumping-off point for wilderness expeditions.

For more information, tune in to North Bay Tourism Radio, **CKTR 104.9 FM,** which started as tourism radio but has evolved into a community radio station highlighting the features of North Bay.

Just southeast of town, Hwy-17 joins Hwy-11, which runs south to Toronto. Near the junction there's a **visitors information center** and the **Dionne Quintuplets Museum** (daily in summer only; C$3.50; 705/472-8480), housed in the cabin that was their 1934 birthplace.

Apart from the Dionne quintuplets, the main attractions of North Bay line up along the Lake Nipissing waterfront park; from here, the *Chief Commanda II* cruises (705/494-8167) follow the old voyageurs' route across the water. In midsummer, the guided tour will likely tell you all about the locally famous **shad flies,** mouthless, fish-smelly bugs (also known as mayflies) that swarm out of the water and make a nuisance of themselves on North Bay sidewalks in their short, 24-hour lives.

Most of the motels are along Main Street and Lakeshore Drive, as are fast-food burger bars, pizza places, and the very good **Indra's Curry House** (454 Main St. E.; 705/478-6000).

Mattawa and the Ottawa River

East of North Bay, Trans-Canada Hwy-17 runs through its wildest and least populated stretch: scenic country largely empty of human habitation. The road hugs the riverside while rolling over steeper hills, past birch and pine for-original cover sheet for *The Maple Leaf Forever,* 1867

ests and many lakes and ponds. In the midst of all this wilderness, the attractive and relatively large town of **Mattawa** (pop. 2,003; "There Is a Story Here Where Rivers Meet") lies at the confluence of the Ottawa and Mattawa Rivers. Surrounded by dense green forest, the riverfront is lined by a very pleasant park (with free hot showers), and the town center is quaint and quiet, with two blocks of brick-fronted buildings along the river just north and west of the main highway.

The Mattawa River is the focus of the expansive **Samuel de Champlain Provincial Park** (705/744-2276), which offers campgrounds, canoeing, and hiking trails.

Algonquin Provincial Park

Between Mattawa and Deep River, Hwy-17 runs along the northern boundaries of the enormous **Algonquin Provincial Park,** which stretches for many miles to the south. Ontario's oldest and most popular park, Algonquin protects 3,000 square miles of almost untouched wilderness, offering a wide variety of wildlife (including moose, bears, beavers, and timber wolves), dozens of lakes, and hundreds of miles of backcountry hiking and canoeing trails. The main **visitors center** (705/633-5572) is at the park's far southwest corner, south of North Bay or west of Pembroke and Renfrew via Hwy-60, the Parkway Corridor, the only road through the park. Here you can get details on the park's abundant camping and cabins and pick up all the necessary permits.

> The Ottawa River marks the border between Ontario and Quebec, the bluffs of which may be seen across the water.

Deep River and Chalk River

The first real town east of Mattawa is **Deep River** (pop. 4,216), Canada's first "Atomic Town," a planned community built for employees of the Chalk River labs just downstream. The real attraction here is the **Laurentian View Dairy Limited** (613/584-3777), featuring homespun Canadian country cooking and homemade ice cream.

Nine miles farther east, you enter **Chalk River.** In 1945, this tiny logging center became the home of the first atomic reactor outside of the United States.

The Dionne Quintuplets

In 1934, during the depths of the Great Depression, in a small house deep in the wilds of north Ontario, five baby girls were born to the Dionnes, a poor rural family. The fact that all the babies—Annette, Cecile, Yvonne, Marie, and Emilie—were born healthy despite being two months premature is noteworthy enough, but what happened in later years verges on the incredible. The babies were cared for at home for the difficult first weeks, but after that, the Ontario government took the infants away from their destitute family. Across from the family home, the government built a zoo-like environment called Quintland, and raised them in public—selling tickets for three shows daily and effectively doing everything possible to keep them from having a normal childhood. At age five (of course) they were introduced to the king and queen of England and later appeared in movies and "wrote" their own autobiography, *We Were Five*. The quints also did product endorsements, promoting soap, toothpaste, cereal, and Carnation milk. During the 1930s, the quintuplets were Canada's number-one tourist attraction—bigger than Niagara Falls, it was said—and by the time they turned 10 years old they had been visited by more than three million people.

After a long and bitter custody battle, the girls were eventually returned to their parents and faded from the public eye. The Ontario government, which earned an estimated half billion marketing the Quints, paid the surviving three girls a settlement of $4 million in 1998. The house where they were born has been moved from Corbeill to North Bay, where it has been rebuilt as the **Dionne Quintuplets Museum** (705/472-8480) and filled with toys, dresses, baby carriages, and photographs that trace their youthful fame. (Continuing the quintuplets' lifelong exploitation, there's a nifty gift shop on the museum premises.)

Seven years later, Atomic Energy of Canada, Ltd. (AECL), a government-owned nuclear research organization, was founded here. It designs and sells commercial and research nuclear reactors around the world and produces most of the world's radioactive isotopes for medical use. In recent years, problems at the Chalk River plant, due to leaks, seismic improvements, and deferred maintenance, caused a serious worldwide shortage of these vital medical products, putting the Chalk River labs in the media spotlight. If you're interested, the **visitors center** lets you "tour the atomic age" (Mon.–Fri. 9 AM–4 PM year-round; free; 613/584-3311 or 800/364-6989), though the radioactive areas are (sensibly enough) off-limits.

Petawawa and Pembroke

Southeast of Chalk River, Hwy-17 crosses the namesake river of the town of **Petawawa,** home since 1905 to a Canadian Forces base. You can visit a number of small military museums on the base; the largest, the **Canadian Forces Airborne Museum,** traces the history of Canadian paratroopers. There's also a riverfront beach and campground, but otherwise the area is strictly off-limits, as the numerous signs along the road warn.

The rather quaint, redbrick town of Petawawa itself is two miles north of Hwy-17 via Hwy-41, well worth the short trip through what seems like one big light-industrial park.

Wrapping around the eastern edge of Algonquin Provincial Park, Hwy-17 nears **Pembroke,** another timber town along the Ottawa River, north of the highway. The main sights here are the more than 30 history-themed murals painted on downtown buildings, the **Champlain Trail Museum** (May–Sept. only; C$5; 1032 E. Pembroke St.), with exhibits on local history, and the friendly ambience and awesome food at the **Nook Creperie Inc.,** right downtown (26 W. Pembroke St.; 613/735-4800).

Arnprior

Midway between Pembroke and Renfrew, you can see the Ottawa River loop north around **Cobden,** a little town on Muskrat Lake. **Renfrew,** another of Ontario's many Scots-founded towns, is now a center of high-tech industry.

Twenty-seven miles east of Renfrew, Hwy-17 approaches the banks of the Ottawa near **Arnprior,** founded in 1823 by Archibald McNab, a despotic Scottish lord who imported dozens of his countrymen and -women to the settlement and ruthlessly exploited them. This reign of terror ended when the townsfolk banded together and drove him away. There's a museum in the old stone post office building, and downtown boasts some moderately priced motels and, best of all, **Wes' Chips** (Mar.–Nov. only; 198 Madawaska Blvd.; 613/623-5492), an open-air chip stand selling the exquisite Canadian delicacy Americans call french fries. Worth planning your day around, for sure!

East of Arnprior, Hwy-17 continues its trek toward Ottawa with a 90-kph (55-mph) maximum speed posted; occasional passing lanes help you get around the timber trucks. The highway curves gradually southward, away from the Ottawa River, through mostly flat woodlands and a few farms, then converts to freeway for the run into Ottawa.

Hwy-17 is fairly boring between Ottawa and Montreal, and you're better off taking the much faster Hwy-417, called the Queensway, or following our two-lane route across Quebec, along the north bank of the Ottawa River.

A quick Québécois sampler for travelers:

arrêt = stop

cul de sac = dead end

bar laitier = ice cream stand

poutine = chili cheese fries

Gatineau and Hull

Offering the best views of Ottawa's dramatic riverside setting, the Francophone town of **Gatineau** (pop. 301,416) is a nice change of pace from the Canadian capital. Known as "Hull" until a civic reorganization in 2002, when it was renamed, Gatineau is older than Ottawa, and French-speaking despite having been founded in 1800 by an American Loyalist (Philemon Wright) fleeing the Revolution.

Montreal

Located on an island in the St. Lawrence River, and first settled as a frontier outpost by fur-trapping French voyageurs, Montreal (pop. 1,934,082) has grown into Canada's second-largest city, and today is easily the most European city in North America, with the largest French-speaking population outside La France. Hotbed of the separatist movement, Montreal tolerates the polyglot federalism of Canada, but the accent here is most definitely on the "French" in French-Canadian; in a wide variety of gourmet restaurants, stylish boutiques, nightclubs, museums, and theaters you can half-close your eyes and pretend you're in Paris.

Montreal city hall

The city takes its name from a 700-foot-high hill, now the very pleasant tree-covered **Mount Royal Park** just north of downtown. Planned by Frederick Law Olmsted and opened in 1876, the park's stairs and paths lead up to a belvedere, from which you have a sweeping view of the city, the St. Lawrence River, the southern suburbs and, on the eastern slope, a huge steel cross that's lit up at night.

At the foot of Mount Royal Park runs Sherbrooke Street, Montreal's most prestigious and majestic street, lined with grand 1920s buildings as impressive as any on Park Avenue. Among the many posh boutiques (Chanel, Armani, et al.) and luxury hotels (like the Ritz-Carlton, where Richard Burton married Elizabeth Taylor), you'll find the **Montreal Museum of Fine Arts** (closed Mon.; free; 1380 Sherbrooke St.; 514/285-2000 or 800/899-6873). The oldest museum in Canada, and one of the finest in the world, the Museum of Fine Arts has a large permanent collection of European, Canadian, and American art, as well as an extensive display of Inuit artifacts. A half mile east, the **McCord Museum of Canadian History** (closed Mon. in winter; open daily in summer; C$13; 690 Sherbrooke St. W.; 514/398-7100) has a wonderful collection of art and artifacts related to Montreal, Quebec, and Canada—everything from Victorian evening gowns to First Nation

Mount Royal Park

masks and carvings. South of the Museum of Fine Arts, the elegantly modern **Canadian Centre for Architecture** (Wed.–Sun.; C$10; 1920 Rue Baile; 514/939-7026) mounts fascinating shows devoted to the built environment.

About a mile southeast of Mount Royal, just off the riverfront, the two-block-long, cobblestone square of **Place Jacques-Cartier** is the heart of Old Montreal, a picturesque neighborhood that was the site of the earliest European settlement. In the summer the square is transformed into an open-air market, and all year-round you can sample the area's excellent cafés and restaurants.

Practicalities

Montreal's airport, known as Dorval, lies 13 miles west of downtown. Numerous freeways crisscross Montreal, and driving around is pretty easy (though all signs, including the complicated parking rules, are in French), but if you want to escape from your car for a day or two, the city is eminently walkable.

For food, Montreal has something for everyone, thanks to the city's truly international population—sizable immigrant communities make Montreal a dining adventure. At lunchtime, workers from the Montreal financial district cram into **Chez Delmo,** formerly Le Nantua (275 Notre Dame St.; 514/288-4288), a contemporary version of traditional Old Montreal seafood restaurants, where dishes are always fresh. There's a nice oyster bar, too. You really must eat French at least once while in Montreal, and French restaurants do not come more traditional than **Le Paris,** in between the art museum and the architecture center (1812 St. Catherine St.; 514/937-4898). Another reliable bet is **L'Express,** east of Mount Royal Park (3927 St. Denis St.; 514/845-5333), open from breakfast until after midnight.

For first-time visitors, one unexpected Montreal specialty is a taste of New York City: the deli sandwich, usually built of slices of rye bread around a classic version of Montreal's beloved "smoked meat," a.k.a. corned beef. Many of the great old delis have gone out of business; one survivor is **Schwartz's Charcuterie Hebraique** (3895 Blvd. St. Laurent; 514/842-4813), which is slightly touristy but serves some of the finest pastrami on the planet.

The best budget place to stay is the large **HI-Montreal Hostel** (C$30–65; 1030 Mackey St.; 514/843-3317), which has dorm beds and private rooms a five-minute walk south of Mount Royal Park. For something a bit more special, **Château Versailles** (C$150 and up; 1659 Sherbrooke St. W.; 514/933-3611) is composed of four Victorian townhouses converted into one charming, antiques-filled hotel.

For tourist information, contact the **Greater Montreal Convention and Tourism Bureau** (1555 Peel St. Ste. 600; 514/844-5400 or 877/266-5687).

The best thing about Gatineau, apart from the chance to walk across the bridges and wander the riverside parks that link it to Ottawa, is the **Canadian Museum of Civilization** (daily, C$12–17; 100 Rue Laurier; 819/776-7000 or 800/555-5621), a huge and fascinating institution, housed in two sinuously curving buildings that are a combined 100,000 square meters (more than one million square feet) on the banks of the Ottawa River, directly across the water from the Parliament Buildings at the foot of the Alexandria Bridge. The main lobby is filled with historic totem poles and canoes made by Canada's diverse native peoples, and galleries elsewhere in the building highlight everything from whaling communities in Labrador to life on the vast western prairies. It's a fun and educational place, well worth half a day at least, and has the added bonus of a nice rooftop restaurant serving lunch), facing across the river to Ottawa's Parliament Hill.

Montebello and Carillon

East from Hull, Hwy-50 runs as a fast freeway along the north bank of the Ottawa River before calming down into a two-lane sojourn along Hwy-148. About an hour east of Ottawa, 80 miles west of Montreal, the town of **Montebello** holds one of the region's most famous landmarks: **Fairmont Le Château Montebello** (C$229 and up; 819/423-6341), an enormous octagonal palace built of red cedar logs that has evolved into one of Canada's most exclusive hotels, frequently hosting international conferences by the likes of NATO, G7, G8, and similar power brokers. The grounds of the hotel hold an even more historic landmark, Papineau Manor, a manor house built in 1850 by a notable French-Canadian politician.

A quiet town and provincial park along the Ottawa River, 32 kilometers (20 miles) west of Montreal, **Oka** gained international prominence in 1990, when native Mohawk Indians, protesting plans to turn a burial ground into a golf course, blocked the main highway to and from Montreal.

Farther east, 72 kilometers (45 miles) west of Montreal via sinuous Hwy-344, the roaring rapids at **Carillon** (pop. 258) have been harnessed by a massive hydropower facility and a lock system that provides the largest single lift of any in Canada—20 meters (65 feet). East of Carillon, Hwy-344 winds through sleepy farming country along the Ottawa River before ending up at the edge of the Montreal metropolis.

Driving Across Montreal

Montreal is as scythed by freeways as any U.S. city, and it helps to be prepared to deal with the sudden shift from quiet countryside to confusing urban madness. If you've followed the rural route across Quebec from Ottawa, you enter the city from the northwest, on the Hwy-640 Autoroute; the freeway route from Ottawa brings you in on the Hwy-40 Autoroute, straight into downtown.

Any east–west freeway you find yourself on will cross the Hwy-15 Autoroute, the main route between Montreal and the U.S. border. Vermont is a quick 30 miles south of Montreal; after crossing the U.S. border, take the second exit off the I-87 freeway and head east along US-11/US-2 to Rouses Point, New York, at the north end of Lake Champlain, to rejoin our two-lane road trip route. Between Vermont and the Canadian border, US-2 nips briefly and uneventfully across the northeast corner of New York State, crossing the international border on the I-87 freeway between the United States and Quebec.

VERMONT

Starting at the state's northwestern corner, US-2 crosses the heart of verdant Vermont. From the shores of **Lake Champlain,** our route winds south to the university town of **Burlington,** then east past Montpelier, the state capital, all the way to New Hampshire, some 150 miles in all. Paralleled for much of the way by the modern I-89 freeway, US-2 makes a slower but much more diverting alternative to the fast lane, passing through some of the state's most attractive small towns and giving an up-close look at its rural charms, not to mention Vermont's untrammeled mountains, forests, lakes, and rivers.

Lake Champlain Islands

After its brief jaunt across New York from the Canadian border, US-2 winds across the sleepy **Lake Champlain Islands.** Pancake-flat and covered with cows, orchards, and pick-your-own fruit farms, this trio of islands is very pretty to drive across, with the Adirondacks rising up to the west and the Green Mountains to the south and east, but there's not a lot to do; far more farm animals than people populate the route, and tractors clog the road, flinging clods of mud and manure (here pronounced "man-OO-ah") with abandon.

From the middle of the Alburg Peninsula, where US-2 crosses from New York into Vermont, a turn west onto Route 129 leads to **Isle La Motte,** home of the first French settlement in Vermont, established in 1666. The site is now occupied by **Saint Ann's Shrine,** a popular pilgrimage destination featuring daily outdoor masses in

> The roaring waterfalls that powered the Champlain Mill have been adapted with a fish lift; in spring and fall you can watch trout and salmon make their way upstream.

summer and a granite statue of the explorer Samuel de Champlain, for whom the lake is named.

Continuing south on US-2, the town of **North Hero** (pop. 810) has a gas station, a stone courthouse, a number of quietly luxurious vacation homes dating from the early decades of the 20th century, and the very handy **Hero's Welcome,** a café and gift shop at the center of the two-block-long town. A mile south along US-2, **Shore Acres Resort** ($85 and up; 802/372-8722) offers tennis courts, boating and swimming, moderately priced lakeside rooms, and a restaurant known to serve up freshly baked fruit pies and white chocolate cheesecake.

A mile north of the town of Grand Isle, along US-2 next to a school, stands the **Hyde Log Cabin,** considered by many to be the country's oldest log cabin, dating from 1783.

Seven miles and another bridge to the south, the town of **Grand Isle** (pop. 2,326) ambitiously claims to be "The Beauty Spot of Vermont." A well-marked turn leads to tiny **Grand Isle State Park** (802/372-4300), on the shores of the lake, where there's a nice campground. At the other end of the island, connected by a causeway to the mainland, **South Hero** is another quaint little place; it and North Hero were named after those famous Vermont Revolutionary War heroes, the Green Mountain Boys, Ira and Ethan Allen.

From South Hero, US-2 rejoins the mainland at the entrance to **Sand Bar State Park,** set in a forest with picnic tables and bathing beaches, surrounded by sprawling, wildfowl-rich marshes on either side. From here US-2 heads east through rolling hills, linking up with the I-89 freeway for the fast route into Burlington, 10 miles to the south.

Winooski

If you have a little time or an abiding interest in America's industrial heritage, get off I-89 at exit 15, or follow Riverside Street (old US-2) north from Burlington to the center of **Winooski,** an old woolen mill town now focusing on the restored Champlain Mill (1 Main St.), downtown. This former woolen mill now houses more than 20 cafés and specialty shops, and the rest of town provides a blue-collar balance to Burlington's somewhat upscale airs. The town green is marred by a bank and large parking lot, but the surrounding buildings hold some interesting spots, including **Sneakers Bistro** (28 Main St.; 802/655-9081), which serves great breakfasts and lunches every day. Another popular spot for home-cooked food and friendly, upbeat service is **Libby's Blue Line Diner** (46 Highpoint Center, Route 7 S.; 802/655-0343), north of Winooski in Colchester, just off I-89 exit 16. The usual diner menu of breakfasts and burgers is enhanced by homemade gravy and sweet Italian sausage.

The worst floods in Vermont's history followed in the wake of Hurricane Irene in August 2011. Streets and buildings were flooded, and many bridges damaged or destroyed, especially between Winooski and Montpelier.

Another reason to visit Winooski is to tour the restored farm of Vermont patriot Ethan Allen, preserved as the **Ethan Allen Homestead** (May–Oct. Thurs.–Mon. 10 AM–4 PM; $7; 802/865-4556) along Route 127 two miles northeast of Winooski.

Burlington

After the original French settlers were ejected from the Lake Champlain region in 1760 at the end of the French and Indian Wars, English settlers soon arrived, and **Burlington** (pop. 42,417) was chartered in 1763. The area was abandoned during the Revolutionary War. Afterward, Ethan Allen, leader of the famous Green Mountain Boys band of guerrillas, and his brothers were granted huge tracts of land along the eastern shore of Lake Champlain. The Allen brothers were ambitious: Not only did they encourage settlement and industry in Burlington, but in 1791 they founded the University of Vermont here. The town boomed, aided by its strategic position on Lake Champlain, which was the quickest

East of the UVM campus, Winooski's historic Centennial Field is home to the Class A **Vermont Lake Monsters** ($7 and up; 802/655-4200), farm club of the Oakland A's.

route between New York's Hudson River and Montreal. Burlington quickly became the center of Vermont industry, finance, education, and culture—a position it has held ever since.

US-2/US-7 passes right through the center of Burlington, following Winooski Avenue to the north, then along Main Street, lined by motels and restaurants on the outskirts but eventually crossing the lively, sprawling campus of the **University of Vermont** (UVM), which stands on a shallow hill on the east side of town. Along Colchester Avenue on the north edge of campus, the **Robert Hull Fleming Museum** (closed Mon.; $5; 802/656-0750) is the main visitor attraction, with a small but varied collection of fine and applied arts from ancient Egypt to the present.

Billings Library on the University of Vermont campus

The Shelburne Museum and Shelburne Farms

One of the most popular and enjoyable stops in the state of Vermont sits just six miles south of downtown Burlington, on the shores on Lake Champlain: the **Shelburne Museum** (mid-May–end-Oct. daily; hours vary $20; 802/985-3346). The museum presents perhaps the best, and certainly the most unusual, agglomeration of fine art, folk art, and general oddities you'll find anywhere. These toys, dolls, trade signs, and weathervanes (and much, much more) really do defy classification, but there's more here than a riot of garage-sale stuff. Assembled over a lifetime by heiress Electra Havemeyer Webb, whose parents introduced America to the art of the French Impressionists, the Shelburne collection includes paintings by European and American masters (Rembrandt, Monet, Manet, and Winslow Homer, to drop a few famous names). However, it is most interesting for its unique Americana: old fire trucks, handmade quilts, and a world-class collection of cigar-store Indians (not to mention a model of a circus parade that's more than 500 feet long).

There are also dozens of historic buildings brought here from all over New England: a covered bridge, a round barn, a lighthouse, a railroad depot, even a complete side-wheeled Lake Champlain steamboat, the *Ticonderoga*. The buildings, which all house different parts of the expansive collection, are spread over 45 acres of lawns and formal gardens, and there's so much to see you may want to save some for another visit, which you can do, since tickets are good for two days.

Northwest of the Shelburne Museum, just over a mile from US-7 via Bay and Harbor Roads, **Shelburne Farms** is a 1,400-acre farm and nonprofit environmental center with eight miles of hiking trails on a promontory jutting out into Lake Champlain. The grounds were laid out by landscape architect Frederick Law Olmsted to take full advantage of the natural topography (and to maximize views across the lake toward the Adirondack Mountains). In recent years, Shelburne Farms has become a leading force in the movement toward sustainable agriculture, and you can taste the results in its fabulously flavorful cheddar cheeses, available nationwide. Free tastings are available here at the Farm Store, where you can also join a 90-minute guided tour ($11; 802/985-8442) and explore the entire property. Included on the tour is a stop at the old mansion at the center of the estate, now the **Inn at Shelburne Farms** (May–Oct.; $155–465; 802/985-8498), where you can stay overnight or enjoy a wonderful meal (or three). There are also concerts, children's programs, and a variety of educational workshops held at Shelburne Farms throughout the summer.

Midway between Lake Champlain and the UVM campus, downtown Burlington is anchored by the **Church Street Marketplace,** a pedestrianized and increasingly chain-dominated shopping district that lies perpendicular to Main Street, north from Burlington's stately old City Hall. From City Hall, Main Street continues west to **Lake Champlain,** where the Burlington Waterfront Park has a strollable boardwalk linking up with Battery Park, home to a collection of cannons pointing menacingly across the lake. In 1813, these cannons were used against British warships that bombarded the town. Bands frequently play here on summer evenings, and a bike path runs along the water. If you feel like getting out on the water, right at the ferry landing at the foot of King Street you can rent a rowboat, kayak, or canoe; hop a ferry across the lake to Fort Kent, New York; take a sunset cruise on board the *Spirit of Ethan Allen* (802/862-8300); or simply have a beer while listening to local bands at the Breakwater Café and Grill (802/658-6276). Whatever you do, keep an eye out for Champ, Vermont's version of the Loch Ness monster, who dwells deep in the waters of Lake Champlain.

Burlington was the home of Dr. Horatio Nelson Jackson, who, in 1903 (along with his chauffeur and a stray dog they picked up along the way), became the first person to cross the country by automobile.

Just south of Burlington is one of the nation's great cultural institutions, the Shelburne Museum.

Burlington Practicalities

Downtown Burlington offers all the delights of a typical college town: bookstores, bars, ethnic food, and trendy shopping. For food, two local favorites—the very popular **Penny Cluse Cafe** (169 Cherry St.; 802/651-8834) and the **Daily Planet** behind Church Street (15 Center St.; 802/862-9647)—stand out among the many offerings around the Church Street Marketplace.

Church Street Marketplace

Thanks to the many students and Vermonters' general love of live music, Burlington has some great nightclubs, ranging from the juke joint ambience of **Nectar's** (188 Main St.; 802/658-4771), where the band Phish was born and bred, to the high-style art deco **Flynn Center for the Performing Arts** (153 Main St.; 802/863-5966), across from City Hall, where bigger-name bands perform.

Places to stay, alas, don't come particularly cheap. The historic and central **Willard Street Inn** ($145 and up; 349 S. Willard St.; 802/651-8710) is a very nice B&B in an 1880s home, and some rooms have views of Lake Champlain. There are also many motels along US-7 south of downtown Burlington, including locally owned ones like the **Bel-Aire Motel** ($79 and up; 111 Shelburne Rd.; 802/863-3116), along US-7.

Richmond and Williston

Between Montpelier and Burlington, US-2 follows the Winooski River Valley, lined with dairy farms. For most of the way, the road parallels the less-than-attractive concrete expanse of I-89, but a few sights along the "old road" make the two-lane route preferable. First and foremost of these is **Al's French Frys** (1251 Williston Rd.; 802/862-9203), east of downtown Burlington on US-2, which has been churning out great fries (sold by the quart!), burgers, hot dogs, and shakes since the 1940s. Al's is open from lunchtime until late (midnight on summer weekends).

To escape the contemporary chaos, turn south from US-2 at the only stoplight in **Richmond,** where the unique **Old Round Church,** a 16-sided, two-story white clapboard structure, stands just east of the road. The church was built in 1813 and is the communal effort of five different Protestant denominations. They eventually parted ways, and the structure lapsed into civic use, becoming the town hall. Today it is used as a meeting house, and on summer weekends the local historical society (802/434-2556) gives guided tours.

Williston (pop. 8,698) sits roughly 10 miles east of Burlington and less than a mile north of the freeway. Although large by local standards, Williston is a classic northern New England town, its streets lined by towering maple trees and white clapboard houses.

If Ben & Jerry's trademark black-and-white splotched ice cream packaging gets you interested in the different bovine breeds, here's a short primer to help you tell them apart:

black-and-white splotches = Holsteins

brown with white splotches = Guernseys

brown all over = Jerseys

Waterbury Center: Ben & Jerry's

Though it's known for beautiful mountains and the brilliant fall color of its hardwood forests, Vermont's number-one tourist attraction is none other than **Ben & Jerry's Ice Cream Factory,** a kind of hippie Disneyland in **Waterbury Center,** on the hillside above Route 100, a mile or so north of I-89. The grounds of the brightly painted factory include a number of large cartoonish artifacts strewn outside to play on—weird vehicles, whimsical picnic tables, and the like. Ben and Jerry began making ice cream in 1978, becoming internationally famous for their ultra-rich ice cream and for their activism, donating a percentage of profits to philanthropies supporting "progressive social change." Now part of Anglo-Dutch conglomerate Unilever, Ben & Jerry's is still a Vermont icon.

You can tour the factory (daily; $3; 866/258-6877), although production is halted on weekends, holidays, and company celebration days—when you get a video presentation. The premises also feature a gift shop and the Scoop Shop, offering all of Ben & Jerry's ice cream, frozen yogurt, and sorbet flavors. Outside are many picnic tables where you can enjoy the ice cream and a view over the valley.

Back on US-2, midway between Montpelier and Waterbury, right on US-2 just west of Middlesex, **Camp Meade** was a Depression-era Civilian Conservation Corps camp that was turned into a shrine to America in the 1930s and 1940s, from the New Deal to D-Day, mostly the latter. The old barracks were turned into a motel, and a fighter plane, a tank, and military trucks once adorned the grounds, but in recent years Camp Meade has evolved into a lively live-work arts and crafts campus, well worth a look.

North of Waterbury Junction on Route 100, the ski resort of **Stowe** was the post–World War II home of the musical von Trapp family, whose escape from the Nazis inspired *The Sound of Music*. Running south, Route 100 travels through the heart of the Green Mountains all the way south to Massachusetts and is one of the state's most popular leaf-peeping drives.

Montpelier

The smallest capital in the country, and the only one without a McDonald's, Vermont's **Montpelier** (pop. 7,855) was settled in 1787 and designated the state capital in 1805. Today, Montpelier's economy is based on government, insurance, and tourism.

As you follow US-2 Business into town, the gold dome of the capitol building hovering over the valley ahead signals your arrival in Montpelier. Constrained by the Winooski River on one side and the narrow valley on the other, Montpelier is so compact that you can park your car and find all the sights within a 10-minute walk. (Thankfully, the I-89 freeway and the main US-2 bypass are well away from downtown.) A quick poll of shops along State and Main Streets reveals the cosmopolitan nature of the town: the magical **Bear Pond Books** (77 Main St.; 802/229-0774), along with coffee bars, wine merchants, and multiple combinations of the same.

In the Montpelier region, alternative music fans will want to tune their car radios to the "The Point," broadcasting Phish, Everclear, Lucinda Williams, Neil Young, and other rowdy rockers at **WNCS 104.7 FM.**

The north side of State Street opens up into a broad lawn fronting the capitol dome, the focal point of the Republic of Vermont—like Texas, the state takes some pride in the fact that it was an independent "country" before joining the rest of the United States. The state legislature is only in session from January to April—being a Vermont politician is a part-time job. The rest of the year they go about being farmers, businesspeople, and so on, but you can tour the building year-round (Mon.–Fri. only).

Above the capitol rises **Hubbard Park,** a 100-year-old, 194-acre green space, with seven miles of hiking trails and a 54-foot observation tower atop the summit, the highest point in Montpelier.

Just west of the capitol is the **Vermont Historical Society Museum** (closed Mon.; $5), where permanent and temporary displays illustrate different aspects of Vermont's history, and you can also find lots of 19th-century furniture and a small bookstore and gift shop. Rising up a hill a few blocks farther west, the **Green Mount Cemetery** is filled with impressive granite monuments. Many of these were carved by the immigrant stone-cutters of nearby Barre for their own family plots, and the well-groomed grounds make ideal picnic spots, especially on a summer afternoon.

Montpelier thrived off the granite quarries of the nearby town of **Barre.** The **Rock of Ages** quarry (June–Oct. Mon.–Sat.; free; 802/476-3119), four miles southeast of Barre, is the world's largest.

Montpelier Practicalities

Montpelier residents take their eating seriously. Very good and fairly inexpensive food is readily available, thanks to the local presence of the New England Culinary Institute, a cooking school

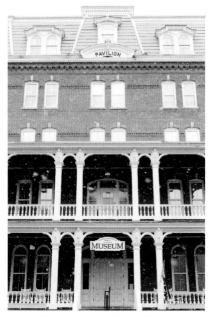

Vermont Historical Society Museum

that operates the **NECI on Main** (118 Main St.; 802/223-3188). A full range of healthy deli food and drink is available at the **State Street Market** (20 State St.; 802/229-9353), and the nearby **Coffee Corner** (802/229-9060), on the corner of State and Main Streets, offers breakfast with cheerful hometown ambience (and hearty home fries).

Near Montpelier, watch sap being turned into delicious maple syrup at the **Morse Farm and Sugarhouse,** three miles northeast from the capitol dome along Main Street.

For upscale lodgings in period surroundings, go to the **Inn at Montpelier** ($165 and up; 147 Main St.; 802/223-2727), two renovated 1820s homes that have been joined into one hotel.

Plainfield

Hitchhikers are common on US-2 between Montpelier and Plainfield, thanks to the presence of **Goddard College,** one of the nation's most renowned countercultural institutes of higher learning. The tiny town of **Plainfield** also boasts the **Maple Valley Country Store,** a combo deli-café-pizzeria that's the local hangout (tie-dye welcome; 802/454-8626). The soups are fantastic, as are the veggie burgers. The store's parking area is built on a foundation of recycled granite, leftovers from the nearby quarries and stonecutters.

If you want to linger, consider a night on the farm: At **Hollister Hill Farm** ($90 and up; 147 Main St.; 802/454-7725), east of town, they make their own maple syrup (and serve it over pancakes at breakfast) and raise all sorts of organic produce (from vegetables to "beefalo" hybrids).

West Danville: Joe's Pond

West Danville, a summer community 20 lovely miles east of Plainfield on the edge of Joe's Pond, is ringed by rustic vacation cabins. The pond, which at sunset in summer is one of the more idyllic spots imaginable, was originally called Indian Joe's Pond, which explains the presence of Injunjoe Court, a set of roadside cabins dating from the pre–politically correct era. At the junction of US-2 and Route 15 in the center of town, you'll see a micro-sized covered bridge and the **Hastings Store** (802/684-3398), the local "if we ain't got it, you don't need it" emporium, selling cheddar cheese, maple syrup, fishing supplies, and other Vermont essentials.

At the hilltop cabins of **Injunjoe Court** ($55 and up; 802/684-3430), guests can borrow pedal boats or canoes from a 300-foot beach and hang out on the water. Injunjoe has a few RV sites, too. You can also stay at the one- or two-bedroom cabins of **Point Comfort** ($55–165; 802/684-3379). Both establishments have weekly rates if you're lucky enough to linger here awhile.

Danville and Peacham

Heading east, the next place you'll pass is **Danville,** yet another picture-postcard Vermont town, set on a hill surrounded by farmland. The center of Danville is a classic New England village green, with a general store and the customary churches. Just off the green you'll find the headquarters of the **American Society of Dowsers** (Mon.–Fri.; 184 Brainerd St.; 802/684-3417), whose members have refined their talents for finding water or mineral deposits using a dowsing rod. The building houses a small exhibit on the history and practice of the art, and a shop where you can buy dowsing books and rods.

South of US-2 from the center of Danville, enjoy the lovely pastoral drive toward **Peacham,** a perennial contender for the "prettiest village in Vermont" title. During the fall color sweeps, the mountaintop village is likely to be crowded with sightseeing tourists, but most of the time it's a somnolent little place. In fact, Peacham is so timeless that the producers of the movie version of Edith Wharton's Victorian fable *Ethan Frome* filmed here (without having to remove any streetlights or other signs of modern life!).

St. Johnsbury

In the 19th century, the economy of **St. Johnsbury** (pop. 7,581) was based on maple products and the manufacture of platform scales. Fairbanks Scales, founded by the inventor of platform scales, still operates a plant here. Today it is the pleasantly peaceful commercial center of Vermont's Northeast Kingdom, at the junction of the US-2 and US-5 highways, the I-91 and I-93 freeways, and the Canadian Pacific and old Maine Central railroad tracks. The economy never regained its Victorian-era prosperity, so the town's extensive stock of historic landmark architecture has been preserved almost totally unchanged. Elegant (and often empty) four- and five-story brick buildings line the riverfront and railroad line along US-2 and US-5. On the hill above the riverfront, a more genteel commercial district surrounded by massive trees and dozens of grand Victorian homes is highlighted by two of the most fascinating institutions in the state, both funded by the largess of the Fairbanks family.

At the center of town stands the **St. Johnsbury Athenaeum, Art Gallery, and Public Library** (Mon.–Fri.; free; 1171 Main St.) in a redbrick 1871 building. The building houses a surprising collection of 19th-century paintings, the jewel of which is Albert Bierstadt's monumental *Domes of Yosemite.*

A block east down Main Street, you'll find my very favorite museum in all New England: the **Fairbanks Museum and Planetarium** (daily; $8; 802/748-2372), a charmingly quirky Victorian-era center of knowledge established by Franklin Fairbanks in 1889. Two menacing stuffed bears greet visitors inside the entrance, followed by a seem-

portrait of Abe Lincoln, made out of 6,399 dried insects by a man named John Hampson in 1916

ingly endless display of taxidermied wildlife—a veritable Noah's Ark of North American fauna. Climb the spiral stairs to the mezzanine of the main gallery, a grand Richardsonian Romanesque space topped by a coffered barrel vault and furnished with fireplaces and other homey touches. You'll find more fascinating oddities: arrowheads and other anthropological artifacts, rocks and fossils, and art made out of bugs (including a portrait of General Pershing made out of flies and moths!). View exhibits on local history, a set of dollhouse furniture made by author Mark Twain, and a very funny letter written by Robert Louis Stevenson in which he gifts his birthday (which he said he was too old to need anymore) to a family friend of the Fairbanks named Annie Ide (whose own birth fell on Christmas, meaning she effectively missed out).

All along US-2, and all over New England for that matter, the old roads are lined by 1940s-style knotty-pine cabins and motor courts, like the photogenic **Wallinda Cabins** east of Plainfield.

St. Johnsbury's eating options include **Hilltopper Restaurant** (802/748-8964), a lunch spot, across the street from the Athenaeum, run by students at the St. Johnsbury Academy, and the excellent **Anthony's Diner** (50 Railroad St.; 802/748-3613) at the US-5/US-2 junction. There's also a good pizza place, the **House of Pizza** (287 Portland St.; 802/748-5144).

For motels, try the **Fairbanks Inn** ($110 and up; 401 Western Ave.; 802/748-5666) on US-2.

Maple Grove Farms

Taking a scenic alternative to the I-93 freeway east from St. Johnsbury, US-2 passes over the Memorial Bridge (1943) spanning the Passumpsic River. One mile east of the bridge you'll find the **Maple Grove Farms** complex. Highlights include the maple museum (and tasting room!) and the so-called "World's Largest Maple Candy Factory." Vermont is the heart of maple-sugar-ing territory, which runs all the way from Maine to Michigan and up into Canada. Maple Grove Farms has been in business here since 1915, and it is the largest packager of maple syrup in the United States. In front of the store, you can have your picture taken in front of the World's Largest Can of Maple Syrup (which is, alas, empty).

Concord and Lunenburg

Near the New Hampshire border, US-2 heads across rolling rocky hills covered with forests, largely pine and birch, with a few scattered farms. This corner of the state, a recreational paradise of hills and lakes and few year-round residents, is known as the Northeast Kingdom. The road drops down into the narrow, pastoral valley of the Moose River before reaching **Concord,** which features a country store and a small historical society.

Fifteen miles east of Concord, along the banks of the broad Connecticut River, **Lunenburg** is a perfect New England village of white clapboard houses clustered around a church—Vermont specializes in this species of quaintness.

From Lunenburg, you can take a highly recommended detour across the Connecticut River on the 266-foot-long Mt. Orne covered bridge, then proceed north along Route 135, rejoining US-2 at Lancaster.

A marker along US-2 points out the site, in nearby **Concord Corner, Vermont,** where the **First Normal School,** America's first teachers' academy, was founded in 1823.

NEW HAMPSHIRE

Crossing the broad Connecticut River, which forms Vermont's 200-mile-long border with New Hampshire, US-2 makes a short but scenic run across the state. From the historic commercial center of **Lancaster,** just east of the state border, US-2 winds along the wide valley of the Israel River before reaching **Jefferson,** home to two of the state's biggest tourist traps. Continuing east, US-2 curves around the northern flank of towering **Mt. Washington** and the rugged White Mountains, an area rich in outdoor recreation and scenic splendor. At **Gorham,** US-2 reaches the valley of the Androscoggin River, which it follows east into Maine.

Lancaster

Across the Connecticut River from Vermont, **Lancaster** (pop. 3,507) is a market town that was first settled in 1764. US-2 becomes Main Street through Lancaster, lined with dozens of attractive old homes and churches, a cemetery on a knoll to the north, and on the south side a redbrick courthouse that dates from 1887.

Two miles south of Lancaster via US-3, the mountaintop estate of the man who saved New Hampshire's forests from the lumber industry has been preserved as **John Wingate Weeks Historic Site** (Wed.–Sun. 10 AM–5 PM in summer only; $4), complete with a tourable mansion and an observation tower

Your welcome to New Hampshire is a sign: Brake for Moose. Apparently, moose are hard to see at night and are involved in many serious collisions because headlights shine through the legs of this towering beast, rather than reflecting off its body.

A roadside marker along US-2 just west of Jefferson commemorates the birth nearby of inventor Thaddeus Lowe, who pioneered balloon aviation during the Civil War.

giving grand views of Mt. Washington and Vermont's Green Mountains.

If you weren't thrilled by the modern bridge that carries US-2 into Lancaster, there are two historic covered bridges in Lancaster that will renew your appreciation of civil engineers. Five miles south of US-2 via Hwy-135 the Mt. Orne covered bridge spans the Connecticut River to Vermont, while just east of US-2 in Lancaster village there's a nifty 148-year-old, 90-foot-long **covered bridge** that spans the Israel River along Mechanic Street.

Jefferson

High above the Israel River on the slopes of the White Mountains, the small resort town of **Jefferson** (pop. 1,107) is good base for exploring the surrounding peaks and is home to two big tourist draws, both ideal for the truly masochistic parent. About a mile west of Jefferson is **Santa's Village** (daily in summer, weekends in the fall; $26; 603/586-4445), with candy canes looming threateningly at the entrance, a Ferris wheel, a roller coaster, the Yule log flume, and, of course, Santa himself. Just east of town is **Six Gun City and Fort Splash** (daily in summer; $21.95; 603/586-4592), an ersatz Wild West town featuring cowboy skits ("Come on out, you varmints!"), frontier shows, a carriage museum, a roller coaster, and a water park.

Outside the town, along US-2 on a crest between Jefferson and Gorham, the **Grand View Lodge** ($85 and up; 603/466-5715) has nice rooms and truly grand views. Two other accommodations in Jefferson deserve mention, starting with the historic **Jefferson Inn** ($85–195; 800/729-7908), which has panoramic views and a swimming pond, right on US-2. A half mile south of Jefferson along Route 115A, the friendly **Applebrook B&B** ($100 and up; 800/545-6504) sits on 35 acres and offers full Victorian splendor gilded with summer raspberries and a hot tub under the stars.

East of Jefferson the road ascends, the valley narrows, and the scenery becomes more spectacular with every mile, as the Presidential Range looms larger and larger to the south.

INTERSECTION

Eight miles south of Gorham, towering Mt. Washington marks the start of our **Appalachian Trail** route, which follows along these landmark mountains all the way south to Atlanta. See page 315.

Gorham

Gorham (pop. 2,848), incorporated in 1836, was another early tourist town. Its boom began when the railroad came through in 1851; the train's story, and the town's, is told at the **Gorham Historical Society** (May–Oct. Tues.–Sat. 10 AM–3 PM; donations; 25 Railroad St.), which stands in the old depot, a half block off Main Street.

Just east of Gorham, the road passes through a famous grove of birch trees, the "world-renowned Shelburne birches." Here you find the big but pleasant **Town & Country Motor Inn** ($58 and up; 603/466-3315) with some spa and resort facilities, such as saunas, a golf course, and a good dining room. This is also where the Appalachian Trail, which runs from Maine's Mt. Katahdin to northern Georgia, crosses US-2.

West of Gorham, right off US-2, the summer-only **Moose Brook State Park** (603/466-3860) has a campground and a swimming hole built back in the 1930s by the New Deal CCC.

MAINE

Following the Androscoggin River across the New Hampshire border, US-2 enters Maine at the forested eastern flank of the **White Mountains.** Winding east along the river, the route passes through alternating mountain resorts and mill towns, starting at sedate **Bethel** and ending up 135 miles later at **Bangor,** once one of the wildest lumber towns in the country. From Bangor the route veers south toward the coast, hitting the Atlantic Ocean at beautiful **Acadia National Park.**

Bethel

At the far west end of its run across Maine, US-2 winds along the south bank of the Androscoggin River through the dense pine and birch forests of the White Mountains National Forest. Ten miles east of the New Hampshire border, along a placid stretch of the Androscoggin, **Bethel** (pop. 2,411) was first settled in 1774. At the tail end of the Revolutionary War, the town, then named Sudbury, suffered the last Indian raid inflicted on New England. The Gould Academy, one of Maine's

Just east of the Maine border, 10 miles west of Bethel, a sign marks a turn south from US-2 onto Route 113 toward **Evans Notch.** This narrow, winding, motorcycle-friendly road runs along Wild River and Cold River up to a stunningly scenic mountain pass.

oldest prep schools, was established at the west end of town in 1836, and after the railroads came through Bethel quickly became a center for White Mountain–area tourism. Founded in 1913, the **Bethel Inn** ($80 and up; 21 Broad St.; 207/824-2175 or 800/654-0125) was one of New England's early health resorts, and it continues that tradition today. The inn is surrounded by 200 acres (including an 18-hole golf course), and if you're looking for upscale lodging at reasonable rates, this is the place to go. Information on Bethel's many other well-preserved old buildings can be found in the 200-year-old **Mason House,** facing the town common, which doubles as a small museum (open July–Aug. Tues.–Sat. 1-4 PM, Sept.–June by appointment; $3; 15 Broad St.; 207/824-2908).

For outdoor enthusiasts, the **Sunday River Ski Area** (800/543-2754), six miles northeast of town, draws thousands of visitors to the area for Aspen-scale skiing in winter, and hiking and mountain biking in summer (there's also a popular "wife-carrying" contest in October). The après-ski party continues year-round, thanks to downtown Bethel's **Funky Red Barn** (19 Summer St.; 207/824-3003), which has a pool table, foosball, food, drink, and good live music.

Back on US-2, which is also known as the Mayville Road, there are a couple of good brewpubs (the **Jolly Drayman Pub** and **Sunday River Brewing Company**), plus one unexpected treat: **Smokin' Good Barbecue,** cookin' up ribs and baked beans in a bright orange trailer (207/824-4744).

Near the well-marked turnoff to Sunday River, there's a nice picnic area with a covered bridge, along US-2 and the Androscoggin River. If you head north from here a mile or so past the ski area, another sign will point you toward the intricately constructed **Artist's Covered Bridge,** which spans the Sunday River.

From US-2 at Bethel, Route 26 runs southeast toward Portland and the coast, passing through the spa town of Poland Spring and the world's last-remaining intact Shaker community at **Sabbathday Lake,** where a small museum gives tours (May–Oct. Mon.–Sat.; $6.50; 207/926-4597).

white pine cone and tassel,
state flower of Maine

Rumford

The biggest and brawniest place along otherwise rural US-2, **Rumford** (pop. 6,472) is a definite change from the leisure-time orientation of many other places in New England. A historic paper-pulp mill town with low brick buildings and a downscale downtown along Waldo Street, Rumford grew up around Androscoggin Falls, which provided the hydro-power that led to the original settlement of the town. Now, enormous steam-puffing smokestacks loom large at New Page, New England's largest paper mill, surrounded by huge piles of logs, chips, and wood residue.

The hard-working, perpetually underpaid realities of Rumford (and its next-door neighbor, Mexico, where the mill is located) are in many ways what makes it remarkable. Clearly this isn't a town designed for tourists, but if you're interested in how Americans live, work, and drink too much in places where heavy industry still rules the roost, Rumford is worth investigating. At the very least, stop for a coffee at **Dick's** (54 Main St.) on US-2 in Mexico.

Away from the center of town, the Rumford area is suddenly semi-pastoral and very pretty. US-2 winds around the valley as the Androscoggin makes an oxbow, and an even nicer route heads north following Route 17 and the Swift River toward the popular Rangeley Lakes resort area.

At a junction in **Dixfield,** a single sign points the way toward Peru and Mexico. Paris, Denmark, Norway, Poland, and Sweden are also within 50 miles—only in America!

Rumford's main claim to fame is as the birthplace of Edmund Muskie, governor, U.S. senator, secretary of state, and vice-presidential and presidential candidate in 1968 and 1972, respectively.

Wilton

West of Farmington and just north of US-2, the town of **Wilton** was the long-time home of famous shoemaker G. H. Bass Company, makers of those leather "Weejuns" so loved by preppies. In 1998 the Bass Company abandoned Wilton for the lower-wage Dominican Republic, but its old mill is still standing. Next to the mill, an old boardinghouse holds the **Wilton Farm and Home Museum** (by appointment only; donation; 207/645-2901), a fascinating muse-um with exhibits on G. H. Bass, its shoe-making operations, and everything from old bottles to the life of the Wilton-born "Maine Giantess," Sylvia Hardy, an 8-foot-tall, 400-pound woman who was a star of P. T. Barnum's famous freak shows.

Wilton is also where you'll find a large windmill marking the **Dutch Treat** restaurant and ice cream stand (63 Magrath), while one of the old G. H. Bass buildings in the historic core is now home to one of

inland Maine's better restaurants: **Calzolaio Pasta Company** (284 Main St.; 207/645-9500).

Farmington

Like many other northern Maine towns, **Farmington** (pop. 7,410) was first settled by soldiers who fought in the Revolutionary War. The rolling hills that surround it still hold a few farms and orchards, but as elsewhere, the economy revolves around trees—both as tourist fodder during the fall color sweeps and as pulp for paper mills (there's a big pulp mill just south of town on US-201). US-2 bypasses the center, but the downtown area has a few blocks of tidy brick buildings housing barber shops, bookstores, and cafés, supported in large part by the presence of the large Farmington campus of the University of Maine.

Farmington's main claim to fame is that way back in 1873 a local teenager, Chester Greenwood, rigged up a pair of beaver-skin pads on a piece of bent wire to create the world's first earmuffs.

On the south edge of downtown, at the US-2/Route 4 junction near where the Farmington Diner used to sit, family-run **Gifford's Ice Cream** (293 Main St.; 207/778-3617) serves silky-smooth "frappes" and luscious high-fat cones.

In the town of Rangeley, an hour northwest of Farmington via Route 4, the **Wilhelm Reich Museum** (207/864-3443) preserves the flat-roofed final home and tomb of the iconoclastic psychoanalyst, who died in 1957.

Between Skowhegan and Farmington, US-2 passes through a pair of quietly quaint places. **Norridgewock** is a historic hamlet, now home to a New Balance shoe factory, and **New Sharon** has a rusty old bridge spanning the Sandy River. The region's real draw is south of US-2: the **Belgrade Lakes,** a chain of seven lakes circled by ageless vacation cabins and summer camps. It was this idyllic location that inspired Ernest Thompson to write the play *On Golden Pond,* later made into that weepy Fonda-family movie. The movie was filmed at New Hampshire's Squam Lake off US-3 in the White Mountains, but you can re-enact real-life scenes here in Maine by taking a ride on the **Great Pond Mailboat,** which departs from the boat house in the village of Belgrade Lakes, along Route 27.

Skowhegan

First settled in 1771 on an island in the Kennebec River, the midsized mill town of **Skowhegan** (pop. 8,824) was the birthplace of Margaret Chase Smith

(1897–1995), one of Maine's most renowned politicians and a 36-year veteran of the U.S. House and Senate. Her home, set on 15 riverside acres, is now the **Margaret Chase Smith Library Center** (Mon.–Fri.; donations; 54 Norridgewock Ave.; 207/474-7133). Northwest of town, the complex includes a museum depicting her life and Cold War times, when Smith was the first U.S. senator to stand up to the red-baiting character assassination of Joe McCarthy's Communist "witch trials."

Skowhegan's other larger-than-life character can be visited off US-201, just north of US-2: the **Skowhegan Indian,** a 62-foot statue sometimes billed as the Largest Wooden Indian in the World, which stands unloved and unmarked in a parking lot near a gas station.

North from Skowhegan, US-201 runs along the Kennebec River, offering some of Maine's greatest fall foliage vistas. One of the prettiest stretches is around the town of **Bingham,** about 25 miles north of Skowhegan. On US-201 a mile south of town, you can catch an alfresco movie at the **Skowhegan Drive-In** (207/474-9277) on weekend nights all summer long.

East of Skowhegan, US-2 veers away from the river across low, rolling hills covered with pine and birch forests, the only signs of habitation a few trailer homes and scraggly farms.

In 1976, the Kennebec River at Skowhegan was the site of the last log drive in Maine.

During the second week of August, Skowhegan is home to the **Maine State Fair.** Celebrated annually since 1818, it is one of the oldest state fairs in the country.

Bangor

Built on the banks of the Penobscot River, **Bangor** (pop. 35,473; pronounced "BANG-gor") is the largest city in northern Maine. This site was an important rendezvous for local tribes, who called it Kendusbeag or "eel-catching place." In 1604 Samuel de Champlain sailed up the Penobscot River as far as Treats Falls here, but long-term settlement did not begin until 1769. Throughout the next century, Bangor was the most important lumber town in the eastern United States. It also developed into a shipbuilding center, and Bangor's lumber circled the globe. The people of Bangor were devoted to providing amusement for the loggers and sailors who would arrive in town with free time and fat wallets. In a riverside neighborhood called the Devil's Half Acre, dozens of bars, bordellos, and gambling dens competed to empty the men's pockets, but now the most prominent sign of life along the water is the Sea Dog Brewery (26 Front St.; 207/947-8009), one of Bangor's most popular bars and restaurants.

In the 19th century, Bangor was as wide open as any town in the Wild West, but traces of rougher days have all but disappeared. Modern Bangor, once a supply center for the northern half of Maine, is still a center for the lumber industry. Coming into town across the Penobscot River, you'll turn right onto Main Street and see a 31-foot statue of a grinning **Paul Bunyan,** erected in 1959. The compact downtown

Bangor, Maine

area, impressive redbrick 19th-century buildings interspersed with church spires, lies a few blocks east of Paul Bunyan.

The **Bangor Museum** (Tues.–Fri. 10 AM–3 PM; $3; 159 Union St.), housed in an 1836 Greek Revival mansion downtown, has exhibits, furnishings, and paintings reflecting 19th-century life. Away from the center of Bangor, car, truck, and tractor fans flock to the **Cole Land Transportation Museum**

Bangor is home to best-selling horror writer Stephen King, who lives in a suitably Gothic and surprisingly visible mansion at 47 West Broadway.

(May–Nov. daily; $7; 405 Perry Rd.), off I-95 and I-395, which displays more than 200 historic vehicles, from wooden wagons to modern 18-wheelers.

Bangor Practicalities

Thanks to the nearby University of Maine, Bangor has a wide variety of places to eat and drink. Unexpectedly, there are a couple of inexpensive Indian and Pakistani places, including **Taste of India** (68 Main St.; 207/945-6865). For whiling away an evening, head down to the **Sea Dog Brewery** (26 Front St.; 207/947-8009).

If you're just passing through Bangor on your way to or from Acadia National Park, you may want to turn off I-95 at exit 180, southwest from downtown (not far from the Land Museum), and soothe your white-line fever at the trucker's favorite stop, **Dysart's** (207/942-4878). This around-the-clock fuel stop and café offers a place to rest where you can dig in to the world's largest sundae, the 18-scoop "18-Wheeler."

Mt. Desert Island, Maine

111—Highest Headland on Atlantic Coast, Great Head, Bar Harbor

The pick of Bangor-area lodging is the **Charles Inn** ($109 and up; 20 Broad St.; 207/992-2820), a restored 1873 hotel downtown. The national chains are out on US-2 near the airport and I-95, a mile or so west of downtown, which is where the fast food is, too.

Ellsworth and Trenton

Ellsworth, chartered in 1763, began as a lumber town but is now a thriving commercial center, located southeast of Bangor at the junction of Route 3 and US-1. Downtown is marked by lots of redbrick buildings and the **Riverside Cafe** (151 Main St.; 207/667-7220), an upscale retro diner that's famous for its weekend brunch and fine slices of pie. The rest of Ellsworth is full of malls and discount stores, car lots, chain motels, and gas stations—harsh reminders of the sprawling suburban America many Maine visitors are trying to escape.

Between Ellsworth and Trenton, gateway to Mount Desert Island and Acadia National Park, there's a short but bittersweet six-mile parade of tacky roadside attractions along Route 3. If you've got kids with you or are in the mood to act like one, you can consider such questionable pleasures as the Great Maine Lumberjack Show in Trenton, plus go-karts, trading posts, miniature golf courses—even a zoo. Just before the bridge, you pass many lobster pounds on this stretch of highway, the best of which is the **Trenton Bridge Lobster Pound** (207/667-2977), open Monday–Saturday and holiday weekends (May–mid-Oct. only) since 1956; just look for the billowing clouds of steam.

From Bangor, US-2 winds northeast along the Penobscot River, ending up near the Canadian border at Houlton. We've opted to head "Down East," ending our cross-country odyssey at **Acadia National Park.**

For local weather and good music, tune in to **WMDI 107.7 FM** in Bar Harbor.

At 1,532 feet, **Cadillac Mountain** on Mount Desert Island is the highest point on the Eastern seaboard of North America. It also shares a namesake with the classy automobile marque.

Bar Harbor

Once a semiprivate enclave of the very rich (can you say Rockefeller?), the town of **Bar Harbor** (pop. 4,820), the largest and busiest on Mount Desert Island, has turned to catering to the less-well-heeled visitor as the old money has retreated to more discreet settlements to the west, such as Northeast Harbor—a.k.a. Philadelphia on the Rocks. Bar Harbor's principal thoroughfares, lined with gift shops, art galleries, bike rental stands, hotels, and restaurants, intersect at the lively and pleasant village green. Since most of Bar Harbor's old mansions were destroyed in a 1947 fire, there aren't all that many sights to search out, although the Tiffany windows of lovely little **St. Saviour's Church** on the west side of the village green give some sense of the wealth that once lingered here.

There are dozens of generally good and relatively inexpensive restaurants clustered together in Bar Harbor's few short blocks, so wander around and

Mount Desert Island

Mount Desert Island is an idyllic, 11- by 14-mile chunk of dense forests, barren peaks, and rocky inlets just off the coast of Maine. (The "desert" in Mount Desert Island is pronounced "dessert.") The island was first inhabited by the Penobscot people and was not explored by Europeans until 1604, when Samuel de Champlain named it Isle de Monts Déserts (Isle of Bald Peaks) and claimed it for France. In 1844, Hudson River School artist Thomas Cole painted a stunning series of scenes featuring Mount Desert Island, which soon became a summer playground for elite Eastern families, many of whom built massive vacation "cottages" here, largely around Bar Harbor. In 1916, the Mount Desert colony, led by the Pulitzer and Rockefeller families, donated most of the island to the federal government to establish the first national park east of the Mississippi—Acadia National Park. The Great Depression and World War II effectively put an end to the Bar Harbor high life, and most traces of the summer colony were either torn down or destroyed by a huge fire that raged through Bar Harbor in 1947.

Today about half of Mount Desert Island remains in private hands, including the villages of Bass Harbor, Northeast Harbor, Seal Harbor, and Southwest Harbor, all of which are exclusive enclaves. These locales offer a much quieter version of island life than you'll get in Bar Harbor. Northeast Harbor is perhaps the most welcoming, with two public gardens, the genteel old **Asticou Inn** ($140 and up; 207/276-3344) on Route 3, and some surprisingly affordable cafés like the **Docksider** (207/276-3965) on Sea Street, where you can munch a lobster roll while waiting for the ferry boats that shuttle across to the picturesque Cranberry Isles.

The upscale environs of **Seal Harbor,** also on Mount Desert Island, are home to one of the country's great luxury car collections, on display inside the **Seal Cove Auto Museum** (May–Oct. only, daily 10 AM–5 PM; 207/244-9242) on Route 102.

take your pick. Many are clearly aimed at the tourist trade, none more so than the amiable **Freddie's Route 66 Restaurant** (21 Cottage St.; 207/288-3708), a pseudo-1950s diner that's absolutely packed with nostalgic memorabilia—jukeboxes, gas pumps, neon signs, you name it. There's a great range of good food, including fab blueberry pie, at **Poor Boy's Gourmet** (300 Main St.; 207/288-4148), and another fun place is **Reel Pizza** (33 Kennebec Place; 207/288-3811), across from the village green, where you can watch a classic or art-house film while kicking back in a recliner, waiting for your pizza. Lobsters, of course, are at the core of Maine cuisine; sample them at a half dozen places on and around the West Street Pier; the most authentic lobster pound around has to be **Thurston's** (207/244-7600), on the water in tiny Bernard, south of Southwest Harbor.

The classic place to stay is the **Bar Harbor Inn** ($89 and up; 1 Newport Dr.; 207/288-3351), which has a lovely historic inn and standard motel rooms right on the water. Other reasonable accommodations include the **Cadillac Motor Inn** (336 Main St.; 207/288-3831).

Acadia National Park

Mount Desert Island's natural glories are preserved in **Acadia National Park,** occupying 41,634 acres of the island's most scenic areas. Route 3 runs through the heart of the park, but the best way to appreciate Acadia is to track the 20-mile-long **Park Loop Road,** which circles the eastern side of the park. (Note that large campers and trailers are prohibited.) Midway along, the loop road pauses at Sand Beach, one of the few sandy beaches in Maine (get here early to find parking in summer), then passes the Thunder Hole

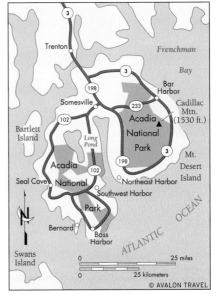

tidal cavern before winding inland past Jordan Pond. If you want to get out and stretch your legs, the best way to see the fantastic ocean views and breathe the fresh ocean air is to walk along the two-mile trail that links Sand Beach, the Thunder Hole, and the 110-foot-high Otter Cliffs. From Jordan Pond, the loop road continues past the turnoff (also accessible directly from Bar Harbor) for the drive to the top of Cadillac Mountain. Here, you'll experience a truly breathtaking panorama over Mount Desert Island, the surrounding inlets and islands, and (on a fog-free day) miles and miles of the Maine coast.

In the summer and fall, when thousands clog the loop road and the streets of Bar Harbor, the most sensible visitors head to the park's hiking trails, which wind among the beautiful inland lakes and mountains. Approximately 57 miles of the unpaved, car-free "carriage roads" constructed (well, paid for) by Edsel Ford and John D. Rockefeller Jr. are open to walkers, bikers, wheelchairs, and baby strollers. Many of these roads leave directly from the main park visitors center, but some of the best (and least crowded) start from Jordan Pond, in the southwest corner of the park. Jordan Pond is also the site of the only restaurant within the park boundary, **Jordan Pond House** (207/276-3316), where you can reserve a table for an idyllic afternoon tea. In winter, when the park is virtually dormant, the carriage roads are kept open for cross-country skiing or snowshoeing, a magical way to get a feel for the place.

Acadia National Park also protects some exemplary places beyond Mount Desert Island, including the southern tip of Isle au Haut, tiny Baker Island (which you can visit on a ranger-guided tour), and the unforgettable Schoodic Peninsula across Frenchman Bay, accessible via US-1 just north of Ellsworth. Three miles northwest of Bar Harbor, on the edge of Hulls Cove, the main **Acadia National Park Visitors Center** (daily; 207/288-3338) is a good place to start.

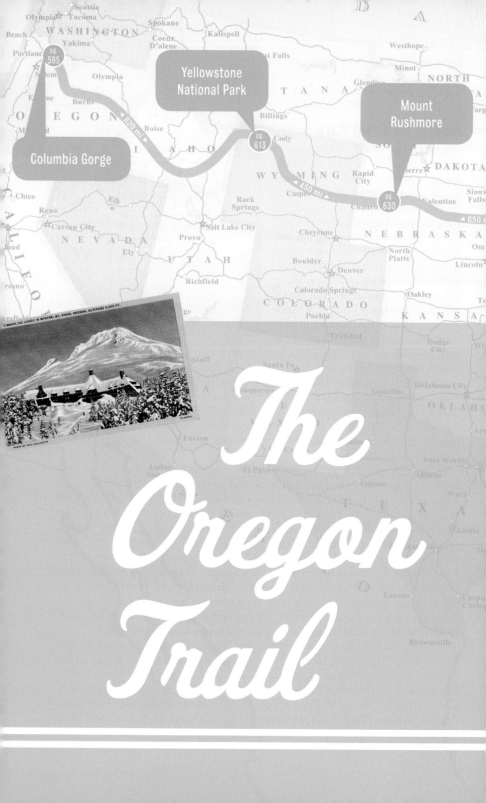

Columbia Gorge

pg. 595

Yellowstone National Park

pg. 613

820 mi

Mount Rushmore

pg. 630

450 mi

650

TIMBERLINE LODGE IN WINTER. MT. HOOD, OREGON. ALTITUDE 11,225 FT.

The Oregon Trail

Field of Dreams

pg. 638

Niagara Falls

pg. 671

Cape Cod

pg. 698

◄ 740 mi ►

◄ 480 mi ►

Following in the footsteps of pilgrims and pioneers, US-20 takes in a little of everything during its two-lane trek from Oregon's rugged coast to the glorious sea and sand of Cape Cod.

BUFFALO BILL'S WILD WEST·
CONGRESS, ROUGH RIDERS OF THE WORLD.

Between the Oregon Coast and Provincetown, Massachusetts

From the wide-open spaces of the West to the dense urban chaos of the East, this route offers the longest and most-involved road trip in this book. Connecting an exceedingly diverse range of places and totaling over 3,300 miles—many more if you count all the potential detours, side trips, and parallel routes—US-20 takes in a little of everything during its two-lane trek from Oregon's rugged coast to the glorious sea and sand of Cape Cod. Superlative sights include at least two wonders of the world, New York's **Niagara Falls** and Wyoming's **Yellowstone National Park;** the great cities of **Boston** and **Chicago;** and two halls of fame, one in Cleveland celebrating rock 'n' roll, the other in Cooperstown idolizing the national pastime, baseball. Odd museums, classic diners, idyllic towns, and poignant post-industrial decay—you'll find it all along this great cross-country highway.

Starting in the West, the route parallels, and in places runs right on top of, the broad path that formed the Oregon Trail. The landscape across **Oregon, Idaho,**

OREGON

Starting at one of the state's most enjoyable small towns, the arts-and-craftsy Pacific Ocean resort community of **Cannon Beach,** this route traverses the heart of Oregon. From the salty cow pastures along the Pacific Ocean, over the evergreen mantle of the Coast Range to culturally vibrant **Portland** and the lush Willamette Valley, the route starts where history says we should end up—amid the bountiful land at the west end of the Oregon Trail. From Portland, the state's largest city, you'll climb into the Cascade Mountains, through the amazing **Columbia Gorge** alongside its signature peak, Mt. Hood. East of the Cascades, the route drops down into the suddenly dry and desert-like landscape of the otherworldly Columbia Plateau, across which the highway rolls and rocks for 300 miles through old mining camps, fossil beds, and wide open, rolling ranch lands before crossing the Snake River into Idaho.

Most of the way across the USA, this Oregon Trail route follows US-20, but here in Oregon we've veered onto US-26, to follow the route of the original Oregon Trail and to visit the beauty spots of Columbia Gorge, Portland, and Cannon Beach.

and **Wyoming** along US-20 and a parallel highway, US-26, is still as lonesome as it was 150 years ago when pioneer families followed this one-way route west to the promised lands of the Pacific Coast. Midway across the country you can visit two notable monuments, **Mt. Rushmore** and **Carhenge.** You also can test the wisdom of Walt Whitman, who wrote, "While I know the standard claim is that Yosemite, Niagara Falls, the upper Yellowstone and the like afford the greatest natural shows, I am not so sure but the Prairies and Plains last longer, fill the aesthetic sense fuller, precede all the rest and make North America's characteristic landscape." Drive across the Sand Hills of northern **Nebraska** on your way past Iowa's Field of Dreams, and see for yourself what's so great about the **Great Plains.**

US-20 crosses the Mississippi River at Dubuque, which, like Galena, on the Illinois side, was one of the oldest settlements on what was once the nation's western frontier. It then stops off for a look at Chicago before winding east through the newly resurgent, former "Rust Belt" along the Great Lakes. This densely populated region also holds some perfectly preserved historic sites, including Amish farmlands and the automobile plants responsible for the country's classiest cars.

In upstate **New York,** we follow US-20 across a historical middle ground, in between the slow boats of the Erie Canal and the high-speed toll road of the I-90/New York Thruway, winding along the north edge of the lovely **Finger Lakes** before crossing the Hudson River into the Berkshires of western **Massachusetts.** The historic Mohawk Trail carries us past Lexington and Concord and into Boston, retracing Paul Revere's historic ride—in reverse—before following old US-6 to the tip of **Cape Cod** at the lovely and lively resort of Provincetown, where the Pilgrims *really* arrived in America, way back in 1620.

US-20 runs farther south, across the center of the state, ending up at the coast at **Newport,** which we cover in the **Pacific Coast** road trip (see page 33). **Cannon Beach** is also part of the trip (see page 29) along scenic US-101's winding route. Complete coverage is on pages 8–113.

Cannon Beach

Unlike most Oregon coast towns, **Cannon Beach** (pop. 1,690) is hidden from the highway, but it's one place you won't want to miss. Though it has long been known as an artists' colony and has grown considerably in recent years thanks to its popularity as a weekend escape from Portland, Cannon Beach retains a rustic quality, a walkably small size, and a coastline that rates second to no other in the state.

Cannon Beach marks the farthest point reached by the Lewis and Clark expedition to the West Coast. From here, they retreated back to their outpost at Fort Clatsop, near the mouth of the Columbia River, where they spent the winter of 1805–1806.

Sunset Highway: Saddle Mountain State Park

Running over the coastal mountains between Cannon Beach and Portland, US-26 is known as the Sunset Highway. Climbing up from the coastal plain, two miles east of US-101, our first stop is the old-growth spruce and fir forest

By state law, there is no self-service gasoline in Oregon; all stations have attendants who pump the gas for you. There's no sales tax, either.

preserved in 25-acre **Klootchy Creek Park.** Until recently, among the many huge firs and spruce trees was the Seaside Giant Spruce. More than 215 feet high, almost 16 feet in diameter, the tree was snapped in two by a storm in December 2007. Safety concerns caused officials to cut down the tree, but the huge stump and fallen sections have been left in place to show how massive the old-timer really was.

About 10 miles east of US-101, an eight-mile side trip to the northeast, along well-signed Saddle Mountain Road, will lift you quickly above the frequent coastal clouds and fog. Named for a geographical saddle that sits high above the surrounding forests, **Saddle Mountain State Park** surrounds the highest point in the Coast Range. A very steep 2.5-mile hiking trail climbs to the summit, with opportunities to view bleeding heart, Indian paintbrush, monkey flowers, and other rare plants and wildflowers. From the 3,283-foot peak, you can often see the mouth of the Columbia River and the spine of the Coast Range. On a clear day, the panorama may include 50 miles of Pacific coastline and Mounts Hood, St. Helens, and Rainier (with more than a few ugly acres of clear-cuts in between). Ten primitive campsites are open March–October ($5; 503/368-5154 or 800/551-6949) on a first-come, first-served basis; RVs should avoid this narrow road.

Camp 18

Continuing east on US-26, 60 miles from Portland, about 18 miles from the coast highway and a mile west of the hamlet of Elsie, the remarkable **Camp 18 Logging Museum and Restaurant** (daily; 503/755-1818 or 800/874-1810) draws

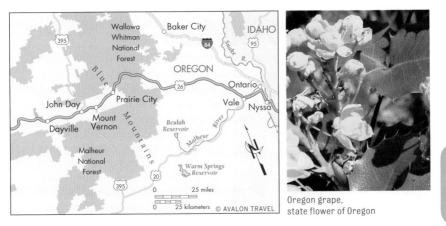

Oregon grape,
state flower of Oregon

travelers for a variety of reasons. Some people come for the absolutely massive portions of very good food, from the gigantic fresh-baked cinnamon rolls and liter jugs of coffee at breakfast to the steaks, chicken, and seafood served up at lunch and dinner. Others are drawn by the playful, Paul Bunyan-esque scale of the place: The front door handle is a hefty old ax, the spacious dining room roof is held up by a single massive Douglas fir log—85 feet long, eight feet thick, and weighing 50,000 pounds—and many of the tables are made from foot-thick planks of planed and polished wood.

The whole room is packed with an amazing collection of old logging gear, but best of all is the setting, overlooking a babbling brook, with dozens of bird-feeders attracting flocks of finches and other colorful songbirds. Outside, an extensive museum in the parking lot lets visitors examine more old logging equipment to get a feel for a bygone era of misery whips, 20-foot handsaws, and steam donkeys. (Surprise, surprise: There's also a good gift shop.)

Banks-Vernonia Linear State Park

Midway between the coast and Portland, US-26 reaches the 1,635-foot crest of Sunset Summit, then winds east through the verdant delights of the leeward Coast Range, zipping through tunnels and sliding down slopes to the farm country of northwest Willamette Valley. **Banks-Vernonia Linear State Park** (free; 503/324-0606 or 800/551-6949), 20 miles or so from downtown Portland, is a 21-mile stretch of abandoned railroad that runs north from US-26 between the town of Banks and the tucked-away timber town of Vernonia. Six well-marked trailheads along Hwy-47 provide access to the fairly level gravel trail, Oregon's first rail-to-trail park. The park is especially lovely, and popular, during October's "fall color" season, when the many ash and maple trees turn gold and red, respectively, while the birds sing and the streams gurgle.

The town of Vernonia (pop. 2,151) has recently played another role in Pacific Northwest tourism, standing in for Forks, Washington, in the movie versions of the teenage vampire *Twilight* saga. (A paper mill credit union office at the center of Vernonia stood in for the film's Forks Police Station, for

Portland

Portland, Oregon's largest city, is located inland from the coast near the confluence of the Willamette and Columbia Rivers. Due to its strategic location,

the pioneer municipality grew so fast it was nicknamed Stumptown for the hundreds of fir stumps left by early loggers, and while railroad tracks and other heavy industrial remnants are still highly visible around town, Portland's riverfront park and numerous winding greenways show that this mini metropolis is not a smokestack town but a community that values art and nature as highly as commerce. Along with one of the largest (5,170-acre Forest Park) and the smallest (24-inches-in-diameter Mill Ends Park) urban parks in the nation, and one of the coolest urban skate parks anywhere (under the Burnside Bridge), Portland also has more movie theaters and restaurants per capita than any other U.S. city, and it ranks high in microbreweries and bookstores per capita as well.

The oldest part of Portland has, over the past few years, been renovated into a lively Old Town district, where cast-iron facades of 120-year-old buildings hold some of the city's most popular bars, clubs, and cafés. (Not to mention general weirdness magnets like the 24 Hour Church of Elvis, most recently found at 408 NW Couch Street.) South of Old Town along the river, an ugly freeway has been torn down to form the Governor Tom McCall Waterfront

Park, and west of the river, downtown Portland centers on lively Pioneer Courthouse Square, at 6th Avenue and Yamhill Street. South of the square, the South Park Blocks between Park and 9th Avenues were set aside as parklands in 1852 and are now bounded by Portland's prime museums. One essential Portland place is north of the square: **Powell's City of Books** (1005 W. Burnside St.; 503/228-4651) is the largest (and certainly among the best) new-and-used bookshop in the world.

One of the largest and oldest ballparks in the minor leagues, the circa-1926 Jeld-Wen Field (formerly PGE Park, Civic Stadium, and Multnomah Stadium), a half-mile west of downtown, saw one of the first outdoor rock concerts when Elvis Presley played here in 1957, and was home to the Portland Beavers ball club until 2010, when baseball was booted out to make room for Portland's pro soccer team, the Timbers.

Along the river 3.5 miles south of town, **Oaks Park** (503/233-5777) is a tiny but wonderful circa-1905 amusement park, with ancient and modern thrill rides and a roller-skating rink, all packed together in a sylvan, oak tree–dotted park.

Practicalities

Air travelers can land at Portland International Airport (PDX), but most long-distance flights here come and go via Seattle's Sea-Tac, which is only about a three-hour drive north, via the I-5 freeway. Getting around public-spirited Portland is a breeze thanks to the combination of an efficient bus system and a light rail train (called MAX; 503/238-7433).

Though it doesn't have a trendy reputation, Portland does have some great places to eat and drink, in all stripes and sizes. **Esparza's Tex Mex Cafe** (2725 SE Ankeny St.; 503/234-7909), hidden away behind a hole-in-the-wall facade a

(continued on next page)

(continued)

VIEW FROM A SKYLINER, PORTLAND, OREGON, MT. HOOD IN THE DISTANCE

© CHAS. R. LAIDLAW

block south of East Burnside Street, is worth searching out for its smoky pork tacos, ice-cold Coronas, and a jukebox featuring Tejano, norteño, and Marty Robbins hits. For more traditional Portland fare, head to **Jake's Famous Crawfish** (401 SW 12th Ave.; 503/226-1419), which for over a century has been the place to go for the finest, freshest seafood. For meat, nothing beats the **RingSide Steakhouse,** a half-mile west of downtown (2165 W. Burnside St.; 503/223-1513), long famous for its great beef, fine fried chicken, monster Walla Walla sweet onion rings, and Hemingway-esque ambience. If your taste happens to run more to Marilyn Manson than Marilyn Monroe, you'll probably prefer to eat across town at **Dots Cafe** (2521 SE Clinton St.; 503/235-0203), a late-night hangout that has comfy dark booths, great black-bean burritos, microbrews, and a pool table. One last must-eat is **Voodoo Doughnut** (22 SW 3rd Ave.; 503/241-4704), which is packed during Old Town Portland's popular Saturday Market but worth a visit any other time (open 24 hours).

There are all sorts of places to stay in Portland, starting with a pair of popular **HI-Portland Hostels,** one east of downtown (3031 SE Hawthorne Blvd.; 503/236-3380) and a newer one in the Northwest District (425 NW 18th Ave.; 503/241-2783). **Hotel deLuxe** ($150 and up; 729 SW 15th Ave.; 503/219-2094) is stylish, comfortable, and close to downtown. If you feel like splurging, try another impeccably restored downtown landmark, **The Heathman Hotel** ($170 and up; 1001 SW Broadway; 503/241-4100 or 800/551-0011), with an elegant lobby and sumptuously appointed (if somewhat small) rooms.

The best source of visitor information on Portland is the **Travel Portland Visitor Information Center** (503/275-8355 or 877/678-5263), on Pioneer Courthouse Square.

example.) Vernonia is very cute, having recovered from a bad flood some years ago, and is a nice destination whether or not you've read the books. After a day of hiking or cycling the Linear Park, recharge your carb-deficits with a Greek gyro, a hoppy pint of homebrew, or some super-sweet baklava at the **Blue House Café,** in the center of town (919 Bridge St.; 503/429-4350).

Across Portland

Coming in from the west on the Sunset Highway (US-26), our route enters Portland next to sylvan Washington Park, then crosses the downtown area along Jefferson and Columbia Streets. Crossing the Willamette River, US-26 follows Powell Boulevard across East Portland.

Mount Hood Highway

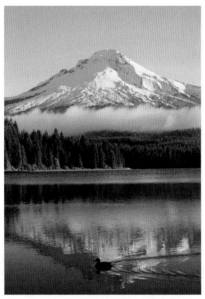

Mount Hood

Starting out along Powell Boulevard east from Portland, US-26—now dubbed the **Mount Hood Highway**—follows, albeit in reverse, the final leg of the historic Oregon Trail. Passing first through the comically named photo-stop town of Boring, the road some 20 miles east of Portland reaches **Sandy** (pop. 9,570), a boisterous gateway to the mountains. Nestled in berry-farm country, Sandy is full of ski shops, pizza parlors, and other enterprises geared for outdoor enthusiasts, but east of Sandy's lively commerce the road ambles through pastureland and into the foothills of the Cascades.

East of Sandy, oddly named towns along US-26 hold good places to eat and drink before or after a day out in the mountains. The **Inn Between Steak House and Lounge** (503/622-5400), east of Wemme in Welches, one of the little wide spots clustered at the base of Mt. Hood, has affordable eats varying from teriyaki chicken to macho nachos.

If you're planning to get out of your car and explore Mt. Hood, make sure you stop beforehand at the **Mount Hood Visitor Center** (daily; 65000 E. US-26; 503/622-3017 or 888/622-4822), in Welches, operated by the USFS and loaded with maps, brochures, and other information on the mountain and surrounding recreational hotspots.

South of US-26 on the western fringes of Portland, the mega-suburb of **Beaverton** is base camp for the high-tech companies of the Silicon Forest and, most famously, corporate headquarters for Nike, the international sports apparel giant.

Government Camp

Just off US-26 at the southern foot of Mt. Hood, **Government Camp** is but another wide spot in the road with a range of food and drink options. For espresso, microbrews,

Enticing though it is, snowcapped **Mt. Hood** is also a difficult and dangerous peak to climb—there is no trail to the 11,247-foot summit, and all routes require a high degree of technical ability and specialized equipment. There are lots of fine hikes around its base, however.

The Columbia River Highway was built by millionaire lawyer Sam Hill, who built the road to link Portland with the Quaker agricultural colony he planned at his 7,000-acre estate at Maryhill, Washington. **Maryhill Museum of Art** is now a fascinatingly eclectic museum (daily; $9; 509/773-3733) near the I-84/US-97 junction. Three miles east of Maryhill, Hill also constructed a concrete replica of Stonehenge, in memory of local men killed in World War I.

sandwiches, pizzas, and pastas, stop at the **Ice Axe Grill** (503/272-3172), part of the Mount Hood Brewing Company premises at the west end of town. Another good stop is the **Huckleberry Inn** (503/272-3325), open 24 hours a day, seven days a week, and famous for its wild huckleberry pies, huckleberry pancakes, and huckleberry shakes. If you're unable to move after a berry feast, the inn also offers rooms for $85 and up a night.

Government Camp's main attraction is the **Mount Hood Skibowl** (503/222-2695), a year-round recreation center with skiing and snowboarding in winter and mountain biking and hiking in summer, plus guided horseback trips, go-karts, paintball games, and a 100-foot bungee jump.

Timberline Lodge

East of Government Camp, near the junction of US-26 and Hwy-35, which comes from Hood River and the Columbia Gorge, be sure to turn off north toward Mt. Hood to visit **Timberline Lodge** ($160 and up; 503/272-3311 or 800/547-1406), an elegantly rustic national landmark dedicated in 1937 by the Depression-era artisans of the Works Progress Administration. The actual hotel seen (from the outside, not the inside) in Stanley Kubrick's creepy 1983 film, *The Shining*, Timberline Lodge is an unforgettable place, with a humongous fireplace in the three-story main lobby, grand dining rooms, and cozy guest rooms decorated in characterful Pacific Northwest motifs, not to mention an unbeatable setting high atop the Cascade Mountains. Even if you don't stay, check out the Cascade Dining Room's award-winning cuisine, the more-casual pizza and sandwiches at the Blue Ox, and the Ram's Head Bar, which has locally brewed beers and ales.

Warm Springs Indian Reservation

East of the Cascades crest, US-26 becomes the Warm Springs Highway as it angles down out of the mountains across the sage and juniper country of eastern Oregon. Most of the land between here and Madras is part of the 600,000-acre **Warm Springs Indian Reservation,** home to the Confederated Tribes of Warm Springs (Wasco, Paiute, and Warm Springs).

Timberline Lodge

Detour: Columbia Gorge

Though our route across Oregon generally follows scenic US-26, the fastest route east from Portland is I-84, which races along the Columbia River, rejoining US-26 at the Idaho border. Freeway the whole way, I-84 is worth considering for its one incredible feature: the **Columbia Gorge,** the deep, verdant basalt canyon through which the mighty river and the freeway, not to mention a busy railroad, run. The heart of the Columbia Gorge is between the small towns of Sandy and Cascade Locks, some 27 and 43 or so miles east of Portland respectively, and is best experienced by driving the **Historic Columbia River Highway**— the oldest scenic route in the country, built beginning in 1913 and still retaining all its old-road character.

Mushroom Rock along the Columbia River Highway, Ore.

The highlight (and approximate midpoint) of this historic highway is the aptly named and recently renovated **Vista House,** built in 1917 to mark the completion of the road, which here rises over 700 feet above the Columbia River. East of Vista House, tremendous waterfalls drop down along the road: First comes **LaTourell Falls,** with water dropping about 249 feet; then the 242-foot cascades of **Wahkeenah Falls;** then, saving the best for last, famous **Multnomah Falls,** which drops around 620 feet into a densely forested canyon, bridged by a delicate concrete arch. Each of these waterfalls is within a short walk of parking areas along the scenic highway, and many smaller falls can be seen cascading from canyon walls.

COLUMBIA RIVER HIGHWAY, OREGON.
343. MULTNOMAH FALLS, SHOWING BENSON FOOT BRIDGE.

The Columbia River Highway rejoins I-84 a few miles east of Multnomah Falls, at the town of Cascade Locks. Another 20 miles east, at the east end of the Columbia Gorge, the outdoorsy town of **Hood River** (pop. 7,167) is packed with brewpubs, espresso bars, bookshops, cafés, and moderate motels. Near the town of Hood River, the historic **Columbia Gorge Hotel** (800/345-1921 or 4000 Westcliff Dr.; 541/386-5566) preserves its Jazz Age elegance, with comfortable rooms and an excellent restaurant.

From US-26, follow signs to **Kah-Nee-Ta High Desert Resort and Casino** (pronounced "ca-NEE-da," all run together despite the odd spelling), a resort complex that cheerfully blends modern and ancient lifestyles. You can soak in the famously soothing hot springs, camp in a tepee, play golf along the banks of the Warm Springs River, and savor salmon fillets cooked over an alderwood fire. The

Vista House on its perch above the Columbia River

resort also includes the large Indian Head casino. Room rates vary tremendously (541/553-1112 or 800/554-4SUN).

Back on US-26, the real attraction of the reservation is the modern, 25,000-square-foot **Museum at Warm Springs** (daily; $7; 541/553-3331). Check out exhibits of more than 20,000 artifacts, replicas of a Paiute mat lodge and a Wasco plank house, recordings of tribal languages, and a pushbutton-activated Wasco wedding scene.

A mile east, at the edge of the reservation, US-26 bridges the deep canyon of the Deschutes River.

The Columbia Gorge west of Hood River is one of the world's best windsurfing spots, and throughout the summer dozens of brightly colored sails can usually be seen racing along the river.

*Around the Warm Springs Reservation, tune to **KWSO 91.9 FM** for an intriguing array of music (from the Eagles to talking drums) and National Native News.*

*One of eastern Oregon's landmarks, and a celebrated challenge to rock climbers, **Smith Rock State Park** ($5; 541/548-7501 or 800/551-6949) stands 17 miles south of Madras along US-97.*

Madras

After crossing the Deschutes River from the Warm Springs reservation, US-26 climbs up a deep canyon, then plateaus at **Madras** (pop. 6,046), birthplace of the late actor River Phoenix and of Boston Red Sox hero Jacoby Ellsbury. By strange coincidence, the town is named for a metropolis in Eastern India (the original Madras is now called Chennai and has a population of eight million), and in the 1980s thousands of orange- and red-clad followers of Indian guru Bhagwan Shree Rajneesh settled near and effectively took over this small Oregon town, but things here have been back to normal for a long while.

There's not a great deal to see or do in Madras, which stands at the junction of US-26 and busy US-97, but there are stores and gas stations and at least one good place to stay, on the south side of Madras: **Sonny's Motel** ($85 and up; 1539 SW US-26/97; 800/624-6137 or 541/475-7217), which has clean rooms and a pool. Best food is at the **Black Bear Diner,** a block west of US-26 (237 SW 4th St.; 541/475-6632).

Prineville

East of Madras, US-26 veers farther away from the Cascades, crossing the **Crooked River National Grasslands,** which mark the geographical center of

End of the Oregon Trail

After long months of hardship and danger, pioneers nearing the end of the Oregon Trail had two options when they reached the narrow gorge of the Columbia River: They could float their wagons down the perilous river to Fort Vancouver or climb over the Cascades to the Willamette Valley via the **Barlow Road,** a route that parallels today's US-26. While much safer than the river route, the Barlow Road had its own precarious moments—emigrants struggled down muddy declines, hanging onto ropes hitched around trees to keep wagons from runaway destruction. Such moments assuredly gave the pioneers second thoughts about their choice of passage. At $5 per wagon and 10 cents a head for cattle, horses, and mules, following the privately owned Barlow Road was also expensive. Nonetheless, in 1845, the first year of operation, records report that 1,000 pioneers in 145 wagons traveled the route.

Heading east, you're going backward along the Barlow Road, so bear that in mind as you take in a few historical sites that record the struggles of pioneers on the last stretch of their 2,000-mile overland journey. The steepest section of the road was the **Laurel Hill Chute,** where wagons skidded down a treacherous grade; a sign and pull-out five miles east of Rhododendron mark the start of a short, steep hike up to the chute. Just

west of Laurel Hill, at Tollgate Campground, you'll find a reproduction of the **Barlow Road Tollgate,** where the road's owner, Sam Barlow, stood with his hand out.

Look for other markers depicting Barlow Road history on Hwy-35, the loop road that traverses the eastern slope of Mt. Hood down to Hood River. The first, **Pioneer Woman's Grave,** is a quarter mile north of the junction with US-26; a sign marks a right turn onto Forest Road 3530 and points toward a gravesite with a brass plaque commemorating the women who traveled the Oregon Trail. Two miles north of the junction is 4,157-foot **Barlow Pass,** where ruts grooved in the Barlow Road lead downhill from a parking area, mute testament to the perseverance of westward-driven settlers.

The "official" western end of the Oregon Trail is at Oregon City, 10 miles south of Portland in the Willamette Valley.

East of the Mt. Hood hamlet of **Zigzag**, US-26 drops to an old-fashioned, undivided two-lane road. Summer-only Lolo Pass Loop (Hwy-18) cuts off north from here on a scenic half-circle around the base of Mt. Hood to Hood River, on the Columbia River and I-84.

Oregon. Strolling the streets of **Prineville** (pop. 9,253), you'll notice plenty of cowboy hats (and "gimme" caps, emblazoned with the logos of the wearer's favorite fertilizer or tractor company) atop the heads of dusty citizens piloting dusty pickup trucks. It's been a rip-snorter of a town since Barney Prine built his blacksmith shop and saloon here in 1868 following the discovery of gold in nearby hills. These days, the people of Prineville are still ranchers, loggers, and miners, plus perhaps 30 employees of social media company Facebook, which in 2011 built a $200 million, 300,000-square-foot "server farm," as its primary U.S. data center. Tourism, too, is slowly but surely making its mark as an economic force.

You can learn more about the region's history at the **A. R. Bowman Museum** (246 N. Main St.; 541/447-3715), two blocks west of the landmark Crook County Courthouse (300 NE 3rd St.). Two floors of exhibits include a campfire setup, a moonshine still, and a country store with a pound of Bull Durham tobacco. A tastier way to get a handle on life here in the middle of Oregon is to chomp down on a juicy steak at **Barney Prine's Steakhouse and Saloon** (380 N. Main St.; 541/447-3333), known for its generous and eclectic menu. Lodging choices include the **City Center Motel** ($45 and up; 509 E. 3rd St.; 541/447-5522), in the middle of the city.

In every U.S. presidential election since Oregon became a state (in 1859), the people of Crook County around Prineville voted for the winner. Until, that is, they voted for George Bush the elder over Bill Clinton in 1992, putting an end to Crook County's reputation as a national bellwether.

The drive along US-26 east of Prineville takes you up into the Ochocos, a low-slung gem of a mountain range once the heartland of the Paiutes. Seven miles from Prineville, US-26 skirts **Ochoco Lake,** a popular recreational reservoir with fishing, boating, hiking, camping, and a picnic bench or two for travelers—but not a lot of shade. The rest of the Ochoco Range, which reaches heights of nearly 7,000 feet, holds acres and acres of lovely meadows, clear streams, pristine pine forests, and views of the jagged Cascade Range, rising on the western horizon.

Mitchell

The only concentration of human habitation near the John Day Fossil Beds National Monument is **Mitchell** (pop. 130), a semi–ghost town 40 miles or so east of Prineville and two miles east of the turnoff for the Painted Hills section of the fossil beds. The main "town" of Mitchell lines up along the three-block stretch of old road signed as the Business Loop, just south of US-26, where Main Street holds the old-fashioned general store **Wheeler County Trading Co.,** capturing the flavor of the 1870s, and a pair of pleasant cafés: The **Little Pine Café and Lodge** (100 E. Main St.; 541/462-3532) and the **Sidewalk** (204 W. Main St.; 541/462-3800) offer good food and great berry pies.

Mitchell also holds one of the more atmospheric old places to stay in this part of eastern Oregon: **The Oregon Hotel** ($30–90; 104 Main St.; 541/462-3027) has genuinely friendly owners and a comfy front porch overlooking the lazy old-road loop.

John Day Fossil Beds National Monument

East of the Ochocos, midway across Oregon, the **John Day Fossil Beds National Monument** documents many millions of years of prehistoric life, from just after the demise of the dinosaurs to delicate aquatic plants. In the 1860s, frontier preacher and amateur geologist named Thomas Condon was the first to recognize the importance of the beds, which contain one of the world's richest and most diverse concentrations of mammalian and reptilian fossils, including saber-toothed cats. Offering a visually attractive and easily accessible record of life on earth, spanning the past 6 million to 54 million years (out of some 4.5 billion since the "Big Bang"), the monument is made up of three distinct units, totaling some 14,000 acres. Needless to say, fossil collecting is strictly prohibited in the park.

The eerie, empty moonscape can be easily toured from US-26. Start in the west with the **Painted Hills Unit,** just west of Mitchell, then six miles north of US-26, where trails and overlooks offer views of striated hills and bluffs formed by fallen ash and brilliantly colored in bands of red, pink, black, and bronze. A life-sized Georgia O'Keeffe landscape, Painted Hills is a popular spot with photographers and painters, especially the short Painted Cove trail, which winds through the most intensely colored section.

About 35 miles east of Mitchell, six miles west of Dayville along US-26, then two miles north on Hwy-19, the **Sheep Rock Unit** is the best place to see fossils up close. The monument headquarters (541/987-2333) and main paleontology museum are

The namesake of the fossil beds, John Day, was a fur-trapper who was robbed of everything, including clothing, near the mouth of a river. People would pass by and mention the incident, so it became known as the John Day River. The river flowed to the fossil area and the city, which were later named after John Day as well. It's likely that John Day was never anywhere near the town and region that now bear his name.

Sheep Rock Unit

ammonite fossil

also here, housed inside an attractive modern building on the grounds of the historic Cant Ranch. East of the turnoff to the Sheep Rock fossil beds, US-26 runs right along the John Day River through the 500-foot-deep basalt canyon of Picture Gorge, so named because of the abundance of Native American pictographs.

A more distant section of the John Day Fossil Beds is the Clarno Unit, along the John Day River some 50 miles northwest of Painted Hills, near the aptly named town of **Fossil,** home of the brand-new and totally fascinating **Oregon Paleo Lands Institute** (333 W. 4th St.; 541/763-4480). This area includes the park's most ancient rocks—ranging from 37 million to 54 million years old—while the very oldest rocks in Oregon, dating back more than 225 million years, can be seen atop volcanic Canyon Mountain, south of John Day village.

John Day: Kam Wah Chung Museum

After gazing at striped hillsides and fossilized remains, regain some perspective by strolling through any of the towns that line the John Day River along this part of US-26—Dayville, Mount Vernon, John Day, and Canyon City. Founded as miners' camps after gold was discovered here in 1862, many now cater mostly to local ranchers—but offer a warm welcome to the few visitors who brave a trip through this uninviting but unforgettable part of the world.

John Day's one and only radio station, **KJDY 1400 AM,** broadcasts country-tinged Top 40 music and local news across eastern Oregon. For truly twangy C&W—à la Waylon, Hank, and Merle—tune to **KFXD 580 AM,** out of Nampa, Idaho.

Starting in the west, **Dayville** (pop. 149) has a great roadside "antiques" store, and what has to be among the world's smallest city halls—a one-room shack at the east edge of town. The town of **John Day** (pop. 1,744), the metropolis in this chain of ghostly gold towns, holds the area's one not-to-be-missed attraction: **Kam Wah Chung Museum** (daily May–Oct. only; $3; 250 NW Canton St.; 800/551-6949 or 541/575-2800), run by the state and located in a nice park just north of US-26 at the center of John Day. Built as a trading post in 1866–1867, in the late 1880s the Kam Wah Chung building became a general store and medical center for the Chinese workers who toiled in the mines, and for 60 years it continued to be the center of the almost exclusively male Chinese community of eastern Oregon, which at times made up a majority of the regional population. Most of the building is preserved intact, displaying a fascinating collection of items ranging from herbal remedies and ornate red Taoist shrines to gambling paraphernalia and ancient canned goods. There's also a bedroom with bunks and a wood stove left as they were by the last residents, Ing Hay and Lung On, the herbalist and storekeeper who lived and worked here until the 1940s.

Right next to the museum is the John Day **swimming pool,** much appreciated on a hot summer afternoon. For food, the **Grubsteak Mining Company** (149 E. Main St.; 541/575-1970) has a sumptuous menu of rib-eyes and other beef entrées. A block away, just north of US-26, the

Dreamers Lodge Motel ($50–100; 144 N. Canyon Blvd.; 800/654-2849 or 541/575-0526) has nice rooms.

Prairie City

The first town east of John Day is tidy little **Prairie City** (pop. 909), an old-fashioned ranching community that is fast becoming a western false-front photo opportunity. For a taste of local life, stay at the 100-year-old **Riverside School House Bed and Breakfast** ($135 cash or check only; 541/820-4731), a white-clapboard two-room schoolhouse, in use until the 1960s and now rented out as a one-of-a-kind B&B, located on a working cattle ranch with delightful views over the headwaters of the John Day River.

Leaving the John Day River watershed, US-26 heads east, climbing over mile-high Dixie Pass (which is just one yard shy of being one mile high—5,277 feet above sea level) while rambling through the **Malheur** and **Wallowa-Whitman National Forests** (541/575-3000; 541/523-6391), where campgrounds, cool mountain lakes, natural hot springs, and dense forests abound.

East of the crest, dropping down from the mountains across the Snake River plain, US-26 crosses another 75 miles of rolling sagebrush, with little more than an occasional cattle ranch, or a golden eagle sitting atop a telephone pole, to attract your attention. Tiny little tavern-and-post-office towns like Unity, Ironside, Brogan, and Willow Creek will make you slow to 45 mph (or risk a ticket), while on a hot summer's day the smell of juniper and sage is so potent it perfumes the dry desert air, unmistakable even if you cruise through at 70 mph with the air-conditioning blasting away.

Vale

The seat of Malheur ("Bad Smell" or "Bad Luck," depending upon who tells it) County, **Vale** (pop. 1,874) sits on the banks of the Malheur River at the junction

Towns in eastern Oregon have taken to decorating their buildings with large and colorful murals, usually with historical or outdoorsy themes.

Halfway between Prairie City and Vale is the dividing line between Pacific and mountain time zones. Adjust clocks accordingly as you head over **Eldorado Pass.**

of US-20 and US-26. The comparatively easy river crossing and the presence of a natural hot spring made it a prime stopping place on the Oregon Trail. Murals and markers around town explain something of the history and point out sights like the **Malheur Crossing,** next to the bridge on the eastern edge of the town, where pioneers dunked their aching bods in the still-hot Malheur River Springs; and Keeney Pass, just south of downtown Vale on Enterprise Avenue, where 150-year-old wagon ruts can still be seen along the roadside. There's more to see inside the **Rinehart Stone House Museum** (255 Main St. S.; 541/473-2070), housed inside a frontier-era stagecoach stop and hotel.

Taking a breather at Vale is an honored tradition—it was here that pioneers rested before climbing out of the Snake River Valley into the Blue Mountains. Today's travelers can opt for a night at the **Bates Motel** (around $50 and up; 101 W. A St.; 541/473-3234), on US-201; it has nothing to do with Hitchcock's *Psycho* but has been run by the Bates family (no Normans among them) for over 30 years, offering clean showers, a pizza restaurant, and a good night's sleep. An unusual option is **The Oregon Trail Inn** (484 N. 10th St.; 541/473-3030), a B&B in a house originally ordered from the Sears & Roebuck catalog back around the turn of the 20th century.

Toward Idaho: Ontario and Nyssa

Approaching the Idaho border, you have two choices: to follow I-84, heading east via **Ontario** (pop. 11,366), the largest of many mid-sized farming and ranching communities in the surrounding area; or to continue along the more atmospheric older roads. The official **Oregon Trail Auto Route** (US-20/26) bends to the south along the Snake River, passing one last Oregon town, **Nyssa,** before crossing into the Land of Famous Potatoes. Nyssa calls itself the "Thunderegg Capital of the World" because of the many geodes found there, but it's primarily a shipping point for the tons of spuds, onions, and sugar beets grown nearby—the different crops are even labeled along the highway for your edification. Along with a very large riverfront sugar beet refinery, Nyssa also offers a great leg-stretch opportunity inside the enjoyable **Sugar Bowl,** a bowling alley off US-20/26 on the north edge of town (909 Park Ave.; 541/372-3592).

IDAHO

US-20's route across southern Idaho cuts through one of the most magnificently empty American spaces, an arid, volcanic region cut by life-giving rivers and isolating mountain ranges, with strange geological outcrops that encourage travelers to stop and explore the inhospitable terrain. Irrigation has altered the look of the land considerably, so much so that vineyards and lush fields now thrive in the otherwise barren, gray-green sagebrush plains, but little else has changed since this region provided the

syringa, state flower of Idaho

greatest challenge to pioneers crossing the country along the Oregon Trail. The provision of visitor services has improved considerably in the intervening centuries, but southern Idaho is still a wild and demanding land. Like much of the American West, it's also an addictively satisfying place to explore.

Parma and Fort Boise

Just as US-20/26 does today, the historic Oregon Trail crosses between Idaho and Oregon at the confluence of the Boise and Snake Rivers, southwest of I-84 at the town of **Parma.** Sugar beets and onions fill the fields around the tiny town, which takes pride in its replica of **Fort Boise,** one of the first European outposts in the Pacific Northwest. Originally established in 1834 by the Hudson's Bay Company, Fort Boise was famous for its frontier hospitality,

> The quickest route across Idaho is the I-84 freeway, though the historic Oregon Trail route, marked by large highway signs, follows a much more scenic route along the Snake River.

entertaining and supplying travelers and traders until the mid-1850s, when it was closed because of declines in demand and an increase in Indian hostilities. The original Fort Boise stood along the banks of the river and was washed away long ago. The site is marked today by an odd, horse-headed stone obelisk festooned with the Hudson's Bay Company flag, which stands along the Snake River at the end of Old Fort Boise Road, two miles west of US-20/26. The less-than-authentic steel-and-stucco reconstruction of the old fort that stands along US-20 near the center of town is the site of the annual **Old Fort Boise Days** in early summer.

Caldwell

East of Parma, US-20/26 runs along the north bank of the Boise River for a dozen miles before crossing I-84 at the city of **Caldwell**—home of the mid-August **Caldwell Night Rodeo** (208/459-2060). A century ago, Caldwell was the site of the 1905 bomb-blast murder of former Idaho governor Frank Steunenberg. Blamed on "Wobbly" left-wing union activists, including "Big Bill" Haywood, who'd been organizing Idaho's miners and loggers, the murder was the story behind Anthony Lukas's sprawling book *Big Trouble: A*

One fun spot out between Caldwell and Boise is the Western Idaho Fairgrounds, home to year-round events and the Class A baseball games of the **Boise Hawks** (208/322-5000).

Murder in a Small Western Town Sets Off a Struggle for the Soul of America.

From Caldwell, you can follow the freeway into Boise, but it's more interesting, and depending on traffic possibly even quicker as well, to stay on US-20/26 (a.k.a. Chinden Boulevard), which runs right atop the old Oregon Trail into downtown, past corn and wheat fields that have been rapidly sprouting golf course estates, a Hewlett-Packard factory, car parts stores, and the usual Asphalt Nation sprawl.

Boise

Capital of Idaho and perennial contender for the title of "most livable" city in the United States, **Boise** (pop. 205,671) is still a very pleasant, medium-sized city, despite growing at a rate of 25 percent per decade. A lush green oasis in the middle of the barren lava lands of the Snake River plain, Boise was so named by fur-trappers for its dense groves of cottonwood trees (*bois* is French for "wood"), which made the area an especially welcome respite before irrigation turned the brown desert much greener than it naturally would be. The presence of the state government and the nearly 20,000 students at Boise State University lend a degree of sophistication and vitality mixed in with the more usual Idaho trappings—more than anywhere else for miles, in-line skates and mountain bikes compete with pickup trucks as the main method of transportation here, and bookshops and espresso bars line the downtown streets.

Downtown Boise focuses on the **state capitol** (closed Sun.; free; 700 W. Jefferson St.), three blocks north of Main Street between 6th and 8th Streets, a typically grand, neoclassical structure, built of local sandstone with a giant eagle atop its landmark dome. The usual exhibits of the state's produce fill display cases, and free guided tours are given upon request.

South of the capitol, restaurants and cafés have reclaimed the blocks of 100-year-old brick buildings around 6th and Main Streets, the historic center of Boise. In the heart of this lively, pedestrian-friendly neighborhood, a block south of Main, the small but intriguing **Basque Museum and Cultural Center** (Tues.–Sat.; $5; 611 Grove St.; 208/343-2671) documents the culture of the Basque people who work in Idaho's ranching industries. A block west stands **Grove Plaza,** home to Boise's convention center and main shopping complex, featuring a large fountain through which daredevils like to skate and cycle. Don't miss **Taters** (249 S. 8th St.; 208/338-1062), which sells all manner of Idaho souvenirs, from postcards and fridge magnets to spud-themed T-shirts and cookbooks describing 100 things you can do with potatoes.

Farther east, where Main Street turns into Warm Springs Road, the **Old Idaho Penitentiary State Historical Site** (daily; $5; 208/334-2844) served as the main state prison for over 100 years after it opened in 1872. High sandstone walls, cut by prisoners, surround the complex, and the old cellblocks are now filled with displays on prison life—from collections of tattoos to the gallows where many prisoners met their end.

Boise Practicalities

By Idaho standards, Boise has a truly exciting range of restaurants, with many good places around 6th and Main Streets and elsewhere in the compact downtown area. For a huge breakfast, or an out-of-this-world milk shake, stop by **Moon's Kitchen Café** (open until 3 PM Sun.–Thurs., until 8 PM Fri. and Sat.; 712 W. Idaho St.; 208/385-0472), recently expanded after 50-plus years operating in the back room of a gift shop that used to be a gun shop. Another favorite stop is **Bar Gernika Basque Pub and Eatery,** near the Basque Museum on the corner of Grove (closed Sun.; 202 S. Capitol Ave.; 208/344-2175), which serves up delicious tastes of Basque-inspired food (lamb sandwiches, chorizo *tapas,* and out-of-this-world shoestring fries), plus Spanish wines and microbrewed beers, in a friendly, unpretentious room—with a sidewalk seating area in summer. And if this doesn't hit the spot, within a few blocks is the excellent **Guido's Pizzeria,** serving classic thin-crust New York–style pies (235 N. 5th St.; 208/345-9011).

Boise's downtown restaurant district doubles as its nightlife zone as well, so after a meal you can stagger between old-fashioned, carved-wood bars like **Pengilly's Saloon** (513 Main St.; 208/345-6344) and nightclubs like the excellent **Blues Bouquet,** hosting frequent live music (1010 W. Main St.; 208/345-6605).

Boise's former best place to stay, the wonderful old Idanha Hotel at 928 Main Street—built in 1901 and featuring ornate corner turrets, opulent public spaces, and Idaho's oldest elevator—has, alas, been converted into apartments, but the **Owyhee Plaza** (around $80 and up; 1109 Main St.; 800/233-4611 or 208/343-4611) is almost as nice. For a cheaper but still restful sleep, head to the **Cabana Inn** ($40 and up; 1600 W. Main St.; 208/343-6000), on the west side of downtown. West of Boise, there's an **HI Hostel** (around $25; 17322 Can-Ada Rd.; 208/467-6858) in Nampa.

Mountain Home and Bruneau Dunes

Northeast from Boise, Hwy-21 makes a very scenic trip through the Sawtooth Mountains to **Stanley.**

Across southern Idaho, the I-84 freeway has effectively replaced the older highways, especially in the area southeast of Boise. The huge **Mountain Home Air Force Base,** 50 miles or so southeast of Boise, is the only thing for miles, which is no doubt by design: The base is home to the latest high-tech weapons systems and aircraft, whose pilots train at the adjacent, 100,000-acre desert bombing range.

Eighteen miles south of Mountain Home and the I-84 freeway via Hwy-51,

The Historic Oregon Trail

In 1993, the 150th anniversary of the opening of the Oregon Trail renewed interest in this best-known of emigrant trails across the Wild West. History buffs got together for summer-long reenactments of the arduous crossing, building authentic wagons and eating, dressing, and sleeping as the pioneers did—with the inestimable comfort of knowing that they, unlike their predecessors, could easily return home at any point.

From 1843 until the 1860s, some 400,000 men, women, and children followed this 2,000-mile trail, averaging four months to make the cross-country journey. Long followed by fur-trappers and traders, and first charted by a series of U.S. Army expeditions led by Kit Carson and John C. Fremont in the early 1840s, the Oregon Trail followed the path of least resistance across the western half of the continent. Beginning at various points along the Missouri River, the trail followed the valley of the Platte River across the Great Plains, crossed the Rockies at Wyoming's gentle South Pass, then set off across the desert of southern Idaho. The most difficult parts were saved for the end, when emigrants had a choice of floating downstream on the turbulent Columbia River or struggling over the rugged Cascades to reach the Willamette Valley. Nearly half of the travelers who set off along the Oregon Trail from Missouri actually had other destinations in mind: More than 100,000 turned off south toward the California gold mines, and some 30,000 Mormons followed the route west to their new colony at Salt Lake City.

The Oregon Trail had many variants and shortcuts and was never a sharply defined track, but clear traces survive in a number of places along the route. Many evocative sites also survive, often as reconstructions of pioneer forts, trading posts, and river crossings. There are also many fine museums along the way.

Many Oregon Trail sites are covered in more detail under our Road Trip routes. As shown on the map, some of the most interesting Oregon Trail sites are:

The Barlow Road: To avoid the treacherous falls of the Columbia Gorge, many emigrants opted to follow this difficult toll road, which cuts inland around Mt. Hood (see page 597).

The National Historic Oregon Trail Interpretive Center: In eastern Oregon, off I-84 near Baker City, Oregon's biggest and most developed Oregon Trail historic site (daily 9 AM–4 PM, until 6 PM in summer; $8; 541/523-1843) has an original Meeker Marker and a 15-mile-long set of well-preserved wagon ruts.

Fort Boise: This fortress, a reconstruction of a fur-trapping post built nearby in 1834, stands along the banks of the Snake River (see page 603).

Three Island State Park: This is one of the best places to get a feel for life as an Oregon Trail pioneer: Camp where they camped and swim where they swam, at one of the most important crossings of the Snake River (see page 608).

Fort Caspar: A credible reconstruction of a frontier fort houses a good museum and the remains of an early ferry and bridge over the Platte River, while a new building in town houses the National Historic Trails Interpretive Center (see page 623).

Fort Laramie: Located 40 miles southeast of Douglas, Wyoming, this re-stored fort is among the best stops on the contemporary trail. The most impressive set of preserved wagon ruts survive in an evocative state park outside Guernsey, upstream from the fort (see page 626).

Santa Fe Trail Junction: For the first few miles, the Santa Fe and Oregon Trails coincided, and a sign here, at what is today the town of **La Junta,** pointed the way: right to Oregon, left to Santa Fe (see page 750).

Independence, Missouri: Where most travelers on the Oregon Trail began, this is also the site of one of the best museums on the subject of the westward migrations (see page 762).

Bruneau Dunes State Park

Bruneau Dunes State Park (208/366-7919) protects the highest free-standing sand dune in North America—rising over 470 feet above the Snake River plain. Since the temperatures can hit 100°F throughout the summer months, mornings or sunsets are the best times to exercise your legs by climbing up and careening back down the white sands.

Glenns Ferry

The tiny town of **Glenns Ferry,** 28 miles southeast of Mountain Home on the Snake River and I-84, would hardly rate a mention were it not the site of one of the most important crossings on the old Oregon Trail. This site, now preserved as **Three Island State Park,** a mile southwest of town, gives one of the strongest impressions of the tough going for Oregon-bound pioneers. A very good **visitors center** (closed Mon. and Tues.; 208/366-2394), with a Conestoga wagon out front, has displays of trail lore and history, and every August enthusiasts get together to reenact the river crossing. Go for a swim to cool off, and feel the powerful currents—more placid here than most anywhere else, which is why it was considered the best place to ford the river. This is also a fine place to camp; the usually clear night sky makes for excellent stargazing, and there's even a very docile herd of buffalo.

At Mountain Home, US-20 cuts off northeast from I-84, following a branch of the Oregon Trail known as Goodale's Cut-off across the harsh volcanic plains. **Bliss** marks the turnoff onto US-30, which follows the old Oregon Trail along the banks of the Snake River along a lovely, waterfall-rich route known as **Thousand Springs Scenic Byway,** rejoining I-84 at Twin Falls.

Bliss and Hagerman

Along with providing the chance to add to your collection of city limits signs, or to send a postcard saying you're in **Bliss** (pop. 318), this idyllically named town is worth a stop to see the deep canyon of **Malad Gorge State Park** (daily dawn–dusk; free; 208/837-4505), well signed southeast of town, off I-84 exit 147. It doesn't look like much until you get out of the car and walk 100 feet down the trail, where you suddenly come upon a truly awesome sight: a 250-foot-deep gorge with a crashing waterfall. The freeway passes overhead, oblivious to the natural wonder directly below.

Across the Snake River from Malad Gorge, **Hagerman Fossil Beds National Monument** contains what's been called "the richest known deposit of Pliocene Age terrestrial fossils," mainly horses *(Equus simplicidens)* that roamed the area some 3.5 million years ago. The undeveloped monument also preserves one of the longest sections of visible wagon ruts in the entire length of the Oregon Trail. The visitors center (208/933-4100) is in Hagerman, five miles south of Bliss and across the river from the fossil beds. The center also has information on visiting the area's other national monument: the **Minidoka Internment National Memorial,** north of Twin Falls (see the *Border to Border* chapter).

US-26: Gooding and Shoshone

In the midst of inhospitable volcanic badlands, a pair of small towns that grew up along the railroad tracks have somehow survived to the present day. Coming from the west along US-26 from Bliss, the first one you reach is

Gooding (pop. 3,567), named for local sheep rancher Frank Gooding, who went from being mayor to Idaho governor to a U.S. senator before his death in 1928.

Shoshone Falls, Idaho.

A straight shot east along the tracks brings you to **Shoshone** (pop. 1,461), another ranching and railroad center with a number of buildings that have been constructed from local volcanic rock. Though it's a fairly timeworn place, Shoshone looks great at sunset, when its steel water tower glows and places like the neon-signed **Manhattan Cafe** (208/886-2142), along the railroad tracks, look especially appealing.

If you're hungry, thirsty, or low on gas, be sure to fill up here, as services are rare between Shoshone and Arco, 75 miles or so to the east.

Shoshone sits at the junction where US-26 crosses Hwy-75, which runs north to Sun Valley, and US-93, which runs south to Twin Falls (see page 143). For more on this **Border to Border** route, see pages 114–173.

Craters of the Moon National Monument and Preserve

Described by writer Washington Irving as a place "where nothing meets the eye but a desolate and awful waste, where no grass grows nor water runs, and where nothing is to be seen but lava," the vast tracts of volcanic fields known as **Craters of the Moon National Monument and Preserve** aren't totally devoid of life—they just look that way. Covering some 750,000 acres at an average altitude of 6,000 feet, the lava fields are but a small part of the extensive

Snake River volcanic plain, a 100-mile-wide, 400-mile-long crescent-shaped swath across southern Idaho from the border with Oregon to northwest Wyoming. The rounded cinder cones and acres of glassy black stone were formed between 2,000 and 15,000 years ago, and despite first impressions,

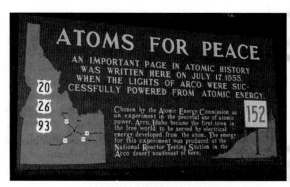

they do shelter a wide variety of plant and animal life, from pines and prickly pears to various raptors and a population of mule deer. May and June see abundant wildflowers, and temperatures stay cool, so it's altogether an ideal time to visit.

Easily accessible from a seven-mile loop road that runs south from US-20/26, the most striking remnants of the region's volcanic activity are the huge cones that rise above the generally flat plain. These huge knolls of light-weight cinder give great views of the overall area, but they're not volcanoes, and there's no crater to look down into. The closest Craters of the Moon comes to real craters is the spatter cones midway along the loop, where the deep openings are often filled with snow late into summer. The most interesting section of the monument is at the end of the loop, where—provided you have a flashlight—you can wander through sub-surface **lava tubes** like Beauty Cave and Indian Tunnel. At 830 feet, Indian Tunnel is the longest in the park.

For further information or to pick up the useful park brochures, stop by the small **visitors center** (daily; 208/527-1335), where you ought to pay the entry fee ($8). In summer there's a basic, 52-site **campground** ($10), offering water and restrooms but no showers, hookups, or dump station.

Arco

"The first city in the free world to be powered by nuclear-generated electricity," **Arco** (pop. 995) sits on the banks of the Big Lost River, so-called because it disappears a few miles downstream, vanishing into the volcanic labyrinth of the Snake River plain. Arco itself, a crossroads town straddling the junction of US-20, US-26, and US-93, is a handy stop for food, gas, or supplies. All over town, signs and historic plaques point out Arco's connections with the early days of nuclear power, including, most unexpectedly, the conning tower from the decommissioned, nuclear-powered Cold War–era submarine, the USS *Hawkbill,* permanently moored along Front Street, a mere 1,000 miles from the nearest ocean.

Northwest of Arco, the highest peak in Idaho, 12,662-foot **Mt. Borah,** was epicenter of a powerful 1983 earthquake that registered 7.3 on the Richter scale.

If you have more than a passing interest in nuclear fission, you'll want to check out the anonymous-looking redbrick structure 18 miles southeast of Arco on the south side of US-20, which holds the inoperative remains of **Experimental Breeder Reactor Number One.** Sitting at the edge of the massive Idaho National Engineering Lab (INEL), the deactivated reactor is open for self-guided tours (daily in summer only; free; 208/526-0050), on which you can get an up-close glimpse of the turbines and control room, even the fuel rods that first produced nuclear power on December 20, 1951. (To put all this in context, the first reaction produced enough electricity to power four small light bulbs.) By 1953 the reactor here was finally able to produce more power through nuclear reactions than it consumed, a much more important achievement. Some 60 years later, INEL is now one of the nation's de facto repositories for nuclear waste and will remain so for the foreseeable future—with a half-life of more than 1,000 years, it will take the next 3 million years or so, by most estimates, until the waste loses its radioactive potency and decays to "safe" levels.

Idaho Falls

Taking its name from the wide but short waterfall completely tamed to form a pleasant green lake at the center of town, **Idaho Falls** (pop. 56,813), at the junction of US-20 and I-15, is a busy, big city with a very attractive, Middle American downtown set along the banks of the Snake River. Grain elevators and stockyards stand along the railroad tracks, train whistles blow throughout the night, and all manner of neon signs line the highways, offering a concentrated dose of rural Americana. The town's hotels, supermarkets, and restaurants make Idaho Falls a handy last stop before heading on to the diverse wilderness areas that rise to the north, east, and west. Apart from the chance to wander around a business district that's hardly changed since 1956, you can stroll along the waterfront park, feeding the geese or just watching the waters tumble over the weirs.

Summer fun in Idaho Falls includes an **Idaho Falls Chukars** Pioneer League baseball game (208/522-8363), at Melaleuca Field along West Broadway (US-20), west of I-15. Games are broadcast on **KUPI 980 AM.**

Though it's rich in small-town Americana, Idaho Falls also has a few pockets of big-city sophistication, no doubt thanks to the well-paid engineers employed at INEL west of town and the skiers bound for Grand Targhee in the mountains to the east. Cafés and bakeries crowd together around Park Avenue and A Street downtown, serving a wide enough range of pastries, coffees, and sandwiches to suit any palate. If you time it so you miss the crowds, the tiny but tasty **The SnakeBite Restaurant** (cash only; 401 Park Ave.; 208/525-2522) is excellent. West of downtown across the river, **Smitty's Pancake and Steakhouse** (645 W. Broadway; 208/523-6450) has been serving "IDF's Best Breakfast" for years, and east of downtown along old US-20, **Bubba's BBQ** has great ribs (118 1st St.; 208/523-2822). For a place to stay, try the aging but inexpensive **Red Lion Inn** (around $85 and up; 475 River Parkway; 208/523-8000 or 800/432-1005), overlooking the falls.

Many of Idaho's famous potatoes are grown in the irrigated "Magic Valley" area along I-84 between Idaho Falls and Twin Falls. Planting takes place in April, while harvest season is usually in fall. To learn everything you ever wanted to know about spuds, take a 20-mile or so trip southwest from Idaho Falls to **Blackfoot** to see the unique **Idaho Potato Museum** ($3; 130 NW Main St.; 208/785-2517).

West of US-20, 15 miles or so north of Idaho Falls, the sleepy town of **Rigby** played a hugely important role in the development of contemporary culture: It was here that young Philo T. Farnsworth, the inventor of the cathode-ray television, grew up and went to school.

Rising to the east of Idaho Falls, the serrated crest of the Grand Tetons stands out along the Idaho/Wyoming border. Though the US-20 route through Yellowstone National Park is closed in winter, you can get across the Rockies by detouring via US-26 through **Jackson Hole, Wyoming**— a beautiful route.

Rexburg

First settled by Mormon homesteaders in the 1880s, the fast-growing town of **Rexburg** (pop. 26,285) still has a pronounced Mormon feel, thanks in part to the thousands of students attending Brigham Young University-Idaho. Apart from the BYU connections, Rexburg is best known for the near-disaster of 1976, when the huge Teton Dam collapsed and unleashed eight billion gallons of floodwater onto the valley below. Fortunately, engineers noticed the warning signs and were able to evacuate the area beforehand; though damage was extensive, fatalities were few. Housed in the basement of the old Mormon tabernacle, the **Teton Flood Museum** (closed Sat. and Sun.; $2; 51 W. Center St.; 208/359-3063) has the usual displays of quilts and cattle brands tracing the history of the region, plus a large section devoted to the great flood of 1976. A short film shows the actual collapse of the dam.

From Rexburg, US-20 runs northeast through the **Targhee National Forest,** climbing from the Snake River plain along Henry's Fork River—one of the country's top fishing streams, loaded with cutthroat trout as big as 10 pounds—into the heart of the Rocky Mountains. On the Idaho/Montana border, 7,072-foot Targhee Pass marks the **Continental Divide.**

West Yellowstone, Montana

Western gateway to Yellowstone National Park, the Montana town of **West Yellowstone** (pop. 1,271; elev. 6,667) sits just over the Idaho border and very nearly on the Wyoming border, offering all the motels, gas stations, and cafés you could ever want, plus a lot more. The primary access point for early tourists visiting Yellowstone on the Oregon Shortline and Union Pacific Railroad, West Yellowstone preserves a great deal of old-style tourist facilities. The rustic old railroad station is now an engaging museum, and the town's many roadside motels (there are more motel rooms than residents!) display a mouthwatering assembly of nifty 1950s-vintage neon signs.

There's also a huge **IMAX theater** ($9; 101 S. Canyon St.; 888/854-5862 or 406/646-4100), in case you prefer the Memorex version to real-life Yellowstone. The IMAX theater is adjacent to the

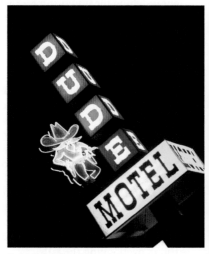

Dude Motel, West Yellowstone

Grizzly and Wolf Discovery Center ($10.50; 201 S. Canyon St.; 800/257-2570 or 406/646-7001), which collects orphaned, abandoned and "problem" bears and wolves and puts them on display rather than kill them, as is otherwise done.

West Yellowstone's main drag, Canyon Street (US-20), is lined by cafés and Wild West souvenir shops. The excellent **Book Peddler** (106 Canyon St.; 406/646-9358) boasts an espresso and sandwich bar along with a wide array of fiction and nonfiction titles.

Most of West Yellowstone's enviable collection of historic motels are off the main highway frontage, so drive around the back streets and take your pick. The arts-and-crafts-style **Stage Coach Inn** ($134 and up; 800/842-2882 or 406/646-7381), at Madison and Dunraven Streets, has been charming visitors for more than half a century, as has the friendly and relaxing **Lazy G Motel** ($68 and up; 123 Hayden St.; 406/646-7586), which has to be one of the world's nicest little motels.

In 1808, when fur-trapper John Colter described the scenes he saw in what's now Yellowstone—gurgling, spouting steam vents and prismatic pools of sulfurous boiling water—nobody believed him, and many thought he was mad, calling the fantastic land "Colter's Hell."

WYOMING

Most visitors to Wyoming have one thing in mind: Yellowstone National Park. This amazing spectacle, which our route takes us right through, is deservedly the state's premier visitor attraction, but the rest of Wyoming holds a surprising variety of interesting places, from Wild West cow towns to the wide open spaces of the Great Plains. The least populated of the 50 states, Wyoming has more wide-open space than just about anywhere else. If you like the idea of traveling for miles and miles without seeing anyone, then coming upon a crossroads outpost where the post office shares space with the general store and gas station, you'll want to take the time to explore Wyoming.

Yellowstone National Park

Sitting astride the Continental Divide, high up in the northern Rockies at the northwest corner of Wyoming, **Yellowstone National Park** is one of the true wonders of the natural world. A veritable greatest hits of Mother Nature, the park is packed full of burbling geysers, magnificent canyons, raging waterfalls, and still-wild wildlife. The country's (and the world's) oldest national park, established in 1872, Yellowstone was first explored by frontiersman John Colter, who passed through in 1808; it's also one of the largest parts of the lower 48 states never to be farmed or fenced.

You probably already know something about what Yellowstone has in store for you: The one essential Yellowstone sight is **Old Faithful Geyser,** in the southwest quarter of the park. One of the world's most famous natural features, Old Faithful is known for its clockwork eruptions, in which thousands of gallons of boiling water are sent over 100 feet into the air, forming a column

Yellowstone's Lower Falls

of steam. Hundreds of people line up around the geyser waiting for it to blow, and rangers are able to predict it with a good deal of accuracy—the visitors center will list the expected times of the day's eruptions, which occur roughly every 90 minutes and last for another two to five minutes. In between eruptions, visit the impressive Old Faithful Visitor Education Center, opened in August 2010, or wander around the other features of the Old Faithful basin. These include a number of other geysers (the Old Faithful area has the greatest concentration in the world), as well as colorful pools and other geothermal features, all linked by well-marked boardwalks and trails along the Firehole River.

the vivid colors of Grand Prismatic Spring in Yellowstone National Park

The other main sight is the **Grand Canyon of the Yellowstone River,** where a pair of powerful waterfalls cascade into a 20-mile-long, half-mile-wide, and 1,000-foot-deep canyon of eroding yellow stone. Parking areas line the north and south rims of the canyon, allowing access to trails along the edge of the gorge. A personal favorite is **Uncle Tom's Trail,** leaving from the south side of the falls. More a staircase than a trail, this route zigzags steeply down the walls of the canyon, bringing you face to face with the falls. Farther along the south rim is Artist's Point, which gives the classic view of the canyon. Also, two "Brink of the Falls" routes lead from the north side down to where the waters plunge.

Along with these two main attractions, there are many more sights to see, so take the time to visit the visitors centers, talk to the rangers, and find out what other wonders await. Covering more than 2.2 million acres, Yellowstone is a big place, plenty big enough to absorb the many tourists who come here during the peak summer season. Whatever you do, don't try to see it all in a day or two; if time is tight, choose one or two places and spend all your time there. Get out of the car, hike a few trails, and enjoy.

Yellowstone Practicalities

The $25 entry fee for each noncommercial vehicle covers seven days and is also good for nearby Grand Teton National Park. (The InterAgency Annual Pass is a better value at around $80—it offers admission to all National Parks and National Historic Sites for an entire family for a full year.) Yellowstone's visitor facilities book up well in advance (sometimes up to a year), so if you want the complete experience, it's best to plan ahead as much as possible. Accommodations are the main thing you ought to sort out as soon as you can, as bed space is at a premium. The first choice is the wonderful **Old Faithful Inn,** next to the famous geyser. Built of split logs and huge boulders and exuding rough-hewn elegance, this delightful inn was completed

One rarely mentioned aspect of life in Yellowstone is the profusion of bison (a.k.a. buffalo) droppings: Everywhere you look—all around the geysers, hot springs, etc.—they've made their mark. And though they may seem placid, bison can be dangerous, so keep your distance.

Note that the Yellowstone visitor season is very short—roads are usually blocked by snow from November until April, May, or even June. US-26 is a year-round alternative through the Grand Tetons and Jackson Hole.

in 1904 and fully renovated in 2005. Rooms in the old lodge, without baths, start at about $67. A newer wing has larger rooms and modern conveniences for around $100–500 a night—some of these rooms have Old Faithful views. Another historic lodge, at Yellowstone Lake, is plusher but architecturally less distinctive. A half dozen other inns, cabins, and motels are scattered around the park, including the still-new **Dunraven Lodge** near the canyon, and the year-round Snow Lodge near Old Faithful, accessible in winter only by tank-like snow cat from West Yellowstone. All rooms are handled through park concessionaire Xanterra (307/344-7311 or 866/439-7375), which also handles reservations for the historic, open-topped Yellow Bus tours and the park's campgrounds, most of which operate on a first-come, first-served basis and tend to fill up by noon daily.

Places to eat include the usual cafeteria-type restaurants at all of the park's hotels and lodges, plus a truly remarkable restaurant at the classic Old Faithful Inn, with a three-story log-cabin dining room and food that's as good as it gets in the national parks.

You'll find gas stations, gift shops, and general stores at just about every road junction in the park. There are ranger stations at most main features and large visitors centers at Mammoth Hot Springs, Old Faithful, and the Canyon. For further information, contact **park headquarters** (307/344-7381).

Cody

Eastern gateway to Yellowstone National Park, and an enjoyable overnight stop in its own right, **Cody** (pop. 9,520) is a self-conscious frontier town and a busy center for local ranching and wood products industries. The outskirts are lined by Wal-Marts, Kmarts, and all the fast-food franchises you could name, but the town center along Sheridan Avenue (US-20) still looks like the Wild West town Cody was built to be.

The annual **Cody Stampede Rodeo** started in 1919 and has been a part of town's 4th of July celebrations ever since, making it the nation's longest-running rodeo. It draws professional cowboys from across the continent. Equally impressive, The **Cody Nite Rodeo** (nightly at 8 PM; $18; 800/207-0744 or 307/587-5155) at the huge rodeo grounds at the west end of town has been held June–September since 1938. Get a seat in the "Buzzard's Roost," close to the chutes where the cowboys mount those bulls and buckin' broncos for this amateur event.

Sitting on the Big Horn Basin plains at the foot of the mountains, Cody was founded in the late 1890s by Wild West showman "Buffalo Bill" Cody, whose name graces most everything in town, including the **Buffalo Bill Historical Center** (daily Mar.–Nov.; Thurs.–Sun. during Dec.–Feb.; $18; 720 Sheridan Ave.; 307/587-4771). One of the country's great museums, and certainly the best in the Wild West, this place tells all you could want to know about the American frontier. The center is divided into five main collections. First stop should be Buffalo Bill's boyhood home, which was moved here from LeClair, Iowa, in 1933; then move on to the Buffalo Bill Museum, which includes a battery of movies and artifacts from his famous Wild West Show, a circus-like extravaganza that toured the world. The Whitney Gallery of Western Art, one of the country's most extensive collections of western art, displays important works by George Catlin, Thomas Moran, Albert Bierstadt, and Frederic Remington, plus some fine contemporary works. Gun freaks will enjoy the Cody Firearms Museum, which displays more than 5,000 historic weapons. Saving the biggest and best for last, the Plains Indian Museum has an amazing collection of art and artifacts created by the diverse Plains Indian peoples, from beadwork dresses to a reconstructed Sioux tepee. Pride of place is given to an extraordinary buffalo robe painted with scenes of the legendary Battle of Little Big Horn.

At the west edge of Cody is **Old Trail Town** (daily mid-May–mid-Sept.; $8; 307/587-5302), a low-key but engaging collection of old buildings moved here from northwestern Wyoming and southern Montana. Wagons, buffalo robes, and other relics are on display. A memorial cemetery holds the remains of Wild West figures, including John Jeremiah "Liver Eating" Johnston, played as Jeremiah Johnson—with no T—by Robert Redford in the 1972 movie named for the man.

Cody Practicalities

You'll find most of Cody's good places to eat on Sheridan Avenue, the main drag. **Silver Dollar Bar and Grill** (1313 Sheridan Ave.; 307/527-7666) serves great burgers and bottles of beer. A block away, the **Proud Cut Saloon** (1227 Sheridan Ave.; 307/527-6905) has a range of sandwiches at lunch and great steaks at dinner. A restaurant and rooms are available at the historic **Irma Hotel** (around $105; 1192 Sheridan Ave.; 800/745-4762 or 307/587-4221), which was built by Buffalo Bill and named for his daughter; it still features a

---

Between Yellowstone and Cody, US-20 drops steeply through lovely **Wapiti Valley**. Teddy Roosevelt supposedly called this area "the most scenic 50 miles in America." Another scenic route, the **Beartooth Highway** (US-212), runs northeast to Red Lodge, Montana, and was rated by Charles Kuralt as "the most beautiful roadway in America."

Though Buffalo Bill gets most of the publicists' ink, another famous Cody figure is the abstract impressionist "action painter" Jackson Pollock, who was born here in 1912.

lovely cherrywood bar given by Queen Victoria, and there's an evening gun-fight on the front porch. Fans of vernacular roadside Americana may want to have a look at the **Buffalo Bill Village** ($100 and up; 1701 Sheridan Ave.; 800/527-5544 ext. 610 or 307/587-5544), which started life in 1914 as a cowboy campout, was developed in the 1930s as a log cabin motor court, and now stands in the heart of Cody amidst the full-service Holiday Inn family resort. The nicest place to stay in Cody may well be the **Big Bear Motel**, near Trail Town ($60–139; 139 W. Yellowstone Ave.; 800/325-7163 or 307/587-3117).

Hwy-120: Meeteetse and Legend Rock

Southeast of Cody, Hwy-120, a prettier alternative to US-20, angles south over the rugged foothill badlands of the Absaroka ("ab-SAR-uh-kuh") Mountains, historic homeland of the Crow Indians but now equal parts cattle ranches and oil wells. Thirty miles along this lonely highway brings you to **Meeteetse** (pop. 327), one of the oldest settlements in central Wyoming and still much the same after 125 years. The broad Greybull River—and an occasional cattle drive—runs right through town, which still retains wooden boardwalks and hitching posts for cowboys' horses.

Besides being wonderfully evocative of an earlier era, Meeteetse also has a great museum documenting diverse aspects of the region's past: the **Charles J. Belden Museum of Western Photography** (Tues.–Sat. 10 AM–3 PM; free; 1947 State St.; 307/868-2423), which holds an extraordinary collection of cowboy photography that includes the first Marlboro Man ads, shot on the nearby Pitchfork Ranch by Mr. Belden, a local rancher and commercial photographer. The building also houses the Meeteetse Museum, which has the stuffed remains of an eight-foot-tall **grizzly bear,** one of the largest ever found in the area.

> Aviator Amelia Earhart was having a cabin built for her near Meeteetse along the Greybull River, but construction stopped in 1937 after she disappeared on her round-the-world flight.

Along with an old but fully stocked general store, tiny Meeteetse has a few restaurants and the **Oasis Motel and RV Park** (around $50 and up; around $20 and up for an RV space; 1702 State St.; 307/868-2551 or 888/868-5270), with RV camping and a Conestoga wagon, right on the Greybull River. The Oasis also owns the Vision Quest Motel (2207 State St.); same rates and same reservation phone numbers.

One of Wyoming's most significant collections of petroglyphs, **Legend Rock** contains over 250 images dating back some 2,000 to 10,000 years, carved into sandstone cliffs in the oil-rich foothills of the Owl Creek Mountains. Legend Rock is administered by **Hot Springs State Park** (538 N. Park St.) in Thermopolis, and you will need a key to a gate and a permit from the State Bath House to view the petroglyphs. It's very hard to get there (follow US-120 for 21 miles from Thermopolis, or 33 miles from Meeteetse, then turn south at the Hamilton Dome turnoff and follow the dirt road for 8.5 miles), but the scene is unforgettable: High above Cottonwood Creek, hundreds of images cover a half-mile long sandstone wall, connecting contemporary visitors with Shoshone Indian ancestors who lived here millennia ago.

Thermopolis

Despite the highfalutin' resonance of its classical-sounding name, **Thermopolis** (pop. 3,009) is a sleepy little retirement town, surrounded by red-rock canyons and centered among a remarkable set of natural hot springs. The land was bought in 1896 from local Shoshone chief Washakie and Arapaho chief Sharp Nose on the understanding that the spring waters be kept open to the public, white and Indian alike. This spring, which flows at a rate of 18,000 gallons of 135°F water daily, was the basis of Wyoming's first state park, **Hot Springs State Park,** which still covers the east bank of the Bighorn River. A state-run bathhouse (daily; free) has showers and changing rooms—you can rent towels and bathing suits for a nominal charge. There are two commercial enterprises in the park—**Hellie's Tepee Pools** and **Star Plunge**—with water slides, saunas, and so on, perfect for families with littler kids.

Across the river in the center of town, the enjoyable **Hot Springs Historical Museum and Cultural Center** (closed Sun.; $4; 700 Broadway St.; 307/864-5183) has a wide-ranging collection of historic photos, farming and oil-drilling implements, and even the cherrywood bar from the Hole-in-the-Wall Saloon where Butch and Sundance supposedly bellied up for a drink or two. The final big draw in Thermopolis—and I mean *big*—is the **Wyoming Dinosaur**

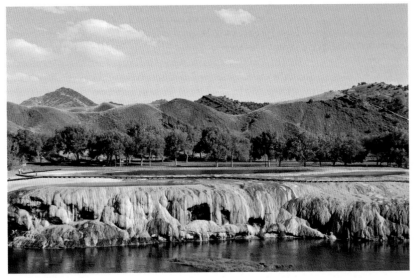

Hot Springs State Park

Center (daily; $10; 100 Carter Ranch Rd.; 307/864-2997 or 800/455-3466), on the east side of town. Follow the green dinosaur footprints from the center of town to a paleontology dig that's open to the public; finds on display include a full T. rex and a triceratops.

velociraptor skeleton at Wyoming Dinosaur Center

Best food in Thermopolis is at **Happy's BBQ,** on the corner of 6th Street and Broadway, next to the Fountain of Youth motel (307/864-2321).

The friendly Thermopolis **visitors center** (307/864-3192 or 800/786-6772), in the same building as the Hot Springs Historical Museum, has more information on the area, including details about the intriguing Legend Rock petroglyphs, north of town.

Wind River Canyon

South of Thermopolis, US-20 winds through **Wind River Canyon,** one of the most memorable drives in a state of memorable drives. The 2,500-foot-deep canyon, with the highway on one side of the broad river and the railroad on the other, reveals millions of years of sedimentary rock. As you drive along heading south, you reach deeper and deeper into the earth; each layer is labeled with signs explaining its geological age and significance, with the oldest layers dating back to the Precambrian era, some 2.5 billion years ago.

Driving along US-20 between the Wind River Canyon and Shoshoni, keep an eye out for the many pronghorn antelope that play on the rolling rangeland.

Due in part to the visual effect of the uplifted sedimentary layers, the river at times gives the illusion of flowing uphill; this may explain why Indians and early explorers thought there were two distinct rivers and called the canyon itself the "Wedding of the Waters." The river still has two distinct names: Upstream from Wind River Canyon, it is called the Wind River; downstream from the canyon, it's called the Bighorn River.

At the south end of the Wind River, Boysen Reservoir, a popular place for fishing and waterskiing, backs up behind Boysen Dam, which was built from 1947 to 1952. The land west of the reservoir forms the 2.2-million-acre **Wind River Indian Reservation,** home to descendants of the Eastern Shoshone and Northern Arapahoe tribes. A woman thought by some to be Sacagawea (the Shoshone guide of Lewis and Clark fame) is buried on the reservation, along the Wind River near Fort Washakie.

Jackson Hole

In winter, Yellowstone is closed to cars, and the only road kept open is US-212 between Gardiner and Cooke City, Montana, at the northern edge of the park.

But if you're here anytime but summer, don't despair: US-26, a very different but still unforgettable route, is open year-round, running south of Yellowstone between Idaho Falls and Casper, through Jackson Hole and the spectacular scenery of Grand Teton National Park.

Climbing up from Idaho Falls along the banks of the Snake River, US-26 crosses into Wyoming on a sinuously scenic route, past cottonwood trees and white-water-running kayakers, before linking up with north–south US-89. The tourist mecca of Jackson Hole, one of the country's most popular "wilderness" destinations, takes its name from the main town, **Jackson** (pop. 9,577), which sits at the center of a broad, mountain-ringed valley. Drawing upward of 35,000 visitors on a summer day, Jackson isn't exactly an idyllic spot, but it has managed to retain its Wild West character, especially in the few blocks around the lively Town Square. Here, false-fronted buildings linked by a raised wooden sidewalk hold upscale boutiques and the wonderfully kitsch likes of the **Million Dollar Cowboy Bar** (25 N. Cache St.; 307/733-2207) on the west side of the square, a huge and always lively hangout with silver dollars implanted in the bar top and real leather saddles instead of bar stools.

Jackson has many very good (and very expensive) restaurants, like the art deco–style **Cadillac Grill** (55 N. Cache; 307/733-3279), which has grilled ahi tuna and similarly sophisticated fare on the Town Square. The Cadillac Grill shares space with Jackson's best burger spot, **Billy's Giant Burgers,** which burger-loving Bill Clinton rated as the best he'd ever tasted. Jackson caters to so many visitors that accommodations, however plentiful, can be booked solid in summer. There's something for everyone here: campgrounds and RV parks, $4,000-a-week dude ranches, B&Bs, and highway motels—including an affordable Motel 6 along US-89, about two miles south of town.

The Jackson Hole area is one of the country's most exclusive winter resorts, with world-class ski areas including **Grand Targhee** (800/827-4433 or 307/353-2300), powder-hound heaven on the Idaho border; and **Jackson Hole Mountain Resort** (888/333-7766 or 307/733-2292), which boasts the longest vertical drop in the United States: an astounding 4,139 feet!

Grand Teton National Park

North of Jackson, south of Yellowstone, the silver peaks of **Grand Teton National Park** cut into the sky, their slopes offering some of the best hiking and mountaineering in the lower 48 states. US-26/89 runs right along the base of the mountains, giving grand views and tempting travelers to stop and explore. West of the main highway, Teton Park Road winds past Jenny Lake, where you can rent a kayak or board a boat ($15/hour or $70/day) and ride across to a short trail that leads up past Hidden Falls to **Inspiration Point,** at the foot of 13,770-foot Grand Teton.

From Grand Teton National Park, US-89 runs north to the heart of Yellowstone National Park.

the Grand Tetons from Snake River Overlook

Details on the abundant hiking, skiing, fishing, and other recreational activities, as well as camping and lodging options, are available by contacting the main Grand Teton National Park **visitors center** (307/739-3600), a mile west of US-26 on Teton Park Road.

Dubois and the National Bighorn Sheep Center

Between Casper and the Grand Tetons, US-26 is a mostly scenic highway, crossing the Continental Divide at 9,658-foot Togwotee Pass before winding along the Wind River through the multicolored badlands that surround the town of **Dubois** (pop. 971; pronounced "dew-BOYS"). A low-key ranching and logging center that's still in its infancy as a tourist destination, Dubois does have one unique attraction: the **National Bighorn Sheep Center** (daily; closed Sun. during winter; $2.50; 307/455-3429 or 888/209-2795), right on US-26 at the west edge of town, documenting the life and times of the thousands of elusive bighorn sheep that congregate in the winter months around Whisky Mountain, south of Dubois. At the center of Dubois, another unique sight is inside historic **Welty's General Store** (free; 113 W. Ramshorn; 307/455-2377), on US-26, where you can see a Colt .44 revolver with the name "Butch Cassidy" carved in the handle; Butch lived and rustled horses here back in the 1880s and in 1890 bought a ranch near Dubois.

On US-26, 18 miles west of Dubois, a roadside monument remembers the work of the "tie hacks" who, from the 1870s until World War II, cut down lodgepole pines to form railroad ties.

There are a few saloons, steakhouses, and fly-fishing shops, and one great place to stay in Dubois: the log-cabin **Twin Pines Lodge** ($95 and up; 218 W. Ramshorn; 800/550-6332 or 307/455-2600), in business since 1934.

Shoshoni: Hell's Half Acre

Named for the Shoshone Indians who once held sway over this part of the Great Plains, the town of **Shoshoni** (pop. 649) sits at the junction of US-20

The Mushroom, Hell's Half Acre, Wyoming.

and US-26, at the southeast edge of the Boysen Reservoir. Though it doesn't look like much if you just race through, Shoshoni has one excellent reason to stop: the **Yellowstone Malt Shop** (502 E. 2nd St.; 307/876-2539), which for years has sold the state's best milk shakes and ice cream floats.

Between Shoshoni and Casper, the only attraction worth mentioning is the odd geology of **Hell's Half Acre,** a 300-acre concentration of grotesquely eroded stone south of US-20 amid the arid badlands landscape. (Scenes in the movie *Starship Troopers* were filmed here in 1996.)

Casper

Like other towns in southern Wyoming, Casper began as a way station on the many frontier trails that followed the North Platte River, first as a ferry crossing (log rafts were run by Salt Lake City–bound Mormons from 1847 to 1852; non-Mormons were charged $1.50) and later toll bridges, culminating with an elaborate plank bridge built by Louis Guinard in 1859. The second-largest city in Wyoming, only slightly smaller than capital city Cheyenne, **Casper** (pop. 55,316) is still dependent upon passing trade. Casper's key location along the I-25 corridor has enabled the local economy to survive the boom-and-bust-and-boom-again variations in its other main industry, oil.

Most of the places of interest in Casper (which was originally spelled Caspar) have to do with the westward migration. Your first stop should be the wonderful **National Historic Trails Interpretive Center,** a cooperative venture between the Bureau of Land Management, the National Historic Trails Center Foundation, and the City of Casper which opened in 2002, just north of I-25 exit 189 (daily in summer, Tues.–Sat. Sept.–Apr.; $4–6; 1501 N. Poplar St.; 307/261-7780). High-tech exhibits are good for younger folks, giving a sight-and-sound tour along the historic Oregon Trail and Pony Express routes, which passed through here on their way west. **Fort Caspar Museum** (daily; $3; 307/235-8462), west of downtown off Hwy-220, is a New Deal–era replica of the original rough log fort and Pony Express station. There's also a reconstruction of the Mormon-operated ferry and displays of pioneer artifacts in the small museum.

While the rest of the city has a definite roughneck feel, downtown Casper is also rich in 1920s Americana, with a pair of great old movie theaters, rusty neon signs, and art deco storefronts, plus one of the country's largest cowboy clothing stores: **Lou Taubert's** (125 E. 2nd St.; 307/234-2500 or 800/447-9378) has over 10,000 pairs of boots and nine floors of blue jeans, rhinestones, and other essential range-riding gear.

Casper was the heart of the oil fields that led to the notorious Teapot Dome scandal of the 1920s, in which Secretary of the Interior Albert Fall went to prison for accepting $400,000 in bribes. It is also the hometown of oil magnate and former vice president Dick Cheney and his high school sweetheart (and wife), Lynne.

Jackalopes 'R' Us

Traveling around the Great Plains, you're bound to come across all sorts of oversized wildlife—giant fish, giant cows, giant bison—plus some more that defy anatomical description. Most of the latter—fur-bearing trout, in particular—are seen primarily on postcards, but at least one species can usually be found mounted on the wall of any self-respecting saloon or taxidermist's shop: the jackalope, Wyoming's "Official State Mythical Creature." So rare that one has never been seen in the wild, the jackalope has the body of a jackrabbit and the horns of an antelope. Dozens of examples are displayed around the Wyoming town of Douglas, with the "world's largest" standing over eight feet head-to-tail in Jackalope Square at 3rd and Center Streets downtown (an even larger one, sometimes wearing a saddle, has been spotted along US-20, a quarter mile west). The enigmatic creature is also celebrated all over Douglas during Jackalope Railroad Days in the middle of June.

The **Pioneer League Casper Ghosts** (307/232-1111) play baseball at community-built Mike Lansing Field, north of I-25 via the Poplar Street exit. A 500-foot home run here would end up in the North Platte River.

East of downtown, one place you really ought to visit is the **Nicolaysen Art Museum and Discovery Center** (closed Mon.; $5; 400 E. Collins St.; 307/235-5247), housed in an imaginatively converted old power plant, along the railroad tracks. The finest contemporary art museum in Wyoming, the Nicolaysen also has a permanent collection of Plains Indian arts and crafts, plus a hands-on art center for children.

Not far from the Nicolaysen museum, the homespun **Cottage Cafe** (116 S. Lincoln St.; 307/234-1157) has good coffees and filling meals for breakfast and lunch. Casper's accommodation options along the I-25 frontage include most of the national chains.

Glenrock: Ayres Natural Bridge

Midway between Casper and Douglas along the south bank of the North Platte River, **Glenrock** (pop. 2,576) was a vital rest stop and supply station on the Oregon and other emigrant trails. Several downtown buildings have endured since its heyday, when Glenrock was known as Deer Creek Station and some 20,000 migrants came through each year, many of them camping overnight at the "rock in the glen" on the west side of town, where a sandstone boulder still holds the names of passing pioneers. Nowadays Glenrock is known for its massive, 800 megawatt coal-fired power plant, one of the largest in the country, and a pair of wind farms intended to generate 100 megawatts of electricity are under construction nearby.

Between Casper and Glenrock, US-26 winds along the river, but between Glenrock and Douglas the old road has been replaced by the I-25 freeway. A dozen miles east of Glenrock, midway to Douglas, turn off I-25 onto Natural Bridge Road and drive five miles south of the freeway to visit one of Wyoming's unsung beauty spots, **Ayres Natural Bridge,** which arches 30 feet above peaceful La Prele Creek, next to a small campground in a pleasant county park.

Douglas

Situated far enough off I-25 to retain its Wild West cowboy character, the enjoyable town of **Douglas** (pop. 6,120) was founded in 1886 across the river

> Douglas's own **KKTY 1470 AM** plays local news, country hits, and Colorado Rockies baseball games.

from Fort Fetterman, which for the previous 25 years had protected traffic on the old Oregon and Bozeman Trails along the North Platte River. The setting of Owen Wister's genre-inventing Western novel *The Virginian* and, more recently, birthplace of that other Wild West icon, the jackalope, Douglas is a quietly picturesque small town with a wild history, and a great place to break your long-distance road trip.

The **Wyoming State Fairgrounds,** along the river at the west end of Center Street, host a livestock-frenzied fair at the end of

1152—Tombstone of George W. Pike

GEORGE W. PIKE

Famous Character of the Early Days in the Wild West

August. The fairgrounds also feature the year-round **Wyoming Pioneer Memorial Museum** (closed Sat. Oct.–May, closed Sun. year-round; free; 307/358-9288), packed full of artifacts from the late 1800s—everything from rifles and a roulette table to fossils and farm implements. It also houses a Sioux-style hide tepee made for the movie *Dances with Wolves.* The wilder side of Douglas history is perhaps most vividly apparent in tombstones in the **cemetery** on the east edge of town at the end of Pine Street, where legendary cattle rustler George Pike is interred beneath an impressive marker that reads, in part:

Underneath this stone in eternal rest sleeps the wildest one of the wayward west.

Lusk

A cattle-ranching and farming center, **Lusk** (pop. 1,567) is the largest town in the least-populated county in the country's least-populated state. It also boasts the only traffic light on US-20 between Douglas, Wyoming, and Chadron, Nebraska. And if those claims to fame don't make you want to stop, the **Stagecoach Museum** (closed Sun.; $2; 322 S. Main St.; 307/334-3444) definitely will, if only to see the sole authentic 1880s Cheyenne-Deadwood

> A marker on the south side of US-20, a mile east of Lusk, stands where US-20 intersects the Texas Trail: In the 1870s over 500,000 head of cattle were driven each year between Fort Worth and the open range of Wyoming and Montana along this route.

Stagecoach—the one Doris Day sang about in *Calamity Jane.* (The only other stagecoach from this legendary route is now in the Smithsonian.) Behind the museum building is another frontier icon—a one-room schoolhouse—and along US-20 at the east edge of town, a plaque points out a redwood water tower dating from 1886, when steam locomotives still chugged across the plains.

Lusk also has a good range of motels, including the **Covered Wagon Motel** (around $100 and up; 730 S. Main St.; 888/338-2836 or 307/334-2836).

Guernsey: Oregon Trail

A worthwhile detour from Douglas or Lusk via I-15 and US-26 takes you 40-plus miles south to the town of **Guernsey** (pop. 1,147) on the North Platte River, where you can visit two of the most evocative Oregon Trail historic sites. The Oregon Trail passed through along the south bank of the river, and a well-signed Guernsey State Park, a mile south of town via Wyoming Avenue, holds the best surviving set of Oregon Trail

Oregon Trail wagon tracks across Guernsey

wagon ruts, cut shoulder-deep in the soft sandstone. Nearby is a small obelisk marking the grave of an unfortunate pioneer, and three miles to the southeast along the same road, **Register Cliff** is carved with the names of over a thousand pioneers and explorers, many dating back to 1840–1860, the heyday of the trail. **Fort Laramie National Historic Site,** another frontier landmark, is a dozen miles east of Guernsey via US-26.

NEBRASKA

In its 430-mile or so trek across Nebraska, US-20 passes through a surprising variety of landscapes. In the west, the highway skirts the edge of the huge and desolate **Sand Hills,** where North America's largest system of sand dunes underlies a grassy pastoral scene. Across the midsection, the road runs parallel to the broad **Niobrara River,** one of the few rivers in the Great Plains not blocked behind a dam, before reaching the bluffs above the Missouri River.

One of the last reaches of the country to be settled and domesticated, northern Nebraska is still sparsely populated and looks like the Great Plains are *supposed* to look. Towns are few and far between, and come and go in the proverbial blink of an eye; the rolling ranch lands are marked every mile or so by spinning Aermotor windmills pumping up water for wandering cattle herds, while historical plaques point out the sites where, barely a century ago, cowboys rode and Indians did battle with the U.S. Cavalry. Besides being rich in Wild West history—and in prehistoric fossil beds—the region has a strong

STATE
OF
NEBRASKA.

literary tradition, thanks to writers such as Mari Sandoz and John G. Neihardt. All in all, few corners of the country pay back time spent with as much interest as does northern Nebraska—hard to believe, perhaps, but true.

Harrison and Agate Fossil Beds National Monument

Just over the Wyoming border, the tiny town of **Harrison** (pop. 251; elev. 4,878) is an attractive wide spot in the road located near the highest point in the state. Though the town is tiny, local appetites are anything but, as hinted at by the huge (28-ounce) Coffeeburgers and silky milk shakes that once filled the menu at Main Street's landmark Sioux Sundries; the drug store has since closed, but the spirit of old-time hospitality is kept alive at the **Harrison House Hotel** and weekend-only restaurant, in an 1888 building at 1st and Main Streets (308/668-2166). Outside of town, on the banks of the Niobrara River 23 miles south of Harrison, the **Agate Fossil Beds National Monument** (daily; free; 308/668-2211 or 308/436-9760) contains the 19- to 21-million-year-old remains of bison-sized pigs, twin-horned proto-rhinos, and other vanished Miocene-era creatures. The acres of grassland here are good for wildflowers and bird-watching, even if you aren't fascinated by old bones. If you are interested in paleontology, the Agate Fossil Beds National Monument and the Hudson-Meng Bison Bonebed in nearby Crawford are both stops along what is being marketed as the "Fossil Freeway" collection of historic sites in Nebraska and South Dakota.

The US-20 highway alignment through Harrison was still unpaved as recently as 1941.

Fort Robinson

Thirty miles east from the Wyoming border, **Fort Robinson State Park** (308/665-2900) was established in 1874 to control the members of the Red Cloud and Pine Ridge Sioux Indian tribes. Now a state park, and planted with groves of mature trees where 100 years ago all was grassland prairie, Fort Robinson has perhaps the most tragic and uncomfortable history of all the many old forts on the Wild West frontier: This is where, in 1877, the unarmed Sioux chief Crazy Horse was stabbed to death with bayonets while in the custody of the U.S. Army. In 1879, the last of the Cheyenne under Morning Star (a.k.a. Chief Dull Knife) escaped from prison and were killed in battle here rather than be taken away to a reservation in Oklahoma.

Knowing this history, it can be hard to take Fort Robinson as the enjoyable respite it is today. The hundreds of hardwood trees make it an oasis on the generally treeless plains, and the whitewashed wooden barracks, many now converted to cultural centers and museums, give it the air of a college campus—especially on summer weekends, when the park turns into a living history museum, complete with cookouts, carriage rides, and evening melodramas.

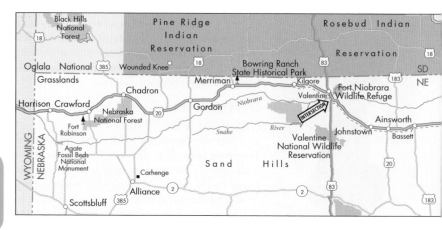

The only part of the park open year-round is the **Fort Robinson Museum** ($2; 308/665-2919) in the old headquarters building, with full displays on the fort's history, plus walking-tour maps of the entire post. Accommodations are offered in the officers' quarters, and there are many good camping spots.

Crawford

Three miles east of Fort Robinson, **Crawford** (pop. 997) has settled into a sedate life as a ranching and farming center. Pines and cottonwoods line the White River at the foot of the weirdly eroded Legend Buttes, making a pretty scene. Even prettier are the **Oglala National Grasslands,** which start six miles north of Crawford via Hwy-2 and occupy nearly 100,000 acres along the Nebraska/Wyoming/South Dakota borders. The grasslands are home to hawks, eagles, and antelope and are highlighted by the eerie landscape of **Toadstool Geological Park,** where ancient fossils can be found amongst weirdly eroded figures. The grasslands also protect an archaeological site known as the **Hudson-Meng Bison Bone Bed** (308/432-0300), a shallow ar-

Fort Robinson State Park

goldenrod,
state flower of Nebraska

royo holding the enigmatic remains of over 600 bison spread over an area the size of a football field. Displays on the site include stone tools and arrowheads dating from approximately 10,000 years ago and a small garden growing native, pre-conquest crops.

Chadron: Museum of the Fur Trade

The largest town in northwest Nebraska, **Chadron** (pop. 5,851) sits at the northern edge of the Sand Hills region, bounded by pine forests to the south and the Pine Ridge Sioux Reservation to the north, across the South Dakota border. The highway frontage along US-20 isn't especially inviting, but the two-block town center preserves its turn-of-the-20th-century character with sandstone and brick-fronted buildings along the south side of the still-used railroad tracks.

Besides giving a good look at the diverse heritage of the Sand Hills region, Chadron makes a handy base for trips north to the Pine Ridge lands and the Black Hills of South Dakota, or south to the marvelous Carhenge. Motels include a Best Western and a Super 8, but the most characterful place to stay is **The Olde Main Street Inn** ($65–95; 115 Main St.; 308/432-3380). Part old railroad hotel, part cozy B&B, the inn has rooms, a popular restaurant and saloon downstairs, and Chadron's only espresso machine. (The hotel has a historical dark side as well: In 1890, General Nelson Miles stayed at this hotel while his soldiers massacred Sioux women and children at Wounded Knee.) Down the street, there's frequent live music and general good times to be had at **Wrecker's Roadhouse** (164 Main St.; 308/432-6773).

Even if you're just passing through, don't miss one of the great stops on the Great Plains, the excellent **Museum of the Fur Trade** (June–Sept. daily, by appointment rest of the year; $5; 308/432-3843), on US-20 three miles east of downtown Chadron. One of the great small museums in the United States, this privately run collection focuses on the material culture of the North

In 1893, Chadron's early boosters found a perfect way to get their town in the news: They sponsored a 1,000-mile horse race from Chadron to Chicago, which made front pages across the country. A plaque in front of the black-and-white Blaine Hotel, a block east of Main Street, marks the start of the race.

Mt. Rushmore, Crazy Horse, and Carhenge

Three of the nation's most distinctive outdoor sculptures stand along US-385 within a manageable drive from US-20. One is perhaps the best-known artwork in the United States: the giant presidential memorial at Mt. Rushmore. Roughly 100 miles north from Chadron, at the far eastern side of the beautiful Black Hills, Mt. Rushmore is graced by the 60-foot heads of four U.S. Presidents—Washington, Jefferson, Lincoln, and Teddy Roosevelt—carved into a granite peak. It's equal parts impressive monument and kitschy Americana, and one of those places you really have to see to believe.

On the way to Mt. Rushmore, be sure to stop and see the ambitious Crazy Horse Memorial, a work-in-progress along US-385 four miles north of Custer, South Dakota, which, when completed, will be around 560 feet tall and 640 feet long—10 times the size of Mt. Rushmore.

Another newer, less-famous monument to America sits in a flat field off US-385, outside the town of Alliance, 62 miles south of Chadron. Built in 1987 as part of a local family reunion, Carhenge is a giant-sized replica of the famous Druid ruin,

Stonehenge; this one, however, is built entirely out of three dozen American cars, stacked on top of one another to form a semicircular temple.

American frontier. Its extensive displays bring to life the first few centuries of interaction between Native Americans and Europeans. Besides giving the overall historical context of the fur trade and its many related enterprises, the collection emphasizes the day-to-day realities of life on the Great Plains in the 18th and 19th centuries. Walls decked with weapons and bottles of whiskey (from the Americans), rum (from the English), and brandy (from the French) document the better-known aspects, but what captures your attention are the little things: packs of playing cards, a checkerboard—even a waterproof parka made out of seal intestines by the Inuit.

Gordon: Mari Sandoz Country

The tiny town of **Gordon** (pop. 1,612), midway between Merriman and Chadron, is a typical northwestern Nebraska ranching town with a strong connection to the "The Story Catcher," Mari Sandoz (1896–1966), whose many books document the lives and times of the surrounding Sand Hills region. Sandoz, who wrote about growing up on a nearby ranch in her first book, the haunting classic *Old Jules,* captured the spirit and history of the Great Plains in her many works of fiction and nonfiction, all of which are available in the **Mari Sandoz Room** (closed Sun.; free; 117 Main St.; 308/282-9972), north of US-20 beyond the grain elevators and railroad tracks at the center of town. The Sandoz museum, which shares space with the Ad-Pad stationery store, has extensive displays of her personal effects and free pamphlets describing a driving tour of Sandoz-related sites in the area. There's another, more municipal-feeling museum dedicated to Mari Sandoz and her stories on the campus of Chadron State College (free; 308/432-6401).

> In north-central Nebraska, an interesting radio alternative is the commercial-free music and news broadcast from the Pine Ridge reservation on **KILI 90.1 FM,** "The Voice of the Lakota Nation."

Gas stations line the US-20 frontage in Gordon, and the one-stop **Hacienda Motel** (605 W. US-20; 308/282-0075) has rooms and a popular restaurant and bar.

Merriman

East of Gordon, US-20 winds along the northern edge of the Sand Hills, coming within a few miles of the South Dakota border. The town of **Merriman** (pop. 128) may not look like much, but it does mark the turnoff north to the nearby **Arthur Bowring Sandhills Ranch State Historical Park** (daily; $4 per car; 308/684-3428), a working cattle ranch preserved pretty much as it was at the turn of the 20th century. The site is lovely, with a sod house surrounded (in springtime, at least) by rolling green hills. A modern visitors center has displays on windmills and other facts of Sand Hills life, plus biographical displays on the politically powerful Bowring family, who lived and worked here from 1895 until 1985. To get there, head 1.3 miles north of town on Hwy-61, then two miles northeast following good signs.

> In Merriman, a block south of US-20, a roadside display shows the many different cattle brands used by Sand Hills ranches.

Between Merriman and Valentine, US-20 passes through flyspeck former railroad towns including Kilgore (pop. 77), Crookston (pop. 69), and Cody (pop. 154).

INTERSECTION

Valentine marks the junction with US-83, **The Road to Nowhere** (see page 199). The full route is described on pages 174–231.

Johnstown

In the village of **Johnstown** (pop. 64), 40 miles southeast of Valentine and eight miles west of Ainsworth, a block of wooden storefronts and boardwalks

Kilgore marks the dividing line between central and mountain time zones; adjust your clocks and watches accordingly.

was gussied up as a backdrop for a TV production of Willa Cather's *O Pioneers!* Behind the contrived facades you'll find a dusty old general store and a beer bar and pool hall complete with backyard privy.

On Norden Road, 16 miles north of Johnstown, the Nature Conservancy protects the nearly 60,000-acre **Niobrara Valley Preserve** (402/722-4440), which has both sand hills and riparian ecosystems stretching west to the Niobrara reserve on the outskirts of Valentine. Self-guided trails wind through the preserve past a slowly expanding herd of some 500 bison, and early spring sees the annual migration of sandhill cranes, some 500,000 of whom rest here and at sites along the North Platte River before continuing north to Canada.

Ainsworth

Roughly the midway point of US-20's long cruise across Nebraska, **Ainsworth** (pop. 1,728) has something of an identity problem, if its slogans ("Welcome to the Middle of Nowhere" and "Where the Sandhills Meet the Niobrara") are any guide. Ainsworth also calls itself the state's "Country Music Capital" and hosts a popular concert and festival in early August. Ainsworth's **Middle of Nowhere Festival,** held in June, is celebrated with a Main Street parade, a Wild West–style trail ride, and a black powder rendezvous—where living-history fans re-enact the muzzle-loading, fur-trapping frontier era. Whenever you come, eat big burgers at **Big John's,** along US-20 (1110 E. 4th St.; 402/387-0500).

windmills in Ainsworth

The grounds of Ainsworth's **Brown County Historical Museum** preserve the weather-beaten shell of a tiny old filling station, with a vintage Phillips 66 pump, right on US-20.

O'Neill

East of Ainsworth, US-20 runs through an especially scenic section of the Sand Hills around the artsy hamlet of Bassett before following the Elkhorn River to the town of O'Neill, 66 miles downstream. Nebraska's official "Irish Capital," **O'Neill** (pop. 3,705) hosts a very popular St. Patrick's Day parade and celebration (the town paints shamrocks on the side of the police station and at the intersection of US-20 and US-281). It also has a fascinating history: The town was founded in 1880 by Irish settlers led by John O'Neill, who commanded a brigade of black infantrymen during the Civil War and afterward became involved in the Fenian invasions of still-British Canada.

Northeast Nebraska

Because it's a fascinating part of the country, fairly detailed coverage has been directed at the places along US-20 across most of northern Nebraska. The same cannot be said of Nebraska's far northeast quarter, but there are a couple of interesting detours.

Six miles north of US-20 via Hwy-59, from a well-signed junction two miles west of the tiny village of Royal (pop. 63), you can watch paleontologists at work uncovering giant fossils at **Ashfall Fossil Beds State Historical Park** (daily; $5 plus $4 park entry permit; 402/893-2000). Unusual for a fossil bed, the skeletons here are preserved completely intact because the original residents—including prehistoric herds of rhinoceros, camels, and saber-toothed deer—got caught in a volcanic eruption some 12 million years ago. Since the bones haven't been disturbed, you can get a clear sense of the creatures' size and the sheer numbers of their populations around a prehistoric watering hole.

If you want to learn more about the fascinating human histories and cultures of the Great Plains, head south of US-20 across the Winnebago and Omaha Indian Reservations to the tiny town of **Bancroft,** where the **John G. Neihardt Center** (daily; free; 888/777-4667 or 402/648-3388) exhibits the personal collection of Nebraska's poet laureate and writer of the Native American classic *Black Elk Speaks.*

> Nearly completed after decades of negotiation and hard labor, the 321-mile-long **Cowboy Trail** is the nation's longest rail-to-trail conversion, following the crushed gravel bed of the old Chicago and Northwestern Railroad along US-20 almost all the way across northern Nebraska. Though the 2011 floods damaged some sections in the east, the trail is open and waiting for your visit all the way from O'Neill to Chadron, with especially nice sections around Valentine.

IOWA

US-20 cuts straight across the midsection of Iowa between the Missouri and the Mississippi Rivers, running along the invisible border that divides the flat, agricultural tableland that distinguishes the northern half of the state from the more heavily industrialized south. The first industry here was lead mining in the 1840s, but the predominant activity these days is livestock raising. Cows and pigs feed on the abundant corn that grows in fields all along the highway. Popcorn is also a major crop.

More than on any other section of its cross-country trek, US-20 across Iowa has been "upgraded" into a fast four-lane freeway, so you may well want to consider alternative routes like old US-30, which preserves some fine stretches of the historic **Lincoln Highway,** the country's first transcontinental road.

Sioux City

The honey-producing and hog-butchering center of **Sioux City** (pop. 82,684) is not most people's idea of a vacation treat, but it does offer a few diversions to the road-tripping traveler. Grain elevators and huge brick warehouses fill the riverfront district, an immaculately restored City Hall dominates downtown, and the gorgeous brick and glass-block **Sioux City**

> Over 86 percent of Iowa is cultivated farmland—the highest percentage of any U.S. state.

Art Center (daily; free; 712/279-6272) at 2nd and Nebraska includes pieces by Grant Wood, Salvador Dali, David Hockney, and James McNeill Whistler. Downtown Sioux City has recently been enhanced by the move here of the **Sioux City Public Museum** (daily; free; 607 4th St.; 712/279-6174), which fills a nicely converted former JCPenney store with comprehensive and engaging displays tracing the Native American, pioneer, and agricultural histories of the area. A select few artifacts are also on display in the museum's previous premises, an 1890s mansion a mile north of downtown (2901 Jackson St.).

Lewis and Clark buffs will also want to stop south of Sioux City at the **Sergeant Floyd Monument Historic Marker,** where a 100-foot stone obelisk marks the place where expedition member Sgt. Charles

Sergeant Floyd Monument

Floyd—the Corps of Discovery's only fatality—died of appendicitis in August 1804, two months after setting off from St. Louis. Besides the historical homage, the site offers a great panorama of the Missouri River. Fact collectors might want to know that this little-known marker was the first official National Historic Landmark in the United States.

Sioux City's favorite daughters were the identical twin sisters and rival advice columnists Ann Landers and Abigail "Dear Abby" Van Buren.

Sioux City Practicalities

Part of the general renaissance of mid-sized American downtowns, the newly renovated two-block section of Sioux City known as **Fourth Street Historic District,** just east of the railroad yards around the intersection of 4th and Court Streets, boasts a large selection of restaurants, brewpubs,

© AVALON TRAVEL

SIOUX CITY EXPLORERS

Sioux City's unaffiliated Northern League baseball team, the **Explorers,** plays throughout the summer in modern Lewis & Clark Park ($5–11; 712/277-WINS). Games are broadcast on **KSCJ 1360 AM.**

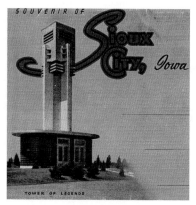

live-music clubs, and specialty shops in a restored commercial district built between 1889 and 1915, many in the Richardson Romanesque style. Just south of historic 4th Street, dine on delicious hot dogs at the beloved **Milwaukee Weiner House** (309 Pearl St.; 712/277-3449).

Away from the historical district, another long-standing local favorite, **Green Gables Restaurant** (1800 Pierce St.; 712/258-4246), a half mile north of downtown, has bountiful, cheap food and very good desserts.

The best in-town accommodation option is probably the pleasant, clean and modern **Stoney Creek Inn** (around $90 and up; 300 3rd St.; 800/659-2220 or 712/234-1100), and the usual chains line the I-29 exits north and south of town.

Sac City and Rockwell City

East of Sioux City, US-20 is pretty much four-lane freeway all the way, racing past acres of farmland and occasional towns. **Sac City** (pop. 2,220) is one of the few places along this stretch where the road is still old-school two-lane, and the town itself seems to want to preserve its past, with a log cabin and preserved Chautauqua Building along US-20 and a small historical museum on Main Street. It also has the nicely maintained **Sac City Motel** (103 Ash Ave.; 712/662-7109), right on US-20.

Twenty miles farther east, in **Rockwell City** (pop. 1,709, "The Golden Buckle on the Corn Belt"), the Leist Oil Company (705 High St.; 712/297-8631) has an incredible collection of old neon and enameled metal roadside signs advertising cars, car parts, soda pop, and sundry other things. Downtown also has a nice old Carnegie Library, a railroad station, and some nifty little shops, well worth a few minutes of wandering.

The Lincoln Highway in Iowa

Iowa may not be everybody's idea of a vacation destination, but fans of old highways are in for a treat here: The state has some of the best-preserved remnants of the nation's first cross-country route, the Lincoln Highway. Running between New York and San Francisco, the Lincoln Highway was the main transcontinental road from its opening in 1915 until 1927, when it was converted to the less-inspiring US-30, which, improvements notwithstanding, it still is today. Much of the original alignment survives, especially in small towns, and the old road makes a fascinating alternative across the state.

Thanks to its many dedicated devotees, the old route is well-marked all across Iowa—just keep an eye out for the red, white, and blue blazes, and the giant "L." Two of the many evocative sites on the Lincoln Highway in Iowa are in the midsection, be-tween Ames and Cedar Rapids. The city of **Belle Plaine** (pop. 2,534), for example, has hardly changed since its 1915 heyday, and in the town of **Tama** (pop. 2,877) a historic bridge, with the words Lincoln Highway spelled out in the concrete guardrails, has been preserved as a river-side park, on 5th Street a block west of the US-30 bypass.

Fort Dodge

Founded in 1850 to protect settlers from roving bands of Sauk and Black Hawk Indians, **Fort Dodge** (pop. 25,206) is today a sleepy Midwestern town, economically dependent upon local farms, gypsum wallboard plants, and a huge Friskies cat food factory. Amid many state-ly homes on the south side of downtown, one

place really worth a look is the **Blanden Memorial Art Museum** (closed Mon. and Sun.; free; 920 3rd Ave. S.; 515/573-2316). Housed inside a grand neoclassical 1930s building, the collections of "Iowa's Oldest Museum" include examples of pre-Columbian pottery, Renaissance sculpture, and Japanese prints. Modern paintings include works by people you wouldn't expect to find in the middle of the Midwest—Max Beckmann, Marc Chagall, and Rufino Tamayo, to name three—along with works by Grant Wood and other Iowa artists.

The famous **Cardiff Giant**, a 10-foot-tall "petrified man" supposedly un-earthed in New York in 1869, was thought by experts to be the body of a prehistoric man. However, the figure, which was kept on prominent display by showman P. T. Barnum for the next 35 years, was later proven to be a hoax, carved from a slab of gypsum quarried at Fort Dodge. A duplicate is on display at the **Fort Museum and Frontier Village** (daily mid-Apr.–mid-Oct.; $6; 515/573-4231) along US-20 on the southwest edge of town.

Cedar Falls and Waterloo

For the eastern half of its run across Iowa, US-20 has been "upgraded" to fast, four-lane freeway most of the way between Dubuque and **Cedar Falls,** a historic industrial town founded in 1845 along the Cedar River. Now home to the University of Northern Iowa, Cedar Falls (pop. 39,260) preserves the remnants of its manufacturing heritage and has some surprisingly upscale bistros tucked away in its sleepy but tidy downtown district. For die-hard road-food types, there is a vintage **Maid-Rite** diner (116 E. 4th St.; 319/277-9748), serving up classic Iowa-style "loose meat sandwiches" in the small industrial section of downtown "CF." Also good, and one of the key forces driving the re-awakening of downtown Cedar Falls, is the **Cup of Joe,** a 1950s-style chrome diner right downtown (102 Main St.; 319/277-1596), whose strong coffee is guaranteed to revive even the most exhausted road-tripper.

Waterloo is worth a look if you can be here on Memorial Day weekend, when vintage car enthusiasts from around the Midwest participate in the **Fourth Street Cruise.**

For a place to stay in Cedar Falls, check out the lovely **Blackhawk Hotel** ($95 and up; 115 Main St.; 800/488-4295 or 319/277-1161), which has a great lobby and oodles of charm.

Downstream from Cedar Falls, and similarly bypassed by the modern US-20 freeway, **Waterloo** (pop. 68,406) is a bigger and busier city, with an almost urban feel and an unexpected ethnic diversity, thanks in particular to the estimated 3,000 Bosnian Muslim refugees who were resettled here by the U.S. government after escaping the genocidal 1990s wars in the Balkans. Waterloo also has a very good museum, the **Grout Museum of History and Science** (closed Mon. and Sun.; $10; 503 South St.; 319/234-6357). Despite the name, it's a general science and history museum—not a collection of great tile-setting materials!

Memorial Day is especially significant in Waterloo, since this was the hometown of the "fighting Sullivan brothers," five young men who were all killed at the World War II Battle of Guadalcanal. The U.S. Navy has named a series of ships after them.

Though it now employs less than half the 25,000 workers it did at its 1960s peak, Waterloo is also home to a massive **John Deere Tractor** assembly plant on the outskirts of town, which is open for free tours (Mon.–Fri. only; 3500 E. Donald St.; 319/292-7697). There's also a small shop where you can stock up on their trademark caps and souvenirs.

Quasqueton: Cedar Rock

Midway between Waterloo and Dyersville, the tiny town of **Quasqueton** (pop. 554) holds **Cedar Rock,** a wonderful riverside house completed in 1950 by architect Frank Lloyd Wright for local-boy-done-good businessman Lowell Walter, who got rich by developing and patenting a method of sealing highway surfaces. Walter died in 1981, and his wife, Agnes, donated it to the state. It is now a state park. Cedar Rock is one of seven houses Wright built in Iowa, and one of only 17 of the 1,000-plus houses Wright built that he "signed" with a signature tile. Cedar Rock is an excellent and complete example of his "Usonian" ideals, and everything in the house—from the soaring roof, the smooth flow of interior space, and the signature hearth, right down to the designs of the carpets and cutlery—embodies Wright's idealized vision of middle-class American houses, designed for simple and stylish living in close accord with nature.

Carved into a limestone ridge overlooking a bend in the Wapsipinicon River, Cedar Rock is five miles south of US-20 and surrounded by acres of rolling woodland. The house and grounds are now owned and managed by the state of Iowa and are open in summer only for guided tours (Thurs.–Sun.; free; 319/934-3572).

Dyersville: The Field of Dreams

"If you build it, they will come. . . ." Ever since the movie *Field of Dreams* came out in 1989, some 65,000 people have flocked each year to **Dyersville** (27 miles west of Dubuque) to reenact the fairy tale baseball movie, major scenes from which were filmed just outside of town. Acres of cornfield surround the rather municipal-looking diamond, where people can play for free. Though privately owned, the attraction is open daily April–November; to get there, take Hwy-136 north from US-20, then follow signs northeast along 3rd Avenue and Field of Dreams Road for about 3.5 miles from US-20.

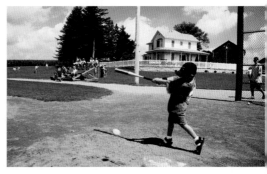

Field of Dreams

Considering it's such a small town, Dyersville has a lot in store. Besides the Field of Dreams, the town boasts one of only a handful of Catholic basilicas in the United States (St. Francis Xavier, that can't-miss gothic pile in the center of town). The **National Farm Toy Museum** (daily; $5; 1110 16th Ave.; 877/475-2727 or 563/875-2727), right off US-20, has over 30,000 miniature tractors and plows showcasing 100 years of toys—from horse-drawn wooden ones to die-cast modern ones—many of them made here in Dyersville by the Ertl Toy Company, which has moved most of its operations overseas.

INTERSECTION

Dubuque marks the junction with our road trip along **The Great River Road** (see page 255). The route is described on pages 232–309.

ILLINOIS

US-20 angles across northern Illinois from the Mississippi River to Lake Michigan, bringing you from the unglaciated scenery of the Driftless Region to the towering city of **Chicago** in less than 200 miles. The western stretches pass through hill-and-valley regions where water power and mineral deposits were harnessed by early industry. Especially around **Galena,** the old two-lane road is still in use, climbing onto stony ridges, then dropping into hardwood-forested valleys across the undulating region that stretches east from the Iowa border. This stretch of old road, officially named and signed as the General Grant Highway, has as great a variety of barns and grain bins as anywhere in the country. However, there's considerable pressure to widen and "improve" it into a four-lane freeway (authorized for completion by 2012), so enjoy it while you can.

Galena

If ever there's a place where you can truly step back in time, **Galena** (pop. 3,429) is it: Pass through the floodgates that protect the town from the namesake river (and the US-20 highway), and it's like entering Brigadoon. Spawned by Wisconsin's mid-19th-century lead-mining rush, Galena became the social and cultural capital of the Upper Mississippi basin. In the 1840s, while Chicago was still a mean collection of tents in a swamp around Fort Dearborn, and the Twin Cities were but a trading post in the woods around Fort Snelling, Galena was producing upwards of 75 percent of the world's lead, and the town was filled with bankers, merchants, and speculators who built mansions, hotels, and emporiums stuffed with fine goods and furnishings from around the world. This part of the Driftless Region saw some of the greatest wealth and commerce of the upper Mississippi, with Galena alone higher in population—some 15,000 lived here during the Civil War—than the entire Minnesota Territory.

From the end of November to the beginning of March, the American bald eagle nests along the middle and upper Mississippi. The best place to catch sight of one is below any of the dams, where turbulence keeps the river from icing over and fish injured or stunned by the dams make easy prey for the great bird.

But the California gold rush, played-out lead mines, a river silting up from miner-induced erosion, and a national economic panic all drove Galena to become a handsome ghost town that nobody bothered to tear down. For 100 years it slumbered, but beginning in the 1980s Galena was resurrected as a quaint tourist town. The brick warehouses were converted into shops and galleries, and anything but the most subtle, hand-carved signage was banned: In Galena, preserving the historical complexion of the streetscape isn't just a good idea, it's the law. The outskirts, especially along the US-20 frontage, are fairly typical roadside sprawl, and there are still a few everyday businesses in the historic core (including a funeral parlor and a large and busy metal foundry), but the overall feel is of a long-ago era. Even the innumerable galleries and shops selling T-shirts and "collectibles" can't spoil the remarkable effect of the place. One essential: Park the car and *stroll*.

Besides the integrity of its mid-19th century buildings, Galena is famous as the town that saw a local store clerk win both the Civil War and the presidency. The modest **Ulysses S. Grant Home** (Wed.–Sun. 9 AM–4:45 PM except major holidays; $4 donation; 815/777-3310) sits up Bouthillier Street in a quiet residential neighborhood across the river from downtown. Given to the general by a grateful group of local Republicans, the house is now a state historic site restored to the period immediately preceding Grant's move to the White House. A small museum behind the house traces Grant's life, from the Civil War to the presidency to his burial in Grant's Tomb.

Commander of the Union Army and President of the United States,
1822–1885

Ulysses S. Grant

Galena Practicalities

Even if you're blind to Galena's manifold aesthetic and historical delights, you'll probably enjoy its wide variety of food and lodging options—the clearest proof of the town's popularity with tourists. The downside of this is that most of the longstanding local cafés have given way to knickknack boutiques and fancy bistros. Unless you're staying at a B&B, the place to get a good breakfast is a half mile west of downtown along US-20, at **Emmy Lou's** (815/777-4732). There is, fortunately, still one great old downtown place for a good, fairly cheap, and always cheerful dinner: the **Log Cabin** (201 N. Main St.; 815/777-0393). Galena's oldest restaurant, with a great big green-and-red sign that predates the town's anti-neon ordinance, the Log Cabin is also known as "The House of Plenty" and has been serving up a mix of industrial-strength Greco-Italian food, steaks, and seafood since 1935. Galena also has a pair of great pizza places: **Cannova's** (247 Main St.; 815/777-3735) and **Procento's** (105 Franklin St.; 815/777-1640).

There are some 60-odd hotels, guest homes, and historic inns here in "the B&B capital of the Midwest." The central **DeSoto House** ($150 and up; 230

common blue violet,
state flower of Illinois

S. Main St.; 815/777-0090) was U. S. Grant's headquarters during his 1868 presidential campaign; the entire place was tastefully modernized during an $8 million renovation back in 1986. Smaller and perhaps more relaxing, the friendly **Farmer's Guest House** ($125 and up; 334 Spring St.; 815/777-3456) is also right downtown. If you're just passing through, the cheapest decent sleep is at the **Grant Hills Motel** (around $89; 9372 E. US-20; 815/777-2116 or 877/421-0924) east of town.

The **Galena/Jo Daviess County Convention and Visitors Bureau** operates an excellent visitors center (877/444-5850 or 800/747-9377), across the river via a pedestrian-only bridge, in the old Illinois Central Railroad depot at the base of Bouthillier Street. Stacks of brochures cover everything from accommodations to bike tours. This is also the best place to park the car, as spaces are at a premium in the often-crowded downtown area.

Galena is also a part of our **Great River Road** trip. The journey along the mighty Mississippi is covered on pages 232–309.

Freeport

Midway between Galena and Rockford, the oddly named town of **Freeport** (pop. 25,638) is neither a port nor even near any body of water. According to the WPA *Guide to Illinois,* the name was bestowed by Elizabeth Baker, the wife of the community's founder, William "Tutty" Baker, to satirize his fondness for providing free river ferry passage and even free room and board to passersby.

There's no free lunch here today, but Freeport does offer at least one good reason to stop: the **Alber Ice Cream Parlor** (126 E. Douglas St.; 815/232-7099), two blocks north of the US-20 Business Loop. Enjoy a creamy, cool milk shake or sundae, then step next

The multinational corporation Kraft Foods got its start in **Stockton, Illinois,** and thanks to the three large cheese plants along US-20, Illinois is the top-ranked Swiss cheese producer in the United States.

Jane Addams (1860–1935), founder of Chicago's reform-minded Hull House and winner of the 1931 Nobel Peace Prize, was born and is buried in the town of Cedarville, six miles north of Freeport.

door to the small park, where an oddly distorted statue marks the site of the second **Lincoln-Douglas debate,** held here on August 27, 1858. A plaque quotes both men equally, with Lincoln's "This government cannot endure permanently half-slave and half-free" opposing Douglas saying, "I am not for the dissolution of the Union under any circumstance."

Rockford

Spreading haphazardly along the leafy banks of the Rock River, **Rockford** (pop. 152,871) is a big, somewhat sprawling, post-industrial city five miles west of the busy I-90 toll road from Chicago. US-20 bypasses the down-at-heel downtown area that, if the denizens wore more hats, would look like a film set on Main Street of

industrial America circa 1949. Unfortunately, many of the classy office buildings and storefronts here have been abandoned in favor of anonymous office parks and shopping malls closer to the I-90 corridor.

North of downtown, along the west bank of the river and away from the frantic highways, one great place to check out (especially if you have creature-loving youngsters with you!) is the **Burpee Museum of Natural History** (daily; $8; 737 N. Main St.; 815/965-3433), where an entire floor of paleontology exhibits is highlighted by the skeleton of a 21-foot-tall, 65-million-year-old T. rex called "Jane."

a friend of Jane's: a Thescelosaurus at the Burpee Museum of Natural History

After exploring Rockford's nooks and crannies, including many nice parks, reward yourself with lunch or dinner at one of Illinois's great road-food haunts, **Der Rathskeller** (1132 Auburn St.; 815/963-2922), off Main Street a mile north of downtown Rockford. Since 1931, this Teutonic institution has been serving up skillets of sausage and potatoes, corned beef sandwiches, and very good desserts. If you'd prefer something a bit more liquid, hoppy, and malty, try the **Carlyle Brewing** pub (215 E. State St.; 815/963-2739).

Rockford has lots of places to stay, from all the main chains along the Interstate to old US-20's characterful **Sweden House Lodge** ($55 and up; 4605 E. State St.; 815/398-4130), a still-thriving icon of 1950s roadside Americana.

Ronald Reagan in Dixon, 1922

Dixon and the Rock River

If you have the time, Hwy-2 follows a lovely route from Rockford along the Rock River southwest to the quaint old town of **Dixon,** where the **Ronald Reagan Boyhood Home** ($5; 816 S. Hennepin Ave.; 815/288-5176) preserves the house where in the early 1920s the late Great Communicator (1911–2004) spent his pre-teen years. Midway along, a rather majestic statue of the great Indian chief Black Hawk stands above the river, outside the town of Oregon.

Union: Illinois Railway Museum

Between Rockford and Chicago, US-20 is a slow, winding, and poorly sign-posted alternative to the high-speed I-90/Jane Addams Memorial Tollway. It's a leisurely route, with few identifiable attractions except for the road itself, which cruises through small towns surrounded by farmlands and lined by fruit-and-vegetable stands. The one real draw here is a mile east of the tiny town of **Union** (pop. 580), where the sprawling **Illinois Railway Museum** (daily; $8 and up; 815/923-4000) displays a great range of track-based transportation: streetcars, interurban trolleys, and railroad cars, with historic engines running weekends throughout the year.

Oak Park

Running parallel to and south of the I-90 Northwest Tollway, old US-20 approaches Chicago from the northwest past Schaumberg and O'Hare Airport, before bending south near **Oak Park** (pop. 51,878), Chicago's most interesting suburb. Just 10 miles west of the Loop, easily reachable at the end of the Lake–Dan Ryan CTA "L" line, this sleepy but well-heeled neighborhood was the boyhood home of Ernest Hemingway, and before that Oak Park was the home and proving ground of America's best-known architect, Frank Lloyd Wright. Visit the **Frank Lloyd Wright Home and Studio** (daily; $15; 951 Chicago Ave.; 312/994-4000) for a

The small town of **Woodstock,** 10 miles northeast of Union, stood in for the Pennsylvania town of Punxsutawney in my favorite Bill Murray movie, *Groundhog Day.*

Chicago

New York may have bigger and better museums, shops, and restaurants, and even Los Angeles has more people, but Chicago is still the most all-American city, and one of the most exciting and enjoyable places to visit in the world. Commerce capital of Middle America, where food processing giants like Kraft Foods, Sara Lee, and Wm. Wrigley Jr. Company are based, Chicago's location at the crossroads between the settled East and the wide-open West has helped it to give birth to many new things we now take for granted: the skyscraper, the blues, and the atomic bomb (not to mention Oprah and Obama!).

Away from the Loop, the skyscraper-spiked lakefront business district that holds North America's tallest and most impressive collection of modern architecture in its oblong square mile, much of Chicago is surprisingly low-rise and residential.

Also surprising, considering its inland location, is that Chicago has a high percentage of immigrants—200,000 Poles form one of the largest communities outside Poland, and Hispanics constitute nearly 29 percent of Chicago's population of close to three million—with a multi-ethnic character readily apparent in numerous enclaves all over the city. Whatever their origin, however, residents take a particular pride in identifying themselves as Chicagoans, and despite the city's rusting infrastructure, their good-natured enthusiasm for the place can be contagious.

For an unbeatable introduction to Chicago, hop aboard a river cruise offered by the **Chicago Architecture Foundation** (daily May–Nov. only; $35; 312/922-3432. Departing from where the Michigan Avenue Bridge crosses the river and Wacker Drive, these informative and enjoyable tours offer an unusual look up at the city's magnificent towers. Enthusiastic expert guides give the city's general historical background as well as pointed architectural history. North from the river, the "Magnificent Mile" of Michigan Avenue is a bustling shopping strip that holds yet more distinctive towers, along with many of the city's top shops, restaurants, and hotels. Starting with the gothic-style Tribune Tower—decorated with bits of famous buildings and monuments stolen by Tribune staffers from around the globe—and running past the circa-1869 Historic Water Tower at its midpoint, the "Mag Mile" ends in the north with the 95-story John Hancock Center.

Along the lakefront at the heart of downtown, the **Art Institute of Chicago** ($18; 111 S. Michigan Ave.; 312/443-3600) boasts one of the world's great collections of 19th- and 20th-century French painting and a broad survey of fine art from all over the world. Among its many fine paintings, the institute gives pride of place to Grant Wood's *American Gothic*, which he painted as a student and sold to the institute for $300. North and east of the

Michigan Avenue Bridge
and skyscrapers

museum is Chicago's latest great claim to fame: **Millennium Park,** a 25-acre public garden full of fabulous sculptures and a magical, Frank Gehry–designed outdoor concert pavilion that's home to numerous summer concerts and events.

More than just another baseball game, watching the **Chicago Cubs** play at Wrigley Field (1060 Addison St.; 773/404-2827) is a rite of passage that taps into the deepest meanings of the national pastime. Ivy covers the redbrick outfield walls and Chicagoans of all stripes root on the perennial not-quite-winners. The "other" Chicago baseball team, the **White Sox,** play at modern U.S. Cellular Field (333 W. 35th St.; 312/674-1000), south of the Loop alongside I-94.

Practicalities

Chicago is home to one of America's busiest and most infuriating airports, O'Hare (ORD), 17 miles northwest of the Loop and well served by Chicago Transit Authority (CTA) subway trains, shuttle services, and taxis. Chicago's other airport, Midway, is closer to the center of town, and Chicago is also the hub of the national Amtrak system, with trains pulling in to Union Station from all over the country. To get around, you'll really be better off leaving the car behind and riding the CTA elevated train—better known as the "El"—which serves the entire city almost around the clock.

Chicago has all sorts of top-quality, cutting-edge-cuisine restaurants, but to get a feel for the city you'll be better off stopping at the many older places that have catered to Chicagoans forever. Near the start of old Route 66, **Lou Mitchell's** (565 W. Jackson St.; 312/939-3111) is one of the greatest breakfast and lunch places on the planet. Along with deep-dish pizza (as served at Uno's, Pizzeria Due, etc.), hot dogs are a real Chicago specialty, best sampled at **Portillo's** (100 W. Ontario St.; 312/587-8910), west of the Mag Mile. One more classic hot dog joint is farther from downtown, toward O'Hare: **Superdawg Drive-In** (6363 N. Milwaukee Ave.; 773/763-0660), where you eat all-beef hot dogs in your car or soak up the 1940s character in a lively dining room.

Places to stay in Chicago include the moderate likes of the **Best Western River North** ($125 and up; 125 W. Ohio St.; 312/467-0800), in the trendy River North gallery district, which offers free parking within a quick walk of the Magnificent Mile along Michigan Avenue. Chicago's classiest older hotel is the **Drake Hotel** ($250 and up; 140 E. Walton Place; 312/787-2200), just off the lake, with elegant public areas and gracious staff. Even if you only soak up the exuberant 1920s Moorish-style lobby, or go for a swim in the palatial 14th floor pool, the most fabulous place to stay could be the **InterContinental** ($200 and up; 505 N. Michigan Ave.; 312/944-4100), though the smallish rooms expose the truth that the building started life as a Shriner's health club.

The best source of detailed information is the **Chicago Office of Tourism** (877/CHICAGO).

fascinating look into the life and work of the great architect. Take a guided tour of the house he designed, remodeling almost constantly between 1889 and 1909 as his practice, and his family, grew. He also completed many other buildings in this turn-of-the-20th-century suburb, including the austere classic Unity Temple.

Oak Park has good transit connections to Chicago and makes a pretty good alternative base, thanks to the **Harvey House B&B** ($185 and up; 107 S. Scoville Ave.; 708/848-6810), which is no relation to the famous 1920s railroad hotels but offers comfortable rooms within walking distance of Frank Lloyd Wright's Unity Temple and the Oak Park CTA "L" station.

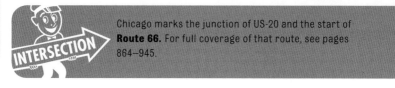

Chicago marks the junction of US-20 and the start of **Route 66.** For full coverage of that route, see pages 864–945.

US-20 Across Chicago

From Oak Park, US-20—which somehow has managed not to be diverted onto one of Chicago's many Interstate freeways—crosses the Des Plaines River and the Chicago Sanitary and Ship Canal, then bends east onto 95th Street, following that road all the way across Chicago to the Lake Michigan waterfront. East of downtown, US-20 bends south along Lake Michigan into Hammond, Indiana, and the industrial districts along the Calumet River.

INDIANA

So close and yet so far away from the excitement of Chicago, northern Indiana can't help but seem a little bit boring. In the northwest, the state is bounded by Lake Michigan, along whose shores Rust Belt hulks of derelict heavy industry stand side by side with the pristine sands of the fascinating and beautiful **Indiana Dunes National Lakeshore.** The northeastern corner, even in the estimation of the state tourist office, offers little more than a few lakes and the so-called "muck lands" around the Fighting Irish homeland of **South Bend.** In between stretch endless acres of rolling farmland, Amish homes, and other tourist-attractive agricultural communities,

as well as some of the most important sites in early American automotive history: the homes of Studebaker, Cord, Duesenberg, and other now-defunct car companies.

Gary

If you ever watched and enjoyed the Hollywood musical *The Music Man*—in which the song "Gary, Indiana" paints a picture of idyllic homespun Americana—you'll be surprised by the reality of the place. In contrast to the

Detour: Indianapolis

Before Detroit came to dominate the industry, **Indianapolis,** a two-hour drive south of South Bend, was an early center of American automobile manufacturing, home to such classy marques as Stutz, Marmon, and Duesenberg, and of course the Indianapolis 500, perhaps the most famous car race in the world. Held the Sunday before Memorial Day almost every year since 1911, the Indianapolis 500 is still the biggest thing in town, drawing upward of a half million spectators to "The Brickyard," the oldest racetrack in the country. The rest of the year, the speedway is open for tours ($5), on a bus that cruises around the legendary 2.5-mile oval. Tours leave

1911: the first Indy 500

from the excellent **Indianapolis Motor Speedway Hall of Fame Museum** (daily; $5; 4790 W. 16th St.; 317/484-6784), which displays some 75 racing cars, from the Marmon "Wasp," which won the inaugural Indy 500 race, to the latest Indy champions. The museum is located on the speedway grounds at in the city of **Speedway** (pop. 11,812), an enclave in the northwest quarter of Indianapolis's pancake-flat sprawl.

rural rest of the state, this far northwest corner of Indiana is among the most heavily industrialized and impoverished areas of the country. In and around **Gary** (pop. 80,294, down from a circa 1960 peak of 178,320), massive petrochemical refineries and factories (including a huge U.S. Steel mill) are surrounded by decaying communities, and the streets are lined by strip malls, strip clubs, stripped-down cars—and signs directing you toward the big new waterfront casinos. During the region's heyday around the middle of the 20th century, the mills, foundries, and factories along the Calumet River pumped out millions of dollars' worth of products every day. The town's more recent products include musical family The Jackson 5, born and raised here in the late 1950s, but nowadays economic times are so hard that local authorities have had to call in the National Guard to police the streets.

Gary's steel heritage is kept alive by the local Northern League baseball team, the **RailCats,** who play at U.S. Steel Yard (around $10; 219/882-BALL), right along the tracks of the South Shore Line, America's oldest inter-urban streetcar system.

Indiana Dunes National Lakeshore

Covering 15,000 acres along 15 miles of Lake Michigan shoreline, 25 miles or so east of Chicago, **Indiana Dunes National Lakeshore** is a striking and

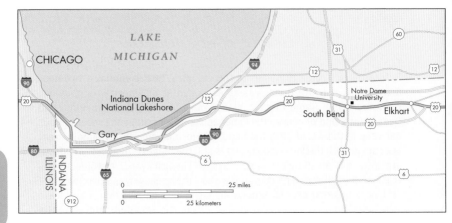

surprising collection of golden sand dunes, freshwater beaches, and dense forests. Chicago poet Carl Sandburg said the dunes "are to the Midwest what the Grand Canyon is to Arizona." Dedicated in 1972, the park includes a huge variety of plantlife—groves of maples and red oaks, pine trees and prickly pear cactus, grasslands and berry bushes—linked by many miles of hiking trails and highlighted by 125-foot Mt. Baldy at the far northeast corner of the park.

Huge steel mills and a number of small vacation home communities share space among the dunes. Also here, two miles northeast of the main visitors center, is the unusual

boardwalk across the interdunal marsh on Miller Wood Trail, Indiana Dunes National Lakeshore

peony,
state flower of Indiana

Beverly Shores, a model community constructed for the "Century of Progress" World's Fair in Chicago in 1933 and reassembled here soon after in an attempt to attract buyers to a new resort community. Six of these then-futuristic structures survive along Lakefront Drive, including three steel-framed, enamel-paneled "Lustron" houses, designed to provide low-cost housing during the Great Depression. Next door is the "House of Tomorrow," an ordinary-looking house designed with an additional garage to hold the private plane every future family was sure to have.

Pick up maps, guides, and other information at the **visitors center** (daily; free; 574/926-7561) on Highway 49, midway between US-20 and I-94 exit 26.

South Bend

The largest city in Indiana's northern tier, **South Bend** (pop. 101,168) is probably best known as the home of the "Fighting Irish" of **Notre Dame University,** and home of the car- and carriage-making Studebaker Company. The Notre Dame campus is most visitors' destination, whether or not it's a Saturday during football season. The 1,250-acre campus, along Michigan Street a mile north of downtown, is worth a stroll to see its many Catholic icons, including a replica of the grotto of Lourdes and the famous "Touchdown Jesus."

The 5,000-seat Coveleski Stadium hosts Midwest League Class A baseball games of the **South Bend Silver Hawks.** Tickets to see these potential Arizona Diamondbacks cost $5–8 (574/235-9988).

For fans of classic cars, the **Studebaker National Museum** (daily; $8; 201 S. Chapin St.; 888/391-5600 or 574/235-9714) is maybe the bigger draw, displaying a comprehensive survey of horseless carriages, stylish cars, fire trucks, and other motor vehicles produced by the South Bend–based company before teh factory closed in 1963.

One of South Bend's best restaurants, **Tippecanoe Place** (620 W. Washington St.; 574/234-9077), is housed in the old Studebaker Mansion. One final piece of car culture history: South Bend was a key stop along the historic Lincoln Highway.

1953 Commander Starliner

The small town of **Peru,** on US-31 midway between South Bend and Indianapolis, was the home base of many traveling circuses during the mid-19-th century, an era remembered in the **Circus City Museum** (154 N. Broadway; 765/472-3918), downtown.

Elkhart

A light industrial center, once famous for producing over half the brass-band instruments made in America, **Elkhart** now makes RVs and pharmaceutical products: Drug giant Miles Laboratories was founded here in 1884 and still has a major presence. In many ways it's a sleepy Midwest town, home to the energetic little **Midwest Museum of American Art** (closed Mon.; $4; 429 S. Main St.; 574/293-6660), downtown in a restored bank building.

Peru was the birthplace of songwriter Cole Porter, who is buried in the town's Mount Hope Cemetery.

Northern Indiana is one of the country's main centers for the manufacture of recreational vehicles, so don't be surprised to find that Elkhart is home to the **RV/MH Hall of Fame** (closed Sun.; $8; 574/293-2344 or 800/378-8694), located east of Elkhart off I-80 exit 96. If you like old machines, it's definitely worth an hour or more, if only for the chance to admire Mae West's 1930s Chevrolet Housecar, the 1950s "canned ham" trailers, the first Winnebago motor home (circa 1967), and the creativity and ingenuity of early hand-made conversions.

Indiana's Amish Country: Middlebury and Shipshewana

East of South Bend, US-20 again becomes a road worth traveling, especially through the quiet agricultural expanses around the towns of **Middlebury** and **Shipshewana,** heartland of Indiana's sizable Amish population. As in other Amish areas, it's the general look of the land, rather than specific attractions, that make it enjoyable to visit; as elsewhere, the few attractions that offer an "authentic Amish experience" leave a lot to be desired. One of the largest tourist traps, the 1,100-seat **Das Dutchman Essenhaus,** looms over US-20 at the west edge of Middlebury, but rather than fight your way through the bus-tour hordes, turn north here into the quiet town center and stop by the **Village Inn** (107 S. Main St.; 574/825-2043). The country café is run by, and popular with, local Amish and Mennonites, who, along with everyone else, enjoy the hearty coffee-shop food—not to mention great homemade pies for around $2 a slice.

Ten miles or so south of Shipshewana via Hwy-5, the tiny town of **Topeka** holds the **Yoder Popcorn Shoppe** (800/892-2170 or 260/768-4051), one of many popcorn sellers whose signs you'll see all around this part of Indiana.

Back on US-20, seven miles east of Middlebury, Hwy-5 runs north just short of a mile to the intriguing **Menno-Hof Mennonite-Amish Visitor Center** (closed Sun.; $6.50; 260/768-4117), outside the hamlet of Shipshewana. Operated by the local Amish and Mennonite communities, who built the large barn that houses the center during a six-day "barn-raising," the center gives an overall introduction to the Amish and Mennonite beliefs and life ways. Surprisingly high-tech multimedia exhibits also tell of their resistance to modern technology, their long struggle for religious freedom, and their love of peace, which has helped them through centuries of torture and abuse—so often, as in the "Dungeon Room" recreated here, at the hands of fellow Christians.

Auburn: Auburn-Cord-Duesenberg Museum

Though it's a bit out of the way (20 miles or so south of US-20 via the I-69 freeway), lovers of vintage American cars will want to make the effort to visit the elegant **Auburn-Cord-Duesenberg Automobile Museum** (daily; $10; 1600 S. Wayne St.; 260/925-1444), in a lovely art deco showroom in the town of Auburn. Considered by most aficionados the finest, most innovative, and most all-around gorgeous automobiles ever produced in America, these instant classics were the brainchild of Auburn industrialist Errett Cord. During the 1920s and 1930s, Cord's company designed and produced the covetable cruisers right here in Indiana—Auburns and the front-wheel-drive Cords were produced in Auburn, while the "Dusies" were made in Indianapolis—and they're now on display inside the original showroom, built in 1930 and immaculately preserved.

The collection here, valued at some $600 million, includes beautifully restored examples of all these classic makes, plus representatives of other classic roadsters—Packards, Cadillacs, even a Rolls-Royce or two—numbering around 150 altogether, and making this one of the top auto museums in the world. It also hosts one of the country's most popular classic car festivals, every Labor Day weekend.

Another lost American industry is remembered near Auburn in **Kendallville,** along US-6: the **Mid-America Windmill Museum** (closed Mon; $4; 260/347-2334), where 40 acres of grounds display over 52 whirring Aermotors, Flint & Wallings, Elgins, and more—the largest collection in the country.

Detour: Detroit

PENOBSCOT BUILDING

Though Detroit (pop. 713,777, down from a 1950 peak population of 1,849,568!) is a ways off our route, no guidebook enamored with American car culture could feel complete without covering the "Motor City," heart of America's automotive industry. Once among the biggest, brawniest and busiest American cities, Detroit has lost more than half its population to suburban sprawl and out-migration. Numerous efforts to "renew" the city by replacing the historic urban fabric with megalithic casinos and sports stadiums have resulted in a cityscape that at times resembles a war zone—the post-apocalyptic *Robocop* movies, for example, were set and filmed in downtown Detroit without much need for an art director. That said, the city's energy is undeniable, and hosting the 2006 Super Bowl put Detroit back in the international spotlight.

One of the best places to get a sense of Detroit, past and present, is at the newly restored **Detroit Institute of the Arts** (Wed.–Sun.; $8; 5200 Woodward Ave.; 313/833-7900), two miles north of downtown. Along with its massive collection of art from around the world—the fifth-largest in the USA—the DIA is well worth a look for its huge and powerful Diego Rivera mural, *Detroit Industry*, celebrating the workers behind the wheels. The other must-see in Detroit is the **Motown Museum** (closed Sun.; $10; 2648 W. Grand Blvd.; 313/875-2264), about three miles northwest of downtown. Dubbed "Hitsville USA," the Motown Museum is contained in the very house where Berry Gordy Jr. produced so many great dance hits in the 1960s. It's surprisingly small and homey, considering the quantity and quality of the music that was born there. Memorabilia galore documents the making of the Motown Sound by the likes of Smokey Robinson, Martha Reeves, Marvin Gaye, Stevie Wonder, the Temptations, and Diana Ross and the Supremes.

Detroit also remembers Joe Louis, the "Brown Bomber," with *The Big Fist,* a 25-foot-high fist looming over the city's main thoroughfare, in the middle of Woodward Avenue at Jefferson Avenue, across from the Renaissance Center downtown.

Baseball fans will want to take in a **Detroit Tigers** (866/66-TIGER) game in the fan-friendly, the faux-retro surrounds of downtown's Comerica Park, where a Ferris wheel and a carousel entertain in between pitches.

In the southwestern suburbs of Detroit, pay homage to the man who made your car affordable at the **Henry Ford Museum & Greenfield Village** (daily; about $30 for both; 20900 Oakwood Blvd.; 800/835-5237 or 313/982-6001), located just off US-12 in Dearborn, about 10 miles southwest of downtown Detroit. The complex has been officially renamed The Henry Ford: America's Greatest History Attraction, and its incredible collection of cars and car-related objects certainly illustrates the massive impact the automobile has had on American history and American life. The adjacent open-air complex of Deerfield Village is a virtual microcosm of American history, holding everything from Abe Lincoln's law office to Thomas Edison's workshop, arranged by Henry Ford and his heirs to form an ideal village of American creativity. Henry Ford's notorious white-supremacist politics are downplayed, but the collection does include one icon of multicultural American history: the bus on which the late, great Rosa Parks refused to give up her seat in 1955, sparking the Civil Rights—era Montgomery Bus Boycott. There's also an IMAX theater showing big-screen films. One of the newest attractions is the chance to tour (for an extra $15) Ford Motor Company's landmark Rouge River automobile factory, home of everything from the Model T to today's F150 pickups. Once the

world's largest factory, "The Rouge" is now a state-of-the-art assembly plant, where you can witness all eras of car-making under one eco-friendly living roof.

Practicalities

The downtown riverfront has been the focus of much of Detroit's reinvention, but the best places to stay, eat, and generally spend time are north of there along Woodward Avenue, in the emerging midtown Cultural District near the DIA and lively Wayne State University. To gain a deeper appreciation of Detroit's past, stay overnight at one of the restored Victorian-era homes that make up the **Inn on Ferry Street** ($160 and up; 84 E. Ferry St.; 313/871-6000), a very comfortable B&B around the corner from the DIA. The same neighborhood also holds **Union Street Saloon,** an old-fashioned tavern (4145 Woodward Ave.; 313/831-3965) with huge portions of good food for

lunch and dinner, and a welcoming if often noisy ambience. For more detailed Detroit information, contact the city's **visitors bureau** (800/DETROIT or 313/202-1800).

the Cleveland Avenue bus made famous when Rosa Parks refused to give up her seat, outside of the Henry Ford Museum

OHIO

The many routes across Ohio along the Lake Erie shore have long been major thoroughfares. Traders and war parties of Iroquois and other Native American tribes regularly passed this way hundreds of years before European and American pioneers started coming through in Conestoga wagons. Nowadays, historical survivors, including colonial-era taverns and other early roadside Americana, and a rapidly decreasing number of vegetable farms and greenhouses fill the flatlands, threatened by ever-expanding suburbia. All over northern Ohio you'll also see Rust Belt remnants of massive industrial activity that took place here from the 1880s to the 1950s, when the Great Lakes were the "Anvil of America," producing the bulk of the nation's—and the world's—iron, steel, and petroleum products.

On I-90 at the Indiana/Ohio border, a very large World's Largest Fireworks Stand also hypes itself as the "8th Wonder of the World."

Rather than try to follow one or another of the many old roads that crisscross the state, it's best to alternate between a variety of routes to either side of the part-tollway, part-freeway known as I-90. In the western half of the state, we follow US-20 from **Toledo** through a rural landscape of gambrel-roofed, red-painted barns, daubed with Chew Mail Pouch signs and made immortal by Sherwood Anderson's classic portrayal in his book *Winesburg, Ohio*. In the middle, we detour north to the lakeshore along US-6, which passes through idyllic summer home communities, gritty old ports, and one of the country's great old amusement parks, **Cedar Point**. East of the metropolitan **Cleveland** area, US-20 veers north along the **Lake Erie** shore, while US-6 zigzags south through the fertile farming country of northeastern Ohio—a region accurately described by the 1939 WPA *Guide to Ohio* as an "enchanting country of tumbling hills, valleys, and forests."

Toledo

One of Ohio's most important industrial centers, **Toledo** (pop. 287,208) is the third-busiest Great Lakes port, with many miles of docks, bridges, warehouses, factories, refineries, and power plants lining the mouth of the Maumee River. That may not sound like a good reason to visit, but Toledo is a fascinating place, big enough to be impressive but small enough to get around and get a feel for. Downtown Toledo has long been a rather anonymous place that empties after 5 PM (that world-renowned expert on tedium, the late John Denver, went so far as to write a song saying, "Saturday night in Toledo, Ohio, is like being nowhere at all"), but the streets just south hold dozens of gorgeous old cast-iron warehouses and commercial buildings around the delightful Fifth Third Field baseball stadium, home of the lovable **Toledo Mud Hens** (419/725-HENS), Class AAA International League affiliate of the Detroit Tigers. The stadium is located not at Fifth and Third Streets (the name comes from a Cleveland bank) but along Huron and Washington Streets.

A mile west of downtown, among the stately homes of the Old West End neighborhood, Toledo's pride and joy is the excellent **The Toledo Museum of Art** (closed Mon.; free; 2445 Monroe St.; 419/255-8000), where works by El Greco (who lived and worked in Toledo, Spain) highlight a survey of European painting. The real strength of the collection is its glassware, with dozens of beautiful goblets and vases dating back to Roman times, housed in a lovely pavilion opened in 2006.

Another truly not-to-be-missed Toledo stop offers a very different feast for the senses: **Tony Packo's Cafe** (1902 Front St.; 419/691-6054), across the river. Packo's addictive chili dogs, made famous by Corporal Klinger (played by real-life Toledo native Jamie Farr) on the long-running TV series *M.A.S.H.*, still pack

the crowds into this East Toledo haunt—despite its location near a huge coal-fired power plant. Tony Packo's also offers some delicious Hungarian specialties, and other signs of Toledo's ethnic mix are on the menu at **Byblos,** an excellent Lebanese restaurant right on US-20 (1050 S. Reynolds Rd.; 419/382-1600).

Architect's Fantasy at The Toledo Museum of Art

In Monroe, Michigan (between Toledo and Detroit), you can kick back in a selection of easy chairs past and present at the **La-Z-Boy Museum,** in the company headquarters! It's free, but by reservation only (734/242-1444).

A good-value place to stay in the region is the **Toledo Hilton** (around $130; 3100 Glendale Ave.; 419/381-6800) on the southwest edge of downtown.

Maumee and Perrysburg

South of Toledo along the Maumee River, a pair of towns preserve important parts of western Ohio's early history. On the west bank of the river, **Maumee** (pop. 14,286; pronounced "MAH-mee") was founded in 1817 at the western edge of settled territory and holds remnants of the Miami and Erie Canal.

Across the river, **Perrysburg** (pop. 20,623) is a pretty little town of white colonial-style houses, with a nice waterfront park and a short strip of restaurants and bars running east along Louisiana Street (US-20). A mile upstream from town, **Fort Meigs** (Wed.–Sun. in summer; $4; 419/874-4121 or 800/283-8916) is a full-scale reconstruction of the wooden fortress that played a key role in defending the frontier against British and Indian attack during the War of 1812.

Fremont

In **Fremont** (pop. 16,734), where in the 1700s native Wyandot Indians established a village along the main trail between Pittsburgh and Detroit, the main attraction is the **Rutherford B. Hayes Presidential Center** (closed Mon.; $13; 1337 Hayes Ave.; 419/332-2081), south of US-20, which encompasses the 25-acre estate of Civil War general and former U.S. president Rutherford B. Hayes, who lived here 1873–1893 and served as president 1877–1881. The nation's first presidential library, the Hayes center includes the rather plain, red-brick family house and a large museum displaying his public and private papers, sundry mementos, and his daughter Fanny's dollhouse collection. Hayes is buried on a wooded knoll on the grounds, alongside his wife and their favorite horses.

Clyde: Winesburg, Ohio

Five miles east of Fremont, the town of **Clyde** (pop. 6,325) is a perfect little place, still very much the typical farm town that the New Deal–era WPA *Guide to Ohio* said might well have served as a model for one of Thomas Hart Benton's murals of rural America: "Old Indian paths and sand ridges are now angular streets; cheek by jowl with an odd assortment of business houses is the railroad cutting across Main Street, gyved with station, elevator, and spur track; around the decorous houses are gardens, flower beds, and shrubbery tended by friendly and loquacious folk."

While downtown "Winesburg" is still a low-key place, the US-20 frontage west of Clyde is dominated by a truly massive factory and distribution center for Whirlpool appliances.

Clyde's brick-paved streets are still quiet, lined by mature trees and most of the same houses as when writer Sherwood Anderson, who was born in southern Ohio in 1876, grew up here in the 1880s and 1890s. Because the people of Clyde took offense at Anderson's sharply drawn and only slightly disguised portraits of them in his groundbreaking book, *Winesburg, Ohio*—which was published in 1919, 20 years after Anderson left Clyde for Chicago—the town doesn't celebrate him in any obvious way. The only real sign of him is in the local **library** (closed Sun.; 222 W. Buckeye St.; 419/547-7174), a block west of the town center, where visitors can check out a collection of his books and a short documentary video of his life and times. The library is also the best place to pick up the pamphlet that points out Anderson's home and the sites of many scenes from *Winesburg.*

In Clyde, the McPherson Cemetery along US-20 holds the remains of Brigadier Gen. James "Birdseye" McPherson, the highest-ranking Union officer killed in the Civil War.

Besides the Winesburg legacy, Clyde also offers a couple of very good road-food stops: **Gary's Diner** (222 W. McPherson Highway; 419/547-9947) and, a block west, the photogenic **Twistee Treat** (daily; 419/547-6996), shaped like an ice-cream cone and serving great shakes. To complete the Sherwood Anderson tour, stay at the AAA-recommended **Winesburg Motel** (214 E. McPherson Hwy.; 419/547-0531).

Sandusky and the Lake Erie Islands

Midway between Toledo and Cleveland, a fine natural harbor has enabled **Sandusky** (pop. 25,793) to remain a busy port, albeit now more for recreational ferries to the offshore islands than for the coal and iron ore it once handled. The waterfront is good for a short stroll, and the town is rich in elaborate mid-1800s houses like the **Follett House Museum** (closed Jan., Feb., and March; free; 404 Wayne St.; 419/625-3834), a well-preserved 1827 Greek Revival house filled with period artifacts and a few displays on the area's history.

On **South Bass Island** in Lake Erie, 15 miles by boat from Sandusky, the 352-foot Perry's Victory and International Peace Memorial (419/285-2184) commemorates the victory of Adm. Oliver Perry, who defeated a British fleet here on September 10, 1813, announcing his success with the laconic words, "We have met the enemy, and they are ours." The second biggest thing on the island, which is a very popular vacation spot, may well be the "World's Longest Bar," a 406-footer running inside the **Beer Barrel Saloon** (324 Delaware Ave.; 419/285-2337) in the town of Put-in-Bay.

If the weather's too bad to brave a boat trip or a ride on the roller coasters of Cedar Point, families may want to head to the **Great Wolf Lodge,** a kid-friendly hotel and massive indoor water park (open to guests only), south of Sandusky (family suites start at around $140; 4600 Milan Rd.; 800/641-9653 or 419/609-6000).

Cedar Point

Northern Ohio's number-one summer attraction is the wonderful, old-time amusement park of **Cedar Point** (hours vary; $49 adults, $30 for children under four feet tall; 419/627-2350), just north of Sandusky. Open since 1892, Cedar Point has the country's biggest and best collection of roller coasters, 17 in all, ranging from fragile-looking old wooden ones to high-speed modern monsters like the **Magnum,** a 15-story colossus; the terrifying **Raptor,** in which riders swing on benches hanging from the track; and the 90-plus-mph **Millennium Force,** which features a stomach-levitating 300-foot drop; or the 42-story **Top Thrill Dragster,** which accelerates from 0 to 120 mph in four seconds. Cedar Point is definitely one of the most popular destinations in the Midwest (and is regularly voted "Best Amusement Park in the World" by its many fans), so expect crowds if you come on summer weekends. The 360-acre park sits on a peninsula across the water from downtown Sandusky and has animal shows, a Lake Erie beach, and a water park, as well as restaurants and on-site camping and hotel accommodations.

Vermilion

One of the more attractive resorts on Ohio's Lake Erie frontage, **Vermilion** (pop. 10,594) took its name from the rich red clay that colors the soil. Along with a fine beach backed by dozens of attractive summer homes, the town also holds the **Inland Seas Maritime Museum** (daily; closed Oct.–Apr.; $6; 480 Main St.; 800/893-1485 or 440/967-3467), along the waterfront. The museum's usual array of scale models and paintings of ships is augmented with preserved timbers from Perry's ship *Niagara* and a 62-foot-tall replica of a Lake Erie lighthouse.

A great old-fashioned ice cream and sandwich parlor, **Granny Joe's Ice Creamatorium** (5598 Liberty Ave.; 440/967-3663), stands at the center of town. For a more complete meal, try the comfortable **Old Prague Restaurant** next door (440/967-7182).

Oberlin

The lovely little town of **Milan** (pop. 1,367), two miles south of I-90 via US-250, was the birthplace in 1847 of the great inventor Thomas Edison. His childhood home at 9 Edison Drive is preserved as a museum.

Away from the lakeshore, 35 miles southwest of Cleveland between I-90 and US-20, the attractive college town of **Oberlin** (pop. 8,286) serves up an idyllic slice of Middle Americana. Founded along with the surrounding town in 1833, Oberlin College has a history of being at the leading edge of American education, despite (or perhaps because of) its location far from the madding crowds. In 1837 Oberlin became the country's first co-educational college. It was also among the first to embrace the education of African Americans: In the 19th century, Oberlin awarded more degrees to black students than all other mainstream American colleges combined.

The Oberlin College campus spreads west of the town's green main square, which is also graced on the east side by the neoclassical facade of the **Allen Art Museum** (closed Mon.; free; 87 N. Main St.; 440/775-8665). The museum displays an overall survey of world art—Japanese prints, Islamic carpets, and modern painting by the likes of Cézanne and Diebenkorn. Architecture fans should take note: The old gallery was designed by Cass Gilbert, who also planned a handful of Romanesque buildings on campus; a new wing was added in 1977 by Robert Venturi. The museum also offers guided tours ($5) of a nearby house designed in 1947 by Frank Lloyd Wright.

The town of Oberlin seems preserved in a time warp, mostly avoiding the trend-swapping café culture of many college towns. Its few blocks are lined by an old five-and-dime, an Army surplus store, a hardware store, and a bookstore, all along the south side of the broad town square. Another block south holds a spacious, modern library (with free Internet access) and a very nice Mediterranean-flavored café, **The Feve** (30 S. Main St.; 440/774-1978), which has fresh falafel, good coffee, and cold Guinness on draught. For a place to stay, try the turquoise green motor court cabins of the **Sunset Motel** ($55 and up; 44077 Old Route 20; 440/375-0808), due east of downtown.

In the past 30 years, much of Ohio has been turned from farmland to suburbia, a development that inspired Pretenders singer and Ohio native Chrissie Hynde to write "My City is Gone"—the beginning strains of which serve as the theme song for Rush Limbaugh's radio program. Some of the song's lyrics: "I went back to Ohio, but my pretty countryside had been paved down the middle by a government that had no pride. The farms of Ohio had been replaced by shopping malls, and Muzak filled the air from Seneca to Cuyahoga Falls."

US-20 Across Cleveland

The nicest old road route into Cleveland from the west is US-6, which winds along Lake Erie as Sandusky Road, Lake Avenue, and Clifton Boulevard. Running right through downtown, past "The Flats" along Shoreway, then east along Superior Avenue, US-6 gives a great taste of the city.

Much of Oberlin's endowment comes from the bequest of Oberlin graduate Charles Hall, who in 1886, a year after graduating, discovered a viable process for refining aluminum and later founded Alcoa Corporation.

US-20, on the other hand, diverges slightly east of downtown Cleveland, following Euclid Avenue past the Cleveland Museum of Art, then crosses to the north of US-6, following the lakeshore all the way into Pennsylvania.

The Cleveland Municipal Airport, Cleveland, Ohio

Kirtland and Mentor

The rolling farmlands of northeastern Ohio around **Kirtland** (pop. 6,866) were, from 1831 to 1837, the center of the Mormon religion. Joseph Smith Jr., along with 1,000 of his followers, settled here and built a large temple—the first Mormon temple anywhere—and developed industries and a bank (known as the "Kirtland anti-BANK-ing Company"). The bank failed in 1838 and Smith fled, first to Liberty, Missouri, and later to Nauvoo, Illinois. He surrendered to the governor in 1844 and was killed by a mob in Carthage, Illnois.

The **Kirtland Temple,** just south of I-90 (9020 Chillicothe Road), is surrounded by pleasant gardens and open to the general public on guided tours (daily; $3; 440/256-1830). The stately Greek Revival structure has a gleaming white interior built in part by Brigham Young, with elaborately crafted woodwork pulpits (one at each end) and an upstairs classroom with more of the

Cleveland

Poor Cleveland. Home base of John D. Rockefeller's Standard Oil monopoly, Cleveland was among the biggest and most prosperous of all the Great Lakes industrial giants for decades on either side of the turn of the 20th century. A century later, the city has lost more than half its population (down from its 1950s peak of almost a million) and spent much of the past 60 years reeling from Rust Belt decay. Even the city's apparent renaissance in the 1990s may have been a false hope: The opening of downtown's Progressive Field briefly made Cleveland feel good about itself, as the **Cleveland Indians** (216/420-4487) baseball team started winning and sold out every game for its first five years. But now even a full house seems to be a thing of the past. The city's spirit has been undermined by the recurring failure of any of its sports teams to win a significant championship. Football's famous Browns defected to Baltimore, and Ohio-born NBA star LeBron James left Cleveland's Cavaliers for Miami.

Cleveland's old heavyweight lakefront industrial district, known as "The Flats," has undergone a successful face-lift: overlaid by a network of bridges (drawbridges, lift bridges, swing bridges, all kinds of bridges) that form a feast for the eyes of any post-industrial amateur archaeologist, with water taxis running back and forth across the river, linking the bars and restau-

Progressive Field, home of the Cleveland Indians

Rock and Roll Hall of Fame and Museum

rants that now fill gigantic old mills, factories, and warehouses. The primal force behind the area's recent rebirth has been the **Rock and Roll Hall of Fame and Museum** (daily; $22; 1100 Rock and Roll Blvd.; 216/781-ROCK), housed in a striking modern I. M. Pei–designed building. A barrage of multimedia exhibits trace the roots and branches of the rock family tree, filling 55,000 square feet of galleries in a 162-foot tower. (Q: Why Cleveland? A: The Hall of Fame was located here because Cleveland DJ Alan Freed is credited with naming the music "rock and roll," way back in 1951.)

In the sedate University Circle neighborhood, away from the waterfront and the rock and roll hype, some of the best things about Cleveland survive from its early 20th century heyday. The most notable cultural institution is the **Cleveland Museum of Art,** just north of US-20/Euclid Avenue (closed Mon.; free; 11150 East Blvd.; 216/421-7350), which in 2010 opened one of the most impressive and enjoyable galleries in the country. Building on a long tradition of excellence in Egyptian and Asian art and sculpture, the museum now fills more than 500,000 square feet with memorable works, including classic paintings by Caravaggio, Botticelli, Zurbarán, and Picasso.

Just east of the museum, another historic treasure is Cleveland's **Lake View Cemetery,** where many of the grandees from Cleveland's prime, including John D. Rockefeller and President James Garfield, now rest in peace among a gorgeously landscaped forest of hardwood trees.

Practicalities

The Cleveland airport, Hopkins International, is 12 miles southwest of downtown, linked by I-71 and the RTA subway (216/621-9500) to central Cleveland. To get a feel for the place, a car is hard to beat, especially since the city tends to sprawl sideways rather than concentrate vertically. In the downtown area, finding your way around the Cuyahoga River waterfront takes patience, as many roads dead-end and some of the old bridges are closed to traffic; on foot, the Ohio City RTA stop is a good place to start exploring.

For food, the **Great Lakes Brewing Company** (2516 Market Ave.; 216/771-4404), in the Cleveland neighborhood of Ohio City, just west of the Cuyahoga River in an artsy low-rent district, has good food, great beer, and a generally convivial crowd. While here, check out the West Side Farmers Market and Allstate Barber College across the street on 26th and Lorain Avenue—20 chairs, no waiting!

(continued on next page)

(continued)

Night Scene, Hotel Cleveland and Terminal Tower.

Cleveland, Ohio

In a light industrial and warehousing district just east of I-90, a half mile from downtown, **Slyman's** (closed Sat. and Sun.; 3106 St. Clair Ave.; 216/621-3760) has the best corned beef in Cleveland, bar none.

For a place to stay, the **DoubleTree Cleveland Downtown-Lakeside** ($125 and up; 1111 Lakeside Ave.; 216/241-5100) is hard to beat. The former Holiday Inn offers the usual comforts and is very near the Rock and Roll museum. Right downtown, across from Claes Oldenburg's *World's Largest Rubber Stamp* statue, the **Renaissance Cleveland Hotel** ($230 and up; 24 Public Square; 216/696-5600) is a 1920s classic that has been immaculately updated into the city's nicest place to stay.

For complete visitor information, contact the **Cleveland Convention and Visitors Bureau** (216/875-6680 or 800/321-1004).

unusual double pulpits. The temple and most of the town have been preserved under the auspices of the Reorganized Church of Jesus Christ of Latter-day Saints, now called Community of Christ, which was set up in 1852 by Joseph Smith Jr.'s oldest son and the Mormons who didn't go west to Salt Lake City with Brigham Young.

North of I-90 along US-20, a half mile from the center of **Mentor,** a large white Gothic-style house is preserved much as it was when James Garfield lived here before assuming the presidency in 1881. Garfield served for only a few months before being assassinated, but his home is now preserved as a national historic site (daily; $5; 440/255-8722).

Ten miles to the northeast in **Painesville,** the **Rider's Inn** (792 Mentor Ave.) is another historic landmark, built in 1812 along the stagecoach route between Buffalo and Cleveland.

Ashtabula

On the shores of Lake Erie, 18 miles from the Pennsylvania border, **Ashtabula** (pop. 19,124) is a large and busy pleasure-boating port, first dredged at the mouth of the Ashtabula River in 1826 and later home to some of the biggest shipyards on the Great Lakes. Now primarily recreation-oriented, Ashtabula still has a few signs of its industrial past, including the lakefront coal conveyor that forms an archway over the river, next to a squat lighthouse and a small local history **museum** housed in the old lighthouse keeper's quarters. The town's lakeside location made it a key transit point for escaping slaves on the Underground Railroad, a history recounted inside the **Hubbard House Museum,** on the corner of Walnut Boulevard and Lake Avenue (Fri.–Sun. afternoons only; $5; 440/964-8168).

A block south of the lakefront, pride of place goes to a burly bascule drawbridge and to the many turn-of-the-20th-century industrial and business premises along Bridge Street that form a three-block parade of gift shops, bars, and restaurants.

Conneaut

A dozen miles east of Ashtabula, just west of the Pennsylvania border, the historic port town of **Conneaut** (pop. 12,841; pronounced "KAH-nee-ut") has an art director's dream of a great road-food restaurant, the **White Turkey Drive-Inn** (388 E. Main Rd.; 440/593-2209), on US-20. Owned and run by the Tuttle family since 1952, this place serves burgers and has a fantastic ambience but is truly famous for two things: shredded turkey sandwiches and root beer floats. Between Mother's Day and Labor Day, sit outside under the red canopy on a warm summer evening watching the fireflies, and everything's guaranteed to feel right with the world.

PENNSYLVANIA

US-20 takes little more than the proverbial blink of an eye to cross the 45 miles of northwestern Pennsylvania, which is part of Pennsylvania only because the country's founding fathers thought it was unfair to deny the Keystone State a share of the Lake Erie shoreline. I-90 is most travelers' route of choice, but US-20 does have a couple of worthwhile stops.

Girard and Erie

Twelve miles east of the Ohio border, the town of **Girard** (pop. 3,104) has the nifty little **Hazel Kibler Museum** (522 E. Main St.; 814/774-3653), documenting local history and the life of circus clown Dan Rice, who posed as Uncle Sam in the famous "I Want You" posters. Girard also has one of the country's oldest Civil War memorials, an eagle-topped obelisk dedicated with great fanfare in November 1865.

Midway across Pennsylvania's short Lake Erie shoreline, the biggest city in these parts, **Erie** (pop. 101,786), is a heavy industrial powerhouse that seems to have escaped the downward spiraling fate of many other Rust Belt cities. Home to

Erie has a Class AA baseball team, the Detroit Tigers–affiliated **Erie Seawolves** (814/456-1300), who play at a neighborly downtown stadium, on 10th Street two blocks east of State Street. Games are broadcast on **WJET 1400 AM.**

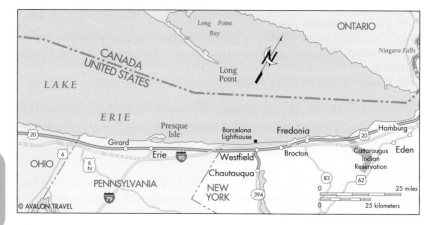

the heaviest of heavy industry, the factory where General Electric produces the world's most powerful locomotives, Erie is re-creating itself around a nice new downtown ballpark, with a replica of Commodore Perry's flagship *Niagara* moored along the Lake Erie waterfront, where the 10-story Bicentennial Tower offers an impressive panorama.

A mile south of the waterfront, along the still-busy train tracks, the art deco Union Pacific depot is now home to a popular brewpub and restaurant, **The Brewerie** (123 W. 14th St.; 814/454-2200). In between, an ornate old firehouse is now home to the restaurant **Pufferbelly's,** a block east of State (414 French St.; 814/454-1557), and the even more opulent **Warner Theater** (811 State St.) is a picture palace par excellence, its 2,250-seat auditorium still in regular use.

marquee of the restored Warner Theater

One more reason to spend time here, especially in the depths of winter, is **Splash Lagoon,** a trio of chain hotels (around $170 and up a night) attached to an 80,000-square-foot indoor water park ($40; 866/3-SPLASH), just south of the I-90 Erie exit.

NEW YORK

From inauspicious beginnings in the marshlands and vineyards of the Lake Erie "grape belt" at the state's far western tip, the portion of US-20 that runs across upstate New York cuts a wide scenic swath through a diverse terrain of flatlands, rippling hills, and spring-fed lakes. This well-maintained, mostly four-lane road glides surreptitiously through four centuries of history, slicing through vast Dutch patroonships, serene Shaker colonies, blood-soaked Revolutionary War battlefields, Native American hunting grounds, the birthplace of the women's movement, Underground Railroad hide-

rose, state flower of New York, at the New York Botanical Gardens

outs, and the long-calmed waters of the once-mighty Erie Canal. Sparkling baseball diamonds, dairy bars by the dozen, petrified creatures, stately long-houses, abandoned motor courts, prancing wooden horses, off-key nose whistles, and succulent, grill-toughened hot dogs are just a few of the countless other reasons to slow down and pull over early and often as you cross the Empire State.

The "Romance Road," as labeled by a 1940s travel writer, follows several old Iroquois Indian trails as it nudges its way through the western Niagara Frontier, then traces the 19th-century Great Western Turnpike through the **Finger Lakes** region before easing down into the historically rich Hudson Valley near **Albany,** where it begins a gradual ascent of the Taconic Mountains and Berkshire foothills that hug the Massachusetts border. All the way across the state, US-20 roughly parallels the crowded, rumbling I-90 New York Thruway toll road—a necessary evil that lures most of the diesel-spewing, view-obscuring 18-wheel traffic away from placid US-20 with a 65-mph speed limit and the promise of uneventful, predictable fast-food rest-stop dining experiences and fluorescent-lit motels.

Westfield: New York's Wine Country

The salt-whitened, snowplow-scraped roadway and endless, slightly hilly expanse of shaggy, kudzu-like vineyards on the south side of the road continue for a dozen monotonous miles between the state line and proud, hardworking **Westfield** (pop. 3,224), known locally as Vine City because of its large Italian American grape-growing community and its proximity to some of Chautauqua County's finest wineries.

The tangy Concord grape was introduced to the region in 1859, but it wasn't until 1897 that Dr. Charles Welch and his father moved to Westfield and founded the factory that led to Westfield's long-standing nickname, the "Grape Juice Capital of the World." Westfield is also in the history books thanks to a local girl who, during the presidential campaign of 1860, urged candidate Abraham Lincoln to grow a beard, which he did to iconic effect.

Westfield's no-frills **Main Diner** (40 E. Main St.; 716/326-4351), in the heart of downtown, is a pleasant place to grab a cup of coffee and sandwich while watching the pickup trucks cruise past; it's open daily 6 AM–3 PM, plus Friday evenings, and has great homemade pies. (For all you diner mavens, the building is a 1929 Ward & Dickinson, originally fabricated in neighboring Silver Creek.)

Across I-90 from Westfield along waterfront Hwy-5, Lake Erie's Barcelona Harbor is home to the landmark **Barcelona Lighthouse,** which was constructed in 1829 and two years later was the first lighthouse in the world to be lit by natural gas. There are a couple of nice cafés nearby, and though the lighthouse itself is prominent even from the road, it stands on private property and is not accessible to visitors.

Comedian Lucille Ball grew up in Jamestown, at the southeast end of Chautauqua Lake. A museum and gift shop ($10; 2 W. 3rd St.; 716/484-0800) displays lots of *I Love Lucy* memorabilia.

West of Fredonia, in the town of **Brocton** ("Home of Don Reinhoudt, World's Strongest Man"), a unique green dome has been hovering over US-20 at the main downtown intersection since 1910.

Fredonia

East of Westfield, US-20 trucks through cherry orchards, vineyards, and dozens of U-pick fruit stands before ebbing into the center of neatly maintained **Fredonia** (pop. 11,230), possible namesake for the Marx Brothers' beloved *Duck Soup* homeland. Site of the first natural gas well in the United States (1825), Fredonia was also—ironically, for a town in the heart of the western New York Wine Belt—the birthplace of the Women's Christian Temperance Union (1873).

Downtown Fredonia boasts the gracefully shaded, New England–style town square, bordered by a restored opera house and a host of Greek Revival, Italianate, Victorian, and gothic 19th-century commercial buildings. A stroll down tree-lined Central Avenue to the north of Main Street (US-20) reveals an equally diverse array of turn-of-the-20th-century homes, which stand in marked contrast to the sterile modernity you encounter up the road in the several I. M. Pei–designed buildings that define the State University of New York (SUNY) Fredonia campus.

The veranda-fronted **White Inn** ($89 and up; 52 E. Main St.; 716/672-2103) has very nice rooms, and its restaurant has been open so long it still boasts of recommendations by 1930s road-food writer Duncan Hines.

East of Fredonia, the vineyards vanish, replaced by the thick stands of scruffy pine trees, used car lots, and cheap-cigarette stands that crowd the

Detour: Chautauqua

One of the few utopian-minded 19th-century communities to survive to the present day, **Chautauqua** (pop. 4,554) is an idyllic, 750-acre Victorian village of quaint pastel cottages, tidy flower gardens, and pedestrian-friendly streets—a genteel model of middle-class, small-town civilization. Chautauqua was founded in 1874 by Lewis Miller, inventor Thomas Edison's father-in-law. It was established as a summer training ground for Methodist Sunday school teachers and is now preserved as a nonprofit, nonsectarian cooperative foundation. In the first decades of the 20th century Chautauqua had an immeasurable effect on American culture, sponsoring correspondence courses and cross-country lecture tours that brought liberal arts education to the masses, especially in the rural Midwest.

Chautauqua, located along Hwy-394 about 20 miles south of Westfield on US-20 (off I-90 exit 60), has hardly changed since its heyday and still welcomes all comers to its summer-long series of lectures and concerts, held in a delightful old open-air amphitheater. Though the emphasis is on education, Chautauqua is not entirely academic: In between broadening their minds, visitors can relax on the white-sand beaches that line the lakeshore. Day visitors to Chautauqua have to pay admission (about $20 and higher, free on Sun.; 716/357-6250) and pass through a set of ancient turnstiles, as if entering a mind-improving amusement park. Others come for a week or two, renting a cottage or staying at the wonderful old **Athenaeum Hotel,** built in 1881 (around $220 and higher with all meals included; 800/821-1881 or 716/357-4444). Along with dozens of quaint Victorian cottages is the Machine Age **Steel Away,** a three-bed Lustron pre-fab (around $2,800 a week; 716/357-3851).

idyllic Chautauqua

For further information, or to request a schedule of Chautauqua classes, lectures, and events, call 800/836-2787.

roadside along US-20's two-mile passage through the northeastern corner of the Cattaraugus Indian Reservation.

Eden: Original American Kazoo Company

US-20 bumps up north along the lakeshore through several miles of scraggly forest, and you won't miss a thing by taking the I-90/NY Thruway to exit 57A, which lands you on a two-lane back road bound right for sleepy downtown **Eden** (pop. 3,516). Eden, a make-your-own-music lovers' paradise that lays claim to an annual summer Eden Corn Festival, is home to the one-and-only **Original American Kazoo Company** museum, gift shop, and factory (closed Mon.; free; 8703 S. Main St.; 716/992-3960). Established in 1916, the company boasts the world's only still-operating metal kazoo factory (most of the ones now made in China and Hong Kong are plastic). A restored, two-story clapboard house contains a gift shop and museum offering an up-close-and-personal view of the factory's belt-and-pulley metal kazoo production line and the opportunity to sign a petition aimed at getting the kazoo declared America's national instrument.

After viewing a video extolling the virtues of one of the few musical instruments invented in the United States, visitors can gaze at a display of antique kazoos, ranging from an original wooden model to the bottle-shaped kazoos churned out to celebrate the repeal of Prohibition. A large sign chimes in with some fascinating kazoo-related trivia, describing the most popular kazoo (the slide trombone), the largest kazoo ever made (the 43-pound Kazoophony), and the number of kazoo bands registered in the United States (15,000 and still counting). You can pick up an adenoid-popping nose flute, a trombone kazoo, and a variety of noisemakers in the gift shop on your way out, or grab some wax paper, rubber bands, and an empty toilet paper roll and create your own kazoo.

Buffalo

Founded as a Niagara frontier outpost in the early 1800s, **Buffalo** (pop. 261,310) exploded into a bustling shipping, manufacturing, and railroad center after the 1825 opening of the Erie Canal. For over a century, especially around World War I, Buffalo was the commercial and industrial linchpin between the Great Lakes, Canada, and the eastern United States. A shrinking population, and the continuing departure of many factories and corporate headquarters to warmer, cheap-labor climes, has dented Buffaloans' self-confidence over the past several decades, but the optimistic made-in-Buffalo spirit captured so eloquently in nonfiction writer Verlyn Klinkenborg's portrait of Polish-American bartender Eddie Wenzek, *The Last Fine Time,* lives on.

A 15-minute drive from downtown up tree-lined Elmwood Avenue takes you to Buffalo's premier attraction, the extensive collection of Picassos, de Koonings, Pollocks, and other important modern masterpieces inside the **Albright-Knox Art Gallery** (closed Mon.; $12; 1285 Elmwood Ave.; 716/882-8700). This world-class museum stands adjacent the grassy expanses and ponds of **Delaware Park,** designed by Frederick Law Olmsted, the landscape architect of New York City's Central Park and Brooklyn's Prospect Park. Across the road you'll see the marble neoclassical structure that has housed the Buffalo and Erie County Historical Society **museum** (closed Mon.; $7; 716/873-9644) since its construction in 1901 for the historic Pan-American Exposition. The non-air-conditioned gallery can be a bit stifling on hot summer afternoons, but the wonderful Made in Buffalo exhibit, on local manufacturing, and Dividing the Land, about immigration, should satisfy most of your local-history thirsts.

A short walk from the Delaware Park brings you to the Frank Lloyd Wright–designed **Darwin D. Martin House** (tours $15 and up; 125 Jewett Parkway; 716/856-3858), well worth a look for anyone interested in American architecture, especially after its recent restoration.

Between Buffalo and Niagara Falls, **North Tonawanda** (pop. 31,568) is a tough-looking factory town concealing one of the Buffalo area's best-kept secrets, the **Herschell Carousel Factory Museum** (closed Jan.–Apr.; $5; 180 Thompson St.; 716/693-1885) a half mile east of Hwy-265. Creators of much-loved landmarks at amusement parks from the Jersey Shore to Santa Monica, the barn-like factory houses a restored 1916 pulley-driven carousel and a stable of immaculately painted wooden steeds, zebras, roosters, ostriches, frogs, bears, and bulls hand-carved by the factory's immigrant artisans for the countless carousels and kiddie rides turned out by the factory in its 1920s to 1940s heyday.

The **Buffalo Bisons,** the New York Mets AAA farm team, play right downtown at 18,025-seat Coca-Cola Park ($8 and up; 716/846-2000). Games are broadcast play-by-play on **WWKB 1520 AM.**

Buffalo Practicalities

Most of Buffalo's many local clubs, films, and offbeat attractions are found in the funky, historic Allentown neighborhood around the junction of Elmwood Avenue and Allen Street, just north of downtown. The "World Famous" **Anchor Bar,** "Birthplace of Buffalo Wings," is here (1047 Main St.; 716/886-8920). Skip the bland Italian entrées in favor of the bar's much-hyped specialty—the saucy, fiery, deep-fried chicken wings, served here since 1964. A long way out Main, about three miles from downtown near the SUNY Buffalo campus, is another even more perfect, only-in-Buffalo pit stop: **Parkside Candy** (3208 Main St.; 716/833-7540), where you can feast on delicious hot fudge sundaes or house-made candies in an opulently decorated 1930s space that looks like a ballroom out of some Jane Austen novel.

Anchor Bar, home of the original Buffalo Wings

Southeast of downtown, another unique Buffalo treat—the Beef on Weck sandwich, a moist and meaty version of a French dip, best eaten with a dash of horseradish—can be sampled at **Schwabl's** (789 Center Rd.; 716/675-2333) in West Seneca.

For a place to stay, most of the national chain motels are clustered east of town around I-90 and the Buffalo airport. The in-town **Best Western** ($140 and up; 510 Delaware Ave.; 888/868-3033 or 716/886-8333) is a bit higher-priced, but its central location saves driving time and grounds you smack in the middle of the city's Allentown bar, restaurant, and club district; there's also a comfy **Hampton Inn** nearby ($144 and up; 220 Delaware Ave.; 716/855-2223). Solo travelers on a small budget will appreciate the immaculate **HI-Buffalo Hostel** ($25; 667 Main St.; 716/852-5222), with dorm beds in a historic downtown building. For more peace and quiet, a tree-lined side street between Allentown and Delaware Park holds the **Belle Fleuve Bed and Breakfast Inn** ($135–175; 242 Linwood Ave.; 800/278-0245 or 716/882-6116), a "Stick Style" 1880s Victorian B&B.

Another arts-and-crafts aesthetic treasure is tucked away in the south Buffalo suburb of East Aurora. In the early 1900s East Aurora was home of Roycroft Campus, a turn-of-the-20th-century arts-and-crafts community of furniture shops and studios, the crown jewel of which was recently restored and opened as **The Roycroft Inn,** a lovely hotel and restaurant ($140 and up; 40 S. Grove St.; 716/652-5552).

For additional information and maps of Buffalo's wealth of significant architecture (Louis Sullivan, H. H. Richardson, Eliel Saarinen, and Frank Lloyd Wright all completed major buildings here), contact the Buffalo/Niagara County **visitors center** (617 Main St.; 716/852-0511 or 800/283-3256).

Niagara Falls

One of the most famous sights in the world, the **Niagara Falls** are a quick trip upriver from Buffalo. They're not the biggest or most powerful waterfall in the world, but they're easy to reach and very easy to get up close and personal with. Once you venture underneath the falls on the famous *Maid of the Mist* boat ride ($14; 716/284-8897), or even stand on the brink at Prospect Park or Goat Island, you won't soon forget the awesome force of the water tumbling in twin, 180-foot-tall torrents.

Much to the despair of the tourism authorities on the American side, where the surprisingly post-industrial town has long suffered from economic decline, the best views are across a bridge on the Canadian side, where all the

Maid of the Mist below American Falls, from Niagara Falls, Canada

major hotels join the Las Vegas–scale **Fallsview Casino Resort** ($189 and up; 888/325-5788) among a barrage of wax museums, water parks, and a Ripley's Believe It or Not! Museum, fronted by a 25-foot statue of King Kong.

The power of Niagara Falls was first used to generate electricity by the remarkable inventor Nikola Tesla in 1896. A monument to him stands near the falls in Prospect Park.

Rochester

There's plenty of culture in the sprawling Genesee River manufacturing center of **Rochester** (pop. 210,565), and the best of it is of the vernacular variety, making the 25-mile detour off US-20 well worth your time and effort. With impressive **High Falls,** a mini Niagara right at the center of town; numerous historic sights (the Erie Canal passed right through Rochester, and Susan B. Anthony and Frederick Douglass both lived here for many years); and an expansive Lake Ontario shoreline boasting long beaches, Rochester is a fine example of how much fun one can have in a "minor league" U.S. city. The best road-trip-worthy attraction is historic **Seabreeze Amusement Park** (around $26; 585/323-1900), which sits on the Lake Ontario shore, complete with the ancient wooden Jack Rabbit roller coaster, the third oldest operating in the USA, and a fun water park.

Start your visit with the vast holdings of the Americana-rich **Strong National Museum of Play** (daily; $12; 585/263-2700), clearly marked off I-490 downtown. This impressive collection includes Victorian-era toys, appliances, dolls, perfume bottles, marbles, salt-and-pepper shakers, and classic board games. It's a must-visit for closet pack rats, pop culture fanatics, and anyone with children in tow. Just inside, but accessible without paying admission, is a lovely circa-1918 Herschell hand-carved carousel (made in nearby

East of Buffalo, US-20 makes a rigidly straight run through the flat corn and hay fields that climb the gradually rising plateau toward the Finger Lakes. This 40-mile-or-so stretch is virtually devoid of traffic, thanks to the faster-moving New York Thruway and serpentine Hwy-5, which links up with US-20 at Avon.

Near the conservatory in Rochester's Frederick Law Olmsted–designed Highland Park, the 1898 memorial to anti-slavery activist Frederick Douglass was the first public statue of an African-American erected in the United States.

The **Rochester Red Wings** Class AAA baseball team play at friendly Frontier Field (around $11; 585/454-1001) downtown. The team had been the Baltimore Orioles' prime farm team since the 1960s (ironman Cal Ripken played for Rochester as a teenager) but now feeds the Minnesota Twins.

South of Rochester, I-390 runs alongside a still-intact section of the original Erie Canal waterway. In other places, the freeway runs right over the old canal, with the old stone locks still visible on the side of the road.

Iroquois legend has it that the **Finger Lakes** (five of which—Cayuga, Onondaga, Oneida, Seneca, Tuscarora bear names of the Six Nations of the Iroquois Confederacy) were created by the handprint of God.

Picturesque, flag-draped downtown Waterloo (pop. 5,171) has an all-American feel, befitting its contentious claim of holding the nation's first observance (in May 1866) of **Memorial Day.**

North Tonawanda), as well as a fully restored 1956 Skyliner diner, serving lunch all day.

The **George Eastman House** (closed Mon.; $12; 900 East Ave.; 585/271-3361) is a 10-minute drive along Rochester's fashionable mansion-lined main boulevard. In addition to relaying the Horatio Alger–like story of workaholic Eastman's success and philanthropy as the founder of the Eastman Kodak Company, the 50-room Colonial Revival mansion in which he lived before his 1932 suicide also houses a fascinating exhibit, Enhancing the Illusion, on the history of photography.

Geneva and Waterloo

Geneva (pop. 13,261) sits at the head of Seneca Lake, the largest of the Finger Lakes, and is linked to this sailboat-flecked jewel by a long, green linear park. For a worthwhile detour off the busy four-lane highway, take a quick pass through the lively downtown along Main Street, perhaps wandering around the twin campuses of Hobart and William Smith Colleges to take in a more long-distance view of the lake. The waterfront is dominated by a solitary high-rise housing the **Ramada Inn** ($130–265; 41 Lakefront Dr.; 315/789-0400), but a much more interesting place to stay is a half mile south of town: the historic **Belhurst Castle** ($140 and up; 4069 S. Hwy-14315/781-0201), a 100-year-old, 14-room B&B and restaurant.

Ten miles east of Geneva, at the edge of **Waterloo,** the unprepossessing **Mac's Drive-In Curb Service Restaurant** (1166 Waterloo-Geneva Rd.; 315/539-3064) has been open every summer since 1961, dishing out creamy Richardson's root beer floats, frosty 16-ounce mugs of Pabst Blue Ribbon, butter-dipped sweet corn, and burgers-in-a-basket at an awning-covered counter or right at your car window.

Seneca Falls: Women's Rights National Historical Park

You'd never think that the diminutive redbrick, blue-collar town of **Seneca Falls** saw the birth of the American women's movement, but it did; the first women's rights convention, spearheaded by Lucretia Mott and Elizabeth Cady Stanton, took place here in July 1848. The remains of the Wesleyan Chapel where the convention was held can still be viewed at the center of town, on a guided tour from the **Women's Rights National Historical Park** (daily; free; 136 Fall St.; 315/568-2991), right on US-20. A brief exhibit on the scandalous pants-like "bloomers" popularized in 1851 by local feminist Amelia Bloomer combines with displays on transcendentalism, abolitionism, temperance, and phrenology to place the rise of this revolutionary movement in historical context.

A block away, the **National Women's Hall of Fame** (76 Fall St.; 315/568-8060) is a reading-intensive monument to the likes of Georgia O'Keeffe, Harriet Tubman, Emily Dickinson, Billie Jean King, and Jane Addams. You can listen to a saucy blues selection from Bessie Smith while dodging an endless stream of group tours.

Auburn

Auburn (pop. 27,687) is a proud industrial city with a solid, hilly downtown and a rich stock of historical homes, including that of William H. Seward, the anti-slavery Whig governor of New York. Seward founded the Republican Party,

At the west edge of Seneca Falls, the emblematic landmark of the long-vanished 1920s-era Windmill Tourist Camp has been kept alive as the local chamber of commerce and visitor information center.

organizers of the first women's rights convention, 1848

was a U.S. senator, served as secretary of state under presidents Abraham Lincoln and Andrew Johnson, and single-handedly negotiated the purchase of Alaska from Russia in 1867. The **Seward House,** on Hwy-34 a block south of US-20 (Tues.–Sat. 10 AM–4 PM; $8; 33 South St.; 315/252-1283), contains all the original furniture and many fascinating historic exhibits. Down the street from the Seward home, you can also tour the home of escaped slave and underground railroad heroine Harriet Tubman, who, from before the Civil War until her death in 1913, lived in the tidy white house (closed Mon. and Sun.; donations; 180 South St.; 315/252-2081). In 1859, Seward, then a U.S. Senator, quietly sold Tubman the home for almost no money, which was both generous and illegal, and he and Tubman are both buried in the town's Fort Hill cemetery, west of South Street between the two homes.

Right downtown, the sparkling, streamlined **Hunter's Dinerant** (18 Genesee St.; 315/255-2282), a 1950s O'Mahony, offers great greasy-spoon breakfasts (24 hours a day Thurs.–Sat.), slices of thick lemon meringue pie, and a panoramic view of the aging Genesee Beer sign that watches over the wide streets of the hill-hugging downtown.

Skaneateles

Roughly midway across New York State, **Skaneateles** (pop. 2,450; pronounced "scan-e-AT-less") is a pristine, sun-dappled resort nestled on the north shore of shimmering Skaneateles Lake. This popular summer family escape houses arts, crafts, and antiques stores along its immaculate Genesee Street (US-20), which fronts a lovely lakeside park where you can enjoy free summer concerts (Fri. at 7 PM) on the quaint bandstand, watch the boats come and go, or hop onboard a historic lake steamer for a scenic tour offered by **Mid-Lakes Navigation** (11 Jordan St.; 800/545-4318 or 315/685-8500). A stroll up the main downtown north–south drag leads you past the unadorned **Skaneateles Bakery** (19 Jordan St.; 315/685-3538) to the Skaneateles Historical Society's **Creamery Museum** (Thurs.–Sat. 1–4 PM; donation; 315/685-1360). Elm-lined side streets are full of well-maintained Greek Revival homes.

If you're hungry for more than a pastry or piece of cake, wait in line at the high-quality but self-effacing **Doug's Fish Fry** (daily; 8 Jordan St.;

315/685-3288), "not famous since 1982" for its fried haddock sandwiches, fried clams, Coney Island hot dogs, and ice-cold beer. Doug's also has creamy, thick Perry's ice cream and milk shakes, plus fresh strawberry sundaes in season. Buy a postcard for a nickel, and Doug's will slap on a stamp and send it on its way.

If the lines at Doug's are too long, or you're not in the mood for fish, try the excellent **Johnny Angel's Heavenly Hamburgers** burger bar (daily; 22 Jordan St.; 315/685-0100).

For something a bit more sit-down and soothing, one of the country's oldest restaurants, **The Kreb** (53 W. Genesee St.; 315/685-5714), has been open since 1899; it will empty your wallet with its pricey-but-hearty lobster, roast beef, and chicken specialties. One of the finest restaurants in upstate New York is the dining room at **Mirbeau Inn and Spa** (851 W. Genesee St.; 877/647-2328 or 315/685-5006), serving classic French meals for around $100 a head; the deluxe inn also has a small number of rooms (around $250).

Right in the center of Skaneateles, the **Sherwood Inn** along US-20 ($150 and up; 26 W. Genesee St.; 800/374-3796 or 315/685-3405) has been welcoming travelers to its lakeside restaurant, good bar, and comfortable rooms since it was built as a stagecoach stop back in 1807.

Syracuse and Utica

A short, 25-minute side trip from US-20 north to **Syracuse** (pop. 145,170) via I-81 yields an informative tour of the fascinating **Erie Canal Museum** (daily; free; 318 E. Erie Blvd.; 315/471-0593) in the shadow of I-690. Housed in an 1850 Weighlock building straddling the mostly paved-over canal bed, the museum has a 65-foot restored 1850s canal boat and offers free guided walking tours of the city that gave birth to the electric typewriter, the loafer, and the turn-of-the-20th-century, arts-and-crafts-style furniture of Gustav Stickley. A short film describes the staggering impact of the canal's 1825

With roots going back to the building of the Erie Canal, the sizable Irish immigrant population of the Tipperary Hill neighborhood in Syracuse insisted that traffic lights in their neighborhoods be turned upside-down so that the "British" red did not sit above the "Irish" green. One traffic light is still "upside down," and a statue at the corner of Tompkins and Milton streets evokes the whole story.

© AVALON TRAVEL

One of the oldest baseball clubs in existence, the **Syracuse Chiefs** (315/474-7833) have been around in various forms since 1858. Now the top farm club for the Washington Nationals, they play at modern Alliance Bank Stadium north of downtown off I-81 exit 25.

Northwest of Utica, the decidedly nonclassical city of **Rome** was the site of Fort Stanwix, which played a decisive role in the struggle for control of upstate New York during the Revolutionary War.

opening on the city, an impact also visible in the cast-iron commercial districts of the historic and still-lively downtown, south and west from the museum around Clinton and Armory Squares.

East of Syracuse down the I-90 NY Thruway, hilly **Utica** (pop. 62,235) is another good detour. Beer fans in particular will want to make the trip: Since 1888, the old West End Brewery **F.X. Matt Brewing Co.** ($5; 811 Edward St.; 315/732-0022), on Brewhouse Square, has pumped out barrels of Matt's trademark Utica Club and Matt's Premium regional beers alongside its soft drinks and premium microbrews. In-depth tours of the compact, family-owned facilities take you through the entire production process and drop you off in a velvet-lined Victorian tavern for your complimentary glasses of Saranac or frothy root beer.

Shake off your post-lager drowsiness with a thick, delicious cheeseburger, coffee, and slice of lemon meringue pie at the timeless **Triangle Coffee Shop** downtown (244 Genesee St.; 315/735-4692). Very friendly and welcoming despite the tight, triangular space (four sit-down tables and a seven-stool counter), the Triangle squeezes and pleases a hungry crowd with breakfast and lunch every weekday.

Cherry Valley

East of I-81, all the way to Albany, US-20 follows the route blazed by the old Great Western Turnpike over gradually steepening roller-coaster hills, past

F. X. Matt Brewing Co.

sweet-corn stands, dairy bars, and cabbage fields, and into the western reaches of picture-perfect Cherry Valley. A tempting place to pause is West Winfield, its streets lined by big trees and well-maintained Victorian-era homes.

Midway between Syracuse and Albany, 15 miles northwest of Cooperstown, **Richfield Springs** (pop. 1,264) is a peaceful crossroads that offers a calmer and less-expensive base for exploring the area. On the south side of US-20, several miles east of Richfield Springs at the crest of a large hill, a private home does double-duty as the **Petrified Creatures Museum of Natural History** (May–Sept. daily, hours vary rest of year; $9, $5 children 5–11, under 5 free; 315/858-2868), an outdoor tour of real 300-million-year-old Devonian-era fossils, plus garishly painted, life-sized "talking" dinosaur sculptures. An added attraction is the option of using a pickaxe to hack out and take home a few fossilized keepsakes from the slate pit—where most of the "petrified creatures" come from. The admission is a bit steep, but the gift shop—packed full of prehistoric-themed knickknacks—is free—though the souvenir shopping could get expensive if you have any dino-loving 10-year-olds with you.

East of Richfield Springs, US-20 makes a roller-coaster ride through the patchwork of hillside cornfields and dairy farms that drape the bubbling landscape through the fertile Cherry Valley region. Just south of the highway, attractive little **Cherry Valley** (pop. 520) contains a small local history museum, **Cherry Valley Museum** (daily in the summer and fall; $5; 49 Main St.; 607/264-3303), that recalls this tiny crossroads' early-19th-century boom period as a rowdy turnpike stagecoach stop. A small monument in the village cemetery on South Main Street pays homage to the residents killed in 1779 in the Cherry Valley Massacre, a British-backed Iroquois raid during the Revolutionary War.

Cherry Valley also holds a more recent landmark: **The TePee** (607/264-3987), a 50-foot-tall, tepee-shaped attraction, which has lured souvenir-starved travelers since 1950 with its array of Native American trinkets, famous TePee Taffy, and "Grand Panoramic View" telescope. A snack bar has hot dogs and very good chili.

Sharon Springs

The 19th-century spa and resort community of **Sharon Springs** (pop. 558), 50 miles or so west of Albany, was once on a par with Saratoga Springs, but for most of the past 75-plus years the silent streets have been lined by the slowly crumbling remains of once-grand wooden Victorian-era hotels. In its pre–Civil War heyday, the spas here attracted as many as 10,000 visitors at a time, but for the past decades Sharon Springs has been kept alive thanks to its unlikely role as a seasonal escape for Orthodox Hasidic Jews fleeing the heat of New York City summers. Throughout the ups and downs, the sulfurous, supposedly health-giving waters have continued to flow, bubbling up into a small fountain in the small park at the center of town.

Sharon Springs offers a high-contrast picture of American architectural history: The characterful hotels and landscaped parks of the old town, just north of US-20, are neighbors to the massive and anonymous beige shed of a Wal-Mart distribution center, on a hill just east.

Detour: Cooperstown

The neat, prosperous village of **Cooperstown** (pop. 1,852), founded in 1786 by the father of *Last of the Mohicans* novelist James Fenimore Cooper, was transformed into a family tourist mecca thanks to the **National Baseball Hall of Fame** (daily; $20; 25 Main St.; 888/425-5633 or 607/547-7200), which opened here in 1939. Recently expanded and upgraded, the Hall of Fame revolves around a beautifully organized time line of dioramas and display cases that walk you through the sport's greatest—and most embarrassing—moments. You'll see Babe Ruth's bat, the pair of cracked, black leather shoes worn by the ill-fated and latterly famous 1919 "Black Sox" player Shoeless Joe Jackson, and rows and rows of bronze plaques naming all the greats of the game. Special exhibits highlight the Negro Leagues, women in baseball, and, of course, baseball cards, all amid a voluminous collection of uniforms, periodicals, programs, player records, scrapbooks, and film and audio holdings. The combination admission ticket (around $30) to the Baseball Hall of Fame also gains you entrance to the other Cooperstown museums.

Cooperstown's many attractions are augmented by the subtler delights of the **Fenimore Art Museum** (daily in summer, Tues.–Sun. spring and fall, closed Jan.–Mar.; $12; 888/547-1450 or 607/547-1400), which, along with memorabilia of the writer, has engaging displays of Native American artifacts, folk art, and Hudson River School paintings. The Fenimore House is on Lake Street a mile north of town along the shores of Otsego Lake—the source of the Susquehanna River, known locally as "Glimmerglass" for its spectacular, sparkling appearance.

Near the Fenimore House, the **Farmer's Museum** (daily in summer, special programs only in winter; $12; 888/547-1450 or 607/547-1450) has illuminating exhibits on 19th-century rural life, with dignified agricultural and local history exhibits occupying most of the sturdy stone structures speck-

In recent years, Sharon Springs has seemed set for a revival. On Main Street, the white-columned hotels have been undergoing total overhauls; the stately **American Hotel** ($200 and up; 192 Main St.; 518/284-2105) now has a very good dining room, with a stylish cocktail bar, and guests can settle into comfy chairs lined up along the spacious front porch and watch the world go by.

Howes Cave: Iroquois Indian Museum

If you're interested in the native history of upstate New York, detour southeast along I-88 to tidy **Howes Cave** (pop. 4,533) and the **Iroquois Indian Museum** (Apr.–Dec. Tues.–Sun. 10 AM–5 PM, Sun. noon–5 PM; $8; 324 Caverns Rd.; 518/296-8949). The imposing, longhouse-shaped structure contains artifacts, arrowheads, and more recent works of art associated with the Native Americans descended from the Six Nations of the Iroquois ling this 1918 farm. The "remains" of the previously encountered Cardiff Giant lie in stony silence.

Avoid the in-town parking hassles and stash your car in one of the free lots near the Fenimore House. Then catch a city-operated trolley ($2 for an unlimited day pass) to downtown.

In the several-block central business district, every other bookstore, restaurant, and variety store seems to be cashing in on their tourist customers' insatiable appetite for baseball-related camp and nostalgia. For example, the **Doubleday Cafe** (93 Main St.; 607/547-5468) has above-average food and a Father-of-the-

National-Pastime theme, while the family-friendly and utterly delicious **Yum Yum Shack,** three miles south of town (4918 Hwy-28; 607/547-8088), has been drawing rave reviews while satisfying visitors from all over the Northeast.

There are literally dozens of motels from which to choose in the Cooperstown area, and the Hall of Fame offers many package deals; be sure to make your reservations far in advance to beat the summer rush. The **Lake Front Motel, Restaurant and Marina** ($65–200; 10 Fair St.; 607/547-9511) has a lakefront beach within walking distance of downtown, while in-town accommodation options include the grand **Hotel Otesaga** ($340 and up; 60 Lake St.; 800/348-6222 or 607/547-9931).

For more information on Cooperstown, including details on the very popular summertime **Glimmerglass Opera Festival,** contact the **visitors bureau** (31 Chestnut St.; 607/547-9983).

Confederacy, as well as an interactive, hands-on children's museum. The museum's collection of contemporary Native American painting and sculpture also asks tough, probing questions about the one-dimensional casino culture that has recently come to dominate reservation life across the United States.

All over this part of New York, massive roadside billboards blare out the competitive presence of Howe Caverns (marked by simple, yellow-and-black Howe Caverns directional signs) and Secret Caverns (on which a Deadhead-ish wizard beckons you onward with pesky lines like "If you haven't seen the underground waterfall, you ain't seen guano!"). Though located within two miles of each other, these two tourist attractions are about as far apart as Pat Boone and Jimi Hendrix.

The sanitized-for-your-protection **Howe Caverns** (daily; $23 and up; 518/296-8900) boast a well-lit, guided elevator and flat-bottomed boat tour of a 156-foot-deep underground cave. Along the same road, you know you're in for something completely different the moment you approach the dark, foreboding **Secret Caverns** (daily in summer; $16; 518/296-8558)—entering through the mouth of a giant, leering bat. Don't let the Abandon Hope All Ye Who Enter Here sign scare you off from taking the twisting (and twisted) 1.5-hour guided trek down into the clammy 180-foot-deep innards along a narrow, randomly lit footpath, which terminates at an impressive, 100-foot waterfall.

Albany

The New York state capital, **Albany** (pop. 304,204) was founded in 1609 when Dutch traders traveling up the Hudson River from New Amsterdam on Henry Hudson's ship *Half Moon* went ashore and established a fur-trading post. As the gateway between upstate New York and the increasingly powerful New York City port, Albany remained an important trading center through the 1820s and 1830s, extending its reach with the opening of the Erie Canal and the city's growth as a central railroad terminus and manufacturing center. Nowadays, the legendary canal has long since vanished, and the glamorous New York Central railroad's French renaissance–style, turn-of-the-20th-century Union Station, at Broadway and Clinton Street, has been transformed into the sleepy corporate headquarters of the Fleet banking group—Amtrak passenger trains now stop at a lonely platform on the opposite side of the Hudson River.

As the seat of the New York state government, however, Albany still wields obvious political power. Its rich array of museums, parks, and tree-lined boulevards—plus a few barely preserved historical neighborhoods that survived the wrecker's balls in the early 1960s—confirm the fact that the Capital City is still very much alive and well. The towering granite slabs and flying saucer–like structures that stick out at the heart of the 98-acre Empire State Plaza government center hold exhibition halls, theaters, a 42-story observation tower, and the excellent **New York State Museum** (daily; free; 518/474-5877), which includes a sensitively organized exhibit on the state's Iroquois and

facade of the cottage at Springside, on exhibit in the New York State Museum

Mohawk Native American cultures, centering on a reconstructed longhouse. The huge area devoted to the history of the metropolitan New York City area is as good or better than anything in "The City That Never Sleeps," with a re-created Upper West Side Hispanic barber shop, a Horn and Hardart Automat food dispenser, a restored 1940s car from the A-train subway line, and a solemn gallery documenting the September 11, 2001, destruction of the World Trade Center. Exhibits on the Empire State fill the rest of the museum, highlighted by a fully functioning (and rideable!) Herschell-Spillman carousel.

Albany Practicalities

If all the high culture and power politics leave you hungry for a back-to-basics road-food experience, head a mile or so west from downtown to **Jack's Diner** (547 Central Ave.; 518/482-9807). This New Jersey–built 1930s chrome-plated diner car attracts a diverse batch of families, local crazies, beat cops (the police station is across the street), and fellow travelers who come for its hearty meat loaf and burgers, bottomless cups of coffee, and friendly, loquacious staff. The **Miss Albany** (893 Broadway; 518/465-9148) is a 1941 Silk City Diner (formerly known as "Lil's") on the National Register of Historic Places.

In between the downtown museums and the green spaces of Washington Park, the blue-collar bohemian Lark Street neighborhood is Albany's answer to Greenwich Village, sporting several cafés, some tattoo parlors, and a number of good restaurants.

Albany's motels congregate off the I-90 Everett Road exit, but one very nice, centrally located place to stay is the **Mansion Hill Inn and Restaurant** ($120–160; 115 Philip St.; 888/299-0455 or 518/465-2038), near the Governor's Mansion, which doubles as a fine restaurant.

Troy

The grave of Uncle Sam and the birthplace of the detachable shirt collar are both across the river in **Troy** (50,129), 10 minutes north via the I-787 freeway. A world removed from downtown Albany, this narrow riverfront city was strategically situated at the point where the Erie Canal headed west from the Hudson River. It rose to national prominence as a manufacturing center in the 19th century, when its foundries and factories cranked out iron for stoves, stagecoaches, bells, and battleships.

Troy's burly factories have given way to a quietly picturesque college town, with Rensselaer Polytechnic Institute rising on the steep hill to the east above the cast-iron business district downtown. In addition to its many impressive buildings, Troy's dense downtown has two great road-food finds: **Manory's Restaurant** (99 Congress St.; 518/272-2422) doles out stuffed combo sandwiches, home-cooked pasta, meat and seafood dinners, and really, really big breakfasts, while **The Famous Lunch** (111 Congress St.; 518/272-9481) is a delightfully worn-down greasy spoon with hand-lettered signs, tall wooden booths, and an eye-opening clientele of cops, winos, RPI

Troy's Astros-affiliated Class A **ValleyCats** (518/ 629-2287), transplanted from Pittsfield, Massachusetts, play on the campus of Hudson Valley Community College.

Downtown Troy's cast-iron buildings are popular with set designers, who transform them into backdrops for films like Martin Scorsese's 1992 adaptation of Edith Wharton's *The Age of Innocence.*

Uncle Sam

Troy's prominent Uncle Sam monument, along the waterfront at River and Front Streets, memorializes bearded local meat-packer Samuel Wilson, who supplied beef to the soldiers quartered at the local Watervliet Arsenal during the War of 1812. Wilson's donations were quickly dubbed "Uncle Sam's beef," and the nickname and character have become the finger-pointing stuff of legend. Wilson himself is buried in the macabre, gothic hillside Oakwood Cemetery, at the head of 101st Street north of Troy via Oakwood Avenue. A health food store around the corner from the monument admonishes passersby with an "I want you…to enjoy good health" window poster.

students, and local businesspeople—nearly all of whom, from noon until late every day but Sunday, chow down on multiple four-inch-long, chili-doused hot dogs served on Styrofoam plates with cold RC Colas on the side.

Mount Lebanon Shaker Village

Heading east from Albany across the Hudson River toward the Massachusetts state line, US-20 follows Columbia Avenue through the warehouse and factory town of **Rensselaer,** then climbs a long, retail-lined hill past innumerable liquor stores, minimarts, gas stations, and motels into the Taconic Mountains. Also here is the full-throttle dirt oval of the **Lebanon Valley Speedway** (518/794-9606), with racing throughout the summer.

After this 25-mile barrage of contemporary culture, the tranquil hillside remains of **Mount Lebanon Shaker Village,** on the south side of US-20 a few hundred yards west of the Massachusetts border, come as a welcome relief. Of the 20 Shaker communities once scattered over the eastern United States,

Shaker Church.

practicing a passionate but celibate form of Christianity, Mount Lebanon was the head ministry, founded here in 1785. The community endured until 1947, and some two dozen historic buildings still stand, including a 192-foot stone barn—the largest stone barn in the world when constructed in 1859—and a no-frills but cleverly constructed 1854 washhouse boasting hidden wall drawers and perfectly fitted floorboards. All the craftsmanship is testimony to the Shaker edict, "Hands to work, hearts to God."

The Mount Lebanon village has been undergoing slow but steady restoration for years, with the announced aim of opening a proper museum here, but in the meantime if you're interested in the Shakers, you may want to make the short detour south of I-90 from Albany or New Lebanon to **Old Chatham,** where an excellent museum (hours vary; 518/794-9100) has the world's most extensive collection of Shaker-related items, from Shaker seed catalogs and pieces of Shaker furniture to the woodworking tools and devices used to make them.

The quickest route east from Troy is Hwy-2, a rural back road across the Taconic Mountains to Williamstown, Massachusetts. Alternatively, you can follow old US-20 east through New Lebanon to Pittsfield, Massachusetts, then follow a short stretch of the **Appalachian Trail** route along US-7 north to Williamstown and North Adams (see page 339). For details on the full route, see pages 310–407.

MASSACHUSETTS

The leafy amble from New York State, up and over the ridge of the Taconics, brings you through a beautiful region dense with visitor appeal, including the Shaker communities along US-20 and the industrial and literary sites of the Berkshires, not to mention Williamstown, a New England poster town if ever there was one. (For full coverage of this region, see the *Appalachian Trail* chapter.)

Across Massachusetts, we follow the very scenic Route 2, also known as the **Mohawk Trail,** across the state's northern tier, rather than US-20, which runs more or less underneath the Massachusetts Turnpike, I-90. Passing across some of the least populous and most deeply forested acres in the whole Commonwealth of Massachusetts, you can easily imagine you're in Vermont rather than the so-called Bay State. Picking its way over the flattened summits of the Hoosac Range foothills to the Green Mountains in the north, Route 2 follows rock-strewn trout streams flecked with white water and shaded by boreal forests of hemlock, yellow birch, and red spruce—including some of the state's only remaining stands of old growth. Midway across Massachusetts, Route 2 bridges the Connecticut River above Turners Falls, lopes through the trees, and emerges at historic **Lexington** and **Concord,** at **Boston**'s back door.

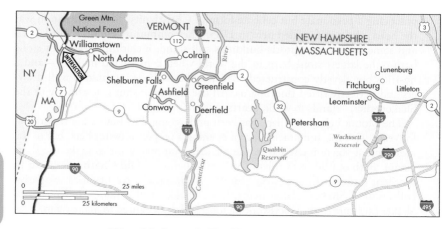

In Massachusetts and the rest of New England, we have adopted the use of "Route" instead of "Hwy-," in keeping with regional practice.

You'll find excellent wooded streamside campsites in **Mohawk Trail State Forest** (413/339-5504) just above where the Cold River empties into the Deerfield. There are six year-round rustic log cabins, too, but make reservations well in advance if you have your heart set on staying in one.

The Mohawk Trail

Running east from North Adams toward Greenfield and I-91, and taking its name from the warpath used for raids against Algonquin settlements along the upper Connecticut River Valley, the **Mohawk Trail** (Route 2) was one of the nation's first scenic highways, improved and paved as early as 1914 as part of a massive state effort to lure tourists into this cash-deprived farm belt of New England. If you're driving an overloaded or underpowered vehicle, you'll appreciate the thrill and radiator-popping risks that once attended the slow switchback grind up around the attention-getting Hairpin Turn at the edge of the Western Summit. The turn is so tight that signs insist on a 15-mph speed limit, and people who don't abide by the rules are likely to find themselves screeching around past the sightseers at the friendly **Golden Eagle Restaurant** (413/663-9834). Farther up, at the top of the hill, the tidy **Wigwam Summit Cottages** (around $75; 413/663-3205), one of many photogenic old motor courts along the route, has been taking in guests since the road was built (though the cottages were undergoing restoration at time of writing). Don't be fooled by the short stretch of gentle ups and downs east of the summit over the glacier-flattened mountain peaks: The route east along the tortuous Cold River ravine quickens the pulse, even in these days of power steering and antilock brakes, especially if you get sandwiched between a pair of 18-wheelers, whose burning brake pads sometimes scent the air all the way down the valley.

mayflower,
state flower of Massachussetts

Big Indian Shop

East of the summit, dropping down into the valley of the Deerfield River, you pass groups of kayakers and some roadside stands offering rentals of inner tubes—the white-water equivalent of a recliner, and the preferred mode of transport for those interested in relaxing and enjoying the ride. More serious river runners may want to sign up for one of the trips offered by **Zoar Outdoor** (800/532-7483). There are also some enticingly kitschy old Indian trading posts, packed full of postcards, plastic tomahawks, and moccasins; my personal favorite is the Big Indian Shop, fronted by a historically inaccurate, politically incorrect, and photogenically irresistible 35-foot-tall statue of a Plains Indian. Another giant Indian statue, a half-ton bronze entitled *Hail to the Sunrise,* stands along Route 2 just west of the town of Charlemont.

Shelburne Falls

Travelers in search of variety should head farther along the historic Mohawk Trail, Route 2, and take a turn at the signs for the lively, artsy little town of **Shelburne Falls,** which is actually two towns, Shelburne and Buckland (combined pop. 1,731), facing one another across the Deerfield River. The two are linked by the **Bridge of Flowers,** a former electric trolley bridge that was converted to a linear display garden after the trolleys closed down in the 1920s. Four score and a few years later, there are mature trees growing out of the concrete arches, and every spring local gardeners add rich displays of annual color. The story of the trolleys is told, and rides are sometimes offered, at the **Shelburne Falls Trolley Museum** (14 Depot Rd.; 413/625-9443), walking distance south of the bridge.

Nearby food and beverage options include espresso concoctions from Bridge Street's **Shelburne Falls Coffee Roasters** (413/625-0116) or the vegetarian-

Bridge of Flowers in Shelburne Falls

friendly deli selections at the rear of **McCusker's Market** (3 State St.; 413/625-9411), facing the south end of the iron bridge. The best cheap grub in town is served up at the homey **Foxtown Coffee and Sandwich Shop** (413/625-6606) on Bridge Street, where you can feast on a short stack of pancakes with real maple syrup for $2 or enjoy a fresh BLT with a packet of potato chips and a pickle on the side for $2.55.

Scenic Route 116: Ashfield and Conway

Come fall, the sugar maples in the surrounding mixed hardwood forest add a blaze of brilliant orange to the landscape, making Route 2 a favorite of leaf-peepers between the end of September and Columbus Day weekend. But if sharing the two-lane road with thousands of rubbernecking drivers becomes wearisome, consider taking a road less traveled. Almost any road will do, but a loop along Route 116 through **Ashfield** and **Conway,** a few miles south of Route 2, passes over several historic covered bridges and offers enough pastoral beauty to more than compensate for the detours.

Shunning the main highway doesn't require skipping meals, either. For instance, there are thin-crust whole pizzas and slices at the **Country Pie Pizza Company** (open daily till 9 PM; 343 Main St.; 413/628-4488) across from Ashfield's public library. Given the fresh fancy toppings available, the prices are a real steal. Fans rate Country Pie as highly as anything north of New Haven, and with delicious whole pies for around $20, it's a great place to stop.

Greenfield and Deerfield

As Route 2 speeds down into the Connecticut River Valley, it veers along I-91 just long enough to skirt the county seat of **Greenfield,** a place once known for its cutlery, tap-and-die, and other metals-related manufacturing. The proximity of the Interstate has endowed Greenfield with some of the few chain motels in western Massachusetts.

A world away from the modern Interstate aesthetic, but just three miles south of Greenfield along Route 5, **Historic Deerfield** (daily; $12; 413/775-7214) is an immaculately preserved ensemble of architecture and agriculture dating back over 350 years. More than a dozen clapboard buildings, shaded by a canopy of stately old elm trees, form a mile-long reminder of the time when this part of Massachusetts formed the frontier of western "civilization," and English settlers waged bloody war against the native Pocumtuck Indians. The adjacent town of Deerfield, and the famous Deerfield Academy prep school, hardly intrude, leaving Historic Deerfield to stand as it was—fanlight windows, wrought iron, well-worn stones, and all. Inside each house, guides discuss the lives, belongings, and historical contexts of the former inhabitants, often with such parental intimacy that you half-expect these long-dead Ebenezers, Jonathans, and Marys to be napping upstairs. One of the finest surviving colonial townscapes in America, Historic Deerfield is well worth a visit, no matter how brief, especially since there's no admission charge if you just want to stop and walk around.

Historic Deerfield also offers the **Flynt Center of Early New England Life** at the edge of a field behind Main Street. The 27,000-square-foot museum, designed to look like a colonial tobacco barn, displays thousands of "fancy goods" and other consumer treasures—pewter teapots, silk waistcoats, and the like—that were keys to civilized life here on the edge of wilderness. For the full historic experience, stay for dinner or overnight at the **Deerfield Inn** ($215 and up; 413/774-5587), right in the historic core.

Route 2: Gardner

About 10 miles east of I-91, Route 2 crosses high over the Connecticut River atop the huge, art deco French King Bridge, giving grand views over the surrounding landscape. From here east, the route becomes a mini freeway as it launches into a 40-mile stretch of almost nothing but forest; though nearly unimaginable today, some two-thirds of the landscape you see out your windows was totally deforested in the early 1800s. After some 150 years, that statistic has been reversed, although much of the forest along this stretch is relatively young, having grown up since a devastating hurricane in 1938 blew down nearly every pine tree in its path.

For most of the way across this part of central Massachusetts, the older two-lane alignment of the Mohawk Trail (Route 2) is still in use as Route 2A, running through a series of small towns like Orange, Athol, Templeton, and **Gardner** (pop. 20,228), which was once one of the busiest chair-making

---

Although early spring is aptly known as mud season throughout New England's back country, it's also when the sugar maple sap starts to flow. Boil away nearly 98 percent of the sap and you have genuine maple syrup delicious enough to make muddy, frost-heaved farm roads positively inviting.

Northeast of Deerfield, near the Vermont border, the town of **Northfield** had the first youth hostel in the United States in 1934. Unfortunately, the hostel closed in 1998, taken over as dormitories by a local college.

It's outside the "historic" core of Deerfield, and not technically in the Berkshires for that matter, but one of New England's great beer-makers, **Berkshire Brewing,** offers tours and tastings in South Deerfield (12 Railroad St.; 413/665-6600).

centers in the United States. The area's industrial history is remembered by the town's pride and joy, the onetime **World's Largest Chair,** which sits on the front lawn of Gardner's Elm Street elementary school.

Leominster

As you approach the Tri-Town area of **Leominster** (pronounced "LUH-minster"), Fitchburg, and Lunenburg, rooftops begin to supplant treetops and Boston radio stations crowd the dial. Although "the Hub" is still some 30 miles away, its gravitational attraction seems to compel a majority of cars to exceed the speed limit. If you already know that you would rather walk barefoot over hot coals than be caught driving in Boston, you can start looking for accommodations now, as you are within the sphere of the MBTA Commuter Rail service to downtown (800/392-6100). Purely by way of an example, the 80-minute journey from end-of-the-line Fitchburg to Boston's North Station, made 10 times daily on weekdays, five times daily on weekends, costs around $12 round-trip—equivalent to a couple of hours' parking in most Boston lots.

Accommodations here, along I-495 on the perimeter of the Boston metropolitan area, are largely geared toward business travelers, though the aptly named **Friendly Crossways Retreat** (247 Littleton County Rd.; 978/456-9386), just north of the Route 2/I-495 junction in the hamlet (not the college) of Harvard, has HI-approved dorm beds and a few private rooms, too.

Practicalities aside, one very positive reason to spend time out here is the presence of **Fruitlands** (May–Oct. daily; $12; 102 Prospect Hill Rd.; 978/456-3924), a 210-acre indoor/outdoor art center. Spiritual heir to the historic Utopian colony that started (and failed) here in 1843, Fruitlands now houses the Harvard College museum of American arts and crafts, Native American life ways, and Shaker design.

Though Lowell is doubtless best known as the home of Jack Kerouac, in recent years the town made the news as the home of boxing brothers Micky Ward and Dicky Ecklund, whose story was the basis of the 2010 film *The Fighter*, which was set and filmed here.

Lowell

At "five o'clock of a red-all-over suppertime" on March 12, 1922, Jack Kerouac—baptized John L. (Jean-Louis) Kirouac by his French Canadian parents—was born in **Lowell** (pop. 106,519), a city sincerely regarded as one of the wonders of the world back when the Industrial Revolution was as fascinating as the Internet is now. Although this original dharma bum is more widely remembered for hanging out with Ferlinghetti in San Francisco and Ginsberg in New York, and for pasting the beat generation firmly across the map of American culture, Kerouac also wrote five novels based on friends and familiar places in his native city. His fictional work, from *On the Road* on, is that much more interesting when read in the context of his real life in this Merrimack River mill town.

Reciprocating Kerouac's lifelong love for Lowell, the National Park Service publishes a walking-tour brochure on Jack and his life in Lowell. It also helps sponsor the annual **Lowell Celebrates Kerouac!** festival the first full weekend in October. Maps and guides to the man and the town are available from the Lowell National Historical Park **visitors center** (246 Market St.; 978/970-5000), but parking is a block west at 304 Dutton Street.

If you want to pay your respects to Kerouac, who died in Florida in 1969, he is buried in Edson Cemetery, two miles south of downtown Lowell via Gorham Street. Fans by the hundreds beat a path to his grave, which is on Lincoln Avenue between 7th and 8th Streets, marked by a pile of beer cans and other ritual offerings.

Even without the Kerouac connection, Lowell—with its working water-powered looms, canal tours, and engaging interpretive tours—would deserve attention. Befitting its blue-collar past, Lowell is home to several classic diners—best of which is the excellent **Arthur's Paradise Diner** (112 Bridge St.; 978/452-8647), a 1937 Worcester diner where the house specialty is the great big Boot Mill sandwich, a two-hands-full combination of eggs, cheese, potatoes, and meat. Lots of meat.

Lowell's other legendary blue-collar landmarks include the **Club Diner** (145 Dutton St.; 978/452-1679) and the **Four Sisters' Owl Diner,** open every day (244 Appleton St.; 978/453-8321).

Concord: The Shot Heard Round the World

Route 2 feels increasingly freeway-like the closer you get to Boston, but there are a few things in the neighborhood you may want to check out if you're not in a hurry to hit the "Hub." A good example is lovely little **Concord** (pop. 17,668), the destination of British Redcoats that fabled day in April 1775 when the war for American independence began. A reconstructed **Old North Bridge,** site of the "shot heard round the world," still arches over the placid Concord River next to open fields and dry stone walls. The superb setting draws artists and picnickers as well as history buffs, and if the crowds aren't too bad, the scene ranks among the most evocative in New England. The **Minute Man National Historical Park** maintains a free year-round visitors

Get to know life in Lowell by watching a Class A baseball game at downtown's riverside LeLacheur Park, home to the Red Sox-affiliated Lowell Spinners (978/459-1702).

Perhaps you haven't got a week—like Thoreau did—to paddle down the Concord River. You can still make your own, albeit abbreviated, journey with a summer or fall canoe rental from **South Bridge Boat House** (around $17/hour; 496-502 Main St.; 978/371-2465), in Concord.

the Minute Man National Historical Park

center (978/369-6993) on the hillside overlooking the famous site. Stop in and pick up a guide to the rest of the park's holdings along the "Battle Road" (a.k.a. Lexington Road and Route 2A) between Concord and Lexington. (And try to turn a deaf ear to the constant stream of small planes flying in and out of nearby Hanscom Field.)

Although it often seems as if you can't toss a stick anywhere in eastern Massachusetts without hitting something of historic significance, this is especially true in and around Concord, where some of the most influential American writers—Ralph Waldo Emerson, Nathaniel Hawthorne, Henry David Thoreau, and Louisa May Alcott, to name the most famous four—lived and/or worked. To get a sense of the lives of these influential and interconnected writers, head to that ancient-looking parsonage alongside the famous Old North Bridge, **The Old Manse** (Apr.–Oct. daily, Feb.–April on Sat. and Sun.; $8; 269 Monument St.; 978/369-3909), whose study window views are

main gate at Sleepy Hollow Cemetery   Ralph Waldo Emerson's marker

Patriots and Poets

One of the more enjoyable rites of springtime in and around Boston is the annual celebration of the events leading up to the American Revolution. Now held on the third Monday in April, but originally occurring on April 18, the state holiday known as Patriot's Day sees all kinds of special events. Most famous is the Boston Marathon, which since 1897 has been run from Hopkinton southwest of the city through Newton to its finish at Copley Square. Although the marathon follows a very different route, it is held on the anniversary of another famous race, the one between British soldiers and patriot Paul Revere, who made his legendary ride on the night of April 18, 1775, to warn his fellow minutemen of the British march on Lexington and Concord.

At the end of his ride, on the morning of April 19, Paul Revere reached the Buckman Tavern in Lexington, where fellow revolutionaries John Hancock and Samuel Adams (he of boutique beer fame) were asleep, awaiting word of the British advance. Revere woke them (and some 70 others), and at 5:30 AM they assembled to meet the redcoats. Although the minutemen backed off, shots were fired and eight Americans were killed. Three hours later, when the British moved on to Concord, they were met by a much larger and better organized force of minutemen, who fired back and started what we now know as the Revolutionary War. This battle, which raged all day and followed the overwhelmed British all the way back to Boston, was remembered in another oft-recited patriotic poem by Concord writer Ralph Waldo Emerson, words from which are inscribed on the base of Concord's *The Minute Man* statue:

> *By the rude bridge that arched the flood,*
> *Their flag to April's breeze unfurled,*
> *Here once the embattled farmers stood,*
> *And fired the shot heard round the world.*

These events and many related ones are all re-enacted each year, either on their actual anniversary or on Patriot's Day, and usually at the historically accurate crack of dawn.

not so very different from what they were when Ralph Waldo Emerson and Nathaniel Hawthorne lived here. And if the mood strikes you, you can visit the final resting place of these literary lions along Author's Ridge in **Sleepy Hollow Cemetery,** off Bedford Street northeast of the town center.

Visitors may be struck by the quantity of No Parking signs lining the streets of Concord, but the reason for this barrage of apparent inhospitality may be seen on any sun-drenched summer weekend, when long columns of cars bound for the beach at nearby **Walden Pond** jam Route 126. Serious fans of

Henry David Thoreau and his little experiment of simple living may be able to overlook its overstressed condition, but more than likely you'll be taken aback by the erosion, the crowds, and the racket of passing commuter trains. Of course, there is still some magic to the place, although it usually takes a near-dawn in late spring or near-dusk in late fall to find any hint of peace or magnificence along the pond's well-worn peripheral path.

For a quick introduction to all this and more, stop by the **Concord Museum** (daily; $10; 978/369-9763 or 978/369-9609), just east of the town green, where the collection contains everything from the lantern used in Paul Revere's famous ride to dozens of household objects (beds, chairs, desks, etc.) belonging to Emerson and Thoreau.

If you want to linger in Concord long enough to have some transcendent moments of your own, stay the night at one of many nice B&Bs, like the **Hawthorne Inn** ($150–350; 462 Lexington Rd.; 978/369-5610), across from Hawthorne's home, The Wayside, which is part of the Minute Man National Park.

Not far from Thoreau's reconstructed cabin at Walden Pond, a very different philosophy of simplicity may be found in the design of the **Gropius House** (Wed.–Sun. 11 AM–4 PM in summer, Sat. and Sun. only the rest of the year; $10; 781/259-8098), on Baker Bridge Road in Lincoln. Built between 1937 and 1938 by and for Bauhaus founder Walter Gropius, this small showcase blends Bauhaus form-is-function precepts with traditional New England simplicity.

One of the most beautiful gardens in the Boston area is **Mount Auburn Cemetery,** along the Charles River in western Cambridge. It has 174 acres of trees, hills, paths, and memorials marking the mortal remains of such luminaries as Henry Wadsworth Longfellow, Winslow Homer, and Buckminster Fuller.

Cambridge

One last stop before you hit Boston proper is erudite **Cambridge** (pop. 105,162), an inseparable sibling to the big city but very much a place in its own right. Best known for its top universities, Harvard and Massachusetts Institute of Technology, Cambridge is a liberal, earthy, and open-minded foil to the big money and social pretension that so often characterize its big brother across the water.

The two universities and their many fine museums (especially Harvard, which boasts world-class collections in the Fogg Art Museum, the Arthur M. Sackler Museum of Far Eastern Art, and the Peabody Museum of Archaeology and Ethnology) are the main draws for visitors, but the "town" away from the "gown" is equally worth exploring, despite the recent outbreak of chain-store disease around Harvard Square. For an antidote, head two stops north on the T subway to Davis Square in neighboring Somerville, where a classic 1941 Worcester diner, **The Rosebud** (381 Summer St.; 617/666-6015), off Elm Street, serves up the highest quality meals all day, with nary a Starbucks in sight.

Driving Across Boston

From Concord, the remaining dozen miles to Boston are most quickly devoured along Route 2, although you can take slower Route 2A if you wish to follow the footsteps of those retreating British redcoats. Either way will bring you to the same gateway for the metropolitan area. Following US-3 will bring you in through wealthy Winchester and eventually onto Memorial Drive along the Charles River, past the campuses of Harvard and MIT. But unless it's

Car Talk

Ever tuned in to your local national public radio station, and instead of hearing breaking news and informed commentary, you got two guys laughing their heads off and making jokes about cars and mechanics? Well, you probably tuned in to *Car Talk*, the Cambridge-based call-in show featuring a pair of MIT-trained auto mechanics, Click and Clack, the Tappet Brothers, otherwise known as Tom and Ray Magliozzi. From its humble beginnings back around 1977, *Car Talk* has become the most popular program at the left edge of the radio dial, reaching more than two million listeners every week. In between bouts of sarcasm and scandal-mongering, Tom and Ray do actually give advice about cars—advice that occasionally helps people—so if you're having trouble with your car, give them a call at 888/227-8255, or send a message through their website, www.cartalk.com. Either way, it's free. And you're safe from the public humiliation for a while at least. The show is not broadcast live but cunningly edited together in a darkened room off Harvard Square (look for a sign saying Dewey, Cheatham, and Howe), with the help of sophisticated technology and an ever-expanding team of contributors with names like Zbigniew Chrysler, Orson Buggy, Rusty Steele, Denton Fender, Alan Greasepan, and Francis Ford Cupholda.

If you're in Cambridge ("Our Fair City") and happen to need some car repair, *Car Talk*'s Ray Magliozzi runs the **Good News Garage** (75 Hamilton St.; 617/354-5383), off Brookline Street midway between Central Square and the Boston University Bridge over the Charles River.

3 AM and the roads are all clear, you would be well-advised to leave your car in the gigantic Alewife T subway station commuter parking garage (about $8 a day) at the Route 2/US-3/Route 16 junction in Arlington, and use the subway to get around the city. (Cyclists note: From the Alewife T, the very nice **Minuteman Bikeway** follows the bed of the old Boston & Lowell Railroad between Cambridge and the edge of Concord—11 idyllic, car-free miles.)

Driving directions across downtown Boston are basically a waste of paper; signs are few and traffic is chaotic, and anyway you'll need to keep your eyes firmly on the road.

Quincy: The Adams Family

South of Boston, Route 3 reemerges from the I-93 freeway at **Quincy** (pop. 92,271), home of the Adams family, the political dynasty that helped shape the early republic. John Adams (1735–1826) signed the Declaration of Independence, served as a diplomat during the Revolutionary War, helped negotiate the Treaty of Paris, then returned home to become George Washington's vice

Playing on the common perception of the Pilgrims as thrifty, reliable, and steadfast, in 1928 the automobile company Chrysler named its now-defunct line of low-priced cars Plymouth.

Boston

CHRIST CHURCH (OLD NORTH), BOSTON, MASS.

THE SIGNAL LANTERNS OF
PAUL REVERE
DISPLAYED IN THE STEEPLE OF THIS CHURCH
APRIL 18, 1775
MARKED THE COUNTRY OF THE MARCH
OF THE BRITISH TROOPS TO
LEXINGTON AND CONCORD

In the nearly 400 years since its founding, Boston (pop. 617,594) has witnessed more historically significant events than any American city even twice its size. The youthful energy of the city's many college students certainly helps cloak its traditional Puritan parochialism, while the high-tech economic boom and the breaking of the "Curse of the Bambino" by the 2004 World Series–champion Boston Red Sox baseball team have helped loosen up a city previously best known for baked beans and banning sexy books.

There are lots of places to start a Boston tour, but a personal favorite is the **Old North Church** (daily; 193 Salem St.; 617/523-6676), a Boston landmark since well before Paul Revere set off on his midnight ride. The steeple has been rebuilt, but almost everything else dates back to colonial times. The **Paul Revere House** (daily; $3.50; 19 North Square; 617/523-2338), the oldest in Boston, is a few blocks away, and the surrounding neighborhood, the predominantly Italian North End, is the city's oldest and most pedestrian-friendly quarter, its narrow streets jutting out toward Boston harbor.

With its abundance of universities, museums, and cultural centers, Boston is packed with places to improve your mind. One of the nicest has to be the **Isabella Stuart Gardner Museum** (closed Mon.; $12; 280 The Fenway; 617/566-1401). In the late 19th century, "Mrs. Jack" Gardner built her home in the style of a Venetian palazzo, crammed it with exquisite art, and then opened it as a museum. And what a museum, now better than ever thanks to the copper-and-glass, Renzo Piano–designed addition, fronting the lushly landscaped interior courtyard. (Note: Anyone named "Isabella" gets in free!) The much bigger **Museum of Fine Arts** (daily; $22; 465 Huntington Ave.; 617/267-9300) is only a short walk away and has more than 200 world-class galleries of just about every type and era of fine art, including world-class Impressionists and perhaps the best Japanese art collection in the United States.

Fenway Park—Home of the Boston Red Sox, Boston, Mass.   78552

For baseball fans, Boston's must-see is **Fenway Park** (tickets at 877/REDSOX-9), home of the Red Sox. Located off Boylston Street at 4 Yawkey Way, this is the oldest, smallest, and arguably most entertaining stadium in the nation. The team is not bad, either.

Practicalities

Boston, a.k.a. "The Hub," sits spider-like at the center of a web of major highways. Air travelers get to deal with the chaos and malfunction of Logan International Airport, the major gateway to New England for U.S. and foreign flights. Logan is very central—just a seven-minute ride across Boston Harbor to downtown if you take the Water Shuttle. Logan is also connected to the city by the Blue Line subway run by Massachusetts Bay Transportation Authority (617/222-3200), the "T," a well-run and nearly comprehensive network of subways, buses, trams, ferries, and commuter trains. Despite the completion of the $15 billion "Big Dig," Boston's 21st-century traffic and 17th-century streets are not for faint-hearted drivers. Narrow, often unidentified, poorly maintained, and laid out in irregular patterns conforming to long-buried topography, the streets of Boston are also home to aggressive, bumper-riding red-light-runners. So park your car, take public transit, and walk.

While nightly rates at top-end hotels run well over $400 a night, places to stay in Boston start with the budget **HI-Boston Hostel** ($35 per person, higher for a private room; 617/536-9455), which will move in 2012 into a new building at 25 Stuart Street at Boston's midtown cultural district, theater district, and Chinatown, close to the Boston Public Garden and adjacent to public transportation. As befitting a historical city such as Boston, the hostel is in National Register of Historic Places building; as befitting the times, it is a LEED building, as well. For a moderate price and a great location, right at the Copley Square finish line of the Boston Marathon, try the popular **Charlesmark Hotel** (around $220 and up; 655 Boylston; 617/247-1212). Many steps up the comfort scale is the well-appointed and very central **Beacon Hill Hotel** ($215 and up; 25 Charles St.; 617/723-7575), a boutique B&B with a popular bistro and rooftop terrace.

Thanks no doubt to Boston's Puritan past, the city has never had a great reputation for its food, but things have definitely changed. If you really have to have an old-fashioned Boston meal, go to **Durgin-Park** (daily; 617/227-2038) in Faneuil Hall Market Place. Open since 1827, this New England eatery serves up Yankee pot roast, clam chowder, and baked beans at shared tables to a mix of tourists and masochistic locals. Boston also has more than few great Mexican, Japanese, and Chinese places, but for another only-in-Boston experience head to **The Daily Catch** (daily; cash only; 323 Hanover St.; 617/523-8567), in the old North End within walking distance of the Haymarket T. This family-run place started in 1973 is so tiny that the cook could shake hands with half his customers without leaving his stove. Calamari (squid) is the house specialty, but the menu's mainstay is Sicilian seafood over linguine (with red or white sauce), served in sauté pans instead of on plates. It takes cash only but doesn't take reservations, so expect a wait after 6 PM.

For further information, contact the **Greater Boston Convention and Visitors Bureau** (888/SEE-BOSTON or 617/536-4100).

night game at Fenway Park

Although the Pilgrims are often given credit for establishing the first permanent white settlement in what later became the United States, they arrived a dozen years after other English settlers established Jamestown, Virginia.

president and successor. His son, John Quincy Adams (1767–1848), served as president from 1825 to 1829. Rather than quit politics after losing the election in 1828, he returned to Washington, serving in the House of Representatives for the next 16 years. The rather modest houses where both men were born, plus a nice garden and a historic church, are preserved as part of the **Adams National Historic Site,** which covers 13 downtown acres starting at a visitors center (daily; $5; 1250 Hancock St.; 617/770-1175).

More recently, Quincy has been home to granite quarries and the truly huge Fore River Shipyard, on Route 3A at the south edge of town, where the massive cruiser **USS *Salem*** (daily; $8; 739 Washington St.; 617/479-7900) is berthed as part of the **United States Naval Shipbuilding Museum.** This dense forest of cranes, derricks, and scaffolding rises along the south side of the 1930s Fore River Bridge, along Route 3A at the south edge of town.

Plymouth Rock and Plimoth Plantation

There's little evidence to back up the story of **Plymouth Rock,** the supposed landing site of those weary *Mayflower* passengers back in 1620, but like the Liberty Bell and Mt. Rushmore, it's something every red-blooded American tourist has to see.

Now protected by a neoclassical granite portico and inscribed with the date 1620, **Plymouth Rock** is right on the waterfront, off Water Street at the south end of North Street in **Plymouth.** The rock is part of pleasant **Pilgrim Memorial State Park,** which also includes the *Mayflower II* (daily; $10), a replica of the Pilgrims' ship, where an onboard exhibit describes the Pilgrims'

Every year, on the Sunday nearest to the anniversary of the **Boston Tea Party** (December 16, 1773), re-enactors dressed as Indians (mimicking the colonists who disguised themselves as Native Americans) throw bales of tea into the harbor from the decks of the Boston Tea Party Ship. It all starts at the Old South Meeting House (daily; $6; 310 Washington Street; 617/482-6439).

two-month transatlantic journey. The *Mayflower* is about the only sign of Plymouth being such a potential tourist trap; the whole place is actually fairly low-key, with a couple of gift shops and snack bars across from the rock. Two blocks inland, downtown Plymouth looks like any other very pleasant New England suburb, with no tacky T-shirt shops to be found.

Two miles south from Plymouth Rock along Route 3A, or off the Route 3 freeway at exit 5, **Plimoth Plantation** (daily; $26; 508/746-1622) is a living history re-creation of the original Pilgrim colony and features costumed inter-preters taking part in planting, harvesting, and other daily chores.

New Bedford

Predominantly Portuguese **New Bedford** (pop. 95,072) is remembered as a capital of the whaling industry back in the days when spermaceti candles and whale oil lamps were ne-cessities, not antiques. The city's harbor at the mile-wide mouth of the Acushnet River was home port for the East Coast's largest commercial fishing fleet until nearly two de-cades of flagrant overfishing brought the industry to col-lapse. The **New Bedford Whaling National Historical Park** showcases the cobblestone streets and brick facades, virtually unaltered since Herman Melville shipped out of here in 1840 aboard a whaler bound for the Pacific. For a good orientation, drop by the well-stocked **visitors center** (508/996-4095), at the corner of William Street and North 2nd Street, and join one of the free hour-long guided walk-ing tours. Before or after a stroll around town, head to the top of Johnny Cake Hill and visit the excellent **New Bedford Whaling Museum** (daily; $14; 508/997-0046). Scrimshaw (carved whale ivory), tools of the whaling trade, historic photos, special maritime exhibits, and an 89-foot ship model are a few of the artifacts found in the not-to-be-missed museum collection maintained by the Old Dartmouth Historical Society. Across the street from the museum, the gorgeous little **Seamen's Bethel,** dedicated in 1832 and featuring a pulpit shaped like a ship's bow, was featured in a chapter of Herman Melville's classic, *Moby Dick.*

To learn more than you ever thought possible about thermometers, pay a visit to the world's largest thermometer collection, proudly on display in the basement of Dick "The Thermometer Man" Porter's home in **Onset;** call 508/295-5504 for directions (and to make sure he's home).

New Bedford's Acushnet Avenue has a significant place in the world of late-19th-century American art: Albert Pinkham Ryder, visionary "painter of dreams," was born here, across from the childhood home of Albert Bierstadt, Romantic painter of the American West.

Diner fans will appreciate New Bedford's offerings, too. The easiest diner to find is **Angelo's Orchid Diner** (805 Rockdale Ave.; 508/993-3172), on old US-6, a 1953 O'Mahony serving solid short-order cookery enlivened by—you guessed it—a Portuguese influence. Or check out another 1950s O'Mahony, the pristine **Shawmut Diner** (943 Shawmut

painting by a New Bedford whaleman, 1840

Ave.; 508/993-3073), at Hathaway near Route 140, open daily from 5 AM; the neon Indian alone makes it worth a visit.

Cape Cod: Sandwich

Although it rides the ridge of Cape Cod's glacial moraine, the forest-clad US-6 freeway (called Mid-Cape Highway) affords few good vistas. Traffic willing, you'll sail between the Sagamore Bridge and the Outer Cape in about 30 minutes, surrounded by more green than blue. One preferred route is parallel Route 6A. Never more than a mile or two away from US-6, this slower road is a good introduction to a part of the Cape that does its utmost to stay quaint without being too cute. Generally, it succeeds.

Take **Sandwich,** for example. When you reach the center of town, you'll come across a small, irregular green bordered by a tall, white church, a stately carriage-stop inn, and the Historical Society's **Sandwich Glass Museum** (Apr.–Oct. daily; $5; 129 Main St.; 508/888-0251). Although the

Massachusetts is one of two states that recognizes private property ownership down to the low tide line, which is why you should respect the No Trespassing signs you may encounter on some beaches. Fortunately, plenty are amended with the words Walkers Welcome.

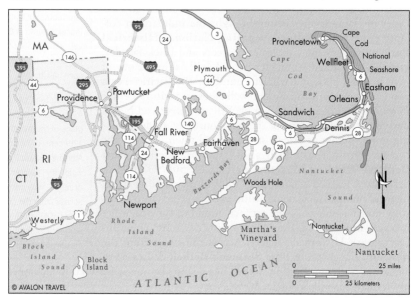

town's various glassworks could and did produce consummate extravagant vases and other artistic pieces, they mostly created inexpensive, mass-market stuff—such as 10-cent oil-lamp chimneys and pressed plates and saucers, hundreds of which are on display.

Nearby on Pine and Grove Streets (follow signs from Route 130) is a more diverse collection of Americana, the **Heritage Museums and Gardens** (May–Oct. daily; $15; 508/888-3300). Here nearly 80 acres of landscaped gardens surround collections of Currier & Ives prints, military miniatures, antique cars, cigar store figures, American primitive portraiture—more unflattering likenesses of children have never been conceived—and even a working 1912 carousel.

If you can't get a ticket to Fenway Park, get a feel for New England baseball by catching a Triple A game at McCoy Stadium (401/724-7300), right in the heart of this historic mill town.

Bayside Route 6A

In total contrast to the high-speed US-6 freeway or the traffic-clogged, overdeveloped, and frequently ugly Route 28 along the south shore, Route 6A along Cape Cod Bay shows off the Cape as it should be seen. Route 6A's winding back roads pass through small historic town after small historic town, and they are lined by seafood shacks, ice cream stands, high-style restaurants, colonial-era homes, village greens, and stately churches—backed all the way by miles of bayfront beaches.

From Sandwich in the west to Brewster in the east, Route 6A offers a taste of what the Cape is all about. **Barnstable** (pop. 45,193), for example, is the second-oldest community on Cape Cod (founded in 1639) and has managed to retain its historic core through the years. A series of quaint villages line the bay between here and **Brewster** (pop. 9,820), which has the 85-acre **Cape Cod Museum of Natural History** (daily; $7; 869 Main St.; 508/896-3867) and the old-fashioned **Brewster Store** (1935 Main St.; 508/896-3744), in a building originally built as a church in 1852.

Midway along, **Dennis,** the terminus of the Cape Cod rail-trail to Wellfleet, is also the setting for the nation's oldest professional summer-stock theater, the **Cape Playhouse** (box office 877/385-3911 or 508/385-3911), on Route 6A just east of the gas station. If you prefer film over stage, the **Cape Cinema** (508/385-2503), on the grounds behind the Playhouse, specializes in movies you won't find at the multiplex. If you arrive late, stick around until the lights go up after the credits or you'll miss one of the Cape's best public artworks, Rockwell Kent's brightly colored, Zodiac-themed mural of Prometheus on the cinema's ceiling.

Dennis also offers the chance to take in excellent Cape Cod views from atop **Scargo Tower;** turn toward South Dennis at the gas station, then follow signs along Scargo Hill Road.

A Cape Cod Primer

To avoid frustration and confusion when visiting Cape Cod, it helps to understand its basic directions and seasons. The compass isn't your friend here, as you will discover when faced with highway signs stubbornly directing you south to Provincetown—when heading south would bring you sooner to Venezuela than to the Cape's northernmost town. Instead, the principal directions are up and down: "Up-Cape" means generally westward, toward the mainland, while "Down-Cape" means roughly east, toward the Outer Cape and Provincetown.

Further confusion arises with the distinctions among the various coasts: "Bayside" faces inward onto Cape Cod Bay, the "South Shore" faces Nantucket Sound, and the "Backside" braves the open Atlantic to the east.

It's a little easier to keep track of Cape Cod's seasons. High season, when Cape-bound traffic can be bumper-to-bumper from near Boston all the way to Hyannis, is basically from Memorial Day to Labor Day. The summer vacation months of July and August see the highest hotel rates, the most crowded beaches, and abysmal traffic on Fridays especially, when most vacation rentals "turn over." That said, even at the worst of times you can still find peace and quiet if you're willing to walk, paddle, or bike a little way from your car.

Cape Cod National Seashore

The outermost stretch of Cape Cod, from Orleans to Provincetown, is protected from commercial development within the **Cape Cod National Seashore,** a 40-mile-long National Park Service property encompassing the whole of the coast.

The park's highlights include miles of gorgeous beaches, harbor seals, and some of the Cape's best waves, which occur here because the south-facing beaches are blocked by the islands of Nantucket and Martha's Vineyard, and the bayside is sheltered by the Cape itself. Pick up information detailing the various nature trails and interpretive programs at the **Salt Pond Visitor Center** in Eastham (daily; free; 508/255-3421) or **Province Lands Visitor Center** in Provincetown (508/487-1256).

Wellfleet

The town of **Wellfleet** (pop. 2,750) is one of the Cape's most picturesque communities, favored for some reason by writers, psychiatrists, and oysters.

Although home to a cluster of fine art galleries, crafts and clothing shops, clam shacks, and pricey restaurants, the place succeeds handsomely in finding a niche between self-conscious quaintness and residential seclusion. It's also blessed by a Cape Cod rarity: **Mayo Beach,** a public beach with year-round free parking, just west of the town pier, where **Mac's Seafood** (508/349-6333) sells fresh fish, shellfish, and ice-cream cones, best eaten just before a glorious sunset over the bay.

Wellfleet also has some of the Outer Cape's more affordable rooms, at the historic **Holden Inn** ($125 and up; 140 Commercial St.; 508/349-3450), where you share bathrooms, the front porch, and yet more bay views.

Truro

One of the finest biking or scenic driving routes on Cape Cod is the stretch of Old County Road that winds between Wellfleet and Truro, on the bay side of US-6. Topography is very varied, with hills and dunes, and traffic is minimal, so you can get a full sense of what the Cape is like beyond parking hassles and bijou restaurants. Like Wellfleet, **Truro** (pop. 2,003) is well off the beaten track and has very little commercial development. From the 1940s through the 1960s, Truro attracted a significant summer artists' colony whose members included painter Edward Hopper. These days, Truro is perhaps best known for the **Head of the Meadow** beach, just north of the landmark Highland Lighthouse on the Atlantic side of the Cape.

The Truro area also has a pair of unique accommodation options. The **HI-Truro Hostel** (late June–early Sept. only; 508/349-3889) is beautifully situated between cranberry bogs and ocean beach in a former Coast Guard station on North Pamet Road. On the calmer bay side, the 1930s beachfront cabins at **Days' Cottages** ($104 and up; 508/487-1062), along Route 6A in North Truro, are photogenic and very popular.

Provincetown

If not for its lack of freshwater, **Provincetown,** not Plymouth, would be the place we immediately equate with the Pilgrims. Way back in 1620, the band of religious travelers and fortune-seeking shipmates aboard the *Mayflower* landed here, expecting warm weather (in November, of all times) and good water. Neither was to be found, and the Pilgrims sailed on, disembarking across the bay at Plymouth Rock. Thus, P-town (as natives and in-the-know locals call it) lost its chance to be enshrined as the cornerstone of Anglo-American civilization and

If you've never watched a movie in the comfort of your own car, it's time you caught up with lost pleasures at the **Wellfleet Drive-In and Cinemas** ($9, cash only; 508/349-7176), on US-6 five miles north of Eastham, a genuine throwback to the era of roller-skating carhops and Mustang convertibles. There's also a four-screen indoor cinema open year-round.

The classic Cape Cod dwelling—a porchless, rectangular, peak-roofed shed not unlike an oversized shingle or clapboard Monopoly piece—is a familiar feature of the Outer Cape landscape.

The fury of the Atlantic constantly reworks Cape topography, borrowing up to 10 feet from the Outer Cape's cliffs each year, and stealing over 30 acres annually through erosion and rising sea levels.

has had to butter its bread with something other than the national creation story.

So P-town took to the water. For much of its history, the sea sustained the town, which became a trading spot, whaling village, and fishing port. As those industries tapered off, new ones arose to take their place. Art and tourism now keep P-town busy.

In 1899 Charles Hawthorne opened an art school here, and the town earned the art colony status that persists to this day. Bohemians followed. Among the artists and writers were John Reed, Eugene O'Neill, and George Cram Cook, whose Provincetown Players made theater history. And on the heels of Greenwich Village's fashionable flock came the car-borne tourists, who have proven themselves as faithful as Capistrano swallows, returning year after year to this tip of the Cape.

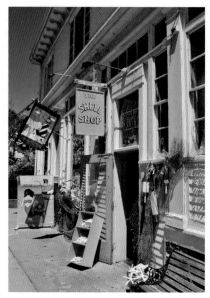

Provincetown shops

Provincetown is a particularly strong magnet for East Coast gays and lesbians, so don't be surprised to see as many rainbow flags as Stars and Stripes waving in the breeze.

That 252-foot tower jutting up over Provincetown is the **Pilgrim Monument and Museum** (Apr.–Nov. 9 AM–5 PM; $7), with the best panorama on the Cape: In clear weather the entire peninsula can be seen, as well as the Massachusetts coast at Plymouth.

Because Cape Cod juts out into the Atlantic, Provincetown is one of the best spots on the East Coast for whale-watching trips. From April through mid-October, boats of the **Dolphin Fleet of Provincetown** leave many times a day on four-hour trips (800/826-9300 or 508/349-1900), traveling out to feeding areas off Stellwagen Bank to see humpback, minke, and finback whales.

The summer trade prompts P-town to do its beach-boardwalk strut, as boatloads of day-trippers from Boston mob aptly named Commercial Street each afternoon, tanned couples mingle among the restaurants and outdoor cafés each evening, and fun-seekers fill up the bars and clubs each night. During any other season, however, the beach shuttle becomes a school bus, the wait for a table is negligible, and there's actually a chance that you'll find a place to park. Meanwhile, the off-season sunsets are still worth a visit to Race Point or Herring Cove Beach, even if they come at an earlier hour and require extra layers of clothing.

Provincetown Practicalities

After a day spent cycling amid dunes speckled with wild roses and beach grasses, or admiring the handiwork of window-box gardeners in P-town's cottage-lined lanes, you'll probably get hungry. Snackers may want to try the sugar-coated *trutas* (sweet potato fritters) from the **Portuguese Bakery** (299 Commercial St.; 508/487-1803). However, if you have a bigger appetite and want a harborside table, consider the moderately priced **Lobster Pot** (321 Commercial; 508/487-0842) just east of MacMillan Wharf for heaping portions of time-tested local favorites such as cioppino or *sopa do mar,* veggie pastas, and of course, lobster every which way you want it. It's open year-round, too—an exception in these parts. Enter through the kitchen.

For livelier, less-expensive dining, check out the multicultural menu—one of the few to please vegetarians—at **Napi's** (7 Freeman St.; 800/571-6274 or 508/487-1145), tucked away behind Tedeschi's. **Spiritus Cafe & Pizzeria** (190 Commercial St.; 508/487-2808) is another good, low-cost savior, dishing up pizza, focaccia sandwiches, ice cream, and lattes to a steady clientele of tattooed young smokers and slackers until 2 AM on summer weekends.

Planning to spend the night? If it's a summer weekend, make reservations or you may spend your time searching for a bed rather than basking on the beach. If you don't mind the occasional bout of late-night laughter from Commercial Street carousers, the **Somerset House Inn** ($120 and up; 378 Commercial St.; 800/575-1850 or 508/487-0383) has comfortable rooms and a very central location in an old Cape Cod manse. Quieter and calmer, the **Inn at Cook Street** ($229 and up; 7 Cook St.; 888/266-5655 or 508/487-3894), in the East End, offers relaxing decks and gardens, and a great breakfast. Rounding out the lodging options are the bargain-priced shared little cottages (and lovely gardens) of the **Outermost Hostel** (May–Oct.; around $25; 508/487-4378) on Winslow Street past the Pilgrim Monument parking lot.

For help with anything to do with Provincetown, from a place to stay to the perfect beach for kite-flying, contact the **visitors bureau** (508/487-3424) office on Lopes Square at the foot of the wharf.

The Loneliest Road

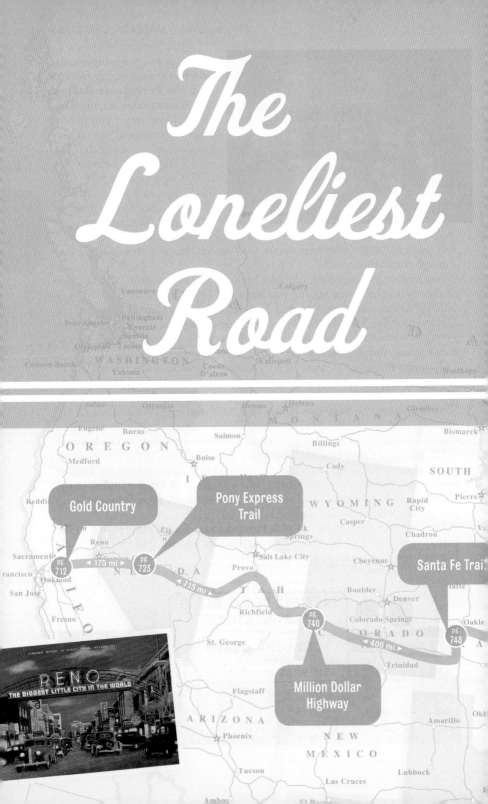

Gold Country

pg. 712

◄ 175 mi ►

Pony Express Trail

pg. 723

◄ 715 mi ►

Santa Fe Trail

pg. 748

Million Dollar Highway

pg. 740

◄ 400 mi ►

RENO
THE BIGGEST LITTLE CITY IN THE WORLD

The backbone of America runs from sea to shining sea, passing through 11 states and some of the country's most magnificent landscapes.

Between San Francisco and the Chesapeake Bay

Running coast-to-coast through the heart of America on a 3,200-mile odyssey from sea to shining sea, US-50 passes through a dozen different states and four state capitals, as well as the nation's capital, Washington, D.C. Along the route are some of the country's most magnificent landscapes: the **Sierra Nevada** and the **Appalachian** and **Rocky Mountains,** the endless farmlands of the **Great Plains,** and the desiccated deserts of **Utah** and **Nevada.** It follows the footsteps of pioneers and gives a reverse time line of national development. Heading west to east, you can travel back in history from the cutting-edge high tech of contemporary Silicon Valley, across the Wild West frontier of the mid-1800s, and through lands the likes of Daniel Boone and countless others pioneered in the 1700s, before arriving at the Atlantic Ocean near some of the oldest and best-preserved colonial-era landscapes in the United States.

All the way across the country, US-50 passes through literally hundreds of time-worn small towns, the great majority of which have survived despite the modern onslaught of Wal-Marts and fast-food franchises. *Blue Highways* author William Least Heat-Moon writes about US-50, "for the unhurried, this little-known highway is the best national road across the middle of the United States." The route offers such a compelling cross-section of the nation that *Time* magazine once devoted an entire issue to telling the story of the road it called the "Backbone of America."

From its start at **San Francisco,** the route cuts across California's midsection, passing the state capital at Sacramento before following the route of the old Pony Express up into the Sierra Nevada to the shores of **Lake Tahoe** and into Nevada. The Nevada portion of the route, dubbed "The Loneliest Road in America" by travel writers and tourist boards, is one of the most compelling long-distance drives in the country—provided you find miles and miles of little more than mountains, sagebrush, and blue sky compelling. The Great Basin desert continues across half of Utah, but then the route climbs over the Wasatch Front and onto the national park–packed red-rock country of the Colorado Plateau.

Continuing east, you cross the Continental Divide atop the Rockies, then follow the Arkansas River along the historic Santa Fe Trail. For fans of vanishing Americana, the route really comes into its own here across the Great Plains, with its hypnotically repetitive landscape of water towers, windmills, railroad tracks, and one small town after another.

After bisecting **Missouri** from Kansas City to St. Louis, US-50 crosses the Mississippi River into a much older and more settled landscape, through the agricultural heartlands of **Illinois, Indiana,** and **Ohio.** After climbing into the Appalachian backwoods of **West Virginia,** US-50 emerges suddenly into the wealth and power of downtown **Washington, D.C.,** before passing through the still perfectly picturesque fishing and farming communities of **Maryland's Eastern Shore.**

CALIFORNIA

Heading east from San Francisco across the heavy-duty Oakland Bay Bridge, the route across California starts off along the busy I-80 freeway through the urbanized San Francisco Bay Area. Passing diverse bayfront towns, including blue-collar **Oakland** and collegiate **Berkeley,** the busy and often congested eight-lane highway heads northeast across the historically important but increasingly suburbanized flatlands of the Sacramento Delta. Beyond **Sacramento,** the state capital of California, US-50 finally emerges, first as a freeway but later as a two-lane mountain road climbing through the heart of the **Sierra Nevada** foothills, where many of the small towns slumber in a gold-rush dream of the 1850s. Continuing east, US-50 winds through endless tracts of pine forest before cresting the Sierra to reach alpine **Lake Tahoe,** a year-round resort lying astride the California/Nevada border.

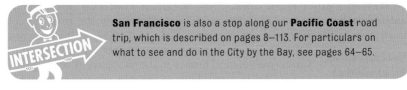

San Francisco is also a stop along our **Pacific Coast** road trip, which is described on pages 8–113. For particulars on what to see and do in the City by the Bay, see pages 64–65.

Oakland

Though it sometimes suffers in comparisons with its richer and better-looking sibling across San Francisco Bay, the hard-working city of **Oakland** (pop. 390,724) is a lively and intriguing place, with a nearly perfect climate and a proudly liberal political heritage. The main attraction for visitors is its waterfront **Jack London Square,** honoring the city's favorite prodigal son. Covering a few blocks at the foot of Broadway, the complex contains a couple

of good restaurants and nightclubs, an transplanted log cabin supposedly lived in by Jack London when he was in the Yukon Territory, and, last but not least, the truly funky **Heinold's First and Last Chance.** This rickety old saloon, serving a very wide variety of good beer, is just about the only survivor from Oakland's wild and woolly past. Jack London Square is a very pleasant to wander, with a

The city's low-budget but high-achieving baseball club, the **Oakland A's** (510/568-5600), play their home games at McAfee Coliseum, south of downtown.

handsome yacht formerly used by President Franklin D. Roosevelt, and ferries ($12.50 round-trip) head across the bay to San Francisco.

Oakland's other main draw is the excellent **Oakland Museum of California** housed in a landmark modernist ziggurat on the east edge of downtown, a block from Lake Merritt (Wed.–Sun.; $12; 1000 Oak St.; 510/238-2200). Inside, exhibits cover everything from California's natural history to the photography of Dorothea Lange. An in-depth look at the state's popular culture is highlighted by a lively display of Hollywood movie posters, neon signs, jukeboxes, and classic cars and motorcycles.

Berkeley

The intellectual, literary, and political nexus of the San Francisco Bay Area, left-leaning **Berkeley** (pop. 112,580) enjoys an international reputation that overshadows its suburban appearance. The town grew up around the attractively landscaped University of California campus, which, during the 1960s and early 1970s, was the scene of ongoing battles between "The Establishment" and unwashed hordes of antiwar, sex-and-drugs-and-rock-and-roll-crazed youth. Today, while its anti-authoritarian traditions are less in-your-face, Berkeley still maintains a typical college town mix of cafés and CD stores, and its site is superb, looking out across the bay to the Golden Gate and San Francisco.

The square-mile **University of California** Berkeley campus sits at the foot of eucalyptus-covered hills a mile east of the University Avenue exit off the I-80 freeway. Wander along Strawberry Creek, admiring the mix of neoclassical and postmodern buildings. Berkeley's cacophonous main drag, Telegraph Avenue, runs south from the heart of campus in a crazy array of tie-dye and tarot.

The busy section of I-80 eastbound from San Francisco has been improved by two new bridges; one is under construction to replace the earthquake-endangered Bay Bridge, while another new span crosses the Carquinez Straits.

To help ease the pain of his baby son's arthritis, in the 1940s a Berkeley machinist named Candido Jacuzzi created the air-bubbling hydro-therapy device that bears his name.

The big "C" above the University of California campus is over 100 years old. It was the first of these giant letters, which have since been repeated on hillsides all over the country.

golden poppy,
state flower of California

There are dozens of great places to eat and drink in Berkeley, including one of the best breakfast joints on the planet, **Bette's Oceanview Diner** (1807 4th St.; 510/644-3230), two blocks north of the I-80 University Avenue exit at the center of a boutique shopping district. Berkeley also has many top-rated restaurants, including world-renowned **Chez Panisse** (reservations essential; 1517 Shattuck Ave.; 510/548-5525), birthplace of California cuisine, located in the heart of Berkeley's gourmet ghetto. Chez Panisse is, not surprisingly, *très très cher,* so mere mortals may decide to take advantage of the more affordable gourmet cheese, bread, and out-of-this-world pizzas made and sold at the **Cheese Board Collective,** across the street (1512 Shattuck Ave.; 510/549-3183), where the California cuisine revolution really started, way back in 1967.

If you want to take the slow road north from Berkeley, follow San Pablo Avenue (Hwy-123), the old US-40/Lincoln Highway/Victory Highway route, which winds uneventfully along the bayfront through El Cerrito (birthplace of 1960s pop group Creedence Clearwater Revival) and industrial Richmond, where the new **Rosie the Riveter National Historical Park** preserves the waterfront's vital World War II–era heritage.

Vallejo

On the north side of the Carquinez Straits, through which the Sacramento and San Joaquin Rivers flow into San Francisco Bay, **Vallejo** is a blue-collar maritime town that made national news by declaring bankruptcy in 2008, in

Vallejo marks the turnoff for Hwy-12, which runs north and west through the Wine Country of the Napa and Sonoma Valleys.

the wake of the sub-prime housing downturn. Longtime home of the huge and historic Mare Island naval shipyard, which from 1854 to 1994 built and maintained many of the country's fighting ships and submarines, Vallejo also served as California's state capital on two different occasions in the gold rush years of the early 1850s. These days, Vallejo's one bona fide attraction is the **Six Flags Discovery Kingdom** theme park (hours vary, daily in summer; around $50; 707/643-6722), on the north side of town just west of I-80. Along with one of California's most intense arrays of high-speed thrill rides (like 65-mph Medusa, or the even-faster Vertical Velocity), Six Flags is surrounded by more than 135 acres of kid-friendly animal attractions, so you can admire tigers, ride on elephants, watch performing dolphins, or feed the tropical birds and butterflies.

the Medusa rollercoaster at Six Flags Discovery Kingdom in Vallejo

I-80 Towns

Between the San Francisco Bay Area and Sacramento, I-80 passes through an ever more suburbanized corridor, where towns like Fairfield and Vacaville have grown almost exponentially, from a few hundred residents in the 1950s to more than 100,000 today. **Fairfield** (pop. 105,321) grew up around busy Travis Air Force Base, and more enjoyably is also home to the **Jelly Belly** jelly bean factory (800/522-3267) and a large Anheuser-Busch beer refinery (June–Aug. Mon.–Sat., Sept.–May Tues.–Sat. 10 AM–4 PM; 707/429-7595 or 800/342-5283), both of which are open for free tours. From the coastal hills the landscape flattens out into the endless plain of the Sacramento Delta, and 80 mph I-80 crosses an unstintingly flat landscape of farmland, housing tracts, and "big box" shopping centers. Just before Sacramento I-80 reaches **Davis,** a bike-friendly former Lincoln Highway town that's now home to a large University of California campus, renowned around the world for its wine-making school.

East of Davis, I-80 is raised on stilts across the Yolo Bypass wetlands, one of the last signs of the natural delta that covered this part of California before the water supply was diverted south to Los Angeles.

Sacramento

Spreading for miles at the heart of California's 500-mile-long, agriculturally rich Central Valley, **Sacramento** (pop. 466,488) is not what most would expect of the capital of the Golden State. Green and suburban, with only the state capitol and a few modern towers rising over fine Victorian houses that line the leafy downtown

California's capitol as it appeared in the early 1900s

streets, Sacramento is a relatively quiet backwater that effectively embodies California's bipolar politics, forming a sort of neutral ground between the liberal urban centers, which contain 90 percent of the state's population, and the conservative, rural rest, which covers 90 percent of the land.

Now scythed by freeways and stretching for miles along the banks of the Sacramento and American Rivers, the city was chosen as the state capital during the gold rush era, when Sacramento was the main jumping-off point for the Sierra Nevada mines. Dozens of buildings dating from that era have been restored to form **Old Sacramento,** a diverting shopping complex and tourist trap along the riverfront, where ersatz paddlewheel steamboats offer sightseeing cruises and the **California State Railroad Museum** (daily; $9; 916/445-6645), boasting one of the world's largest collections, documents the history of western railroads. Along with the wealth of gold rush architecture, "Old Sac" also has memorials to the Pony Express and the Transcontinental Railroad, both of which had primary stations here.

One of the most popular minor league baseball teams in recent years has been the Oakland A's Class AAA farm club, the Sacramento **River Cats** (916/376-4700), who play all summer long at Raley Field, across the bridge from Old Sacramento. Games, which frequently sell out, are broadcast on **KSTE 650 AM.**

Two other museums are nearby. The **Crocker Art Museum** (closed Mon.; $10; 216 O St.; 916/808-7000), two blocks from the riverfront, is the oldest art gallery west of the Mississippi, with a broad range of European and Californian paintings. A half mile south of Old Sacramento, underneath the I-80/I-5 interchange at Front and V Streets, the **California Automobile Museum** (daily 10 AM–6 PM; $8; 916/442-6802) displays hot rods and muscle cars (from Corvettes to a Lamborghini Countach), alongside examples of just about every Ford made before 1952, from Model Ts to massive Ford V-8s.

A half mile inland from the riverfront, standing at the west end of a pleasantly landscaped park, the impressive **California State Capitol** (daily; free) has publicly accessible legislative chambers of the state's Senate and Assembly, and hallways full of exhibits on the Golden State's diverse counties.

Two miles east of the waterfront, at 27th and L Streets, Sacramento's main historic attraction is **Sutter's Fort** (daily; $5; 916/445-4422), a reconstruction of the frontier outpost established here in 1839 by Swiss settler Johannes Sutter. The first commercial settlement, as opposed to religious, in Alta California, Sutter's Fort played a vital role in early West Coast history—this is where the Donner Party was headed, and where the gold rush really began, when Sutter's employee James Marshall discovered flakes of gold at Sutter's Mill, in the Sierra Nevada foothills above Sacramento. The grounds of Sutter's Fort also hold the small but interesting **California State Indian Museum** ($3), which has displays of baskets and other California Native American handicrafts.

During Memorial Day weekend, Old Sacramento hosts the **Sacramento Jazz Jubilee** (916/372-5277), which draws an enormous crowd intent on hearing the dozens of very different jazz bands-everything from Dixieland and "trad" bands to cutting-edge contemporary players.

Sacramento Practicalities

The Old Sacramento area has some good but touristy restaurants and bars, but the Midtown neighborhood south of Sutter's Fort holds Sacramento's best range of restaurants, including the tasty but inexpensive **Cafe Bernardo** (2726 Capitol Ave.; 916/443-1180), with fresh salads, pizza, and sandwiches; **Paesano's** (1806 Capitol; 916/447-8646) has great cheap pizzas and a nice sidewalk terrace.

Another lively spot is the **Tower Café** (1518 Broadway; 916/441-0222), attached to the landmark 1920s Tower Theater (which plays art-house hits) and serving healthy, multiethnic food with a world-beat attitude. (The café is where the now-defunct Tower Records got its start.)

Though Sacramento can't compete with San Francisco for cutting-edge cuisine, it does excel in one culinary niche: hamburgers. There are some truly great old burger places in and around downtown Sacramento, like **Ford's Real Hamburgers,** on the south side of expansive Land Park (1948 Sutterville; 916/452-6979), and funky little **Jim-Denny's** (816 12th St.; 916/443-9655), a 1930s burger stand downtown between H and I Streets.

Places to stay include the wonderful **HI-Sacramento International Hostel** ($28; 925 H St.; 916/443-1691), in a fabulous Victorian mansion right downtown. For an unusual experience, how about staying the night in a 1920s paddlewheel riverboat? The **Delta King** ($120–175; 916/444-5464) is permanently moored on the Old Sacramento riverfront.

Placerville and Coloma: Gold Country

The main US-50 stop in the Sierra Nevada foothills, **Placerville** (pop. 10,389; elev. 2,187) takes its name from the placer gold deposits recovered from the South Fork of the American River, which flows just north of town. The historic core of Placerville is well preserved, with a few cafés and bars paying homage to its rough-and-tumble past. A reminder of the town's gold-rush heritage is the nation's only municipally owned gold mine: **Gold Bug Mine** (daily in summer, weekends only rest of the year; $5; 530/642-5207), a mile north of US-50 off the Bedford Avenue exit. A stamp mill and other mining equipment stand outside the entrance to the mine tunnel, which you can explore on a self-guided tour.

If you want to explore the region's many evocative gold-rush-era remnants, Placerville makes a good base, with its handful of motels (including a Best Western and a Days Inn) fronting the highway. Placerville also has one very good place to eat, the **Old Town Grill** (444 Main St.; 530/622-2631).

North and south of Placerville, Hwy-49 runs along the Sierra Nevada foothills through the heart of the Gold

Between Sacramento and Placerville, US-50 is an eight-lane freeway—and one of the California Highway Patrol's most lucrative speed traps, especially for westbound (downhill) travelers.

Throughout the gold-rush era, Placerville was known as Hangtown, with a reputation for stringing up petty thieves and other law-breakers. An effigy still hangs at the center of town, in front of a bar.

Country. Starting in the north beyond beautiful Nevada City, Hwy-49 winds through one historic town after another, all the way to the gates of Yosemite National Park, 150 miles to the south. One great old Gold Country haunt can be reached within a short drive of US-50 from Placerville. The ancient and very popular **Poor Red's Barbecue** (530/622-2901), housed in a gold-rush-era stagecoach station in the hamlet of El Dorado, five miles south of Placerville on Hwy-49, has full lunches and dinners (and great margaritas) for very little money. If you have the time and inclination to take a longer detour, head south along Hwy-49 to the stately town of Sutter Creek, then climb up into the mountains via winding Hwy-88, which passes by the intriguing semi-ghost town of Volcano before linking up again with US-50 near Lake Tahoe and Carson City.

A half-hour north of Placerville via Hwy-49, the original site of the discovery of gold, **Sutter's Mill,** has been reconstructed as part of **Gold Discovery State Historic Park** (daily; $5 per car; 530/622-3470) in **Coloma,** now an idyllic place along the banks of the American River, nine miles north of Placerville along Hwy-49. The 273-acre park, set aside in 1890 as the state's first historic monument, is also a prime spot for white-water rafting and kayaking, especially on weekends, so don't be surprised to find the place thronged with wet-suited and Teva-shod hordes. For a restful or romantic place to stay, try the gold-rush-era **Coloma Country Inn** ($120 and up; 345 High St.; 530/622-6919), set in two and a half acres of gardens.

The American River and Lover's Leap

Some 20 miles east of Placerville, US-50 changes suddenly from a four-lane freeway into a twisting, narrow, two-lane road over the crest of the Sierra Nevada. The usually busy highway, which every year is battered and frequently closed by winter storms, runs right alongside the steep banks of the American River. The lushness of the western Sierra Nevada is immediately apparent as the road passes luxuriant groves of pine, fir, and cedar, with numerous old resorts and vacation cabins lining the highway.

About six miles west of the summit, the towering granite cliff of **Lover's Leap** stands out to the south of the highway, its 1,300-foot face attracting rock climbers, while to the north the delicate cascade of **Horsetail Falls** offers a more serene pit stop. Climbing east up US-50's steepest set of hairpin turns, you'll reach 7,365-foot Echo Summit, which gives great views of the Lake Tahoe basin—the shining blue waters beckoning you along another steep stretch of US-50, downhill to the lakeshore itself.

South Lake Tahoe

One of the biggest (12 miles wide, 22 miles long, and 72 miles of coastline) and deepest (over 1,000 feet in places) lakes in the country, straddling the Nevada/California border at 6,220 feet above sea level, Lake Tahoe is a beautiful sight from any angle—from the crest of the alpine peaks surrounding it, from a car or bicycle as you cruise along the shoreline roads, or from a boat out on the lake itself.

Sitting, as the name suggests, at the southern end of Lake Tahoe, the ungainly resort community of **South Lake Tahoe** is a place of multiple personalities. On the California side, low-rise motels line the US-50 frontage, and the atmosphere is that of a family-oriented summer resort, with bike-rental stands and T-shirt shops clogging the roadside. Across the Nevada border, glitzy 20-story casinos rise up in a sudden wall of concrete and glass, ignoring the surrounding beauty in favor of round-the-clock "adult fun"—gambling, fine dining, racy nightclub revues, and more gambling. A few strategically placed pine trees work hard to retain a semblance of the natural splendor, but in peak summer season it's basically a *very* busy stretch of road, on both sides of the state line.

To get away from it all, head along Hwy-89 around the west side of the lake to the magnificent state parks around Emerald Bay. Acres of shoreline forest and numerous mansions built as summer resorts back around the turn of the 20th century, like the **Tallac Historic Site** ($5–10; 530/541-5227), three miles west of US-50, have been preserved and are open for tours. In winter, the Tahoe area turns into an extremely popular ski resort—**Heavenly** (775/586-7000) on the south shore and **Squaw Valley** (530/583-6985) in the north are among the largest and busiest ski areas in the United States; both have sight-seeing chair lifts in summer.

Despite the lake's great popularity, year-round prices for Tahoe accommodations are surprisingly low; with a couple of Best Westerns (530/541-6722 or 530/542-1101) and dozens of others to choose from, you shouldn't have trouble finding something suitable. For a carb-loading breakfast head to the circa 1959 **Red Hut Cafe** (2723 Lake Tahoe Blvd.; 530/541-9024) on US-50. Red Hut has three other locations along US-50 in South Lake Tahoe, but this is the original.

NEVADA

Between Lake Tahoe in the west and **Great Basin National Park** on the Utah border, US-50 crosses more than 400 miles of Nevada's corrugated country, climbing up and over a dozen distinct mountain ranges while passing through four classic mining towns and the state capital, **Carson City.** Early explorers mapped this region, Pony Express riders raced across it, and the long-distance Lincoln Highway finally tamed it, but the US-50 byway has always played second fiddle to the I-80 freeway, the more popular northern route across the state. Besides being a more scenic alternative to the mind-numbing, and therefore accident-prone, I-80, US-50 across Nevada has gained a measure of notoriety in its own right—it's known as the "Loneliest Road in America." As you travel along it you'll see road signs, T-shirts, and bumper stickers proclaiming it as such.

Inspired by the July 1987 story in *Life* magazine that dubbed US-50 "The Loneliest Road," the state-run Nevada Commission on Tourism (775/687-4322 or 800/NEVADA-8) sponsors a tongue-in-cheek promotion in which trans-Nevada travelers can earn themselves a certificate saying "I Survived the Loneliest Road in America." Get your official US-50 travel passport stamped at visitors centers along the highway.

sagebrush, state flower of Nevada

Stateline

Right where US-50 crosses from California into Nevada, the casino complex at **Stateline** forms, for a few short blocks, a mini Las Vegas, with four 20-story resort hotels towering over the lakeshore. **Harveys** ($89 and up; 775/588-6611), the largest with 742 rooms, started it all in the 1940s with six nickel slot machines. **Harrah's** ($135 and up; 775/588-6611), across US-50, is the most opulent, with luxurious 500-square-foot suites. Altogether, over 2,000 rooms are available, combined with at least that many more across the California border. The multitudes of game-hungry visitors that converge here create a definite charge in the rarefied atmosphere when the casino tables are turning at full

I SURVIVED

HWY 50

The Loneliest Road

speed, and it's also a great place to catch your favorite music and comedy performers (particularly ones whose popularity peaked in the 1980s) or a Vegas-style floor show.

Nevada Beach and Zephyr Cove

From the casino district at Stateline, US-50 winds along Lake Tahoe's southeastern shore for over 20 miles, passing by a pair of waterfront parks at **Nevada Beach** and **Zephyr Cove,** where you can ride the faux paddlewheeler **MS Dixie II** on a variety of cruises ($39 and up; 775/589-4906) across the lake. Otherwise, lakeshore access is severely limited, since most of the waterfront is privately owned, though numerous roadside turnouts (most easily accessible to westbound, lakeside travelers) offer ample opportunities to take in unforgettable views.

Midway along the lake's eastern shore, US-50 turns sharply and begins climbing up and over the 7,140-foot crest of Spooner Summit, all the way giving great views of the tantalizing blue gleam below. At the summit, stretch your legs on the Tahoe Rim Trail, a work-in-progress that will eventually circumnavigate the entire Lake Tahoe basin. Dropping down swiftly from Spooner Summit into the Great Basin desert, US-50 links up with US-395 for the final few miles into Carson City.

Genoa

Between Stateline and Carson City, a delightful little back-door route takes you through **Genoa,** the oldest city in Nevada. Founded by Mormon farmers way back in 1851, Genoa still retains its rural frontier feel, especially since most of the 20th-century development was focused elsewhere, leaving Genoa pleasantly far behind the times—for the time being, at least, though new faux-Victorian houses for Carson City commuters have been springing up around the historic downtown.

At the center of town is **Mormon Station State Historic Park** (daily; 775/782-2590), which has a small museum and a stockade dating back to the

1850s. Across the way, at Main and 5th streets, the **Genoa Courthouse Museum** (May–Oct. daily; 775/782-4325) has more comprehensive displays of historical items—everything from Native American baskets to the keys of the old jail, with an especially interesting exhibition on Wild West legend John A. "Snowshoe" Thompson, who carried the mail over the mountains between Genoa and Placerville. There's also a little tidbit on mining engineer and native son George Ferris, who designed and built the first of his namesake Ferris wheels for the 1893 World's Fair in Chicago. Much of old Genoa has burned down over the years, but the **Genoa Bar** (2282 Main St.; 775/782-3870) is full of character and fairly claims to be the oldest bar in the state. A nice place to stay is the **Genoa House Inn** ($135 and up; 180 Nixon St.; 775/782-7075), a quaint historical B&B.

To get to Genoa from Stateline and Lake Tahoe, go east on Hwy-207, down the very steep Kingsbury Grade, then turn north on Hwy-206. From Carson City, turn off US-395 south of the US-50 junction onto Jacks Valley Road (Hwy-206), and follow that for 12 miles.

Carson City

Nevada's state capital and 10th largest city, **Carson City** (pop. 55,274) was named in honor of Wild West explorer Kit Carson. Nestled at the base of the sheer eastern scarp of the Sierra Nevada, the city was founded in 1858—just a year before the discovery of the Comstock Lode riches, and six years before Nevada became a state.

Carson City is a hard place to characterize. Considering it's the capital, life is very slow, with the main buzz being the **Carson Nugget** (507 N. Carson St.; 775/882-1626) on the main US-50/395 route through town. It features roulette, craps, and blackjack tables, and an army of senior citizens feeding banks of slot machines.

In 1861, Orion Clemens was appointed secretary to the governor of Nevada Territory, and his younger brother Sam came with him to Nevada. Sam submitted dispatches of his mining and travel adventures to Virginia City's largest daily newspaper, the *Territorial Enterprise*, and began perfecting his unique brand of humor under the pen name Mark Twain.

Gambling aside, the one place to stop in Carson City is the excellent **Nevada State Museum** (daily; $8; 600 N. Carson St.), which stands across the street from the state capitol—and catercorner from the Nugget. The solid old U.S. Mint, built in 1870 to make coins from Comstock silver, houses displays on mining (including a large, full-scale mock-up of a working mine), a Native American gallery called Under One Sky, and gives an overview of Great Basin natural history. Also worth a look: the old Virginia & Truckee steam engines at **Nevada State Railroad Museum** (2180 S. Carson St.), south of town along US-50/395, where vintage trains run on warm-weather weekends.

Good Mexican meals are the order of the day at **El Charro Avitia,** south of town (4389 S. Carson St.; 775/883-6261), while the best and most expensive fare is served at **Adele's** (1112 N. Carson St.; 775/882-3353), where power brokers broker their power. Motels line Carson Street north and south of the capitol; try the classic 1950s-style **Frontier Motel** (1718 N. Carson; 775/882-1377).

Nevada State Railroad Museum

Virginia City

In 1859, prospectors following the gold deposits up the slopes of Mt. Davidson discovered one of the richest strikes in world history: the **Comstock Lode.** Almost overnight, the bustling camp of Virginia City grew into the largest settlement between Chicago and San Francisco, and over the next 20 years nearly a billion dollars in gold and silver (in 19th-century money!) was grubbed from deep underground. Afterward the town very nearly dried up and blew away, but thanks in part to the 1960s TV show *Bonanza,* in which Hoss and company were always heading over to Virginia City for supplies or to fetch the sheriff, tourists discovered the town and gave it a new lease on life.

The dress of the Silver Queen in Virginia City contains over 3,000 silver dollars.

These days **Virginia City** (pop. 1,000) is both a tacky tourist trap and one of the most satisfying destinations in the state. Reachable via a very steep (grades in excess of 15 percent) eight-mile drive up Hwy-341 from US-50, dozens of hokey but enjoyable attractions—like the amiable **Bucket of Blood Saloon,** which offers a panoramic view down the mountain—line the five-block-long main drag, C Street. The streets above and below—and I do mean above and below: The town clings to such a steep slope that C Street is a good three stories higher than neighboring D Street—hold some of the most authentic sites. B Street, for example, has the elegant **Castle,**

Nevada's premier mansion, with all the original furnishings and fittings, a block south of the ornate Victorian **Storey County Courthouse** and the landmark **Piper's Opera House.** Down the hill on D Street was once a more raucous quarter, where brothels and opium dens shared space with railroad tracks, cemeteries, and the mines themselves: the Gold & Curry, the Ophir, and the Consolidated Virginia.

Before or after a wander around town, be sure to stop in to the excellent museum on the ground floor of the **Fourth Ward School** (May–Oct. daily; 775/847-0975), the Victorian gothic landmark at the south end of C Street. Exhibits inside recount the lively history of Virginia City, from mining technology to Mark Twain, who made his start as a journalist with Virginia City's *Territorial Enterprise.* An intact classroom is preserved as it was in its heyday through the late 1880s to 1936, when the last class graduated.

Another not-to-be-missed spot is the **Red Light Museum** (daily; 5 C St.; 775/847-9288), which displays an amazing barrage of antique condoms, pornographic postcards, opium pipes, and other sexually explicit historical oddities. The museum is in the basement of a former saloon, now the Mandarin Gardens Chinese restaurant, adding to the weirdness factor.

Unless you're tempted by the many places to eat hot dogs and drink sarsaparilla along C Street, food options in Virginia City are limited. C Street is home to the Red Dog Saloon, which played a crucial role in the development of West Coast psychedelic music in the years before the "Summer of Love," and the nearby **Delta Saloon** (18 C St.).

Reno

Nothing helps heighten the contrast between the rest of the world and life along the "Loneliest Road" more than making a stop in **Reno** (pop. 225,221), "The Biggest Little City in the World," as the bold archway over Virginia Street downtown proclaims. An ancient city by Nevada standards, dating back to pioneer days (the Donner Party camped here on their ill-fated way west),

National Automobile Museum

Reno first came to national prominence in the 1930s as a center for quickie divorces. It now has all the gambling of its much-larger sibling, Las Vegas, but at a pleasantly homey, settled-down scale.

Besides taking advantage of Reno's cheap hotel rooms, cheap food deals ($1 hot-dogs-and-Heinekens!), and 24-hour fun, car culture fans may want to visit the $10 million, 100,000-square foot **National Automobile Museum** (daily; $10; 10 S. Lake St.; 775/333-9300), on the south bank of the Truckee River, perhaps the best and probably the most extensive car collection in the country, assembled primarily by casino magnate William Harrah. Over 220 classic cars, including the 1949 Mercury James Dean drove in *Rebel Without a Cause,* are on display, and there's a great gift shop, too. Reno's other national attraction is the **National Bowling Stadium** (300 N. Center St.), a state-of-the-art 78-lane extravaganza. The parking garage is at Center and 4th Streets.

Reno's famous arch, which spans Virginia Street at 3rd Street downtown, was first erected in 1926 to mark the Lincoln Highway route through town. The current arch, the third to stand on the site, was built in 1987; an older version has been rebuilt next to the National Auto Museum.

Dayton

Though the roadside east of Carson City is increasingly lined by trailer parks and convenience stores, just a half block north of the highway sits **Dayton,** one of the oldest settlements in Nevada. Gold was first discovered here in 1849, and later the town's massive stamp mills pounded the ore carried through the massive Sutro Tunnel from the fabulous Comstock Lode in the mountains above. The historic town center is little more than the two blocks of Main Street north from the traffic light on US-50; choose from a couple of combination café-saloons, including the nicely renovated **J's Bistro** (30 Pike St.; 775/246-4400). Formerly named the Old Corner Bar, it was the rumored hangout of John Huston, Marilyn Monroe, and Arthur Miller, when they were in Dayton in 1960 during the filming of *The Misfits.*

Fallon

Coming into Fallon, especially after crossing the Great Basin deserts of Utah and Nevada that stretch to the east, can be a shock to the system. First, relative to Nevada's other US-50 towns, **Fallon** is big: upward of 7,000 residents, with all the attendant shopping malls, traffic lights, and fast-food franchises. Second, but perhaps more striking, Fallon is green: alfalfa, onions, garlic, and cantaloupe grow as far as the eye can see. Otherwise, Fallon offers ATMs, gas stations, and motels lining US-50, as well as the usual Pizza Huts and Subways, and a handy 24-hour Safeway.

About the only radio station along this stretch of US-50 is Fallon's **KVLV 980 AM,** which plays a standard array of country hits.

Besides agriculture, Fallon's main employer is the U.S. Navy, whose air base and target range is an important training center for carrier-based fighters and bombers—the "Top Guns" like Tom Cruise.

While it's not an especially attractive place, Fallon does have what they accurately call "The Best Little Museum on the Loneliest Road in America," the eclectic and engaging **Churchill County Museum** (closed Sun.; free; 1050 S. Maine St.; 775/423-3677), less than a mile south of US-50. Filling an old Safeway supermarket, the exhibits contain native Paiute basketry, clothing and hunting gear, and the usual array of pioneer quilts and clothing, and the gift shop sells a wide range of books and historical postcards.

Forty-five miles east of Fallon, Hwy-361 heads south to the magnesium-mining company town of Gabbs. East of Gabbs lies fascinating **Berlin-Ichthyosaur State Park** (775/964-2440), which holds an only-in-Nevada combination: the 100-year-old ghost town of Berlin and a 225-million-year-old marine fossil quarry. Camping is available year-round, and guided tours of the town and the fossil beds are given weekends in summer.

Grimes Point and Sand Mountain

The 110 miles of US-50 between Fallon and Austin, the next town to the east, look pretty empty on most maps, but there's more to see than you might think. In the midst of a U.S. Navy target range, where supersonic fighters play electronic war games across the alkali flats, there are historical plaques marking Pony Express and Butterfield Stage way stations, a dusty old brothel, and two unique attractions—a singing sand dune and an extensive petroglyph site.

Grimes Point petroglyphs

Ten miles east of Fallon, the extraordinary grouping of petroglyphs at **Grimes Point** is not to be missed. Just 100 yards north of US-50, a self-guided trail leads past hundreds of images etched into the lichen-covered, espresso-brown basalt boulders. Some 8,000 years ago, when the carvings were made, Grimes Point was on the shores of

At the turnoff to Sand Mountain, a battered sign marks the official (solar-powered!) Loneliest Phone on the Loneliest Road in America.

now-vanished Lake Lahontan, a prime hunting and fishing ground for prehistoric Great Basin peoples. These days, fast and fierce lizards, and the occasional antelope, share the arid setting with the shiny rocks, into which a huge array of abstract and figurative images have been pecked and chiseled. If you're intrigued and want to know more, stop by the excellent Churchill County Museum in Fallon; guided tours (every other Sat.) are available of nearby **Hidden Cave,** where significant archaeological remains have been uncovered.

Sand Mountain, 15 miles east of Grimes Point, 84 miles west of Austin, and just a half mile north of US-50, is a giant sword-edged sand dune that makes a deep booming sound when the cascading crystals oscillate at the proper frequency—somewhere between 50 and 100 hertz. On weekends you're more likely to hear the sound of unmuffled dirt bikes and dune buggies, but at other times the half-hour trudge to the top is well worth making to watch the swirls of sand dance along the ridges.

Austin

Some 110 miles east of Fallon and 70 miles west of Eureka, tiny **Austin** (pop. 340) huddles well above 6,000 feet on the north slope of the mighty Toiyabe Mountains. The steep incline of Main Street (US-50) as it passes through town attests to the precariousness with which Austin has clung to life since its 10-year mining boom ended—in 1873. Austin hangs on to the rustic, steadfastly un-whitewashed nature that was once—and in some places, remains—central to Nevada's character. Austin takes its central assignment seriously, since the state's exact geographical center is a mere 12 miles to the south (near the hard-to-find but very pleasant Spencer Hot Springs).

According to local legend, a Pony Express rider accidentally discovered silver ore here in 1862, and the rush was on. Prospectors fanned out from Austin, which was named after the Texas hometown of one of its founders, to establish Belmont, Berlin, Grantsville, Ione, and dozens of other boomtowns-turned-ghost towns; roughly $50 million in gold and silver was shipped out over the next 10 years. Since then Austin has experienced a long, melancholy decline, though recent efforts to mine the abundant turquoise in the region have met with some success.

If the "Loneliest Road" nickname makes you think that road maintenance may have suffered, it hasn't; the road surface is actually mostly all smooth champagne asphalt, much to the delight of the hundreds of motorcyclists who ride the road every summer.

A two-minute drive (at 10 mph) along Main Street takes you past all there is to see in Austin today, but you could easily spend hours wandering around the place or hanging out in its quirkily populated junk shops, cafés, and bars. The impressive steeples of the Catholic, Methodist, and Episcopal churches dominate the townscape, while at the western (downhill) end of town you can glimpse **Stokes Castle,** a three-story stone sentinel built in 1897 and lived in for all of a month. It looks best from a distance, looming

The Pony Express

Of all the larger-than-life legends that animate the annals of the Wild West, none looms larger than that of the Pony Express. As is typical of frontier adventures, accounts of the Pony Express are often laced with considerable exaggeration, but in this case the facts are unusually impressive. Beginning in April 1860, running twice a week between St. Joseph, Missouri, and Sacramento, California, where it was linked with San Francisco by steamship, the Pony Express halved the time it took to carry news to and from the West Coast, making the 1,966-mile trek in just 10 days. Eighty riders (including teenaged William "Buffalo Bill" Cody, who made the record single run of 322 miles) were employed to race between the 190 stations en route, switching horses every 10–15 miles and averaging 75 miles per run—day or night, in all kinds of weather, across 120°F deserts or snowbound Sierra passes.

Covering nearly 2,000 miles of the wildest and ruggedest land on the frontier, the Pony Express established the first high-speed link between the two coasts. At a time when the nation was divided against itself, with the Civil War looming on the horizon, the Pony Express connection played a key role in keeping the valuable mines of California and Nevada in Union hands. A private enterprise that lasted just 18 months and lost considerable amounts of money before being put out of business for good, the Pony Express proved that overground connections across the still-wild western United States were both necessary and possible.

The completion on October 28, 1861, of the transcontinental telegraph made the Pony Express obsolete overnight, and not so much as a saddle survives from this legendary endeavor, apart from a few postmarked letters. Along with the various statues and plaques marking the Pony Express route, the most evocative sites survive in the dry Nevada desert, within easy access of the US-50 highway. East of Fallon, for example, the highway runs right on top of the old Pony Express route, and the remains of two relay stations can still be seen. One is at **Sand Springs,** at the foot of Sand Mountain. More substantial remains survive at **Cold Springs,** 32 miles east, where plaques recount the history and a trail brings you to what was once among the most isolated and dangerous of the Pony Express stations.

Every June, Wild West aficionados recreate the era in the **Pony Express Reride,** in which a team of 550 riders follows the old route as closely as possible, alternating direction each year.

1860
1861

PONY EXPRESS
TRAIL

over the nearby cemeteries, but if you want to get closer, follow Castle Road for about a half mile south from US-50.

For its 300 or so residents, Austin has two gas stations (it's a very long way to the next town, so fill up here) and three motels—including the clean but basic mobile home trailers of the **Cozy Mountain Motel** (around $45; 40 Main St.; 775/964-1433). Two cafés are right on US-50/Main Street; both open early (around 6 AM) and both close around 9 PM: the ancient **International Café and Bar,** moved here board by board from Virginia City in 1863, and the **Toiyabe Cafe.**

Hickison Petroglyph Recreation Area

Bookended by 7,000-foot mountain ranges at either end, the route between Austin and Eureka is perhaps the longest, flattest, straightest stretch of the entire trans-Nevada length of US-50, over 70 miles of Great Basin nothingness. Cattle ranches fill the plains, which were crisscrossed by early explorers like John C. Fremont, who passed through in 1845, as well as by the Pony Express and the Butterfield Stage. Such recent history, however, pales in comparison to the relics from the region's prehistoric past, particularly the fine petroglyphs carved into the rocks on the eastern side of 6,594-foot Hickison Summit, 28 miles east of Austin and 46 miles west of Eureka.

Now protected as part of the BLM-operated **Hickison Petroglyph Recreation Area,** the petroglyphs stand in a shallow sandstone draw on the north side of the highway. A half-mile trail loops through sagebrush, junipers, and piñon pines from the parking area and campground past dozens of these enigmatic figures, some of which are thought to date back as far as 10,000 BC. Somewhat surprisingly, so far they are graffiti-free.

Eureka

Right in the middle of a 100-mile stretch of spectacular Great Basin scenery, **Eureka** is one of the most engaging and enjoyable stops in the state. Unlike a lot of places along the Loneliest Road, Eureka is fairly thriving, thanks to numerous gold mines still in operation in Eureka County.

The four blocks of 100-year-old buildings lining the steeply sloping, franchise-free Main Street (US-50) are a mix of well-restored brick and wood storefronts alongside less fortunate ruins, some merely sets of cast-iron pilasters holding up false fronts. The focal point, the grand 1879 **Eureka County Courthouse,** is still in use, and behind it the **Eureka Sentinel Museum** (daily May–Oct., closed Sun. Nov.–Apr.; free; 775/237-5010) has displays tracing the lively local history as well as typesetting equipment and printing presses of the newspaper published here from 1870 to 1960.

Besides being an intriguing place to stroll around (walking-tour booklets are available from the Sentinel Museum and many local shops), Eureka is also a good place to break a journey. A Best Western ($100 and up; 775/237-5247) has modern rooms and is conveniently located on Main Street. The liveliest place to drink and be merry is the **Owl Club** café and casino, down Main Street; fast food can be had from **DJ's Drive-In Diner,** at the east end of town (509 S. Monroe).

historic Eureka

Ely

Ely (pop. 4,255; pronounced "EE-lee") is a sprawling crossroads community where US-6, US-50, and US-93 all intersect. For nearly 100 years, Ely was a boomtown flush with the wealth from the massive Kennecott-owned Liberty Pit copper mines, Nevada's largest and longest-lived mining venture, which produced over a billion dollars' worth of ore while employing nearly 10,000 people at its peak during the 1950s. After the main mines closed down in 1982, the railway that had shuttled pay dirt from the mines to the smelter was abandoned—track, stock, and depot. In 1985 the entire railroad operation was turned into **Nevada Northern Railway Museum** (Wed.–Sun. in summer; 775/289-2085), and now you can take a two-hour tour aboard the Ghost Train, pulled by a 1910 Baldwin Steamer locomotive. The train leaves from the depot at the north end of East 11th Street and uses a ton of coal and 1,000 gallons of water; tickets cost around $25.

Ely's other main stop is the **White Pine Public Museum**

Across Nevada, US-50 follows the route of the Lincoln Highway, the nation's first transcontinental route.

mural of macho miners in Ely

(daily; free; 2000 Aultman St./US-50; 775/289-4710), which has a wide-ranging collection of minerals, mining implements, and Pony Express memorabilia on display.

Along with extensive mining history, Ely has motels, gas stations, the only supermarket for the next 250 miles east, and dozens of vivid, building-sized **murals** depicting various aspects of the town's heritage. The heart of town is a neon-rich few blocks of Aultman Street (US-50) west of the US-93 junction, centering upon the landmark **Hotel Nevada** ($35 and up; 775/289-6665), with its giant cowboy and neon-lit slot machines. Inside there are real (as opposed to video) slot machines, pool tables, a café, and a bar. Also nice is the quiet **Four Sevens Motel** ($35 and up; 500 High St.; 775/289-4747), a block north of Aultman.

For food, Ely has three coffee shops along US-50, plus the chance to down a milk shake at the soda fountain inside **Economy Drug**, Aultman and 7th Streets (775/289-4929).

The route east of Ely toward Great Basin National Park is an official "scenic route," rolling across sagebrush plains and climbing over the Schell Creek and Snake Mountain ranges through dense groves of pine and juniper.

Mountains of mine tailings tower over US-50 west of Ely, and five miles west of town a short detour south takes you to **Ruth,** which sits alongside the huge crater where hundreds of tons of ore were dug. A mining company is currently leaching the metal out of the previously discarded ore, so there's no longer access to the crater itself.

Ely marks the junction of US-50 and our **Border to Border** route along US-93 (see page 150). Running between the Canadian Rockies and the desert Southwest, US-93 is covered on pages 114–173.

Connors Pass and Majors Place

East of Ely, US-50, spliced together with US-6 and US-93 into a single two-lane highway, continues for 25 miles before crossing the narrow waist of the Schell Creek Range at 7,729-foot **Connors Pass.** As you ascend toward the pass, the air cools and freshens, while the single-leaf piñon and Utah juniper appear and increase, and as you crest the summit, the mighty Snake Range, including 13,063-foot Wheeler Peak, comes into view.

East of the pass, at **Majors Place** (where there's a roadhouse with cold beer and "loose slots" but no reliable gas), US-93 cuts due south, heading 80 long, solitary miles to the next contact with humans at Pioche, while US-50 heads east across open rangelands toward Great Basin National Park.

Great Basin National Park

Approaching Nevada from the east, travelers are greeted by the towering silhouette of **Wheeler Peak,** at 13,063 feet the second-highest and most impressive mountain in the state; from the west, similarly sheer escarpments tower over lush green open range for miles and miles along US-50. In 1987 the 77,000 acres around Wheeler Peak were designated **Great Basin National Park,** but its remote location has made it one of the least-visited national parks in the United States. Hikers and campers will have no trouble finding solitude amidst the alpine forests, ancient bristlecone pines, delightful annual wildflowers, glacial lakes, and small ice field.

The world's oldest known bristlecone pine, dubbed Prometheus, was cut down on Wheeler Peak in 1964 by a graduate student researcher who discovered too late that, at 4,900 years old, the tree had been the oldest living thing on earth. A cross-section of the trunk is displayed at the **Bristlecone Convention Center** (150 6th St.) in Ely.

Wheeler Peak in Great Basin National Park

Lehman Caves, Great Basin National Park

Thanks to the well-maintained **Wheeler Peak Scenic Road** climbing to over 10,000 feet, the wilderness areas are easily accessible to people willing to take a short hike, though many visitors go no farther than the park's centerpiece, **Lehman Caves.** Geological forces have been sculpting Lehman Caves for roughly 70 million years, but they weren't noticed until homesteader Absalom Lehman stumbled upon the small entrance to the caves in 1885. They were declared a national monument in 1922, and since then only minor improvements have been made, leaving the mind-bending limestone formations alone—no flashy light-and-sound show, just hundreds of delicate stalagmites, stalactites, helictites, aragonites, and the like. A variety of guided tours ($8–10) are conducted at intervals throughout the day; on some summer evenings at 4:30 PM, there's a memorable candlelight tour. Tours leave from the small **visitors center** (775/234-7331), which has details of hiking and camping options as well as exhibits on Great Basin wildlife—from birds and bats to mountain lions. There's even a small summer-only café.

If you're not camping and self-relying, or if you are and want a break, the nearest food and drink are at the foot of the park in the tiny, artsy, friendly "town" of **Baker** (pop. 68), which boasts a gas station, a great place to stay—the seven-room **Silver Jack Inn** ($49–69; 775/234-7323)—as well as good food, beer, wine, and occasional free movies at the **LectroLux Café.**

Back on US-50, straddling the Utah/Nevada border, the **Border Inn** is a much more functional café/gas station/motel, open 24 hours a day (775/234-7300). From here, the only other reliable services are in Ely, 70 miles west, or in Delta, 85 miles to the east, so pass by at your peril.

UTAH

For most of the way across Utah, the high-speed I-70 freeway has replaced US-50, but if you have time to take a couple of detours you'll be rewarded with some of the most incredible scenery in the world. Most of this is concentrated in the southeastern corner of the state, where a number of national parks, including **Canyonlands** and **Arches,** preserve the sandstone "Canyon Country" of the Colorado Plateau. In the west a few old mining towns stand amidst the arid desert of the Great Basin. Distances are huge and services few and far between, but if you have the time and plan ahead, this is one of the most satisfying and memorable corners of the country.

Delta

About 85 miles east of the Nevada border, the landscape changes suddenly from barren desert to lush pastures around the town of **Delta,** which is irrigated by the green Sevier River. Delta bills itself the "Gateway to Great Basin National Park," and it does have a **Best Western** and other motels, gas stations, and a large supermarket—but very little else to attract visitors. One place worth a stop is the small **Great Basin Museum** (Mon.–Sat. only; free; 328 West 100 North; 435/864-5013), a block north of Main Street. The museum features minerals, arrowheads, and local history exhibits, including a display of artifacts relating to **Topaz Camp,** an internment camp set up in the desert west of Delta by the U.S. government to imprison more than 8,000 American men, women, and children of Japanese descent during World War II.

North of Delta, the horizon is split by the belching smokestack of the 1,800-megawatt coal-fired Intermountain Power Plant.

From Delta, US-50 officially cuts southeast across I-15, linking up with I-70 at Salina for the trip east to Grand Junction. Our route, however, follows US-6 (old US-50) toward the Great Salt Lake area, then east over the Wasatch Front, rejoining official US-50 (now I-70) at Green River.

Little Sahara Recreation Area

From Delta, the route follows the Sevier River northwest, racing across the featureless desert for 32 miles before reaching the well-posted turnoff north to the **Little Sahara Recreation Area.** Visible from the highway, to the north of US-6, the Little Sahara Recreation Area holds 60,000 acres of sand dunes and sagebrush flats, the prettiest parts of which are preserved for hikers and campers, though motorcyclists and ATVers can overwhelm any sense of peace and tranquility, turning it into a campground from hell.

Eureka

Fifty miles east of Delta, 20 miles west of the I-15 freeway, the weather-beaten town of **Eureka** (pop. 750) climbs steeply up surrounding mountainsides at the heart of the once-thriving Tintic Mining District, where, as recently as the 1930s, thousands of miners dug millions of dollars' worth of gold, silver, copper, and lead out of the ground every year. Now the massive wooden headframes of long-closed mine shafts stand high above the houses and prefab trailers that cling to the slopes, while fading signs advertise abandoned businesses along Main Street.

Though diehard residents still speak of plans to reopen one or more of the mines, prosperity seems a distant dream in Eureka, and while it's not quite a ghost town, it seems well on its way there. The glory days are recounted in the small **Tintic Mining Museum** (435/433-6842), next to city hall on Main Street. At the west edge of town a historical plaque stands alongside the heavy timber head-frame of the Bullion-Beck Mine, one of the area's most productive.

Heading east from Eureka, our route bends across rock-strewn sagebrush hills around the southern shore of Utah Lake toward I-15. **Utah Lake,** which is freshwater in contrast to the briny expanse of the Great Salt Lake to the north, used to be much larger than it is now, before so much of it was diverted to water the apple, peach, and cherry orchards that line US-6 around **Santaquin**—whose three gas stations are the last reliable source of fuel for westbound travelers until Delta, 70 miles to the southwest. From Santaquin, follow the I-15 freeway north to **Springville,** from where the Salt Lake City megalopolis stretches north along I-15 for nearly 100 miles.

Park City, in the mountains above Salt Lake City, is home to the annual **Sundance Film Festival,** and nearby ski resorts hosted the 2002 Winter Olympics.

Helper earned its name in 1892 when the Denver and Rio Grande Railroad built a depot and roundhouse here to hold the "helper" engines that were added to trains to help push them over Soldier Summit, 25 miles to the west.

Castle Gate and Helper

Heading east from Springville, the drive along US-6 (old US-50) up and over 7,477-foot **Soldier Summit** is truly beautiful, as the two-lane highway twists alongside pines and cottonwoods to the crest, then passes through bright red sandstone canyons along the stark eastern side of the towering Wasatch Range. Dropping down from Soldier Summit, US-6/191 winds along the Price River through **Castle Gate,** a steeply walled sandstone canyon lined with working coal mines, many of which you see from the highway. While most now rely on heavy machinery to do the dirty work of digging out the coal, the Castle Gate area has been the site of the two worst mining disasters in Utah history: 171 men and boys killed in a 1924 explosion, and 200 killed at nearby Scofield on May Day, 1900.

Tiny **Helper** (pop. 2,201), at the downstream edge of

sego lily,
state flower of Utah

Main Street in Helper, Utah

Castle Gate six miles northwest of Price, is a classic railroad town preserved almost unchanged for nearly a century. The six-block downtown area, fronting onto the tracks, includes so many turn-of-the-20th-century brick- and stone-fronted buildings that it's been declared a national historic district—though the sad truth is that most of these have stood abandoned since the railroad switched to diesel power in the 1950s.

Relive the glory days at the excellent **Western Mining and Railroad Museum** (Tues.–Sat. in the winter, closed Sun. in the summer; 294 S. Main St.; 435/472-3009), which contains enough raw material on railroading and coal mining, not to mention the region's diverse immigrant cultures, to keep you occupied for an hour or more. There's also a display recounting the exploits of Butch Cassidy and his gang, who raided banks and rustled cattle throughout the region in the late 1890s, hiding out in the surrounding hills. Behind the museum, an outdoor lot displays some of the giant machines used in the coal mines, which, unlike the railroad, still employ a large number of local people.

Price

The largest city in eastern Utah, **Price** (pop. 8,715) is located roughly midway between the I-15 and I-70 freeways, 65 miles northwest of Green River. Coal is so prevalent in the area that road cuts reveal solid black seams, but the town itself is lush and green, thanks to irrigation provided by the Price River, which flows south from town into the Green and Colorado Rivers.

Detour: Salt Lake City

With no other city for some 500 miles in any direction, **Salt Lake City** (pop. 186,440), an hour north of Springville via the I-15 freeway, seems like the oasis it naturally is. Taking its name from the undrinkable alkaline Great Salt Lake, the city is actually blessed with abundant fresh water, thanks to the rain- and snow-making properties of the Wasatch Range, which rises knife-like to the east. Founded by Mormons in 1847, and effectively controlled by Mormon elders ever since, Salt Lake City is clean and pleasant, and unusual enough to merit a detour. Most of what there is to see has to do with the Mormons, better known as the Church of Latter-day Saints, which has its worldwide headquarters at **Temple Square** downtown (street numbers and addresses are measured from here, not the nearby state capitol, which goes to show just how predominant the LDS church is in local life). On the west side of Temple Square are the amazing genealogical libraries the Mormons maintain; a block east of Temple Square is the **Beehive House,** preserved as it was in the 1850s, when Brigham Young lived here.

Given its Mormon roots and Midwest temperament, Salt Lake City is not exactly a food-lover's paradise, but there are a number of good restaurants. One truly fine place to dine is **Bambara** (202 S. Main St.; 801/363-5454), whose eclectic menu and stylish décor would feel at home in New Orleans or San Francisco. The same 1920s building houses a nice place to stay: the boutique **Hotel Monaco** ($129 and up; 801/595-0000).

For more information, contact the **Salt Lake City visitors bureau** (800/541-4955).

In June 1925, Price saw the lynching of a black man, Robert Marshall, an itinerant miner who was hanged by vigilantes for allegedly killing a coal company guard. A crowd of over 1,000 people witnessed the lynching, but no one was willing to testify against the 11 men accused of murder. In 1998 a small memorial, describing Marshall as "A Victim of Intolerance—May God Forgive" was erected on his grave in the Price cemetery.

Coal mining and, to a lesser extent, agriculture still power Price, where the kid-friendly **Prehistoric Museum** (Tues.–Sat. 9 AM–5 PM; $5; 155 E. Main St.; 435/613-5060) is worth a look for its extensive displays on the Native American cultures of the region, and for its range of full-sized dinosaur skeletons, including a stegosaurus and a utahraptor. Many of these were reassembled from fossils collected from the **Cleveland-Lloyd Dinosaur Quarry,** 30 miles south of town.

Price also has all the highway services travelers might need: numerous gas stations, places to eat, and six motels, including the nice **Best Western Carriage House Inn** ($80 and up; 435/637-5660).

Southwest from Price, bound for Green River and the I-70 freeway, US-6/191 runs alongside the busy

Denver and Rio Grande mainline railroad through a region of arid plateaus highlighted every few miles by brilliantly colorful, weirdly sculpted sandstone mesas. Though barren and empty at first glance, the region is particularly rich in two things: coal mines and, more unusually, dinosaur bones. (Why do you think they call them fossil fuels?)

SALT LAKE BEES

The LA Angels Triple A farm club, Salt Lake Bees (801/325-2273) play right downtown at West Temple and 1300 South Street.

Green River

Straddling the eponymous river on the north side of I-70, **Green River** (pop. 952) makes a handy base for exploring southeastern Utah, but it offers very little in and of itself. The town holds numerous 24-hour gas stations, a handful of motels, and a couple of good places to eat—try the **Tamarisk** (870 E. Main St.; 435/564-8109), overlooking the Green River.

Just south of Main Street, the most characterful place to eat and drink in Green River is **Ray's Tavern** (25 S. Broadway; 435/564-3511), with good beers, a pool table, and dining tables made out of tree trunks.

Even if you don't need fuel, food, or a place to sleep, Green River offers one very compelling reason to stop: the spacious, modern **John Wesley Powell River History Museum** (daily in summer, closed Sun. in winters; $4; 1765 E. Main St.; 435/564-3427), above the east bank of the river. In 1869 Powell and his crew were the first to travel the length of the Colorado River through the Grand Canyon; though the legendary explorers started their epic adventure in Green River, Wyoming, not here in Utah, the spacious modern museum, on old US-50 along the east bank of the Green River, is the best single repository of artifacts relating to their feat. The collection concentrates on Powell in particular and on waterborne transport in general, but there are also displays chronicling the adventures of other early explorers (including Juan de Oñate in 1605 and the Domínguez and Escalante expedition of 1776), and of fur-trappers, miners, and Mormons—all of whom contributed to the exploration and mapping of the American West.

The otherworldly aspects of the Utah landscape south of Green River have tempted would-be space colonizers to establish the **Mars Desert Research Station** here, to test equipment and train potential Mars-bound astronauts.

To get some sense of what Powell and crew experienced, take a raft, canoe, or kayak trip down the Green or Colorado River. Dozens of outfitters offer equipment rentals, shuttles, and guided trips, from all-day to weeklong tours.

aerial view of the Green River

Butch Cassidy and the Hole-in-the-Wall Gang

Long before Paul Newman played him alongside Robert Redford's Sundance Kid, Butch Cassidy was one of the great outlaw legends of the Wild West. Thanks to his habit of sharing the proceeds from his crimes with the widows and children of men killed or ruined by bankers and cattle barons, Butch Cassidy earned a reputation as the Robin Hood of the Wild West. That, plus the fact that he never killed anyone while committing his crimes, gained him popularity and admiration from the cowboys, miners, and homesteading pioneers among whom he worked his trade.

Born Robert Leroy Parker to a family of Mormon farmers in Beaver, Utah, on Friday the 13th of April, 1866, the man who came to be known as Butch Cassidy spent his youth as a ranch hand in Utah, Colorado, and southern Wyoming. The first major crime attributed to Butch Cassidy is the robbery of a bank in Telluride, Colorado, in 1889, which netted him and his three accomplices some $20,000. From 1894 to 1896 he was imprisoned in Wyoming for cattle theft, and following this he joined up with Harry Longabaugh (a.k.a. The Sundance Kid) and the rest of the gang. Together they robbed over a dozen banks, trains, and stagecoaches throughout the West, netting an estimated $350,000 in five years. One of their many daring heists was the daylight robbery of a coal-mining company in Castle Gate, Utah, in April 1897; while the payroll was being taken from a train, Butch simply grabbed the satchel and rode off in a cloud of dust, $9,000 richer.

According to many sources, Butch and Sundance died in 1908, in a shootout in South America (as depicted in the 1969 movie *Butch Cassidy and the Sundance Kid*). But some people (including his sister, who lived until the 1970s) say that Butch survived to a ripe old age, living in Spokane, Washington, under the name William T. Phillips until his death in 1937.

Canyonlands National Park

The largest and least-visited park in the Southwest, **Canyonlands National Park** is both breathtakingly beautiful and totally inhospitable, an arid wilderness of high plateaus and deep canyon carved by the mighty Green and Colorado Rivers. The park is divided into several very different areas, each of which is at least a 100-mile drive from the others, so it pays to plan ahead. The most popular section, the **Island in the Sky,** stands high above the confluence of the rivers and gives the most sweeping panoramas—100 miles in every direction from over 6,000 feet above sea level. South of the rivers, **The Needles** district holds 50 square miles of spires, arches, and canyons and is the best place to undertake lengthy hikes. One trail leads from the end of the road down to the mouth of Cataract Canyon on the Colorado River. Another area of Canyonlands, **The Maze,** is west of the rivers and virtually inaccessible.

Uranium mined from **Temple Mountain,** west of Canyonlands, was used to make the first atomic bombs.

There's one **visitors center** near the entrance to Island in the Sky and another near the entrance to The Needles. The Canyonlands **headquarters** (125 West 200 South; 435/259-7164) in Moab also has extensive information. Adjacent to Canyonlands are two state parks, **Dead Horse Point** in the north and **Newspaper Rock** in the south, both of which are also well worth a look.

Arches National Park

Taking its name from the hundreds of naturally formed sandstone arches scattered here, **Arches National Park** is the most feature-packed of southern Utah's national parks. Ranging in size from around three feet to nearly 300 feet in span, the arches are the result of erosion over millions of years, the same agent that formed the thousands of brilliantly colored spires, pinnacles,

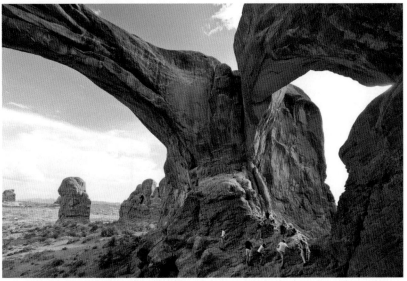

Double Arch formation at Arches National Park

and canyons that cover southeast Utah. Piñon pines and junipers add a splash of green to the red and brown backdrop, but mostly what you see are red stone and blue sky—lots and lots of both.

The park's highlights can be easily reached from the 18-mile paved road that runs through the center of the park. A **visitors center** (hours vary by season; 435/719-2299) at the entrance, east of US-191 and five miles north of Moab, has maps, pamphlets, and displays on the geology and natural history of Arches.

From the entrance, the road switchbacks uphill past the sandstone skyline of "Park Avenue" before reaching a turnoff east to **The Windows,** whose dense concentration of arches and spires is required viewing, no matter how little time you have. Four miles beyond The Windows, a dirt road leads east to Wolfe Ranch, trailhead for **Delicate Arch,** the park's most postcard-worthy feature, a three-mile round-trip hike. Three miles farther along the main road, **Fiery Furnace** is an otherworldly collection of narrow canyons, that, despite the name, is quite cool and shady; park rangers give guided walks here throughout the summer. At the far end of the road there's a two-mile trail leading to **Devil's Garden,** where you can see **Landscape Arch,** the park's largest (and the world's second-largest)—291 feet across and 105 feet high.

Moab

Driving across southern Utah, you have two main options: Race along I-70 and get somewhere else in a hurry, or slow down and search out the truly unforgettable scenery the state has to offer. One of the best places to base yourself for an exploration of the region is **Moab** (pop. 5,046), an old uranium mining town located 30 miles south of the freeway, surrounded by two na-

Arches National Park

tional parks (Arches and Canyonlands) and hundreds of thousands of acres of desert wilderness.

Thanks to *Outside* magazine and the recent mania for outdoor athleticism, Moab has experienced a massive tourist boom in the past decade—Edward Abbey, cantankerous poet of the Southwest who wrote his first book, *Desert Solitaire,* about a season he spent at nearby Arches National Park, would probably turn in his grave if he saw the gangs of Lycra-clad mountain bikers milling around Moab's Main Street T-shirt stores and brewpubs. But despite the addition of fast-food franchises and hundreds of new motel rooms, Moab is still a dusty little back-of-beyond hamlet, albeit one that gives easy access to the wilds nearby.

If you're not prepared to camp out in the backcountry (if you are, the nearby state and national parks have a full range of possibilities), Moab has the usual national motels plus local ones like the **Apache** ($45 and up; 166 South 400 East; 435/259-5727 or 800/228-6882), where John Wayne slept while filming *Rio Bravo* near Moab in 1958.

For breakfast or lunch, try the excellent **Jailhouse Café** (101 N. Main St.; 435/259-3900) or the **Moab Diner,** two blocks away (189 S. Main St.; 435/259-4006). After a day on the trails, treat yourself to a gourmet dinner at the **Desert Bistro** at Moab Springs Ranch (1266 N. Hwy 191; 435/259-0756).

For more information on visiting the Moab area, including all the surrounding parks, contact the very helpful **Moab Information Center** (daily; 435/259-8825 or 800/635-6622) at Main and Center in the middle of town.

The prettiest route east from Moab, Hwy-128, winds along the broad and

The annual Fat Tire Festival, which is now the **Moab Ho-Down Mountain Bike Festival,** held the week before Halloween, brings mountain bikers from all over the world to Moab.

A word of warning: Even if you're not planning to venture from your car, it's a good idea to carry at least a gallon of water per person when traveling in the desert.

Behind the Rocks Trail, Moab

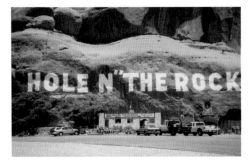

brown Colorado River past 25 miles of swimming, kayaking, and camping spots. Hwy-128 links up with I-70 23 miles west of the Colorado border at junction 212, near the former sheep-ranching center of **Cisco,** a ghostly old US-50 crossroads abandoned after completion of the Interstate, where old gas station buildings are slowly decaying into a post-apocalyptic art installation.

Fifteen miles south of Moab along US-191, one of Utah's oddest attractions is the **Hole N" The Rock** (daily; $5; 435/686-2250) a 5,000-square-foot home carved out of a sandstone cliff over a 20-year period, beginning in the 1940s, by Albert and Gladys Christensen. Now open to tourists, the site also includes a large carving of FDR's face.

COLORADO

Driving across southern Colorado on US-50 takes you through almost every landscape landlocked North America has to offer. From the geological wonderland of the Colorado River plateau, which stretches west into Utah, the route climbs up and over the 14,000-foot **Rocky Mountains,** which form a formidable wall down the center of the state. Continuing east, the alpine meadows, deeply etched river canyons, and snow-covered peaks of the southern Rockies fade away into the flat, agricultural prairies that stretch east across the middle of the country. While there is considerable ranching and farming, outdoor recreation—fishing, hiking, skiing, and mountain biking—is the basis for the economy, and the region is well provided with tourist facilities, especially in the mountainous middle.

Grand Junction

Thirty miles east of the Utah border, US-50 diverges from high-speed I-70 at the city of **Grand Junction** (pop. 58,556) on the Colorado River. After all the desert that surrounds it, Grand Junction feels much bigger than you'd expect, with its thriving old downtown, complete with cobblestone streets, odd bits of outdoor sculpture, great antiques shops, neon signs—and tons of free parking. Catering to passing traffic, Grand Junction's I-70 frontage has all the motels and places to eat you could want, but downtown holds one really

fresh peaches at a roadside market east of Grand Junction

nice older place, the clean and comfortable **Melrose Hotel** ($50 and up; 337 Colorado Ave.; 970/242-9636), a block south of Main Street—just look for the red neon sign.

Like the rest of western Colorado and eastern Utah, the Grand Junction area is rich in two things: the scenic splendor of rivers and red-rock canyons, and fossilized dinosaurs. The scenery is everywhere, and a fine array of the latter are on display west of town along I-70 at Fruita, in the Museum of Western Colorado's wonderful **Dinosaur Journey** (daily; $8.50; 970/858-7282). Kids can have fun pushing buttons to control gigantic audio-animatronic mechanical critters, while learning a little about Triassic, Jurassic, and other period details.

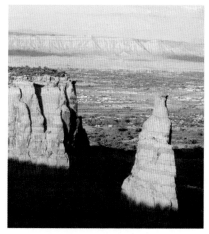

Colorado National Monument

Colorado National Monument

Rising south and west of Grand Junction, nearly 2,000 feet above the Colorado River, the brilliantly colored cliffs of **Colorado National Monument** are simply impossible to miss. Deep canyons, alive with piñon pines and cottonwood trees, nestle at the foot of sheer rock walls, at the top of which you get panoramic views over miles and miles of the Colorado Plateau. The 23-mile-long **Rim Rock Drive** winds along the tops of the cliffs, giving quick access to numerous trails for up-close looks at the various layers and hues of sandstone and shale, which have eroded over the eons into masses of sculpted stone.

There's a large **visitors center** (970/858-3617) at the main entrance, four miles southeast of town, and there's another entrance off I-70 in Fruita, at the northern end of the park.

Delta

From Grand Junction, US-50 briefly becomes a four-lane freeway, then reverts to two lanes following the Gunnison River as far as **Delta** (pop. 9,250). The half dozen building-sized murals of elk and local agricultural products support Delta's claim that it is "The City of Murals," but the biggest attraction to travelers is the reconstructed **Fort Uncompahgre** (pronounced "un-com-PA-gray"; Apr.–Oct. Mon.–Fri.; $3.50; 970/874-1718), at the confluence of the Gunnison and Uncompahgre Rivers on the northwest side of town. The small, city-sponsored fort re-creates the lifestyles of trappers and traders who first settled in the western Rocky Mountains in the early 1820s, explaining the historical context of the fur trade while introducing visitors to the arts and skills necessary for frontier life: metalworking, tanning, and tomahawk-throwing, not to mention hunting, shooting, and fishing.

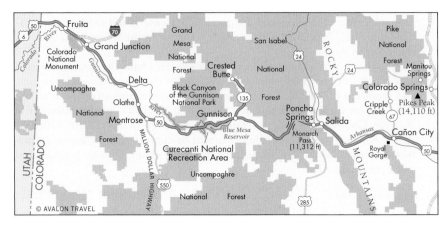

Delta has one great old landmark, the 1920s **Egyptian Theater** movie palace (452 Main St.; 970/874-9770), along with its fair share of motels (including a **Best Western**) and fast-food places. It's also home to a classic piece of roadside Americana: the log-and-stone cabins of the **Westways Court Motel** ($40–74; 1030 Main St.; 970/874-4415), on US-50 in the center of town.

Montrose: The Million Dollar Highway

With the San Juan Mountains standing out to the south, and Black Canyon just up the road, **Montrose,** a fast-growing farming community of some 20,000 souls that spreads from the heart of the fertile Uncompahgre Valley, makes a good base for exploring the region. The town itself has an appealing, still-in-business business district and a historical museum housed in the old railroad depot; the US-50 frontage has plenty of motels and places to eat.

memorial to snowplow drivers killed on the Million Dollar Highway

Eight miles east of Montrose, Hwy-347 turns off north from US-50 toward the Black Canyon of the Gunnison National Park, but Montrose also marks the start of one of the best-loved roads in the country, the **Million Dollar Highway,** a classic stretch of two-lane blacktop that forms a swirling ribbon through the San Juan Mountains, the wildest and ruggedest peaks in the Colorado Rockies. Marked on maps and by road signs as US-550, which runs south from the Gunnison River ranch lands around Montrose to the Southern Ute Indian Reservation, the "Million Dollar" tag is generally applied to the 25 steep and twisting miles that link Ouray and Silverton, a pair of remote gold- and silver-mining communities, but it's also an appropriate nickname for the entire 110 miles of US-550 that link US-50 with Ouray and Durango.

Rocky Mountain columbine,
state flower of Colorado

No matter what you want from a scenic drive, the Million Dollar Highway has it in spades. Loaded with sublime natural scenery, historically fascinating and visually appealing small towns, and, most of all, sheer driving pleasure, the road more than lives up to its name. As you might expect of a road born in a Wild West mining country animated by tales of million-dollar fortunes earned, lost, and hoped for, the history of the Million Dollar Highway is rife with legend. The route was first blazed by the so-called "Pathfinder of the San Juans," a five-foot-tall Russian immigrant named Otto Mears who was working as a U.S. mail carrier between Silverton and Telluride. By 1882 Mears had created a lucrative toll road that he parlayed into a sizable empire of roads and railroads, but his original hand-carved route through the mountains formed the basis of today's Million Dollar Highway.

Even the origin of the "Million Dollar" name is clouded in myth. Some say it was first used after an early traveler, complaining of the vertigo-inducing steepness of the route, said, "I wouldn't go that way again if you paid me a million dollars." Others claim that it derives simply from the actual cost of paving the route in the 1930s. But the favorite explanation is also the most likely: When the highway was first constructed, the builders used gravel discarded by nearby gold and silver mines, only to find out later that this dirt was actually rich in ore and worth an estimated million dollars.

The New Deal–era documentary photography project, which produced many indelible images from the likes of Walker Evans and Dorothea Lange, was directed by Roy Stryker, who spent his youth on a ranch outside Montrose.

Black Canyon of the Gunnison National Park

Some of the hardest and oldest rocks on earth form the sheer walls of 2,000-foot-deep **Black Canyon of the Gunnison,** the deepest and most impressive gorge in the state. The river cutting through the canyon falls faster than any other in North America—dropping 2,150 feet in under 50 miles—and the canyon bottom is so rugged that there are no trails along it. Unless you're a serious mountaineer, you'll have to content yourself with looking down into it from the rim, which is accessible on the north side via Hwy-92 and from

US-50 on the south via Hwy-347. The **visitors center** (970/641-2337) on the south rim provides details on hiking trails and camping and can tell you more than you ever wanted to know about the canyon's unique geology: For instance, unlike the Grand Canyon with its layers of exposed rock, the Black Canyon is basically one solid hunk of stone, a half-mile-thick chunk of two-billion-year-old Precambrian gneiss (pronounced "nice").

Upstream from the Black Canyon, US-50 parallels the Gunnison River, renowned for its excellent trout and landlocked salmon fishing, though sadly the once-raging waters have been backed up behind dams to form a series of reservoirs, jointly managed as the **Curecanti National Recreation Area.**

Gunnison and Crested Butte

A crossroads cattle town with a rapidly growing recreational aspect and the only commercial airport for miles, **Gunnison** (pop. 5,585, elev. 7,707) is made livelier than many Colorado towns by the presence of Western State College, whose ski-bumming students are responsible for the town's many bike shops and Internet cafés, not to mention the huge "W" that marks a mountainside south of town. To get a feel for Gunnison, stop by the lively **W Cafe** and nearby coffeehouse, **The Bean** (120 N. Main St.), a half block north of US-50, which runs through the redbrick heart of old downtown Gunnison. Later in the day, pig out at the **Trough** (970/641-3724), on US-50 a mile west of downtown. Motels line up along US-50, making Gunnison a handy base for exploring the region.

If you're taken with the scenery around Gunnison and want to see more, head north along Hwy-135 and the Gunnison River to the area's skiing and mountain biking center, **Crested Butte** (pop. 1,750), 25 miles away. As in Telluride and Aspen, this 100-year-old gold-mining camp won a second lease on life thanks to tourism, though compared to other Colorado places Crested Butte is low-key and somewhat off the beaten path. Skiers in search of solitude flock here in winter to cruise the 1,100-plus acres of Mt. Crested Butte, while in summer Crested Butte is a mountain bike mecca, home to the **Mountain Bike Hall of Fame** (331 Elk Ave.) and miles upon miles of mining roads and single-track trails winding through the mountains. (The ski lifts convert to bike lifts, to save you suffering on the climb back uphill.)

For a non-commercial, "wide-spectrum" audio taste of Crested Butte, tune in to **KBUT 89.9 FM** and **90.3 FM.**

The first European explorers to pass through this part of the Rockies were the Spanish missionaries Domínguez and Escalante, in 1776.

Relax while you recharge your batteries with a burger and a beer or two at the **Wooden Nickel** (222 Elk Ave.; 970/349-6350) or the adjacent **Idle Spur Grill and Brewery** (226 Elk Ave.; 970/349-5026).

Three blocks north of Elk Avenue, the **HI-Crested Butte International Hostel** ($18–28 pp; 615 Teocalli Ave.; 970/349-0588) has dorm beds and family rooms. There are also hotels and condos available through the ski resort (970/349-2262 or 800/544-8448).

Monarch Pass

East of Gunnison, the landscape changes swiftly as US-50, along with a few masochistic cyclists, climbs steeply through a gorgeous alpine landscape of

Detour:
Movie Manor and Colorado Gators

Some 75 miles southwest of US-50, the potato-farming town of Monte Vista is home to the **Movie Manor** ($104 and up; 2830 W. US-160; 719/852-5921 or 800/771-9468), a unique combination of drive-in movie theater, restaurant, and Best Western motel. You can watch movies (for free!) from the comfort of your motel room, though the screen is so far away it's about the same size as watching movies on TV. Fun, though, and unique, for sure—where else can you snuggle down beneath the covers, gazing out the window as the sun sets and the lights come up on the big-screen figures swaggering through their latest Hollywood hits against a backdrop of snowcapped, 14,000-foot peaks?

Other good reasons to loop south from US-50 include the **Great Sand Dunes National Park** and the even more unlikely sight of some 400 alligators enjoying the geothermal hot springs at **Colorado Gators** (daily; $15; 719/378-2612), an hour south of US-50 on Hwy-17, near the turnoff east to the Great Sand Dunes.

Great Sand Dunes National Park

meadows and cattle ranches toward 11,312-foot **Monarch Pass.** The pass marks the highest point on US-50 and straddles the Continental Divide: The 30 feet of annual snowfall on the east side of the pass end up in the Atlantic, while (in theory, at least) moisture falling farther west makes its way to the Pacific. There's a ski and snowboarding area here in winter, and in summer you can ride a tram or hike to a nearby summit for a 360-degree view over the Rocky and Sangre de Cristo Mountains.

Salida

Sitting alongside the Arkansas River east of Monarch Pass, **Salida** (pop. 8,710; elev. 7,038) is a riverfront railroad town gradually switching over to the tourist trade. Close your eyes to the sprawl of Wal-Mart and McDonald's along

US-50, and head a dozen blocks north to the historic downtown. Here along the riverfront, a half dozen brick buildings line up along 1st Street, where the **Laughing Ladies** serve excellent (and rightly popular) lunches, dinners, and Sunday brunches (128 W. 1st St.; 719/539-6209). Right along the river you'll find outdoor recreation shops like **Headwaters** (102 N. F St.; 719/239-2009), which rents and sells mountain bikes and kayaks and is the best source of information on the area's wealth of recreational opportunities.

The **Salida Hot Springs,** next to the visitors bureau, are the largest in the state. The naturally heated, WPA-built indoor pool and baths are open year-round (around $10; 410 W. Rainbow Blvd./US-50; 719/539-6738).

East of Salida, river rafters can be seen riding the rapids of the Arkansas River for most of the next 45 miles. Over a dozen different rafting companies have operations along this beautifully scenic stretch, where steeply walled sandstone gorges alternate with broad meadows and sagebrush plains all the way to Royal Gorge and Cañon City.

Royal Gorge

It would be easy to object to the rampant commercialism of **Royal Gorge** (daily; around $30; 719/275-7507), owned and operated by Cañon City, but if you don't mind seeing impressive works of humankind amidst a stupendous show of nature's prowess, I heartily recommend a visit. The gorge itself is unforgettable, its sheer, red granite cliffs dropping over 1,000 feet straight down to the Arkansas River. The experience is enhanced by a barrage of civil engineering feats, including aerial trams, incline railways, and an impossibly delicate suspension bridge, all enabling visitors to experience the area in diverse ways. You can look down from the rim, dangle from a gondola on your way across to the other side, and from there follow a short nature trail that offers

River rafters and a railroad share Royal Gorge.

bridge over Royal Gorge

good views of Pike's Peak. Walk back across the wooden planks of the bridge—the highest in the world, feeling uncomfortably like a rickety old seaside pier—then drop down on a funicular to the gorge's bottom, where you can stand alongside the raging river, listening to the roar or admiring the famous Denver and Rio Grande Railroad line that passes through the gorge, in places suspended out over the river from the solid rock walls.

Cañon City

One of the last remaining Wild West towns in the lower 48 states, **Cañon City** (pop. 15,723) is carved out of the eastern flank of the Rocky Mountains. Over a mile high and surrounded by a ring of 14,000-foot peaks, Cañon City's short Main Street, a block north of US-50, is lined by workaday saddle shops, gun shops, bookshops, and saloons (eight in four blocks!). But the local economy prospers not so much from tourism as from prisons—a dozen in all, including the famous federal maximum-security penitentiary, nicknamed "Supermax." Built in the 1990s, the top-security Supermax prison has held some 500 of the nation's most notorious inmates, including numerous organized crime kingpins and terrorists like Oklahoma City bomber Terry Nichols; Atlanta Olympics bomber Eric Rudolph; the "Unabomber," Ted Kaczynski; and Al Qaeda "Shoe Bomber" Richard Reid.

All along US-50 west of Cañon City, you can see rafters racing along the wild Arkansas River. Many companies offer guided trips, including **Royal Gorge Rafting** (719/275-7238).

Despite the notoriety of its many prisons, Cañon City's main attraction is the surrounding scenery, particularly the views along **Skyline Drive,** accessible from just west of town. It's a three-mile, one-way drive across the top of an 800-foot hill, as close to riding a roller coaster as you're ever likely to get while inside a passenger car. Royal Gorge to the west is another major draw, and Cañon City makes a good base for explorations, with a few moderately priced motels. The best place for cheap food and drink is **The Owl** (626 Main St.; 719/275-9946), a combo cigar store, soda fountain, diner, and pool hall at the heart of the lively Main Street business district just north of US-50.

Pike's Peak and Manitou Springs

One of the highest points you can drive to in the continental United States, **Pike's Peak** has been a road trip destination since 1901 when the first car (a two-cylinder Locomobile Steamer) made its way to the 14,110-foot summit. Opened as a toll road in 1915, the Pike's Peak Highway now winds its way to the top—climbing nearly 7,000 vertical feet in under 20 miles, with no guardrails to comfort you or block the amazing 360-degree Rocky Mountain panorama. The road is now owned and operated by the city of Colorado Springs,

Detour: Denver

Though it's 100 miles north of Pueblo via the I-25 freeway, **Denver** (pop. 600,158) has the biggest, newest, and coolest airport in the Rockies, which may make it a handy starting or stopping point. The airport, which opened in 1995, is in the middle of nowhere, 25 miles northeast of town. The main lobby has a soaring fabric roof that from the outside looks like a Plains Indian encampment; inside is a

pair of artworks, called *America: Why I Love Her,* which trace artist Gary Sweeney's childhood memories of road trips to see the "World's Largest Ball of Twine" and other all-American icons.

Other reasons to visit Denver include the **U.S. Mint** (Mon.–Fri.; free; 320 W. Colfax Ave.), right downtown, where you can watch and hear coins being pressed into shape; **Coors Field** (303/292-0200 or 800/388-ROCK), lively home of the Colorado Rockies baseball team; and **Lakeside Amusement Park** (4601 Sheridan Blvd.; 303/477-1621), off I-70, a very nifty and not expensive (unlimited rides cost $13.75 on weekdays and $19.75 on weekends and holidays!) summer-only amusement park with art deco architecture, a wooden Cyclone roller coaster, and other rides dating back over 100 years.

On the west side of the **Colorado State Capitol,** a benchmark at the unlucky 13th step lets you stand exactly 5,280 feet above sea level—a mile high.

In downtown Denver, eat at **Dixon's Downtown Grill** (1610 16th St.; 303/573-6100), a family-friendly haunt serving great breakfasts, afternoon sandwiches (try the Reuben), and drinks all night long in a historic building. There is the usual range of hotels and motels in and around Denver, plus one unforgettable classic dating from the 1890s: President Dwight Eisenhower's favorite hotel, the **Brown Palace** ($189 and up; 321 17th St.; 303/297-3111). The lobby is worth a look even if you stay the night somewhere else.

For details on these or anything else to do with Denver, contact the **visitor information center** (1600 California St.; 303/892-1505 or 800/645-3446).

Pike's Peak

which charges a $10 per person toll; go early, before the clouds and haze build up, for the best long-distance views.

And if the views aren't enough, another good reason to climb Pike's Peak is that to get there you pass through the delightful old resort town of **Manitou Springs.** A national historic district, Manitou Springs has all the grand hotels, hot springs, tourist traps, and cave tours you could want, plus what may be my very favorite pinball arcade in the entire world: The barely advertised **Penny Arcade** (free; 900 Manitou Ave.; 719/685-9815) houses dozens of ancient machines in perfect working order, all still charging the same penny, nickel, or dime that they did in the 1920s, '30s, and '40s.

Besides places to play, Manitou Springs also has some classic places to stay, like the historic motor court cabins of the **El Colorado Lodge** ($65 and up; 23 Manitou Ave.; 719/685-5485), arrayed around four acres of pine trees, with fireplaces, a pool, and a horseshoe pit!

North of Manitou Springs, the 1,350-acre **Garden of the Gods** (daily; free) is a photogenic geological outcropping of red sandstone spires, some rising to heights of 300 feet.

After a visit to the top of Pike's Peak in 1893, Katharine Lee Bates wrote the words to "America the Beautiful."

The **Pike's Peak International Hill Climb** has been held around the 4th of July almost every year since 1916. Top drivers often compete, hitting speeds of up to 100 mph on the twisting mountain road.

Pueblo

At the foot of the mountains, 38 miles east of Cañon City and 150 miles west of the Kansas border, the heavily industrialized city of **Pueblo** (pop. 104,877) spreads to both sides of the Arkansas River. Colorado's seventh-largest city, Pueblo was founded by legendary black fur-trapper Jim Beckwourth in 1842, but the town really grew in the 1870s following the arrival of the railroad and the discovery nearby of vast amounts of coal. Steel mills, including some of the largest west of the Mississippi, still stand around the fringes of the pleasant,

Santa Fe Trail

For over half a century, beginning in the 1820s and lasting until the railroads were completed in the 1880s, the Santa Fe Trail was the primary link between the United States and the Spanish and Mexican Southwest. Running from the Missouri River ports around present-day Kansas City, the trail angled along the banks of the Arkansas River, splitting west of what's now Dodge City into two routes: the Mountain Branch, which US-50 follows, and the quicker but more dangerous Cimarron Cut-Off, across the arid plains of the Jornado del Muerto. The two branches rejoined before climbing the Sangre de Cristo Mountains into what was then, as it is now, the capital of the Southwest, Santa Fe.

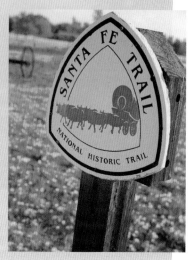

Unlike many of the routes across the Wild West frontier, the Santa Fe Trail was established by commercial traders rather than emigrant pioneers, and travel along it was active in both directions: Merchants from the United States brought manufactured goods by the wagon load, which they exchanged for Mexican silver. First blazed by trader William Becknell in 1821, the year the newly independent Republic of Mexico opened the border (which Spain had kept closed), the 750-mile-long trail was surveyed by the U.S. government in 1826, and traffic increased slowly until the Mexican-American War brought Santa Fe, and all the land in between, under U.S. control. Military forts were established to protect traders from the marauding Comanche and other native tribes; at the time of the Civil War, commerce along the trail reached a peak, with over 5,000 wagons making the trek to Santa Fe, carrying over $50 million worth of trade goods. The extension of the railroads across the Great Plains in the 1870s diminished the importance of the trail, and by 1880, when the Santa Fe railroad reached Santa Fe itself, the trail became a part of history.

Though US-50 follows the Santa Fe Trail almost exactly, from Las Animas east to Kansas City, very little remains, apart from outposts like Bent's Fort and Fort Larned and a few all-but-invisible stretches of old wagon ruts. Numerous plaques mark historic sites, and it's still possible to get a powerful sense of what the trail might have been like—provided you take the time to park the car and walk even a few hundred yards in the footsteps that crossed here a century ago.

The following are some of the most evocative sites along the Santa Fe Trail, west to east.

Santa Fe, New Mexico: The second-oldest city in North America preserves a vivid taste of its Spanish, Mexican, and American past (see page 908-909).

Bent's Old Fort, Colorado: A reconstructed adobe trading post sits along the banks of the Arkansas River in the Rocky Mountain foothills (see page 750).

Dodge City, Kansas: On one of the best-preserved remnants of the original Santa Fe Trail, wagon ruts stretch across the rolling farmlands just west of this Wild West landmark town (see page 753).

Fort Larned, Kansas: This well-preserved U.S. Army fortress, intact since the 1850s, protects a fine set of wagon ruts (see page 755).

Council Grove, Kansas: The last American town on the trail west has hardly changed since the heyday of the trail (see page 759).

Westport, Missouri: Now surrounded by suburban Kansas City, this was the real start of the trail from the 1840s on (see page 764).

Independence, Missouri: The original start of the Santa Fe and the Oregon Trails offers a fine museum detailing the westward frontier movements (see page 762).

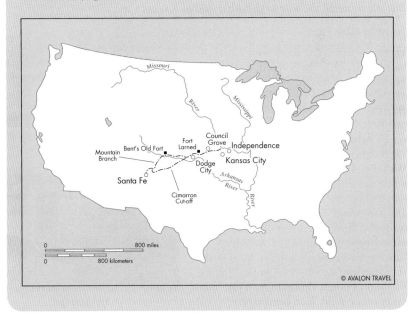

© AVALON TRAVEL

From US-50, one of the West's most scenic drives (unpaved but easily passable), **Phantom Canyon Road,** 25 miles west of Pueblo and seven miles east of Cañon City, winds north to the old mining camp, and now prosperous gambling town, of **Cripple Creek.**

On the west side of the Colorado State Capitol, a benchmark at the unlucky 13th step lets you stand exactly 5,280 feet above sea level—a mile high.

tree-lined downtown area, but Pueblo is increasingly more bucolic than brawny, and the historic areas are slowly filling up with artsy cafés, bookshops, and antiques stores, especially along Union Avenue on the south side. For great fresh-made Mexican food, try **Papa Jose's Union Café** (320 S. Union Ave.; 719/545-7476); for pizza, go to **Angelo's** (105 E. Riverwalk; 719/544-8588).

La Junta

For eastbound travelers, **La Junta** (pop. 7,046), a busy railroad town on the banks of the Arkansas River, is where we begin tracing the historic Santa Fe Trail. The name La Junta, which means "the junction," is apt, since the town has long been a key crossroads, first on the Santa Fe Trail and now as the main Amtrak stop south of Denver. Besides gas stations, a good range of places to eat (Mexican restaurants are a particular strength), a two-screen movie theater, and an ancient-looking barber shop, La Junta also offers the excellent **Koshare Indian Museum** (daily; $5; 719/384-4411), on the campus of Otero Junior College on the south side of town. Sleep cheap at the clean and friendly **Midtown Motel** ($45–67; 215 E. 3rd St.; 719/384-7741).

La Junta also marks the spot where the Mountain Branch of the Santa Fe Trail finally cuts away to the south, following what's now US-350 through the Comanche National Grassland and continuing over Raton Pass into New Mexico and on to Santa Fe. Eastbound travelers are in luck, as we follow this historic route all the way to the other side of Kansas City.

Bent's Old Fort

From La Junta, an interesting quick detour off US-50, Hwy-194 runs along the north bank of the Arkansas River to one of Colorado's most evocative historic sites, **Bent's Old Fort** (daily; $3; 719/383-5010). It lies eight miles east of La Junta, or 15 miles west of Las Animas. From 1833, when it was built by the fur-traders William and Charles Bent, until 1848, when war with Mexico and increasing unrest among the local Arapahoe, Apache, and Cheyenne tribes put an end to their business, Bent's Fort was the Southwest's most important outpost of American civilization, and a stopping place for travelers, trappers, and explorers including John C. Fremont, Francis Parkman, and just about every other Wild West luminary.

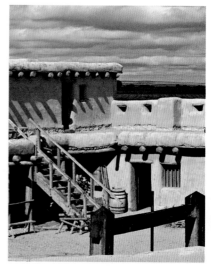

Bent's Old Fort

Though it was abandoned and left to decay for over 100 years, the large adobe fort was authentically rebuilt by the National Park Service in 1976 and now stands as a palpable reminder of the early years of the frontier era. Thick adobe walls, 15 feet tall with circular bastions at the corners, protect a roughly 100-square-foot compound. Rangers dressed in period clothing work as wheelsmiths, coopers, and carpenters, or process the many buffalo robes and beaver pelts piled up in storerooms.

Las Animas

The farming community of **Las Animas** (pop. 4,000) takes its name from the Arkansas River tributary originally known as Río de las Animas Perdidas en Purgatorio (River of Lost Souls). Las Animas is also the place where, on November 15, 1806, Lt. Zebulon Pike first laid eyes on the Rocky Mountain peak that now bears his name—Pike's Peak, 120 miles to the northwest.

Beyond Las Animas, US-50 continues its gradual descent across the Rocky Mountains foothills. The area was first known as Big Timbers for the tall cottonwoods that grew here along the Arkansas River, though most of these trees were cut down soon after the arrival of white settlers. In the 1840s and 1850s, local Cheyenne, Arapaho, Kiowa, and Apache tribes bartered bison hides at William Bent's trading post, and Wild West explorer Kit Carson died here on May 23, 1868, in his family home at what was then the U.S. Army's Fort Lyon, south of present-day US-50. Carson's remains were later moved to Taos, New Mexico, and his lands were flooded after the Arkansas River was dammed to form the large John Martin Reservoir, which stretches most of the way downstream to Lamar.

Lamar

Following the Arkansas River downstream toward the Kansas border, US-50 runs along what was known as the Mountain Branch of the Santa Fe Trail, a longer but safer alternative to the main route along the Cimarron Cut-Off. There's little to see here apart from acres and acres of irrigated farmlands, feedlots, and cattle ranches, though the region's main town, **Lamar** (pop. 7,953), is worth a quick stop, if only to admire the "World's Oldest Gas Station" (501 N. Main St.). Built out of blocks of 175-million-year-old petrified wood, the structure opened as a gas station in 1932. Although the building still attracts tourists, it is now used for storage.

At the heart of town, next to the old depot, a stately *Madonna of the Trail* stands as a reminder of the indefatigable spirit of the pioneers. Standing nearly 20 feet tall atop an engraved plinth, this statue is one of 12 identical memorials erected in the 1920s by the Daughters of the American Revolution (D.A.R.). From Bethesda, Maryland,

Lamar's **KLMR 93.3 FM** plays a broad mix of chart-topping pop and country music.

Lamar's *Madonna of the Trail*

to Upland, California, the memorials were placed along the original National Old Trails Highway, which followed the National Road (US-40) and later Route 66 on the westward path of Manifest Destiny.

North of Lamar then east of US-287, the **Sand Creek Massacre National Historic Site** (daily; free; 719/438-5916) preserves and interprets the place where, in November 1864, volunteer U.S. soldiers opened fire on a camp of Cheyenne and Arapahoe Indians, killing some 160 unarmed women and children.

All the way across Kansas, we follow almost exactly in the footsteps of the trappers and traders who braved the Santa Fe Trail along the western frontier, stopping at preserved old outposts like Fort Larned and Council Grove while tracking the few more evocative remnants of this pioneer Wild West corridor.

KANSAS

In its nearly 500 miles across Kansas, US-50 and its selected variants pass across the agricultural heartland of America, winding through dozens of small farming towns that dot the generally level landscape. (Locals definitely seem to prefer the word "level" to the equally accurate "flat," if only because it sounds less boring.) This is the heart of the "Wheat Belt," where most of the country's grain is grown—as much as half the bread baked in America is made from Kansas wheat—and it's also prime cattle country, with towns like **Dodge City** and many less famous ones maintaining their historic dependence on cows and cowboys.

The dividing line between central and mountain time zones is 15 miles west of **Garden City.** Set your clocks and watches accordingly.

Holcomb

Apart from numerous feedlots fattening cattle for slaughter, and a few wheat, corn, and beet farms fed by water diverted from the Arkansas River, there's not much to see in the 120 miles of barren plains that stretch east from

At **Garden City,** 50 miles west of Dodge City, US-50 crosses US-83, **The Road to Nowhere,** which follows the 100th meridian from Canada to Mexico. See pages 174–231 for details on this route. Garden City is described on pages 211–212.

the Colorado border. On the western outskirts of Garden City, the region's biggest town, US-50 runs through the meat-packing town of **Holcomb,** notorious as the site of the *In Cold Blood* murders documented by Truman Capote and in a pair of mid-2000s Hollywood bio-pics (*Capote* and *Infamous*). In 1959, Perry Smith and Richard Hickock ruthlessly killed all four members of the Clutter family during a robbery attempt. Both killers were eventually captured, convicted, and executed.

Santa Fe Trail Tracks

One of the best-preserved sections of Santa Fe Trail **wagon ruts** is along this stretch of US-50, nine miles west of Dodge City. Marked by a large sign, just west of the Howell grain elevator, these wheel tracks, or ruts, lie in a rolling field 100 yards north of the parking area and are basically a broad depression in the soil, approximately 800 yards wide and two miles long. Farther west, at Cimarron, 32 miles east of Garden City and 16 miles west of Dodge City, the main track of the Santa Fe Trail crossed the Arkansas River and headed southwest across the waterless plain of the Jornada del Muerto on what was known as the **Cimarron Cut-Off.** This desolate region is also where, in 1831 during the earliest days of the trail, legendary mountain man Jedediah Strong Smith was killed by a band of Comanche warriors.

Dodge City

One of the most notorious places on the Wild West frontier, **Dodge City** (pop. 27,340) can be something of a disappointment if you come here looking for a rip-roaring frontier town. In its heyday, which lasted roughly from 1872, when the railroad arrived, to 1884, when the cattle drives were effectively

sunflower,
state flower of Kansas

Tornadoes

Driving across the Great Plains heartland, especially in late spring and early summer, be prepared to encounter Mother Nature's most potent force: a tornado, whose swirling winds can reach 150–300 mph or more. The Midwest has been dubbed Tornado Alley, for the frequency of storms that can hit the region. While the tornado at the start of *The Wizard of Oz* touched down in Dorothy's home state, Kansas, they are just as likely to occur in Michigan, Missouri, or Alabama.

Each year there are more than 1,000 tornadoes across the United States, and on average 50 or so people are killed by them, though in recent years storms seem to have become more frequent and more deadly: More than 500 people were killed by tornadoes in the U.S. in 2011, and the powerful tornado that tore through Joplin, Missouri, in May killed more than 150 people. Tornadoes can last from several seconds to more than an hour, but most last around 10 minutes.

If confronted by a tornado, you can greatly reduce the chance of injury by doing a few simple things. First, be aware of the possibility of severe weather; most tornado-related deaths and injuries happen to people who are caught unaware and uninformed, so tune into local TV and radio stations for current information. If a **tornado watch** has been issued, it means that a tornado is considered likely. Once a **tornado warning** is issued, it means that a tornado has actually been spotted, and if you are nearby you should seek shelter immediately.

If you are in a car and spot a tornado, it is not a good idea to try to escape by driving away from it. Tornadoes have been known to blow cars off the road or hurl them hundreds of feet in the air. If there is no time to find shelter somewhere solid and indoors, get out of the car and lie down in a ditch or low-lying area, away from the vehicle. Though it might look safe, experts say it's best not to seek shelter under a highway overpass, which can act like a wind tunnel, making the winds even stronger.

banned, Dodge City was the undisputed capital of the buffalo-hunting, cattle-driving Wild West, with as many as 100 million bison hides and seven million head of cattle shipped out from here in that decade alone. At the same time, Dodge City was known as "Hell on the Plains," famous for its gunfights and general lawlessness, despite marshals like Bat Masterson and Wyatt Earp keeping order and planting bad guys in the Boot Hill cemetery above town.

However, almost nothing in Dodge City survives from that era. Boot Hill, for example, was bought by the city and is now the site of a small office building. (A statue of a cowboy, erected in 1927, says somewhat mournfully: "On the ashes of my campfire this city is built.") Most of what you see in Dodge City dates from the 1920s at the earliest, and Dodge City is by and large a busy farming and cattle-ranching community, with extensive stockyards sur-

Historic Front Street
Dodge City, Kansas

rounding the small downtown area. Because of the low-profit economics of the beef industry, most of the 4,000–5,000 people who work in the feedlots and slaughterhouses today are immigrant workers from Mexico—which explains the predominance of Mexican cafés and grocery stores around town.

For travelers, there's little here apart from one of the Midwest's more heavily hyped tourist attractions, the fake but fun **Boot Hill Museum** (daily; $10; 620/227-8188) and its re-created Front Street, where actors stage gunfights and "medicine shows" throughout the day. There's also an evening burlesque show, featuring Miss Kitty and her Can Can Girls; a reconstructed sod house; the old (circa-1865) jail; and a one-room schoolhouse. A historic Santa Fe locomotive completes the Boot Hill collection; not surprisingly, Boot Hill is hard to miss, well marked on the west side of town, just north of the railroad tracks along Wyatt Earp Boulevard (US-50/56), the main route through town.

Kinsley: Midway USA

Paralleling the mainline Santa Fe Railroad across the flattest, emptiest 50 miles of Kansas cornfields, east of Dodge City we follow US-50 as far as **Kinsley,** where we switch onto US-56 (which used to be known as "US-50 North") to follow the Santa Fe Trail. Kinsley, which calls itself "Midway USA," lies equidistant from New York and San Francisco: 1,561 miles from either place. This geographical fact is pointed out by a large sign outside the entertaining (and free!) **Edwards County Historical Museum,** at the US-50/56 junction on the west side of town, surrounded by an old locomotive and a variety of old farming and ranching equipment.

Fort Larned

One of the best-preserved vestiges of the Santa Fe Trail, and the whole "Wild West" for that matter, **Fort Larned** (daily; free; 620/285-6911), six miles west of US-56 via Hwy-156, was established in 1859, and for the next 20 years troops stationed here protected travelers on the Santa Fe Trail from the threat of attack by local Arapahoe and Cheyenne tribes. The fort also served a vital role in the many Indian Wars of 1860s, but by 1878, when the trail was no longer in active use, the fort was deactivated. It was sold and used as a ranch until 1960 but has survived the intervening years in excellent condition. Careful restoration by the National Park Service has made Fort Larned an excellent place to experience what the frontier really looked like, albeit from the U.S. military perspective.

Detour: The Garden of Eden

If you're one of those bi-coastal types who thinks the Midwest is full of conventional-minded folks leading ordinary lives as contented consumers, you owe it to yourself to visit the **Garden of Eden** (daily during the summer; $6; 785/525-6395), one of the country's oldest and oddest folk-art environments. Located in the tiny town of **Lucas, Kansas** (pop. 436), the Garden of Eden is the sort of place that puts the gothic back in American Gothic, a front-yard forest of biblical scenes and Populist political allegories—Adam and Eve, Cain and Abel, and the Crucifixion of Labor at the Hands of Preachers, Bankers, and Lawyers—created out of concrete from around 1910 to 1930 by one Samuel Dinsmoor. An Ohio native and Civil War veteran, Dinsmoor actively promoted his garden as a tourist attraction, managing to draw many hundreds of visitors to this distant and fairly inaccessible corner of Kansas. Dinsmoor died at age 89 in 1932 and is preserved in a glass-covered tomb on the property, yet carried on his hucksterism even after death, insisting in his will that no one be allowed "to go in and see me for less than $1."

This all-American Garden of Eden (305 E. 2nd St.) is at the corner of 2nd and Kansas in **Lucas,** which is on Hwy-18 north of Great Bend and 15 miles north of I-70. Homespun Lucas is also home to the **Grassroots Art Center** (213 S. Main St.; 785/525-6118), a gallery showing and selling artworks created by other self-taught "outsider" artists. Outside the gallery is a courtyard full of carved limestone masonry sculptures, many salvaged from demolished buildings around the area.

Sandstone buildings, which replaced the original adobe after the end of the Civil War, surround a 400-square-foot parade ground, and interior rooms have been filled with accurate reproductions of original fixtures and fittings, ranging from barracks to blacksmith's shops to a large storehouse. A nearby farm preserves a set of ruts surviving from the Santa Fe Trail days, though you really need to have an active imagination to get much from them.

In between Fort Larned and US-56, the **Santa Fe Trail Center** (closed Mon.; $4; 620/285-2054) is a private, nonprofit museum focusing on the overall history of the Santa Fe Trail region. Diorama-like exhibits feature full-scale mock-ups of wagons and frontier trading posts, and behind the main building are a sod house and a one-room schoolhouse.

Pawnee Rock

Just eight miles northeast of Larned, a half mile north of US-56 and the Arkansas River, **Pawnee Rock** was once one of the most important landmarks on the Santa Fe Trail. However, so much of the original 60-foot-high tower of Dakota sandstone has been quarried—to build houses as well as the roadbed of the Santa Fe railroad—that it's little more than a stubby hump. But you can still get a grand view of the surrounding countryside from the easy trail that leads to the rock's much-diminished summit.

Great Bend

Spreading along the northern bank of the Arkansas River at the northernmost point on its sweep across central Kansas, **Great Bend** (pop. 15,995) was originally established as a fort along the Santa Fe Trail, but it really began to grow after the railroad came through. As with Dodge City to the southwest, the arrival of the railroad in 1872 attracted cattle drovers from the Chisholm Trail, who turned Great Bend into a raucous Wild West town. It's now a quiet, rural city, earning its livelihood from wheat farms and, since the 1930s, oil.

Downtown Great Bend has a number of building-sized murals, especially the blocks along Main Street perpendicular to US-56, and the outskirts of town have the engaging **Barton County Historical Society Museum** (closed Mon.; $4; 620/793-5125), just south of the railroad tracks and the river along US-281. Farther afield, the Great Bend area holds two of the largest wildlife refuges in Kansas, **Cheyenne Bottoms** to the northeast and **Quivira** to the southeast, both of which offer excellent bird-watching (and hunting) opportunities.

Great Bend does have a fairly good range of places to eat, with franchise fast food supplemented by a handful of local restaurants. Best breakfast place: **Granny's Kitchen** (925 10th St.; 620/793-7441).

Along with the national chains, one reliable place to stay in Great Bend is the **Traveler's Budget Inn** ($37 and up; 4200 W. 10th St.; 620/793-5448).

Lyons

The farming, oil-drilling, and salt-mining town of **Lyons** (pop. 3,732), 30 miles due east of Great Bend, doesn't look much different from most other Kansas towns, but it has an unusually impressive history—and a very nice courthouse square downtown. There's a 150-foot-long intaglio serpent carved into the prairie eight miles northeast of town, and some Santa Fe Trail ruts, but the most compelling remains are those left behind by Coronado's expedition through the region in 1541, in search of the fabled Golden City of Quivira. Exhibits on all of these, as well as on Indian and pioneer American cultures, are displayed inside the modern, purpose-built **Coronado-Quivira Museum** (closed Mon.; $2; 105 W. Lyon St.; 620/257-3941), two blocks south of the landmark county courthouse off US-56.

Two miles west of Lyons along US-56, a large cross marks

Great Bend was the boyhood hometown of Jack Kilby, the Texas Instruments electrical engineer who helped invent the integrated circuit and the pocket calculator. Kilby was awarded the Nobel Prize for Physics in 2000, and he died in 2005.

The next town east of Great Bend along US-50 is **Ellinwood,** where a couple of antiques shops mark the historic downtown area. Ellinwood sits atop a series of tunnels used as tornado shelters and occasionally as storerooms for contraband. They are sometimes open for guided tours by **Underground Ellinwood** ($5; 620/564-2400).

If you happen upon one, check out a public auction, held irregularly in towns across the rural Midwest. Fast-talking auctioneers take bids on various lots, ranging from real antiques to boxes of junk and cast-off clothes.

the site where Father Padilla, who accompanied Coronado on his expedition and returned the following year to convert the natives, was killed by unreceptive Indians, thereby becoming the first "Christian martyr" in the present-day United States.

For a place to stay, try the **Lyons Inn** ($50 and up; 817 W. Main St.; 620/257-5185), on US-56.

US-50: Hutchinson

If you've opted to follow US-50 rather than the Santa Fe Trail tour along US-56, be sure to check out **Hutchinson** (pop. 42,080), a large and lively city that's home to the world's longest grain elevator (over a half mile long). The town's old salt mines, some 600 feet below ground, are now used for storage of important archives, including the original negatives of many classic Hollywood films. The mines aren't open to visitors, but Hutchinson does have another surprising attraction: the **Kansas Cosmosphere and Space Center** (daily; $17; 1100 N. Plum St.; 620/662-2305 or 800/397-0330). The center boasts a great collection of historic air- and spacecraft, including Mercury, Gemini, and Apollo capsules; a Lockheed SR-71A Blackbird spy plane; and a pair of German V-1 and V-2 rockets; plus two planetarium shows and an IMAX theater.

McPherson

From a distance across the flat plains, the towering grain elevators make **McPherson** (pop. 13,155), 35 miles east of Lyons and marking the junction of US-56 and I-135 between Salina and Wichita, look more impressive than it really is. You can fill the gas tank or get a bite to eat (all the usual franchise food places and gas stations are here) or just stretch your legs wandering around the four-block Main Street business district.

The small **McPherson Museum** (Tues.–Sun. 1–5 PM; $3; 1130 E. Euclid St.; 620/241-8464), well marked in a residential district, displays rooms furnished in typical turn-of-the-20th-century Kansas style. It also holds the world's first man-made diamond, produced by Willard Hershey, a local chemistry teacher.

Mennonite Country

One of the centers of the sizable local Mennonite community, **Hillsboro** (pop. 2,491), 13 miles west of US-77, serves as market center for the area's highly productive farmlands. Tabor College, on the east side of town, is the most visible sign of the Mennonite presence; although it's a coed nondenominational college, about half the students are local Mennonites.

The tidy town of **Goessel** (pop. 539), 15 miles southwest of Hillsboro, was also founded by Mennonite farmers and now holds the worthwhile **Mennonite Heritage and Agricultural Museum** (Tues.–Sat.; $4; 200 N. Poplar St.; 620/367-8200), where numerous buildings, including two schools, a barn, and a bank, have been moved for preservation. The flat, black earth around Goessel is among the world's greatest producers of wheat, in particular the hardy hybrids able to withstand the Midwest winter. The original seed, known

Mennonite church in Goessel

as "Turkey Red," was brought to Kansas in the early 1870s by Russian Mennonites who immigrated here after their 100-year exclusion from military service was rescinded.

Zigzagging east from Hillsboro and then north along US-77/US-56, after another 37 "level" miles US-56 reaches the town of **Herington,** whose central square holds a monument to Father Padilla, who passed through southern Kansas in search of the mythical Golden City of Quivira as part of Coronado's expedition.

Council Grove

Just 75 miles southwest of the suburban sprawl of Kansas City, 25 miles west of the I-335 Kansas Turnpike, **Council Grove** (pop. 2,182) still looks much as it did over a century ago, when, from the 1830s to the 1860s, it was the most important of all way stations on the Santa Fe Trail. Council Grove's lush maples and oaks were the last hardwoods available on the long route west across the treeless plain, which meant traders and travelers could make final repairs and stock up on spare axles and other essentials. It was also the western extent of "safe territory"; beyond here travelers were subject to frequent attacks by hostile Indians.

The **Kaw Mission State Historic Site,** in Council Grove five blocks north of Main on Mission Street, was built by Methodist missionaries in 1851 as a school for local Indian children. Students included Charles Curtis, who served as U.S. vice president from 1929 to 1933.

Nowadays the town proudly preserves its many historic sites, and in many ways serves as the most not-to-be-missed stop for modern travelers heading along the Santa Fe Trail. Though by now the trees themselves are little more than desiccated stumps, the sites of two of the most important trail icons are marked along Main Street (US-56), east of the bridge over the small Neosho River: the **Council Oak,** under which, in 1825, the native Kansa and Osage Indians agreed to allow Americans to cross their territory, and the **Post Office Oak,** which served as a natural message center for early travelers. Four blocks west, the **Last Chance Store** at Main and Chautauqua Streets has served as a bank and a post office since it was built in 1857.

In between, the banks, cafés, and stores along Main Street, which the Santa Fe Trail followed through town, make little obvious effort to cater to tourists, and the town basically goes about its day-to-day business without forgetting its extraordinary past. The **Hays House** (112 W. Main St.; 620/767-5911), in the center of town, lays fair claim to being the oldest restaurant west of the Mississippi; originally built as a frontier home, and later serving as a saloon, supply post, courthouse, and hotel, it has stood on this site since 1847. Now modernized, it is still the focus of the town's social and political life and is open all day—with excellent fried chicken. Across Main, the soda fountain inside the **Aldrich Apothecary** (115 W. Main St.; 620/767-6731) serves famous "Santa Fe Trail" root beer floats. And ice cream. The best place to stay is the comfortable **Cottage House Hotel** ($60–190; 25 N. Neosho; 620/767-6828).

US-50: Tallgrass Prairie National Preserve

The delights of the Flint Hills landscape are pastoral in the extreme, with few roaring waterfalls or towering cliffs to take your breath away or make you pull out the camera, but the unique ecosystem has enough admirers that a section of it was recently set aside as the **Tallgrass Prairie National Preserve.** Located along Hwy-177 about 17 miles south of Council Grove, or two miles north of Strong City and US-50, the 11,000-acre preserve protects a large remaining portion of the extensive tallgrass prairie that once covered the Great Plains—most of the present-day Midwest. While the building that houses the visitors center (daily; 620/273-8494) is currently under construction, interpretive facilities are available. Also available are exhibits and videos on the natural flora, fauna, and geography of the area. A 1.5-mile nature trail starts here,

winding along to the historic one-room Fox Creek Schoolhouse while giving an up-close look at the head-high (or taller) flowering grasses that give the tallgrass prairie its name. Park rangers also guide bus tours of the grassland ecosystem. Call ahead as times may vary.

The best base for a visit to the Tallgrass Prairie National Preserve is **Cottonwood Falls,** two miles south of Strong City and US-50 via Hwy-177. The town boasts the beautiful Chase County Courthouse, the oldest still in use in the state, standing like a French château at the south end of a sleepy Main Street business district. In the business district, you'll also find a couple of cafés and crafts shops, and the elegant 10-room **Grand Central Hotel** ($160 and up; 215 Broadway; 620/273-6763), which has a fine, subtly Western-

Chase County Courthouse in Cottonwood Falls is the oldest operating courthouse in Kansas.

Blue Highways to PrairyErth

Writing about US-50, author William Least Heat-Moon has said that "for the unhurried, this little-known highway is the best national road across the middle of the United States." After traveling 13,000 miles of back road through the nooks and crannies of 38 states to write his first book, the road-trip classic *Blue Highways*, Heat-Moon began work on a very different study. Straying no farther than the 744 square miles of Chase County, Kansas, he embarked upon what he termed a "deep map" of the area that sits atop the lush rolling Flint Hills, the nation's last remaining grand expanse of tallgrass prairie, split by US-50 and the Santa Fe Railroad.

The result was the 1991 book *PrairyErth*, a 600-plus-page evocation of history and contemporary life in this otherwise unremarkable corner of the country, which Heat-Moon describes as being "five hours by Interstates from home, eight hours if I follow a route of good café food." Combining folk history and contemporary anecdotes with captivating quotes from sundry novels, Native American legends, travel guides, essays, and old newspaper clippings, this unique project—which has been described as the nonfiction equivalent of the Great American Novel—manages to capture the rhythms of ranching life here in the middle of the great American nowhere.

themed restaurant. For a night out in the country, consider the **1874 Stonehouse on Mulberry Hill** ($95–150; 620/273-8481), located on 60 rolling acres just outside town, on the banks of the Cottonwood River.

Burlingame and Baldwin City

Between Council Grove and Kansas City, US-56 passes through the lovely cattle-ranching grasslands of the northern Flint Hills, zigzagging at 90-degree angles through onetime coal-mining towns like Worden, Overbrook, and Scranton. **Burlingame** (pop. 934), the largest of this bunch, is noteworthy for its very broad, brick-paved, 20-mph Main Street (US-56), lined by diverse 100-year-old buildings painted with a barrage of signs advertising player pianos as well as the usual liquor, food, and auto parts.

At the northeast edge of the Flint Hills, 13 miles west of the I-35 freeway from Kansas City, US-56 skirts the leafy, brick-paved streets of **Baldwin City** (pop. 4,515), a small town that was once a main rest-and-repair stop on the Santa Fe Trail—four days' travel west of Independence, Missouri. In 1858, the first college on the western frontier was founded here in a three-story sandstone building now preserved as "The Old Castle," alongside a combination general store and post office on the east side of the pleasant campus of Methodist-run Baker University. The library (Mon.–Fri. only; free) three blocks west displays the Quayle Collection of rare religious texts, including clay tablets dating from Old Testament times and a range of hand-bound bibles, arranged to trace the development of printing techniques and typography styles.

For the rest of the way east to Kansas City, US-56 parallels I-35 across lush rolling grassland pastures and farms, marked in places by signs reading Old US-50. Along this route, two miles west of Gardner, a historical marker stands on the site where the Santa Fe and Oregon Trails once divided. For many years, a crude wooden sign pointed westbound travelers in the proper direction: left to Santa Fe, right to Oregon.

MISSOURI

From **Kansas City,** and its noteworthy neighboring towns of Independence and Liberty, US-50 makes a lazy trek across Missouri's rolling-prairie farmlands, stopping at the historic railroad town of **Sedalia** before reaching the state capital, **Jefferson City,** roughly midway across. Continuing east, climbing through hardwood forests of the Ozark uplands, US-50 leads to a number of similarly slow but more interesting old roads like Hwy-100, which winds through a number of historic towns along the banks of the Missouri River before approaching **St. Louis,** at the eastern edge of the state.

US-50: Across Kansas City

US-50 is now submerged beneath the Interstates and runs west–east around Kansas City via I-35, I-435, and I-470. The older, pre-Interstate route also avoided downtown, following what's now signed as US-169 along Park Avenue and 47th Street, past the Country Club Plaza and the Nelson-Atkins Museum of Art, before dipping south again on the Swope Parkway to Lee's Summit, where the old alignment rejoins the current US-50 routing.

To reach the downtown area from US-50, you can follow any of many north–south streets, like Troost Avenue, the down-at-the-heels old main drag, or the parkway-like El Paseo.

Independence

A quiet suburb lying on the eastern fringe of greater Kansas City, **Independence** (pop. 116,830) doesn't look like a special place, but it is. One of the country's most history-rich small cities, Independence came to life during the early years of the westward expansion, serving as the jumping-off point for the Santa Fe and, later, Oregon and California Trails. A century later, Independence again gained prominence as the hometown of President Harry Truman, who lived here from boyhood until his death in 1972.

The city-run **National Frontier Trails Museum** (daily; $6; 318 W. Pacific St.), four blocks south of the town square, is one of the best museums dedicated to America's pioneers. Beginning with a brief account of Lewis and Clark, the exhibits explore the heyday of the Santa Fe Trail, which throughout the 1820s and 1830s made Independence the leading town on the western frontier. The later Oregon Trail, on which some 300,000 people left Independence for the West Coast, is recounted through an engagingly displayed series of diary entries and drawings made by pioneers.

While very little remains from the pioneer days, Independence has hardly changed since Harry Truman grew up here around the turn of the 20th century. The soda fountain where he held his first job, and the courtroom where he presided as judge, still stand in the town square. His home, northwest of the square, is open for **tours** (daily; $4; 219 N. Delaware St.), and the large **Harry S Truman Library and Museum** (daily; $8) four blocks north contains his presidential papers, a replica of his White House office, and the gravesites of Truman and his wife, Bess.

Clinton's Soda Fountain, "Where Harry Had His First Job" (100 W. Maple St.; 816/833-2046), still serves milk shakes and sandwiches. For a place to stay, try the historic **Serendipity B&B** ($45 and up; 116 S. Pleasant St.; 816/833-4719), within a short walk of all the Independence attractions.

Liberty

Another ideally named small town on the suburban fringes of Kansas City, **Liberty** (pop. 29,149) is worth a visit for rather different reasons. This is where,

Outlaw Jesse James grew up near Liberty.

having finished fighting for the Confederacy in the Civil War, on February 13, 1866, **Jesse James** and his brother Frank staged the first-ever daylight bank robbery, getting away with over $60,000. The bank building itself, on the northwest corner of the preserved-in-amber town square, is pretty much as it was, complete with the vault, safe, and banknotes; it's now a small **museum** (Mon.–Sat.; $6; 103 N. Water St.).

A block north of the square stands another historic site, the oxymoronic **Liberty Jail** (daily; free; 216 N. Main St.), where Mormon prophet Joseph Smith and his followers were imprisoned during the winter of 1838–1839. It's a significant site for Mormons and has been faithfully reconstructed.

Clay Savings, the site of Jesse James' first bank robbery

Kansas City

Though it covers a huge area, stretching for some 20 miles on both sides of the Missouri/Kansas border, and nearly 30 miles north to south, Kansas City (pop. 459,787) never really feels like a big city. It's more like a conglomeration of small towns, once separate from each other but now joined together by tract-house sprawl and the 100-mile-long I-435 Beltway. The historic center of Kansas City lines the south bank of the Missouri River, where 30-story sky-scrapers stand above hefty brick warehouses, huge stockyards, railroad tracks, and banks of grain elevators all testifying to Kansas City's role as the main distribution point for Midwestern farm products.

Southwest of the city center, off Main and 40th Streets, **Westport** is the birthplace of Kansas City. Before the Kansas River switched course and left it high and dry, Westport was the westernmost steamboat landing in the United States, and it quickly grew into a prime supply point on the Santa Fe and Oregon Trails. For a better taste of old-time riverfront Kansas City, head down-town to the **Steamboat Arabia Museum** (daily; $14.50; 400 Grand Blvd.; 816/471-1856), in the historic City Market, which displays the fascinating contents of a steamboat that sank in 1856: hardware, guns, clothes, booze, canned and bottled food, and all sorts of things that made life on the west-ern frontier livable.

Steamboat Arabia Museum

Located on the south side of Westport, the remarkable **Nelson Atkins Museum of Art** (closed Mon.–Tues.; free; 4525 Oak St.; 816/561-4000) would do any city proud, with strong surveys of both Asian and American art, in-cluding in-depth coverage of K.C.-based Thomas Hart Benton and the nation's larg-est collection of Henry Moore sculptures. The museum's translucent Bloch Building addition has been lauded as one of the world's Top 10 most interesting new buildings. Two blocks west is another architectural innovation: **Country Club Plaza,** one of the country's first shopping malls, its opulent Spanish Revival styling still attracting the upscale likes of Armani, Saks, and the Body Shop.

Right downtown, the **Hallmark Visitors Center** (closed Sun.; free; 2450 Grand Blvd.; 816/274-3613) tells the story of the $4 billion greeting card com-pany, which is based here. Across Main Street, the historic tower of the Liberty Memorial has been joined by the thought-provoking **National World War I Museum** (daily in the summer, closed Sat. rest of the year; $12; 816/784-1918), which pays tribute to the soldiers while putting the conflict into its com-plicated political context.

A mile east of downtown K.C. is the revitalizing 18th and Vine neighborhood, heartland of Kansas City's prolific African American 1930s–1940s music scene, a golden age that spawned jazz greats Charlie Parker, Lester Young, Count Basie, and Jo Jones, all of whom are honored in the **American Jazz Museum** (1616 E. 18th St.). The neighborhood was also site of Municipal Stadium, where the Kansas City Monarchs (and the Beatles!) played, which explains why the jazz museum shares space with the marvelous **Negro Baseball Leagues Museum** (closed Mon.; $8; 816/221-1920), dedicated to documenting the players and culture of the various professional baseball leagues that existed side-by-side with the "majors" before the color barriers began to be broken down in the late 1940s.

Today, the **Kansas City Royals** (816/921-8000) play at the very pleasant, 40,000-seat Kauffman Stadium off I-70 at the I-435 junction. Games are broadcast on **KCSP 610 AM**.

Practicalities

To get around Kansas City, drive. As in Los Angeles, which Kansas City resembles more than residents of either city are likely to admit, cars rule the roads. Distances are huge and public transportation is basically nonexistent.

In downtown Kansas City, there are a number of very nicely restored, very grand 1920s hotels: the **Hilton President** ($159 and up; 1329 Baltimore Ave.; 816/221-9490) is a block away from the **Holiday Inn Aladdin** ($109 and up; 1215 Wyandotte St.; 816/421-8888). Budget-conscious travelers can choose from a slew of highway motels lining the Interstates.

For food, there's no better introduction to the delights of K.C. cuisine than **Arthur Bryant's** (1727 Brooklyn Ave.; 816/231-1123), east of downtown near the Negro Baseball Leagues Museum. Meat-eaters drive for miles to eat at this classic, no-frills rib shack, where heavenly barbecue sauces come in plain plastic bottles. For burgers, fries, malts, and shakes (and a killer cherry limeade!), look no farther than **Winstead's,** across from the art museum, near Country Club Plaza (101 Brush Creek Blvd.; 816/753-2244).

Kansas City's once-vaunted nightlife is nothing like it was during the jazz and R&B heyday of the 1940s and 1950s, though there's always something

going on in the ambitious **P&L,** the "Power and Light District," where bars, clubs, restaurants, and street performers cover eight downtown blocks around 13th and Main Street. One other place to go: The historic **Kelly's Westport Inn** (500 Westport Rd.; 816/561-5800) is a great place to enjoy a budget-priced beer while soaking up some old K.C. ambience.

In 1867, the militant prohibitionist Carrie Nation moved to the village of **Holden,** nine miles south of US-50 via Hwy-131, with her alcoholic first husband, Dr. William Gloyd, who died the following year.

Twenty miles west of Sedalia, south of US-50 near the town of Knob Noster, **Whiteman Air Force Base** is the home of the 509th Bomb Wing, which operates and maintains the entire fleet of B-2 Stealth bombers. Whiteman AFB was named after 2nd Lt. George A. Whiteman, a Sedalia resident and fighter pilot who was killed in action during the attack on Pearl Harbor.

Sedalia

East of Kansas City, the roadside along fast, four-lane US-50 is endless open, rolling prairie, most of it planted in wheat and corn. As in most of the West, early development here occurred along the railroad lines, which were constructed beginning in the 1850s. Towns boomed when the trains arrived, but most went bust as the tracks were extended westward to Kansas City and beyond.

Sedalia (pop. 21,250), 75 miles east of Kansas City, was one of the few that survived, growing into a small city thanks to its position straddling the main line between St. Louis and Kansas City. Sedalia reached its peak of prosperity around 1900, an era evoked by the ragtime music of Sedalia's own Scott Joplin. The tracks through town, and most of the way across Missouri, have been converted into the hiking and bicycling Katy Trail.

Along with ragtime music and railroad history, Sedalia offers an unexpected treat: modern galleries of excellent contemporary art, courtesy of the **Daum Museum** (closed Mon.; free; 3201 W. 16th St.) on the campus of the local community college, a half mile south of US-50.

Sedalia also has many great places to stop and eat. **Eddie's Drive-In** (115 W. Broadway; 660/826-0155), on US-50, has been a Sedalia establishment since 1937, serving steak burgers—with meat ground fresh each day. For a taste of Cajun country without the 600-mile drive down US-65 to the Louisiana bayous, try **Le Maire's Cajun Catfish** (3312 S. Limit Ave.; 660/827-3563), which has great fried

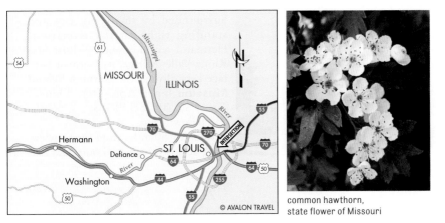

common hawthorn,
state flower of Missouri

catfish, boiled shrimp, crab legs, frog legs, crayfish, and other swamp, creek, and seafood fare.

At the heart of the historic downtown, a few blocks from the Katy Trail, the **Hotel Bothwell** ($75 and up; 103 E. 4th St.; 660/826-5588) is a nicely restored 1920s hotel, now part of the Clarion Hotel group.

The old railroad depot downtown has been brought back to life as the town's **welcome center** (600 E. 3rd St.; 660/826-2222).

Jefferson City

Roughly at the center of the state, 130 miles west of St. Louis and 140 miles east of Kansas City on the south bank of the Missouri River, **Jefferson City** (pop. 43,079) is a strangely small and somnolent place. The handsome neoclassical **state capitol** (daily; free), modeled on the U.S. Capitol and completed in 1917, is the central landmark, rising above the river at the heart of town. Inside, the rotunda and ground floor area is packed with informative exhibits tracing the state's political and natural history, while hourly **guided tours** take in the entire building, including a famous mural by Thomas Hart Benton on the walls of the third-floor House Lounge.

The small, surprisingly quiet downtown area has a couple of places worth searching out: start with **Arris Pizza** (117 W. High St.; 573/635-9225), which has been serving great pizzas and a range of Greek specialties since 1961. Afterwards, enjoy freshly churned ice cream at **Central Dairy** (610 Madison St.; 573/635-6148). And if all that makes you want to linger, stay the night at the historic but recently remodeled **Hotel DeVille/Baymont Inn,** right downtown, a block off US-50 ($69 and up; 319 W. Miller St.; 573/636-5231), the main alternative to the national chains.

Hwy-100: Hermann and Washington

Running along the south bank of the Missouri River, Hwy-100 is the most interesting route between Jefferson City and St. Louis. Midway along, the town of **Hermann** (pop. 2,706) was founded by German immigrants in 1837.

It was at Westminster College in the town of **Fulton,** 20 miles northeast of Jefferson City, that Winston Churchill made his famous "Iron Curtain" speech in 1946.

Missouri State Capitol, Jefferson City, Missouri

Surrounded by small wineries and standing right on the riverfront, Hermann reminds some visitors of a Rhine Valley village, its German heritage kept alive at the **German School Museum** (open Apr.–Oct. Thurs.–Tues.; $5; 312 Schiller St.; 573/486-2389) downtown.

Roughly 50 miles from the Gateway Arch at downtown St. Louis, the red-

Scott Joplin: The King of Ragtime

Music is among the most mobile of the arts, equally affecting anywhere and anytime, but many forms are strongly identified with a given place and era. New Orleans means jazz, the Delta has the blues, Detroit will always be equated with the Motown sound, and if credit were given where credit is due, Sedalia, Missouri, would join the above places as the source of another classic African American music—ragtime. The first ragtime tunes, so-called because of their ragged, syncopated rhythms, were played in the early 1890s but later came into full flower out of the musical mind of Scott Joplin, the universally acclaimed king of ragtime.

Born in 1868 near Texarkana, Texas, to a former slave and freeborn mother, Scott Joplin was one of six children in a musical family. After moving around the Midwest throughout his youth, in the late 1890s Joplin settled in Sedalia, which was then a raucous railroad town, where he studied music theory at Sedalia's small black college. To pay his way, Joplin played piano at many of the clubs that lined Main Street in Sedalia, which had a reputation both for multiracial harmony and as an adult playground of bars and brothels catering to the many itinerant men passing through. One of these nightclubs gave its name to the "Maple Leaf Rag," the composition that made Joplin's reputation and which, at a penny-per-sheet royalty, earned around $500 a year—enough to support him, but far from a fortune. As late as 1940, *Life* magazine said Sedalia still had one of the "most notorious red-light districts" in the Midwest, but very little remains here today to give a taste of the rowdy, ragtime era. Sedalia remembers its favorite son with a **Scott Joplin Ragtime Festival** (660/826-2271) every June. There's also a Scott Joplin mural, downtown at Ohio and 2nd Streets, near the site of the Maple Leaf club.

brick town of **Washington** (pop. 21,200) rises on narrow streets above the broad Missouri River. Like Hermann, the town was settled by German immigrants in the mid-1800s and is now full of restaurants and B&B inns catering to weekend visitors. The small **Washington Historical Society Museum** at 4th and Market Streets has exhibits on early settlers and the town's current main industry (after tourism, that is): manufacturing corn-cob pipes.

The great frontiersman Daniel Boone settled along the northern banks of the Missouri River in 1799 and lived near what's now the town of **Defiance** for the next 20 years until his death in 1820. His home, five well-signed miles outside Defiance, is now owned by his descendants and open for tours (Mon.–Sat. 9 AM–5 PM and Sun. noon–5 PM; $7–12; 636/798-2005).

West of St. Louis, Hwy-100 and US-50 merge into the high-speed I-44 freeway in Eureka, very near the massive Six Flags amusement park ($32–47; 636/938-4800), which has great roller coasters and various "theme" areas evoking aspects of Missouri's past: the wooden Colossus Ferris wheel is decorated with scenes from the 1904 World's Fair.

St. Louis is the only city where three of our routes coincide—US-50, The **Great River Road** (page 271), and **Route 66** (page 875). For details on visiting **St. Louis,** see pages 272–273.

ILLINOIS

US-50 runs straight across over 150 miles of southern Illinois's pancake-flat farmlands—acres of corn and soybeans as far as the eye can see, with small towns dotting the roadside every 10 or so miles. For much of the way, US-50 follows the Trace Road, a slightly raised causeway originally traced across the swampy marshlands by the same prehistoric people who built the enigmatic mounds at Cahokia, which still stand in the eastern suburbs of St. Louis. Midway across Illinois, US-50 passes through the quirkily historic town of **Salem** (birthplace of two American icons: William Jennings Bryan and Miracle Whip), then crosses over the Wabash River into Indiana.

Lebanon

US-50 follows I-64 east from St. Louis across the flat prairie, whose fertile alluvial soil has earned it the nickname Little Egypt. The highway parallels the Illinois Central Railroad through a dozen small towns, the most significant of which is **Lebanon** (pop. 3,458), 20 miles east of the Mississippi River. An attractive town with a number of stately, mansard-roofed, Victorian-era commercial buildings now housing antiques shops along Main Street and St. Louis Street (US-50), Lebanon grew up around the bucolic campus of McKendree University, founded here in 1828, making it one of the oldest in Illinois.

The best reason to stop, however, is the small **Mermaid House Hotel,** on US-50 (114 E. St. Louis St.). Charles Dickens, who visited the area to see the

© AVALON TRAVEL

rich but muddy prairie east of town, stayed here for a night in 1842 and described it in *American Notes* as comparing "favorably with any village ale house of a homely kind in England." After spending most of the past 150 years as a private home, the building is now undergoing restoration but is open for tours (Sat.–Sun. 10 AM–4 PM; donations).

Salem

Halfway across Illinois, just east of the busy I-57 freeway, US-50 cuts through the center of **Salem** (pop. 7,909), a historically fascinating if visually less-than-thrilling city best known as the birthplace and boyhood home of William Jennings Bryan. The turn-of-the-20th-century politician and orator, who served as leader of the Democratic Party for 15 years, prosecuted the so-called "Monkey Trial" of 1925 and led the successful attack on Tennessee schoolteacher John Scopes (who, coincidentally, was also born and raised in Salem) for breaking a local ban on teaching evolution. Bryan was born in 1860 in the small frame house 408 S. Broadway, four blocks south of Main Street (US-50). It has been preserved as a small **museum** (hours by appointment only; free). There's a statue of Bryan, crafted by Mt. Rushmore sculptor Gutzon Borglum, on Broadway a half mile north of Main Street, in front of the Roller Palace skating rink.

Salem has also given America the **G.I. Bill of Rights.** Also known as the G.I. Bill, this law entitles military veterans to subsidized education and other services. It was first proposed by the local American Legion branch before being signed into law in 1944.

Salem is an interesting place to linger, and if you want to stay overnight try the inexpensive **Continental Motel** ($40–60; 1600 E. Main St.; 618/548-3090), on US-50, next door to an enjoyable bowling alley.

Olney and Lawrenceville

The flat farmlands of southeast Illinois are dotted with occasional oil wells and signs painted on barn sides encouraging travelers to Chew Mail Pouch Tobacco or See Rock City, but towns are few and far between. The first of these is the attractive town of **Olney** (pop. 7,994). Besides boasting a large number of grand old mansions set behind broad green lawns along quiet, leafy streets, Olney has the singular attraction of **albino squirrels,** which were set loose in town around the turn of the 20th century. By 1940, the WPA *Guide to Illinois* noted that "thousands of the little animals now scamper about the parks and courthouse square, and frisk over lawns, trees, and rooftops," though these days there are fewer than 100 white squirrels, and you're most likely to see them if you head to the **city park** north of the courthouse square.

Perhaps the best reason to detour through Olney is to sample the incredibly good cheeseburgers, onion rings, and milk shakes at **Hovey's** (412 E. Main St.; 618/395-4683)

East of Olney, US-50 reverts to two-lane highway, running for 23 miles before passing by **Lawrenceville** (pop. 4,954), which was named for U.S. Navy Capt. James Lawrence, best remembered for his dying words, "Don't give up the ship," during the War of 1812.

East of Lawrenceville, follow the old road south of the modern freeway, crossing the Wabash River into Indiana at historic Vincennes.

Miracle Whip was created at Max Crosset's Cafe on Main Street before being sold to Kraft Foods (for $300!) in 1931. The birthplace of Miracle Whip is now a parking lot at the center of Salem.

On the east side of Carlyle, 22 miles west of Salem, the very delicate **General Dean Suspension Bridge** was built in 1859 and has been preserved in a riverside park, on the northeast side of where US-50 crosses the Kaskaskia River.

The Wabash River between Indiana and Illinois marks the boundary between the central and eastern time zones. Subtract an hour heading west, add an hour heading east. At the west end of the bridge over the river, a roadside memorial recounts the westward migration of young Abraham Lincoln and his family.

INDIANA

From the Wabash River at its western end to the Ohio River in the east, the 170 miles of southern Indiana that lie in between present an immensely varied landscape. The hilly eastern sections are surprisingly rugged, though the central and western reaches are comparatively flat and largely agricultural. Besides numerous well-preserved historic Ohio River towns like

Madison and **Aurora,** there are a number of unlovely industrial sections, especially around **Bedford** and the famous limestone quarries in the central parts of the state.

Vincennes

First settled by the French in 1732, and intensely fought over during the Revolutionary War, **Vincennes** (pop. 17,385) remained a lawless frontier until 1803, when it was named the territorial capital. A handful of early buildings, including a bank, a church, and a newspaper office, have been restored at 1st and Harrison Streets in the historic downtown area. Nearby, overlooking the Wabash River,

George Rogers Clark Memorial

the **George Rogers Clark National Historical Park** ($3) is a classical dome honoring Revolutionary War general George Rogers Clark, who led local militiamen in the capture of Vincennes from the British in 1779. (George Rogers Clark was the older brother of William Clark, of Lewis and Clark fame.)

The monument, built as a WPA project during the Great Depression, wouldn't look out of place in D.C., but the rest of Vincennes is decidedly down-to-earth, with grain elevators, five-and-dime stores, and cafés along the busy railroad tracks.

The area around Vincennes is very flat farming country, notable for its large Amish communities (and numerous roadside "Amish Kountry Korner" stores and cafés), especially around **Loogootee,** 30 miles east of Vincennes.

French Lick and Mitchell

Between Vincennes and Bedford, US-50 winds its way through the hilly groves of the Hoosier National Forest, but a worthwhile detour heads south through the hometowns of two of Indiana's best-known sons. The first of

West Baden Springs Hotel's atrium

these, on Hwy-56 just south of US-150, is **French Lick** (pop. 1,807), where 1980s Boston Celtics basketball star Larry Bird, who famously called himself "The Hick from French Lick," learned to play.

The town itself is now little more than a two-block-long business district, but a century ago the surrounding area was a popular vacation resort, as thousands of Midwesterners (including Al Capone and other Chicago mobsters) came here to stay and play. After many years of neglect, the resorts have been reborn as part of the inevitable casino complex but still retain oodles of historic character. The fabulous **West Baden Springs Hotel** closed decades ago but was fully restored and reopened in 2007; it is now operated as part of the opulent **French Lick Resort Casino** ($219 and up; 812/936-9300), where you can take the mineral-rich waters that still flow from local Pluto Springs.

The other famous southern Indiana hometown, **Mitchell,** is about six miles south of Bedford and was the boyhood home of astronaut Virgil "Gus" Grissom, who captained Mercury and Gemini space flights before dying in the Apollo 1 disaster. There's an impressive memorial—a 44-foot-high limestone statue of a Redstone rocket—to Grissom south of Main Street on 6th Street, next to the police station.

West Baden Spring No. 5

Bedford

Nicknamed "Stone City" because it holds some of the largest and most famous limestone quarries in the country, **Bedford** (pop. 13,413) is a busy, industrial-looking city, the largest on the Indiana stretch of

Detour: Louisville

Home of the world's greatest horse race (the Kentucky Derby), the world's biggest baseball bat (a 120-foot-tall Louisville Slugger), and the man who was and is simply "The Greatest" (boxer Muhammad Ali, who grew up here, and who is now featured in a riverfront museum), Louisville (pronounced "LOO-a-vil") is a characterful midsized city on the south bank of the Ohio River. During Kentucky Derby week, the mint julep–fueled party leading up to the first Saturday in May, the whole city comes alive, but Louisville is an enjoyable place to explore any time of year. Lining up within a short walk of the Muhammad Ali museum is an expansive riverfront park hosting indoor and outdoor concert and events, a pair of intriguing science and history museums, and one of the country's top pop-culture destinations: the **Louisville Slugger Museum** (daily; $10; 800 W. Main St.; 502/588-7228 or 877/775-8443), marked by that giant baseball bat and full of memorabilia on big hitters from Babe Ruth to Hank Aaron. Thanks to the Louisville Slugger connection, the local baseball team is called the **Louisville Bats** (502/212-2287), a Class AAA farm club for the Cincinnati Reds. The Bats play at Louisville Slugger Field, right downtown on Main Street. Games are broadcast on **WKRD 790 AM.**

Though Louisville suffers from the legacy of 1960s freeway-building and "urban renewal" as much as any American city, it has managed to preserve a great number of its fine old homes, including some unusual brick-built mansions from the 1870s. They now form the heart of the **Old Louisville** neighborhood, south of downtown along 4th Street, near the expansive University of Louisville campus. For a walking tour, pick up a map at 1217 South 4th Street (502/637-2922). Another fascinating corner of Louisville is Cave Hill cemetery, east of downtown, where diverse luminaries, including soldier George Rogers Clark, early settler George Keats (brother of the English poet John Keats), and Kentucky's famous "Colonel" Harlan Sanders.

There's lots of unexpected interest, good food, and fun all over Louisville, but if you're only here for a short time make sure you stop for breakfast or brunch at **Lynn's Paradise Café** (984 Barret Ave.; 502/583-3447). For more information, contact the **visitors bureau** (401 W. Main St.; 502/584-2121 or 800/626-5646), in the convention center.

Outside Louisville, along US-31 30 miles to the southwest, you can cruise past another icon, **Fort Knox,** and dream about the 150 million ounces of gold locked inside.

Louisville Slugger Museum

US-50. The quarries that earned Bedford's reputation are still in use, producing the durable stone that has clad many high-profile structures, including the Empire State Building. Though you can see the limestone *in situ* at many road cuts along US-50, perhaps the most prominent examples in Bedford are the monuments and gravestones in the cemeteries lining the highway through town.

Triple A farm club for the Cincinnati Reds, the enjoyable Louisville Bats (855/BAT-TIXS) play at downtown's Louisville Slugger stadium.

Bedford's main hard-rock attraction is **Bluespring Caverns** (May–Oct. daily; $14; 812/279-9471), five miles west of downtown on US-50, where you can descend into a cave and take an hour-long boat tour along the largest underground river in the United States.

Brownstown, Seymour, and North Vernon

Roughly 27 miles east of Bedford and 10 miles west of the I-65 freeway, **Brownstown** (pop. 2,947) is an unusually pretty Indiana town set around a large central square shaded by 100-year-old maple trees—and a war surplus tank. An old-fashioned general store and a couple of down-home restaurants make it worth a brief stop, particularly during the annual **Watermelon Festival** in the fall.

East of Brownstown, it's a scenic 10 miles to **Seymour** (pop. 17,503), with its many motels (including a Holiday Inn and an EconoLodge), fast-food franchises, 24-hour gas stations, and an absolutely *huge* Wal-Mart distribution center marking the junction with I-65. Blue-collar Seymour is the birthplace of rock star John Mellencamp and Indiana's first Miss America (2009 winner Katie Stam), and you can get a good feel for the place by stopping for a meal at the **Town House Cafe** (206 E. 4th St.; 812/522-1099).

Twelve miles east of Seymour, turn south from US-50 at neat little **North Vernon** onto Hwy-7, which runs toward the Ohio River town of Madison across miles of rolling farmland, closely paralleling the route of Morgan's Raid, when Gen. John Morgan and 2,000 Confederate soldiers invaded Indiana during the Civil War.

One thing to see along US-50 is 10 miles east of North Vernon, in **Butlerville,** where a roadside plaque marks the 1885 birthplace of Hannah Milhous Nixon, Richard's mother.

Madison and the Ohio River Towns

The route east along US-50 is uneventful, so if you have some time, loop to the south along **Hwy-56,** which curves along the north bank of the broad Ohio River. The riverside here is rich in history, and the 60-mile drive passes by modest tobacco farms and timeless small towns, the pastoral scene marred only by occasional power plants, most of them across the water on the Kentucky side.

Though the drive is nice enough in itself, it's most worthwhile because it brings you to **Madison** (pop. 11,967), one of the best-preserved historic Ohio River towns, thanks in large part to the National Trust for Historic Preservation, which used Madison as a case study in how to keep small-town America alive and well in the modern age. Now a popular vacation destination,

The quaint town of **Vevay,** 20 miles east of Madison, was the birthplace of Edward Eggleston, author of *The Hoosier Schoolmaster.* Another important area native was engineer Elwood Mead, the man for whom Lake Mead is named.

especially during the **Chautauqua Arts Festival** in late September and the rowdier **Madison Regatta** around the 4th of July, when 200-mph hydroplanes race along the river, Madison has managed to stay alive economically without sacrificing its small-town charms. Wandering around a few blocks of the franchise-free Main Street, you can enjoy a meal, listen to the town gossip while getting a haircut at the chrome and red-leather barber shop, or tour the many historic homes. The best of these is the impressive Greek Revival mansion of Civil War financier James Lanier ($4; 601 W. 1st St.), near the river. Also worth a look is the perfectly preserved Victorian-era doctor's office (120 W. 3rd St.), which served as the only hospital between Cincinnati and Louisville.

Along with its wealth of Americana, Madison has a number of good places to eat along the three blocks of Main Street, including the 1930s-era **Hinkle's** (204 W. Main St.; 812/265-3919), open 6 AM–10 PM on weekdays and 24 hours on Friday and Saturday (closed Sun.) for great greasy-spoon burgers, traditional breakfasts, and fresh fried fish. There's the very romantic **Riverboat Inn** ($60 and up; 906 E. 1st St.; 812/265-2361). Best value are the motel-type rooms at the **Clifty Inn** ($82–192; 812/265-4135) in wooded Clifty Falls State Park, a mile west of town on Hwy-56.

Rising Sun

Farther along Hwy-56, nine miles south of Aurora and US-50, the village of **Rising Sun** holds a handful of frontier-era structures as well as one of the state's biggest riverboat casinos, the **Grand Victoria** (800/472-6311), which opened in 1996 with 1,300 slot machines. The adjacent hotel offers 201 rooms ($69 and up). The historic parts of town have managed to stay quaint despite the influx of gamblers, and the old-fashioned (but newly repaved) downtown area has the very good **Ohio County Historical Museum** (212 S. Walnut St.). Along with the usual array of local history, the museum also recounts the Ohio River's unique heritage of hydroplane racing.

Aurora and Lawrenceburg

Our Ohio River detour along Hwy-56 rejoins US-50 at **Aurora** (pop. 4,029), a small riverside town that's well worth at least a brief stop. The highlight here is the handsome **Hillforest Mansion** (closed Mon. Apr.–Dec.; $5; 213 5th St.), an exuberant survivor from the steamboat era whose colonnaded facade is topped by a circular lookout tower from which residents could gaze out at river

Lawrenceburg's signs of the old road

traffic up and down the Ohio. Built in 1852 and preserved in fine condition, the hillside mansion gives a strong sense of how comfortable and sophisticated life was for the wealthy, even on the so-called frontier.

East from Aurora, approaching the Ohio state line, US-50 forms a seedy gauntlet of roadside motels, diners, cut-rate liquor stores, and fireworks stands, all competing via giant billboards for the tri-state trade. **Lawrenceburg** (pop. 5,042), along the I-275 freeway three miles west of the Indiana/Ohio/Kentucky border, seems to revolve around the sale of cheap booze, perhaps be-

Hillforest Mansion, also called the Thomas Gaff House

cause for years the main employer was the massive redbrick **Seagram's** distillery at the north end of Main Street—among the largest and oldest in the United States, dating from 1847. Nowadays Lawrenceburg embraces another vice, gambling, as evidenced by the sprawling Argosy Casino that spreads south of US-50 on the east side of town.

Lawrenceburg as seen from US-50 is less than scenic, with railroad tracks and a huge levee cutting off the town from the waterfront. However, the historic town center, south of the highway along Walnut Street, holds a number of interesting old buildings dating from the steamboat era of the early 1800s, when Lawrenceburg was a favorite Ohio River port of call. Among the many church spires competing for preeminence is that of the Presbyterian church, where in 1837 orator Henry Ward Beecher (brother of Harriet Beecher Stowe, she of *Uncle Tom's Cabin* fame) held his first pastorate.

Places to eat in old-town Lawrenceburg emphasize the 80-proof aspects of local life: **Whisky's** (334 Front St.; 812/537-4239), for example, serves steaks in an old button factory on Front Street.

While Lawrenceburg embraces its heritage of gambling and booze, a detour across the river into Kentucky will bring you to a very different place: the fundamentalist **Creation Museum,** off I-275 in Petersburg, where 70,000 square feet of high-tech galleries ($25; 888/582-4253) let you "walk through" a biblical history of the world.

OHIO

Winding along the Ohio River from Indiana, US-50 cuts east from Cincinnati across the hill-and-valley country of southern Ohio before finally crossing the Ohio River into West Virginia. The 220 miles US-50 takes to cross the state are a fairly constant mix of upland forest and bottomland farms, with a single industrial district in the middle, around **Chillicothe,** and a refreshing small college town, **Athens,** farther east.

Cincinnati

Spreading along the north bank of the Ohio River, Cincinnati, whose nicknames range from "Queen City" to "Porkopolis," was once the largest and busiest city on the western frontier. During the heyday of steamboat travel in the first half of the 19th century, the city's riverside location made it a prime transportation center, but as the railroad networks converged on Chicago, Cincinnati was eclipsed as the prime gateway to the western United States. Procter & Gamble, the world's largest consumer products company, started here in the 1830s, making soap out of the abundant animal fat from the city's hundreds of slaughterhouses. In recent years, the city has welcomed some cutting-edge art and architecture, most notably in the unforgettable form of Zaha Hadid's **Contemporary Arts Center,** downtown (closed Tues.; $7.50; 44 E. 6th St.; 513/345-8400). But Cincy has been in the news for a variety of less salubrious things: race riots, the fall from grace of baseball hero Pete Rose, and the TV antics of Jerry Springer. (Onetime mayor of Cincinnati, Springer started his media career here in the 1970s as a hard-rock radio DJ.)

Cincinnati's modest population, just under 300,000 people, ranks it just ahead of Toledo as Ohio's third largest city, which from a traveler's point of view makes it an easily manageable and usually stress-free place to visit. A good first stop in Cincy is the **Museum Center** (daily; $12.50; 513/287-7000 or 800/733-2077), west of downtown in the former Union Terminal off I-75 exit 1. This 1930s art deco railroad station has been converted into an enjoyable complex of science and history museums, plus an Omnimax Theater. Nearby Eden Park holds the respected **Cincinnati Art Museum** (closed Mon.; free; 513/721-ARTS), as well as a planetarium and conservatory amidst acres of greenery.

Unfortunately, most of Cincinnati's once vibrant waterfront area, known as "The Basin," has been torn down in the name of urban renewal. What the 1940 WPA *Guide to Ohio* called "a museum of city history and the building styles of the past century," has been demolished in favor of a stadium each for the Reds (513/381-REDS) and Bengals, which loom on either side of the Freedom Center, a contentiously flashy, $110 million museum about the anti-slavery **Underground Railroad** (closed Mon. and Sun.; $12; 513/333-7500). The sole survivors of old Cincinnati are found across the river in Covington, Kentucky. You can get there by crossing the Roebling Bridge, built in 1865 as a precursor to the more famous Brooklyn Bridge. East of the bridge, a line of well-preserved

45:—Aeroplane View, Ohio River and Bridges connecting Kentucky and Cincinnati, Ohio.

1820s houses, many of which served as way stations on the actual Underground Railroad, overlook the historic Ohio River boundary between "slave" and "free" states.

Along with art and history, Cincinnati is also home to a museum embracing a more unusual subject: The **American Sign Museum,** housed in an old parachute factory in the Camp Washington area, holds hundreds of actual, full-sized signs: painted signs, sculpted signs, neon signs—you name it, they're here. The museum has been in flux in recent years, so check in before you arrive ($10; 2515 Essex Place; 513/258-4020).

Practicalities

Most major airlines fly into the Cincinnati/Northern Kentucky International Airport, which lies southwest of downtown in Kentucky. Getting around town is best done by car, if only so you can drive back and forth across the Ohio River on the Roebling Bridge. There are hundreds of rooms available in national chain motels along the I-71 and I-75 freeways. The handy and spacious **Embassy Suites** ($139 and up; 859/261-8400) overlooks the Ohio River from Covington on the Kentucky side of the Roebling Bridge. Downtown, nicest place to stay is the classic art deco **Hilton Netherland Plaza** ($129 and up; 35 W. 5th St.; 513/421-9100). One of the country's grandest old hotels, its lovely lobby is often clogged with ad execs courting Procter & Gamble business.

No road-tripper in his or her right mind should pass through Cincinnati without sampling its excellent road food—mounds of chili and/or stacks of melt-in-your-mouth ribs, finished off with a scoop or two of Graeter's ice cream (available all over the city, both at its own parlors and at most good restaurants). Cincinnati-style chili is poured over spaghetti and served either "3-Way" (spaghetti, chili, and grated cheese); "4-Way" (add onions); or "5-Way" (add beans). One road-food landmark, **Camp Washington Chili** (513/541-0061), three miles north of downtown at 3005 Colerain, right off I-75 exit 3, is famous for it. Over 100 other places around town serve this subtly spiced local specialty. Downtown, **Arnold's** (210 E. 8th St.; 513/421-6234) is a fine old place, a cozy circa-1860 tavern and deli that also features good live music. East of downtown along the river, **Montgomery Inn at the Boathouse** (925 Riverside Dr.; 513/721-7427) serves some of the best barbecue ribs in America in a very pleasant, river-view setting. The original **Montgomery Inn** (9440 Montgomery Rd.; 513/791-3482) can be found about 12 miles northeast of downtown, off I-71. (In tandem, these two restaurants manage to serve over 200 tons of ribs annually, more than anywhere else in the country.)

The main source for visitor information is the **Greater Cincinnati Visitors Bureau** (513/621-2142 or 800/543-2613).

North Bend

East from the Indiana line, US-50 winds along the partly industrial, partly rural Ohio River waterfront, without much to detain you before Cincinnati. The one place really worth a stop is the hamlet of **North Bend** (pop. 720), five miles east of the state border. A tall sandstone obelisk, overlooking the river and US-50 amidst a 14-acre park, marks the final resting place of William Henry Harrison (1773–1841), the ninth president of the United States, who lived here for many years when North Bend was a thriving frontier port. Born in Virginia, Harrison came to fame fighting Shawnee tribes in and around the Ohio Valley, and he served in Congress for many years before he was elected president; he died of pneumonia after only a month in office. His grandson Benjamin Harrison, who became president in 1889, was born in the nearby family home in 1833.

Continuing along US-50, five miles west of downtown Cincinnati and just three miles north of the main Cincy airport, the tiny **Anderson Ferry** ($4 per car, 50 cents for foot passengers) has been chugging back and forth since 1817, though the broad Ohio River is nothing like the busy river it was back then. But as recently as 1940, the WPA *Guide to Ohio* wrote that "fleets of barges pushed by snub-nosed towboats crawl along the motionless water; and now and then appears one of the Greene Line packets, all white and triple-decked."

US-50: Across Cincinnati

US-50 survives pretty much intact across Cincinnati, though most of its former traffic now follows the freeways that loop around and cut through the city. West of downtown, US-50 follows the Ohio River along River Road, but the old alignment veers away from the freeway-sliced waterfront along State Avenue, running through downtown along 7th, 8th, and 9th Streets. East of downtown, old US-50 rejoins the riverfront around Mt. Adams, then follows the Columbia Parkway east to the garden city of Mariemont, where we rejoin it.

Mariemont

From Cincinnati, US-50 follows surface streets through the warehouse and residential districts along the Ohio River before becoming a freeway for the

red carnation,
state flower of Ohio

quick drive east to **Mariemont** (pop. 3,196). Built in the mid-1920s as one of the nation's first planned "Garden City" communities, Mariemont's mock-Tudor downtown centers on the historic and very comfortable **Best Western Mariemont Inn** ($150 and up; 6880 Wooster Pike; 513/271-2100), right on US-50. Across the street there's a branch of the excellent local ice-cream chain, **Graeter's,** and the sole surviving neighborhood of Mariemont's original 1920s half-timbered arts-and-crafts homes is an easily walkable block to the southeast.

East of Mariemont, US-50 crosses the Little Miami River at the scenic, 25-mph town of **Milford**—where there's a **Frisch's Big Boy** restaurant (840 Lila Ave.; 513/831-0111) with a great old Big Boy sign, straight out of *American Graffiti*—before racing east across 40 miles of flat and sparsely settled farming country to Hillsboro.

Hillsboro

Hillsboro (pop. 6,605), 60 miles east of Cincinnati and 40 miles west of Chillicothe, is the biggest and busiest town along the way. Besides the Greek Revival landmark Highland County Courthouse, second oldest in Ohio, Hillsboro has a unique, alcohol-related history: During Christmas in 1873, the town's 13 saloons were closed down by one of the country's earliest temperance movements, and more recently, late great country singer Johnny "Take This Job and Shove It" Paycheck did time in prison for shooting a man in Hillsboro's North High Saloon. (Even more recently, that saloon was torn down to make way for a new city office building.)

Midway between Chillicothe and Hillsboro, the nice little town of **Bainbridge** was the site of the first dental school in the United States, now a dental museum along US-50 (208 W. Main St.).

Serpent Mound

Across southwestern Ohio, US-50 winds past whitewashed farmhouses and broad cornfields flanked by low hills. The region also holds two fascinating remnants of the Mound Builder people who once lived here. Just west of the sleepy village of Bainbridge, heading 20 miles south onto Hwy-41 (or following Hwy-73 south from Hillsboro) brings you to the **Serpent Mound** (in

The Mound Builders

The broad area between the Mississippi River and the Appalachian crest is rich in early American history, but the human story here goes back way beyond Daniel Boone and Abraham Lincoln to an era not often discussed in textbooks. From around 800 BC until AD 1500, this region was home to two successive prehistoric cultures that were roughly simultaneous with the legendary Mayans and Aztecs of Mexico but are now all but forgotten, remembered solely for the massive earthen mounds they left behind.

The older of these two prehistoric peoples is known as the Hopewell culture, since the first scientific studies were conducted in 1891 at a farm owned by a man named Hopewell. Some 50 years earlier, the mounds had already become famous, as stories spread tracing their construction back to a "lost race" of mysterious origin, not unlike the Anasazi of the desert Southwest. As the Hopewell culture began to decline, around AD 500, another culture, called the Mississippian, came into being. Similarities between these two hunter-gatherer cultures, with their far-flung trading networks and hierarchical societies, are much greater than their differences, but archaeologists consider them to be completely distinct from one another. A key difference: Almost all of the Hopewell mounds were rounded or conical, and built as burial sites, while Mississippian sites tended to be more rectilinear, with the mounds serving not as interments but as bases for long-vanished wooden structures built atop them. In Hopewell sites, buried along with the usually cremated human remains, archaeologists have recovered a compelling array of artifacts—obsidian tools (from the Pacific Northwest), shell beads (from the Gulf of Mexico), and silver and copper objects (from the Great Lakes)—which give some hint of the quality of ancient Native American life.

Ohio is particularly well provided with these enigmatic earthworks; at the **Hopewell Culture National Historic Park** near Chillicothe, five prehistoric earthworks complexes have been preserved by the National Park Service. West of Chillicothe, the low-lying **Serpent Mound** stretches for a quarter mile along a river, and over 100 other sites have been identified across the state.

Farther west on US-50, along the Mississippi at **Cahokia Mounds State Historic Site** (see page 873), the remnants of the largest prehistoric city in North America now sit across the river from St. Louis. North along the river, the **Effigy Mounds National Monument** in Iowa across from Prairie du Chien (see page 251) preserves yet more burial mounds, while down south, the Natchez Trace Parkway features the prehistoric **Emerald Mound** (see page 296).

summer daily 10 AM–5 PM, weekends only the rest of year; $7 per car; 937/587-2796), which stretches in seven sinuous curves alongside a creek for nearly a quarter mile. There's a small museum on the site, and to see the snake-shaped earthworks—the largest and finest effigy mound in the country—visitors climb up a turn-of-the-20th-century vintage lookout tower.

Another of these prehistoric sites, the **Seip Mound,** two miles east of Bainbridge and 14 miles west of Chillicothe, is over 200 feet long and 30 feet tall, surrounded by 10 acres of pasture. To prevent early farmers from plowing them into oblivion in the 1880s, many of these evocative monuments were purchased and preserved through the efforts of Harvard University archaeologists. Harvard owned the land for many years and later donated the sites to the state of Ohio.

Chillicothe and Mound City

In the middle of the state, **Chillicothe** (pop. 21,847; pronounced "chill-a-COTH-ee") comes as a sudden surprise after the pastoral landscape that surrounds it. It is one of the state's oldest industrial centers; since 1812 Chillicothe's economy has revolved around the massive paper mill on the south side of town, whose red-and-white striped smokestack belches a pungently steaming white cloud around the clock.

Chillicothe served as capital of the Northwest Territory from 1800 to 1802, and later as the first capital of Ohio.

Heavy industry aside, Chillicothe has done an admirable job of preserving its history, most notably in the recently spruced-up "First Capital" district along Main Street (US-50) downtown. Dozens of elaborate, late-Victorian commercial buildings and Greek Revival–style mansions, mostly dating from the mid-1850s, surround the overwrought Ross County Courthouse, which has a different entrance for each government department.

"Mound City", or Hopewell Culture National Historic Park

While the downtown area is worth a quick stroll, specific sights are few, and the area's real attraction is three miles north of town via Hwy-104. Officially known as the **Hopewell Culture National Historical Park,** but usually called **Mound City,** this complex of prehistoric burial sites sits on the west bank of the Scioto River, just beyond a huge prison complex. Two dozen distinct, grass-covered mounds, the largest of which is about 15 feet high, are reachable on a mile-long trail that starts at the **visitors center** (daily; free; 16062 Hwy-104; 740/774-1126), where films and exhibits explore aspects of this 2,000-year-old culture.

Chillicothe is known throughout Ohio as the site of *Tecumseh,* an outdoor pageant dramatizing the life of the Shawnee Indian warrior. Shows are at 8 PM Monday–Saturday in summer only ($23; 740/775-0700). More fun, and cheaper, are the baseball games played by the Prospect League **Chillicothe Paints** ($6; 740/773-8326), who play from June through August on the grounds of the VA Hospital, near Mound City.

Athens

East of Chillicothe, US-50 passes through Vinton County, one of the state's poorest and least-developed regions. Hidden amidst forested hills, the remains of coal mines and overgrown, rail-fenced cornfields line the next 50 miles, and little has changed (for the better, at least) since the WPA *Guide to Ohio* described the scene in 1939: "Abruptly the road sweeps into a rock-bound gorge dotted with the rickety houses of hill-folk...who make a living by seasonal mining, moonshining, trapping, or on Government relief projects."

After all this rural poverty, US-50 finally arrives at **Athens** (pop. 23,832), one of the most attractive small towns in Ohio. Set, like its classical namesake, on a series of hills, Athens is an idyllic little town that has grown up around the leafy campus of Ohio University, which opened here in 1809 and has developed a reputation as the liveliest small party school in the country. Brick-paved streets lined by bookstores, copy shops, and clothing stores, mostly catering to the college's 18,000 well-groomed twentysomethings, fill the eight-block Uptown neighborhood along College and Court Streets on the north side of the neoclassical college green, a national historic landmark dating from 1816.

Southeastern Ohio has one of the country's greatest concentrations of barns painted with signs reading Chew Mail Pouch Tobacco.

US-50 follows the Hocking River and bypasses the heart of town, so follow Stimson Avenue or State Street from the highway, past the cafés and shops that fill the few blocks around the campus, where **The Pub** (39 N. Court St.; 740/592-2699) has Athens's best cheap burgers and happy hour specials. Accommodations in Athens include a **Hampton Inn** (986 E. State St.; 740/593-5600), just east of campus, and many other motels along Columbus Road (US-33) on the north side of town.

Kennedy Museum of Art on the Ohio University campus

East of the Athens area, US-50 passes through 40 miles of scrubby second-growth forests and the abandoned but enticingly named coal-mining towns of Guysville and Coolville, before reaching the West Virginia border at the Ohio River and Parkersburg.

WEST VIRGINIA

The slowest part of US-50's transcontinental crossing is the 150-mile section across West Virginia, which twists and turns its way over the rugged **Allegheny Mountains.** Starting along the Ohio River in the western, more-developed half of the state, US-50 runs briefly as a fairly fast freeway before beginning its climb into the rugged hill country. Though there are many fine hardwood forests and white-water rivers, including some of the most extensive semi-wilderness areas left in the eastern states, this part of West Virginia is mostly rural, with more than a few corners where things seem straight out of a Depression-era Walker Evans photograph. Rusting appliances and broken-down cars fill more than a few front yards, but around the next bend you may come across a lovely old covered bridge, or a waterfall that takes your breath away. The few towns along the route, formerly bustling thanks to the railroads or coal mines, are still dominated by the empty remnants of industries that have vanished, never to return, and most places are populated by people who seem to have lived there forever. The self-reliant, "mountaineer" ethos still runs strong in West Virginia, but the lingering impression a visit leaves behind is of taking a step back in time to a world where men work hard in mines and mills, women raise the kids, and everybody goes to church on Sunday.

Parkersburg

Northern West Virginia's largest and most heavily industrialized city, **Parkersburg** (pop. 31,492) is located strategically at the junction of the Ohio and Little Kanawha Rivers. The town's economy is based on an unusual pair of employers: the federal Bureau of the Public Debt, which redeems U.S. Savings Bonds, and a massive DuPont Teflon factory.

Though the first impression can be fairly bleak, Parkersburg does merit a closer look. The **Blennerhassett Museum** (closed Mon.; $4; 304/420-4800), housed in a turn-of-the-20th-century brick warehouse at 2nd and Juliana Streets, traces regional history, with a focus on the escapades of the Irish aristocrat Harman Blennerhassett, who in 1806 conspired with Aaron Burr to establish an independent fiefdom in Texas and the Southwest. If you're interested, you can ride a paddlewheeler to and from the Ohio River island on which Blennerhassett built the palatial home where the plot was hatched. The house has been reconstructed as a state park (tours $4), and boats ($8) leave hourly for the island from Point Park, which is two blocks west of the museum, under the railroad bridges and on the far side of the 25-foot concrete flood walls at the confluence of the rivers.

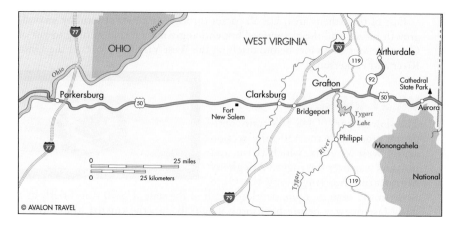

Parkersburg also has a good range of motels and a couple of coffee shops along US-50, like the 24-hour **Mountaineer Family Restaurant** (4006 E. 7th St.; 304/422-0101), near I-77 on the east side of town. If you want to linger, stay overnight at the delightful **Blennerhassett Hotel** ($125 and up; 320 Market St.; 304/422-3131).

Fort New Salem

Between Parkersburg and Clarksburg, US-50 winds along as a fast, four-lane freeway through a mountainous onetime oil- and gas-producing region dotted with tiny, all-but-forgotten towns. The small farms are cultivated by descendants of Scotch-Irish immigrants who settled here in the late 18th century. One place that's well worth a short stop is **Fort New Salem** (Wed.–Sun.; $5–7; 304/695-2220), 14 miles west of Clarksburg. Just south of US-50, near the campus of Salem International University, the fort consists of 18 historic log cabins relocated here in the 1970s.

Clarksburg houses the FBI's national center for fingerprint and high-tech biometric security operations, located here thanks to the machinations of West Virginia's long-serving U.S. Senator, Robert Byrd.

Clarksburg

Birthplace of Confederate Civil War hero Thomas "Stonewall" Jackson, and now a national center for law enforcement biometric data analysis, **Clarksburg** (pop. 16,743) is a tidy railroad town sitting on a branch of the Monongahela River. The downtown area is a sampler of turn-of-the-20th-century commercial buildings, great for taking pictures of old signs and brick walls. The house where Jackson was born is marked by a plaque (326 Main St.).

The town's large Italian population, estimated at around 40 percent, supports numerous good restaurants, like **Minard's Spaghetti Inn** (813 E. Pike St.; 304/623-1711) on old US-50, at the Joyce Street exit off the US-50 freeway. Another good old-fashioned place to eat is the **Ritzy Lunch** (465 W. Pike St.; 304/622-3600), selling famous chili dogs since 1933.

On the east side of Clarksburg, US-50 climbs a steep hill before becoming suddenly busy at **Bridgeport,** which straddles the I-79 freeway, around which the highway is lined by a two-mile sprawl of motels and fast food.

rhododendron,
state flower of West Virginia

Grafton: International Mother's Day Shrine

Grafton (pop. 5,614), the first large town west of Winchester, Virginia, grew up as a bustling B&O railroad town beginning in the 1850s but is now among the most economically and socially depressed places in the state. Dozens of architecturally interesting but run-down houses and churches drop on brick-paved streets down the steep hills to the Tygart River and the railroad tracks, where a monumental station and a grand but boarded-up hotel are grim reminders of Grafton's formerly busy self.

Besides its impressive physical setting, Grafton's main claim to fame is as the birthplace of Mother's Day, first celebrated here in 1908 in a Methodist church that's now been converted into the **International Mother's Day Shrine** (Fri.–Sun.; donations; 11 E. Main St.), across from the old train station.

East of Grafton, the landscape becomes more mountainous, and isolated villages replace the small towns that line the western half of the route.

Arthurdale

Northeast of Grafton, a half hour north of US-50 via Hwy-92, the homestead community of **Arthurdale** was the first and perhaps the most important of the many anti-poverty rural resettlement projects initiated during the Depression-era New Deal. Though not the largest, Arthurdale was prominent because of the personal involvement of First Lady Eleanor Roosevelt, who not only helped plan the project but also visited many times, handing out diplomas at school graduations.

Beginning in 1934 with the construction of some 165 homes, plus schools and factories, a cooperative farm, a health center, and a small hotel, Arthurdale was an ideal community set up to relieve the dire living conditions of unemployed

The Grafton area saw the first fatality of the Civil War, when Union soldier Bailey Brown was killed by Confederate forces during the battle of Philippi.

South of Grafton, US-119 passes through the town of **Philippi,** where the largest covered bridge in West Virginia spans the Tygart River. Originally constructed in 1852, the 285-foot-long red-and-white bridge was badly burned in 1989 but has been totally restored.

Across West Virginia, US-50 follows the approximate route of the colonial-era Northwest Turnpike, which was surveyed in 1748 by a 16-year-old George Washington.

Morgantown coal miners. Most of the houses are still intact and still inhabited by the original homesteaders or their descendants. The old community center is being restored and now holds a small **museum** ($8; 304/864-3959) that chronicles the whole story.

Cathedral State Park

Four miles west of the Maryland border, US-50 runs right through **Cathedral State Park,** where over 130 acres of stately maples and hemlocks constitute one of the few first-growth stands left in this lumber-hungry state. Beyond here, US-50 makes a quick seven-mile jaunt across a corner of Maryland before crossing the north branch of the Potomac River back into West Virginia.

From the bridge, US-50 climbs steeply up the densely wooded Alleghenies, twisting over 3,000-foot-high ridges with turns so tight the posted speed limit is 15 mph—the going is very slow, and not much fun if you're prone to car sickness.

Romney and the Eastern Gateway

The oddly shaped arm of eastern West Virginia, which juts between Maryland and Virginia at the headwaters of the Potomac River, is promoted as the "Eastern Gateway" and offers quick access to the mountainous wilderness of Monongahela National Forest that stretches south of US-50, and to the raging white water of the Cheat and Gauley Rivers. Originally inhabited by Shawnee Indians, the region was settled during colonial times as part of the six-million-acre Virginia estate of Lord Fairfax.

The B&O railroad came through in the 1850s, which made the region strategically important during the Civil War, nowhere more so than around **Romney** (pop. 1,971), the Eastern Gateway's largest town, which changed hands over 50 times in four years of fighting. In the center of Romney, at the corner of Main Street and Bolton, the **Davis History House** (hours vary; 304/822-3185) is a well-restored log cabin packed full of pioneer and Civil War artifacts. Romney also has the oldest Confederate War Memorial, erected on the west side of town in Indian Mound Cemetery semi-secretly in 1866, since West Virginia was officially a "northern" state.

Heading east toward Winchester, US-50 passes through mountain hamlets like **Capon Bridge** (on the West Virginia side) and **Gore** (on the Virginia side), which consist of little more than a gas station, a tavern, and a post office, plus one or two antiques stores selling everything from colonial-era furniture to old highway signs. It's hard to help feeling light years from the modern world, even though Washington, D.C., is only 90 miles away.

VIRGINIA

Dropping from the Allegheny and Appalachian Mountains of West Virginia, US-50 enters Virginia at the northern tip of the **Shenandoah Valley,** passing through the center of the quietly attractive small city of **Winchester.** Continuing east, in short order the road climbs the foothills of the Blue Ridge Mountains and crosses the Shenandoah River, delighting John Denver fans and carrying travelers through the heart of the ultra-wealthy "Hunt Country" of northern Virginia, a rural and unspoiled landscape of small towns, horse farms, and vineyards that's home to more well-connected millionaires than just about anywhere in the United States.

Approaching the outer suburbs of the nation's capital, however, US-50 swiftly loses its luster, and while you *can* follow it through miles of suburban sprawl on both sides of the I-495 Beltway, you might prefer to follow the misleadingly numbered I-66 freeway—which has nothing at all to do with the *real* Route 66—into the city. US-50's final approach takes you past the powerful Iwo Jima Memorial, arriving in **Washington, D.C.** at the Lincoln Memorial.

Winchester

Northern Virginia's largest city, **Winchester** (pop. 26,203) is a surprisingly quiet and very pleasant small city, best known for the extensive apple orchards that fill the surrounding countryside. The I-81 freeway, complete with the usual sprawl of shopping malls and fast-food franchises, cuts across US-50 along the east side of Winchester, but the downtown district is eminently strollable, especially the pedestrianized Old Town area around Loudon Street, between Piccadilly (US-50) and Cork Street, where you can visit George Washington's office or Stonewall Jackson's Civil War headquarters.

After apples and American history, Winchester is probably most famous as the hometown of Patsy Cline, the inimitable country singer who died in a plane crash on March 5, 1963, at age 30. Cline, whose greatest hits include "Crazy," "Sweet Dreams," and "Walking After Midnight," lived in Winchester from

Patsy Cline (Sept 8, 1932–March 5, 1963)

© AVALON TRAVEL

On Winchester's town square you'll find the "World's Largest Apple," a 5,200-pound rival to another "World's Largest Apple" in Cornelia, Georgia (which was actually a 1927 gift from the city of Winchester).

age 3 to age 16 in a small house near downtown (608 S. Kent St.) and dropped out of high school to earn money making milk shakes at **Gaunt's Drug Store,** south of downtown at Loudon Street and Valley Avenue. She's buried in **Shenandoah Memorial Park,** a mile southeast of town.

US-50 crosses our **Appalachian Trail** route near 1,100-foot-high Ashby Gap, 15 miles east of Winchester. **Harpers Ferry,** West Virginia, is just 26 miles north of US-50 via US-340 (see page 372). **Shenandoah National Park** is just south of US-50 (see page 376).

Middleburg

Located at the heart of northern Virginia's "Hunt Country," where senators, ambassadors, and aristocrats mix at multimillion-dollar country estates, **Middleburg** (pop. 976) is a small but immaculate town with a four-block business district packed with antiques shops, art galleries, and real estate agencies.

Many of Middleburg's brick- and stone-fronted buildings date from colonial times, including the **Red Fox Inn** ($170 and up; 2 E. Washington St.; 540/687-6301 or 800/223-1728), on US-50 at the center of town. Originally built in 1728 as a coach inn and tavern, it's now a comfortable and upscale B&B and restaurant. There are a couple of other good places to eat, including the zesty Italian cooking at the **Backstreet Cafe** (4 E. Federal St.; 540/687-3122) and the **Upper Crust Bakery** (4 N. Pendleton St.; 540/687-5666), a local favorite offering cookies and sandwiches among the usual array of baked goods.

East of Middleburg, US-50 winds through gently rolling farmlands for a dozen miles before hitting the outlying suburbs of Washington, D.C.

Manassas National Battlefield Park

Site of the first major land battle of the Civil War, **Manassas National Battlefield Park** has been preserved intact despite the suburbanizing pressures of the surrounding towns. The prospect of battle-view executive homes still looms in the future, but for now, Manassas (which in the North was also known as Bull Run) is among the most evocative of all the Civil War sites, its five square miles of rolling hills and woodlands kept as they were, with few intrusions of modern life.

Manassas, which controlled transportation links between Washington, D.C., and the Shenandoah Valley, was the site of two major battles. The first battle, fought here on July 21, 1861, was strategically inconclusive, though the fact that the Confederates forced the overconfident Union army into a panicked retreat surprised the many onlookers who had traveled out from Washington to watch the fighting and foreshadowed the next four years of war. The second battle, fought August 28–30, 1862, followed the instatement of Robert E. Lee as commander of the Confederate forces. That conflict marked the beginning of the bloodiest year of fighting, culminating in the battle of Gettysburg the following July.

Monuments and memorials dot the grassy hills, pointing out the many key moments of the battles, and rows of artillery are set up along battle lines. A loosely structured 1.4-mile walking tour begins at the **Henry Hill Visitor Center** ($3; 703/361-1339), where audiovisual displays and collections of military artifacts give a sense of what the war was like.

To reach Manassas Battlefield, follow the I-66 freeway from Washington, D.C., or the Lee Highway (US-29) west from Fairfax. From US-50, follow US-15 or the smaller Hwy-659 south.

Arlington National Cemetery

Across the Potomac River from Washington, D.C., one of the most compelling and thought-provoking places in the capital region is **Arlington National Cemetery** (daily; free), a 600-acre hillside that contains the mortal remains of over 250,000 U.S. soldiers, sailors, and public servants. Row after row of nearly identical, unadorned white tablets cover most of the cemetery, but special plots are dedicated to the most prominent people, such as John F. and Jacqueline Kennedy, who are buried together beneath an eternal flame, 200 yards straight beyond the main gate. Bobby Kennedy's grave is adjacent.

Located high on a ridge at the top of Arlington Cemetery, the neoclassical mansion of **Arlington House** was the antebellum home of Confederate general Robert E. Lee. Besides providing great views of the Mall and the heart of monumental Washington, the house serves as a vivid reminder of the deep rift caused by the Civil War. During the war, the grounds of the house were made into a cemetery for war dead, which formed the basis for Arlington National Cemetery. Washington's French-born designer, Pierre L'Enfant, lies in front of the mansion in a tomb marked by his plan for the city. The somber **Tomb of the Unknowns** is a quarter mile south of Arlington House, where a U.S. Army honor guard is formally "changed" every half hour during hot summer days, every hour on cold winter nights.

Confederate hero Thomas "Stonewall" Jackson earned his nickname at the first battle of Manassas, where his steadfastness under fire helped rally rebel troops.

A dozen miles north of Manassas, just north of US-50 on the western fringes of Washington, D.C., the grounds of Dulles International Airport are home to the Smithsonian Air and Space Museum's **Udvar-Hazy Center** (703/572-4118), which displays hundreds of over-sized airplanes and spaceships that cannot be exhibited on the National Mall. The two sites together showcase the largest collection of aviation and space artifacts in the world.

Tomb of the Unknown Soldier, Arlington National Cemetery, Va.

HERE RESTS IN HONORED GLORY AN AMERICAN SOLDIER KNOWN BUT TO GOD

To explore the cemetery more completely, stop first at the **visitors center** (703/607-8585) near the cemetery entrance for a map of the grounds that identifies the gravesites of many other famous people interred here, including boxer Joe Louis, explorer Robert Peary, civil rights martyr Medgar Evers, and

Washington, D.C.

Even if you slept through high school civics and have less than zero interest in national politics, visiting Washington, D.C. (pop. 601,723), is still an unforgettable experience. The monuments and monoliths that line the city's many grand avenues embody nearly two centuries of American political history, and museums show off everything from ancient art to the first flying machines. Best of all, almost everything is free, though there are a few caveats every would-be tourist should know: Parts of D.C. can be dangerous after dark, and the weather here varies tremendously, from freezing cold in winter to swelteringly hot and humid in summer (though both spring and fall can be lovely).

During your visit to D.C., you'll probably spend the bulk of your time at the many great museums that line up along the National Mall, at the center of town. Along with the Air and Space Museum, you ought to spend a few hours at the **National Museum of American History** (daily; free; 202/633-5285), on the north side of the Mall between 12th and 14th Streets. Part of the huge Smithsonian Institution, this huge and endearingly quirky museum is the best example of its role as the "Nation's Attic," displaying a little of everything: the giant flag that inspired Francis Scott Key to write the "Star-Spangled Banner," the ruby slippers Judy Garland wore in *The Wizard of Oz,* even a 40-foot stretch of historic Route 66, part of the massive "America on the Move" transportation exhibit.

In recent years, a trio of impressive and sometimes controversial museums and monuments have opened along the National Mall, ranging from the stunning **National Museum of the American Indian,** closest to the Capitol, through the eight-acre **FDR Memorial,** at the west end of the Mall, which traces the journey of our longest-serving U.S. president from his elite childhood through his midlife affliction by polio, up through the Great Depression and

National Museum of the American Indian

Thomas Jefferson Memorial at Night, Washington, D. C.

World War II. World War II is also the background for the intensely moving **Holocaust Memorial Museum,** south of the Washington Monument (free timed tickets required for admission; 800/400-9373).

If you're not the most serious student of historical *globalpolitik*, your favorite memory of visiting Washington may turn out to be watching workers pushing wheelbarrows full of money across the floors of the **Bureau of Engraving and Printing** (Mon.–Fri.; free, but tickets required in peak season; 202/874-2330), south of the Holocaust Memorial Museum at 14th and C Streets SW. This high-security printing plant is where your hard-earned cash—some $300 billion a year—is born. Postage stamps, too.

Washington's long-awaited baseball team, the **Nationals** (888/632-NATS), play at a nice new $600 million riverfront stadium, near the Navy Yard metro station.

Practicalities

Ronald Reagan National Airport (DCA) is D.C.'s main airport, very near downtown and easily accessible on the Metro subway system. The second D.C. airport is Dulles (IAD), way out in the western suburbs, which handles most international flights (and has a large branch of the Smithsonian Air and Space Museum nearby). Thanks to Southwest Airlines, the cheapest D.C.-area airport is Baltimore/Washington International (BWI), midway between D.C. and Baltimore to the northeast. By road, D.C. lies on the busy north–south I-95 corridor, encircled by the I-495 Beltway. US-50, redubbed I-595 east of D.C. and supplemented in the west by the I-66 freeway, is the main east–west artery.

The basic layout of D.C. is fairly simple, as the entire diamond-shaped city is

President Obama throws the ceremonial first pitch to launch the 2010 Nationals season.

(continued on next page)

(continued)

divided into four quadrants (NE, NW, SE, and SW) with the Capitol at the center. However, because of D.C.'s baroque street plan, with its extensive one-way systems, driving can be very confusing. To get around, you'll do well to avail yourself of the handy Metro subway, which serves most of the places you'll want to go. It may also help to know that the Mall, where most of the museums and memorials are located, is roughly two miles long, from the Capitol west to the Potomac River.

The cheapest and most convenient place to sleep is the modern **HI Hostel** (1009 11th Street NW; 202/737-2333), within walking distance of the White House. It has dorm beds (around $30), private rooms ($90), and many amenities (like air-conditioning, essential in a D.C. summer). At the plushest end of the price and comfort spectrum, the **Hay Adams Hotel** ($250 and up; 1 Lafayette Square NW; 202/638-6600), directly across from the White House, is a well appointed old hotel, with a grand lobby and discreet Off The Record cocktail bar full of expense-account lobbyists. The nicest midrange place to stay has to be the **Woodley Park Guest House** ($145 and up; 2647 Woodley Road NW; 202/667-0218 or 866/667-0218), which has clean, nicely furnished rooms and helpful staff in a convenient location near the Zoo Metro stop and trendy Adams-Morgan neighborhood.

To wine and dine with the movers, shakers, and wannabes of Washington, head to Wisconsin Avenue in Georgetown, at the northwest edge of the district, or take a giant leap back to a time when polished wood bars and brass spittoons were the order of the day at the **Old Ebbitt Grill,** east of the White House (675 15th Street NW; 202/347-4800). Open early until late, this casual grill serves everything from breakfasts and burgers to oysters and filet mignon. For a more down-home taste of D.C., head north on the Green Line Metro to the U Street station, near which you can enjoy Bill Cosby's favorite chili dogs at **Ben's Chili Bowl** (1213 U St.; 202/667-0909); Ben's also has a stand at the new Nationals ballpark.

For more information, contact the **Washington, D.C. visitors bureau** (202/789-7000 or 800/422-8644).

Old Ebbitt Grill

writer Dashiell Hammett. Arlington is ideal for wandering around, but if it's hot and humid (as it often is in D.C.'s swampy summers), you might want to hop on a Tourmobile tram (unlimited rides for $8.50; $7.50 for those over 65) and take a guided ride up the hill.

Driving D.C.

Following US-50 across Washington, D.C., takes you through the heart of the nation's capital. Starting in the west, alongside Arlington National Cemetery at the **Iwo Jima Memorial** (which sits in the middle of a traffic circle and is all-but-impossible to reach), US-50 crosses the Potomac River, entering "The District" on the Theodore Roosevelt Bridge—making a beeline toward the State Department. US-50 then follows Constitution Avenue along the north side of The Mall, running past the Lincoln and Vietnam Veterans memorials and between the White House and the Washington Monument, before zigzagging northeast along 7th Street and New York Avenue. Heading east of D.C., US-50 turns into a freeway and runs east to Annapolis and the Chesapeake Bay.

One place worth stopping in the D.C. suburbs is the **29 Diner** (10536 Lee Hwy.; 703/591-6720), off US-50 on US-29 (hence the name), in Fairfax. A national landmark, chrome-and-blue enamel, 1947 Mountain View diner, it's open 24 hours every day except Monday.

MARYLAND

Racing out of Washington, D.C., on a high-speed multi-lane freeway, US-50 accesses one of the state's most popular destinations, the colonial Chesapeake Bay port town of **Annapolis.** From Annapolis, heading toward the Atlantic coast and the massively popular beach resort of **Ocean City,** the final leg of US-50's 3,200-mile transcontinental trek is a mad dash across 100 miles of Maryland's Eastern Shore. This is one of the more captivating areas in the northeastern United States, but the four-lane US-50 freeway doesn't

Recent versions of D.C. license plates read Taxation without Representation, a symbol of the District's quest for full representation in the U.S. Congress.

encourage sightseeing, so if you want to get a feel for the *real* Eastern Shore of piney woods, cornfields, and fishing fleets, you'll have to follow the many back roads and search out the many historic towns and villages—many of which we point out as worthwhile detours, including some that are among the oldest and most carefully preserved in the nation.

Between D.C. and Annapolis, the town of **Bowie** is home to the Baltimore Orioles' Class AA farm team, the **Bowie Baysox** (301/464-4865).

Annapolis

State capital of Maryland, and one of the most attractive and well-preserved historic cities in the United States, **Annapolis** (pop. 38,394) is one place you won't want to miss. First settled in 1649 and chartered in 1708, Annapolis makes fair claim to being the oldest city in the country. The nation's first capital, it's now best known for its maritime heritage, both as a yachting center and as home of the U.S. Naval Academy, which stands guard along the Chesapeake Bay waterfront.

The historic center of Annapolis is just south of US-50 via Hwy-70, which leads straight to the **State House** (Mon.–Fri.; free), where the U.S. Congress met in 1783–1784 and ratified the Treaty of Paris, thus ending the Revolutionary War. This is the oldest legislative building in America, and well worth some time. From the State House, Main Street drops downhill to the City Dock waterfront, where a **visitors center** has walking-tour maps and guides to the wealth of historic buildings, including the beautiful colonial-era **Hammond Harwood House** (closed Mon.; $6; 19 Maryland Ave.; 410/263-4683).

In Annapolis, **WRNR 103.1 FM** is an anarchic modern rock station, playing everything from The Animals to Frank Zappa.

Annapolis has a number of good places to eat, including the venerable **Chick & Ruth's Delly** (165 Main St.; 410/269-6737), a longstanding local fave.

To fully absorb the colonial-era ambience, stay a night or two at the **Historic Inns of Annapolis** ($160 and up; 410/263-2641 or 800/847-8882), a trio of historic homes right across from the State House, or any of the town's many characterful B&Bs.

Bay Bridge

Before the four-mile-long **Bay Bridge** was completed in the early 1950s, Maryland's Eastern Shore was physically and spiritually an island, protected by the broad Chesapeake Bay from the sprawling modern cities of Washington and Baltimore, and cut off at its neck by the Chesapeake and Delaware Canal. Despite the completion of a parallel span in the 1970s, the bridge gets clogged solid each summer by vehicles headed for coastal resorts like Rehoboth Beach ("The Beltway by the Bay") and Ocean City.

At the west end of the bridge, US-50 lands at **Sandy Point State Park,** where you can swim, hike, or launch a boat. At the eastern end, US-50 is joined by US-301, and together the two roads race along as a six-lane freeway as far as **Queenstown,** a busy port in the early 1800s but now little more than an upscale suburb of the greater Baltimore/Washington urban area.

Detour: Baltimore

The best description I've ever heard of Baltimore's quirky charms came from film director John Waters, who has drawn considerable inspiration from his offbeat hometown. In his book *Shock Value*, Waters wrote: "I would never want to live anywhere but Baltimore. You can look far and wide, but you'll never discover a stranger city with such extreme style. It's as if every eccentric in the South decided to move north, ran out of gas in Baltimore, and decided to stay." Signs of this can be seen at the **American Visionary Art Museum** (Tues.–Sun. 10 AM–6 PM; $15.95; 800 Key Hwy.; 410/244-1900), which displays an array of works by "outsider" and self-taught artists in every medium imaginable—painted packing crates, "art cars," and so on—south of the popular Inner Harbor waterfront redevelopment.

Location for the nostalgic 1980s film *Diner,* as well as the acclaimed TV shows *Homicide* and *The Wire*, Baltimore is not as faded or gritty as that might sound. For typically Baltimorean food and drink, head to historic **Fell's Point,** a mile east of the Inner Harbor. One of a dozen good places to eat here is **Bertha's** (734 S. Broadway; 410/327-5795), a friendly little café famed for (grit-free!) mussels and other seafood specialties. To sample the other local specialty, Chesapeake Bay crab served with a black peppery spice, head to **Obrycki's** (1727 E. Pratt St.; 410/732-6399).

If you're interested in catching a ballgame, the **Baltimore Orioles** play at Camden Yards (888/848-BIRD) right downtown. For more information, contact the **Baltimore visitors bureau** (877/BALTIMORE).

Easton

Midway across Maryland, 20 miles southeast of the Chesapeake Bay Bridge, turn off the freeway and head a half mile west to explore the well-preserved heart of **Easton** (pop. 14,677), where the stately Talbot County Courthouse overlooks a compact business district that could easily pass as an English country High Street. Besides the many 18th-century structures, including a Federal-style town house that's been converted into the Talbot County historical society **museum** (free; closed Sun.; 25 S. Washington St.), the most interesting place to stop is the white, wood-frame **Third Haven Friends Meeting House,** on the edge of town on South Washington Street, built in 1684 and still in use by a Quaker congregation.

Maryland's Eastern Shore is excellent bicycling country, with generally flat, quiet roads winding through farmlands, forests, and waterfront fishing villages.

The most impressive place to stay in Easton is the stately **Tidewater Inn** ($119 and up; 101 E. Dover St.; 410/822-1300 or 800/237-8775), a well restored landmark in the center of town, which offers guests free carriage rides around town and the option of a 4:30 AM breakfast—designed for early-rising duck-hunters. Easton also holds the comfortable (and bike-friendly!) **Bishop's** log canoe Edmee S. with the Point Lookout Tower at the Chesapeake Bay Maritime Museum

House B&B ($185 and up; 214 Goldsborough St.; 410/820-7290) and the usual range of motels and fast-food places along the US-50 frontage.

St. Michaels and Oxford

The pride and joy of the Eastern Shore is the Chesapeake Bay village of **St. Michaels,** a colonial-era shipbuilding center turned yachting haven that's home to the excellent **Chesapeake Bay Maritime Museum** (daily; $13; 410/745-2916). Located right on the waterfront at the center of town, the museum has extensive displays of skipjacks and other historic sailing vessels, which you can watch being restored in the museum workshops. There are also diverse pieces of fishing and hunting gear, plus a working lighthouse, all displayed to conjure up traditional Eastern Shore maritime life.

West of St. Michaels, at the far end of Hwy-33, **Tilghman Island** is home port for Chesapeake Bay's sole surviving fleet of skipjacks, the unique sail-powered vessels used to harvest oysters from the bay.

Though full of lovingly maintained old houses and commercial buildings as well as working wharves, chandlers, and sail lofts, St. Michaels, it has to be said, is definitely a major tourist trap, with the usual array of souvenir shops, overpriced restaurants, and over-quaint B&Bs.

After seeing the museum and wandering around the town, if you want to get a feel for the unspoiled Chesapeake, follow the signs southeast from St. Michaels to the historic **ferry** (daily 9 AM–sunset; $18/car round-trip, $5/pedestrian round-trip) that shuttles across the Tred Avon River every half hour or so between Bellevue and Oxford. **Oxford** (pop. 700), a truly sleepy little Eastern Shore town, has hardly changed since the 1760s, when it was one of two authorized ports-of-entry into colonial-era Maryland. Wander along the waterfront or south along Morris Street to the village center, through what may be the best-preserved colonial townscape left in America. No less an authority than James Michener (who lived in St. Michaels for many years) did go so far as to say that the crab cakes served inside the circa-1710 **Robert Morris Inn** ($135 and up; 410/226-5111) opposite the ferry dock were among the best he'd ever tasted.

Cambridge

Founded in 1684 on the south bank of the broad Choptank River, unlike sleepy Oxford, busy **Cambridge** (pop. 12,326) is a market town for the surrounding farmlands. Still somewhat industrial in feel, thanks to its now-closed canning and packing plants, Cambridge does have some attractive corners, though its one apt but unique sight is the decaying old **Cape Charles ferry,** which once sailed south to Norfolk but has long since been abandoned on the northwest side of the US-50 bridge over the Choptank River.

HARRIET TUBMAN.

US-50 through Cambridge is the **Harriet Tubman Highway.** Her birthplace is eight miles west of town.

Cambridge is also home to the Eastern Shore's most bizarre range of annual festivals, from February's **National Muskrat Skinning Championship** to powerboat and antique-airplane fairs held throughout the summer.

Salisbury

Though largely modern and commercial, **Salisbury** (pop. 30,343) has preserved part of its older townscape in a pedestrianized downtown shopping district and in the Newton Historic District, a collection of dainty Victorian-era houses along Elizabeth Street. The one place to stop is the **Ward Museum of Wildfowl Art** (daily; $7; 900 S. Schumaker Dr.), on the Salisbury University campus, which has a comprehensive collection of carved decoys and other hunting-related arts and crafts. Though this may not sound immediately enticing, the museum does explore varying aspects of the engagement between people and the "natural" world, and the items on display, ranging from Native American reed figures to highly collectible decoys, are all beautifully crafted.

Throughout the summer, Salisbury is home to the popular **Delmarva Shorebirds,** the Baltimore Orioles' Class A farm team, who play at the modern Perdue Stadium ($8, $2 on Mon.; 410/219-3112) off US-50 on Hobbs Road.

Crossing the coastal wetlands and estuaries, US-50 races east from Salisbury, bypassing a few small towns like Willards and Whaleyville, which are best seen by following the Hwy-346 frontage road. The two routes run parallel, joining each other 30 miles east in the old-time beach resort of Ocean City.

INTERSECTION Ocean City is also a stop along the **Atlantic Coast** route (see pages 408–491). Full coverage of **Ocean City** begins on page 421.

From deserts to bayou swamps and Tex-Mex to barbecue, this route offers a full-spectrum taste of America.

U.S. 80
SAN DIEGO TO SAVANNAH
VIA VICKSBURG, MISS.

By Crossing the Mississippi River Via U.S. 80 at Vicksburg, Miss. You have the Benefit of the Only All Year, All Weather Route from Coast to Coast. All Paved from San Diego, California, - Savannah, Georgia.

U.S. 80

COMPLIMENTS OF
VICKSBURG BRIDGE COMPANY
VICKSBURG, MISS.

U.S. 61

Bonnie and Clyde

Hank WIlliams Memorial

Tybee Island, Georgia

◀ 600 mi ▶

pg. 837

◀ 420 mi ▶

pg. 850

◀ 375 mi ▶

pg. 863

Between San Diego, California, and Savannah, Georgia

Following old US-80 and its contemporary equivalents across the nation's southern tier takes you through more varied cultural and physical landscapes than you'll find along any other cross-country route. Throughout this roughly 3,000-mile journey you can shift from one world to another in the time it takes to watch a football game. Heading east from the golden sands of San Diego, within a few hours you reach the harshly beautiful Southwest deserts, their trademark saguaro cacti creating a backdrop straight out of a Roadrunner cartoon. The route's central segment crosses the thousand-mile, "you can see for two days" plains of New Mexico and Texas, where pumpjacks jig for oil and cattle graze beneath a limitless sky. To the east spreads another land, starting at the cotton-rich Mississippi Delta and continuing along the foot of the Appalachians to the bayous and sea islands surrounding the country's grandest little city, Savannah.

Especially memorable is the diversity of people and prevailing customs along the route, all highlighted by a range of accents and lingos. For travelers, this cultural diversity is perhaps most accessible in the food. Many regional American cuisines—Tex-Mex, Cajun, Creole, and barbecue, to name a few—were originally developed somewhere along this route, and roadside restaurants continue to serve up local specialties that lend new meaning to the word "authentic." Along the open borders between Texas and New and old Mexico, in unselfconscious adobe sheds

CALIFORNIA

From the Pacific bays and golden beaches of **San Diego,** you can choose between two routes as you head east across Southern California: the high-speed I-8 freeway up and over pine-forested mountains, or a winding drive along the Mexican border. We've covered the slower, more southerly route that follows the remnants of old US-80 through sleepy border towns and past a pair of unique roadside attractions—the funky old **Desert View Tower** and the oddly endearing "Official Center of the World" at tiny **Felicity.** Also included is a quick side trip south of the border to beer-making **Tecate.** But no matter which way you choose, eventually you'll have to cross many monotonous miles of the **Mojave Desert,** a barren, dry, and inhospitable land.

with corrugated metal roofs, chile-powered salsa accompanies roast-steak fajitas; in Louisiana, entrées featuring catfish fillets or bright red boiled shrimp grace most menus; and everywhere you turn, roadside stands dish out reputedly the best barbecue in the universe. We've noted favorite places along the route, but all you really need to do is follow your nose, or look for a line of pickup trucks, and you'll find yourself in culinary heaven.

On an equal footing with the fine food is the incredible variety of music you'll hear, whether it's in a Texas honky-tonk or in the juke joints and gospel-spreading churches of Mississippi and Alabama. Along the Mexican border, from San Diego well past El Paso, radio stations blast out an anarchic mix of multilingual music, part country-western, part traditional Mexican, with accordions and guitars and lyrics flowing seamlessly from one language to the other and back—often in a single line of a song. Along the way, you can visit the hometowns of Buddy Holly, Little Richard, and Otis Redding, or pay your respects at the final resting places of Hank Williams, Jimmie Rodgers, and Duane Allman. After dark, listen to the current and next generation making music in roadside bars and clubs.

A wealth of distinctive literature has grown out of these regions, and you can visit dozens of characteristic literary scenes, live and in the flesh: Carson McCullers's "Ballad of the Sad Cafe" and other tales, which capture 1920s life in Columbus, Georgia; Cormac McCarthy's wide-open tales of the Texas frontier; the diner from *Fried Green Tomatoes*; and the original God's Little Acre and Tobacco Road. But there's also sober history, from Wild West Tombstone and Bonnie and Clyde's death site, to the **Dallas** intersection where JFK was assassinated, to the streets of **Selma,** where the civil rights movement burst forth onto the nation's front pages. Best of all, many of the most fascinating places along the way remain refreshingly free of the slick promotion that greets you in more-established tourist destinations. The relatively low profile of tourism here, and the fact that only a few big cities lie in wait to swallow your vacation dollars, help make this part of the country relatively inexpensive for visitors—but even at twice the price, it would be well worth experiencing.

Point Loma: Cabrillo National Monument

The sturdy headland that protects San Diego's extensive harbor from the open Pacific Ocean, Point Loma has long been occupied by the military, whose many fences, radio towers, and gun emplacements all seem to disappear at the very tip, where the **Cabrillo National Monument** (daily 9 AM–5 PM; $5 per car; 619/557-5450) protects a breathtaking 160 acres of cliffs and tidepools. It was set aside in 1913 to remember the efforts of conquistador Juan Cabrillo, who explored the California coast in 1542, sailing under a Spanish flag. There's also an old lighthouse, some nice trails, and a visitors center describing the whole shebang.

Across San Diego: Old US-80

From Point Loma and the Pacific Ocean, old US-80 bends south past the San Diego International Airport (sometimes referred to as Lindbergh Field, named

San Diego is at the southern end of our **Pacific Coast** road trip, which is described on pages 8–113. For details on visiting **San Diego,** see pages 110–111.

for Charles Lindbergh and featuring one of the most hair-raising landing patterns of any big American airport) and through downtown along 12th Avenue and Market Street, then veers north again along the Cabrillo Freeway (one of the oldest in the country) through historic **Balboa Park,** home to the San Diego Zoo, a replica of London's old Globe Theater, and many grand Spanish colonial buildings that have been standing here since the 1915 Panama-California Exposition.

East of San Diego, old US-80 follows El Cajon Boulevard past San Diego State University and a dozen miles of old motels, cafés, and gas stations before it reaches the foothill town of La Mesa, where you can leave old US-80 (which runs alongside the high-speed I-8 freeway) and turn onto the two-lane blacktop of Hwy-94. Twisting to the southeast around the 4,000-foot peaks of this part of the Cleveland National Forest, Hwy-94 traverses classic Southern California landscape: rolling, chaparral-covered hillsides rising above grassy ranch lands and stately valley oaks.

Tecate, Mexico

After passing through **Jamul** and **Dulzura,** two quiet ranching towns that appear on the verge of extinction due to San Diego's rapidly approaching sprawl, some 40 miles east of downtown San Diego along Hwy-94, you'll spot a sign marking the turnoff south to the Mexican border town of **Tecate** (pop.

border crossing at Tecate

64,764). Known around the world as the source of tangy Tecate beer—by most accounts, the brew that started people drinking beer with a squeeze of fresh lime—Tecate is in the top tier of enjoyable border towns, if only by virtue of being cleaner, quieter, safer, and much less "touristy" than Tijuana. Potential stops include a nice park, three blocks south of the border; the usual restaurants, cantinas, and souvenir shops; plus one unique stop: **Tecate Brewery** (closed Sun.; 665/654-9490). The brewery offers free tours, but make sure to call ahead for a reservation.

Campo (pop. 2,684) marks the southern end of the **Pacific Crest Trail,** which winds for 2,638 or so miles between Canada and Mexico.

Because of insurance concerns and Homeland Security hassles, it's a good idea to leave your car on the U.S. side of the border and cross into Mexico on foot, passport in hand. East of the Tecate area, Hwy-94 runs along the U.S. side of the border for 41 miles before joining the I-8 freeway.

Campo

Set in a broad valley midway between Tecate and the I-8 freeway, tiny **Campo** (pop. 2,684) has one main attraction, the **Pacific Southwest Railway Museum** (Sat.–Sun. and holidays 9 AM–5 PM; $5; 619/478-9937), at the west end of town on Forrest Gate Road. Along with an extensive outdoor collection of old locomotives and carriages, the museum offers rides (11 AM and 2:30 PM; $15) on restored steam- and diesel-powered trains, including a 12-mile round-trip through the surrounding countryside. Occasionally, the museum also offers all-day trips south to Tecate, Mexico.

Jacumba and the Desert View Tower

South of the I-8 freeway on a surviving stretch of the old US-80 highway, **Jacumba** (pop. 561) is a former spa and resort town where Clark Gable, Marlene Dietrich, and countless others soaked themselves silly in the free-flowing natural hot springs. Established in 1852 as a station on the stagecoach mail route across the desert, Jacumba had its heyday during the 1920s, and while little remains apart from the water, it makes a great place to stop. The

Anza-Borrego State Park

When driving in the desert, always keep the gas tank as full as possible, and always carry at least one gallon of drinking water per person. In case of trouble, stay with your car. Don't walk off in search of help; let it find you.

For more information on visiting Anza-Borrego State Park, which covers some 600,000 acres of desiccated desert, contact the ranger station in Borrego Springs (760/767-5311).

mineral-rich hot springs still flow into outdoor pools and private hot tubs at **Jacumba Hot Springs Spa** ($15; 44500 Old US-80; 619/766-4525), which includes motel rooms for around $75, a good on-site restaurant, and a popular "locals" bar.

Southern gateway to the splendid, 600,000-acre **Anza-Borrego State Park,** the largest and wildest desert park in the country, the Jacumba area is also home to one of the great road-trip stops in southern California: the **Desert View Tower** (daily 9 AM–dusk; $3; 619/766-4612). The four-story, cut-stone structure was built in 1922 to commemorate the pioneers who struggled across the arid desert.

Inside the tower, a small but interesting museum displays a haphazard collection of desert Americana such as Navajo blankets and Native American artifacts, with similar items on sale in the gift shop. You can't beat the price of admission, and at the top of the tower, an observation platform offers views across 100 miles of desert landscape, sliced by the I-8 freeway. (You can also see places where the excavations for I-8 have left sections of the old US-80 roadway stranded on man-made mesas, 50 feet or so higher than the modern freeway.)

Across the parking lot from the Desert View Tower, a hillside of quartzite granite boulders has been carved with dozens of three-dimensional figures. Most of the figures are of skulls, snakes, and lizards—with real lizards sometimes racing each other across the rocks. The whole ensemble was created during the Depression by an out-of-work engineer named W. T. Ratliffe.

The Desert View Tower stands at a cool 3,000 feet above sea level, three miles east of Jacumba, on the north side of I-8 at the In-Ko-Pah Road exit; billboards point the way.

El Centro

Located some 50 feet below sea level, midway across California at the heart of the agricultural Coachella Valley, **El Centro** (pop. 42,598) was founded in 1906 and has since bloomed into a bustling small city, thanks to irrigation water diverted from the Colorado River. Melons, grapefruit, and dates are the region's prime agricultural products, along with alfalfa grown to feed the many dairy cows. There's not a lot here that doesn't depend upon farming.

Though not much of a destination, El Centro is still the best place to break a journey between San Diego and the Arizona border, so fill your gas tank if nothing else. All the national food and lodging chains are here, along with neon-signed local ones along the I-8 Business Loop. Local character and tasty Mexican food abound at the very good **La Fonda,** two miles north of I-8 (548 Broadway St.; 760/353-6450).

El Centro is the winter home of the aerial acrobats of the U.S. Navy's Blue Angels, who can sometimes be spotted practicing their loops and rolls in the skies around the city. It is also the birthplace of Cher.

Algodones Dunes

In the middle of the southern Mojave Desert, 42 miles east of El Centro, a rest area south of the I-8 freeway at the Gray's Well Road exit gives access to the enticing pink-hued sands of the **Algodones Dunes,** which stretch to both sides of the freeway for over 50 miles. The slender dunes, which measure at most 10 miles across and reach heights of 200 to 300 feet, have been seen in Hollywood movies from *Beau Geste* to *Star Wars* and often cover the highway in blowing sandstorms. Though you can amble around on foot, be aware that the dunes themselves are under constant abuse from hordes of motorcycles and dune buggies.

If you're really, really interested in old highways, you won't want to miss the reconstructed remnants of a wooden plank road, built across the sands in 1915 and later replaced by the original US-80 highway. Preserved by the dry desert air and arranged to form a 100-foot section across the dunes, this fenced-off museum piece is along the south side of I-8, two miles west of the Gray's Well Road exit. The All-American Canal, which waters the Coachella Valley, snakes alongside the freeway.

Felicity: The Center of the World Pyramid

One of the odder sites in the Southwestern deserts—and competition for this title is pretty fierce—sits just north of the I-8 freeway in the tiny but happily named town of **Felicity** (pop. 4). Local resident Jacques-Andre Istel— author of a children's fairy tale concerning a scholarly, fire-breathing dragon

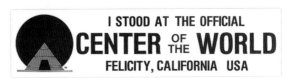

I STOOD AT THE OFFICIAL
CENTER OF THE WORLD
FELICITY, CALIFORNIA USA

From 1858 to 1861 the original Butterfield Stage, which carried mail and passengers from St. Louis to San Francisco, followed the approximate route of I-8 across Southern California. The route was originally blazed by Spanish explorer Juan de Anza, on his way to found San Francisco in 1775.

named Coe who lives at the center of the world reading fire-proof books and eating the nearby Chocolate Mountains—named the "town" after his wife Felicia and somehow convinced France, China, and Imperial County to recognize that Felicity is, legally and officially, the center of the world.

A 25-foot-high pink terrazzo pyramid stands above the exact spot, which you can visit on regular guided tours (late Nov.–mid-April daily; $3 donation; 760/572-0100); the fee also buys a certificate saying you've stood at "The Official Center of the World." You can climb a set of stairs that used to belong to the Eiffel Tower and sift through sundry souvenirs in the gift shop.

ARIZONA

Between the Colorado River, which divides Arizona from California, and the Phoenix–Tucson megalopolis in the middle of the state, there is not very much to attract the traveler off the freeway. However, the rather complete absence of interesting places in southwestern Arizona is more than made up for by the wealth of fascinating things to see in the state's southeast corner. Here you'll find such legendary sites as **Tombstone**—home of the OK Corral—and other finely presented reminders of the state's Wild West heritage, along with some of Arizona's most beautiful natural scenery.

The Colorado River forms the border between California and Arizona, and it marks the line between the Pacific and Mountain time zones. Arizona, however, doesn't observe daylight saving time, so in summer both states are on the same time.

Yuma

Among the hottest, driest, and fastest-growing areas in the country, **Yuma** (pop. 195,751) was first settled in the 1770s at the site of one of the few good crossings along the

Colorado River. Dozens of decaying old adobe buildings around town testify to Yuma's lengthy history, and a select few places are preserved as historic parks. The **Yuma Quartermaster Depot State Historic Park** (daily; $4; 928/329-0471), along the river and I-8 at the north end of 4th Avenue, includes buildings that have been restored to their appearance prior to the arrival of the railroad in 1877, when supplies for U.S. troops throughout the Southwest arrived here by steam-

Along with dozens of Spanish-language stations north and south of the Mexican border, Yuma's **KBLU 560 AM** offers a healthy dose of news/talk radio.

407 OCEAN TO OCEAN HIGHWAY AND SOUTHERN PACIFIC BRIDGES.

ACROSS THE COLORADO RIVER, YUMA, ARIZONA

boat from the Gulf of California.

Around the time the railroad arrived, a full century after its founding by Spanish missionaries, Yuma was the site of Arizona Territory's main prison. Convicts struggled in the 120°F heat to build the stone and adobe prison, which earned a reputation as the "Hellhole of Arizona," due in large part to the summer heat and the brutality of its regime, though park rangers emphasize the fact that prisoners had access to a library and other facilities unusual at the time. It operated 33 years until it was closed in 1909 and is now preserved as the state-run **Yuma Territorial Prison State Historic Park** (closed Tues.–Wed.; $5; 928/783-4771), well posted along the north side of I-8 at the 4th Avenue exit; the site consists of a few of the cells and the main gate, as well as a small museum.

From the prison, a rickety pedestrian-only steel bridge (formerly part of US-80) leads across the Colorado River to California and the **St. Thomas mission church** on the Quechan Fort Yuma Indian Reservation.

Along with the usual national franchises, Yuma has a number of decent places to eat, ranging from the big breakfasts and afternoon barbecue at **Brownie's Cafe** (1145 S. 4th Ave./old US-80; 928/783-7911) to the pool tables, burgers, and sandwiches at ancient **Lutes Casino** (221 S. Main St.; 928/782-2192) in the historic old downtown area. Voted the "Best Place to Stop in Yuma" by the *Arizona Republic* newspaper, Lutes is a barn-like hall full of old photos, political posters, street signs, and all manner of junk, well worth a look at least for its passionately played domino games.

Along with the national chains, places to sleep in Yuma include the pleasant **Yuma Cabana** (around $40 and up; 2151 S. 4th Ave.; 928/783-8311 or 800/874-0811), with palm trees, a nice pool, and a recliner in every room.

Yuma to Gila Bend: I-8

Spanning 110 miles of barren desert east of Yuma, between the U.S. Air Force's 2.7-million-acre Barry M. Goldwater Bombing Range and a U.S.

Twelve miles or so west of Gila Bend, off I-8 at exit 102, Painted Rocks Road leads 11 miles north to a BLM-managed site where petroglyphs, carved into the boulders by the Hohokam people around AD 1400 and earlier, cover the rocks.

From Gila Bend, Hwy-85 runs south to the beautiful and totally deserted **Organ Pipe Cactus National Monument** (daily, 520/387-6849) before linking up with Hwy-86 to loop east to Tucson. Be aware that the area is subject to road closures.

Army Proving Ground, the I-8 freeway follows the route of early Spanish explorers and settlers on the flat but forbidding Camino del Diablo, along the banks of the usually dry Gila River.

East of 767-foot-high Telegraph Pass, 20 miles outside Yuma, the old US-80 highway reappears along the north side of the freeway, running through old-time desert outposts. If you're hungry, the flyspeck ranching community of **Tacna** has a great place to eat burgers, lamb chops, and a full menu of other Mexican and American dishes: **Basque Etchea** (closed Mon.; 928/785-4027). Take I-8 exit 42, then head north across the railroad tracks.

Another great middle-of-nowhere desert oasis, along I-8 at milepost 67, is **Dateland,** 65 miles or east of Yuma or 48 miles west of Gila Bend. Dateland has a 24-hour gas station, café (928/454-2772), RV park, and gift shop selling dates in all possible forms, including refreshing milk shakes. The top-quality, hand-pollinated Medjool dates are grown in the adjacent nine-acre grove.

Gila Bend

The only place approaching a town between Yuma and Phoenix or Tucson, **Gila Bend** (pop. 1,922) is regularly the "Hottest Spot in the Country"—a title of which it is so proud that, more than once, it's been caught inflating the numbers. First settled as a main stop on the Butterfield Stage route, Gila Bend doesn't offer much relief for the senses, though it does have some photogenic old motels and all the gas stations, restrooms, and restaurants you could reasonably expect to find in the middle of the Arizona desert.

One place to eat is the **Outer Limits Coffee Shop** (401 E. Pima Ave.), downtown off exit 115. Marked by a flying-saucer-shaped sign, it's part of the **Best Western Space Age Lodge** motel ($90 and up; 928/683-2273 or 866/683-7722). Both are essential stops for any Jetsons-aged traveler, though the refurbishment after a fire has diminished the 1960s Space Age charm.

Old US-80 via Phoenix

I-8 is by far the fastest way east from Gila Bend to Tucson and beyond, but if you have the time and inclination to follow the old road, it took the long way around: From Gila Bend US-80 veers north across the usually dry Gila River

Between Phoenix and Tucson, I-10 parallels our US-93 **Border to Border** road trip route, which runs about 20 miles to the east, along Hwy-79 (see page 165). From **Phoenix,** the route passes such enticing desert oddities as the famous Biosphere 2 and a memorial to cowboy actor Tom Mix. Phoenix and Tucson, and the alternative route between them, are covered on pages 166–171.

along what's now an unmarked county road, then east through the towns of Arlington, Palo Verde, and **Buckeye,** where a 40-odd-foot statue of "Hobo Joe" stands along Baldy Street downtown. US-80 runs through downtown Phoenix on Van Buren Street (which was also US-60 and US-70) before heading south to Tucson.

If you're interested in following the route of old US-80 across California and western Arizona, pick up a copy of the entertaining and informative *Old US-80 Highway Traveler's Guide,* by Eric J. Finley.

Saguaro National Park: Tucson Mountain Park

The saguaro cactus, whose creamy white blossoms are the Arizona state flower, blooms in May.

Northwest of Tucson, the more popular half of **Saguaro National Park** protects extensive stands of saguaro cactus as well as ancient petroglyphs, spring wildflowers, and generally gorgeous desert scenery. From I-10 at Cortaro (exit 246), a loop road runs southwest, then back east through rugged, mountainous terrain, which, though popular,

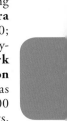

is a great place to get a feel for the Sonora Desert landscape. A **visitors center** (daily; 520/733-5158) has details of the many hikes here, like the popular Hugh Norris Trail, which winds along a mountain ridge to the 4,687-foot summit of Wasson Peak.

There's more hiking, plus camping and the excellent **Arizona Sonora Desert Museum** (daily; $12–14.50; 520/883-2702)in the adjacent county-owned **Tucson Mountain Park** (520/877-6000), where **Old Tucson Studios** ($16.95; 520/883-0100) has movie sets used to film more than 300 movies and TV shows. These days, however, the "action" is mostly staged gunfights and dance-hall revues.

Saguaro National Park

Across Tucson: Old US-80

From the north and west, the best old road introduction to Tucson is the so-called **Miracle Mile,** a few blocks of slightly seedy old neon-signed motels, right off the I-10 freeway at exit 255. From here, old US-80 follows a series of one-way surface streets into compact downtown Tucson, first following 5th Avenue, then 6th Avenue, the pre-Interstate main highway.

Tucson marks the junction with our **Border to Border** road trip along US-93, covered on pages 114–173. **Tucson** and nearby attractions are covered on pages 170–171.

Saguaro National Park: Rincon Mountains

A dozen miles east of Tucson, on the slopes of the Tanque Verde and Rincon Mountains, the eastern half of **Saguaro National Park** covers nearly 58,000 acres of rolling desert landscape. Named in honor of the anthropomorphic saguaro cactus, which here reaches heights up to 50 feet and lives as long as 200 years, the monument is best seen by following eight-mile Cactus Forest Drive, along which numerous hiking trails give close-up looks at the multi-limbed succulents. For more information and details of hiking opportunities, stop at the **visitors center** (520/733-5153).

Colossal Cave

Beyond the Rincon Mountains section of Saguaro National Park, 20 miles or so from downtown Tucson via the Old Spanish Trail, **Colossal Cave** (daily; $5 per car, plus $12 and up per tour; 520/647-7275) is another great place to stop. A huge old limestone cavern that offers a cool (in every sense of the word!) escape from the sweltering summer heat, this is one of the state's most enduring tourist attractions. (Avid cavers will appreciate comparing Colossal Cave, a "dry" cave, with the newly opened Kartchner Caverns, a "wet" cave where the humidity will have you dripping with perspiration.) Colossal Cave was used in Wild West times by train robbers who escaped here with $72,000 in gold and currency. Most of the very limited "development" here (footpaths, museum, and gift shop) was done as a Civilian Conservation Corps project during the New Deal 1930s.

The surrounding ranch land has been opened as a nature reserve with hiking, horse-riding, and mountain-bike trails, and the ranch buildings have been preserved as a museum of early Arizona life.

Kartchner Caverns State Park

On the other side of I-10 from Colossal Cave, one of Arizona's most long-awaited "openings" was that of **Kartchner Caverns State Park,** a massive limestone cavern—over two miles long—that is rated by experts as one of the 10 most beautiful in the world. Discovered by a pair of avid cavers, Randy Tufts and Gary Tenen, back in 1974, it then took 25 years of negotiation and more than $28 million worth of careful construction of tunnels and facilities before the cave was opened to the general public. Advance reservations for one of the guided tours are all but required if you want to enter the cave to see the 150-foot-square Throne Room, with its 60-foot ceiling, or the larger but less lofty Rotunda, or any of the other phantasmagorical sights. The caverns, which are kept at near 100 percent humidity by a set of airlocks at the entrance, are remarkable for their diverse and delicate formations, including over 30 different types of stalactites, stalagmites, columns, draperies, shields, and helictites, not to mention the longest "soda straw" in the United States—a thin tube of limestone over 21 feet long but only a quarter-inch in diameter.

Kartchner Caverns State Park is just west of Benson, nine miles south of I-10 exit 302, along Hwy-90. If you don't manage to join a tour, it's still worth stopping at the 23,000-square-foot **visitors center** (daily; $6 per vehicle; 520/586-4100) to see the movie describing the cave and its discovery. There are also some full-scale replicas of the cave's features, along with an above-ground hiking trail through native hummingbird habitat and a 63-site campground with full hookups.

Benson and the Amerind Foundation

Off I-10 along the banks of the San Pedro River, **Benson** (pop. 5,105) was founded as a Santa Fe railroad connection to booming Tombstone and the Mexican harbor town of Guaymas. Trains still rumble through town, but there's not much to see apart from fading roadside signs. **Reb's Cafe and Coffee Shop** (1020 W. 4th St.; 520/586-3856) and the **Horseshoe Cafe** (154 E. 4th St.; 520/586-3303), across from the railroad tracks, are where locals go to eat. Thanks in part to the popularity of Kartchner Caverns, Benson has a number of motels congregating around I-10 exit 304.

> Benson radio station **KAVV 97.7 FM** plays lots of good Waylon-and-Willie-type country hits, plus captivating accounts of local news and activities.

From Benson, our route cuts south on old US-80 (now Hwy-80), while I-10 races east over the mountains that 100-plus years ago were a stronghold of Apache warriors under Geronimo and Cochise. If you're following the Interstate, a couple of sights are worth looking for. The more satisfying of these, the **Amerind Foundation Museum** (closed Mon.; $8; 520/586-3666), lies 12 miles or so east of Benson, off Dragoon Road a mile southeast of I-10 exit 318. Started in 1937, the private, nonprofit museum is devoted to the study of local Native American cultures, with everything from ancient arrowheads to contemporary Pueblo pottery on display in the spacious mission-style buildings. Not surprisingly, the best collections are of Hopi, Navajo, and Apache artifacts, with well-presented exhibits of ceremonial and domestic objects—kachina dolls, rugs, and ritual costumes.

I-10: The Thing?

Advertised by signs all along the freeway, one of the country's odder roadside attractions stands atop 5,013-foot Texas Summit, along I-10 at exit 322: **The Thing?** ($1; 520/586-2581). A gas station, a gift shop, and a Dairy Queen stand in front of a prefab shed full of stuff ranging from a Rolls Royce once used by Adolf Hitler to The Thing itself, a mummified corpse whose "secret identity" has yet to be revealed. "What is it?" the signs ask.

re-enacters at Tombstone role-play the famous shoot-out

Tombstone

While I-10 races east over the mountains, our more scenic route, promoted by tourism authorities as the "Cochise Trail," winds south on old US-80 through the Wild West town of Tombstone, "The Town too Tough to Die." The route loops along the Mexican border before rejoining I-10 across the New Mexico border.

Though it's just 22 miles south of the freeway, and regularly inundated by bikers, RVers, and busloads of tourists, the rough-and-ready mining town of **Tombstone** (pop. 1,380) has kept itself looking pretty much as it did back in the 1880s, when 10,000 miners called it home and one of the more mythic events of the Wild West took place here: the shootout at the OK Corral.

Historians, and everyone in Tombstone, still debate the chain of events of October 26, 1881. Was Wyatt Earp a sharpshooting savior, out to make Tombstone safe for decent society? Or was he really a grandstanding cowboy whom history has romanticized? Decide for yourself after hearing all sides of the story. The **OK Corral** is still there, a block south of Fremont Street (old US-80), on Allen Street between 3rd and 4th Streets, with life-sized, black-leather-clad statues taking the places of Virgil and Wyatt Earp facing down the Clanton brothers. Nearby, in a fenced-off outdoor theater, gunslinging actors stage re-creations of the shootout. To see any or all of this, you have to buy a ticket at the entertaining **Historama** (daily; $10; 520/457-3456), adjacent to the OK Corral.

The dead men, and many hundreds of others, ended up at **Boot Hill Cemetery** (daily; free; 520/457-3300), along

About 20 miles southeast of Tombstone, three miles west of Bisbee at the 6,033-foot Mule Pass summit of old US-80, the much-abused stone obelisk of the **Divide Monument** commemorates the convict-laborers who first constructed the road in 1913. The monument stands in a somewhat scruffy parking area directly above the modern tunnel, and from it you get a great panoramic view of the surrounding Mule Mountains.

the highway at the northwestern edge of town, where you can wander among 300 wooden grave markers inscribed with all manner of rhyming epitaphs. The Boot Hill Cemetery is the real thing, and the souvenirs in the large gift shop at the entrance are as wonderfully tacky as they come.

Though the OK Corral and Boot Hill are both fun, the best place to learn about Tombstone's real, as opposed to mythic, history is at the **Tombstone Courthouse State Historic Park,** at 3rd and Toughnut Streets ($5; 520/457-3311). Built in 1882, this old courthouse building holds 12,000 square feet of artifacts documenting and describing the *real* Wild West.

Despite the huge numbers of people who descend upon Tombstone every day, and the gauntlet of T-shirt and knickknack shops catering to them, the town is still a very appealing place to visit. Enjoy a cool drink at the truly historic **Big Nose Kate's Saloon** (520/457-3107), right at the center of things on Allen Street; named for, owned, and run by Doc Holliday's brothel-keeper girlfriend, the very authentic old saloon now hosts live music and serves the very tasty "Reuben That Won the West."

Every day in summer, just about every hour on the hour, historic gunfights are reenacted all around Tombstone, and during the third week in October, the whole town comes alive with a weekend of shootouts and parades during **Helldorado Days.** Places to stay are not extensive, nor very expensive: Try the centrally located **Tombstone Motel** ($50 and up; 502 E. Fremont St.; 888/455-3478 or 520/457-3478), on the main road.

Bisbee

A classic boom-and-bust mining town, **Bisbee** (pop. 5,575) is one of the most satisfying offbeat destinations in Arizona, combining scenic beauty, palpable history, and a good range of places to eat, drink, and enjoy yourself. Climbing up winding streets lined by 100-year-old structures—Victorian cottages, board shacks, and stately brick churches—Bisbee has attracted a diverse population of desert rats, bikers, working artists, and New Age apostles, all of whom mix amiably in the town's cafés and bars.

The heart of Bisbee lies north of old US-80 along Main Street, stretching west from the **Bisbee Mining and Historical Museum** (daily 10 AM–4 PM; $7.50), which displays dioramas, old photos, and sundry artifacts inside the old Phelps Dodge company headquarters.

For visitors, the main event in Bisbee is the **Queen Mine.** Put on a hard hat and a miner's lamp and take a train ride down into the mine shafts and tunnels, which

One of the more infamous events in Bisbee's busy history occurred in July 1917, when Industrial Workers of the World representatives presented demands for better conditions. Tensions grew and a few weeks later 1,186 men—not all of them miners on strike for better pay and conditions—were forcibly deported and literally railroaded out of town and dumped in the desert outside Columbus, New Mexico.

Every summer since 1910, Bisbee has hosted the 4th of July **Bisbee Coaster Race Soap Box Derby,** part of a generally excellent Independence Day party.

Fly's Photos

The work of Wild West photographer Camillus S. Fly forms one of the primary records of life in frontier Arizona. Fly was born in Missouri and raised in Napa, California. After marrying Mary "Mollie" Goodrich in 1879, he moved to Arizona to open a portrait studio in Tombstone, now restored as part of the OK Corral Historama complex. His iconic images, displayed in the small gallery, include some of the earliest photos taken of Chiricahua Apache warrior Geronimo, photographed soon after his 1886 surrender. Fly's studio also displays his images of Wyatt Earp, "Doc" Holliday, and many others. What Matthew Brady was to the Civil War, Camillus S. Fly was to Tombstone in its 1880s heyday.

were in operation until 1975. Hour-long tours (daily; $13; 866/432-2071 or 520/432-2071) leave every 90 minutes from the Queen Mine building, just south of downtown along old US-80. Temperature down in the mine is a cool 47°F, so dress appropriately.

One of Arizona's most unforgettable sights, the massive **Lavender Open Pit** forms a gigantic polychrome crater along Hwy-80, just south of the Queen Mine. Named not for its color—which is more rusty red than purple—but for a mine superintendent, Harrison Lavender, this was a true glory hole with ore deposits that provided the bulk of Bisbee's eight billion pounds of copper before being shut down in 1974. The Queen Mine also offers hour-long tours ($7; 520/432-2071) of this mile-wide, 900-foot-deep pit.

Bisbee Practicalities

Lined by characterful old brick buildings, Bisbee's winding Main Street has many cafés, antiques shops, art galleries, and restaurants. At the center of town, the **Copper Queen Hotel** ($125 and up; 520/432-2216), looming over downtown along Howell Street, has been the best place to stay since it opened in 1902. Most of the rooms have been upgraded to include modern conveniences without losing their old-fashioned charm.

Bisbee also offers what has to be the most unusual accommodation option in Arizona: the **Shady Dell RV Park** (1 Douglas Rd.; 520/432-3567). Located a mile east of downtown, behind the Chevron station at the Hwy-80/Hwy-92 traffic circle, the Shady Dell welcomes you to stay the night—or longer—in one of 12 well-restored 1940s and '50s Airstream, Silver Streak, and Spartanette trailers, or a pleasure boat, all filled with period furnishings. Rates are a reasonable $55–145 per night and include use of a VCR stocked with classic B-movies; you can also pitch a tent or pull up your own RV. And if that's not enough to tempt you, the Shady Dell is also home to **Dot's Diner** (520/432-1112), which serves out-of-this world Cajun-spiced food for breakfast and lunch Tuesday–Saturday.

Back in Bisbee proper, the Copper Queen Hotel has a good restaurant and popular bar, while the nicest place in town is the gourmet **Cafe Roka** (35 Main St.; 520/432-5153). Brewery Gulch, which runs north from Main Street at the east side of downtown Bisbee, once held over 50 different saloons and gambling parlors; it's considerably quieter now but still home to such fun haunts as **The Stock Exchange Saloon,** inside the old Bisbee Stock Exchange (15 Brewery Ave.; 520/432-1333) and **St. Elmo's Bar** (36 Brewery Ave.; 520/432-5578), which has live music most weekend nights.

For further information, walking-tour maps, or details of special events, contact the Bisbee **visitors center** (520/432-3554), located next to the Copper Queen Hotel.

Much of southeastern Arizona is still open range, so keep an eye out for livestock on the highway.

The Border: Douglas and Agua Prieta

Like Bisbee, the border town of **Douglas** (pop. 17,378) grew up on copper mining, which here lasted until fairly recently: The Phelps-Dodge smelter a mile west of town was in operation until 1987, processing ores from mines in Bisbee and Mexico. Now most of the economy revolves around the many *maquiladora* plants in its much larger Mexican neighbor, **Agua Prieta** (pop. 77,254), which feels surprisingly calm and quiet, considering its border-town location.

There's not a lot to see in either Douglas or Agua Prieta, though Douglas does boast one fabulous attraction: the landmark **Gadsden Hotel** ($60 and up; 1046 G Ave.; 520/364-4481). Rebuilt in 1929 after a fire destroyed the 1907 original, the spacious gold-leafed lobby—one of the grandest public spaces in the state—has a pretty Tiffany-style stained-glass mural decorating its mezzanine. The small and basic rooms are bargain-priced, and there's also a good Mexican-American restaurant, the El Conquistador Dining Room, and a very popular bar, the Saddle and Spur Tavern, its walls decorated with over 200 cattle brands from area ranches.

Travel along the Mexican border is enlivened immeasurably by the many radio stations, varying from the country twang of Douglas's **KDAP 96.5 FM** to the many south-of-the-border stations, like Radio Sonora, **101.3 FM,** that play a part-English, part-Spanish Tejano mélange typified by songs like "Mama, No Deje Que Sus Hijos Grow Up To Be Vaqueros."

Agua Prieta was the site of skirmishes between revolutionary Pancho Villa and the Mexican army.

Cave Creek Canyon and Chiricahua National Monument

For the 50-odd miles between Douglas and the New Mexico state line, old US-80 cuts diagonally across the southeast corner of Arizona, a rugged country of mountains, canyons, and volcanic outcrops rising above sagebrush plains. There's not much to see along the highway, but to the northwest rise the enticing Pendregosa Mountains, whose forested peaks, now protected as part of the Coronado National Forest, long served as sanctuary to Chiricahua Apaches and sundry outlaws and wanted men.

While you can also reach them from the north off I-10, the best access to the mountains from the south is via the aptly named hamlet of **Portal,** west of old US-80 from the New Mexico border, where the **Portal Peak Lodge, Store, and Cafe** (2358 Rock House Rd.; 520/558-2223) is a welcoming oasis, offering fresh food and comfortable rooms (around $85).

Big Balanced Rock in Chiricahua National Monument

Above Portal rise the sheer cliffs of **Cave Creek Canyon,** which writer William Least Heat-Moon described in *Blue Highways* as "one of the strangest pieces of topography I've ever seen," its pale sandstone walls looking like a sun-bleached twin of Utah's Zion National Park. A narrow but passable (except in winter) 20-mile dirt road from Cave Creek climbs over the mountains' pine-covered, 7,600-foot-high crest, ending up in the west at the foot of intriguing **Chiricahua National Monument,** a veritable "Wonderland of Rocks" whose contorted shapes were formed out of soft volcanic rhyolite by eons of erosion.

NEW MEXICO

Between Arizona and Texas, the I-10 freeway crosses above the part of New Mexico known as the Bootheel, for the way it steps down toward Old Mexico. Until the Gadsden Purchase of 1853, all this was part of Mexico, and the Hispanic influence still dominates the Anglo-American. The few towns here, like **Lordsburg** and **Deming,** were founded and remain primarily based on the railroad and offer little for the passing traveler. However, at least one place is definitely worth a stop: the historic village of **Mesilla,** set around a dusty plaza just south of the region's one big city, **Las Cruces.**

Lordsburg and Shakespeare

Coming in from southeastern Arizona, old US-80 rejoins I-10 at a crossroads community aptly called "Road Forks" (near the tin-roofed ghost town of Steins), and 15 miles farther east the freeway swerves south to bypass the town of **Lordsburg** (pop. 2,797). Named not from any religious conviction but in honor of the Southern Pacific railroad engineer who plotted it in 1880, Lordsburg has one great attraction—a taste of New Mexican home cooking at the family-run **El Charro** (daily 8 AM–10 PM; 209 Southern Pacific Blvd.; 575/542-3400), along the train tracks at the center of town.

Like something out of *The Andromeda Strain,* Lordsburg feels oddly abandoned, as if everyone has just packed up and left town. In fact, the other main draw is New Mexico's best-preserved ghost town, **Shakespeare,** three miles south of Lordsburg on a well-marked dirt road. Briefly home to some 3,000 silver miners during the early 1870s, Shakespeare was abandoned when the mines dried up, only to be reborn during another brief mining boom in the 1880s. By the 1930s it was turned into a ranch by the Hill family, whose descendants still live here, care for the buildings, and conduct irregularly scheduled guided tours (weekends 10 AM and 2 PM; $5; 575/542-9034) of the Grant House saloon, a former Butterfield Stagecoach station, and the Stratford Hotel, where Billy the Kid washed dishes as a young boy.

After delving into Texas at El Paso, this route enters New Mexico again near Carlsbad Caverns National Park.

Silver City, an evocative old mining town high in the mountains 45 miles northeast of Lordsburg, was another early stomping ground of Wild West outlaw Billy the Kid and makes an excellent side trip between Lordsburg and Deming. In the wilderness north of Silver City, the **Gila Cliff Dwellings National Monument** (575/536-9461) is well worth setting aside a full day.

Deming

Some 60 miles east of Lordsburg, halfway to Las Cruces, the dusty ranching and farming community of **Deming** (pop. 14,855) advertises itself as "Deming—Home of Pure Water and Fast Ducks." This odd motto makes more sense than it may at first seem: Deming's water comes from the underground Mimbres River, and

For The *Rest* of Your Life *Stop* at
Hub Motel and Cafe
On Hiways 70 and 80   Deming, New Mexico

every year at the end of August the town hosts the Great American Duck Race (888/345-1125 or 575/544-0469)—for living ducks, not the rubber kind, racing 20 feet in less than two seconds!

Deming's own **KNFT 102.9 FM** *plays Top 40 country hits of the past 25 years.*

All this may be little more than a cheap ploy to get hapless (or bored stiff, or both) travelers to turn off tedious I-10 and visit the city, but fortunately, Deming's not a bad place, boasting the excellent **Deming-Luna-Mimbres Museum** (daily; donations; 301 S. Silver Ave.; 575/546-2382), three blocks south of Pine Street (old US-80), Deming's main drag. Besides the usual range of old pottery, sparkling rocks, and pioneer artifacts, the museum displays an endearing collection of old toys, dolls, quilts, and dental equipment—well worth a quick look at the very least. Don't be worried by the big tank parked out front—the museum is housed in the old Armory building.

Deming also offers great Mexican food (*chorizo y huevos, fajitas,* etc.) at **La Fonda** (601 E. Pine St.; 575/546-0465).

Rooms range from local places like the neon-signed **Butterfield Stage Motel** (309 W. Pine St.; 575/544-0011) to the national chains. The best place to camp is southeast of town in **Rockhound State Park** ($5 for day use, $8 per night for primitive campsite, $10 for developed site; 575/546-6182), where, besides finding nice sites with hot showers, you can collect up to 15 pounds of geodes, agates, or quartz crystals—something the rangers urge you to do.

Las Cruces

Spreading along the eastern banks of the Rio Grande, at the foot of the angular Organ Mountains, **Las Cruces** (pop. 97,618) is the commercial center of a prosperous agricultural and recreational region. Named for a concentration of pioneer grave markers, Las Cruces was first settled by Spanish missionaries but is now a thoroughly modern, American-looking place, with all the motels you could want, and a youthful vitality made possible by the presence of the large New Mexico State University campus. One place worth searching out is **Nellie's Cafe** (1226 W. Hadley St.; 575/524-9982), a Mexican restaurant famed for spicy salsas and delicious green-chile cheeseburgers, housed in a little brown box off Valley Boulevard on the northwest edge of downtown. For a unique place to stay, consider **The Lundeen Inn of the Arts** ($80 and up; 618 S. Alameda Blvd.; 575/526-3326), which offers B&B rooms in a 140-year-old restored Mexican territorial inn.

Along US-70 some 60 miles northeast of Las Cruces, **White Sands National Monument** *protects over 73,600 acres of gleaming white gypsum dunes.*

A Tortilla by Any Other Name

Carne adovada, calabacitas, posole, sopapillas...Menu items like these put you squarely in the lower left-hand quadrant of any U.S. map. But how do you know whether you're eating traditional New Mexican cooking, Southwestern cuisine, or the popular hybrid known as Tex-Mex? Truth is, they're all hybrids, launched nearly five centuries ago when the Spanish brought European spices and domestic animals to combine with indigenous ingredients. As Spanish and Mexican settlers followed El Camino Real north from Chihuahua to Santa Fe, culinary distinctions grew out of regional variations in locally grown products along the way.

What's new is the categories: A generation ago, folks just helped themselves to "Mexican food." Tex-Mex, as its name implies, draws from both sides of the international border, from grazing lands where vaqueros roast meat over mesquite fires. In New Mexico, it's the chiles that set the dishes apart—and set your taste buds afire. When you order a local specialty, the server may ask, "Red or green?"—referring to red or green chile. Red chiles are usually sun-dried, while green chiles are fresh, but the flavor and spiciness varies depending on which of the 200 or more different chile varieties are used to make it. Try a little of each, and enjoy.

One more rare treat: West of town along I-10, the Las Cruces rest area is home to a giant-sized statue of the New Mexico state bird, the roadrunner, crafted entirely from recycled material (or what used to be called "trash").

Mesilla

The best thing about Las Cruces is its nearness to a truly neat little place, the historic village of **Mesilla,** three miles southwest of Las Cruces via Hwy-28. Low-slung adobe buildings set around a shady central plaza include the landmark 1855 adobe church of San Albino, an old jail from which Billy the Kid escaped in 1880, and a former Butterfield Stage station that's now home to the very popular **La Posta** restaurant (daily for lunch and dinner; 575/524-3524).

Across Hwy-28 from the plaza, the **Gadsden Museum** (by appointment only; 575/526-6293) traces local history from pre-conquest to current times.

Mesilla was founded across the Rio Grande on the Mexican side of the border in 1848, after the agreement of the Mexican-American War gave everything to the north to the Americans. Six years later, Mesilla became (legally at least) American again, after the Gadsden Purchase bought the entire, nearly 30,000-square-mile "Bootheel" region for $10 million.

Juan de Oñate, for whom Hwy-28 and numerous other places in the Southwest are named, was a Spanish conquistador and colonial commander. His name is infamous in Native American circles because of his role in ordering the mutilation of 24 captive warriors from Acoma, whose right feet were cut off in 1599.

It's a private collection, pulled together over five generations of the same family; the folk art (dozens of hand-crafted *retablos* and *santos*) is wide-ranging and powerfully evocative of life in the harsh Southwest.

Hwy-28: Juan de Oñate Trail

Southeast from Las Cruces and Mesilla, our route dips south across the Texas border to El Paso, then continues on US-180 for some 130 miles east before re-entering New Mexico at Carlsbad Caverns National Park. For the run to El Paso you have your choice between I-10 or slower and more scenic Hwy-28, the **Juan de Oñate Trail,** which avoids the freeway and runs through the pecan groves, pepper fields, and dusty small towns that spread along the west bank of the Rio Grande.

This part of New Mexico is chili country, and there's no better place to sample the great variety of spicy peppers than at **Chope's Bar and Cafe** (575/233-3420), an unpretentious cinderblock café along Hwy-28 in La Mesa, roughly midway between Mesilla and El Paso. House specialty here is *chiles rellenos*—whole chiles stuffed with cheese and deep-fried.

TEXAS AND NEW MEXICO

Mileage-wise, the haul across Texas is the longest part of this coast-to-coast route, but as far as things to see, the state doesn't offer a very high quotient per gallon. In the far-western stretches near **El Paso,** to maximize scenic interest follow the slower but significantly more attractive route along US-180 past the beautiful **Guadalupe Mountains,** and veer across a corner of New Mexico to see the remarkable **Carlsbad Caverns.**

From Carlsbad it's a straight shot across the painfully flat **Llano Estacado,** or Staked Plains, which stretches to both sides of the New Mexico/Texas border; this section of the route is one of the least action-packed in the country—there's almost nothing for miles on end, apart from oil derricks, cattle ranches, and cotton plantations. Only a few of the sporadic towns here have any historic claim or aesthetic interest; it's basically a long day's drive across the open plains. If you're in a hurry, you won't miss much by following the route of old US-80, alongside the I-20 freeway between El Paso and the **Dallas/Fort Worth** metropolitan area, through roughneck oil towns like **Odessa** and **Midland.**

In eastern Texas, the landscape gradually evolves into that of the Deep South, the dense pine woods doing their best to disguise the historic dependence on the oil industry—with profits far more apparent in the towers of Dallas than here at the often poverty-stricken source. Again, the Interstates offer a faster way across, and you can turn off where you want to visit the few sites of interest, like tiny **Kilgore,** home of the "World's Richest Acre."

El Paso

Part of the largest and fastest-growing international community in North America, **El Paso** (pop. 649,121) was originally settled because of its site at one of the safest crossings of the Rio Grande. It later grew into a vital way station on the transcontinental Butterfield Stage and Southern Pacific Railroad. As its name suggests, for most people El Paso is a place to pass through, but there are many things here for visitors to enjoy.

One of the most interesting aspects of El Paso is the border itself, which for years followed the Rio Grande (known as the Río Bravo in Mexico), whose frequent changes in course caused innumerable

The independent **El Paso Diablos** ($7; 915/755-2000) play baseball April–August at Cohen Stadium, north of I-10 via the US-54 "Patriot Freeway."

El Paso's hard-to-find **Concordia Cemetery** (it's just northwest of the I-10/US-54 junction) is the final resting place of John Wesley Hardin, the "Fastest Gun in the West" before he got killed in 1895.

bluebonnet,
state flower of Texas

For the first 35 miles east of El Paso, US-180 runs along the southern edge of gigantic Fort Bliss, which stretches north for 50 miles into New Mexico and is home to about 35,000 U.S. troops.

From 1858 to 1861, the legendary Butterfield Overland Mail ran between St. Louis and San Francisco by way of El Paso, carrying mail and passengers across the country in 24 days. Running twice a week in both directions, the Butterfield line had some 140 relay stations along the route, each supplied with a Concord stagecoach and a fresh team of horses.

problems for the two governments. Finally, in 1968, the river was run through a concrete channel so it could not change course. El Paso has at least three other unique claims to fame: It's the home of Tony Lama boots, which are available at significant discounts at four showrooms around town; the "World's Largest Harley-Davidson Dealership," Barnett's (8272 Gateway Blvd. E.; 800/453-1513), is along I-10; and the UTEP (University of Texas El Paso) campus, along I-10 west of town, has the only buildings in North America designed to look like Tibetan monasteries. College basketball fans may also know that in 1966 UTEP (then called Texas Western) became the first all-black team to win the NCAA championships, a story told in the book and film *Glory Road*.

Hidden away amidst El Paso's horizontal sprawl are the oldest Spanish colonial missions that still stand in what is now the United States. These three churches—Ysleta, Socorro, and San Elizario—stand along the well-signed "Mission Trail," southeast of downtown between the Rio Grande and I-10.

Places to eat in and around El Paso tend, not surprisingly, to specialize in Tex-Mex food. One unique stop for breakfast or lunch is at the very friendly **H&H Car Wash and Coffee Shop** (701 E. Yandell Ave.; 915/533-1144), just north of downtown, where you can enjoy delicious scrambled eggs and chorizo or *chile relleno* burritos while getting your car cleaned at the adjacent car wash. Another classic is **Forti's Mexican Elder** (321 Chelsea St.; 915/772-0066), east of downtown near the Paisano Avenue exit off I-10.

El Paso's finest place to stay is the grand old **Camino Real Hotel** ($99 and up; 101 S. El Paso St.; 915/534-3000), one of the classiest hotels anywhere, with a beautiful bar off the lobby. All the usual midrange chains are here too: There's a nice old-fashioned **Travelodge** ($50 and up; 6400 Montana Ave.; 915/772-4231), as well as a handy HI-approved youth hostel at the historic **Gardner Hotel** (311 E. Franklin St.; 915/532-3661), downtown.

Hueco Tanks State Historic Park

In the 100 miles of arid West Texas desert between El Paso and the Guadalupe Mountains, don't miss tiny **Hueco Tanks State Historic Park** (daily 8 AM–dusk; $5; 915/857-1135). Located on the eastern fringes of sprawling Fort Bliss, some 25 miles east of El Paso, then eight miles north on Hwy-2775, the 860-acre park was established to preserve the approximately 3,000 pictographs painted on the syenite basalt boulders. The "tanks" of the title are naturally formed rock basins, which collect rainwater and have made the site a natural stop for passing travelers, from prehistoric natives to the Butterfield stagecoach, which stopped here in the 1850s. Unfortunately, sometimes

The 70-mph section of US-180 east of El Paso is also signed as Camino Buena Suerte, the "Good Luck Highway."

Q: Why do they call it Texas?
A: Because it "Texas" so long to drive across.

Detour: Ciudad Juárez

Largest by far of the Mexican border cities, **Ciudad Juárez** (pop. 1.6 million, and growing fast) is a compelling, disturbing, exciting, and unforgettable place to visit, though the recent rash of drug-related violence (and an annual average of 2,500 murders) has made the city off-limits to most sensible travelers. The city sprawls through miles and miles of some of the worst pollution and direst poverty in Mexico, and if you feel brave a half-hour walk can take you very far away from the United States. From the El Paso side, don't drive; park and walk down Stanton Street from downtown and cross the bridge on foot. This crossing drops you at the head of Avenida Juárez, the main drag, lined by cantinas and nightclubs and stalls and stores selling everything from mass-produced "crafts" to knock-off designer goods and Cuban cigars, which will likely be confiscated if you try to bring them back into the United States.

About a half mile south of the border, at the junction with Avenida 16 de Septiembre, Avenida Juárez brings you to the heart of Juárez, where the very good historical museum, housed in the old customs building, and a large, often-packed cathedral give glimpses into the city's history and culture. Among the many restaurants and bars along Avenida Juárez, a couple to check out are the **Kentucky Club** (629 Avenida Benito Juárez), a 1930s-looking bar that could be used as a set for some Raymond Chandler underworld adventure. Legend has it that Marilyn Monroe got drunk here, celebrating her Juárez divorce from playwright Arthur Miller. Next door, **Martino's** is a very popular Mexican restaurant. Be warned, however, that many Juárez bars double as brothels—these tend to have giveaway names like "The Pink Lady."

Food and drink aside, the best thing about a trip south is the chance to enjoy some **Lucha Libre**—professional wrestling, Mexican style. Theatrical and impassioned bouts (about US$8 for a ringside seat) are often held on Sunday nights, in the large municipal auditorium near the cathedral, and there's been talk of someone establishing a *salón de fama* or Wrestling Hall of Fame.

the "historic" graffiti is overwhelmed by more contemporary spray-paint versions, but the site is pleasant enough, with a popular campground and excellent opportunities for bird-watching and rock climbing.

Some 35 miles east of the Hueco Tanks turnoff, the tiny highway town of **Cornudas** has a nice café—"Home of the World Famous Cornudas Burger"—and a row of false-fronted Wild West buildings.

road through Guadalupe Mountains National Park with El Capitan

Guadalupe Mountains National Park

One of the few un-hyped wonders of Texas, **Guadalupe Mountains National Park** covers the rugged peaks that rise along the New Mexico border, 110 miles east of El Paso. Formed as part of the same Capitan Reef of 250 million-year-old limestone as the great caverns of Carlsbad, the Guadalupe Mountains, a cool contrast to the surrounding desert, rise in sheer faces about 2,000 feet above the desert floor and offer the chance to experience many different and contrasting ecosystems side by side, within easy reach of the highway.

Even if you're not prepared to do any serious hiking—which is really the best way to experience the grandeur of the park or to see signs of the abundant wildlife (including mountain lions)—the quickest way to get a feel for the Guadalupes is to walk the half-mile **nature trail** that runs between the main visitors center (daily; $5 park entry fee; 915/828-3251) and the remains of a Butterfield stagecoach station, passing well-signed specimens of all the major desert flora. If you have more time, head to **McKittrick Canyon,** off US-62/180 in the northeast corner of the park. From the ranger station at the end of the road, a well-marked, well-maintained, and generally flat trail winds along a stream, through a green landscape that changes gradually from the cactus of the Chihuahuan Desert to the oaks, walnuts, and maples of the inner canyon. Rated by many as the most beautiful spot in Texas, it's best in spring, when the desert wildflowers bloom, or in autumn, when the bigleaf maple hardwoods turn color.

Along with New Mexico, El Paso and the Guadalupe Mountains area are in the mountain time zone. The rest of Texas is on central time.

If you're feeling fit, climb **Guadalupe Peak,** at 8,749 feet the highest point in Texas, via a very steep 8.5-mile round-trip trail from the main visitors center. Be aware that the change in elevation makes the mountains subject to serious weather, with great booming thunderstorms in late summer.

Roswell: UFO Central

Seventy-five miles or so north of Carlsbad, the New Mexico ranching town of Roswell (pop. 48,366) has become a catch-word for flying saucers, UFOs, extraterrestrials, and a complicated U.S. government cover-up of all the above. The cover-up is the one thing that's pretty much a given, since the Air Force has gone so far as to deny officially that anything ever happened in Roswell—which is equivalent to a confession, in the minds of UFO believers. Everything else about Roswell is, so to speak, up in the air.

The Roswell story goes something like this: In 1947, at the start of Cold War hysteria, something strange and metallic crashed into a field outside town, and the Army Air Corps (teams of tight-lipped operatives wearing special suits and dark glasses, no doubt) came and recovered it. Reports to the effect that a flying saucer had landed in Roswell appeared in the local paper, and then quickly spread around the globe, only to be denied by the government, which claimed the "flying saucers" were actually weather balloons.

Thirty-three years later, a retired military intelligence officer from the Roswell base sold a story to the *National Enquirer,* repeating details of the 1947 "flying saucer" crash and telling of his subsequent capture of extraterrestrial beings. This in turn spawned countless other stories, books, and videos, and spurred the growth of a battery of tourist attractions and

souvenir stores in and around Roswell. To learn more, stop at the **International UFO Museum and Research Center** ($5; 114 N. Main St.; 800/822-3545 or 505/625-9495), which fills an old movie theater in downtown Roswell. There are plans for a new museum several blocks north of the present location—across the street from the only UFO-themed McDonald's in the world.

Camping is available on a first-come, first-served basis at Pine Springs Campground, near the main visitors center, and at numerous sites in the backcountry.

Carlsbad Caverns National Park

Carved out of the solid limestone of Capitan Reef by eons of dripping water, the Carlsbad Caverns National Park contains over 110 miles of underground caves, some 1,500 feet across. A mile-long trail drops steeply from the large visitors center, or you can board an elevator and ride 750 feet straight down to the Big Room, where the floor area totals more than eight acres (daily; $6 for park entrance and self-guided tours, more for ranger guided tours;

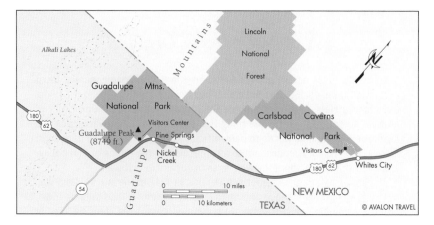

575/785-2232). After wandering among the countless stalactites, stalagmites, and other formations, you can chow down on cheeseburgers at a classic 1950s-style cafeteria. Everyone has to ride the elevator back to the surface.

The Big Room is only one of many cave formations protected at Carlsbad; some more delicate features can be found in the King's Palace, and the park also has many more exotic and hard-to-reach caves (like Spider Cave, which you have to explore on hands and knees, or Slaughter Canyon, which is 23 miles away). These other caves can be enjoyed (if that's the word . . .) on the many longer guided **tours** available ($7–20; 877/444-6777). These ranger-guided tours provide all the specialist caving gear (helmets, headlamps, knee pads, etc.) that you'll need if you want to explore some of the more delicate features of the caverns or clamber around through more-confined reaches of the caves.

the Dome Room in Carlsbad Caverns National Park

Lubbock: Panhandle Music Mecca

The largest city in northwest Texas, Lubbock (pop. 229,573) is a busy agricultural center, best known for having given the world Buddy Holly, whose songs ("Peggy Sue," "That'll Be The Day," "Rave On") helped pave the way for rock 'n' roll. Music fans make the trip downtown to pay homage at the statue of Buddy and to learn about his brief but influential life in the **Buddy**

Holly Center, just west of I-27, off 19th Street (Tues.–Sat. 10 AM–5 PM, Sun. 1–5 PM; $5; 1801 Crickets Ave.; 806/775-3560).

Buddy Holly's sudden, tragic death at age 22 in a 1959 plane crash also took the lives of fellow American rock and roll pioneers Ritchie Valens and J. P. "The Big Bopper" Richardson, and inspired the Don McLean song "American Pie," remembering "The Day the Music Died." Holly is buried near the entrance of Lubbock Cemetery, at the east end of 31st Street (his grave stone uses the "real" spelling of his family name, "Buddy Holley"). The Buddy Holly Center also houses a small "Hall of Fame," which tells about the lives and times of Lubbock's other musical boys and girls made good, including Roy Orbison, Waylon Jennings, Tanya Tucker, and Joe Ely.

Even if you just opt for the main cavern, be aware that the trail down to the Big Room closes early in the afternoon (usually around 3 PM) so that visitors don't interrupt the increasingly popular spectacle of the **Bat Flight,** in which hundreds of thousands of Mexican freetail bats swirl out of the caverns at sunset. Every summer evening (usually around 7 PM, except in winter when the bats have migrated to Mexico), rangers give a brief free talk about bats—proselytizing about how really great and harmless they are—while waiting for them to set off into the night. For more details, call 575/785-3012.

The nearest places to stay and eat are at **White's City and Water Park** (575/785-2291 or 800/228-3767), a historic complex of motels, RV park, restaurants, pinball arcades, and souvenir shops along Hwy-180 at the turnoff to the park.

Carlsbad

Twenty miles or so northeast of the Carlsbad Caverns, the town of **Carlsbad** (pop. 26,138) makes its living from the 750,000 tourists who visit the caves every year. Lining Canal Street (a.k.a. US-180, the National Parks Highway), the main road through Carlsbad, you'll find most national motel chains and funkier local counterparts like the **Stagecoach Inn** (around $50 and up; 1819 S. Canal St.; 575/887-1148). There's also one very good Mexican restaurant,

As part of a federal program known as WIPP—the **Waste Isolation Pilot Plant**—the 250 million-year-old salt beds east of Carlsbad have been adapted into a contentious disposal site for some of the nation's nuclear waste. You can't visit the plant itself, 2,150 feet below the desert, but there is a small museum describing the project at the WIPP Information Center in Carlsbad (4021 National Parks Hwy.; 800/336-WIPP).

The Llano Estacado town of Gail and the county (Borden) are named in memory of pioneer surveyor and newspaper editor Gail Borden, who is perhaps best known as the inventor of condensed milk and founder of Borden Foods.

the **Casa de Cortez** (506 S. Canal St.; 575/885-4747), a plain brown-brick building where locals come for heaping helpings of *frijoles refritos* and *chiles rellenos;* there is no booze and no credit cards are accepted, but try the great fresh *sopapillas.*

Apart from the caverns, the one other wonderful thing to see in the Carlsbad area is the **Living Desert State Park** (daily; $5; 575/887-5516), four miles northwest off US-285, which shows off the plant and animal life of the arid Chihuahuan Desert region. Foxes, wolves, hawks, and eagles are kept in re-creations of their natural environments and can be seen along a 1.5-mile nature trail.

US-180: The Llano Estacado

From Carlsbad, US-180 crosses the Pecos River, then snakes across the barren **Llano Estacado** (Staked Plains), which covers most of eastern New Mexico and the Texas Panhandle. Supposedly named by early explorers who drove wooden stakes into the ground to mark their way, the Llano Estacado area is pretty much the same on both sides of the border—flat, dry, and mostly devoid of settlement. For eastbound travelers, this is the place where oil first becomes noticeably important—pumpjacks can be seen pumping away from here all the way to Alabama.

This is also cowboy country, thanks to the extensive pastures irrigated by water pumped up from aquifers deep underground. For travelers, however, the dominant image is of land stretching out far and wide: mile after mile after mile of endless flat cotton fields, interrupted every now and then by brilliant green alfalfa fields and a few surprisingly large towns, like **Hobbs,** New Mexico (pop. 34,122). Right on the border, its main street lined by various drilling supply companies and huge piles of old pipe. Because the plains get a huge amount of summer sunshine, which generates a lot of thermal lift, this part of the world is ideal for gliding, which is why the **Soaring Society of America** (575/392-1177) is located here.

The Texas part of the drive is dotted with towns like **Lamesa** (pop. 9,422; pronounced "la-MEE-sa"), which after the miles of open, red-earth prairie around it can seem like a bustling hive of activity. Lamesa also has all the All-American makings of a location from the high-school-football book, movie, and TV show *Friday Night Lights:* sports-mad families and an intact old Dairy Queen Drive-in, right on the main drag (512 N. 4th St.; 806/872-8155). To make a perfect all-American adventure, add in the smoky barbecue at **K-Bob's Steakhouse,** on the north side of town (2200 US-87/Lubbock Hwy.; 806/872-6531), and the open-air movies at the **Sky-Vue Drive In,** on US-87 a mile south of town ($5; 806/872-7004). (The Sky-Vue is said to be the site of Buddy Holly's first performance outside his native Lubbock.)

At the town of **Anson,** US-180 crosses US-83, **The Road to Nowhere** (see page 217). That road trip is described on pages 174–231.

Albany

Albany (pop. 2,034), one of the more interesting-looking towns in this part of Texas, started as a stagecoach stop on the Butterfield Overland Mail in 1854. It's still a tiny place, but it has a lively feel, the oldest county courthouse in the state, and, more surprisingly, a small but intriguing **Old Jail Art Center** (closed Mon.; free; 201 S. 2nd St.; 325/762-2269) in the Old City Jail. A big surprise in the middle of the ranch lands, the museum contains an outstanding permanent collection of art by Modigliani, Picasso, and others, and also displays Chinese ceramics from the Tang and Ming dynasties. If you're here the last two full weekends in June, make plans to see a production of "The Longest-Running Outdoor Musical," the ***Fort Griffin Fandangle*** (tickets around $15; 325/762-3838), which began as a school play in 1938 and has grown to involve a cast of some 300, mostly local performers.

Coming from the west, US-80/180 makes one last small-town stop in **Weatherford** (pop. 25,250), where an opulent old courthouse anchors a lively town square. For a last taste of small town Americana before or after a trip across Dallas, stop for a breakfast, or a bite of chicken-fried steak, or just a cup of coffee at the **Weatherford Downtown Café,** a block south of the square (101 W. Church St.; 817/594-8717).

I-20: Sweetwater and Cisco

If you've decided to take the high-speed route along I-20, midway across Texas you'll pass **Sweetwater** (pop. 10,906), where, every March during the **Jaycees Rattlesnake Round-Up,** townspeople get together and collect hundreds of rattlers from the surrounding ranch lands, winning prizes for the biggest, shortest, and most snakes handed in. The town, 25 miles or so west of Abilene, also has shops selling all manner of rattlesnake-related souvenirs, and any time of year, Sweetwater—which was first settled in the 1850s and now earns its livelihood mining gypsum for use in wallboard—is worth a stop for some of the best fried chicken in West Texas, at **Allen Family Style Meals** (lunch and dinner Tues.–Sat.; 1301 E. Broadway; 325/235-2060), along old US-80.

Northwest of Fort Worth, 22 miles south of Wichita Falls, writer Larry McMurtry has been turning his hometown of **Archer City** (pop. 1,834) into the world's largest used-book store. Housed in a number of downtown buildings, many of which are featured in McMurtry's *The Last Picture Show* and other works, his **Booked Up** bookstore (closed Sun.; 940/574-2511) has more than 400,000 titles, mostly rare and out-of-print editions.

Another highlight of the drive west of Dallas is **Snyder** (pop. 12,195), where a life-sized statue of an albino buffalo stands on the courthouse square.

The I-20 town of **Cisco** (pop. 3,899), 45 miles east of Abilene, is where **Conrad Hilton** bought and ran his first hotel, the Mobley, in 1919; the hotel is now the chamber of commerce office, and a couple of rooms have been restored to their circa-1919 appearance.

East of Cisco, the town of **Eastland** (pop. 3,960) has two world-class oddities. The middle entrance to the county courthouse displays the embalmed body of "Old Rip" the horny toad, who survived 30 years embedded in the cornerstone of the old courthouse before supposedly being discovered, alive, when the building was being torn down. A few blocks away, the post office (411 W. Main St.) contains a huge stamp-themed mural made entirely of 11,217 postage stamps, created over a seven-year period by former postmistress Marene Johnson. (A postcard of the mural is available.)

Old US-80 Across Fort Worth and Dallas

From Weatherford and the west, it's easiest to approach Fort Worth and Dallas via I-20 and I-30, which separate west of the city. From I-30, old US-80 enters Fort Worth on Camp Bowie Boulevard, running right past the museums of the Cultural District to the heart of downtown. East of Fort Worth, the older roads disappear under the modern freeways, so hop onto I-30 and beeline past Arlington, where the stadiums for the Texas Rangers and Dallas Cowboys stand around the Six Flags over Texas amusement park before reaching Dallas.

The salt deposits under **Grand Saline,** 60 miles east of Dallas, are estimated to be over 20,000 feet thick and nearly a mile and a half across, enough to supply the world's needs for the next 20,000 years.

The old road between Fort Worth and Dallas, now signed as Hwy-180, approaches downtown Dallas on Commerce Street, passing the notorious Texas School Book Depository before heading down Main Street. East of Dallas, the old main road passes through Deep Ellum neighborhood before leaving town past the historic Cotton Bowl football stadium, on the grounds of the Texas State Fair (held here in October).

Kilgore: Oil!

The pine-covered, red-earth hills of East Texas are covered with creaking old pumpjacks, still sucking up the crude oil that has kept the region economically afloat since the 1930s. The oil business here has gone through numerous booms and busts since it gushed into existence in December 1930 at a well outside **Kilgore** (pop. 12,975), on the south side of I-20, 10 miles southwest of Longview via US-259. This comparatively small and quiet oil town has street lamps disguised as oil rigs and a set of 100-foot-tall derricks standing along the railroad tracks in memory of the "World's Richest Acre," a plot of downtown land that produced over 2.5 million barrels of oil through the 1960s. The site was so productive and so valuable that one of the wells was drilled through the terrazzo floor of a local bank, and over a thousand derricks once loomed over the downtown area.

The history of the local petroleum industry is recounted in entertaining detail at the **East Texas Oil Museum** (closed Mon.; $5; 903/983-8295) on the campus of Kilgore College, on Ross Street off US-259. The museum includes displays of drilling equipment and old gas stations, plus a simulated "elevator ride" a mile deep into the earth to show off the oil-bearing geology. Also on the Kilgore College campus, in the Physical Education Complex, is a small free museum devoted to the **Kilgore Rangerettes** (1100 Broadway; 903/983-8265), a highly trained precision drill and dance cheerleading team that performs at college and professional football games.

South of I-20, the city of **Tyler** grows thousands and thousands of roses, including the famous yellow ones.

Back on US-80, well north of the I-20 freeway, the booming oil-fueled city of **Longview** (pop. 80,455) holds one of the best places to eat in this part of East Texas: New Orleans-style Creole-spiced **Johnny Cace's Seafood** (closed Mon.; 1501 E. Marshall Rd.; 903/753-7691), east of downtown.

Marshall and Jefferson

North of I-20 some 25 miles west of the Louisiana state line, **Marshall** (pop. 23,523) is one of the older towns in Texas, and once among its wealthiest.

Dallas and Fort Worth

D-25   The Gateway to Dallas, Texas

The Triple Underpass

Like warring branches of an extended family, Dallas and Fort Worth are inseparable arch-rivals. Both towns lay fair claim to being capitals of their respective industries: Fort Worth (pop. 741,206) calls itself "Cowtown" but has a surprisingly sophisticated range of cultural centers and feels like an altogether more "Texan" place; it was founded during the heyday of the Chisholm Trail and still retains much of its Wild West past. Meanwhile, Dallas (pop. 1,197,816), which boomed after the discovery of oil in east Texas during the 1930s, plays the role of nouveau riche to the nth degree, home to luxury department store Neiman Marcus (not to mention the eponymous 1980s TV soap opera).

In terms of things to see and do, Fort Worth holds the winning hand. The wonderful **Kimbell Art Museum** (closed Mon.; free; 3333 Camp Bowie Blvd.; 817/332-8451) is one of the most perfectly beautiful modern buildings on the planet, designed as a series of vaulted galleries by Louis Kahn. This small museum, which has an impressive collection of pre-Columbian art and some notable post-Impressionist paintings, stands at the heart of the Fort Worth Cultural District, which encompasses another wonderful work of architecture, the Tadao Ando–designed **Modern Art Museum of Fort Worth** (closed Mon.; $10; 3200 Darnell St.; 817/738-9215), and, across the street, the **Amon Carter Museum** (closed Mon.; free; 3501 Camp Bowie Blvd.; 817/738-1933), displaying the country's finest collection of Wild West and other American art.

Two miles north of downtown Fort Worth, head to the Stockyards, on Main and Exchange Streets (817/624-4741). For a taste of how Texas used to be, spend some time wandering these two short blocks of turn-of-the-20th-century buildings, stretching west from the still-busy Fort Worth Stockyards and housing some of the city's most popular places to eat, drink, and be merry. After dark, check out **Billy Bob's Texas** ($12 and up; 817/624-7117), the "World's Largest Honky-Tonk," which has live music almost every night, often featuring famous names such as Willie Nelson, Merle Haggard, and Ted Nugent.

Farther out on the north side of Fort Worth is the U.S. government's Bureau of Engraving and Printing's **Western Currency Facility** (daily; 9000 Blue Mound Rd.; 817/231-4000), where you can see billions of dollars being printed as you walk along an enclosed walkway suspended over the production floor. Be sure to factor in time needed to get through security for this tour.

In Dallas, sightseers head to **The Sixth Floor Museum at Dealey Plaza** in the **Texas School Book Depository** (daily; $14; 411 Elm St.; 214/747-6660), on the west side of downtown. Besides the gruesome novelty value of looking out from the very same place where Lee Harvey Oswald shot (or didn't shoot . . .) President John F. Kennedy on November 22, 1963, this extensive museum describes the historical context and discusses the myriad conspiracy theories. Amidst the forest of skyscrapers downtown, the **Dallas Museum of Art** (closed Mon.; $10; 1717 N. Harwood St.; 214/922-1200) and the elegant **Nasher Sculpture Center** (closed Mon.; $10; 2001 Flora St.; 214/242-5100) are soothing refuges from all the Texas-sized commerce.

In between Dallas and Fort Worth, the **Texas Rangers** (817/273-5222) play at retro-modern Rangers Ballpark, off I-30 at the Ballpark Way exit in Arlington. Games are broadcast on **103.3 ESPN.**

Practicalities

Linked (or is it divided?) by a trio of fast freeways (I-20, I-30, and Hwy-183), Dallas and Fort Worth lie some 25 miles or so apart across the plains of northeast Texas. Each city is circled by its own ring road, and two north–south freeways (I-35W through Fort Worth and I-35E through downtown Dallas) complete the high-speed network.

Food in Fort Worth, not surprisingly, tends to the beefy. **Cattlemen's Steak House,** in the historic Stockyards (2458 N. Main St.; 817/624-3945), has steaks of all cuts and sizes, plus barbecue and some seafood. **Joe T. Garcia's** (cash only; 2201 N. Commerce St.; 817/626-4356) may or may not be the world's biggest Tex-Mex restaurant, but it sure can feel like it. Finally, the very friendly (and often busy) **Paris Coffee Shop** (closed Sun.; 700 W. Magnolia; 817/335-2041) has great breakfasts, fried chicken, and delicious fresh fruit pies.

In Dallas, east of the I-35E Central Expressway from downtown, "Deep Ellum" is a slightly scruffy-looking, post-industrial district of boutiques, restaurants, and nightclubs and biker bars like **Reno's Chop Shop,** a block north of Elm Street (210 N. Crowdus St.; 214/742-1200). For a stylish place to stay, **The Adolphus Hotel** ($152 and up; 1321 Commerce St.; 214/742-8200) is a historic four-star downtown hotel, built in 1912 by beer magnate Adolphus Busch.

In Fort Worth, the newly renovated **Sheraton** ($170 and up; 1701 Commerce St.; 800/325-3535 or 817/335-7000) is centrally located, just across from the convention center and the magical Fort Worth Water Gardens. Bonnie and Clyde (both of whom grew up and are buried in Dallas, in different cemeteries) stayed in the **Stockyards Hotel** ($190 and up; 109 E. Exchange Ave.; 817/625-6427), a turn-of-the-20th-century hotel that has been restored and redecorated according to various themes, including the Depression-era bank robbers. The downstairs bar is fun, too: It has saddles instead of bar stools.

For maps and more extensive information, contact the visitors centers in **Dallas** (800/232-5527 or 214/571-1000) or **Fort Worth** (800/433-5747 or 817/336-8791).

Now a fairly quiet place, in its early years Marshall was the commercial capital of the East Texas cotton country, and during the Civil War two local residences served as the Confederate capital—of Missouri. This anomaly, along with general regional history, is chronicled in the **Harrison County Historical Society Museum** (Wed.–Fri. only; $2; 903/935-8417), housed in the supremely ornate, yellow Old Harrison County Courthouse on Peter Whetstone Square.

If you have the time and inclination to get a more palpable sense of the varied culture and history of East Texas, take US-59 15 miles or so north of Marshall to **Jefferson** (pop. 2,106), an almost perfectly preserved bayou town that looks much as it did during the 1870s when, with a population of nearly 7,300, it was the busiest inland port west of the Mississippi. Among the most prominent of the hundreds of historic structures here is the 1858 **Excelsior House** (around $100 and up; 211 W. Austin St.; 903/665-2513 or 800/490-7270); across the street, you can tour Jay Gould's private railroad car, the Atalanta, or simply explore the many good antiques shops, cafés, and restaurants.

Back on the main road, just before the Louisiana border, the stretch of old US-80 that runs parallel to I-20 is home to the ever-welcoming **New Waskom Café** (230 E. Texas Ave.; 903/687-3113), open weekdays for breakfast and lunch since the 1920s.

LOUISIANA

Northern Louisiana, which covers some 200 miles of forested, rolling hills between Texas and Mississippi, is a far cry from the Cajun fun of the southern half of the state. A Baptist-dominated "Bible Belt" heartland, it's also a very diverse place—part heavily industrial, part poor rural backwater, with a mix of people and products that encapsulates its transitional position between the agricultural Deep South and the petrochemical plants of Texas.

The main city here is the oil town of **Shreveport,** which has recently become a prime place for gamblers, with flashy casinos lining the riverfront. However, you'll mostly find small towns ranging from **Gibsland** (where Bonnie and Clyde met their doom) to the college town of **Ruston** (home to Louisiana Tech and Grambling Universities).

Shreveport and Bossier City

Shreveport is named in honor of Capt. Henry Shreve, who in the 1830s cleared the Red River of a 165-mile-long logjam known as the Great Raft that had blocked navigation. He then "bought" the land from native Caddo Indians.

A King Cotton town that thrived in the antebellum years and survived the war physically, though not economically, unscathed, **Shreveport** (pop. 199,311) is now a busy industrial city rising on the west bank of the Red River. Along with its ugly stepbrother, **Bossier City** (pop. 61,315; pronounced "BO-zyur") across the river, Shreveport is a center of the Louisiana oil business, which is small only when compared to that of Texas and is still hugely important. Also, the cities emerged in recent years as two of the hot spots of Louisiana's nascent gambling industry, with a line of major resort-casinos along the riverfront attracting people from all over the tri-state "Ark-La-Tex" region—including the lively **Horseshoe,** a 25-story Harrah's hotel (711 Horseshoe Blvd.; 800/789-0711) and four-story faux riverboat floating in a shallow pond on the Bossier City side.

Downtown Shreveport is the usual mix of turn-of-the-20th-century brick buildings and boarded-up shopfronts, loomed over by a solitary 10-story glass office tower, with a handful of interesting structures surviving near the riverfront.

The nicest part of town is the leafy Highland Historic District, stretching south from the end of Market Street, south of I-20 between the river and the I-49 freeway. This is where you'll find the grand old houses of the landed gentry, many of which look like they belong in *Gone With the Wind,* despite the fact that almost all of them date from the 20th century. The Highland district also holds a couple of Shreveport's better places to eat: the homey **Strawn's Eat Shop,** serving yummy hash browns, biscuits, fried chicken, and seasonal strawberry pies (125 Kings Hwy.; 318/868-0634), and the comparatively upscale **Columbia Cafe** (3030 Creswell Ave.; 318/425-3862), serving eggs benedict brunches and bistro-style pasta dishes.

All the usual hotel and motel chains line I-20.

Gibsland: Bonnie and Clyde

East of Shreveport, the old US-80 highway winds through dozens of somnolent little towns, following the rolling land while crisscrossing back and forth under the high-speed I-20 freeway. After passing the pawn shops and girlie bars outside Barksdale Air Force Base, the route parallels railroad tracks along the remains of a historic log turnpike, built in the 1870s to provide all-weather passage across the muddy bogs and bayous.

Apart from the usual barrage of roadside businesses, there's not a lot to stop for until you reach the tiny town of **Gibsland** (pop. 979), just south of I-20, 45 miles east of Shreveport. This pleasantly unremarkable little hamlet has one unique claim to fame: It was here, in 1934, that the notorious Depression-era criminals Clyde Barrow and Bonnie Parker were ambushed and killed by a posse of police. A small,

North of Shreveport on Hwy-1, **Oil City** has one of the region's better history museums, housed inside the old railroad depot and displaying a wonderful collection of old postcards.

The independent **Shreveport-Bossier Captains,** formerly known as the Shreveport Sports ($5; 318/636-5555), play Central League baseball at Fair Grounds Field (2901 Pershing Blvd.).

From 1948 to 1969 and again from 1973 to 1987, Shreveport and Bossier City hosted the *Louisiana Hayride,* a country-western radio program (and later television show) on which Hank Williams and Elvis Presley both started their careers. The same sort of music can still be heard on **KWKH 94.5 FM** or **1130 AM,** your best bet for late-night bluegrass in northwest Louisiana.

Clyde and Bonnie, c. 1933

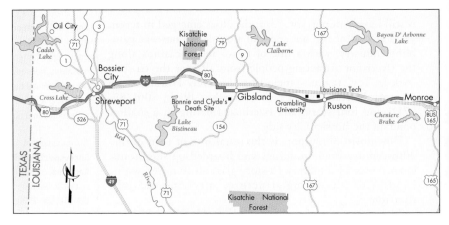

town-run **Bonnie and Clyde Ambush Museum** and gift shop (closed Wed.; $7; 2419 Main St.; 318/843-1934) tells their story and sells gruesome postcards of their bullet-riddled bodies, while every May locals dress up for the Bonnie and Clyde Festival and stage gun battles and car chases—more for

cops-and-robbers fun than out of any real dedication to historical accuracy.

A battered stone marker, eight miles south of Gibsland along Hwy-154, stands on the site where the desperate duo were riddled with bullets by Texas and Louisiana law enforcement officers. The late-1960s Arthur Penn movie *Bonnie and Clyde* enveloped him in Hollywood glamour, but as far as most accounts describe him, the real-life Clyde was a nasty, twisted, cold-blooded murderer, nothing like the romantic hero played by Warren Beatty. Bonnie, who like Clyde grew up desperately poor, may or may not have ever shot anyone, and she definitely was a romantic figure; at her funeral, the newspapers of Dallas donated the most impressive floral tribute, and some 20,000 people lined the streets to say farewell.

Ruston and Monroe

Roughly halfway across the state, **Ruston** (pop. 21,859) calls itself the "Peach Capital" but is best known for two major colleges: Louisiana Tech (where local boy Terry Bradshaw played college football) and smaller Grambling University, one of the nation's top historically African American schools, three miles west in the town of Grambling (pop. 4,949), just south of I-20.

Considering that it is one of the largest towns in northern Louisiana, **Monroe** (pop. 48,815) feels strangely abandoned, even though the downtown area has a number of classic commercial buildings dating from the period be-

magnolia, the state flower of
Louisiana and of Mississippi

One of the oldest, largest,
and most significant
concentrations of archaeological
remains in North America has
been protected as **Poverty Point
National Monument** ($2;
888/926-5462 or 318/926-5492),
18 miles north of I-20 off Hwy-17
near **Epps,** Louisiana. These
3,000-year-old burial mounds
are jointly managed by federal
and state authorities.

tween the two World Wars, and Victorian-era warehouses and hundreds of ancient-looking shotgun shacks line the railroad tracks and US-80. Celtics
basketball star Bill Russell, in 2011 awarded the Presidential Medal of
Freedom winner for his role in desegregating professional sports, was born in
Monroe, as was Black Panther Huey Newton.

Apart from its photogenic architecture and fading roadside signs, Monroe
doesn't really offer much reason to stop, though the gorgeous greenery of the
Louisiana Purchase Gardens and Zoo (daily; $5; 1405 Bernstein Park Rd.;
318/329-2400), south of I-20 off US-165, makes it a great place to stretch your
legs, ride a steam train, or go for a boat ride (Mar.–Oct.; $3) among the moss-
draped oaks and cypress trees.

East of Monroe, it's an hour's drive across the bayous before you reach the
fascinating city of Vicksburg, across the Mississippi River.

MISSISSIPPI

US-80, which for much of the way has been replaced by the I-20 freeway, cuts
across the middle of Mississippi, passing through its three largest cities—
Meridian, Jackson, and **Vicksburg**—whose small sizes show how rural and

diffuse the state still is. Only Jackson, the capital and by far the biggest city in the state, is anything like an urban center, with a couple of "skyscrapers" and nearly 200,000 people. Mostly what you see along this stretch is small farms and Civil War battlefields, the most extensive and important of which rises above the Mississippi River in Vicksburg.

The Mississippi River town of **Vicksburg** marks the junction with **The Great River Road** (see page 291). That route is covered in full detail on pages 232–309.

Clinton and the Natchez Trace

The onetime Choctaw Indian agency of **Clinton** (pop. 25,216), north of I-20 10 miles west of Jackson, was renamed in 1828 in honor of New York governor DeWitt Clinton, who oversaw construction of the Erie Canal. Now a small cotton-growing and shipping center, with a few blocks of "olde towne" around the Baptist-run Mississippi College along Leake and Jefferson Streets, in its early years Clinton sat on the notorious Natchez Trace, now followed by the blissfully pleasant **Natchez Trace Parkway,** which runs southwest to Port Gibson (see *The Great River Road* chapter) and northeast all the way to Nashville.

Though it survived the Civil War relatively unscathed, Clinton later saw some of the worst Reconstruction-era race riots in the state, with an estimated 50 unarmed blacks killed during a single rampage in 1875. More recently, Clinton has also suffered through the painful fallout of the MCI/WorldCom scandal: The multinational telecom company had its world headquarters here, and CEO Bernie Ebbers, convicted in 2005 of overseeing a multibillion-dollar fraud, was a Mississippi College graduate.

Jackson

Spreading west from the banks of the Pearl River, **Jackson** (pop. 173,514) was established as state capital in 1822. Named for Andrew Jackson, hero of the Battle of New Orleans during the War of 1812 and later president of the United States, it was destroyed during the Civil War but is now Mississippi's political and commercial heart and its biggest city—though you wouldn't know it by the somnolent look of the place.

The very attractive Greek Revival **Old State Capitol,** built in 1839 and used until 1903, rises at the center of town at State and Capitol Streets and is open for free self-guided tours of the building (closed Mon.; 601/576-6920) and the well-pre-

The tiny town of **Vaughan,** 30 miles north of Jackson via the I-55 freeway, was the site of the crash that killed legendary train engineer John Luther "Casey" Jones. A small museum, a mile east of I-55 exit 133, has exhibits on Casey and the history of railroading in the South.

the Old State Capitol building in Jackson

sented historical exhibits that fill it. Substantial floor space is given over to the 20th century, including a thoughtful (and thought-provoking) examination of the civil rights movement. The few other fine old antebellum buildings—under a dozen altogether—that survive around Jackson were used by Union forces and were thus spared destruction. These include the art-filled **Governor's Mansion** (Tues.–Fri. 9:30–11 AM; free; 300 E. Capitol St.; 601/359-6421), a short walk east of the old capitol, and **The Oaks House Museum** (closed Sun.–Mon.; $5; 823 N. Jefferson St.; 601/353-9339), in which General Sherman lived. Restored to prewar splendor,

Double A affiliate of the Atlanta Braves, the Mississippi Braves (601/932-8788) play baseball in Pearl, just east of Jackson.

Father of Country Music

The collision of Mississippi's rural past with the early stages of industrial development was embodied in the life and work of Meridian's favorite son, Jimmie Rodgers, whose original mixing of black Delta blues and white Appalachian folk songs earned him the title Father of Country Music. What Elvis Presley was to the 1950s, Rodgers was to the previous generation. Born in Meridian on September 8, 1897, Rodgers worked briefly on the railroad, lost his job after coming down with tuberculosis, then became the original overnight success. After he was discovered by an RCA talent scout in 1927, Rodgers's first record, "Sleep, Baby, Sleep," sold over a million copies. For the next five years he called himself the "Singing Brakeman" and was the world's best-selling recording artist. Rodgers's life and legend are honored in the small **Jimmie Rodgers Museum** (Tues.–Sat. 10 AM–4 PM, Sun. 1–5 PM; $8; 1725 Jimmie Rodgers Dr.; 601/485-1808) in Highland Park, well signed two miles northwest of downtown. It con-

tains all manner of odd Rodgers-related memorabilia, plus his boots and his custom Martin guitar. Jimmie Rodgers died of tuberculosis in May 1933 and is buried alongside his wife in Oak Grove Cemetery, two miles south of Meridian. On the centenary of Rodgers's birth, an excellent tribute album of his songs was recorded by the likes of Bono, Bob Dylan, Jerry Garcia, and Willie Nelson, all of whom rated Rodgers as a major influence on their music.

How times change, Mississippi style: Jackson's main streets have been renamed to honor civil rights movement martyrs Martin Luther King Jr. and Medgar Evers.

After burning Jackson to the ground during the Civil War, Gen. Ulysses S. Grant is said to have coined the expression "War is Hell."

The Oaks is furnished with period antiques and, surprisingly for the South, a sofa from Abraham Lincoln's law office.

On the south side of downtown Jackson, the new home of the **Mississippi Museum of Art** (closed Mon.; $5; 380 S. Lamar St.; 601/960-1515) has established an international reputation as one of the top museums in the USA.

Away from downtown, the main attraction is the **Mississippi Agriculture and Forestry Museum** (closed Sun.; $5; 601/432-4500), a 40-acre complex on Lakeland Drive northeast of downtown, off I-55 exit 98B. Despite the dull name, it's a hugely engaging and entertaining place, with a composite "Crossroads Town" made up of authentic buildings, including a general store, filling station, and sawmill brought here from all over Mississippi.

For more local flavor, head to the north side of Jackson east of US-51/State Street, where the home of Pulitzer Prize–winning writer Eudora Welty (1909–2001) is now open as an atmospheric museum of her life and work. For more than 76 years, she lived and worked here, and you can visit the **Eudora Welty House** (Tues.–Fri. only; $5; 1119 Pinehurst St.; 601/353-7762).

For food and drink, a good place to get a taste of Jackson is the **Elite Restaurant** (141 E. Capitol St.; 601/352-5606) near the Mississippi Museum of Art, a friendly, old-timey local favorite serving up a wide range of inexpensive but great-tasting food. For fried catfish (the Mississippi state dish), good beer, and great live music, make your way to **Hal & Mal's** (closed Sun.; 200 S. Commerce St.; 601/948-0888), in an old warehouse perched along the abandoned railroad tracks above the Pascagoula Street underpass.

Places to stay in Jackson tend to be either rough-but-cheap highway motels lining old US-80 or anodyne chains along the I-20 and I-55 Interstate frontages. One grand exception is the 1920s beaux arts classicism of the **King Edward Hotel,** now operated as a Hilton Garden Inn (around $150 and up; 235 W. Capitol St.; 877/STAY-HGI or 601/353-5464). After nearly 40 years of neglect, the hotel has been reborn, with a great bar, good food, and oodles of ambience. For complete information, or details on driving the nearby Natchez Trace Parkway (see *The Great River Road* chapter), contact the **visitors bureau** (111 E. Capitol St.; 601/960-1891 or 800/354-7695).

Meridian

Meridian's former Public Library now houses the Meridian Museum of Art.

At the junction of US-80, I-20, and I-59, the main route to and from New Orleans, modern **Meridian** (pop. 41,148) is a medium-sized industrial center that started from rubble in the aftermath of the Civil War, and owes its existence to strategic geography: After the native Choctaw Indians were removed in 1831, Meridian became a railroad junction and served as a Confederate stronghold until Sherman destroyed it in February 1864, saying afterward, "Meridian with its depots, storehouses, arsenals, hospitals, offices, hotels, and cantonments no longer exists." Despite this, the town recovered with a vengeance, and from the 1890s until the 1930s Meridian was the largest and most prosperous city in this very poor state, as shown by the many fine Edwardian and art deco buildings that still stand (in varying stages of repair) around the leafy and clean downtown area.

Roadside Shrines

Among the many pleasures of traveling around rural America is the likelihood of coming upon a striking monument in the middle of nowhere. Winding back roads that for miles and miles have run quietly through woodlands or along cotton fields will be suddenly marked by giant crosses or a pylon of hand-lettered signs. In the Midwest, you'll often see a fiberglass dinosaur or other giant creature constructed by some well-intentioned civic organization and intended to draw highway traffic to local businesses. In the South, however, what you see are intensely personal creations, built by eccentric and often outcast individuals (99 percent of them men), and instead of acting as an advertising gimmick, they usually spout chapter and verse of scripture, warning about the impending Apocalypse or the inevitable coming of Judgment Day.

Among the Deep South roadside shrines, don't miss the one that completely covers the cinderblock and plywood shell of **Margaret's Grocery** (4535 N. Washington St.; 601/638-1163), along Business US-61 on the north side of Vicksburg, Mississippi. At a glance, the assemblage of huge hand-lettered signs

Margaret's Grocery, north of Vicksburg

Two of Meridian's most intriguing stops are two miles northwest of downtown, in **Highland Park** on 41st Avenue at State Boulevard/Highland Park Drive. First is the **Dentzel Carousel** (daily in June and July, Sat.–Sun. only the rest of the year, 1–5 PM; $0.50), a cheerful and historic wooden merry-go-round manufactured in 1896 by Gustav Dentzel of Philadelphia, Pennsylvania, for the 1904 St. Louis Exposition and later sold to the City of Meridian, preserved in its original condition. Nearby is the **Jimmie Rodgers Museum** (Tues.–Sat. 10 AM–4 PM, Sun. 1–5 PM; $8; 1725 Jimmie Rodgers Dr.; 601/485-1808).

The incidents recounted in the film *Mississippi Burning* (the murders of civil rights activists by Ku Klux Klan members in June 1964) took place in the small town of **Philadelphia,** 30 miles northwest of Meridian.

Another offbeat but interesting Meridian "attraction" is the gravesite of the "King and Queen of the Gypsies," Emil and Kelly Mitchell, whose 1915 plot in Rose Hill Cemetery (west of downtown on 40th Avenue between 8th and Davis Streets) is a place of pilgrimage for Gypsies from all over atop various red-and-white constructions resembles a fanatical Legoland, but the biblically inspired injunctions are worth at least a pause. Hurry, though: Owner Margaret died in 2010, and her preacher husband Reverend Dennis moved into sheltered housing, so their creation may well fade away, fast.

The best known of these "Gardens of Revelation," as scholar John Beardsley has called them in his excellent book of the same name, is Howard Finster's **Paradise Garden** (Sat.–Sun. 10 AM–5 PM; donations; 706/859-1452), near Summerville in the Appalachian foothills of northwest Georgia. Famous for his primitivist paintings, which appeared on album covers by rock bands like R.E.M. and Talking Heads, Finster (who died in 2001) created a series of Gaudí-esque shrines, embedding seashells, bits of tile, and old car parts into concrete forms. Only two hours from Atlanta, the Paradise Garden is now one of the more popular attractions in the area. To get there, make your way to Summerville, then head north on US-27 for three miles to Pennville. At Howard Finster's Paradise Garden, pictures of Henry Ford, Hubert Humphrey, and Hank Williams are arrayed alongside dozens of signs quoting scripture, but the spirit of the place is best summed up by Finster's own verse: *"I built this park of broken pieces / to try to mend a broken world of people / who are traveling their last road."*

These roadside shrines are by no means limited to states south of the 35th parallel. More northerly states have their share as well, including two of the most intense: the **Garden of Eden** in Lucas, Kansas (see page 756), and the **Dickeyville Grotto** in Iowa (see page 253).

America. Marked by a set of wrought-iron patio furniture and traditional headstones, the grave is often piled high with strands of beads, fruit, and other offerings.

Thanks to its location at the I-20 and I-59 junction, there's no shortage of places to eat and sleep in Meridian.

Continuing its musical traditions, Meridian is also the birthplace and corporate headquarters of Peavey Electronics, amplifier- and instrument-makers to the stars.

ALABAMA

Our route across the midsection of Alabama cuts through the rural Black Belt—a name that comes from the richly fertile but often swampy lowland soil, but which also reflects its predominantly African American population. Prime cotton-growing country, central Alabama was feverishly supportive of slavery and secession—Montgomery, the state capital, was also the first capital of the Confederacy—and later became a crucible in the civil rights battles of the 1950s and 1960s.

Events of both of these historical moments provide most of

what there is to see and do in the state, but the intimate scale of things—even the biggest city, **Montgomery,** feels like a sleepy, small town—makes for an enjoyable tour, as does the fact that for most of its 230-odd miles, US-80 alternates between old-style two-laner and newer-style four-lane freeway, far away from the anodyne Interstates and passing through some of the South's most interesting places.

Demopolis and Faunsdale

Standing just north of US-80 on a bluff at the confluence of the Black Warrior and Tombigbee Rivers, **Demopolis** (pop. 7,483) has an interesting history to explain its unusual name—which means "City of the People" in Greek. In 1817, a band of French aristocrats in exile for their allegiance to Napoleon arrived here after the U.S. Congress granted them the land to found a colony based on growing grapes and olives. Not surprisingly, the colonists, a group of soldiers and courtiers whom the WPA *Guide to Alabama* described as "cultured people...from the glittering drawing rooms of the French aristocracy...none of whom had ever set foot in a plowed field," failed miserably; they survived thanks only to the local Choctaw Indians, who gave them food and taught them to grow viable crops.

*The Tombigbee River at Demopolis comes to life the first weekend of December for **Christmas on the River,** when lighted, animated "floats that really float" parade downstream.*

By the 1820s the last of the French had quit, and the lands were swiftly taken over by slave-owning American cotton planters, whose mansions still stand in and around town. Though it's not overly imposing from the outside, the biggest and best of these is **Gaineswood** (Tues.–Fri. 10 AM–4 PM, Sat. 10 AM–2 PM; $5; 805 S. Cedar St.; 334/289-4846), just north of US-80. The finest antebellum mansion in Alabama, and one of the top three in the country according to the *Smithsonian Guide to Historic America,* Gaineswood began as a rough cabin in 1821 and over the next 40 years grew into a classic Greek Revival manor, built by slave laborers according to pattern-

Gaineswood antebellum mansion

book designs. Most unusually, it is still decorated with the original furniture, fixtures, and fittings. Today it is a national historic landmark owned and operated by the Alabama Historical Commission.

The other well-maintained plantation home still standing in Demopolis is **Bluff Hall** (closed Mon.; $5; 405 N. Commissioners Ave.; 334/289-9644), overlooking the river at the west edge of town. Smaller than Gaineswood but more attractively situated, Bluff Hall contains a wider array of furniture, with pieces dating from throughout the 19th century; the kitchen in particular is packed with Victorian-era gadgets.

Demopolis's franchise-free downtown fills four blocks of Washington Street east from Bluff Hall and the river. It's centered upon one of the South's oldest public squares, with a cast-iron fountain and many comfy benches.

The most enjoyable place to eat near Demopolis is about 15 miles east of town in tiny **Faunsdale** (pop. 98), on the south side of US-80. Though little more than a speck on the map, Faunsdale is worth a stop to enjoy the gorgeous home-cooked food and frequent live music at the **Ca-John's Faunsdale Bar and Grill** (Wed.–Sun. 5–9 PM only; 334/628-3240) in the block-long center of town. In spring, the restaurant hosts the annual **Alabama Crawfish Festival,** which sees hundreds of visitors turn out for bands, beers, and some 20 tons of "mudbugs."

Selma

A full century before it played a seminal role in the civil rights movement of the 1960s, **Selma** (pop. 20,756) was second only to Richmond as an industrial arsenal for Confederate forces—Selma's foundries and forges produced weapons, ammunition, and ironclad warships, including the legendary CSS *Tennessee*—and altogether accounted for nearly half of Confederate-made munitions. As in Richmond, the factories were destroyed by Union forces toward the end of the war in April 1865, but a few blocks of downtown's Water Avenue were spared and now form one of the few intact antebellum business districts left in the South. Hundreds of Civil War–era houses line Selma's streets, marked by blue shields and forming one of the largest collections of historic houses in the country.

Along the north bank of the broad Alabama River, Water Avenue's five blocks of well-maintained commercial structures, many now housing antiques shops, include the **St. James Hotel** ($95 and up; 1200 Water Ave.; 334/872-3234), the oldest hotel still standing in the South, built in 1837 and restored in 1997 to its original grand stature, with wrought-iron balconies, views of the river, and well-restored rooms and suites arrayed around a gorgeous garden atrium. At the west end of Water Avenue, the humpbacked landmark **Edmund Pettus Bridge** still carries old US-80 over the river, and at the north foot of the bridge the small but significant **National Voting Rights Museum** (closed Sun.; $6; 6 US-80 E.; 334/418-0800), near the US-80 intersection with Cosby

Edmund Pettus Bridge

Avenue, uses photographs and handbills to tell the story of the civil rights struggles of the 1950s and 1960s. While most accounts focus on the high-profile political leaders, the story here is of the local grassroots activists who struggled for years to win the right to vote. The big names, particularly Rev. Martin Luther King Jr., clearly played key roles, but the sense you get from visiting the Voting Rights Museum is that it was the many brave but uncelebrated heroes who really made the civil rights movement happen.

Five blocks east, at the other end of the Water Avenue historic district, on the site of Selma's largest Civil War foundry, the **Old Depot Museum** (closed Sun.; $4; 4 Martin Luther King Jr. St.; 334/874-2197) traces regional history from before the Civil War up through the civil rights movement and features a large selection of Confederate currency, much of which was printed in Selma. The depot also marks the juncture of Selma's Civil War history with the more recent battles for civil rights: North along Martin Luther King Jr. (formerly Sylvan) Street, markers point out the unchanged sites of key moments in the civil rights movement up to the 1965 March to Montgomery fronted by Dr. King. Twenty different displays explain the significance of Selma and point out the historic importance of such sites as the Brown Chapel AME church, where marchers set off toward Montgomery before being violently turned back at the Edmund Pettus Bridge, and the simple brick public housing of the George Washington Carver Homes, where most of the original activists lived.

Civil Rights Movement National Historic Trail

Dozens of sites in Selma and Montgomery, and the entire 54-mile length of US-80 between them, are being documented, preserved, and protected as part of the **Civil Rights Movement National Historic Trail.** It's a challenging story to tell, and so far two of three planned National Park Service interpretive centers are opened, on the north side of US-80 near **Hayneville** (daily; free; 334/877-1984) and in Selma (daily; free; 2 Broad St.; 334/872-0509). The centers have information on the Selma-to-Montgomery marches and explore the larger context of Civil Rights Movement through interactive displays and a film.

Just east of Hayneville is the place where Viola Liuzzo, a white housewife from Detroit who volunteered to help shuttle marchers between Montgomery and Selma, was murdered by the KKK. A small memorial stands on the site, on the south side of US-80 between Petronia and Lowndesboro.

Responding to the civil rights marches of 1965, President Lyndon Johnson said, "At times, history and fate meet at a single time, in a single place to shape a turning point in man's unending search for freedom. So it was at Lexington and Concord. So it was a century ago at Appomattox. So it was last week in Selma, Alabama."

Alabama's original state capital, **Cahawba,** was founded along the Alabama River in 1820 but was totally abandoned by the 1860s. Its few buildings and other remains are preserved as a state historic park (daily 9 AM–5 PM; free; 334/872-8058), 13 miles southwest of Selma via Hwy-22 and Hwy-9.

Montgomery

Original capital of the Confederate States of America, and now the state capital of Alabama, **Montgomery** (pop. 205,764) is among the more engaging destinations in the Deep South. Not surprisingly, much of what there is to see has to do with the Civil War, which officially started here when Jefferson Davis gave the order to fire on Fort Sumter. Montgomery survived the war more or less unscathed and is now a very pleasant little city with lovely houses lining leafy streets and an above-average range of restaurants, thanks to the presence of politicos and the nearly 6,000 students at Alabama State College.

Montgomery's Maxwell-Gunter Air Force Base, originally established as a flight school by the Wright Brothers in 1910, is now home to the **Air University and War College,** national finishing school for fighter pilots and military tacticians. Tuskegee, just east, was the training base of the Tuskegee Airmen, black pilots who fought in World War II.

Montgomery's landmark is the circa-1851 **Alabama State Capitol** (closed Sun.; free; 334) 242-3935), which served as the Confederate capitol for four months in 1861 and is still in use. A bronze star on the west portico marks the spot where Jefferson Davis took the oath of office as President of the Confederate States of America on February 18, 1861, and twin cantilevered spiral staircases surrounded by historical murals climb the three-story domed rotunda. Moved to a site across the street from the capitol in 1921, the **White House of the Confederacy** is where Jeff Davis and family lived before moving from Montgomery to Richmond. Yet more Confederate memorabilia is on display next door at the **State Archives and History Museum** (closed Sun.; free; 334/242-4435), which has displays tracing Alabama history from Creek Indian and pioneer times up through today.

The building behind the Civil Rights Memorial houses the nonprofit Southern Poverty Law Center, a nationally important force for fighting all forms of racial and religious hatred. Along with numerous legal battles, the center has targeted racism on the Internet via its website, www.tolerance.org.

A single block west of the state capitol complex—mind-bogglingly close, considering the historically huge gulf between whites and blacks in Alabama—stands the **Dexter Avenue King**

Memorial Baptist Church, a simple brick building where Martin Luther King Jr. served as pastor from 1954 to 1960. One of the key landmarks of the civil rights movement, it was here that supporters rallied around Rosa Parks in the Montgomery bus boycott of 1955–1956, leading to an end to official segregation. Right downtown, a small **museum** (closed Sun.; $6; 252 Montgomery St.; 334/241-8615) dedicated to Rosa Parks and the bus boycott opened in the new Troy University library, next to the site of the bus stop where Mrs. Parks refused to give up her seat for a white passenger, sparking the struggle.

Dexter Avenue King Memorial Baptist Church

Around the corner from the Dexter Avenue King Memorial Baptist Church, Montgomery's most powerful site may be the **Civil Rights Memorial** (400 Washington Ave.), two blocks west of the state capitol at the entrance to the Southern Poverty Law Center. Designed by Vietnam Veterans Memorial architect Maya Lin, the monument consists of a circular black granite table inscribed with the names of 40 people killed in the struggle for civil rights, with a brief description of how and when they died radiating like the hands of a clock from a central water source, which flows gently over the edges of the stone. Behind the table, a waterfall tumbles over a marble wall inscribed with Martin Luther King's favorite biblical passage, which says that we will not be satisfied "until Justice rolls down like water, and righteousness like a mighty stream."

Montgomery also has sights to see that have nothing at all to do with the Civil War or the civil rights movement. The first of these is the **Hank Williams Memorial,** marking his final resting place on the northeast side of downtown in Oakwood Cemetery Annex (1304 Upper Wetumptka Rd.). Hank Williams was an Alabama native, and singer and writer of such enduring classics as "Your Cheating Heart," "Jambalaya," "Hey, Good Lookin'," "I'm So Lonesome I Could Cry," and "Lost Highway." Williams's last concert in Montgomery took place on December 28, 1952, three days before his death; he died in the back of his

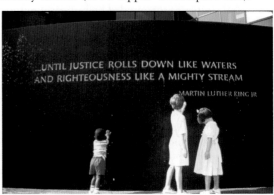

Civil Rights Memorial

Cadillac while en route from Knoxville, Tennessee, to a scheduled New Year's Day concert in Canton, Ohio. His song, "I'll Never Get Out of This World Alive," was rising up the charts at the time of his demise. His grave is on the east side of the central circle, and his baby blue 1952 Cadillac convertible is one of the prime exhibits inside the Hank Williams **museum,** across from City Hall (daily; $8; 118 Commerce St.; 334/262-3600).

Another notable local was Zelda Fitzgerald, who was born and raised in Montgomery and later lived here with her husband F. Scott while he wrote *Tender Is the Night* during the winter of 1931–1932. The house they shared, south of downtown, has been converted into apartments, one of which (Apt. B, on the ground floor) is now a small **museum** (Wed.–Fri. 10 AM–2 PM, Sat. and Sun. 1–5 PM; donations; 919 Felder Ave.; 334/264-4222) that details their lives and works through videos and memorabilia—press clippings, twin typewriters, first editions, photographs, and more. It's the only museum dedicated to either of them, anywhere.

The **Montgomery Biscuits,** Class AA farm club of the Tampa Bay Devil Rays, play at a nice new riverfront stadium, right downtown (200 Coosa St.; 334/323-2255).

Montgomery Practicalities

At the east end of downtown, there's a clutch of very good "Authentic Southern" restaurants within a short walk of the state capitol, including the cacophonously huge, and hugely popular, cafeteria-style **Farmers Market Cafe** (315 N. McDonough St.; 334/262-1970 or 334/262-9163). Another great, traditional Deep South place is on the south side of town: **Martin's Restaurant,** southeast of the Alabama State University campus (closed Sat.; 1796 Carter Hill Rd.; 334/265-1767), gets votes for making the "World's Best Fried Chicken," and they also bake some pretty fine pies. Montgomery even has great fast food: **Chris' Hot Dogs,** located three blocks west of Dr. King's church (closed Sun.; 138 Dexter Ave.; 334/265-6850), is famous across the state for its spicy chili dogs and crispy fries.

Places to stay in Montgomery include the usual national chains, plus two good choices in downtown: a comfy **Hampton Inn,** in a restored older building (around $100 and up; 100 Commerce St.; 334/265-1010), and the luxurious **Renaissance** ($140 and up; 201 Tallapoosa St.; 334/481-5000).

Tuskegee

Midway between Montgomery and the Georgia border, **Tuskegee** (pop. 9,865) is a medium-sized town that has grown up around **Tuskegee University** (334/727-8347), founded in 1881 by the industrious former slave, Booker T. Washington, in order to help black Americans rise up the economic ladder, and now a national historic site. Many of the early buildings built by student laborers still stand around the university's 5,000 acres, which include the campus, farm, and forest land, but the main points of interest are close to the entrance off Old Montgomery Road. Here you'll find the **George Washington Carver Museum** (daily; free; 334/727-3200), which is part of the Tuskegee Institute National Historic Site and traces the career of Tuskegee teacher George Washington Carver, with displays of the various products Carver developed during his lifelong tenure at Tuskegee.

Facing the Carver Museum across the lawn is the strikingly modern Tuskegee University Chapel, designed by noted architect Paul Rudolph and built from 1967 to 1969. The graves of both Booker T. Washington and George Washington Carver are next to the chapel.

Across the Chattahoochee River from Georgia, the oddly spelled **Phenix City** is where thousands of native Creek Indians were gathered in 1836 before being forced west to new territory in Oklahoma, along what became known as the **Trail of Tears.**

Southeast of the college campus, the center of Tuskegee is a broad square dominated by the large Macon County Courthouse. At the Rexall Drug Store on the west side of the square, the store windows are filled with lessons in African American history, illustrated by a "Tuskegee Airman" edition of GI Joe.

East of Tuskegee, the I-85 freeway races up to Atlanta, while US-80 rolls its way east to the engaging old industrial city of Columbus, across the Georgia border.

GEORGIA

Running across the middle of Georgia, US-80 follows the "fall line," a geological divide where rivers drop in a series of rapids from the higher Piedmont Plateau to the lower coastal plain. Because the fall line marked the limits of navigation in from the sea, settlements naturally sprung up along it: **Columbus** was founded on the banks of the falling Chattahoochee, while in the middle of the state, **Macon** was built along the Ocmulgee River.

These, the second- and third-biggest cities, respectively, in this still-rural state, are the only real cities our route passes through, and both are fascinating places in very different ways. For the rest of its trip across Georgia, US-80 takes in more than 300 miles of rolling countryside, speckled here and there with dozens and dozens of small towns. Runs along ancient-looking two-lane blacktop wind through thick hardwood-and-pine forests, past stately white-columned farmhouses with wide lawns and run-down tin-roofed shacks with yards full of rusting refrigerators and old bangers-on-blocks.

In the western half of Georgia, you can detour to explore the surprisingly simple homes of two U.S. presidents, Franklin Delano Roosevelt at **Warm Springs,** and Jimmy Carter at **Plains.** At the heart of Georgia, Macon is home to the engaging **Georgia Music Hall of Fame** and a large but little-visited prehistoric Mound City. Continuing east toward Savannah and the Atlantic Coast, US-80 has been replaced by the much faster I-16 freeway, bypassing numerous small towns across an agricultural region that was devastated during General Sherman's Civil War "March to the Sea." Fortunately, Sherman spared the colonial capital, **Savannah,** a lushly verdant gem generally considered among the most beautiful cities in North America.

Columbus

Crossing the Chattahoochee River between Alabama and Georgia, look north to see the rushing waterfalls around which the city of **Columbus** (pop. 189,885) grew. Built on the site of a Creek Indian village, Columbus ("Home of the 2006 Little League World Series Champions") is now Georgia's second-largest city and home of the brutal Army Ranger training school at Fort Benning. During the Civil War, its iron foundries and water-powered factories converted to munitions production, but Columbus was untouched until Union general James H. Wilson stormed across the Chattahoochee in 1865; unaware that the treaty of Appomattox had already ended the war, "Wilson's Raiders" destroyed much of the city. The huge brick textile mills now lining the river's eastern bank date from the post-Reconstruction years up through the turn of the 20th century, when Columbus emerged as an industrial giant, an era captured in the stories of Columbus author Carson McCullers and in the recordings of blues singer Gertrude "Ma" Rainey. Her home has been preserved, and now houses **The Gertrude "Ma" Rainey House and Blues Museum** (Tues.–Sat.; 805 5th Ave.; 706/653-4960).

Most city sights are conveniently located in a compact riverside district. Stroll along the Riverwalk promenade for a close-up look at the river (or the kid-friendly science museum), or rumble down the cobblestone lanes of Broadway and Front Street past block after block of graceful old homes and fountain-studded parks. The elegant little **Springer Opera House** (103 10th St.) is the highlight of the adjacent commercial district, where beautifully renovated buildings mix with funky shops selling wigs and voodoo trinkets.

On a hill east of downtown, a half mile from the river, the **Columbus Museum** (closed Mon.; free; 1251 Wynnton Rd.; 706/748-2562) is the major cultural center for the region, with engaging displays tracing the history of the river valley from the time of the Creek Indians—don't miss the 20-minute movie *Chattahoochee Legacy,* which screens frequently throughout the day. A wide-ranging collection of fine and folk art is on display in the spacious galleries. Overall, this is one of the state's more captivating small museums, well worth an hour at least.

On the site of the former Confederate shipyard at Port Columbus, south of downtown at the foot of 4th Street, the **National Civil War Naval Museum**

Especially in the western half of the state, US-80 runs across rolling Piedmont countryside past extensive orchards at the heart of Georgia peach country. Follow U-pick signs in early summer for a field-fresh selection, or stop at roadside stands along the route selling this Georgia specialty along with other local fruits and vegetables, including, of course, peanuts.

The Chattahoochee River between Alabama and Georgia officially marks the line between the central and eastern standard time zones, though Phenix City, Alabama, also observes eastern time.

(daily; $7.50; 1002 Victory Dr.; 706/327-9798) contains the charred remnants of two Civil War ironclad ships, mock-ups of early submarines and mines, and tons of naval memorabilia.

Columbus Practicalities

At either end of historic downtown, restaurants span the range from down-home to upper-crust. **Country's on Broad** (1329 Broadway; 706/596-8910) serves up classic country cookin' and fabulous hickory-smoked barbecue in a spruced-up 1940s bus depot. At the other end of town, **Bludau's Goetchius House** (405 Broadway; 706/324-4863), overlooking the river, serves upscale dinners Monday through Saturday—if the seafood and chateaubriand are too rich for your blood, stop for a mint julep at its speakeasy downstairs. On old US-80 east of downtown, the adventurous might try the lunch counter of the **Dinglewood Pharmacy** (1939 Wynnton Rd.; 706/322-0616), for a Scrambled Dog, a hot dog buried under chili, onions, and Oysterette crackers.

Most of the national chains line up along the I-185 freeway, but the nicest place to stay in Columbus is the **Marriott** ($110 and up; 800 Front Ave.; 706/324-1800) downtown, impressively carved out of a former foundry. The Ironworks next door has been converted into a convention center and performance space and is the site of the city's major festival, the **RiverFest,** in April. Southeast from downtown, Victory Drive winds toward Fort Benning, passing most of Columbus's budget accommodations.

For more information on Columbus, contact the **visitors center** (900 Front Ave.; 706/322-1613 or 800/999-1613).

Warm Springs: FDR's Little White House

About 15 miles north of Columbus, an hour southwest of Atlanta, the rising, forested flanks of Pine Mountain attract flatlanders in search of cooler temperatures and an overlook of the surrounding countryside. In 1924, the therapeutic natural hot springs here also drew the future president Franklin Delano Roosevelt, who, in between losing the election for vice president in 1920 and winning the governorship of New York in 1928, was struck with

azalea,
state wildflower of Georgia

polio and left unable to walk. Roosevelt loved the area so much he built a wooded, three-bedroom retreat here later called the **Little White House** (daily; $8; 706/655-5870). He established a treatment center nearby for himself and fellow polio sufferers, funded a charity that grew into today's March of Dimes, and returned regularly over the next two decades. After being elected president in 1932 he formulated much of the "New Deal" and managed the conduct of World War II while staying here. And on the afternoon of April 12, 1945, FDR collapsed suddenly and died at Warm Springs, leaving an unfinished portrait propped on an easel.

The surprisingly small and unpretentious house is very much as it was when Roosevelt died, with the recent addition of an excellent 11,000-square-foot museum telling all about Roosevelt's life and times. Many of the displays concentrate on his political career, but many of the objects are personal and

FDR's Little White House

vividly moving, such as the heavy leg braces FDR wore during public appearances, the wall full of walking canes crafted for FDR by disabled people all over the world, and the dark blue Ford V-8 convertible (with hand controls) that he drove around the Warm Springs countryside.

At nearby 9,049-acre **F.D. Roosevelt State Park,** on land donated by Roosevelt, you can take in the terrific views, swim at the pool, hike a portion of the 26-mile Pine Mountain Trail, or stay the night in one of the many rustic cabins (800/864-7275 for reservations). In the small town of **Warm Springs** (pop. 425), a half mile north of the Little White House park, **Mac's Bar-B-Q** (daily; 706/655-2472), at the corner of Spring and Main Streets a block east of Hwy-41, has hickory-smoked ribs and chicken. Home-style comfort food is on the menu at warm and friendly **Bulloch House Restaurant,** in a gorgeous old Victorian home a short walk down Spring Street (47 Bulloch St.; 706/655-9068). Right in the heart of Warm Springs, the historic **Hotel Warm Springs** ($75–150; 47 Broad St.; 800/366-7616 or 706/655-2114) offers B&B accommodations (with 12-foot ceilings!). There are also plenty of craft, gift, and antiques stores to browse through.

One last area attraction, west of Warm Springs off US-27, is perhaps the biggest draw in north Georgia: **Callaway Gardens** (daily; $18 adults; 800/225-5292 or 706/663-2281), which has 13,000 lushly landscaped acres covered in topiary gardens, a lakeside swimming beach, and dazzling displays of colorful flowers. The **Day Butterfly Center,** a 7,000-square-foot atrium with 50 exotic species of free-flying butterflies, is surrounded by four more acres of butterfly-friendly gardens, and restaurants, a golf course, and overnight accommodations are also available.

Plains: Jimmy Carter

Another stop along central Georgia's "Presidential Trail," 45 miles southeast of Columbus via US-285, **Plains** (pop. 776), the home of former president Jimmy Carter, stands as a living monument to small-town America. Here, in a town that's small and remote even by South Georgia standards, the 39th president of the United States was raised, mounted his presidential campaign, and now officiates on matters of international diplomacy—that is, when he isn't teaching Sunday School at the Maranatha Baptist Church. Though the Carter family compound is off-limits, visitors can see Carter's high school, stop by late brother Billy's old gas station (the only one in town), and buy a bag of peanuts at the general store.

Much of Plains has been proclaimed the **Jimmy Carter National Historic Site,** and self-guided touring maps are available at the **visitors center** (daily; 300 N. Bond St.; 229/824-4104), inside the old Plains High School. Another major part of the Plains experience is the family farm, preserved in the pre-electricity, circa-1937 state described in Carter's evocative memoir, *An Hour Before Daylight: Memories of a Rural Boyhood*. Finally, there's the old train depot downtown, which served as Carter's campaign headquarters in 1976 and again in 1980, when he was trounced by Ronald Reagan.

Ten miles northeast of Plains, in the market town of **Americus** (pop. 17,041), the wealth generated by the region's cotton plantations is embodied the 39th president and former first lady in their hometown

in the towering brick **Windsor Hotel** ($100–200; 125 W. Lamar St.; 229/924-1555 or 800/780-7234). A truly elegant Victorian-era hotel with a three-story atrium lobby— one of the grandest interior spaces in the state—the Windsor is worth a look and makes a great base for exploring central Georgia.

The town of **Americus** is worldwide headquarters of **Habitat for Humanity,** which helps provide basic shelter for people all over the world.

Andersonville Prison

Ten miles or so northeast of Americus via Hwy-49, the **Andersonville National Historic Site** (daily; free; 229/924-0343) stands on the site of the largest and most notorious Confederate military prison. During the final 18 months of the Civil War, more than 32,000 Union soldiers were imprisoned here in overcrowded conditions, and 13,000 died as a result of disease, poor sanitation, and exposure. Once this was uncovered, public outrage was so great that the camp's commandant, Capt. Henry Wirz, the only Confederate officer tried for war crimes, was convicted of murder and hanged in Washington, D.C. Historians generally agree that there was little he could have done to alleviate the suffering. Thousands of closely packed gravestones fill the Andersonville National Cemetery, just north of the prison site.

Only a few parts of the prison have been reconstructed, but the prisoners' harrowing stories are told in one part of the adjacent **National Prisoners of War Museum,** which was dedicated in 1998 and recounts the stories of American POWs during wars up through the present day. Perhaps surprisingly, the tone of the museum is neither vindictive nor especially patriotic, focusing instead on the instances of individual bravery in the face of impossible difficulties.

Macon

Near the geographic center of the state, the city of **Macon** (pop. 91,350) was founded along the Ocmulgee (pronounced "oak-MUL-gee") River in 1823, and flourished with the cotton trade. The downtown area was energized by opening of the Georgia Music Hall of Fame, which

In early spring, Macon's nearly 300,000 cherry trees come into bloom, drawing flower lovers from all over the region.

stood alongside dozens of well-preserved, historically significant
public buildings, including the
110-year-old **Grand Opera House**
(651 Mulberry St.) and the turn-
of-the-20th-century **Douglass
Theater** (355 Martin Luther King
Jr. Blvd.) west of Mulberry Street,
where such Macon-born music legends as Lena Horne, Otis Redding,
and Little Richard got their start.

A generation later, the Allman Brothers' "Ramblin' Man" was "born in the
back seat of a Greyhound Bus, rolling down Highway 41," and old US-41 is
now home to the **Big House,** a mile west of downtown Macon (Thurs.–
Sun., 11 AM–6 PM; $7; 2321 Vineville Ave.; 478/741-5551), where a museum
and memorial occupies the same 16-bedroom mansion the innovative bluesy,
jazzy rock-and-roll band called home during their 1970s heyday. Band members Duane Allman and Berry Oakley are both buried in Rose Hill
Cemetery, off Riverside Drive; Oakley's epitaph reads ". . . and the road goes
on forever."

Another aspect of Macon heritage, the city's collection of well-preserved antebellum mansions, stands on a low hill at the north end of downtown, having
survived the Civil War unscathed apart from one brief battle: While most of
Sherman's troops skirted by to the north, a band of Union soldiers engaged
young Confederate soldiers at the city limits and fired a cannonball that landed in the foyer of a stately residence, now known as the **Cannonball House.** A
small museum (closed Sun.; $6; 856 Mulberry St.; 478/745-5982) behind the
house displays the usual barrage of Confederate memorabilia, and inside the
house you can see the dented floor and original cannonball. A block away, the
stunning **Hay House** (Tues.–Sun.; $9; 934 Georgia Ave.; 478/742-8155) is
among the most beautiful antebellum houses in the state. You can see these
two and many more on a meandering walk led by a
Macon tour guide posing as Sidney Lanier, the city's
famous 19th-century poet; call the **visitors bureau**
(478/743-1074 or 800/768-3401) for details.

Knoxville, Georgia, 25 miles
west of Macon and just north
of US-80, is built around a
typical Southern courthouse
square, which holds a unique
monument to the local girl,
Joanna Troutman, who
designed the Lone Star flag
of Texas. She gave the flag,
which featured a blue star
on a white background but
which was otherwise
identical to the current one,
to a battalion of Macon
volunteers heading west to
fight for the Texas Republic.

Macon Practicalities

One of the world's greatest places to eat, downtown
Macon's **Len Berg's,** closed down after nearly 100
years in business, but for visitors its heritage (if not its
menu!) has been adopted by another Macon institution, the original **Nu Way Weiners** hot dog stand
(closed Sun.; 430 Cotton Ave.; 478/743-1368). A wider
range of American classics—tuna melts, meat loaf
sandwiches, Cobb salad, chicken gumbo—is on the
menu at the cheerful **Market City Cafe** (502 Cherry
St.; 478/257-6612), and if you want something a little

Macon Music

Many people dismissed the creation of Macon's Georgia Music Hall of Fame as simply another symptom of the state's desperate urge to create tourist attractions to complement Atlanta's hosting of the Olympic Games, way back in the summer of 1996. While Olympic enthusiasm was clearly a key to raising $6.5 million in seed money from the state, the end result was one of the most engaging and enjoyable music museums in the entire country: 12,000 square feet of guitars, amps, albums, posters, costumes, jukeboxes, sunglasses, and blue suede shoes, with just enough curatorial explanation to let you piece together the whole crazy story of Georgia music. The displays were anything but dry, using all manner of artifacts to memorialize their subjects. And best of all, the Hall of Fame was free from the "music industry" bias that says sales equal success—unlike Cleveland's Rock and Roll Hall of Fame, not all of the artists honored in the Macon center were by any means world-famous or commercial superstars.

The Georgia Music Hall of Fame developed a strong reputation within the music world, but unfortunately it never really caught on with the general public, at least not enough to support itself, and in the summer of 2011, the Hall of Fame closed suddenly. It's a shame, because while Macon may not have the legendary status in music circles as say, Memphis or Detroit, its claims to fame goes beyond its location at the center of the state. The Macon music scene had its heyday in the 1950s and 1960s, when it gave birth to such diverse artists as Ray Charles, Little Richard, Otis Redding, and the Allman Brothers, all of whom were enshrined there. Display cases were packed with instruments and memorabilia donated in many cases by the artists themselves, which lent an air of personality to the place. It's an especially big loss, because besides telling the musical life and times of Georgia musicians, the museum did an admirable job of evoking the social, racial, and economic contexts in which the different forms of music were

created, and gave long-overdue credit to the many people working behind the scenes, casting the spotlight on songwriters, producers, and engineers, not to mention diverse promoters, hucksters, and hangers-on. By documenting the contributions of everyone from Ma Rainey to R.E.M., and genres from jazz to rap, the museum made a strong case for Georgia as the true musical crossroads of America.

Little Richard, among others, got his start in Macon.

more exotic try the Italian pastries, salads, and sandwiches at **Adriana's,** a block away (359 3rd St.; 478/742-2255).

For a place to stay, choose from the many motels lining Riverside Drive north of town along the I-75 frontage, or splurge a little on the very comfortable **1842 Inn** ($139–255; 353 College St.; 800/336-1842 or 478/741-1842), a white-columned antebellum mansion converted into a bed-and-breakfast with tons of historical ambience.

Ocmulgee National Monument

Across the Ocmulgee River, well signed from I-16 exit 4, two miles east of Macon along the Emory Highway (US-80), the settlement now preserved as the **Ocmulgee National Monument** was a center of pre-conquest Native American culture. By the mid-1500s,

entrance to the earth lodge at Ocmulgee National Monument

when DeSoto and the first colonists arrived, Ocmulgee had been inhabited for over 800 years, with some remains dating from AD 900.

From the small, WPA-era **visitors center** (daily; free; 478/752-8257), where you can watch a short film and admire pieces of elaborate pottery found on the site, a short trail leads you to a restored earth lodge (complete with thinly disguised air-conditioning ducts!), where you walk through a narrow tunnel to the center of the circular, kiva-like interior. The trail continues past the excavated remains of a Creek Indian trading post, then crosses a set of railroad tracks before climbing a 45-foot-high Great Temple Mound, where you can see downtown Macon across the rumbling I-16 freeway—2,000 years of culture in one very pleasant half-mile walk.

Juliette: *Fried Green Tomatoes at the Whistle Stop Café*

Tucked away upriver on the Ocmulgee, in the heart of the Piedmont forests of middle Georgia, sits the town of **Juliette,** somewhat revived after a long slumber because of its **Whistle Stop Cafe** (443 McCrackin St.; 478/992-8886). The café, town, and river were the backdrop for the 1991 film *Fried Green Tomatoes,* based on Fannie Flagg's novel. (The novel, it should be said, was based upon the Irondale Café outside Birmingham, Alabama.)

You can taste Whistle Stop barbecue, along with a plate of fried green tomatoes, every day of the week. Juliette lies due north of Macon along US-23, or 10 miles east of the I-75 town of Forsyth via Juliette Road.

All across the Deep South, but across Georgia in particular, US-80 is lined by the photogenic remains of long-abandoned filling stations, many of them built with accommodations on the upper floor—right above the old gas pumps.

Off I-16: Dublin and Vidalia

Named by its Irish founders in 1812, **Dublin** (pop. 16,201) continues to celebrate its Irish heritage with shamrocks painted on the center dividers, and an all-out St. Patrick's Day festival that lasts most of two months. The historic district is centered along Bellevue Avenue, where you can note the prominent Confederate Memorial, glimpse the town's many graceful old homes, and look inside the local historical museum (Tues.–Fri. 1–4:30 PM; free; 478/272-9242) at Bellevue and Academy Streets.

The Dublin area hosts an increasingly popular, very-tongue-in-cheek annual celebration of rural America: the **Redneck Games.** Started by local radio DJ Mac Davis as a joking response to Atlanta's preparations for the 1996 Olympics, the Redneck Games competitions include such questionable "country-style" events as bobbin' for pigs' feet, a mud-pit belly-flop contest, bug-zapping, and an armpit serenade in which contestants play TV theme songs by cupping hands under their arms. The games take place in July; admission is around $5 per person.

Southeast of Dublin, around 15 miles south of I-16, **Vidalia** (pop. 10,473) is known to food-lovers around the world as the home of the delectable Vidalia onion, so sweet it can be eaten raw, like an apple. In late April and early May, follow the scent to the **Vidalia Onion Festival** (912/538-8687) for taste treats.

Statesboro and Claxton

Twelve miles north of I-16, **Statesboro** (pop. 28,422) was also one of Sherman's stops on his notorious March to the Sea. Here in 1864 his troops torched the courthouse; today's historic courthouse dates from the late 19th century. Georgia Southern University, with an enrollment of more than 19,000, dominates the town, especially during the fall football season. In Statesboro, Main Street runs in four different directions: north, east, south, and west. In the late 1920s the town inspired Georgia-born Blind Willie McTell to write "Statesboro Blues," a blues classic later recorded by Taj Mahal and the Allman Brothers.

For barbecue, head over to **Vandy's Barbeque** (closed Sun.; 22 W. Vine St.; 912/764-2444), a white-painted breezeblock local landmark a block south from the center of Statesboro on that omni-directional Main Street, then a block west.

Ten miles south of I-16 at the intersection of US-280 and US-301, the town of **Claxton** (pop. 2,746) bills itself as the "Fruitcake Capital of the World." In the fall fruitcake-making season, the **Claxton Bakery** (800/841-4211 or 912/739-3441), right along the railroad racks in the center of town, offers free samples of the 3,000 tons of fruitcake it pounds out each year.

Dublin's **WQZY 96 FM** plays popular country and NASCAR, but it is most famous for the annual **Redneck Games** it organizes every July.

Around Dublin, you can tune to one of the greatest old-time country stations I've found anywhere: **WXLI 1230 AM,** broadcasting Hank Williams, Hank Snow, Johnny Cash, and other country pioneers "from a little building just off the Interstate."

North of US-80 via US-1, the town of **Wrens** (pop. 2,187) was the boyhood home of Erskine Caldwell, author of the classic stories *Tobacco Road* and *God's Little Acre,* both of which were set in this part of rural Georgia.

The beautiful city of Savannah marks the junction of our US-80 route with the **Atlantic Coast** road trip, which begins on page 408. **Savannah** is covered in full on pages 456–457.

US-80 across Savannah

Old US-80 comes into Savannah on Louisville Road, past the Savannah-Hilton Head International Airport on the northwest edge of town. The old road turns into Bay Street for the final approach, then runs south across the historic downtown area before turning east onto Victory Drive, which runs along the southern foot of Savannah, then across to the barrier islands. If you'd rather save Savannah for another day, you can follow I-16 and Victory Drive around the south side of downtown.

The drive east from Savannah to the Atlantic Ocean passes by the beautiful Bonaventure Cemetery, a stately Civil War fort, and a number of picturesque fishing villages on its way across the serene marshlands, where a maze of riverlets and creeks weaves through the tall green reeds, and fishing boats bob along the tidal waters as they head off to harvest shrimp and oysters.

Bonaventure Cemetery

Whether or not you got obsessed with *Midnight in the Garden of Good and Evil,* the book that put Savannah back on the map in the 1990s, you'll enjoy visiting **Bonaventure Cemetery** (daily; free; 330 Bonaventure Rd.), which features prominently in the story. Located east of Savannah proper, north of US-80 via Whatley Avenue, it is simply one of the most evocative corners of this characterful part of the country, where majestic old trees draped in mossy strands stand over abundant azaleas and all manner of monuments and memorials. No less a figure than naturalist John Muir, who camped here for a while immediately after the Civil War, called it "one of the most impressive assemblages of animal and plant creatures I have ever met." Songwriter Johnny Mercer of "Moon River" fame is buried here, along with centuries' worth of other Savannahians.

Fort Pulaski

East of Savannah the landscape gets peaceful very quickly, and amidst the contemporary calm stands **Fort Pulaski National Monument** (daily; $5; 912/786-5787), 15 miles east of Savannah on US-80, a well-preserved stone-and-brick fortress completed in 1848 at a commanding site at the mouth of the Savannah River. Its prominent island site originally held colonial-era fortifications, which were demolished by a hurricane in 1804 and replaced by the architecturally impressive, pentagon-shaped bulwark that survives in its battered and breached state today, surrounded by a moat and many acres of grassy lawn. Beautiful and endlessly photogenic, besides the military history Fort Pulaski preserves abundant natural habitat for all sorts of splendid creatures: eagles, falcons, and songbirds fly about, while manatees and turtles cruise through the lazy waters.

Tybee Island

Less than 20 miles southeast of central Savannah, spreading lazily over the easternmost of many islands filling the delta at the mouth of the Savannah River, the town of **Tybee Island** (pop. 2,990) is a funky old family-oriented resort, with four blocks of burger stands, taverns, and broad clean sands at the eastern end of US-80. Increasingly grown-up and genteel, Tybee still has one last remnant of a rowdier era, in a fun amusement arcade/batting cage/go-kart/mini-golf combo, **Island Miniature Golf and Games** (912/898-3833), on US-80 just west of the Bull River Bridge. Locally famous for the annual **Beach Bum's Parade** before Memorial Day (912/786-5444 or 800/868-2322), Tybee Island's main attraction is its endless, and usually uncrowded, powdery white-sand beaches, which spread from either side of the pier and pavilion at the east end of Tybrisa Street (also known as 16th Street).

> Beginning in 1829, construction of **Fort Pulaski,** proclaimed "as strong as the Rocky Mountains," took 18 years, used 25 million bricks, and cost just over a million dollars (which is equivalent to something close to $5 billion these days, as a share of the U.S. GDP!). During the Civil War, its seven-foot-thick walls withstood bombardment by the Union forces' new rifled cannon for only 30 hours, prompting the fort's surrender in April 1862.

At the north end of Tybee Island, from whence the Union forces bombarded Fort Pulaski during the Civil War, a centuries-old lighthouse stands next to the World War II–era concrete bunkers that house the **Tybee Island Light Station and Museum** (closed Tues.; $8; 912/786-5801), which includes the old lighthouse keeper's cottage among its collections tracing the island's history.

Other draws here are the wacky, slightly ersatz, diner-style **Breakfast Club** (1500 Butler Ave.; 912/786-5984), right at the center of things, open daily for breakfast or an early lunch; if the line is too long, pop across the road to the **Sunrise** (912/786-7473).

Tybee Island's stretch of US-80, Butler Avenue, was home to the world's first Days Inn motel, but these days inexpensive accommodations can be hard to find. There's an older but comfortable **Howard Johnson's** near the beach ($95 and up; 1501 Butler Ave.; 800/793-7716 or 912/786-0700). For a more memorable stay, try the **Tybee Island Inn,** built in 1902 and set in lovely gardens at the north end of the island, on the grounds of historic Fort Screven ($190 and up; 24 Van Horne Ave.; 866/892-4667 or 912/786-9255).

Tybee Island Light Station and Museum

If you're looking for great displays of neon signs, mom-and-pop motels in the middle of nowhere, or kitschy Americana, do as the song says and "get your kicks on Route 66."

pg. 867
Chicago

pg. 871
175 mi
Land of Lincoln

pg. 887
465 mi
Will Rogers Memorial

400 mi

Between Chicago, Illinois, and Los Angeles, California

The romance of Route 66 continues to captivate people around the world. Running between Chicago and Los Angeles, "over two thousand miles all the way" in the words of the popular R&B anthem, this legendary old road passes through the heart of the United States on a diagonal trip that takes in some of the country's most archetypal roadside scenes. If you're looking for great displays of neon signs, rusty middle-of-nowhere truck stops, or kitschy Americana, do as the song says and "get your kicks on Route 66."

But perhaps the most compelling reason to follow Route 66 is to experience the road's ingrained time line of contemporary America. Before it was called Route 66, and long before it was even paved in 1926, this corridor was traversed by the National Old Trails Highway, one of the country's first transcontinental highways. For three decades before and after World War II, Route 66 earned the title **"Main Street of America"** because it wound through small towns across the Midwest and Southwest, lined by hundreds of cafés, motels, gas stations, and tourist attractions. During the Great Depression, hundreds of thousands of farm families, displaced from the Dust Bowl, made their way west along Route 66 to California, following what John Steinbeck called **"The Mother Road"** in his vivid portrait, *The Grapes of Wrath*. After World War II, many thousands more expressed their upward mobility by leaving the industrial East, bound for good jobs in the suburban idyll of Southern California—again following Route 66, which came to embody the demographic shift from the Rust Belt to the Sun Belt.

ILLINOIS

Heading diagonally across the state between Chicago and St. Louis, what remains of Route 66 is a surprisingly rural cruise through endless fields of corn. Despite the urban conglomerations at both ends, for most of its nearly 300-mile trek here, Route 66 and its modern usurper, I-55, pass along flat prairies with nary a smokestack or skyscraper as far as the eye can see.

The heavy industrial and poverty-stricken hinterlands of Chicago and East St. Louis aren't terribly rewarding for travelers in search of the Mother Road, but a couple of intriguing attractions—one

Beginning in the late 1950s and continuing gradually over the next 25 years, old Route 66 was bypassed section by section as the high-speed Interstate highways were completed. Finally, after the last stretch of freeway was completed in 1984, Route 66 was officially decommissioned. The old route is now designated Historic Route 66.

Though it is no longer a main route across the country, Route 66 has retained its mystique in part due to the very same effective hype, hucksterism, and boosterism that animated it through its half-century heyday. It was a Route 66 sight, the marvelous Meramec Caverns, that gave the world the bumper sticker, and it was here on Route 66 that the great American driving vacation first flourished. Billboards and giant statues along the highway still hawk a baffling array of roadside attractions, tempting passing travelers to view giant blue whales, to see live rattlesnakes and other wild creatures on display in roadside menageries, or to stay at "Tucumcari Tonite."

The same commercial know-how and shameless self-promotion has helped the towns along the old route stay alive. Diners and motels play up their Route 66 connections, and many bona fide Route 66 landmarks are kept in business by nostalgic travelers intent on experiencing a taste of this endlessly endangered American experience. That said, many quirky old motels and cafés hang on by a thread of hope, sit vacant, or survive in memory only—all for want of an Interstate exit. In fact, of all the roads covered in this book, Route 66 has perhaps felt the greatest impact from the modern Interstate world; for many stretches you'll be forced to leave the old two-lane and follow the super slabs that have been built right on top of the old road.

Route 66 passes through a marvelous cross-section of American scenes, from the cornfields of Illinois all the way to the golden sands and sunshine of Los Angeles, passing by such diverse environs as the **Grand Canyon,** the Native American communities of the desert Southwest, the small-town Midwest heartlands of **Oklahoma** and **the Ozarks,** as well as the gritty streets of **St. Louis** and **Chicago.** Whether you are motivated by an interest in history, feel a nostalgic yearning for the "good old days" Route 66 has come to represent, or simply want to experience firsthand the amazing diversity of people and landscapes that line its path, Route 66 offers an unforgettable journey into America, then and now.

a prehistoric city, the other a water tower shaped like a catsup bottle—are worth searching out. The only real city along Route 66 is the Illinois state capital, **Springfield,** which has preserved its sections of Route 66 alongside a wealth of places connected to the namesake president here in the "Land of Lincoln." Dozens of small towns across the state play up their Route 66 connections, and most boast at least one true old-road landmark.

Route 66 Across Chicagoland

Following the first (or last) leg of Route 66 across Chicago and its hinterlands is really not worth the effort for anyone except the most die-hard end-to-ender—even Jack Rittenhouse, in his original 1946 *A Guide Book to Highway 66,* didn't bother to describe the route until it reached Plainfield, 35 miles southwest

At Plainfield, a little piece of highway history happened when the original version of Route 66 crossed the even older Lincoln Highway, America's first transcontinental road.

of the Loop. For a symbolic starting point, you can use the grand old Art Institute of Chicago in Grant Park along the lakeshore, since the last US-66 shield used to hang from a streetlight just south of the gallery. If Chicago is your "end of the road," you'll probably prefer to avoid the final few miles of surface streets and make your way to town as quickly as possible via I-55.

From Lake Michigan, the old road ran west via Adams Street (take Jackson Boulevard eastbound; both are one-way) before angling southwest along Ogden Avenue—a long, diagonal exception to the city's main grid of streets. **Cicero** prides itself on having been a haven to Al Capone and other mobsters during the Prohibition era and now enjoys its Route 66 connections at **Henry's Drive-In** (6031 W. Ogden Ave.; 708/656-9344), where you can snack on excellent Polish hot dogs smothered with a pile of french fries. Neighboring **Berwyn** has lined old Route 66 with a series of glass-block markers but didn't do much to save its most remarkable work of art: **The Spindle,** a tower of ruined cars impaled on a 50-foot steel spike, which stood in the parking lot of a shopping mall until mid-2008, when it was removed in the middle of the night to make way for yet another Walgreens. (You may have seen The Spindle in the 1990s comedy *Wayne's World*.)

To continue south and west, you have to follow I-55, which was built right on top of old Route 66. In Willowbrook, off Hwy-83 on the north side of I-55 about 20 miles from the Loop, **Dell Rhea's Chicken Basket** (645 Joliet Rd.; 630/325-0780) is a welcoming old roadside tavern, with famously fabulous chicken dinners and frequent live music.

Chicago marks the junction of Route 66 and our cross-country route along **The Oregon Trail,** detailed on pages 584–703. The city of **Chicago** itself is covered on pages 644–645.

Joliet

Joliet, the "City of Steel and Stone," has a rough reputation that doesn't really reflect its welter of historic attractions. Route 66 through this once-mighty industrial enclave is a feast for fans of post-industrial scenery: Loads of old warehouses and commercial buildings line the route, while stalwart bridges cross the historic Illinois & Michigan Canal, which, beginning in the 1840s, connected Chicago with the Mississippi River. Also in Joliet: the now-closed state prison from which John Belushi (a.k.a. "Joliet Jake") is released at the beginning of the 1980 movie *The Blues Brothers.*

South of Joliet, following old Route 66 (Hwy-53) across the I-80 superslab brings you past the massive **Chicagoland Speedway** and the **Route 66 Raceway** (815/722-5500), where NHRA drag races, NASCAR stock car races, and occasional pop music concerts are held.

Midewin National Tallgrass Prairie Preserve

Along Route 66 between Joliet and Wilmington, a unique undertaking is working to re-create the natural ecosystem on one of the most environmentally damaged areas imaginable: 20,000 acres of the old Joliet ammunition factory are being converted into the **Midewin National Tallgrass Prairie Preserve** (trails open daily, welcome center open Mon.–Sat. in summer, Mon.–Fri. in winter; 815/423-6370). Since 1996, when the land was transferred from the U.S. Army to the U.S. Forest Service, the change from producing TNT to re-growing the native tallgrass prairie has been slow and steady. After more than 15 years of toxic cleanups and careful husbandry, more than half the old plant has been returned to its natural state and now offers more than 20 miles of hiking and biking trails on both sides of Hwy-53 (old Route 66). Midewin (pronounced "mi-DAY-win") is a native Potawatomi word meaning "healthy balance," and a visit here gives a good feeling for the flora and fauna that would have existed naturally in places like this all over the Midwest.

Hwy-53: Wilmington and Dwight

From Joliet, you can follow old Route 66 southwest through a series of nice small towns along Hwy-53, which runs along the southeast side of I-55. Though the route is sometimes a bit obscure and not all that rich in history or aesthetic delights, the towns here offer a very pleasant taste of what old Route 66 had to offer: **Wilmington** is semi-famous for the 30-foot-tall Gemini Giant statue that stands outside the **Launching Pad Drive-In** (810 E. Baltimore St.; 815/476-6535), and **Braidwood** has the popular, retro-1950s **Polk-A-Dot Drive-In,** on old Route 66 (222 N. Front St.; 815/458-3377).

Continuing along Hwy-53, there are a couple more classic Route 66 scenes along the old road northwest of Pontiac, the next biggish town. **Dwight** is leafy and quaint, well known a century ago for its Keeley Institute treatment center for alcoholics, and now famous for its fine old Texaco station, which stands at the main crossroads (near the reliable Old Route 66 Family Restaurant). The Dwight Texaco station opened in 1933 and managed to stay in business until 1999, earning it a reputation as the oldest surviving gas station on the Mother Road (retiring at the ripe old age of 66 was a clever marketing move!). The station has been restored to its original look and now serves as Dwight's welcome center. To my eye, an even more picturesque old Standard Oil gas station stands just down Hwy-53 in the next Route 66 town, **Odell.**

Pontiac

Some 90 miles southeast of Lake Michigan, the former coal-mining town of **Pontiac** (pop. 11,931) surrounds the stately circa-1875 Livingston County Courthouse. The courthouse's green lawns hold the usual battery of monuments, including one to the namesake Ottawa chief whose visage also graced the General Motors marquee. According to the WPA *Guide to Illinois,* another

A short stretch of original, circa 1926-era Route 66 near **Lexington,** right off the south side of I-55 exit 178, has been decorated with replicas of old billboards and Burma-Shave advertisements, and dubbed **Memory Lane.** It's officially a pedestrian and bike-only section of Morris Street.

of these monuments, the Soldiers and Sailors Monument, received the shortest presidential dedication in history when, in 1902, it was "dedicated with a few hasty words by President Theodore Roosevelt, before an audience of less than a dozen people, who congregated briefly under a terrific downpour."

Though the old road ran around rather than right through Pontiac, the town has become one of the main stops on the Illinois Route 66 tour, thanks to the presence here of the **Route 66 Hall of Fame Museum,** in the old main fire station (daily; free; 110 W. Howard St.; 815/844-4566). Along with the usual displays of gas pumps, enamel and neon advertising signs, and old photos documenting the road's heritage, the Pontiac museum is worth a look for its tribute to iconic Route 66 artist Bob Waldmire (1945–2009), whose delicate line drawings and large murals are reproduced here, next to the 1972 VW camper and the big old Chevy schoolbus RV Bob traveled and lived in for much of his prolific life. (Bob's van, and Bob himself, inspired the character "Fillmore" in the movie *Cars,* which was voiced by comedian George Carlin.)

Pontiac is also home to a Pontiac car museum, the "Wall dogs" sign and mural museum, and a long-lived Route 66 landmark, the **Old Log Cabin Inn** (18700 N. Aurora St.; 815/842-2908) on the north edge of town. When Route 66 was redirected behind the original location, this restaurant was jacked up and flipped around, and the old, old road, which dates from 1918, is still there, behind the café along the railroad tracks.

Bloomington-Normal

Hometown of politician Adlai Stevenson (and Col. Henry Blake of TV's *M*A*S*H*), **Bloomington-Normal** sits at the middle of Illinois, surrounded by five different Interstate freeways and miles of cornfields. Its main claim to fame is in being the only place in the world where that classic bar snack, **Beer Nuts,** is made; for a free sample (but no tour, alas), stop by the factory (103 N. Robinson St.; 800/BEER-NUT). The "Twin Cities" are also the corporate home of insurance company State Farm and birthplace of another all-American icon, the Midwest-based burger chain Steak 'n Shake, which started here in 1934. Good food is available at characterful **Lucca Grill,** which has been serving pizza and pasta dishes since the 1930s (116 E. Market St.; 309/828-7521).

Funks Grove

Heading on from Bloomington-Normal, westbound drivers will encounter the next two towns in sonorous order—Shirley and McLean—but wordplay aside, the stretch of Illinois farmland between Bloomington and Springfield is rich in Route 66–related heritage. In McLean, 47 miles from Springfield and 15 miles southwest from Bloomington, old Route 66 emerges from the shadow of I-55 and you can follow old Route 66 along the west side of the freeway for just over four miles past the delightful anachronism of **Funks Grove** (309/874-

3360), where the friendly Funk family has been tapping trees and selling delicious maple sirup (that's how they spell it) since 1891. If you're here in late winter or early spring you can watch them tap the trees and hammer in the spouts; each tree can produce up to four gallons of sap a day, but it takes 50 gallons of sap for each gallon of the final product. Free tastings are available, and a full range of bottles is on sale.

Lincoln

The only town named for Honest Abe in his lifetime, **Lincoln** (pop. 14,504) took his name before he became a famous figure. As a young lawyer, Abraham Lincoln drew up the legal documents for founding the town but warned developers that he "never knew of anything named Lincoln that amounted to much." At the dedication ceremonies, Lincoln supposedly "baptized" the place by spitting out a mouthful of watermelon seeds—hence the plaster watermelon and historical plaque remembering the great event, next to the Amtrak-serviced train station at Broadway and Chicago Streets in the center of town. Lincoln was also home to Harlem Renaissance poet Langston Hughes (1902–1967), who was elected Class Poet while in the 8th grade here.

Springfield

As the Illinois state capital, **Springfield** (pop. 118,033) embodies the rural small-town character of most of the state and feels much farther away from Chicago than the three-plus-hour drive it actually is, traffic willing. Springfield is also the place that takes the "Land of Lincoln" state's obsession with Abraham

Lincoln to its greatest extreme, for it was here that Honest Abe worked and lived from 1837 to 1861. He left Springfield after being elected president and was buried here after his assassination at the end of the Civil War.

There are all manner of Lincoln sights to see all over Springfield, but the newest and best place to start your homage is at the state-run **Abraham Lincoln Presidential Library and Museum** (daily; $12; 212

Lincoln's Tomb

N. 6th St.; 217/782-5764), across from Union Square Park. Once you've toured this comprehensive, reverential yet thought-provoking, over $100 million, 200,000-square-foot exhibition, other sights include the only home Lincoln ever owned, his law offices, and of course his tomb. Located in Oak Ridge Cemetery, two miles north of downtown, Lincoln's tomb also includes the remains of his wife and three of four children. Legend has it that if you touch the nose on the bronze bust of Lincoln, good luck will follow.

Though quite sincere and understated, the Lincoln homage can overwhelm, and if you need a change of pace from Lincoln Land there is the beautiful **Dana-Thomas House** (Wed.–Sun.; $5; 301 E. Lawrence Ave.; 217/782-6776), a half mile south of the state capitol. Designed by Frank Lloyd Wright in 1902, it is the most luxurious, best preserved, and most fully furnished of his houses. Actually a complete remodel of a house that already stood on the site, the Dana-Thomas house was built for socialite Susan Dana, who lived here until the late 1940s, when it was sold to a publishing company and used as offices until the state of Illinois purchased it in 1981.

Also worth a look: Housed in what some say is the oldest gas station on Route 66, **Shea's Gas Station Museum** (Wed.–Sat.; 2075 N. Peoria Rd. 217/522-0475) is curated by the ever-engaging Bill Shea, who has spent the past 50 years right here on Route 66. This petroliana and Route 66 museum displays a photogenic collection of vintage gasoline pumps, signs, shields, and anything else related to sale and use of our favorite fossil fuel.

Springfield also has a favorite Route 66 watering hole, the **Cozy Dog Drive-In** (2935 S. 6th St.; 217/525-1992), on the old road south of downtown. The birthplace of the corn dog, which here goes by the nicer name "Cozy," was founded in 1949 by Ed Waldmire, father of noted Route 66 artist Bob

Waldmire. So come on in and chow down—two Cozy Dogs, a drink, and a big basket of fries cost around $7.

Complete your Route 66 Americana tour by taking in a flick or two at the **Route 66 Twin Drive-In,** west of Sixth Street southwest of the I-72/I-55 junction (1700 Recreation Dr.; 217/698-0066).

Almost all the national chain hotels and motels have operations in Springfield, so you shouldn't have trouble finding a room. For a bit of character across from the Lincoln House, and close to everything else in Springfield, consider the **Henry Mischler House,** a Victorian-era B&B ($95 and up; 802 E. Edwards St.; 217/525-2660).

Litchfield and Mount Olive

Between Springfield and Cahokia Mounds, the most interesting stretch of old Route 66 runs along the east side of the freeway for about a dozen miles, between Litchfield and Mount Olive. First stop is **Litchfield,** an old coal-mining center that is home to one of the best and most stylish Route 66 restaurants, the **Ariston café** (Tues.–Sun.;413 Old Route 66; 217/324-2023), right in the heart of town at the junction of old Route 66 and Hwy-16. The food is a step or two up from the usual roadside fare, and the white linen and refined decor have earned it a spot in the Route 66 Hall of Fame. The rest of Litchfield reeks of the old road, with cafés, motor courts, and old billboards aplenty, plus another old "ozoner," the **Sky-View Drive-In** on old Route 66 two miles north of town (217/324-4451).

Some seven miles southwest of Litchfield, the hamlet of **Mount Olive** (pop. 2,052) was a bustling coal-mining center in the early 20th century. It's now a sleepy little community, where the only signs of its mining past are in the Union Miners Cemetery, along old Route 66 at the northwest edge of town. Near the rear is a granite shaft rising from an elaborate pedestal, which serves as a memorial to Mary Harris "Mother" Jones (1830?–1930), the celebrated union activist (and liberal-minded magazine namesake) who died here, possibly aged 100, while supporting a miners' strike. Famous for her passionate oratory, like the phrase "Pray for the dead, and fight like hell for the living," she is buried nearby, her grave marked by a simple headstone.

For old-road fans, Mount Olive is also home to the oldest surviving service station on Route 66, the immaculate restored (but no longer in business) Shell station downtown, long owned by Russell Soulsby.

Collinsville: Cahokia Mounds

Old Route 66 followed today's I-270 around the north side of St. Louis, crossing the Mississippi River on the restored Chain of Rocks Bridge, but one of southern Illinois's biggest attractions sits directly east of the Gateway Arch, off the I-55/70 freeway at exit 6. Clearly visible to the south side of the Interstate, the enigmatic humps of **Cahokia Mounds State Historic Site** are the remains

South of Springfield, on the stretch of old Route 66 that forms the frontage road at I-55 exit 63, near the town of Raymond, a marble statue of the Virgin Mary forms a shrine that has become known as **Our Lady of the Highways.**

Parts of the old road survive between Springfield and Litchfield, but the route is incomplete and can be confusing to follow. I-55 makes much shorter work of the 45-mile drive.

Cahokia Mounds sit in the middle of the American Bottom, a floodplain whose gunpowder-black alluvial soils have long been considered among the richest and most productive in the world. However, Charles Dickens called it an "ill-favored Black Hollow" after enduring its mud, which, as he wrote in *American Notes,* had "no variety but in depth."

of the largest prehistoric Indian city north of Mexico. Over 100 earthen mounds of various sizes were built here by the indigenous Mississippian culture while Europe was in the Dark Ages; the largest covers 14 acres—more ground than the Great Pyramid of Cheops. But don't expect the works of the pharaohs: Symmetrical, grass-covered hills sitting in flat, lightly wooded bottomlands are what you'll find here. The view of the Gateway Arch in distant St. Louis from the 100-foot top of Monks Mound lends an odd sense of grandeur to the site, and a sophisticated Interpretive Center (hours vary; 618/346-5160) is a recommended first stop for its exhibits, award-winning multimedia orientation show, and guided and self-guiding tours.

The nearest town to the Cahokia Mounds is **Collinsville,** a pleasant little place that's nearly world-famous for its 170-foot-high **World's Largest Catsup Bottle,** which rises high above Hwy-159 a quarter mile south of Main Street, on the grounds of what used to be the Brooks Catsup Company (800 S. Morrison Ave.). This decorated water tower was constructed in 1949 and restored by the people of Collinsville in 1993; it has since been adopted by Collinsville as a super-size symbol of local pride and perseverance.

Chain of Rocks Bridge

If you have the time and the inclination to stretch your legs and breath deeply, make your way to the northeast edge of St Louis, where instead of following the 75-mph I-270 freeway, you can cross the Mississippi between Illinois and Missouri on the historic **Chain of Rocks Bridge.** The bridge has been renovated for use as a mile-long bike and hiking trail (daylight hours only; 314/741-1211), decorated with an array of old gas pumps and neon signs, just south of the modern I-270 freeway. If you're driving, the best parking is on the Illinois side of the bridge, but cyclists or energetic walkers can cross the bridge and continue all the way to the Gateway Arch in St. Louis, following an 11-mile Riverfront Trail.

Not quite on the same scale as the Cahokia Mounds, the Chain of Rocks Bridge, or even the Collinsville catsup bottle, the nearby Route 66 town of Mitchell holds one more Route 66 landmark: 85-year-old **Luna Café,** a onetime casino, speakeasy, and brothel that's now a pretty seedy but very "atmospheric" bar, north of the I-270 freeway exit 6, along old Route 66 (201 E. Chain of Rocks Rd.; 618/931-3152).

MISSOURI

The Ozark Highlands of southern Missouri, which Route 66 crosses in its 300-odd-mile journey between Illinois and Kansas, are about the only significant hills the road crosses east of the Sandia Mountains in New Mexico. This plateau region, though not by any means alpine or breathtaking, is visually dynamic in a way the broad flatlands of Illinois or Oklahoma rarely are. Though the I-44 freeway has replaced the old road all the way across the state, there are many signs of older alignments, and just about every Interstate exit drops you within a moment's drive of the Mother Road. Missouri also holds some great old motels and one of the greatest of the old Route 66 tourist attractions—**Meramec Caverns,** an extensive set of limestone caves offering the most over-the-top underground tour you can take.

Route 66 Across St. Louis

It can be maddening to follow old Route 66 across St. Louis, but its many great spots—Ted Drewe's Frozen Custard Stand, in particular— make it well worth the effort. One route crossed the Mississippi River right into downtown from Collinsville, Illinois, while another "City 66" route headed across the Chain of Rocks Bridge before running into downtown St. Louis along Florissant Avenue and Riverview Drive.

Heading southwest out of downtown, the old road followed Gravois Avenue, Chippewa Street, and Watson Road, just south of the parallel I-44 freeway.

St. Louis, the only place where three of our Road Trip routes coincide, marks the junction of old Route 66; US-50, the cross-country **Loneliest Road** (page 769); and **The Great River Road** (page 271). **St. Louis** itself is covered on pages 272–273.

Times Beach: Route 66 State Park

There's no plaque or notice proudly marking the spot, but the story of **Times Beach** (pop. 0) deserves mention. Founded in the 1920s as a weekend getaway a dozen miles west of St. Louis along the Meramec River, thanks to Route 66 the town grew into a working-class commuter suburb, with some 2,000 people but no paved streets except for the not-yet-famous highway that passed through the center of town. Times Beach remained a quiet hamlet until 1982, when the federal government discovered that the industrial oil sprayed on streets to keep down dust had in fact been contaminated with toxic dioxin. The toxic waste, combined with a Meramec River flood that buried the town for over a week, made Times Beach uninhabitable.

In 1984 the government paid $33 million to buy Times Beach and tear it down, and 15 years later the cleanup was declared complete. Four hundred acres of what was once Times Beach have since been reopened as the **Route 66 State Park,** north of I-44 exits 264, 265, and 266 (daily; free; 636/938-7198), with hiking trails, river access, and a nice little museum on Times Beach and Route 66, housed in a 1930s roadhouse.

Eureka and Gray Summit: I-44

Heading south and west out of St Louis, the I-44 freeway has pretty well obliterated old Route 66 as far as Eureka, where the sprawling amusement park **Six Flags St. Louis** (around $45; 636/938-5300) effectively marks the city's suburban edge. The park has all the thrill rides and water park fun you could want, and often hosts concerts and special events.

A very different experience can be had at Gray Summit, just west of Six Flags, where the Missouri Botanical Garden tends to the magical **Shaw Nature Reserve** (daily; $3; 636/451-3512), a 2,500-acre semi-wilderness of native plants, cultivated orchards, and wildflower meadows, just 35 miles from the Gateway Arch. And if you like animals, especially dogs and cats, you'll want to check out the well-trained pets showcased across I-44 at **Purina Farms** (closed Mon.; free; 314/982-3232). Dogs catch Frisbees and do all sorts of amazing tricks, while cats sit there and look pretty.

In between Six Flags and the Shaw Nature Reserve, Route 66 re-emerges from the shadows of I-44, winding through the hamlet of Pacific, where the Red Cedar Inn served dinner every evening from 1935 to 2007, when it closed. West of Pacific, Route 66 climbs toward Gray Summit past the faded old Route 66 sign for the Diamonds Truck Stop and the Gardenway Motel.

From Gray Summit, Hwy-100 runs northwest from I-44 toward the Missouri River to the historic towns of **Washington** and **Hermann,** which are covered in our US-50 road trip, **The Loneliest Road.** See page 767.

For most of the 30 miles between Gray Summit and Meramec Caverns, old Route 66 is overwhelmed by the I-44 freeway, so most Route 66 aficionados opt for the freeway and save their exploring for better stretches, like Devil's Elbow.

Meramec Caverns

The best stop along old Route 66's trek across Missouri, and one of the most enjoyable and charming roadside attractions along the entire Mother Road, **Meramec Caverns** (daily; $20; 573/468-2283) is a set of limestone caves advertised by signs on barns and buildings all along the route, and all over the Midwest. First developed during the Civil War, when the natural saltpeter was mined for use in manufacturing gunpowder, the caves were later popularized as a place for local farmers to get together for dances;

Among its many other claims to fame, Meramec Caverns is known as the birthplace of the bumper sticker.

Detour: Branson

A middle-American Las Vegas, Branson is a century-old Ozark resort town that hit the big time in the 1980s through clever promotion and cunning repackaging of country-and-western music and God-fearing recreation. There are well over 50 major performance venues in Branson, and looking down the list of people who make a living playing here—the Osmond Brothers, Tony Orlando, and Jim "I Don't Like Spiders and Snakes" Stafford—you'd think that anyone who had a hit record or a TV show, or who can sing in a twang and impersonate a country-western star, can have their own showcase theater. The range of shows keeps expanding, so these days you can also take in such exotic offerings as Acrobats of China or the Beatles-themed Liverpool Legends.

Bus tours throng and clog the streets and highways around Branson all summer long, and the experience can seem to sum up everything that's annoying and disappointing about the mass-merchandising of "pop culture"—then again, millions of people like it, so Branson must be doing something right.

What originally put Branson on the tourist map was not music but a book: *The Shepherd of the Hills,* by Harold Bell Wright. Set in and around Branson and published in 1907, it was a huge bestseller, with a hugely complicated plot. Adapted in the 1930s into an outdoor stage play ($37; 800/653-6288), featuring more than 80 actors if not quite a cast of thousands, *Shepherd of the Hills* has been drawing millions to Branson ever since.

The Ozark Mountains area around Branson is still a lovely place to explore; just about any road south, east, or west will take you through beautifully scenic mountain landscapes. One of the most popular spots in Branson is **Silver Dollar City** (daily; $55 and up; 417/338-2611), nine miles west of Branson via Hwy-76, a turn-of-the-20th-century theme park devoted to Ozark arts, crafts, and music—and roller coasters.

Meramec Caverns: nature's best sculpture and a disco light show!

the largest room in the caves is still used for Easter Sunrise services, occasional crafts shows, and even the occasional chamber of commerce meeting. An hour west of St. Louis, Meramec Caverns was opened as a tourist attraction in 1935 by Lester Dill, who guided visitors through the elaborate chambers and, more importantly, was a true master of the art of garnering cheap but effective publicity for his tourist attraction. An example: After World War II, Dill sent his son-in-law to the top of the Empire State Building dressed up as a caveman and had him threaten to jump off unless everyone in the world visited Meramec Caverns.

Fact and fiction mix freely at Meramec Caverns, adding to the pleasures of seeing the massive caves. Jesse James used these caverns as a hideout, and at least once took advantage of the underground river to escape through the secret "back door." Though Meramec is not huge compared to other caves, the natural formations are among the most sculptural and delicate of any cave you can visit, and the man-made additions are all low-tech and kitschy enough to be charming: The hand-operated sound-and-light show ends with a grand finale of Kate Smith singing "God Bless America," while the red, white, and blue of Old Glory is projected onto a limestone curtain. For the full Meramec experience, add in a canoe ride or a zip-wire ride, or stay the night in the pleasant riverside campground.

Meramec Caverns is near the town of **Stanton,** 55 miles west of St. Louis, three miles south of I-44 exit 230. There's a small café and a motel on the grounds, which spread along the banks of the Meramec River. At the I-44 exit, the odd little **Jesse James Museum** (weekends only April–May and Sept.–Oct.; $5) insists, despite all evidence to the contrary, that a 100-year-old man who turned up in Stanton in 1948 was in fact Jesse James.

Cuba and Rolla

Along I-44 west of Meramec Caverns, the old Route 66 roadside is lined by ramshackle wooden stands, which, toward the end of summer, sell sweet Concord grapes from local Rosati vineyards. The stands are located along the frontage roads (which in many cases are the remnants of the original Route

white hawthorn,
state flower of Missouri

66), but people park along the freeway and walk to them. At the eastern edge of this grape-growing district, the small town of **Cuba** has a vintage Phillips 66 gas station and a dozen colorful murals covering large areas of downtown buildings with scenes from Cuba's history (depicting everything from the Civil War to the day in 1928 when Amelia Earhart made an emergency landing in a farmer's field).

Cuba also makes it onto many Route 66 itineraries thanks to the friendly **Wagon Wheel Motel,** which for many years was famous for offering 1930s charm at 1970s prices. Recently remodeled under new ownership, the Wagon Wheel still allows travelers to sample a kinder, gentler, less complicated era—even while taking advantage of free Wi-Fi. The Wagon Wheel Motel is right on Route 66 ($60 and up; 901 E. Washington St.; 573/885-3411). An added bonus: good barbecue right next door, at the **Missouri Hick** (573/885-6791).

Twenty miles west of Cuba, about midway between St. Louis and Springfield, one of the liveliest towns along the Ozark Mountains stretch of Route 66 is **Rolla** (pop. 18,488; pronounced "RAW-la"). In the center of town, right along old Route 66 on the campus of the Missouri University of Science and Technology (MUST), one big draw is the half-scale replica of that ancient Druidical observatory, **Stonehenge.** (Alas, Rolla's Stonehenge now stands surrounded by buildings, so you can't do any solstice sunrise celebrations). If you have trouble finding Rolla's Stonehenge, this miniature Wonder of the World stands across Route 66 from the **Great Wall of China,** a pretty good Chinese restaurant on Route 66 (1505 N. Bishop Ave.; 573/341-9922). Talk about "small world."

Adding to the surprising mix of international flavors is another Rolla tradition: a wild and crazy St. Patrick's Day party, held every year since 1908, during which students paint the streets of Rolla green, slay rubber snakes, and drink just about anything they can find, all in homage to the Emerald Isle.

Amongst the I-44 freeway clutter of Waffle Houses and Shoney's at the west end of Rolla, there's still a sign for the fireworks and moccasins on sale at the landmark **Totem Pole Trading Post – since 1933,** but the real enduring draw here is the food and drink served up for breakfast, lunch, and dinner every day, just south of the Totem Pole at **Tommy's Tater Patch,** a stone's throw off Route 66 (103 Bridge School Rd.; 573/368-3111).

Old Route 66: Devil's Elbow

West of Rolla on in to Springfield, I-44 has been built right on top of the old Route 66 corridor, and dozens of mostly abandoned old motels, motor courts, gas stations, and other highway-dependent businesses line the remains of the old road, which still serves as a freeway frontage road for most of the way. There are plenty of antiques shops and cafés to make detours interesting, and the longish detour along old Route 66 through the **Devil's Elbow** district is especially memorable, but if you're pressed for time even the Interstate superslab offers a plenty-scenic drive through these upland Ozark Mountains, much of which are protected from development within the Mark Twain National Forest.

This is the most ruggedly picturesque stretch of Route 66 across Missouri; the name "Devil's Elbow" comes from a section of the Big Piney River that turns so acutely it caused repeated logjams. The earliest incarnations of Route 66 followed what's now signed as "Teardrop Road," and up until 1981 the last alignment of Route 66 followed what's now the very hilly, four-lane **Hwy-Z,** some of the last Missouri sections of the old road to be bypassed by I-44 (all this is between I-44 exits 163 and 169).

Besides the old road itself, a great reason to tour this 10-mile stretch of old Route 66 is the chance to sample some fine Missouri barbecue at the **Elbow Inn,** just south of the junction of Hwy-Z and Teardrop Road (573/336-5375), a lively, good-natured biker bar with cans of cold beer and lots of bras pinned to the ceiling. If you're a barbecue fan, you can vote for mid-Missouri's best ribs by comparing the Elbow Inn with its nearest competitor, the **Sweetwater BBQ** (573/336-8830), on Hwy-Z just southeast of I-44 exit 163.

West of here, the scenic old road crashes suddenly back into the franchised fast food of I-44 at the twin towns of St. Robert and Waynesville, where 30,000-plus soldiers and dependents at the nearby Fort Leonard Wood U.S. Army base, headquarters of the U.S. Army military police school (and a small museum), have generated a rash of Wal-Marts and shopping malls.

Lebanon: Munger Moss and Laura Ingalls Wilder

West of Waynesville, in **Lebanon** (pop. 14,292), the stretch of old Route 66 running along the north side of I-44 holds the marvelous **Munger Moss Motel** ($45; 1336 E. Route 66; 417/532-3111), a landmark since 1946, where Ramona Lehman and family offer clean rooms, a wonderful neon sign, and a swimming pool. Across Route 66 from the Munger Moss is a bowling alley with a snack bar and a set of batting cages (5 cents a pitch!), making Lebanon something of a perfect Route 66 destination.

While the good food and warm Munger Moss hospitality is more than reason enough to visit

Lebanon, the town also marks the turnoff for a trip to visit another American institution, the Ozark Mountain homestead where author Laura Ingalls Wilder wrote the famous *Little House* books. Though it's an hour detour south via Hwy-5, or 45 miles due east of Springfield via US-60, Wilder's Rocky Ridge Farm has been preserved as the **Laura Ingalls Wilder Home and Museum,** on a hill two miles southeast of the town of Mansfield (daily; $8; 3068 Highway A; 417/924-3626). Unlike the many reconstructed Little House sights elsewhere, this museum has a direct and intimate connection with the woman who, for generations of readers, brought the American frontier to life. Born in 1867, Wilder grew up with the country, her iconic "little house" moving ever westwards from the "big woods" of Wisconsin on to the "prairie" of Kansas and South Dakota. Wilder moved to the Ozarks in 1894 and worked to establish a successful apple and dairy farm, and it was not until the economic downturns of the 1930s, when Wilder was in her 60s, that she began publishing her books, which have since sold millions (some of the royalties go to support the Mansfield library, where there is also a small museum). The home the Wilders lived in most of their adult lives forms the heart of the museum, and they are buried in the town cemetery, alongside their daughter Rose, who urged on (and some say collaborated on) Laura's autobiographical stories.

Springfield

The largest city in southern Missouri, **Springfield** (pop. 157,630) doesn't feel nearly as big as it is, though it does sprawl for many miles in all directions. Despite the ongoing growth and development, Springfield has preserved much of its old Route 66 frontage, along St. Louis Street east of downtown, as well as the grandly named Chestnut Expressway west of downtown. The 20-mph speed limit on downtown streets—along with tons of free parking—enables Route 66 pilgrims to pay homage to the town's Arabesque landmark **Shrine Mosque** theater (601 E. Saint Louis St.), which still hosts occasional concerts.

Springfield is also celebrated as the place where "Wild Bill" Hickok killed fellow gambler Dave Tutt, apparently because Tutt wore the watch he'd won from Hickok playing cards. A plaque in the central square, three blocks west of the Shrine Mosque, tells one of many variations on the tale.

One place you have to see to believe—though the fisherman or hunter in your family will already know about it, for sure—is "The World's Greatest Sporting Goods Store," **BASS Pro Shops Outdoor World** (1935 S. Campbell St.; 417/887-7334). Along with acres of floor space, this granddaddy of all sporting goods stores, birthplace of what is now an international chain, has eight different fish tanks totaling 140,000 gallons, a 40-foot waterfall, and even its own restaurant, called Hemingway's, and a snack bar.

Springfield has at least one fine old Route 66 motel: the **Route 66 Rail Haven** ($65 and up; 203 S. Glenstone Ave.; 417/866-1963), on the corner of

Springfield is home to the Class AA Texas League **Springfield Cardinals,** who play off US-65 at one of the country's most attractive ballparks, Hammons Field (417/863-2143).

A great stretch of old Route 66, renumbered Hwy-96, runs for 50 miles along the north side of I-44 between Springfield and Carthage, passing rolling pastures and little towns like Halltown and Avilla, with antiques shops and abandoned cafés lining the old highway frontage.

Carthage was the boyhood home of naturalist Marlin Perkins, host of Mutual of Omaha's *Wild Kingdom* TV show. A life-sized statue of him stands in Central Park, three blocks southwest of the courthouse square. Carthage was also the girlhood home of Wild West outlaw Belle Starr.

old Route 66 and US-65. Open since 1938, it has been fully modernized and now is a Best Western affiliate with a railroad theme. A mile away on old Route 66 is one of the earliest and most stylish models of the **Steak 'n Shake** burger chain (1158 E. St. Louis St.; 417/866-6109); open 24 hours, this is one of the last ones where carhops still bring your food to your car (during daylight hours).

Carthage

Just shy of the Kansas border, six miles north of I-44 and right on old Route 66, **Carthage** (pop. 14,378) is a perfect little town, looking for all the world like the model for the idyllic though fictional town of Hill Valley from the *Back to the Future* movies. The center of Carthage is dominated by the outrageously ornate, circa-1895, limestone Jasper County Courthouse, which features a local history mural and an open-cage elevator in the lobby. (On Thursdays and Fridays the elevator is hand-operated by a charming and friendly young woman, Geraldine Bunn, who serves as Carthage's unofficial ambassador.) Away from the courthouse square area, the rest of the town is fairly franchise-free—away from the Interstate at least—and the residential areas hold well-maintained Victorian houses.

For fun on the road, there's a bowling alley, **Star Lanes** (219 E. 3rd St.; 417/358-2144), just east of the square. A mile or so west of downtown on Old Route 66, enjoy a double feature of Hollywood blockbusters in the comfort of your car at the **66 Drive-In** (weekends only; 17231 Old 66 Blvd.; 417/359-5959).

If you have a soft spot for hyperbolic sentimentality, one not-to-be-missed monument is the **Precious Moments Chapel** (daily; free; 417/358-7599), featuring the wide-eyed characters from the religious figurine series. The chapel is well signed, west of US-71 on the southwest edge of Carthage.

The 1940s stainless steel landmark **Iggy's Diner** (Mon.–Sat.; 2400 Grand Ave.; 417/237-0212) is on the south side of town, while downtown Carthage has another good place to eat, the **Carthage Deli** (301 S. Main St.; 417/358-8820), which serves sandwiches and milk shakes in a 1950s-style soda fountain on the northwest corner of the courthouse square.

Also in Carthage is an old Route 66 landmark: the glowing pink-and-green neon sign of the **Boots Motel** (107 S. Garrison St.). Clark Gable stayed here, and it remained a welcoming, family-run place until the late 1990s, but Boots changed hands a few times, started offering longer-term housing, and eventually fell into foreclosure. At the time of writing, local Route 66 fans were working with a new owner to renovate and reopen the property.

Joplin

If you want to travel the old Route 66 alignment across Kansas, you'll also pass through **Joplin** (pop. 50,15), a border town that's the industrial center of the tri-state region. Formerly a lead- and zinc-mining town, in May 2011 Joplin made the national news in the worst possible way when it was hit by one of the most powerful tornados in recent U.S. history, 200-mph winds tearing a swath of destruction and killing more than 150 people in less than 10 minutes of terror. Before the tornado, Joplin was better known for its high-quality limestone quarries than for its history, though highway heritage is well served at Schifferdecker Park, west of downtown off 7th Street, a pre–Route 66 rest area that now has a mining museum, small Route 66 museum, and a public swimming pool (daily; $1; 417/625-4750) that is much appreciated on a sweltering late summer day. Though the tornado destroyed dozens of homes and businesses, Joplin's downtown area does hold one unlikely attraction, a vibrant mural by artist Thomas Hart Benton depicting life in Joplin at the turn of the 20th

On the Kansas/Missouri border, tune to **KRPS 89.9 FM** for classical music.

George Washington Carver National Monument (daily; free; 417/325-4151) preserves the farm where the eminent agricultural scientist, educator, and self-sufficiency advocate grew up in the 1860s.

One of the Lead and Zinc Mines in the Tri-State Mining District of Missouri-Kansas-Oklahoma

Massive lead mines like this have disappeared from Kansas.

century. The over-70-square-foot mural, which turned out to be the artist's final complete work, is in the lobby of the Joplin City Hall (602 S. Main St.).

Downtown Joplin has a number of good places to eat, including the Greek-accented, family-owned and -run **Arde's Main Street Bistro,** which is just a short walk away from City Hall (407 S. Main St.; 417/624-3536).

KANSAS

The shortest but perhaps best-signed stretch of Route 66's eight-state run is its 13.2-mile slice across the southeast corner of Kansas. Be careful not to blink your eyes, or you'll be saying, as Dorothy did in *The Wizard of Oz,* "I have a feeling we're not in Kansas anymore."

Coming from Missouri, your first town in Kansas is **Galena,** where the funky **Galena Mining and Historical Museum** (hours vary; 319 W. 7th St.; 620/783-2192), just off the main drag and marked by a big Old 66 sign, is stuffed with old newspaper clippings and other items that give a glimpse of town life during its 1920s-era mining heyday. At its peak, Galena had a population near 30,000 (10 times the current number), and various rusting tools and machines testify to the work that once went on here. That said, the hospitable Route 66 spirit lives on, most obviously at **Women on the Route,** inside the old Kan-O-Tex gas station (119 N. Main St.; 620/783-1366), now serving sandwiches and selling souvenirs related to Pixar's animated Route 66 movie *Cars*. (The early 1950s International Harvester tow truck that apparently inspired the *Cars* character "Tow Mater" is parked outside, though they've had to change its name to avoid the wrath of Disney's lawyers.)

Baxter Springs soda fountain

Another appetizing attraction awaits in **Riverton,** the next town to the west, where the **Old Riverton Store** (620/848-3330), a.k.a. "Eisler Brothers," has been open since the 1920s. Across the highway from a big power plant, the old store has a good deli counter, with sandwiches and a soda fountain. The last of the Eislers passed away in 2009, but the store is still in good hands, headquarters of the small but active Kansas Route 66 Association and an essential stop for fans of the old road.

Heading west towards Oklahoma, the newer highway bypasses a fine old rainbow-arched Route 66 concrete bridge, just east of **Baxter Springs,** where locals point with pride at the circa 1870 Crowell Bank, which was said to have been robbed by Jesse James and now houses the popular **Café on the Route** (1101 Military Ave.; 620/856-5646),

Baxter Springs information center

which has been featured on the Food Network's national TV shows, and handily rents B&B rooms upstairs. A block away, the nicely restored 1930s Phillips 66 filling station is now a useful museum and Baxter Springs **information center** (620/856-2066) at 10th Street and Military Avenue (a.k.a. Route 66).

Though it's pretty quiet these days, during the Civil War Baxter Springs saw one of the worst massacres in the country's history, when more than 100 unarmed Union soldiers, including many African Americans, were captured and killed by William Quantrill's rebel Confederate raiders (including the aforementioned Jesse James), who had disguised themselves by wearing blue Union uniforms. A monument to the murdered soldiers stands in **Baxter Springs Soldiers' Lot** in the Baxter City Cemetery, off US-166 two miles west of town.

OKLAHOMA

Apart from occasional college football teams, Oklahoma doesn't often get to crow about being the best in the country, but as far as Route 66 is concerned, the state is definitely number one. Containing more still-drivable miles of the old highway than any other state, Oklahoma is definitely mecca for old-roads fans.

Underneath the promotional hoopla that Route 66 generates everywhere it ever went, all over the state you can see signs that barely a century ago all of Oklahoma was Indian Territory, last refuge of Kiowa, Apache, Comanche, and other tribes before the U.S. government took even this land away from them during "land rushes" in the 1890s. A few years later, oil was discovered and the state started on one of a series of boom-and-bust cycles. The Dust Bowl exodus of the 1930s was the greatest downturn, as thousands of Oklahoman families headed west on Route 66, though many of the towns along the road take bittersweet pride in *The Grapes of Wrath* connections.

Oklahoma has the longest and most intact stretches of old Route 66, and if you really want to explore it to the full, get your hands on a copy of the essential map-packed road guide *Oklahoma Route 66*, by Arcadia, Oklahoma's own Jim Ross.

Northeast Oklahoma: The Sidewalk Highway

In the far northeastern corner of Oklahoma, old Route 66 runs through a hardscrabble former lead- and zinc-mining region, from the Kansas border to Vinita on the I-44 Turnpike. Three miles southwest of the Kansas border, **Quapaw** could be the first or last Oklahoma town you visit, depending upon your direction, but either way it's worth a look for the many murals painted on the walls of downtown businesses. The next town along, **Commerce** (pop. 2,473), was another old mining town, noteworthy as the boyhood home of the late, great Yankee player Mickey Mantle, in whose honor the old Route 66 alignment down Main Street has been renamed.

Four miles to the south via old Route 66 (now signed as US-69), **Miami** holds the magnificent Spanish Revival–style Coleman Theater, built in 1929 when the

old-style Conoco station, Commerce

town was still luxuriating in the riches coming out of the surrounding mines. Two blocks down Route 66 from the opulent theater, fans of 1970s motorcycle daredevil Evel Knievel or motorcycle-loving 1960s movie star Steve McQueen will want to spend some time at **Vintage Iron** (free; 128

S. Main St.; 918/542-6170). Here old Harleys rub fenders with classic 1960s Triumphs, rare Bultacos, and the 400cc Husqvarna that McQueen rode in his classic movie, *On Any Sunday.* The "museum" is basically an expensively decorated motorbike shop, selling all sorts of riding gear plus lots of desirable vintage-looking T-shirts. (If you like bikes, you'll want to check out Oklahoma's other great Route 66 motorcycle museum, Seaba Station, west of Chandler.)

Still following US-69, now roughly parallel to (and eventually crossing under) I-44 between Miami and Afton, some of the earliest paved stretches of old Route 66 were constructed only one lane wide, because in 1926 the state of Oklahoma did not have enough money to build a full-width version. Not surprisingly, these lengths of the road became known as the "Sidewalk Highway." The easiest stretch to find runs parallel to US-69—turn west at the Northeast Technology Center vocational school along an increasingly narrow country lane, and look out for the 66 shields painted on the pavement. This "Sidewalk Highway" rejoins the main Route 66 alignment at Afton, where a convenience store now stands on the site of the fabled Buffalo Ranch Trading Post. For more on Afton, the Buffalo Ranch, Route 66, or help finding the Sidewalk Highway, head down to **Afton Station** (12 SE 1st St.; 918/257-4044), a nicely renovated 1930s-era gas station that has been brought back to life as a gift shop and museum of mostly old Packard cars.

Vinita

Old Route 66 crosses the Interstate (a.k.a. the Will Rogers Turnpike) again at **Vinita,** where the region's Native American heritage is brought into focus at the **Eastern Trails Museum** (hours vary; free; 215 W. Illinois St.; 918/256-2115), next to the public library. The exhibits center on the Cherokee Trail of Tears, which brought the tribe here after a forced march from North Carolina in the 1830s, but the museum also covers the general history of the surrounding area.

Vinita is home to the **Will Rogers Memorial Rodeo,** held here each August since 1935, the year he died; Rogers attended secondary school in Vinita after growing up near Claremore. Vinita also hosts the annual **World's Largest Calf Fry Festival** in late-August. (Calf fries are prairie oysters, otherwise

Totem Pole Park

known as beef testicles. Just so you know.) Contact the visitors center (918/256-7133) for details on any of these.

Vinita also has a great old Route 66 restaurant: **Clanton's Cafe** (319 E. Illinois Ave.; 918/256-9053), right at the center of town. "Oklahoma's oldest family-owned and -operated restaurant," since 1927 Clanton's has been famous for its chicken-fried beefsteak, served here with mashed potatoes and slathered in peppery white gravy. Clanton's also has good burgers and, in case you miss the festival, calf fries. (See above for a disclaimer.)

Foyil

Between Vinita and Claremore, old Route 66 survives in regular use as the "free road" alternative to the I-44 Turnpike, alternating between two-lane and divided four-lane highway. The most interesting wide spot along this stretch of hallowed road is **Foyil,** where in the 1940s and 1950s retired fiddle-maker and folk artist Ed Galloway sculpted an outdoor garden of giant totem poles—the tallest is over 90 feet—and other Native American–inspired objects out of concrete. After fading and weathering for many years, the poles, four miles east of town via Hwy-28A, were restored in 1993–1994 as **Totem Pole Park** (daily dawn–dusk; free), and now it's a fascinating place to stop for a picnic or to simply admire the effort that went into these "Watts Towers of the Plains."

> Foyil was the hometown of Andy Payne, the Cherokee youth who in 1928 won the "Bunion Derby," a coast-to-coast foot race that followed Route 66 from Los Angeles to Chicago, then headed east to New York City—equivalent to running a marathon and a half every day for the 84 days it took him to finish.

Claremore: Will Rogers Memorial

Twenty miles northeast of Tulsa, **Claremore** (pop. 18,581) is a bigger-than-average Route 66 town, one that will be forever connected with its favorite son, Will Rogers (1879–1935). Rogers was born nearby in a rough log cabin "halfway between Claremore and Oologah before there was a town at either place." He rose from a vaudeville career as a sideshow rope-tricks artist to become one of the most popular figures in America, thanks to his folksy humor.

Will Rogers starred on Broadway for 10 years in the *Ziegfield Follies,* wrote an immensely popular national newspaper column, and acted in more than 70 Hollywood movies. Sadly, before he could retire back home to Claremore, Rogers was killed in a plane crash in 1935; his land here was later turned into the **Will Rogers Memorial** (daily; donations; 918/341-0719), a mile northwest of downtown Claremore on a hill overlooking the town. A statue of Rogers greets visitors at the front door, and his tomb is here, along with a small archive and museum that recounts his life story, showing off his collections of saddles, lariats, and other cowboy gear.

Will Rogers Memorial

Another popular Claremore stop is the **J. M. Davis Arms and Historical Museum** (closed Sun. in winter; donations; 330 N. J.M. Davis Blvd.; 918/341-5707), right off Route 66. Besides one of the largest and most comprehensive gun collections anywhere in the world (just under 14,000 firearms!), the museum has antique musical instruments, hundreds of posters dating back to World War I, and 1,200 German beer steins.

For good food and out-of-this-world pies (over a dozen different kinds), stop by the **Hammett House,** west of downtown next to the Rogers Memorial (1616 W. Will Rogers; 918/341-7333).

Catoosa: The Blue Whale

One of Tulsa's premier Route 66 attractions was the giant **Blue Whale,** in the suburb of **Catoosa,** northeast of Tulsa along the stretch of the old road that runs from I-44 exit 240. The park, built as an animal-themed tourist attraction in the 1970s by Hugh Davis, a curator at the Tulsa Zoo, closed down long ago and was left to crumble. Unlike so many other long-suffering Route 66 landmarks, however, the Blue Whale has been lovingly restored by the family of its original creators (with a little help from the Hampton Inn brand of Hilton Hotels).

Catoosa, surprisingly, is also a major port, linked, by way of impressively engineered improvements to the Arkansas River system, to the Gulf of Mexico.

Tulsa

Home to fine art deco buildings built during the 1920s boom years of the Oklahoma oil industry, as well as the Gilcrease Museum, one of the country's top art museums, **Tulsa** (pop. 391,906) is a bustling big city that doesn't make a song-and-dance out of its many treasures. It's a fascinating place to explore, but

Books on Route 66

Considering the old road's great fame, it's hardly surprising that over a dozen different books in print deal with the Route 66 experience. Some are travel guides, some folk histories, others nostalgic rambles down what was and what's left along the Mother Road. Photographic essays document the rapidly disappearing architecture and signage, and at least one cookbook catalogs recipes of dishes served in cafés on the route. Even in the age of GPS coordinates, online maps, and Twitter feeds (like the timely and accurate Route 66 News), nothing beats a good book. The following is a sampling of favorite titles, most of which can be found in stores along the route if not in your local bookstore.

The Grapes of Wrath, John Steinbeck (Penguin Books). The first and foremost Route 66–related story, this compelling tale traces the traumatic travels of the Joad family from Dust Bowl Oklahoma to the illusive Promised Land of California. Brutally vivid, *The Grapes of Wrath* was an instant bestseller at the tail end of the Depression and was the source of Route 66's appellation, "The Mother Road."

A Guide Book to Highway 66, Jack Rittenhouse (University of New Mexico). A facsimile reprinting of the self-published 1946 book that the late author sold door-to-door at truck stops, motor courts, and cafés along the route.

EZ 66: Route 66 Guide for Travelers, Jerry McClanahan (National Historic Route 66 Federation). The most-detailed driver's guide to old Route 66, packed with maps and mile-by-mile instructions and information, spiral-bound for on-the-road ease of use.

Route 66: The Mother Road, Michael Wallis (St. Martin's Press, 1987). This richly illustrated and thoroughly researched guide to the old road is more armchair companion than practical aid, but the book captures the spirit of Route 66, and the writer has been a key promotional force behind the road's preservation and rediscovery. (Wallis also does the voice of the sheriff in *Cars*.)

Route 66 Sightings, Jerry McClanahan, Jim Ross and Shelle Graham (Ghost Town Press, 2011). By far the best Route 66 photo book, this lush new volume captures the Mother Road in all its moods.

Searching for 66, Tom Teague (Samizdat House, 1996). More personal than other titles on Route 66, this poignant book of vignettes, illustrated with the fine pen-and-ink drawings of Route 66 artist Bob Waldmire, describes the author's interactions with the many people along Route 66 who made it what it was. Sadly, both the author and the artist (and almost everyone profiled) have since passed away, making the stories here all the more important and affecting.

Tulsa is the home of **Oral Roberts University,** marked by a futuristic, 15-story tower and an 60-foot-high pair of praying hands along Lewis Avenue, six miles south of downtown.

if your time is limited, spend it at the **Gilcrease Museum** (closed Mon.; 918/596-2700), on the northwest edge of Tulsa. Bought with the fortune benefactor Thomas Gilcrease made when oil was discovered on his land, the collection includes some of the most important works of Western American art and sculpture, with major works by Thomas Moran, George Catlin, and others, plus Native American artifacts and early maps that put the frontier region into its historical context. The expansive grounds include a lovely series of gardens and Mr. Gilcrease's old house.

South of the Tulsa airport, not too far from Route 66, the **Admiral Twin Drive-In** in Tulsa burned in 2010 and was rebuilt by donations in 2011, and in the 1960s it played a starring role in S. E. Hinton's bestselling coming-of-age novel, *The Outsiders.*

For dinner or a drink, the liveliest part of Tulsa is the Brookside district, south of downtown around 34th Street and Peoria Avenue, where there's a handful of trendy cafés, nightclubs, and restaurants. There's hardly anything left along old Route 66, but you can get a feel for the old days downtown at the retro 1920s **New Atlas Grill** (415 S. Boston St.; 918/583-3111), serving full breakfasts plus soups, salads, and lunchtime sandwiches in an art deco tower. If you want a taste of the 1950s, you'll probably enjoy the good honest food at **Tally's Good Food Café,** a retro-Route 66 diner just off Midtown Tulsa's 11th Street alignment, east of the University of Tulsa campus (1102 S. Yale Ave.; 918/835-8039).

The usual chain hotels and motels line all the freeways around Tulsa. There's a big **Holiday Inn** ($100 and up; 17 W. 7th St.; 918/585-5898) downtown. For the full Route 66 experience, try the saguaro-signed **Desert Hills Motel,** just east of Tally's Good Food ($40 and up; 5220 E. 11th St.; 918/834-3311), and there's also the newly renovated and very stylish **Campbell Hotel,** formerly the Casa Loma, which reopened in 2011 ($99 and up; 2636 E. 11th St.; 918/744-5500).

Old Route 66: Stroud

Between Sapulpa, on the suburban fringes of southwest Tulsa, and the next main stop, Chandler, old Route 66 zigzags back and forth along the freeway for the next 50 miles. Near the east end of this stretch, three miles west of Sapulpa, the circa-1921 **Rock Creek Bridge** is a reminder of what the old roads were really like: 120 feet long yet only 12 feet wide, the truss is rusty but the bridge still stands as a proud reminder of the original 1920s Route 66. Across the bridge is another evocative reminder: an abandoned drive-in movie theater, long closed but with the screen and the fan-shaped parking lot still intact.

Another stop to keep in mind, **Russ's Ribs** (233 S. Main St.; 918/367-5656) in the brick-paved heart of **Bristow,** is home to some of the best barbecue sandwiches on the planet. A full slab (enough meat to feed three people, so long as I'm not there to hog it all) will set you back around $25, and Russ's also makes some excellent deli sandwiches and "family packs" with all the fixin's for a roadside picnic.

Continuing west, old-roads fanatics will probably want to follow the winding alignment of Route 66, which continues along the south side of the turnpike for over 40 miles. On the west side of **Stroud** (pop. 2,690; "Home of Daneka Allen, Miss OK 1999"), check out the **Rock Cafe** (114 W. Main St.; 918/968-3990), a Route 66 relic built in 1939 out of local stone quarried when the original highway was cut in the 1920s, and still churning out its better-than-average roadside fare. The Rock Café (whose bathroom featured original graffiti by *Toy Story* creator John Lasseter, who modeled some scenes in his Route 66 movie *Cars* on the Rock Café's inimitable architecture) suffered from a fire in 2008 but got back up and running in no time. Stroud also has the classic old **Skyliner Motel** ($50 and up; 717 W. Main St.; 918/968-9556).

Chandler and Warwick

West of Stroud, as for most of the way between Tulsa and Oklahoma City, old Route 66 continues along the south side of the I-44 Turnpike, which has another of its very rare exits at Chandler. **Chandler** (pop. 3,100) is one of the most pleasant old Route 66 towns in Oklahoma and stands out from its top-notch colleagues for a number of good reasons, not least of which is the classic **Lincoln Motel** ($45; 740 E. 1st St.; 405/258-0200), along old Route 66 at the east edge of town. It's a little time-worn, for sure, but still as neat and tidy as the day it opened in 1939—two dozen two-room cabins, each with a green bench for watching the world whiz by. Chandler's solid-looking WPA-era Armory has been done up to house the lively and engaging **Route 66 Interpretive Center** (closed Sun. in winter and Mon. year-round; $5; 400 E. Route 66/1st St.; 405/258-1300), which gives a eye-opening introduction to the enterprising and welcoming Route 66 spirit, and the small town also has a well-restored cottage-style Phillips 66 station.

Heading west toward Oklahoma City, old Route 66 continues along the south side of I-44, passing a metal-roofed barn emblazoned with a photogenic "Meramec Caverns—Stanton MO" sign west of Chandler and crossing under the freeway about three miles west of Warwick. From here, one of the state's best surviving stretches of Route 66, known locally as the "free road," runs for over 30 miles along the north side of the turnpike, passing by horse and cattle ranches as it rolls across the red earth.

At **Warwick,** on old Route 66 about seven miles west of Chandler, and a few miles east of where Route 66 again crosses the I-44 Turnpike (at exit 158), the old highway town of Warwick has a small gem: the **Seaba Station Motorcycle Museum** (closed Wed., free), a simple 1920s filling station, recently and thoughtfully renovated to house a covetable collection of motorcy-

cles, memorabilia, fan magazines, and more—my favorite item is a 1970s Evel Knievel pinball machine. Altogether there are around 60 motorbikes on display, mostly one-of-a-kind racing and moto-cross machines. (If you like this, check out Oklahoma's other great Route 66 motorcycle museum, Vintage Iron in Miami.)

North of OKC, Route 66 ran through the town of **Edmond,** the place where aviator Wiley Post is buried (he was the pilot killed in the same crash as Will Rogers). Edmond is also notorious for the fact that a disgruntled post office employee killed 14 of his co-workers here in 1986, inspiring the expression "going postal."

Following old Route 66 across Oklahoma City can be confusing, but keep an eye peeled for a bottle-shaped building on Classen Boulevard at 23rd Street.

Arcadia

About 10 miles east of the I-35 freeway through OKC, the main stop along this idyllic rural cruise is the old highway town of **Arcadia** (pop. 247), which holds a wonderfully restored, very large red **round barn.** The ground floor of this much-loved landmark, originally built way back in 1898, is now a mini museum and gift shop (405/396-0824) selling some highly collectible original Route 66 memorabilia.

A half mile east of the round barn, Arcadia's other Route 66 landmark is bright, shiny, and comparatively new: **Pops** (405/928-7677), a gas station and small café fronted by a giant (66-foot-tall) soda pop bottle–shaped sign (not neon, but multicolored energy-efficient LEDs). Built by Aubrey McClendon, an Oklahoma-born natural gas billionaire, Pops opened in 2007 and sells over 500 different varieties of soda pop (including around 100 brands of root beer!), as well as the requisite burgers and fuel, plus silky milkshakes. Even if you're not all that hungry or thirsty, the exuberant, bottle-shaped tower, with its rainbow of colors, makes it worth hanging around till nightfall.

Oklahoma City

Now tragically synonymous with the anti-government terrorist bombing carried out by Timothy McVeigh in 1995, **Oklahoma City** (pop. 579,999) has long been one of the primary stops along the Mother Road. In the Bobby Troup song, it was the only place along the route he singled out for praise, no doubt more for the easy rhyme ("Oklahoma City is mighty pretty") than for its less obvious visual charms. The city was the biggest boomtown of the 1889 Land Rush, when Oklahoma was opened for white settlement after being set aside "for eternity" as Indian Territory. Between noon and sundown on April 22, over 10,000 people raced here to claim the new lands—many of them having illegally camped out beforehand, earning the nickname "Sooner," which is still applied to the state's college football team.

A second boom took place during the Depression years, when oil was struck; there are still producing wells in the center of the city, including some on the grounds of the state capitol. The collapse of the oil industry in the 1980s hit hard, but the shock of the 1995 bombing seems to have galvanized the city, which has since revitalized itself with a gorgeous new baseball stadium, an exciting NBA basketball team, a concert arena, and canal-side cafés in the Bricktown warehouse district south of downtown.

Just off old Route 66 across from the capitol, a good first stop is the **Oklahoma History Center** (closed Sun.; $7; 800 Nazih Zuhdi Dr.; 405/521-

2491), which has exhibits tracing the state's history, with special collections on the Native American presence, on pioneers, and on the oil industry. There's also a wide-ranging oral history of the Mother Road.

For poignant balance to a nostalgic Route 66 tour, pay your respects to the 168 men, women, and children killed in the April 19, 1995, bombing of the Alfred P. Murrah Federal Building. Between the capitol and Bricktown, the site of the bombing has been preserved as a **memorial park** (open 24 hours; free), landscaped with a shallow pool around which are arrayed a series of 168 sculpted chairs. Each chair represents a person killed in the blast, and the chairs range from very small to full-sized, marking the varying ages of the dead (who included 19 kids from the building's day-care center). An adjacent **museum** (daily; $10; 405/235-3313) tells the story of the bombing, its perpetrators, and its victims.

The Class AAA **Oklahoma RedHawks** (405/218-1000) play at ever-pleasant Bricktown Ballpark, south of downtown near the junction of I-35 and I-40.

The exciting young **Oklahoma City Thunder** NBA basketball team (405/208-4600) plays at City Arena, a half mile west of Bricktown.

Oklahoma City Practicalities

Downtown OKC spreads northwest from the busy I-35/I-40 junction ("The Crossroads of America"), where a massive new **American Indian Cultural Center** (405/239-5500) is under development. On the west side of the freeway, the Bricktown district is home to many fun restaurants and bars like **Tapwerks Ale House** (121 E. Sheridan Ave.; 405/319-9599), which has great beers, good food, and frequent live music. Oklahoma City also has more barbecue stands and steakhouses than just about anywhere in the country: One old Route 66 landmark, the Kentucky Club speakeasy and roadhouse (1226 NE 63rd St.), once frequented by Pretty Boy Floyd, survived until 2010. Its closing narrowed the field of candidates for OKC's Best BBQ to three: traditional **Jack's BBQ** (4418 NW 39th St.; 405/605-7790); the bigger and more accessible **Iron Starr Urban BBQ,** just off 36th Street (3700 N. Shartel Ave.; 405/524-5925); or **Earl's Rib Palace,** with six locations including one in Bricktown (215 Johnny Bench Dr.; 405/272-9898). For great, non-barbecue food right on old Route

66, go to the popular **Ann's Chicken Fry House** (405/943-8915)—look for the classic Caddies and fake police cars in the parking lot. Or if you're feeling adventurous, step inside the bottle-shaped building of **Saigon Baguette** (2426 NW Classen; 405/524-2660), which serves delicious Vietnamese food at the heart of OKC's rapidly expanding Asia District (In the mid-1970s, OKC served as a resettlement center for more than 10,000 Vietnamese refugees).

Accommodation options in and around OKC are provided by the usual motel chains, plus a very nice **Hampton Inn** in Bricktown ($90 and up; 300 E. Sheridan Ave.; 405/232-3600).

For westbound travelers, El Reno marks the first appearance of one of the longest-running ad campaigns along Route 66: dozens of billboards advertising "Tucumcari Tonite," this one 350 miles from its New Mexican subject.

West of Oklahoma City, old Route 66 runs along the north side of I-40; in places it's a three-lane road, with a dangerous passing lane in the center. The first real town beyond the OKC suburbs is **Yukon,** hometown of country crooner Garth Brooks and of a giant "Yukon's Best Flour" grain mill, whose huge sign lights up the night sky and draws shutterbugs off the highway.

El Reno: Hamburger City

Established as Fort El Reno in 1874 as part of U.S. Army efforts to subdue the Cheyenne, **El Reno** (pop. 16,749) later saw duty as a POW camp during World War II. More recently, the town earned a measure of fame as the site of a motel seen in the offbeat road movie *Rain Man.* (In the movie, the motel was in Amarillo, but the "real" one, called the Big Eight, sat along old Route 66 at the east edge of El Reno.)

For hungry road-trippers, especially those fond of all-American burger joints, El Reno offers an abundance of choices. Three great old places stand within a block of old Route 66, which followed Wade Street across downtown. The oldest, **Robert's** (300 S. Bickford St.; 405/262-1262), has been cooking since 1926, and should be a national model for short-order cooking. A block to the west is **Sid's Diner** (300 S. Choctaw St.; 405/262-7757), which has become insanely popular since it was featured on the TV show *Man vs. Food.* Finally, a block to the east is **Johnnie's Grill** (daily; 301 S. Rock Island; 405/262-4721), famed for its Fried Onion Burgers. (On the first weekend in May, El Reno gets together to cook up the "World's Largest Fried Onion Hamburger," a 750-pound behemoth that inspires an all-day festival.)

Hydro: Lucille's Road House

There's no clearer contrast between the charms of the old road and the anonymity of the Interstate than tiny **Hydro,** about midway between Oklahoma City and Clinton on the west bank of the Canadian River. A wonderful length of old Route 66 runs along the north side of I-40 exit 89, right past the ancient service station and souvenir stand operated by Lucille Hamons from 1941 until her death, at age 85, in August 2000. Though it's just 50 yards from the fast lane of the freeway, visiting Lucille's place to buy a soda or a postcard and have a quick hello with the energetic proprietor was a Route 66 rite of passage. Lucille's inspired the creation of a replica roadhouse on the north side of I-40 in the next town to the west, Weatherford; called **Lucille's Roadhouse** (580/772-8808), but without the energy and drive of Lucille herself, it lacks a little sparkle (though the burgers can be pretty tasty).

West of Lucille's, a surviving six-mile stretch of old Route 66 pavement follows the lay of the land up and down, offering a better sense of the landscape than does the faster but duller new road, which was completed in 1966.

Clinton

Named for Judge Clinton Irwin and not for former president Bill, **Clinton** (pop. 9,033) started life as a trading post for local Cheyenne Arapahoe people and is now in the spotlight as home of the official **Oklahoma Route 66 Museum** (daily, closed Sun. and Mon. in winter; $4; 2229 W. Gary Blvd.;

Oklahoma Route 66 Museum

580/323-7866), near the west end of town. Unlike many other "museums" along the route, this one is a true showcase and not just another souvenir stand. Funded by a variety of state and local sources, the museum reopened in late 1995 after undergoing a massive, million-dollar expansion and improvement and is one of the better museums of the old road along the old road. Collectors from all over the country, including Clinton's own Gladys Cuthbert, whose husband, Jack Cuthbert, was the primary promoter of Route 66 throughout its glory years, donated signs, artifacts, and memorabilia, which have been organized into a comprehensive exhibition of Mother Road history and culture not to be missed by any Route 66 aficionado. (There's a good gift shop, too.)

Childhood home of country-western star Toby Keith, Clinton also has the very nice McLain Rogers public park, with a swimming pool and water slides, at the center of town along 10th Street (old Route 66), next to the Route 66 Miniature Golf Course.

For food, west of town along the I-40 frontage, just north of exit 62, **Jiggs Smoke House** (580/323-5641) is a tiny cabin selling deliciously smoky barbecue sandwiches but specializing in travel-friendly beef jerky. Alas, Clinton's longtime favorite Route 66 restaurant, Pop Hick's, burned to the ground in 1999, with no insurance and no real chance of being rebuilt. Another blast from the past, Elvis Presley, stayed at least four times at the slightly faded **Trade Winds Inn** ($50 and up; 2128 Gary Blvd.; 580/323-2610), across from the Route 66 museum. Elvis's room has been "preserved" as a mini shrine, and you can stay in it (for around $100) and experience a time warp back to the mid-1960s. There's also a Hampton Inn and many other national chains.

Elk City

The last—or first, depending on your direction—sizable town east of the Texas border is **Elk City** (pop. 11,693), "Home of Susan Powell, Miss America 1981," and also childhood home of songwriter Jimmy Webb, who penned such all-time classics as "Galveston," "Wichita Lineman," "MacArthur Park" and "Up, Up and Away"). It was a popular stopover on Route 66, as evidenced by the many old motels along the various alignments of the old highway through town. Long before Elk City had its Route 66 heyday, it was a wild frontier town along the cattle trails from Texas to Dodge City, Kansas. The area's cowboy and pioneer history is recounted in the **Old Town Museum** (daily; $5; 580/225-6266), on the far west side of town, where there's a re-created Wild West town, complete with doctor's office, schoolhouse, tepee, and rodeo museum. A newer addition to Old Town Museum is the official **National Route 66 Museum,** which has a *huge* Route 66 shield outside; inside there's an old pickup truck decorated to look like the one from *The Grapes of Wrath* and lots of other old-road memorabilia.

Just east of the Texas/ Oklahoma border, **Texola** (pop. 36) has dried up and all but blown away since it was bypassed by I-40, but a few remnants still stand, awaiting nostalgic photographers. The only signs of life hereabouts are the shouts and swears emanating from the combination pool hall and beer bar housed in the large metal shed on the south side of the old highway, where you're welcome to watch the most passionate domino games this side of Yuma, Arizona.

Welcome to Texola.

During the 1940s oil and gas were discovered underground in the Anadarko Basin, and the town experienced another short boom, a time remembered by the towering "Rig 114," a record-breaking, 180-foot-tall drilling rig, installed after its retirement in the park next to the Casa Grande Hotel (107 E. 3rd St.). Though fossil fuels have had their ups and downs, in recent years the industry has been on the upswing, leading city fathers to proclaim Elk City the "National Gas Capital of the World."

Elk City has two more surefire Route 66 attractions: excellent, Okie-style onion burgers at **Billy's** (210 N. Madison; 580/225-3355) and the delectable French Silk pie (butter, sugar, and vanilla served in a graham cracker crust) baked at the **Country Dove Tea Room** (610 W. 3rd St.; 580/225-7028).

Sayre

If you want a quick flashback to the dark days of Steinbeck's *The Grapes of Wrath*, turn north off I-40 into sleepy **Sayre** (pop. 4,375). The landmark Beckham County Courthouse, which looms over the east end of Main Street, was prominently featured in the movie version as Henry Fonda and the rest of the Joads rattled down Route 66 toward California. The Depression era also lives on in the cool and pleasant WPA-era swimming pool in Sayre City Park, in between the old Route 66 alignments. Just off the old road, take a look in the ever-expanding **Shortgrass Country Museum** (Tues.–Fri.; free; 106 E. Poplar St.), housed in the old Rock Island Line railroad depot, with changing displays documenting regional history from Cheyenne times to the arrival of homesteading settlers during the great Land Rush of 1892. East of the museum stands a giant grain elevator that has rusted into a gorgeous orange glow.

Erick

In Jack D. Rittenhouse's original *A Guide Book to Highway 66*, published in 1946 and now widely available in reprinted versions, he described Erick as "the first town you encounter, going west, which has any of the true 'western' look,

with its wide, sun-baked street, frequent horsemen, occasional sidewalk awnings, and similar touches." His description still rings true today (apart from
the horses, which have been replaced by pickup trucks). Along with main
streets named for hometown musical heroes Sheb "Flying Purple People Eater"
Wooley and Roger "King of the Road" Miller, **Erick** (pop. 1,052) has another
unique draw: All the buildings at the main intersection, and the only stoplight
in town, have chamfered corners, filed off to give a sense of consistency and
improve the view. One of the original buildings is gone, so it's not perfect, but
another has been resuscitated to house the **Roger Miller Museum** (closed
Mon.–Tues.; 580/526-3833). Established by the widow of the original "King
of the Road," it shows off many old photos, posters, and personal items.

A mile south of the I-40 freeway (exit 7), a nice stretch of late-model Route
66 continues west from Erick as a four-lane divided highway, all the way to
Texas through the borderline ghost town of Texola.

TEXAS

Known as the Panhandle because of the way it juts north
from the rest of Texas, this part of the route is a nearly 200-
mile stretch of pancake-flat plains. Almost devoid of trees
or other features, the western half, stretching into New
Mexico, is also known as the Llano Estacado or "Staked
Plains," possibly because early travelers marked their route by
driving stakes into the earth. The Texas Panhandle was the southern
extent of the buffalo-rich grasslands of the Great Plains, populated by roving
bands of Kiowa and Comanche Indians as recently as 100 years ago. Now oil
and gas production, as well as trucking and Route 66 tourism, have joined
ranching as the region's economic basis.

Even more so than in New Mexico or Oklahoma, old Route 66 has been replaced by I-40 most of the way across Texas, though in many of the ghostly
towns, like **McLean, Shamrock,** or **Vega,** and the sole city, **Amarillo,** old
US-66 survives as the main business strip, lined by the empty remains of roadside businesses. A select few are still open for a cup of coffee and a sharp taste
of the living past.

Midway between McLean and the Oklahoma border, the town
of Shamrock marks the junction of Route 66 and US-83, **The
Road to Nowhere** along the 100th meridian, which is
described in full on pages 174–231. **Shamrock** is covered on
pages 215.

McLean

Founded around the turn of the 20th century by an English rancher, Alfred
Rowe, who later lost his life on the *Titanic* in 1912, considering its minimal
size **McLean** (pop. 778) is now perhaps the most evocative town along the
Texas stretch of Route 66. Bypassed only in the early 1980s, the old main drag

East of McLean along the old Route 66 frontage, north of the freeway near exit 148, a skeletal sign still spells out the command: Rattlesnakes Exit Here.

is eerily silent, with a few businesses—such as a boot shop and a fine Texas-shaped neon sign—still standing on despite the near-total drop in passing trade.

McLean is headquarters of the state's Old Route 66 Association, and efforts are being made to preserve the town in prime condition, which explains the lovingly restored Phillips 66 station at 1st and Gray Streets (on the westbound stretch of old Route 66—the pumps price gas at 19 cents a gallon!) and the many other odds and ends on display around town. The center of activity here is the wonderful **Devil's Rope Museum** (closed Sun.; free; 100 S. Kingsley St.; 806/779-2225) at the east end of downtown, which has a huge room full of barbed wire—the "devil's rope"—and some of the most entertaining and educational collections of Route 66 memorabilia you'll find anywhere. No hype, just lots of good stuff and friendly people telling you all about it.

Besides the barbed wire museum, a pair of places next to each other at the west end of McLean offer good food and reliably clean and pleasant rooms: Try the thick steaks, juicy catfish, and weekend barbecue at the **Red River Steak House** (101 W. Route 66; 806/779-8940), or sleep at the **Cactus Inn** (806/779-2346).

Groom

The town of **Groom** (pop. 574), 40 miles east of Amarillo on the north side of I-40 at exit 113, holds two of the more eye-catching sights along old Route 66. One of these is a water tower that leans like the Tower of Pisa, causing drivers to stop and rub their eyes, then stop and pull out the camera to take some snapshots to show the folks back home. The other landmark is even harder to miss, a gigantic stainless steel cross—just shy of 200 feet tall and weighing 1.25 tons. This was the largest cross in the western hemisphere until a competitive copycat erected a slightly taller one along I-70 in Effingham, Illinois. Erected by a religious group in 1995, the Groom cross stands above a series of sculptures depicting biblical scenes and the evils of abortion.

Amarillo

At the heart of the Llano Estacado, midway across the Texas Panhandle, **Amarillo** (pop. 191,000; pronounced "am-uh-RILL-o") is a busy, big city that retains its cowboy roots. Center of the local ranching industry that handles some two million head of cattle each year, Amarillo handles nearly 90 percent of all the beef in Texas and some 25 percent of the national total.

Old Route 66 followed 6th Street through Amarillo, past the brick-paved streets of the Old San Jacinto district around Western Avenue, where you can wander amongst ancient-looking gun and saddle shops, numerous Wild West–themed clothing shops, and kitsch-minded antiques shops. To eat and drink with the Coors-drinking cowboys and cowgirls of Amarillo, head west to the **Golden Light Cafe** (2908 W. 6th Ave.; 806/374-9237), a fairly funky roadhouse famed for burgers, homemade hot sauce, green-chile stew, and Frito pies. Next door, the Golden Light Cantina hosts frequent live music. Amarillo is best known for its many good steakhouses, the most famous of which has to be the 450-seat **Big Texan Steak Ranch,** which started in 1960 along historic Route 66 and now stands on the east side of Amarillo, off I-40 exit 74, marked by a false-front Wild West town and a giant cowboy atop a billboard. This is the place where they offer a free 72-ounce steak, provided you eat it all—plus a table full of salad, baked potato, and dessert—in under an hour. If you don't finish everything, the cost is around $72; regular meals and very good "normal" steaks are available as well.

There's a nice motel featuring a Texas-shaped swimming pool at the **Big Texan** ($60 and up; 806/372-5000), and dozens of moderate chain motels stand along the I-40 and I-27 frontages, so rooms shouldn't be hard to find.

Most of the Texas Panhandle's 20 inches of annual rain falls during summer thunderstorms that sweep across the plains between May and August.

The Great Plains region, and Amarillo in particular, was one of the few places on earth where lighter-than-air helium has been found in an easily recoverable form. An estimated 90 percent of the world's supply once came from here.

Cadillac Ranch

No, you're not seeing things—there really are nearly a dozen Cadillacs up-ended in the Texas plain west of Amarillo, roughly midway between Chicago and Los Angeles. Two hundred yards south of I-40 between the Hope Road and Arnot Road exits (numbers 62 and 60, respectively), some six miles west of Amarillo where old US-66 rejoins the Interstate, the rusting hulks of 10 classic Caddies are buried nose-down in the dirt, their upended tail fins tracing design changes from 1949 to 1964.

A popular shrine to America's love of the open road, Cadillac Ranch was created by the San Francisco–based Ant Farm artists' and architects' collective in May 1974, under the patronage of the eccentric Amarillo helium millionaire Stanley Marsh III. The cars were all bought, some running, some not, from local junkyards and used car lots at an average cost of $200 each. Before the Cadillacs were planted, all the hubcaps and wheels were welded on, a good idea since most of the time the cars are in a badly vandalized state. Every once in a while advertising agencies and rock bands tidy them up for use as backdrops during photo shoots, and in recent years many of the cars have rusted through, requiring some oxy-acetylene

TLC. In August 1997, the Cadillacs got another 15 minutes of fame when Marsh decided to dig them up and move them two miles west from where they'd been—to escape the ever-expanding Amarillo sprawl and preserve the natural horizon.

There's a well-worn path from the frontage road if you want a closer look, and visitors are allowed any time, day or night.

In addition to his Cadillac Ranch, patron Stanley Marsh is the brain behind a series of surreal street signs placed around Amarillo, nicknamed the Dynamite Museum, that say things like "Road Does Not End," "Lubbock is a Grease Spot," and "Remember You Promised Yourself This Would Be a Good Day."

Palo Duro Canyon State Park

Lovely **Palo Duro Canyon** (daily, $5), one of the most beautiful places in all Texas, is just 25 miles southeast of Amarillo, east of the town of Canyon off the I-27 freeway. Cut into the Texas plain by the Prairie Dog Town Fork of the Red River, Palo Duro stretches for over 100 miles, with canyon walls climbing to 1,000 feet. Coronado and company were the first Europeans to lay eyes on the area, and numerous Plains tribes, including Apache, Kiowa, and Comanche, later took refuge here. From the end of Hwy-217, a well-paved road winds past the Palo

Palo Duro Canyon State Park

Duro park visitors center (daily; 806/488-2227), from where a short trail leads to a canyon overlook. Beyond here the road drops down into the canyon and follows the river on a 15-mile loop trip through the canyon's heart. It's prettiest in spring and fall, and fairly popular year-round.

On your way to or from Palo Duro Canyon, be sure to stop by the excellent **Panhandle-Plains Historical Museum** (daily; $10; 2503 4th Ave.; 806/651-2244) in the neighboring town of Canyon. One of the state's great museums, this has extensive exhibits on the cultural and economic life of the Panhandle region and its relations with Mexico, the Texas Republic, and the United States. The museum, which is housed in a WPA-era building on the campus of West Texas A&M University, has a special section on rancher Charles Goodnight (1836–1929), who once owned a half million acres here, invented the "chuck-wagon," and was an early advocate of saving the bison from extinction.

Vega and Adrian: Midpoint Cafe

Between Amarillo and the New Mexico border, the landscape is identical to what lies east of the city: endless flat plains dotted with occasional oil derricks and Aermotor windmills. The one biggish town, **Vega** (pop. 884), has a very photogenic collection of former and still-functioning businesses, including the **Hickory Café** (806/267-2569) and the **Boot Hill Saloon and Grill** (806/267-2904), both on Route 66 (Vega Boulevard) at the center of town, and a nicely preserved 1920s Magnolia service station.

West of Vega, the main event hereabouts is both a geographical and culinary magnet: the hamlet of **Adrian** (pop. 166) and the unmiss-able **Midpoint Cafe** (daily Mar.–Jan.; 806/538-6379). One of the route's most enjoyable places to eat, located more or less at the halfway point in Route 66's long ride between Chicago and Los Angeles—both of which are 1,139 miles away—the Midpoint is friendly, has great food, and basically epitomizes all that old-fashioned hospitality that makes Route 66 such a special experience. Be sure to check out the fine selection of Route 66 books and "midpoint" souvenirs, or just stop by for a piece of baked-from-scratch Ugly Crust pie. As more than one satisfied customer has said, you can taste the happiness.

NEW MEXICO

Following old Route 66 across New Mexico gives you a great taste of the Land of Enchantment, as the state calls itself on its license plates. There is less of the actual "old road" here than in other places, but the many towns and ghost towns along I-40, built more or less on top of Route 66, still stand. Route 66 runs around the historic heart of the state's cultural and political capital, **Santa Fe,** and right through the heart of its sprawling Sun Belt commercial center, **Albuquerque,** while in other places finding the old road and bypassed towns can take some time, though the effort is usually well rewarded.

Western New Mexico has the most to see and the most interesting topography, with sandstone mesas looming in the foreground and high, pine-forested peaks rising in the distance. Paralleling the Burlington Northern Santa Fe Railway, the route passes through the heart of this region, and numerous detours—to **Inscription Rock** and **Chaco Canyon,** among others—make unforgettable stops along the way. In the east, the land is flatter and the landscape drier as the road transitions from the Great Plains.

The border between Texas and New Mexico marks the boundary between central and mountain time zones. Set your clocks and watches accordingly.

Tucumcari

Subject of one of the most successful advertising campaigns in Route 66's long history of roadside hype, **Tucumcari** (pop. 5,363) looks and sounds like a much bigger place than it is. Also known as "the town that's two blocks wide and two miles long" (though Tucumcari Boulevard, which follows the route blazed by old Route 66 through town, stretches for closer to seven miles between Interstate exits), Tucumcari does have a little of everything, including a great range of neon signs, but it can be hard to explain the attraction of the town that hundreds of signs along the highways once trumpeted as Tucumcari Tonite—2,000 Motel Rooms. (A new ad campaign plays on this legacy, but signs now say Tucumcari Tonite—1,200 Motel Rooms.)

Hype or no hype, Tucumcari is a handy place to break a journey, and even if you think you can make it to the next town, you will never regret stopping here for a night.

Buddy Holly, Clovis Man

South of Tucumcari, at the edge of the desolate Llano Estacado that stretches south and east across the Texas Panhandle, the city of Clovis is a large railroad and ranching town that has two unique claims to fame. One is that it was the site where some of the oldest archaeological remains ever found in North America were unearthed: In the 1930s, archaeologists dug up bones and arrowheads that proved human habitation dating back as early as 9000 BC Some of these artifacts, belonging to what archaeolo-

gists have dubbed "Clovis Man," are on display at the **Blackwater Draw Museum** (daily; $3; 575/562-2202), on US-70 about 10 miles south of Clovis.

Clovis is also semi-famous for having played a part in early rock 'n' roll: Buddy Holly came here from Lubbock, across the Texas border, in the late 1950s to record "Peggy Sue," "That'll Be The Day," and other early classics. You can tour the restored **Norman Petty Recording Studios,** open only by appointment (1313 W. 7th St.; 575/763-3435). Buddy's contributions to western culture are also well documented in his hometown of **Lubbock,** which is described on page 829.

Especially if you stop at the famous **Blue Swallow Motel** ($50 and up; 815 E. Tucumcari Blvd.; 575/461-9849), which no less an authority than *Smithsonian* magazine called "the last, best, and friendliest of the old-time motels." Thanks to the warm hospitality of longtime owner Lillian Redman, few who stayed there during her long reign would disagree, and more recent owners have kept up the old spirit while improving the plumbing and replacing the mattresses. Each room comes with its own garage, and the neon sign alone is worth staying awake for. If the Blue Swallow is full, as it often is, try one of Tucumcari's other old-fashioned motels: the **Motel Safari,** a block away ($50 and up; 722 E. Route 66 575/461-1048), has Wi-Fi and flat-screen TVs, while the **Route 66 Motel** ($40 and up; 575/461-1212) is clean and simple, as the name suggests.

Across Route 66 from the Blue Swallow stands another survivor, the landmark tepee fronting the historic **Tee Pee Curios** (924 E. Tucumcari Dr.; 575/461-3773), where friendly owners Mike and Betty Callens will tempt you to add to your collection of Southwest or Route 66 souvenirs (or "Damn Fine Stuff," as their business cards have it). The Tee Pee has one of the coolest neon signs anywhere, so time your visit to see it in its full glory. For a place to eat,

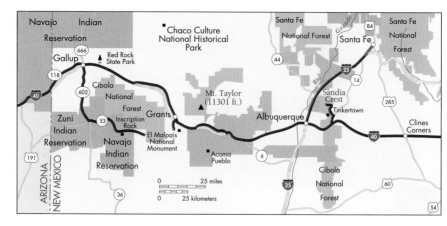

try the Mexican food at **La Cita** (575/461-7866), under the turquoise, yellow, and brown sombrero on the corner of 1st Street and old Route 66.

Three newer additions fill out Tucumcari's roster of attractions: one is a chromed steel **Route 66 sculpture,** welcoming travelers at the west edge of town; another is the vivid Route 66 mural painted on the corner of 2nd Street. The third is the unique **Mesalands Dinosaur Museum** (closed Sun. and Mon.; $6.50; 211 E. Laughlin St.; 575/461-3466), two blocks north of Route 66. Housed inside Mesa Community College, the museum boasts "the largest collection of life-sized bronze prehistoric skeletons in the world," plus real fossils, unusual minerals, and the unique *Torvosaurus,* a very rare carnivorous cousin of legendary *Tyrannosaurus rex.*

Santa Rosa

The I-40 freeway has bisected the town of **Santa Rosa** (pop. 2,750) and cut its old Route 66 frontage in two, but for over 65 years, travelers crossing New Mexico along Route 66 and I-40 made a point of stopping here for a meal at Club Cafe, "The Original Route 66 Restaurant Since 1935." Thanks to signs lining the road for miles in both directions, emblazoned with the smiling face of the "Fat Man," the Club Cafe was

scuba diver in the Blue Hole

nationally famous for its always-fresh food until it closed in 1992.

Just off the freeway, right on Route 66 and marked by a hard-to-miss bright yellow hot rod perched atop a 30-foot pole, the **Route 66 Auto Museum** (2866 W. Route 66; 505/472-1966) has a wide-ranging exhibit on "anything to do with wheels," highlighted by some tricked-out old Fords and Chevys and a totally cherry 1957 T-Bird convertible.

© AVALON TRAVEL

Along the Pecos River via US-84, some 50 miles southeast of Santa Rosa, the gravesite of Wild West legend Billy the Kid lies just steps from the **Old Fort Sumner Museum** ($5; 575/355-2942) in Fort Sumner, where 7,000 Navajo people were imprisoned from 1864 to 1869. A visit to the grave is free, but to learn more about the Kid, stop by the private museum about two miles from downtown Fort Sumner.

Santa Rosa's other main attraction is unique: the **Blue Hole,** an 80-foot-wide, 80-foot-deep artesian well filled with water so crystal-clear that it draws scuba divers from all over the western states to practice their underwater techniques here. The water of the Blue Hole, at around 61°F, is too cold for casual swimming, but in the summer heat it's a great place to cool your heels. The Blue Hole is well signed at the end of Blue Hole Road, a half mile south of old Route 66; for purists, Blue Hole Road is *old, old* Route 66, since it formed the early (pre-1937) alignment of the Mother Road across Santa Rosa, the rest of which is used as a runway at the city's airport (no cars allowed!). East of here, running along the south side of I-40, one of the oldest stretches of Route 66 is only partly paved, and best done in a 4WD or on a mountain bike. Here you get an indelible sense of what travel was like in the very early days, when less than half the route's 2,400-odd miles were paved.

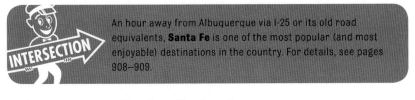

INTERSECTION

An hour away from Albuquerque via I-25 or its old road equivalents, **Santa Fe** is one of the most popular (and most enjoyable) destinations in the country. For details, see pages 908–909.

Tinkertown and the Sandia Crest

Not that there's any shortage of wacky roadside Americana along what's left of Route 66, but one of the most endearing of them all, **Tinkertown** (daily Apr.–Oct.; $3; 505/281-5233), is a quick 10-minute drive north of the old road. Like an old-fashioned penny arcade run riot, Tinkertown is a marvelous assembly of over a thousand deli-

Clines Corners, midway between Albuquerque and Santa Rosa off I-40 exit 218, is a truck stop café that dates back to 1934 and is, as the signs say, Worth Waiting For—for the huge gift shop if not for the unexciting food.

cately carved miniature wooden figures, arranged in tiny stage sets to act out animated scenes—a circus Big Top complete with side show, a Wild West town with dance-hall girls and a squawking vulture—all housed in a ram-shackle building made in part out of glass bottles and bicycle wheels, created over the past 50-odd years by Ross and Carla Ward and family. It's impossible to describe the many odds and ends on show here—one display case holds over 100 plastic figures taken from the tops of wedding cakes, for example—especially since the whole thing is always being improved and "tinkered" with, but the spirit of the place is aptly summed up in the Tinkertown motto: "We Did All This While You Were Watching TV." The Dalai Lama loved it, and so will you.

To get to Tinkertown, turn off I-40 at exit 175, six miles east of Albuquerque, and follow Hwy-14 for six miles, toward Sandia Crest. Tinkertown is on Hwy-536, 1.5 miles west of the Hwy-14 junction, hidden off the highway among the juniper trees.

Tinkertown

Sandia Crest itself is another 12 miles uphill at the end of Hwy-536 National Scenic Byway; the ridge offers a phenomenal panorama from an elevation of 10,678 feet. Back on Hwy-14, south of Tinkertown some four miles north of I-40 in Tijeras, the **Sandia Mountain Hostel** (12231 N. Hwy-14; 505/281-4117) offers clean bunks in a ski- and bike-friendly environment.

Albuquerque

Roughly located at the center of New Mexico, the sprawling city of **Albuquerque** (pop. 545,852) spreads along the banks of the Rio Grande and east to the foothills of 10,000-foot Sandia Crest. By far the state's biggest city, Albuquerque is a young, energetic, and vibrantly multicultural community, which, among many features, boasts a great stretch of old Route 66 along Central Avenue through the heart of the city—18 miles of diners, motels, and sparkling neon signs.

Though most people associate computer giant Microsoft with Seattle, the company actually began here in Albuquerque in 1975, in a series of dingy Route 66 motels.

One of the best parts of town is **Old Town,** the historic heart of Albuquerque. Located a block north of Central Avenue, at the west end of Route 66's cruise through downtown, Old Town offers a quick taste of New Mexico's Spanish colonial past, with a lovely old church, the 300-year-old San Felipe de Neri, as well as shops and restaurants set around a leafy green park. An information booth in the park has maps of Old Town and other information about the city. Another Old Town attraction, one that carries on the Route 66 tradition of reptile farms and private zoos, is the **Rattlesnake Museum** (daily; $5; 202 San Felipe St.), southeast of the main square, where you can see a range of rattlers from tiny babies to full-sized diamondbacks, about 50 all together, plus fellow desert-dwellers like tarantulas and a giant Gila monster.

A very different look into New Mexico's varied cultural makeup is offered at the **Indian Pueblo Cultural Center** (daily; $6; 2401 12th St.; 505/843-7270), a block north of I-40 exit 158. The center is owned and operated by the state's 19 different Pueblo communities; its highlight is a fine museum tracing the history of the region's Native American cultures, from Anasazi times up to the Pueblo Revolt of 1680, with the contemporary era illustrated by video presentations and a mock-up of a typical tourist—camera, shorts, and all. On most weekends ceremonial dances are held in the central courtyard—free and open to the general public. There's also a small cafeteria where you can sample food like fry bread and Navajo tacos, and a smoke shop selling discount cigarettes.

Downtown Albuquerque has been under reconstruction seemingly forever, with an ambitious mixed-use project surrounding the train station and massive old Santa Fe Railroad yards. Despite budget shortfalls, the state has pledged money for it, so someday the area may feature the enticing-sounding Wheels Museum (1501 SW 1st St.; 505/243-6269), tracing (surprise, surprise . . .) transportation in New Mexico.

Albuquerque was also the home of the great travel writer and World War II war correspondent Ernie Pyle. His old house at 900 Girard Avenue, a half mile south of Central Avenue, is now the city's oldest public library, which includes his collected works and a few personal items in a small display.

New Mexico's long relationship with radioactivity is reflected in the name of Albuquerque's very popular L.A. Dodgers–affiliated Class AAA baseball club, the **Isotopes** (505/924-2255), who play just south of downtown. Games are broadcast on **KNML 610 AM.**

Albuquerque Practicalities

The largest city in New Mexico, Albuquerque makes a very handy point of entry for tours of the southwestern United States. For old-road fans, the best stretch of Route 66 through Albuquerque is probably the section along Nob Hill, east of downtown and Old Town near the University of New Mexico. Here you'll find vintage neon and some great places to eat and drink, including **Kelly's Brew Pub** (3222 E. Central Ave.; 505/262-2739), housed in a 1930s Streamline Moderne auto dealership, and the upscale **Monte Vista Fire Station** (3201 E. Central Ave.; 505/255-2424). Between Nob Hill and downtown, the excellent **66 Diner** (1405 E. Central Ave.; 505/247-1421) serves top-quality burgers and shakes, and regional specialties like blue-corn pancakes.

Another good range of places to eat lies within walking distance of Old Town. Enjoy a delicious mix of Mexican and American diner food at **Garcia's** (1736 W. Central Ave.; 505/842-0273), beneath a glorious neon sign. For a taste of 1950s Americana (and good root beer), head to the **Route 66 Malt**

Santa Fe

New Mexico's state capital, and one of the prime vacation destinations in the country, Santa Fe (pop. 67,947) has been at the center of Southwest life for centuries, and the cultural cross-roads of a region that has been set-tled for thousands of years. From the east, detour north from Clines Corners via US-285, or for the full "Historic Route 66" tour follow US-84 north near Santa Rosa toward Las Vegas (the original one, here in New Mexico), then continue west on I-25, parallel to the pioneer-era Santa Fe Trail.

Despite its swirling hordes of vacationers, and its vast infrastructure of hotels, restaurants, art galleries, and souvenir shops, Santa Fe remains one of the most enjoyably un-American small cities. It makes the most sense to begin your tour of Santa Fe at its center, the **Plaza.** This will help you get not only your geographical bearings but also a historical context with which to appreciate the rest of Santa Fe. On the north side of the Plaza, the **Palace of the Governors** (closed Mon.; $9) is the oldest continuously used public building in America. Dating from 1610, the pal-ace served as residence for Spanish, Mexican, and, later, American territorial gov-ernors until 1909, when the New Mexico legislature voted to turn the building into the Museum of New Mexico. The museum contains an excellent overview of the building's and the city's tumultuous history, numerous artifacts and documents, and an exhaustive collection of regional photographs.

To get a sense of the life and work of the woman who did as much as anyone to fix Santa Fe in the American mind, walk two blocks west and one block north from the Plaza to the **Georgia O'Keeffe Museum** (daily; $10; 217 Johnson St.; 505/946-1000), which contains 1,149 pieces of the late artist's work. Many of the paintings here depict the landscape in and around her home at Abiquiu, north of Santa Fe, where she lived for 40 years.

Shops, shops, and more shops (plus a few cafés and restaurants) line the streets emanating from the Plaza. Many of these have a decidedly upscale bent; there are about 200 art galleries alone in Santa Fe, for instance (though the most engaging and scenic stretch of them is found along narrow and tree-lined Canyon Road, which runs east from Paseo de Peralta up into the foothills above town). Once you penetrate Santa Fe's Paseo de Peralta, the histor-ic ring road encircling the 17th-century city center, leave your car at one of the many parking lots or garages and see Santa Fe on foot. Another downtown street, Old Pecos Trail, carried Route 66 for its first dozen years before Santa Fe was bypassed in favor of Albuquerque in 1937.

Santa Fe's central Plaza

If you're interested in classical music,

the **Santa Fe Chamber Music Festival** (505/983-2075) performances take place in July and August in a variety of atmospheric old Santa Fe buildings.

Practicalities

It's a pleasant surprise that only moderately deep pockets are needed to find good food or memorable accommodations in Santa Fe. With recipes that show the influence of more than 2,000 years of Native American culture (which contributed three major staples: beans, corn, and squash), some 400 years of Catholic inclusion (chiles, cilantro, cumin, onions, garlic, wheat, rice, and both beef and pork), and a liberal dash of American inventiveness, Santa Fe restaurants serve the world's oldest, newest, and, some say, tastiest cuisines—often all side by side on the very same plates. Menu offerings include dishes like a buttermilk corn cake with smoky chipotle-chile shrimp (and a side of red chile onion rings), *chiles rellenos* stuffed with roast duck and black bean mole sauce, or blue corn turkey enchiladas, meaning that Santa Fe's fine food is at least as much a draw as its rich history and magical mountain light.

To ease your way into Santa Fe food, start on the Plaza at the **Plaza Cafe** (54 Lincoln Ave.; 505/982-1664), which has been serving no-nonsense meals since it opened in 1918. Part of the fun here is the constant clatter of dishes and silverware, the old-fashioned tile floor, and a rear wall with a giant mural map of the Southwest. If you don't have time for a full meal (the Plaza meatloaf is a specialty), pop in for a helping of **Frito pie,** which is quite the local delicacy (although the recipe allegedly originated in Texas in the 1930s, when Daisy Doolin, the mother of the Dallas-based founder of Frito-Lay, poured chili over her Fritos and found that she liked it).

Another outstanding source of filling New Mexican breakfast fare is **Tecolote Cafe,** a mile southwest of the Plaza (1203 Cerrillos Rd.; 505/988-1362). Closer in, and well worth a visit for its addictive breakfast quesadilla (with scrambled eggs, applewood-smoked bacon, Jack cheese, and guacamole), is **Cafe Pasqual's,** just off the Plaza (121 Don Gaspar Ave.; 505/983-9340), which has deliciously inventive dishes at lunch and dinner, too.

After a meal elsewhere (unless someone else is paying your expenses!), join Santa Fe's old guard at the **Pink Adobe,** also called simply "The Pink" (406 Old Santa Fe Trail; 505/983-7712), a very deluxe, retro-minded supper club that's also home to the kitschy Dragon Room bar, a popular late-night hangout.

For a convenient and memorable place to stay, a pair of small B&B gems are within a short walk of the Plaza: **Adobe Abode** ($125 and up; 202 Chapelle St.; 505/983-3133) and the **Casa del Toro** ($125 and up; 229 McKenzie St.; 505/820-6177). The former, as the name suggests, consists of several large adobe-style rooms and casitas, and both have modern baths, upscale amenities, and eclectic antiques and folk furnishings.

If you prefer to park within sight of your room, there's a nice motor inn, with a location that's hard to beat: **Garrett's Desert Inn,** a few blocks off the Plaza ($95 and up; 311 Old Santa Fe Trail; 505/982-1851). If all the desirable places are full, or if you're tight on funds, cruise along busy Cerrillos Road (Hwy-14), where you'll find all the major chains.

For complete listings of accommodation options, and for information on anything else to do with Santa Fe, contact the **Santa Fe Convention and Visitors Bureau** (201 W. Marcy St.; 505/955-6200 or 800/777-2489).

Shop, originally housed in an old gas station and motor court but now occupying a new purpose-built home (3800 E. Central Ave.; 505/242-7866). Another old Route 66 landmark, **Mac's La Sierra,** serves up Steak in the Rough and other beefy specialties in a cozy, dark wood dining room a long ways west of town (6217 W. Central Ave.; 505/836-1212).

Like most of New Mexico, Albuquerque has a ton of inexpensive accommodations, with all the usual chain motels represented near the airport and along the Interstate frontage roads, plus a lot of fading or extinguished old stars of the Route 66 era, like the famous El Vado (2500 W. Central Ave.), which has been threatened with demolition for decades. Recently purchased by the city of Albuquerque, the El Vado likely will be redeveloped in some fashion. For Route 66 character, consider the still neat and tidy, Del Webb–built **Hiway House Motel,** in the Nob Hill district ($65 and up; 3200 E. Central Ave.; 505/268-3971) or the unimaginatively but accurately named **Monterey Non-Smokers Motel,** near Old Town (around $75; 2402 W. Central Ave.; 505/243-3554). Since its 2008 renovation, the nicest old hotel has got to be the grand **Hotel Andaluz,** previously known as La Posada ($150 and up; 125 2nd St.; 505/242-9090), a block off old Route 66 downtown, one of the first inns built by New Mexico–born hotel magnate Conrad Hilton.

Old Route 66: Bernalillo

True fans of the full Route 66 tour, and anyone interested in the art and architecture (and food!) of the American Southwest, will want to make the trip to the state capital, Santa Fe. The original Route 66 alignment ran north from Albuquerque along the I-25 corridor, then curved back south from Santa Fe along what's now US-84, to rejoin I-40 west of Santa Rosa.

The best sense of this old route across old New Mexico comes just north of Albuquerque, at the historic town of **Bernalillo.** Route 66 here follows the much older El Camino Real, which linked these Spanish colonies 400 years ago. The heart of Bernalillo contains two great stops, poles apart from each other in ambience but together capturing the essence of the place. First of these is ancient-feeling **Silva's Saloon** (955 Camino del Pueblo; 505/867-9976), whose walls, coated in layers of newspaper clippings, old snapshots, and other mementos, form a fabulously funky backdrop for a cold beer, a burger, or an evening listening to local live music alongside cowboys, bikers, and other characters. Up the street is the stylish **Range Cafe** (925 S. Camino del Pueblo; 505/867-1700), where a spacious dining room has very good "New New Mexican" food (try the bread pudding!) and a sophisticated, big-city air.

Rio Puerco and the Route 66 Casino

Between Albuquerque and Acoma Pueblo, a fine old stretch of old Route 66 survives, passing crumbling tourist courts and service stations across the Laguna Indian Reservation. The photogenic Route 66 highlight here is the graceful old steel truss **Rio Puerco Bridge,** which spans a usually dry river, right alongside the I-40 superslab about 10 miles west of Albuquerque. The old road ambience is also overwhelmed by the huge new **Route 66 Casino,** south of the freeway, the largest of many gambling complexes that have sprung up on Indian reservations across this part of New Mexico. Besides the jinglingly huge, 50,000-square-foot casino (which has the usual card tables, craps, and roulette), the complex also has a 2,800-seat theater, a roadside café, a smoke shop offering cheap (tax-free) tobacco, and a large hotel ($80 and up; 866/711-STAY).

The heart of the historic Laguna Pueblo, where some 500 people live in adobe buildings around a church that dates from 1699, is not really open to travelers, but just west of the pueblo the old Route 66 frontage runs past an old road landmark: **Budville,** where the remnants of an old trading post and café still stand in atmospheric silence along the south side of the highway.

Acoma Pueblo: Sky City

A dozen miles east of Grants and 50 miles west of Albuquerque, one of the Southwest's most intriguing sites, **Acoma Pueblo,** stands atop a 350-foot-high sandstone mesa. Long known as "Sky City," Acoma is one of the very oldest communities in North America, inhabited since AD 1150. The views out across the plains are unforgettable, especially toward Enchanted Mesa on the horizon to the northeast.

Acoma Pueblo

Few people live on the mesa today, though the many adobe houses are used by Pueblo craftspeople, who live down below but come up to the mesa-top to sell their pottery and other crafts to tourists. To visit this amazing place, you have to join a guided **tour** (daily, closed Mon.–Thurs. in winter; $20; 800/747-0181), which begin with a bus ride to the mesa-top and end with a visit to **San Esteban del Rey Mission,** the largest Spanish colonial church in the state. Built in 1629, the church features a roof constructed of huge timbers that were carried from the top of Mt. Taylor on the backs of neophyte Indians—a distance of more than 30 miles.

Acoma Pueblo, or "Sky City"

Acoma Pueblo is 15 miles south of I-40, from exit 108 (westbound) or exit 96 (eastbound). Start your visit by appreciating the artifacts displayed in the beautiful **Haak'u Museum,** at the base of the mesa, where tours of the ancient Sky City begin. The Acoma tribe also operates the money-spinning **Sky City Casino and Hotel** ($80 and up; 888/SKY-CITY), sited well away from the historic core of the pueblo, right off I-40 exit 102.

US-60: Pie Town and the Lightning Field

A long way south of Grants, an old mining camp was so famous for fine desserts it became known as **Pie Town.** After many years of pielessness, local meringue-lovers lucked out when baker Kathy Knapp opened the **Pie-O-Neer Cafe** (closed Tues.—Thurs.; 505/772-2711), on old US-60 at milepost 59.

East of Pie Town off US-60, more than 20 miles outside Quemado (the next "town" to the west), the **Lightning Field** (May–Oct. only; 505/898-3335) is an outdoor "land art" installation by Walter De Maria, who implanted a grid of steel tubes into the high-elevation (7,200 feet above sea level) New Mexico plain with the intention of attracting lightning strikes. The sculpture consists of 400 stainless steel poles, ranging height from 16 to 27 feet, placed 200 feet apart in a rectangular grid that is roughly one mile by one kilometer. The engineering feat here was to set the poles so that their tops form an exactly level plane. Despite the name, the experience is meant to be about contemplation, rather than spectacle; casual visitors are not allowed, and for the full Lightning Field experience you have to stay overnight in a nearby cabin, and meals and transportation to the site are included in the $150 to $250 per person fees. The Lightning Field is maintained by the same foundation that curates the intriguing Dia-Beacon museum, north of New York City.

Grants

Along with the usual Route 66 range of funky motels and rusty neon signs, the former mining boomtown of **Grants** (pop. 9,182) has the unique attraction of the **New Mexico Mining Museum** (closed Sun; $3; 505/287-4802), right downtown on old Route 66 (Santa Fe Avenue) at the corner of Iron Avenue. Most of the exhibits trace the short history of local uranium mining, which began in 1950 when a local Navajo rancher, Paddy Martinez, discovered an odd yellow rock that turned out to be high-grade uranium ore. Mines around Grants once produced half the ore mined in the United States, but production has ceased (pending renewed interest in nuclear power). From the main gallery, ride the elevator down (only one floor, but it feels like 900 feet) to the highlight of the mining museum: a credible

New Mexico Mining Museum

re-creation of a uranium mine, complete with an underground lunch room emblazoned with all manner of warning signs.

The landmark Uranium Café, with its atomic neon sign across Route 66 from the mining museum, has been going in and out of business for years. Its latest incarnation is family-run **Nana's Cafe** (519 W. Santa Fe Ave.; 505/285-3446), serving very good Mexican food.

Inscription Rock and El Malpais: Hwy-53

Western New Mexico is among the most beautiful places on the planet. South of I-40 and Route 66, one of the best drives through it, Hwy-53, loops between Gallup and Grants across the Zuni and Navajo Nation Indian Reservations. Skirting the southern foothills of the 9,000-foot Zuni Mountains, along the edge of the massive **El Malpais** lava flow—thousands of acres of pitch-black, concrete-hard, glassy sharp rock sliced and diced by lava tubes and collapsing craters. Formed between 10,000 and 115,000 years ago, most of the Malpais is wild and undeveloped, but on the slopes of Bandera Volcano, you can tour the privately run **Ice Cave** (daily; $10; 505/783-4303), where the cool temperatures are very welcome on a hot summer's day.

West from El Malpais, the route follows ancient Indian trails that Coronado used on his ill-fated 1540 explorations, winding past piñon-covered hills, open grasslands, and the fascinating graffiti collection of El Morro National Monument. Better known as **Inscription Rock,** the 200-foot-high sandstone cliffs of El Morro have been inscribed by travelers like Juan de Oñate, who wrote his name with a flourish in 1605, after he "discovered" the Gulf of California.

Atop the cliffs are the partially excavated remains of a small pueblo dating from around AD 1200. A two-mile loop trail to the inscriptions and the ruins starts from a small **visitors center** (daily; $3 trail fee; 505/783-4226), where exhibits outline the history of the site. The trails are closed an hour before sunset, so get here early enough in the day to enjoy the beautiful scenery. There is also a small campground (no showers, pit toilets) amidst the junipers.

Gallup

Though it's not exactly scenic, **Gallup** (pop. 20,209) is a fascinating place. Founded in 1881 when the Santa Fe Railroad first rumbled through, and

Midway between Grants and Gallup, I-40 crosses the 7,250-foot Continental Divide, where the Top O' the World dance hall used to tempt travelers off old Route 66. From here (exit 47), it's possible to follow the old road for 30 miles, running east along I-40 as far as Grants.

Much less developed, but every bit as memorable as the cliff dwellings of Mesa Verde, the extensive archaeological remains protected inside **Chaco Culture National Historical Park** are well worth your time. Though it's an hour's drive from I-40 via unpaved roads, the park is one of the wonders of the Southwest desert.

Southwest of Inscription Rock, animal lovers may want to visit the **Wild Spirit Wolf Sanctuary** (closed Mon.; $7; 505/775-3304), where over two dozen wolves and wolf-dogs live on a 100-year-old moonshiner's ranch.

calling itself "The Gateway to Indian Country" because it's the largest town near the huge Navajo and other Native American reservations of the Four Corners region, Gallup has some of the Southwest's largest trading posts and one of the best strips of neon signs you'll see anywhere on old Route 66.

For travelers intent on experiencing a little of the charms of old Route 66, Gallup also has **El Rancho** ($80 and up; 1000 E. Route 66; 505/722-2285), a delightful old hotel lovingly preserved in its 1930s glory. Built by a brother of movie director D. W. Griffiths, El Rancho feels like a national park lodge, with a large but welcoming lobby dominated by a huge stone fireplace. All the rooms in the old wing are named for the movie stars who have stayed here over the years—the W. C. Fields Room, the John Wayne Room, the Marx Brothers Room (which sleeps six), even the Ronald Reagan Room—and signed glossies of these and many more actors and actresses adorn the halls. El Rancho also has a good restaurant serving regional food, and a gift shop selling souvenirs and locally crafted jewelry, pottery, and rugs.

Gallup also hosts the annual **Inter Tribal Ceremonial,** perhaps the largest Native American gathering in the country, held early in August at Red Rock State Park, eight miles east of Gallup, and culminating in a parade that brings some 30,000 people out to line old Route 66 through town. Festivities include a rodeo, powwows, and a beauty show; call for the latest details (505/863-3896).

In the heart of historic downtown, the old Santa Fe train depot (still in use by Amtrak), houses the **Gallup Cultural Center** (201 E. Route 66; 505/863-4131). Free dance shows are staged at the nearby courthouse square nightly in summer, next to a statue of a World War II Navajo Code Talker. Another place worth spending some time is **Richardson's Cash Pawn and Trading Post** (222 W. Route 66; 505/722-4762). Family-run since 1913, this busy but friendly space is crammed to the rafters with arts, crafts, and pawned goods—Navajo rugs and jewelry, ornately tooled leather saddles, pearl-inlaid guitars, and more—that give a better sense of local lifestyles (and all their ups and downs) than any museum ever could.

ARIZONA

If you're not yet a die-hard Route 66 fan, traveling the old route across Arizona is bound to convert you. The high-speed I-40 freeway gives quick access to some of the best surviving stretches of the old road, and these are some of the most captivating parts of Route 66 anywhere. Between the red-rock mesas of New Mexico and the arid desert along the Colorado River, the route runs past dozens of remarkable old highway towns along some of the oldest and longest still-driveable stretches of the Mother Road.

East of **Flagstaff,** the old road is effectively submerged beneath the freeway, which drops down to cross desolate desert, passing through desiccated towns and **Petrified Forest National Park.** Remnants of numerous old roadside attractions—Indian trading posts, wild animal menageries, and **Holbrook's** famous "Sleep in a Teepee" Wigwam Village—all survive in varying degrees of preservation along Arizona's section of Route 66.

Midway across the state, the route climbs onto the forested (and often snowy) Kaibab Plateau for a look at the mighty **Grand Canyon,** one of the true wonders of the natural world.

Painted Desert and Petrified Forest National Park

Right along the New Mexico border, Arizona welcomes westbound travelers with an overwhelming display of trading-post tackiness—huge concrete tepees stand at the foot of brilliant red-rock mesas, while gift shops hawk their souvenirs to passing travelers. The gift shops themselves may not be all that attractive, but the old Route 66 frontage road along here, a.k.a. Hwy-118 between exit 8 in New Mexico and exit 357 in Arizona, is truly spectacular, running at the foot of red-rock cliffs. If you like rocks, gems, and petrified wood, a fine collection is for sale at the endearingly strange **Stewart's Trading Post,** marked by a family of animated dinosaurs at I-40 exit 303.

A great introduction to the Four Corners region, the **Hubbell Trading Post National Historic Site** ($2; 928/755-3254), 38 miles north of I-40 from

I-40 and old Route 66 trace the southern edge of the massive Navajo Nation Indian Reservation, home to radio station **KTNN 660 AM,** which broadcasts a fascinating mélange of Navajo chants and Jimi Hendrix riffs on a "clear" signal that (especially at night) reaches all over the western USA. KTNN is also the only station in the United States that broadcasts pro football games—in Navajo.

purple sands in the Painted Desert

saguaro cactus blossom,
state flower of Arizona

exit 333 and a mile west of the town of
Ganado, is a frontier store preserved as it
was in the 1870s, when trader John
Hubbell began buying the beautiful rugs
made by local Navajo weavers.

The easternmost 60-mile stretch of I-40
across Arizona is little more than one long
speedway, since almost any sign of the old
road has been lost beneath the four-lane
Interstate. One place that's worth a stop
here is **Petrified Forest National Park**
(daily dawn–dusk; $10 per car; 928/524-
6228). The polished petrified wood on display in the visitors center is gorgeous to
look at, but seeing 93,000 acres of the stuff
in its raw natural state is not, to be honest,
particularly thrilling. The story of how the
wood got petrified is interesting, though:
About 225 million years ago, a forest was
buried in volcanic ash, then slowly em-

Petrified Forest National Park

balmed with silica and effectively turned to stone. Alongside the visitors center at
the entrance to the park, there's a handy restaurant and a gas station.

While the park contains a vast array of prehistoric fossils and pictographs as
well as the petrified wood, one of the more interesting sights is the old **Painted
Desert Inn,** a Route 66 landmark during the 1920s and 1930s that was converted into a museum and bookstore after the Park Service took it over in the
1960s. The pueblo-style building, now restored to its 1920s splendor with
lovely murals, Navajo rugs and sand paintings, and handcrafted furnishings, is
perched on a plateau overlooking the spectacularly colored **Painted Desert**
that stretches off toward the northern horizon.

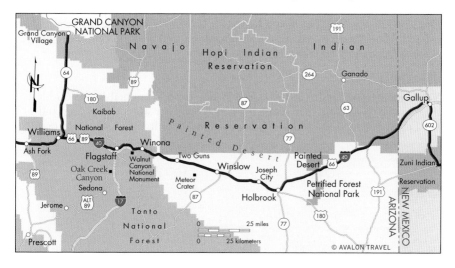

Holbrook: Wigwam Village

Holding a concentrated dose of old Route 66 character, **Holbrook** (pop. 5,100) is definitely worth a quick detour off the I-40 freeway. More than the other Route 66 towns in the eastern half of Arizona, it still feels like a real place, with lively cafés and some endearing roadside attractions around the center of town, where Route 66 alternates between Hopi Drive and Navajo Boulevard. Along with the many rock shops—be sure to check out the huge dinosaur collection outside the **Rainbow Rock Shop,** a block south on Navajo Boulevard near the railroad tracks—and trading post tourist traps, another worthwhile place to stop is the **Navajo County Museum** (daily; free) in the old Navajo County Courthouse, about a quarter-mile south of I-40 at the corner of Navajo Boulevard (old Route 66) and Arizona Street. The collections are wide-ranging and include a walk downstairs to the old county jail, in use from 1899 until 1976 (the graffiti is great).

In and around Holbrook, you'll come across a series of concrete dinosaurs rescued from the old International Petrified Forest Dinosaur Park, which used to stand along I-40 near exit 289.

Best of all, stop for the night at the marvelous **Wigwam Village** (around $55; 811 W. Hopi Dr.; 928/524-3048) at the western edge of town and sleep in a concrete tepee. Based on the original circa-1936 Wigwam Village motor court built in Cave City, Kentucky, Holbrook's was one of seven franchises across the country; this one opened in 1950 but closed down when the Interstate came through in 1974. The family of original owner Chester Lewis fully renovated the buildings and reopened the place after his death in 1988; original bentwood hickory furniture, a small curio shop, and a handful of historic American cars parked outside help complete the ambience of classic roadside Americana. Especially if you want to introduce the younger generations to the joys of old-road travel, you really should stay here at least once in your life.

After you've checked in to the Wigwam, be sure to wander down the road for a friendly, filling Route 66 meal at **Joe and Aggie's Cafe** (120 W. Hopi

Dr.; 928/524-6540) or **The Wayside,** serving delicious green-chile cheeseburgers and other Mexican and American favorites a mile west on old Route 66 (1150 W. Hopi Dr.; 928/524-3167).

Winslow

Winslow, Arizona, didn't make it into Bobby Troup's original Route 66 hit list, but the town more than made it a generation later when Glenn Frey and the Eagles recorded the Jackson Browne tune "Take It Easy," whose second

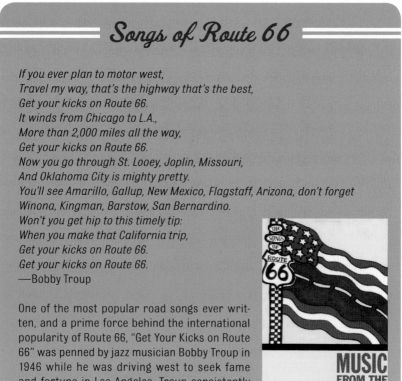

Songs of Route 66

If you ever plan to motor west,
Travel my way, that's the highway that's the best,
Get your kicks on Route 66.
It winds from Chicago to L.A.,
More than 2,000 miles all the way,
Get your kicks on Route 66.
Now you go through St. Looey, Joplin, Missouri,
And Oklahoma City is mighty pretty.
You'll see Amarillo, Gallup, New Mexico, Flagstaff, Arizona, don't forget
Winona, Kingman, Barstow, San Bernardino.
Won't you get hip to this timely tip:
When you make that California trip,
Get your kicks on Route 66.
Get your kicks on Route 66.
—Bobby Troup

One of the most popular road songs ever written, and a prime force behind the international popularity of Route 66, "Get Your Kicks on Route 66" was penned by jazz musician Bobby Troup in 1946 while he was driving west to seek fame and fortune in Los Angeles. Troup consistently credited his former wife Cynthia, with whom he was traveling, for the half dozen words of the title and refrain. The rest of the song simply rattled off the rhyming place-names along the way, but despite its apparent simplicity, it caught the ear of Nat King Cole, who made it into a hit record and also established the pronunciation as "root" rather than "rout," as repeated in later renditions by everyone from Bob Wills to the Rolling Stones.

If you haven't heard the song for a while, there's a jazzy version by Bobby Troup, along with some lively Route 66–related songs, on the compilation CD, *The Songs of Route 66—Music from the All-American Highway,* available at souvenir stores en route.

verse starts with "Standin' on a corner in Winslow, Arizona," a line that has caused more people to turn off in search of the place than anything else. Right downtown in between the two strips of Route 66, which runs one-way in each direction down 2nd and 3rd Streets, the funky **Old Trails Museum** (Tues.–Sat.; free; 212 Kinsley Ave.; 928/289-5861) sells a range of "Standin' on the Corner" T-shirts and displays a few reminders of Winslow in its heyday. Standing on the corner of 2nd and Kinsley, where a little sign stakes a claim to being *the* corner the Eagles sang about, there's a statue of a guy with a guitar and a mural of a girl (my lord!) in a flatbed Ford, slowing down to take a look.

The usual chain motels and fast-food franchises stand at either end of town around Winslow's I-40 exits, but in between is a great landmark of Southwest style: the elegant **La Posada Hotel** ($110 and up; 303 E. 2nd St.; 928/289-4366). Designed in the late 1920s for Fred Harvey by architect Mary Colter, who considered it her masterpiece, the hotel was closed for 40 years before being fully and lovingly restored and reopened in 1998. Near a busy rail line but surrounded by very pleasant gardens, the luxurious hotel is also home to a stylish cocktail bar and one of the finest restaurants for miles, the Turquoise Room. If you have the time and inclination to appreciate its old-fashioned, handcrafted charms, La Posada is an unforgettable stop.

West of Holbrook along I-40, **Joseph City** is noteworthy for two things. East of town, the giant 995-megawatt Cholla power plant consumes more than 100 tons of coal every hour. At the west end of town, on the south side of I-40 at exit 269, there's the **Jackrabbit Trading Post,** the one whose signs you've probably noticed over the past hundred miles—take a picture or buy a postcard of the giant jackrabbit, one of a long line of creatures who have stood here since 1949.

Meteor Crater

Between Winslow and Winona, three miles east of Two Guns and six miles south of I-40 exit 233, sits **Meteor Crater** (daily; $15; 928/289-2362), Arizona's second-most-distinctive hole in the ground. Formed by a meteorite some 50,000 years ago and measuring 550 feet deep and nearly a mile across, the crater is a privately owned tourist attraction. The Astronaut Wall of Fame plays up the crater's resemblance to the surface of the moon (Apollo moonwalkers practiced here). You can't climb down into it, but (weather permitting) you can join a guided rim tour, walking a half mile there and back across the desert to gaze down into the crater.

aerial view of Meteor Crater

Back along I-40, at the Meteor City exit, the **Meteor City Trading Post** boasts the usual range of souvenirs plus "The World's Largest Map of Route 66." Stretching 100 feet from end to end, the mural/map was originally created by noted Route 66 artist Bob Waldmire, but after fading and flaking it was "restored" by volunteers and the Hampton Inn Hilton motel chain back in 2002, without Bob's quirky charm.

Two Guns and Twin Arrows

Heading west from Meteor Crater toward Flagstaff, the route climbs swiftly from the hot red desert up into the cool green pines, but old-road fanatics will want to take the time to explore what remains of two old-time tourist traps lining the next 20 miles of highway. Keep your eyes peeled approaching I-40 exit 230: The freeway crosses deep Diablo Canyon, where an old Route 66 bridge still spans the dry wash, and the walls of a half dozen bleached buildings are all that's left of the **Two Guns Trading Post.** A roadside attraction par excellence, Two Guns had a zoo full of roadrunners, Gila monsters, and coyotes, and one building still has a sign saying Mountain Lions—all for the entertainment of passing travelers. For a while in the 1970s, Two Guns was a KOA Kampground (with swimming pool!), and according to various reports down the Route 66 grapevine, Two Guns has been on the verge of reopening many times, most recently after reports circulated that the whole shebang had been purchased by Australian actor Russell Crowe. But most of the time Two Guns is dead quiet, with the old access road blocked by a sign reading "No Trespassing by Order of Two Guns Sheriff Department." Probably a good thing, since the old buildings are all dangerously close to collapse. It's an evocative site, nonetheless, and photogenic in the right light.

A dozen miles west of Two Guns is another double attraction: **Twin Arrows,** where a pair of giant and surprisingly well-preserved red and yellow arrows point toward a long-closed café and trading post, last seen alive in the 1990s movie *Forrest Gump.*

Don't Forget: Winona

East of Flagstaff, in fact across most of eastern Arizona, following old Route 66 can be a frustrating task, since much of the roadway is blocked, discontinuous, torn up, or all three. Unlike the long stretches found in the western half of the state, here the old road exists only as short segments running through towns, and most of the way you're forced to follow the freeway, stopping at exit after exit to get on and off the old road. Among the places worth considering is the one town mentioned out of sequence in the Route 66 song: "Flagstaff, Arizona, don't forget Winona," which, alas, is now little more than a name on the exit sign along I-40.

Walnut Canyon National Monument

The most easily accessible of the hundreds of different prehistoric settlements all over the southwestern United States, **Walnut Canyon National Monument** (daily 9 AM–5 PM, 8 AM–5 PM in summer; $5; 928/526-3367) is also one of the prettiest places imaginable, with piñon pines and junipers clinging to the canyon walls, and walnut trees filling the canyon floor. On the edge of the canyon, a small visitors center gives the historical background, but the real interest lies below, on the short but very steep Island Trail, which winds through cliff dwellings tucked into overhangs and ledges 400 feet above the canyon floor. Winter storms sometimes dislodge boulders that wipe out parts of the trail, so check with the rangers to make sure the trail is open, and ask about weather, water supplies, and other safety issues. The rim of Walnut Canyon is nearly 7,000 feet above sea level, and the altitude can make the climbing especially strenuous.

The entrance to the Walnut Canyon monument, which contains some 300 identified archaeological sites, lies seven miles east of Flagstaff, accessible from I-40 exit 204.

Flagstaff

An old railroad and lumber-mill town given a new lease on life by an influx of students at Northern Arizona University, and by the usual array of ski bums and mountain bikers attracted by the surrounding high mountain wilderness, **Flagstaff** (pop. 68,870) is an enjoyable, energetic town high up on the Colorado Plateau. The natural beauty of its forested location has meant that, compared to other Route 66 towns, Flagstaff was less affected by the demise of the old road. That said, it still takes pride in the past, notably in the form of the **Museum Club** (3404 E. Route 66; 928/526-9434), an old roadhouse brought back to life as a country-western nightclub and ad hoc nostalgia museum.

Along with a great but slowly shrinking range of classic neon signs, Flagstaff also has a pair of non–Route 66 related attractions. First and foremost of these stands high on a hill on the west side of downtown Flagstaff, reachable from the west end of Santa Fe Avenue (old Route 66): the **Lowell Observatory,** established in 1894 by Percival Lowell and best known as the place where, in 1930, the onetime planet Pluto was discovered. A **visitors center** (daily in summer; $10; 928/774-3358) has descriptions of the science behind what goes on here—spectroscopy, red shifts, and expanding universes, for example—and the old telescope, a 24-inch refractor, is open for viewings 8–10 PM most nights in summer. Not exactly consistent with its neon-lit Route 66 reputation, Flagstaff has since the 1950s been a pioneer in combating light pollution; to help preserve the dark sky at night, here at the

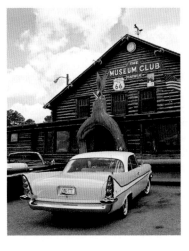

Way back in 1946, in his classic *A Guide Book to Highway 66,* Jack Rittenhouse wrote that "Cowboys and Indians can be seen in their picturesque dress on Flagstaff streets year-round," but these days he'd probably notice the lycra-clad cyclists who crowd into the college town's many cafés.

Flagstaff's San Francisco Street was named not for the California city but for the nearby volcanic peaks, so called by early Spanish missionaries and still held sacred by the native Hopi Indians.

Flagstaff very nearly became an early movie center, when young Cecil B. DeMille stopped here briefly while scouting locations to shoot the world's first feature-length film, a Western called *The Squaw Man.* It was snowing in Flagstaff that day, so he moved on to Los Angeles.

observatory and also at the surrounding natural sights, Flagstaff has proclaimed itself the world's first (and so far only) "International Dark Sky City."

Flagstaff's other main draw, the **Museum of Northern Arizona** (daily; $7; 928/774-5213), perches at the edge of a pine-forested canyon three miles northwest of downtown via US-180, the main road to the Grand Canyon; extensive exhibits detail the vibrant cultures of northern Arizona, from prehistoric Puebloans to contemporary Hopi, Navajo, and Zuni.

Downtown Flagstaff has more than enough espresso bars—probably a half dozen within a two-block radius of the train station—to satisfy its many multiply pierced, twenty-something residents.

the telescope that discovered Pluto, Lowell Observatory

There are also ethnic restaurants specializing in Greek, Thai, German, or Indian cuisine, so finding suitable places to eat and drink will not be a problem. Grab a cup of good coffee at **Macy's** (14 S. Beaver St.; 928/774-2243), a cozy café two blocks north of the Northern Arizona University campus, or wander two blocks farther north and east, past the train station and across Route 66 to **MartAnne's Burrito Palace,** a tiny and very popular little hole-in-the-wall serving authentic Mexican specialties (*posole, chilaquiles,* etc.) alongside more Americanized palate-pleasers like *chimichangas* (10 N. San Francisco St.; 928/773-4701). Hungry road-food fans may prefer to cruise west down Route 66 to the authentic-feeling **Galaxy Diner,** open since 1959 (931 W. Route 66; 928/774-2466).

Accommodations, too, are plentiful, and you can pick either the motel with the most appealing sign or step back into an even earlier time and stay at the classy railroad-era **Hotel Monte Vista** ($65–175; 100 N. San Francisco St.; 928/779-6971), right off old Route 66. It was good enough for Gary Cooper, and it has been restored to its Roaring '20s splendor.

Sunset Crater and the Grand Canyon

While 90 percent of visitors approach the Grand Canyon from the south, a better and less crowded approach follows US-89 and Hwy-64, climbing up from the Navajo Nation deserts onto the Kaibab Plateau. The views are amazing in any direction—north across the desiccated Colorado Plateau, east across the colorful Painted Desert, west to the forests of the Kaibab Plateau, or south to the angular San Francisco Peaks, including 12,663-foot Mount Humphreys, the highest point in Arizona.

This route is somewhat longer than the US-180 route to the Grand Canyon, but in most other ways it's far superior—not least because it gives access to a huge variety of scenery and historic sites. The first of these, 12 miles north of

Flagstaff and three miles east of US-89, is **Sunset Crater,** a 1,000-foot-tall black basalt cone tinged with streaks of oranges and reds and capped by a sulfur-yellow rim—hence the name, which was bestowed by explorer John Wesley Powell in 1892. You can hike through the lava field that surrounds the cone, but the cone itself is off limits.

Sunset Crater marks the start of a scenic loop that winds around for some 30 miles through neighboring Wupatki National Monument (daily; $5; 928/679-2365). The monument protects the remains of a prehistoric Native American community, thought to have been ancestors of the Hopi, who lived here between AD 1100 and 1225 and now inhabit the broad mesas rising to the northeast. Hundreds of ruins—most in very fine condition—are spread over the 35,000-acre monument. The largest ruin, 100-room **Tall House,** stands near a ceremonial amphitheater and a very rare ball court, which may indicate a link with the Mayan cultures of Central America.

> Cameron is named in memory of a cantankerous prospector-turned-early-promoter of the Grand Canyon. Ralph Cameron blazed the Bright Angel Trail (then charged tourists $1 to use it) and did everything he could to obstruct the government from taking over "his" canyon—even going so far as to get elected U.S. senator (in 1920) so he could try to eliminate the newly established national park.

Back on US-89, 20 miles north of the north entrance to Wupatki, the crossroads settlement of Cameron stands at the junction with Hwy-64, which heads up (and up) to the east entrance of **Grand Canyon National Park.** A mile north of the Hwy-64 junction, along the south bank of the Little Colorado River, historic **Cameron Trading Post** (which also has a $120-a-night motel and an RV park; 928 /679-2231) stands next to an equally historic one-lane suspension bridge, built in 1911 (and now carrying an oil pipeline). Cameron makes a good alternative to Tusayan, in case all the Grand Canyon's in-park accommodations are full.

From Cameron, Hwy-64 runs west along the Little Colorado River Gorge, which Hopi cosmology considers to be the place where man emerged into the present world. This deep canyon leads into the much larger Grand Canyon, while Hwy-64 climbs up the plateau for 30 miles to the east entrance of Grand Canyon National Park. Your first overlook is a desert view, where the photogenic 1930s Watchtower gives a great taste of the canyon from the highest point on the South Rim.

Williams

The last Route 66 town to be bypassed by I-40, **Williams** (pop. 2,842; elev. 6,780 feet) held out until the bitter end, waging court battle after court battle before finally surrendering on October 13, 1984. Despite the town's long

INTERSECTION

Arizona's biggest attraction, in every sense of the word, is the **Grand Canyon,** a geological spectacle carved by the Colorado River through an astonishing array of solid rock over the past 1.5 billion years—and counting. More coverage and tips on visiting the Grand Canyon are on pages 924–927.

Grand Canyon National Park

One of the wonders of the natural world, the Grand Canyon of the Colorado River—200 miles long, a mile deep, and anywhere from 5 to 15 miles across—defies description, and if you're anywhere nearby you really owe it to yourself to stop for a look. The most amazing thing about the Grand Canyon, apart from its sheer size and incredible variety of shapes and colors, is how different it looks when viewed from different places (artist David Hockney has said that the Grand Canyon is the only place on Earth that makes you want to look in all directions—up, down, and side to side—at the same time), so be sure to check it out from as many angles, and at as many different times of day, as you can. A book like this one can do little more than hint at all there is to see and do, but if you have time for nothing else, take a quick hike down into the canyon to get a real sense of its truly awesome scale.

The great majority of the nearly five million people who visit the Grand Canyon each year arrive at the South Rim and gaze down into the Grand Canyon from Mather Point, where the entrance road hits the edge of the gorge. The park visitors center and most of the food and lodging are located a mile west at Grand Canyon Village. Beyond Grand Canyon Village, West Rim Drive winds west, leading past the J. W. Powell Memorial at Hopi Point (from where you get great views of the Colorado River, which otherwise can be surprisingly hard to see) and a series of other viewpoints before ending up at Hermit's Rest, eight miles from Grand Canyon Village—where there are yet more stupendous views as well as restrooms, drinking fountains, and a gift shop.

The **West Rim Drive,** which was built for tourists by the Santa Fe Railroad in 1912, is closed to cars throughout summer, but frequent shuttle buses stop at all the viewpoints. A six-mile hiking trail runs west from the Powell Memorial to Hermit's Rest, and a three-mile paved nature trail links the Powell Memorial with Grand Canyon Village.

view of Grand Canyon looking to the North Rim including Bright Angel Trail

East from Mather Point, **East Rim Drive** runs for 25 miles, stopping first at aptly named Grandview Point, 12 miles from Grand Canyon Village and a half mile north of the East Rim Drive. This is, literally and figuratively, a high point of any Grand Canyon tour, giving a 270-degree panorama over the entire gorge. Continuing east, the road passes a small prehistoric pueblo at Tusayan Ruins before ending with a bang at **Desert View Watchtower,** an Anasazi-style tower set right at the edge of the canyon. Though it looks ancient, the tower was created for tourists in 1932, designed by Mary Colter, also the architect of the Bright Angel Lodge and most of the wonderful old Harvey House hotels that lined Route 66 across the Southwest.

From the watchtower, the road continues along the rim through the east entrance, then drops down to the crossroads town of Cameron and the Little Colorado River.

Grand Canyon Hikes

To get a real feel for the Grand Canyon, you have to get out of the car, get beyond the often overcrowded viewpoints that line the South Rim, and take a walk down into the depths of the canyon itself. The most popular and best-maintained path, the **Bright Angel Trail,** descends from the west end of Grand Canyon Village, following a route blazed by prospectors in the 1890s. It's an 18-mile hike down to the Colorado River and back. There are rest stops (with water) along the way; however, the park does not recommend anyone walking from rim to river in one day. A shorter day hike cuts off to **Plateau Point,** 1,300 feet above the river and a 12-mile round-trip from the South Rim. If you can finagle a reservation, you can stay overnight at **Phantom Ranch,** on the north side of the Colorado River, which is accessed from the South Rim by a pair of suspension bridges. Camping at nearby **Bright Angel Campground,** which has space for more than 100

(continued on next page)

(continued)

people, requires an advance permit from the park. Permit information is available at www.nps.gov/grca or by calling the main visitors center for details.

Another interesting old trail drops down from Grandview Point to Horseshoe Mesa, where you can still see the remnants of an old copper mine that closed in 1907. This is a six-mile round-trip and gives an unforgettable introduction to the Grand Canyon.

No matter where you go, when hiking down into the canyon remember that it will take you twice as long to hike back up again, that the rim can be covered in snow and ice as late as June, and *always carry water*—especially in summer—at least a quart for every hour you're on the trail. The very good **visitors center**

Lower Ribbon Falls

(928/638-7888) in Grand Canyon Village has information about the park's many hiking trails, the canyon's geology, the burro rides that take you down and back up again, and anything else to do with the Grand Canyon.

Practicalities

It may give a sense of the immensity of the Grand Canyon to know that, while the North Rim is a mere 6–10 miles from the South Rim as the crow flies, to get there by road requires a drive of at least 215 miles.

Most of what you'll need to know to enjoy your Grand Canyon visit is contained in the brochure you're given at the entrance, where you pay the $25-per-car fee (national parks passes are accepted).

To make advance reservations for accommodations—a good idea at any time of year but essential in the peak summer months—phone the park concessionaire, **Xanterra** (888/297-2757 in advance, 303/297-2757 same-day), which handles reservations for the six very different lodges in Grand Canyon Village. The most characterful and best-value place to stay is the **Bright Angel Lodge,** which overlooks the canyon; the cheapest rooms share bathrooms, while others have canyon views and fireplaces. The coffee shop here is open all day, there's a pretty nifty soda fountain right on the edge of the canyon, and the lobby fireplace shows off the rock strata, in proper chronological order, that form the walls of the Grand Canyon. The other historic lodge is the **El Tovar Hotel,** built in 1905 but recently renovated; rooms here start around $150 and top out at more than $300 a night. The El Tovar also has the park's best restaurant—and a comfy piano bar to help while away the night.

For a basic motel bed, there are four other lodges in Grand Canyon Village, offering more than 750 rooms altogether, costing $81–184 a night. There's also a very nice lodge at the North Rim, open usually mid-May to mid-October.

It's more of an effort to reach, but the best place to get a feel for the Grand Canyon is splendid **Phantom Ranch,** a rustic complex of cabins and dormitories way down in the canyon, on the north side of the Colorado River. Space here is usually taken up by people on overnight burro-ride packages (which cost around $400), but in off-season particularly you may be able to get a bed without the standard six months' (or more) advance reservation. Ask at the desk in the Bright Angel Lodge, or call 303/297-2757.

Reservations for camping (877/444-6777 or online at www.recreation. gov) at the South Rim are also essential in summer. The largest facility, **Mather Campground,** is near Market Plaza, the park's general store and commerce area, and is open year-round, with more than 300 sites (no hookups, $18 a night) and coin-operated showers; sites with RV hookups are available nearby at the Xanterra-run **Trailer Village.** There's another National Park Service campground at Desert View, near the east entrance, and backcountry camping (overnight permits required) is available at established sites down in the canyon.

If all the in-park accommodations are full, thousands of rooms are available in Williams and Flagstaff, and right outside the park's southern boundary at **Tusayan,** where you can choose

from a Best Western, a Holiday Inn Express, and a Quality Inn. Tusayan (which has a summer shuttle bus to the South Rim, and the third-busiest airport in Arizona) is also headquarters for a half dozen companies offering airplane and helicopter tours of the canyon; you can't miss their billboards, but details of prices (think $200 per hour) and trips can be got from operators such as **Papillon** (928/638-2419) or **Grand Canyon Airlines** (928/638-2359).

A FREE GOVERNMENT SERVICE
GRAND CANYON
NATIONAL PARK
U.S. DEPARTMENT NATIONAL PARK
OF THE INTERIOR SERVICE

opposition, in the end Williams gave in gracefully, going so far as to hold a cel-
ebration-cum-wake for the old road, highlighted by a performance atop a new
freeway overpass by none other than Mr. Route 66 himself, Bobby "Get Your
Kicks" Troup.

Williams today is primarily a gateway to the Grand Canyon, but it also
takes full tourist advantage of its Route 66 heritage: The downtown streets
sport old-fashioned street lamps, and every other store sells a variety of Route
66 souvenirs, making the town much more than a pit stop for Grand Canyon–
bound travelers. Apart from the Route 66 connections, Williams's pride and
joy is the vintage **Grand Canyon Railway,** which whistles and steams its way
north to the canyon every morning March–December, taking roughly two
hours each way. Call for current schedules and fares (round-trip costs around
$70; 800/843-8724), or stop by the historic depot, a former Harvey House
hotel restored in 1990.

If you hanker after a slice of pie and a cup of coffee, or simply appreciate
good food and a warm welcome, you'll want to save time and space for the
Pine Country Restaurant, serving breakfast, lunch, dinner, and famous fresh
pies near the train station (107 N. Grand Canyon Blvd.; 928/635-9718).
Williams is also home to a landmark old Route 66 restaurant, **Rod's Steak
House** (301 E. Bill Williams Ave.; 928/635-2671), in business since 1946.

For a place to stay—and there are many, thanks to the nearby Grand
Canyon—there are a couple of old motor court motels, one disguised as an
EconoLodge ($60 and up; 302 E. Route 66; 928/635-4085), another branded
as a **Rodeway** ($100 and up; 928/635-4041). At the upper end of the scale, try
the plushly renovated **Lodge on Route 66** ($125 and up; 200 E. Route 66;
928/635-4534), or look into that historic Harvey House hotel, now known as
the **Grand Canyon Railway Hotel** ($150 and up; 800/843-8724), a very
plush overnight that's ideal for passengers taking the vintage train to the
Grand Canyon.

Grand Canyon Railway

Sedona

Most Arizona visitors head for the Grand Canyon, but smaller and still scenic Oak Creek Canyon, just south of Flagstaff, has one great advantage over its world-famous neighbor: you can drive through it, on scenic Hwy-89A. Starting right at the edge of Flagstaff, this red sandstone gorge has been cut into the surrounding pine and juniper forests by eons of erosion. The most popular place to enjoy Oak Creek Canyon, **Slide Rock State Park** (daily, $20, 520/282-3034), 18 miles south of Flagstaff and seven miles north of Sedona, is a 55-acre, day-use-only area focused on the long, natural rock chute for which the park is named. Nearby **Slide Rock Lodge** (520/282-3531) has peaceful motel rooms starting around $100 in summer. No Wi-Fi is provided, but there are barbecue grills for the do-it-yourself cook.

Cathedral Rock

At the south end of Oak Creek Canyon, 25 miles from Flagstaff, the otherworldly landscape surrounding **Sedona** (pop. 10,031) has made it one of the nation's most popular vacation destinations, particularly for New Agey visitors, who in the past 20 years have made Sedona into a upmarket center for psychic channeling, soul travel, and the like. Sedona first came to attention in the 1950s, when the red-rock spires that dominate the local landscape were seen in a wide variety of Hollywood westerns (including *Johnny Guitar*). Despite the rampant sprawl—and the high hotel rates, which can reach $200 a night—Sedona is still well worth a look, especially if you can get away from the town and explore some of the surrounding wilderness.

Jerome

South of Route 66 and I-40 from Ash Fork, or west from Sedona, Hwy-89A makes a wonderfully scenic loop, winding past 7,815-foot Mingus Mountain into photogenic **Jerome** (pop. 378; elev. 5,400 feet), the liveliest and most interesting "ghost town" in Arizona. Set on steep streets that switchback up the mountainside, Jerome is an old copper mining camp that has turned itself into a thriving artists' community, with many nice shops, galleries, and cafés, and almost no touristy schlock. Park wherever you can and walk around, enjoying the incredible views out over the Verde Valley to the San Francisco Peaks and beyond.

At the north (uphill) edge of town, a mile off Hwy-89 at the end of fairly rough Perkinsville Road, the **Gold King Mine** (928/634-0053, daily 10 AM–5 PM; $5) has a misleading name but is still a great place to go. Not so much a mine as an anarchic collection of ancient-looking machinery (sawmills, pumps, hoists, trucks, cars, and ore cars), most of which is kept in working order, plus an intact old gas station dating from Jerome's 1920s heyday.

At the heart of Jerome, enjoy food or a fine shot of espresso at the **Flatiron Cafe** (416 Main St.; 928/592-3625), or for a full meal with a great view, try the delicious Asylum dining room inside the huge old **Jerome Grand Hotel,** a former hospital ($125 and up; 200 Hill St.; 928/634-8200).

Seligman

One of best places to stop and get a feel for the spirit of old Route 66, the sleepy little town of **Seligman** (pop. 510; pronounced "SLIG-man") is a perfect place to take a break before or after rejoining the Interstate hordes. The town retains a lot of its historic character—old sidewalk awnings and even a few hitching rails—and offers lots of reasons to stop, including Angel Delgadillo, the town barber, whose shop (217 E. Route 66) has been a pilgrimage point for old-roads fans for decades. His brother, Juan Delgadillo, created and ran the wacky **Snow Cap Drive-In** (928/422-3291) a half block to the east, where the sign says Sorry, We're Open, and the menu advertises Hamburgers without Ham. Behind the restaurant, in snow, rain, or shine, sits a roofless old Chevy decorated with fake flowers and an artificial Christmas tree. Juan died in 2004 (at the ripe old age of 88), but his family carries on the Snow Cap traditions, and the burgers, fries, and milk shakes (not to mention the jokes!) are worth driving miles for.

Seligman, which in the 1940s was the location of Andreas Feininger's classic Route 66 photograph, also has some very good places to eat, such as the kitschy **Road Kill Café** near the Rusty Bolt junk shop. Seligman also some more unexpected combinations, like the German-American barbecue at **Westside Lilo's,** good coffee served behind the bright-green facade of **Seligman Sundries,** and the cold beer typically downed by cowboys and truckers at the **Black Cat Bar.** All are within stumbling distance of each other along Historic Route 66. For an overnight, choose from a half dozen motels (but not the Unique Motel, which is now a sign only), like the nice, clean, and friendly **Historic Route 66 Motel** ($60 and up; 500 W. Route 66; 928/422-3204).

Between I-40 exit 139, just west of Ash Fork and the wonderful town of Seligman, a very nice section of the old Route 66 two-lane runs all the way to Seligman along the railroad tracks just north of, and parallel to, the I-40 freeway. Coming into Seligman on this stretch of Route 66, you'll be greeted by the fantastic Rusty Bolt junk shop and oddball emporium, impossible to miss along the north side of the old highway.

Probably the most evocative stretch of old Route 66 runs between Seligman and Kingman through the high-desert Hualapai (pronounced "WALL-ah-pie") Reservation, along the Santa Fe Railroad tracks through all-but-abandoned towns bypassed by the "modern" Interstate world.

Delgadillo's Snow Cap Drive-In

Grand Canyon Caverns

Far, far away from the high-speed freeway frontage, 22 miles northwest of Seligman and a dozen miles east of Peach Springs, a large green sign marks the entrance to **Grand Canyon Caverns** (daily; $15; 928/422- 3223), which has somehow managed to survive despite being bypassed by the I-40 superslab. Once one of the prime tourist draws on the Arizona stretch of Route 66, the Grand Canyon Caverns were discovered and developed in the late 1920s and still have the feel of an old-time roadside attraction. Tours start every half hour at the gift shop, where you hop on the elevator that drops you 300 feet to underground chambers, including the 18,000-square-foot Chapel of the Ages. Tours last around 45 minutes. There's also a gas station and a motel, and if you want a truly unique experience, the owners may let you stay overnight in their Cave Suite, a fully furnished two-bed suite dating back to the 1962 Cuban Missile Crisis, when a corner of the caverns was set up as a fallout shelter.

Just west of the Grand Canyon Caverns, Hwy-18 cuts off 65 miles to the northeast toward the **Havasupai Indian Reservation,** which includes one of the most beautiful and untrammeled corners of the Grand Canyon. No roads, just red rocks, green canyons, cobalt-blue waterfalls, and the **Havasupai Lodge** ($145; 928/488-2111).

Old Route 66 Loop: Grand Canyon Skywalk

Midway along the Historic Route 66 loop between Seligman and Kingman, the road comes close to the Grand Canyon as it passes through the large and lonely Hualapai Indian Reservation. The 2,100-strong Hualapai tribe has its community center at the town of **Peach Springs,** which marks the halfway point of this 90-mile, old-roads loop and offers at least one reason to stop: the comfortable **Hualapai Lodge** ($70–115; 928/769-2230) hotel and Diamond Creek restaurant, right on Route 66. Apart from this, Peach Springs is mostly a prefab Bureau of Indian Affairs housing project with few services, though there is a photogenic old Route 66 filling station at the center of town.

Peach Springs is the starting point for the 19-mile drive along Diamond Creek Road—all the way to the "bottom" of the Grand Canyon. Get a permit and detailed info at the Hualapai Lodge.

The lodge was the first sign of tourism in Peach Springs, but the Hualapai tribe seems to have embraced commerce in a big way: 2007 saw the opening of the much-hyped (and much-troubled) **Grand Canyon Skywalk,** a glass-floored steel horseshoe that juts out from the edge of the Grand Canyon, 4,000 feet higher than the Colorado River. Installed at a cost of $30 million, the very daring and impressive Skywalk is certainly unique, but it's also very expensive (count on it costing close to $100 per person, including lots of annoying fees and charges to park and ride the bus out to the Skywalk itself). The Skywalk is most popular as a day-trip destination from Las Vegas, but you can get here from Peach Springs via 75 miles of rough roads. The recommended route is to take I-40 or Route 66 to Kingman (50 miles southwest of Peach Springs), then head north via US-93, Pierce Ferry Road, and Diamond Bar Road, sections of which are still unpaved.

A Skywalk museum is planned and facilities are supposed to start being improved once the money rolls in, but for now there isn't much apart from the Skywalk itself. There's an ambitious long-term plan to develop the entire western end of the Hualapai Reservation into "Grand Canyon West," with all sorts of water-rafting tours and outdoor activities on offer; time will tell if the Skywalk endures once the novelty wears off.

US-93 is covered in our **Border to Border** road trip. See pages 114–173.

West of Peach Springs, Route 66 winds along the railroad tracks, passing through a few ghost towns (like Hackberry, where the old gas station still stands in rusting splendor) before zooming into Kingman.

Kingman

The only town for miles in any direction since its founding as a railroad center in 1880, **Kingman** (pop. 27,521) has always depended upon passing travelers for its livelihood. Long a main stopping place on Route 66, and still providing the only all-night services on US-93 between Las Vegas and Phoenix, and along I-40 between Flagstaff and Needles, the town remains more a way station than a destination despite the increasing number of people who have relocated here in recent years, attracted by the open space, high desert air, and low cost of living.

The best first stop in Kingman is **The Powerhouse,** 120 W. Andy Devine Ave.; 928/753-9889), a hulking old power plant that's been inventively reused to house a very good Route 66 museum, with galleries full of enough old cars, postcards, and mementos to occupy you for an hour or more. Best of the bunch is a nifty relief map of the entire path of Route 66 (the many mountain ranges make you realize why old cars needed so many service stations!), and the displays do a good job of evoking and exploring the deep romance many Americans seem to feel for the old Mother Road.

The stretch of Route 66 through Kingman has been renamed in memory of favorite son Andy Devine, who was born in Flagstaff in 1905 but grew up here, where his parents ran the Beale Hotel. One of the best-known character actors of Hollywood's classic era, the raspy-voiced Devine usually played a devoted sidekick. Devine's most famous role was as the wagon driver in the classic 1939 John Ford western *Stagecoach;* he also did the voice of Friar Tuck in Disney's version of Robin Hood and remained active in films and TV until his death in 1977.

Be sure to contact the **visitors center** here (928/753-6106), to pick up a copy of the town's very good Route 66 brochure, then pop across Route 66 for a burger, some fries, and a milk shake at the very good **Mr. D'z Route 66 Diner** (105 E. Andy Devine Ave.; 928/718-0066), impossible to miss thanks to its bank of neon.

The blocks off Route 66 hold Kingman's most interesting older buildings—Beale Street, north of Route 66, has dozens of 100-year-old railroad era storefronts now housing an array of junque and antiques shops. Besides the usual chain motels along I-40, accommodation options in Kingman include the pleasant **Hill Top Motel** ($40 and up; 1901 E. Andy Devine Ave.; 928/753-2198), forever infamous as the place where evil Timothy McVeigh stayed for a week before blowing up the Federal Building in Oklahoma City.

To escape the summer heat, Kingmanites head east and south along a well-marked 14-mile road to **Hualapai Mountain Park,** where pines and firs cover the slopes of the 8,417-foot peak. Hiking trails wind through the wilderness, where there's a campground and a few rustic cabins ($55–125) built by the Civilian Conservation Corps during the New Deal 1930s. Contact the ranger station (928/757-3859) near the park entrance for detailed information or to make reservations.

Cool Springs and Black Mountains

Midway between Kingman and Oatman, set against the angular **Black Mountains** high above the desert plain, **Cool Springs** is a nifty old rough stone service station resurrected as a Route 66 gift shop and mini museum. Built in the 1920s, abandoned in the 1960s, and brought back to life in 2005, Cool Springs is a nice place to stop, buy a soda, and soak up the Route 66 spirit.

Between Cool Springs and Oatman, old Route 66 twists and turns past recently reactivated gold workings while climbing up and over the angular Black Mountains. Steep switchbacks and 15-mph hairpin turns carry the old road on a breathtaking 2,100-foot change in elevation over a very short eight miles of blacktop.

Old Route 66: Oatman

One of the most demanding, desolate, and awesomely satisfying stretches of the old road loops north from the I-40 freeway, between Kingman and the California border. Climbing over steep mountains while cutting across a stretch of desert that brings new meaning to the word "harsh," the narrow roadway passes few signs of life on this 50-mile loop, so be sure you and your car are prepared for the rigors of desert driving.

Crossing the Colorado River between Arizona and California, look downstream (south) from the I-40 freeway to see the arching silver steel bridge that carried Route 66 up until 1966. It's still in use, supporting a natural gas pipeline; beyond it, the red-rock spires for which Needles is named rise sharply out of the desert plains.

Westbound drivers have it the easiest—simply follow the well-signed Historic Route 66 west from Kingman, exit 44 off I-40. From the west heading east, take exit 1 on the Arizona side of the river, then head north. Whichever way you go, you can't avoid the steep hills that lead to **Oatman** (elev. 2,700 feet), an odd mix of ghost town and tourist draw that's one of the top stops along Route 66. A gold mining town whose glory days had long faded by the time I-40 passed it by way back in 1952, Oatman looks like a Wild West stage set, but it's the real thing—awnings over the plank sidewalks, bearded roughnecks (and a few burros) wandering the streets, lots of rust, and slumping old buildings. The gold mines here produced some two million ounces from their start in 1904 until they panned out in the mid-1930s; at its peak, Oatman had a population of over 10,000, with 20 saloons lining the three-block Main Street. One of these, the old **Oatman Hotel** (181 N. Main St.), was where Clark Gable and Carole Lombard were said to have spent their first night after getting married in Kingman in 1939. You can sample some highly recommended Navajo tacos and have a beer in the downstairs bar (which is thickly wallpapered in years and years worth of dollar bills!), or peer through a Plexiglas door at the room where Clark and Carole slept, hardly changed for half a century.

Saloons and T-shirt shops line the rest of Main Street, where on weekends and holidays Wild West enthusiasts act out the shootouts that took place here only in the movies. Oatman does get a considerable tourist trade, but after dark and outside of the peak summer tourist season, the town reverts to its rough-and-tumble ways, and the conservative, libertarian bent of most of the local population ensures that nothing is likely to change Oatman's crusty charms.

The crossing over the Colorado River at the California/Arizona border was the site of illegal but effective roadblocks during the Dust Bowl era, when vigilante mobs turned back migrant Okies if they didn't have much money.

Lake Havasu City and London Bridge

The first stop east of the Colorado River, just across the border and 23 miles south of I-40, **Lake Havasu City** is a thoroughly modern vacation town built around a thoroughly odd centerpiece: **London Bridge,** brought here stone by stone between 1967 and 1971. Terribly tacky souvenir shops and faux London pubs congregate around the foot of the bridge, which spans a man-made channel to a large island, but the bridge itself is an impressive sight.

Unless you plan to retire here—or simply rent a houseboat and relax on the water—there's not a lot to do at Lake Havasu. That said, the area has become a popular spring break destination for western college kids, thousands of whom flock to **Lake Havasu State Park** (928/855-2784)

London Bridge

It may not have stood out as the finest piece of engineering art when it spanned the Thames, but London Bridge is a marvelous sight in the middle of the Arizona desert. A replacement for a series of bridges that date back to medieval times, inspiring the children's rhyme, "London Bridge Is Falling Down," this version of London Bridge was constructed in the 1830s. When it was no longer able to handle the demands of London traffic, the old bridge was replaced by a modern concrete span and its stones were put up for sale in 1967.

Bought by property developer Robert McCulloch for $2.4 million, the 10,246 blocks of stone were shipped here and reassembled at a cost of another $7 million. After a channel was cut under the bridge to bring water from the Colorado River, the Lord Mayor of London flew in to attend the rededication ceremonies in October 1971; the bridge now stands as the centerpiece of a fast-growing retirement and resort community that's home to more than 50,000 residents.

There's no admission charge to see this oddly compelling sight. If you have a taste for surreal experiences, walk across the bridge and sample the Ye Olde England ambience of Barley Brothers brewpub. Even more schizoid is the adjacent, all-suite **London Bridge Resort** ($125 and up; 928/855-0888), where the "original" medieval turrets and Arthurian design flourishes have been redecorated with palm trees for that unforgettable tropical island experience.

for fun-in-the-sun and who-knows-what after dark. For the rest of us—have an English muffin and a cup of tea, pay your respects and take a photograph or two, then hit the road again.

CALIFORNIA

From the demanding **Mojave Desert,** over mountains and through lush inland valleys, to the beautiful beaches of **Santa Monica,** Route 66 passes through every type of Southern California landscape. The old road, which survives intact almost all the way across the state, is marked for most of its 315 miles by signs declaring it Historic Route 66. Across the Mojave Desert the route is also marked as the National Old Trails Highway, its title before the national numbering system was put into effect in the late 1920s.

Needles

Founded soon after the Santa Fe Railroad came through in 1883 and named for the group of sharp stone spires that stand near where I-40 crosses the Colorado River from Arizona, **Needles** (pop. 4,844) is one of the hottest places in the country, with summertime highs hovering between 100°F and 120°F for months on end. Though often unbearable in summer, Needles is a popular place with winter snowbirds escaping colder climes; it also has a very rich Route 66 heritage. The stretch of old Route 66 through Needles runs along Broadway, alternating along both sides of the freeway. The magnificent El Garces Hotel is undergoing long-term renovation into a restaurant, hotel, historical museum and visitors center, and until it is back open for business, the best place to stop and soak some Route 66 personality is the Wagon Wheel Restaurant, west of downtown (2420 Needles Hwy.; 760/326-4305), open all day for good fresh food, and on Friday nights for all-you-can-eat fish 'n' chips.

If you're set on traveling as much of the old road as possible, another stretch of Route 66 runs west of Needles and north of I-40 through the near-ghost towns of Goffs and Fenner, on a roller coaster of undulating two-lane blacktop, parallel to the railroad tracks.

Needles was the boyhood home of Snoopy and Charlie Brown cartoonist Charles Schulz and is featured in the comic strips as the desert home of Snoopy's raffish sibling, Spike. Needles now features Spike and Snoopy in a series of Route 66–themed murals around town, as at the Chevron station on Needles Highway.

From Needles, it's a quick 25-mile drive north along the Colorado River into Nevada to visit the gambling center of **Laughlin.** Since the mid-1980s Laughlin has boomed into a sparkling city with huge casinos and over 10,000 cheap rooms.

Old Route 66 Loop: Ludlow and Amboy

Thanks to the orderly planners of the Santa Fe Railroad, which first blazed this route across the desert in 1883, many of the place-names on this old Route 66 loop come in alphabetical order: from west to east, you have Amboy, Bristol, Cadiz, Danby, Essex, Fenner, Goffs, Home, Ibis, Java, and Klinefelter. Yes, Klinefelter.

Huge chunks of the Mojave Desert have been used as military training grounds since World War II, when General George Patton used this area to prepare his tank battalions for battle in the North African desert. As many as 90,000 soldiers were based here during the war years; the remains of the camp can still be seen in the desert along Crucero Road, just north of the I-40 Ludlow exit.

If you want a quick and convincing taste of what traveling across the Mojave Desert was like in the days before air-conditioning and cellular phones, keep your eyes peeled for Historic Route 66 signs, and turn south off I-40 and follow the National Old Trails Highway, one of the many monikers Route 66 has carried over the years, on a 75-mile loop along the old road. Heading west, the loop leaves I-40 about 25 miles beyond Needles; heading east, the old road turns off I-40 at **Ludlow,** 50 miles east of Barstow, where two gas stations, a coffee shop, and a motel represent a major outpost of civilization.

While the drive alone is worth the extra time it takes, the real attraction comes midway along this old road loop: **Amboy** is synonymous with **Roy's Motel and Café,** a museum-worthy assembly of roadside architecture that has survived solely due to the willpower of its longtime lord and master, Buster Burris, who ran the place from 1938 (when he married the daughter of owner Roy Crowl) until 2000, when Buster died at the age of 92. In the late 1940s, Roy's was the prime stop between Needles and Barstow, and as many as 90 people staffed the café, the motel, and the car repair shop, working around the clock to cater to the thousands of passing cars. Roy's fell on hard times after the opening of I-40 in 1974, but the whole town—complete with a huge "Roy's" sign, a classic late-1940s roadside café, a set of simple motor court cabins, and a pair of gas pumps—has hung on. Now, thanks to owner Albert Okura (who also owns the San Bernardino-based restaurant chain Juan Pollo and the "First McDonald's" museum), the café and gas station are open as often as possible, and Amboy is used as a film and photo-shoot location as well as being a photogenic reminder of the heyday of Route 66.

From Amboy, you can leave Route 66 and head south to the lovely high desert of **Joshua Tree National Park** and the newly re-energized, 1950s Rat Pack–era resorts of Palm Springs. Staying on Route 66, you'll pass the lava flows around Amboy Crater, and you may see and hear helicopters and Warthog fighters playing war games on the huge Twentynine Palms Marine Corps base, which stretches off to the south. At nearly 1,000 square miles, it's the largest base in the country and often the last U.S. stop for personnel bound for battle in the Middle East.

Mojave National Preserve

Spreading north of old Route 66, more than 1.5 million acres between I-40 and I-15 have been set aside as the **Mojave National Preserve,** a harsh desert landscape of volcanic cinder cones and sand dunes, desert tortoises, and Joshua trees. One evocative landmark here in the middle of desert is the **Kelso Depot** (760/252-6165), a restored train station that sits on the main L.A. to Las Vegas Union Pacific railroad line. Trains still rumble past, and the depot, featuring a variety of interpretive exhibits and a very nice lunch room called The Beanery, re-creates the sense of life here in the 1920s, before air-conditioning and cell phones made life in the desert so much more agreeable. Kelso is on Kelbaker Road, about 22 miles north of I-40, midway between Fenner and Ludlow.

Another of the many places in the Mojave Preserve that's worth the trip is **Mitchell Caverns** ($6; 760/928-2586) at the center of **Providence Mountains State Recreation Area,** 25 miles north of I-40 at the end of Essex Road. At the time of this writing, the park was closed due to state budget cuts. Call before you make the drive.

Newberry Springs: Bagdad Cafe

Running alongside the I-40 freeway for about 50 miles east of Barstow, old Route 66 survives as a sort of frontage road, passing little more than an occasional lava flow (like Pisgah Crater, where there's a pair of I-40 rest areas).

Northeast of Barstow, **Calico Ghost Town** is an enjoyable resurrection of the silver mining camp that boomed here during the 1890s.

About 20 miles east of Barstow is the place that for many people symbolizes the quirky personality of Route 66: **Newberry Springs,** where the popular Percy Adlon movie *Bagdad Cafe* was shot at the town's one and only café, now also known as the **Bagdad Cafe** (760/257-3101). Welcoming and appropriately weird, considering its connections with the oddly endearing movie (which features a cast of drifters, a fat German magician, and Jack Palance!), the real-life Bagdad Café is not so much a restaurant as it is a semi-catered film set, staying in business as a pit stop for fans of off-beat European cinema who happen to find themselves in the middle of the Mojave Desert. Be sure to read and sign the guest book, which features heartfelt comments from hundreds of people who've made the trek here from all over the world. (Scandinavians and other Teutonic types seem especially well represented.)

Between the Bagdad Café and Barstow, old Route 66 runs past the region's other unique claim to fame: the semi-successful **Solar One** and **Solar Two** power plants, experimental, 10-megawatt electricity generating stations north of I-40 that are now used as an astronomical gamma-ray observatory.

Barstow

The burly railroad and transportation center of **Barstow** (pop. 22,639) is located in the middle of the Mojave Desert, at the point where I-40 disappears into I-15, midway between Los Angeles and Las Vegas. Trucks and trains are the main business in town—even the McDonald's pays homage to trains, with its dining rooms housed in old passenger cars from a train—and Barstow is scruffy and a little scary in the way railroad towns can be. Along Main Street, the old Route 66 corridor, many of the old cafés and motels are now closed and boarded up, but just north of old Route 66, the circa-1911 Harvey House **Casa del Desierto** hotel next to the train station is a survivor from an earlier age. Looking like the Doge's Palace in Venice (if the Doge's Palace faced the wide-open desert instead of an intricate network of canals . . .), the gothic-style arcades are a substantial reminder of a time when travel meant more than just getting somewhere. The long-abandoned building has been brought back to use as a railroad and Route 66 **museum** (Fri.–Sun. 11 AM–4 PM; free; 760/256-9276).

The Mojave Desert is one of the driest places on the planet; parts of it receive less than three inches of rainfall in an average year, sometimes going for more than two years without getting a drop.

Oro Grande: Bottle Tree Ranch

Between Barstow and Victorville, old Route 66 survives as an "old roads" trek across the Mojave Desert. The 36-mile route, called the National Old Trails Highway, parallels the railroad tracks and the usually parched Mojave River, passing through odd little towns like **Oro Grande,** which is still home to a huge cement plant and an array of roadside junk shops. The cement plant, processing local limestone, follows on from the optimistic prospectors who gave the town its "Big Gold" name back in the 1850s. The cemetery here is one of the oldest in southern California, and Oro Grande is also home to some long-abandoned roadside businesses, relics of Route 66. One relic lives on: A 1930s tractor dealership now houses the popular **Iron Hog Saloon,** which serves cold beers and big steaks (and rattlesnake!) at 20848 Old Route 66 (760/843-0609).

Outside Barstow at the west end of Main Street, keep an eye out for the Christian Motorcycle club sign welcoming you to **Lenwood,** a crossroads near where the old road reconnects with I-15.

The Oro Grande boasts an impressive silver steel bridge over the bed of the Mojave River and is getting famous for another more colorful sight: the hard-to-miss **Bottle Tree Ranch** (24266 Route 66), where thousands of green, blue, brown and clear glass bottles have been dangled from a forest of mostly metal "trees" by a white-bearded local retiree named Elmer Long. There's no admission charge for the Bottle Tree Ranch, which Elmer has dedicated to "those who have lived and died on the Mother Road." Elmer's not shy (he has his own Facebook page!), so stop and say "hi."

Victorville

Take the "old road" between Barstow and Victorville to be sure to enter Victorville on old Route 66 and see Victorville at its best. At the **California Route 66 Museum,** right on old Route 66, in Old Town across from the train station (daily; 16825 D St.; 760/951-0436), a small but growing collection of road signs, photographs, and reminiscences help preserve the life and times of this great old highway. The museum also holds most of the surviving pieces of Hula Ville, an outdoor sculpture park and oddball art gallery that once stood west of Victorville. Most of its paintings and hand-lettered memorials to sundry bums, hobos, and other travelers were moved here after Hula Ville's 100-year-old creator and caretaker, former carnival worker "Fry Pan" Miles Mahan, passed away in 1996.

pointing the way to the 66 Motel in Victorville

Without its Route 66 connections, Victorville would be just another distant SoCal commuter suburb. In fact, ever since the departure of Hula Ville, not to mention the wonderful Roy Rogers and Dale Evans Museum, which—along with its much-loved celebrity subjects—had a home here, Victorville just hasn't seemed the same. Fortunately old Route 66 can still be traced through town: From the Route 66 Museum, turn south onto 7th Street, which runs past a few neon-signed old motels like the **New Corral** ($50; 14643 7th St.; 760/245-9378) with its animated bucking bronco.

There's also a worthwhile stop two miles east of downtown: Join the truckers and bikers at family-run **Emma Jean's Holland Burger Café** (17143 N. D St.; 760/243-9938), rated best in the country by the *Diners, Drive-ins and Dives* TV show.

South and west of Victorville, heading toward Los Angeles and the seemingly distant Pacific Ocean, a number of very picturesque but generally dead-end stretches of old Route 66 go over **Cajon Pass,** but the main road is definitely I-15. At the top of the pass, turn off the freeway at the Oak Hills exit and stop for a burger and fries at the **Summit Inn** (760/949-8688), one of the few survivors of the old road businesses along this stretch of highway.

San Bernardino

Sometimes known as "San Berdoo," in the 1940s and 1950s the city of **San Bernardino** (pop. 210,000) was where Maurice and Richard McDonald perfected the burger-making restaurant chain that bears their name. In 1961, the McDonald brothers sold their company to Ray Kroc, and the rest is fast-food history. Though the original buildings were demolished decades ago, the location is now home to an unofficial, ad hoc museum, displaying McDonalds and Route 66 memorabilia (free; 1398 N. E St.; 909/885-6324).

San Bernardino County, which covers over 20,000 square miles (most of it desert), is the largest in the United States.

From downtown San Bernardino, which somewhat confusingly is actually a dozen miles east of the I-15 freeway, the old Route 66 alignment headed west along Foothill Boulevard, where a remnant of old Route 66 road culture still survives: the 19 concrete tepees that form the **Wigwam Motel** (around $70; 2728 W. Foothill Blvd.; 909/875-3005). Once as seedy as its "Do It In A TeePee" sign suggested, this Wigwam (one of three in the world—another sits along Route 66 in Holbrook, Arizona) has been fully updated and once again welcomes travelers interested in offbeat accommodations (with free Wi-Fi, a swimming pool, and barbecue grills).

San Bernardino is home to the Class A farm club of the Anaheim Angels, and the team name plays up the Route 66 connections: They're called the **Inland Empire 66ers.** The stadium is right off the old road ($6 and up; 280 S. E St.; 909/888-9922). Games are broadcast on **KCAA 1050 AM.**

From the Wigwam Motel, Foothill Boulevard runs west through the post-industrial city of Fontana, birthplace of the Hell's Angels' Motorcycle Club (and L.A. culture critic Mike Davis), before passing by another great old road landmark: **Bono's Giant Orange,** an orange-shaped stand that, during the 1920s, offered thirsty Route 66 travelers "All The Orange Juice You Can Drink—10¢." The original orange grove is now a Wal-Mart, and the Giant

Orange was moved next to **Bono's Restaurant and Deli** (15395 Foothill Blvd.), where it's in good shape—and slated for possible reopening as a juice stand. Bono's Giant Orange is one of the last of the dozens of giant orange-shaped roadside businesses all over California, which used to tempt passersby to stop and sample their wares.

The San Gabriel Valley takes its name from old **Mission San Gabriel Arcangel,** which still stands (daily 9 AM–4:30 PM; $5; 537 W. Mission Dr.; 626/457-3035). Despite suffering extensive earthquake damage, the mission is an interesting spot, though not as evocative as others in the chain.

the first McDonald's, now a museum

San Gabriel Valley

Winding between Pasadena and San Bernardino, along the foothills of the sometimes-snowcapped San Gabriel Mountains, old Route 66 links a number of once-distinct communities like **Azusa,** home of the classic Foothill Drive-In, whose marquee was saved when the land was recently developed, and collegiate **Claremont.** In **Upland,** where the old road features a number of recently installed retro–Route 66 streetlamps, there's a grass median strip graced by a statue of the pioneer Madonna of the Trail, which officially marked the western end of the National Old Trails Highway, the immediate precursor to Route 66.

The city of **Monrovia** (pop. 37,000) holds another Route 66 survivor: the groovy, Mesoamerican-style art deco exuberance of the **Aztec Hotel** (311 W. Foothill Blvd.; 626/358-3231), better for its popular bar Brass Elephant (which hosts frequent live music) than for its unrestored rooms, but well worth a look. Monrovia was home for many years to quixotic author Upton Sinclair (1878–1968) and is now the headquarters of the cult-favorite grocery store Trader Joe's. The company, which started in 1958 as Pronto Markets, opened its first Trader Joe's store in Pasadena in 1967.

Rancho Cucamonga (pop. 165,269) is now best known as the home of the Epicenter, where the very popular **Cucamonga Quakes** (909/481-5000), an L.A. Dodgers farm club, play Class A baseball, and a statue of Jack Benny welcomes you through the turnstiles. (If you ever heard Benny's log-running radio and TV show, which featured Mel Blanc reading the tag line "Anaheim, Azusa, and CU-CA-MON-GA," you'll know why he's there.)

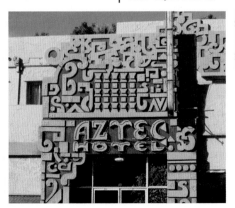

Though it's now effectively swallowed up in Southern California's never-ending sprawl, the San Gabriel Valley used to be the westbound traveler's first taste of Southern California. After crossing the Mojave Desert and the high mountains, Route 66 dropped down into what might have seemed like paradise: orange groves as far as the eye could see, a few tidy towns linked by streetcars, and houses draped in climbing roses and bougainvillea.

In the next town to the west, **Sierra Madre,** Foothill Boulevard runs past the landmark racetrack at **Santa Anita,** designed by Hoover Dam stylist Gordon Kaufmann. In 1937 the Marx Brothers filmed *A Day at the Races* here, but the art deco facades have been ruined by the track's ongoing "development" into a Las Vegas–scale gaming and shopping complex.

Huntington Library, Museum and Gardens

East of Pasadena, at the west end of the San Gabriel Valley, old Route 66 runs along Huntington Drive, which takes its name from one of the most important figures in early Los Angeles, Henry Huntington. Nephew of Southern Pacific Railroad baron Collis P. Huntington, from whom Henry inherited a huge fortune (as well as a wife, Arabella), Henry Huntington controlled most of southern California's once-extensive public transit system. He is now most remembered for creating and endowing one of the world's great museums, the **Huntington Library, Museum and Gardens,** located in the exclusive community of San Marino (closed Tues.; $15 and up; 1151 Oxford Rd.; 626/405-2141).

The Huntington Library contains all sorts of unique books and documents and preserves thousands more for the benefit of scholars, but the real draw is the art gallery, which displays an excellent collection of British and European painting and sculpture, with major works by Reynolds, Gainsborough, and others. There are also fine assemblages of American art, including Gilbert Stuart's familiar portrait of George Washington. Perhaps the best part of the Huntington is its splendid **gardens,** which cover 120 acres in a series of mini-ecosystems, distilling the essence of Australia, Japan, South America, and, in one of the country's largest cactus gardens, the American Southwest.

Pasadena

Heading out of downtown Los Angeles, the historic Pasadena Freeway (Hwy-110) drops you off unceremoniously short of **Pasadena,** but following Figueroa Street brings you in with a bang on the soaring **Colorado Boulevard Bridge,** an elegantly arching, circa-1913 concrete bridge at the western edge of Pasadena, which long marked the symbolic entrance to Los Angeles from the east.

Aloe saponaria and blue stick succulents (*Senecio mandraliscae*), Huntington Library Desert Garden

Recently restored, the bridge spans **Arroyo Seco** along the south side of the Ventura Freeway (Hwy-134). Arroyo Seco itself is full of significant sights, including college football's Rose Bowl and some of the most important architecture in Southern California, notably the **Gamble House,** a 100-year-old arts-and-crafts gem (Thurs.–Sun. afternoons; $10; 4 Westmoreland Place; 626/793-3334). Above the arroyo, on old Route 66, the **Norton Simon Museum** (closed Tues.; $10; 411 W. Colorado Blvd.; 626/449-6840) has a medium-sized but impeccably chosen collection of western and southeast Asian art, ranging from Hindu sculpture to one of the world's foremost collections of Degas paintings, drawings, and sculptures.

Colorado Boulevard in Pasadena holds the annual **Tournament of Roses Parade,** every New Year's Day before the famous Rose Bowl football game.

Just a few blocks east of Arroyo Seco and the Norton Simon Museum down old Route 66, Old Pasadena is the name for the old center of town, where locals congregate for evening fun and daytime shopping. Start your morning with breakfast at **Marston's** (151 E. Walnut St.; 626/796-2459), just north of Old Pasadena, or detour two blocks south of old Route 66 to enjoy the fine neon sign and classic soda-fountain milk shakes at the **Fair Oaks Pharmacy** (1526 Mission St.; 626/799-1414). There are quite a few old motels along this stretch of Route 66; one good bet is the **Saga Motor Hotel** ($99 and up; 1633 E. Colorado Blvd.; 626/795-0431).

Route 66 Across Los Angeles

Diehard old-road fans will be pleasantly surprised to know that Route 66 across Los Angeles still exists, almost completely intact. West from Pasadena

Los Angeles is a stop along our **Pacific Coast** route, which begins on page 8. Some classic L.A. sights, scenes, and drives are described on pages 100–101.

Besides all the sights, Route 66 across L.A. also holds two of the city's best bookshops: **Book Soup**, in West Hollywood (8818 Sunset Blvd.), and **Vroman's**, in Pasadena (695 E. Colorado Blvd.).

into downtown L.A., you have your choice of Route 66 routings. You can hop onto the Pasadena Freeway (Hwy-110) for a trip back to freeways past: Opened in 1939, when it was called the Arroyo Seco Parkway, this was California's first freeway and featured such novel (and never repeated) concepts as 15-mph exit ramps and stop signs at the entrances. Or, you can follow Figueroa, which in L.A. lingo is known as a "surface street," running parallel to the freeway past some fascinating pieces of Los Angeles new and old, including the concrete-lined Los Angeles River, hilltop Dodger Stadium, and the excellent **Autry National Center** at Griffith Park (closed Mon.; $10; 323/667-2000), a phenomenally wide-ranging collection featuring Native American art and artifacts from all over western North America, as well as Wild West ephemera and pop culture icons. (The center is the result of a merger between the Southwest Museum of the American Indian and the Museum of the American West, established by Hollywood's "Singing Cowboy," Gene Autry, a media magnate who is the only person ever awarded five stars on the Hollywood Walk of Fame.)

Now marked by prominent beige road signs reading "Historic Route 66 1935–1964," old Route 66 follows Sunset Boulevard from the historic core of the city, starting at Olvera Street and the El Pueblo de Los Angeles State Historic Park before winding west to Hollywood. In Hollywood itself, Route 66 turns onto Santa Monica Boulevard, then runs past the cemetery-cum-theme park **Hollywood Forever**

Johnny Ramone's final resting place in the Hollywood Forever cemetery

(daily; free; 323/469-1181), where such luminaries as Rudolf Valentino and Mel Blanc are entombed, overlooked by the water tower of legendary Paramount Studios. It's a unique experience by day, and even more so on nights when the cemetery is host to outdoor screenings of its residents' works.

Continuing west to the Pacific, old Route 66 follows Santa Monica Boulevard through the heart of West Hollywood and Beverly Hills, where "Mr. Route 66" himself, the Oklahoma-born comedian Will Rogers, once was honorary mayor.

Santa Monica

Old Route 66 had its western terminus at the edge of the Pacific Ocean in **Santa Monica,** on a palm-lined bluff a few blocks north of the city's landmark pier. The pier holds a small amusement park and a lovely old Looff carousel (as carousel at the historic Looff Hippodrome on the Santa Monica Pier

seen in the movie *The Sting*). A beachfront walkway heads south of the pier to Venice Beach, heart of bohemian L.A., but near where Santa Monica Boulevard dead-ends at Ocean Avenue, a brass plaque marks the official end of Route 66, the "Main Street of America," also remembered as the Will Rogers Highway, one of many names the old road earned in its half century of existence. The plaque remembers Rogers as a "Humorist, World Traveler, Good Neighbor"—not bad for an Okie from the middle of nowhere.

Two blocks east of the ocean, stretch your legs at Santa Monica Place and the adjacent Third Street Promenade, an indoor/outdoor shopping area and icon of contemporary Southern California (sub)urban culture. The surrounding streets are among the liveliest in Southern California; people actually walk, enjoying street performers, trendy cafés, bookshops, and movie theaters.

Enjoyable in its own right, Santa Monica also makes a very good base for seeing the rest of the L.A. area. For the full retro-luxury experience, check in

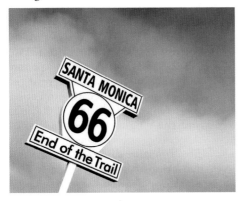

to the art deco **Georgian Hotel** ($225 and up; 1415 Ocean Ave.; 310/395-9945). Or you can save your money for food and fun by staying at the very popular **HI-Santa Monica Hostel** (around $38 per person; 1436 2nd St.; 310/393-9913).

Road Trip Resources

ORGANIZATIONS

The American Automobile Association (AAA) (1000 AAA Drive, Heathrow FL 32746, 800/922-8228, www.aaa.com) is an indispensable resource. No traveler in his or her right mind should hit the road without a membership card. Besides the free roadside assistance (24 hours a day across the country), AAA also offers free maps, useful guidebooks, and tons of related information. Check their website or look in the Yellow Pages to find a local office.

The Lincoln Highway Association (136 N. Elm St., P.O. Box 308, Franklin Grove, IL 61031, 815/456-3030, www.lincolnhighwayassoc.org) is a group of old-roads aficionados who work to preserve remnants of the nation's first coast-to-coast highway and to promote its memory. They also get together for annual meetings to retrace the route.

The National Historic Route 66 Federation (P.O. Box 1848, Lake Arrowhead, CA 92352-1848, 909/336-6131, www.national66.org) is the only nationwide, nonprofit organization committed to revitalizing Route 66 and to promoting awareness of its historic role as the Main Street of America. Members receive a high-quality quarterly magazine. All dues go directly toward lobbying governments to preserve what's left of Route 66.

The National Trust for Historic Preservation (1785 Massachusetts Avenue NW, Washington DC 20036, 800/944-6847, www.preservationnation.org) is a nonprofit organization dedicated to protecting the irreplaceable historic buildings and the neighborhoods and landscapes they anchor. One of the benefits of membership ($20 a year) is a subscription to the wonderful bimonthly magazine *Preservation*.

The Society for Commercial Archeology (P.O. Box 45828, Madison, WI 53744-5828, www.sca-roadside.org) is an all-volunteer organization working to preserve and interpret roadside culture. Anyone interested in the cultural landscape lining America's highways and byways will want to join the SCA. The enterprise is geared toward appreciation and enjoyment of quirks and crannies of the highway environment. Studies cover everything from diners to giant roadside dinosaurs. Dues are $45 a year, and members receive a full-color magazine and a quarterly newsletter that details preservation efforts as well as get-togethers for annual tours of different regions.

PRACTICALITIES
Hotel and Motel Chains

Best Western: 800/780-7234, www.bestwestern.com

Clarion: 877/424-6423, www.clarionhotel.com

Comfort Inn: 877/424-6423, www.comfortinn.com

Courtyard: 888/236-2427, www.marriott.com/courtyard

Days Inn: 888/440-2021, www.daysinn.com

Econo Lodge: 877/424-6423, www.econolodge.com

Embassy Suites: 800/EMBASSY, embassysuites.hilton.com

Hampton Inn: 800/HAMPTON, hamptoninn.hilton.com

Hilton: 800/HILTONS, www.hilton.com

Holiday Inn: 888/HOLIDAY, www.holidayinn.com

Howard Johnson: 888/637-4861, www.hojo.com

Hyatt: 888/591-1234, www.hyatt.com

Marriott: 888/236-2427, www.marriott.com

Motel 6: 800/4-MOTEL-6, www.motel6.com

Radisson: 800/967-9033, www.radisson.com

Ramada Inn: 888/228-4982, www.ramada.com

Ritz-Carlton: 800/542-8680, www.ritzcarlton.com

Rodeway Inn: 877/424-6423, www.rodewayinn.com

Sheraton: 800/325-3535, www.starwoodhotels.com/sheraton

Super 8: 888/8288-5081, www.super8.com

Westin: 800/937-8461, www.starwoodhotels.com/westin

W Hotels: 877/WHOTELS, www.starwoodhotels.com/whotels

Wyndham: 877/999-3223, www.wyndham.com

Camping

One essential purchase for anyone traveling around the USA, especially in the western states, is a pass from the **National Parks Service.** The cost for a general **InterAgency Annual Pass** is around $80. This card gives free admission (for an entire family for a full year), to all National Parks and National Historic Sites. The **Senior Pass** is a $10 lifetime pass that gives free admission to any U.S. citizen or permanent resident over the age of 62. The free **Access Pass** makes the National Parks available to people with permanent disabilities. Other passes offer discounts on campgrounds. For more information, call (888/GO-PARKS) or visit their website at www.nps.gov. For information on camping and recreation in other federal lands, a great starting point is the www.recreation.gov website.

Car Rental Companies

Alamo: 877/222-9075, www.alamo.com

Avis: 800/230-4898, www.avis.com

Budget: 800-527-0700, www.budget.com

Enterprise: 800/261-7331, www.enterprise.com

Hertz: 800/654-3131, www.hertz.com

National: 877/222-9058, www.nationalcar.com

Thrifty: 800/367-2277, www.thrifty.com

U.S. STATE TOURISM AND ROAD CONDITIONS

Alabama
Tourism Info: 800/ALABAMA,
www.alabama.travel

Arizona
Tourism Info: 888/275-5816
Road Conditions: 888/411-7623,
www.highwayconditions.com/az

Arkansas
Tourism Info: 800/NATURAL,
www.natural.com
Road Conditions: 800/245-1672,
www.arkansashighways.com

California
Tourism Info: 800/TO-CALIF,
www.visitcalifornia.com
Road Conditions: 800/427-7623,
www.dot.ca.gov

Colorado
Tourism Info: 800/COLORADO,
www.colorado.com
Road Conditions: 303/639-1111,
www.cotrip.org

Connecticut
Tourism Info: 800/CT-BOUND
Road Conditions: 860/594-2650

Delaware
Tourism Info: 800/441-8846
Road Conditions: 302/760-2080,
www.roadcondition.us/delaware

Florida
Tourism Info: 888/7-FLA-USA,
www.visitflorida.com
Road Conditions: 800/475-0044,
www.usroadconditions.com/fl

Georgia
Tourism Info: 800/VISIT-GA,
www.exploregeorgia.org
Road Conditions: 404/635-6800,
www.roadcondition.us/georgia

Idaho
Tourism Info: 800/635-7820

Illinois
Tourism Info: 800/226-6632
Road Conditions: 800/452-4368,
www.usroadconditions.com/il

Indiana
Tourism Info: 888/365-6946,
www.enjoyindiana.com
Road Conditions: 800/261-7623,
www.in.gov/indot

Iowa
Tourism Info: 800/345-IOWA
Road Conditions: 515/288-1047,
www.iowaroadconditions.org

Kansas
Tourism Info: 800/2-KANSAS
Road Conditions: 800/585-7623

Kentucky
Tourism Info: 800/225-TRIP,
www.kentuckytourism.com

Louisiana
Tourism Info: 800/33-GUMBO

Maine
Tourism Info: 888/624-6345,
www.visitmaine.com
Road Conditions: 207/287-3427,
www.511maine.gov

Maryland
Tourism Info: 800/543-1036
Road Conditions: 800/327-3125,
www.chart.state.md.us

Massachusetts
Tourism Info: 800/227-MASS,
www.massvacation.com
Road Conditions: 617/374-1234

Michigan
Tourism Info: 888/78-GREAT,
www.michigan.org
Road Conditions: 800/381-8477

Minnesota
Tourism Info: 800/657-3700
Road Conditions: 800/542-0220,
www.511mn.org

Mississippi
Tourism Info: 800/WARMEST

Missouri
Tourism Info: 800/877-1234
Road Conditions: 800/222-6400

Montana
Tourism Info: 800/VISIT-MT,
www.visitmt.com
Road Conditions: 800/332-6171

Nebraska
Tourism Info: 800/228-4307
Road Conditions: 402/471-4533

Nevada
Tourism Info: 800/NEVADA-8,
www.travelnevada.com
Road Conditions: 877/687-6237

New Hampshire
Tourism Info: 800/FUN-IN-NH,
www.visitnh.gov
Road Conditions: 603/271-6900

New Jersey
Tourism Info: 800/JERSEY-7

New Mexico
Tourism Info: 800/733-6396
Road Conditions: 800/432-4269

New York
Tourism Info: 800/CALL-NYS
Road Conditions: 800/847-8929

North Carolina
Tourism Info: 800/VISIT-NC,
www.visitnc.com
Road Conditions: 877/368-4968

North Dakota
Tourism Info: 800/435-5663,
www.ndtourism.com
Road Conditions: 701/328-7623

Ohio
Tourism Info: 800/BUCKEYE,
www.discoverohio.com
Road Conditions: 614/644-7031

Oklahoma
Tourism Info: 800/652-6552,
www.travelok.com
Road Conditions: 405/425-2385

Oregon
Tourism Info: 800/547-7842,
www.traveloregon.com

Pennsylvania
Tourism Info: 800/VISIT-PA
Road Conditions: 814/355-6044

Rhode Island
Tourism Info: 800/556-2484

South Carolina
Tourism Info: 800/346-3634

South Dakota
Tourism Info: 800/S-DAKOTA,
www.travelsd.com
Road Conditions: 605/367-5707

Tennessee
Tourism Info: 800/GO-2-TENN,
www.tnvacation.com
Road Conditions: 800/858-6349

Texas
Tourism Info: 800/888-8TEX,
www.traveltex.com
Road Conditions: 800/452-9292

Utah
Tourism Info: 801/538-1030,
www.travel.utah.gov
Road Conditions: 801/964-6000

Vermont
Tourism Info: 800/VERMONT,
www.vermontvacation.com

Virginia
Tourism Info: 800/VISIT-VA,
www.virginia.org
Road Conditions: 800/367-7623

Washington
Tourism Info: 800/544-1800,
www.experiencewa.com
Road Conditions: 800/695-7623

West Virginia
Tourism Info: 800/225-5982,
www.wvtourism.com
Road Conditions: 877/982-7623

Wisconsin
Tourism Info: 800/432-TRIP
Road Conditions: 800/762-3947

Wyoming
Tourism Info: 800/225-5996,
www.wyomingtourism.org
Road Conditions: 307/772-0824

CANADIAN PROVINCIAL TOURISM AND ROAD CONDITIONS

Alberta
Tourism Info: 800/661-8888
Road Conditions: 403/246-5853

British Columbia
Tourism Info: 800/663-6000
Road Conditions: 250/953-9000

Ontario
Tourism Info: 800/668-2746
Road Conditions: 416/235-4686

Quebec
Tourism Info: 800/363-7777
Road Conditions: 418/684-2363

RECOMMENDED READING
Roadside America

American Diner: Then and Now by Richard J. S. Gutman (Johns Hopkins University, 2000): Lushly illustrated, encyclopedic history of that great American roadside institution, from its humble beginnings in the lunch wagons of the late 1880s to the streamlined stainless-steel models so beloved by art directors everywhere.

Asphalt Nation: How the Automobile Took Over America and How We Can Take It Back by Jane Holtz Kay (University of California, 1998): An enthusiastic and informative account of how cars, and the commuter culture they've spawned, have sapped the strength of the nation's communities. Not as histrionic as the title might lead you to believe, this is an engaging and insightful book that aims to help us cut down on the billions of annual hours Americans spend stuck in traffic.

Colossus of Roads: Myth and Symbol Along the American Highway by Karal Ann Marling (University of Minnesota Press, 2000): If you're interested in the stories behind America's many roadside giants—Paul Bunyan statues, supersized fruits and vegetables, and myriad concrete dinosaurs—you'll love this informative and funny study. Packed with pictures, but a little lacking in details on how to find these giant figures in the flesh, it's bound to inspire more than a few detours.

Flattened Fauna: A Field Guide to Common Animals of Roads, Streets, and Highways by Roger M. Knutson (Ten Speed Press, 1987): Lighthearted look at that under-studied ecosystem, the highway. Besides being a helpful guide to identifying the sundry dead objects along the roadside, the book also details the natural life and habitats of the unfortunate road-killed creatures.

The Lincoln Highway: Main Street Across America by Drake Hokanson (University of Iowa Press, 1999): The bible of Lincoln Highway history, tracing America's first transcontinental highway from its beginnings in 1915 to its gradual fadeout in the post-Interstate world. If you want to travel along the granddaddy of old roads, look for *Greetings from the Lincoln Highway,* a fully illustrated mile-by-mile guide by Brian Butko (Stackpole Books, 2005).

Main Street to Miracle Mile: American Roadside Architecture by Chester H. Liebs (New York Graphic

Society, 1985): This lushly illustrated historical survey of roadside design is the best single introduction to the familiar, yet fascinating environment that lines the nation's highways.

Open Road: A Celebration of the American Highway by Phil Patton (Simon and Schuster, 1986): An energetic account of how the American roadside landscape came to look the way it does today, masterfully blending a discussion of the economic and political forces behind the nation's highway network with a contagious enthusiasm for the inherent democracy the automobile embodies.

Pump and Circumstance: Glory Days of the Gas Station by John Margolies (Little, Brown, 1993): Profusely illustrated coffee-table book that uses photographs, advertising, enamel signs, road maps, and brief but revealing text to track the development of that essential feature of the American highway landscape, the gas station. The same author/photographer has produced many other great books, including **Hitting the Road,** about road maps; **Fun Along the Road,** about roadside amusements; and **See the USA,** which explores the graphic world of travel brochures and posters.

Roadside America by Doug Kirby et al. (Fireside Books, 1993): The best guidebook to the wackiest and weirdest attractions along the Great American Roadside. Organized by theme rather than by location, but still an entertaining and agreeable travel companion; check it out "live" at www.roadsideamerica.com.

Travel Guidebooks

The American Guide: A Source

Book and Complete Travel Guide for the United States in Four Volumes (Hastings House Publishers, 1949): Invaluable documents of the state of the nation during the 1930s and 1940s, these state-by-state, road-by-road, somewhat socialist-minded guidebooks were compiled during the Depression and later by teams of writers put to work under the auspices of the New Deal Works Project Administration (W.P.A.). Many great writers, including Saul Bellow, Richard Wright, Studs Terkel, Ralph Ellison, Kenneth Patchen, Nelson Algren, and Jim Thompson contributed to the series, selected volumes of which have been brought back into print.

The Amusement Park Guide by Tim O'Brien (Globe Pequot, 2003): The subtitle says it all: Coast to Coast Thrills. Contains full descriptions and practical information for 275 small, medium, and large amusement parks all over the United States and Canada.

Ballpark Vacations by Bruce Adams and Margaret Engel (Fodor's, 2002): Enjoyable and informative travel guide detailing the best minor and major league baseball parks in the country, with details on the teams and well-chosen suggestions of places to eat and sleep in 75 different cities and towns. Baseball fanatics should also pick up a copy of the annual *Baseball America* directory, which gives details of every professional and semi-pro team in the United States and Canada.

Eat Your Way Across the USA by Jane and Michael Stern (Broadway Books, 1997): Handy, cross-country compendium of All-American diners, drive-ins, lobster shacks, and barbecue stands, put together by the road-food experts and *Gourmet* magazine correspondents.

Watch It Made in the U.S.A. by Karen Axelrod and Bruce Brumberg (Avalon Travel Publishing, 2006): A travel guide that takes you to watch the manufacture of such all-American products as Crayola crayons, Louisville Slugger baseball bats, Hershey's chocolates, and Harley-Davidson motorcycles.

Travelogues

Blue Highways: A Journey Into America by William Least Heat-Moon (Little, Brown and Company, 1982): One of the best-selling travel books ever written, this intensely personal yet openhearted tale traces the path of a part-Indian English teacher who travels the back roads "in search of places where change did not mean ruin and where time and men and deeds connected."

Drive, They Said: Poems About Americans and Their Cars edited by Kurt Brown (Milkweed Editions, 1994): If you like to drive, and like to read or write poetry, you'll love this thick volume of contemporary verse, which samples the work of over 100 poets.

Elvis Presley Boulevard: From Sea to Shining Sea, Almost by Mark Winegardner (Atlantic Monthly Press, 1987): An energetic mix of road trip journal and coming-of-age autobiography, this short book recounts a summer-long tour around the southern and central United States. The Elvis obsession hinted at by the title is only a small part of the book, which looks at many of the odder corners of America.

Fear and Loathing in Las Vegas by Hunter S. Thompson (Random House, 1972): Subtitled "A Savage Journey to the Heart of the American Dream," this riotous blast of a book starts with the words "We were somewhere around Barstow on the edge of the desert when the drugs began to take hold," and goes on to tell the story of a lost weekend in Sin City, and much, much more.

Great Plains by Ian Frazier (Farrar, Straus and Giroux, 1989): In-depth, top-to-bottom study of the wide-open land where the buffalo roamed, tracing historical themes like water, cowboys, and Indians, while capturing the contemporary scene.

Let Us Now Praise Famous Men by James Agee, photographs by Walker Evans (Mariner Books, 2001): A classic. The talented collaborators spent the summer of 1936 living with three families of poor white cotton sharecroppers in the Appalachian foothills of northwest Alabama, and together created a vivid and compassionate portrait of rural America during the depths of the Great Depression.

The Lost Continent: Travels in Small Town America by Bill Bryson (Harper Perennial, 1990): Iowa-born British transplant returns to America in search of material for his sarcastic commentary on contemporary life. Hilariously funny in parts, mean-spirited in others, and packed with trivial truths about life in the land of liberty.

On the Road by Jack Kerouac (Viking, 1957): What the Beatles were to music, the Beats were to literature, and this wild ramble of a road story was Kerouac's first number-one hit, inspiring a generation or two to hightail it along America's highways in the tracks of Sal Paradise and Dean Moriarty.

Out West: American Journey Along the Lewis and Clark Trail by Dayton Duncan (Viking Penguin, 1987): The best travel book since *Blue Highways,* this marvelous tale retraces the route blazed by the Corps of Discovery on their epic adventure. With a combination of concise history lessons, captivating storytelling, and wry humor, Duncan vividly points out what has and hasn't changed in the 200-odd years since the captains first trekked across the country and back.

Road Trips, Head Trips, and Other Car-Crazed Writings edited by Jean Lindamood (Atlantic Monthly Press, 1996): An introduction and description of a road trip along the Mexican border by P. J. O'Rourke sets the tone for this compilation of car-and-driver tales, which also features pieces by Jack Kerouac, John Steinbeck, and Hunter S. Thompson.

Spirit of Place: The Making of an American Literary Landscape by Frederick Turner (Sierra Club Books, 1989): A multi-layered tapestry of biography, travel writing, and literary criticism, this wonderful book explores how different locales have inspired and defined many of America's greatest writers.

Travels with Charley: In Search of America by John Steinbeck (Viking, 1962): Rambling around "this monster of a land" in his camper Rocinante, accompanied only by the eponymous French poodle, Steinbeck returns to his California haunts from self-imposed exile in New York to find that, even if you can't go home again, there are many intriguing things along the way.

Zen and the Art of Motorcycle Maintenance: An Inquiry into Values by Robert M. Pirsig (William Morrow and Company, 1974): The subtitle points out this big book's more ponderous aspects, but at its best this is a captivating, full-throttle ride down America's back roads in search of meaning in the modern age.

INDEX

A

abalone: 58
Abbey, Edward: 168
Aberdeen: 21–22
Abilene: 217
Abilene Zoo: 218
Abraham Lincoln
  Presidential Library and
  Museum: 872
Acadia National Park: 583
Acadian immigrants: 303
Accomac: 426
Acoma Pueblo: 911
Adams family: 693
Adams National Historic
  Site: 696
Adamson House: 98
Addams, Jane: 642
Adrian: 901
advertising, notable roadside:
  Burma-Vita Company 245,
  870; Rockwell City 635;
  Tucumcari Tonite 894;
  Wall Drug 196–197
African American history/
  sites: Charles Town 373;
  City Market, Charleston
  450; Civil Rights
  Movement National
  Historic Trail 848;
  DuBois, W. E. B. 346; Fort
  McKavett State Historic
  Site 222; Harpers Ferry
  372; Mound Bayou 289;
  Museum of Afro-American
  History and Culture 297;
  National Civil Rights
  Museum 280; National
  Voting Rights Museum
  847; Price lynching
  732; Sea Islands 452;
  Washington, Booker T.
  384, 851
Agar: 194
Agate Fossil Beds National
  Monument: 627
Agness: 40
agriculture: Central Valley,
  California 72; Crystal City
  spinach 226; Deerfield
  687; Dust Bowl 210, 211;
  El Centro 807; fairs 318;
  Farmer's Museum 678;
  flower seeds 91–92; Fredonia

666; Historic Ditch Walk
  221; Kansas 752; melon 256,
  257; Mississippi Agriculture
  and Forestry Museum
  842; peaches 268, 853;
  Rio Grande Valley 228;
  sustainable 332;
  Wenatchee 502
Agua Prieta: 817
Ainsworth: 632
aircraft manufacturing: 495
Aitkin: 240
Alabama: 845–852
Alamo, the: 153, 225
Alaska Highway: 119
Albany, New York: 680–681
Albany, Texas: 831
Albinger Archaeological
  Museum: 96
Albright-Knox Art Gallery:
  668
Albuquerque: 906
Alcatraz: 64
Algodones Dunes: 807
Algonquin Provincial Park:
  557
Allegheny Mountains: 785
Allen Art Museum: 658
Allentown: 361
Alligator Farm: 467
alligators: 379, 445, 448, 467,
  470, 483
Alsea Bay Historic
  Interpretive Center: 35
Alton: 270
Amarillo: 899
Amelia Island: 462
American River: 713
American Sign Museum: 779
American Visionary Art
  Museum: 797
Amerind Foundation
  Museum: 813
Amish Country: 650
amusement and theme
  parks: Balboa Pavilion,
  105; Belmont Park, 113;
  Cedar Point, 657; Dinosaur
  Journey, 739; Dinosaur
  Land, 374; Disneyland,
  103–104; Dollywood,
  396; Funland Amusement
  Park, 419; GatorLand, 470;
  Gillian's Wonderland Pier/

Water Park, 415; Great
  Wolf Lodge water park,
  657; Island Miniature
  Golf and Games, 863;
  Lakeside Amusement
  Park, 746; Legoland, 109;
  Marineland, 467; Oaks
  Park, 591; Ocean City,
  421; Paul Bunyan Land,
  244; Santa Cruz Beach
  Boardwalk, 70, 71; Santa
  Monica, 944–945; Santa's
  Land Theme Park and Zoo,
  395; Santa's Village, 574;
  Schlitterbahn Waterpark
  Resort, 231; Seabreeze
  Amusement Park, 671;
  Seaside boardwalk, 28;
  Silver Dollar City, 877;
  Six Flags Discovery
  Kingdom, 710; Six Flags
  St. Louis, 876; Story
  Land, 317; Stratosphere
  Tower, 157; Tinkertown,
  905; Walt Disney World,
  470; Wildwood, 416;
  Yooperland, 546
Anaheim: 103
Anastasia State Recreation
  Area: 467
Ancient Spanish Monastery:
  478
Anderson Valley: 56
Anderson Valley Brewing
  Company: 57
Andersonville Prison: 857
Andrew Molera State Park:
  80
Andy Griffith Show: 387
Angola: 301
Annapolis: 796
Año Nuevo State Reserve: 69
Anson: 217
Antietam National
  Battlefield: 371
Anza-Borrego State Park:
  806
Apache Trail: 164
Apostle Islands National
  Lakeshore: 537
Appalachian Trail: 310–407;
  Massachusetts 337–348;
  New Hampshire 312–327;
  New York 351–357;

North Carolina 386–399; Pennsylvania 357–370; Vermont 327–337; Virginia 374–386; West Virginia 371–373

apples: 502, 789

aquariums: Aquarium of the Pacific 102; Birch Aquarium 112; Bogue Bank 438; Feiro Marine Life Center 14; Guttenberg 252; Monterey Bay Aquarium 72, 73; Montshire Museum of Science 327; National Mississippi River Museum and Aquarium 254; Oregon Coast Aquarium 34; South Dakota Discovery Center and Aquarium 195; Tennessee Aquarium 397; Virginia Aquarium 428; Wetlands Institute 416

Aquarius: 161

Arcadia: 892

Arcata: 46

archaeological sites: Cahokia Mounds State Historic Site 873–874; Caliente 152; Casa Grande Ruins National Monument 168; Clovis Man 903; Cross Ranch Nature Preserve 186; Emerald Mound 296; Grimes Point 721; Hickison Petroglyph Recreation Area 724; Hudson-Meng Bison Bone Bed 628; Knife River Indian Village National Historic Site 181; Legend Rock 618; Ocmulgee National Monument 860; Paint Rock Pictographs 220; Poverty Point 839; Serpent Mound 781; Sunset Crater 923; Wahkpa Chu'gn "Buffalo Jump" Archaeological Site 520; Walnut Canyon National Monument 921; Winterville Mounds 289; *see also* petroglyphs; pictographs

Arches National Park: 735

architecture: Adamson House 98; Art Deco 478–479; Balboa Park 110; Bauhaus 692; Bavarian 501; Biltmore Estate 392; Canadian Centre for Architecture 561; Cedar Rock 637; Charleston, South Carolina 450; Chicago 644; Cincinnati 778; Coral Castle 482; County Courthouse, Santa Barbara 94; Daly mansion 135–136; Darwin D. Martin House 669; Deerfield 687; Demopolis 846; Elsah 270; Figge Art Museum 259; Fort Worth 834; French Lick Resort Casino 773; Gamble House 943; Gardner Museum of Architecture and Design 264; Gateway Arch 272; Glacier Park Lodge 516; Great Barrington 346; Hearst Castle 84; Henry Morrison Flagler Museum 475; Hillforest Mansion 776; Hotel del Coronado 111; Las Vegas 154–155; Macon 858; Madonna Inn 90; Natchez antebellum 296–297; National Museum of the American Indian 792; Nelson Atkins Museum of Art 764; Nitt Witt Ridge 86; Pacific County Courthouse 23; Plantation Alley 304–309; Port Gamble 13; Principia College 270; Rock and Roll Hall of Fame and Museum 660; Santa Barbara 93; Solvang 92; Spokane 506; St. Augustine 466; St. Johnsbury 571; Vicksburg antebellum 293; Villa Louis 250; Walker Art Center 242; West Feliciana Historical Society Museum 300; Wright, Frank Lloyd 166, 248, 643, 872

Arco: 610

Area 51: 156

Arizona: 160–173, 808–818, 914–935

Arizona Sonora Desert Museum: 171

Arizona State Museum: 170

Arkansas Blues and Heritage Festival: 285

Arlington National Cemetery: 791

Arnprior: 559

Art & Pumpkin Festival: 67

Arthur Bowring Sandhills Ranch State Historical Park: 631

Arthurdale: 787

artichokes: 72

Art Institute of Chicago: 644

Arts and Heritage Museum: 229

Asheville: 389, 392

Ashland, Wisconsin: 538

Ash Springs: 153

Ashtabula: 662

Asilomar Conference Grounds: 76

Assateague Island National Seashore: 423

Astoria: 25, 26

Astoria Column: 26

AT&T Pebble Beach National Pro-Am: 76

Athabasca Falls: 121

Athens, Georgia: 406

Athens, Ohio: 784

Atlanta: 400–401

Atlantic City: 412–414

Atlantic Coast: 408–491; Delaware 418–420; Florida 461–491; Georgia 455–460; Maryland 420–423; New Jersey 411–418; North Carolina 430–442; Old Baldy Lighthouse 443–453; Virginia 424–430

atomic testing: 153, 156

ATVs: 37

Auburn: 673

Auburn-Cord-Duesenberg Automobile Museum: 651

Audubon State Historic Site: 300

Aurora: 776

Austin, Nevada: 722

Avenue of the Giants: 51, 53

Avon: 435

Ayres Natural Bridge: 625

B

Babe the Blue Ox: 237

backpacking: 16, 81, 121, 123

Bagdad Cafe: 937–938

Bahia Honda State Park: 488

Bailey Yard: 202

Balboa Park: 110, 804

Balboa Pavilion: 105

Baldwin, Thomas: 264

Baldwin City: 761

Bal Harbour: 478

Ball, Lucille: 666
Ballinger: 219
Baltimore: 797
Bandon: 38
Bandon Driftwood Museum: 38
Bandon Dunes Golf Resort: 39
Bandon Historical Society Museum: 38
Banff: 125
Banff National Park: 122
Banff Park Museum: 126
Bangor: 579
Banks-Vernonia Linear State Park: 589
barbed wire: 898
barbecue: Athens 406; Bristow 890; Brunswick 458, 459; Cairo 277; Clarksdale 287; Devil's Elbow 880; Fort Lauderdale 477; Jay's Barbecue 303; Jiggs Smoke House 895; Jonesboro 276; Mackay free 139; Memphis 281; Placerville 713; Santa Maria 91; Statesboro 861; Texan 218; Warm Springs 856; *see also specific place*
Bar Harbor: 581
Barnstable: 699
Barstow: 938
Bartholomew's Cobble: 346
Barton, Clara: 371
baseball: Albuquerque Isotopes, 907; Arizona Diamondbacks, 166; Asheville Tourists, 393; Baltimore Orioles, 797; Boise Hawks, 604; Bowie Baysox, 796; Buffalo Bisons, 669; Burlington Bees, 261; Chattanooga Lookouts, 398; Chicago Cubs and White Sox, 645; Cleveland Indians, 660; Colorado Rockies, 746; Cucamonga Quakes, 941; D.C. Nationals, 793; Delmarva Shorebirds, 799; Detroit Tigers, 652; Erie Seawolves, 663; Everett AquaSox, 495; Fenway Park, 694, 696; Gary Railcats, 647; Gwinett Braves, 407; Idaho Falls Chukars, 611; Inland Empire 66ers, 940; Jackson, "Shoeless Joe", 267; Jacksonville Suns, 465;

Kansas City Royals, 765; L.A. Dodgers, 100; Las Vegas 51s, 158; Los Angeles Angels, 104; Louisville Bats, 774; Lowell Spinners, 689; Minnesota Twins, 242; Missoula Ospreys, 133; Montgomery Biscuits, 851; Myrtle Beach Pelicans, 445; National Baseball Hall of Fame, 678; Negro Baseball Leagues Museum, 765; New York Mets, 475; Norfolk Tides, 429; Oakland A's, 707; Oklahoma RedHawks, 893; Pawtucket Red Sox, 699; Pioneer League Casper Ghosts, 624; Quad Cities River Bandits, 259; Rochester Red Wings, 672; Sacramento River Cats, 711; Salt Lake Bees, 733; San Antonio Missions, 227; San Diego Padres, 110; San Francisco Giants, 64; Savannah Sand Gnats, 455; Seattle Mariners, 498; Sioux City Explorers, 635; South Bend Silver Hawks, 649; Spokane Indians, 506; Springfield Cardinals, 882; Spring Training Cactus League, 163; Spring Training Grapefruit League, 472; St. Louis Cardinals, 272; St. Paul Saints, 242; Syracuse Chiefs, 676; Toledo Mud Hens, 655; Troy ValleyCats, 681; Tucson Padres, 169; Vero Beach 474
Bash Bish Falls: 348
basket-making: 449
Basque culture: 149, 604
Bass, Rick: 510
Baton Rouge: 301–302
bats: 829
Battle of Bad Axe: 249
Battle Rock: 39
Bavarian immigrants: 190–191
Baxter Springs: 884
Bay Bridge: 796
Bayfield: 537
bayous: 305
beaches: Anastasia State Recreation Area 467; Boca Raton 476; Cannon Beach

30; Cape Cod National Seashore 700; Carmel 77; Chincoteague NWR 425; Crystal Cove State Park 105; Fort Lauderdale 477; Garrapata State Park 80; Gaviota State Park 93; Guadalupe-Nipomo Dunes NWR 91; Haulover Beach 478; Little Talbot Island 463; Long Beach Peninsula 23; Long Key State Park 487; Miami Beach 478–479; Newport Beach 105; Olympic National Park 20; Oswald West State Park 30; Outer Banks 433, 434; Pacific Coast Highway Beaches 97; Pescadero 68; Pfeiffer Beach 81; Point Lobos State Natural Reserve 80; Point Reyes National Seashore 62; Port Townsend 10; Ruby Beach 20; Santa Cruz 70; "sleeper" waves 60; Sonoma Coast State Park 60; South Carlsbad State Beach 109; Sunset Bay State Park 38; Torrey Pines State Natural Reserve 112; Tybee Island 863; Westport 22
Beale Street: 280
Beard, James: 28
Bear Mountain: 353
bear shows: 322–323
Beaufort, North Carolina: 438
Beaufort, South Carolina: 449
Bedford: 773
beef industry: 755, 899
beer: 57, 247, 272, 676, 687
bees, killer: 230
Belgrade Lakes: 578
Bellevue: 256
Belmont Park: 113
Bemidji: 237
Ben & Jerry's: 568
Bennington: 336
Bennington College: 336
Benson: 813
Bent's Old Fort: 750
Berkeley: 708
Berlin: 423
Berlin-Ichthyosaur State Park: 721
Bermuda Triangle: 477
Bernalillo: 910
berries: 69

Bethel: 575
Bethlehem: 360
Beverly Shores: 649
Biedenharn, Joseph: 293
Big Basin Redwoods State
    Park: 69
Big Fish Supper Club: 239
Bigfork: 132
Big Hole National Battlefield:
    136
bighorn sheep: 153
Big Sur: 11, 78
Big Sur Village: 80
biking: Everglades National
    Park 483; Jekyll Island 460;
    La Framboise Island Nature
    Area 195; Lake Chelan
    503; Lake Itasca State Park
    236; Little Talbot Island
    463; Mackinac Island 545;
    Père Marquette State Park
    269; RAGBRAI 254; Sam
    Vadalabene Bike Trail
    269; Trempealeau 246;
    Truro 701; Utopia 100K
    223; Valentine 201; *see also*
    mountain biking
Biltmore Estate: 392
Biosphere 2: 168
The Birds: 60, 61
"Birdman of Alcatraz": 278
bird-watching: Assateague
    Island National Seashore
    423; bald eagles 268, 639;
    Bartholomew's Cobble
    346; Bentsen-Rio Grande
    Valley State Park 228; Bird
    Island 41; Canadian 214;
    Cape Romain NWR 448;
    Delaware Seashore State
    Park 420; Devils Lake
    529; Fort Pierre National
    Grasslands 195; Fort
    Pulaski 862; Great Bend
    area 757; Hassayampa
    River Preserve 164; Hawk
    Ridge 533; Horseshoe Lake
    Conservation Area 276;
    Lake Bowdoin NWR 522;
    Leadbetter Point State
    Park 24; Niobrara Valley
    Preserve 632; northern
    spotted owl 18, 34; Pea
    Island NWR 435; peregrine
    falcons 87; Sabal Palm
    Grove Sanctuary 230;
    Shenandoah National Park

378; Siletz Bay 32; Vermont
    Institute of Natural Science
    328; Wetlands Institute
    416; white pelicans 523
Bisbee: 815
Biscayne Bay: 482
Bismarck: 186
Bitterroot Mountains: 136
Bitterroot Valley: 135
Bix Beiderbecke Memorial
    Jazz Festival: 259
Bixby Creek Bridge: 81
Blackbeard: 437
black bears: 395
Black Canyon of the Gunnison
    National Park: 741
Black Coulee National
    Wildlife Reserve: 523
Black Elk Speaks: 633
Blackfeet Indian Reservation:
    517
Black Hawk: 249
Black Hawk War: 250
Black Kettle National
    Grassland: 214
Black River Road: 541
Black Rock Mountain State
    Park: 403
Blandin Paper Mill: 239
Blarney Stone: 215
Blennerhassett Museum: 785
Bloomington-Normal: 870
blowholes: 35, 55
Blowing Rock: 388
Blue Angels: 807
Blue Highways: 761
Blue Hole: 905
Blue Ridge Parkway: 378–
    379, 385, 390–391
blues music: 284–287, 290, 853
Bluff Hall: 846
Boardwalk, Atlantic City: 413
Boca Raton: 476
Bodega: 60
Bodega Bay: 60
Bodie Island Lighthouse: 434
bodysurfing: 105
Boeing plant: 496
Bogachiel State Park: 19
Bogue Bank: 438
Bohemian Grove: 59
Boise: 604
Bolinas: 62
Bonaventure Cemetery: 862
"Boneyard," the: 170
Bonners Ferry: 509
Bonneville Salt Flats: 148, 149

Bonnie and Clyde: 837–838
"Boontling" language: 56
Boot Hill: 814
Boot Hill Museum: 755
border crossing, Mexico: 229,
    817
Border to Border Route:
    115–173; Arizona 160–173;
    Canadian Rockies 116–128;
    Idaho 137–146; Montana
    128–136; Nevada 146–159
Boston: 694–695
Bottle Tree Ranch: 939
Bottle Village: 96
Boulder City: 158
Bowie, Jim: 221
Bow Lake: 122
bowling: 720
Bow Summit: 122
Bow Valley Parkway: 126
Boyce Thompson Arboretum
    State Park: 165
Brainerd: 241
Branson: 877
Bretton Woods: 320
Brewster tours: 121
bridges, notable: Bay
    Bridge 796; Chesapeake
    Bay Bridge-Tunnel 427;
    Colorado Boulevard Bridge
    942; Duluth 534; Golden
    Gate Bridge 66; Jonesboro
    suspension 276; Mackinac
    Bridge 545; Rock Creek
    Bridge 890; Rock Island
    Line Railroad Bridge 212;
    Roebling Bridge 357; Royal
    Gorge 745; Sault Ste. Marie
    551; Seven Mile Bridge 487;
    Sunshine Bridge 304
Brookgreen Gardens: 445
Brookings: 41
Brown, John: 372, 373
Brownsville: 230
Browstown: 775
Bruneau Dunes: 605
Brunswick: 459
Brussels: 268
Bryan, William Jennings: 770
Bubble Gum Alley: 90
Buellton: 92
buffalo: 194, 211, 615, 632
Buffalo: 668–670
Buffalo Bill Museum: 258
Buffalo Bill Ranch State
    Historical Park: 203
Buffalo Gap: 219

buffalo jumps: 520
"Buffalo Soldiers": 222, 526
Buffalo Trails Museum: 527
Bunyan, Paul: 237, 238, 579
Bureau of Engraving and
   Printing: 793
Burlingame: 761
Burlington, Iowa: 261
Burlington, Vermont: 565
Burma-Vita Company: 245,
   870
Burns, Julia Pfeiffer: 83
Burnside: 305
Burpee Museum of Natural
   History: 642
butterflies: 76, 80, 166, 230,
   856

C

Cabrillo National Monument:
   803
cacti: 162, 165, 226, 261, 811
Cactus League: 163
Cadillac Ranch: 900
Caesars Palace: 155
Cahokia Mounds State
   Historic Site: 873–874
Cain, James M.: 97
Cairo: 277
Cajun Country: 303
Caldwell: 603
Calhoun County: 268
Caliente: 152
California: 10, 41–113, 707–
   715, 802–808, 935–945
California Adventure: 104
Calvin Coolidge Country:
   334–335
Cambria: 85
Cambridge, Maryland: 799
Cambridge, Massachusetts:
   692
Camp 18: 588
Camp David: 370
Camp Lejeune: 439
Camp Meade: 569
Campo: 805
Camp Pendleton: 108, 109
Canada: 549–563
Canadian, Texas: 213–214
Canadian Rockies: 116–128
Canadian War Museum: 554
Cannery Row: 73, 75
Cannon Beach: 29, 587
Cannon Mountain: 322
canoeing/kayaking: Assateague
   Island National Seashore

423; Colorado River 738;
Concord River 689; Cross
Ranch State Park 186;
Delaware Water Gap NRA
359; Fort Niobrara NWR
201; Front Royal 375; Gold
Discovery State Historic
Park 713; Grand Teton
National Park 621; Green
and Colorado Rivers 733;
Hanover 326; Housatonic
Meadows State Park 350;
La Framboise Island Nature
Area 195; Long Lake Canoe
Trail 246; Pictured Rocks
National Lakeshore 547; sea
kayaking 55, 56, 87; Snow
Hill 423; South Llano River
State Park 222
Cañon City: 745
Canyonlands National Park:
735
Cape Arago State Park: 38
Cape Blanco: 39
Cape Canaveral: 472
Cape Cod: 698–701
Cape Disappointment: 24, 25
Cape Fear: 442
Cape Flattery: 18
Cape Foulweather: 33
Cape Girardeau: 276
Cape Hatteras Lighthouse: 435
Cape Hatteras National
Seashore: 433
Cape Henlopen State Park: 418
Cape Kiwanda: 32
Cape Lookout: 31
Cape Lookout National
Seashore: 437
Cape Lookout State Park: 32
Cape May: 417
Cape May–Lewes Ferry: 417
Cape Meares: 31
Cape Perpetua: 35–36
Cape Romain National
Wildlife Refuge: 448
Cardiff Giant: 636
Carhenge: 202, 630
Carillon: 562
Carlsbad: 109, 829
Carlsbad Caverns National
Park: 827
Carmel-by-the-Sea: 77
Carmel Mission: 88
car museums: 582, 711, 720,
904
carousel factory: 669

car racing: Bonneville Salt
Flats 148, 149; Daytona
Beach 469, 470; Indy
500 647; Joliet 868; Lime
Rock Park 349; Nazareth
Speedway 360; Pike's Peak
International Hill Climb 747
Cars (film): 884
cars, antique: Fourth Street
Cruise 637; Hemmings
Motor News 337; Henry
Ford Museum 652; Lime
Rock Park 349; National
Automobile Museum
720; Pioneer Auto Show
198; Studebaker National
Museum 649; Wheels of
Yesterday 423
Carson City: 717
Carson Mansion: 48
Car Talk: 693
Carter, Jimmy: 856
Carthage: 882
Carver, George Washington:
852, 883
Casa Grande Ruins National
Monument: 165, 168
Cashmere: 501
Casper: 623
Cassidy, Butch: 522, 734
Castillo de San Marcos: 467
Castle Gate: 730
Castroville: 72
Cat Head Blues and Folk Art:
287
Cathedral Gorge State Park: 152
Cathedral State Park: 788
Catocin Mountain Park: 370
cattle industry: 198, 216, 217
Cave and Basin National
Historic Site: 125
Cave Creek Canyon: 818
caves: Apostle Islands
National Lakeshore 538;
Carlsbad Caverns National
Park 827–828; Colossal
Cave 812; Grand Canyon
Caverns 930; Howe and
Secret Caves 679–680;
Ice Cave 913; Kartchner
Caverns State Park 812;
Leakey 223; Lehman Caves
728; Lost River Gorge 324;
Luray Caverns 378; Mark
Twain Cave Complex 266;
Meramec Caverns 876, 878;
Shoshone Ice Caves 143

Cayce, Edgar: 429
Cayucos: 86
cedar, Port Orford: 40
Cedar Falls: 637
Cedar Point: 657
Cedar Rock: 637
Center for Creative
 Photography: 170
Center for the Study of
 Southern Culture: 288
Chaco Culture National
 Historical Park: 913
Chadron: 629
Chain of Rocks Bridge: 874
Chalk Pyramids: 208
Chalk River: 557
Challis: 138
Chandler: 891
Channel Islands National
 Park: 95
Charles A. Lindbergh House
 and History Center: 244
Charles J. Belden Museum of
 Western Photography: 618
Charleston, Oregon: 38
Charleston, South Carolina:
 450–451
Charles Town: 373
Charlottesville: 380–381
Chattanooga: 397
Chautauqua: 667
cheese: 31
Cherokee: 394
cherries: 132
Cherry Valley: 676
Chesapeake Bay Bridge-
 Tunnel: 427
Chesapeake Bay Maritime
 Museum: 798
Chester: 275
Chesterwood: 346
Chez Panisse: 709
Chicago: 644–645, 867–868
Childress: 216
Childress County Heritage
 Museum: 216
Chillicothe: 783
Chimney Rock: 394
Chincoteague: 424
Chincoteague National
 Wildlife Refuge: 425
Chinese culture: 600
Chinook: 520
Chiricahua National
 Monument: 818
Chittenden, Larry: 219
Chloride: 161–162

Christian fundamentalism:
 217, 777
Chrysler Museum: 429
Church of the Golden Hand:
 295
Cimarron Cut-Off: 753
Cincinnati: 778–779, 780
Cisco: 831
Citizen Kane: 85
City Hall: 12
Ciudad Juárez: 825
Ciudad Miguel Alemán: 227
Civil Rights Memorial: 850
Civil Rights Movement: 280,
 290, 847, 848–850
Civil Rights Movement
 National Historic Trail: 848
Civil War: Andersonville
 Prison 857; Antietam
 National Battlefield 371;
 Baxter Springs 884; Fort
 Fisher State Historic Site
 442; Fort Pulaski 863; Fort
 Sumter National Monument
 449; Gettysburg National
 Military Park 369; Jackson,
 "Stonewall" 383, 786,
 791; Manassas National
 Battlefield Park 790;
 National Civil War Naval
 Museum 853; Picacho Peak
 165; Vicksburg National
 Military Park 291, 293–294;
 War Correspondents
 Memorial 370; Wilmington,
 North Carolina 441
clamming: 22, 423
Claremore: 887
Clark, William: 183
Clark Art Institute: 339
Clark County Museum: 157
Clarkesville: 405
Clarksburg: 786
Clarksdale: 287
Clark's Trading Post: 322
Clarksville: 267
classical music: 335, 344
Claxton: 861
Clayton: 140, 404
Cleveland: 660–661
Cleveland Museum of Art: 660
Cline, Patsy: 789
Clingman's Dome: 396
Clinton, Mississippi: 840
Clinton, Oklahoma: 894
clocks: 366
Club Del Monte: 75

Clyde: 656
Coal Creek Station: 180
coal plants: 624
coastal walking: 60
Cobain, Kurt: 22
Coca-Cola: 293
Cocoa Beach: 473
Cody: 616
Cody, Buffalo Bill: 203, 258,
 616, 617
Colorado: 738–752
Colorado Belle: 161
Colorado National
 Monument: 739
Colossal Cave: 812
Columbia Basin: 505
Columbia Falls: 511
Columbia Gorge: 594
Columbia Icefield: 121
Columbia River: 26
Columbia River Maritime
 Museum: 27
Columbus: 853
Comstock Lode: 718
Concord: 573, 689
condor, California: 82
Confluence Project: 25
Confusion Hill: 53
Conneaut: 663
Connors Pass: 727
Conrad Mansion: 131
Contemporary Arts Center: 778
Continental Divide: 121, 139
Conway: 318
Coolidge, Calvin: 334–335
Cool Springs: 933
Cooperstown: 678–679
Coos Bay: 37
Copper Peak Ski Flying Hill:
 541
copper smelters: 150
Coral Castle: 482
Coral Gables: 482
Cornucopia: 536
Cornudas: 825
Coronado-Quivira Museum:
 757
Cottonwood Falls: 760
Coulee City: 504
Council Grove: 759
covered bridges: Drift
 Creek Covered Bridge 32;
 Jackson 317; Lancaster 574;
 Philippi 787; Vermont 333;
 Woodstock 330
Cowboy Poetry Gathering:
 149

Cowboys' Christmas Ball: 218–219
"Cowboy Trail": 201
cows: 568
Cozad: 204
crab, Dungeness: 14
Craters of the Moon National Monument and Preserve: 609
crawfish: 304
Crawford: 628
Crawford Notch: 319
Crayola Crayon Factory Tour: 360
Crazy Horse: 627
Crescent City: 43
Crested Butte: 742
Croft Mine Historical Park: 241
Crookston: 532
Crosby: 241
cross-country skiing: Galena Lodge 142; Hurricane Ridge 16; Izaak Walton Inn 513; Lost Trail Hot Springs 136; Stanley 140
Cross Ranch Nature Preserve: 186
Cross Ranch State Park: 186
Crow Wing State Park: 244
cruises: 95
Crystal City: 224
Crystal Cove State Park: 105
Crystal Falls: 541
Cuba: 878
Cumberland Island National Seashore: 460
currency, Canadian: 118
currency, U.S.: 344
Custer: 140
Custer, General: 189
Custer Motorway: 140
Customs House: 73
Cut Bank: 518
cypress, Monterey: 79

D
daiquiri bars: 301
Dallas: 831, 834–835
Daly, Marcus: 135–136
dams: Dry Falls Dam 504; Fort Peck Dam 523; Garrison Dam 180; Grand Coulee Dam 504; Hoover Dam 158; Libby 510, 511; Mississippi River locks and 246, 256, 258, 267; Teton Dam 612
Dana-Thomas House: 872

Dancing Leaf Earth Lodge: 205
Danville: 571
Darby: 136
daredevil jumps: 145
Darien: 455
Dartmouth College: 325, 326
Davenport: 505
Davenport Roadhouse at the Cash Store: 69
Davis: 710
Davis, Jefferson: 300, 849
Day, John: 599
Dayton: 720
Daytona Beach: 469
Dean, James: 87
Decatur County/Last Indian Raid Museum: 207
decoy museums: 799
Deep River: 557
deer, key: 488
Deerfield: 687
Deetjen's Big Sur Inn: 83
Defiance: 769
Delaware: 418–420
Delaware Park: 668
Delaware Seashore State Park: 420
Delaware Water Gap National Recreation Area: 358
Deliverance: 404
Del Mar: 112
Del Norte Coast Redwoods State Park: 43
Delta, Colorado: 739
Delta, Mississippi: 282, 287
Delta, Utah: 729
Delta Blues Museum: 287
Delta Cultural Center: 285
Deming: 820
Deming-Luna-Mimbres Museum: 820
Demopolis: 846
Dennis: 699
Dentzel Carousel: 844
Denver: 746
Depoe Bay: 32
Depression: 210
Desert Botanical Garden: 166
Desert Caballeros Western Museum: 163
Desert National Wildlife Refuge: 153
Desert View Tower: 805, 806
Detroit: 652–653
Detroit Institute of the Arts: 652

Devil's Elbow: 880
Devils Lake: 529
Devil's Punchbowl: 33
Devil's Rope Museum: 898
Dexter Avenue King Memorial Church: 849–850
Dia: Beacon: 352
Dickeyville Grotto: 253
Dillard: 399
diners: general discussion, 330–331; Albany, 681; Albuquerque, 906; Apple Pan, 101; Arthur's Paradise Diner, 689; Blue Benn Diner, 337; Blueberry Hill, 273; Boca Diner, 476; Collin's Diner, 348; DJ's Drive-In Diner, 724; Dot's Diner, 817; Eat-Rite Diner, 273; Farmers Diner, 328; '59er Diner, 500; Fog City Diner, 65; Gary's Diner, 657; Hi-Way 101 Diner, 14; Iggy's Diner, 882; Joe's Diner, 345; Louis', San Francisco, 66; Maid-Rite, 237, 261, 265, 637; Main Diner, Westfield, 666; Majestic Diner, 402; Miami Beach, 481; Midpoint Cafe, 901; Milford Diner, 358; Miss Adams Diner, 338; Moab Diner, 737; Mr. D'z Route 66 Diner, 932; New Bedford, 698; Old School Diner, 454; 101 Café, 109; Oxford, Mississippi, 289; Polka Dot Diner, 328; Rock Cafe, 891; Rudy's, 247; Savannah, 457; Shorty's Diner, 143; Sid's Diner, 894; Spokane, 507; Sunny Day Diner, 323; Tally's Good Food Café, 890; 29 Diner, 795; White Turkey Drive-Inn, 663; Winooski, 564; Wright's Dairy-Rite, 382; York, 367
Dinosaur Land: 374
dinosaurs: *see* fossils
Dionne Quintuplets: 556, 558
Dipsea: 66
Discovery Trail: 25
Disneyland: 103–104
diving: Biscayne National Park 483; Blue Hole 905; Carmel 77; Key Largo

Coral Reef National Marine Sanctuary 485; La Jolla 112; Salt Point State Park 58
Dixon: 643
Dodge City: 753
dollars, Canadian: 118
Dollywood: 396
Dolphin Research Center: 487
Douglas, Arizona: 817
Douglas, Wyoming: 625
dowsing: 571
Drift Creek Covered Bridge: 32
Drift Creek Wilderness: 34
Driftless Region: 245
drinking and driving: 301
drive-ins: 383, 701, 743, 830, 868, 869, 873, 882, 930
Dry Falls: 504
Dry Tortugas National Park: 491
Dublin: 861
Dubois: 622
DuBois, W. E. B.: 346
Dubuque: 253
dude ranches: 163
Dull Knife, Chief: 207, 209
Duluth: 534
Dune (film): 37
dunes, sand: Algodones Dunes 807; Bruneau Dunes 608; Great Sand Dunes National Park 743; Indiana Dunes National Lakeshore 648; Lewes 418; Little Sahara Recreation Area 729; Mojave National Preserve 937; Nebraska Sand Hills 201–202; Oregon 37; Pictured Rocks National Lakeshore 547; Pismo Beach 91; Sand Mountain 722; Wright Brothers National Memorial 431
Dungeness: 13–14
Dunseith: 177–178
Dust Bowl: 210, 934
Dutch community: 92
Dvorak, Antonin: 252
Dwight: 869
Dyersburg: 278
Dyersville: 255, 638
Dyerville Giant: 51
Dylan, Bob: 534

E

Earp, Wyatt: 814
earthquakes: Ferndale 49;

Lost River Valley 140; Mt. Borah 610; New Madrid 278
East Glacier Park: 516
East Humboldt Range: 148
Eastman, George: 672
Easton, Maryland: 797
Easton, Pennsylvania: 360
Eastside Highway: 135
Eastville: 427
Eastwood, Clint: 77
Ecola State Park: 29
Eden: 667
Edison, Thomas: 658
Effigy Mounds National Monument: 251
Egremont: 348
Eisenhower National Historic Site: 369
El Camino Real: 88–89
El Centro: 807
El Cuartelejo: 209
elephant seals: 69, 85
Elk: 57
elk, Roosevelt: 19, 44
Elk City: 895
Elkhart: 650
Elko: 148
Ellinwood tunnels: 757
Ellsworth: 581
El Malpais: 913
Elmo: 132
El Paso: 823
El Reno: 894
Elsah: 269
Ely: 725
Emerald Lake Lodge: 123
Emerald Mound: 296, 298
Enders Beach Road: 43
Enola Gay: 148
environmental issues: 510
environmental research: 168
Ephrata: 363
Epping: 527
Erick: 896
Erie: 663
Erie Canal Museum: 675
Erskine: 533
Esalen Institute: 83
Escanaba: 543
Essex: 513
Eureka, California: 46–48
Eureka, Missouri: 876
Eureka, Montana: 129
Eureka, Nevada: 724
Eureka, Utah: 729
Evans, Dale: 224
Everett: 495

Everglades National Park: 483
Extraterrestrial Highway: 156

F

Factor's Walk: 456
Fairbanks Museum and Planetarium: 572
Fairfield: 710
Fairlawn Mansion: 535
Fairmont Banff Springs Hotel: 125
Fairmont Chateau Lake Louise: 124
Fairmont Hotels: 124
Fairmont Le Château Montebello: 562
fall color: Banks-Vernonia Linear State Park 589; Bemidji 237; Cove Hardwood Nature Trail 396; Farmington 578; Kancamagus Highway 319; Lake Michigan 544; Larch Valley 125; Peacham 573; Shenandoah National Park 376; Tumwater Canyon 500
Fallon: 721
farmers markets: 90, 364
Farmington: 578
farm toys: 638
Faulkner, William: 288
Fayette State Park: 543
F.D. Roosevelt State Park: 856
FDR's "Little White House": 854
Feiro Marine Life Center: 14
Felicity: 807
Fenimore Art Museum: 678
Fenwick Island Lighthouse: 420
Ferndale: 49
Ferriday: 297
ferries: Balboa Island 105; Cape Charles ferry 799; Cape May–Lewes Ferry 417; Los Ebanos ferry 228; Port Angeles to B.C., Canada 17; Seattle area 13
festivals and events: Alabama Crawfish Festival, 847; Arkansas Blues and Heritage Festival, 285; Art & Pumpkin Festival, 67; AT&T Pebble Beach National Pro-Am, 76; Bach Festival, 361; Banff Film, 126; Beach Bum's Parade, 863; Big Top Chautauqua,

537; blues music, 286; Bumbershoot, 498; Confederate Pageants, 297; Cowboy Poetry Gathering, 149; Cowboys' Christmas Ball, 217, 218–219; film, 126, 730; Fish House Parade, 240; Inter Tribal Ceremonial, 914; Irrigation Festival, 14; Jaycees Rattlesnake Round-Up, 831; Jim Bowie Days, 221; Juke Joint Festival, 287; Kinetic Grand Championship, 47; Lavender Festival, 14; Liberal's International Pancake Day race, 212; Loggers PlayDay bash, 21; Lowell Celebrates Kerouac!, 689; Madison, Indiana, 776; Maine State Fair, 579; Marlboro Music Festival, 335; Melon Days, 256; Middle of Nowhere Festival, 632; Milk River Indian Days, 522; Mini-Sapa Days, 207; Minot, 178; Mississippi Delta Blues and Heritage Festival, 290; Missouri River Bluegrass Festival and Kid Fest, 186; Moab Ho-Down Mountain Bike Festival, 737; Monterey Jazz Festival, 73; Muskrat Skinning Championship, National, 799; Nauvoo Grape Festival, 263; Nauvoo LDS pageant, 263; Northern Plains Indian Culture Fest, 181; OzFest, 212; Pageant of the Masters, 106; Patriot's Day, 691; Pebble Beach Concours d'Elegance, 77; Pennington Balloon Championship, 302; Pony Express Reride, 723; Popeye Picnic, 275; Punkin' Chunkin', 420; Quechee Hot Air Balloon, Craft and Music Festival, 328; Redneck Games, 861; sand castle competition, Cannon Beach, 30; Spoleto Festival USA, 451; Sultan Summer Shindig and Logging Show, 496; Sundance Film Festival, 730; Tanglewood, 344;

Tom Sawyer Days, 266; Tournament of Roses Parade, 943; Vidalia Onion Festival, 861; Watermelon Festival, 775; Westport seafood, 22; Woodstock Festival of Music and Art, 357; World's Largest Calf Fry Festival, 886
Field, Darby: 319
Field of Dreams: 638
Figge Art Museum: 259
firefighting: 134
fire lookouts, lodging in: 129, 509, 511
Fisher: 532
Fisher, Carl: 479
Fisherman's Wharf: 73
fish frys: 235, 674
fish hatcheries: 180
Fish House Parade: 240
fishing: Astoria 26; Bemidji 237; Cape Kiwanda 32; Delaware Water Gap National Recreation Area 359; Fort Bragg 54; Islamorada 486; Lake Chelan 503; Lake Sakakawea 180; Makah Indian Reservation 18; Moss Landing 72; Ochoco Lake 598; salmon 22; Waldport 34–35; walleye 239; world-record catfish 271
Fitzgerald Marine Reserve: 67
Flagler, Henry: 464, 476
Flagstaff: 921
Flathead Indian Reservation: 132
Flathead Lake: 132
Flavel, George: 26
Flavel House Museum: 26
flooding: 299, 306, 329, 439, 529, 564, 612
Florence, Arizona: 165
Florence, Oregon: 36
Florida: 461–491
Floyd: 386
Floyd Monument: 183
Fly, Camillus S.: 816
Flynt Center of Early New England Life: 687
folk art: American Visionary Art Museum 797; Bottle Village 97; Cat Head Blues and Folk Art 287; Dickeyville Grotto 253;

Folk Art Center 391; Gehrke Windmill Garden 505; Mission San Xavier del Bac 169; Moses, Grandma 336; Nitt Witt Ridge 86; Romano Gabriel Wooden Sculpture Garden 48; Shelburne Museum 566; Southern 288
food, Mexican: 821
forests: Allegheny Mountains 785; Berkshire County 338; Delaware Water Gap National Recreation Area 358; forest fires 134; Forest History Center 240; Gifford Woods State Park 333; Joshua Forest Parkway 162; Porcupine Mountains Wilderness 541; Shawnee National Forest 275; Targhee National Forest 612; *see also* old-growth forests
Forks: 18–19
Forks Timber Museum: 18
Fort Abraham Lincoln State Park: 189
Fort Belknap Indian Reservation: 520–522
Fort Boise: 603
Fort Bragg: 54
Fort Buford: 526
Fort Canby: 183
Fort Clark: 184
Fort Clatsop: 27
Fort Clatsop National Memorial: 27, 183
Fort Clinch State Park: 463
Fort Cody Trading Post: 204
Fort Defiance State Park: 277
Fort Dodge: 636
Fort Fisher State Historic Site: 442
Fort Frederica National Monument: 458
Fort Jackson: 309
Fort Larned: 755
Fort Lauderdale: 476
Fort Lincoln Trolley: 189
Fort Macon State Park: 439
Fort Mandan: 183, 184
Fort McKavett State Historic Site: 222
Fort Moultrie: 448
Fort New Salem: 786
Fort Niobrara National Wildlife Refuge: 200

Fort Peck: 523
Fort Peck Dam: 523
Fort Peck Indian Reservation: 523
Fort Pierce: 475
Fort Pierre: 195
Fort Pierre National Grasslands: 195
Fort Point: 64
Fort Pulaski National Monument: 862
Fort Raleigh National Historic Site: 432
Fort Robinson: 627
Fort Ross State Historic Park: 58
Fort Steele Heritage Town: 128
Fort Stevens: 27
Fort St. Joseph National Historic Park: 551
Fort Sumter National Monument: 449
Fort Totten: 529
Fort Uncompahgre: 739
Fort Union Trading Post: 525
Fort Worden: 12
Fort Worth: 831, 834–835
49-Mile Drive: 66
Fort Yates: 189–190
fossils: Agate Fossil Beds National Monument 627; Ashfall Fossil Beds State Historical Park 633; Berlin-Ichthyosaur State Park 721; Burpee Museum of Natural History 642; Cleveland-Lloyd Dinosaur Quarry 732; Fick Fossil Museum 208; Fort Peck 523; Hagerman Fossil Beds National Monument 609; John Day Fossil Beds National Monument 599; Toadstool Geological Park 628
Founder's Grove: 51
Fountain of Youth: 465
Foxfire Museum: 403
Foyil: 887
Franconia: 321
Franconia Notch: 321
Franklin: 398
Fredonia: 666
Freeport: 641
Fremont: 656
French Lick: 773
Fried Green Tomatoes: 860

Friedlander, Lee: 22
Frio Canyon: 223
Frontier Culture Museum: 382
frontier history: 272
Frontier Trails Museum, National: 762
Front Royal: 375
Frost Place: 321
fruitcake: 861
Fryeburg: 318
Funks Grove: 870
fur-trapping outposts: Bent's Old Fort 750; Crow Wing 244; Fort Clark 184; Fort Pierre National Grasslands 195; Fort Ross State Historic Park 59; Fort Union Trading Post 525; Museum of the Fur Trade 629; Sainte Genevieve 274

G

Gabriel, Romano: 48
Gadsden Hotel: 817
Gaineswood: 846
Galena: 639, 883
Galena Lodge: 142
Galena Mining and Historical Museum: 883
Galena Summit: 141
Gallup: 913
gambling: Alton 270; Atlantic City 413; Dubuque 255; French Lick Resort Casino 773; Kah-Nee-Ta High Desert Resort and Casino 596; Las Vegas 154; Laughlin 161; northwest Mississippi 284; Prairie Knights Casino and Resort 190; Reno 720; riverboat casinos 776; South Lake Tahoe 714; Stateline 716
game calls: 221
Garberville: 52
Garden City: 211
Garden of Eden: 756
gardens: Boyce Thompson Arboretum State Park 165; Bridge of Flowers 685; Brookgreen Gardens 445; Carmel Mission 79; County Courthouse, Santa Barbara 94; Daly mansion 136; Desert Botanical Garden 166; Esalen Institute 83;

Golden Gate Park 64; Heritage Museums and Gardens, Cape Cod 699; Huntington Library, Museum and Gardens 942; Kruse Rhododendron State Natural Preserve 58; Mendocino Coast Botanical Gardens 55; Mount Desert Island 582; Naumkeag 345; Ohme Gardens County Park 502; Ramirez Canyon Park 98; Roosevelt Park 179; Rosedown Plantation 300; Rosemont Plantation 299; Rural Life Museum 302; San Juan Capistrano 107; Santa Barbara Mission 89; Sequim lavender 14; Shaw Nature Reserve 876; Shore Acres State Park 38
Gardner: 687
Garfield, James: 662
Garland, Hamlin: 248
Garland, Judy: 240
Garner, John Nance: 224
Garrapata State Park: 80
Garrison: 180
Garrison Dam: 180
Gary: 646
gas stations, Oregon: 26
Gateway Arch: 272, 273
Gatineau: 559
GatorLand: 470
gay community: 59, 702
Gearhart: 28
Gehlen House: 255
gemstones: 389, 391, 398
Geneva: 672
Genoa: 716
geodes: 264, 602
geography, New England: 325
geologic formations: Arches National Park 735; Bartholomew's Cobble 346; Black Canyon of the Gunnison National Park 741; Canyonlands National Park 735; Chalk Pyramids/Monument Rocks 208; Chiricahua National Monument 818; Craters of the Moon National Monument and Preserve 610; Dry Falls 504; Garden of the Gods 747; Grand

Canyon National Park 924–927; Haystack Rock 30; Hell's Half Acre 623; John Day Fossil Beds National Monument 599; Natural Bridge 383; Natural Bridges State Beach 70; Rugby 179; Shoshone Ice Caves 143; Toadstool Geological Park 628; Weaver's Needle 164; Yellowstone National Park 613; *see also* gorges
George Eastman House: 672
Georgetown: 446
George Washington Carver Museum: 852
George W. Norris Home: 205
Georgia: 455–460, 852–863
Georgia Aquarium: 400
Georgia Music Hall of Fame: 852, 859
Georgia O'Keeffe Museum: 908
Georgia Sea Turtle Center: 460
German heritage: 252, 768
Gettysburg: 368
Gettysburg National Military Park: 368–370
Getty Villa: 99
geysers: 613
Giant Dipper: 71
G.I. Bill of Rights: 771
Gibsland: 837
Gifford Woods State Park: 333
Gila Bend: 810
Gilcrease Museum: 890
Girard: 663
Girl Scouts of America: 457
Glacier National Park: 514–516
Glacier Park Lodge: 516
glaciers: 120, 121–122
Gladys Porter Zoo: 230
Glasgow: 522
glass making: 698
Glen: 317
Glenns Ferry: 608
Glenrock: 624
gliding: 830
Goessel: 758
Gogebic Range: 540
Going-to-the-Sun Road: 514
Gold Bar: 497
Gold Beach: 40
Gold Bluffs Beach: 44
Gold Country: 712
Gold Discovery State Historic Park: 713

Golden Eagle: 268
Golden Gate Bridge: 66
Golden Gate Park: 64
Golden Isles: 458
Gold Rush: 711
golf: 39, 76, 109
gondolas: 125, 506
Gooding: 609
Goodnight-Loving Trail: 216
The Goonies: 26
Gorda: 84
Gordon: 631
Gorge: 404
gorges: Cathedral Gorge State Park 152; Columbia Gorge 595; Lost River Gorge 324; Malad Gorge State Park 608; Moses Coulee 504; Piers Gorge 543; Quechee Gorge 328; Royal Gorge 744; Salmon River Gorge 137, 138; Tallulah Gorge State Park 405; Wind River Canyon 620
Gorham: 575
gospel music: 287
Government Camp: 593
Graceland: 283
Grace Museum: 217
Grafton: 269, 787
Grafton Notch State Park: 316
Grand Canyon Caverns: 930
Grand Canyon National Park: 923, 924–927
Grand Canyon of the Yellowstone River: 615
Grand Canyon Skywalk: 931
Grand Coulee Dam: 504
Grand Forks: 529
Grand Isle: 564
Grand Junction: 738
Grand Rapids: 239
Grand Strand: 443
Grand Teton National Park: 621
Grant, Ulysses S.: 640
Grants: 912
Granville Gulf: 334
The Grapes of Wrath: 210
Grays Harbor: 12, 21–22
Grays Harbor Historical Seaport: 22
Gray Summit: 876
Great Barrington: 346
Great Basin National Park: 715, 727
Great Bend: 757

Great Northern Brewing Company: 130
Great Northern route: 492–583; Idaho 507–509; Maine 575–583; Michigan 540–549; Minnesota 531–535; Montana 509–525; New Hampshire 573–575; North Dakota 525–531; Vermont 563–573; Washington 494–507; Wisconsin 535–540
Great Platte River Road Archway Monument: 204
Great River Road: 232–309; Illinois, Iowa, and Missouri 250–278; Kentucky and Tennessee 278–282; Louisiana 300–309; Minnesota 235–245; Mississippi 282–299; navigating 236; Wisconsin 245–250
Great River Road State Park: 289
Great Sand Dunes National Park: 743
Great Smoky Mountains National Park: 395
Greenfield: 686
Green Mount Cemetery: 570
Green River: 733
Greenville: 290
Greyfield Inn: 460
Grimes Point: 721
Groom: 898
Gropius House: 692
Ground Zero Blues Club: 287
Guadalupe: 91
Guadalupe Mountains National Park: 826
Guadalupe-Nipomo Dunes National Wildlife Refuge: 91
Gualala: 57
Guerneville: 59
Guernsey: 626
guitars: 360
gun museum: 888
Gunnison: 742
Guttenberg: 252

H
Hagerman: 608
Hagerman Fossil Beds National Monument: 609
Hailey: 143
Half Moon Bay: 67
Hallam: 366

Hallmark Visitors Center: 764
Hamburger City: 894
Hamilton: 135
Hamlim: 217
Hampton Plantation: 447
Hancock Shaker Village: 342
hang-gliding: 112, 431
Hank Williams Memorial: 850
Hannibal: 265
Hanover: 325
Hard Rock Hotel and Casino: 155
Harley-Davidson motorcycles: 367, 824
Harold Warp Pioneer Village: 204
Harpers Ferry: 372
Harrah's: 161
Harriman State Park: 353
Harris Beach State Park: 41
Harrison: 627
Harte, Bret: 46
Hassayampa River Preserve: 164
Havre: 520
Hayes, Rutherford B.: 656
Haystack Rock: 30, 32
Heard Museum: 166
Hears, William Randolph: 84
Hearst Castle: 84
Hearst family: 84
Heat-Moon, William Lease: 761
Heceta Head: 36
Helena, Arkansas: 285
Hell's Half Acre: 623
Helper: 730
Hemingway, Ernest: 142, 489
Hemingway House: 489
Henderson: 157
Henry Miller Memorial Library: 82
Henry Morrison Flagler Museum: 475
Henson, Jim: 290
Hermann: 767
Herschell Carousel Factory Museum: 669
Hiawatha National Forest: 543
Hickison Petroglyph Recreation Area: 724
Hickman: 278
Hidalgo: 230
High Plains Museum: 205
Highway 101: 25
Highway 105: 22–23
Highway 112: 17

Highway 61: 290
Higuera Street: 90
hiking: Acadia National Park 583; Anastasia State Recreation Area 467; Andrew Molera State Park 80; Apostle Islands 537; Appalachian Trail 312; Assateague Island 423; Battle Rock 39; Big Basin Redwoods 69; Black Kettle National Grassland 214; Canyonlands National Park 735; Cape Disappointment 25; Cape Perpetua 35–36; Chain of Rocks Bridge 874; Chincoteague NWR 425; Crawford Notch 319; Cross Ranch State Park 186; Cumberland Island 460; Delaware Water Gap 358; Fort Clatsop National Memorial 27; Glacier National Park 515; Grand Canyon National Park 925; Grand Teton National Park 621; Great Basin National Park 727; Guadalupe Mountains National Park 826; Harriman State Park 353; Housatonic Meadows State Park 350; Icefields Parkway 120–121; Indiana Dunes 648; Jedediah Smith Redwoods State Park 42; Kootenai Falls 510; Kootenay National Park 127; Lake Crescent 16; Lake Quinault 20–21; La Purisima Mission 92; Little Sahara Recreation Area 729; Little Talbot Island 463; Lost Coast 49–50; Lost Maples 223; Marin Headlands 66; Mount Olympus 19; Mt. Hood 594; Oregon Coast Trail 29; Oregon Dunes 37; Oswald West State Park 30; Père Marquette State Park 269; Peyto Lake 122; Pfeiffer Big Sur State Park 81; Pike's Peak State Park 252; Point Reyes 62; RiverPark 284; Russian Gulch State Park 55; Sabino Canyon 171; Saddle Mountain 588;

Saguaro National Park 812; Salt Point State Park 58; Santa Monica Mountains 98; Shelburne Farms 566; South Llano River State Park 222; Stanley 140; Torrey Pines State Natural Reserve 112; Wallace Falls 497; Whitefish Mountain Resort 130
Hiko: 152, 153
Hillforest Mansion: 776
Hillsboro: 781
Hilton Head Island: 452
hippie enclaves: 52, 99
Hitchcock, Alfred: 60, 61
Hobcaw Barony: 446
Hockaday Museum of Art: 131
Hofwyl-Broadfield Plantation: 455
Hoh Rainforest: 19–20
Holbrook: 917
Holcomb: 752
Hole-in-the-Mountain Peak: 148
Hole-in-the-Wall Gang: 734
Holly, Buddy: 829, 903
Hollywood elite: 97–98
Hollywood Forever: 944
Holocaust Memorial Museum: 793
Homestead: 482
Hood Canal: 13
Hood Museum of Art: 326
Hoopa Valley Indian Reservation: 44
"hoosiers": 648
Hoover Dam: 158
Hoover Dam Museum: 158
Hopewell Culture National Historic Park: 782, 783
Hoquiam: 20, 21–22
Hoquiam's Castle Bed & Breakfast: 21
horseback-riding: 80, 120, 123, 594
Horse Hollow Wind Energy Center: 219
horse racing: 112
Horseshoe Lake Conservation Area: 276
hot-air balloons: 302, 328
Hotel del Coronado: 111
Hotel del Sol: 65
hot springs: Banff 125; Jacumba 806; Lolo Hot Springs Resort 135; Lost

Trail 136; Manitou Springs 747; Nat-Soo-Pah 146; Panaca Spring 152; Radium 128; Salida 744; Sharon Springs 677; Sleeping Buffalo 522; Sunbeam 140; Thermopolis 619; Warm Springs 854
Hot Springs State Park: 619
Houmas House: 305
Housatonic Meadows State Park: 349
House of Mystery: 512
House on the Rock: 166
Hoven: 194
Hualapai National Park: 932
Hueco Tanks State Historic Park: 824
Humboldt Redwoods State Park: 50–51
Humbug Mountain State Park: 40
Hungry Horse: 512
hunting: 221, 522, 757
Huntington Beach: 103
Huntington Beach State Park: 445
Huntington Library, Museum and Gardens: 942
Huron Mountains: 547
Hurricane Ridge: 15, 16, 367
hurricanes: 432, 439
Hutchinson: 758
Hwy-13: 536
Hwy-1806: 188
Hwy-2: 202
Hwy-23: 309
Hwy-35: 250
Hwy-61: 533
Hwy-79: 165
Hyde Log Cabin: 564
Hydro: 894

I
ice-climbing: 122
ice cream: 568
Icefields Parkway: 116, 120, 121
ice-fishing: 237, 240
Idaho: 137–146, 507–509, 602–613
Idaho Falls: 611
Illinois: 256–278, 639–646, 769–771, 866–874
Illinois Railway Museum: 643
Illinois River: 269
Independence: 762

Index: 497
Indiana: 646–651, 771–777
Indiana Dunes National Lakeshore: 647
Indianapolis Motor Speedway Hall of Fame Museum: 647
Indian Pueblo Cultural Center: 907
Indy 500: 647
Inscription Rock: 913
International Surfing Museum: 103
Iowa: 250–278, 633–638
Irish culture: 215
iron industry: 363
Iron Mountain: 542
Ironwood: 540
Isabella Stuart Gardner Museum: 694
Isla La Motte: 563
Islamorada: 486
Itasca Heritage and Arts Center and Judy Garland Exhibit: 240
Iwo Jima Memorial: 229
Izaak Walton Inn: 513

J
jackalopes: 624
Jack London Square: 707
Jackpot: 147
Jackson, Mississippi: 841
Jackson, New Hampshire: 316
Jackson, Wyoming: 621
Jackson, Joseph Jefferson "Shoeless Joe": 267
Jackson, Michael: 92
Jackson, "Stonewall": 383, 786, 791
Jackson Hole: 620
Jackson Square: 306
Jacksonville Beach: 465
Jacumba: 805
James, Jesse: 763, 878, 884
James Dean Memorial: 87
Japanese internment camps: 144, 289, 729
Jasper: 118
Jasper National Park: 120–121
Jasper Tramway: 118
jazz: American Jazz Museum 765; Bix Beiderbecke Memorial Jazz Festival 259; Monterey Jazz Festival 73; New Orleans 306, 307; Sacramento Jazz Jubilee 711
Jedediah Smith Redwoods

State Park: 42
Jeffers, Robinson: 77
Jefferson: 574, 833
Jefferson, Thomas: 380
Jefferson City: 767
Jefferson National Expansion Memorial: 183
Jekyll Island: 459
Jenner: 59
Jerome: 929
Jessie M. Honeyman Memorial State Park: 37
Jimmy Carter National Historic Site: 856
Jimmy Rodgers Museum: 842, 844
Jim Thorpe: 362
Jockey's Ridge State Park: 431
Joe's Pond: 571
John Day Fossil Beds National Monument: 599
John Deere Tractor plant: 637
John Nance Garner Museum: 224
Johnson, Robinson: 284
Johnston Canyon Resort: 126
Johnstown: 631
John Wesley Powell River History Museum: 733
Joliet: 868
Jones, C. J. "Buffalo": 211
Jonesboro: 276
Joplin: 883
Joplin, Scott: 768
Joseph, Chief: 520, 521
Joshua Forest Parkway: 162
Joshua Tree National Park: 936
J. Paul Getty Museum: 99
Juan de Fuca Strait: 17
Juan de Oñate Trail: 822
juke joints: 287
Julia Pfeiffer Burns State Park: 83
Junction: 222
Jupiter: 475

K
Kalaloch: 20
Kalispell: 131
Kam Wah Chung Museum: 600
Kancamagus Highway: 318
Kansas: 206–213, 752–762, 883–884
Kansas City: 762, 764–765
Kansas Cosmosphere and Space Center: 758

Karen Beasley Sea Turtle Rescue & Rehabilitation Center: 440
Kartchner Caverns State Park: 812
Kaskaskia: 274
kayaking: *see* canoeing/kayaking
kazoos: 668
Kenel: 192
Kennedy Space Center: 472
Kent: 350
Kentucky Derby: 774
Kerouac, Jack: 688
Kerrville Folk Festival: 222
Kesey, Ken: 34
Ketchum: 142
Key Largo: 484
Key Largo Coral Reef National Marine Sanctuary: 485
Key Lime Products: 485
Key West: 489
Kid, Billy the: 905
Kilgore: 833
Killington: 333
Kimbell Art Museum: 834
Kinetic Grand Championship: 47, 49
King, Stephen: 580
King Jr., Martin Luther: 849–850
Kingman: 932
Kingsley Plantation: 463
Kinsley: 755
Kirtland: 659
kite-surfing: 69, 434
Kitty Hawk: 430
Klamath: 43
Knievel, Evel: 145
Knife River Indian Village National Historic Site: 181, 183
Kootenai Falls: 510
Kootenay National Park: 117, 127
Kruse Rhododendron State Natural Preserve: 58
Kutztown Folk Festival: 362

L

La Casa Pacifica: 108
Lackawaxen: 357
La Costa: 109
La Crosse: 247
Lady Bird Johnson Grove: 45
Lady Washington: 21, 22

Laguna Beach: 106
La Jolla: 112–113
La Junta: 750
Lake Champlain: 567
Lake Champlain Islands: 563
Lake Chelan: 503
Lake City: 246
Lake Crescent: 15, 16
Lake Crescent Lodge: 17
Lake Erie Islands: 657
Lake Havasu City: 934
Lake Hiddenwood State Park: 194
Lake Huron: 551
Lake Itasca State Park: 235
Lake Louise: 123, 124
Lake Mead: 159
Lake Mead Recreation Area: 160
Lake Michigan: 544
Lake Oahe: 187
Lake Quinault: 20–21
Lake Sakakawea: 180
Lake Scott State Park: 209
Lake Tahoe: 714
Lamar: 751
Lancaster: 366, 573
Land of the Yankee Fork State Park: 138
La Purisima Mission: 88, 91
Larch Valley: 125
Laredo: 226
La Salle: 269
Las Animas: 751
Las Cruces: 820
Las Vegas: 153–155
Latin American culture: 481
Latter-Day Saints: 261–263, 659, 716, 732
Laughlin: 161
Laura: 308
lava tubes: 143, 610, 913
lavender: 14
Lawrenceburg: 777
Lawrenceville: 771
Lawrence Welk Birthplace: 190
Leadbetter Point State Park: 24
Leakey: 223
Lear, Bill: 267
Leavenworth: 501
Lebanon, Illinois: 769
Lebanon, Vermont: 327
Lebanon Valley: 682
Le Claire: 258
Lee Richardson Zoo: 211
Legend Rock: 618
Leggett: 52
Legoland: 109

Lehman Caves: 728
Lemhi Pass: 183
Lenox: 344
Leo Carrillo State Park: 97
Leominster: 688
León, Ponce de: 465–466
lesbian communities: 59, 702
Lewes: 418
Lewis, Jerry Lee: 297
Lewis, Meriwether: 182
Lewis and Clark sites: Bitterroot Valley 135; Camp Disappointment 517; Clark, William 274; Continental Divide crossing 139; expedition history 182–183; Fort Clatsop National Memorial 27; Fort Mandan 184; Kenel 192; Lewis & Clark Historical Site (Alton) 271; Lewis & Clark Interpretive Center 186; Lewis and Clark Interpretive Center 24; Lewis and Clark National Historic Trail 182; Long Beach Peninsula 23; Seaside 28; Sergeant Floyd Monument Historic Marker 634
Libby: 129, 510
Liberal: 211
Liberal's International Pancake Day race: 212
Liberty: 763
Life-Saving Station Museum: 422
lighthouses: Apostle Islands National Lakeshore 537; Barcelona Lighthouse 666; Barnegat Lighthouse 412; Cape Disappointment 24–25; Cape Hatteras National Seashore 433–434, 435; Escanaba 543; Heceta Head 36; Mark Twain Memorial Lighthouse 266; Okracoke 436; Old Baldy Lighthouse 442; Pigeon Point Lighthouse 68; Point Arena 57; Point Sur 80; Seul Choix Pointe 544; Tillamook Rock Lighthouse 29; Tybee Island 863
Lightning Field: 912
Lime Rock Park: 349
Lincoln, New Hampshire: 323
Lincoln, Illinois: 871

Lincoln, Abraham: 871, 872
Lincoln City: 32
Lincoln County Courthouse: 151
Lincoln County Museum: 203
Lincoln-Douglas debate: 642
Lincoln Highway: 369, 636
Lindberg, Charles A.: 244
Linton: 191
Lion Country Safari: 476
Litchfield: 873
Litchfield Hills: 348
Litchfield Plantation: 446
literature: on Chase County, Kansas 761; Faulkner, William 288; Grey, Zane 357; Hemingway, Ernest 142, 489; Jupiter 475; Kerouac, Jack 688; Lanier, Sidney 458; Melville, Herman 343; Miller, Henry 82; Pound, Ezra 143; on Route 66 889; Steinbeck, John 75; Twain, Mark 265–266; Welles, Orson 82, 85; Welty, Eudora 843; Wharton, Edith 344; Wolfe, Thomas 392
Lititz: 366
Little A'Le'Inn: 156
Little Falls: 244
Little House in the Big Woods: 246
Little Sahara Recreation Area: 729
Little Switzerland: 389
Living Desert State Park: 830
living history centers: Hancock Shaker Village 342; Oliver H. Kelley Farm 244; Plimoth Plantation 697
Llano Estacado: 830
locks, Soo: 548–549
Loggers PlayDay bash: 21
logging: Bemidji 237; Camp 18 Logging Museum 588; Forks Timber Museum 18; Scotia 50; sustainable 23
Lolo Hot Springs Resort: 135
Lompoc: 91
London Bridge: 934
Loneliest Road: 704–799; California 707–715; Colorado 738–752; Illinois 769–771; Indiana 771–777; Kansas 752–762; Maryland 795–799;

Missouri 762–769; Nevada 715–728; Ohio 777–785; road conditions 722; start of 67; Utah 728–738; Virginia 788–791; West Virginia 785–788
Long, Huey: 301
Long Beach: 23, 102
Long Beach Island: 412
Long Beach Peninsula: 23
Longhorn Bar and Grill: 173
Long Key State Park: 487
Lordsburg: 819
Los Angeles: 99–102, 943–944
Los Angeles International Airport (LAX): 100
Lost Coast: 49–50
Lost Dutchman State Park: 164
Lost Maples: 223
Lost River Gorge: 324
Lost River Valley: 139
Louisiana, Illinois: 267
Louisiana: 836–839
Louisiana Purchase Gardens and Zoo: 839
Louisville: 774
Lovejoy, Elijah: 271
Lover's Leap: 266
Lowell: 688
Lowell Observatory: 921
LSU Tigers: 302
Lubbock: 829
Lucia: 84
Lucille's Road House: 894
Lucy the Elephant: 415
Ludlow: 936
lumber mills: 37, 50, 237, 495
Lunenburg: 573
Luray Caverns: 378
Lusk: 625
Luxor: 155
Lyme: 325
Lyons: 757

M

MacArthur Memorial: 429
Mackay: 139
MacKerricher State Park: 54
Mackinac Island: 545
Maclean, Norman: 134
Macon: 852, 857
Madison: 775
Madonna Inn: 90
Madras: 596
Maggie Valley: 394

Mahaiwe Performing Arts Center: 346
Maiden Rock: 246
Maine: 575–583
Makah Indian Reservation: 18
Makah Museum: 18
Malad Gorge State Park: 608
Malibu: 97
Malibu Colony: 98
Malibu Pier: 98
Mall of America: 243
Malmberg Prairie: 532
Malta: 522
Mammoth Cave: 143
Manassas National Battlefield Park: 790
Mandan: 188
Mandarin Oriental: 65
Manitoulin Island: 552
Manitou Springs: 746
Manteo: 433
Manzanita: 30
Maple Grove Farms: 572
maple syrup: Billings Farm 331; Funks Grove 870–871; Maple Grove Farms 572; maple season 687; Morse Farm 570; Plainfield 570; Sugar Hill 321
Marathon: 487
Marble Canyon: 127
Marbles Hall of Fame: 416
Mardi Gras: 306
Margaret Chase Smith Library Center: 579
Margaret's Grocery: 844
Margate: 414
Mariemont: 780
Marin County: 61
Marineland: 467
Marin Headlands: 66
maritime museums: 27, 429, 438, 449, 490, 658, 798
Mark Twain Boyhood Home: 266
Mark Twain Museum: 266
Marquette, Iowa: 251
Marquette, Michigan: 546
Mars Desert Research Station: 733
Marshall: 833
Marsh-Billings-Rockefeller National Historical Park: 331
Marsh's Free Museum: 24
Martin Guitar Company: 360
Maryland: 420–423, 795–799

Marymere Falls: 16
Massachusetts: 337–348, 683–703
Massey: 552
Matador Ranch: 216
Matamoros, Mexico: 230
Mateel Community Center: 52
Mattawa: 556
Mavericks: 67
McAllen: 228
McClellanville: 447
McCook: 205
McCord Museum of Canadian History: 560
McGill: 150
McGregor: 251
McLean: 897
McPherson: 758
Meeteetse: 618
Mel Fisher Maritime Museum: 490
Melville, Herman: 343
Memphis: 280–281
Menard: 220
Menardville Museum: 221
Mendocino: 55–56
Mendocino Coast Botanical Gardens: 55
Mendocino Headlands State Park: 55
Menno-Hof Mennonite-Amish Visitor Center: 651
Mennonite Country: 758
Meramec Caverns: 876, 878
Meridian: 843
Mesilla: 821
Meteor Crater: 919
Metropolis: 277–278
Mexican food: 821
Mexico 85: 226
Miami: 480
Miami Beach: 478
Miccosukee Indian Village: 483
Michigan: 540–549
Mid-America Air Museum: 212
Middleburg: 790
Midewin National Tallgrass Prairie Preserve: 868
Midway: 454
Midway USA: 755
Milford: 358
military bases: Air University and War College 849; "Boneyard," the 170; Camp Lejeune 439; Camp

Pendleton 108; Canadian 559; Dyess Air Force Base 218; Fallon 721; Fort Bliss 824; Jacksonville Beach 465; Kings Bay U.S. Navy Base 460; Mid-America Air Museum 212; Minot Air Force Base 177; Mountain Home 605; Newport News 428; Point Loma 803; Point Mugu 97; Rock Island 258; Twentynine Palms 937; U.S. Naval Academy home 796; Whiteman Air Force Base 766; Yuma area 809
Milk River Valley: 522
Millennium Park: 645
Miller, Henry: 82
Million Dollar Highway: 740
Mingus, Charles: 173
Minidoka Internment National Monument: 144
mining: Bisbee 815–816; coal 730; Comstock Lode 718; copper 150, 551, 816; Cornish Pump and Mining Museum 542; Dubuque 254; Ely 725, 726; Eureka, Utah 729; Galena 639; Gold 712; iron 239, 241; Land of the Yankee Fork State Park 139; Libby 510; Nevada State Museum 717; New Mexico Mining Museum 912; Sudbury pollution 552; Sutter's Mill 711, 713; Western Mining and Railroad Museum 731
Minneapolis: 242–243
Minnesota: 235–245, 531–535
Minot: 178
mint juleps: 294
Minute Man National Historical Park: 689
Miracle Mile: 811
Miracle of America Museum: 132
Mirage, The: 155
Mission: 198
missions, California: general discussion 88–89; Carmel 77; La Purisima Mission 91, 92; Mission San Antonio de Padua 84, 88; Mission San Antonio de Pala 108; Mission San Gabriel

Arcangel 941; Mission San Luis Obispo de Tolosa 87; Old Mission San Luis Rey de Francia 108; Old Mission Santa Inés 93; San Buenaventura 95–96; San Juan Bautista 72; San Juan Capistrano 89, 106; Santa Barbara 94
missions, outside California: Mission San Xavier del Bac 169; San Esteban del Rey Mission 911; San Saba Mission 221
"Mississippi," defined: 282
Mississippi: 839–845
Mississippi Museum of Art: 842
Mississippi Palisades: 257
Mississippi River: clean-up of 269; French explorers sight 250; headwaters 235; locks and dams 267; National Mississippi River Museum and Aquarium 254; New Orleans as below 309; Old River Control Project 299
Missoula: 129, 133
Missouri: 256–278, 762–769, 875–883
Missouri River: 184, 186, 188
Mitchell: 598, 773
Mix, Tom: 168
Moab: 736
Mobridge: 192
Moby Dick: 697
Moby Dick Hotel and Oyster Farm: 24
Modern Art Museum of Fort Worth: 834
Mohawk Trail: 684
Mojave National Preserve: 937
Monarch Pass: 742, 743
Money: 290
Monroe: 838
Monroe, Marilyn: 72
Monrovia: 941
Montana: 128–136, 509–525
Montara: 67
Montebello: 562
Monterey: 73
Monterey Bay: 72
Monterey Bay Aquarium: 73
Monterey cypress: 79
Monterey Jazz Festival: 73
Monterey Peninsula: 74
Montgomery: 849

Monticello: 380
Montpelier: 569
Montreal: 560–561
Montreal Museum of Fine Arts: 560
Montrose: 740
Montshire Museum of Science: 327
Monument Rocks: 208
Moon Lake: 284
moose crossings: 323, 574
Moraine Lake: 124
Morehead City: 438
Mormons: 261–263, 659, 716, 732
Morro Bay: 87
Mo's: 34
Moses Coulee: 504
mosques: 528
mosquitoes: 446, 483
Moss Landing: 72
Mother's Day: 787
motorcycle rallies: 198, 471
motorcycles: 885–886, 891
Motown Museum: 652
Mound Bayou: 289
Mound Builder people: 289, 782
Mound City: 783
Mount, The: 344
mountain biking: Big Basin Redwoods State Park 69; Hurricane Ridge 16; inventors 63; Lake Crescent 16; Marin Headlands 66; Moab 737; Mountain Bike Hall of Fame 742; Mount Greylock 341; Point Reyes National Seashore 62; Schweitzer Mountain Resort 508; South Llano River State Park 222; Stanley 140; Whitefish Mountain Resort 130
Mountain City: 403
Mountain Home: 605
mountain lions: 19
Mount Airy: 387
Mount Baldy Fire Lookout: 511
Mount Desert Island: 582
Mount Greylock: 341
Mount Hood Highway: 593
Mount Lebanon Shaker Village: 682
Mount Locust: 298
Mount Olive: 873

Mount Olympus: 19
Mount Pleasant: 449
Mount Royal Park: 560
Mount Washington: 312–314, 315, 319
Mount Washington Auto Road: 314
Mount Washington Cog Railway: 314, 320
Mount Washington Hotel: 320
Movie Manor: 743
Mt. Borah: 139
Mt. Edith Cavell Road: 120
Mt. Emily: 40
Mt. Hood: 594
Mt. Katahdin: 316
Mt. Tamalpais: 63
Mt. Washington Valley: 316
Muddy Waters: 291
Mud Island: 281
Muir Woods: 63
Mulholland Drive: 100
Munson Creek Falls: 31
murals: brick 200; Cape Girardeau 276; Delta, Colorado 739; eastern Oregon 601; Ely 726; Quapaw 885
Murdo: 198
Murrells Inlet: 443
Museum of Contemporary Art: 113
Museum of Fine Arts, Boston: 694
Museum of Northern Arizona: 922
Museum of the Southern Jewish Experience: 296
Museum of Westward Expansion: 272
music: Branson 877; Delta, Mississippi 282; Delta blues 286, 287, 290; Dvorak, Antonin 252; Georgia Music Hall of Fame 852, 859; Hank Williams Memorial 850; jazz 259, 306, 307, 711, 765; Johnson, Robinson 284; Joplin, Scott 768; Macon 858, 859; Memphis 280; Ole Miss Blues Archive 288; Rainey, Gertrude "Ma" 853; Reggae Sunsplash 246; River Music Experience 259; Rodgers, Jimmy 842; see also festivals and events

Myers Flat: 51
Myrtle Beach: 443
Myrtle Beach Pelicans: 445
Mystery Spot: 71

N
Nacimiento-Fergusson Road: 84
Nags Head: 431
Nahcotta: 24
Naples: 508
NASA: 472
Natchez: 296
Natchez Trace Parkway: 296, 298, 840
National Automobile Museum: 720
National Bighorn Sheep Center: 622
National Bison Range: 133
National Bowling Stadium: 720
National Canal Museum: 360
National Civil Rights Museum: 280
National Civil War Naval Museum: 853
National Gallery of Canada: 554
National Historic Trails Interpretive Center: 623
National Mississippi River Museum and Aquarium: 254
National Museum of American History: 792
National Museum of the American Indian: 792
National Prisoners of War Museum: 857
National Steinbeck Center: 75
National Women's Hall of Fame: 673
Native American Reservations: Bad River Indian Reservation 539; Blackfeet Indian Reservation 517; Cherokee Indian Reservation 394; Flathead Indian Reservation 132; Fort Belknap Indian Reservation 520–522; Fort Berthold Indian Reservation 528; Fort Peck Indian Reservation 524; Fort Totten Sioux Indian Reservation 529; Havasupai

Indian Reservation 931; Hoopa Valley Indian Reservation 44; Makah Indian Reservation 18; Rosebud Indian Reservation 198; Standing Rock Indian Reservation 189–190; Warm Springs Indian Reservation 594; Wind River Indian Reservation 620
Native American sites/history: Acoma Pueblo 911; Amerind Foundation Museum 813; Autry National Center 944; Big Hole National Battlefield 136; Black Hawk War 249; Buechel Memorial Lakota Museum 199; Canadian Museum of Civilization 562; Cass Lake 239; Chaco Culture National Historical Park 913; Chief Joseph 520, 521; Eastern Trails Museum 886; Effigy Mounds National Monument 251; El Cuartelejo 209; Flathead Indian Museum and Trading Post 133; Fort Buford 526; Fort Robinson 627; Inter Tribal Ceremonial 914; Iroquois Indian Museum 678; Koshare Indian Museum 750; Makah Museum 18; Miccosukee Indian Village 483; Mound Builder people 781–783; Museum of Ojibwa Culture 545; Museum of the Cherokee Indian 395; Museum of the Plains Indian 517; National Museum of the American Indian 792; Native American Museum 435; Northern Plains Indian Culture Fest 181; Oberlin 207; Oñate, Juan de 822; Sand Creek Massacre National Historic Site 752; Scherr-Howe Arena 192; Sitting Bull Memorial 192; South Dakota Cultural Heritage Center 194; Trail of Tears State Park 277; Wellfleet 205; see also archaeological sites

Nat-Soo-Pah Hot Springs: 146
Natural Bridge: 383
Natural Bridges State Beach: 66
Naumkeag: 345
Nauticus National Maritime Center: 429
Nauvoo: 261–263
Nauvoo Temple: 263
Navy SEALS: 474
Neah Bay: 18
Neahkahnie Mountain: 30
Nebraska: 199–206, 626–633
Nebraska National Forest: 202
Nebraska Sand Hills: 201–202
Needles: 935
Negro Baseball Leagues Museum: 765
Nehalem Bay State Park: 30
Nellis Air Force Range: 156
Nelson Atkins Museum of Art: 764
Nepenthe: 82
Netarts: 31
Nevada: 146–159, 715–728
Nevada Open Road Challenge: 153
Neverland Ranch: 92
New Hampshire: 312–327, 573–575
New Jersey: 411–418
New Mexico: 818–836, 902–914
New York: 351–357, 665–683
New Bedford: 697
New Bedford Whaling Museum: 697
New Bedford Whaling National Historical Park: 697
New Boston: 260
New Camaldoli Hermitage: 84
New Jersey Shore: 412
New Madrid: 279
New Orleans: 306–307, 309
Newport, Oregon: 33–34
Newport, Washington: 507
Newport Beach: 105
New York City: 354–355
New York State Museum: 680
Nez Percé: 521
Niagara Falls: 671
Nicolaysen Art Museum and Discovery Center: 624
Niota: 261

Nitt Witt Ridge: 86
Nixon, Richard: 104, 108
Nogales: 173
Norfolk: 349, 429
Norris, George: 205
Norsk Hostfest: 178
North Carolina: 386–399, 430–442
North Dakota: 177–184, 525–531
North Adams: 338
North Bay: 556
North Bend: 780
North Canaan: 348
North Conway: 317
North Dakota Heritage Center: 188
North Haverhill: 324
North Head Lighthouse: 25
North Miami Beach: 478
North Platte: 202
North Vernon: 775
North Woodstock: 323
Norway: 543
Norwich: 327
Notre Dame University: 649
Nottoway: 305
nuclear power: 246, 610, 735
nuclear waste: 830
nude beaches: 81, 478
Nye Beach: 34
Nyssa: 602

O
Oak Alley: 308
Oakland: 707
Oakland Museum of California: 708
Oakley: 207
Oak Park: 643
Oak Springs Summit: 152
Oatman: 933
Oberlin: 206, 658
Oberlin College: 658
Ocean City: 421
Ocean Drive: 415
Ocean Road State Natural Site: 35
Oceanside, California: 108
Oceanside, Oregon: 31
Ochoco Lake: 598
Ocmulgee National Monument: 860
Odwalla: 69
Oglala National Grasslands: 628
Ohio: 654–663, 777–785

Ohio River Towns: 775
Ohme Gardens County Park: 502
oil industry: 833, 837, 892, 896
OK Corral: 814
O'Keeffe Museum, Georgia: 391
Oklahoma: 212–213, 885–897
Oklahoma City: 892
Okracoke: 436
Old Depot Museum: 848
Old Faithful Geyser: 613
Old Fort Sumner Museum: 905
old-growth forests: Cathedral State Park 788; Del Norte Coast Redwoods State Park 43; Drift Creek Wilderness 34; Humboldt Redwoods State Park 50–51; Jedediah Smith Redwoods State Park 42; Klootchy Creek Park 588; Lake Quinault 20; Prairie Creek Redwoods State Park 44; Samuel H. Boardman State Scenic Corridor 41
Old Jail Art Center: 831
Old Spanish Trail: 466
Old Town Bandon: 38
Old Town Eureka: 48
Old Town Florence: 36
Olney: 771
Olympic National Park: 10, 15, 18, 19
Onancock: 426
On-A-Slant Indian Village: 183, 189
One Flew Over the Cuckoo's Nest: 34
O'Neill: 632
Onida: 194
Ontario, Oregon: 602
Onward: 292
Oquawka: 263
Oregon: 10, 25–41
Oregon Coast Trail: 29
Oregon Dunes National Recreation Area Visitors Center: 37
Oregon Trail: 584–703; historic 203, 606–607; Idaho 602–613; Illinois 639–646; Indiana 646–651; Iowa 633–638; Massachusetts 683–703;

National Historic Trails Interpretive Center 623; Nebraska 626–633; New York 665–683; Ohio 654–663; Oregon 586–602; Pennsylvania 663–665; wagon ruts 626; western end of 597; Wyoming 613–626
Organ Pipe Cactus National Monument: 810
Orick: 45
Original American Kazoo Company: 668
Orlando: 470
Oro Grande: 939
Oswald West State Park: 30
Ottawa River: 556
Otter Crest Loop: 33
Ottowa: 554–555
Outer Banks: 433, 434
Overseas Highway: 484–485
owl, spotted: 18, 34
Oxford, Maryland: 798
Oxford, Mississippi: 288
oysters: Hood Canal 13; Nahcotta and Oysterville 24; Raymond 23; Seattle 499; skipjacks 798; Swan Oyster Depot 65; Tomales Bay 61; Yaquina Bay 33
Oysterville: 24

P

Pacifica: 67
Pacific Coast: 10–113; California 41–113; Oregon 25–41; Washington 10–25
Pacific County Courthouse: 23
Pacific Grove: 75
Pacific Lumber Company: 50
Pacific Way Bakery & Cafe: 28
Paducah: 216
Pageant of the Masters: 106
Painted Desert: 915
Painted Hills Unit: 600
Paint Pots: 127
Paint Rock Pictographs: 220
Palace of the Governors: 908
Palm Beach: 475
Palo Duro Canyon State Park: 900
pampas grass: 84
Panaca: 151
Panaca Spring: 152
Panhandle-Plains Historical Museum: 901
paper mills: 239, 241, 783

Paradise Garden: 845
Parchman: 287
Park City: 730
Parkersburg: 785
Parliament Hill: 554
Parma: 603
Pasadena: 942
Patrick's Point State Park: 45
Patriot's Day: 691
Paul Revere House: 694
Pawleys Island: 446
Pawnee Rock: 756
Peacham: 571
Pea Island National Wildlife Refuge: 434
Pearce, Simon: 329
Pebble Beach: 76
Pebble Beach Concours d'Elegance: 77
pecans: 294
Pelican Bay State Prison: 43
Pennsylvania: 357–370, 663–665
Pennsylvania Dutch Country: 364–365
Penny Arcade: 747
Pepin: 246
Pepperdine University: 98
peregrine falcons: 87
Père Marquette State Park: 269
Perrysburg: 656
Perryton: 213
Pescadero: 68
Petawawa: 556, 559
Petrified Creatures Museum of Natural History: 677
Petrified Forest National Park: 916
petrified wood: 751, 915
petroglyphs: 618, 721, 724, 811
Petrolia: 49
Peyto Lake: 122
Pfeiffer Beach: 81
Pfeiffer Big Sur State Park: 81
pheasants, wild: 192
Phoenix: 166–167
photography: 618, 672
Picacho Peak: 165
pictographs: 213, 220, 270, 600, 824, 916
Pictured Rocks National Lakeshore: 547
Piedras Blancas: 85
Pierre: 194–195
Pigeon Key: 487
Pigeon Point Lighthouse: 68

Pike Place Market: 498
Pike's Peak: 746
Pike's Peak State Park: 252
Pilgrim Monument and
  Museum: 702
Pima Air and Space Museum:
  170
Pinal County Historical
  Museum: 168
pine, bristlecone: 727
Pinkham Notch: 314
Pinnacle Peak: 267
Pioche: 151
Pioneer Auto Show: 198
Pioneer Square: 498
piracy: 437
Pismo Beach: 90
Pittsfield: 334, 341
Place Jacques-Cartier: 561
Placerville: 712
Plainfield: 570
Plains: 856
Plains Indians: 205
planetariums: 572
Plantation Alley: 300,
  304–305
plants, invasive: 84
Plimoth Plantation: 697
Plymouth Notch: 334
Plymouth Rock: 696
Pocono Mountains: 359
Point Arena: 57
Point Dume State Beach: 97
Point Lobos State Natural
  Reserve: 79
Point Loma: 803
Point Mugu: 96
Point Reyes: 61
Point Reyes National
  Seashore: 62
pollution: 376, 510, 552
Polson Museum: 21, 132
Pomfret: 327
Pompeo Coppini's Charles H.
  Noyes Statue: 219
ponies, wild: 425
Ponte Vedra Beach: 465
Pontiac: 869
Pony Express: 723
pop culture: 469, 479, 671
Popeye: 275
Porcupine Mountains
  Wilderness: 541
Port Angeles: 12, 14–16
Port Gamble: 13
Port Gibson: 295
Port Jervis: 356

Portland: 28, 590–591
Port Orford: 39
Port Townsend: 10, 12–13
Post Ranch Inn: 82
*The Postman Always Rings
  Twice*: 97
potatoes: 611
Pound, Ezra: 143
poverty: 282, 784, 785
Powell, John Wesley: 733
Powell's City of Books: 591
Powerhouse, The: 932
powwows: Bad River
  Indian Reservation 539;
  Cornucopia 537; Fort Peck
  Indian Reservation 524;
  North American Indian
  Days Powwow 517; Rosebud
  Sioux Tribal Fair and
  Powwow 199
Prairie City: 601
Prairie Creek Redwoods State
  Park: 44
Prairie Dog Town: 207
Prairie du Chien: 250
Prairie Island Nuclear Power:
  246
prairies: 760, 868
PrairyErth: 761
Prefontaine, Steve: 37
Prehistoric Gardens: 40
Preservation Hall: 307
Presidio: 66
Presley, Elvis: 283
Price: 731
Princeton: 67
Principia College: 270
Prineville: 596
prisons: 43, 64, 165, 287, 490,
  605, 745, 809, 857
Prohibition era: 284
Provincetown: 701
Pueblo: 747
Pueblo Indians: 209
pumpkins: 67
Purina Farms: 876
Pygmy Forest: 56

Q-R
Quad Cities: 258
Quakers: 797
Quechee Gorge: 328
Queen Mary: 102
Quinault Loop Trail: 21
Quincy: 264, 693
races, foot: 66
Rachel: 156

Radium Hot Springs: 128
RAGBRAI: 254
ragtime music: 768
railroads: Agawa Canyon Tour
  Trains 551; Barstow 938;
  Caliente 152; California
  State Railroad Museum 711;
  Canadian Pacific Railway
  124; Conway Scenic
  Railroad 318; Fenelon Place
  Elevator 254; Florida 464;
  Grand Canyon Railway
  928; Great Northern 500;
  Illinois Railway Museum
  643; Nevada Northern
  Railway Museum 725;
  Nevada State Railroad
  Museum 717; North Dakota
  State Railroad Museum
  188; North Platte 202–203;
  Pacific Southwest Railway
  Museum 805; Quad Cities
  258–259; Skunk Trains
  54; Wells 147; Western
  Gateway Heritage State
  Park 338; Western Mining
  and Railroad Museum 731;
  Whitefish 130
Rainey, Gertrude "Ma": 853
Ramirez Canyon Park: 98
Rancho del Cielo: 93
rattlesnakes: 831, 907
Ravalli County Museum: 136
Raymond: 23
Reading: 362
Reagan, Ronald: 93, 96, 643
Red Light Museum: 719
Redway: 52
Redwood National Park:
  44–45
Reedsport: 37
Reelfoot Lake: 278
Refugio State Beach: 93
Reggae on the River: 52
Rehoboth Beach: 419
R.E.M.: 406
Reno: 719–720
Return of the Jedi: 45
Revolutionary War: Allen,
  Ethan and Ira 564; armory
  for 349; Bennington Battle
  Monument 337; Cherry
  Valley 677; Clark, George
  Rogers 772; Florida's role
  in 462; Kaskaskia 275;
  Lexington 382; Liberty
  Bell Shrine 362; Minute

Man National Historical Park 689; Patriot's Day 691; Vincennes 772

Rexburg: 612

rhododendrons: 37, 55, 58

Rice Museum: 447

Richard Nixon Presidential Library: 104

Richmond: 568

Rincon Mountains: 812

Rio Grande Valley: 228

Rio Puerco: 910

Ripley's Believe It or Not!: 467

Rising Sun: 776

A River Runs Through It: 134

Riverfront Park: 506

River of No Return: 183

Riverside Resort Hotel: 161

River Street: 456

Riverton: 884

River Valley Pioneer Museum: 214

road rules, Canada: 550

Road to Nowhere: 175–231; Illinois, Iowa, and Missouri 256–278; Kansas 206–213; Nebraska 199–206; North Dakota 177–184; South Dakota 191–199

Roadside America: 363

roadside art, attractions, and curiosities: Anderson's Pea Soup, 92; Big Nickel, 553; Bono's Giant Orange, 940; Bottle Tree Ranch, 939; brontosaurus sculpture, 215; Cadillac Ranch, 900; Carhenge, 202, 630; Catoosa Blue Whale, 888; Center of the World, 808; Chloride folk art, 162; Columbia Falls and Hungry Horse, 512; Crazy Horse Memorial, 630; drive-thru trees, 52, 53; "Eat Beef Keep Slim" sign, 211; Enchanted Highway, 185; Garden of Eden, 756; Gehrke Windmill Garden, 505; giant chessboard, 87; Groom, 898; Haystack Rock, 30; Margaret's Grocery, 844; Mt. Rushmore, 630; Munger Moss Motel, 880; old-growth redwoods, 51; Paradise Garden, 845; Prairie Dog Town, 207; Radio Flyer wagon, giant, 506;

Radium Wood Carvers, 128; Roadside America, 363; Roy's Motel and Café, 936; sculpture, North Dakota, 530; Sign Post Forest, 119; Skowhegan Indian, 579; South of the Border, 444; Stonehenge, 879; the Tepee, 677; "The Tree That Owns Itself", 406; The Thing?, 813; Wee'l turtle, 177; Wildwood, 416; World's Largest Catsup Bottle, 874; World's Largest Chair, 688; World's Largest Cow, 187; World's Largest Free-Standing Man-Made Star, 385; World's Largest Frying Pan, 24; World's Largest Lobster, 486; World's Largest Six-Pack, 247; World's Largest Spruce Tree, 21; World's Largest Van Gogh, 208; World's Oldest Gas Station, 751

Roanoke: 384

Roanoke Island: 432

Robinsonville: 284

Rochester, New York: 671

Rochester, Vermont: 334

Rock and Roll Hall of Fame and Museum: 660

Rock City: 397, 399

rock climbing: 501, 713

Rockefeller Forest: 51

Rockford: 642

Rock Island Line Railroad Bridge: 212

Rockport: 52

Rockwell, Norman: 345

Rockwell City: 635

rodeos: Buffalo Bill Rodeo 203; Caldwell 603; Cody 616–617; Fort Peck Indian Reservation 524; Will Rogers Memorial Rodeo 886

Rodgers, Jimmy: 842

Roger Miller Museum: 897

Rogers, Will: 887–888

Rogue River: 40

Rolla: 879

Roma: 227

Romano Gabriel Wooden Sculpture Garden: 48

Romney: 788

Ronald Reagan Presidential Library: 96

Roosevelt, Franklin D.: 352, 854

Roosevelt, Teddy: 179

Rosebud: 199

Rosebud Indian Reservation: 198

Rosedown Plantation: 300

Rosemont Plantation: 299

Rosie the Riveter National Historical Park: 709

Ross: 528

Roswell: 827

Route 100: 334, 335

Route 116: 686

Route 66: 864–945; Arizona 914–935; California 935–945; California Route 66 Museum 939; Illinois 866–874; Kansas 883–884; literature on 889; Missouri 875–883; National Route 66 Museum 895; New Mexico 902–914; Oklahoma 885–897; Oklahoma Route 66 Museum 894; Route 66 Auto Museum 904; Route 66 Hall of Fame Museum 870; Route 66 Interpretive Center 891; Shea's Gas Station Museum 872; songs 918; St. Louis diners 273; Texas 897–902; Western terminus of 99

Route 66 Casino: 910

Route 66 State Park: 876

Route 6A: 699

Route 9: 335

Royal Gorge: 744

Ruby Beach: 19

Ruby Mountains: 148

Rugby: 179

Ruins of Windsor: 296

Rumford: 577

Running Fence: 60

Rural Life Museum: 301

Russell-Colbath Historic House: 319

Russian Gulch State Park: 55, 56

Ruston: 838

S

Sabal Palm Grove Sanctuary: 230

Sabinal Canyon Museum: 223

Sabino Canyon: 171

Sabula: 256

Sacagawea: 180, 181, 183, 187, 529
Sac City: 635
Sacramento: 710
Saddle Mountain State Park: 587
Saguaro National Park: 811, 812
sailboarding: 69, 434
Sainte Genevieve: 274
salamanders: 396
Salem: 770
sales tax: 26
Salida: 743
Salinas: 75
Salisbury: 799
Salk Institute: 112
Salmon: 137
Salmon River, North Fork: 137
Salmon River Gorge: 137, 138
salt deposits: 149, 832
Salt Lake City: 732
Salt Point State Park: 58
Samoa: 48
Samoa Cookhouse: 48
Sam's Grill: 65
Samuel H. Boardman State Scenic Corridor: 41
San Antonio: 225
San Bernardino: 940
San Clemente: 108
Sand Hills: 631
Sandia Crest: 906
San Diego: 110–111, 803–804
San Diego Padres: 110
San Diego Zoo: 110
Sandland Adventures: 37
Sand Mountain: 722
Sandoz, Mari: 631
Sandpoint: 508
Sandsage Bison Range and Wildlife Area: 211
Sandusky: 657
Sandwich: 698
Sandwich Glass Museum: 698
Sandy: 593
San Francisco: 64–65
San Francisco Giants: 64
San Francisco Solano: 88
San Francisco Zoo: 66
San Gabriel Arcángel: 89
San Gabriel Valley: 941
San Juan Bautista: 72, 88
San Juan Capistrano: 89, 106
San Juan Mountains: 740
San Luis Obispo: 87
San Miguel Arcángel: 88
San Saba Mission: 221

San Simeon: 84
Santa Barbara: 89, 93–95
Santa Cruz: 70
Santa Fe: 908–909
Santa Fe Trail: 748–749, 753, 759
Santa Fe Trail Center: 756
Santa Maria: 91
Santa Monica: 944–945
Santa Monica Mountains Recreation Area: 98
Santarella: 346
Santa Rosa: 904
San Xavier: 169
Sapelo Island: 454
Sappho: 18
Sault Ste. Marie, Michigan: 548
Sault Ste. Marie, Ontario: 551
Savanna: 257
Savannah: 456–457, 862
Save the Redwoods League: 51
Sawtooth National Recreation Area: 141
Sayre: 896
Scandinavian festivals: 178
Scandinavian Heritage Park: 178
Scherr-Howe Arena: 192
Schlitterbahn Waterpark Resort: 231
Science North: 553
Scotia: 50
Scott City: 209
sculpture: Brookgreen Gardens 445; Chesterwood 346; Dallas 835; Douglass, Frederick 671; Garden of Eden 756; Huntington Library, Museum and Gardens 942; Lightning Field 912; Millennium Park 645; Minneapolis Sculpture Garden 242; Pompeo Coppini's Charles H. Noyes Statue 220; roadside, North Dakota 530; Romano Gabriel Wooden Sculpture Garden 48; Route 66 sculpture 904; Savannah 456; Storm King Art Center 352; Superman 278; *see also* roadside art, attractions, and curiosities
Seabreeze Amusement Park: 671
Seagram's distillery: 777
Sea Islands: 452
sea kayaking: 55, 56, 87
Seal Harbor: 582

Sea Lion Caves: 36
seals, elephant: 69
Sea Ranch: 58
Sears Fine Foods: 65
Seaside: 28
Seattle: 12, 498–499
Seattle Art Museum: 498
Seattle Center: 498
Sedalia: 766
Sedona: 929
Seip Mound: 783
Selby: 193
Seligman: 930
Selma: 847
Seneca Falls: 672
Sequim: 13–14
Serpent Mound: 781
7 Cedars Casino: 14
17-Mile Drive: 76
Seward House: 674
Seymour: 775
shad flies: 556
Shakers: 342, 682
Shakespeare: 819
Shamrock: 215
Sharon Springs: 677
Shawnee National Forest: 275
Shay's Rebellion: 348
Shelburne Falls: 685
Shelburne Falls Trolley Museum: 685
Shelburne Inn: 23
Shelburne Museum: 566
Shelby: 518
Shelter Cove: 49–50
Shenandoah National Park: 376–378
The Shining: 594
shipwrecks: 433, 442, 547
Shoe House: 366
Shore Acres State Park: 38
Shoshone: 144, 609
Shoshone Falls: 146
Shoshone Ice Caves: 143
Shoshoni: 622
Shoup: 137
Shreveport: 836
Sidewalk Highway: 885–886
Sign Post Forest: 119
Siletz Bay: 32
Silver State Challenge: 153
Simi Valley: 96
Sioux City: 633
Sioux Lookout: 204
Sitting Bull Memorial: 192
Siuslaw River Bridge: 36
Skaneateles: 674

skiing: Bridgewater 332; Crested Butte 742; Ironwood 540; Jackson Hole 621; Killington 333; Lost Trail 136; Mount Hood Skibowl 594; Norheim, Sondre 529; Schweitzer Mountain Resort 508; Skiers' Highway 335; South Lake Tahoe 714; Stevens Pass 500; Sunday River 576; Sun Valley 142; Whitefish Mountain Resort 130
ski jumping: 541, 542
Skowhegan: 578
Sky City: 911
skydiving: 264
Skykomish: 497
Skyline Drive: 377
Skyline Parkway: 533
sled dog racing: 547
sleeper waves: 60
sleigh rides: 317
Slide Rock State Park: 929
Sloane-Stanley Museum: 350
Smallest Church in America: 453
Smith, Jedediah Strong: 42
Smith, Joseph: 659
Smith, Jr., Joseph: 262
Smokejumpers Base Aerial Fire Depot: 134
Snake River Canyon: 145
Snohomish: 496
snorkeling: 483, 485, 488
Snow Hill: 423
Snyder's of Hanover: 367
Soldier Summit: 730
Sol Duc River: 18
Solvang: 92
Somers: 132
Sometimes a Great Notion: 34
Sonoma Coast State Park: 60
Soo Locks: 548–549
The Sound of Music: 569
South Carolina: 443–453
South Dakota: 191–199
South Bass Island: 657
South Bend, Indiana: 649
South Bend, Washington: 23
South Carlsbad State Beach: 109
South Dakota Cultural Heritage Center: 194
South Dakota Discovery Center and Aquarium: 195
Southern Jews: 296
Southern Pacific route:

800–863; Alabama 845–852; Arizona 808–818; California 802–808; Georgia 852–863; Louisiana 836–839; Mississippi 839–845; New Mexico 818–836; start of 113
South Lake Tahoe: 714
South Llano River State Park: 222
South of the Border: 444
South Padre Island: 230–231
space center, NASA: 472–473
Space Needle: 498
speeding tickets: 275
speed limits: 519
Spillville: 252
spinach: 226
Spiral Tunnel Viewpoint: 123
Spokane: 505–507
sporting good stores: 881
spotted owl, northern: 18, 34
Springfield, Illinois: 871–873
Springfield, Missouri: 881
Spring Green: 248
square dancing: 228
Stagecoach Museum: 625
Standing Rock Indian Reservation: 189–190, 192
Stanley, Idaho: 140
Stanley, North Dakota: 528
Stanley, William: 347
Stanton: 181
Stateline: 716
Statesboro: 861
Statue of Liberty: 411
St. Augustine: 465
Staunton: 379
Stax Records: 280
St. Donatus: 255
Steamboat Arabia Museum: 764
Stearns Wharf: 93
Steinbeck, John: 75, 186, 210
Stevens Pass: 500
Stevensville: 135
St. Francis: 199
St. Francisville: 300
St. Ignace: 545
St. Ignatius: 133
St. Ignatius Mission church: 133
Stinson Beach: 62
St. Johnsbury: 571
St. Joseph Island: 551
St. Louis: 271–273, 875
St. Louis County Heritage and Arts Center: 535

St. Lucie County Historical Museum: 475
St. Mary: 516
St. Michaels: 798
Stockbridge: 345
Stokes Castle: 722
Stone Mountain: 407
St. Orres: 57
Stout Grove: 42
St. Paul: 242–243
Strait of Juan de Fuca: 17
Strasburg: 190
Stratosphere Tower: 157
Strip, Las Vegas: 153
Strong National Museum of Play: 671
Sturgis: 198
Sudbury: 552
sugarcane: 303
Sugar Hill: 321
Sula: 136
Sunbeam: 140
Sundance Film Festival: 730
Sunflower River Blues and Gospel Festival: 287
Sun Records: 280
Sunset Bay State Park: 38
Sunset Boulevard: 100
Sunset Crater: 923
Sunset Highway: 587
Sunshine Bridge: 304
Sun Valley: 142
Superior: 535
Superior Falls: 539
Superman: 277–278
Superstition Mountains: 164
surfing: Boca Raton 476; bodysurfing the Wedge 105; Cape Kiwanda 32; Cocoa Beach 474; Huntington Beach 103; La Jolla 112; Mavericks 67; Oswald West State Park 30; Pacific Beach 112; Paskowitz Surf Camp 112; Port Orford 39; Westport 22
Surfing Museum: 70
surf-kayaking: 22
Surfrider Beach: 98
Sutro Baths: 66
Sutter, John: 364
Sutter's Fort: 711
swamp tours: 305
Swanton Berry Farm: 69
Sweetwater: 831
Syracuse: 675

T

Tabasco: 304
Tahkenitch Lake: 37
Takakkaw Falls: 123
Taliesin West: 166
Tallgrass Prairie National
   Preserve: 760
Tallulah Falls: 404
Tallulah Gorge State Park: 405
Tangier Island: 426
Tanglewood: 344
Tappet brothers: 693
Tatoosh Island: 18
Tecate, Mexico: 804
teddy bears: 292
Temple Gemiluth Chassed:
   295, 732
Teton Flood Museum: 612
Texas: 213–231, 897–902
Texas Hill Country: 223, 225
Texas Square Dance
   Jamboree: 228
Texas Vietnam Veterans
   Memorial Highway:
   213–231
Theatricum Botanicum: 99
Thedford: 202
Theodore Roosevelt National
   Park: 528
thermometers: 697
Thermopolis: 619
The Thing?: 813
Thomson: 256
Three Capes Loop: 31
ticks: 136
tidepools: Bolinas 62; Cabrillo
   National Monument 803;
   Cape Perpetua 35; Half
   Moon Bay 67; Leo Carrillo
   State Park 97; Lost Coast 49;
   Olympic Peninsula 15, 20;
   Patrick's Point State Park 45;
   Torrey Pines State Natural
   Reserve 112
Till, Emmett: 290
Tillamook: 31
Tillamook Air Museum: 31
Tillamook Cheese Factory: 31
Tillamook Head: 29, 183
Tillamook Rock Lighthouse: 29
Tillman, Pat: 159
Times Beach: 875
Titan Missile Museum: 169, 172
Tobacco Valley Historical
   Village: 129
Tokeland: 22–23

Toledo: 654
Toledo Museum of Art: 655
tolerance, racial: 849–850
Tomales Bay: 61
Tomb of the Unknowns: 791
Tombstone: 814
Tom Sawyer: 266
Tom's Coin & Gem Shop: 178
Tonto National Forest: 164
Tony Packo's Cafe: 655
tool museum: 350
Topanga Canyon: 99
tornadoes: 754, 883
Torrey Pines State Natural
   Reserve: 112
Tortilla Flat: 164
Totem Pole Park: 887
Tourism Victoria: 17
trading posts: Cameron 923;
   Clark's Trading Post 322;
   Fort Cody Trading Post
   204; Gallup 914; Hubbell
   Trading Post National
   Historic Site 915; Jackrabbit
   Trading Post 919; Meteor
   City Trading Post 919;
   Stewart's Trading Post 915;
   Totem Pole Trading Post
   879; Two Guns and Twin
   Arrows 920
Trail of Tears: 276, 277, 852,
   886
trams: Cannon Mountain
   322; Franconia Notch 321;
   Jasper National Park 118;
   Pioche 151; Royal Gorge 744
transportation museums: 204,
   384, 580, 643
Trapp family: 569
Traveler's Rest: 183
Trees of Mystery: 43, 53
Trempealeau: 246
Trenton: 581
Trimper's Amusements: 421
Trinidad: 46
Triple U Buffalo Ranch: 194
trolleys: 189
Troy, Montana: 510
Troy, New York: 681
Truman Library: 763
Truro: 701
Tubac: 172
Tucumcari: 902
Tulsa: 888
Tumácacori National Historic
   Park: 172

Tumwater Canyon: 500
turtles, sea: 435, 440, 460,
   475
Tucson: 169, 170–171, 811
Tuskegee: 851
Tuskegee University: 851
Twain, Mark: 265–266, 267,
   719
Twilight saga: 18, 589
Twin Falls: 144
Tybee Island: 863
Tyringham: 346

U

UDT Navy SEALs Museum:
   474
UFO tourism: 156, 827
Ulysses S. Grant Home: 640
Umpqua Dunes: 37
Uncle Sam: 682
Underground Atlanta: 400
Underground Railroad: 663,
   778
Underwood: 180
Union: 643
Union Pacific Depot: 152
United States Naval
   Shipbuilding Museum: 696
University of Arizona: 170
University of California: 112,
   708
University of Mississippi: 288
University of Montana: 134
University of Virginia: 380
U.P. 200: 547
US-299: 46
US-83: 175–231
US-93: 129, 133, 137, 139
U.S. southernmost point: 490
Utah: 728–738
Utah Lake: 730
Utica: 296, 676
Utopia: 223
utopian communities: 667
Uvalde: 224

V

Vacherie: 308
Vale: 601
Valentine: 199
Valentine National Wildlife
   Refuge: 201
Valentine's Day cards: 199
Vallejo: 709
Valley Ford: 60
Vega: 901

Ventana Inn & Spa: 82
Ventana Wilderness: 81
Ventura: 95
Verendrye Museum: 198
Vermilion: 658
Vermilion Crossing: 127
Vermont: 327–337, 563–573
Vero Beach: 474
Versace, Gianni: 478
Vicksburg: 282, 291
Vicksburg National Military
　Park: 293–294
Victoria, British Columbia: 17
Victoriana: 250
Victorville: 939
Vidalia: 861
Vieux Carré: 306
Villa de San Agustín
　Historical District: 226
Vincennes: 772
Vinita: 886
Virginia: 374–386, 424–430,
　788–791
Virginia Beach: 428
Virginia City: 718
Vulture Mine: 163

W
Wabasha: 246
Waddell Beach: 69
wagon ruts: 753, 757
Walden Pond: 691
Waldport: 34–35
Walker Art Center: 242
Wall Drug: 196–197
Walnut Canyon National
　Monument: 920
Walt Disney World: 470
The Waltons: 379
Wapiti Valley: 617
Warm Springs: 854
Warm Springs Indian
　Reservation: 594
Warsaw: 263
Washburn: 185
Washington, Virginia: 375
Washington, Booker T.: 384,
　851
Washington, D.C.: 792–795
Washington: 10–25,
　494–507
Washington Monument State
　Park: 371
watches: 366
waterfalls: Athabasca Falls
　121; Bash Bish Falls 348;
　Bow Glacier Falls 123;

Columbia Gorge 595;
Crawford Notch 319;
Crystal Falls 541; Deception
Falls 500; Franconia Notch
321, 322; Grand Canyon
of the Yellowstone 615;
Great Smoky Mountains
National Park 396; Julia
Pfeiffer Burns State Park 83;
Kent 350; Kootenai Falls
510; Lake Louise area 124;
Malad Gorge State Park
608; Moss Glen Falls 334;
Munson Creek Falls 31;
Niagara Falls 671; Pfeiffer
Big Sur State Park 81;
Sabbaday Falls 319; Sabino
Canyon 171; Santa Monica
Mountains Recreation Area
98; Shenandoah National
Park 376; Spokane 506;
Tahquamenon Falls State
Park 547; Takakkaw Falls
123; Thousand Springs
Scenic Byway 608;
Transylvania County 398–
399; Twin Falls 145–146;
underground 680; Wallace
Falls 497; Weeping Wall 122
Waterloo: 637
watermelons: 256
water skiing: 159
water-skiing: 237
Waterville: 503
Watsonville: 72
waves, sleeper: 60
weather: hurricanes 432,
439; Laughlin, Nevada
161; Mojave Desert 938;
Montana 523; Mount
Washington 315; Olympic
Peninsula 16; Texas
Panhandle 899; tsunami
effects 43; Tucson 170;
Wisconsin snow 536
Wedge, The: 105
Weeping Wall: 122
Welk, Lawrence: 190
Welles, Orson: 82, 85
Wellfleet, Massachusetts: 700
Wellfleet, Nebraska: 205
Wellington: 215
Wells: 147
Welty, Eudora: 843
Wenatchee: 502
Wendover: 148
Wendover Air Force Base: 148

Wendover Will: 148
West Virginia: 371–373,
785–788
West Cornwall: 349
West Danville: 571
Westfield: 665–666
West Glacier: 512
West Hartford: 327
Westhope: 177–178
West Point: 351
Westport, California: 52
Westport, Oregon: 22–23
Westport, Kansas City: 764
West Salem: 248
West Yellowstone: 612
Wetlands Institute: 416
whale-watching: Cape
Lookout 31; Garrapata
State Park 80; Leo Carrillo
State Park 97; Mendocino
Coast Botanical Gardens 55;
Ocean Road State Natural
Site 35; Patrick's Point
State Park 45; Point Lobos
State Natural Reserve 79;
Provincetown 702; Santa
Barbara 94; Westport 22
whaling: 697
Wharton, Edith: 344
Wheeler Peak: 727
Whistle Stop Cafe: 860
Whitefish: 130
Whitefish Mountain Resort:
130
White House of the
Confederacy: 849
White Mountains National
Forest: 317
White River Junction: 328
white-water rafting:
Chattooga River 404;
Deerfield River 685; Gold
Discovery State Historic
Park 713; Royal Gorge 745;
Tumwater Canyon 500
Whitingham: 335
Whyte Museum of the
Canadian Rockies: 126
Wickenburg: 162
Wickliffe: 278
Wikieup: 162
Wilbur: 505
Wilder, Laura Ingalls: 881
wildflowers: Bartholomew's
Cobble 346; Boyce
Thompson Arboretum State
Park 165; Craters of the

Moon National Monument and Preserve 610; Del Norte Coast Redwoods State Park 43; Great Basin National Park 727; Guadalupe Mountains National Park 826; Icefields Parkway 121; Lost Maples 223; Olympic National Park 15; Saguaro National Park 811; Santarella 346; Shaw Nature Reserve 876; Shenandoah National Park 376; White Mountains National Forest 320

wildlife viewing: albino squirrels 771; Algonquin Provincial Park 557; bison 186; Cajun Country 303; Cape Lookout 31; Desert National Wildlife Refuge 153; elephant seals 69, 85; elk, Roosevelt 19, 44; Elkhorn Slough 72; Eureka, Montana 129; Fort Niobrara National Wildlife Refuge 200; Fort Pierre National Grasslands 195; Goat Lick 513; Kootenay National Park 127; National Bighorn Sheep Center 622; National Bison Range 133; Niobrara Valley Preserve 632; Sea Lion Caves 36; seals 38; Sullys Hill National Game Preserve 529; Tahkenitch Lake 37; *see also* whale-watching

Wildwood: 416

Willapa Bay: 23
Williams, Arizona: 923
Williams, Hank: 850
Williams, Tennessee: 284, 285
Williams College Museum of Art: 339
Williamstown: 339
Williston: 527, 568
Willow Creek: 46
Will Rogers Memorial: 887
Wilmington, Illinois: 869
Wilmington, North Carolina: 441
Wilmington, Vermont: 335
Wilton: 577
Winchester: 789
wind energy: 219
Wind River Canyon: 620
windsurfing: 434, 467, 596
wineries: 56, 263, 665–666
Winona: 920
Winooski: 564
Winslow: 918
Winterville Mounds: 289
Wisconsin: 245–250, 535–540 212, 240
Wolfe, Thomas: 392
Wolfsonian: 479
Women's Rights National Historical Park: 673
Woodrow Wilson Presidential Library and Museum: 382
Woodstock: 329
Woodville: 299
World of Coca Cola: 400
World's Largest Catsup Bottle: 874

World's Largest Spruce Tree: 21
World War II: 27, 144
Wright, Frank Lloyd: 166, 248, 872
Wright Brothers National Memorial: 430
Wrightsville Beach: 439
Wynn Las Vegas: 155
Wyoming: 613–626
Wyoming Pioneer Memorial Museum: 625

XYZ

Yachats: 35
Yellow Banks: 260
Yellowstone National Park: 613–616
Yoho National Park: 123
York: 367
Young, Brigham: 335, 732
Yuma: 808
Yuma Quartermaster Depot State Historic Park: 809
Zane Grey Museum: 357
Zapata: 227, 228
Zephyr Cove: 716
ziplines: 320
zoos: Abilene Zoo 218; Alligator Farm 467; Gladys Porter Zoo 230; Lee Richardson Zoo 211; Lion Country Safari 476; Louisiana Purchase Gardens and Zoo 839; Luray Zoo 378

Photo and Illustration Credits

All vintage postcards, photographs, and maps in this book are from the private collection of Jamie Jensen, unless otherwise credited.

Photos © Jamie Jensen pages 17, 44, 46, 47, 48, 83, 93, 109, 128, 139, 145, 173, 178, 181 (bottom), 188, 212, 221, 226, 239, 245, 246, 275, 292, 295 (detail), 299, 310, 331, 332, 334, 430 (top), 454, 491 (top), 505, 515, 518, 519 (top), 528, 537, 539, 541, 566, 574, 588, 610, 621, 630 (bottom), 636 (top), 654, 667, 685, 689, 713, 721, 722, 723, 738 (top), 740, 755, 770, 774, 776, 783 (top), 809, 812 (bottom), 813, 817, 819, 829, 851, 857, 866, 874, 880, 888 (bottom), 896, 899, 901 (bottom), 902, 913, 920, 937.

United States Quarter-Dollar Coin Images

State quarter-dollar coin images from the United States Mint. Used with permission.
page 410: 2007 Presidential $1 Coin image from the United States Mint. (www.usmint.gov/pressroom/index. cfm?flash=no&action=photo#Pres)

United States Postage Stamps

All postage stamps © United States Postal Service. All rights reserved. Used with permission. Written auhtorization from the postal service is required to use, reproduce, post, transmit, distribute, or publicly display these images. Pages 10, 26, 41, 128, 137, 148, 160, 177, 191, 199, 206, 212, 213, 235, 245, 250, 258, 278, 282, 300, 314, 327, 338, 348, 351, 357, 370, 372, 374, 386, 399, 411, 418, 443, 461, 540, 575, 613, 646, 654, 728, 738, 818, 845 Greetings from America Series Stamp Designs © 2002 United States Postal Service; 91 Dorothea Lange © 2002 United States Postal Service; 104 Walt Disney © United States Postal Service; 284 Tennessee Williams © 1995 United States Postal Service. Reproduction of the Tennessee Williams postage stamp by special permission of the U.S. Postal Service, Michael Deas, and The University of the South, Sewanee, Tennessee; 292 Teddy Bears © 1998 United States Postal Service. Reproduction of the Teddy Bear stamp by special permission of the U.S. Postal Service and Gund, Inc.; 812 Sonoran Desert Issue: Cactus Wren, brittlebush, teddy bear cholla © 1999 United States Postal Service; 812 Sonoran Dessert Issue: Western diamondback rattlesnake, cactus mouse, © 1999 United States Postal Service; 852 George Washington Carver © 1998 United States Postal Service.

Minor League Baseball Logos

All Minor League Baseball logos are Registered Trademarks of their organizations. Used with permission. Pages 133, 158, 169, 227, 259, 261, 352, 362, 398, 407, 429, 445, 455, 465, 475, 495, 506, 565, 604, 611, 635, 649, 654, 663, 669, 672, 676, 689, 699, 711, 733, 775, 796, 841, 882, 893, 907, 940, 941.

The following images were sourced from www.123rf.com:

12 © Travis Manley, 18 © Harry Hu, 28 (top) © Steve Estvanik, 39 © Jill Battaglia, 42 © iofoto, 59 © Julia Nelson, 63 © Mariusz Jurgielewicz, 68 © Mariusz Jurgielewicz, 78 © Andrew Zarivny, 81 © Mariusz Jurgielewicz, 83 © Mike Norton, 98 © Byron Moore, 100 © StrangerView, 101 © Andrew Kazmierski, 107 © Wayne Geisler, 110 © Deepa Vaswani, 111 © Andrew Zarivny, 121 © Rieke Photo, 122 © Jennifer Barrow, 123 © Elena Elisseeva, 133 © Sergey Andrianov, 141 © Matthew Pintar, 155 © Songquan Deng, 157 © Cecilia Lim, 158 © Amy Harris, 159 © Andrew Zarivny, 160 © Dave Broberg, 168 © William Silver, 189 (both) © George Burba, 208 (bottom) © Deron Rodehaver, 225 © Brandon Seidel, 231 © Mike Norton, 272 © Henryk Sadura, 275 © Carlos Santa Maria, 283 © Steve Kingsman, 318 © Richard Semik, 320 © Patricia Hofmeester, 321 © Chee-Onn Leong, 368 © Todd Thatcher, 376 © S. Borisov, 381 © Rollie, 391 © Timothy Mainiero, 411 © P. Orbital, 428 © Tom McNemar, 463 (top) © Iofoto, 463 (bottom) © Carolina K. Smith, M.D., 468 (bottom) © Rui Dios Aidos, 477 © Ivan Cholakov, 483 (top) © William Silver, 483 (bottom) © Oleg Zinkovetsky, 488 (top) © Natalia Bratslavsky, 488 (bottom) © Varina and Jay Patel, 490 © Chris Cifatte, 499 © Gino Rigucci, 501 © William Perry, 503 (top photo) © Travis Manley, 503 (bottom photo) © Frank L. Junior, 514 © Snehit, 516 © Robert Brown, 538 © Scott

Nesvold, 544 © Snehit, 546 © Michael G. Smith, 548 © Snehit, 549 © Phillip O'Brien, 550 © Keith Levit, 553 (top) © CityLights, 554 © Mark Spowart, 555 (bottom) © Steve Kingsman, 560 (top) © CityLights, 560 (bottom) © Stefanos Kyriazis, 570 © Richard Semik, 593 © DesignPics, 614 (top) © Crystal Garner, 614 (bottom) © Jason Ross, 619 © Sascha Burkhard, 622 © pdmai, 645 © Frank Romeo, 665 © Avi Kenny, 719 © Natalia Bratslavsky, 727 © DesignPics, 735 © Jarno Gonzalez, 736 © Harris Shiffman, 806 © Patrick Poendl, 826 © Peter M., 828 © Marcos Casiano, 841 © Henry K. Sadura, 860 © William Silver, 863 © William Mahnken, 911 (bottom) © Ralf Broskvar, 915 © Steven Love, 916 (bottom) © Susan Peterson, 919 © Mitch Aunger, 925 © Scott Griessel, 945 (top) © Kay DeBoer, 945 (bottom) © Walter Arce.

State flag and Canadian flag images:
© Juergen Priewe at www.123rf.com, pages 117, 420, 424, 430, 453, 494, 507, 509, 525, 531, 535, 563, 573, 586, 626, 633, 639, 663, 665, 693, 707, 715, 752, 762, 771, 777, 785, 808, 822, 836, 840, 885, 902.

Public Domain images:
The following images are in the public domain because one of the following applies:
- The work is a work of a U.S. government soldier or employee, taken or made during the course of the person's official duties. As a work of the U.S. federal government, the image is in the public domain.
- The work was published in the United States between 1923 and 1977 and without a copyright notice. Unless its author has been dead for several years, it is copyrighted in jurisdictions that do not apply the rule of the shorter term for US works, such as Canada (50 p.m.a.), Mainland China (50 p.m.a., not Hong Kong or Macao), Germany (70 p.m.a.), Mexico (100 p.m.a.), Switzerland (70 p.m.a.), and other countries with individual treaties.
- The copyright has expired, often because the first publication of the image occurred prior to January 1, 1923.
- The copyright holder of the work has released the work into the public domain. This applies worldwide. In some countries this may not be legally possible; if so: The copyright holder grants anyone the right to use the work for any purpose, without any conditions, unless such conditions are required by law.
- The work is a postage stamp published before 1978.
See http://copyright.cornell.edu/resources/publicdomain.cfm for further explanation.

9, 115, 175 shields Courtesy of SPUI/Wikimedia Commons; 28 stamp courtesy of United States Postal Service; 64 (bottom) Courtesy of Two+two=4/Wikimedia Commons; 71 (photo) Courtesy of Jacob Kearns/Wikimedia Commons; 82 Courtesy of Scott Frier/Nikon/U.S. Fish & Wildlife Service; 95 and 96 digital files Courtesy of Kevin Roe Collection; 105 Courtesy Nixon Presidential Library and Museum, original taken July 9, 1972; 166 Courtesy of Dave Pape/Wikimedia Commons; 177 Courtesy of the United States Air Force; 182 and 183 portraits by Charles Willson Peale, c. 1807, Courtesy of North Dakota Tourism; 189 Courtesy of the State Historical Society of North Dakota; 190 Courtesy of ABC Television, 1969; 193 Courtesy of Malchow/Wikimedia Commons; 197 (top) Courtesy of Minnesota Jones/Wikimedia Commons; 197 (bottom) Courtesy of Jllm06/Wikimedia Commons; 203 Courtesy of Wyoming Division of Cultural Resources; 210 Courtesy of Library of Congress's Prints & Photographs Division (digital ID ppmsc.00241); 227 map by Henry Wellge, 1892. *Laredo, Texas. The Gateway to and From Mexico.* Published by American Publishing Co., Milwaukee, Wis., Amon Carter Museum, Fort Worth.; 228 Courtesy of Library of Congress/Bain News Service; 251 (both) Courtesy of the National Park Service/bottom image by Kristen Maxfield; 259 detail from 1924 photo of The Wolverines, digitized and retouched by Hans Eekhoff; 267 Courtesy of steamboattimes.com, photo by A.F. Bradley, New York, 1907; 281 Courtesy of Jeffrey Rohan/Wikimedia Commons; 287 Courtesy United States Postal Service; 325 Courtesy of Kane5187/Wikimedia Commons; 326 Courtesy of Library of Congress's Prints & Photographs Division (LC-USZ62-3924), Lithograph of Stodart & Currier, N.Y. published by B.O. Tyler, [1834 or 1835]; 328 originally published by the Green Mountain Card Company, White River Junction, Vermont, c. 1910; 336 (both) Courtesy of Hunter Kahn/Wikimedia Commons; 338 Courtesy of Library of Congress's Prints & Photographs Division (LC-USZ62-23933); 339 Courtesy Clark Art Institute/Wikimedia Commons; 342 (top) Courtesy of Eranb/Wikimedia Commons; 343 Courtesy of Library of Congress, original painting by Joseph O. Eaton, 1870; 353 Courtesy of Disputantum/Wikimedia Commons; 371 Courtesy National Park Service, original photo by Mathew Brady, c. 1865; 373 Courtesy National Park Service/Doug Coldwell; 382 Courtesy Library of Congress's Prints & Photographs Division (digital ID cph.3a04218), original photograph by Pach Brothers, New York, 1912; 384 Courtesy Library of Congress's Prints & Photographs Division (digital ID ppmsca.23961), original photograph by Harris & Ewing, 1905; 366 Courtesy of Ken Thomas/Wikimedia Commons (http://kenthomas.us); 402 Courtesy Scott Ehardt/Wikimedia Commons, 407 (photo) Courtesy of Bloodfox at en.Wikipedia; 422 (bottom) Courtesy Tex Jobe, U.S. Army Corps of Engineers/Wikimedia Commons; 425 (bottom) Courtesy United States Coast Guard, PA2 Christopher Evanson; 429 (stamp) Courtesy of the United States Postal

Service; 430 (bottom) Courtesy Library of Congress's Prints & Photographs Division (LC-DIG-ppprs-00626), original authors: Orville Wright and John T. Daniels, 1903; 431 (both) Courtesy Library of Congress's Prints & Photographs Division (LC-DIG-ppprs-00680 and LC-DIG-ppprs-00683); 437 Courtesy of www.neatorama. com, original painting: *Capture of the Pirate, Blackbeard, 1718* by Jean Leon Gerome Ferris, 1920; 439 Courtesy FEMA Photo Library/Cynthia Hunter; 440 Courtesy of Ken Thomas/Wikimedia Commons (http://kenthomas. us), 441 Courtesy US Navy, USN photo # DN-ST-89-00322, by Don S. Montgomery; 442 Courtesy www. learnnc.org/lp/multimedia/12418, original map by Union soldier Robert Knox Sneden, 1865; 449 Courtesy United States Postal Service, 464 (top) Courtesy of Mike Horn/Wikimedia Commons; 473 Courtesy NASA/ Tony Gray and Tom Farrar/Wikimedia Commons; 490 (top) digital file Courtesy of Downtowngal/Wikimedia Commons; 491 (bottom) digital file Courtesy Domini Dragoone; 493 digital file Courtesy Doug Pappas; 502 (top) Courtesy Wenatchee Valley Museum & Cultural Center; 511 Courtesy of the U.S. Army Corps of Engineers Digital Visual Library; 519, 602, 753, 787 "Our State Flowers: The Floral Emblems Chosen by the Commonwealths", *National Geographic Magazine*, XXXI (June 1917), paintings by Mary E. Eaton; 521 Courtesy National Archives, photo by William H. Jackson, before 1877; 522 Courtesy Wyoming State Museum; 523 Courtesy Harry Weddington, U.S. Army Corps of Engineers; 530 (bottom) Courtesy Only/Wikimedia Commons; 547 Courtesy Brenda St. Martin/National Park Service; 557 Courtesy Toronto Public Library; 616 from Wikimedia Commons, photo by Burke, c. 1892; 627 from Wikimedia Commons; 628 Courtesy Ammodramus/ Wikimedia Commons; 643 Courtesy Ronald Reagan Presidnetial Library; 648 Courtesy of Visviva/Wikimedia Commons; 658 Courtesy Library of Congress's Prints & Photographs Division (digital ID cph.3c31044), original photo by Hunt, Ft. Myers, FL, 1914; 661 Courtesy Derek Jensen/Wikimedia Commons; 673 Courtesy National Park Service; 676 Courtesy F.X. Matt Brewing Company/Wikimedia Commoons; 679 Courtesy Library of Congress's Prints & Photographs Division; 682 (top) Courtesy Library of Congress's Prints & Photographs Division (LC-USZC4-3859), poster by James Montgomery Flagg; 682 (bottom) Courtesy New York Public Library Digital Library (ID G91F085_024F), photo by James E. Irving, c. 1880; 690 (bottom left) Courtesy Midnightdreary/Wikimedia Commons; 690 (bottom right) © Allowishus/Wikimedia Commons; 694 Courtesy Boston Public Library; 705 digital file Coutesy Doug Pappas; 764 Courtesy Charvex/Wikimedia Commons; 766 Courtesy U.S. Air Force; 768 from Wikimedia Commons, originally published by Seminary Music Co., New York, 1908; 773 from Wikimedia Commons, originally published Baker-Meyer & Co., Importers & Publishers, West Baden, Ind.; 784 Courtesy Leslie K. Dellovade/Wikimedia Commons; 793 Courtesy U.S. Navy/Mass Communication Specialist 2nd Class William Selby; 799 originally printed by W.J. Moses in *Scenes from the Life of Harriet Tubman*, pre 1869; 801 digital file Courtesy Doug Pappas; 811 Courtesy Jörn Napp/Wikimedia Commons; 816 (both) Courtesy National Archives, photos by Camillus S. Fly; 820 and 821 Courtesy Boston Public Library; 827 Courtesy J. Dykstra/Wikimedia Commons; 833 Courtesy Bob Smith/EPA/Wikimedia Commons; 837 United States Library of Congress's Prints & Photographs Division (digital ID cph.3c34474); 843 (bottom) Courtesy of the Mississippi Department of Archives and History; 846 © Carol Highsmith/Wikimedia Commons; 847 Library of Congress's Prints & Photographs Division (digital ID highsm.07312), photo by Carol Highsmith; 859 Courtesy Anna Blecker/Wikimedia Commons; 888 (top) Courtesy OkiefromOkla/Wikimedia Commons; 895 Courtesy Count Calen/Wikimedia Commons; 901 (top) Courtesy Leaflet/Wikimedia Commons; 908 (top) Courtesy Boston Public Library, Prints Division; 912 Courtesy Anna Foxlover/Wikimedia Commons; 926 Courtesy Kkaufman11/Wikimedia Commons; 927 Courtesy Library of Congress's Prints & Photographs Division (digital ID ppmsca.13397), original poster by NPS employee, 1938.

GNU and/or Creative Commons images:

21 photo © Miso Beno (http://commons.wikimedia.org/wiki/File:Lady_Washington_Commencement_Bay.jpg), 34 © PFFY (http://commons.wikimedia.org/wiki/File:Aquarium_tunnel.jpg), 54 © Robert Campbell/www. chamoismoon.com (http://commons.wikimedia.org/wiki/File:Fort_Bragg_California_aerial_view.jpg), 85 (top photo) © Urban (http://commons.wikimedia.org/wiki/File:Hearst_Castle_Casa_Grande1.jpg), 96 (bottom photo) © Los Angeles/Wikimedia Commons (http://commons.wikimedia.org/wiki/File:Grandma_ Prisbrey%27s_Bottle_Village_(3).jpg), 113 © David S. Roberts (http://commons.wikimedia.org/wiki/

Wyoming_Dinosaur_Center.jpg), 629 © Daryl Mitchell (http://commons.wikimedia.org/wiki/File:Goldenrod_ Flowers.jpg), 642 © Ben Jacobson (Kranar Drogin (http://commons.wikimedia.org/wiki/File:Burpee_-_ Thescelosaurus.JPG), 653 © femaletrumpet02 (http://commons.wikimedia.org/wiki/File:Rosa_Parks_bus_full_ shot_by_femaletrumpet02.jpg), 660 © Andrew (http://commons.wikimedia.org/wiki/File:We_Win!.jpg), 664 © Pat Noble (http://commons.wikimedia.org/wiki/File:Warner_Theatre_Erie_Marquee.jpg), 670 © Darmon (http://commons.wikimedia.org/wiki/File:AnchorBar.jpg), 680 © UpstateNYer (http://commons.wikimedia.org/ wiki/File:SpringsideCottageFacade2.jpg), 685 (top) © Nancy (http://commons.wikimedia.org/wiki/File:Epigaea_ repens.jpg), 686 © ToddC4176 (http://commons.wikimedia.org/wiki/File:Bridge_of_Flowers.JPG), 690 (top) © Daderot at en.wikipedia (http://commons.wikimedia.org/wiki/File:Hartwell_Tavern_Lexington_Massachusetts. jpg), 696 © werkunz1 on Flickr (http://commons.wikimedia.org/wiki/File:Fanway_Park_2009.jpg), 707 © Calibas (http://commons.wikimedia.org/wiki/File:Heinolds.jpg), 709 (top) © Magnus Manske (http:// commons.wikimedia.org/wiki/File:Eschscholzia_californica_%27californian_poppy%27_2007-06- 02_%28flower%29.jpg), 710 (top) © Tinned Elk (http://commons.wikimedia.org/wiki/File:Medusa_%28Six_ Flags_Discovery_Kingdom%29_01.JPG), 715 (bottom) © Ragesoss (http://commons.wikimedia.org/wiki/ File:Small_twisted_sagebrush.jpg), 720 © Tobias (http://commons.wikimedia.org/wiki/ File:USA_2005_%28October_1st%29_Nevada,_Reno,_National_Automobile_Museum.jpg), 725 (top) © Davemeistermoab (http://commons.wikimedia.org/wiki/File:Eurekanv.JPG), 728 © Wing-Chi-Poon (http:// commons.wikimedia.org/wiki/File:Calabash_Shaped_Stalactites_that_Resemble_Chinese_Red_Lanterns.jpg), 731 (top) © Maylett (http://commons.wikimedia.org/wiki/File:Sego_lily_cm.jpg), 731 (bottom) © Tricia Simpson (http://commons.wikimedia.org/wiki/File:HelperUtah.jpg), 733 © Signalhead (http://commons. wikimedia.org/wiki/File:Green_river_utah_from_sky.jpg), 745 © Hustvedt (http://commons.wikimedia.org/ wiki/File:Royal_Gorge_Bridge_2010.jpg), 747 © MarekWK (http://commons.wikimedia.org/wiki/File:Pike_ Peak_1.JPG), 750 © Ealdgyth (http://commons.wikimedia.org/wiki/File:Bent%27s_Old_Fort_buildings.jpg), 759 © Jon Harder (http://commons.wikimedia.org/wiki/File:Alexanderwohl-church-2.jpg), 760 © Ichabod (http://commons.wikimedia.org/wiki/File:Chase_county_kansas_courthouse_sideview_2009.jpg), 763 (bottom) © Americasroof at en.wikipedia (http://commons.wikimedia.org/wiki/File:Clay-savings.png), 773 © Sarah Wilkerson Poole from Bedford, USA (http://commons.wikimedia.org/wiki/File:West_Baden_Springs_Hotel_ atrium.jpg), 777 © Cédric Boismain from France (http://commons.wikimedia.org/wiki/File:Thomas_Gaff_ House_%28Hillforest%29.jpg), 781 © Rick Kimpel (http://commons.wikimedia.org/wiki/File:Red_Carnation_ Flower.jpg), 783 (bottom) © Rdikeman at en.wikipedia (http://commons.wikimedia.org/wiki/ File:Hopewell_culture_nhp_mounds_chillicothe_ohio_2006.jpg), © Albert Herring (http://commons. wikimedia.org/wiki/File:Virginia_State_Capitol_complex_-_state_seal_on_doorknob.jpg), 792 © Phillip Ritz (http://commons.wikimedia.org/wiki/File:National_Museum_of_the_American_Indian_in_ Washington,_D.C.jpg), 794 © Tim1965 (http://commons.wikimedia.org/wiki/File:Metropolitan_Square_-_ Washington_DC_-_Old_Ebbitt_Grill.JPG), 798 © Acroterion (http://commons.wikimedia.org/wiki/ File:Log_Canoe_Edmee_S_and_Point_Lookout_Tower.jpg), 805 © Marriedtofilm at en.wikipedia (http:// commons.wikimedia.org/wiki/File:Tecate_Border_Crossing.jpg), 807 © Nick Seibert (http://commons. wikimedia.org/wiki/File:Blue_angels_flyover.jpg), 818 © Sascha Brück (http://commons.wikimedia.org/wiki/ File:Chiricahua_balanced_rock.jpg), 823 (bottom) © Dave at Dave's Garden (http://commons.wikimedia.org/ wiki/File:Texas_Bluebonnet_%28Lupinus_texensis%29.jpg), 838 © Billy Hathorn (http://commons.wikimedia. org/wiki/File:MVI_2654_Bonnie_%26_Clyde_Ambush_Museum_%28Revised%29_.jpg), 850 (top) © Colin Mutchler from Brooklyn, United States (http://commons.wikimedia.org/wiki/File:Montgomerychurch.jpg), 855 © Jim Clark (http://commons.wikimedia.org/wiki/File:Little_White_House_HIstoric_Site.jpg), 872 (top) © Robert Lawton (http://commons.wikimedia.org/wiki/File:Lincoln%27s_Tomb.JPG), 877 © T. Sujatha (http:// commons.wikimedia.org/wiki/File:Cavern_2.jpg), 879 © Vladimer Shioshvili (http://commons.wikimedia.org/ wiki/File:Crataegus_flowers_in_Martkophi.jpg), 884 (top) © The White Pelican (http://commons.wikimedia. org/wiki/File:Baxter_Springs_Soda_Fountain.jpg), 884 (bottom) © Vanessa Ezekowitz (http://commons. wikimedia.org/wiki/File:Baxter_Springs_Independent_Oil_and_Gas_Service_Station.jpg), 885 © The White Pelican (http://commons.wikimedia.org/wiki/File:Old_Conoco_Station_-_Commerce.jpg), 887 © Abe Ezekowitz (http://commons.wikimedia.org/wiki/File:Totem_Pole_Park.jpg), 898 © Venturist/Wikimedia Commons; 900 © Ralf Kiepert (http://commons.wikimedia.org/wiki/File:USA_Texas_Amarillo_Cadillac_ Ranch_Side_09-10-15.jpg), 903 © Wordbuilder (http://commons.wikimedia.org/wiki/File:Norman_Petty_Stu- dios.jpg), 904 © Autopilot (http://commons.wikimedia.org/wiki/File:Blue_Hole_-_New_Mexico.jpg), 908 (bottom) © http://www.flickr.com/photos/blmurch/157779639/ (http://commons.wikimedia.org/wiki/ File:Santa_Fe_Plaza.jpg), 911 (top) Ian McKellar (http://commons.wikimedia.org/wiki/File:Acoma_Pueblo_-_ Wooden_Ladders.jpg), 914 © Bernard Gagnon (http://commons.wikimedia.org/wiki/File:Great_Seal_of_the_ State_of_Arizona.jpg), 916 (top) © Ken Bosma (http://commons.wikimedia.org/wiki/File:Saguaro_cactus_blos- soms.jpg), 922 © James Jones (http://commons.wikimedia.org/wiki/File:The_Telescope_that_Discovered_Pluto.

jpg), 928 © Spbear (http://commons.wikimedia.org/wiki/File:Grandcanyon_railroad.jpg), 930 © PMDrive1061 (http://commons.wikimedia.org/wiki/File:Snow_cap_seligman.jpg), 934 © Ken Lund from Las Vegas, Nevada, USA (http://commons.wikimedia.org/wiki/File:London_Bridge,_Lake_Havasu_City,_Arizona_(3227888290). jpg), 938 © Vicente Villamon (http://commons.wikimedia.org/wiki/File:Bagdad_Cafe._(4054050230).jpg), 939 © Doug Wertman (http://commons.wikimedia.org/wiki/File:Route_66_Motel_Sign_-_Victorville,_CA.jpg), 941 (top) © Cogart Strangehill (http://commons.wikimedia.org/wiki/File:First_McDonalds,_San_Bernardino,_ California.jpg), 941 (bottom) Flickr user Living in Monrovia (http://commons.wikimedia.org/wiki/File:Aztec_ Hotel.jpg), 943 © Pamla J. Eisenberg from Anaheim, USA (http://commons.wikimedia.org/wiki/ File:Aloe_%26_blue_stick_succulents,_Huntington_Desert_Garden.jpg), 944 © Sean Russell (http://commons. wikimedia.org/wiki/File:Johnny_Ramone_-_Hollywood_Forever_Cemetary_1.jpg).

Additional Credits:

14 © Sequim Lavender Festival, 19 © State of Washington Tourism Division, 21 logo Courtesy Grays Harbor Historical Seaport, 29 Courtesy of Oregon Tourism Division, 37 © Bob Race, 50 Courtesy Eel River Brewery, Inc., 51 logo is a registered trademark of Save the Redwoods League, 53 © Drive-Thru Tree Park, 54 logo Courtesy North Coast Brewing Co., 55 © California Department of Parks and Recreation, 56 © The Boonville Hotel, 60 © Redwood Empire Association, 61 © Robert Holmes/California Division of Tourism, 62 © Michael Schwab Studio, 63 © Michael Schwab Studio, 64 (top) © Domini Dragoone, 65 (top) © Domini Dragoone, 69 © Swanton Berry Farm, 73 © Domini Dragoone, 75 © National Steinbeck Center, 85 (bottom) © California Department of Parks and Recreation, 90 © San Luis Obispo Convention & Visitors Bureau, 92 © California Travel and Tourism Commission/Robert Holmes, 103 © Disney, 106 © Festival of Arts of Laguna Beach, 119 © Andrew Hempstead, 125 © Andrew Hempstead, 130 © Donnie Sexton / Montana Office of Tourism, 131 © Montana Historical Society, 132 © Erika Howsare, 135 (both) © Erika Howsare, 142 © Sun Valley Co., 144 © Erika Howsare, 148 © Todd Clark, 150 © Western Folklife Center, 154 (top) © Las Vegas News Bureau, 154 (bottom) © Domini Dragoone, 156 © Nevada Commission on Tourism, 162 © Mildred Wheeler, 185 (photo) © Fred Walker/North Dakota Tourism, 192 © Kelly Krabbenhoft/North Dakota Tourism, 198 © Rosebud Casino, 204 © J. Nabb/Nebraska Department Of Economic Development, 208 (top) © Kansas Division of Travel & Tourism/Meredith Corporation/Mitch Kezar, 211 © Mike LeMasters, 215 © Bob Waldmire, 218 Courtesy of Frontier Texas, 219 © Elizabeth Grivas/Texas Dept. of Commerce, 231 (top) Courtesy of Seven Seas Gift Shop, 238 © Mississippi River Parkway, 238 © Adam Rademacher/This Old Farm, 240 © Turner Entertainment, 244 Courtesy of the Cradle of Aviation Museum, 247 La Crosse Lager® is a registered trademark of City Brewery, La Crosse WI, 252 © Barnum & Bailey, 254 and 255 Courtesy of Dubuque Area CVB, 261 Courtesy of Iowa Tourism Office, 264 Courtesy of Quincy CVB, 268 © Calhoun Ferry Company, 270 © Quad City CVB, 278 © Metropolis Convention & Visitors Bureau, 286 © Kap Stann, 290 © Doug Pappas, 291 © Mississippi Development Department, 296 (both) © Mississippi State Department of Tourism, 301 © Louisiana Office of Tourism, 315 © David Brownell/NHOTTD, 322 © Priscilla Carton/Clark's Trading Post, 328 Courtesy of The Hanover Inn, 345 Printed by permission of the Norman Rockwell Family Agency. Copyright © 1960 the Norman Rockwell Family Entities., 348 Courtesy Santarella Museum & Gardens, 349 © Ben Thompson, 380 Photo supplied by, and reproduced with the permission of, Binney & Smith, maker of Crayola products., 374 photo © Julian Smith, 382 Courtesy of Mrs. Rowe's, 388 © Mayberry Motor Inn, 396 Courtesy of Dollywood, 397 © Steve Freer, Tennessee Valley Railroad Museum, 401 Courtesy Atlanta History Center, 413-415 Courtesy Atlantic City Convention & Visitors Authority, 416 © Doug Pappas, 419 Courtesy Delware Tourism Office, 427 Courtesy of the Chesapeake Bay Bridge-Tunnel, 449 (bottom) Courtesy Charleston Area CVB - http://ExploreCharleston. com, 456 and 457 Courtesy http://www.SavannahVisit.com, 460 Courtesy Georgia Sea Turtle Center, 472 logo is a Registered Trademark of NASA, 475 Ron Jon Surf Shop logo and tagline are Registered Trademarks of Ron Jon Surf Shop, 503 (logo) the Apple Logo is a registered trademark of the Washington Apple Commission, 506 (photo) © State of Washington Tourism Division, 517 © Donnie Sexton / Montana Office of Tourism, 524 © Bob Race, 525 © Jason Lindsey / North Dakota Tourism, 527 logo is a trademark of the Buffalo Trails Museum, 530 (top) © North Dakota Tourism Department/Dawn Charging, 540 © Tom Huhti, 542 Courtesy Ontonagen Chamber of Commerce, 558 © Dionne Quintuplets Museum, 572 Courtesy Fairbanks Museum, 577 © Keith Kanoti/Maine Forest Service/Bugwood.org, 579 © Maine Office of Tourism, 585 Courtesy Buffalo Bill Historical Center, Cody, WY, 596 Courtesy of the Oregon Tourism Commission, 601 "The New Arrivals" by Don Gray is Courtesy of The Vale Mural Society, 612 © Donnie Sexton / Montana Office of Tourism, 616 (top) Courtesy Xanterra, 618 © Wyoming Division of Cultural Resources, 624 © Doug Pappas, 626 © Wyoming Division of Tourism, 630 (top) © South Dakota Tourism, 630 (middle) © Crazy Horse Memorial Archives, 632 Courtesy Nebraska Department of Economic Development, 634 Courtesy Iowa Tourism Office, 636 and 637 (signs) © Kevin Roe, 638 Courtesy Iowa Tourism Office, 641 © Charles Brutlag, 647 © IMS Properties, 649 © Fang

Hong/Wikimedia Commons, 650 © Studebaker National Museum, 655 Courtesy of the Toledo Museum of Art, 674 © Doug's Fish Fry, 677 © Kevin Roe, 702 and 703 (top) © Tim Grafft / Massachusetts Office of Travel and Tourism MOTT, 709 (bottom) © Domini Dragoone, 710 (bottom) © California Deptartment of Parks and Recreation, 718 (top) © Nevada Tourism Comission, 725 (bottom) © Wei Luan/Ely Renaissance Society/Photo by Jamie Jensen, 734 © Buffalo Bill Historical Center, Cody WY, 737 © Utah Office of Tourism, 738 (bottom), 739, 743, 744, 748 © Matt Inden/Weaver Multimedia/Colorado Tourism Office, 751 © Erika Howsare, 765 © Kansas City Convention & Visitors Association, 814 © by James G. Howes, 2008., 815 © Arizona Office of Tourism, 839 (bottom) © Louisiana Office of Tourism, 842 © Jimmie Rodgers Museum, 844 (top) © Bill Swislow, 844 Courtesy of Mississippi Development Authority, 850 (bottom) © Dan Brothers/Alabama Bureau of Tourism & Travel, 855 © The Green J/Wikimedia Commons, 869 © Shellee Graham, 872 (bottom) © Bob Waldmire, 891 © Trust Authority, 906 both images Courtesy of Tinkertown Museum, 918 © Lazy SOB Records, 921 Courtesy of Flagstaff Convention & Visitors Bureau, 929 Courtesy of Arizona Department of Tourism/Photograph by Hoshino.

Cover Images:

Map photo © Domini Dragoone.

Cover postcards from the private collections of Domini Dragoone, Jamie Jensen and Kevin Roe.

Original publishers:

R: "New Overseas Highway, Above 'Pigeon Key', on the Way to Key West, Florida", Tichnor Bros.,Inc., Boston, MA

O: J.C. Bardell, San Francisco, CA, artwork © Moulin Studios

A: "Causeway, Coast Highway, Between Ventura and Santa Barbara, Along the Coastal Highway California", Western Publishing & Novelty Co., Los Angeles, CA

D: "Mt. Rushmore Memorial, Black Hills, So. Dak.", Curt Teich & Co.,Inc., Chicago, IL. Photography by Bell Studio. Distributed by Black Hills Postcard Co., Deadwood, S.D.

T: "Skyline, Detroit, Mich.," Metropolitan, Everitt, MA

R, I: "Along the Coastal Highway California", Western Publishing & Novelty Co., Los Angeles, CA

P: "Shepperd's Dell, Columbia River Highway, Oregon", American Art Post Card and Lipschuetz & Katz, artwork © Weister Co.

U: "Japanese Cherry Blossoms, Riverside Drive, Potomac River, Washington, D.C.", Curt Teich & Co., Inc., Chicago, IL., B.S. Reynolds Co., Washington D.C.

S: "Oversea Highway to Key West, Florida looking S.W. from lower Matecumbe", Tichnor Brothers, Boston, MA.

A: "The Watchman, Zion National Park, Utah", De Witt Bros., Ogden, UT

Ready to hit the open road?

Visit roadtripusa.com for trip ideas, maps, road trip routes, a Driver's Almanac of monthly trip suggestions, and more.

Web-exclusive features include Jamie Jensen's Road Tripper blog and free downloadable podcasts.

roadtripusa.com—the online source for road trippers!

www.moon.com

DESTINATIONS | ACTIVITIES | BLOGS | MAPS | BOOKS

MOON.COM is ready to help plan your next trip! Filled with fresh trip ideas and strategies, author interviews, informative travel blogs, a detailed map library, and descriptions of all the Moon guidebooks, Moon.com is all you need to get out and explore the world—or even places in your own backyard. While at Moon.com, sign up for our monthly e-newsletter for updates on new releases, travel tips, and expert advice from our on-the-go Moon authors. As always, when you travel with Moon, expect an experience that is uncommon and truly unique.

KEEP UP WITH MOON ON FACEBOOK AND TWITTER
JOIN THE MOON PHOTO GROUP ON FLICKR

Acknowledgments

Keeping tabs on the life and times along more than 40,000 miles of all-American highways is a lot of fun—and a lot of work. For those who've helped make this latest edition more of the former than the latter, I'd like to send out a huge and heartfelt "thank you."

First and foremost I'd like to acknowledge the tremendous contributions from the whole team at Avalon Travel, for their usual but nonetheless extraordinary efforts in fact-checking and map-making. Specific shout-outs go to ace designer Domini Dragoone, and eagle-eyed editor Kevin McLain, without whom this book would not be the attractive and engaging object you're holding in your hands.

I am also indebted to the many intrepid travelers, local historians, business owners and others who have provided images for inclusion, from the best burger joints to the biggest murals. Special thanks go to Sandra Hebert at Minor League Baseball, Jill Barnett in Cuba Missouri, Stacy Lane in Cape Girardeau, and Betsy Coy at Jekyll Island's Georgia Sea Turtle Center.

And to all of you who have got in touch with suggestions, ideas and intriguing questions: please keep those postcards, trip reports, and emails coming!

After more than 20 years of wanderlust, there's still no place I'd rather be than alongside my wife Catherine Robson and our boys Tom and Alex, with whom I always look forward to our next trip

Getting to know these miles of highways, and the wonderful places they can take us, has been a dream come true, but tracking the changes has a bittersweet side as well. I would like to dedicate this sixth edition to a man who helped open my eyes (and those of many others) to the abundance of life along Route 66 and other great roads: the late, great artist and adventurer Bob Waldmire of Illinois, Arizona, and all points in between.

ROAD TRIP USA
Cross-Country Adventures on America's Two-Lane Highways
6th Edition

Jamie Jensen

Avalon Travel
a member of the Perseus Books Group
1700 Fourth Street
Berkeley, CA 94710, USA
www.travelmatters.com
Editor: Kevin McLain
Fact checkers: Christine des Garennes (Route 66), Joshua Lawrence Kinser (Atlantic Coast), Keith Michaud (The Road to Nowhere, The Appalachian Trail, The Oregon Trail, Southern Pacific), Haley Shapley (Pacific Coast), Maggie Thach (Border to Border, The Great River Road, The Great Northern, The Loneliest Road)
Copy Editor: Deana Shields
Cover and Interior Designer: Domini Dragoone
Graphics and Production Coordinator: Domini Dragoone
Map Editor: Mike Morgenfeld
Cartographers: Mike Morgenfeld and Kaitlin Jaffe
Proofreader: Danielle Miller
Indexer: Rachel Kuhn

ISBN: 978-1-59880-925-1
ISSN: 1085-7036

Printing History
1st Edition — 1996
6th Edition — May 2012
5 4 3 2 1

ROAD TRIP 7

The Great Northern

INCLUDING: Seattle, Washington 498 • Glacier National Park 514 • Roadside Giants 530 • Michigan's Upper Peninsula 540 • The Big Nickel 553 • Acadia National Park 583

ROAD TRIP 8

The Oregon Trail

INCLUDING: Columbia Gorge 595 • Yellowstone National Park 613 • Mount Rushmore 630 • Field of Dreams 638 • Niagara Falls 671 • Cape Cod 698

ROAD TRIP 9

The Loneliest Road

INCLUDING: Gold Country 712 • Pony Express Trail 723 • Million Dollar Highway 740 • Santa Fe Trail 748 • Independence, Missouri 762 • Louisville, Kentucky 774 • Annapolis, Maryland 796

ROAD TRIP 10

Southern Pacific

INCLUDING: Desert View Tower 805 • Felicity: Center of the World 807 • The Thing? 813 • Buddy Holly Monument 829 • Bonnie and Clyde 837 • Hank Williams Memorial 850 • Tybee Island, Georgia 863

ROAD TRIP 11

Route 66

INCLUDING: Chicago 867 • Land of Lincoln 871 • Will Rogers Memorial 887 • Cadillac Ranch 900 • Tinkertown 905 • London Bridge 934 • Hollywood 944